80.00

D1432921

The
Schirmer
Guide to
Schools
of Music
and
Conservatories
Throughout
the
World

THE SCHIRMER GUIDE TO SCHOOLS OF MUSIC AND CONSERVATORIES THROUGHOUT THE WORLD

Nancy Uscher

SCHIRMER BOOKS
A Division of Macmillan, Inc.
NEW YORK
Collier Macmillan Publishers
LONDON

Schirmer Books
A Division of Macmillan, Inc.
866 Third Avenue, New York, N.Y. 10022

Collier Macmillan Canada, Inc.

Library of Congress Catalog Card No.: 88-1518

Printed in the United States of America

printing number
1   2   3   4   5   6   7   8   9   10

Library of Congress Cataloging-in-Publication Data

Uscher, Nancy.
    The Schirmer guide to schools of music and conservatories
  throughout the world / Nancy Uscher.
        p. cm.
    Includes indexes.
    ISBN 0-02-873030-5
    1. Conservatories of music—Directories. I. Title.
ML12.U8 1988
780 '.7'29—dc19   88-1518
                                                      CIP
                                                       MN

**To my dear parents,
Ida and Milton Uscher,
who introduced me to music at Tanglewood
during my fifth year.**

CONTENTS

Preface ix
Introduction xi
How to Use This Guide xiii
Main Entries

UNITED STATES
Alabama 1
Alaska 7
Arizona 9
Arkansas 13
California 19
Colorado 50
Connecticut 56
Delaware 63
District of Columbia 65
Florida 68
Georgia 75
Hawaii 82
Idaho 84
Illinois 87
Indiana 106
Iowa 115
Kansas 120
Kentucky 127
Louisiana 134
Maine 142
Maryland 144
Massachusetts 149
Michigan 160
Minnesota 169
Mississippi 177
Missouri 182
Montana 190
Nebraska 192
Nevada 195
New Hampshire 197
New Jersey 199
New Mexico 207
New York 210
North Carolina 236
North Dakota 243
Ohio 245

Oklahoma 263
Oregon 270
Pennsylvania 276
Puerto Rico 290
Rhode Island 291
South Carolina 293
South Dakota 297
Tennessee 298
Texas 303
Utah 324
Vermont 327
Virginia 329
Washington 338
West Virginia 345
Wisconsin 348
Wyoming 356

INTERNATIONAL
Albania 361
Algeria 361
Argentina 361
Australia 363
Austria 367
Belgium 368
Bolivia 371
Brazil 371
Bulgaria 375
Burma 375
Canada 376
Chile 391
China, People's Republic of 392
Colombia 396
Costa Rica 397
Cuba 398
Czechoslavakia 399
Denmark 401
Dominican Republic 402
East Germany (German Democratic Republic) 402
Ecuador 404
Egypt 405
El Salvador 405
Ethiopia 405

CONTENTS

Federal Republic of Germany (West Germany) 481
Finland 406
France 409
German Democratic Republic (East Germany) 402
Ghana 410
Greece 411
Guatemala 412
Haiti 412
Honduras 413
Hong Kong 413
Hungary 414
Iceland 416
India 416
Indonesia 420
Iran 421
Iraq 422
Ireland 422
Israel 422
Italy 424
Ivory Coast 428
Jamaica 428
Japan 429
Kampuchea 433
Kenya 433
Korea (Democratic People's Republic) 434
Korea, Republic of 434
Kuwait 437
Lebanon 437
Liberia 438
Luxembourg 438
Mexico 438
Monaco 439
Morocco 439
Netherlands 440
New Caledonia 442
New Zealand 442
Nicaragua 444
Nigeria 444
Norway 444
Oman 446

Panama 446
Paraguay 446
Peru 447
Philippines 447
Poland 450
Portugal 453
Qatar 454
Romania 454
Saudi Arabia 455
Senegal 455
South Africa, Republic of 455
Spain 456
Sri Lanka 457
Sudan 458
Sweden 458
Switzerland 460
Syria 463
Taiwan (Republic of China) 464
Tanzania 464
Thailand 465
Tunisia 465
Turkey 465
Uganda 467
United Kingdom 467
Uruguay 473
U.S.S.R. 473
Venezuela 480
Vietnam 481
West Germany (Federal Republic of Germany) 481
Yemen Arab Republic 490
Yugoslavia 490
Zaire 492
Zambia 492
Zimbabwe 493

Institution Index 495
Index of Program Areas 507
Index of Instruments Taught 557
Appendix: International Telephone Codes 635

PREFACE

In 1983, while on sabbatical from my position as co-principal violist of the Jerusalem Symphony Orchestra, I held a master class and presented a recital of American music at the Cairo Conservatory of Music. That same year I visited the Lebanese Conservatory of Music in Beirut as well as several European conservatories. Fascinated by what I saw and heard at these music schools, I sought more information about them. To my surprise, it soon became apparent that no comprehensive reference book about music conservatories existed. Sensing that others would have a need for the kind of information I was seeking, I decided to write such a book.

Getting material was not always easy. While institutions in the United States, Canada, Western Europe, and some parts of Asia and Australia usually have printed catalogs or brochures, schools in other regions of the world provide little or no documentation. Occasionally the cultural, educational, or information attaché at a nation's Washington embassy or New York consular office had a few addresses or telephone numbers. Far more often these diplomatic channels had no reference materials about cultural institutions in their own countries.

A basic tool for gathering data worldwide was a questionnaire that was translated into several languages, including Chinese. However, even in their translated versions, questionnaires were often returned unopened because addresses that had been obtained from basic reference works were no longer valid.

Offsetting the difficulties and disappointments was the excitement of discovery inherent in any serious research project. At the Academy library in Katowice, Poland, buried among the treasures of Silesian culture, librarians unearthed an all-but-forgotten English-language document about the institution, an anniversary publication produced several years before, which they presented to me in a parcel filled with other materials and facsimiles of scores from the school's archives. I also had an opportunity to study firsthand other institutions listed in the book. It was enthralling to attend concerts at the Franz Liszt Academy and see the significant impact this institution has on the cultural life of Budapest, exciting to visit the Instituto Superior de Arte in Havana and have the opportunity to observe the students preparing for their professional lives, and nothing short of awe-inspiring to behold the magnificent buildings, themselves museums of artworks and instruments, in which many of the European academies are housed.

A number of secondary sources helped me significantly in exploring uncharted territory. I gratefully acknowledge consulting the following: *Commonwealth Universities Yearbook 1987*, 4 vols. (London: The Association of Commonwealth Universities, 1987); *Directory of Music Faculties in Colleges and Universities, U.S. and Canada, 1986–88* (Boulder: The College Music Society, 1986); *Directory of Music Research Libraries*, 5 vols. (Kassel: Barenreiter-Verlag, 1983); *The Great Soviet Encyclopedia*, 31 vols. (New York: Macmillan, 1973–1983); *The New Grove Dictionary of Music and Musicians*, 20 vols., edited by Stanley Sadie (London: Grove's Dictionaries of Music, Inc., 1980); *International Directory of Music Education Institutions* (Paris: UNESCO, 1968); *International Handbook of Universities*. 10th ed., edited by D.J. Aitken (New York: Stockton Press, 1986); *Studying Music in the Federal Republic of Germany* (Mainz: Schott, 1987); and *World of Learning* (London: Europa Press, 1986).

Despite hundreds of questionnaires transmitted by mail, endless phone calls to heads of music schools and departments, scores of follow-up letters, some sent through diplomatic pouch all over the world, and extensive research of related literature and reference materials, various countries still eluded clarification. Consequently some entries, those of Poland and Hungary, for example, are longer and more substantive than those of countries such as Argentina, Venezuela, or Portugal. This imbalance will be corrected in future editions of the work. I will be grateful to be informed of any errors or omissions found in this first edition.

Without friends, colleagues, and acquaintances who furnished me with all kinds of information, financial assistance for research trips, advice, and emotional support, this book would never have been written.

I would like to express my deepest gratitude to William E. Burgess and his company, Modoc Press, Inc., in Santa Monica, California, for designing the format of this reference book, helping to compile the data, and generously advising and guiding me through a number of difficult moments. Mr. Burgess and his colleague, Frank E. Lobaugh Jr., worked tirelessly to put vast amounts of material emanating from every corner of the globe into logical, clear order.

Further thanks are in order for my editors, Maribeth Payne and Michael Sander; my agent, Susan Zeckendorf; Mansour Ajami, Lois Anderson, Michael Beckerman, Gerard Béhague, Rina Harrison Birnbaum, George Bock, Christian Botha, May Brooks, Charles Capwell, Cecile Clayton, Richard Colwell, Constantine D. Constantinides, Douglas Crow, Monika Darron, Laurence Dreyfus, Emine Ayşegül Durakoğlu, Jon Eichenberger, John Eric Floreen, Kate and Hans Freyhan, Debbie Galant, Janice L. Gorn, R.I.P. Hayman, Jim and Jo Ann Hutcheson, Robert Jesselson, Jafran Jones, Ashenofi Kebede, Florence Koffler, Malena Kuss, John Laughton, Richard K. Levitz, Ming Fang Li, Weigang Li, William Lincer, Jan Maegaard, William P. Malm, Menachem Meir, Ignatius Mudzimba, Bruno Nettl, Lisa Pleskow, Jihad Racy, Annie Saulnier, Cynthia Schmidt, Sergiu Schwartz, The Soros Foundation, Simon Shaheen, Phillip Schuyler, Ruth Stone, Sridevi Upadhya, Helga Storck, William Street, Anderson Sutton, Maria Szwajger-Kułakowska, Susan Teicher, Donald Thompson, Ludmila Tschakalova-Verheyen, Witold Turant, Homer Ulrich, Ginni Walsh, Ray Wang, Mrs. James P. Warburg, Marvin Williamsen, and Adam Zemła. Lot Polish Airlines, Malev Hungarian Airlines, Finnair, and SAS generously awarded me travel grants to visit the music schools in the countries within their service areas. Finally, my husband, Bill Barrett, provided support and loving encouragement when I most needed it.

Nancy Uscher

INTRODUCTION

This *Guide* presents the histories, curricula, special programs, tuition, admission requirements, and other pertinent pieces of information about more than 750 music institutions throughout the world. It will be of use to high school students seeking information about undergraduate music study, undergraduates scrutinizing graduate music programs, and students interested in studying abroad on fellowships such as the Fulbright. It should be helpful to faculty performers and musicologists contemplating cultural exchanges with institutions of other countries. In addition, it will aid cultural and information attachés in consulates and embassies of those countries where specific information about cultural institutions is difficult to obtain.

The first section covers institutions in the United States, arranged alphabetically by state. The remainder of the book catalogs schools by countries arranged in alphabetical order. Schools included in the *Guide* are not evaluated for excellence or lack thereof. However, some institutions' entries include a *commentary* section, which is the author's note on an unusual, newly inaugurated, or noteworthy program of a particular conservatory or university music department.

Although every effort was expended to make all the entries, and the indexes derived from them, as complete as possible, institutions sometimes failed to report, for example, programs of study in which they are particularly strong. Such omissions will be rectified in future editions of the *Guide*.

Among countries throughout the world, the terms "faculty," "conservatory," and "school of music" denote several kinds of institutional entities. "Conservatory" in some European countries refers to the preparatory school to college, while in other places, including the United States, it is usually a college-level school interchangeable in designation with "music department" and "school of music." In the United States "music faculty" signifies the list of individuals who teach at a particular institution, whereas "faculty of music" in other parts of the world means the actual music department or music division of a university. In the United States, musicology, composition, and performance disciplines are often taught in the same university music department. However, in many parts of Europe there is a clear division of study. Performance is taught in the conservatory while the academic disciplines of music come under the aegis of the university, which has the sole authority to grant university degrees and recognized postgraduate status.

These differences made it necessary to vary from country to country the criteria for inclusion in the book. In the United States I have focused on institutions that offer at least a Master's degree in music, or that have more than 10 full-time members of the music faculty above the rank of instructor. Institutional lines between academic and practical music disciplines are especially difficult to discern in the United States and Canada. For this reason, I have included institutions emphasizing both. In most countries of Europe, however, the guidelines are different. A music school (academy, college, *Hochschule für Musik*), in the majority of European countries, exists specifically to prepare students for the professional life of a musician, while a university department (faculty) focuses on the academic disciplines of music in a context devoid of the professional or practical, performance-oriented goals of the music college or academy. As this book is directed to institutions training students for lives as professional musicians, university music divisions in those countries have not been included. Countries such as Liberia and Kenya have no university-level music schools, although other programs in which music plays a significant role have been included. In New Zealand, where there are no independent conservatories, university music faculties (departments) are listed. In Finland, Qatar, and Venezuela important research institutions have been included, although they do not fit the description of most of this work's entries. In Czechoslovakia and Finland, where the curricula of the middle schools, directly below the level of university, are closely connected to the music academies, they, too, have been included.

Generally, names of faculty members do not appear. To some this might seem a grave short-coming. After all, a school is only as good as the people teaching there, especially since one-to-one relationships between teacher and student figure so significantly in the study of music. However, listing teachers would be unrealistic in the light of year-to-year faculty turnover and the lengthy lead time required to compile a directory of this kind, which render any such listing immediately obsolete. Faculty information for the United States and Canada is already published in the College Music Society's *Directory of Music Faculties in Colleges and Universities, U.S. and Canada,* 1986–88 edition, updated biennially, or can be obtained by writing directly to the institutions of interest.

HOW TO USE THIS GUIDE

Arrangement

The main entries for institutions in the United States are arranged alphabetically within state and appear before entries for other countries throughout the world, ranging from Albania to Zimbabwe. Beginning page numbers for the main entries for all countries can be found by referring to the *Contents* on page vii.

Content

The various elements of the main entry are self-explanatory and appear only when the information is available: Chief Administrator, Accreditation, Enrollment (Music Majors), Music Faculty, Term System, Entrance Requirements, Admission Procedure, Music Degrees Offered, Music Degree Requirements, General Program Areas, Instruments Taught, Practice Facilities, Concert Facilities, Community Facilities, Concerts/Musical Activities, Music Library, Featured Programs, Performance Groups, Foreign Programs, Affiliated Programs, Costs, Financial Aid, Commentary.

Telephone numbers do not include the country code for international dialing. A list of these international codes appears in the Appendix. For those not shown, dial Operator for assistance. In some cases, particularly for European schools, a city code appears in parenthesis before the main telephone number. Telephone numbers vary in the form of presentation; they are printed here in the sequence and spacing as supplied by the institution. Additional telephone numbers and extensions are often appended to the main number.

Costs

The tuition fees and costs for room and board generally reflect those in effect for the 1986–87 school year. These expenses continue to rise each year and all institutions state that costs are subject to change without notice. A 5 to 10 percent annual increase in costs is not unusual.

Costs for institutions outside the United States are given in the local currency when available. U.S. equivalents fluctuate with the times and caution is recommended in attempting to arrive at actual costs. For Australia and Canada, amounts are expressed in Australian and Canadian dollars, respectively.

Indexes

This *Guide* includes three indexes. The *Institution Index* is a complete listing of every conservatory and school of music that appears in this *Guide*. It lists the school's department or school of music, and the geographic location.

The *Index of Program Areas* is an alphabetical listing by subject. It is designed to indicate the schools that offer study in particular subject areas in the field of music, based on the institutions' responses to questionnaires. Beneath each subject heading is an alphabetical listing of the institutions including the geographic location for each. Referral to the main entry under that location will yield the full information available about the school offering the program area.

The *Index of Instruments Taught* is an alphabetical listing of instruments taught by the schools and conservatories. The index includes individual instruments as well as the general term covering a family of instruments (i.e., trumpet as well as brass; viola as well as stringed instruments).

The
Schirmer
Guide to
Schools
of Music
and
Conservatories
Throughout
the
World

UNITED STATES

UNITED STATES

ALABAMA

University of Alabama
School of Music
University
Alabama 35486

Telephone. (205) 348-7110

Chief Administrator. Dr. Dennis C. Monk, Director.

The University of Alabama began classes in 1831 in response to the state legislature's call to "establish a seminary of learning." In April of 1865, Federal troops burned all but four buildings, and the campus lay dormant until 1871. Today, the University is a campus of 645 acres and enrolls more than 14,000 students annually. The university is situated in Tuscaloosa (population 127,000), 60 miles southwest of Birmingham and 100 miles northwest of Montgomery.

The program of the School of Music provides intensive professional training and offers the non-musician an introduction to music. It also offers all members of the University community the opportunity to participate in performing organizations.

Accreditation. Southern Association of Colleges and Schools; National Association of Schools of Music; National Council for Accreditation of Teacher Education.

Academic Information

Enrollment, Music Majors. (Total University) 14,005.

Music Faculty. 21.

Term System. Semester.

Entrance Requirements. Admission at the freshmen level is based on the probability of success as determined by high school grade point average used in combination with scores on the ACT; completion of 16 units including 12 academic required; audition on major instrument or voice.

Admission Procedure. Application with $15 nonrefundable fee to Admissions Office.

Music Degrees Offered. Bachelor of Music; Bachelor of Arts; Bachelor of Science; Master of Music; Master of Arts; Doctor of Musical Arts.

Music Degree Requirements. The School of Music offers the following degree programs: the Bachelor of Music in performance, composition, theory, arranging, and music therapy; the Bachelor of Arts in music and music administration. The degree Bachelor of Science in education is offered by the College of Education with majors in instrumental music education and vocal/choral music education. The music education programs satisfy academic requirements for the certificate to teach music in elementary and secondary schools. The baccalaureate programs require the completion of a minimum of 128 semester hours.

The School of Music offers programs leading to the Master of Music and the Doctor of Musical Arts degrees. The Master of Arts in music education is offered through the College of Education.

General Program Areas. Choral Music, Conducting, Music Administration, Music Education, Performance.

Instruments Taught. Bass, Bassoon, Clarinet, Euphonium, Flute, French Horn, Harpsichord, Oboe, Organ, Percussion, Piano, Saxophone, Trombone, Trumpet, Tuba, Viola, Violin, Violoncello, Voice.

Musical Facilities

Concert Facilities. Marian Gallaway Theatre, seating 338; Cadek Recital Hall.

Concerts/Musical Activities. The School of Music presents a regular series of concerts by faculty and students, University ensembles, and guest artists.

Music Library. The library contains the Byron Arnold Folksong Collection.

Special Programs

Performance Groups. Jazz Ensembles, Brass Ensemble, Alabama Brass Quintet, Cadek Trio, Capstone Wind Quintet, Piano Ensemble, Trombone Choir, Opera Theatre, Percussion Ensemble, Alabama Wind Ensemble, Concert Band, Million Dollar Marching Band, Symphonic Band, University Chorus, University Singers, University Symphony Orchestra, String Chamber Ensemble, Alabama Festival Chorus, Contemporary Music Ensemble.

Financial

Costs. Per academic year: Tuition in-state resident $1,-304, out-of-state $2,798. Private applied study fee $210 for music majors, $170 for non-majors. Room $1,000. Board $1,300.

Financial Aid. The School of Music has its own scholarship fund as well as several endowed scholarships which are awarded on the basis of performing or creative talent. Music students are also eligible for University financial aid. In addition to scholarships, students are eligible for Band and Orchestra Grants. These are awarded at the end of each semester and students need not make special application. A number of opportunities under the College Work-Study program are also available to music students. These include work in the music library and various secretarial and clerical jobs.

Alabama State University
School of Music
Montgomery
Alabama 36195

Telephone. (205) 293-4341

Chief Administrator. Dr. Laurence M. Hayes, Acting Dean.

Alabama State University was established in 1887. The campus is situated on a 40-acre site with 27 buildings in Montgomery, the capital of Alabama.

The objectives of the School of Music are to provide students with the necessary background in music theory, music history and literature, keyboard, and sight reading; to provide those students who are interested in teaching careers the requisite professional knowledge and skills, and to provide the foundation needed for a career in music business or performance.

Accreditation. Southern Association of Colleges and Schools; National Association of Schools of Music; National Council for Accreditation of Teacher Education.

Academic Information

Enrollment, Music Majors. (Total University) 3,629.

Music Faculty. 14.

Term System. Quarter.

Entrance Requirements. High school graduation with 16 units including 3 units of English and the remaining 13 from among mathematics, foreign language, science, and social science; ACT or SAT; audition required; tests related to musical achievement and knowledge of music theory; arrangements for auditions are made by the Dean of the School.

Admission Procedure. Application with supporting documents to Admissions Office.

Music Degrees Offered. Bachelor of Arts; Bachelor of Music Education; Master of Arts; Master of Music Education.

Music Degree Requirements. The Bachelor of Arts in music degree has areas of concentration in performance, theory, and history. The areas of specialization in performance are voice, keyboard, and orchestral instruments. The Bachelor of Music Education degree is designed for students who desire public school music teaching as a career. The degree program has areas of specialization in vocal/choral music and in instrumental music; it leads toward state certification for teaching in Alabama public schools. The baccalaureate degrees require the completion of 192 to 198 quarter hours.

The Master of Arts degree is offered in theory/composition, performance, and history/literature. A Master of Music Education degree is also offered. The degrees require the completion of 45 to 48 quarter hours consisting of a common core and 28 hours in the major subject and electives.

General Program Areas. Composition, Music Education, Music History, Music Literature, Music Theory, Performance.

Instruments Taught. Brass, Organ, Percussion, Piano, Stringed Instruments, Voice, Woodwinds.

Musical Facilities

Practice Facilities. Tullibody Hall has facilities for band and choir, classrooms, practice rooms, and a recital hall.

Concert Facilities. Recital Hall, seating 200; Thelma M. Glass Auditorium.

Concerts/Musical Activities. Student/faculty concerts and recitals.

Music Library. The Music Library and listening library are located in Tullibody Hall.

Special Programs

Featured Programs. The School of Music Summer Camp features marching band activities, flag corp instruction, percussion instrument drills, and a number of other musical activities.

Performance Groups. University Choir, Concert Choir, Male Glee Club, Women's Glee Club, Marching Band, Symphonic Band, University Orchestra, Woodwind Ensemble, Brass Ensemble, Percussion Ensemble, Jazz Band, String Ensemble, ROTC Band, Pep Band, Saxophone Ensemble, Trumpet Quartet, Jazz Combo.

Financial

Costs. Per academic year: Tuition in-state resident $960, out-of-state $1,920. Fees $75. Room and board $1,620.

Financial Aid. Financial aid is awarded on the bases of financial need and musical ability. Both institutional and state/federal aid available. Scholarship/financial aid application due August 15. Part-time employment and a College Work-Study program also available.

Auburn University
Department of Music
101 Goodwin Music Building
Auburn
Alabama 36849

Telephone. (205) 826-4164

Chief Administrator. Dr. Harold A. Kafer, Department Head.

Auburn University was chartered in 1856 by the Methodist Church. It became part of the State University System in 1872. It enrolls over 16,000 students and has a faculty of over 1,100. The 1,872-acre campus includes 73 major buildings in the city of Auburn (population 28,000), 120 miles southeast of Birmingham.

The major goal of the Department of Music is to train students in performance. The Department offers programs leading to the bachelor's and master's degrees.

Accreditation. Southern Association of Colleges and Schools; National Association of Schools of Music.

Academic Information

Music Faculty. Full-time 22, part-time 1.

Term System. Quarter. 10-week summer session. Academic year October to June.

Entrance Requirements. High school graduation or equivalent with 2.5 minimum GPA and 16 units including English, mathematics, social studies, science, and foreign languages; ACT score of 18 or higher; audition required.

Admission Procedure. Application with supporting documents to Admissions Office; contact Department for audition.

Music Degrees Offered. Bachelor of Music; Bachelor of Arts; Bachelor of Music Education; Master of Music.

Music Degree Requirements. The bachelor degrees require the completion of approximately 200 quarter hours including requirements in general education, core curriculum, and the major concentration. The master's degree requires a minimum of 48 quarter hours. Recitals are required for the degrees.

General Program Areas. Church Music, Composition, Jazz Studies, Music Education, Music Theory, Performance, Piano Pedagogy.

Instruments Taught. Brass, Organ, Percussion, Piano, Stringed Instruments, Voice, Woodwinds.

Musical Facilities

Practice Facilities. 3 organs (1 Schantz, 2 Hammond). 26 practice rooms. 26 practice pianos (Hamilton); 1 grand piano reserved for piano majors.

Concert Facilities. Concert Hall, seating 1,275.

Concerts/Musical Activities. Recitals, large and small ensembles; 130 performances per year.

Music Library. Music materials are housed in the main University library. Listening facilities (stereo).

Financial

Costs. Per academic year: Tuition in-state resident $1,284, out-of-state $2,937. Room $1,350.

Financial Aid. Both institutional and federal/state financial aid available.

Jacksonville State University
Department of Music
Mason Hall
Jacksonville
Alabama 36265

Telephone. (205) 231-5781

Chief Administrator. Dr. James Fairleigh, Department Head.

Jacksonville State University, located in northeast Alabama, primarily serves the citzens of that area, with an enrollment of 5,355 students. It was established by the Alabama Legislature in 1883 as Jacskonville State Normal School, a two-year college for elementary teacher training. For many years the college was located in downtown Jacksonville and in 1908 moved to its present location, a 150-acre campus with 45 buildings on the northern edge of the city. In 1929, the institution became a four-year state teacher's college and in 1957 the name was changed to Jacksonville State College. University status was achieved in 1966.

Jacksonville, with a population of 13,000, is 100 miles from Atlanta (GA) and 75 miles from Birmingham. Anniston, 12 miles from the campus, is served by AMTRAK, Atlantic Southeast Airways, Greyhound and Continental Trailways bus lines.

The goals of the Department of Music are to provide balanced curricula for the graduate and undergraduate degrees in music with emphasis in music education and/ or performance; to provide an adequate curriculum for music minors emphasizing basic music fundamentals and applied music; to provide introductory elective courses and playing opportunities to all university students.

Accreditation. Southern Association of Colleges and Schools; National Association of Schools of Music; National Council for Accreditation of Teacher Education.

Academic Information

Enrollment, Music Majors. Undergraduate 153, graduate 27. Foreign students 2.

Music Faculty. Total 18 (all full-time).

Term System. Semester. Summer session.

Entrance Requirements. Graduation from an approved high school with a total of 15 units including 3 English, 1 mathematics, 1 laboratory science, 1 social studies. ACT or SAT. GED accepted. *For foreign students:* TOEFL (minimum score 500) must be on file before application materials may be submitted; mini-

3

mum deposit of $1,000 must be made with the University.

The regular University entrance requirements apply to the candidate for any degree offered by the Department of Music, plus special placement examination in applied music and music theory, given at the time of matriculation.

Admission Procedure. Apply at least 3 months before beginning of term of enrollment. Submit completed application with nonrefundable $10 fee and complete high school transcript. Students transferring from a junior college may have an unlimited number of hours accepted but must earn a minimum of 64 semester hours in residence at Jacksonville State University. Early admission, early decision available. Advanced placement through CLEP, AP, and Credit by Challenge. Audition before professors in major applied music area required before becoming music major and studying an instrument.

Music Degrees Offered. Bachelor of Science in Music Education; Bachelor of Arts in Music Performance; Bachelor of Arts in Music with a required minor in an academic area outside of music. The B.S. in Music Education fulfills the requirements for the professional certificate to teach music in the public schools in Alabama on both the elementary and secondary levels. The B.A. in Music Performance allows a student to stress various music subjects in preparation for a career in professional performance. Students pursuing this degree must consult the department head for academic advisement. The B.A. in Music with a non-music minor offers a program designed for the study of music within a liberal arts curriculum.

Music Degree Requirements. The Bachelor of Arts degree with a major in music requires the completion of 128 semester hours of which 44 are in the major; the Bachelor of Arts degree with a major in music performance (piano, vocal, brass, woodwind, percussion) requires the completion of 136 semester hours, of which 58 are in the major and 28 in supportive music courses.

Courses in applied music include individual and class instruction in voice, piano, or band and orchestral instruments. The student may elect the area of individual instruction best adapted to individual needs. Class instruction is designed to cover all phases and activities of vocal and instrumental music in order that the student may receive a practical and broad musical experience. All students majoring in music are required to appear in recital performance.

A student who is not a major or minor may take courses if qualified. Entrance is determined by a placement test prior to the student's registration.

General Program Areas. Applied Music, Conducting, Ensemble Music, Music Education, Music History, Music Theory.

Instruments Taught. Bassoon, Clarinet, Flute, French Horn, Oboe, Organ, Percussion, Piano, Saxophone, Trombone, Trumpet, Tuba, Voice.

Musical Facilities

Practice Facilities. One organ available on campus (local churches used for organ instruction and practice); 3 practice rooms for percussionists; 40 practice pianos (upright models of Yamaha, Baldwin); total of 60 practice rooms available.

Concert Facilities. Performance Center on campus has an audience capacity of 300.

Community Facilities. Local churches are used for organ instruction and practice.

Music Library. Music holdings: 7,500 volumes; 4,600 scores; 40 periodicals; 400 microfiche; 6,500 recordings (music holdings are housed in the central library; the music department maintains a separate library of recordings). Listening facilities located in the music building include 8 cassette decks, 8 stereo turntables, 8 compact disc players. Central library staff of 35 includes a music librarian.

Special Programs

Performance Groups. The Department of Music supports a 300-member band (The Marching Southerners) that enjoys a distinguished reputation throughout the southeastern United States. The Department also supports a 100-member chorus (The J.S.U. A Capella Choir).

Affiliated Programs. Dual degree program available.

Financial

Costs. Per academic year: Tuition in-state resident $950, non-resident $1,350. Room $550 to $700. Board $950.

Financial Aid. 50% of student body receives some form of financial aid. 75 music scholarships ranging from $400 to $800 per year; apply by March 31. College Work-Study program.

University of Montevallo
Department of Music
Station 291
Montevallo
Alabama 35115

Telephone. (205) 665-6030

Chief Administrator. Joan Cowan, Department Head.

The University of Montevallo is a state institution with an enrollment of over 2,500 students. It was established as the Alabama Girls' Industrial School in 1896. The name was changed to Alabama College in 1924 and it became a coeducational institution in 1955. The present name was adopted in 1969. The 164-acre campus has 74 buildings, including 7 residence halls. Montevallo (population 3,500) is located near the center of the state, 32 miles south of Birmingham and 68 miles north of Montgomery.

The Department of Music offers programs in music education and performance.

Accreditation. Southern Association of Colleges and Schools; National Association of Schools of Music.

Academic Information

Enrollment, Music Majors. Undergraduate 75, graduate 5. 4 foreign students.

Music Faculty. Full-time 13, part-time 12.

Term System. Semester. Summer session.

Entrance Requirements. High school graduation or equivalent; completion of 15 units, including 4 English, 2 mathematics, 2 laboratory science, 4 social studies; ACT required; GRE required for graduate school. TOEFL of 500 or better required of foreign students plus affidavit of financial support, completed health form, and transcript of U.S. equivalent of secondary school. Audition required on an informal basis; more formal for scholarship assistance.

Admission Procedure. Application due 10 days prior to registration with $10 nonrefundable fee.

Music Degrees Offered. Bachelor of Music; Bachelor of Arts; Bachelor of Science; Bachelor of Music Education; Master of Music.

Music Degree Requirements. The bachelor degrees require the completion of a core curriculum, general education courses, and a major concentration for a total of 138 semester hours. The Master of Music requires the completion of 33 semester hours of study.

General Program Areas. Choral Music, Music Education, Pedagogy, Performance.

Instruments Taught. Brass, Harpsichord, Organ, Percussion, Piano, Stringed Instruments, Voice, Woodwinds.

Musical Facilities

Practice Facilities. 2 practice organs (Flentrop, Holtkamp). Special practice facilities for percussionists. 50 practice pianos (Everett, Knight, Yamaha); 4 grand pianos reserved for piano majors. Electronic music studio; LeBaron sound booth with recording facilities.

Concert Facilities. Recital Hall, seating 245; Palmer Auditorium, 1,300; Reynolds Theater, 150.

Music Library. 4,000 scores; 13 music periodicals; 2,116 recordings. Listening facilities (2 cassette decks; 6 stereo turntables, 2 compact disc players). Other music materials housed in the main University library.

Financial

Costs. Per academic year: Tuition in-state resident $1,092, out-of-state $1,904. Fees $110. Room $1,062. Board $1,160.

Financial Aid. 25 to 30 music scholarships ranging from $300 to full tuition. Scholarship application due 6 months prior to admission. Other sources of financial aid include grants, loans, part-time employment, and a College Work-Study program.

Samford University
School of Music
800 South Lakeshore Drive
Birmingham
Alabama 35229

Telephone. (205) 870-2851

Chief Administrator. Dr. L. Gene Black, Dean.

Samford University is a privately supported university owned and operated by the Alabama Baptist State Convention. It was founded in 1841 at Marion, Alabama and moved to Birmingham in 1887. The present site was occupied in 1957. The University offers 20 degree programs in seven colleges. An International Study Centre in London, England, is part of the University.

The School of Music offers bachelor's and master's degree programs in music within a liberal arts curriculum. It considers its major strengths to be in voice, piano, church music, and music education.

Accreditation. Southern Association of Colleges and Schools; National Association of Schools of Music.

Academic Information

Enrollment, Music Majors. Full-time 77 men, 82 women. 1 foreign student.

Music Faculty. Full-time 17, part-time 10. Artists in residence: Magnolia String Quartet.

Term System. Semester. Academic year from September to May.

Entrance Requirements. Accredited high school graduation or equivalent; completion of 16 units including 4 English, 8 in other academic areas; ACT score of 16 or SAT combined score of 750 required; audition required in performance area; theory placement examination; interview.

Admission Procedure. For admission procedure, contact the School of Music.

Music Degrees Offered. Bachelor of Music; Bachelor of Arts; Master of Music; Master of Music Education.

Music Degree Requirements. The Bachelor of Music degree requires the completion of a liberal arts core and a major concentration for a total of approximately 140 semester hours. Concentrations are offered in performance, church music, music education, and theory/composition. The Bachelor of Arts degree is offered with a major in music. Specific baccalaureate requirements include piano proficiency and a recital.

The Master of Music and Master of Music Education degrees require the completion of 34 semester hours with courses primarily in music education, and/or religion. Music history, analytical techniques, oral examination, and comprehensive examination are required.

General Program Areas. Church Music, Composition, Conducting, Music Education, Music Theory, Performance.

Instruments Taught. Baritone, Bass, Carillon, Clarinet, Flute, French Horn, Harpsichord, Organ, Percussion, Piano, Piccolo, Saxophone, Trombone, Trumpet, Tuba, Viola, Violin, Violoncello, Voice.

Musical Facilities

Practice Facilities. 30 practice rooms. 5 organs (Aeolian-Skinner, Holtkamp, Schlicker, 2 von Beckerath). 30 practice pianos (28 Baldwin, 2 Yamaha); 2 grand pianos reserved for piano majors. Studios for conducting, carillon, organ.

Concert Facilities. Concert Hall, seating 2,800; Reid Chapel, 700; Recital Hall, 180.

Concerts/Musical Activities. 40 to 50 concerts per semester including chamber music, solo performances, operas, orchestra concerts.

Music Library. 2,935 scores; 159 audiovisual titles; 17 microform titles; 4,774 phonograph recordings; 1,899 audiocassettes. 25 listening stations. Special collections include: Lorenz Hymnal Collection; American and British hymnals; gospel hymn collection; sacred tunebooks. The Birmingham City Library, Birmingham Southern College Library, and the University of Alabama in Birmingham Library are other resources for music students.

Special Programs

Foreign Programs. London Study Centre (England), owned and operated by Samford University.

Financial

Costs. Per academic year: Tuition $6,300. General music fees $400. Room $1,100. Board $1,400.

Financial Aid. Financial aid is awarded on the basis of academic merit, financial need, and musical ability. Both institutional and state/federal aid available. 90 music students receive some form of aid (average award $500). Financial aid/scholarship application due February 1. College Work-Study program available.

Commentary

Alexander technique workshops, outside the curricular framework, take place at the University.

Troy State University
Department of Music
School of Fine Arts
Troy
Alabama 36082

Telephone. (205) 566-3000

Chief Administrator. Dr. John M. Long, Chairman.

Troy State University began as a normal school in 1887 and became a four-year college in 1929. It achieved university status in 1967. The 433-acre campus is situated one mile from the center of the city of Troy and 50 miles from the city of Montgomery, the state capital.

The Department of Music is a unit in the School of Fine Arts. Courses are offered to the general university student body as well as a minor in music (for non-teaching degrees only) and a major in music education.

Accreditation. Southern Association of Colleges and Schools.

Academic Information

Enrollment, Music Majors. (Total University) 6,423.

Music Faculty. 12.

Term System. Quarter.

Entrance Requirements. High school graduation or equivalent; completion of 15 units including 3 English; minimum ACT score 13 required.

Admission Procedure. Application with nonrefundable $10 fee to Admissions Office.

Music Degrees Offered. Bachelor of Music Education.

Music Degree Requirements. The Bachelor of Music Education is offered with emphases in comprehensive nursery-grade 12; instrumental music and comprehensive nursery-grade 12; vocal-choral music.

General Program Areas. Conducting, Music Education, Music History, Music Theory.

Instruments Taught. Bass, Bassoon, Clarinet, Euphonium, Flute, Horn, Oboe, Organ, Percussion, Piano, Saxophone, Trombone, Trumpet, Tuba, Viola, Violin, Violoncello, Voice.

Musical Facilities

Practice Facilities. John Maloy Long Hall is a modern music support facility.

Concert Facilities. Charles Bunyan Smith Hall Auditorium, seating 1,228.

Concerts/Musical Activities. Student concerts and recitals.

Music Library. The Troy State University Library supports the music programs of the Department.

Special Programs

Featured Programs. The National Band Association Hall of Fame is housed on the campus.

Performance Groups. University Band, University Choir, Collegiate Singers

Financial

Costs. Per academic year: Tuition in-state resident $1,086, out-of-state $1,629. Room $738. Board $1,117.

Financial Aid. Financial aid is awarded on the basis of need. Both institutional and state/federal aid available. Financial aid applications accepted on a rolling basis. Part-time employment and a College Work-Study program available.

ALASKA

University of Alaska
Music Department
312 Tanana Drive
Fairbanks
Alaska 99775

Telephone. (907) 474-7555
Chief Administrator. Dr. David A. Stech, Department Head.

In 1917, the Territorial Legislature created the Alaska Agricultural College and School of Mines. In 1922, the College opened with six faculty members and six students. In 1935, the college became the University of Alaska and in 1974 a Tanana Valley Community College was established on the university campus. The University, now part of a statewide system, has expanded to three colleges and four professional schools. Degrees are currently offered in 65 major areas. The campus is located four miles from Fairbanks on a 2,250 site. The city of Fairbanks is 100 miles south of the Arctic Circle.

The Department of Music offers programs for those desiring a broad liberal education, preparation for teaching training with sufficient time to develop skills in performance, and intense professional training in music performance. As the University is part of large statewide systems, students often have access to facilities such as free computer time. The Department specializes in preparing teachers for small rural communities.

Accreditation. Northwest Association of Schools and Colleges; National Association of Schools of Music.

Academic Information

Enrollment, Music Majors. Full-time 256 men, 248 women.
Music Faculty. Full-time 12, part-time 7.
Term System. Semester.
Entrance Requirements. High school graduation with 11 units including 3 English, 2 mathematics, 2 laboratory science, 2 social studies; ACT required; audition required.

Admission Procedure. Application due August 1 or December 1 with nonrefundable $20 fee.
Music Degrees Offered. Bachelor of Music; Bachelor of Arts; Master of Arts; Master of Arts in Teaching.
Music Degree Requirements. The Bachelor of Music degree requires the completion of 127 hours; the Bachelor of Arts degree 130 hours, including specific general education curriculum and the major and minor complex of courses. The Master of Arts degree requires the completion of 30 hours; the Master of Arts in Teaching degree requires 36 hours.
General Program Areas. Ethnomusicology, Music Education, Music History, Music Theory, Performance.
Instruments Taught. Bass, Clarinet, Cornet, Flute, French Horn, Guitar, Oboe, Organ, Piano, Saxophone, Trombone, Trumpet, Tuba, Viola, Violin, Violoncello.

Musical Facilities

Practice Facilities. 2 organs (1 Gress-Miles pipe organ, 1 Rodgers electronic). Percussion-equipped practice room. 10 practice pianos; 2 grand pianos reserved for piano majors.
Concerts/Musical Activities. Full schedule of performances during each semester; Associated Student Body sponsors concerts several times per year.
Music Library. Holdings in the Elmer E. Rasmuson Library consist of more than 1 million volumes, including books, periodicals, serial titles, government documents, microfilm, microcards, microfiche, maps, phonograph recordings, and cassettes. Listening facilities in reserve room of main library; Department has some listening equipment for ear training. Special collections include the Fairbanks Symphony Association Orchestra Collection.

Financial

Costs. Per academic year: Tuition in-state resident $960, out-of-state $2,520. Practice room fee $120. Room and board $2,420.
Financial Aid. 6 music students receive scholarships ranging from $250 to $1,000 (average $400). Scholarship applications due January 15 and March 15. Part-time

employment available.

Commentary

The University of Alaska uses its unique location to enhance the study of Alaskan ethnomusicology, a major for the master's degree. The curriculum for the M.A.T. is designed primarily to prepare public school teachers for jobs in Alaskan rural areas. Neither harp nor percussion is presently taught, although the department hopes to increase the offerings in performance.

ARIZONA

University of Arizona
School of Music
Tucson
Arizona 85721

Telephone. (602) 621-1655

Chief Administrator. Dr. David G. Woods, Director.

The University of Arizona was established in 1885. It has an annual enrollment of 30,000 students. The purpose of the University is to provide the inhabitants of Arizona with the means of acquiring a thorough knowledge of the various branches of literature, science, and the arts. The University has 12 colleges. The 320-acre campus has 131 buildings in the city of Tucson which is located 65 miles north of the Arizona-Mexican border.

The primary goal of the School of Music is to create valuable educational opportunities on and off the campus for the training of performers, teachers at all levels of instruction, scholars, and technicians. The School seeks to provide a broadbased experience for each student.

Accreditation. North Central Association of Colleges and Schools; National Association of Schools of Music.

Academic Information

Term System. Semester. 3 summer sessions (one 3-week presession, two 5-week terms).

Entrance Requirements. High school graduation with rank in upper half of class; completion of 16 units including 4 English, 2 mathematics, 1 laboratory science; 2 social studies, 7 electives; state residents ACT minimum 21 or SAT minimum 930 required; nonresidents ACT minimum 23 or SAT minimum 1010 required; no audition, but entrance exams are required.

Admission Procedure. Application due one month prior to registration with $10 fee (refundable to out-of-state applicants only).

Music Degrees Offered. Bachelor of Music; Bachelor of Arts; Master of Music; Doctor of Musical Arts; Doctor of Philosophy.

Music Degree Requirements. The Bachelor of Music degree is offered with concentrations in performance, music education, jazz studies, and theory/composition. The Bachelor of Arts degree is offered with the major in music. The bachelor's degrees require the completion of a general education curriculum and a major concentration for a total of 122 to 132 semester hours. Specific requirements in the major include class piano, musical skills and structure, music literature, 20th century music (form and structure), history of Western music, plus courses specific to area of specialization.

The Master of Music degree requires the completion of 30 semester hours of study. The degrees Doctor of Musical Arts and Doctor of Philosophy require 90 semester hours of study.

General Program Areas. Composition, Jazz Studies, Music Education, Music History, Music Theory, Performance.

Instruments Taught. Baritone, Bass, Bassoon, Clarinet, Flute, Guitar, Harp, Harpsichord, Horn, Oboe, Organ, Percussion, Piano, Saxophone, Trombone, Trumpet, Tuba, Viola, Violin, Violoncello, Voice.

Musical Facilities

Practice Facilities. 23 practice rooms. 2 organs (MacDowell, Tucson organ builder). 3 percussion-equipped practice rooms. 42 practice pianos (35 uprights, 7 grands); 5 pianos reserved for piano majors. 2 electronic music studios; recording studio; piano laboratory.

Concert Facilities. Crowder Hall.

Concerts/Musical Activities. Over 250 concerts and recitals presented each academic year by faculty, visiting artists, and students.

Music Library. 55,152 scores; 27,000 books; 65,562 pieces of sheet music; 210 periodicals; 2,000 microfiche; 26,500 recordings. Listening facilities (16 cassette, 16 stereo). Special collections include: popular sheet music; Gutkind and Medicus collections of early flute music; National Flute Association; International Trombone Association Resource Library; music relating to Mexico-U.S. border. Most books and periodicals housed in main University library.

Special Programs

Featured Programs. Center for Music and Technology; Music Experience Laboratory Program for Children.

Performance Groups. Various instrumental and vocal ensembles; orchestra; band.

Financial

Costs. Per academic year: Tuition in-state resident $1,136, out-of-state $4,260. Room $1,023. Board $1,529.

Financial Aid. 301 scholarships ranging from $50 to $8,000. Applications for scholarships accepted on a rolling basis. Other sources of financial aid include institutional grants, state/federal loans, part-time employment, and a College Work-Study program.

Commentary

A new Ph.D. in Music Education has been proposed at University of Arizona and is awaiting final approval.

Arizona State University
School of Music
Tempe
Arizona 85287

Telephone. (602) 965-9011

Chief Administrator. Dr. George E. Umberson, Director.

Arizona State University was founded in 1885 as a Normal School. It now enrolls over 30,000 students annually. The main campus comprises more than 600 acres near the heart of metropolitan Phoenix in the city of Tempe (population 140,000).

The School of Music offers curricula which provide a conceptual understanding of the components of music—sound, rhythm, melody, harmony, texture, and form—and their interrelationships. The programs also provide opportunities for students to try out the different roles of listener, performer, composer, scholar, and teacher. The curricula cover a music repertory from all cultures and historical periods.

Accreditation. North Central Association of Colleges and Schools; National Association of Schools of Music; National Council for Accreditation of Teacher Education.

Academic Information

Enrollment, Music Majors. (Total University) 30,342.

Music Faculty. 60.

Term System. Semester. 3 summer sessions.

Entrance Requirements. High school graduation with rank in upper 50 percent; completion of 16 units including 3 English, 2 mathematics, 2 science, 2 foreign language, 2 social studies, 5 electives; ACT or SAT; audition in primary performing medium required.

Admission Procedure. Application with supporting documents to Office of Admissions; out-of-state students include nonrefundable $10 fee.

Music Degrees Offered. Bachelor of Music; Bachelor of Arts; Master of Music; Master of Arts; Master of Education; Doctor of Musical Arts; Doctor of Philosophy; Doctor of Education.

Music Degree Requirements. The Bachelor of Music degree program includes fields of specialization in choral-general music, instrumental music, performance, music therapy, and theory and composition. Choral-general music and instrumental majors are provided for students wishing to meet certification requirements for teaching in the public schools. The Bachelor of Arts degree is offered with a major in music. It requires the completion of 50 credit hours of music courses. All baccalaureate degrees require the completion of a minimum of 126 credit hours.

The Master of Arts degree provides advanced studies in history and literature of music. The Master of Music degree has majors in the fields of performance (voice, keyboard, instrumental, piano accompanying, pedagogy, music theatre musical direction, choral music, and theory and composition. The Master of Education degree in secondary education (with focus on choral, general, or instrumental music), the Doctor of Musical Arts degree, the Doctor of Education degree in secondary education (music education), and the Doctor of Philosophy degree in secondary education (music) are offered in cooperation with the College of Education.

General Program Areas. Choral Music, Composition, Instrumental Music, Music History, Music Literature, Music Theory, Music Therapy, Performance.

Instruments Taught. Brass, Organ, Percussion, Piano, Stringed Instruments, Voice, Woodwinds.

Musical Facilities

Concert Facilities. Gammage Center for the Performing Arts Auditorium, seating 3,000; recital hall, 125.

Concerts/Musical Activities. Student/faculty concerts and recitals; visiting artists.

Music Library. The Music Library contains a large collection of music scores, recordings, and music reference materials, plus listening facilities for individuals and groups. Special collections include the Wayne King Collection; the Pablo Casals International Cello Library (not his personal library); and the International Percussion Reference Library.

Special Programs

Performance Groups. Chamber Orchestra, Symphony Orchestra, Choral Union, Concert Choir, University Choir, Men's Chorus, Women' Chorus, Marching Band, Concert Band, Chamber Music Ensembles, Collegium Musicum, New Music Ensemble, Brass Choir, Percussion Ensemble, Stage Band.

Financial

Costs. Per academic year: Tuition in-state resident $1,-136; out-of-state $4,260. Private music instruction $80 (1/2 hour of instruction weekly); instrument rental $20. Room and board $2,400.

Financial Aid. Financial aid is awarded on the basis of academic merit, financial need, musical ability. Institutional and state/federal aid available. 30 music scholarships (average award $990). Financial aid/scholarship applications due March 1. Part-time employment and a College Work-Study program available.

Commentary

Arizona State University has attractive buildings to house the activities of its School of Music. The Gammage Center for the Performing Arts, one of the last creations of Frank Lloyd Wright, contains an auditorium modeled after Bayreuth's Wagnerian Theatre and a recital hall which opens into a rooftop courtyard. The Music Building, an eight-level circular structure, was designed to complement Wright's structural concept.

Northern Arizona University
Music Department
College of Creative Arts
Flagstaff
Arizona 86001

Telephone. (602) 523-9011
Chief Administrator. P. Curry, Departmental Chair.

Northern Arizona University was founded in 1899 as a normal school, became a four-year institution in 1925, and achieved University status in 1966. The 698-acre campus is located in the city of Flagstaff, 80 miles from Grand Canyon National Park.

The purpose of the Music Department is to provide students with training in general musicianship and aesthetic awareness. It also seeks to prepare students for traditional performance and teaching careers, alternative careers, or for graduate study.

Accreditation. North Central Association of Colleges and Schools; National Association of Schools of Music; National Council for Accreditation of Teacher Education.

Academic Information

Enrollment, Music Majors. (Total University) 10,393.
Music Faculty. 22.
Term System. Semester. 2 summer sessions.
Entrance Requirements. High school graduation with rank in upper 50 percent; completion of 16 academic units; ACT or SAT; audition required.
Admission Procedure. Application with supporting documents and nonrefundable $10 fee to Admissions Office.

Music Degrees Offered. Bachelor of Music; Bachelor of Music Education; Bachelor Science.

Music Degree Requirements. The Bachelor of Music degree is offered with majors in vocal performance, instrumental performance, music history and literature, choral music education, and instrumental music education. The degree requires the completion of 125 semester hours including the University liberal studies program of 44 semester hours. The Bachelor of Music Education degree is offered with emphases in choral music education or instrumental music education. Education courses totaling 25 hours including student teaching are also required for this degree. The Bachelor of Science degree in secondary or elementary education with music emphasis is also available. A Bachelor of Science program in arts management with music emphasis is also offered. This program, administered by the Department of Humanities and Religious Studies, prepares students for management of orchestras, choral societies, and other music organizations and companies.

General Program Areas. Arts Management, Choral Music Education, Instrumental Music Education, Music Education, Music History, Music Literature, Music Theory, Performance.

Instruments Taught. Baritone Horn, Bass, Bassoon, Clarinet, Flute, French Horn, Guitar, Harp, Oboe, Organ, Percussion, Piano, Saxophone, Trombone, Trumpet, Tuba, Viola, Violin, Violoncello, Voice.

Musical Facilities

Practice Facilities. The Creative Arts Center houses the music studios, rehearsal rooms, classrooms, and workrooms.

Concert Facilities. Creative Arts Theatre, seating 360; Ardrey Auditorium, 1,500.

Concerts/Musical Activities. Student/faculty concerts and recitals; visiting artists.

Music Library. Media Center has collections of phonograph recordings, audiocassettes, tapes, books, and scores. Listening facilities.

Special Programs

Performance Groups. University Orchestra, Flagstaff Symphony, Wind Ensemble, Symphonic Band, Marching Band, Pep Band, University Chorale, University Singers, Oratorio Choir, Flagstaff Chorale, Opera Theater, String Ensemble, Woodwind Ensemble, Brass Ensemble, Percussion Ensembles, Piano Ensemble, Vocal Chamber Ensemble, Vocal Jazz Ensemble, Vocal Show Ensemble.

Financial

Costs. Per academic year: Tuition in-state resident $1,-136, out-of-state $3,692. Room $970. Board $1,430.

Financial Aid. Scholarship awards are available from the College of Creative Arts. Scholarship/financial aid application due April 15. Sources of financial aid include

institutional scholarships, grants, loans, and work programs.

ARKANSAS

University of Arkansas
Department of Music
201 Fine Arts Annex
Fayetteville
Arkansas 72701

Telephone. (501) 575-4701

Chief Administrator. James R. Greeson, Chairman.

The University of Arkansas was established with a public land-grant act of the U.S. Congress which was accepted by the General Assembly of the State in 1871. The University currently enrolls 12,826 students.

The J. William Fulbright College of Arts and Sciences, consisting of 21 departments and 10 interdisciplinary programs, is committed to provide a broad, liberal education to all students within the University community, and to furnish specialized knowledge at the upper division and graduate levels.

The University of Arkansas campus is situated on 351 acres and includes 149 buildings. Fayetteville has a population of 36,000 and is served by air and bus transportation.

The Department of Music provides studies in performance, music history and literature, theory, composition, and music education. Both the Bachelor and Master's degrees are offered.

Accreditation. Southern Association of Colleges and Schools; National Association of Schools of Music; National Council for Accreditation of Teacher Education.

Academic Information

Enrollment, Music Majors. 122 undergraduate; 21 graduate.

Music Faculty. Full-time 25, part-time 4.

Term System. Semester. Summer session.

Entrance Requirements. Undergraduate: Graduation from a state-accredited high school with a grade point average of at least 2.50 (on a 4.00 grading system) or an ACT composite score of at least 18 or an SAT score of at least 770-800; completion of 4 units English, 3 social studies, 3 natural sciences (must include at least 2 years to be chosen from biology, chemistry, and physics), 3 mathematics (at least 1 year of algebra and 1 year from among algebra, geometry, trigonometry, precalculus, or calculus). Graduate: Baccalaureate degree from an accredited university with cumulative grade point average of 2.70 or above for all coursework attempted prior to receipt of the baccalaureate degree or a 3.20 cumulative grade point average on the last 60 hours of coursework attempted prior to receipt of the baccalaureate degree.

To achieve junior standing in the curriculum leading to the Bachelor of Arts degree with a major in Music and the Bachelor of Music degree, the student must have completed 56 hours and must have maintained a cumulative grade point average of C in all music courses (with the exception of ensemble) by the end of the fourth semester. The student must also have earned a grade point average of not less than B in the major applied field of study during the sophomore year. All students majoring in music must pass a piano proficiency examination upon entering the University of Arkansas or must register in piano class until this requirement is met.

Admission Procedure. Undergraduate: Apply to Office of Admissions with completed application, transcripts, and $15 nonrefundable application fee. Foreign students whose native language is not English must submit a TOEFL score of 550 or above if they have not completed grades 10-12 at a U.S. accredited high school. Credit established by CLEP examination will be applied to any degree program. The Director of Admissions shall determine the amount of transfer credit awarded. Graduate: Apply to Graduate School Admissions Office with completed application, $15 nonrefundable application fee, and all transcripts. All students seeking admission to the program of Master of Music must show evidence of satisfactory proficiency in aural and written theory, and in music history and literature. This shall be done by means of GRE music scores and in aural and written theory and history examination administered by the department. Applicants in applied music will present a repertoire (instrumental or vocal) corresponding to that required for the Bachelor of Music degree.

13

Music Degrees Offered. Bachelor of Music; Bachelor of Science in Education with a major in Music Education; Bachelor of Arts with a major in Music; Master of Music; Master of Education in Music Education.

Music Degree Requirements. The major leading to a Bachelor of Music degree requires a minimum of 90 semester hours in all major emphases except voice performance and piano accompanying to allow for 9 and 6 hours respectively in 2 additional foreign languages appropriate to vocal repertoire.

The Departmental Honors Program in music provides upper-division undergraduate students with an opportunity to participate formally in scholarly music activities. Honors candidates carry out independent study and research under the guidance of the music faculty and participate in special honors classes and seminars. The student may select one of the four major areas of music concentration: Performance, Music History and Literature, Theory, or Composition.

The Master of Music degree requires the completion of 36 semester hours. Required courses are dependent upon the program of study.

General Program Areas. Applied Music, Ensemble, Music Education, Music History, Music Literature, Music Pedagogy and Techniques, Theory.

Instruments Taught. Alto Saxophone, Baritone, Bass, Bassoon, Clarinet, Cornet, Flute, French Horn, Harpsichord, Oboe, Organ, Percussion, Piano, Recorder, Trombone, Trumpet, Tuba, Viola, Violin, Violoncello, Voice.

Musical Facilities

Practice Facilities. 4 organs available; 2 practice rooms for percussionists; 30 practice pianos (6 practice grands; others upright). Electronic music and piano laboratories; 3 harpsichord practice rooms.

Concert Facilities. Fine Arts Concert Hall with audience capacity of 350; Arkansas Union Ballroom, 1,000; Arkansas Union Theatre, 300; Center for Continuing Education, 500.

Music Library. Music students use the Fine Arts Library and Audiovisual Library. The Department maintains orchestra, choral, opera, and band music libraries. Other music holdings are housed in the main library.

Financial

Costs. Per academic year: Tuition undergraduate in-state resident $1,000, out-of-state $2,512; graduate in-state resident $1,100, out-of-state $2,360. Music maintenance fee $20 per semester. Room and board $1,133 to $1,163 per semester; off-campus lodging ranges $150 to $300 per month.

Financial Aid. Scholarships and financial aid in the categories of grants, work, and loans are available.

Arkansas State University
Department of Music
College of Fine Arts
P.O. Box 779
State University
Arkansas 72467

Telephone. (501) 972-2094
Chief Administrator. Dr. William D. Holmes, Chairman.

Arkansas State University developed from one of the four state agricultural schools established in 1909 by an act of the Arkansas General Assembly. The institution opened as a vocational high school in 1910 and was reorganized as a junior college in 1918. The name of the institution was changed in 1925 to State Agricultural and Mechanical College and in 1933 to Arkansas State College. The current name was adopted in 1967. The campus occupies an area of 800 acres in the city of Jonesboro.

The Department of Music at Arkansas State University offers the Bachelor of Music Education and Bachelor of Music degrees. The Bachelor of Music Education curriculum qualifies a student for the state teaching certificate, while the Bachelor of Music degree emphasizes composition, performance, or sacred music. The Department serves a large area of the state with clinics and concerts by faculty members, students, and ensembles. Departmental requirements include recital attendance, performance proficiency, and participation in one or more of the performing organizations.

Accreditation. North Central Association of Colleges and Schools; National Association of Schools of Music; National Council for Accreditation of Teacher Education.

Academic Information

Enrollment, Music Majors. (Total university) Full-time 2,896 men, 3,221 women; part-time 804 men, 1,525 women.

Music Faculty. 21.

Term System. Semester. Two 5-week summer terms.

Entrance Requirements. High school graduation or GED; 15 units (3 English, 1 mathematics, 1 laboratory science, 2 social studies); ACT.

Admission Procedure. Applications accepted on a rolling basis. Audition not required.

Music Degrees Offered. Bachelor of Music; Bachelor of Music Education; Bachelor of Arts; Master of Music; Master of Music Education.

Music Degree Requirements. The Bachelor of Music degree requires the completion of 44 semester hours of a general education curriculum, 63 hours in the major, and special emphasis area requirements of 26 hours each for instrumental, voice, or composition and 28 to 29 hours for keyboard. A total of 133 hours is required for the degree. The major in sacred music must complete 44 hours of general education plus 90 hours in the major. The Bachelor of Music Education degree requires the completion of 139 hours including 24 hours in professional education requirements and 7 hours in additional certification requirements. The Bachelor of Arts with a major in music, Master of Music, and Master of Music Education are also offered by the Department.

General Program Areas. Composition, Music Education, Music Theory, Performance, Sacred Music.

Instruments Taught. Brass, Organ, Percussion, Piano, Stringed Instruments, Voice, Woodwinds.

Musical Facilities

Practice Facilities. 30 practice rooms. 1 percussion-equipped practice room. 3 organs (Wicks, Hammond, Baldwin). 40 practice pianos (Baldwin); 2 grand pianos reserved for piano majors.

Concert Facilities. Recital Hall.

Community Facilities. Forum in downtown Jonesboro used for some concerts and recitals.

Concerts/Musical Activities. Recitals, concerts by students and faculty; Department Guest Artist Series; University Concert Series.

Music Library. 5,100 books; 1,100 scores; 154 periodicals; 6,377 microfiche; 1,900 phonograph recordings.

Special Programs

Performance Groups. Marching Band, Laboratory Band, Concert Band, Jazz Ensemble, Wind Ensemble, ASU Concert Choir, Madrigal Singers, Opera Production.

Financial

Costs. Per academic year: Tuition in-state $790, out-of-state $1,740. Room $870. Board $985.

Financial Aid. Forms of financial aid include scholarships, grants, loans, student employment, and College Work-Study program. Scholarship/financial aid applications due April 1.

Commentary

The University has plans to build a new theater and rehearsal hall. The University Museum features a collection of instruments from Arkansas settlers and the Civil War era.

Arkansas Tech University
Department of Music
Russellville
Arkansas 72801

Telephone. (501) 968-0389
Chief Administrator. Dr. Robert L. Casey, Department Head.

Arkansas Tech University was established in 1909 as Arkansas Polytechnic College. It achieved university status and assumed its present name in 1976. The 475-acre campus has 56 major buildings.

The objectives of the Department of Music are to train accredited music teachers for the public schools; to prepare students who wish to work toward professional performance and/or teaching in higher education; to provide opportunities for the cultural growth and development of all college students; to offer a solid musical background for students working in highly specialized programs such as music therapy and church music; and to provide a basic background to those who are preparing for a profession (elementary education, parks and recreation) requiring some knowledge of music.

Accreditation. North Central Association of Colleges and Schools; National Association of Schools of Music; National Council for Accreditation of Teacher Education.

Academic Information

Enrollment, Music Majors. (Total University) 2,776.
Music Faculty. 13.
Term System. Semester. Summer session of 2 terms.
Entrance Requirements. Graduates of Arkansas high schools may be admitted by presenting an official transcript; students from other states must also present certification of class rank in their graduating class; recommend completion of 4 units English, 3 mathematics, 8 from science, social studies, and electives; ACT required for placement purposes; audition required.

Admission Procedure. Application with supporting documents to Office of Admissions.

Music Degrees Offered. Bachelor of Arts.

Music Degree Requirements. The Bachelor of Arts degree is offered with curricula in music and music education. The degree requires the completion of 133 semester hours of specified courses depending on the curriculum pursued. Private instruction in the student's major performance area is required as well as a senior recital.

General Program Areas. Composition, Music Education, Music History, Music Theory, Performance.

Instruments Taught. Bass, Bassoon, Clarinet, Euphonium, Flute, French Horn, Harpsichord, Oboe, Organ, Percussion, Piano, Saxophone, Trombone, Trumpet, Tuba, Viola, Violin, Violoncello, Voice.

Musical Facilities

Concert Facilities. Witherspoon Auditorium, seating 742.

Concerts/Musical Activities. Student/faculty recitals and concerts.

Music Library. The Tomlinson Library supports the programs of the Department of Music.

Special Programs

Performance Groups. Opera Workshop, Jazz Ensemble, Band, Brass Choir, Woodwind Ensembles, Brass Ensembles, Percussion Ensembles, String Ensembles, Orchestra, University Choir, Concert Chorale, Vocal Ensembles, Instrumental Ensembles.

Financial

Costs. Per academic year: Tuition in-state resident $880, out-of-state $1,760. Fees $40. Room and board $1,900.

Financial Aid. Financial aid is awarded on the basis of academic merit, financial need, and musical ability. 25 music awards totaling $20,000 (average award $800). Part-time employment and a College Work-Study program available.

University of Central Arkansas
Department of Music
Conway
Arkansas 72032

Telephone. (501) 450-3163

Chief Administrator. Dr. Sam Driggers, Chairman.

Established in 1907 with emphasis on teacher education, the character of the University of Central Arkansas has changed along with the multipurpose nature of its currently varied curricula. The 220-acre campus is located in the southwestern part of Conway within 30 minutes driving time from Little Rock.

The specific aims of the Department of Music are: (1) to prepare professional musicians in the field of teaching and performance, (2) to meet the requirement of the general education program, (3) to provide courses that meet specific requirements in such fields as elementary education, and (4) to enrich the cultural life of the campus and the community by the presentation of recitals, concerts, and musical-dramatic performances.

Accreditation. North Central Association of Colleges and Schools; National Association of Schools of Music.

Academic Information

Enrollment, Music Majors. (Total University) 5,829.

Music Faculty. 21.

Term System. Semester. Two summer sessions.

Entrance Requirements. High school graduation or GED; ACT required; audition in major applied field; series of music screening tests.

Admission Procedure. Applications accepted on a rolling basis.

Music Degrees Offered. Bachelor of Music; Bachelor of Music Education; Master of Music; Master of Music Education.

Music Degree Requirements. The Bachelor of Music degree requires successful completion of 138 hours including the general education component and courses in applied music, theory, music history and literature, pedagogy, and electives. The Bachelor of Music Education degree requires the successful completion of 137 hours including the general education component and prescribed music requirements.

For a Master of Music degree the student must complete a 30-hour program with a concentration from among performance, choral conducting, instrumental conducting, or music theory. The Master of Music Education degree requires the completion of 30 hours in major courses, supporting music courses, professional education courses, and electives.

General Program Areas. Applied Music, Choral Conducting, Music Education, Music History, Music Literature, Music Theory, Orchestral Conducting, Performance.

Instruments Taught. Bassoon, Clarinet, Euphonium, Flute, French Horn, Guitar, Oboe, Organ, Percussion, Piano, Saxophone, Trumpet, Tuba, Viola, Violin, Violoncello, Voice.

Musical Facilities

Practice Facilities. 13 teaching studios. 2 organs (Moeller, 2-manual Allen concert). 50 pianos (3 grand and 2 concert grand). 1 harpsichord. Recording and listening laboratory.

Concert Facilities. Recital hall, theater, small and large rehearsal halls.

Concerts/Musical Activities. Recitals, concerts, visiting artists.

Music Library. Most music materials are housed in the Torreyson Library.

Special Programs

Performance Groups. Marching Band, Symphonic Wind Ensemble, Concert Band, UCA Symphony, Conway Civic Orchestra, Jazz Band, Dixieland Band, Brass Choir, Brass Quintet, Flute Choir, Clarinet Choir, Saxophone Choir, Woodwind Quintet, Percussion Ensemble, Student String Quartet, Concert Choir, Chamber Singers, Women's Chorus, Men's Chorus, Opera Workshop, Piano Ensemble.

Financial

Costs. Per academic year: Tuition in-state resident $900, out-of-state $1,800. Room and board $1,800 to $2,000.

Financial Aid. The University offers scholarships for talented students in Band, Choir, Orchestra, and Keyboard. Auditions for scholarships are held each spring and at other times by appointment. Scholarship application due March 30. Other sources of financial aid include grants, loans, part-time employment, and a College Work-Study program.

Henderson State University
Department of Music
1100 Henderson Street
Arkadelphia
Arkansas 71923

Telephone. (501) 246-5511

Chief Administrator. Wendell O. Evanson, Department Head.

Henderson State University was first established as Arkadelphia Methodist College in 1890. It became a state institution in 1929; graduate study was inaugurated in 1955. The University adopted its current name in 1968 when university status was achieved. It now enrolls over 2,700 students and has a faculty of 140. The 100-acre campus has 25 major buildings in the city of Arkadelphia, 70 miles southwest of Little Rock and 35 miles south of Hot Springs.

The Department of Music has the basic purpose of developing each student musically, academically, and personally. It is concerned that the student be prepared to participate and compete in the professional world and be accepted into the Graduate School of his/her choice. The Department believes its strength is applied music instruction in winds, percussion, piano, organ, and voice.

Accreditation. North Central Association of Colleges and Schools; National Association of Schools of Music.

Academic Information

Enrollment, Music Majors. Undergraduate 76, graduate 12.

Music Faculty. Full-time 13, part-time 1.

Term System. Semester. Graduate courses and workshops available during summer session.

Entrance Requirements. Open enrollment policy; completion of 15 units including 3 English, 2 mathematics, 2 laboratory science, 2 social studies; ACT required. GRE required for graduate students. Audition required through appointment.

Admission Procedure. Application due within a reasonable time prior to the semester of enrollment.

Music Degrees Offered. Bachelor of Music; Bachelor of Music Education; Master of Music Education.

Music Degree Requirements. The Bachelor of Music degree is offered with concentrations in piano, organ, voice, winds, and composition. A piano proficiency test is usually taken at the end of the sophomore year. The degree requires the completion of 144 semester hours. The degree Bachelor of Music Education is offered with options in keyboard, vocal, or instrumental. The degree requires the completion of 149 to 154 semester hours of prescribed general education courses and the major concentration.

The degree Master of Music Education requires the completion of 36 semester hours of study.

General Program Areas. Choral Conducting, Choral Music, Composition, Music Education, Music History, Music Literature, Music Theory, Performance.

Instruments Taught. Brass, Harpsichord, Organ, Percussion, Piano, Voice, Woodwinds.

Musical Facilities

Practice Facilities. 26 practice rooms. 3 organs (35-rank Moeller, 3-rank Moeller, 19-rank Schantz). Special practice facilities for percussionists. 4 grand pianos reserved for piano majors. Electronic composition laboratory; recording laboratory.

Concert Facilities. Arkansas Hall, seating 900; Fine Arts Recital Hall, 240.

Concerts/Musical Activities. Concerts and recitals throughout the year.

Music Library. 3,200 books; 3,000 scores; 50 music periodical titles; 1,535 microfiche; 3,600 phonograph recordings. Listening facilities (5 cassette decks, 5 stereo turntables). The library resources of Ouachita Baptist University are available to students.

Special Programs

Performance Groups. Madrigal Singers, Chamber Chorale, Symphonic Band, Marching Band, Jazz Band.

Financial

Costs. Per academic year: Tuition in-state resident $872, out-of-state $1,744. Student fees $220. Room $664. Board $912.

Financial Aid. 116 music scholarships ranging from $200 to $1,000. Scholarship applications accepted on a rolling basis. Other sources of financial aid include institutional grants, state/federal loans, student employment, and a College Work-Study program.

Ouachita Baptist University
School of Music
410 Ouachita Street
Arkadelphia
Arkansas 71923

Telephone. (501) 246-4531

Chief Administrator. Dr. Charles W. Wright, Dean.

Ouachita Baptist University was founded in 1885 by the Arkansas Baptist State Convention.

The School of Music seeks to prepare students for careers in the fields of musical performance, music education, theory-composition, and church music. A curriculum combining the various areas of performance with study in theory, music history, analysis, and literature prepares students for careers in music or for the pursuit of music as an avocation. All music students are required to take courses in the humanities, social sciences, and subjects related to their major areas of study.

Accreditation. North Central Association of Colleges and Schools; National Association of Schools of Music.

Academic Information

Enrollment, Music Majors. (Total University) 1,161.
Music Faculty. 16.
Term System. Semester.
Entrance Requirements. Open enrollment policy; C average; completion of 15 units including 3 English, 2 mathematics, 2 science, 1 social studies; ACT required (minimum score 15).
Admission Procedure. Application with nonrefundable $25 fee to Admissions Counselor by August 15 for Fall term.
Music Degrees Offered. Bachelor of Music; Bachelor of Music Education; Bachelor of Arts.
Music Degree Requirements. The Bachelor of Music degree is offered with curricula in applied music, church music, and theory-composition. The Bachelor of Music Education degree is offered with instrumental and choral majors. The Bachelor of Arts degree is offered with a major in music. The baccalaureate degrees require the completion of a minimum of 128 semester hours. The School of Music also offers a program leading to the Master of Music Education degree.
General Program Areas. Applied Music, Church Music, Composition, Music Education, Music Literature, Music Theory.
Instruments Taught. Brass, Organ, Percussion, Piano, Stringed Instruments, Voice, Woodwinds.

Musical Facilities

Concert Facilities. Mabee Fine Arts Center.
Concerts/Musical Activities. Student and faculty concerts and recitals; visiting artists.
Music Library. A branch of the Riley Library is located in Mabee Fine Arts Center and serves the School of Music. Special collections include the microfiche reprint series of complete works of music and the microcard collection of early writings on music from Eastman School of Music.

Special Programs

Performance Groups. University Choir, Ouachita Singers, Ouachi-Tones, Chamber Singers, Opera Workshop, Singing Men, Piano Ensemble, University Marching Band, Concert Band, Stage Band, Woodwind Ensemble, Brass Ensemble, Percussion Ensemble, Handbell Ringers, String Ensemble.

Financial

Costs. Per academic year: Tuition $3,100. Fees $50. Room $670. Board $1,080.
Financial Aid. The School of Music awards a limited number of scholarships based on auditions. Other financial aid in the form of grants, loans, and part-time employment are available. Scholarship/financial aid application due March 3. A College Work-Study program is also available.

CALIFORNIA

Azusa Pacific University
School of Music
Citrus and Alosta
Azusa
California 91702

Telephone. (818) 969-4995
Chief Administrator. Dr. Gary Bonner, Dean.

Azusa Pacific University is an independent, church-related university. Six religious organizations—Brethren in Christ, Church of God, the Free Methodist Church, the Missionary Church, the Salvation Army, and the Wesleyan Church—have chosen to affiliate with the University and have representatives on the Board of Directors. Many individual churches representing various segments of the conservative Biblical tradition actively support Azusa Pacific University. The student body represents over thirty religious backgrounds.

In 1965 Azusa Pacific College emerged as a new name among institutions of higher learning in Southern California. Two independent schools, Azusa College and Los Angeles Pacific College, merged to form the new College. For sixty years they had administered academic programs as private, church-related colleges. Their goals, curricula, and mission were similar and Azusa Pacific College inherited this legacy. The merger made it the official college for the Free Methodist Church in the Southwestern United States. In 1968 Arlington College of Long Beach, California affiliated with Azusa Pacific College. Arlington had been founded in 1954 by the Church of God in Southern California (headquarters in Anderson, Indiana). By 1981, Azusa Pacific's program and curriculum had developed to the place that university status was adopted.

The University is located in the San Gabriel Valley communities of Azusa and Glendora, 25 minutes east of Los Angeles. Situated on the 50-acre valley campus are the University administrative facilities, library, classrooms, student center, gymnasium, residence halls, and student apartments.

The School of Music offers degrees in music performance, music education, music theory, church music, and conducting. Built on the understanding that music is for the masses, not to be hidden and savored by only an elite few, the School of Music continually strives to offer its students and audiences a balance of music ranging from highly treasured music of the past to the most exciting music of the present. A new School of Music building is planned for the future.

Accreditation. Western Association of Schools and Colleges.

Academic Information

Enrollment, Music Majors. Total 50 men, 80 women (all full-time).

Music Faculty. Full-time 11, part-time 3.

Term System. Semester. Academic year September to May.

Entrance Requirements. Admission to the University requires graduation from an accredited high school with courses in English, social studies, mathematics, science (including one laboratory science), and a foreign language; ACT or SAT; two references. Prospective music majors are required to take placement examinations in piano, voice, and music theory. The theory examinations will include key signatures, major and minor scales, meter signatures, and intervals. Those who are deficient in theory are required to take Music Fundamentals before proceeding with first year theory. Students who have a keyboard deficiency must enroll in class or private piano. Each student must pass a piano proficiency examination or enroll in a piano class until the requirement is met. Placement auditions are held for all performance areas.

Admission Procedure. Application form and statement of agreement with two photographs; nonrefundable $30 application fee; transcripts of high school and each college or university attended.

Music Degrees Offered. Bachelor of Arts in Music Performance, Music Education, Music Theory, Church Music; Master of Music in Conducting.

Music Degree Requirements. The minimum unit requirement for the Bachelor of Arts degree is 126. In addition to the 58 units in music, each applicant for graduation must have completed the minimum of 68 units in General Studies requirements; all students must earn a minimum cumulative grade point average of 2.0 in all university work attempted. The Master of Music degree requires the completion of 36 units; 3.0 grade point average; graduate recital; written comprehensive examinations must be passed at the conclusion of the program.

General Program Areas. Applied Music, Church Music, Conducting, Music Education, Music History, Music Literature, Music Theory.

Instruments Taught. Brass, Organ, Percussion, Piano, Stringed Instruments, Voice, Woodwinds.

Musical Facilities

Practice Facilities. Moeller pipe organ; 23 practice pianos (grands and consoles); 19 practice rooms. Special studios: piano lab; electronic music lab.

Music Library. The Marshburn Memorial Library has holdings of 360,000 cataloged items, including microforms. The Media Center houses an extensive collection of non-print materials, including disc recordings, audiotapes, and videotapes.

Special Programs

Performance Groups. 12 ensembles ranging from 7 to 125 students in each, including the Male Chorale, Concert Band, Reflection, Bel Canto Choir, Innermission, Chancel Singers, Triumphant Review, Jazz Ensemble, University Choir.

Financial

Costs. Per academic year: Tuition $5,500. Fees $200 to $400. Room $1,600. Board $1,600. Off-campus housing approximately $400 per month.

Financial Aid. Financial aid is awarded on the basis of academic merit, financial need, musical ability. Institutional and state/federal aid available. 90% of students receive financial aid. Part-time employment and College Work-Study program available.

Biola University
Department of Music
13800 Biola Avenue
La Mirada
California 90639

Telephone. (213) 944-0351

Chief Administrator. Dr. Jack Schwarz, Chair.

Biola University is a privately supported, interdenominational Christian university enrolling over 2,500 students annually. The 95-acre campus is located 22 miles southeast of Los Angeles.

The objectives of the Department of Music are to provide opportunities for all students to study music as an essential part of a liberal education; to prepare well-trained musicians for teaching, graduate study, performance, the ministry of church music, and other careers in music; and to involve all graduates in contributing to the musical life of the evangelical church. Biola requires a minimum of 30 units of Biblical studies regardless of major.

Accreditation. Western Association of Schools and Colleges; National Association of Schools of Music.

Academic Information

Enrollment, Music Majors. (Total University) 2,577.

Music Faculty. 14.

Term System. Semester.

Entrance Requirements. High school graduation or equivalent; completion of 16 units including 3 English, 3 mathematics, 2 social sciences, 2 foreign language, 2 science; SAT or ACT. All students seeking admission must demonstrate musical background and performance strengths necessary for successful completion of the curriculum. Provisional acceptance is granted for the first year of study. Upon entrance, students will be given placement examinations and auditions in music history, music theory, keyboard skills, and performance.

Admission Procedure. Application with supporting documents may be filed on a rolling admissions basis.

Music Degrees Offered. Bachelor of Music; Bachelor of Arts.

Music Degree Requirements. The Bachelor of Music degree is offered in the areas of performance, composition, and music education. The Bachelor of Arts degree in music is offered in the context of a liberal arts program. All music majors must complete a basic core of 35-36 units of music. The baccalaureate degrees require the completion of a minimum of 130 semester hours.

General Program Areas. Church Music, Composition, Music Education, Music Theory, Performance.

Instruments Taught. Brass, Harpsichord, Organ, Percussion, Piano, Stringed Instruments, Voice, Woodwinds.

Musical Facilities

Concert Facilities. Lansing Auditorium; Concert Hall, seating 450.

Concerts/Musical Activities. The music department concert series features guest artists as well as faculty performances. Individual performance opportunities are offered through weekly student recitals and junior/senior recitals.

Music Library. The Biola University Library and the Media Center support the programs of the Department of Music.

Special Programs

Performance Groups. Biola Chorale, Chamber Music Ensemble, Chamber Orchestra, University Singers, La Mirada Symphony, Stage Band, Symphonic Band, Handbell Choir.

Financial

Costs. Per academic year: Tuition $5,604. Room $1,-580. Board $1,438.

Financial Aid. Music scholarships and performance awards in varying amounts are available to qualified students. The Los Angeles metropolitan area offers many opportunities for remunerative service in music. There are frequent openings for organists, church choir directors, soloists, accompanists, and instrumentalists. Other sources of financial aid are institutional scholarships and state/federal grants and loans.

University of California, Berkeley
Department of Music
Berkeley
California 94720

Telephone. (415) 642-2678

Chief Administrator. Dr. Bonnie C. Wade, Chairman.

The Berkeley campus is the oldest and largest of the University of California campuses. Founded in 1868, it awards undergraduate and graduate degrees through 14 colleges and schools. With 30,000 students, a distinguished faculty, nearly 300 degree programs, and alumni in positions of national and international leadership, Berkeley today is a large and complex institution, offering students a vast range of scholarly endeavor and an unusual depth of inquiry both for personal growth and individual involvement with others. The campus is surrounded by wooded, rolling hills and by the town of Berkeley (population 112,000). Students study, work, and relax among academic buildings, wooded glens, and parklands spread across 1,232 scenic acres overlooking San Francisco Bay. The majority of students are Californians, but people come from every part of the United States and 100 foreign countries to study at Berkeley.

The Department of Music, one of the oldest in the country, offers the serious student of music a wealth of resources while maintaining its traditional balance between musical scholarship and musical performance. The permanent professorial ranks, comprised of composers, musicologists, and performer/scholars, are regularly supplemented by distinguished visitors, most notably through the Department's Ernest Bloch Visiting Professorship. The creative work of the faculty is often aligned with the performing forces of the Department in productions of special musical or historical significance, such as the revival of an early opera using a performance edition published by a faculty scholar, or the first perfor-

mance of a major contemporary work for chorus, orchestra, dancers, and soloists.

The music buildings, Morrison Hall and adjacent Hertz Hall, bring all of the Department's resources together in a centralized, communal setting. A complete collection of modern orchestral instruments is available. Harpsichords, fortepianos, and other early keyboard instruments, and an exceptional collection of modern and antique organs provide an excellent resource for keyboard players. Students interested in early music may play antique wind and stringed instruments or modern reproductions. Advanced string players may perform on some of the fine instruments in the Salz Collection of rare violins and violas. A Javanese gamelan highlights the growing collection of authentic instruments from non-Western musical traditions such as those of India, Africa, and East Asia.

Accreditation. Western Association of Schools and Colleges.

Academic Information

Enrollment, Music Majors. Undergraduate 100, graduate 45.

Music Faculty. Full-time 20, part-time 31.

Term System. Semester. Minimal summer instruction in music.

Entrance Requirements. To enter the University of California as an undergraduate, a student must complete a set of requirements which demonstrates as accurately as possible whether an applicant has sufficient intellectual knowledge, skills, and interests to pursue a university degree. High school graduation required with 4 years English, 3 mathematics, 1 history, 1 laboratory science, 2 foreign language, 4 electives; 3.3 grade point average; SAT or ACT. The Graduate Program requires a bachelor's degree; 3 letters of recommendation; Graduate Record Examination; departmental placement examinations in musicianship, harmony and counterpoint, history of music, and analysis.

Admission Procedure. Application and $35 nonrefundable fee to the Office of Admissions and Records between November 1 and 30 of year prior to enrollment for Fall semester; and between July 1 and 31 for the Spring semester. Graduate students admitted in the Fall semester only; apply with all supporting materials by January 10.

Music Degrees Offered. Bachelor of Arts; Master of Arts; Ph.D.

Music Degree Requirements. The Bachelor of Arts degree program involves an intensive two-year program of musicianship, theory, and keyboard skills, after which students may concentrate in areas of special interest such as performance, musicology, composition, or ethnomusicology. Private instruction in voice or instrument is available to music majors. The Master of Arts degree is offered with specialties in musical composition and musical scholarship (musicology and ethnomusicology).

The period of study is from three to four semesters (24 units) ending with the M.A. comprehensive examination. The Ph.D. degree is awarded for original, creative achievement, not for the completion of a course of study; course and unit requirements are not rigidly prescribed.

General Program Areas. Composition, Conducting, Ethnomusicology, Music History, Music Literature, Musicology, Performance, Theory.

Instruments Taught. Brass, Javanese Gamelan, Organ, Piano, Stringed Instruments, Voice, Woodwinds.

Musical Facilities

Practice Facilities. Special practice facilities for organists. 33 piano practice rooms; 50 pianos (upright and grand). Electronic studio; transcription lab.

Concert Facilities. Hertz Hall seating 700; Eikus Hall seating 100.

Concerts/Musical Activities. Weekly Noon Concert Series; Friday Afternoon Concerts; regular concerts of the Department's performing organizations.

Music Library. The Music Library contains a collection of about 125,000 books, scores, and serials; 33,000 sound recordings; 5,000 reels of microfilm. Under the late Vincent Duckles, author of the standard *Music Reference and Research Materials, an Annotated Bibliography,* the library became one of the major centers for research in the United States, with important collections of manuscripts, early printed music, and opera libretti as well as a number of archival collections. Listening facilities include 15 cassette decks, 31 turntables, 2 compact disk players.

Special collections include: Ernest Bloch memorabilia; Romantic music materials; nineteenth century opera scores; seventeenth and early eighteenth century opera materials from library of Alfred Cortot; Tartini Collection; seventeenth century instrumental music and music treatises; harp music; Danish materials; Franz Liszt materials; ethnomusicological sound recordings.

Special Programs

Performance Groups. University Symphony, University Chorus, Chamber Music Ensemble, Contemporary Chamber Music Ensemble, African Music Ensemble, Collegium Musicum.

Financial

Costs. Per academic year: State resident student fee $1,346, nonresident tuition $5,162 plus $1,346 student fee. Room and board $3,807.

Financial Aid. 30 music scholarships available ranging from $500 to $3,000. Applications due February 6. Part-time employment and Work-Study program available.

University of California, Davis
Department of Music
Davis
California 95616

Telephone. (916) 752-0666
Chief Administrator. D. Kern Holoman, Chairman.

This campus of the University of California was originally known as the University Farm in 1909 when the student body consisted of 28 young men who wanted to become farmers. The Davis campus now has over 19,500 students enrolled in six colleges and the graduate division. The campus is situated on a 3,600-acre campus in the Central Valley, thirteen miles west of Sacramento and 65 miles north of San Francisco.

The Department of Music offers a balanced major in music (theory and composition, history and criticism, and performance) as well as courses for the general undergraduate program. The graduate curriculum includes specialization in musicology. The Department considers its major strengths to be in nineteenth- and twentieth-century studies, electronic music, composition, voice, piano, and conducting. A Ph.D. program is planned which will emphasize theory-based composition and nineteenth- and twentieth-century studies.

Accreditation. Western Association of Schools and Colleges.

Academic Information

Enrollment, Music Majors. Undergraduate 35, graduate 2.

Music Faculty. Full-time 10, part-time 35.

Term System. Quarter. Summer session for elementary theory and music appreciation courses.

Entrance Requirements. High school graduation with 15 units including 4 English, 3 mathematics, 1 laboratory science, 1 U.S. history, 4 college preparatory electives, 2 foreign language; SAT or ACT. GRE required for graduate school. Audition required for instrument major (scales, sight-reading, prepared piece).

Admission Procedure. Application with $35 nonrefundable fee due November for Fall Quarter, July for Winter Quarter, October for Spring Quarter.

Music Degrees Offered. Bachelor of Arts; Master of Arts.

Music Degree Requirements. The Bachelor of Arts degree with a major in music requires the completion of 180 quarter hours of prescribed courses, core music curriculum, and major concentration. The degrees Master of Arts and Master of Arts in Teaching are also offered.

General Program Areas. Applied Music, Electronic Music, Musicology, Nineteenth Century Music, Performance, Twentieth Century Music.

Instruments Taught. Brass, Organ, Percussion, Piano, Stringed Instruments, Woodwinds.

Musical Facilities

Practice Facilities. 12 practice rooms. 2 organs (Schlicker pipe organ, Brombaugh positive organ). 17 pianos (9 Baldwin uprights, 8 grands); 8 grand pianos reserved for piano majors. Electronic music studio; recording studio.

Concert Facilities. Freeborn Hall, seating 2,000; Kleiber Hall, 250; Wyatt Pavilion, 300; Music Building, 150; Main Theatre, 500.

Concerts/Musical Activities. Ensemble recitals; student performances.

Music Library. Music materials are housed in the Music Department and Main Library. 40,000 books, scores, periodicals; 20,000 recordings. Listening facilities (35 cassette decks; 20 stereo turntables; 5 compact disc players).

Special collections include: historical instruments; Severin Saphir Memorial Collection of Chamber Music; Bernard Storch Collection of Theater Music; Edward O. Dannreuther Collection of Nineteenth Century Music; tapes of first performances of Darius Milhaud works. The offices of the journal, *19th-Century Music,* are located in the Music Building.

Financial

Costs. Per academic year: Fee in-state resident $1,286, tuition and fee nonresident $5,372. Room and board $3,345.

Financial Aid. Sources of financial aid include scholarships, grants, loans, student employment, and a College Work-Study program.

Commentary

The University of California at Davis offers the five-year B.A./M.A. double degree program.

University of California, Irvine
School of Fine Arts
Department of Music
Irvine
California 92717

Telephone. (714) 856-6615
Chief Administrator. Joseph B. Huszti, Chair.

The Irvine campus of the University of California opened in 1965. It was planned from the beginning with the intention that five fundamental Schools would represent five fundamental areas of knowledge, as well as provide an academic structure for related studies. The campus is five miles from the Pacific Ocean and near Newport Beach, 40 miles south of Los Angeles.

The School of Fine Arts directs its energy toward the refinement, enhancement, and encouragement of the artistic and creative talent of the students who enter the School and the development of their understanding of related theory and history. The requirements for the student of music include extensive studio and workshop experiences, essential theoretical and historical background studies, and exercises in criticism. All new students are assigned or may choose their own faculty advisors and are encouraged to meet with them during orientation week and periodically throughout the year to plan programs of study and to discuss educational and career objectives.

Accreditation. Western Association of Schools and Colleges.

Academic Information

Enrollment, Music Majors. Full-time 50 men, 70 women; part-time 2 men, 2 women. Foreign students 10.

Music Faculty. 32.

Term System. Quarter. Two summer sessions.

Entrance Requirements. Undergraduate admission requires high school graduation with a minimum of 15 units including English 4, history 1, mathematics 3, laboratory science 1, foreign language 2, electives 4; SAT or ACT; 3 College Board Achievement Tests; high school scholarship requirements. Graduate admission requires baccalaureate degree; admission of graduate students for the fall quarter only. Entering baccalaureate students should have ensemble experience in chorus, orchestra, or band. Basic keyboard experience desirable; some experience as a solo performer; knowledge of scales, chords, arpeggios; sight reading; 3 to 6 years of private instruction; solo repertory (sonata and chamber literature, art song, or oratorio).

Admission Procedure. Application packets for undergraduate admission to the University are available from the counseling office of any California high school or community college, or from the Admissions Office. Submit application with nonrefundable $35 fee. Filing dates for Winter quarter July 1-30, Spring October 1-30, Fall November 1-30. Graduate application must be completed by March 1. Applicants are advised to arrange for audition, interviews, and the submission of portfolios, compositions, and dossiers by March 11.

Music Degrees Offered. Bachelor of Music; Bachelor of Arts; Fifth-Year Option to obtain the California Teaching Credential; Master of Fine Arts.

Music Degree Requirements. The degrees Bachelor of Music and Bachelor of Arts with a major in music require the completion of university requirements, core requirements, and performance requirements. All students receive lessons on instruments or in voice and participate in various choral or instrumental ensembles (these requirements vary for the B.A. and B.Mus. degrees). All students must complete two years of work in sight-singing, one to four-part dictation, and keyboard harmony. Basic to the program for all majors are keyboard skills.

The Master of Fine Arts degree is offered with emphasis in composition, choral conducting, voice, piano performance, and instrumental performance. Normally, two years of residence are required. The degree requires a total of 72 quarter hours with courses specified depending on area of concentration.

General Program Areas. Music Composition, Music Theory, Performance.

Instruments Taught. Bass, Bassoon, Clarinet, Flute, French Horn, Guitar, Lute, Oboe, Percussion, Piano, Trombone, Trumpet, Tuba, Viola, Violin, Violoncello, Voice.

Musical Facilities

Practice Facilities. 2 practice rooms for percussionists. 20 practice rooms. 40 pianos (Steinway, Young Ching); 10 pianos reserved for piano majors. Electronic music studio.

Concert Facilities. The Village Theatre seating 420; Concert Hall, 230.

Concerts/Musical Activities. Artist Series, student/faculty recitals, ensembles, jazz and folk performers.

Music Library. The UCI Main Library contains more than 1,200,000 volumes. Students have access from other libraries in the University of California system. A music listening facility is located in the Fine Arts Village.

Special collections include: collected published works of Peter Odegard.

Special Programs

Performance Groups. University Concert Choir, Chamber Singers, Men's Chorus, Women's Chorus, Freshmen Singers, UCI Symphony Orchestra, UCI Pep Band, Song Leaders, ensemble groups.

Financial

Costs. Per academic year: Tuition undergraduate in-state resident $1,404, graduate $1,452; out-of-state undergraduate $5,490, graduate $5,538. Room and board $4,386.

Financial Aid. Students who demonstrate that they need financial assistance in order to attend are eligible for financial aid through the Financial Aid Office. In addition to awarding aid on the basis of financial need, the Office also offers some scholarships based on academic excellence.

University of California, Los Angeles
Department of Music
College of Fine Arts
405 Hilgard Avenue
Los Angeles
California 90024

Telephone. (213) 825-4321
Chief Administrator. Robert H. Gray, Dean, College of Fine Arts.

The University of California, Los Angeles (UCLA) was established in 1881 as a normal school. In 1919, the Los Angeles State Normal School was replaced by the Southern Branch of the University of California and in 1927 it became the University of California at Los Angeles (the "at" was replaced by a comma in 1958). The UCLA campus lies at the foot of the Santa Monica mountains in the residential community of Westwood, five miles from the Pacific Ocean.

The Department of Music is housed in Schoenberg Hall and Annex, named in honor of composer Arnold Schoenberg, Professor of Music at UCLA from 1936 to 1944. The Department offers a four-year undergraduate curriculum comprising practical, theoretical, and historical studies, with related performance and academic studies in non-Western music. The major is based on a core curriculum of theory, history, analysis, and individual and group performance. Given in the context of a liberal arts education, this provides a foundation for an academic or professional career. At the graduate level, specialized studies are offered in composition, ethnomusicology, historical musicology, music education, and systematic musicology as well as all orchestral instruments, voice, opera, and conducting.

Accreditation. Western Association of Schools and Colleges.

Academic Information

Enrollment, Music Majors. (Total University) 31,051.
Music Faculty. 91.
Term System. Quarter. 2 summer sessions.
Entrance Requirements. To qualify for admission as a freshman, the applicant must present a high school academic record of 15 units including 1 history, 4 English, 3 mathematics, 1 laboratory science, 2 foreign language, 4 college preparatory electives; combination of grade point average and ACT or SAT scores; 3 College Board Achievement Tests; music aptitude and achievement tests; piano skills test.

Admission Procedure. Application with supporting documents and nonrefundable $35 fee due July, October, November.

Music Degrees Offered. Bachelor of Arts; Master of Arts; Master of Fine Arts; Doctor of Philosophy.

Music Degree Requirements. The Bachelor of Arts degree is offered with specialization in composition and theory, history and literature, ethnomusicology, performance, music education, or systematic musicology. The degree requires the completion of a minimum of 180 units (45 courses).

The Master of Arts and Doctor of Philosophy degrees are offered in the fields of historical musicology, ethnomusicology, systematic musicology, composition, and music education. The Master of Fine Arts degree (performance practices) is offered in all classical solo instruments, voice, opera, and conducting. All Master of Arts students must use the thesis plan except those specializing in music education who may follow either the thesis or comprehensive examination plan.

General Program Areas. Composition, Conducting, Ethnomusicology, Music Education, Music History, Music Literature, Music Theory, Musicology, Opera, Performance.

Instruments Taught. Bass, Bassoon, Clarinet, Flute, French Horn, Guitar, Harp, Harpsichord, Lute, Oboe, Organ, Percussion, Piano, Saxophone, Trombone, Trumpet, Tuba, Viola, Viola da Gamba, Violin, Violoncello, Voice.

Musical Facilities

Concert Facilities. Royce Hall, seating 1,900; Schoenberg Auditorium, 525; Jan Popper Theatre, 150.

Concerts/Musical Activities. Student/faculty recitals and concerts; extensive visiting artist series. The Center for the Performing Arts stages more than 200 public concerts and events each year.

Music Library. The Walter H. Rubsamen Music Library contains 50,000 volumes of books, 60,000 volumes of scores from Greek and Roman times to the present, 35,000 disc and tape recordings, and more than 5,000 operas, operettas, and musical comedies. Audio facilities are available which seat 40 listeners. The Library houses historical musicology and ethnomusicology materials, musical scores, recordings, and the personal collections of such composers as Henry Mancini, Alex North, and Ernst Toch. Instrument collections include ethnic instruments, banjos, mandolins, guitars, and rare clarinets. Other special collections include: English seventeenth and eighteenth century culture; rare books and music, especially original editions and librettos of vocal works, English Baroque treatises, letters of prominent nineteenth century composers; ethnomusicology archive; popular American sheet music; the American Film and Television Music Archives. The Ethnic Instrument Collection contains over 1,000 non-Western instruments and ethnic art objects. The Archive of American Popular Music (which includes the Meredith Willson Library of Popular Sheet Music), the Henry Roth Library of American Theater Music, and the Erich Lachmann Collection of Historical Stringed Instruments are also housed in the Library.

Special Programs

Performance Groups. A Capella Choir, University Chorus, Madrigal Singers, Opera Workshop, Symphony Orchestra, Concert Band, Symphonic Wind Ensemble, Collegium Musicum, Men's Glee Club, Women's Glee Club, Musical Comedy Workshop, Marching Band, Varsity Band, Jazz Ensemble, Ethnomusicology Performance (American Indian, Bali, Bulgaria, China, Ghana, India, Japan, Java, Korea, Mexico, Persia, Thailand, Near East, Afro-American).

Financial

Costs. Per academic year: Tuition in-state resident none, out-of-state $4,086. Fees $1,406. Room and board $2,740.

Financial Aid. Financial aid is awarded on the basis of academic merit and financial need. Scholarships, grants, loans, part-time employment, and a College Work-Study program are available. Financial aid/scholarship application due February 10.

Commentary

Master of Business Administration degrees in arts management and entertainment are offered by UCLA's Graduate School of Management.

University of California, Riverside
Department of Music
College of Humanities and Social Sciences
Riverside
California 92521

Telephone. (714) 787-3683
Chief Administrator. Dr. Edward H. Clinkscale, Chair.

In 1948, the Regents approved the establishment of the College of Letters and Science in Riverside and it opened for classes in 1954. By act of the Regents, the Riverside campus in 1959 was declared a general campus of the University of California with a mandate to develop appropriate areas of study. In 1960, the Graduate Division was established and graduate and professional programs were added. Enrollment on the campus is presently about 5,200 students.

The 1,200-acre Riverside campus is located 50 miles east of Los Angeles. It is virtually equidistant from the desert, the mountains, and the ocean. The city of Riverside is accessible by several main highways and is served by the nearby Ontario International Airport.

The major in music is designed to help the student explore music through its history, theory, and performance. Flexibility is provided by means of electives to permit students to follow individual interests and to choose special fields of emphasis. Each student is assigned to a member of the department for individual counseling each quarter. Because of their additional performance requirements music majors have been granted an exemption from the 80-unit limit on courses in the major, so that 102 music units may be counted toward the Bachelor of Arts degree. The graduate program at Riverside further develops the music student with specialization in theory/composition, history, and performance practice.

Accreditation. Western Association of Schools and Colleges.

Academic Information

Term System. Quarter. Academic year September June.

Entrance Requirements. To enter the University of California as an undergraduate, a student must complete a set of requirements which demonstrates whether the applicant has sufficient intellectual knowledge, skills, and interests to pursue a university degree. High school graduation is required with 4 years English, 3 mathematics, 1 history, 1 laboratory science, 2 foreign language, 4 electives; 3.3 grade point average; SAT or ACT. The Graduate program requires a bachelor's degree and undergraduate background equal to that of a music major at the University of California, Riverside, including piano proficiency and musicianship (ear training). An advisory examination is required.

Admission Procedure. Application and $35 nonrefundable fee to the Office of Admissions and Records; opening dates November 1, July 1, and October 1 of year prior to enrollment.

Music Degrees Offered. Bachelor of Arts; Master of Arts.

Music Degree Requirements. The Bachelor of Arts degree requires the completion of a prescribed curriculum with 80 to 102 units in the major. The Master of Arts degree requires the completion of 36 units with either a thesis or comprehensive examination.

General Program Areas. Composition, Music History, Music Theory, Performance.

Instruments Taught. Bass, Bassoon, Carillon, Clarinet, Flute, French Horn, Guitar, Harpsichord, Lute, Oboe, Organ, Percussion, Piano, Recorder, Saxophone, Trombone, Trumpet, Viola, Viola da Gamba, Violin, Violoncello, Voice.

Musical Facilities

Practice Facilities. 12 practice rooms, 6 teaching studios. 12 pianos (Steinway, Yamaha). Electronic music studio.

Concert Facilities. University Theatre.

Concerts/Musical Activities. More than 50 formal and informal concerts and recitals by campus ensembles, students, members of the performance faculty, and distinguished visiting artists.

Music Library. Located in the Music Wing of the Humanities Building. 16,500 scores; 10,500 sound recordings. Long-playing records or cassettes are played from high fidelity sound equipment in the central control room to 36 listening stations. Over 16,000 music titles are housed in the main library collection; 200 musical journals. Historical collection of 13,000 phonograph recordings and a media library containing 2,500 videotapes and laser disk recordings. Special departmental instrument collection of historical replicas of 3 Baroque organs, 2 harpsichords, a fortepiano, lutes, a theorbo, viols, and a large representative group of smaller Renaissance and Baroque instruments.

Special collections include: Organology collection, with materials related to bells and carillons; record sound archive; Heinrich Schenker Archive; 500 first and early editions of eighteenth and nineteenth century composers.

Special Programs

Featured Programs. The UC Riverside Music Festival is staged annually.

Performance Groups. Orchestra, Collegium Musicum, Choral Society, Madrigal Group, University Band, Chamber Music, Carillon Guild.

Financial

Costs. Per academic year: Fees undergraduate resident $1,329, nonresident $4,086. Housing $3,400 to $3,700.

Financial Aid. Scholarships, grants, and loans are available.

University of California, San Diego Department of Music
110 Mandeville Center for the Arts
La Jolla
California 92093

Telephone. (619) 452-3230

Chief Administrator. Dr. Edwin Harkins, Chairman.

The University of California, San Diego is one of the newest of the nine campuses which make up the University of California system. It celebrated its twenty-fifth anniversary during the 1985-86 academic year. Graduate and undergraduate programs are offered in a wide range of disciplines. Undergraduates enjoy the benefits of a great university without the disadvantages of "bigness." The master plan conceived by UCSD's planners borrowed from the Oxford and Cambridge concept to provide a "family" of colleges, each with its own special academic and social "flavor." Presently, there are four colleges: Reveille, John Muir, Third, and Earl Warren. Each of the four is designed to accommodate 2,500 students. Each has its own dining halls, commons, and classrooms. Each college has its own educational philosophies and traditions, its own set of general-education requirements, and its own administrative and advising staff. Although independent, the colleges are interrelated as all university and academic support facilities are available to all students, regardless of their college affiliation. The campus is located in La Jolla, immediately north of the city of San Diego.

The Department of Music is dedicated to the development of musical intelligence. The goal of its undergraduate program is to enhance the musical intelligence of students in the appreciation of the music-making process; its graduate program aims to educate researchers who will extend the musical intelligence of the entire musical community. The special characteristic of the undergraduate program in music has been its attempt to coordinate graduate activity with undergraduate studies. By involving undergraduate students whenever possible with faculty and graduate students, undergraduates are offered special opportunities for enlarging their musical abilities and understanding.

Accreditation. Western Association of Schools and Colleges.

Academic Information

Enrollment, Music Majors. Undergraduate 50, graduate 73. Foreign student 15.

Music Faculty. Full-time 19, part-time 18.

Term System. Quarter. Summer session.

Entrance Requirements. To enter the University of California as an undergraduate, a student must complete a set of requirements which demonstrates as accurately as possible whether an applicant has sufficient intellectual knowledge, skills, and interests to pursue a university degree. High school graduation is required with 4 years English, 3 mathematics, 1 history, 1 laboratory science, 2 foreign language, 4 electives; 3.3 grade point average; SAT or ACT. The Graduate Program requires a bachelor's degree, 3 letters of recommendation; Graduate Record Examination; departmental advisory examinations, demonstration of level of vocal and/or instrumental performance.

Admission Procedure. Application and $35 nonrefundable fee to the Office of Admissions and Records between November 1 and 30 of year prior to enrollment for Fall quarter; and between July 1 and 31 for the Spring quarter. Graduate applications should be submitted by January 15 of the admission year.

Music Degrees Offered. Bachelor of Arts; Master of Arts; Ph.D.

Music Degree Requirements. The Bachelor of Arts music major degree program is intended for students interested in music as one of the fine arts and who may wish later to engage in music as a profession. Most of the courses in this major involve the student in the performance as well as the analysis of music. This major requires extensive development of technical musical skills. The music/humanities program is intended for students interested in music as one of the liberal arts and who wish to gain extensive knowledge and appreciation of music that will enable them to form part of an understanding, sophisticated musical public. The program does not require training in music prior to entrance into UCSD nor extensive time-consuming training in musicianship skills. The degree programs required the completion of 180 quarter units.

The Master of Arts degree program places emphasis on composition, performance, computer music, or theoretical studies. The degree requires the completion of at least 36 quarter units of graduate courses, including 6 units of advanced research projects and independent study bearing directly on completion of the master's thesis. All graduate students are expected to attend regularly the departmental colloquia and concerts aimed at extending and sharing their musical experience. They are encouraged to use these as opportunities to present their own work, research, and creative interests.

Students of superior musical competence may pursue a program with emphasis in composition or in theoretical studies leading to the Ph.D. degree in music. The normative time for the Ph.D. degree in music is four years (with master's degree), six years (without master's degree).

General Program Areas. Composition, Computer Music, Music Theory, Performance.

Instruments Taught. Bass, Bassoon, Clarinet, Flute, French Horn, Harp, Oboe, Piano, Saxophone, Trombone, Trumpet, Violin, Violoncello, Voice.

Musical Facilities

Practice Facilities. 19 practice rooms; 2 rooms equipped for percussionists. Wersi and Hammond, Allen Full organs; 25 pianos (upright, grand, electric); 4 grand pianos reserved for piano majors. 3 recording studios.

Concert Facilities. Mandeville Center Auditorium, seating 800; Recital Hall, 180; B-210 recital hall, 150.

Concerts/Musical Activities. Visiting artists, student/faculty recitals, concerts.

Music Library. The Central University Library houses an extensive separate collection of holdings in contemporary music, including an archive of recordings of most Department of Music performances. 15,000 books; 25,000 scores; 125 music periodicals. Listening facilities include 17 cassette decks; 5 stereo turntables; 4 compact disc players. Special manuscript collections of Ernest Krenik, Pauline Oliveros, Peter Yates.

Special Programs

Performance Groups. Symphony Orchestra, Concert Choir, Symphonic Chorus, Chamber Orchestra, Collegium Musicum, Gospel Choir, Chamber Opera, Music Theatre, Jazz Ensemble, Chamber Singers, Wind Ensemble, Madrigal Singers.

Financial

Costs. Per academic year: Estimated expenses for on-campus undergraduate residents of California $7,814; out-of-state students $12,976.

Financial Aid. All financial assistance is administered by the Student Financial Services Office. Scholarships, fellowships, and loans are available.

University of California, Santa Barbara
Department of Music
Santa Barbara
California 93106

Telephone. (805) 961-2311

Chief Administrator. Dolores M. Hsu, Department Chair.

The Anna S.C. Blake Training School, established in 1891, became the Santa Barbara State Normal School in 1909, and Santa Barbara State College in 1935. This school became a part of the University of California in 1944 and was designated a general campus in 1958. UCSB is located in Goleta on the Pacific shore, nine miles from the city of Santa Barbara.

The Department of Music undergraduate major programs are designed to serve as background for professional careers in music, as preparation for graduate studies, or as an area of concentration for a liberal arts education. Graduate programs are also offered. Performance ensembles are available for all qualified students, and a wide range of undergraduate courses is offered for nonmajors.

Accreditation. Western Association of Schools and Colleges.

Academic Information

Enrollment, Music Majors. (Total University) 17,415.
Music Faculty. 40.

Term System. Quarter. Six-week summer session.

Entrance Requirements. To qualify for admission as a freshman, the applicant must present a high school academic record of 15 units including 1 history, 4 English, 3 mathematics, 1 laboratory science, 2 foreign language, 4 college preparatory electives; combination of grade point average and ACT or SAT scores; 3 College Board Achievement Tests; theory placement test; placement audition in class piano and performance.

Admission Procedure. Application with supporting documents and nonrefundable $35 fee due July, October, November.

Music Degrees Offered. Bachelor of Music; Bachelor of Arts; Master of Arts; Doctor of Philosophy.

Music Degree Requirements. The Bachelor of Music degree is open by audition to specially qualified students in performance. The Bachelor of Arts degree program is offered with concentrations in composition, history, theory, and performance. The baccalaureate degrees require the completion of a minimum of 180 quarter units.

The Master of Arts degree is available in the areas of musicology, composition, theory, and musical performance. The latter program requires a recital and a supporting document; the other concentrations require a thesis or composition.

The Doctor of Philosophy degree is offered in the areas of musicology, composition, or theory.

General Program Areas. Composition, Music History, Music theory, Musicology, Performance.

Instruments Taught. Bass, Bassoon, Carillon, Clarinet, Flute, French Horn, Guitar, Harp, Harpsichord, Oboe, Organ, Percussion, Piano, Trombone, Trumpet, Viola, Violin, Violoncello, Voice.

Musical Facilities

Practice Facilities. 110 pianos (41 grands, 2 concert grands); 3 harpsichords; 4 organs; 2 harps. 1 percussion studio.

Concert Facilities. Lotte Lehmann Concert Hall, seating 467.

Concerts/Musical Activities. Each year more than 30 professional artists and ensembles perform; student/faculty concerts and recitals.

Music Library. The Arts Library is a full-service branch library that supports academic programs in art and music. The music collection is located on the second floor and contains 35,000 books, 10,000 discs, and a special archival collection of 78 rpm opera recordings. A multichanneled listening facility has 82 positions.

Special Programs

Performance Groups. Gold 'n Blues Band, Men's Chorus, Schubertians, Collegiate Chorale, Opera Workshop, Guitar Ensemble, New Music Ensemble, Piano Ensemble, Orchestra, Flute Choir, Chamber Music Ensemble, Brass Choir, Woodwind Ensemble, Symphonic Band, Jazz Ensemble, Collegium Musicum, Percussion Ensemble.

Financial

Costs. Per academic year: Tuition in-state resident none; out-of-state $4,086. Fees $1,320. Room and board $3,124.

Financial Aid. Financial aid funds are made available by the federal government, the State of California, the Board of Regents of the University of California, and various private organizations, corporations, and donors. Scholarship/financial aid application due March 15.

Commentary

Of particular note on the UCSB campus is the Center for Music and Research Acoustics, a new six-room, multi-media center housing studios with advanced equipment such as the VAX 11/750 mini-computer.

University of California, Santa Cruz
Music Board, Division of the Arts

Porter College
1156 High Street
Santa Cruz
California 95064

Telephone. (408) 429-2292

Chief Administrator. Dr. John Hajdu, Head.

Since it opened in 1965, the University of California, Santa Cruz has established a reputation within the UC system as a university devoted primarily to excellence in undergraduate education, enriched by a selected range of graduate programs and major research units. The academic plan and physical design of the campus combine the advantages of a small-college setting with the research and scholarship strengths of the University of California. The campus offers a full range of major programs with three academic divisions—Humanities and Arts, Natural Sciences, and Social Sciences—as well as a considerable number of interdisciplinary programs. The major programs are administered by boards or committees of studies, similar to departments at other universities. The Santa Cruz campus occupies 2,000 acres on the west side of the city of Santa Cruz, on Monterey Bay, about 75 miles south of San Francisco and 35 miles southwest of San Jose.

The music program provides courses for both general education and the major curriculum. The former serves all students, regardless of major, and encourages them to enroll in music courses, including performing groups and private instruction. The latter is designed to develop musicians whose knowledge of the discipline integrates scholarship and performance. It is expected that a music major will gain considerable experience in both these areas and will establish a broad and substantial foundation for further academic or performing studies, a teaching career, or other vocations that involve music. Students may prepare for advanced study and careers in scholarship, performance, or composition. While the core of the curriculum primarily focuses on music of Western civilization, it also embraces the traditions of non-Western cultures.

Accreditation. Western Association of Schools and Colleges.

Academic Information

Enrollment, Music Majors. 100. Foreign students 2.

Music Faculty. Full-time 15, part-time 20.

Term System. Quarter. No summer session.

Entrance Requirements. High school graduation with 16 units, including 4 English, 3 mathematics, 1 laboratory science, 1 social studies (U.S. history), 7 electives; SAT (preferred) or ACT; 3 College Board Achievement Tests (English, mathematics, and one from social sciences, foreign language, science, or literature). Audi-

tion required on arrival, or by appointment or tape in special circumstances; theory placement examinations.

Admission Procedure. Complete application with supporting documents and $35 nonrefundable fee. Applications accepted November 1 for following Fall quarter.

Music Degrees Offered. Bachelor of Arts.

Music Degree Requirements. The Bachelor of Arts degree with a major in music requires the completion of 180 quarter hours of prescribed courses. Music majors must successfully complete the language, keyboard proficiency, and senior comprehensive requirements, as well as the proficiency audition.

General Program Areas. Electronic Music, Ethnomusicology, Music History, Music Theory, Performance.

Instruments Taught. Bass, Bassoon, Clarinet, Flute, French Horn, Guitar, Harpsichord, Javanese Gamelan, Oboe, Percussion, Piano, Trombone, Trumpet, Tuba, Viola, Violin, Violoncello, Voice.

Musical Facilities

Practice Facilities. 18 practice rooms. 2 percussion-equipped practice rooms. 20 practice pianos; 4 grand pianos reserved for piano majors. Electronic music studio.

Concert Facilities. Concert Hall, seating 225.

Community Facilities. Several churches in the community and Carmel Mission.

Concerts/Musical Activities. The Arts and Lectures Program presents an annual series of performances by highly acclaimed artists and companies in theater, dance, music, and performance art; student/faculty recitals and ensemble groups.

Music Library. The music section of the McHenry Library contains 20,500 volumes; 8,000 scores; 10,000 music books; 11,000 phonograph recordings. Listening stations include 30 cassette decks and 6 stereo turntables. Library staff includes a music bibliographer, music cataloger, and a recordings room unit head. The Music Board has a special collection of gamelan instruments. Libraries at Stanford University and the University of California, Berkeley are available to students.

Special Programs

Performance Groups. Chamber Music, Chamber Singers, Ethnic Performing Ensemble, Javanese Gamelan Ensemble, University Concert Choir, Early Music Consort, University Orchestra.

Financial

Costs. Per academic year: Tuition in-state resident $1,394, out-of-state $5,481. Room and board $4,065. Fees charged for private music lessons.

Financial Aid. The University maintains a broad-based financial aid program of scholarships, loans, grants, and part-time employment. 9 music scholarships (average award $135 to $405) for music lessons; auditions are held each May. Part-time employment (range of earnings $4.25 to $6.30 per hour). College Work-Study program available.

California Institute of the Arts
School of Music

24700 McBean Parkway

Valencia

California 91355

Telephone. (805) 253-7818

Chief Administrator. Frans van Rossum, Dean.

The California Institute of the Arts (CalArts) was founded in 1961 as the first fully-accredited, degree-granting institution of higher learning in the United States created specifically for students of the visual and performing arts. The Institute was established through the vision and generosity of Walt Disney and the merger of two well-established professional schools, the Los Angeles Conservatory of Music, founded in 1883, and Chouinard Art Institute, founded in 1921. In 1970, CalArts opened its new campus and seven years later began its annual Contemporary Music Festival. In 1987, the CalArts Twentieth Century Players started a New Music Series in downtown Los Angeles in collaboration with the Los Angeles Philharmonic New Music Group. The Institute has awarded honorary doctoral degrees to Ravi Shankar, John Cage, Jan de Gaetani, Henry Mancini, and others.

The campus is situated on 60 acres of rolling hills 35 miles north of Los Angeles and reached via the Golden State Freeway.

Accreditation. Western Association of Schools and Colleges.

Academic Information

Enrollment, Music Majors. Full-time 65, part-time 53. 32 foreign students.

Term System. Semester. Academic year from Thursday after Labor Day to third Friday in May.

Entrance Requirements. High school graduation or equivalent; audition required (live or tape); portfolio for composers only; live interview; written statement of projected goals; evidence of talent in a particular area of concentration outweighs results of tests and transcripts. Foreign students required to have TOEFL and statement of financial competency.

Admission Procedure. Application and supporting documents to Admissions Office.

Music Degrees Offered. Bachelor of Fine Arts; Master of Fine Arts; Certificate; Advanced Certificate.

Music Degree Requirements. For the Bachelor and Master degree performance majors: 1 year residency, completion of all class requirements, mid-residence and graduation recitals, jury exam. For composer majors: 2 compositions each semester (Bachelor degree); 1 composition each semester (Master degree).

General Program Areas. Balinese Music, Composition, Electro-acoustic Composition, Euramerican Performance, Javanese Music, Jazz Composition, Jazz Performance, North Indian Music, West African Music, World Music Performance.

Instruments Taught. African Drum, Brass, Gamelan, Harp, Indian Flute, Percussion, Piano, Sitar, Stringed Instruments, Tabla, Voice, Woodwinds.

Musical Facilities

Practice Facilities. 21 practice rooms. Special practice facilities for percussionists. 6 grand pianos reserved for piano majors. Electro-acoustic music studios (analog and state-of-the-art digital).

Concert Facilities. Roy O. Disney Hall, seating 120; Modular Theatre, 320; Main Gallery, 300.

Concerts/Musical Activities. Faculty concerts (8 per year); Twentieth Century Players (8 per year); Chamber Music concerts (6 per year); Contemporary Music Festival (11 concerts per year); approximately 100 student recitals per year.

Music Library. 2,750 volumes; 12,300 scores; 133 current periodical subscriptions; 75 audiovisual items; 11,-950 phonograph recordings; 8,000 audiocassettes. 5 listening stations (stereo). Special collection of manuscripts and rare editions of contemporary scores.

Special Programs

Foreign Programs. Exchange program with the Hochschule der Kuenste in West Berlin, Germany.

Financial

Costs. Per academic year: Tuition $8,500. Room $1,-800 to $2,250. Board $1,600.

Financial Aid. Financial aid is awarded on the basis of academic merit, financial need, and musical ability. Institutional and state/federal aid as well as part-time employment and a College Work-Study program are available. 78 students receive aid (average award $6,000). Financial aid/scholarship application due February 1.

Commentary

California Institute of the Arts describes itself as a place where "everything is possible except narrow-mindedness." In many ways, it lives up to its reputation as a school of the future. Among its strengths are bachelor's and master's programs in jazz and non-Euroamerican (African, Indonesian, and North Indian) music. A more traditional aspect of the curriculum is a special woodwind quintet program offering intensive chamber music study.

The Internship program, administered by the Institute's Internship Program Office, gives a student the opportunity to take a job connected to his or her major academic interest. Some internships are paid positions while others are "brokered" for academic credit.

California State University, Chico
Department of Music
School of Humanities and Fine Arts
First and Normal Streets
Chico
California 95929

Telephone. (916) 895-5152
Chief Administrator. Raymond Barker, Department Chair.

California State University, Chico was established in 1887. The 126-acre campus is located in Chico at the northern end of the Sacramento Valley. The city is 90 miles north of Sacramento, eight miles from the Sacramento River, and two miles from the foothills of the Sierra Nevada.

The Department of Music offers wide curricular choices corresponding to particular student career objectives. All music majors take the music core consisting of a four-semester sequence of basic theoretical studies embodying harmony, counterpoint, analysis, instrumentation, conducting, and composition plus a two-semester sequence of music history. The objective of the core program is to provide theoretical training and historical knowledge basic to musicianship. To complete the baccalaureate requirements, students choose a curricular "pattern" fulfilling their personal goals and needs.

Accreditation. Western Association of Schools and Colleges; National Association of Schools of Music.

Academic Information

Enrollment, Music Majors. (Total University) 12,892.
Music Faculty. 20.
Term System. Semester.
Entrance Requirements. High school graduation or equivalent with a B average; SAT or ACT; audition required.
Admission Procedure. Application with supporting documents and nonrefundable $35 fee to Director of Admissions.
Music Degrees Offered. Bachelor of Arts; Master of Arts.
Music Degree Requirements. The Bachelor of Arts degree program offers "patterns" in the performance (instrumental, vocal, keyboard). These patterns are intended for students whose career goal is professional performance. Students planning careers in public school teaching follow the single subject credential pattern. The general pattern is a flexible program designed to serve the student who desires to study music as the focus of a broadly based liberal arts education as well as the student whose career goals lie in the realm of composer-

theorist or music historian. The baccalaureate degree requires the completion of a total of 124 units.

The Master of Arts degree in music, requiring the completion of 30 units, is available in two areas of emphasis: performance and music education.

General Program Areas. Composition, Music Education, Music History, Music Theory, Performance.
Instruments Taught. Brass, Harpsichord, Organ, Percussion, Piano, Stringed Instruments, Voice, Woodwinds.

Musical Facilities

Practice Facilities. The Department of Music is housed in the Performing Arts Center. 30 practice rooms, each with a piano. 2 harpsichords; clavichord, pedal clavichord. Electronic piano classroom; composition studio.
Concert Facilities. Harlan Adams Theatre; Ruth Rowland-Taylor Recital Hall; Lawrence Wismer Arena Theatre.
Concerts/Musical Activities. Frequent student/faculty concerts and recitals; visiting artists.
Music Library. Listening library.

Special Programs

Performance Groups. A Cappella Choir, Band, Marching Band, University Chorus, Orchestra, Symphonic Wind Ensemble, Brass Choir, Woodwind Quintet, Collegium Musicum, Mixed Ensembles, Jazz Ensemble, Opera Workshop, Chamber Singers.

Financial

Costs. Per academic year: Tuition in-state resident none, out-of-state $3,906. Fees $710. Room and board $2,434.
Financial Aid. Financial aid is awarded on the basis of academic merit, financial need, musical ability. Institutional and state/federal aid available. Financial aid/scholarship application due March 1. Part-time employment and a College Work-Study program available.

California State University, Fresno
Department of Music
School of Arts and Humanities
Shaw and Cedar Avenues
Fresno
California 93740

Telephone. (209) 294-4240
Chief Administrator. Phyllis A. Irwin, Chairman.

California State University, Fresno is the sixth oldest in the California State University system. It began as the first junior college in California in 1910, becoming a state normal school in 1911 with an enrollment of 150 students. University status was achieved in 1972 and the current name adopted. The 1,410-acre campus is located in the northeast section of Fresno (population 500,000) in the San Joaquin Valley.

The Department of Music provides undergraduate instruction in music for those planning professional careers as performers, composers, and teachers, as well as those preparing for advanced degrees in performance, composition, and musicology. The Department also strives to give non-music majors a background in music appreciation.

Accreditation. Western Association of Schools and Colleges; National Association of Schools of Music; National Council for Accreditation of Teacher Education.

Academic Information

Enrollment, Music Majors. (Total University) 13,904.
Music Faculty. 16.
Term System. Semester.
Entrance Requirements. High school graduation in upper one third of graduating class; SAT or ACT required.
Admission Procedure. Application with supporting documents and nonrefundable $35 fee to Admissions Office.
Music Degrees Offered. Bachelor of Arts; Master of Arts.
Music Degree Requirements. The Bachelor of Arts degree program is offered with two options. The Option 1 program is preparation for performance, composition, musicology, and careers in music other than public school teaching. Option 2 is a waiver program for single subject credential preparing students to teach music in grades K-12. A minimum of 124 semester units is required for the baccalaureate degree.

The Master of Arts degree program is designed to increase the candidate's professional competence, to increase the ability for continued self-directed study, and to provide opportunity for greater depth in the chosen area of concentration within the field of music. A total of 30 units is required for the degree.

General Program Areas. Composition, Music Education, Musicology, Performance.
Instruments Taught. Brass, Harp, Organ, Percussion, Piano, Stringed Instruments, Voice, Woodwinds.

Musical Facilities

Practice Facilities. The Music Building consists of faculty studios, offices, classrooms, practice rooms, rehearsal halls, and a recital hall. Special facilities include an electronic studio and a computer-assisted instruction laboratory.
Concert Facilities. Recital hall.
Concerts/Musical Activities. Student/faculty recitals and concerts; visiting artists.
Music Library. The Henry Madden Library supports the programs of the Department of Music through its Music Department.

Special Programs

Performance Groups. Community Chorus, Concert Choir, Chamber Singers, Musical Theatre Workshop, Jazz Singers, University Men's Chorus, University Women's Chorus, Brass Ensemble, Percussion Ensemble, String Ensemble, Woodwind Ensemble, Keyboard Ensemble, Orchestra, Concert Band, Marching Band, Jazz Ensemble.

Financial

Costs. Per academic year: Tuition in-state resident none, out-of-state $3,906. Fees $721. Room $1,439. Board $1,497.
Financial Aid. Financial aid is awarded on the basis of academic merit, financial need, musical ability. Institutional and state/federal aid available. Financial aid/ scholarship application due March 1. Part-time employment and a College Work-Study program available.

California State University, Fullerton
Department of Music
School of the Arts
800 North State College Boulevard
Fullerton
California 92634

Telephone. (714) 773-3511
Chief Administrator. David Thorsen, Department Chair.

California State University, Fullerton was founded in 1959. The 225-acre campus is located in Orange County, 35 miles from downtown Los Angeles.

The Department of Music offers a wide spectrum of degree programs with an overall emphasis in performance. The curriculum, designed to provide a balanced music education, offers basic preparation for careers in music or further graduate study. The Department strives to develop each student's musical and intellectual potential to the highest possible level.

Accreditation. Western Association of Schools and Colleges; National Association of Schools of Music; National Council for Accreditation of Teacher Education.

Academic Information

Enrollment, Music Majors. (Total University) 16,652.
Music Faculty. 28.
Term System. Semester. Two 6-week summer sessions.
Entrance Requirements. High school graduation with combined grade point average and test score placement in upper third of California high school graduates; SAT or ACT; audition required.
Admission Procedure. Application with supporting documents and nonrefundable $35 fee to Office of Admissions and Records.

Music Degrees Offered. Bachelor of Music; Bachelor of Arts; Master of Music; Master of Arts.

Music Degree Requirements. The Bachelor of Music and Bachelor of Arts degree programs are offered with an emphasis in liberal arts, music history and theory, music education, performance, composition, or accompanying. A minimum of 124 semester units is required for the baccalaureate degree.

The Master of Music degree program provides an avenue of graduate study for the composer or performer tailored to each student's demonstrated talent and to each student's professional development. The Master of Arts in music degree program provides advanced studies in breadth as well as in an area of specialization, either music education or music history and literature. The master's degree requires a minimum of 30 units of graduate study.

General Program Areas. Accompanying, Composition, Conducting, Music Education, Music History, Music Theory, Performance.

Instruments Taught. Brass, Organ, Percussion, Piano, Stringed Instruments, Voice, Woodwinds.

Musical Facilities

Concert Facilities. UC Theatre.

Concerts/Musical Activities. Student/faculty recitals and concerts; visiting artists.

Music Library. The Phonorecord and Tape Library includes a representative selection of classical and semi-classical music. The Music Listening Room in the University Center has a wide selection of the latest releases of rock, jazz, classical, and country-western music.

Special Programs

Performance Groups. Symphony Orchestra, University Choir, University Concert Band, Opera Theatre, University Singers, Wind Ensemble, Women's Choir, Jazz Band, Varsity Band, Chamber Singers, Percussion Ensemble, Brass Ensemble, Horn Ensemble, Chamber Orchestra, Renaissance Ensemble, Guitar Ensemble, Keyboard Ensemble, String Ensemble, Saxophone Ensemble, Collegium Musicum.

Financial

Costs. Per academic year: Tuition in-state none, out-of-state $5,115. Fees $744.

Financial Aid. Financial aid is awarded on the basis of academic merit and financial need. Institutional and state/federal aid available. Financial aid/scholarship application due March 1. Part-time employment and a College Work-Study program available.

California State University, Hayward
Department of Music
Hayward
California 94542

Telephone. (415) 881-3135

Chief Administrator. William G. Wohlmacher, Chair.

California State University, Hayward was founded in 1959 with an enrollment of 303 students. Today it enrolls over 9,000 students each year. The 354-acre campus overlooks the San Francisco Bay area.

The Department of Music offers undergraduate and graduate programs, providing training in public school or private teaching, careers in performance, and preparation for more specialized study in graduate school. A number of performance groups present public performances. The Department also offers a number of courses designed especially for non-music majors.

Accreditation. Western Association of Schools and Colleges; National Association of Schools of Music; National Council for Accreditation of Teacher Education.

Academic Information

Enrollment, Music Majors. (Total University) 9,460.

Music Faculty. 19.

Term System. Quarter.

Entrance Requirements. High school graduation or equivalent; California residents in upper third of all California high school graduates; SAT or ACT required; majors entering with composition as their applied area are required to be proficient in an instrumental medium; audition required.

Admission Procedure. Application with supporting documents and nonrefundable $35 fee to Office of Admissions and Records.

Music Degrees Offered. Bachelor of Arts; Master of Arts.

Music Degree Requirements. The Bachelor of Arts degree is offered with emphasis in keyboard, voice, orchestral or band instrument, guitar, or composition. The program requires the completion of 186 quarter units, including the general education and other graduation requirements and courses in music.

The Master of Music degree curriculum provides an opportunity for advanced study for school and college music teachers who wish to increase their professional effectiveness, and for students who plan to continue graduate study. The degree is offered with a choice of four areas of emphasis: theory-composition, history and literature, performance, and music education. Completion of 45 quarter units is required.

General Program Areas. Composition, Jazz Studies, Music Education, Music History, Music Literature, Music Theory, Performance.

Instruments Taught. Baritone, Bass, Bassoon, Clarinet, Flute, French Horn, Guitar, Harp, Harpsichord,

Oboe, Organ, Percussion, Piano, Saxophone, Trombone, Trumpet, Tuba, Viola, Violin, Violoncello, Voice.

Musical Facilities

Concert Facilities. Theatre, seating 500.

Concerts/Musical Activities. Student and faculty concerts and recitals; visiting artists.

Music Library. The University Library supports the programs of the Department of Music. Listening facilities.

Special Programs

Performance Groups. University Chorus, University Orchestra, University Singers, Opera Workshop, Chamber Ensemble, Men's Chorus, Jazz Workshop, Symphonic Band, University Oratorio.

Financial

Costs. Per academic year: Tuition in-state none, out-of-state $4,497. Fees $633.

Financial Aid. Financial aid in the form of scholarships, grants, loans, and part-time employment is available. Financial aid/scholarship application due April 15.

California State University, Long Beach
Department of Music

School of Fine Arts
1250 Bellflower Boulevard
Long Beach
California 90840

Telephone. (213) 498-4781

Chief Administrator. Dr. Wayne M. Sheley, Dean, School of Fine Arts.

California State University, Long Beach, was founded in 1949. It enrolls over 23,000 students annually. The 322-acre campus has 67 buildings in the city of Long Beach, 20 miles south of Los Angeles.

The undergraduate curriculum provides programs in performance, teaching, and music therapy, and to prepare for graduate studies. There is also a program for non-music majors. The Department offers graduate degrees.

Accreditation. Western Association of Schools and Colleges; National Association of Schools of Music.

Academic Information

Enrollment, Music Majors. (Total University) 23,376.

Music Faculty. 16 plus applied music staff.

Term System. Semester. 3 summer sessions.

Entrance Requirements. High school graduation; top one third of graduating class; ACT or SAT; all entering freshmen and transfer students are required to take a theory placement test and performance auditions which are regularly administered in May and December and are also available at the beginning of registration week each semester. GRE required for graduate study.

Admission Procedure. Application with all supporting documents and nonrefundable $35 fee to Office of Admissions and Records.

Music Degrees Offered. Bachelor of Music; Bachelor of Arts; Master of Arts.

Music Degree Requirements. The Bachelor of Music degree is offered with concentrations in history and literature, composition, instrumental music, choral-vocal music, and performance. The degree requires a total of 132 units which must include a minimum of 40 upper division units. The Bachelor of Arts degree with a major in music is offered in the context of a liberal arts program.

The Master of Arts degree in music requires the completion of a minimum of 30 units.

The Music Therapy Certificate Program is also offered by the Department.

General Program Areas. Choral Music, Composition, Instrumental Music, Music History, Music Literature, Music Therapy, Performance.

Instruments Taught. Accordion, Brass, Guitar, Organ, Percussion, Piano, Stringed Instruments, Voice, Woodwinds.

Musical Facilities

Practice Facilities. The Music Department is housed in facilities dedicated in 1982 which provide accommodations for group lessons, private practice, and development of electronic music.

Concert Facilities. 2 performance halls.

Concerts/Musical Activities. Student and faculty concerts and recitals; visiting artists.

Music Library. The University Library houses over 900,000 volumes. Special collections include: Wesley Kuhnle Repository concentrating on historic tunings and temperaments; oral history of the arts in Southern California.

Special Programs

Featured Programs. The Summer Institute of Chamber Music is a comprehensive program devoted to the study and performance of chamber music.

Performance Groups. New Music Ensemble, Marching Band, Chamber Music, Brass Ensembles, Percussion Ensemble, String Quartet, Collegium Musicum, Vocal Ensembles, University Choir, Forty-Niner Chorus, Men's Chorus, Women's Chorus, Band, Orchestra.

Financial

Costs. Per academic year: Tuition in-state none, out-of-state $3,906. Fees $656. Room and board $3,500.

Financial Aid. Institutional and state/federal aid in the form of scholarships, grants, loans, and part-time employment is available. Financial aid/scholarship application due March 15.

California State University, Los Angeles
Department of Music
5151 State University Drive
Los Angeles
California 90032

Telephone. (213) 224-3448
Chief Administrator. Dr. Donald Para, Chair.
California State University, Los Angeles, was founded in 1947. Located at the eastern edge of Los Angeles, the campus occupies 200 acres.

The undergraduate programs in music are designed to provide students with a broad, general foundation in the theoretical branches of music, competence in artistic performance, and professional preparation for graduate study.

Accreditation. Western Association of Schools and Colleges; National Association of Schools of Music; National Council for Accreditation of Teacher Education.

Academic Information

Enrollment, Music Majors. (Total University) 13,919.
Music Faculty. 20.
Term System. Quarter.
Entrance Requirements. High school graduation with a rank in upper third of class; SAT or ACT required; audition required. GRE required for graduate programs.
Admission Procedure. Application with supporting documents and nonrefundable $35 application fee to Office of Admissions and Records.
Music Degrees Offered. Bachelor of Music; Bachelor of Arts; Master of Arts.
Music Degree Requirements. The Bachelor of Music degree curriculum is designed to provide professional training for serious, talented musicians seeking preparation for careers in performance. A total of 198 units is required for the degree including a core program, the major, and general education requirements. Options are available in keyboard performance for piano, organ, or harpsichord; instrumental performance in solos, small ensembles, bands, or orchestras; solo and group vocal performance; and jazz music performance, production, composition, recording, and conducting. The Bachelor of Arts degree curriculum emphasizes history, theory, composition, and literature of music, with a foundation in performance. Included are courses in keyboard, instrumental, and vocal performance; conducting; with opportunity for development in one of the areas of specialization (choral teaching, instrumental teaching, performance, or composition). A total of 186 units is required for the degree.
General Program Areas. Choral Teaching, Commercial Music, Composition, Instrumental Teaching, Jazz Studies, Music Education, Music History, Music Literature, Music Recording Arts, Music Theory, Performance.

Instruments Taught. Brass, Organ, Percussion, Piano, Stringed Instruments, Woodwinds.

Musical Facilities

Concerts/Musical Activities. Student and faculty recitals and concerts; visiting artists.
Music Library. The University Library houses more than 820,000 books and bound periodicals and serves the goals and programs of the Department of Music. Special collections include: performing scores of Otto Klemperer; Roy Harris Archive.

Special Programs

Featured Programs. The Department of Music, in cooperation with the Departments of Electrical and Computer Engineering and Technology, offers a credit certification program in music recording arts.
Performance Groups. Symphonic Band, Symphony Orchestra, Glee Club, Concert Choir, Chorus, String Ensemble, Woodwind Ensemble, Brass Ensemble, Percussion Ensemble, Jazz Ensemble, Chamber Singers.

Financial

Costs. Per academic year: Tuition in-state none, out-of-state $4,320. Fees $738. Room $1,800.
Financial Aid. Financial aid is awarded on the basis of academic merit and financial need. Institutional and state/federal aid available as well as part-time employment and a College Work-Study program. Financial aid/scholarship application due April 15.

California State University, Northridge
Music Department
18111 Nordhoff Street
Northridge
California 91330

Telephone. (818) 885-3184
Chief Administrator. Dr. Clarence E. Wiggins, Chair.
California State University, Northridge, formally known as San Fernando State College, now enrolls over 20,000 students annually. The 350-acre campus is located north of Los Angeles in the San Fernando Valley, 20 miles from the Pacific Ocean.

The Music Department offers a curriculum designed for students who plan to teach music in the public schools and/or privately or who desire a liberal arts education with emphasis in music. It also offers a program for students who plan musical careers as performers, directors, composers, arrangers, or college teachers. A graduate program is also offered.

Accreditation. Western Association of Schools and Colleges; National Association of Schools of Music.

Academic Information

Enrollment, Music Majors. (Total University) 20,701.
Music Faculty. 37.

Term System. Semester. 2 summer sessions.

Entrance Requirements. High school graduation with a composite scholastic average and ACT or SAT score in the upper third of California high school graduates; audition required.

Admission Procedure. Application with supporting documents and nonrefundable $35 fee to Office of Admissions and Records.

Music Degrees Offered. Bachelor of Music; Bachelor of Arts; Master of Music; Master of Arts.

Music Degree Requirements. The Bachelor of Music degree is offered with options available in each of the following performance areas: strings, winds and percussion, voice, keyboard, studio music, and composition/theory. The program requires the completion of 132 semester units. The Bachelor of Arts degree provides a broad base and thorough grounding in all aspects of music history, appreciation and literature, theory and composition, applied music, musical organizations and ensembles, and music education.

The Master of Arts degree is available in music education, musicology, and theory. A minimum of 30 units is required.

General Program Areas. Choral Conducting, Composition, Instrumental Conducting, Music Education, Music History, Music Literature, Music Theory, Music Therapy, Musicology, Performance.

Instruments Taught. Brass, Guitar, Percussion, Piano, Stringed Instruments, Voice, Woodwinds.

Musical Facilities

Practice Facilities. The Department is housed in the Music Building.

Concerts/Musical Activities. Student/faculty recitals and concerts; visiting artists.

Music Library. The University Libraries house over 900,000 volumes. An Instructional Media Center, located in the Oviatt Library, provides a full range of media services.

Special Programs

Performance Groups. University Chorus, Jazz Vocal Ensemble, University Singers, Oratorio, Chamber Singers, Opera Chorus, Women's Glee Club, Symphonic Wind Ensemble, Concert Band, Jazz Ensemble, Symphony Orchestra, Matador Field Band, Chamber Orchestra, Brass Ensemble, Studio Orchestra, Percussion Ensemble, Jazz Ensemble, Opera Workshop, Wind Chamber Ensemble, Piano Ensemble, Collegium Musicum.

Financial

Costs. Per academic year: Tuition in-state none, out-of-state $4,371. Fees $752. Room and board $2,910.

Financial Aid. Institutional and state/federal scholarships, grants, loans, and part-time employment are available. Financial aid/scholarship application due March 1.

California State University, Sacramento
Department of Music

6000 J Street
Sacramento
California 95819

Telephone. (916) 278-6514

Chief Administrator. Dr. Lorna Adams, Chairman.

Founded in 1947, California State University, Sacramento is the seventh largest of the 19 State University campuses. It is a regional multipurpose institution of public education, serving 13 counties of north-central California. Formerly named Sacramento State College, the present name was adopted in 1972. The 300-acre campus is situated along the American River in Sacramento, the capital of California.

The Department of Music believes that its particular strength is in instrumental performance.

Accreditation. Western Association of Schools and Colleges; National Association of Schools of Music.

Academic Information

Enrollment, Music Majors. 212, including graduate students.

Music Faculty. Full-time 24, part-time 10.

Term System. Semester.

Entrance Requirements. High school graduation with a composite scholastic average and SAT or ACT score placing the applicant in the upper third of California high school graduates; for nonresidents, upper sixth; audition required;

Admission Procedure. Submit application with supporting documents to Admissions Office. During the first week of classes, auditions are held to place the student in an 8-semester sequence.

Music Degrees Offered. Bachelor of Music; Bachelor of Arts; Master of Arts.

Music Degree Requirements. The Bachelor of Music degree is offered with concentrations in piano technology, theory/composition, and history and literature. The Bachelor of Arts degree with a major in music is offered in the context of a liberal arts curriculum. The Master of Arts degree is offered in four areas: theory/composition, history and literature, performance, and music education.

General Program Areas. Choral Conducting, Composition, Music Education, Music History, Music Literature, Music Theory, Performance.

Instruments Taught. Bass, Flute, French Horn, Guitar, Oboe, Organ, Piano, Trombone, Trumpet, Viola, Violin, Violoncello, Voice.

Musical Facilities

Practice Facilities. 50 practice pianos. Special practice facilities for percussionists. Electronic music studio.

Concert Facilities. Recital Hall, seating 346.

Concerts/Musical Activities. Large and small performing ensembles; solo and chamber recitals.

Music Library. Most music materials are housed in the main library. Separate collection of phonograph recordings maintained in the Music Building. Listening facilities (audiocassettes, stereo).

Special Programs

Performance Groups. Ensembles, choral groups, orchestra.

Financial

Costs. Per academic year: Fee in-state resident $677, out-of-state tuition and fee $4,061. Room $1,640. Board $1,460.

Financial Aid. Financial aid in the form of state/federal loans available.

The Claremont Graduate School
Music Department
Harper Hall 160
150 East 10th Street
Claremont
California 91711

Telephone. (714) 621-8081

Chief Administrator. Dr. Roland Jackson, Chairman.

The Claremont Graduate School, founded in 1925, is a private institution devoted to study beyond the bachelor's degree. Association with five distinguished undergraduate colleges in a cluster known as The Claremont Colleges enables the Graduate School to offer the facilities of a university while retaining the flexibility and close faculty-student relationships of a separate college of graduate studies. The city of Claremont is a residential community of 34,000 people located 35 miles east of Los Angeles. Situated at an elevation of 1,150 feet on the lower slopes of the San Gabriel Mountains, Claremont is an unusually attractive city, with tree-lined streets and 140 acres of parks.

The Music Department offers courses of study leading to the Master of Arts, the Master of Musical Arts in Church Music, the Doctor of Musical Arts, and the Doctor of Philosophy degrees. In addition to studies during the regular academic year, the Music Department participates in the Three-Summer Master's Degree program. This program is designed primarily for prospec-

tive and current teachers in secondary schools and junior colleges. Candidates seeking initial certification in the public secondary schools of California may also participate in the Claremont Secondary Internship Program. The Music Department also accepts for the Three-Summer M.A. degree program applicants wishing to specialize in music history, composition, and performance.

Accreditation. Western Association of Schools and Colleges.

Academic Information

Enrollment, Music Majors. Full-time men 14, women 21.

Music Faculty. Full-time 3, part-time 12.

Term System. Semester. Summer session. Academic year from early September to early May.

Entrance Requirements. Criteria for admission include the high probability of success in graduate study and subsequent teaching, research, or professional careers; the admissions decision is individualized and based on a wide range of information about the applicant; bachelor's degree granted by a university or college of recognized standing is requisite to admission.

Admission Procedure. Application with nonrefundable $30 fee; transcripts, biography, 3 letters of recommendation; GRE score; TOEFL for foreign students. Auditions (tape recordings may be accepted in lieu of personal appearance in the case of applicants who live a considerable distance from the Graduate School); compositions or published articles for other sub-fields.

Music Degrees Offered. Master of Arts; Master of Musical Arts; Doctor of Musical Arts; Doctor of Philosophy.

Music Degree Requirements. The degree Master of Arts in Music requires a minimum of 30 semester units of coursework, 16 of which are basic courses. The remainder are to be taken in the student's area of concentration. Concentrations available are performance (including conducting), composition, music history, and music education. The degree Master of Musical Arts in Church Music with a major in either organ or choral conducting requires the completion of 60 semester units, 40 in musical subjects and 20 in the field of theology. All students must pass examinations in two languages, including German and either French, Italian, or Latin. The project component of the degree is fulfilled by two public concerts and a substantial paper.

The Doctor of Musical Arts degree may be pursued in one of two majors: performance or composition. Either major requires a minimum of 72 units beyond the bachelor's degree. Proficiency is required in two foreign languages. The ability to read and perform fluently from Medieval or Renaissance musical notation may be substituted when appropriate by performance majors in place of reading proficiency in the second foreign language. Qualifying examinations and a project are also required. The degree Doctor of Philosophy in Musicology requires a minimum of 72 units beyond the bachelor's degree. Course requirements include historical era courses emphasizing performance practices; performance; electives; dissertation research, and a non-music minor (all in one field). Language requirements, preliminary examinations, qualifying examinations, and a dissertation are required.

General Program Areas. Composition, Conducting, Music Education, Music History, Musicology, Performance.

Instruments Taught. Bass, Bassoon, Clarinet, Flute, Guitar, Harp, Harpsichord, Horn, Oboe, Organ, Piano, Saxophone, Timpani, Trombone, Trumpet, Tuba, Viola, Violin, Violoncello, Voice.

Musical Facilities

Practice Facilities. Special practice facilities for organists, pianists, and percussionists.

Concert Facilities. Ten halls are available for musical performances at The Claremont Colleges, ranging in seating capacity from 125 to 2,500.

Concerts/Musical Activities. Numerous student/faculty recitals throughout the academic year.

Music Library. Students have access to campus libraries with musical literature and score collections numbering some 26,780 items as well as 10,300 recordings. Special research holdings at the Claremont Colleges are the Janssen Collection of musical instruments, the Seymour Collection of operatic scores, the McCutcheon Collection of hymnology, and the Schumann-Heink Collection of music and memorabilia. Important research collections such as those at the Huntington Library in San Marino are within easy reach of the campus.

Special Programs

Featured Programs. The Clavier Workshop is a two-semester workshop in which the student has the opportunity to build, or work on, a copy of a baroque keyboard instrument.

Performance Groups. Collegium Musicum, Baroque Instrumental Ensemble, Orchestra, Chamber Choir, Concert Choirs (two).

Financial

Costs. Per academic year: Tuition $8,730. Fees $100. Housing $195 to $495 per month.

Financial Aid. Fellowships and research/teaching assistantships are available.

Mills College
Music Department
5000 MacArthur Boulevard
Oakland
California 94613

Telephone. (415) 430-2171

Chief Administrator. David Rosenboom, Department Head.

Mills College is a privately supported, residential liberal arts college for women. Men are permitted to enroll in the graduate school. The College was founded in 1852 as a Young Ladies Seminary in Benicia, California. In 1854, Mary Atkins, a graduate of Oberlin College, took over the school. It was purchased by Cyrus Mills in 1865 and the College moved to its present campus in 1871. The 127-acre campus is surrounded by the city of Oakland and within 30 minutes of downtown San Francisco.

The Music Department curriculum is drawn from the expertise of a small faculty of active professionals in performance, research, and composition. The undergraduate music major at Mills is directed toward the acquisition and development of knowledge and skills that are basic to all musicians. Through course electives, it provides opportunities for the student to follow a special interest, whether in music history, Indonesian gamelan, ethnomusicology, improvisation, composition, or performance.

Accreditation. Western Association of Schools and Colleges.

Academic Information

Enrollment, Music Majors. Undergraduate 40, graduate 37.

Music Faculty. Full-time 4, part-time 8; instrumentalists 32.

Term System. Semester. No summer session.

Entrance Requirements. High school graduation or GED; recommend 4 units English, 3 mathematics, 2 laboratory science, 2 to 4 foreign language, 2 social studies; SAT (average combined score 1050-1100); audition required.

Admission Procedure. Priority application due February 1 for freshmen, April 1 for transfer students; nonrefundable application fee $25.

Music Degrees Offered. Bachelor of Arts; Master of Arts; Master of Fine Arts; Master of Liberal Studies.

Music Degree Requirements. The Bachelor of Arts degree program requires the completion of 34 semester course credits including requirements in general distribution, writing, and the major. The major includes 14½ semester course credits in prerequisites, theory, history and literature, letters, and additional music courses. A comprehensive examination, senior project, or independent study is also required.

The Master of Arts degree is offered with concentrations in composition, music history and literature, and performance. The programs include two years of residence and 8 to 9 semester course credits. The Master of Fine Arts degree in electronic music and the recording media can be pursued with concentrations in composition and performance utilizing electronic media; interdisciplinary work based on music but involving a variety of media forms such as video and film production, staging, lighting, and scriptwriting; research in instruments or systems design, emphasizing fine arts computation; and research in music languages, algorithmic composition, and aspects of formal perception and modelling. The degree requires the completion of 9 semester course credits.

Teaching credentials may also be pursued at Mills College. The one-year program may be combined with the master's degree program. Courses stress the integration of theory and practice to develop a highly skilled and reflective professional educator as teacher.

General Program Areas. Baroque Music, Composition, Electronic Music, Ethnomusicology, Music Education, Music History, Music Literature, Performance, Recording Media.

Instruments Taught. Bassoon, Clarinet, Clavichord, Flute, Gamelan, Guitar, Harp, Harpsichord, Oboe, Organ, Percussion, Piano, Saxophone, Trumpet, Viola, Violin, Violoncello, Voice.

Musical Facilities

Practice Facilities. 30 practice rooms; 4 studios. 2 organs (Holtkamp free standing pipe organ; Baldwin electric 2 manual and pedal board). 1 percussion-equipped practice room. 58 pianos (7 Steinway grands, 5 Baldwin grands, 7 miscellaneous grands; 39 uprights (Baldwin, Ivers and Pond, Chickering, Yamaha); 5 grand pianos reserved for piano majors.

Concert Facilities. Concert Hall, seating 530; Greek Theatre, 500; Chapel, 150; Ensemble Room, 80.

Concerts/Musical Activities. Concerts and recitals.

Music Library. The main library houses 190,000 volumes, 12,000 of which are musical scores located in the music building. 35 music-related periodicals; 4,000 phonograph recordings. Listening facilities (cassette, stereo). The Bender Room containing rare books and manuscripts also displays a Petrus Guarnerius violin, circa 1690.

Special collections include: extensive Darius Milhaud collection; chamber music manuscripts of works dedicated to Elizabeth Sprague Coolidge.

Special Programs

Featured Programs. The Center for Contemporary Music maintains a variety of electronic equipment, instruments, studios, and laboratories. It provides instruction and technical assistance, and houses valuable recorded archives. As part of the Music Department, the Center offers many new music and allied arts concerts each year, plus a seminar series on Formal Methods in which guest artists share the latest ideas in language research, experimental aesthetics, music perception, arts, and technology.

Foreign Programs. Study Abroad Programs available for sophomores and juniors.

Affiliated Programs. Cross-registration under special circumstances with the University of California at Berkeley, California College of Arts and Crafts, Holy Names College, St. Mary's College, and a few other selected colleges.

Financial

Costs. Per academic year: Tuition $8,400. Fees $250. Room and board $4,100.

Financial Aid. Financial aid in the form of scholarships, grants, loans, student employment, and College Work-Study program. Financial aid/scholarship applications due February 1 and April 1.

Commentary

Mills College has attained a prominent place in twentieth century music history, beginning with the thirty-one-year tenure of celebrated French composer Darius Milhaud (1940-1971). Over the years, it has attracted visits by distinguished composers and performing artists from all over the world.

University of the Pacific
Conservatory of Music
3601 Pacific Avenue
Stockton
California 95211

Telephone. (209) 946-2415
Chief Administrator. Dr. Carl Nosse, Dean.

The University of the Pacific was established in 1851 as California's first chartered institution of higher learning. Undergraduate programs are offered through six divisions of the University: the College of the Pacific (liberal arts), the Conservatory of Music, the School of Business and Public Administration, the School of Engineering, the School of Education, and the School of Pharmacy. Located in a residential area of Stockton, the architecture and landscaping of the 150-acre main campus provide the University with a pleasant educational setting. A majority of the 3,400 undergraduate students, who come from 38 states and 60 foreign countries, live on campus.

The Conservatory of Music, founded in 1878, was one of the first conservatories west of the Mississippi River. For over 100 years, the University of the Pacific's Conservatory of Music has been engaged in training students for the music profession. In addition to a strong emphasis upon performance, the Conservatory offers programs in theory and composition, music education, music history, music therapy, and music management. Students from other schools and colleges in the University, for whom music is an enjoyable avocation, have enrolled in Conservatory classes and activities, learning to play instruments, to sing, and to understand and appreciate fine music as a fundamental part of their education in the humanities.

Conservatory programs stress not only the artistic values of creativity and experimentation, but also the disciplined attributes of scholarship and skill. Small classes and one-on-one applied music and vocal instruction are offered.

Accreditation. Western Association of Colleges and Schools; National Association of Schools of Music; National Association of Music Therapy.

Academic Information

Enrollment, Music Majors. Full-time 55 men, 86 women; part-time (graduate) 14 men, 3 women. Foreign students 1.

Music Faculty. Full-time 25, part-time 14. 13 artists currently in residence.

Term System. Semester. Academic year from August to May. Three summer sessions from May to August.

Entrance Requirements. High school graduation or equivalent with strong college preparatory program and B average or better; SAT preferred, ACT accepted; counselor's recommendation required; GRE required for graduate school. All prospective Conservatory students must pass an audition, either in person or via a tape recording; auditions are held on the Stockton campus in the spring, and personal auditions are held off campus and out of state during the month of February. Auditions are held in such cities as Honolulu, San Francisco, Los Angeles, San Diego, Phoenix, Chicago, Minneapolis-St. Paul, Portland (Oregon), Denver, Seattle, Albuquerque, St. Louis, and Oklahoma City. Applicants for the theory and composition major are also required to submit an original composition; those applying for the music history major must prepare a 500-word essay on a subject provided by the Conservatory. All entering music students take placement examinations in theory and music history and audition in keyboard and applied music during Orientation Week.

Qualified transfer students may enter the Conservatory at the beginning of any semester.

Admission Procedure. Application due no later than March 15 for Fall and December 15 for Spring; $25 nonrefundable application fee.

Music Degrees Offered. Bachelor of Music, Bachelor of Arts emphasizing a general overview of music, Master of Arts in Music, Master of Music in Performance, Master of Arts in Theory and Composition, Master of Arts in Music Therapy, Master of Arts in Teaching in Music Education, Doctor of Education in Music Education.

Music Degree Requirements. The degree requirements include a balance of four elements: core curriculum, general education, internship and performance, and the major.

General Program Areas. Composition, Music Education, Music History, Music Management, Performance, Theory.

Instruments Taught. Baritone, Bass, Bassoon, Cello, Clarinet, Cornet, Flute, French Horn, Guitar, Harp, Harpsichord, Oboe, Organ, Percussion, Piano, Saxophone, Trombone, Trumpet, Tuba, Viola, Violin, Voice.

Musical Facilities

Practice Facilities. Special practice facilities for organists; 5 organs (Esty, Schlicker, Moeller, Wicks, Schoenstein). Practice rooms for percussionists. 57 practice rooms for piano majors; 38 practice pianos (6 Yamaha grand, 4 Kawai grand; Hamilton, Baldwin, Kimball uprights); 5 grand pianos reserved for piano majors. Music therapy labs, music education labs, electronic music studio, recording studio.

Concert Facilities. Faye Spanos Concert Hall seats 1,000; Long Theatre seats 500; Recital Hall seats 120.

Community Facilities. Local professional recording studio.

Concerts/Musical Activities. Resident Artist Series, Student Recital Series, Alumni Recital Series, Guest Artist Series.

Music Library. The music collection is shelved as a distinct collection within the main library. (A new Music Library was scheduled for completion in 1987.) 5,000 books; 7,000 musical scores; 110 current periodical subscriptions; 20 audiovisual materials; 30 microforms; 6,000 phonograph recordings; 50 audiocassettes; 25 listening booths. Some early editions and rare books housed in Special Collections Department. Other large music libraries located in San Francisco Bay area at University of California, Berkeley and Stanford University.

Special Programs

Performance Groups. Concert Band, Pacific Wind Ensemble, Tiger Marching Band, Varsity Band, Jazz Band, A Cappella Choir, Women's Chorus, Concert Chorus, Conservatory Opera Theatre, Symphony Orchestra, Pacific Arts Woodwind Quintet, Sierra Chamber Players, Pacific Chamber Players.

Financial

Costs. Per academic year: Tuition $9,992. Applied music lessons $35 to $200 depending on instrument and number of units. Room and board $3,928. Off-campus housing approximately $400 per month.

Financial Aid. Financial aid is awarded on the basis of academic merit, financial need, musical ability. Institutional and state/federal aid available. 111 students currently receive some form of financial aid (average award

$9,726). Financial aid/scholarship application due February 11. College Work-Study program available.

Pomona College
Music Department
Claremont
California 91711

Telephone. (714) 621-8155

Chief Administrator. Dr. Jon D. Bailey, Department Chair.

Pomona College is a privately supported, coeducational liberal arts college established in 1887. It is one of the founding members of the Claremont Colleges. The campus is located 35 miles east of Los Angeles.

The Music Department offers instruction for students who wish to study music as one of the liberal arts as well as for those who are seeking professional training in musical performance, scholarship, or related fields. Courses without prerequisites are designed specifically for students who possess little or no musical background; courses in the concentration curriculum are intended primarily for music majors and others with musical training and experience.

Accreditation. Western Association of Schools and Colleges.

Academic Information

Enrollment, Music Majors. (Total College) 1,359.

Music Faculty. 11 plus performance music faculty.

Term System. Semester.

Entrance Requirements. High school graduation with superior academic grades and outstanding personal qualifications; college-preparatory courses recommended (4 units English, 3 mathematics, 2 science, 2 foreign language, 2 social science); SAT or ACT; 3 Achievement Tests recommended.

Admission Procedure. Application with supporting documents and nonrefundable $30 fee to Office of Admissions.

Music Degrees Offered. Bachelor of Arts.

Music Degree Requirements. The Bachelor of Arts degree in music is offered in the context of a liberal arts program. Students interested in a concentration combining music with a related field may work out a special program in consultation with professors in the respective departments. The baccalaureate degree requires the completion of 32 courses, normally accomplished in eight semesters.

General Program Areas. Conducting, Music History, Music Theory, Performance.

Instruments Taught. Bass, Bassoon, Clarinet, Flute, Harpsichord, Oboe, Organ, Percussion, Piano, Saxophone, Trombone, Trumpet, Tuba, Viola, Violin, Violoncello.

Musical Facilities

Practice Facilities. The Thatcher Music Building was completed in 1970 and includes offices and studios for the Department; Bryant Hall for orchestra and band. Bridges Hall houses a four-manual Moeller organ; Thatcher Hall houses a two-manual Moeller practice organ, a three-manual von Beckerath baroque organ with tracker action, and a ten-rank Flentrop tracker-action practice organ.

Concert Facilities. Ralph H. Lyman Hall; Greek Theatre in Blanchard Park.

Concerts/Musical Activities. Student and faculty recitals and concerts; visiting artists.

Music Library. Victor Montgomery Music Library is housed in the Thatcher Music Building.

Special Programs

Performance Groups. Pomona College Choir, Symphony Orchestra, Pomona College Band, Chamber Music, Jazz Ensemble, Pomona College Glee Club, String Arts Ensemble.

Financial

Costs. Per academic year: Tuition $10,150. Fees $270. Room $1,850. Board $2,350.

Financial Aid. Various memorial music scholarships and prizes are awarded annually. A limited number of financial grants for applied music lessons are available through the Department of Music. Other sources of financial aid include grants, loans, and part-time employment. Financial aid/scholarship application due February 11.

University of Redlands
School of Music
1200 East Colton Avenue
Redlands
California 92374

Telephone. (714) 793-2121

Chief Administrator. Philip Swanson, Director.

The University of Redlands was founded in 1907 by the American Baptists. It is a privately supported liberal arts university composed of three colleges: University College, Whitehead College, and Johnston College. Enrollment exceeds 1,200 full-time and 1,000 part-time students. The 100-acre campus is located two miles from downtown Redlands and 63 miles east of Los Angeles.

The School of Music was established with the founding of the University. Training programs in voice, piano, and violin were gradually extended until, by mid-century, the School became a comprehensive institution offering instruction in all traditional areas of music study. The University was one of the first schools in the western United States to grant the professional degrees Bachelor of Music and Master of Music. The School of Music is a professional school for those who wish to pursue undergraduate and master's level music studies and a cultural resource for all University students.

Accreditation. Western Association of Schools and Colleges; National Association of Schools of Music.

Academic Information

Enrollment, Music Majors. Full-time 33 men, 48 women; part-time 1 man, 2 women. 5 foreign students.

Music Faculty. Full-time 12, part-time 22.

Term System. Semester (4-1-4 plan). 2 summer sessions (only private instruction offered).

Entrance Requirements. High school graduation with a B average or class rank in upper 30% of graduating class; recommend 4 units English, 2 mathematics, 1 laboratory science, 2 foreign language, 3 social studies. SAT or ACT required; audition scheduled through School of Music office or via tape if 200 miles from Redlands; portfolio for prospective composition majors.

Admission Procedure. Application with $25 nonrefundable fee due at least one month before classes begin each term.

Music Degrees Offered. Bachelor of Music; Bachelor of Arts; Master of Music.

Music Degree Requirements. The Bachelor of Music degree is offered with concentrations in performance, composition, music education, and musical studies. The degree requires the completion of 30 units of core liberal arts requirements plus 90 units of music courses. The Bachelor of Arts degree with a major in music is also available.

The degree Master of Music is offered with concentration in composition or performance. A total of 34 units is required.

General Program Areas. Composition, Conducting, Music Education, Performance.

Instruments Taught. Bass, Bassoon, Clarinet, English Horn, Flute, Guitar, Harp, Harpsichord, Horn, Jazz Guitar, Oboe, Percussion, Piano, Saxophone, Trombone, Trumpet, Tuba, Viola, Violin, Violoncello, Voice.

Musical Facilities

Practice Facilities. 17 practice rooms. 5 organs (Casavant, Schlicker, Goodwin, Wicks, Stevens). Percussion-equipped practice room. 15 pianos (Yamaha, Steinway, Kimball uprights; 5 Steinway grands, 1 Yamaha grand); 5 grands reserved for piano majors. Electronic music studio.

Concert Facilities. Concert halls seating 200 and 1,500, respectively.

Concerts/Musical Activities. More than 200 concerts and recitals presented on campus each year by students, faculty, and guest artists.

Music Library. 4,660 scores; 2,500 books; 14,020 phonograph recordings. 8 listening stations (cassette, stereo).

Special Programs

Performance Groups. Ensembles; choral groups; orchestra.

Foreign Programs. University of Redlands Center in Salzburg, Austria (for second semester of junior year); Vienna, Austria for junior year.

Financial

Costs. Per academic year: Tuition undergraduate $8,410, graduate $5,040. Room $1,920. Board $1,585.

Financial Aid. Variable number of music scholarships available ranging from $500 to $2,500 (average $1,500). Scholarship applications for first priority due before April 1. Graduate assistantships available. Other forms of financial aid include state/federal loans, part-time employment, and a College Work-Study program.

San Diego State University
Music Department
5300 Campanile Drive
San Diego
California 92182

Telephone. (619) 265-6031

Chief Administrator. Dr. Greg Steinke, Chairman.

San Diego State University is the largest of the 19 campuses of the California State University system. It offers undergraduate, graduate, and joint doctoral degrees. The university is housed on a 300-acre campus.

The music curricula are designed to provide professional training, a foundation for graduate music study, preparation for one of the several state teaching credentials, and music study as a minor or elective.

Accreditation. Western Association of Schools and Colleges; National Association of Schools of Music.

Academic Information

Music Faculty. Full-time 30, part-time 25.

Term System. Semester. 6-week summer session from late June to early August. Academic year from late August to May.

Entrance Requirements. High school graduation with a composite scholastic average and SAT or ACT score in upper third of California high school graduates; higher score for non-California residents; audition required on instrument; music theory and music history examinations. TOEFL score and financial statement required for foreign students.

Admission Procedure. Submit application with supporting documents to Admissions Office; write to Music Department concerning program information.

Music Degrees Offered. Bachelor of Music; Bachelor of Arts; Master of Arts; Master of Music.

Music Degree Requirements. The Bachelor of Music degree requires the completion of 49 units in general education and 73 to 76 units in music. Concentrations are offered in performance, composition, and music history and literature. The Bachelor of Arts degree with a major in music requires the completion of general education courses and the music major. A minor is not required. To qualify for upper division study, music majors must pass a Junior Level Examination. This is a more intensive solo performance before a faculty jury at the close of the fourth semester of study. Each semester of private instruction concludes with a solo performance. Students must also participate in at least one ensemble each semester. The bachelor's degree (music major) single-subject teaching credential is also offered.

The Master of Arts and Master of Music degrees require the completion of 30 units of studies in various emphases.

General Program Areas. Composition, Ethnomusicology, Jazz Studies, Music Education, Music History, Music Literature, Music Theory, Non-Western Instruments, Performance.

Instruments Taught. Baritone Horn, Bass, Bassoon, Cello, Clarinet, Early Instruments, Flute, French Horn, Guitar, Harp, Harpsichord, Oboe, Organ, Percussion, Piano, Saxophone, Trombone, Trumpet, Tuba, Viola, Violin, Voice.

Musical Facilities

Practice Facilities. Special practice facilities for percussionists. 40 practice pianos. Electronic music studio.

Concert Facilities. Concert Hall, seating 450.

Concerts/Musical Activities. Student concerts and recitals.

Music Library. Music materials are housed in the main library. Recordings located in Music Department. Special collections include: twentieth century operas; works of local composers; nineteenth century U.S. sheet music; Czech and Slavic materials.

Financial

Costs. Per academic year: Fee in-state resident $661; out-of-state tuition and fee $4,891. Room and board $3,414.

Financial Aid. Music scholarships are awarded by audition; approximately 30 are awarded per year (average award $300). Other sources of financial aid include state/federal aid, student employment, and a College Work-Study program.

San Francisco Conservatory of Music
1201 Ortega Street
San Francisco
California 94122

Telephone. (415) 564-8086
Chief Administrator. Milton Salkind, President.

When two young women founded the Ada Clement Piano School in 1917, San Francisco was still recovering from the devastating earthquake and fire of eleven years earlier. Ada Clement and Lillian Hodghead believed the city was ready to support a serious school of music. By 1924, their piano school became the San Francisco Conservatory of Music, and a year later they convinced the eminent composer Ernest Bloch to become the young conservatory's director. Among the early students at the Conservatory were Isaac Stern and Yehudi Menuhin. Since becoming president in 1966, Milton Salkind has guided the Conservatory, the only major independent college of music in the West, through its greatest expansion. The collegiate program has grown from 42 to 200 students.

The Conservatory is located in the Sunset District of San Francisco, a quiet residential neighborhood close to the ocean and Golden Gate Park. The city of of some 700,000 people offers arts and culture that compares favorably with any of the large cities in the U.S. Both the traditional and innovative arts thrive here.

Accreditation. Western Association of Schools and Colleges; National Association of Schools of Music. Founding member of the Association of Independent Colleges of Music.

Academic Information

Enrollment, Music Majors. Full-time 85 men, 102 women; part-time 13 men, 19 women. 35 foreign students.

Music Faculty. Full-time 18, part-time 50.

Term System. Semester.

Entrance Requirements. High school graduation; SAT or ACT. Foreign students must demonstrate proficiency in English (TOEFL). Graduate students are expected to hold a bachelor's degree in the field of music from an accredited college, university, or conservatory.

Admission Procedure. Application due July 1 with $35 nonrefundable fee; earlier application urged. Audition required; audition schedule published in fall; out-of-town undergraduate applicants may submit audition tape; graduate applicants must audition in person. High level of music proficiency required.

Music Degrees Offered. Bachelor of Music; Master of Music; Music Diploma.

Music Degree Requirements. The Bachelor of Music degree is planned to extend over a period of four years. The areas of concentration offered include keyboard instruments, orchestral instruments, classical guitar, voice, composition, and instrumental conducting. A performance pedagogy major is available to qualified undergraduates after their freshmen year. The degree requires the completion of 130 credits including the major area of concentration and core curriculum requirements. The Music Diploma is not an academic degree; it is a certification by the Conservatory that the student has successfully completed that course of study in music. It is planned to extend over a period of three to four years and is identical to the requirements for the Bachelor of Music degree except that the candidates are not required to complete Humanities courses beyond the introductory course.

The Master of Music degree is offered in keyboard instruments, orchestral instruments, classical guitar, voice, composition, instrumental conducting, piano accompanying, and chamber music. The minimum requirement is 30 semester hours of credit. Candidates other than voice majors may complete the degree in one academic year.

General Program Areas. Accompanying, Applied Music, Baroque Music, Chamber Music, Composition, Instrumental Conducting, Music Theory, Performance, Performance Pedagogy.

Instruments Taught. Bass, Bassoon, Clarinet, Flute, French Horn, Guitar, Harp, Harpsichord, Oboe, Organ, Percussion, Piano, Trombone, Trumpet, Tuba, Viola, Violin, Violoncello, Voice.

Musical Facilities

Practice Facilities. 62 practice rooms. 3 percussion-equipped practice rooms. 70 pianos. Electronic music studio; early music studio.

Concert Facilities. Hellman Hall, seating 333.

Concerts/Musical Activities. 300 recitals and concerts per year; 500 community concert off-campus performances per year. Chamber Music West is an annual three-week festival that features internationally acclaimed artists.

Music Library. The Bothin Library is known throughout the Bay Area for its wide-ranging collection of scores and parts in performing editions. 25,000 volumes; 19,000 scores; wide selection of periodicals featuring nearly all English-language music journals. Daniel E. Koshland Listening Room offers more than 6,000 recordings, tapes of both professional and student performances, ear-training exercises and language lessons. Listening equipment includes turntables, cassette and reel-to-reel tape decks.

Special Programs

Featured Programs. Summer Music West, a comprehensive day camp instituted in 1984. Full program of evening classes. The Conservatory sponsors the annual *Sing-It-Yourself Messiah* during the December holiday season. The Music Marathon, which celebrates the work of one composer or a specific genre of music, began in 1979 and is an annual event.

Performance Groups. Conservatory Orchestra, Opera Theatre, Brass Choir, Brass/Woodwind Ensemble, Cantata Singers, Chamber Music Ensemble, Guitar Ensemble, New Music Ensemble, Ortega Ensemble, Percussion Ensemble, Woodwind Ensemble.

Financial

Costs. Per academic year: Tuition $6,250. Room and board $3,000 to $3,700.

Financial Aid. Scholarship awards ranging from $300 to $6,250; application due April 1.

Commentary

The San Francisco Conservatory has initiated a two-year graduate program in chamber music culminating in an artist's certificate. The small size of the student body gives an intimate, informal ambience to the school. To maintain this atmosphere, the Conservatory intends to keep the size of the student body at 225.

San Francisco State University Department of Music

School of Creative Arts
1600 Holloway Avenue
San Francisco
California 94132

Telephone. (415) 469-1431

Chief Administrator. Richard A. Webb, Chair.

San Francisco State University was established in 1899 primarily to train elementary school teachers. It is now a multipurpose university enrolling over 18,000 students annually in eight schools. The 130-acre campus is located in southwest San Francisco.

The courses and curricula of the Department of Music are designed to provide both professional strength and liberal arts breadth; and to develop musical and intellectual excellence combined with social and humanistic responsibility and sensitivity. Elective courses for non-majors form an important function of the music program, in addition to the majors and minors composed of balanced offerings in music literature, performance, and theory.

Accreditation. Western Association of Schools and Colleges; National Association of Schools of Music; National Council for Accreditation of Teacher Education.

Academic Information

Enrollment, Music Majors. (Total University) 18,413.

Music Faculty. 43.

Term System. Semester.

Entrance Requirements. High school graduation with scholastic average in the upper third of California high school graduates; SAT or ACT; audition required.

Admission Procedure. Application with supporting documents and nonrefundable $35 fee to Office of Admissions and Records.

Music Degrees Offered. Bachelor of Music; Bachelor of Arts; Master of Music; Master of Arts.

Music Degree Requirements. The Bachelor of Music degree is offered with emphases in music education, piano, organ, voice, orchestral instruments, composition, and history and literature. Students who select the music education emphasis must complete a concentration from among vocal, instrumental, or keyboard/choral. The degree requires the completion of 132 units. The Bachelor of Arts degree in music is offered in the context of a liberal arts program.

The Master of Music degree curriculum is designed to provide graduate study for the performer and to allow for maximum development of specialized skills in the particular areas of talent. The program is offered with emphases in music education, music history, and music theory-composition. The degree requires the completion of a minimum of 30 units. The Master of Arts degree in music is also offered in the same areas of emphasis.

General Program Areas. Composition, Music Education, Music History, Music Literature, Music Recording Industry, Music Theory, Performance.

Instruments Taught. Bass, Bassoon, Clarinet, Flute, Guitar, Harp, Horn, Oboe, Organ, Percussion, Piano, Saxophone, Trombone, Trumpet, Tuba, Viola, Violin, Violoncello, Voice.

Musical Facilities

Concert Facilities. The School of Creative Arts facilities include four theaters and a modern concert hall.

Concerts/Musical Activities. Student and faculty concerts and recitals; visiting artists. The Chamber Music Center, supported by a grant from the May T. Morrison Foundation, regularly schedules recitals and concerts featuring well-known instrumental artists.

Music Library. The J. Paul Leonard Library contains over 675,000 volumes. The Media Access Center serves as the central distribution point for the University's non-print materials for students. It also houses the library's microcomputer lab and the Audio/Music collection.

Special collections include: sixteenth and seventeenth century vocal music; rare recorded sound archive, with concentrations on singers of the "Golden Age;" opera scores and chamber music scores.

Special Programs

Featured Programs. The Music/Recording Industry program is designed for those who want to learn more about the music and recording industry through a structured course of study. The program integrates technical skills in recording, business and legal aspects, and productive elements to provide foundations in the music and recording field. The program requires the completion of 22 semester units and is offered through the Division of Extended Education.

Performance Groups. Orchestra, Symphonic Band, Concert Choir, Concert Band, Opera Workshop, Instrumental Ensembles, Chamber Music, Choral Union, Chamber Orchestra, Chamber Choir, General Chorus, Piano Ensemble, Collegium Musicum, Jazz Ensemble, New Music Ensemble.

Financial

Costs. Per academic year: Tuition in-state resident none; out-of-state $4,371. Fees $682. Room and board $3,198.

Financial Aid. The Department of Music offers a variety of scholarships, both performance and scholastic, including the Janis D. Getz Scholarship, an annual award for talented piano majors with strong academic records, and the Peter Frampton Contemporary Music Award, among many others. Other sources of financial aid include institutional and state/federal grants, loans, and part-time employment.

San Jose State University
Department of Music
One Washington Square
San Jose
California 95192

Telephone. (408) 277-2905

Chief Administrator. Dr. Gus C. Lease, Chairman.

San Jose State University is the oldest institution of the California State University System. It was founded in 1857 as Minns' Evening School in San Francisco and in 1862 became the California State Normal School. In 1871, the school moved to San Jose and in 1881 opened a branch campus in Los Angeles (later to become UCLA). The name of the institution was changed to San Jose State Normal School in 1887, to San Jose Teachers College in 1921, to San Jose State College in 1935, and to San Jose State University in 1974. The campus is located 50 miles south of San Francisco in the Santa Clara Valley.

The Department of Music was established in 1918. All music majors must demonstrate an acceptable level of performance ability in an applied area offered in the curriculum. Each degree concentration within the Department has some requirements which are applicable only to that particular concentration.

Accreditation. Western Association of Schools and Colleges; National Association of Schools of Music.

Academic Information

Enrollment, Music Majors. Full-time 99 men, 65 women; part-time 66 men, 46 women. 4 foreign students.

Music Faculty. Full-time 28, part-time 18.

Term System. Semester. 8-week summer session from June to August. Academic year from late August to late May.

Entrance Requirements. High school graduation with 2.5 GPA; 4 years English, 2 mathematics; SAT or ACT; audition and placement/theory interview. Separate criteria for foreign students (limited filing periods; TOEFL with minimum score of 500).

Admission Procedure. Application with supporting documents to Admissions Office.

Music Degrees Offered. Bachelor of Music; Bachelor of Arts; Master of Arts.

Music Degree Requirements. The Bachelor of Music degree is a 132-unit program designed for students who plan musical careers as performers, composers, and/or teachers. Options are available in orchestral instruments (including keyboard), voice, and composition. The Bachelor of Arts in Music degree program provides a broad base and thorough grounding in all aspects of music history and literature, theory and composition, applied music, large and small ensemble participation, jazz studies, and music education. The 124-unit curriculum is designed for students who (1) plan to teach music in the public schools and/or private studios or (2) desire a liberal arts education with an emphasis in music.

The Master of Music degree is a 30-credit program with 12 credits in core courses, 12 in electives, and 6 in performance or written documents (or combination of these two). The program requires advanced work in specialized areas culminating in a final performance or performances, with or without documentation, or final thesis.

General Program Areas. Applied Music, Composition, Jazz Studies, Music Education, Music History, Music Literature, Music Theory, Performance, Vocal Music.

Instruments Taught. Asian Percussion Instruments, Baroque Instruments, Bass, Bassoon, Clarinet, Flute, French Horn, Guitar, Harpsichord, Oboe, Organ, Percussion, Piano, Piccolo, Saxophone, Trombone, Trumpet, Violin, Violoncello, Voice.

Musical Facilities

Practice Facilities. 50 practice rooms. 2 organs (pipe, electronic). 120 pianos (Kimball, Everett); 6 grand pianos reserved for piano majors. Electronic music studio; recording studio.

Concert Facilities. Concert Hall, seating 545.

Concerts/Musical Activities. Approximately 6 concerts per week (student performances, faculty recitals, guest performances, ensembles, studio recitals).

Music Library. Music collection in the Music Building is an extension of the regular library's collection. 500 volumes; 15,000 scores; 5 current music periodicals; microforms of outdated titles; 5,000 phonograph recordings. Listening stations in main library. The main library also has a Beethoven Center; complete works on microfilm of Harry Partch and Hugo Kauder.

Special Programs

Featured Programs. A Music Honors Program is designed for the superior student who has outstanding talent and scholastic ability. The program may follow one of three general plans: (1) A senior recital with an accompanying project paper; (2) a major written project on some aspect of history, literature, or music education; (3)

a major project in the field of music composition.

Performance Groups. Symphony Orchestra, Symphony Band, Concert Choir, University Chorus, Choraliers, Collegium Musicum, Gamelan, Opera Theatre, Concert Band, University Jazz Chorus, Jazz Singers, Spartan Marching Band, Modern Jazz Ensemble, Recording Studio Orchestra, Percussion Ensemble, Wind Ensemble, Pep Band.

Foreign Programs. Students may participate in study abroad at a campus in one of 12 foreign nations with which the California State University system has a cooperative arrangement.

Financial

Costs. Per academic year: Fees in-state resident $731; tuition and fees out-of-state resident $4,241. Practice room fee $30. Room $1,738. Board $1,268 to $1,768.

Financial Aid. Financial aid is awarded on the basis of financial need. Both institutional and state/federal aid available (average award $2,699). Scholarship/financial aid application due March 1. Part-time employment and College Work-Study program available.

University of Southern California
School of Music
University Park
Los Angeles
California 90007

Telephone. (213) 743-6935

Chief Administrator. Larry Livingston, Dean.

The University of Southern California, founded in 1880, is a privately supported institution enrolling over 23,000 students. The 100-acre campus is located near the center of downtown Los Angeles, three miles from the Civic Center.

Since its founding in 1884, the growth of the School of Music has been parallel to the development of the city of Los Angeles as an international center of musical activity. Los Angeles is the home of numerous musical organizations whose performances contribute to the cultural life of the region, and also the home of the nation's major recording, radio, film, and television industries.

The School of Music offers professional and academic degrees at the undergraduate and graduate levels.

Accreditation. Western Association of Schools and Colleges; National Association of Schools of Music; National Council for Accreditation of Teacher Education.

Academic Information

Enrollment, Music Majors. 367 men, 305 women. 58 foreign students.

Music Faculty. 67; adjunct 81.

Term System. Semester. Academic year late August to early May. 3 Summer sessions.

Entrance Requirements. High school graduation (with 3.0 GPA) or equivalent; minimum of 12 academic units (3 English, 2 mathematics, 2 social studies, 1 laboratory science, 2 foreign language); ACT or SAT required (SAT preferred, with score of 1000 combined); audition required.

Admission Procedure. Application with supporting documents and nonrefundable $25 fee to Admissions Office; supplementary application to School of Music.

Music Degrees Offered. Bachelor of Music; Bachelor of Arts; Master of Music; Master of Music Education; Master of Arts; Doctor of Musical Arts; Doctor of Philosophy.

Music Degree Requirements. The Bachelor of Music degree is offered with specializations in accompanying, composition, theory, music education, instrumental performance, jazz studies, and vocal arts. Students may take either a single major program or a double major in several combinations. The degree requires the completion of 132 units. The Bachelor of Arts degree is for students with a strong music background but who do not have professional performance aspirations. For this degree, students enroll in the College of Letters. A combined Bachelor of Arts and Bachelor of Music program is offered in a combined curriculum requiring a total of 160 units.

The Master of Music degree allows specialization in choral music, church music, composition, conducting, music education, accompanying, guitar, harpsichord, jazz studies, organ, piano, voice, or instrumental performance. A total of 30 graduate units is required for the degree. The Master of Music Education degree is offered jointly with the School of Education. It is intended for persons who are now or who plan to be school or community music specialists. The Master of Arts degree, offered in conjunction with the Graduate School, stresses music history or theory with emphasis on scholarly research.

The Doctor of Musical Arts is the highest professional degree offered by the School of Music. Students may specialize in choral music, church music, composition, music education, vocal or instrumental performance. The Doctor of Philosophy degree is offered through the Graduate School. It is an academic degree in the fields of historical musicology or music theory.

The non-degree Artist Diploma is awarded to those working toward soloist careers through full-time study for 3 to 5 years.

General Program Areas. Accompanying, Choral Music, Church Music, Composition, Conducting, Jazz Studies, Music Education, Music Theory, Musicology, Vocal Arts.

Instruments Taught. Bass, Brass, Guitar, Harp, Organ, Percussion, Piano, Stringed Instruments, Voice, Woodwinds.

Musical Facilities

Practice Facilities. Booth Hall, winds and percussion teaching and practice studios; Raubenheimer Music Faculty Building, classrooms, rehearsal halls, recording studio, electronic music studio; Virginia Ramo Hall of Music, vocal arts, accompanying, strings, piano, harpsichord, and guitar facilities.

Concert Facilities. Bovard Auditorium, seating 1,450; Bing Theatre of the Arnold Schoenberg Institute, 200; Music Faculty Building; United University Church.

Music Library. Located in the University's Doheny Library, the Music Library contains over 33,000 items of standard works; historical sets; collected editions; a comprehensive collection of basic research materials; 150 current music periodicals; most books on music education; 18,000 recordings on disks and cassettes; microcards and microfilms. Listening and microfilm reader facilities are in the music library. Special collections include manuscripts of film composers. A new program for Armenian Musical Studies has been developed.

Additional resources include The Alfred Newman Memorial Library and The Polish Music Reference Center.

The Arnold Schoenberg Institute, a unique resource houses the complete archives, library, and memorabilia of Arnold Schoenberg. It is located on the USC campus near the School of Music. Since its establishment in 1973, the Institute has become an international center for Schoenberg studies, attracting the foremost international scholars and musicians. The Institute Archives have served as a primary resource for numerous doctoral dissertations throughout the country. The Institute sponsors a Twentieth Century Concert Series emphasizing music of the Second Viennese School in combination with other contemporary masters. The Institute offers master classes by artists, special lectures by visiting scholars, and weekly composition forums and Contemporary Music Ensemble concerts sponsored by the Composition Department of the School of Music. The Institute also publishes *The Journal of the Arnold Schoenberg Institute,* with articles by well-known scholars researched primarily in the Institute Archives and devoted to Arnold Schoenberg's life, work, and legacy.

Special Programs

Performance Groups. Hoover Street Music Company, University Chorus, University Men's Chorale, University Women's Chorale, Concert Choir, Chamber Singers, Opera Chorus, Chamber Orchestra, Symphony Orchestra, Community Orchestra, Trojan Marching Band, Trojan Concert Band, University Wind Orchestra, Wind and Percussion Chamber Music, Guitar Ensemble, String Chamber Music, Keyboard Ensemble, Contemporary Music Ensemble, Jazz Chamber Music, Vocal Chamber Music, Early Music Ensemble, Keyboard Chamber Ensemble, Collegium Musicum.

Financial

Costs. Per academic year: Tuition $12,064. Fees $1,-000. Room and board $4,080.

Financial Aid. Financial aid programs include scholarships, fellowships, grants, loans, College Work-Study program, and part-time employment. Financial aid/scholarship application due December 31.

Commentary

The University of California's School of Cinema-Television offers a program for cinema composition where composers have the opportunity to work in real-film dubbing situations. The School of Music, in which Jascha Heifetz and Gregor Piatagorsky once taught, has always had a first-rate performance faculty.

Stanford University
Department of Music
Stanford
California 94305

Telephone. (415) 723-3811
Chief Administrator. Dr. Albert Cohen, Chairman.

Stanford University is a privately supported university established in 1885 with a gift of more than $20,000,000 from the Stanford family. The campus of 8,000 acres was created on the land of Leland Stanford in Palo Alto, 32 miles south of San Francisco. The University enrolls over 13,000 students.

The Department of Music aims to promote understanding and enjoyment of music in the University at large and to provide specialized training for those who plan careers in music as composers, performers, teachers, or research scholars. It was founded in 1947 as part of the School of Humanities and Sciences, and in 1984 moved into its new home in Braun Music Center. The Department has a large time-sharing digital computer on which work is done in sound synthesis, acoustical analysis, composition, digital recording, and music manuscript. The computer will benefit advanced students interested in electronic music and use of the computer in composition. Students with a particular interest in acoustics are encouraged to make use of this facility.

Accreditation. Western Association of Schools and Colleges.

Academic Information

Enrollment, Music Majors. Full-time 55 men, 45 women. Foreign students 9.

Music Faculty. Full-time 15, part-time 27.

Term System. Quarter. One 6-week summer session.

Entrance Requirements. High school graduation or equivalent; completion of four-year college preparatory course; SAT or ACT required; CEEB Achievement Tests in English and any two others are strongly recom-

mended; graduation in upper 10% of graduating class recommended. GRE required for graduate students. Personal audition (tape acceptable) required.

Admission Procedure. Application with supporting documents and $35 nonrefundable fee due January 1.

Music Degrees Offered. Bachelor of Arts; Master of Arts; Doctor of Musical Arts.

Music Degree Requirements. The Bachelor of Arts degree may be planned in one of three ways (1) with a concentration in composition, performance, or music history; (2) as preparation for secondary school teaching; or (3) a general program of studies without special emphasis on any particular branch of music. The plan in each case is drafted by the student and advisor to include certain required work.

The Master of Arts degree requires a minimum of three quarters of full-time study in residence. The student may concentrate in composition or performance (including conducting). A total of 36 units of coursework must be completed plus three quarters of ensemble performance. Depending on the concentration, a Master of Arts project will be an investigative essay, a composition, or a demonstration of performance supported by a written commentary on the performance practices that are involved.

The purpose of the Doctor of Musical Arts program is to offer advanced training in the practice and pedagogy of music. Students may concentrate in composition, or performance (including conducting)—the latter concentration to be centered on the investigation of performance practices from medieval to modern times. A limited number of students with superior qualifications are accepted by the Department for work toward the Ph.D. degree in Music. In addition to a minimum of 3 years of full-time work, the program requires: (1) seminars in musical notation, analysis, performance practice, and musicology; (2) readings in music theory; (3) dissertation research; (4) foreign language requirements; (5) departmental examinations.

General Program Areas. Baroque Music, Composition, Conducting, Music History, Music Theory, Performance, Performance Practices, Renaissance Music.

Instruments Taught. Baroque Instruments, Brass, Harpsichord, Organ, Percussion, Piano, Renaissance Instruments, Stringed Instruments, Woodwinds.

Musical Facilities

Practice Facilities. Special practice facilities for organists; 4 organs. 1 practice room for percussionists. 22 practice rooms. 7 uprights, 13 grand pianos.

Concert Facilities. Dinkelspiel Auditorium; Campbell Recital Hall; two theaters for concert and operatic productions.

Concerts/Musical Activities. Student recitals; ensemble groups; visiting artists.

Music Library. Comprehensive collection of complete editions, scores, books, and records (78,000 items). Supplementing these holdings is the Stanford Memorial Library of Music which is an invaluable collection of musical manuscripts and first editions. The Harry R. Lange Historical Collection of rare instruments is available for student use.

Financial

Costs. Per academic year: Tuition $11,210. Room and board $4,700.

Financial Aid. Institutional and state/federal aid is available.

COLORADO

University of Colorado at Boulder
College of Music
Box 301, UC
Boulder
Colorado 80309

Telephone. (303) 492-6352

Chief Administrator. Robert R. Fink, Dean.

At its first session in 1861, the Territorial Legislature of Colorado passed an act providing for a university at Boulder. The University was formally founded in 1876, the same year that Colorado became a state. The cornerstone for Old Main, the first University building, was laid in 1875 and students began study in 1877. Today the University system includes four campuses: the main campus at Boulder and those at Colorado Springs, Denver, and the Health Sciences Center in Denver. The campuses have a combined enrollment of almost 35,000 students. The 600-acre Boulder campus is situated at the base of the Rocky Mountains at an altitude of over 5,000 feet. There are 160 buildings in a rural Italian architectural style. The city of Boulder (population 80,000) is 36 miles northwest of Denver.

The College of Music was established by the Regents of the University of Colorado in 1920. The College is organized to provide specialized training in music to prepare for professional work or advanced study, a background in music education that will prepare the student to teach music in the schools, and training in music as the basis for general cultural enrichment. Each curriculum is designed to present music as an integrated whole. Solo performance and techniques, ensemble performance, historical and theoretical studies, concert and recital opportunities, and elective courses both inside and outside the college are intended to give the student a balanced approach to musical understanding and musicianship. After a first year of study and counseling with a principal professor, students determine the particular area in which they are qualified and in which they wish to work.

The Music Building and Macky Auditorium contain studios, classrooms, rehearsal rooms, and practice rooms.

Accreditation. North Central Association of Colleges and Schools; National Association of Schools of Music; National Council for Accreditation of Teacher Education.

Academic Information

Enrollment, Music Majors. Full-time 210 men, 200 women; part-time 30 men, 30 women. 15 foreign students from England, Australia, China, Japan, and Mexico.

Music Faculty. Full-time 42, part-time 6.

Term System. Semester. Two 5-week summer sessions.

Entrance Requirements. High school graduation in top half of graduating class; combined SAT score of 1000; ACT 23; GED accepted. Audition in person or 10-minute tape; some keyboard and theory recommended.

Admission Procedure. Application with $30 nonrefundable fee due by February 1.

Music Degrees Offered. Bachelor of Music; Bachelor of Music Education; Bachelor of Arts; Master of Music; Master of Music Education; Doctor of Musical Arts; Doctor of Philosophy.

Music Degree Requirements. The curriculum leading to the Bachelor of Music degree is a professional training course with concentration areas of voice, piano, organ or church music, string instruments, guitar, wind and percussion instruments, composition, or history and literature. A minimum of 244 credit points and 122 semester hours must be earned for the Bachelor of Music in Performance degree. The Bachelor of Music Education degree is designed to provide preparation for the teaching of music in the schools. Three basic curricula are provided: choral emphasis, general music emphasis, and instrumental emphasis. A minimum of 134 semester hours must be earned for the degree, including 40 semester hours in liberal arts. Performance in organizations (orchestra, band, choir) is required of all undergraduates for seven semesters. The degree Bachelor of Arts in Music has as its goal a broad education in music within a liberal arts context. The curriculum is designed to give the student competency and knowledge to deal with music within the cultural milieu of present-day society. A minimum of 124 semester hours is required, 72 of which must be in nonmusic courses and 40 to 54 in music courses.

The Master of Music degree is offered with emphases in performance, church music, music literature, composition, conducting, and pedagogy. The Master of Music Education degree offers emphasis in vocal or instrumental music. The program is designed to augment the student's undergraduate preparation in music education with the more advanced training required for service as both a teacher and a supervisor. The minimum requirement for the master's degree is 30 semester hours.

The Doctor of Musical Arts degree is a professional degree for creative and performing students who possess the talent as well as the breadth of knowledge, background, outlook, and scholarly capacity requisite to a doctoral program. Areas of study include composition; literature and performance of choral music; instrumental conducting and literature; organ performance; performance, literature, and pedagogy of piano, voice, strings, winds, and percussion; performance, literature, and pedagogy of piano; process of group environments. Beyond the master's degree a minimum of 30 hours, including dissertation, is required. The Doctor of Philosophy degree in music, with music education or musicology as fields of specialization, is also offered.

General Program Areas. Choral Music, Church Music, Composition, Conducting, Music Education, Music History, Music Literature, Music Theory, Musicology, Performance, Piano Pedagogy.

Instruments Taught. Bass, Bassoon, Euphonium, Flute, Guitar, Harp, Harpsichord, Horn, Oboe, Organ, Percussion, Piano, Saxophone, Trombone, Trumpet, Tuba, Viola, Violin, Violoncello, Voice.

Musical Facilities

Practice Facilities. 86 practice rooms. 8 practice organs plus 4-manual Austin and Casevant tracker (Organ Department has special facilities in Macky Auditorium). 6 percussion-equipped practice rooms. 86 pianos; 22 grand pianos reserved for piano majors. Electronic music studio; group piano studio; opera theatre.

Concert Facilities. 6 auditoriums; 54 studios.

Concerts/Musical Activities. Solo recitals; concerts; visiting artist series; class recitals held each week.

Music Library. Located in the Music Building. 40,000 scores; 40,000 sound recordings; 20,000 books; 250 periodicals. Computerized listening facilities; computer-based reference searching. Special collections include: performing editions of 18th and 19th century chamber music; archives of the College Music Society; country and folk music including hillbilly and Western music recorded 1923-1932; Ben Gray Lumpkin Collection of Colorado Folklore; two musical instrument collections.

Special Programs

Performance Groups. Ensembles, University Symphony Orchestra, University Chamber Orchestra, band, choral groups.

Foreign Programs. The College of Music participates in international study programs as well as a special music program in Regensburg, Germany.

Financial

Costs. Per academic year: Tuition in-state resident $2,000, out-of-state $6,600. Room and board $2,900 to $3,500.

Financial Aid. There are several scholarships designed specifically for students of the College of Music. Other sources of financial aid are grants, state/federal loans, part-time employment, and a College Work-Study program.

University of Colorado at Denver
College of Music
1100 Fourteenth Street
Denver
Colorado 80202

Telephone. (303) 556-2727

Chief Administrator. Roy Pritts, Acting Resident Dean.

The urban campus of the University of Colorado at Denver was founded in 1912 as an extension division and given status as a separate campus in 1972. It offers programs in 41 undergraduate fields and 40 graduate areas in the liberal arts and professional degree programs. The University shares the new 169-acre Auraria Campus located next to the Denver Center for the Performing Arts.

The music program at the University of Colorado at Denver prepares students for professional careers in the music broadcasting, recording, business, and entertainment industries.

Accreditation. North Central Association of Colleges and Schools; National Association of Schools of Music.

Academic Information

Enrollment, Music Majors. (Total University) 2,832.

Term System. Semester. 1 summer session.

Entrance Requirements. High school graduation or GED; 15 academic units; SAT or ACT; top 50 percent of high school graduating class; audition required.

Admission Procedure. Application with supporting documents and nonrefundable $20 fee to Admissions Office.

Music Degrees Offered. Bachelor of Science.

Music Degree Requirements. The Bachelor of Science degree is offered in four areas of study: scoring and arranging; performance; elective studies in music management; and elective studies in sound synthesis and recording. Also available is a five to five and one-half year track for qualified students culminating in the Bachelor of Science in Music Management and the Master of Business Administration degrees.

Graduate study in music is presently offered through several cooperative programs with the University of Colorado at Boulder. Varying amounts of coursework toward the Master of Music and the Master of Music Education degrees may be taken on the Denver campus.

General Program Areas. Arranging, Music Management, Performance, Recording Industry, Sound Synthesis.

Instruments Taught. Brass, Percussion, Piano, Stringed Instruments, Voice, Woodwinds.

Musical Facilities

Concerts/Musical Activities. Special workshops, clinics, seminars, and symposia are offered periodically by the College, e.g., National Association of Recording Arts and Science, National Music Publishers' Association, National Public Radio, and performers appearing in the Denver area.

Music Library. The Auraria Library provides a variety of learning resources for the students and faculty. It supports the academic programs of all participating institutions (Community College of Denver, Metropolitan State College, University of Colorado at Denver).

Special Programs

Performance Groups. Electronic Music Ensemble, Jazz Ensemble, New Music Ensemble, New Singers, Fusion Ensemble, Dixie Ensemble, Chamber Music Ensembles, Percussion Ensemble, Brass Ensemble, Jazz-Rock Groups.

Financial

Costs. Per academic year: Tuition in-state resident $1,036, out-of-state $4,530. Facilities fee $48.

Financial Aid. Scholarships, grants, loans, and part-time employment are available. Financial aid/scholarship application due March 1.

Commentary

A new Master of Science in Music degree with emphases in music technology and music management has been proposed. A principal goal of this program is to provide skills for alternative careers in music.

Colorado State University
Department of Music, Theatre, and Dance
Fort Collins
Colorado 80523

Telephone. (303) 491-1101, 491-5528

Chief Administrator. Dr. James E. McCray, Department Chairman.

Colorado State University was established in 1970. The land-grant concept of a balanced program of teaching, research, extension, and public service provides the foundation for the University's programs. The three campuses of the University are located in or near the city of Fort Collins, 65 miles north of Denver.

The program goals of the music curricula are to encourage, develop, and offer high standards of teaching, scholarship, research, and performance in music; to provide a stimulating musical environment for the campus and the community; and to prepare and educate music teachers, music therapists, and performers. Nonmusic majors with musical skills and aptitudes may participate in chorus, band, or orchestra and enroll in selected music classes.

Accreditation. North Central Association of Colleges and Schools; National Association of Schools of Music; National Council for Accreditation of Teacher Education.

Academic Information

Enrollment, Music Majors. (Total University) 18,084.
Music Faculty. 25.
Term System. Semester. Three summer terms.
Entrance Requirements. Admission decision is based on secondary school grades, class rank, pattern of high school academic units, trend in quality of high school performance, SAT scores, and personal recommendations; most significant factor is scholastic achievement during high school; upper 50 percent of graduating class; audition required.

Admission Procedure. Application with supporting documents and nonrefundable $25 fee to Admissions Office.

Music Degrees Offered. Bachelor of Music; Bachelor of Arts; Master of Music.

Music Degree Requirements. The Bachelor of Music degree is offered with concentrations in music education or performance. Music education prepares students for teaching vocal, instrumental, or general music in elementary and secondary schools. The performance concentration is available with an instrument or vocal option. The Bachelor of Arts degree is offered with concentrations in music therapy or performing arts. Successful completion of the curriculum in music therapy plus a six-month clinical internship qualifies the candidate to sit for the National Certification Examination and for eligibility for admission to the National Registry maintained by the National Association for Music Therapy.

Programs leading to the degree Master of Music are available in applied music (performance), conducting (choral or orchestral), music education, music history and literature, music theory, music therapy, and composition.

General Program Areas. Choral Conducting, Music Education, Music History, Music Literature, Music Theory, Music Therapy, Orchestral Conducting, Performance.

Instruments Taught. Bass, Bassoon, Clarinet, Euphonium, Flute, French Horn, Guitar, Harp, Harpsichord, Oboe, Organ, Percussion, Piano, Saxophone, Trombone, Trumpet, Tuba, Viola, Violin, Violoncello, Voice.

Musical Facilities

Concerts/Musical Activities. Student/faculty concerts and recitals; visiting artists.

Music Library. The William E. Morgan Library houses approximately 1.5 million items and supports the academic programs of the Department of Music, Theatre, and Dance.

Special Programs

Performance Groups. Women's Chorus, Marching Band, University Chorus, University Orchestra, Symphonic Band, Jazz Ensemble, University Chamber Singers, Opera Theatre, Chamber Orchestra, Symphonic Wind Ensemble.

Financial

Costs. Per academic year: Tuition in-state resident $1,-275, out-of-state $4,411. Fees $238. Room and board $2,682.

Financial Aid. President's Scholarships are awarded to Colorado residents with outstanding academic records. Creative and Performing Arts Awards are given each year on the basis of outstanding talent in art, music, drama, forensics, creative writing, or dance. Other sources of financial aid are grants, loans, and a College Work-Study program. Financial aid/scholarship application due April 1.

University of Denver
Lamont School of Music
Houston Fine Arts Center
7111 Montview
Denver
Colorado 80220

Telephone. (303) 871-6400

Chief Administrator. Dr. Anne M. Culver, Director.

The University of Denver was established in 1864 by a group of pioneers led by Dr. John Evans, an outstanding Methodist layman. It was originally chartered as Colorado Seminary and adopted its present name in 1880. The main 100-acre campus has 60 buildings and is located in the south central part of Denver, the state capital. There is a university shuttle bus which transports students between this main campus and the northeast campus (site of the Lamont School of Music).

The Lamont School of Music was founded in the 1920s and was housed in a small 3-story building in downtown Denver. In the early 1960s the School was moved into a renovated apartment building on the main campus of the University of Denver. In August 1985, the School moved again to the Houston Fine Arts Center, formerly the Colorado Women's College. This facility now houses the entire School of Music. Each year the School hosts a May Week festival featuring prominent musical artists.

Accreditation. North Central Association of Colleges and Schools; National Association of Schools of Music.

Academic Information

Enrollment, Music Majors. Full-time 58 men, 65 women; part-time 2 men, 8 women. Foreign students 6.

Music Faculty. Full-time 20, part-time 15.

Term System. Quarter. One summer session. A wide variety of workshops offered during the summer quarter.

Entrance Requirements. High school graduation with a minimum C average and rank in upper half of graduating class; completion of 15 units including 4 English, 3 mathematics, 2 science, 2 social science; ACT or SAT required; prospective music majors must audition. Requirements for the graduate program include GRE Aptitude Test; entrance examinations in theory, history, and performance.

Admission Procedure. Formal application to the University of Denver; all prospective students must audition, music theory test, piano proficiency for all entering freshmen except piano majors; students with no piano background will be placed in a beginning level class.

Music Degrees Offered. Bachelor of Music; Bachelor of Music Education; Master of Arts.

Music Degree Requirements. The Bachelor's degree program requires the completion of a core curriculum and specific division requirements. Divisions include strings, piano, voice, organ, winds and percussion, piano pedagogy, composition and theory, and accordion. Total credit hours vary depending upon major pursued. Junior and Senior recitals are also required.

The degree Master of Arts in Music is offered with concentrations in composition, music education, music education - Orff Schulwerk, piano pedagogy, theory, conducting, music history and literature, piano performance, performance, Suzuki Pedagogy.

General Program Areas. Composition, Conducting, Music Education, Music History, Music Literature, Music Theory, Orff Schulwerk, Performance, Piano Pedagogy, Suzuki Pedagogy.

Instruments Taught. Accordion (Concert), Baritone, Bass, Bassoon, Clarinet, Flute, Guitar, Harp, Harpsichord, Horn, Oboe, Organ, Percussion, Piano, Saxophone, Trombone, Trumpet, Tuba, Viola, Violin, Violoncello, Voice.

Musical Facilities

Practice Facilities. Special practice facilities for organists. 3 practice rooms for percussionists. 25 practice pianos; 2 grand pianos reserved for piano majors. Electronic music lab; piano lab.

Concert Facilities. Two concert halls.

Concerts/Musical Activities. Ten Lamont-sponsored concerts per quarter are required for each student.

Music Library. Music holdings are contained in the University library holdings. Listening facilities available (6 stereo cassette players, 6 stereo phonographs).

Financial

Costs. Per academic year: Tuition $7,560. Fees $360. Room and board $3,135.

Financial Aid. 96 students receive some form of financial aid. Scholarships range from $150 per quarter to full tuition; average $400 per quarter. Scholarship applications accepted January 25 to February 15 for top priority; otherwise deadline of March 15.

Commentary

The University's Lamont School of Music has proposed new degree programs in arts management, record engineering, music industry, music therapy, piano technology, accompanying, and jazz studies.

University of Northern Colorado
School of Music
Frasier Hall 102
Greeley
Colorado 80639

Telephone. (303) 351-2678

Chief Administrator. Dr. Shirley Howell, Director.

The University of Northern Colorado, formerly Colorado State College, was founded in 1890. Although teacher education was its original purpose, the University now offers programs in the liberal arts, preprofessional, and vocational programs. The 380-acre campus is located in a residential area of Greeley, an agricultural county in northern Colorado midway between Denver and Cheyenne, Wyoming.

The Department of Music was created in 1895. In 1918, it was designated a Conservatory of Music, and in 1934, it was renamed a Division of Music. Concurrent with the emergence of the University of Northern Colorado from Colorado State College, the title School of Music was applied.

From the very beginning of its existence, the School of Music has had an active role in music education and cultural development of the region. In 1911, music professor John Kendel led a group of college musicians, students, and townspeople in his home basement studio to establish the Greeley Philharmonic Orchestra which

is today the oldest symphony orchestra in the Rocky Mountain Region. The UNC Performing Arts, begun in 1934 as the Little Theatre of the Rockies, was joined in 1954 by the Opera Guild (now Opera Theatre), and by the Dance Program in 1966. The cooperative efforts of music, theatre, and dance faculty have produced an interdisciplinary preprofessional training program for talented music and theatre students.

The primary goal of the School of Music is to develop skilled musicians in the following disciplines: performance, conducting, education, composition, history, theory, and administration.

Accreditation. North Central Association of Colleges and Schools; National Association of Schools of Music; National Council for Accreditation of Teacher Education.

Academic Information

Enrollment, Music Majors. Total 400. Foreign students 92.

Music Faculty. Full-time 38, part-time 2.

Term System. Quarter. Summer session.

Entrance Requirements. High school graduation with 15 units (recommended 4 English, 2 mathematics, 2 laboratory science, 2 foreign language, 2 social studies); SAT or ACT recommended. Music students must audition on their instruments or voice for admission; non-music majors may take private lessons with permission of the instructor only; some ensembles are open only by audition. GRE required for doctoral programs.

Admission Procedure. Application due 3 weeks prior to enrollment with $15 nonrefundable fee.

Music Degrees Offered. Bachelor of Music; Bachelor of Music Education; Bachelor of Arts; Master of Music; Master of Music Education; Doctor of Arts; Doctor of Music Education.

Music Degree Requirements. The Bachelor of Music degree prepares specialists in the various music professions including performers, theorists, and composers. The degree requires the completion of 180 quarter hours including 125-163 hours in the area of emphasis (instrumental, voice, piano, theory and composition). The Bachelor of Arts degree with a major in music is designed to provide a comprehension of music as a humanistic study within the framework of a broad, liberal arts education. It provides for the development of performance skills and competence in the structure and forms of music. Emphasis is placed on the development of scholarly skills in music and on the musical heritage of Western civilization. The degree requires the completion of 180 quarter hours minimum including an 87-hour major. The Bachelor of Music Education program is designed to produce broadly educated and skilled school music teachers. The degree requires the completion of a minimum of 180 quarter hours including specific courses in music and professional teacher education.

The Master of Music program offers study in the areas

of performance, conducting, theory, and composition, and is designed to broaden and deepen scholarly abilities, research, and pedagogical techniques. The degree requires the completion of a minimum of 45 quarter hours including specific departmental requirements. The Master of Music Education degree has been developed for the music teacher who has made a professional commitment to effective music instruction in grades K-12.

The Doctor of Arts degree in music is designed to prepare professional, academically well-qualified teaching scholars for the junior and senior college level. The degree is available in the areas of music history and literature, theory and composition, music performance, conducting or performance, and pedagogy. The degree requires the completion of a minimum of 96 quarter hours including specific departmental requirements. The Doctor of Music Education program prepares students as educator musicians, and develops expertise in teaching, consulting, and administration within public schools, college music education, and community cultural responsibilities.

General Program Areas. Conducting, Ensemble, Instrumental Techniques, Jazz Studies, Music Composition, Music Education, Music History, Music Literature, Music Theatre, Music Theory, Pedagogy, Performance.

Instruments Taught. Brass, Guitar, Harp, Harpsichord, Organ, Percussion, Piano, Stringed Instruments, Voice, Woodwinds.

Musical Facilities

Practice Facilities. Special practice facilities for organists; Layton pipe organ. 4 practice rooms for percussionists. 41 piano practice rooms; 28 Hamilton Baldwin uprights; 5 grand pianos reserved for piano majors. Electronic and computer music studio.

Concert Facilities. Foundation Hall is the music concert hall; a recital hall seating 300 is contained within the James Michener Library and is used for smaller recitals; other campus buildings are used from time to time.

Community Facilities. Local churches (First United Methodist, First Presbyterian, and Trinity Episcopal) are used for organ recitals.

Concerts/Musical Activities. Summer Festival Orchestra, Mixed Concert Choir, Women's Glee Club, Women's Concert Choir, Men's Glee Club, Summer Symphonic Band, Wind Ensemble, Symphony Band, Concert Band, University Brass Choir, University Symphony Orchestra.

Music Library. 13,000 volumes; 23,000 scores; 11,500 recordings. 4 cassette listening stations; 23 stereo listening stations. Special collections include popular songs, programs, clippings, choral music, tapes, band music, orchestral music.

Special Programs

Performance Groups. Performance organizations include Small Jazz Ensembles, Contemporary Small Jazz Ensemble, Dixieland Jazz Band, Jazz Bebop Quintet, Jazz Octet, Jazz Quartet, Jazz Rock Ensemble, Jazz Sextet, Jazz Trombone Quintet, Jazz Tuba Ensemble, Vocal Jazz Ensemble, String Ensemble, Brass Ensemble, Woodwind Ensemble, Percussion Ensemble, Piano Ensemble, Classical Guitar Ensemble, Reading Jazz Band, Sinfonia, University Singers, Opera Workshop, Opera Orchestra, Concert Orchestra. Faculty performance groups include The Rocky Mountain Brass Quintet, the Ginsberg Art Woodwind Quintet, the Baroque Ensemble, Faculty String Quartet, Faculty Jazz Ensemble, and Saxophone Quartet.

Financial

Costs. Per academic year: Tuition in-state resident $1,110 to $1,170, out-of-state $4,285 to $4,498. Fees $252. Room and board $2,550.

Financial Aid. Scholarship applications due April 30. Scholarships range from $200 to $2,000 (average $500).

CONNECTICUT

University of Connecticut
Department of Music
School of Fine Arts
876 Coventry Road
Storrs
Connecticut 06268

Telephone. (203) 486-3728

Chief Administrator. Dorothy J. Payne, Department Head.

The University of Connecticut was founded in 1881 as the Storrs Agricultural School, and in 1933 was named Connecticut State College. It achieved university status in 1939 and assumed its present name. Over 24,000 students are enrolled each year. The campus is situated on 3,844 acres in Storrs, a rural area 25 miles east of Hartford.

The Department of Music was founded in 1932 and became a component of the School of Fine Arts when it was established in 1965. The Department offers curricula designed for students majoring in music as well as courses for the general student.

Accreditation. New England Association of Schools and Colleges; National Association of Schools of Music; National Council for Accreditation of Teacher Education.

Academic Information

Enrollment, Music Majors. Full-time 92 men, 138 women.

Music Faculty. Full-time 24, part-time 28.

Term System. Semester. Academic year from early September to mid-May. Two 6-week summer sessions from late May to early August.

Entrance Requirements. High school graduation in upper 50 percent of graduating class; completion of 12 units including 4 English, 3 mathematics, 1 science, 2 foreign language; SAT required; audition; theory placement examination; composition portfolio as appropriate.

Admission Procedure. Apply to Admissions Office; Department will contact applicant for audition.

Music Degrees Offered. Bachelor of Music; Bachelor of Science; Bachelor of Fine Arts; Master of Music; Master of Arts; Doctor of Philosophy.

Music Degree Requirements. The Bachelor of Music degree is offered with majors in applied music, music history, music theory, and composition. The curriculum with a major in music education is offered through the School of Education (students spend the first two years in the School of Fine Arts and the last two years in the School of Education) and leads to the Bachelor of Science degree. A non-professional curriculum with a concentration in music leads to the Bachelor of Fine Arts degree in music. The baccalaureate degrees require the completion of a minimum 120 credits. Each degree has special requirements plus the academic credits.

The Department offers the Master of Music and Master of Arts degrees requiring 24 credits with thesis or 30 credits without thesis (e.g., in performance). The Doctor of Philosophy degree in music requires a minimum of 24 to 30 credits beyond the master's degree plus a dissertation.

General Program Areas. Applied Music, Composition, Conducting, Music Education, Music History, Music Theory, Psychomusicology.

Instruments Taught. Bass, Bassoon, Euphonium, Flute, French Horn, Guitar, Harp, Oboe, Organ, Percussion, Piano, Saxophone, Trombone, Trumpet, Tuba, Viola, Violin, Violoncello, Voice.

Musical Facilities

Practice Facilities. 25 practice rooms. 2 organs (Fiske tracker). Special practice facilities for percussionists. 3 grand pianos reserved for piano majors. Electronic music studio; computer music studio.

Concert Facilities. J. Louis Von der Mehden Recital Hall, seating 550; Jorgenson Auditorium, 3,000.

Concerts/Musical Activities. Approximately 125 concerts and recitals performed on campus per year.

Music Library. 9,500 volumes; 10,400 musical scores; 568 microform titles. 13 listening stations. Additional listening facilities in Main Library.

Special Programs

Performance Groups. Marching Band, Band, Chorus, Orchestra, Chamber Ensembles, Jazz Ensemble.

Financial

Costs. Per academic year: Tuition in-state resident $1,-350, out-of-state $2,345. Private applied music lessons $25 for one-half hour lesson per week or $50 for a one-hour lesson per week per semester. Fees in-state $800, out-of-state $1,360. Room $1,320 to $1,400. Board $1,-200 to $1,450.

Financial Aid. Financial aid is awarded on the basis of academic merit, financial need, musical ability. Institutional scholarships, state/federal grants and loans, part-time employment, and a College Work-Study program are available.

Commentary

An unusual feature of the Department of Music at the University of Connecticut is a program in psychomusicology, the study of listener response to musical and related stimuli. The Music Performance Analysis Laboratory on campus is the research facility for this discipline.

University of Hartford
Hartt School of Music
200 Bloomfield Avenue
West Hartford
Connecticut 06117

Telephone. (203) 243-4467

Chief Administrator. Donald Harris, Dean.

The University of Hartford is an independent, comprehensive university which provides educational programs in liberal arts and professional disciplines for undergraduate and graduate students. The 200-acre campus is located in a suburban area of West Hartford, four miles from the center of Hartford.

The Hartt School of Music, one of the founding institutions of the University of Hartford, was established in 1920. The original music school became a college department in 1927, and the Hartt College of Music in 1951. In 1957, Hartt joined with Hillyer College and the Hartford Art School to found the University. In 1980, the College was renamed the Hartt School of Music and its noncredit unit, the Julius Hartt School, became known as the Community Division.

Accreditation. New England Association of Schools and Colleges; National Association of Schools of Music; National Council for Accreditation of Teacher Education.

Academic Information

Enrollment, Music Majors. (Total University) 7,611. The Hartt School of Music admits approximately 160 new students each fall.

Music Faculty. 113.

Term System. Semester. Summer term offers graduate courses, special workshops, master classes, and selected performance activities.

Entrance Requirements. High school graduation with rank in upper 40 percent; completion of 16 units including 4 English, 2-3½ mathematics, 2 foreign language, 2 science, 2 social science; SAT or ACT required; audition and interview required.

Admission Procedure. Application with supporting documents and nonrefundable $30 fee to Director of Admission.

Music Degrees Offered. Bachelor of Music; Bachelor of Arts; Bachelor of Science; Master of Music; Master of Music Education; Doctor of Musical Arts.

Music Degree Requirements. The Bachelor of Music degree is offered with majors in applied music, jazz studies, musical theater, opera, theory, composition, music history, music education, and music management. The Music Management Program is designed to enable students to complete both a bachelor's degree and a master's degree (MBA) in five years. Qualified students who wish to take a liberal arts curriculum with special emphasis on music may apply to the College of Arts and Sciences. The Bachelor of Science degree in Engineering with a major in acoustics and music is a combined option available within the Interdisciplinary Engineering Studies program of the College of Engineering. The program includes a basic engineering core as well as a major concentration of courses offered by the Hartt School of Music.

The Master of Music degree is offered in instrumental performance and teaching, liturgical music, choral conducting, voice, opera, composition, theory, and music history. The Master of Music Education degree curriculum provides emphases in performance, conducting, theory, composition, history, Kodaly method, and special education.

The Doctor of Musical Arts degree may be earned in applied music, composition, or music education. The curricula prepares the candidates to become effective teachers, performers, and compsoers. A core program is augmented by a selection of courses fitting specific needs and interests as indicated by the student's specialization and previous training.

General Program Areas. Applied Music, Composition, Jazz Studies, Kodaly Method, Music Education, Music History, Music Management, Music Theory, Musical Theater, Opera.

Instruments Taught. Baritone, Bass, Clarinet, Flute, French Horn, Guitar, Harp, Harpsichord, Lute, Oboe, Organ, Percussion, Piano, Recorder, Saxophone, Trombone, Trumpet, Tuba, Viola, Violin, Violoncello, Voice.

Musical Facilities

Practice Facilities. The Hartt School of Music is located in the Alfred C. Fuller Music Center, a three building complex. Paranov Hall houses classrooms, teaching studios, rehearsal rooms, recording studio, library, faculty and administrative offices, and lounges. O'Connell Hall houses the Organ Studio, Berkman Recital Hall, practice rooms, teaching studios.

Concert Facilities. Millard Auditorium, seating 428; Lincoln Theater, 700; Berkman Recital Hall.

Concerts/Musical Activities. Faculty Artist Series; Winter Chamber Music Series; Hartt Opera-Theater; student concerts and recitals

Music Library. The Mildred P. Allen Memorial Library provides circulating and reference materials. Included in the collection of 54,000 catalogued volumes are 16,000 recordings and 1,900 tapes. The 25,000-volume music collection includes standard works and a growing number of historical sets and scholarly editions. Two listening rooms, plus eight phonographs, thirteen cassette players. Special collections include: letters of Ernest Bloch; contemporary American Composers' Library project.

Special Programs

Featured Programs. The Institute of Contemporary American Music has been in residence at Hartt since 1948, bringing to the school each year many major figures of today's music. The Institute has provided a forum for the confrontation and comparison of various styles and trends in new music.

Performance Groups. Mixed Ensemble, Guitar Ensemble, String Ensemble, Woodwind Ensemble, Brass Ensemble, Percussion Ensemble, Baroque Ensemble, Collegium Musicum, Chorale, Women's Chorus, Opera Chorus, Collegiate Singers, Madrigal Consort, Vocal Arts Ensemble, Orchestra, Contemporary Players, Concert Band, Symphonic Wind Ensemble, Concert Jazz Band, Choraleers.

Affiliated Programs. A Hartt/Kodaly Musical Training Institute cooperative program makes it possible for an undergraduate to earn a KMTI Certificate while pursuing an undergraduate music education degree at the Hartt School of Music.

Financial

Costs. Per academic year: Tuition $8,240. Fees $345. Room and board $4,123.

Financial Aid. In addition to the awards made through the University Office of Admission and Student Financial Assistance, Hartt students are eligible for a number of talent-based music scholarships. These annual scholarships, which range from several hundred to several thousand dollars, are awarded by a faculty/administration committee to outstanding students. No special ap-

plications are need. State/federal aid and part-time employment also available.

Commentary

The Emerson Quartet has recently joined the performance faculty of Hartt School of Music.

Wesleyan University
Department of Music
High Street
Middletown
Connecticut 06457

Telephone. (203) 347-9411

Chief Administrator. William Barron, Jr., Department Head.

Wesleyan University has had a tradition of educational innovation and experimentation since its founding in 1831 as a school dedicated to the preparation of young men for the ministry and the professions. No longer affiliated with any religious denomination, the University offers only one undergraduate degree, the Bachelor of Arts, and master's degrees in eight fields of study, and doctoral degrees in five. Today the faculty is composed of more than 300 teacher-scholars and the student body numbers 3,100. The 100-acre campus has 62 buildings in the city of Middletown (population 40,000), located 15 miles south of Hartford and 24 miles north of New Haven. It lies halfway between Boston and New York.

The major goals of the Department of Music are to integrate the scholarly and performing components of music education; expose musicians to the world's music; and join music to the liberal arts. The Department of Music expects each major to strike a balance between classroom and performance modes of work and to show evidence of an awareness of more than one musical tradition. The Department offers an array of major programs, among which are concentrations in Javanese music, composition and performance of experimental music, Western art music (instrumental or vocal), Afro-American music, and historical musicology.

Accreditation. New England Association of Schools and Colleges.

Academic Information

Enrollment, Music Majors. Full-time 25. Foreign students 4.

Music Faculty. Full-time 15, part-time 2.

Term System. Semester.

Entrance Requirements. High school graduation with 4 units English, 3 mathematics, 2 laboratory science, 2 social studies, 3 foreign language; or GED. SAT and 3 Achievement Tests required; personal interview. No audition required.

Admission Procedure. Application with supporting documents and $40 nonrefundable application fee. 35% of applicants accepted. Application due Jan 15.

Music Degrees Offered. Bachelor of Arts; Master of Arts; Doctor of Philosophy.

Music Degree Requirements. The Bachelor of Arts degree with a music major includes three units of required courses. All majors must complete a senior project by the end of the senior year. The degree requires the completion of a minimum of thirty-four courses, of which about one-third are devoted to the student's major field of concentration. The Master of Arts and Doctor of Philosophy degrees are offered in the field of ethnomusicology.

General Program Areas. Afro-American Music, Composition, Ethnomusicology, Folk Music, Historical Musicology, Javanese Music, Jazz Studies, Performance, Western Art Music.

Instruments Taught. Baroque Instruments, Bonang, Brass, Javenese Gamelan, Kendhang, Organ, Percussion, Piano, Stringed Instruments, Voice, Woodwinds.

Musical Facilities

Practice Facilities. Special practice facilities for organists and percussionists. 23 practice rooms. 8 grand and 6 upright pianos.

Concert Facilities. Center for the Arts is a modern complex of 11 buildings housing the departments of art, music, and theater; includes theater, cinema, gallery, concert hall, and a smaller recital hall for the World Music programs.

Music Library. The Wesleyan University Library contains 956,000 volumes; 3,100 periodicals; students have complete access to the stacks. Music collection includes 18,000 scores; 6,000 volumes; 67 periodical titles; 7,500 phonograph recordings. Listening facilities in main library with 21 cassette decks, 16 stereo turntables, 16 compact disk players. World Music Archives contain 3,000 items, mostly field recordings, for enthnomusicological research.

Special collections include: World Music Archives.

Special Programs

Affiliated Programs. Academic cooperative plans with several other colleges, including Smith, Amherst, Trinity, Dartmouth, Vassar, Mt. Holyoke, Wellesley, and others.

Financial

Costs. Per academic year: Tuition $10,860. Fees $510. Room $2,220. Board $1,975.

Financial Aid. Financial aid is awarded on the basis of academic merit and financial need. Institutional and state/federal aid available.

Yale College (Yale University)
Department of Music
143 Elm Street
New Haven
Connecticut 06520

Telephone. (203) 432-2985

Chief Administrator. Dr. Craig Wright, Chairman, Department of Music.

See Yale University, School of Music.

The Department of Music offers introductory and advanced instruction in the history of music, the theory of music, and composition. Undergraduates interested in musical performance may obtain individual instruction at the School of Music. Students, whether majoring in music or not, who are qualified for instruction in performance, may offer up to four terms of instruction in performance for academic credit toward the thirty-six course credit requirement for the bachelor's degree.

Accreditation. New England Association of Schools and Colleges.

Academic Information

Music Faculty. 20.

Term System. Semester. Academic year early September to late April.

Entrance Requirements. Graduation from secondary school. Recommend units from wide variety of subjects. SAT; 3 Achievements. TOEFL required for foreign students. For graduate study, the faculty looks for the candidate who possesses musical talent, a strong background in the liberal arts, experience with foreign languages, and an interest in pursuing scholarly research. Grades, samples of work, letters of recommendation, and scores from the GRE (the Advanced Music Test is not necessary) are evaluated. No admission test in music is administered by the Department.

Admission Procedure. For Fall acceptance, apply as early as September 1 of previous year, but not later than January 2 of year of enrollment. Students are notified of acceptance in April. Apply by November 12 for early decision; must limit application to Yale. Early acceptance available.

Music Degrees Offered. Bachelor of Arts; Master of Arts; Bachelor of Arts/Master of Music (combined degree program); Doctor of Philosophy.

Music Degree Requirements. The Music major, leading to the Bachelor of Arts degree, is designed to provide a general music program in the humanities, as well as preparation for graduate studies or for careers in music. The standard major consists of at least ten term courses. The *intensive* major is designed for students of high standing who are qualified to do independent and original work in the history or theory of music, or in composition.

Majors in music in Yale College possessing outstanding ability in performance and composition may anticipate, through their undergraduate programs, one year of the Master of Music program in the School of Music without altering the present Yale College Music major. The Master of Arts in music curriculum is for students who wish either to augment previous graduate study or to go on to further study in one of the musical disciplines such as music history, theory, librarianship, or performance; or to prepare for non-academic careers in journalistic criticism, curatorship, or arts administration.

The Department of Music offers programs of study in music history and theory leading to the degree Doctor of Philosophy. Normally, four years are needed to complete the requirements for the degree, and these include two years of coursework, qualifying examinations, and a doctoral dissertation.

General Program Areas. Archival and Manuscript Studies, Baroque Music, Chamber Music, Medieval Music, Music History, Music Theory, Performance, Renaissance Music, Tonal Music.

Instruments Taught. Bassoon, Brass, Clarinet, Flute, French Horn, Guitar, Harp, Harpsichord, Oboe, Organ, Piano, Stringed Instruments, Trombone, Trumpet, Voice, Woodwinds.

Musical Facilities

Practice Facilities. See Yale University, School of Music.

Concert Facilities. See Yale University, School of Music.

Music Library. See Yale University, School of Music.

Special Programs

Affiliated Programs. Publications include *The Yale Collegium Musicum Series* (ed. Leon Plantinga); *Journal of Music Theory* (ed. Martha Hyde); *Music Theory Translation Series* (ed. Claude Palisca); and *Composers of the Twentieth Century Series* (ed. Allen Forte). The latter two series are published by Yale University Press.

Financial

Costs. Per academic year: Tuition $11,340. Room and board $4,700.

Financial Aid. Scholarships, grants, loans, and a College Work-Study program are available. For graduate students, tuition fellowships for either half or full tuition, and living stipends ranging from $1,000 to $5,000 are available for qualified students. Teaching fellowships and assistantships for up to $6,000 are regularly assigned to third- and fourth-year students.

Commentary

Yale University has two separate music divisions. Although they function independently of one another, undergraduates from Yale College may study an instrument or voice at the Yale School of Music. The combined B.A./M.M. program between the Department

and the School allows a student to complete two degrees in five years instead of the usual six. While students at the School of Music have always been able to take courses at the Department, the Department is now offering chamber music courses to its own undergraduates. In addition, the School and Department have collaborated in combined symposia and festivals. Yale's musical resources include the Yale Music Library, The Archive of Historical Sound Recordings (located in Sterling Memorial Library), and the Yale Collection of Musical Instruments, one of the most important American collections of historical instruments.

Yale University
School of Music
Stoeckel Hall
96 Wall Street
New Haven
Connecticut 06520

Telephone. (203) 432-1960, 432-4160

Chief Administrator. Dr. Frank Tirro, Dean.

Yale University was founded in 1701 and is comprised of 12 schools and colleges. It was the first university in the United States to grant the Doctor of Philosophy degree. Over 10,000 undergraduate and graduate students are enrolled each year. The campus is located in the city of New Haven on Long Island Sound.

In 1854, the sum of $5,000 was presented to Yale College by Joseph Battell "for the support, as far as it may go, of a teacher of the science of music to such students as may avail themselves of the opportunity." In April of the following year the Yale Corporation approved the appointment of Gustave Jacob Stoeckel as an instructor in church music and singing, and as director of the Chapel Choir and other musical activities at Yale College. Mr. Stoeckel's active campaign to establish a department of music at Yale led to its creation in 1889. Mr. Stoeckel was appointed as Battell Professor of Music in 1890, and in that year Yale's first credit courses in music were offered. The Yale School of Music was eventually established in 1894. The School of Music became exclusively a graduate professional school in 1958, requiring an undergraduate degree for admission and conferring only the Master of Music degree. Additional programs of graduate professional studies for performers and composers, leading to the degrees of Master of Musical Arts and Doctor of Musical Arts, were introduced in 1968. In 1973, the Institute of Sacred Music was established at Yale as an interdisciplinary graduate center for the study of music, liturgy, and the arts.

Most of the Yale Music Campus is located in the block bounded by College, Wall, Temple, and Elm streets.

Accreditation. New England Association of Schools and Colleges; National Association of Schools of Music.

Academic Information

Enrollment, Music Majors. Full-time 74 men, 56 women; part-time 2 men, 8 women. 22 foreign students.

Music Faculty. Full-time 23, part-time 37. Artists in residence: Tokyo String Quartet.

Term System. Semester. Yale Summer School of Music and Art (6 weeks, noncredit). Academic year early September to late April.

Entrance Requirements. Bachelor's degree; applicant must be qualified for undertaking advanced professional studies in performance in the individual's special field; tapes and auditions required.

Admission Procedure. Application, transcripts, audition tapes, letters of recommendation; GRE for all Master of Musical Arts applicants as well as composition, organ, choral, and orchestral conducting applicants. Materials are reviewed by the faculty for decision on whom to invite for audition. Foreign students must have TOEFL score of at least 550; if accepted for admission, must submit statement proving financial resources available to cover expenses; tape may be accepted in lieu of audition in some cases.

Music Degrees Offered. Master of Music; Master of Musical Arts; Doctor of Musical Arts; Certificate in Performance.

Music Degree Requirements. The Master of Music degree requires two years of residence and students must pass a minimum of 72 term hours with an average grade of B; degree recital or its equivalent in the second year of study. The Master of Musical Arts degree is awarded to candidates who successfully complete the three-year program (normally 18 hours per term) of predoctoral studies. The program is designed to provide intensive training in the student's major field, either performance or composition, supported by studies in theoretical and historical subjects. Degree requirements include the public presentation of recitals and/or compositions during the student's enrollment in the program. A thesis, as well as a public lecture based on the thesis is required of all candidates. Comprehensive written and oral examinations must be passed during the last term in residence. A total of 108 term hours is required for the degree.

The Doctor of Musical Arts degree is awarded to those who have earned the Master of Musical Arts degree at Yale in a three-year program of predoctoral studies with a major in either performance or composition, and who have subsequently demonstrated their qualification for the doctorate through distinguished achievement in the profession. Candidates may apply for the doctorate whenever they feel that their achievements subsequent to receiving the Master of Musical Arts degree warrant consideration. Formal applications will not be accepted from candidates prior to March 15 of the second year after which they have received the Master of Musical Arts degree.

The Certificate in Performance is a three-year program resulting in 96 credits, designed for gifted students who do not hold a bachelor's degree. This program is directed primarily toward string players.

Students in Yale College possessing outstanding ability in performance and composition may apply to the Bachelor of Arts/Master of Music program.

General Program Areas. Choral Conducting, Composition, Orchestral Conducting, Performance.

Instruments Taught. Bass, Bassoon, Brass, Clarinet, Flute, French Horn, Guitar, Harp, Harpsichord, Oboe, Opera, Organ, Percussion, Piano, Stringed Instruments, Trombone, Trumpet, Tuba, Viola, Violin, Violoncello, Voice, Woodwinds.

Musical Facilities

Practice Facilities. 30 practice rooms. 14 organs (Holtkamp, Flentrop, Schantz, Casavant, Moeller, Skinner, Von Beckerath, Charles Fisk). 60 practice pianos (mostly Steinways). Electronic music studio; recording studio; film music studio.

Concert Facilities. Woolsey Hall, seating 2,700; Sprague Hall, 728; Battell Chapel, 1,200; Dwight Chapel, 350.

Concerts/Musical Activities. Student degree recitals (75); opera performances (2); Orchestra concerts (6); jazz concerts (4); composer performances (6); Contemporary Ensemble concerts (2); professional organ series (6); professional Chamber Music Society concerts (6); faculty chamber music concerts (4); faculty recitals (4).

Music Library. The John Herrick Jackson Music Library contains over 117,000 bound scores and books and 14,500 phonograph records, in addition to several thousand titles on microfilm and a large file of unbound sheet music. The collection has been designed for scholarly study and reference, as well as to meet the needs of performing musicians. Special collections include theoretical literature of the sixteenth, seventeenth, and eighteenth centuries; chamber works of all periods for various instrumental combinations; an extensive collection of musical iconography; the Galeazzi collection of Italian manuscripts; the manuscripts and papers of Lehman Engle, Henry Gilbert, Thomas de Hartmann, J. Rosamond Johnson, Carl Ruggles, Alec Templeton, Virgil Thomson, and Kurt Weill; the manuscripts of Leo Ornstein and Hershey Kay; and the works of noted composers formerly associated with Yale University as teachers or students. The last-named area includes the complete manuscript collection of Charles E. Ives (B.A., 1898); the collection of documents concerning Paul Hindemith's career while in the United States; and the complete papers and manuscripts of David Stanley Smith, Horatio Parker, Richard Donovan, and Quincy Porter. The library also houses the extensive Lowell Mason Library of Church Music, noted for its collection of early American hymn and tune books. 28 listening stations are available.

The Yale University Collection of Musical Instruments is an independent member of the Yale community of museums devoted to the documentation of the history of music and organology through historical instruments. The Collection contains over 800 instruments of which the majority document the Western European art music tradition, especially the period from 1550 to 1850.

Special Programs

Performance Groups. Philharmonia Orchestra of Yale, Yale Symphony, University Marching Band, Concert Band, Yale Divinity School Choir, Yale Glee Club, Battell Chapel Choir, Yale Camerata, Yale Opera, Yale Jazz Ensemble, Yale-New Haven Jazz Repertory Dance Band, Yale Russian Chorus, Yale Slavic Chorus, Bach Society, Collegium Musicum.

Affiliated Programs. The Institute of Sacred Music is a distinct graduate center within Yale University for the interdisciplinary study of worship, theology, music, and related arts. Through the joint Institute/School of Music course of study, the Master of Music, Master of Musical Arts, and Doctor of Musical Arts may be granted. In addition to general music study in organ performance, choral conducting, composition, and history, Institute students participate in courses at the Yale Divinity School designed to enrich their understanding of the theological and liturgical disciplines.

Financial

Costs. Per academic year: Tuition $9,275. Room $2,-090 to $2,370. Board $951 for first term, $973 for second term. Off-campus housing $400 per month (estimated).

Financial Aid. The Yale School of Music Scholarship is made to students based on need, merit, and potential in the music profession. Students awarded scholarship funds are committed to three hours per week assisting in different areas of the School of Music where needed. Part-time employment, loans, and College Work-Study grants are available. Financial aid/scholarship application due February 1.

DELAWARE

University of Delaware
Department of Music
College of Arts and Sciences
Newark
Delaware 19716

Telephone. (302) 451-2577

Chief Administrator. Dr. Larry W. Peterson, Chairperson.

The University of Delaware was established in 1743. It currently enrolls over 18,000 full-time and part-time students. The campus in Newark occupies 1,300 acres.

The Department of Music provides a wide variety of educational programs ranging from opportunities for general cultural enrichment to preparation for professional careers. For the University at large, the Department offers courses in the fundamentals of music, music literature, electronic music, and class study of voice and piano. All courses in the Department, except private lessons, are available to any University student who can meet course prerequisites.

Accreditation. Middle States Association of Colleges and Schools; National Association of Schools of Music.

Academic Information

Enrollment, Music Majors. (Total University) Full-time 6,269 men, 7,797 women; part-time 4,096.

Music Faculty. 30. Artists-in-residence: Delos String Quartet.

Term System. Semester. 2 summer sessions.

Entrance Requirements. High school graduation; recommended completion of 4 units English, 3 mathematics, 2 foreign language, 3 science, 4 social science; SAT required; placement auditions and musicality tests.

Admission Procedure. Application with supporting documents and nonrefundable $25 fee to Office of Admissions.

Music Degrees Offered. Bachelor of Music; Bachelor of Arts.

Music Degree Requirements. The Bachelor of Music degree programs are for those students who intend to become professional musicians. There are opportunities to major in music education, theory-composition, or applied music (band or orchestral instruments, organ, piano, classical guitar, and voice). The Bachelor of Arts degree provides a basic program in music theory, literature, ensembles, and applied music. All baccalaureate programs are preparatory to graduate study.

General Program Areas. Applied Music, Composition, Music Education, Music Literature, Music Theory.

Instruments Taught. Brass, Organ, Percussion, Piano, Stringed Instruments, Voice, Woodwinds.

Musical Facilities

Concerts/Musical Activities. The academic year includes many opportunities for students to participate in and attend musical events, including concerts, recitals, and musical theatre productions; faculty concerts and recitals.

Music Library. The collections of the University of Delaware Library contain over 1,500,000 volumes.

Special Programs

Featured Programs. The National Consortium for Computer-Based Music Instruction, founded by the Department of Music, includes member institutions in the United States and Europe.

Performance Groups. Choral Union, Chorale, University Singers, Concert Choir, Marching Band, Wind Ensemble, Symphonic Band, Concert Band, Jazz Ensemble, Chamber Ensembles, University-affiliated Orchestra.

Financial

Costs. Per academic year: Tuition in-state resident $2,100, out-of-state $4,800. Fees $94. Room $1,484. Board $1,022.

Financial Aid. Scholarships, grants, loans, and part-time employment are available. A limited number of Music Merit Awards offered by the Department of Music allow continuing study in private music instruction for upperclass students. Financial aid/scholarship application due May 1.

DISTRICT OF COLUMBIA

The Catholic University of America
The Benjamin T. Rome School of Music
Fourth Street and Michigan Avenue, N.E.
Washington
District of Columbia 20064

Telephone. (202) 635-5414
Chief Administrator. Dr. Elaine R. Walter, Dean.

Catholic University was was founded in 1887 and is a privately supported Roman Catholic institution. The 181-acre campus has 58 buildings in Washington, D.C.

Although music has been an important part of campus life since 1927 when the first courses were offered under the auspices of the Catholic Sisters College and in the University's summer session, it was not until 1950 that a Division of Music was established within the College and Graduate School of Arts and Sciences. The Division was elevated to the status of a Department in 1952, and to a school in 1965. The School was named The Benjamin T. Rome School of Music in 1984 in honor of alumnus, Trustee emeritus, and longtime benefactor, Benjamin T. Rome.

The specific objectives of the School, derived directly from the aims and goals of the University, are to foster excellence in faculty and student musical research, creativity, and performance, serving the cultural needs of the Church and the nation.

Accreditation. Middle States Association of Colleges and Schools; National Association of Schools of Music; National Council for Accreditation of Teacher Education.

Academic Information

Enrollment, Music Majors. (Total University) Full-time 2,105 men, 2,100 women; part-time 2,428.

Music Faculty. 39.

Term System. Semester.

Entrance Requirements. High school graduation with rank in upper third; recommend 4 units English, 3 college preparatory mathematics, 2 foreign language; SAT and English Composition Achievement Test required;

audition required.

Admission Procedure. Application with supporting documents and nonrefundable $20 fee (graduate $30) to Office of Admissions.

Music Degrees Offered. Bachelor of Music; Master of Music; Master of Arts; Master of Liturgical Music; Doctor of Musical Arts.

Music Degree Requirements. The Bachelor of Music degree program provides majors in composition, general-choral music education, combined general-choral and instrumental music education, music therapy, orchestral instruments, organ, piano, and voice. Specific curricula are followed for each major.

The Master of Music degree is offered in accompanying and chamber music (piano), choral conducting, composition, instrumental conducting (wind ensemble concentration), music education, music education with an emphasis on the Kodaly method, music therapy, orchestral instruments (performance: violin, viola, violoncello, string bass, solo woodwind and brass instruments, percussion, harp, classical guitar, and harpsichord), organ performance, piano performance, piano pedagogy, vocal pedagogy, and vocal performance.

The Master of Arts degree in musicology is offered with an emphasis in music history or theory. A joint degree program in music librarianship (Master of Arts in musicology and Master of Science in Library Science) and the Master of Liturgical Music degree are also available.

The Doctor of Musical Arts degree is offered to selected, qualified students as a recognition of high professional attainment in some branch of performance, in original composition, liturgical music, or in the field of music teaching. The objective of the degree is to provide an opportunity for advanced study at the highest artistic and pedagogical level.

General Program Areas. Chamber Music, Choral Conducting, Choral Music Education, Instrumental Conducting, Instrumental Music Education, Kodaly Method, Liturgical Music, Music History, Music Librarianship, Music Theory, Music Therapy, Orchestral Instruments, Performance, Piano Pedagogy, Vocal

Pedagogy.

Instruments Taught. Bass, Bassoon, Clarinet, Euphonium, Flute, Guitar, Harpsichord, Horn, Oboe, Organ, Percussion, Piano, Saxophone, Trombone, Trumpet, Tuba, Viola, Violin, Violoncello, Voice.

Musical Facilities

Concerts/Musical Activities. More than 300 concerts, opera productions, and recitals are presented each year on the campus and throughout the Washington area. An annual concert of the University Orchestra and Chorus is presented at the John F. Kennedy Center for the Performing Arts.

Special Programs

Featured Programs. The Latin American Center for Graduate Studies in Music was created to: promote the study and research of Latin American music; compile a complete and specialized library of scores, books, and recordings of Latin American music; and foster the exchange of students, scholars, performers, composers, and music educators between the United States and Latin American countries.

Performance Groups. University Chorus, University Symphony Orchestra, University Wind Ensemble, A Cappella Choir, Trombone Choir, Percussion Ensemble, Guitar Ensemble, Contemporary Chamber Ensemble, Cardinalaires

Financial

Costs. Per academic year: Tuition $7,900. Fees $200. Music lesson fee $30 per half-hour lesson per semester, $60 per one hour lesson; music practice fee per hour for organ or grand piano $40, other $30. Room $2,240. Board $1,830.

Financial Aid. Scholarships, fellowships, and other forms of financial support are available to United States citizens. Federal grant and loan programs and a College Work-Study program available. Awards based on musical ability, academic record, and financial need are available each year to students in the School of Music. Among these awards are the John Paul Music Scholarship and the David Burchuk Memorial Scholarship. A scholarship for study in the School of Music is awarded to the winner of the annual opera competition. High school seniors and college freshmen and sophomores are eligible. Scholarship/financial aid application due February 15.

Howard University
Department of Music
College of Fine Arts
2400 Sixth Street, N.W.
Washington
District of Columbia 20059

Telephone. (202) 636-7082

Chief Administrator. Doris Evans McGinty, Chairman.

Howard University, founded in 1867, is a privately supported university with an enrollment exceeding 11,000 students. The 89-acre main campus has 67 buildings in the center of Washington, D.C. A 22-acre West Campus is located near Rock Creek Park in the northwest section of the city.

The College of Fine Arts came into existence in 1960 when the School of Music, the Department of Art, and the Department of Drama were merged. The School of Music (now Department of Music) began with a few courses offered in 1870, was organized as a department of the Normal School in 1892, and was established as an independent conservatory in 1914. The Department of Music offers undergraduate and graduate programs.

Accreditation. Middle States Association of Colleges and Schools; National Association of Schools of Music.

Academic Information

Enrollment, Music Majors. (Total University) Full-time 4,138 men, 5,103 women; part-time 1,943.

Music Faculty. 60.

Term System. Semester. 3 summer sessions.

Entrance Requirements. High school graduation; completion of 16 units; SAT; 2 Achievement Tests; audition required.

Admission Procedure. Application with supporting documents and nonrefundable $25 fee to Admissions Office.

Music Degrees Offered. Bachelor of Music; Bachelor of Music Education; Master of Music; Master of Music Education.

Music Degree Requirements. The Bachelor of Music degree may be earned in one of five major areas: applied music, composition, history and literature, jazz studies, and music therapy. Options within the applied music major include piano, voice, organ, guitar, saxophone, or orchestral instruments. The Bachelor of Music Education is available in Urban Music. The Bachelor of Music Education and the Master of Music Education degrees may be earned with an emphasis in piano, voice, organ, saxophone, guitar, or an orchestral instrument. The degree Master of Music is offered in applied music, composition, history, and musicology. The degree in musicology includes the option of a concentration in Afro-American music studies.

General Program Areas. Afro-American Music, Applied Music, Composition, Jazz Studies, Music Education, Music History, Music Literature, Musicology.

Instruments Taught. Baritone, Bass, Bassoon, Clarinet, Flute, French Horn, Guitar, Harp, Oboe, Organ, Percussion, Piano, Saxophone, Trombone, Trumpet, Tuba, Viola, Violin, Violoncello, Voice.

Musical Facilities

Concert Facilities. University Center Auditorium.

Concerts/Musical Activities. Student/faculty concerts and recitals.

Music Library. The Channing Pollock Theatre Collection, one of three special collections in the University Libraries system, contains materials on the performing arts; it also documents the Black experience in that area. Special collection of books on Blacks in the arts; jazz records; musical instrument collection. The Fine Arts Branch of the Libraries includes materials supporting the academic programs of the College of Fine Arts.

Special Programs

Featured Programs. The Center for Ethnic Music, formerly called The Project in African Music, is committed to research and its dissemination on African and African-derived music. The Center has a collection of over 50 African and Asian instruments. In conjunction with the Department of Music, the Center assists individuals through consultant services and the use and loan of resource materials on Black music.

Performance Groups. Chamber Ensemble, String Ensemble, Woodwind Ensemble, Saxophone Ensemble, Brass Ensemble, Marching Band, Concert Band, Jazz Ensemble, Orchestra, University Choir, University Chorale, University Collegium.

Financial

Costs. Per academic year: Tuition $3,500. Fees $415. Room $1,500. Board $1,630.

Financial Aid. Financial aid is awarded on the basis of academic merit and financial need. Institutional and state/federal aid as well as part-time employment and a College Work-Study program available. Financial aid/scholarship application due April 1.

Commentary

In Howard University's Artist/Scholar program, the Bachelor's degree can be earned through a variety of independent educational experiences. International travel and other forms of outside study can be part of this individualized curriculum plan.

FLORIDA

University of Central Florida
Department of Music
Box 25000
Orlando
Florida 32816

Telephone. (305) 275-2869
Chief Administrator. B. Whisler, Chairman.

The University of Central Florida is part of the State University System of Florida. The campus of 1,227 acres is located 13 miles east of downtown Orlando.

The Department of Music offers undergraduate programs leading to the baccalaureate degree.

Accreditation. Southern Association of Schools and Colleges; National Association of Schools of Music.

Academic Information

Enrollment, Music Majors. (Total University) 8,106 men, 8,338 women.

Music Faculty. Full-time 13, part-time 13.

Term System. Semester. 3 summer sessions.

Entrance Requirements. High school graduation; academic units to include 4 English, 3 mathematics, 3 natural science, 3 social science, 2 foreign language, 4 electives; SAT or ACT; audition required.

Admission Procedure. Application with supporting documents and nonrefundable $15 fee to Admissions Office.

Music Degrees Offered. Bachelor of Arts.

Music Degree Requirements. The Bachelor of Arts degree is offered with options in applied music, piano pedagogy, instrumental music education, choral music education, and elementary school education. The music education programs are approved by the Florida State Department of Education. Courses leading to teacher certfication are offered cooperatively with the College of Education.

General Program Areas. Applied Music, Music Education, Piano Pedagogy.

Instruments Taught. Baritone, Bass, Bassoon, Clarinet, Flute, French Horn, Guitar, Harp, Oboe, Organ, Percussion, Piano, Recorder, Saxophone, Trombone, Trumpet, Tuba, Viola, Violin, Violoncello, Voice.

Musical Facilities

Concerts/Musical Activities. Student/faculty concerts and recitals; visiting artists.

Music Library. The University Library houses a collection of over 500,000 volumes.

Special Programs

Performance Groups. Marching Band, Pep Band, Concert Band, Wind Ensemble, Community Orchestra, University Choir, Madrigal Singers, Chamber Chorus, Oratorio Choir, String Ensemble, Percussion Ensemble, Piano Ensemble, Jazz/Pop Ensemble, Opera Workshop.

Financial

Costs. Per academic year: Tuition in-state resident $895, out-of-state $2,942. Room $900 to $1,228. Board $687 to $1,477.

Financial Aid. Financial aid in the form of scholarships, grants, loans, and part-time employment is available.

University of Florida
Department of Music
College of Fine Arts
West University Avenue and 13th Street
Gainesville
Florida 32611

Telephone. (904) 392-0223
Chief Administrator. James Pierce Hall, Professor of Music.

The University of Florida is a combined state university and land-grant college enrolling over 32,000 students annually. The campus is located in Gainesville in north-central Florida.

The Department of Music within the College of Fine Arts offers undergraduate and graduate programs.

Accreditation. Southern Association of Colleges and Schools; National Association of Schools of Music.

Academic Information

Enrollment, Music Majors. (Total University) 32,453.
Term System. Semester. 2 summer sessions.
Entrance Requirements. High school graduation with rank in upper 40 percent; minimum of 18 academic units including 4 English, 2 foreign language, 3 mathematics, 2 laboratory science, 3 social science, 4 electives; SAT or ACT; audition required.
Admission Procedure. Application with supporting documents and nonrefundable $15 fee to Office of Admissions.
Music Degrees Offered. Bachelor of Music; Bachelor of Music Education; Master of Fine Arts; Master of Education; Master of Arts; Doctor of Education; Doctor of Philosophy.
Music Degree Requirements. The Bachelor of Music degree is offered with majors in performance, theory and composition, history, and church music. The Bachelor of Music Education degree is offered in cooperation with the College of Education. The degree Master of Fine Arts with a major in music is designed primarily for those who wish to become teachers in colleges and universities, performers, music historians, music critics, church musicians, composers, and conductors. The Department of Music cooperates with the College of Education in offering graduate degrees in education: Master of Education in music education (thesis or nonthesis), Specialist in Education, Doctor of Education degree in college music, and the Doctor of Philosophy degree in college music teaching (emphasis in music history, literature and criticism, music theory and composition, performance practices, and music education).
General Program Areas. Church Music, Composition, Conducting, Music Criticism, Music Education, Music History, Music Literature, Music Theory.
Instruments Taught. Bass, Bassoon, Brass, Carillon, Clarinet, Euphonium, Flute, French Horn, Harpsichord, Oboe, Organ, Percussion, Piano, Saxophone, Trombone, Trumpet, Tuba, Viola, Violin, Violincello, Voice, Woodwinds.

Musical Facilities

Concerts/Musical Activities. Student and faculty concerts and recitals; visiting artists.
Music Library. The Music Library has an extensive collection of published and recorded music of all types. Music listening facilities are available.
Special collections include: American Liszt Society Archives; eighteenth and nineteenth century music imprints; Belknap Collection for the Performing Arts.

Special Programs

Performance Groups. Marching Band, Concert Band, Symphonic Band, University Orchestra, University Choir, Women's Chorale, Men's Glee Club, Choral Union, Chamber Music Ensemble, Musical Theatre Ensemble, Jazz Bands, Vocal Jazz Troupe, University Chamber Singers, Renaissance Ensemble.

Financial

Costs. Per academic year: Tuition in-state resident $889, out-of-state $2,549. Room $1,194. Board $1,575.
Financial Aid. Sources of financial aid include part-time employment, assistantships, fellowships, grants, scholarships, loans, prizes, and awards. Scholarship/financial aid application due March 1.

Florida State University School of Music
Tallahassee
Florida 32306

Telephone. (904) 644-3424
Chief Administrator. Robert Glidden, Dean.
Founded in 1851 and designated as The Florida State University in 1947, the University has built a reputation as a center for research both in the sciences and in the humanities. Presently there are more than 21,000 students enrolled of which over 4,000 are graduate students enrolled in the University's 98 programs of graduate study.
The 347-acre campus has 75 buildings that range in architectural design from collegiate Gothic to the ultra-modern. Dormitory facilities accommodate 1,322 men and 2,579 women. The campus is located in the city of Tallahassee in northwestern Florida. All forms of transportation serve the area.
The School of Music is an integral component of the Florida State University community. It serves as an agency for the cultural development of the state and offers a comprehensive program of instruction for all students who expect to become professional musicians: composers, performers, scholars, teachers. For the general university student, it offers a wide spectrum of opportunities for disciplined personal growth and creative achievement.
Strengths of the Department include disciplines in performance, music education, music therapy, Center for Music Research, and ethnomusicology (Center for Music of the Americas).
Accreditation. Southern Association of Colleges and Schools; National Association of Schools of Music.

Academic Information

Enrollment, Music Majors. Undergraduate 410, graduate 266; full-time 295 men, 335 women; part-time 27 men, 19 women.

Music Faculty. Full-time 63, part-time 10.

Term System. Semester. One thirteen-week and two six-week summer sessions.

Entrance Requirements. Undergraduate: Graduation from an accredited high school with approximately a 2.5 (on a 4.0 scale) grade point average in all academic subjects (grades 9 through 12) and test scores of 21 (composite) on the ACT or 950 (verbal plus math) on the SAT. GED acceptable. Foreign students must have a TOEFL score of 550.

Selective admission within curricular, space, and fiscal limitations. Separate application required by School of Music. All entering students are required to take a placement audition in applied music. All applicants must meet appropriate minimum standards through this audition before being granted admission to the School of Music. This audition is heard by a faculty jury and is closed to all except the area faculty concerned. Students are expected to be prepared to play or sing representative works of an acceptable repertoire. A live audition on campus is preferred; taped audition may be accepted.

Admission Procedure. Application for admission and a nonrefundable $15 fee. For fall term applications should be filed the preceding October and November, but preferably no later than March.

Music Degrees Offered. Bachelor of Music in performance, music theory, composition, music history and literature, music theatre, music therapy; Bachelor of Music Education in choral, instrumental, general music; Master of Music in performance, accompanying, choral conducting, wind ensemble and band conducting, music theory, composition, musicology, music therapy, opera; Master of Music Education; Doctor of Philosophy in music education and music theory; Doctor of Education in music education; and Doctor of Music in composition or in performance (piano, organ, voice, guitar, violin, viola, violoncello, double bass, flute, oboe, clarinet, saxophone, bassoon, trumpet, horn, trombone, tuba, or percussion).

The Bachelor of Arts degree with an emphasis in Music and the Doctor of Philosophy degree in humanities with an emphasis in music are available in the College of Arts and Science.

A Certificate is also awarded in performance, church music, jazz studies, piano pedagogy, piano technology, special music education, and computers in music.

Music Degree Requirements. Baccalaureate degree: 120 semester hours; 2.0 grade point average; 30 hours in residence; 49 hours in liberal studies. Master's degree: 30 semester hours; 3.0 grade point average, thesis or equivalent (recitals) or additional coursework. Doctoral degree: 70 semester hours; 3.0 grade point average;

dissertation or equivalent (recitals); one academic year in residence.

General Program Areas. Church Music, Computers in Music, Jazz Studies, Music Education, Music Therapy, Performance, Piano Pedagogy, Piano Technology.

Instruments Taught. Bass, Bassoon, Cello, Clarinet, Euphonium, Flute, Guitar, Harpsichord, Horn, Oboe, Organ, Percussion, Piano, Saxophone, Trombone, Trumpet, Tuba, Viola, Violin, Voice.

Musical Facilities

Practice Facilities. 4 organs (Holtcamp) and 1 Hill and Davison English Chamber Organ; 9 practice rooms for percussionists; 134 practice room pianos and 39 office and classroom upright pianos (Baldwin, Steinway, Yamaha, Everett & Grinnell); 67 studio and recital hall grand pianos (Steinway, Baldwin, Bosendorfer). 10 Steinway "L" grand pianos reserved for piano majors. 134 practice rooms (sound attenuated); average size 80 square feet.

Concert Facilities. Three, including a 530-seat recital and concert hall and a 200-seat recital and lecture hall. *Special studios:* Computer-based music instruction classroom; 2 digital electronic studios; computerized music formatting and printing studio; analog electronic music studio; perception research laboratory; multimedia production laboratory; 2 computer software laboratories; electronic hardware laboratory (used for both analog and digital electronics). 25 classrooms.

Community Facilities. Tallahassee-Leon County Civic Center.

Music Library. Music Library collection of 17,000 books; 42,000 scores; 23,800 recordings; 175 current periodical subscriptions; 2,100 microforms. Annual budget for books and other materials approximately $65,000.

Special collections include: scores and manuscripts of Ernest von Dohnanyi, Carlisle Floyd, Howard Wilson.

Special Programs

Featured Programs. Center for Music Research; Center for Music of the Americas.

Performance Groups. Baroque Ensemble, Brass Ensembles, Chamber Chorus, Chamber Orchestra, Chamber Winds, Choral Union, Collegians (Men's Glee Club), Concert Bands, Early Music Ensembles, Jazz Ensembles, Madrigal Singers, Marching Chiefs, Music Theatre Ensemble, New Music Ensemble, Opera Chorus, Opera Orchestra, Percussion Ensembles, String Ensembles, Symphonic Band, University Chorale, University Singers, University Symphony, Wind Orchestra, Woodwind Ensembles, Women's Glee Club, and World Music Ensembles. In addition there are numerous student and faculty ensembles including the Faculty Brass Quintet and several faculty string chamber music groups.

Foreign Programs. International study centers in London, England and Florence, Italy; programs for undergraduates in Costa Rica, Switzerland, and Yugoslavia.

Financial

Costs. Per academic year: Undergraduate tuition and fees in-state $1,111, out-of-state $3,636. Campus housing $1,167 to $1,318. Board $1,082.

Financial Aid. 114 music students received some form of financial aid. Scholarships range from $200 to $1,965 (average $830). Scholarship applications due mid-March.

Commentary

Florida State University, whose music school is one of the largest and best-rounded in the region, has a good performance program supported by impressive facilities. The interesting library collections include scores and manuscripts of E. von Dohnanyi and Carlisle Floyd, and nineteenth-century flute music. In addition, the Department of Anthropology maintains an ethnic instruments collection.

University of Miami
School of Music
Coral Gables
Florida 33124

Telephone. (305) 284-2161

Chief Administrator. Dr. James William Hipp, Dean.

The University of Miami was chartered in 1925. It is a private, nonsectarian institution that enrolls over 9,000 full- and part-time undergraduates and over 4,500 graduate. The 273-acre campus contains 183 buildings in Coral Gables, a city in the metropolitan Miami area.

The School of Music has four primary objects: to provide its majors with a high quality of preprofessional education and training in preparation for entering music and music-related fields, and at the same time, promote the values inherent in a liberal education; to serve the general students of the University through the offering of specially designed courses and performance opportunities, with the aim of increasing their understanding of and appreciation for various musical repertoires; to foster advancements in musical performance, creativity, research, scholarship, and teaching; and to serve as an educational and cultural resource for the university community, the Greater Miami area, and the South Florida region.

Accreditation. Southern Association of Colleges and Schools; National Association of Schools of Music.

Academic Information

Enrollment, Music Majors. (Total University) Full-time 4,669 men, 3,832 women; part-time 1,094; graduate students 4,883.

Music Faculty. 88.

Term System. Semester. Two 5-week summer sessions.

Entrance Requirements. High school graduation or GED; recommend 16 academic credits including 4 English, 3 mathematics, 2 foreign language, 1 laboratory science, 2 social science; SAT (combined scored 840) or ACT (minimum score 20); live audition or tape (cassette); placement tests upon entrance in theory, piano, instrument.

Admission Procedure. Application to University plus supplementary application to School of Music upon declaring major; priority deadline March 1; nonrefundable application fee $30.

Music Degrees Offered. Bachelor of Music; Master of Music; Doctor of Musical Arts; Doctor of Philosophy. Bachelor of Science and Bachelor of Arts with major in music offered by other schools and colleges in the University.

Music Degree Requirements. The Bachelor of Music degree is offered with majors in the areas of applied music, music education, music engineering technology, music merchandising, musical theatre, music therapy, studio music and jazz, and theory-composition. The degree requires the completion of 120 to 137 semester hours of general education, core curriculum, and the major area.

The Master of Music degree, administered by the Graduate School, is offered with majors in music education, music therapy, theory-composition, applied music (voice, piano, conducting, organ, harp, woodwinds, multi-woodwinds, brass, percussion, or stringed instruments), musicology, accompanying, music librarianship, jazz performance, jazz pedagogy, music merchandising, studio jazz writing, studio writing and production, and musical theatre. The degree requires the completion of 30 to 37 semester hours depending on concentration. The degrees Doctor of Musical Arts and Doctor of Philosophy in music are also administered by the Graduate School and enrollment is limited. The degrees require the completion of 60 semester hours beyond the master of Music degree.

General Program Areas. Accompanying, Applied Music, Composition, Conducting, Jazz Pedagogy, Jazz Studies, Music Education, Music Engineering Technology, Music Librarianship, Music Merchandising, Music Theory, Music Therapy, Musical Theatre, Musicology, Performance, Studio Jazz Writing.

Instruments Taught. Baritone Horn, Bass, Clarinet, Flute, French Horn, Guitar, Harp, Harpsichord, Oboe, Organ, Percussion, Piano, Saxophone, Stringed Instruments, Trombone, Trumpet, Tuba, Viola, Violin, Violoncello, Voice, Woodwinds.

Musical Facilities

Practice Facilities. Bertha Foster Memorial Music Building has 65 practice rooms and teaching studios. Pipe organ studio; electronic music studio; recording studio. Percussion Building contains teaching-practice studio. Other buildings include Nancy Greene Symphony Hall, Caroline Broby Choral Hall, Henry Fillmore Band Hall; Arnold Volpe Building.

Concert Facilities. Maurice Gusman Concert Hall; Brockway Hall.

Community Facilities. Knight Convention Center is used for some performance activities.

Concerts/Musical Activities. More than 300 student forums, student and faculty recitals, concerts, lectures, and music festivals are presented during the academic year.

Music Library. Albert Pick Music Library houses a collection of 28,000 scores, 18,000 recordings, current issues of music periodicals, and a selected group of reference books. Special collections include: jazz music; Latin American music; Yiddish music; Handleman Institute of Recorded Sound. All other books about music are kept in the nearby Otto G. Richter Library.

Special Programs

Featured Programs. Workshops and clinics to enrich the music knowledge of professional teachers and musicians are offered during the academic year. Enriched opportunities for high school keyboard, choir, band, orchestral, and jazz students are provided in annual summer music campus and workshops.

Performance Groups. Avant Garde Ensemble, Brass Chamber Music, Brass Choir, Brass Quintet, Chamber Orchestra, Chamber String Ensemble, Classical Guitar Ensemble, Collegium Musicum, Concert Band, Contemporary Music Ensemble, Electric Bass Ensemble, Electronic Music Ensemble, Flute Choir, Jazz Band, Jazz Guitar Ensemble, Mallet Ensemble, Marching Band, Marimba Ensemble, Percussion Ensemble, Rock Ensemble, String Quartet, Symphonic Band, Symphonic Orchestra, Tuba Ensemble, Wind Ensemble, Woodwind Chamber Music, Woodwind Doublers Ensemble, Woodwind Quintet, Chamber Singers, Concert Choir, Graduate Chorale, Miami Civic Chorale, Musical Theatre, Opera Workshop, Recital Chorale, Singing Hurricanes, University Mixed Chorus, University Singers.

Financial

Costs. Per academic year: Tuition $8,740. Fees $75. Room and board $3,850.

Financial Aid. Financial aid is available in the form of scholarships, grants, state/federal loans, part-time employment, and a College Work-Study program.

Commentary

The University of Miami was the first university in the country to offer a degree in music engineering. The M.M. degree is available in a diverse selection of areas, and jazz is not only prevalent in the curriculum, it dominates the performing groups on campus, with the Funk, Bebop, and Monk/Mingus Ensembles. Annual tuition and room and board are expensive for this part of the country.

University of South Florida
Department of Music
College of Fine Arts
4202 Fowler Avenue
Tampa
Florida 33620

Telephone. (813) 974-2311

Chief Administrator. Dr. Jack J. Heller, Chairman.

The University of South Florida was founded in 1956 and regional campuses were opened in St. Petersburg in 1965, Fort Myers in 1974, and Sarasota in 1975. The University enrolls over 27,000 students each year. The Tampa campus of the University is located on a 1,695-acre tract of land ten miles northeast of downtown Tampa, a city of over a quarter of a million people on the west coast of Florida on the Gulf of Mexico.

The Department of Music offers a comprehensive program providing students opportunities to develop their interests and talents to the highest level. Candidates for a major in music are required to pass an entrance examination (audition) in their respective performance area. Composition candidates are required to submit appropriate scores and/or tapes of their compositions for faculty appraisal. All students seeking a degree in music are required to complete successfully the piano proficiency and music theory, history, and literatures requirements; present a partial public recital during the junior year (except composition majors); present a full public recital during the senior year; and present a record of satisfactory recital attendance during each of the semesters of study at the University.

Accreditation. Southern Association of Colleges and Schools; National Association of Schools of Music.

Academic Information

Enrollment, Music Majors. Full-time 90 men, 120 women; part-time 40 men, 60 women. 10 foreign students.

Music Faculty. Full-time 35, part-time 8.

Term System. Semester. Two 7-week summer sessions from mid-May to mid-August. Academic year from August to May.

Entrance Requirements. High school graduation rank combined with SAT score used as criterion; audition on principal instrument or voice.

Admission Procedure. Application with supporting documents to Admissions Office; contact Director of Admission, Department of Music for audition schedule.

Music Degrees Offered. Bachelor of Music; Bachelor of Arts; Master of Music; Master of Arts; Doctor of Philosophy.

Music Degree Requirements. The Bachelor of Music degree is offered with concentration in performance (voice, piano, organ, harp, guitar, and orchestral instruments), composition, and piano pedagogy. The degree requires the completion of 132 credits including general education requirements, core curriculum, and major courses. Credits required for the concentration vary with program pursued. The Bachelor of Arts degree in music education requires an audition in the student's performance area. Special requirements include completion of the piano proficiency requirement, participation in a major performing ensemble each semester the student is enrolled in applied music, and the presentation of a one-half hour recital in the major performing medium during the senior year. Requirements of the College of Education must also be met. The Master of Music degree is offered with concentrations in performance, composition, piano pedagogy, theory, choral conducting, and wind instrument conducting. Degree requirements will vary (32 to 36 credits) according the the program chosen and the student's needs and interests. The Master of Arts degree offers plans in both instrumental and vocal music. The student may complete either 35 hours of coursework, 32 hours plus recital, or 30 hours plus thesis. The degree Doctor of Philosophy in music education is offered in conjunction with the College of Education.

General Program Areas. Applied Music, Conducting, Jazz Studies, Music Education, Music History, Music Theory, Piano Pedagogy.

Instruments Taught. Bass, Bassoon, Euphonium, Flute, Guitar, Harp, Oboe, Organ, Percussion, Piano, Saxophone, Trombone, Trumpet, Tuba, Viola, Violin, Violoncello, Voice.

Musical Facilities

Practice Facilities. 30 practice rooms. Special practice facilities for percussionists. 20 pianos; 5 grand pianos reserved for piano majors. Electronic music studio.

Concert Facilities. 2 theatres, seating 300 and 500 each; Recital Hall, 225.

Community Facilities. Several churches in the community used for organ practice; professional concert hall.

Concerts/Musical Activities. Over 250 recitals and ensemble events are presented each year; INTERMUSE, a new music/media festival.

Music Library. Music materials are housed in the main library. 7,785 music books; 4,500 scores; 20 music-related periodicals; 13,700 phonograph recordings; 7,385 cassettes. 114 listening stations (stereo) in Listening Laboratory. The Tampa Public Library is also available to students.

Special Programs

Featured Programs. The Systems Complex for the Studio and Performing Arts (SYCOM) provides instructional services and state-of-the-art reproducing, mixing, editing, and electronic sound generating and processing equipment (digital and analog) for development and implementation of explorative research and creative activity by artists, scientists, and students generally enrolled in related classes.

Performance Groups. Choral, orchestral, wind, and jazz ensembles.

Financial

Costs. Per academic year: Tuition in-state $1,000, out-of-state $4,000. Fees $100. Room $1,200. Board $1,500.

Financial Aid. The University has made available to highly qualified undergraduate students a number of Music Service awards. Usually these awards cover in-state tuition fees, and are distributed following open auditions held in February and March. Out-of-state tuition waiver is also possible. Also available are scholarships awarded in specified areas. Available to graduate students who show special potential for creative contribution to the profession are the Graduate Council Fellowships and graduate assistantships and fellowships. Additionally, loans, grants, and work programs are available to qualified students. Financial aid is granted on the basis of need, academic promise, and character.

Stetson University School of Music
North Boulevard
Deland
Florida 32720

Telephone. (904) 734-4121

Chief Administrator. Dr. James E. Woodward, Dean.

Stetson University, a church-related institution founded in 1883 by Henry A. DeLand, a Baptist layman, is Florida's first university. Known first as DeLand Academy, the name was changed in 1889 to honor John B. Stetson, the well-known Philadelphia hat manufacturer who had a winter home in Deland and became a generous supporter of the young institution. The University is affiliated with the churches of the Florida Baptist State Convention. The campus has a physical plant of 35 buildings on nearly 100 acres in the city of Deland, a community in central Florida 22 miles from the Atlantic Ocean.

The School of Music is an undergraduate professional school that seeks to prepare its graduates for professional careers and for graduate study. The degree programs stress training in basic musical disciplines and include a liberal arts requirement.

Accreditation. Southern Association of Colleges and Schools; National Association of Schools of Music.

Academic Information

Enrollment, Music Majors. Full-time 54 men, 59 women; part-time 1 man, 3 women.

Music Faculty. Full-time 19, part-time 9.

Term System. Semester (4-1-4 plan). One 8-week summer session.

Entrance Requirements. High school graduation with rank in upper 40% of graduating class; completion of 16 units, including 4 English, 3 mathematics, 2 laboratory science, 2 foreign language, 2 social studies, 3 general academic electives; SAT or ACT. In addition to general University admission requirements and academic regulations, applicants must be auditioned and interviewed by a faculty committee.

Admission Procedure. Application with $20 non-refundable fee due March 1. Write to the Dean of the School of Music for audition and interview appointments.

Music Degrees Offered. Bachelor of Music; Bachelor of Arts; Bachelor of Music Education.

Music Degree Requirements. The Bachelor of Music degree is offered with majors in piano, organ, voice, orchestral instruments, church music (organ, voice, instrumental), musical theatre, theory. The degree requires completion of general education (liberal arts) courses, a core curriculum, and prescribed curriculum in the major area for a total of 128 semester hours. The Bachelor of Music Education degree is offered with emphases in instrumental and vocal (principals in voice and piano). The Bachelor of Arts degree with a major in music is also offered. It is not a professional degree program; it is a cross-disciplinary program, jointly offered between the College of Liberal Arts, which grants the degree, and the School of Music.

General Program Areas. Applied Music, Church Music, Music Education, Music History, Music Theory, Musical Theatre.

Instruments Taught. Brass, Guitar, Harpsichord, Organ, Percussion, Piano, Stringed Instruments, Voice, Woodwinds.

Musical Facilities

Practice Facilities. 43 practice rooms. 5 organs (Beckerath). 2 percussion-equipped practice rooms. 21 pianos (14 uprights, 7 grands); 7 grands reserved for piano majors. Electronic music studio.

Concert Facilities. Elizabeth Hall Auditorium.

Concerts/Musical Activities. Approximately 100 concerts and recitals presented each year.

Music Library. 5,720 books; 8,750 scores; 36 music periodicals; 5,691 recordings. Listening facilities include 4 cassette decks; 10 disc players; 4 reel-to-reel tape players. Special collections include historical organ recordings; Haig Gudenian Collection of violin music. Books other than reference and scores are housed in the duPont-Ball Library.

Special Programs

Featured Programs. Honors courses are available to academically superior music students. These are designed to replace the Freshman and Sophomore comprehensive musicianship and music history courses currently required of all students in the School of Music.

It is intended that these courses will stress the integration of aural training, keyboard skills, theory and philosophy of music, and the history of music.

Performance Groups. Ensemble groups, Stetson Orchestra, Concert Choir, Stetson Opera Workshop, Symphonic Wind Ensemble, Stetson Jazz Ensemble.

Foreign Programs. The University has centers in Germany, France, and Spain.

Affiliated Programs. Reciprocal tuition waiver affiliations with some neighboring colleges.

Financial

Costs. Per academic year: Tuition $6,100. General fee: $250. Room $1,295. Board $1,300.

Financial Aid. 28 music scholarships ranging from $500 to $5,500 (average $2,550). Other forms of financial aid include state/federal loans, grants, student employment, and a College Work-Study program.

GEORGIA

Columbus College
Department of Music
School of Arts and Letters
Algonquin Drive
Columbus
Georgia 31993

Telephone. (404) 568-2049

Chief Administrator. L. Rexford Whiddon, Chairman, Department of Music.

Columbus College was established in 1958 as a junior college, and became a four-year institution in 1966. The 147-acre campus is located in the city of Columbus, 100 miles south of Atlanta on the Georgia-Alabama border.

The Department of Music offers programs designed for the student who plans to teach at the college level or perform professionally.

Accreditation. Southern Association of Colleges and Schools; National Association of Schools of Music; National Council for Accreditation of Teacher Education.

Academic Information

Enrollment, Music Majors. (Total University) 3,872.

Music Faculty. 15.

Term System. Quarter.

Entrance Requirements. High school graduation; SAT; audition required.

Admission Procedure. Application with supporting documents and nonrefundable $10 fee reviewed on a rolling admission basis.

Music Degrees Offered. Bachelor of Music; Bachelor of Arts.

Music Degree Requirements. The Bachelor of Music degree is offered with majors in performance and music education. The major in performance can be pursued with a concentration in piano, piano pedagogy, organ, voice, flute, oboe, clarinet, saxophone, bassoon, trumpet, horn, euphonium, trombone, tuba, violin, viola, violoncello, string bass, guitar, or percussion. The performance degree with a concentration in piano pedagogy offers a comprehensive four-year program which includes su-

pervised teaching experience and the study of teaching theory. The major in music education is offered with a concentration in either choral or instrumental music. The degree leads to teacher certification by the Georgia State Department of Education. The Bachelor of Arts degree with a major in music is a broad, liberal arts degree with a curriculum that includes the standard music theory and music history courses but encourages diversification through many electives outside of music. The degree provides preparation for further study in careers other than performance or public school teaching.

General Program Areas. Music Education, Music History, Music Theory, Performance, Piano Pedagogy.

Instruments Taught. Brass, Percussion, Piano, Stringed Instruments, Voice, Woodwinds.

Musical Facilities

Practice Facilities. Fine Arts Hall contains studios, practice rooms, and rehearsal areas.

Concert Facilities. Fine Arts Auditorium, seating 1,000.

Concerts/Musical Activities. Student and faculty recitals and concerts; visiting artists.

Music Library. The Simon Schwob Memorial Library has a book collection exceeding 195,000 volumes.

Special Programs

Performance Groups. College Choir, College Orchestra, College Band, Chamber Choir, String Ensemble, Wind Ensemble, Brass Choir, Jazz Band, Percussion Ensemble, Flute Ensemble, Opera and Music Theatre Workshop.

Financial

Costs. Per academic year: Tuition in-state resident $960, out-of-state $2,880. Fees $126.

Financial Aid. Music scholarships include the Ruth S. Schwob Scholarship Fund, the Schwob Foundation Scholarship Program, and the Virginia Cook Lee and Kathy Lee Cook Scholarship Fund. Other sources of financial aid include Regents' scholarship, state/federal grants and loans, and part-time employment.

University of Georgia
School of Music
Fine Arts Building
Athens
Georgia 30602

Telephone. (404) 542-3737

Chief Administrator. Dr. Ralph Verrastro, Head.

Established in 1785, The University of Georgia was the first state-supported university in the United States. In 1931, the General Assembly of Georgia placed all state-supported institutions of higher education, including The University of Georgia, under the jurisdiction of a single board. This organization, known as the University System of Georgia, is governed by the Board of Regents. The University of Georgia has developed its curriculum from a program of classical studies to over 170 fields of study in 13 schools and colleges. The Athens campus contains 219 buildings and covers approximately 3,500 acres within Clarke County. The city of Athens is 70 miles northeast of Atlanta.

Since its establishment in 1928, the Department of Music has made a significant contribution to the cultural life of the University community and the State of Georgia. The Department offers programs at the undergraduate and graduate levels designed to prepare students for professional careers in performance, teaching, therapy, composition, research, and related musical fields. Programs of study and participation also are provided for the musical amateur through Department of Music general music courses open to all members of the University community.

In addition to formal programs of instruction, the Department of Music recognizes and welcomes its responsibility as a university-affiliated music unit in the extension and development of knowledge related to the several aspects of the musical art. As such, the Department is committed to the performance and composition of music; to the scholarly and creative exploration and investigation of the origins, development, and potential of music as an aural expression of the life experience; and to the therapeutic, psychological, philosophical, and physiological nature of music learning and perception.

Through the presentation of a wide variety of musical programs, the discovery and publication of knowledge, and the creation and dissemination of new music, the Department of Music contributes to the cultural vitality of the state and region.

Accreditation. Southern Association of Colleges and Schools; National Association of Schools of Music.

Academic Information

Enrollment, Music Majors. (Total university) 25,000. Foreign students 1,200.

Music Faculty. (Total university) 2,200.

Term System. Quarter. One summer session.

Entrance Requirements. High school graduate with units including 4 English, 4 mathematics, 4 laboratory science, 4 foreign language, 4 social studies; 3.0 GPA (B average); 1,000 SAT combined score; musical audition.

Admission Procedure. Application and $15 nonrefundable fee due 20 days prior to quarter of desired enrollment. All applicants are required to give evidence of musical ability through vocal performance or performance on a major instrument before an examining committee.

Music Degrees Offered. Bachelor of Music; Bachelor of Arts; Master of Music; Master of Music Education; Doctor of Musical Arts.

Music Degree Requirements. The Bachelor's degree requires the completion of 190 quarter hours including general education and core music curriculum. Areas of concentration include music history and literature, music education, music therapy, jazz studies, and applied music. Students in applied music should expect to participate in weekly seminars in their major performance media, and to attend recitals and concerts.

The Master of Music degree offers concentrations in performance, choral conducting, woodwinds, composition, and music literature. Each concentration requires an approved program with a minimum of 50 quarter hours of graduate coursework and a five-credit hour final project. The final project is satisfied by a solo recital which indicates graduate quality, a large original composition, or by an approved research project. The degree Master of Music Education offers a concentration in music education or music therapy.

The Doctor of Musical Arts degree provides advanced professional, academic, and research preparation for music careers in teaching, performing, composing, and conducting. Major concentrations are offered in music education, performance, composition, and choral conducting.

General Program Areas. Choral Conducting, Composition, Jazz Studies, Music Education, Music History, Music Literature, Performance.

Instruments Taught. Brass, Guitar, Harp, Organ, Percussion, Piano, Stringed Instruments, Voice, Woodwinds.

Musical Facilities

Practice Facilities. Special practice facilities for organists; 3 organs. 4 percussion practice rooms. 28 practice rooms. 100 pianos (65 Steinways; 30 grand pianos); 10 grand pianos reserved for piano majors. Electronic music laboratory; recording studio.

Concert Facilities. 3 concert halls.

Concerts/Musical Activities. 300 programs are presented each year; all but five are free of charge.

Music Library. 253,265 volumes; 33,616 scores; 215 periodicals; 2,138 microfiche; 13,650 recordings. Listening facilties for cassette, compact disc, and stereo. Special collections include the Guido Adler Collection; Olin Downes Papers; Rudolph Kratina Collection; American Sheet Music Collection; National Trumpet Guild Archive; and Serge Prokofiev Collection.

Special collections include: Olin Downes Papers; Serge Prokofiev Collection.

Special Programs

Performance Groups. Men's Glee Club, Women's Glee Club, Concert Band, Chamber Music Ensemble, Contemporary Chamber Ensemble, Afro-American Choral Ensemble, University Symphony Orchestra, University Chorus, Concert Choir, University Band, Symphonic Wind Ensemble, University Chamber Orchestra, Collegium Musicum.

Affiliated Programs. Certain courses may be completed at other colleges in the University System of Georgia at various locations.

Financial

Costs. Per academic year: Tuition in-state resident $1,554, out-of-state $4,054. Room $975. Board $1,230.

Financial Aid. Financial aid is awarded on the basis of academic merit and financial need. Institutional and state/federal aid available. Scholarships range from $150 to $1,200. Scholarship application due February 22. College-Work Study program available.

Commentary

The University of Georgia is planning to build a new music building and performance complex.

Georgia Southern College
Department of Music
School of Arts and Sciences
Statesboro
Georgia 30460

Telephone. (912) 681-5396

Chief Administrator. Dr. Raymond C. Marchionni, Department Head.

Georgia Southern College was established in 1906. It originated as one of the ten district agricultural and mechanical schools established by an act of the Legislature. The First District Agricultural and Mechanical School opened in 1908 and continued as such until 1924 when it was converted into the Georgia Normal School. In 1929, the name was changed to South Georgia Teachers College. The institution was placed under the control of the University System of Georgia in 1931 and in 1939 became Georgia Southern College. The 300-acre campus has 49 buildings and is located in Statesboro, a town of 17,500, approximately 60 miles northwest of Savannah.

Enrollment in applied music is mandatory for all music majors. Prior to performing a junior or senior recital, the candidate must pass a recital approval examination, and all music majors must pass the piano proficiency and music theory examinations.

Accreditation. Southern Association of Colleges and Schools; National Association of Schools of Music.

Academic Information

Enrollment, Music Majors. Full-time 32 men, 30 women.

Music Faculty. Full-time 11, part-time 5.

Term System. Quarter. Academic year September to June.

Entrance Requirements. High school graduation or equivalent; C average and completion of 16 units including 4 English, 3 mathematics, 2 science, 3 social studies; SAT combined score 800; prior musical experience and training; audition required.

Admission Procedure. Application with supporting documents to Admissions Office; students wishing to pursue a degree in music must complete an application for admission to the Department of Music as well as perform an entrance audition.

Music Degrees Offered. Bachelor of Music; Bachelor of Arts; Bachelor of Science; Master of Education; Master of Science.

Music Degree Requirements. The Bachelor of Music degree requires the fulfillment of the core curriculum, completion of all requirements in music, and two hours of health and five hours of physical education. A minimum of 190 quarter hours is required for graduation. Majors are offered in band/orchestral instruments, church music, keyboard, school music (keyboard and vocal), music theory/composition, voice, jazz performance, and music merchandising. The Bachelor of Science in Education degree is offered through the School of Education. This program prepares the student to teach music as well as other forms of the arts. Studies selected from the musical arts curriculum provide the background and appropriate perspective of the other areas. The Bachelor of Arts degree with a major in music is also offered to students in the liberal arts curriculum.

The Master of Science for Teachers degree program requires a minimum of 60 quarter hours of study. The program includes a prescribed minimum of 20 quarter hours in professional education with the remaining to be selected from courses offered by the Department of Music.

General Program Areas. Applied Music, Church Music, Composition, Music Education, Music History, Music Merchandising, Music Theory, Performance, Piano Pedagogy.

Instruments Taught. Brass, Organ, Percussion, Piano, Stringed Instruments, Voice, Woodwinds.

Musical Facilities

Practice Facilities. 15 practice rooms. 2 organs. Special practice facilities for percussionists. 18 pianos (Steinway studio uprights); 1 grand piano reserved for piano majors. Electronic music studio.

Concert Facilities. Recital hall, seating 400.

Concerts/Musical Activities. Approximately 60 concerts of varied programs presented per year.

Music Library. Music materials are housed in the main library. 3,645 volumes; 2,655 scores; 83 current periodical subscriptions; 3,285 phonograph recordings. 5 listening stations (stereo).

Special Programs

Performance Groups. Vocal Ensemble, Opera Theater, Woodwind Ensemble, Brass Ensemble, Percussion Ensemble, Wind Ensemble, Jazz Ensemble, String Ensemble, Collegium Musicum, Jazz Combo, Chorus, Symphonic Band, Orchestra, Marching Band.

Affiliated Programs. A cooperative program with the University of Georgia for the Doctor of Education degree.

Financial

Costs. Per academic year: Tuition in-state resident $1,242, out-of-state $3,162. Room $840. Board $1,050. Off-campus housing $100 to $300 per month.

Financial Aid. Financial aid is awarded on the basis of academic merit, financial need, and musical ability. Average music scholarship $500. Sources of financial aid include scholarships, grants, loans, part-time employment, and a College Work-Study program.

Georgia State University
School of Music
University Plaza
Atlanta
Georgia 30303

Telephone. (404) 658-3676

Chief Administrator. Dr. Steven Winick, Director.

In 1913, Georgia State University's direct ancestor was founded by Georgia Tech and at first was called the Georgia Tech Evening School of Commerce. The institution became an independent college of the University System of Georgia during the 1930s and in 1947 it was incorporated into the program of the University of Georgia with the title Atlanta Division of the University of Georgia. In 1955, the school once more became independent with its current name. The campus is located in Atlanta, the capital of Georgia and a major commercial, industrial, financial, and cultural center of the southeast.

The School of Music prepares the student for a professional career in music. It provides a comprehensive education for students in music education, performance, theory, or history and literature. The curricula of the School are designed so that all students attain performance skills, acquire tools for analyzing and comprehending music, possess a thorough knowledge of music history and literature, and demonstrate research skills. For those students who wish to teach music in public schools, the School provides special programs in teaching choral music, instrumental music, and general classroom music. These programs require the student to demonstrate teaching competencies through field-based experiences. In addition, the School offers public concerts and lectures to the general student body and the community.

Accreditation. Southern Association of Colleges and Schools; National Association of Schools of Music; National Council for Accreditation of Teacher Education.

Academic Information

Music Faculty. Full-time 23, part-time 34.

Term System. Quarter. 6- and 8-week summer sessions from June 17 to Aug 23.

Entrance Requirements. High school graduation or equivalent; C average and 16 units including 4 English, 2 mathematics, 2 science, 2 social science; SAT required. Applicants to the music program are expected to have had previous musical training; diagnostic tests required; audition.

Admission Procedure. Application and supporting documents to Admissions Office; upon acceptance, arrange with School of Music for audition and theory placement test.

Music Degrees Offered. Bachelor of Music; Master of Music; Specialist in Education.

Music Degree Requirements. The Bachelor of Music degree is offered with a concentration in performance, jazz studies, music theory, music history and literature, or music education. The degree requires the completion of general degree requirements in humanities, natural sciences, and social sciences (60 quarter hours). A total of 205 to 210 quarter hours is required for the degree, depending on area of concentration and program pursued. The concentration in music education prepares students for teaching in elementary and secondary schools in the specialties of choral/general music and instrumental music.

The Master of Music degree is offered with concentrations in music education, performance, music theory, choral conducting, piano pedagogy, and sacred music. The programs require the completion of 50 to 58 quarter hours of study depending on the concentration. The Specialist in Education degree with a major in music education is a 50-hour program and leads to TS-6 Certification. The program is offered by the College of

Education in conjunction with the School of Music.

General Program Areas. Choral Conducting, Jazz Studies, Music Education, Music History, Music Literature, Music Theory, Performance, Piano Pedagogy, Sacred Music.

Instruments Taught. Brass, Organ, Percussion, Piano, Stringed Instruments, Voice, Woodwinds.

Musical Facilities

Practice Facilities. 35 practice rooms. 1 organ (Moeller 36-rank). Special practice facilities for percussionists. 40 pianos (Steinway, Baldwin, Yamaha); 5 pianos reserved for piano majors. Electronic music studio; computer room; music media room.

Concert Facilities. GSU Recital Hall, seating 400.

Community Facilities. Atlanta Civic Center; Woodruff Memorial Arts Center - Symphony Hall.

Concerts/Musical Activities. 40 concerts per quarter including symphonic, opera, wind ensemble, choral, orchestra, jazz, and chamber music.

Music Library. Music materials are housed in Pullen Library. 50,000 volumes; 10,000 scores. 20 listening stations (stereo). Reference music collection housed in School of Music.

Special Programs

Featured Programs. Internship program with Georgia Retardation Center for music therapy courses.

Performance Groups. Jazz Band, Choral Ensemble, Instrumental Ensemble, Marching Band, Orchestra, Chamber Ensemble.

Affiliated Programs. The Department of Commercial Music/Recording offers a Bachelor of Science degree designed with a concentration in the business or recording/production aspects of the music industry. An Associate of Science degree is also offered.

Financial

Costs. Tuition in-state resident $30 per quarter hour, out-of-state $104 per quarter hour. Activity fee $69 per academic year. No on-campus housing.

Financial Aid. Scholarships available for music students include the American Society of Composers, Authors, and Publishers (ASCAP) Music Scholarship; the Atlanta Music Club Performance Scholarship; the Haskell L. Boyter Choral Music Scholarship; the Montgomery Music Scholarship; the Presser Scholarship; the Helen Riley Smith Voice Scholarship; the Harris M. Taft Memorial Music Scholarship; and the Charles Thomas Wurm Music Scholarship. In addition, the School of Music provides scholarships to students who have outstanding musical ability, who have financial need, and whose talents meet the current needs of the School. Other sources of financial aid include state/federal loans, student employment, and a College Work-Study program.

Commentary

Georgia State University produces a Summer Opera Workshop.

Shorter College
Department of Music
Shorter Hill
Rome
Georgia 30161

Telephone. (404) 291-2121

Chief Administrator. Dr. John Ramsaur, Department Head.

Shorter College was founded in 1873 as the Cherokee Baptist Female College. The name was changed to Shorter Female College in 1877 and the present name was adopted in 1923. The private liberal arts college became coeducational in the 1950s and is controlled by the Georgia Baptist Convention. The 150-acre campus has 19 buildings in the city of Rome, 68 miles northwest of Atlanta.

The Department of Music is treated as an organic part of the work of the institution and music in all its branches is regarded as having an academic as well as vocational and cultural value. The aim of the Department includes the following interests: intensive professional training in a performance field; a solid foundation of thorough musicianship; a broad cultural and intellectual background for the music major, and music appreciation for students of other arts and sciences.

Accreditation. Southern Association of Colleges and Schools; National Association of Schools of Music.

Academic Information

Enrollment, Music Majors. (Total College) Full-time 268 men, 368 women; part-time 37 men, 53 women.

Music Faculty. 12.

Term System. Semester. One summer session.

Entrance Requirements. High school graduation with 4 units English, 2 mathematics, 2 history, 1 science, plus foreign language and/or additional acceptable academic subjects; SAT required; recommendation of high school counselor and/or principal; audition and theory placement test.

Admission Procedure. Application with $15 nonrefundable fee due no later than August.

Music Degrees Offered. Bachelor of Music; Bachelor of Music Education; Bachelor of Church Music; Bachelor of Arts.

Music Degree Requirements. The Bachelor of Music degree is a professional program with concentrations in piano, organ, voice, and piano pedagogy. The Bachelor of Music Education and the Bachelor of Church Music are also four-year professional programs with specific curricular requirements. The Bachelor of Arts degree with a major in music requires four years of applied music in one instrument or voice in addition to the general liberal arts requirements. A minimum of 126 semester hours is required for the baccalaureate degree.

General Program Areas. Applied Music, Church Music, Music Education, Piano Pedagogy.

Instruments Taught. Organ, Piano, Voice.

Musical Facilities

Practice Facilities. 26 practice rooms. 2 organs (Holtkamp, Beckerath). 26 pianos (6 Yamaha upright, 20 Kawai grand).

Concert Facilities. Chapel, Recital Hall.

Concerts/Musical Activities. Faculty, alumni, and student recitals; choral and opera programs; visiting artists.

Music Library. The Caroline Gray Memorial Music Library contains an extensive collection of books, records, and scores.

Special Programs

Performance Groups. Madrigal Singers, Vocal Jazz Ensemble, Chorale, Mixed Chorus.

Financial

Costs. Per academic year: Tuition $4,030. Room $816. Board $1,634.

Financial Aid. Academic scholarships are awarded to freshman students who graduated in the top 15% of their high school senior class. Special music scholarships are also available. Scholarship applications due February 1. Other sources of financial aid include state/federal aid and loans.

Valdosta State College
Department of Music
School of the Arts
North Patterson Street
Valdosta
Georgia 31601

Telephone. (912) 333-5804

Chief Administrator. J. David Morris, Head.

Valdosta State College was established in 1913 as the Georgia State Normal College for Young Ladies and a four-year curriculum for the institution was authorized in 1922. The college became coeducational and adopted its present name in 1950. There are two campuses located less than a mile from each other in the city of Valdosta in south-central Georgia.

The Department of Music offers undergraduate and graduate programs.

Accreditation. Southern Association of Colleges and Schools; National Association of Schools of Music; National Council for Accreditation of Teacher Education.

Academic Information

Enrollment, Music Majors. (Total College) 5,592.

Music Faculty. 11.

Term System. Quarter.

Entrance Requirements. High school graduation with completion of 16 units including 3 English, 2 mathematics, 2 science, 2 social science; SAT required; audition required.

Admission Procedure. Application with supporting documents and nonrefundable $10 fee to Office of Admissions.

Music Degrees Offered. Bachelor of Music; Bachelor of Arts; Master of Music Education.

Music Degree Requirements. The Bachelor of Music is a professional music degree and is available with majors either in music education or in the applied music performance areas of organ, piano, voice, or orchestral instruments. The Bachelor of Music degree in music education meets the requirements of the Georgia State Department of Education for T-4 teacher certification in music. The Bachelor of Arts with a major in music is a liberal arts degree.

The program of courses for the Master of Music Education degree is planned in terms of individual needs. Students entering this degree program must take a classification examination which covers the areas of music theory, analysis of music, music history, and performance in the student's major applied area.

General Program Areas. Music Education, Performance.

Instruments Taught. Brass, Organ, Percussion, Piano, Stringed Instruments, Voice, Woodwinds.

Musical Facilities

Practice Facilities. The Fine Arts Building houses the School of the Arts.

Concert Facilities. Whitehead Auditorium; Sawyer Theater.

Concerts/Musical Activities. Student/faculty concerts and recitals; visiting artists.

Music Library. The Library houses over 275,000 volumes and serves the academic programs of the School of Fine Arts.

Special Programs

Performance Groups. Chamber Singers, Concert Choir, The Spotlighters, Opera and Musical Theatre, Concert Band, Jazz Ensemble, Marching Band, Basketball Pep Band, Instrumental Ensembles, Jazz Combo, College Community Band, Vocal Chamber Ensembles

Financial

Costs. Per academic year: Tuition in-state resident $1,200, out-of-state $3,120. Room and board $1,836.

Financial Aid. Financial aid is awarded on the basis of academic merit and financial need. Institutional and state/federal aid available as well as part-time employment and a College Work-Study program. Financial aid/scholarship application due April 15.

West Georgia College
Department of Music
Carrollton
Georgia 30118

Telephone. (404) 836-6516

Chief Administrator. Dr. Robert M. Coe, Chairman.

West Georgia College is a coeducational, residential, liberal arts institution. It originated in 1906 as the Fourth District Agricultural and Mechanical School and in 1933 became West Georgia College, a junior college established by an act of the Board of Regents of the University System of Georgia. The college became a senior college unit in 1957.

The college, with a student body of over 6,000, is situated on the western side of Carrollton, the county seat of Carroll County and one of Georgia's fastest growing industrial areas. The campus includes more than 60 structures on 393 acres of wooded land. Presently under construction is a Performing Arts Center which will house a 500-seat theatre-concert hall and a 250-seat experimental theatre.

The goal of the Department of Music is to prepare students as performers and as teachers of music. The Department seeks to develop in each student an overall comprehension of the meaning of music, and an understanding of the evaluation of the art.

Accreditation. Southern Association of Colleges and Schools; National Association of Schools of Music; National Council for Accreditation of Teacher Education.

Academic Information

Music Faculty. Full-time 10, part-time 5.

Term System. Quarter. Academic year from mid-September to early June. Summer session of 6 weeks from mid-June to early August.

Entrance Requirements. High school graduation with overall 2.8 grade point average; SAT score 680. Applicants for graduate study must hold a baccalaureate degree from an accredited college or university.

Admission Procedure. Submit a formal application with $10 nonrefundable fee. Graduate students must submit application with $10 nonrefundable fee; letters of recommendation; test scores (GRE or Miller Analogy).

Music Degrees Offered. Bachelor of Music with major in performance, music education, or theory-composition; Bachelor of Music with majors in both music education and performance; Master of Music with majors in performance or music education.

Music Degree Requirements. The Baccalaureate degree requires completion of a minimum of 190 quarter hours with 50 of those earned in residence, 70 in upper division courses; student must pass Regents' Examination and constitution and history test; completion of specific music requirements; minimum 2.0 grade point average. All music majors must be in an ensemble each quarter enrolled, for a minimum of eleven quarters.

The Master's degree program requires completion of 60 quarter hours for performance major and 61 quarter hours for music education major; comprehensive examination, oral or written; performance majors must meet recital requirements.

General Program Areas. Music Education, Performance, Theory-Composition.

Instruments Taught. Brass, Organ, Piano, Stringed Instruments, Voice, Woodwinds.

Musical Facilities

Practice Facilities. Special practice facilities for organists; 1 Reuter organ and 1 Allen organ available. 14 practice pianos (1 Mason & Hamlin grand; 1 Steinway grand). 2 pianos reserved for piano majors; 12 practice rooms. Special studios: 1 computer lab, 1 electronic piano lab.

Concert Facilities. 235-seat recital hall; 225-seat auditorium.

Community Facilities. 650-seat High School Auditorium; local church for choral/orchestral concerts.

Concerts/Musical Activities. Events featuring students, faculty, and professional artists and musicians fill the calendar with recitals, concerts, art exhibits, musical theatre productions, lectures, book reviews, and films.

Music Library. The Irvine Sullivan Ingram Library houses over 260,000 volumes; 3,000 musical scores; 17,000 films; 726,000 microforms.

Special Programs

Featured Programs. Annual Fine Arts Festival has been held since 1964.

Performance Groups. Various ensembles, Concert Choir, Concert Band, Marching Band.

Financial

Costs. Per academic year: Tuition state resident $1,131, nonresident $3,213. Activity fee $186, applied music fee $50 per hour. Room $840 to $960. Board $960. Off-campus housing approximately $300 monthly.

Financial Aid. Financial aid is awarded on the basis of academic merit, financial need, musical ability. Institutional and state/federal aid available. 50% of students receive financial aid; average award per student $1,857. Financial aid/scholarship application due date March 1. Part-time employment and College Work-Study program; average earnings $1,000 per academic year.

HAWAII

University of Hawaii at Manoa
Music Department

2411 Dole Street
Honolulu
Hawaii 96822

Telephone. (808) 948-7756

Chief Administrator. Dr. John Mount, Chairman.

The University of Hawaii at Manoa is the founding campus of a multicampus system. It was established in 1907 as the College of Hawaii, a land-grant college of agriculture and mechanic arts. The first classes were held at a temporary site in downtown Honolulu and in 1912 the school moved to its permanent location in the Manoa Valley. The campus took its present name in 1972 to distinguish it from the other units of the university system. The campus is located on 300 acres in a residential section close to the heart of metropolitan Honolulu, the state capital situated on the island of Oahu.

The Music Department of the College of Arts and Humanities is located at the western end of the campus in a complex of buildings which includes rehearsal halls, classrooms, studios, practice rooms, a listening facility, archives, and the Mae Zenke Orvis Auditorium. The Department offers the Bachelor of Music and the Bachelor of Arts degrees. A coordinated program has been established with the College of Education to prepare music teachers for the intermediate and high schools.

Accreditation. Western Association of Colleges and Schools; National Association of Schools of Music.

Academic Information

Music Faculty. Full-time 23, part-time 34.

Term System. Semesters. Summer session. Academic year from August to May.

Entrance Requirements. High school graduation with rank in upper 40%; 15 units including 3 English, 1 algebra, 6 science; SAT; audition required.

Admission Procedure. Application with supporting documents to Admissions Office.

Music Degrees Offered. Bachelor of Music; Bachelor of Arts; Master of Music; Master of Arts.

Music Degree Requirements. The Bachelor of Music degree is offered with concentrations in composition, guitar, instrumental, piano, voice. The degree requires the completion of 124 semester hours of general education courses, core curriculum, and the major area of concentration. The Bachelor of Arts degree with a major in music is offered with concentrations in dance ethnology, ethnomusicology, music literature, theory, or a general program.

The Master of Music degree is offered with concentrations in composition and performance (voice, piano, and certain orchestral instruments). The degree Master of Arts in music is available with concentrations in dance ethnology, ethnomusicology, music education, musicology, and theory. A minimum of 30 credits is required.

General Program Areas. Composition, Ethnomusicology, Music History, Music Literature, Music Theory, Musicology, Performance.

Instruments Taught. Bass, Bassoon, Clarinet, Euphonium, Flute, French Horn, Guitar, Harp, Javanese Gamelan, Oboe, Organ, Percussion, Piano, Recorder, Trombone, Trumpet, Tuba, Viola da Gamba, Violin, Violoncello.

Musical Facilities

Practice Facilities. 30 practice rooms. 2 organs (Schlicker). Special practice facilities for percussionists. 73 pianos (3 Baldwin, 16 electric Baldwin, 14 Steinway grand, 20 Steinway upright, 7 Yamaha, 1 Hamilton, 5 Story and Clark, 6 Everett, 1 Chickering); 4 grand pianos reserved for piano majors. Electronic music lab.

Concert Facilities. Orvis Auditorium, seating 409.

Community Facilities. Neal Blaisdell Concert Hall; Lutheran Church of Honolulu; Kennedy Theatre on campus.

Concerts/Musical Activities. 12 faculty concerts per year; 24 student recitals annually; 40 non-departmental recitals; Honolulu Chamber Music Series, 8 concerts per year.

Music Library. All music library and listening materials are housed in the main Sinclair Library where there is an Audio Center. Special collections include: Asian, Hawaiian, and Pacific Collection.

Special Programs

Performance Groups. Hawaiian Chorus, University Chamber Singers, Jazz Ensemble, Ethnic Music Ensembles, University Concert Choir, University Symphony Orchestra, Opera Workshop, Hula/Chant Ensemble, Collegium Musicum, University Band, University Chorus.

Financial

Costs. Per academic year: Tuition undergraduate in-state $1,880, out-of-state $3,370; graduate in-state $1,-110, out-of-state $4,020. Room and board $2,445.

Financial Aid. Financial aid is awarded on the basis of academic merit. Both institutional and state/federal aid available. College Work-Study program.

Commentary

The University of Hawaii Music Department features the study in music of Pacific cultures in the ethnomusicology program.

IDAHO

Boise State University
Music Department
College of Arts and Sciences
1910 University Drive
Boise
Idaho 83725

Telephone. (208) 385-1771

Chief Administrator. Dr. Wilber D. Elliott, Chairman.

Boise State University, founded in 1932 by the Episcopal Church as a junior college, was the first institution of higher education located in the state's capital. The Episcopal Church discontinued its sponsorship of the school in 1934 when the Boise Junior College became a nonprofit private corporation sponsored by the Boise Chamber of Commerce and the community. The junior college was granted four-year status and named Boise College in 1964, brought into the state system of higher education in 1969, and renamed Boise State University in 1974. The 110-acre campus consists of 49 buildings.

The Music Department was first instituted as a department in the late 1930s. Its goal is to train and educate professional musicians as public school teachers, as teachers/performers, and as composers at the baccalaureate level. The Department offers two bachelor's degree programs and one graduate degree program.

Accreditation. Northwest Association of Schools and Colleges; National Association of Schools of Music; National Council for Accreditation of Teacher Education.

Academic Information

Enrollment, Music Majors. Undergraduate 120, graduate 10.

Music Faculty. Full-time 16, part-time 10.

Term System. Semester. 5-week summer session (general music and limited private lessons).

Entrance Requirements. High school graduation or GED; SAT, ACT, or WPL is required. Audition not required. Foreign students must have a minimum score of 500 on TOEFL or similar test of English competence; financial proof of responsibility; valid visa.

Admission Procedure. Application with nonrefundable $10 fee accepted on a rolling basis.

Music Degrees Offered. Bachelor of Music; Bachelor of Arts; Master of Arts.

Music Degree Requirements. The Bachelor of Music degree is a professional music degree with emphasis in performance, theory-composition, or music education. The emphasis in performance or theory-composition is designed to train performers, performing artist teachers, and composers. The emphasis in music education is designed to prepare students for music teaching careers in the secondary and elementary educational systems and also to prepare students for graduate work in music. The degree requires the completion of 128 semester hours of general education and specific departmental requirements. The Bachelor of Arts degree with music as a major is a general liberal arts degree designed for the student who wants a general music major within a broader-based program.

The Master of Arts in Education with music education emphasis is designed to meet the needs of practicing junior or senior high school music specialists. The degree requires the completion of 30 to 33 semester hours.

General Program Areas. Composition, Music Education, Music History, Music Theory, Performance.

Instruments Taught. Bass, French Horn, Guitar, Organ, Percussion, Piano, Trombone, Trumpet, Tuba, Viola, Violin, Violoncello, Voice, Woodwinds.

Musical Facilities

Practice Facilities. 14 practice rooms. 2 organs (pipe organ, 3-manual Austin). 3 percussion-equipped practice rooms. 14 pianos (uprights). Electronic music laboratory.

Concert Facilities. Morrison Center Main Hall, seating 2,000; Recital Hall, 180; Special Events Center, 400.

Concerts/Musical Activities. Concerts, student recitals; faculty members perform in the Faculty Artist Series each month; visiting artists.

Music Library. Music materials are housed in the main library. 8,649 monographs and scores; 63 music periodicals; 6,080 recordings; Listening facilities include 10 cassette decks, 8 stereo turntables, and 1 compact disc player. The Music Department has a small library of recordings and scores and some listening facilities for records and tapes.

Special Programs

Performance Groups. Symphonic Band, University Singers, Meistersingers, Orchestra Music Theatre, Jazz Band, Vocal Ensemble, Opera Theatre, Brass Ensemble, Symphony Orchestra, Woodwind Ensemble, Percussion Ensemble, String Ensemble, Guitar Ensemble, Duo-Piano Ensemble.

Financial

Costs. Per academic year: Tuition in-state resident $1,658, out-of-state $2,960. Room and board $2,400.

Financial Aid. Financial aid in the form of scholarships, state/federal loans, student employment, and a College Work-Study program is available.

University of Idaho
School of Music
Moscow
Idaho 83843

Telephone. (208) 885-6231

Chief Administrator. Dr. Greg Steinke, Director.

The University of Idaho was created in 1889 by a statute of the 15th territorial legislature, commonly known as the university charter. Each year approximately 9,000 students from all the states and 55 foreign countries enroll at the University to choose programs from 130 fields of study. The main campus includes approximately 50 educational and residential buildings on 320 acres of land. Other university land includes the nearby farms and experimental forests exceeding 8,000 acres.

Music has been part of the University of Idaho curriculum from its early years. A department of music was created in 1893. The present School of Music was so designated in 1969 as a unit of the College of Letters and Science. The courses and curricula in music seek to prepare elementary, secondary, and college teachers of music; to train professional musicians; to enrich the cultural environment of the university community. Students in the School of Music learn by performing, listening, analyzing, and creating music. Emphasis is on the understanding of musical style and techniques of all eras.

Accreditation. Northwest Association of Schools and Colleges; National Association of Schools of Music; National Council for Accreditation of Teacher Education.

Academic Information

Music Faculty. 20.

Term System. Semester. 8-week summer sessions with terms of varying lengths.

Entrance Requirements. Open enrollment policy for state residents; completion of 15 units including 3 English, 2 mathematics, 2 social science, 2 laboratory science; SAT or ACT; audition may be required.

Admission Procedure. Application with supporting documents and $15 nonrefundable fee to Admissions Office.

Music Degrees Offered. Bachelor of Music; Bachelor of Arts; Master of Music; Master of Arts; Master of Arts in Teaching.

Music Degree Requirements. The baccalaureate degree programs are offered in vocal or instrumental performance, vocal or instrumental music education (including a combined degree in both), composition, and elementary music. The Bachelor of Music degree is professionally oriented and is the normal preparation for graduate study in music or for teacher certification. The Bachelor of Arts degree emphasizes a broad liberal education and is offered with majors in applied music (performance), music history and literature, and music theory. The baccalaureate degrees require a minimum of 128 semester hours.

The Master of Music, Master of Arts, and Master of Arts in Teaching degrees are available in performance (vocal and instrumental), composition, theory-composition, music literature, music education, and piano pedagogy and performance studies. The Master of Arts option is in music history. The Master of Arts in Teaching is a final degree for students whose preparation is the equivalent of an undergraduate teaching minor. The master's degree requires the completion of 32 semester hours of prescribed courses, depending on the option pursued.

General Program Areas. Choral Music, Composition, Conducting, Music Education, Music History, Music Literature, Music Theory, Performance, Piano Pedagogy.

Instruments Taught. Bass, Bassoon, Clarinet, Flute, French Horn, Oboe, Organ, Percussion, Piano, Saxophone, Trombone, Trumpet, Viola, Violin, Violoncello, Voice.

Musical Facilities

Practice Facilities. 32 practice rooms. 2 organs (Cassavant, Schoenstein). 1 percussion-equipped practice room. 30 pianos; 4 grand pianos reserved for piano majors. Electronic music studio.

Concert Facilities. 1 concert hall.

Concerts/Musical Activities. Recitals, concerts; visiting artists.

Music Library. The Music Building houses a record and score library, a music education materials center, and a record and tape listening center.

Special Programs

Performance Groups. Concert Choir, Chorus, Orchestra, Band, Chamber Orchestra, Festival Choir, Jazz Ensemble, Chamber Ensemble, Collegium Musicum, Percussion Ensemble, Opera Workshop.

Affiliated Programs. Some affiliated programs with Washington State University.

Financial

Costs. Per academic year: Fee in-state resident $485, out-of-state tuition and fee $2,970. Room and board $2,-225.

Financial Aid. Financial aid in the form of scholarships, state/federal loans, student employment, and a College Work-Study program is available.

ILLINOIS

American Conservatory of Music
116 South Michigan Avenue
Chicago
Illinois 60603

Telephone. (312) 263-4161
Chief Administrator. Charles Moore, President.

Founded in 1886, the American Conservatory of Music is an independent institution situated in the center of Chicago. The Conservatory is able to use this major cultural center as an integral part of its educational process, with such internationally renowned organizations as the Chicago Symphony Orchestra, the Chicago Lyric Opera, and the Art Institute of Chicago in close proximity.

The philosophy of the Conservatory is to develop the musician as composer/performer/listener. The emphasis lies always in performance. The studies of the major performance areas as well as involvement in ensembles, repertoire classes, and recitals continue throughout the degree programs.

Accreditation. National Association of Schools of Music.

Academic Information

Enrollment, Music Majors. Full-time 65 men, 37 women; part-time 61 men, 25 women. 15 foreign students.

Music Faculty. 14 department chairpersons with supporting faculty.

Term System. Semester. One summer session.

Entrance Requirements. High school graduation or GED; 15 units including 3 English, 3 mathematics, 3 social studies, 6 music/art/foreign language; audition required (material as designated by Audition Requirement Sheet); theory diagnostic test. Foreign students required to submit affidavit of financial support.

Admission Procedure. Applications with nonrefundable $15 fee accepted on a rolling basis.

Music Degrees Offered. Bachelor of Music; Bachelor of Music Education; Master of Music; Master of Music Education; Doctor of Musical Arts. Certificate, Associate degree, and Basic Musicianship Diploma also awarded.

Music Degree Requirements. The Bachelor of Music degree is offered with majors in composition, classical guitar, jazz and commercial music, orchestral instruments, organ, percussion, piano, voice, theory. A total of 133 to 135 semester hours is required for the degree including specified ensemble and adjunct requirements. The Bachelor of Music Education degree is offered with a performance major.

The degree Master of Music offers majors in performance (instrument or voice), composition, and theory. Students in the program for the Master of Music Education degree are required to do intensive research work. The master's programs require the completion of 34 semester hours.

The Doctor of Musical Arts degree is offered with major fields of study in composition, performance and literature in piano, organ, voice, violin, and other orchestral instruments. The degree requires the completion of 64 semester hours plus a comprehensive examination and thesis.

General Program Areas. Commercial Music, Composition, Jazz Studies, Music Education, Music History, Music Literature, Music Theory, Musicology, Performance, Piano Pedagogy, Piano Technician.

Instruments Taught. Bass, Bassoon, Clarinet, Flute, Guitar, Harp, Oboe, Orchestral Instruments, Organ, Percussion, Piano, Saxophone, Trombone, Trumpet, Viola, Violin, Voice.

Musical Facilities

Practice Facilities. 10 practice rooms. 4 organs. 4 percussion-equipped practice rooms. 5 practice pianos (uprights). Recording studio.

Concert Facilities. Edward J. Collins Hall.

Concerts/Musical Activities. Concerts; student/faculty recitals.

Music Library. 9,392 volumes; 5,895 scores; 2,006 recordings. Listening facilities (cassette, stereo). Special collections include Bach Gesellschaft Ausgabe; Nene Bach Ausgabe; Nene Mozart Ausgabe; Haydn Werke.

Nearby libraries include the Newberry Library, University of Chicago, and Northwestern University.

Special Programs

Performance Groups. Chamber Ensemble, Chamber Singers, Chorus, Concert Band, Guitar Ensemble, Vocal Jazz Ensemble, Instrumental Jazz Ensemble, New Music Ensemble, Opera Workshop, Orchestra, Organ Ensemble, Percussion Ensemble, Steel Band Ensemble.

Affiliated Programs. Consortium agreements with Roosevelt University and Art Institute of Chicago.

Financial

Costs. Per academic year: Tuition $5,500. No on-campus housing; students may make arrangements at nearby dormitories and residence houses, average cost $3,500 to $5,000 per school year.

Financial Aid. Applicants for scholarship must show a high degree of talent and give evidence of need and integrity of purpose. To be eligible to receive a scholarship award, undergraduate students must enroll for a minimum work load of 8 semester hours, graduate student for a minimum of 6 semester hours, and must maintain a B average. Other sources of financial aid include state/federal grants and loans, part-time student employment, and a College Work-Study program.

Commentary

The American Conservatory of Music has special five- and eight-week seminars on the music business, with such titles as "Inside the Music Business," "Music Publishing," and "Public Relations."

Bradley University
Division of Music and Theatre Arts
Constance Hall
Peoria
Illinois 61625

Telephone. (309) 677-2660

Chief Administrator. Dr. Alex Sidorowicz, Director.

Bradley University was founded in 1897 by Mrs. Lydia Moss Bradley in memory of her husband and children. It is a nonsectarian, privately endowed institution. The campus of the University contains 33 buildings on 35 acres in Peoria, central Illinois' largest metropolitan area. The University community consists of some 5,500 undergraduate and graduate students.

The Division of Music and Theatre Arts (formerly separate divisions but merged in 1985) offers programs in music designed to prepare music students for successful careers as teachers or administrators in music; as professional performers; as composers; or as executives in the music industry. It also prepares students who are not music majors for lifelong pleasure in music.

Accreditation. North Central Association of Colleges and Schools; National Association of Schools of Music; National Council for Accreditation of Teacher Education.

Academic Information

Enrollment, Music Majors. Total university: 4,246.

Music Faculty. Total university: 110.

Term System. Semester. Two summer sessions.

Entrance Requirements. Accredited high school graduation or equivalent with completion of 4 units in English, 2 mathematics, 1 laboratory science, 2 foreign language, 2 social science; SAT or ACT required. Foreign students must submit certified financial statement and TOEFL score. Advanced placement through CLEP general and subject examinations. Students must have a minimum of 2 years' experience in orchestra, band, chorus, or private lessons in piano, voice, or instrument; audition required (performance of 3 classical pieces); applicants chosen on basis of musicianship.

Admission Procedure. Applications accepted on a rolling basis; submit application with supporting documents and $20 nonrefundable fee.

Music Degrees Offered. Bachelor of Music; Bachelor of Music Education; Bachelor of Arts; Bachelor of Science; Master of Music; Master of Music Education.

Music Degree Requirements. The Bachelor of Music degree is designed for students whose vocational objective is in the field of professional performance or studio teaching. Candidates for the degree will be required to play on recital laboratory at least once each semester during the freshman and sophomore years at the discretion of the major teacher. They are also required to present a half-recital during the junior year and a formal, full recital during the senior year. Concentrations are offered in piano, piano-accompanying, violin, voice, orchestral and band instruments, and composition or theory. The Bachelor of Music Education degree requires the completion of a minimum of 66 to 80 hours in music, 28 hours in professional education, and 37 hours in general education. The Bachelor of Arts and Bachelor of Science degrees are offered in interdisciplinary programs that combine music with a business option or a speech/theatre option.

The Master of Music and the Master of Music Education degrees require a minimum of 30 hours beyond the bachelor's degree.

General Program Areas. Accompanying, Applied Music, Composition, Conducting, Music Business, Music Theory, Pedagogy, Performance.

Instruments Taught. Bass, Bassoon, Clarinet, Flute, French Horn, Harpsichord, Oboe, Organ, Piano, Recorder, Saxophone, Traverso, Trombone, Trumpet, Tuba, Viola, Viola da Gamba, Violin, Violoncello, Voice.

Musical Facilities

Practice Facilities. Special practice facilities for organists; 1 organ. 2 practice rooms for percussionists. 16 practice rooms. 13 pianos; 6 grand pianos reserved for piano majors. Electronic music studio.

Concert Facilities. Concert Hall.

Community Facilities. Peoria Civic Center and local churches are available to the University.

Concerts/Musical Activities. Concerts, recitals.

Music Library. 11,000 scores; 8,000 recordings; music books are primarily housed in the main Bradley University Library. Listening facilities available. The Peoria Public Library is also available to students.

Special Programs

Performance Groups. Concert Band, Chorus, Chorale, Chamber Orchestra, Peoria Symphony.

Financial

Costs. Per academic year: Tuition $6,300. Room and board $1,430 to $1,480.

Financial Aid. Financial aid/scholarship applications due March 1. Scholarships range from $200 to $8,560. State/federal loans and College Work-Study program are available.

University of Chicago
Department of Music
5845 South Ellis Avenue
Chicago
Illinois 60637

Telephone. (312) 702-8484

Chief Administrator. Dr. Robert P. Morgan, Chairman.

The University of Chicago was founded in 1891 through the generosity of a diverse number of donors, including the American Baptist Education Society, Marshall Field, and John D. Rockefeller. The University is composed of the College, four graduate Divisions, and six professional schools. The campus is comprised of over 130 buildings on 170 acres in a residential neighborhood along the shore of Lake Michigan, fifteen minutes from the downtown area of Chicago, the third largest city in the United States.

The Department of Music was founded within the Division of the Humanities in 1930. The Graduate School offers four programs of advanced study in music. Students may also pursue a liberal arts undergraduate degree with a major in music through the College of the University. The Department is administered by a Chairman who yearly appoints a number of advisors and committees responsible for academic policies and matters relating to graduate study. The Department does not offer study in applied music, music education, or conducting. Students are expected to be able to perform creditably on some instrument or to sing, and candidates are encourage to participate in one or more of the performance organizations supported by the Department.

Accreditation. North Central Association of Colleges and Schools.

Academic Information

Enrollment, Music Majors. Full-time 31 men, 19 women; part-time 19 men, 21 women.

Music Faculty. Full-time 13, part-time 4.

Term System. Quarter. Academic year from late September to mid-June.

Entrance Requirements. Undergraduate students applying for the College must meet university-wide requirements which include high school graduation; SAT or ACT. GRE scores (verbal and quantitative) required for graduate students plus sample of writing skills or compositions. TOEFL required for foreign students.

Admission Procedure. Graduate students should apply to the Department at least one month before the beginning of the quarter in which they wish to enroll.

Music Degrees Offered. Bachelor of Arts; Master of Arts; Doctor of Philosophy.

Music Degree Requirements. The Department of Music offers courses intended for students in the College who wish to enhance their understanding and enjoyment of music. A more specialized program leads to the Bachelor of Arts degree with a major in music. Two tracks are offered: (1) preparation for graduate work in music history, theory, or composition; (2) a liberal arts program with a concentration in music.

The Master of Arts degree is offered with emphasis in the history and theory of music and in composition. The degree requires the completion of 18 courses, knowledge of 2 foreign languages, 6 practicum skills, and a comprehensive examination.

The Doctor of Philosophy degree requires the completion of 27 courses, knowledge of 3 foreign languages, 6 practicum skills, comprehensive examination, special field/qualifying examination, and a doctoral dissertation.

General Program Areas. Composition, Music History, Music Theory.

Musical Facilities

Practice Facilities. 9 practice pianos (1 Kawai upright; 8 grands, Steinway and Yamaha). Electronic music studio available for students who take the introductory class.

Concert Facilities. Goodspeed Recital Hall, seating 150; Leon Mandel Hall, 900.

Community Facilities. Various area churches are used for choir concerts.

Concerts/Musical Activities. All performance activities are extracurricular. Eight performance organizations perform 3 to 5 times per year; noontime recital and extra concerts are offered about 40 times per year.

Music Library. Music materials are housed on one floor of the main library. 95,000 volumes; 10,000 phonograph recordings. 10 listening stations. Rare music books are housed in Special Collections department of main library. Department has a large, as yet uncatalogued, Jazz Archive.

Special collections include: emphasis on the history of Western music, Renaissance music (with large microform holdings), and contemporary music; large collection of Chopaniana; in the John U. Nef and Elinor Castle Nef Collection are letters to Schoenberg and more than 100 of Arthur Schnabel; Chicago Jazz Archives; musical instrument collection; manuscripts of Ralph Shapey, Donald Martino, Jean Martinon, and Easley Blackwood; Fromm Collection of American compositions on microfilm.

Special Programs

Performance Groups. University Symphony Orchestra, University Chamber Orchestra, New Music Ensemble, University Chorus, Chamber Choir, Collegium Musicum.

Affiliated Programs. Member university of the Newberry Library Consortium of Chicago.

Financial

Costs. Tuition undergraduate $3,784 per quarter; graduate $3,800 per quarter. Activity fee $30.

Financial Aid. Financial aid is awarded on the basis of academic merit and financial need. Scholarship/financial aid applications due January 5. Institutional and state/federal aid, student employment, and a College Work-Study program are available.

Commentary

University of Chicago collections include manuscripts of composers who have taught at the University, i.e., Easley Blackwood, Ralph Shapey, and an ethnic instrument collection at the Oriental Institute.

DePaul University
School of Music
804 West Belden Avenue
Chicago
Illinois 60614

Telephone. (312) 341-8373
Chief Administrator. Dr. Frederick Miller, Dean.

DePaul University, founded in 1898 by the Vincentian Fathers, is one of the ten largest Catholic universities in the world. The main campus is located near the Loop area of Chicago; the Lincoln Park campus is 15 minutes away by rapid transit.

The purpose of the School of Music is to develop each student's potential to its highest level. As a division of a university concerned with professional preparation, emphasis is placed on specific career requirements in music.

Accreditation. North Central Association of Colleges and Schools; National Association of Schools of Music; National Council for Accreditation of Teacher Education.

Academic Information

Enrollment, Music Majors. (Total University) 8,948.
Music Faculty. 93.
Term System. Quarter.
Entrance Requirements. High school graduation or equivalent; recommend completion of 4 units English, 2 mathematics, 1 science, 2 social science; SAT or ACT required; audition required.
Admission Procedure. Application with supporting documents and nonrefundable $20 fee to Admissions Office.
Music Degrees Offered. Bachelor of Music; Bachelor of Arts; Master of Music.
Music Degree Requirements. The Bachelor of Music degree requires the completion of specified core requirements and a major from the areas of performance, composition, music therapy, music education, and jazz studies. The Bachelor of Arts is a non-professional degree intended for students interested in incorporating the study of music into a broad course of humanistic study. The program contains emphasis on liberal studies, and is not directed at preparing students for careers in music as performers or teachers.

The Master of Music degree is offered with emphasis in performance, church music, music education, music theory, and music composition.

General Program Areas. Church Music, Composition, Jazz Studies, Music Education, Music Theory, Music Therapy, Performance.

Instruments Taught. Baritone, Bass, Bassoon, Clarinet, Flute, French Horn, Guitar, Harp, Oboe, Organ, Percussion, Piano, Saxophone, Trombone, Trumpet, Tuba, Viola, Violin, Violoncello, Voice.

Musical Facilities

Practice Facilities. The Fine Arts Building contains teaching studios, ensemble rehearsal rooms, classrooms, and faculty offices.

Concert Facilities. Lecture-Recital Hall, seating 140; Concert Hall, seating 500.

Concerts/Musical Activities. Student/faculty concerts and recitals; visiting artists.

Music Library. The Lincoln Park Campus Library supports the programs of the School of Music. Listening facilities available; extensive collection of music recordings and scores.

Special Programs

Performance Groups. Concert Band, University Chorus, Orchestra, Guitar Ensemble, Trombone Choir, Wind Ensemble, Chamber Choir, Brass Quintet, Chamber Music, Saxophone Quartet, Percussion Ensemble, Woodwind Ensemble, Jazz Ensemble, Jazz Chamber Ensemble.

Financial

Costs. Per academic year: Tuition $5,352. Fees $50. Room $1,800. Board $1,260.

Financial Aid. Students may apply for financial assistance based on family need through the Office of Financial Aid. Incoming freshmen may also compete for several privately funded music scholarships in the annual Music Scholarship Contest. The number and amount of these music awards vary each year. Financial aid/scholarship application due April 22.

Eastern Illinois University
Department of Music
College of Fine Arts
Charleston
Illinois 61920

Telephone. (217) 581-3010

Chief Administrator. Professor Duwayne Hansen, Chairperson.

Eastern Illinois University is a state institution founded in 1895. It now has 35 departments and enrolls over 9,500 students annually. The 317-acre campus is located in Charleston, 50 miles west of the Indiana border.

The Department of Music of the College of Fine Arts offers baccalaureate programs in music and music education.

Accreditation. North Central Association of Colleges and Schools; National Association of Schools of Music; National Council for Accreditation of Teacher Education.

Academic Information

Enrollment, Music Majors. (Total University) 9,748.

Music Faculty. 28.

Term System. Semester.

Entrance Requirements. High school graduation or GED; open enrollment for summer session; SAT or ACT required; audition required for entering freshmen and transfer students in performance area.

Admission Procedure. Application with supporting documents to Office of Admissions at least 10 days prior to registration.

Music Degrees Offered. Bachelor of Music; Bachelor of Music Education.

Music Degree Requirements. The Bachelor of Music degree is offered with options in performance or theory-

composition. Students in the performance option may choose emphasis in string, wind, or percussion instruments; keyboard (piano primary, organ or harpsichord primary, accompanying primary); or vocal. The Bachelor of Music Education degree is offered with emphasis in instrumental, vocal, and general music.

General Program Areas. Composition, Music Education, Music Theory, Performance.

Instruments Taught. Baritone, Bass, Bassoon, Clarinet, Flute, Harpsichord, Horn, Oboe, Organ, Percussion, Piano, Recorder, Saxophone, Trombone, Trumpet, Tuba, Viola, Violin, Violoncello, Voice.

Musical Facilities

Practice Facilities. The Department of Music is housed in the Quincy V. Doudna Fine Arts Center.

Concerts/Musical Activities. Student/faculty concerts and recitals; visiting artists.

Music Library. The Mary J. Booth Library houses the main library collection. There is a Music Room, a self-study materials center, and an audiovisual center.

Special Programs

Performance Groups. Cecillian Singers, Chamber Singers, Collegium Musicum, Concert Band, Concert Choir, Jazz Band, Lab Band, Jazz Combo, Marching Band, Marimba Orchestra, Mixed Chorus, Music Theater/Opera, Oratorio Chorus, Pep Band, Percussion Ensemble, Steel Band, String Orchestra, Studio Clarinet Choir, Wind Ensemble.

Financial

Costs. Per academic year: Tuition in-state resident $1,020, out-of-state $3,060. Fees $394. Room and Board $2,148.

Financial Aid. Financial aid is available in the form of scholarships, grants, loans, and part-time employment. Financial aid/scholarship application due April 15.

University of Illinois
School of Music
1114 West Nevada
Urbana
Illinois 61801

Telephone. (217) 333-2620

Chief Administrator. Dr. Robert Bays, Director.

The University of Illinois at Urbana-Champaign was founded in 1867 as a state-supported land grant institution with a three-fold mission of teaching, research, and public service. There are approximately 35,000 students and 11,000 faculty and staff members in the University community. Located in the adjoining cities of Urbana-Champaign, approximately 130 miles south of Chicago, the University has a central campus of 705 acres with

180 major buildings.

The School of Music was founded in 1895 and became a School within the College of Fine and Applied Arts in 1931. The School of Music prepares students primarily for careers as performers, composers, scholars, and teachers. The curriculum in music offers music history, ethnomusicology, and music theory/composition options leading to the Bachelor of Music degree and six areas of specialization leading to the degree of Bachelor of Science in Music Education. A program in the College of Liberal Arts and Sciences leading to the Bachelor of Arts degree with a field of concentration in music is offered to qualified students. Although students in the program are encouraged to pursue all phases of the study of music, including applied music, the emphasis is on historical, cultural, and theoretical aspects of music rather than on professional training. Graduate courses are offered under the regulations of the Graduate College.

Accreditation. North Central Association of Colleges and Schools; National Association of Schools of Music; National Council for Accreditation of Teacher Education.

Academic Information

Enrollment, Music Majors. Full-time 275 men, 335 women. 33 foreign students.

Music Faculty. Full-time 82, part-time 9.

Term System. Semester. One 8-week summer session of two 4-week terms.

Entrance Requirements. High school graduation or equivalent; completion of 15 units including minimum 3 English, 2 mathematics; SAT or ACT required; beginning freshmen are selected on a best-qualified basis using a combination of class rank plus score on SAT or ACT. GRE required for graduate school. TOEFL required for foreign students. Audition required; theory placement examination for transfer students.

Admission Procedure. Application with $20 non-refundable fee accepted by Admissions Office on a rolling basis. All applicants for music curricula are also required to satisfy a qualifying audition in the major performance area prior to approval for admission to the School. Applicants for music composition or history of music programs are required to submit original scores or other pertinent writings to substantiate their ability to pursue work in their chosen program of studies. Auditions are held on designated dates during the academic year; tape recordings may be permitted.

Music Degrees Offered. Bachelor of Music; Bachelor Arts; Bachelor of Science; Master of Music; Master of Science; Advanced Certificate; Doctor of Education; Doctor of Philosophy.

Music Degree Requirements. The Bachelor of Music degree is offered with major options in instrumental, composition, history of music, and voice. The Bachelor of Science degree in music education prepares graduates for teaching music in grades K through 12. The Bachelor

of Arts degree with a major in music is offered through the College of Liberal Arts and Sciences. All baccalaureate degrees require the completion of a minimum of 130 semester hours.

Graduate courses leading to the degrees Master of Music, Master of Science in music education, Advanced Certificate in music education, Doctor of Education in music education, Doctor of Philosophy in musicology, and Doctor of Musical Arts in composition, choral music, and performance are offered through the Graduate College. The master's degree programs require the completion of a minimum of 32 semester credits and the doctoral programs have specific requirements including comprehensive examinations and a dissertation.

General Program Areas. Applied Music, Choral Music, Composition, Ethnomusicology, Music Education, Music History, Music Literature, Musicology, Performance.

Instruments Taught. Bass, Bassoon, Clarinet, Cornet, Euphonium, Flute, French Horn, Harp, Harpsichord, Oboe, Organ, Percussion, Piano, Saxophone, Trombone, Trumpet, Tuba, Viola, Violin, Violoncello, Voice.

Musical Facilities

Practice Facilities. 110 practice rooms. 7 organs (2 concert, Casavant and Buzard tracker; 5 practice). 5 percussion-equipped practice rooms. 120 practice pianos; 40 grand pianos reserved for piano majors. 5 experimental music studios; computer music studio.

Concert Facilities. 6 concert halls.

Concerts/Musical Activities. Approximately 360 concerts, recitals, operas produced by the School of Music; 26 guest artist events.

Music Library. 35,000 books; 135,000 scores; 8,500 microforms; 40,000 records. Listening stations include 12 carrels for cassettes; 48 carrels with stereo. About 14,000 additional volumes of music books in main University Library and its Rare Book Room.

Special collections include: comprehensive music collection; John Philip Sousa Collection; Rafael Joseffy collection of piano music; Joseph Szigeti collection (library) of violin music; Harry Partch Archive; 78-rpm records; piano rolls.

Special Programs

Performance Groups. University Orchestras, University Bands, choral ensembles, jazz bands, New Music Ensemble, Oratorio Society, University Chorus, Opera Chorus.

Financial

Costs. Per academic year: Tuition in-state resident undergraduate $1,406 to $1,652, graduate $1,960; out-of-state undergraduate $4,218 to $4,956, graduate $5,880. Room and board $3,026 to $3,162.

Financial Aid. Sources of financial aid include scholarships, grants, loans, student employment, and a College

Work-Study program. 110 music students awarded scholarships ranging from $500 to $4,000 (average award $1,200).

Commentary

The University of Illinois is one of the few American institutions to offer the option of ethnomusicology—with emphases available in American Indian cultures, India and Middle Eastern culture, and African and Afro-American cultures—at the Bachelor level. The University's music program, both undergraduate and graduate, is well balanced in its strengths, supported by an outstanding faculty. The School of Music hopes to expand its graduate studies, adding the disciplines of conducting, early music performance, and jazz studies.

Illinois State University
Department of Music
College of Fine Arts
230 Centennial East
Normal
Illinois 61761

Telephone. (309) 438-7631
Chief Administrator. Arthur Corra, Chairperson.

Illinois State University, established in 1857, was the first institution of higher education in Illinois. It has an enrollment of over 18,000 students. The University is comprised of 50 buildings on 850 acres located near the geographical center of Illinois.

The Department of Music offers undergraduate program leading to the baccalaureate degree. Students who intend to major in music are expected to have previous music experience. All majors must pass the senior college examination which evaluates the student's mastery of musicianship and performance skills.

Accreditation. North Central Association of Colleges and Schools; National Association of Schools of Music; National Council for Accreditation of Teacher Education.

Academic Information

Enrollment, Music Majors. (Total University) 18,873.
Music Faculty. 45.
Term System. Semester. 2 summer sessions.
Entrance Requirements. High school graduation; SAT or ACT; performance audition on major instrument or voice.
Admission Procedure. Application with supporting documents reviewed on a rolling admissions basis.
Music Degrees Offered. Bachelor of Music; Bachelor of Music Education; Bachelor of Arts; Bachelor of Science.
Music Degree Requirements. The Bachelor of Music degree program offers six area sequences: music theory-

composition; music history-literature; keyboard instrument-performance pedagogy (piano, organ, harpsichord); voice; band and orchestra instruments performance; and music therapy. The Bachelor of Music Education degree program includes four area sequences: choral-general-vocal; choral-general-keyboard; instrumental-band; instrumental-orchestra. The Bachelor of Arts and the Bachelor of Science degrees are liberal arts programs with the major in music. All baccalaureate degree programs require the completion of a music core, general education courses, and the major sequence.

General Program Areas. Composition, Music History, Music Literature, Music Theory, Music Therapy.

Instruments Taught. Brass, Guitar, Harpsichord, Organ, Percussion, Piano, Stringed Instruments, Voice, Woodwinds.

Musical Facilities

Concert Facilities. Auditorium, seating 3,500.
Concerts/Musical Activities. Student/faculty recitals and concerts; visiting artists.
Music Library. A collection of 21,800 recordings is available. The various collections of the University Library include over 1 million catalogued books.

Special collections include: strengths in performance, music education, and music therapy; George K. Jackson collection; circus band scores; musical instruments collection.

Special Programs

Performance Groups. Symphonic Band, Concert Band, University Band, Pep Band, Marching Band, Symphony Orchestra, Chamber Wind Ensemble, Concert Choir, University Glee Club, Treble Choir, Civic Chorale.

Financial

Costs. Per academic year: Tuition in-state resident $1,116, nonresident $3,348. Fees $783. Room $1,028. Board $1,256.

Financial Aid. The Financial Aid Office administers and coordinates more than thirty million dollars annually in aid to approximately sixty-five percent of the student population. Scholarship/financial aid application due March 1.

Illinois Wesleyan University
School of Music
College of Fine Arts
Presser Hall
Bloomington
Illinois 61701

Telephone. (309) 556-3061

Chief Administrator. Dr. Charles G. Boyer, Director.
Illinois Wesleyan University is a privately supported
liberal arts university founded in 1851. It is affiliated
with the United Methodist Church and enrolls over 1,-
500 students annually. The 42-acre campus has 40 buildings in the northern residential district of Bloomington.

The School of Music provides a program designed to
equip the student with the skills necessary to meet the
demands placed upon today's musician/teacher and to
serve as a basis for continued professional growth. The
School also provides music courses to the general college
student.

Accreditation. North Central Association of Colleges
and Schools; National Association of Schools of Music;
National Council for Accreditation of Teacher Education.

Academic Information

Enrollment, Music Majors. (Total University) 1,568.
Music Faculty. 20 plus adjunct faculty.
Term System. Semester. One summer session.
Entrance Requirements. High school graduation or
GED; rank in upper 40 percent of graduating class; completion of 15 college preparatory units with minimum of
4 English, 2 mathematics, 2 foreign language, 2 science,
3 social studies; SAT or ACT; recommendations of high
school counselors; audition required.
Admission Procedure. Application with supporting
documents reviewed on a rolling admissions basis.
Music Degrees Offered. Bachelor of Music; Bachelor
of Music Education; Bachelor of Sacred Music; Bachelor
of Arts.
Music Degree Requirements. The Bachelor of Music
degree is offered with majors in piano, piano pedagogy,
organ, voice, orchestral instruments, and composition.
The Bachelor of Music Education degree program requires completion of courses in general education, music
and music education, and courses from the Department
of Education. Upon satisfactory completion of the requirements for the degree, the student must make application to the Illinois State Certification Board in order
that a certificate may be issued granting authority to
teach music, grades K-12, in the public schools of Illinois. The degree Bachelor of Sacred Music is offered
with a concentration in organ and voice. The Bachelor
of Arts degree is a liberal arts program with a major in
music.
General Program Areas. Church Music, Composition,
Music Education, Performance, Piano Pedagogy.
Instruments Taught. Baritone, Bass, Bassoon, Clarinet, Flute, French Horn, Harpsichord, Oboe, Organ,
Percussion, Piano, Saxophone, Trombone, Trumpet,
Tuba, Viola, Violin, Violoncello, Voice.

Musical Facilities

Practice Facilities. Presser Hall contains 25 teaching
studios, 56 practice rooms, seminar rooms, electronic
music laboratory, recording studio, rehearsal rooms for
small and large ensembles, and an electronic piano
laboratory. Major equipment items include 92 pianos, 5
organs, 2 harpsichords, a pianoforte, and stereo playback
installations in all classrooms. The New Music Building
provides additional studios.
Concert Facilities. Recital Hall, seating 600.
Concerts/Musical Activities. Faculty and student recitals; concerts by University organizations and ensembles;
programs presented by guest artists and performing
groups.
Music Library. Thorpe Music Library is located in
Presser Hall and contains books and periodicals relating
to music. The score collection of performing editions of
works for solo instruments and chamber ensembles is
supplemented by editions of major composers and other
historical sets in printed form as well as microfilm. Music education curriculum materials constitute an important part of the collection. A non-circulating collection
of disc and tape recordings complements the score collection. Listening facilities offer individual disc, cassette,
and reel-to-reel tape listening and pre-recorded programs for class assignments.

Special Programs

Featured Programs. A Symposium of Contemporary
Music is sponsored each year by the School of Music in
conjunction with the University-wide Fine Arts Festival.
The program of lectures, recitals, and concerts centers
around the presentations and works of a prominent guest
composer who is brought to the campus.

A limited number of pre-college students are accepted
in piano and stringed instruments for instruction in music performance and musicianship skills. The work is
normally in a combination of group and private lessons.
These students serve as a laboratory group for college
students who are preparing to become music teachers.

A Summer Music Camp Program provides qualified
junior high and high school students with a concentrated
period of musical study.
Performance Groups. University Orchestra, Concert
Band, Collegiate Choir, Titan Band, Festival Choir,
Chamber Ensembles (Strings, Brass, Woodwinds, Per-
cussion, Voice, Piano), Chapel Choir, Women's Chorus,
Jazz Ensemble, Collegium Musicum, University Singers.

Financial

Costs. Per academic year: Tuition $7,130. Fees $60.
Room $1,345. Board $1,535.
Financial Aid. Scholarships, grants, loans, part-time
employment, and a College Work-Study program are
available. Scholarship/financial aid application due May
1.

Millikin University
School of Music
1184 West Main Street
Decatur
Illinois 62522

Telephone. (217) 424-6211

Chief Administrator. Dr. A. Wesley Tower, Dean.

Millikin University is a privately supported institution affiliated with the Presbyterian Church U.S.A. Millikin was founded in 1901 as the Decatur College and Industrial School and together with nearby Lincoln College was known for 50 years as the James Millikin University. This identity was dissolved in 1953 when the separate institutions of Lincoln College and Millikin University were established.

The major objectives of the School of Music are to develop professional musicians in the areas of teaching, performance, church music, and commercial music; to foster the growth of musicianship through the development of skills and of insights into the structure of music and to provide opportunities for nonmusic majors to participate in musical activities as part of their liberal arts education.

Accreditation. North Central Association of Colleges and Schools; National Association of Schools of Music; National Council for Accreditation of Teacher Education.

Academic Information

Enrollment, Music Majors. (Total University) 1,478.

Music Faculty. Full-time 15, adjunct 12.

Term System. Semester. One summer session.

Entrance Requirements. High school graduation or equivalent with rank in upper half of graduating class and completion of 15 units; SAT or ACT required; audition required; personal interview recommended.

Admission Procedure. Application with supporting documents and nonrefundable $15 fee to Office of Admissions.

Music Degrees Offered. Bachelor of Music; Bachelor of Science; Bachelor of Arts.

Music Degree Requirements. The Bachelor of Music degree is offered with a major in applied music (instrumental, vocal, or jazz emphasis), church music, and music education (instrumental, vocal, or jazz emphasis). Students in the music education degree programs with a vocal or instrumental emphasis may take music electives that prepare them to teach in a second area. The Bachelor of Science degree with a major in music and a minor in business administration is also offered. The Bachelor of Arts degree is offered as a liberal arts program with a major in music.

General Program Areas. Applied Music, Church Music, Jazz Studies, Music Business, Music Education.

Instruments Taught. Bass, Bassoon, Clarinet, Euphonium, Flute, French Horn, Guitar, Oboe, Organ, Percussion, Piano, Saxophone, Trombone, Trumpet, Tuba, Viola, Violin, Violoncello, Voice.

Musical Facilities

Practice Facilities. The School of Music Building contains 28 soundproof practice rooms, classrooms, and studios. Music facilities include a 3-manual organ, a 2-manual organ, 2-manual practice organs. Kirkland Fine Arts Center includes rehearsal areas.

Concert Facilities. Kaeuper Hall, seating 175; Kirkland Auditorium, 2,000.

Concerts/Musical Activities. Faculty concerts, student recitals, music workshops, festivals, Christmas oratorios.

Music Library. The Staley Library houses over 154,-000 volumes and supports the academic programs of the School of Music.

Special Programs

Featured Programs. Applied music and class piano instruction is available for students not enrolled in the University or not eligible for college credit.

Performance Groups. University Orchestra, University Band, University Chorus, Opera Workshop, Opera Theatre, University Choir, Chamber Singers, Jazz Band, Instrumental Ensembles, Vocal Ensembles, Jazz Ensemble.

Financial

Costs. Per academic year: Tuition $6,410. Fees $61. Room $1,410. Board $1,440.

Financial Aid. Scholarships, grants, loans, part-time employment, and a College Work-Study program are among the types of financial aid available. Scholarship/financial aid application due August 1.

Northeastern Illinois University
Department of Music
5500 North St. Louis
Chicago
Illinois 60625

Telephone. (312) 583-4050

Chief Administrator. Helen Engler, Chairperson.

Northeastern Illinois University, one of the first teacher training institutions in Illinois, was founded in 1867 in Englewood as the Cook County Normal School. The present name, after a number of previous versions, was adopted in 1971. The University is an urban, commuter university serving the Chicago metropolitan area. Total graduate and undergraduate enrollment is over 10,000. In addition to offering traditional programs in the arts, sciences, and education, Northeastern has a strong commitment to innovative, nontraditional education such as special programs for adults.

The Department of Music offers undergraduate and graduate programs which enable students to acquire understanding of historical/theoretical analysis, compositional/performance techniques, and critical/aesthetic aspects of music and dance. The major in music offers a choice of six areas of emphasis and is designed as background for personal enrichment, and to prepare for professional music careers, graduate study, studio or private teaching, and teaching music in the secondary schools.

Accreditation. North Central Association of Colleges and Schools; National Council for Accreditation of Teacher Education.

Academic Information

Enrollment, Music Majors. (Total University) full-time 1,840 men, 2,510 women; part-time 2,475 men, 3,850 women.

Music Faculty. Full-time 18, part-time 10.

Term System. Trimester. Academic year from September to August.

Entrance Requirements. High school graduation or equivalent with rank in upper half of graduating class; ACT required; GRE required for graduate school; music background assumed (deficiencies may be fulfilled in coursework). Audition required in performance area. TOEFL for foreign students.

Admission Procedure. Application with supporting documents to Office of Admissions.

Music Degrees Offered. Bachelor of Arts; Master of Arts.

Music Degree Requirements. The Bachelor of Arts degree in music in the liberal arts sequence is offered with emphases in vocal or instrumental performance, music theory, piano pedagogy, and music history and literature. The secondary education sequence is offered with emphases in secondary education/vocal music, secondary education/instrumental music. There are three minor programs: (1) elementary music, as part of the elementary education major; (2) an individualized minor in music; and (3) an individualized minor in dance. The baccalaureate degree requires the completion of a minimum of 120 credit hours including general education requirements, core curriculum, and the major/minor requirements.

The Master of Arts degree in music offers two areas of emphasis: music education and applied music pedagogy. The master's program provides advanced study for elementary and secondary teachers of music, and preparation to teach music in colleges and universities. It also provides additional study for private studio teachers, for students who wish to pursue further graduate study, and for students who wish to increase their levels of musical accomplishment. The master's degree requires completion of 36 hours of study.

General Program Areas. Applied Music Pedagogy, Music Education, Music History, Music Theory, Performance, Piano Pedagogy.

Instruments Taught. Brass, Percussion, Piano, Stringed Instruments, Voice, Woodwinds.

Musical Facilities

Practice Facilities. Percussion-equipped practice facilities; piano practice rooms; computer music/synthesizer laboratory.

Concert Facilities. Auditorium, seating 650; Recital Hall, 150.

Concerts/Musical Activities. Each season, student, faculty, and guest performers present afternoon and evening concerts on campus.

Music Library. Music materials are housed in the central Library; learning resources lab in Department of Music includes records, tapes, and computer-assisted instruction equipment.

Special Programs

Performance Groups. Collegium Musicum, Concert Choir, Instrumental Ensembles, Jazz Ensemble, Madrigal Singers, New Music Ensemble, Opera Workshop, Orchestra, Pep Band, University Chorus, University Concert Band, Wind Band, Chamber Singers, Recorder Ensemble, University Dance Ensemble.

Financial

Costs. Per trimester: Tuition in-state resident lower division $698, out-of-state $1,826; in-state resident upper division $710, out-of-state $1,875; graduate in-state $684, out-of-state $1,931.

Financial Aid. Financial aid is awarded on the basis of academic merit, financial need, and musical ability. State/federal and institutional aid is available as well as part-time employment and a College Work-Study program. Scholarship/financial aid applications due in Financial Aid Office by May 1.

Northern Illinois University
School of Music
DeKalb
Illinois 60115

Telephone. (815) 753-1551

Chief Administrator. Donald J. Funes, Chair.

Northern Illinois University is a state-assisted coeducational institution of 25,000 students. It offers programs on the campus in DeKalb and at a number of outreach centers throughout northern Illinois. The 449-acre main campus in DeKalb, a community of 35,000, is located 65 miles west of Chicago's Loop.

The School of Music provides professional training at the bachelor's and master's levels in performance, theory, composition, history, and music education at the undergraduate and graduate levels.

Accreditation. North Central Association of Colleges and Schools; National Association of Schools of Music.

Academic Information

Enrollment, Music Majors. Full-time 126 men, 96 women; part-time 45 men, 26 women.

Music Faculty. Full-time 42, part-time 8.

Term System. Semester. 8-week summer session from mid-June to mid-Aug. Academic year from August to May.

Entrance Requirements. Accredited high school graduation with rank in upper half of high school class and ACT of 18; students must pass a performance audition and complete an interview and aural skills test. Foreign students must provide sufficient financial support for themselves; scholarship and tuition waivers are available and may be applied toward their financial support.

Admission Procedure. Application and supporting documents to Admissions Office; students must be accepted by the University and the School of Music.

Music Degrees Offered. Bachelor of Music; Bachelor of Arts; Master of Music.

Music Degree Requirements. The Bachelor of Music degree is offered with a comprehensive major in music education for students preparing for public school teaching. This program is offered with emphases in instrumental music, vocal music, and general music. Also offered is the major in music with emphases in keyboard instruments, voice, band or orchestral instruments, history and literature of music, and theory and composition. A comprehensive major in music for students whose interests lie in acquiring a broad, liberal education is also offered and leads to the Bachelor of Arts degree. The baccalaureate programs require the completion of a minimum of 124 semester hours including general education, core curriculum, and departmental requirements.

The School of Music offers graduate programs in music education, performance, and individualized programs leading to the Master of Music degree.

General Program Areas. Composition, Music History, Music Literature, Music Theory, Performance.

Instruments Taught. Brass, Guitar, Organ, Percussion, Piano, Stringed Instruments, Voice, Woodwinds.

Musical Facilities

Practice Facilities. 85 practice rooms. 4 organs (W. Zimmer & Sons Opus 150, 16 rank and Opus 151, single rank; Flentrop 12 rank; Martin Ott 36 rank). Special practice facilities for percussionists. 20 pianos (10 Yamaha uprights, 10 Wurlitzer uprights); 20 pianos reserved for piano majors. Piano lab; 2 electronic music studios; recording studio; world music studio.

Concert Facilities. Music Building Concert Hall, seating 750; Recital Hall, 150.

Community Facilities. Egyptian Theatre.

Concerts/Musical Activities. Faculty solo recitals; chamber music programs; student recitals; large ensemble concerts. The School of Music presents 200 programs per year.

Music Library. 12,500 volumes; 18,400 scores; 160 periodicals; 2,500 microforms; 24,100 phonograph recordings; 500 audiocassettes. 35 listening stations (stereo). Special collections include the Kaltenbach-Sorensen collection of 1,700 78-rpm recordings of jazz and dance band music. The NIU Library maintains the Chicago Civic Opera Archives; the Charles Elliott Fouser manuscripts; and the Wurlitzer Archives.

Special Programs

Featured Programs. World Music.

Performance Groups. Instrumental Ensembles (string, woodwind, brass, percussion, keyboard, mixed, neoteric, jazz), Collegium Musicum, Chamber Orchestra, Wind Symphony, All-University Band, Marching Band, University Chorus, Concert Choir, Philharmonic, String Orchestra, World Music Ensemble (gamelan, Chinese Orchestra, African Ensemble, Steel Band, tabla).

Foreign Programs. The School of Music has an informal relationship with the Shanghai Conservatory of Music. Several faculty have visited that institution to present recitals and a number of students from Shanghai have attended the School of Music.

Financial

Costs. Tuition in-state resident undergraduate $46.50 per credit hour, graduate $47.50 per credit hour. Fees $18. Room $1,162.

Financial Aid. Institutional and state/federal aid available. 60 music students receive financial aid. Scholarship application due April 1. Part-time employment and a College Work-Study program available.

Commentary

The Vermeer Quartet, one of America's premiere chamber ensembles, is in residence at Northern Illinois University. A small music department, reasonable tuition, good string teaching, and a serious chamber music program make this university an excellent college choice for young string players.

**Northwestern University
School of Music**
711 Elgin Road
Evanston
Illinois 60201

Telephone. (312) 491-7575
Chief Administrator. Dr. Thomas Miller, Dean.

Northwestern University is a privately supported university chartered in 1851. It is one of the nation's largest independent institutions of higher learning. It is nondenominational and enrolls over 10,000 students. The University is located on two separate campuses fronting on Lake Michigan. The larger campus, running a mile along the shoreline and bordered on the other three sides by the suburban city of Evanston, contains 145 buildings on 170 acres. Twelve miles south, on a 14-acre lakefront site one mile from Chicago's downtown Loop, is the Chicago campus.

The Northwestern University School of Music, established in 1895, is one of the oldest degree-conferring schools of music in the United States. Its origin dates back to the Northwestern Female College in 1855, which changed its name in 1871 to Evanston College for Ladies. In 1873, Northwestern University incorporated the Evanston College for Ladies, becoming a coeducational institution. At the same time, plans were announced for the foundation of a Conservatory of Music on the European plan. The Conservatory of Music appears for the first time in the University catalog of 1876. In 1895-96 the department was transformed and advanced from a Department of Music to a School of Music. The early years emphasized church and choral music. The 1930s and 1940s emphasized music education and the strong role that music plays in the nation's culture. The School then sought to expand its role in other areas—training performers, inviting prominent guests to the campus, and otherwise broadening the base of the School. Since then there has been a strengthening of the basic education in music for the undergraduate and a development of a professional program at the graduate level.

Accreditation. North Central Association of Colleges and Schools; National Association of Schools of Music.

Academic Information

Enrollment, Music Majors. Full-time 281 men, 253 women; part-time 10 men, 9 women. Foreign students 19.

Music Faculty. Full-time 53, part-time 19.

Term System. Quarter. Academic year begins September. Six-week summer session from late June to early August.

Entrance Requirements. Top fifth of high school class; SAT score 1000, ACT score 21; completion of 15 college preparatory courses including a minimum of 4 English, 3-4 mathematics, 2-4 foreign language, 2-3 science, 2-4 social science. High quality performance audition required (personal auditions are conducted in 26 cities throughout the United States). Graduate students must have baccalaureate degree; 3.00 GPA from previous program of study. Foreign students must meet regular admission requirements; evidence of ability to speak, read, and write the English language and to meet the financial obligations; students for whom English is a second language must present the results of TOEFL; must have

achieved outstanding school records to be considered.

Admission Procedure. Submit application and fee with supporting documents. Master of Music students recommendations, transcripts, and other specifications depending on emphasis to be pursued. Doctoral candidates must submit recommendations, transcripts; also required is a campus audition and examination in music history and literature, music theory, and departmental diagnostic examinations for application in piano, organ and church music, and conducting; other materials depending on emphasis pursued.

Music Degrees Offered. Bachelor of Arts; Bachelor of Music; Master of Music; Doctor of Music, Doctor of Philosophy.

Music Degree Requirements. The Bachelor degrees require the completion of 192 quarter hours with an overall 2.75 GPA. Emphasis in music education requires student teaching, in composition an original work, and in performance a full recital.

The Master's degrees are offered with emphases in music history and literature, music theory, music composition, conducting, church music and organ, piano, stringed instruments, winds and percussion, and voice. The Master's degrees require the completion of 48 quarter hours with an overall 3.00 GPA plus proficiency in music theory, music history, and aural skills; a terminal project; final assessment.

The Doctor of Music degree may be pursued with emphasis in music education, music history and literature, music theory, music composition, conducting, church music, organ, piano, stringed instruments, winds and percussion, and voice. The degree requires the completion of 72 quarter hours with an overall 3.00 GPA plus proficiency in music theory, music history, and aural skills; English proficiency; language requirements; research document/dissertation or other final project.

The Certificate in Performance for organ, piano, stringed instruments, woodwind/brass/percussion, voice and opera are also awarded.

General Program Areas. Church Music, Composition, Conducting, Music Education, Music History, Music Literature, Music Theory, Pedagogy, Performance.

Instruments Taught. Bassoon, Clarinet, Flute, Guitar, Harp, Horn, Oboe, Organ, Percussion, Piano, Saxophone, String Bass, Trombone, Trumpet, Tuba, Viola, Violin, Violoncello, Voice.

Musical Facilities

Practice Facilities. Special practice facilities for organists; 9 organs (3 Roderer, 1 Wilhelm, 1 Ott, 2 Schantz, 1 Holtkamp, 1 Flentrop. Practice facilities for percussionists. 97 practice rooms. 195 pianos (Baldwin, Baldwin Electric, Knight, Yamaha, Mason & Hamlin, Kurtzman, Conover, Wurlitzer Electric, Cembalo, Krakauer, A.B. Chase, Stieff, Schimmel, Kawai, Kranich & Bach, Everett, Weaver Hoffman, Hamilton, Bosendorfer). Electronic music studio; computer music studio.

Concert Facilities. Lutkin Hall, seating 400; Regenstein Master Class Recital Hall, 200; Pick-Staiger Concert Hall, 1,000; Kahn Auditorium, 1,150; Alice Millar Chapel.

Concerts/Musical Activities. Performing Arts Series (7 to 8); 140 guest recitals, master classes, student ensembles, student operas, and faculty ensembles; 280 student recitals; 15 to 20 summer performances.

Music Library. 26,500 volumes; 418 current periodical subscriptions; 39,000 audiovisual materials (in addition to those under the jurisdiction of the University Library Media Center); 4,000 microforms; 42,000 phonograph recordings; 300 audiocassettes. 60 listening stations (stereo). Special collections include: Twentieth Century Music; Fritz Reiner Library; John Cage Notation Collection; John Cage Archive; manuscripts of Jean Martinon; Ricordi Collection; ethnomusicological recordings emphasizing African music.

Special Programs

Affiliated Programs. Two-year double program with Rosary College yielding a Master of Arts in Library and Information Science and a Master of Music in Music History.

Financial

Costs. Per academic year: Tuition Undergraduate $11,031, graduate $10,314. Room and Board undergraduate $3,884, graduate $4,390 to $5,985.

Financial Aid. Financial aid is awarded on the basis of academic merit, financial need, and musical ability. Institutional and state/federal aid available. 80% of undergraduates and 91% of graduates receive financial aid; average award per Master's student $4,358, Certificate student $7,417, Doctoral student $8,384. Financial aid/ scholarship application due March 1. Part-time employment (average earnings per academic year $900 to $1,- 000) and College Work-Study program available.

Commentary

The School of Music at Northwestern University enjoys an enviable reputation in many of its disciplines. The brass department in particular, whose faculty includes principal players of the Chicago Symphony Orchestra, attracts outstanding students. Five-year undergraduate double degree programs are available. The School houses the highly regarded Computer Music Studio, and holds a collection of fine string instruments, the Cage Archive, and the Ricordi collection of nineteenth-century music.

Roosevelt University
Chicago Musical College
430 South Michigan Avenue
Chicago
Illinois 60605

Telephone. (312) 341-3782
Chief Administrator. William F. Bonch, Dean.

Roosevelt University was founded in 1945 as an independent, nonsectarian, institution. The student enrollment is approximately 6,000, of which about one-third are pursuing graduate studies. A large percentage of Roosevelt students also work full-time. Since 1947, Roosevelt University's home has been the Auditorium Building on Michigan Avenue overlooking Grant Park and Lake Michigan. The building is considered to be the masterpiece of architects Dankmar Adler and Louis Sullivan.

Founded in 1867 by Florenz Ziegfeld, Chicago Musical College has served the art of music for more than a century. In 1954, the University's School of Music was combined with the original Chicago Musical College and the name was retained. In order to meet the needs of all those who apply for admission, the College is organized in two parts, the College and the Non-Credit Division. The goals of the College are (1) to develop students' individual professional excellence; (2) to provide a well-rounded education in music and related fields; (3) to acquaint all students with the musical traditions of the past, as well as the music of today; (4) to stress creative musical performance and compositional skills; (5) to prepare graduates for demands made for successful employment in all fields of music; and (6) to discover and train young talent in the Non-Credit Division.

Accreditation. North Central Association of Colleges and Schools; National Association of Schools of Music.

Academic Information

Enrollment, Music Majors. 238. 28 foreign students.
Music Faculty. Full-time 22, part-time 44.

Term System. Semester. Two summer sessions including intensive courses for full academic credit in shorter term; workshops.

Entrance Requirements. Accredited high school graduation with rank in upper 75% of graduating class; 15 units of college preparatory work; SAT, ACT, or Roosevelt Entrance Examination; personal or taped audition; theory placement test.

Admission Procedure. Application with supporting documents and $20 nonrefundable fee ($30 for graduate school applicants) accepted on a rolling basis.

Music Degrees Offered. Bachelor of Music; Bachelor of Music Education; Bachelor of Arts; Master of Music; Master of Music Education.

Music Degree Requirements. The Bachelor of Music degree is offered with majors in performance (keyboard, guitar, orchestral instrument, or voice), piano pedagogy, music theory, composition, music history, jazz studies (performance or composition), music education (choral, instrumental, comprehensive, jazz, or music in special education), or music business. The degree requires the completion of at least 120 semester hours of credit including general education, core curriculum, and departmental requirements. The Bachelor of Music Education degree program has the ultimate goal of helping students gain an understanding of music and the relationship of music to the education of students in elementary and secondary schools. The five curricula offered include instrumental, choral, comprehensive concentration, special education (double certification or music only), and jazz studies. The College also offers a major in music for students seeking a Bachelor of Arts degree. Concentrations are possible in music history and literature, music theory, and applied music.

The Master of Music degree is offered with majors in performance (keyboard, guitar, voice, orchestral instruments), opera, vocal pedagogy, theory, composition, and musicology. The Master of Music Education degree is offered with emphases in performance, general music, elementary/junior high/senior high, choral music, instrumental music, music supervision and administration, and music in special education. The master's degrees require the completion of 30 semester hours of prescribed courses.

General Program Areas. Applied Music, Choral Music, Commercial Music, Composition, Jazz Studies, Music Business, Music Education, Music History, Music Literature, Music Theory, Musicology, Piano Pedagogy, Vocal Pedagogy.

Instruments Taught. Brass, Gamelan, Guitar, Organ, Percussion, Piano, Stringed Instruments, Voice, Woodwinds.

Musical Facilities

Practice Facilities. 38 practice rooms. 2 organs (Wicks). 5 percussion-equipped practice rooms. 35 pianos (8 grands). Electronic/computer music studio.

Concert Facilities. Auditorium Theatre, seating 4,200; small concert hall.

Concerts/Musical Activities. 130 recitals offered on campus during the academic year. College is within walking distance of all major concert halls.

Music Library. 28,000 books; 10,000 recordings; 92 microfiche titles; 90 periodicals; 7,000 pieces of sheet music; 300 librettos. Listening facilities (3 cassette stations, 11 stereo stations). The Chicago Music College Archives are housed in the Music Library. Audio-Visual and Television Center with recording studio and various instructional aids.

Special Programs

Performance Groups. Roosevelt University Symphony Orchestra, Symphonic Band, Training Band, Chorus, Concert Choir, Opera Theatre, Jazz Ensemble, Javanese Gamelan Ensemble, New Music Ensemble, Electric Guitar Ensemble, Classic Guitar Ensemble, Percussion Ensemble, Saxophone Ensemble, Woodwind Ensemble, Brass Ensemble, Two Piano Ensemble.

Affiliated Programs. The Bachelor of Fine Arts in Musical Theatre is an intercollegial degree program offered jointly by the Chicago Musical College and the College of Arts and Sciences. It is designed to prepare the student to become a professional performer in all areas of musical theater except opera. Cooperative programs with Spertus College of Judaica and School of the Art Institute of Chicago.

Financial

Costs. Tuition $168 per credit (full-time $5,040 per academic year). Housing approximately $3,200 per year.

Financial Aid. A number of special music scholarships are granted each year by competition or recommendation. 43 music students have scholarships ranging from $350 to $3,800. Scholarship applications due March 1. Other sources of financial aid include state/federal aid, part-time employment, and a College Work-Study program.

Southern Illinois University at Carbondale School of Music
Carbondale
Illinois 62901

Telephone. (618) 536-7505
Chief Administrator. Dr. Robert Ronbos, Director.
Southern Illinois University, chartered as a normal school in 1869, opened in 1874. University powers were granted in 1943 and the present name was adopted in 1947. SIU is a comprehensive university with a diverse offering of graduate programs and a commitment to research. In fiscal year 1985, the University awarded a total of 5,630 degrees. The campus is located in Carbondale, a city of 26,400 people, approximately 60 miles north of the southern tip of Illinois.

Potential music majors without an extensive background will be required to complete preparation which may extend the time to graduation. Music credits earned at other accredited institutions will apply toward requirements but the transfer student will be evaluated for proper placement in the music curriculum. A number of students choose to complete coursework outside the field of music, which may result in a minor, double major, or a specifically designed program combining music with other areas of interest. Examples of outside areas that students have used in the past include radio-television, theater, business and economics, language education, dance, and art.

Accreditation. North Central Association of Colleges and Schools; National Association of Schools of Music.

Academic Information

Enrollment, Music Majors. 142.

Music Faculty. Full-time 22, part-time 1.

Term System. Semester. Summer session of 8 weeks from mid-June to mid-August.

Entrance Requirements. All applicants must have graduated from high school before beginning classes; ACT score of 18 or above (or SAT combined score of 780 or above) *or* ACT score between 15 and 17 (SAT combined of 700-770) and class rank in the upper half; audition not required.

Admission Procedure. Application with supporting documents accepted as early as 15 months prior to the date of enrollment.

Music Degrees Offered. Bachelor of Arts; Bachelor of Music; Master of Music.

Music Degree Requirements. The Bachelor of Arts degree program, essentially a double major, offers a liberal arts degree with considerable flexibility. Within the framework of 40 hours of music, 40 hours in general education, and 40 hours in a core area of choice, the degree can be tailored to meet individual needs. Some areas that might be combined with music include business, religion, language education, dance, art, radio-television, theater, graphic arts, and visual communications. The Bachelor of Music degree program offers several well-defined specializations: performance, jazz performance, piano pedagogy, theory-composition, music business, music education. The musical core required gives a strong background in an applied area (keyboard, voice, band or orchestral instrument) as well as in theory, ear training, history, and literature. A Total of 120 hours is required for the degree. The professional education sequence is carried out in cooperation with the College of Education and includes courses in psychology, evaluation, and classroom management.

In addition to the bachelor's degrees in music, SIU offers the Master of Music degree with several concentrations: performance, music education, music history and literature, music theory and composition, piano pedagogy, opera/theater.

General Program Areas. Applied Music, Composition, Conducting, Jazz Performance, Music Business, Music Education, Music History, Music Literature, Music Theory, Opera, Performance, Piano Pedagogy.

Instruments Taught. Baritone, Bass, Bassoon, Clarinet, Flute, Guitar, Harpsichord, Horn, Oboe, Organ, Percussion, Piano, Recorder, Saxophone, Trombone, Trumpet, Tuba, Viola, Violin, Violoncello, Voice.

Musical Facilities

Practice Facilities. 25 practice rooms. 3 organs. Special practice facilities for percussionists. 5 grand pianos reserved for piano majors.

Concert Facilities. Shryuck Auditorium, seating 1,400; Old Baptist Foundation Recital Hall, 300; Quigley Auditorium, 200.

Concerts/Musical Activities. Ensemble recitals; concerts; the Marching Salukis play regularly at St. Louis Cardinals baseball and Chicago Bears football games.

Music Library. The Morris Library houses over 1.7 million volumes; 2.1 million units of microfilm. Collections of recordings are located here as well as in the School of Music. Listening facilities (stereo).

Special Programs

Featured Programs. SIU has active chapters of music societies including Phi Mu Alpha, Mu Phi Epsilon, Music Educators National Conference, Pi Kappa Lambda, and the Beethoven Society for Pianists.

Performance Groups. Marching Salukis, Symphonic Band, Concert Wind Ensemble, Jazz Ensemble, Brass and Percussion Ensemble, Symphony, Choral Union, Chamber Choir, Madrigal Singers, Concert Choir, Vocal Jazz Ensemble, Male Glee Club.

Financial

Costs. Per academic year: Tuition in-state resident $1,603, out-of-state $3,741. Out-of-state students can qualify for in-state tuition rates after 80 days. Room and board $2,580.

Financial Aid. Special grants and awards are available to students enrolled in the School of Music who are qualified and in need of financial assistance. Opportunities for employment in the student work program; tuition awards and loan programs available through the Office of Student Work and Financial Assistance.

Southern Illinois University at Edwardsville Department of Music

School of Fine Arts and Communications
Edwardsville
Illinois 62026

Telephone. (618) 692-3900

Chief Administrator. Dr. William D. Claudson, Chairman.

Southern Illinois University at Edwardsville traces its origin to a recommendation in 1956 to the Southwest Illinois Council of Higher Education. The Council was convinced that higher education facilities were needed in counties bordering Missouri in the greater St. Louis area. It was recommended that Southern Illinois University, one hundred miles south in Carbondale, establish satellite campuses. In 1957, "residence" centers were established in Alton and East St. Louis. In 1968, Southern Illinois University at Edwardsville moved onto its new campus. It is now a completely autonomous university with an enrollment of 10,000 students. The campus is located fifteen miles from the city of St. Louis.

The faculty of the Department of Music believes that students at the undergraduate level should receive a comprehensive musical background which includes individual performance, ensemble performance, scholarly studies in music theory and history/literature, teacher preparation (if applicable), and a sound cultural background through the General Studies program. The ultimate aim is to develop skilled and informed musicians, able scholars, and/or competent and enthusiastic teachers.

Accreditation. North Central Association of Colleges and Schools; National Association of Schools of Music.

Academic Information

Enrollment, Music Majors. Full-time 100 men, 160 women; part-time 20 men, 30 women.

Music Faculty. Full-time 23, part-time 20.

Term System. Quarter. 8-week summer session from June 15 to August 15. Academic year from September 20 to June 7.

Entrance Requirements. High school graduation in upper half of graduating class or ACT of 18 or above; demonstrated potential in performance and musical aptitude; audition required. Baccalaureate degree and GRE for graduate students.

Admission Procedure. Application with supporting documents to Office of Admissions.

Music Degrees Offered. Bachelor of Music; Bachelor of Arts; Master of Music.

Music Degree Requirements. The Bachelor of Music degree is a curriculum designed to prepare students for professional careers in music and/or advanced graduate studies. The degree is offered with specializations in performance, music education, theory/composition, and studio music and jazz performance. The degree requires the completion of general studies, electives, and major requirements for a minimum total of 192 quarter hours. The Bachelor of Arts degree is designed for students who wish to specialize in music within a liberal arts curriculum. It may also serve as the foundation for advanced studies in music.

The Department of Music offers graduate work leading to the Master of Music degree with majors in performance and in music education. The minimum number of graduate hours required for the degree is 48. All students must satisfactorily complete placement examinations in music theory, music history/literature, and music education or performance audition, whichever is appropriate to the candidate's major. A proficiency in foreign language is required of performance majors. Graduate curricula are designed to prepare the student for professional work as a teacher and/or performer.

General Program Areas. Applied Music, Composition, Conducting, Jazz Studies, Music Education, Music History, Music Literature, Music Merchandising, Music Theory, Performance, Studio Music.

Instruments Taught. Baritone, Bass, Bassoon, Clarinet, Flute, French Horn, Guitar, Harp, Harpsichord, Oboe, Organ, Percussion, Piano, Saxophone, Trombone, Trumpet, Tuba, Viola, Violin, Violoncello, Voice.

Musical Facilities

Practice Facilities. 15 practice rooms. 2 organs. 28 pianos (20 Steinway uprights, 8 grands); 5 pianos reserved for piano majors. Computer laboratory; recording studio; keyboard laboratory.

Concert Facilities. Theater, seating 400; Recital Hall, 150.

Community Facilities. Local ballroom and gymnasium.

Concerts/Musical Activities. 150 concerts and recitals per year; visiting artists.

Music Library. 6,000 volumes; 2,000 band, orchestra, and choral scores; 50 periodical subscriptions; 40 audiovisual titles. 16 listening stations.

Special collections include: American hymnals and songbooks; Walter Damrosch memorabilia; Kiburz flute music collection; archives of Suzuki Association of America; jazz archive.

Special Programs

Performance Groups. University Band, University Chorus, Symphonic Band, Jazz Combo, Piano Ensemble, University Symphony Orchestra, Wind Ensemble, Concert Jazz Band, Concert Chorale, Chamber Orchestra.

Financial

Costs. Per academic year: Tuition in-state resident $1,200, out-of-state $3,300. Fees $300. Housing $1,600.

Financial Aid. Financial aid is awarded on the basis of academic merit, financial need, musical ability. Institutional and state/federal aid available as well as part-time employment and a College Work-Study program.

Commentary

Southern Illinois University at Edwardsville has a newly installed music computer lab to assist composition, analysis, and music-printing activities. Among noteworthy University holdings is a flute collection dating back to the mid-eighteenth century, an African instrument collection, and a collection of Western and Oriental instruments.

VanderCook College of Music
3209 South Michigan Avenue
Chicago
Illinois 60616

Telephone. (312) 225-6288

Chief Administrator. James Gilworth, President.

VanderCook College of Music is a privately supported professional college. It was founded in 1909 by Mr. H.A. VanderCook to train professional musicians, directors, and teachers. In 1928, the school was incorporated as a nonprofit teacher training institution and its curriculum was approved by the Illinois State Department of Public Instruction. In 1931, the College became one of the first institutions in the United States to offer a degree in music education. The mission of the school is to prepare prospective music teachers to teach all aspects of choral, vocal, instrumental, orchestral, and general music in the public schools.

Accreditation. North Central Association of Colleges and Schools; National Association of Schools of Music.

Academic Information

Enrollment, Music Majors. Full-time 67 men, 31 women; part-time 5 men, 2 women. 5 foreign students.

Music Faculty. Full-time 12, part-time 30.

Term System. Semester. One summer session primarily for graduate students and 20 different workshops.

Entrance Requirements. Accredited high school graduation or GED; SAT or ACT recommended; applicants expected to have been active in their high school bands, choirs, and/or orchestra programs; special entrance examinations required including audition. If an on-campus audition is not possible, a good quality tape will be expected.

Admission Procedure. Application with $25 nonrefundable fee accepted on a rolling basis.

Music Degrees Offered. Bachelor of Music Education; Master of Music Education.

Music Degree Requirements. The Bachelor of Music Education degree requires the completion of 139 semester hours. It is a four-year program and students must pass all coursework; have no grades below a C in any course in the junior and senior years; pass all jury examinations on major instrument; pass senior year comprehensive examinations; complete all recital and cultural event requirements; pass all student teaching requirements; and pass U.S. Constitution test for teacher certification.

The Master of Music Education degree requires the completion of 32 semester hours. It can be accomplished in four summer sessions or full-time in one academic year.

General Program Areas. Music Education, Music Theory, Performance.

Instruments Taught. Baritone, Bass, Bassoon, Clarinet, Flute, French Horn, Guitar, Oboe, Percussion, Piano, Saxophone, Trombone, Trumpet, Tuba, Viola, Violin, Violoncello, Voice.

Musical Facilities

Practice Facilities. 29 practice rooms. 3 percussion-equipped practice rooms. 15 practice pianos (uprights); 2 grand pianos reserved for piano majors. Piano laboratory; listening laboratory.

Concert Facilities. Concert hall.

Concerts/Musical Activities. There is a complete set of yearly recitals; weekly required assembly that presents a host of outside recital guests; students are required to attend a number of concerts offered in Chicago.

Music Library. 18,898 volumes; 24,260 scores; 68 current periodicals; 1,841 microfiche titles; 1,874 record albums; 2,538 discs. 14 listening stations (cassette, stereo). Special collection of instrumental, band, and orchestral method books.

Special Programs

Featured Programs. The College is founder (1946) and co-host of the MidWest Band and Orchestra Clinic, an annual gathering of some 11,000 music educators from all over the world.

Performance Groups. Performance ensembles, orchestra, band, choral groups.

Affiliated Programs. The College has had a thirty-year working relationship with Illinois Institute of Technology whereby the bookstore, dormitories, and cafeterias are made available to IIT students.

Financial

Costs. Per academic year: Tuition $5,234. Room $3,415.

Financial Aid. 32 scholarships ranging from $200 to $2,500 (average $1,500). Other sources of financial aid include loans, part-time employment, and a College Work-Study program.

Western Illinois University
Department of Music
College of Fine Arts
900 West Adams Street
Macomb
Illinois 61455

Telephone. (309) 298-1544.

Chief Administrator. Dr. James A. Keene, Chair.

Western Illinois University was originally founded in 1899 as a normal school and teacher education has remained an important mission of the institution. The campus, extending over 1,000 acres with 52 buildings, is located in Macomb, 200 miles southwest of Chicago.

The Department of Music offers baccalaureate programs with options in applied music, music therapy, and teacher certification. Certification as a music therapist is available through the national accrediting associations. Students seeking teacher certification are qualified for K-12 Special Certification.

Accreditation. North Central Association of Colleges and Schools; National Association of Schools of Music; National Council for Accreditation of Teacher Education.

Academic Information

Enrollment, Music Majors. (Total University) 10,028.
Music Faculty. 32.
Term System. Semester.
Entrance Requirements. High school graduation with rank in upper two-thirds of graduating class; GED accepted; ACT or SAT required; audition required.
Admission Procedure. Application with supporting documents reviewed on a rolling admissions basis.
Music Degrees Offered. Bachelor of Arts.
Music Degree Requirements. The Bachelor of Arts degree in music is offered with options in applied music, music therapy, and teacher certification. The teacher certification option prepares students to teach in the public schools of Illinois. All music education students must appear before the Student Teaching Committee for evaluation of competencies and skills prior to student teaching. A total of 120 semester hours is required for the baccalaureate degree.
General Program Areas. Applied Music, Music Education, Music Therapy.
Instruments Taught. Bass, Bassoon, Clarinet, Euphonium, Flute, Guitar, Horn, Oboe, Organ, Percussion, Piano, Saxophone, Trombone, Trumpet, Tuba, Viola, Violin, Violoncello, Voice.

Musical Facilities

Concerts/Musical Activities. Students and faculty perform numerous concerts and recitals; Summer Musical Theater.
Music Library. The Music Library in Browne Hall contains books, journals, recordings, and scores.

Special Programs

Performance Groups. University Chorus, University Singers, Madrigal Choir, Swing Choir, Men's Glee Club, Women's Glee Club, Western Community Chorus, University Band, University Marching Band, Symphonic Wind Ensemble, Jazz Band, Clarinet Choir, Brass Ensemble, Woodwind Quintet, Saxophone Ensemble, Flute Ensemble, Recreational Band, University Orchestra, Chamber Orchestra, String Ensemble, Percussion Ensemble, Mixed Ensemble.

Financial

Costs. Per academic year: Tuition in-state resident $1,080, out-of-state $3,240. Fees $415. Room and board $2,255.
Financial Aid. The Financial Aid Office administers a variety of student assistance programs including grants, employment, tuition waivers, and low interest student loans. Scholarship/financial aid application due March 15.

Wheaton College Conservatory of Music
Wheaton
Illinois 60187

Telephone. (312) 260-5098
Chief Administrator. Dr. Harold M. Best, Dean.

The forerunner of Wheaton College was Illinois Institute, a preparatory school established in 1852 on the present campus site by the Wesleyan Methodists. Assets were transferred to a new board of trustees who appointed Jonathan Blanchard to begin a new Christian liberal arts college which opened in 1860 as Wheaton College. The nondenominational Christian college has a student body of over 2,100 undergraduates and 300 graduate students. The 80-acre campus is located in a residential suburb, 25 miles west of Chicago.

The Conservatory of Music functions both as a professional school and as a department of the college. It seeks to bring each of its students to an intellectual understanding of the theoretical, historical, and stylistic aspects of musical practice and to relate each of these to the vast literature of music. Most importantly, the Conservatory seeks to undertake this task in a biblical perspective which describes the making of music as an act of worship, relating all of man's creativity to the Creatorhood of God. Elective courses and private lessons are available to students in other departments of the College, as well as to those of all ages from the community.

Accreditation. North Central Association of Colleges and Schools; National Association of Schools of Music.

Academic Information

Enrollment, Music Majors. Full-time 152.
Music Faculty. Full-time 20, part-time 6.
Term System. Semester. Two 4-week summer sessions.
Entrance Requirements. High school graduation with rank in upper half of graduating class; completion of 16 college-preparatory units with 13 from academic subjects; SAT or ACT required; 3 Achievement Tests; audition required (arrangements made after receipt of application); two professional musician appraisals.
Admission Procedure. Application with supporting documents with $50 nonrefundable fee to Director of Admissions by January 1 for fall entrance.

Music Degrees Offered. Bachelor of Music; Bachelor of Music Education; Bachelor of Arts.

Music Degree Requirements. The Bachelor of Music degree in performance (piano, organ, voice, or orchestral instrument) is designed for those who are contemplating a variety of graduate programs or careers in music. In addition to music performance, courses in theory, music history and literature, conducting and cultural subjects are included to give the student a thorough preparation in complete musicianship. A theory, history-literature, ethnomusicology, or church music emphasis may be undertaken through careful use of free electives. The major in composition stresses advanced work in theory, literature, and composition. The major in history and literature is designed to prepare the student for entrance into graduate programs and careers in musicology and college teaching, in addition to music criticism, broadcasting, publishing, and library/archival science. The major also offers opportunities for interdisciplinary study. The ethnic music theory program provides an exposure to the musics of the world, and extends musical perception and analysis beyond that of Western tradition. Special emphasis is given to the investigation of cultures with oral traditions and to the development of music for Christian worship, including an ethnic hymnody. In addition to its potential for work in music and missions, the program attempts to provide a solid foundation for graduate study in ethnomusicology and opportunity for studies in linguistics, Bible translation, cross-cultural communication and computer related studies in musical analysis. The degree requires 127 to 129 semester hours including general education, conservatory, and other requirements.

The Bachelor of Music Education degree program meets the principal requirements for teaching in elementary and secondary school systems. Minor modifications may be made in education subjects to meet specific state requirements. Instrumental, vocal, or keyboard emphases are available, each preparing for a particular area of work. Certification is granted upon successful completion of all requirements. The degree requires a total of 135 semester hours. The Bachelor of Arts degree is offered by the College Department with emphases in performance, theory, history-literature, conducting, or ethnomusicology. The large number of general electives available enables the student to build a program in a second field as well, such subjects as Christian education, science, or a language.

General Program Areas. Composition, Ethnomusicology, Music Education, Music History, Music Literature, Musicology, Performance.

Instruments Taught. Brass, Guitar, Harp, Harpsichord, Organ, Percussion, Piano, Stringed Instruments, Voice, Woodwinds.

Musical Facilities

Practice Facilities. 35 practice rooms. 2 organs. 2 percussion-equipped practice rooms. 53 pianos (Yamaha, Hamilton); 2 grand pianos reserved for piano majors. Digital electronic music studio.

Concert Facilities. Edman Chapel, seating 2,400; Pierce Chapel, 1,200; Barrows Hall, 500.

Concerts/Musical Activities. Faculty Recital Series; Artists Series; student recitals and performance classes each week; junior and senior recitals presented throughout the school year.

Music Library. 5,928 books; 7,218 scores; 43 current periodicals; 31 microfiche titles; 5,442 recordings. Listening facilities (cassette, stereo, compact disc). Special collection of 1,818 hymnals.

Special Programs

Featured Programs. The West Suburban Choral Union is composed of members of the College and civic communities. Major performances are presented twice a year.

Performance Groups. Concert Choir, Men's Glee Club, Women's Chorale, Symphony Orchestra, Concert Band.

Financial

Costs. Per academic year: Tuition $6,652. Room $1,486. Board $1,466.

Financial Aid. 27 music scholarships ranging from $500 to $2,750 (average $1,430). Other sources of financial aid include state/federal loans, student employment, and a College Work-Study program.

INDIANA

Ball State University
School of Music
College of Fine Arts
Muncie
Indiana 47306

Telephone. (317) 285-5400
Chief Administrator. Dr. Joe B. Buttram, Director.
Ball State University was founded in 1918 and currently features liberal arts, teacher education, and various professional programs. The 690-acre campus has 41 buildings in the city of Muncie located in east-central Indiana.

The School of Music comprises Academic Studies in Music and Applied Studies in Music. The divisions of music education, music history and musicology, and music theory and composition are in Academic Studies in Music; the divisions of keyboard, voice and guitar, symphonic instruments, and ensembles and conducting are in Applied Studies in Music.

Accreditation. North Central Association of Colleges and Schools; National Association of Schools of Music; National Council for Accreditation of Teacher Education.

Academic Information

Enrollment, Music Majors. (Total University) 15,653.
Music Faculty. 47.
Term System. Quarter.
Entrance Requirements. High school graduation in top 50 percent of class.
Admission Procedure. Application with supporting documents and nonrefundable $15 fee must be submitted at least thirty days prior to the beginning of the quarter.
Music Degrees Offered. Bachelor of Music; Master of Music.
Music Degree Requirements. The Bachelor of Music degree is offered with majors in music theory and composition (options in music theory, music composition, music engineering technology), organ, piano, symphonic instruments or guitar, and voice. Teaching programs require additional courses in educational methods. A Master of Music degree program is also available.
General Program Areas. Applied Music, Composition, Music Education, Music Engineering Technology, Music History, Music Theory, Musicology.
Instruments Taught. Brass, Organ, Percussion, Piano, Stringed Instruments, Voice, Woodwinds.

Musical Facilities

Practice Facilities. The Robert Hargreaves Music Building houses the School of Music rehearsal rooms, practice rooms, and studios.
Concert Facilities. John R. Emens College-Community Auditorium, seating 3,605; John J. Pruis Hall, seating 800.
Concerts/Musical Activities. Student/faculty concerts and recitals; visiting artists.
Music Library. The Bracken Library houses more than one million volumes; it serves the academic programs of the School of Music and maintains a collection of music scores and recordings.

Special collections include: performing library for T.U.B.A. (tuba literature); International Horn Society; saxophone collection (original and historical instruments; manuscripts and first editions of saxophone literature; Hewitt A. Waggener Collection of historic instruments.

Special Programs

Performance Groups. Wind Ensemble, Symphonic Band, Marching Show Band, Symphony Orchestra, Jazz Ensemble, University Concert Band, Variety Band, Training Band, Training Orchestra, Concert Choir, Opera Chorus, University Singers, Women's Chorus, Statesmen, University Chorus.

Financial

Costs. Per academic year: Tuition in-state resident $1,662, out-of-state $3,825. Room and Board $2,190.
Financial Aid. Financial aid is available in the form of scholarships, grants, loans, part-time employment, and a College Work-Study program. Financial aid/scholar-

ship application due March 1.

Butler University
Jordan College of Fine Arts
College of Music
4600 Sunset Avenue
Indianapolis
Indiana 46208

Telephone. (317) 283-9231

Chief Administrator. Dr. Louis F. Chenette, Dean.

Butler University opened its doors in November 1855. In at least three ways, the institution was unusual. First, it was coeducational, the first college or university in Indiana, and the third in the nation, to admit women on an equal basis with men. In 1858, the University took another innovative step by appointing women to the faculty. Third, it was the first institution in Indiana to allow its students, with parental consent, to elect subjects suited to their needs, under a new "elective system." The University is a privately-supported institution offering undergraduate and graduate programs through its five colleges. It enrolls approximately 4,000 students.

The 254-acre campus is located in a residential area seven miles from the heart of Indianapolis. The campus physical plant is comprised of 19 buildings valued at over $90 million. On-campus dormitories and fraternity/sorority houses are available.

The Jordan College of Fine Arts has a tradition extending from the year 1895 when the Metropolitan School of Music was founded. The school merged in 1928 with the Indiana College of Music and Fine Arts to become the Arthur Jordan Conservatory of Music. In 1951, after twenty-three years of close affiliation, the Conservatory became a part of Butler University as Jordan College of Music. The change of title to Jordan College of Fine Arts in 1978 reflected the expansion of programs facilitated by the new Eiteljorg Gallery of Ethnographic Art. The goals of the school are to prepare undergraduate students for professional careers in music, radio and television, dance, and theatre; to encourage understanding in the arts, humanities, and sciences; to provide students the skills needed for careers in education; and to offer graduate study leading to increased professional competency.

Accreditation. North Central Association of Colleges and Schools; National Association of Schools of Music.

Academic Information

Enrollment, Music Majors. Full-time 110 men, 131 women; part-time 9 men, 7 women. Foreign students 2.

Music Faculty. Full-time 19, part-time 34.

Term System. Semester. May session, regular summer session, post-summer session.

Entrance Requirements. Undergraduate: Applicant must present satisfactory high school transcript (15 units including 4 in English, 2 mathematics, 2 laboratory science, 2 foreign language, 2 social studies) and SAT scores (ACT accepted); GED accepted; must audition for admission to programs in Jordan College of Fine Arts. Graduate: Baccalaureate degree from an accredited institution in the United States or proof of equivalent training at a foreign institution; audition required for official acceptance as a performance major; composition majors must submit scores and/or tapes of their music; applicants planning to major in music history, music theory, or music education are urged to arrange for a personal interview with the Director of Graduate Music Studies.

Admission Procedure. All credentials for admission (application form with $20 nonrefundable application fee and transcripts of high school or college/university) must be in the office of the Director of Admissions before the student's application can be processed.

Music Degrees Offered. Bachelor of Music; Bachelor of Arts; Bachelor of Science in Arts Administration; Master of Music.

Music Degree Requirements. All baccalaureate degrees require the completion of 136 credits; students are required to participate in vocal and instrumental organizations; last year of major must be earned in residence; recital appearances during each year of principal or major study; all applied music majors are required to present a complete graduation recital; a minimum of one substantial composition is to be performed from memory on all required recitals; proficiency examinations are required for degrees and specific courses.

The Master of Music requires the completion of 30-36 credits and completion of specific course requirements of the program pursued; a thesis is required for 30-hour programs; comprehensive examination.

General Program Areas. Applied Music, Arts Administration, Composition, Conducting, Music Education, Music History, Performance, Theory.

Instruments Taught. Bassoon, Cello, Clarinet, Contrabass, English Horn, Euphonium, Flute, Harp, Harpsichord, Oboe, Organ, Percussion, Piano, Saxophone, Trombone, Trumpet, Tuba, Viola, Violin, Voice.

Musical Facilities

Practice Facilities. Special practice facilities for organists (Allen Electric organ, small pipe organ). 3 practice rooms for percussionists. 35 Steinway upright pianos; 50 piano practice rooms; 6 grand pianos reserved for piano majors. Special electronic studio.

Concert Facilities. The Hilton U. Brown Theatre, located at the south end of the Butler Bowl, is a 4,200-seat facility and the site of University events and summer Starlight Musical programs. Clowes Memorial Hall seats 2,210 and is designed as a multi-purpose hall for the performing arts as well as university programs for other cultural and civic purposes.

Concerts/Musical Activities. Numerous recitals and ensemble groups.

Music Library. The Irwin Library houses approximately 200,000 volumes. The music collection includes over 10,000 volumes, 14,000 scores, and 8,650 recordings.

Special Programs

Performance Groups. Contemporary Ensemble (Chamber Music), Baroque Ensemble, University Choir, University Chorale, University Marching Band, University Symphonic Band, University Symnphony, Jazz Ensemble, Women's Choir, Men's Choir.

Financial

Costs. Per academic year: Tuition full-time $6,340. Room and board $2,720.

Financial Aid. Butler University offers a variety of financial assistance programs based on the demonstration of academic excellence, performance, or financial need. The Ruth L. Elias Scholarship Fund and The Elma Jackson Lemley Memorial Scholarship are two programs specifically available to students of the Jordan College of Fine Arts.

DePauw University
School of Music
Performing Arts Center
600 South Locust Street
Greencastle
Indiana 46135

Telephone. (317) 658-4816

Chief Administrator. John D. Vander Weg, Director.

DePauw University was founded by Indiana Methodists in 1837 as Indiana Asbury University, in honor of Francis Asbury, pioneer Methodist bishop in America. It was to be an ecumenical institution of national stature. Most important, the college was "forever to be conducted on the most liberal principles, accessible to all religious denominations, and designed for the benefit of our citizens in general." DePauw University remains committed to the goals of the founders and has continued its relationship with the United Methodist Church.

The University is located in Greencastle, a residential town of 9,000 citizens, 40 miles west of Indianapolis.

The School of Music, established in 1884, is one of the oldest professional music schools in the United States. In its performance-oriented program of study, the School offers students playing opportunities in band, choir, orchestra, and chamber music and provides private instruction in all orchestral instruments, voice, piano, and organ. The School is located in the Performing Arts Center. Built in 1976, this complex houses classrooms,

practice rooms, faculty offices, rehearsal facilities, and three performance halls.

Accreditation. North Central Association of Colleges and Schools; National Association of Schools of Music; National Council for Accreditation of Teacher Education.

Academic Information

Enrollment, Music Majors. Full-time 40 men, 85 women. 2 foreign students.

Music Faculty. Full-time 16, part-time 17.

Term System. Semester. Academic year August 31 to May 20. January winter term.

Entrance Requirements. High school graduation; SAT or ACT; interview strongly encouraged. Students must perform 2 or 3 contrasting pieces that best demonstrate ability by March 15 of their senior year in high school; auditions should be performed on campus if possible. TOEFL required for foreign students.

Admission Procedure. Application deadline dates November 1, December 1, and March 1 with notification on a rolling basis.

Music Degrees Offered. Bachelor of Music.

Music Degree Requirements. The Bachelor of Music degree is offered with majors in performance, area performance, music/business, music education, or composition. A double major curriculum and the Bachelor of Music/plus curriculum are offered for students wishing to incorporate an academic or preprofessional major within the Bachelor of Music program that provides students an opportunity for dual preparation in graduate study and/or career. A Bachelor of Arts degree with a music major is also offered by the College of Liberal Arts. The degrees require the completion of a total minimum of 31 to 32 course credits. Any student on the campus, regardless of major, may audition for membership in the University concert organizations.

General Program Areas. Applied Music, Choral Music, Church Music, Composition, Music Business, Music Education, Music History, Music Theory, Performance.

Instruments Taught. Bass, Bassoon, Clarinet, Flute, French Horn, Harpsichord, Oboe, Organ, Percussion, Piano, Piano Pedagogy, Trombone, Trumpet, Tuba, Viola, Violin, Violoncello, Voice.

Musical Facilities

Practice Facilities. 53 practice rooms. Special practice facilities for organists and percussionists. 7 organs including 4 contemporary tracker-action instruments built by Charles Fisk and Rudolf von Beckerath, four-manual 80-stop Moeller organ, and the gallery organ of classical design in the Gobin Memorial United Methodist Church. 10 electronic pianos.

Concert Facilities. Kresge Auditorium, seating 1,500; Moore Theatre, 440; Thompson Recital Hall, 220.

Community Facilities. Gobin United Methodist Church used for organ recitals.

Concerts/Musical Activities. Approximately 120 concerts/recitals from September to May; performing arts series sponsors 6 non-university events.

Music Library. 3,275 volumes; 2,700 scores; 31 current periodical subscriptions; 3,300 phonograph recordings; 1,100 audiocassettes. Listening stations (stereo).

Special Programs

Performance Groups. University Band, Orchestra, Choir, The Century Singers, University Festival Choir.

Foreign Programs. Semester programs in Vienna, Austria, and New York City.

Affiliated Programs. DePauw University is a member of the Great Lakes College Association.

Financial

Costs. Per academic year: Tuition $8,800 (includes fees and Winter Term). Room and board $3,300. Private instruction in applied music $200 or $300 (1 lesson a week or 2 lessons a week).

Financial Aid. Financial aid is awarded on the basis of academic merit, financial need, musical ability. 75% of students receive institutional and/or state/federal aid; average award $6,894 per student. Aid application due February 15. Part-time employment and College Work-Study program available.

University of Evansville
Music Department

College of Fine Arts
Evansville
Indiana 47702

Telephone. (812) 479-2754
Chief Administrator. Dr. Edwin V. Lacey, Head.

The University of Evansville, a privately supported institution affiliated with the United Methodist Church, was founded in 1854 as Moores Hill Male and Female Collegiate Institute. It moved to Evansville as Evansville College in 1919, and the present name was adopted in 1967. The 75-acre suburban campus is located in southwestern Indiana.

Music Department curricula are designed to prepare students for a variety of professional careers in music, to give all students opportunities for increasing their enjoyment and knowledge of music, and to contribute to the cultural and artistic life of the community.

Accreditation. North Central Association of Colleges and Schools; National Association of Schools of Music; National Council for Accreditation of Teacher Education.

Academic Information

Enrollment, Music Majors. (Total University) 4,033.
Music Faculty. 17.
Term System. Quarter. Two summer sessions.
Entrance Requirements. High school graduation with 16 units, including 4 English, 2 mathematics, 2 laboratory science, 2 social studies; SAT or ACT; counselor's recommendation; audition required. GRE required for graduate study.

Admission Procedure. Application with supporting documents and nonrefundable $20 fee to Office of Admissions.

Music Degrees Offered. Bachelor of Music; Bachelor of Music Education; Bachelor of Arts; Bachelor of Science; Master of Music; Master of Arts.

Music Degree Requirements. The Bachelor of Music degree is offered with concentration in performance or music therapy. The performance program is designed to permit a concentration in the area of performance for those who are seeking careers in performance-related fields. The music therapy program includes courses in health-related and mental health-related fields. Successful completion of this program leads toward certification as registered music therapists by the National Association for Music Therapy. Successful completion of the Bachelor of Music Education degree program qualifies students for teacher certification in Indiana and most other states. The program includes choral, general, and instrumental emphases and prepares students for teaching all areas of music, K-12. The Bachelor of Arts degree in music is designed for those students who elect to pursue the broadest possible education while maintaining music as the area of interest. The Bachelor of Science degree in music management combines music and business studies for the student interested in working in the music industry. The Bachelor of Science degree in music and associated studies offers a variety of career directions to those interested in studying music without pursuing the traditional performance degree or music education degree. A career program directed toward a position in a music-related field can have music combined with engineering, commercial art, journalism, computing science, theatre, or communication.

A Master of Music degree is also offered with emphases in performance, music education, or church music. A Master of Arts degree ia a flexible, general program for advanced study in music.

General Program Areas. Church Music, Music Business, Music Education, Music History, Music Literature, Music Theory, Music Therapy, Performance.

Instruments Taught. Brass, Guitar, Harp, Harpsichord, Lute, Organ, Percussion, Piano, Stringed Instruments, Voice, Woodwinds.

Musical Facilities

Concerts/Musical Activities. Student/faculty recitals and concerts; visiting artists.

Music Library. The Clifford Memorial Library contains more than 170,000 bound books and journals. The Library supports the academic programs of the College of Fine Arts.

Special Programs

Performance Groups. Symphonic Band, Football Band, Aces Brass, Jazz Ensemble, Saxophone Ensemble, Clarinet Ensemble, Woodwind Ensemble, Flute Ensemble, Jazz Ensemble, University Orchestra, String Ensemble, Brass Ensemble, Percussion Ensemble, University Choir, Singing Aces, Choral-Ayres, Chapel Choir, Opera Workshop, Chamber Chorus, Choral Society.

Financial

Costs. Per academic year: Tuition $6,442. Fees $150. Room $1,188. Board $1,624.

Financial Aid. Financial aid is awarded on the basis of academic merit and financial need. Institutional and state/federal aid plus part-time employment and a College Work-Study program are available. Financial aid/scholarship application due March 1.

Indiana State University Department of Music
Terre Haute
Indiana 47809

Telephone. (812) 237-2771

Chief Administrator. Dr. Robert L. Cowden, Chairman.

Indian State University is the outgrowth of the Indiana State Normal School which was created by an Indiana statute in 1865. Its primary purpose was to be "the preparation of teachers for teaching in the common schools of Indiana." The first bachelor's degrees were awarded in 1908. In 1929, the school was renamed Indiana State Teachers College in recognition of its broadened instructional program. In 1961, the name of the institution was changed to Indiana State College, and in 1965 the present name was adopted upon achieving university status. The main campus adjoins the north side of Terre Haute's downtown business district and covers 91 acres.

The Department of Music has as its primary purpose the preparation of musicians who will perform, teach privately, teach in public or parochial schools, or pursue careers in the music industry. The Department provides instruction in voice and in the various instruments, experiences in choral and instrumental groups, and listening opportunities for all interested students.

Accreditation. North Central Association of Colleges and Schools; National Association of Schools of Music; National Council for Accreditation of Teacher Education.

Academic Information

Enrollment, Music Majors. (Total University) Full-time 7,789, part-time 2,870.

Music Faculty. 34.

Term System. Semester. Summer session of 3 terms.

Entrance Requirements. High school graduation or equivalent; SAT for state residents required, ACT for out-of-state students; audition required (in person or by tape, scales, sight reading, two contrasting solos). GRE required for graduate school. Foreign students must submit TOEFL score and proof of financial stability.

Admission Procedure. Application with $10 nonrefundable fee accepted on a rolling basis.

Music Degrees Offered. Bachelor of Music, Bachelor of Arts, Bachelor of Science.

Music Degree Requirements. The Bachelor of Music degree is offered with concentration in performance. The Bachelor of Arts and the of Bachelor of Science degrees with a major in music in a liberal arts curricula are also available. A concentration in merchandising is offered as part of the liberal arts program. Candidates for the baccalaureate degrees must satisfy all University requirements for graduation, including general education and the minimum of 124 semester hours.

Graduate offerings in the Department of Music are designed to further the development of musical and professional proficiencies. Individual programs are prepared for those intending to pursue more advanced study as well as those expecting to terminate their graduate study at the master's degree level. A student interested in further study after obtaining an Indiana Teacher Certificate may enroll in a Master of Arts or a Master of Science degree program. Specializations in Music History and Literature, Music Theory, or Composition may be pursued through the Master of Arts degree, and the Music Performance specialization through the Master of Science degree. The master's degrees require the completion of 32 semester hours of study.

General Program Areas. Choral Music, Music Education, Music Merchandising, Music Theory, Performance.

Instruments Taught. Bass, Bassoon, Clarinet, Euphonium, Flute, Horn, Oboe, Percussion, Piano, Saxophone, Trombone, Trumpet, Tuba, Viola, Violin, Violoncello, Voice.

Musical Facilities

Practice Facilities. 35 practice rooms. 1 organ (Schlicker two-manual 19 rank). 7 percussion-equipped practice rooms. 28 practice pianos (20 uprights, 8 grands); 8 grand pianos reserved for piano majors. 2 piano laboratories.

Concert Facilities. Tilson Music Hall, seating 1,732; Recital Hall, 170.

Concerts/Musical Activities. Concerts, recitals, visiting artists.

Music Library. 11,800 books; 6,700 scores; 446 microfiche titles; 2,800 recordings. Listening stations (cassette, stereo). Special collections include the Kirk collection of popular music and the early 20th century.

Special Programs

Performance Groups. Marching Band, Sycamore Singers, Women's Glee Club, Basketball Band, Varsity Band, Chorale, University Singers, Brass Ensemble, Madrigal Singers, Percussion Ensemble, Music Theatre, Woodwind Ensemble, University Symphony, Symphonic Band, Jazz Ensemble.

Financial

Costs. Per academic year: Tuition in-state resident $1,542, out-of-state $3,622. Applied music fee $25 per semester hour. Room and board $2,176.

Financial Aid. Scholarships, grants, loans, part-time employment, and a College Work-Study program are available. Scholarship/financial aid application due March 1.

Indiana University - Bloomington
School of Music
Bloomington
Indiana 47405

Telephone. (812) 335-1582

Chief Administrator. Dr. Charles H. Webb, Dean.

Indiana University was created in 1820 by the Indiana General Assembly and now provides a statewide system of public higher education. Statewide, it has grown until it now is ranked the tenth largest university in the United States in terms of full-time enrollment. The 2,000-acre main campus is located in Bloomington (population 50,000) in southern Indiana, 50 miles east of Indianapolis.

The School of Music serves as a professional school preparing music majors for careers in music, and provides opportunities for all students to study music as an essential part of a liberal arts education. Music instruction dates from the year 1893, although it was not until 1910 that a Department of Music was organized with Charles Campbell as Head. In 1947, the appointment of Wilfred C. Bain as Dean marked the beginning of a period of rapid growth and expansion. The School offers majors in performance, area performance, music/business, music education, piano pedagogy, and composition. The School is housed in its own building, the Performing Arts Center, with modern facilities for all facets of music study.

Accreditation. North Central Association of Colleges and Schools; National Association of Schools of Music.

Academic Information

Enrollment, Music Majors. Undergraduate 1,000, graduate 600.

Music Faculty. Full-time 137, part-time 4.

Term System. Semester. 2 summer sessions.

Entrance Requirements. An Indiana resident who graduates from an accredited high school, ranks in the top one-half of high school class, scores above average for a high school senior on the SAT or ACT, and completes application proceedings at the appointed time may expect admission to the University; nonresidents must have SAT combined score of 1000 or minimum ACT score of 24; audition required (students are responsible for arranging the audition or sending a tape). Baccalaureate degree in music required for graduate students.

Admission Procedure. Application with nonrefundable $20 fee due March 20 for fall entrance.

Music Degrees Offered. Bachelor of Music; Bachelor of Music Education; Bachelor of Science; Master of Music; Master of Music Education; Doctor of Music; Artist Diploma.

Music Degree Requirements. The Bachelor of Music degree is offered with concentrations in piano, early instruments, organ, orchestral instruments, woodwind instruments, piano accompanying, composition, music theory, and music history and literature. The Bachelor of Music Education degree is offered with concentrations in choral/general teaching and instrumental teaching. The Bachelor of Science in music and an outside field (business, speech, theatre, journalism, radio and television, audio technology, costume construction technology, string instrument technology, stage technology, languages, mathematics) is offered as well as with a concentration in opera scenic technique. The baccalaureate degrees require a minimum of 130 semester hours of general education, core curriculum, departmental, and university requirements. The Artist Diploma course is a performance curriculum for outstanding students in applied music who show promise of becoming performing concert artists and who do not wish to pursue study leading to an academic degree. The purpose of the program is to provide concentrated study in solo and chamber music literature and it requires the completion of a minimum of 60 semester hours.

The School of Music offers the Master of Music degree in applied music, conducting (choral and instrumental), early music, jazz studies, organ and church music, composition, musicology, music theory, and electronic and computer music. The degree Master of Music Education is also available. The Master of Arts degree with a major in composition, musicology, music theory, or arts administration and the Master of Arts for Teachers with a major in music education are available through the Graduate School. The master's degree programs require the completion of 35 semester hours.

The Graduate Division of the School of Music offers coursework leading to the degree Doctor of Music with a major in music literature and performance (double bass, brass, early music, flute, harp, oboe, organ and church music, percussion, piano, saxophone, viola, violoncello, voice, woodwinds) or with a major in composition, conducting (choral, instrumental, or operatic), or music literature and pedagogy (brass, piano); the degree Doctor of Music Education, and through the Graduate School, the degree Doctor of Philosophy with a major in musicology, music education, or music theory. The doctoral degree may be conferred upon completion of at least 90 hours of advanced study (including the master's degree), at least 30 hours of which must have been completed at Indiana University.

General Program Areas. Accompanying, Applied Music, Chamber Music, Church Music, Composition, Computer Music, Conducting, Early Music, Electronic Music, Ethnomusicology, Jazz Studies, Music Education, Music History, Music Literature, Music Theory, Musicology, Opera Coaching, Opera Scenic Technique, Performance.

Instruments Taught. Baritone, Baroque Instruments, Bass, Bassoon, Carillon, Clarinet, Cornet, English Horn, Euphonium, Flute, French Horn, Guitar, Harp, Oboe, Organ, Percussion, Piano, Piccolo, Saxophone, Trombone, Trumpet, Tuba, Viola, Violin, Violoncello, Voice, Woodwinds.

Musical Facilities

Practice Facilities. 178 practice rooms. Reuter and Schantz studio organs; 11 practice organs and a four-manual recital organ of 79 ranks in the University Auditorium. 15 percussion-equipped practice rooms. 471 practice and teaching pianos (237 uprights, 234 grands); 103 grand pianos reserved for piano majors. Electronic and computer music studio.

Concert Facilities. School of Music Recital Hall, Musical Arts Center.

Concerts/Musical Activities. 1,000 recitals per year; classical and popular concerts in the Auditorium.

Music Library. 75,000 scores; 50,000 books; 12,000 microfiche; 40,000 records; 30,000 tapes. Performing Ensembles Division has 200,000 scores. Listening facilities (cassette, stereo).

Special collections include: opera; early keyboard works; contemporary music; Fritz Busch Archive; taped performances by Hoagy Carmichael; taped rehearsals by Leopold Stokowski; library of Tibor Kozma; Willi Apel collection of photocopies of early keyboard music and violin music; musical instruments collection; Archives of Traditional Music; Saul Starr collection of American sheet music; scores of 20th century broadway musicals. The Latin American Music Center and the Early Music Institute have special collections of music and instruments. There is a Black Music Center. The Lilly Library includes a collection of Handel scores and first editions

of opera scores.

Special Programs

Performance Groups. Marching Hundred Band, Symphonic Band, Concert Band, University Civic Band, Basketball Pep Band, Chamber Singers, Pro Arte Ensemble, Singing Hoosiers, University Chorale, Opera Chorus, University Singers, Women's Chorus, Orchestral Ensembles, University Instrumental Ensembles, Early Music Ensembles, University Choral Ensembles, Contemporary Music Chamber Group, Guitar Ensemble, Jazz Chamber Music Ensemble, Brass Chamber Music, Brass Choir, Piano Ensemble, Schola Cantorum, Electronic Music Ensemble, Harp Ensemble, Chamber Orchestra, String Instrumental Ensemble, Woodwind Ensemble, Flute Ensemble, Percussion Ensemble, Doctoral String Quartet.

Financial

Costs. Per academic year: Tuition undergraduate in-state resident $1,760, out-of-state $4,850; graduate in-state resident $1,835, out-of-state $4,907. Room $1,116. Board $1,310.

Financial Aid. School of Music financial assistance is based on performance skills as demonstrated in an audition. Amounts range from $500 to $3,000 (average award $1,500). Scholarship applications due February 15 for returning students; March 15 for incoming students. Other sources of financial aid include state/federal aid, part-time employment, and a College Work-Study program.

Commentary

Indiana University's School of Music, one of the most important music institutions in the world, offers unique opportunities outside the traditional conservatory curriculum. Among the faculty are many artists-scholars with international reputations, and a wide range of program options is available. The Bachelor's degree in early instruments includes opportunities to study lute and viola da gamba, among many others. Jazz studies, opera scene technique (for which a music background is not a prerequisite), and piano accompanying are other innovative bachelor majors. Associate of Science programs are offered in audio technology, costume-construction technology, stagecraft technology, and string-instrument technology.

All the traditional music fields are available on the graduate level, as well as degrees in music and library science, arts administration, music theater scenic techniques, and stage direction for opera.

Ethnomusicology studies take place in the University's Folklore Institute, which is not part of the School of Music. The Archives of Traditional Music, connected with the Folklore Institute, have particularly strong collections of North and South American Indian music and African music. The Hoagy Carmichael Collection is a recent acquisition. Instrument collections include hundreds of non-Western instruments from American Indian tribes, Africa, Asia, and the Pacific.

University of Notre Dame
Department of Music
College of Arts and Letters
Notre Dame
Indiana 46556

Telephone. (219) 239-6211
Chief Administrator. Dr. Calvin M. Bower, Chairman.
The University of Notre Dame operates under the auspices of the Roman Catholic Church, enrolling over 9,500 students each year. The campus is located 3 miles north of the community of South Bend.

The Department of Music has two objectives: (1) to provide for all students, regardless of their major, knowledge and training in music through introductory, historical, and theoretical courses; through participation in large and small ensembles; and through applied instrumental or vocal study; and (2) to provide intensive curriculum and training for the student who chooses music as a major area of concentration.

Accreditation. North Central Association of Colleges and Schools; National Association of Schools of Music.

Academic Information

Enrollment, Music Majors. (Total University) 9,686.
Music Faculty. 15.
Term System. Semester.
Entrance Requirements. High school graduation in top 10 percent of graduation class with an A- average and 16 units including 4 English, 3 mathematics, 1 laboratory science, 2 foreign language, 1 social studies; SAT required. GRE required for graduate study.
Admission Procedure. Application with supporting documents by March 1 for Fall semester.
Music Degrees Offered. Bachelor of Arts; Master of Music; Master of Arts.
Music Degree Requirements. The Bachelor of Arts degree in music is built around three years of music theory, two years of musicianship, and one year of music history. The major program therefore must be begun by at least the sophomore year and is ideally begun in the freshman year. The study of applied music, ensembles, and electives completes the various programs leading to the major in music. In addition to the baccalaureate programs leading to degrees appropriate for further professional study in the field, the Department offers a program in music as a second major, a program in which the student maintains a primary major in a department other than music, but studies the basic foundations of the discipline of music.

Within the Master of Music degree program the student may pursue programs in music and liturgy, or performance and literature. Within the Master of Arts degree program the student may specialize in historical musicology, music theory, or liturgical music.
General Program Areas. Liturgical Music, Music History, Music Theory, Musicology, Performance.
Instruments Taught. Brass, Guitar, Organ, Percussion, Piano, Violin, Violoncello, Voice, Woodwinds.

Musical Facilities

Concert Facilities. Crowley Hall of Music.
Concerts/Musical Activities. Student/faculty recitals and concerts; visiting artists.
Music Library. The University Library contains more than 1.5 million volumes and supports the academic programs of the College of Arts and Letters.

Special Programs

Performance Groups. Varsity Marching Band, Orchestra, Glee Club, Sacred Heart Church Chapel Choir, Concert Wind Ensemble, Collegium Musicum, Jazz Ensemble, Chorale, Brass Ensemble, Woodwind Ensemble.

Financial

Costs. Per academic year: Tuition $7,985. Fees $140. Room and board $2,530.
Financial Aid. Financial aid is available in the form of scholarships, grants, loans, part-time employment, and a College Work-Study program. Financial aid/scholarship application due March 1.

Valparaiso University
Department of Music
Valparaiso
Indiana 46383

Telephone. (219) 464-5454
Chief Administrator. Robert Roland Bergt, Chair.
Valparaiso University, a private institution affiliated with the Lutheran Church-Missouri Synod, was founded in 1859 as one of the first coeducational institutions. The 310-acre campus has 70 buildings and is located in Valparaiso, a community 50 miles southeast of Chicago.

The Department of Music offers undergraduate and graduate programs leading to careers in teaching, performance, composition, church music, music merchandising, and music administration.
Accreditation. North Central Association of Colleges and Schools; National Association of Schools of Music.

Academic Information

Enrollment, Music Majors. (Total University) 3,603.
Music Faculty. 11.
Term System. Semester.
Entrance Requirements. High school graduation; recommend 4 units English, 3 mathematics, 3 laboratory

science, 2 or 3 social studies; SAT required; entrance test in musicianship and applied music.

Admission Procedure. Application with supporting documents and nonrefundable $20 fee to Director of Admissions.

Music Degrees Offered. Bachelor of Music; Bachelor of Music Education; Bachelor of Arts; Master of Music; Master of Arts.

Music Degree Requirements. The Bachelor of Music degree requires the completion of 128 credits in a prescribed curriculum. The Bachelor of Music Education degree requires the completion of 138 credits including general education, core curriculum, and other requirements in the teacher licensing areas of choral, general, and instrumental. The Bachelor of Arts degree program is designed so that the student may earn a basic major in music and a major or minor in other disciplines. A Bachelor of Arts program in music enterprises is a four-year interdisciplinary program in music and business.

The Master of Music degree program is intended for performers, music teachers in the public and parochial schools, studio teachers, church musicians, and others who wish to continue their professional studies at the graduate level. A Master of Arts degree in liberal studies with concentration in music is also offered.

General Program Areas. Church Music, Composition, Electronic Music, Music Business, Music Education, Music History, Music Theory, Performance.

Instruments Taught. Baritone, Bass, Bassoon, Clarinet, Flute, French Horn, Guitar, Harp, Harpsichord, Oboe, Organ, Percussion, Piano, Saxophone, Trombone, Trumpet, Tuba, Viola, Violin, Violoncello, Voice.

Musical Facilities

Concert Facilities. The Chapel of the Resurrection is frequently the site for concerts and recitals.

Concerts/Musical Activities. Visiting artists and lecturers are brought to the campus from time to time to conduct seminars and workshops in various fields of music. The Church Music Seminar, instrumental and vocal clinics, master classes by guest artists, and other such events are also scheduled.

Music Library. Recordings are available in the Music Record Library, a collection of 4,300 recordings and tapes.

Special Programs

Performance Groups. Chapel Choir, Concert Choir, Kantorei, Treble Choir, Show Review, Choral Society, Symphonic Band, Jazz Band, Marching Crusaders Band, University Band, University Symphony Orchestra, Opera Workshop, Collegium Musicum, Brass Ensemble, Percussion Ensemble, Jazz Combo.

Financial

Costs. Per academic year: Tuition $6,380. Fees $200. Room $1,300. Board $1,130.

Financial Aid. Financial aid is awarded on the basis of academic merit and financial need. Institutional and state/federal aid available through scholarships, grants, loans, and part-time employment. Financial aid/scholarship application due March 1.

IOWA

Drake University
Department of Music
College of Fine Arts
26th and University Avenue
Des Moines
Iowa 50311

Telephone. (515) 271-3879
Chief Administrator. Dr. Marion A. Hall, Chairperson.

Drake University is an independent, comprehensive university founded in 1881. The 70-acre campus is located in Des Moines, the state capital of Iowa.

The Department of Music offers undergraduate programs for students preparing for careers in professional performance or teaching as well as programs for liberal arts students. Advanced degrees in music are offered through the School of Graduate Studies.

Accreditation. North Central Association of Colleges and Schools; National Association of Schools of Music; National Council for Accreditation of Teacher Education.

Academic Information

Enrollment, Music Majors. (Total University) 4,459.
Music Faculty. 21.
Term System. Semester. 2 summer sessions.
Entrance Requirements. High school graduation or equivalent; rank in upper half of high school class; completion of 15 units; SAT or ACT required; audition required.
Admission Procedure. Application with supporting documents and $25 nonrefundable fee to Office of Admissions.
Music Degrees Offered. Bachelor of Music; Bachelor of Arts; Bachelor of Music Education; Master of Music; Master of Music Education.
Music Degree Requirements. The Bachelor of Music degree is offered with majors in applied music, church music, piano pedagogy, composition, and with a business concentration in marketing/retailing. The Bachelor of Arts degree with a major in music is designed for those students wishing to balance music training with liberal arts and sciences and other academic courses. The degree Bachelor of Music Education is also available.

The Master of Music degree may be pursued with majors in applied music or composition. The Master of Music Education degree is also offered.

General Program Areas. Applied Music, Church Music, Composition, Music Education, Music Merchandising, Piano Pedagogy.

Instruments Taught. Baritone, Bass, Bassoon, Clarinet, Flute, French Horn, Harpsichord, Oboe, Organ, Percussion, Piano, Saxophone, Trombone, Trumpet, Tuba, Viola, Violin, Violoncello, Voice.

Musical Facilities

Practice Facilities. The Henry G. Harmon Fine Arts Center includes 58 practice rooms; a variety of band and orchestral instruments for the use of students in instrumental methods; Holtkamp and Reuter organs; two large teaching studios for organ; band, orchestra, and choral library rooms; uniform storage area; instrumental ensemble rehearsal rooms; choral classrooms; music education classroom; 26 applied teaching studios.

Concert Facilities. Hall of Performing Arts, seating 600; Monroe Recital Hall; Studio Theatre.

Concerts/Musical Activities. Visiting artists of national and international reputation are invited to the campus each year to give workshops and discuss their work with students and faculty; concerts and recitals by students and faculty.

Music Library. The College of Fine Arts serves the Department of Music. Special collections include over 3,000 sound recordings in the Dixon Media Resource Center where there are individual and group listening-viewing stations.

Special Programs

Performance Groups. Drake Choir, University-Community Chorus, Opera Theatre, University Band, Wind Ensemble, Concert Band, Symphonic Wind Ensemble, Marching Band, Drake Jazz Lab Bands, Drake Symphony Orchestra, String Ensemble, Percussion Ensemble, Chamber Chorale, Drake Fine Arts Trio

Financial

Costs. Per academic year: Tuition $7,130. Room and board $2,970.

Financial Aid. Scholarships, grants, loans, and part-time employment are available. Financial aid/scholarship application due March 1.

University of Iowa
School of Music
Iowa City
Iowa 52242

Telephone. (319) 353-3445
Chief Administrator. Marilyn Somville, Director.

The University of Iowa was founded in 1847 and is the state's oldest institution of higher education. It was the country's first state university to admit women and men on an equal basis, which it did from its opening in 1855. The University consists of ten colleges and offers liberal arts programs and a broad spectrum of graduate and professional studies. The 1,300-acre campus is located in Iowa City, 30 miles south of Cedar Rapids.

The School of Music offers all qualified students an opportunity to study music toward either professional or avocational goals. Programs are offered in all areas of specialization. Approximately 50 percent of the school's undergraduate students earn certification to teach. Most of those who earn certification do enter teaching, where there are also opportunities to pursue interests in performing, composing, and other related activities. Students in the School of Music are actively and directly involved in all of the aspects of music that will contribute effectively to their musical maturation. The present home of the School of Music opened in 1971-72.

Accreditation. North Central Association of Colleges and Schools; National Association of Schools of Music.

Academic Information

Enrollment, Music Majors. 600.
Music Faculty. Full-time 52, adjunct 3.
Term System. Semester. One summer session.
Entrance Requirements. High school graduation in the upper half of graduating class or have a 24 ACT composite score. All music enrollments at Iowa require School of Music approval as well as fulfillment of the general requirements for undergraduate admission. The School has no specific requirement of previous instruction or performance experience; however, the entering student should have sufficient background, ability, and interest to anticipate that with normal progress the student will be able to perform satisfactorily the required senior recital. All prospective students are expected to audition, either in person or by tape recording, in ad-

vance of registration.

Admission Procedure. Submit application with supporting documents and nonrefundable $10 fee to Office of Admissions. Contact the School of Music for scheduling audition.

Music Degrees Offered. Bachelor of Music; Bachelor of Arts; Master of Arts; Master of Fine Arts; Doctor of Musical Arts; Doctor of Philosophy.

Music Degree Requirements. The Bachelor of Music and the Bachelor of Arts degrees are offered by the School. Curricula are the same for both, except that candidates for the B.M. degree may, and candidates for the B.A. may not, count more than 50 semester hours of coursework in music toward the 124 semester hours required for graduation; and the foreign language requirement for the B.M. is one year of college-level study, while the requirement for the B.A. is two years. Areas of concentration offered in both programs are performance, music education, music therapy, composition/theory, and music history.

A wide range of graduate programs is available: (1) Master of Arts in performance (all standard instruments, composition, voice, and conducting), music theory, composition, musicology, and music education; (2) Master of Fine Arts is available for superior ability in the areas of composition, instrumental or vocal performance, conducting, and opera theatre directing; (3) Doctor of Musical Arts in performance and conducting; (4) Doctor of Philosophy in composition, musicology, music education, music theory, and music literature.

General Program Areas. Applied Music, Composition, Conducting, Jazz Studies, Music Education, Music History, Music Literature, Music Theory, Music Therapy, Musicology, Opera, Performance, Sacred Music.

Instruments Taught. Bass, Bassoon, Clarinet, Euphonium, Flute, Harp, Horn, Oboe, Organ, Percussion, Piano, Saxophone, Trombone, Trumpet, Tuba, Viola, Violin, Violoncello, Voice.

Musical Facilities

Practice Facilities. 55 teaching studios; 73 practice rooms. 2 electronic music laboratories; ear-training and listening facilities with 50 listening stations; recording studio. Cassavant tracker organ in Clapp Recital Hall.

Concert Facilities. Hancher Auditorium, seating 2,684; Clapp Recital Hall, seating 720; Harper Hall, 200.

Concerts/Musical Activities. In a given year, faculty artists and the many student ensembles of the school present about 100 major concerts, plus an additional 270 to 300 student vocal and instrumental recitals. Faculty ensembles in residence include the Stradivari String Quartet, the Iowa Woodwind Quintet, the Iowa Brass Quintet, the Percussion Quartet, the Vocal Quartet, and the Baroque Players.

Music Library. 50,000 volumes of music and books; 2,100 reels of microfilm; 300 microcard titles; 175 periodicals; 5,000 recordings. 24 study carrels. Special collections include: Goldman Band Library and memorabilia, one of the world's most famous collections of band music; 18th and 19th century keyboard treatises, keyboard works, and chamber music; Anthony L. Scarmolin compositions; Edwin Ford Piper Collection of ballads and folk songs.

Special Programs

Featured Programs. The Center for New Music provides an environment for innovative composition and a vehicle for the performance of new works. Its repertoire includes the works of little-known young composers as well as compositions by recognized modern composers.

Performance Groups. Symphony Band, Hawkeye Marching Band, Jazz Band, Wind Ensemble, Concert Band, University Symphony, Chamber Orchestra, Sinfonietta, Symphonic Choir, University Choir, Kantorei, Camerata Singers, Opera Theater, Old Gold Singers, Percussion Ensemble, Collegium Musicum.

Financial

Costs. Per academic year: Tuition undergraduate in-state resident $1,390, out-of-state $4,080; graduate in-state resident $1,646, out-of-state $4,256. Applied music fee $160 (1-hour lesson per week), $300 (2-hour lesson per week). Room $1,117. Board $1,127.

Financial Aid. In addition to the assistance available to University students through the Office of Student Financial Aid, music activity scholarships are available. These scholarship awards range from applied music fees to full resident tuition and are available to music majors on the basis of ability (demonstrated by audition), academic standing, and need.

Commentary

The University's Center for New Music, which for decades has sponsored performances and recordings of twentieth century music, has earned a distinguished reputation for its innovative activities.

Iowa State University
Department of Music
Music Hall
Ames
Iowa 50011

Telephone. (515) 294-5364

Chief Administrator. Dr. Arthur G. Swift, Department Head.

Iowa State University is a land-grant institution that opened its doors in 1868. The institution was chartered as the Iowa Agricultural College. The expansion of the college's programs was recognized with the adoption in 1896 of the more inclusive name, Iowa State College of Agriculture and Mechanic Arts. Since 1959 the formal name of the institution has been Iowa State University of Science and Technology. The University is situated on a campus of 1,000 acres in Ames, 30 miles north of Des Moines.

Music has been an important part of the Iowa State University curriculum since its establishment. The first catalogue included instruction in music as an elective for the general student body. Although this service remains an important element today (approximately one-third of the students participate in music activities), the Department's mission since 1967 has been to provide strong baccalaureate programs. The Department of Music's program is twofold: (1) to provide opportunities for any student to develop an understanding and appreciation of music as part of a liberal education through courses in music literature, theory, and areas of performance and (2) to offer a four-year course of professional studies to students who wish to prepare for careers in teaching, performance, composition, and graduate studies in music or related areas.

Accreditation. North Central Association of Colleges and Schools; National Association of Schools of Music; National Council for Accreditation of Teacher Education.

Academic Information

Enrollment, Music Majors. Full-time 32 men, 44 women.

Music Faculty. Full-time 26, part-time 1.

Term System. Semester. 8-week summer session from early June to late July. Academic year from late August to mid-May.

Entrance Requirements. High school graduation or equivalent with rank in upper half of high school class; minimum ACT score of 24; theory placement test; performance audition.

Admission Procedure. Submit application with supporting documents and $10 nonrefundable fee to Admissions Office.

Music Degrees Offered. Bachelor of Music; Bachelor of Arts.

Music Degree Requirements. The Bachelor of Music degree requires the completion of 124.5 to 139.5 semester credits including general education, music core curriculum, and the major concentration. Major areas of concentration include history and literature, performance (organ, piano, string instruments, theory and composition, voice, wind or percussion instruments). Music education certification options are available in vocal 7-12, vocal K-12, instrumental K-12, instrumental K-6, vocal K-6.

General Program Areas. Composition, Music Education, Music History, Performance.

Instruments Taught. Bass, Bassoon, Carillon, Clarinet, Cornet, Euphonium, Flute, French Horn, Guitar, Harpsichord, Oboe, Organ, Percussion, Piano, Saxophone, Trombone, Trumpet, Tuba, Viola, Violin, Violoncello, Voice.

Musical Facilities

Practice Facilities. 29 practice rooms plus 2 small ensemble rooms, carillon rehearsal room, 3 organ practice rooms, harpsichord room, percussion-equipped room. Concert organ by John Brombaugh; 2 practice organs by Lynn Dobson, 1 by Wolfe, and 1 portafif by Noack. 26 electronic pianos in piano laboratory (24 consoles and 2 master consoles), 6 Steinway Grands (2 in small ensemble rooms), 22 uprights, and 4 additional Steinway grands; 4 grand pianos reserved for piano majors. Organ studio; harpsichord studio; percussion studio; electronic piano laboratory; opera studio; electronic music studio; carillon studio.

Concert Facilities. C.Y. Stephens Auditorium, seating 2,700; Fisher Theatre, 450; Great Hall-Memorial Union, 800; McKay Auditorium, 400; Music Hall Recital Hall, 350; Benton Auditorium, 400.

Community Facilities. Collegiate Methodist Church, Collegiate Presbyterian Church, and Octagon.

Concerts/Musical Activities. Faculty and student solo recitals; chamber music concerts; combined concerts/recitals, guest recitals. 150 events per year.

Music Library. Most music materials in Parks Library. 500 volumes; 5,000 musical scores; 60 periodical subscriptions; 5,000 recordings; 50 audiocassettes. 16 listening stations. Library has a first edition score of Haydn's *Te Deum* and an autographed edition of a Gretchaninov piano work.

Special Programs

Featured Programs. Extension and outreach programs include the Cyclone Honor Band, AIOFA Festival Youth Symphony, and Honor Choir.

Performance Groups. Iowa State Singers, Chamber Singers, Symphony Orchestra, Cardinal Keynote Singers, Men's Glee Club, Marching Band, Jazz Ensemble, Concert Band, Wind Ensemble, Chamber Groups; faculty ensembles include the Ames Quartet (piano), Musica Antiqua (Renaissance/Baroque consort), Dickson Schilling Duo (oboe and harpsichord).

Financial

Costs. Per academic year: Tuition in-state resident $1,-304, out-of-state $3,830. Applied music fee $180 (1-hour lesson), $120 (1/2-hour lesson). Room $900 to $1,200. Board $1,050. Off-campus housing $200 to $600 per month.

Financial Aid. Approximately 50 music majors receive financial aid (average award $600). Financial aid is awarded on the basis of financial need and musical ability. Scholarship/financial aid applications due January 1 of year student intends to enroll. Sources of financial aid include institutional and state/federal aid, part-time employment, and a College Work-Study program.

University of Northern Iowa
School of Music
College and West 23rd Streets
Cedar Falls
Iowa 50614

Telephone. (319) 273-2024

Chief Administrator. Dr. Ronald D. Ross, Director.

The University of Northern Iowa was established as the Iowa State Normal School in 1876 by enactment of the Iowa General Assembly. It was renamed the Iowa State Teachers College in 1909 and then the State College of Iowa in 1961. The current name was adopted in 1967. The academic structure of the University includes four instructional Colleges, the School of Business, and the Graduate College. The campus is comprised of 44 buildings in Cedar Falls, an industrial community on the Cedar River in northeast Iowa.

The School of Music provides undergraduate and graduate training of musicians as prospective teachers and performers. As a former "Teachers College," music teacher training has always been a staple offering in the curriculum.

Accreditation. North Central Association of Colleges and Schools; National Association of Schools of Music; National Council for Accreditation of Teacher Education.

Academic Information

Enrollment, Music Majors. Undergraduate full-time 62 men, 91 women; part-time 6 men, 6 women; graduate 30. 4 foreign students.

Music Faculty. Full-time 33, part-time 3.

Term System. Semester. Two 4-week summer sessions from early June to late July. Academic year from late August to mid-May.

Entrance Requirements. High school graduation with rank in upper half of high school graduating class; SAT or ACT; complete core of course requirements to include 4 years English, 3 mathematics, 3 social science, 2 science, 2 electives; audition required. TOEFL required for foreign students; admission of international students is monitored by the Foreign Student Adviser who certifies the students' credentials necessary for entry to the United States. Baccalaureate degree in music required for graduate school.

Admission Procedure. Submit application with supporting documents and nonrefundable $10 fee to Office of Admissions.

Music Degrees Offered. Bachelor of Music; Bachelor of Fine Arts; Bachelor of Arts; Master of Music; Master of Arts.

Music Degree Requirements. Majors in the Bachelor of Music degree program have the choice of an educational major or two professional majors; each requires a total of 130 semester hours. The music education major carries certification to teach music in grades K-12. The performance major with emphases in voice, piano, organ, and band-orchestral instruments and the theory-composition major are professional programs designed to prepare students for careers as artist-performers or composers, or for entrance to graduate schools where further excellence in a performance area might be pursued. The Bachelor of Fine Arts degree is offered as an interdisciplinary major in music theatre combining courses from the School of Music and Speech-Theatre of the Department of Communication and Theatre Arts. A minimum total of 130 semester hours is required for the degree. The Bachelor of Arts degree is offered with a major in music and requires the completion of 124 semester hours. This degree is a liberal arts program for the student interested in combining the discipline of music training with the breadth offered by a liberal arts curriculum. Music majors in all baccalaureate programs must choose an area of applied music for specialization and must meet proficiency standards of the School of Music.

The Master of Music degree is offered with majors in composition, conducting, music history, and performance. The degree requires the completion of a minimum of 30 semester hours (opera emphasis requires 32 semester hours). The Master of Arts degree with majors in music or music education are also available on either a thesis or non-thesis basis.

General Program Areas. Applied Music, Audio Recording Technology, Composition, Conducting, Jazz Studies, Music Education, Music History, Music Literature, Music Theory, Musical Theater, Performance.

Instruments Taught. Bass, Bassoon, Clarinet, Cornet, Euphonium, Flute, French Horn, Guitar, Harp, Harpsichord, Oboe, Organ, Percussion, Piano, Saxophone, Trumpet, Tuba, Viola, Violin, Violoncello, Voice.

Musical Facilities

Practice Facilities. 34 practice rooms. 2 organs (Noehren, Casavant). Special practice facilities for percussionists. 29 pianos (3 Steinway grands; uprights include 9 Story & Clark, 5 Baldwin, 1 Gulbransen, 4 Cable, 1 Yamaha, 2 Wurlitzer, 2 Everett, 2 Hamilton); 3 grand pianos reserved for piano majors. Recording studio.

Concert Facilities. Russell Hall Auditorium, seating 600; UNI Auditorium, 1,000.

Concerts/Musical Activities. 80 student recitals per year; 20 faculty recitals per year.

Music Library. Main collection in UNI Library; partial collection in Music Hall. 22,731 volumes; 60 periodical subscriptions; 499 microforms; 8,950 phonograph recordings; 733 audiocassettes; 71 compact discs. 34 listening stations (stereo). Annex in Russell Hall has record collection and listening stations. Special collections include: ethnomusicological sound recording collection; musical instrument collection; 70 books; 25 rare books. Cedar Falls and Waterloo Public Libraries also have

resources for music students.

Special Programs

Performance Groups. Concert Chorale, University Chorus, Varsity Men's Glee Club, Women's Chorus, Ensemble, Band, Jazz Band, Orchestra.

Financial

Costs. Per academic year: Tuition in-state undergraduate $1,324, out-of-state $3,194; graduate in-state undergraduate $1,476, out-of-state $3,542. Room $878. Board $1,072. Off-campus housing $175 to $250 per month.

Financial Aid. Financial aid is awarded on the basis of academic merit, financial need, and musical ability. Scholarship/financial aid applications due March 1. Institutional, state/federal aid, part-time employment, and a College Work-Study program are available.

KANSAS

Emporia State University
Division of Music
1200 Commercial Street
Emporia
Kansas 66801

Telephone. (316) 343-1200

Chief Administrator. Dr. Kenneth W. Hart, Division Chair.

Founded in 1863 as Kansas Normal School, the institution has since been known as Kansas State Teachers College, Emporia Kansas State College, and since 1977 as Emporia State University. It is one of seven institutions under the Kansas Board of Regents System. The 200-acre campus is located in Emporia, close to the geographical center of the United States.

In general, the music division curriculum contributes to the academic environment by giving all students the opportunity to study music according to their interests and their needs; they may acquaint themselves with music as appreciative listeners, as inquisitive scholars, or as performing participants. A varied selection of courses provides for those who wish to major or minor in music along with offerings that furnish musical experiences for any student in the university community. Specifically, state-approved degree programs are offered that prepare teachers of music for the elementary and secondary schools of Kansas. Also, they train performers, arrangers, and composers for professional careers. Further, music programs are offered that will qualify and enable students to function as music merchants, church organists, choirmasters, or private teachers.

Accreditation. North Central Association of Colleges and Schools; National Association of Schools of Music; National Council for Accreditation of Teacher Education.

Academic Information

Enrollment, Music Majors. (Total University) 2,438 men, 2,457 women.

Music Faculty. Full-time 15, part-time 6.

Term System. Semester. 9-week summer session from early June to early August. Academic year from mid-August to mid-May.

Entrance Requirements. Accredited high school graduation or GED; open enrollment policy for Kansas residents; ACT required. GRE required for graduate studies.

Admission Procedure. Application with supporting documents to Office of Admissions accepted on a rolling basis.

Music Degrees Offered. Bachelor of Music; Bachelor of Music Education; Bachelor of Arts; Bachelor of Science; Master of Music.

Music Degree Requirements. The Bachelor of Music is offered with concentrations in performance and composition and is designed for the student interested in a career as a professional musician or as an independent teacher of music. The Bachelor of Music Education degree is organized for students who propose to teach music in the elementary and the secondary schools. Satisfactory completion of the requirements for this degree entitles the graduate to a three-year certificate, issued by the Kansas State Department of Public Instruction, to teach all phases of music at any level. The Bachelor of Arts degree is for the musician who wants an emphasis on the liberal arts. The Bachelor of Science degree with a major in music merchandising is designed to prepare students for careers in music retailing. This degree is also offered in elementary education with a music concentration. All baccalaureate degrees require the completion of 124 semester hours including general education, core curriculum, the major concentration, and other specified courses.

The Master of Music degree is offered with thesis or non-thesis options. It requires the completion of 30 hours (thesis) or 36 hours (non-thesis) of study.

General Program Areas. Composition, Music Education, Music Merchandising, Musicology, Performance.

Instruments Taught. Bass, Bassoon, Clarinet, English Horn, Euphonium, Flute, Guitar, Harp, Harpsichord, Horn, Oboe, Organ, Percussion, Piano, Saxophone,

Trombone, Trumpet, Tuba, Viola, Violin, Violoncello, Voice.

Musical Facilities

Practice Facilities. 26 practice rooms. 2 organs (Reuter). 26 pianos (20 uprights, 6 grands); 6 grand pianos reserved for piano majors. Electronic music studio.

Concert Facilities. Beach Music Hall, seating 370; Albert Taylor Hall, 1,360; Bruder Theatre, 760; Social Lecture Hall, 900.

Community Facilities. White Auditorium, seating 2,-500.

Concerts/Musical Activities. Solo and ensemble performances (140 per year).

Music Library. Music materials are housed in the William Allen White Library. Special collection of collegium musicum instruments.

Special Programs

Performance Groups. College Orchestra, Opera Workshop, Marching Band, Symphonic Band, Symphonic Choir, Men's Chorale, Treble Clef, Jazz Workshops, A Capella Choir, Madrigals, Jazz Chamber Music, Gospel Choir, Brass Quintet, Woodwind Quintet.

Financial

Costs. Per academic year: Tuition in-state resident $1,-123, out-of-state $2,373. Room $940. Board $1,110.

Financial Aid. Financial aid is awarded on the basis of academic merit, financial need, musical ability. Average award $500. Sources of financial aid include scholarships, state/federal loans, part-time employment, and a College Work-Study program.

Fort Hays State University
Department of Music
600 Park Street
Hays
Kansas 67601

Telephone. (913) 628-4226

Chief Administrator. Dr. John E. Huber, Chairman.

Fort Hays State University was established in 1902 on the abandoned Fort Hays Military Reservation. The campus is located adjacent to and southwest of the Hays city limits.

The Department of Music provides a full range of degree programs at the undergraduate level and graduate programs leading the the master's degree. The Department also offers study opportunities for non-music majors and serves as a center of musical activity for the community.

Accreditation. North Central Association of Colleges and Schools; National Association of Schools of Music; National Council for Accreditation of Teacher Educa-

tion.

Academic Information

Enrollment, Music Majors. (Total University) 4,258.
Music Faculty. 15.
Term System. Semester.
Entrance Requirements. High school graduation or equivalent; open enrollment policy; ACT or SAT acceptable.

Admission Procedure. Application with supporting documents reviewed on a rolling admissions basis.

Music Degrees Offered. Bachelor of Music; Bachelor of Arts; Master of Music.

Music Degree Requirements. The Bachelor of Music degree is offered with concentrations in music education, music theory and composition, and performance.

Graduate study leading to the Master of Music degree is offered with concentrations in music education, music history and literature, music theory and composition, and performance in voice, piano, organ, strings, wind instruments, and percussion.

General Program Areas. Composition, Music Education, Music Literature, Music Theory, Performance.

Instruments Taught. Brass, Guitar, Percussion, Piano, Stringed Instruments, Voice, Woodwinds.

Musical Facilities

Practice Facilities. Malloy Hall houses the Department of Music.

Concert Facilities. Malloy Auditorium.

Concerts/Musical Activities. Student and faculty recitals and concerts; visiting artists.

Music Library. Forsyth Library serves the academic programs of the Department of Music; Media Center.

Special Programs

Performance Groups. Men's Glee Club, Women's Glee Club, Collegium Chorale, Concert Choir, Marching Band, Symphonic Band, Hays Symphony, String Orchestra, Brass Choir, Clarinet Choir, Jazz Ensemble, Fort Hays Singers, Recorder Ensemble, String Ensemble, Brass Ensemble, Woodwind Ensemble, Percussion Ensemble.

Financial

Costs. Per academic year: Tuition in-state resident $1,-193; out-of-state $2,410. Room $1,250. Board $648.

Financial Aid. Financial aid is awarded on the basis of academic merit and financial need. Scholarships, grants, loans, and part-time employment are available. Financial aid/scholarship application due March 15.

University of Kansas
School of Fine Arts
Department of Music
Lawrence
Kansas 66045

Telephone. (913) 864-3436

Chief Administrator. Dr. Stanley N. Shumway, Chairman.

The University of Kansas was established in 1864 and is the largest of the Regents institutions in Kansas. The 1,000-acre main campus has 87 major buildings. Since 1981, the University has completed construction and renovation projects worth $38 million on the Lawrence campus. The faculty includes 1,900 full-time members and the student enrollment approaches 25,000. Students come from every state in the nation and from nearly 100 foreign countries. Lawrence (population 55,000) is on the banks of the Kansas River and is forty minutes by expressway from Kansas City.

The School of Fine Arts offers courses which will help students to acquaint themselves with the fine arts, either as members of the public or as trained performers. In cooperation with the School of Education, it trains teachers of music and art in the elementary and secondary public schools and institutions of higher education. The Department of Music seeks to provide sound professional training in music in a comprehensive university environment, featuring music performance and studies in music history and theory.

Accreditation. North Central Association of Colleges and Schools; National Association of Schools of Music; National Association for Music Therapy; National Council for Accreditation of Teacher Education.

Academic Information

Enrollment, Music Majors. 400.

Music Faculty. 54.

Term System. Semester. One summer session.

Entrance Requirements. Accredited Kansas high school graduation; limited number of well-qualified graduates of out-of-state high schools who rank in the upper 50% of their high school class may admitted; GED accepted; ACT required. Students desiring to major in performance (e.g., voice, violin, piano) must demonstrate a satisfactory level of proficiency in the major field; theory placement test.

Admission Procedure. Application with supporting documents due March 15.

Music Degrees Offered. Bachelor of Music; Bachelor of Music Education; Bachelor of Arts; Bachelor of Fine Arts; Master of Music; Master of Music Education; Doctor of Musical Arts, Doctor of Philosophy.

Music Degree Requirements. The Bachelor of Music degree requires a major in performance, theory, composition, or music history. All undergraduate music pro-grams except the major in voice have a minimum ensemble requirement of six semesters. The major fields have other specific curricular requirements. The Bachelor of Music Education degree, offered through the School of Education, affords skill development in the entire spectrum of general music education; individual emphasis is reflected in the choice of major performance medium and performance ensembles; it prepares students for application to the state for testing for teacher certification. The program requires a minimum of 126 semester hours of credit distributed among general studies, the major, and professional education class work. Each student must participate in appropriate performing ensembles, demonstrate proficiency in a major applied performance medium and in other performance areas, and participate in at least ten appropriate and acceptable individual public performances. The Bachelor of Music Education-Therapy degree prepares individuals for general music therapy practice in hospitals, institutions for exceptional children, community health programs, geriatric institutions, and private and group settings. Specific course requirements must be completed. The program requires a minimum of 133 semester hours of credit in required subjects. The Bachelor of Arts degree with a major in music requires the satisfactory completion of 124 credit hours of required subjects. The Bachelor of Fine Arts degree in theatre/voice has similar requirements with courses dependent on the major concentration.

The Master of Music, Master of Music Education, and doctoral degrees may also be pursued. A total of 30 credit hours is required for the master's, 60 or above for the doctorate. Other requirements vary with the degree program.

General Program Areas. Church Music, Composition, Jazz Studies, Music Education, Music History, Music Theory, Music Therapy, Performance.

Instruments Taught. Bassoon, Clarinet, Double Bass, Euphonium, Flute, French Horn, Harp, Oboe, Organ, Percussion, Piano, Saxophone, Trombone, Trumpet, Tuba, Viola, Violin, Violoncello, Voice.

Musical Facilities

Practice Facilities. Special facilities for organists; 6 organs (4 Reuter, 2 Cassavant). 5 practice rooms for percussionists. 82 practice rooms. 60 practice pianos; 5 grand pianos reserved for piano majors. Music synthesizer laboratory.

Concert Facilities. Crafton-Preyer Theatre seating 1,-188; Swarthout Recital Hall, 396; William Inge Memorial Theatre.

Concerts/Musical Activities. 200 concerts/recitals per year; opera workshop performances, musical theatre.

Music Library. The Thomas Gorton Music Library has an extensive collection of over 37,000 items such as scores, recordings, and microfiche. Listening facilities include 12 stations in the library and 7 in classrooms. Special collections in jazz and opera are maintained.

Special collections include: Gershwin materials (on Lawrence campus). Books on music and medicine, acoustics, physics, physiology, and diseases as they relate to musical subjects; seventeenth century imprints (in Medical Center on Kansas City Campus).

Special Programs

Performance Groups. University Symphony Orchestra, University Chorus, University Symphonic Band, Concert Band, University Band, University Marching Band, Jazz Ensemble, Jazz Choir, Chamber Choir, Concert Choir, Concert Chorale, University Singers, Men's Glee Club, Percussion Ensemble, Collegium Musicum, Oread Trio, Kansas Brass Quintet, Kansas Woodwinds.

Financial

Costs. Per academic year: Tuition in-state resident $1,-290, out-of-state $3,200. Room and board $2,465.

Financial Aid. Most scholarship and loan awards on the Lawrence campus are administered through the Office of Student Financial Aid. College Work-Study program available.

Commentary

The University of Kansas is the only institution in the state granting the D.M.A. and Ph.D. in music.

Kansas State University
Department of Music
Manhattan
Kansas 66502

Telephone. (913) 532-5740

Chief Administrator. Dr. Robert A. Steinbauer, Department Head.

Kansas State University was founded in 1863 under the Morrill Act, by which land-grant colleges came into being. At first the University was located on the grounds of the old Bluemont Central College, chartered in 1858, but in 1875 most activities of the University moved to its present site. The 315-acre campus is situated in Manhattan, a city in the northeastern part of the state, 125 miles west of Kansas City.

When the University opened in 1863, melodian and piano lessons were offered. Vocal music was introduced in 1864 and music groups performed in conjunction with calisthenics classes. Much of the early music taught was in the preparatory department and not at the college level. In 1867, the first diploma was awarded for completing a course in music and in 1882 the first college orchestra was formed followed by the college band in 1886. By 1916 there was a three-year curriculum in applied music and by 1918 a two-year curriculum in public school music instruction. A four-year curriculum in music was introduced in 1920. The Department of Music's present major goal is to produce gifted, well-rounded performers, teachers, and composers.

Accreditation. North Central Association of Colleges and Schools; National Association of Schools of Music; National Council for Accreditation of Teacher Education.

Academic Information

Enrollment, Music Majors. 60 men, 100 women.

Music Faculty. Full-time 23, part-time 5.

Term System. Semester. Academic year from late August to mid-May.

Entrance Requirements. High school graduation or GED; ACT or SAT referred to for scholarship assistance. Audition required only for scholarship assistance.

Admission Procedure. Application with supporting documents to Office of Admissions.

Music Degrees Offered. Bachelor of Music; Bachelor of Music Education; Bachelor of Arts; Master of Music.

Music Degree Requirements. The Bachelor of Music is a four-year program in performance and is offered with concentrations in voice, keyboard, strings, wind, percussion instruments, or theory/composition. The degree requires the completion of 128 hours for graduation. The program leading to the Bachelor of Music Education degree is a nine-semester curriculum designed to prepare music teachers for grades K-12. With careful planning and enrollment during summer sessions(s) all requirements may be completed in four years. Within this curriculum there are three options—one leading to certification in vocal/choral music, another to certification in instrumental music, and a third which permits both instrumental and vocal certification. The degree requires the completion of 135 to 139 hours, depending on emphasis. The Bachelor of Arts degree with a major in music emphasizes the liberal arts tradition. The program provides enough flexibility in electives for the student to meet other preprofessional requirements. This degree requires the completion of 120 hours for graduation.

The Master of Music degree is offered with emphases in music education, performance, pedagogy, theory and composition, and music history and literature. All areas of emphasis center on a common core of study with ample flexibility for the development of personal interests. The degree requires the completion of a minimum of 32 hours, including a master's report (or recital) or master's thesis. Students emphasizing music education may choose a 36-hour degree without report or thesis.

General Program Areas. Applied Music, Composition, Music Education, Music History, Music Literature, Music Theory, Performance.

Instruments Taught. Baritone, Bass, Bassoon, Clarinet, Early Wind Instruments, Flute, Harpsichord, Horn, Oboe, Organ, Percussion, Piano, Saxophone, Trombone, Trumpet, Tuba, Viola, Viola da Gamba, Violin, Violoncello, Voice.

Musical Facilities

Practice Facilities. 12 practice rooms. 5 organs (2 Reuter, 1 Bosch, 1 Austin, 1 Allen Electronic). Special percussion practice facilities. Pianos include Kawai, Baldwin, Story & Clarke uprights; Steinway grands; 3 grand pianos reserved for piano majors. Electronic music studio; harp studio; gamba studio.

Concert Facilities. McCain Auditorium, seating 1,800; All Faiths Chapel Auditorium, 550; Choral Room, 120 to 150; Forum Hall, 350.

Community Facilities. Various local churches.

Concerts/Musical Activities. Student and faculty recitals; solo and small ensemble performances; Artists Series.

Music Library. Most materials are housed in main library. 11,145 volumes; 14,690 scores; 40,337 items including films, discs, compact discs, tapes; 556 microform titles; 12,000 phonograph recordings; 91 audiocassettes; 458 reel-to-reel tapes; 181 compact discs; 5 videocassettes. 33 listening stations (stereo). 1,075 rare books collection; private record collection in Department of Music.

Special Programs

Performance Groups. Concert Choir, Marching Band, Concert Band, Symphonic Wind Ensemble, Chamber Singers, Collegiate Chorale, K-State Singers, Symphony Orchestra, Theatre Orchestra, Men's Glee Club, Women's Glee Club, Instrumental Ensemble, Concert Jazz Ensemble, Vocal Ensemble, Jazz Instrumental Ensemble, String Ensemble, Brass Ensemble, Wind Ensemble, Opera Workshop, Collegium Musicum.

Financial

Costs. Per academic year: Tuition in-state resident $1,290, out-of-state $3,200. Room and board $2,135.

Financial Aid. Music scholarships are awarded on basis of musical ability. Average award $300 to $800 per year (renewable). Other sources of financial aid include institutional, private individual, state/federal loans, part-time employment, and a College Work-Study program. Scholarship/financial aid application priority deadline June 15.

Commentary

Among the resources at Kansas State University are a collection of harpsichords and a chest of matched viols. The University's electronic music studio with ARP synthesizer is one of the best in the Midwest.

Pittsburg State University
Department of Music
1701 South Broadway
Pittsburg
Kansas 66762

Telephone. (316) 231-7000

Chief Administrator. Gene E. Vollen, Chairperson.

Pittsburg State University is a multipurpose state university enrolling over 4,000 students each year. The 234-acre campus is comprised of 41 buildings in Pittsburg, a community in southeast Kansas.

The Department of Music prepares students for elementary and secondary music teaching and serves students pursuing careers in college teaching and professional performance.

Accreditation. North Central Association of Colleges and Schools; National Association of Schools of Music; National Council for Accreditation of Teacher Education.

Academic Information

Enrollment, Music Majors. (Total University) 4,404.

Music Faculty. 14.

Term System. Semester. One summer term.

Entrance Requirements. High school graduation or equivalent; open enrollment for Kansas residents; non-residents must rank in upper half of graduating class; ACT required; audition required. GRE required for graduate study.

Admission Procedure. Application with supporting documents reviewed on a rolling admissions basis.

Music Degrees Offered. Bachelor of Music; Bachelor of Music Education; Bachelor of Arts; Master of Music.

Music Degree Requirements. The Bachelor of Music degree program is offered with emphasis in piano, organ, harpsichord, voice, string, wind, or percussion instruments. It is designed for the musical performer who aspires to college or private teaching or to professional performance. The program is considered as preparation for study at the master's level and beyond. The Bachelor of Music Education degree is offered with emphasis in either instrumental or vocal music for elementary or secondary public school teaching. The Bachelor of Arts degree program offers the major in either music or piano technology.

Courses leading to the Master of Music degree are offered with emphases in applied music, theory/composition, music history, instrumental music education, vocal music education, and choral conducting.

General Program Areas. Applied Music, Choral Conducting, Composition, Music Education, Music History, Music Theory.

Instruments Taught. Bass, Bassoon, Clarinet, Euphonium, Flute, Harpsichord, Horn, Oboe, Organ, Piano, Saxophone, Trombone, Trumpet, Tuba, Viola,

Violin, Violoncello, Voice.

Musical Facilities

Concerts/Musical Activities. Student and faculty concerts and recitals; Major Attraction Series; Solo and Chamber Music Series.

Music Library. The Leonard H. Axe Library supports the programs of the Department of Music. The holdings exceed 500,000 items.

Special Programs

Performance Groups. Band, Jazz Ensemble, Orchestra, Symphonic Choir, University Chorale, Collegiates.

Financial

Costs. Per academic year: Tuition in-state resident $1,098, out-of-state $2,348. Room and board $2,152.

Financial Aid. Financial aid is awarded on the basis of academic merit and financial need. Scholarships, grants, loans, part-time employment, and a College Work-Study program are available. Scholarship/financial aid application due March 15.

Wichita State University
School of Music
College of Fine Arts
185 Fairmount
Wichita
Kansas 67208

Telephone. (316) 689-3500

Chief Administrator. Dr. William Mathis, Chairman.

Wichita State University began as Fairmount College in 1895 with 16 students and three instructors. Founded by the Congregational Church, the college was governed by the church until 1926 when the citizens of Wichita voted to make Fairmount College the Municipal University of Wichita. The University was then placed under the direction of what eventually would be known as the Board of Trustees. After 38 years as a municipal institution, the University again changed its status in 1964 and officially entered the state system of higher education. The 320-acre campus is located in the northeastern section of Wichita (population 400,000), the largest city in Kansas.

The Division of Music of the College of Fine Arts includes the Departments of Music Education, Music Performance, and Musicology-Composition. These Departments offer programs designed to train and educate students who are planning professional careers in music. In addition, the Division's curriculum allows students in other colleges to gain an understanding of music as a humanistic study. Recitals by students, faculty, and guests augment community programs in the fine arts.

Accreditation. North Central Association of Colleges and Schools; National Association of Schools of Music.

Academic Information

Enrollment, Music Majors. (College of Fine Arts) 456.

Term System. Semester. Four summer sessions.

Entrance Requirements. High school graduation or equivalent; rank in upper half of graduating class; completion of 12 college-preparatory units recommended; ACT; open enrollment for Kansas residents.

Admission Procedure. Application with supporting documents accepted on a rolling basis.

Music Degrees Offered. Bachelor of Music; Bachelor of Music Education; Master of Music; Master of Music Education.

Music Degree Requirements. Students pursuing the Bachelor of Music degree choose either a performing medium (piano, organ, voice, strings, wind, or percussion) or theory-composition as their major area of concentration. The degree requires the completion of 127 to 133 semester hours including general university and departmental requirements. The degree Bachelor of Music Education is offered with emphases in instrumental, vocal, special music education, or piano pedagogy. A student teaching semester is required. Students in Fairmount College of Liberal Arts and Sciences who wish to major in music leading to a Bachelor of Arts degree are required to elect 41 hours in various areas of music as well as satisfying the general education and liberal arts requirements.

The Master of Music degree allows for specialization in history-literature, piano pedagogy, theory-composition, and performance. The degree requires the completion of a minimum of 30 graduate hours, including a thesis or recital. The Master of Music Education allows for concentration in elementary music, choral music, instrumental music (with recital option), music in special education, and voice. Conducting options may be elected in the choral and instrumental programs. The degree requires the completion of 31 to 35 hours including 13 hours of a core curriculum.

General Program Areas. Applied Music, Choral Music, Composition, Conducting, Instrumental Music, Music Education, Music History, Music Literature, Music Theory, Musicology, Performance, Piano Pedagogy.

Instruments Taught. Bass, Bassoon, Clarinet, Euphonium, Flute, French Horn, Guitar, Harp, Oboe, Organ, Percussion, Piano, Saxophone, Trombone, Trumpet, Tuba, Viola, Violin, Violoncello, Voice.

Musical Facilities

Practice Facilities. 25 practice rooms. 5 organs (Marcussen, Cassavante, 2 Moeller, Phelps). 3 percussion-equipped practice rooms. 60 pianos (45 uprights; 15 electronic pianos in class piano laboratory); 14 grand pianos reserved for piano majors.

Concert Facilities. 2 concert halls.

Concerts/Musical Activities. 200 concerts per year.

Music Library. 23,000 scores; 12,000 recordings. 3 turntables; 3 cassette decks. Special collections include Thurlow Lieurance Archives (former dean and composer who incorporated North American Indian music in his work).

Special Programs

Performance Groups. Orchestra, Concert Band, Marching Band, Symphony Band, Wichita Community Band, Wind Ensemble, Choral Union, Women's Glee Club, Men's Glee Club, A Cappella Choir, University Singers, Concert Chorale, Opera Theater, Madrigal Singers, Chamber Singers, Woodwind Ensemble, Saxophone Quartet, Brass Chamber Ensemble, Percussion Ensemble, String Ensemble, Jazz Arts Ensembles, Guitar Ensemble.

Financial

Costs. Per academic year: Tuition undergraduate in-state resident $1,040, out-of-state $2,950; graduate in-state resident $1,160, out-of-state $3,070. Room and board $2,078 to $2,260.

Financial Aid. Financial aid is available in the form of scholarships, state/federal loans, part-time employment, and a College Work-Study program. Scholarship applications due March 15 for next academic year.

KENTUCKY

Eastern Kentucky University
Department of Music

Foster Music Building
Richmond
Kentucky 40475

Telephone. (606) 623-3266

Chief Administrator. Dr. John A. Roberts, Chairman.

Eastern Kentucky University was established as Eastern Kentucky State Normal School in 1906. It became the Eastern Kentucky State Normal School and Teachers College in 1922 and was renamed the Eastern Kentucky State Teachers College in 1930. The word "Teachers" was removed from the name in 1935 and the present name was adopted in 1966 when the institution gained university status. The 375-acre campus is located in the heart of the Kentucky Bluegrass region in the city of Richmond, 26 miles southeast of Lexington.

The primary function of the Department of Music is to prepare music specialists to teach in the public schools, to prepare students for careers in church music, private studio teaching, concert performance, professional ensemble performance, teaching in colleges and universities and other aspects of professional musicianship, and to provide instruction to the university-at-large in courses for the elementary classroom teacher and by offering courses which contribute to the general education and cultural development of all students on campus. The Department of Music offers a variety of undergraduate degrees and options.

Accreditation. Southern Association of Colleges and Schools; National Association of Schools of Music.

Academic Information

Enrollment, Music Majors. 160.

Music Faculty. Full-time 22, part-time 9.

Term System. Semester. 8-week summer session. Academic year from late August to mid-May.

Entrance Requirements. High school graduation or GED; out-of-state applicants must rank in upper half of graduating class; ACT required; audition and theory placement examination.

Admission Procedure. Application with supporting documents to Admissions Office.

Music Degrees Offered. Bachelor of Music; Bachelor of Music Education; Bachelor of Arts; Master of Music; Master of Arts in Education; Master of Music Education; Rank 1 Certification (Education).

Music Degree Requirements. The Bachelor of Music degree is offered with options in performance and church music. The option in performance requires 70 hours of courses in the major; the church music option requires the completion of 69 hours in the major area. The Bachelor of of Arts degree is offered with options in theory/composition (52 hours), music history and literature (52 hours), and performance (48 hours). The Bachelor of Arts degree with a major in music merchandsing requires the completion of 66 hours in the major. The Bachelor of Music and Bachelor of Arts degrees require the completion of a total of 128 semester hours, including general education, electives, and the major concentration. The Bachelor of Music Education degree requires the completion of a minimum of 125½ semester hours. The program includes 48 hours of major requirements, 28 hours of professional education courses, 41 hours of general education requirements, and 8 hours of elective courses. Teacher certification plans are available and require 144½ to 146½ semester hours for completion.

The Master of Music degree is offered with options in performance, theory/composition, and choral conducting. The Master of Arts in Education with an option in music, the Master of Music Education, and Rank 1 Certification are offered in the College of Education with the cooperation of the Department of Music.

General Program Areas. Applied Music, Choral Conducting, Composition, Music Education, Music History, Music Merchandising, Music Theory, Performance.

Instruments Taught. Brass, Guitar, Organ, Percussion, Piano, Stringed Instruments, Voice, Woodwinds.

Musical Facilities

Practice Facilities. 72 practice rooms. 3 organs. 68 pianos (Baldwin studio); 5 grand pianos reserved for piano majors. Electronic music studio.

Concert Facilities. Gifford Hall, seating 270; Brock Hall, 1,600; Posey Hall, 730; Buchanan Hall, 150.

Concerts/Musical Activities. 89 concerts and recitals per year.

Music Library. 8,963 volumes; 8,700 scores; 101 periodical subscriptions; 22 audiovisual items; 7,839 recordings; 160 audiocassettes. 8 listening stations (stereo).

Special Programs

Performance Groups. Opera Workshop, Chamber Music, Chamber Singers, Concert Choir, Madrigal Singers, Oratorio Chorus, Women's Ensemble, Bell Ensemble, Show Choir, Orchestra, String Orchestra, Brass Choir, Percussion Ensemble, Stage Band, Clarinet Choir, Concert Band, Symphonic Band, Wind Ensemble, Marching Band.

Financial

Costs. Per academic year: Tuition in-state resident $1,070; out-of-state $2,700. Applied music fee $100.

Financial Aid. Financial aid is awarded on the basis of academic merit, financial need, and musical ability. Sources of aid include scholarships, state/federal grants and loans, part-time employment, and a College Work-Study program.

University of Kentucky
School of Music
College of Fine Arts
8 Limestone
Lexington
Kentucky 40506

Telephone. (606) 257-8181

Chief Administrator. Dr. Alan Hersh, Director.

The University of Kentucky was established in 1865 as the Agricultural and Mechanical College of Kentucky. In 1878, when the people of Kentucky decided to establish a state institution of higher learning, the Agricultural and Mechanical College was separated from Kentucky University and reestablished on land donated by the city of Lexington. In 1899, the legislature changed the name of the institution to State University, Lexington, Kentucky. In 1916, the present name was adopted. As the state's comprehensive institution, the University of Kentucky is charged with the missions of teaching, research, and service. The institution has an enrollment of more than 20,000 students. The campus of 100 major buildings is located in Lexington, a city noted for its tobacco market and surrounding horse farms.

The College of Fine Arts was established in September 1976 and includes the Department of Art, the Department of Theatre, and the School of Music. Baccalaureate programs are offered to students interested in a professional career in performance, preparation for graduate school, or studies in music education. Students from any college may choose to minor in music or music performance.

Accreditation. Southern Association of Colleges and Schools; National Association of Schools of Music.

Academic Information

Enrollment, Music Majors. 158.

Music Faculty. Full-time 34, part-time 6.

Term System. Semester. Academic year from August to May. 8-week summer session from June to August.

Entrance Requirements. Accredited high school graduaton or equivalent; open enrollment policy for state residents; ACT required; audition required; theory placement examination.

Admission Procedure. Application and supporting documents to Admissions Office.

Music Degrees Offered. Bachelor of Music; Bachelor of Music Education; Bachelor of Arts; Master of Music; Doctor of Musical Arts.

Music Degree Requirements. The degree Bachelor of Music in performance requires the completion of 120 credit hours with a 2.0 grade point average. At the conclusion of the sophomore year and before continuing in music performance at the upper division level, each student must perform before the music performance faculty for approval. Each student must also present a full recital during the senior year. Students must complete a concentration in an instrument, piano, organ, or voice. The Bachelor of Music Education degree is the joint concern of the School of Music and the College of Education. Music education majors in the School of Music who wish to receive a teaching certificate must meet the certification requirements of the College of Education as well as the requirements of the School. To qualify for student teaching and teacher certification, a student must be officially admitted into the Teacher Education Program. The Bachelor of Arts degree with a major in music is offered. Admission to the program is granted only after the successful completion of an audition in the student's performance area. Students must also take a theory placement test.

The Master of Music and the Doctor of Musical Arts degrees are offered through the Graduate School.

General Program Areas. Applied Music, Composition, Conducting, Music Education, Music History, Music Literature, Music Theory, Musicology, Performance.

Instruments Taught. Bass, Bassoon, Clarinet, Early Instruments, English Horn, Euphonium, Flute, French Horn, Guitar, Harp, Harpsichord, Oboe, Organ, Percussion, Piano, Saxophone, Trombone, Trumpet, Tuba, Viola, Violin, Violoncello, Voice.

Musical Facilities

Practice Facilities. 33 practice rooms. Special practice facilities for organists and percussionists. 20 pianos; 7 grand pianos reserved for piano majors.

Concert Facilities. The Center for the Arts Concert Hall, Recital Hall.

Concerts/Musical Activities. Student and faculty recitals and concerts; faculty ensembles include the Faculty Brass Quintet, the Kentucky Wind Quintet, and the Concord Trio; University Artist Series; Central Kentucky Chamber Music Society annually presents a series of concerts; the Lexington Philharmonic Orchestra gives performances on the University campus.

Music Library. The University of Kentucky Libraries collection contains more than 2 million volumes. Specialized collections (including music) are housed separately and include the Alfred Cortot Collection.

Special Programs

Performance Groups. Symphony Orchestra, Symphonic Band, University Choristers, University Chorus, Jazz Ensemble, Opera Workshop, Collegium Musicum, Wind Ensemble, Marching Band, String Orchestra.

Financial

Costs. Per academic year: Tuition undergraduate in-state resident $1,332, out-of-state $3,812; graduate in-state resident $1,452, nonresident $4,172. Room and board $2,249 to $2,543.

Financial Aid. Financial aid is available in the form of scholarships, grants, loans, part-time employment, and a College Work-Study program.

Commentary

The University of Kentucky has a collection of Appalachian and other early American instruments, a Music Education Curriculum Center, and a new performance facility, the Center for the Arts. This structure, housing two concert halls and a rehearsal room, has been lauded for its fine acoustical engineering.

University of Louisville
School of Music
Belknap Campus
Louisville
Kentucky 40292

Telephone. (502) 588-6907

Chief Administrator. Jerry W. Ball, Dean.

The University of Louisville is a publicly supported liberal arts university founded in 1798 as Jefferson Academy. It was later known as Louisville College and in 1846, upon attaining university status, adopted its present name. The 140-acre campus, situated in the northwestern Kentucky's city of Louisville on the Ohio River, has 90 buildings.

The School of Music was founded in 1932 and now occupies a building on the northwest corner of the University's Belknap Campus. The goals of the School are to train students for careers in music and to enhance the quality of life for the University and surrounding community through performances, compositions, research, and instruction.

Accreditation. Southern Association of Colleges and Schools; National Association of Schools of Music; National Council for Accreditation of Teacher Education.

Academic Information

Enrollment, Music Majors. (Total University) 15,150.

Music Faculty. 43.

Term System. Semester.

Entrance Requirements. High school graduation or equivalent with completion of 12 academic units; SAT or ACT; qualifying applied music entrance examinations.

Admission Procedure. Application with supporting documents to Admissions Office; reviewed on a rolling admissions basis.

Music Degrees Offered. Bachelor of Music; Bachelor of Music Education; Master of Music; Doctor of Philosophy.

Music Degree Requirements. The major subject in the Bachelor of Music degree program may be piano, voice, organ, guitar, band or orchestral instruments, music history, theory-composition, piano pedagogy, or voice pedagogy. Bachelor of Music Education degree students may elect to pursue a curriculum with vocal or instrumental emphasis.

The major subject in the Master of Music degree curriculum may be applied music, music history, or theory-composition. The Master of Music Education degree program allows an applied music minor in instrument or voice.

The Doctor of Philosophy degree in musicology is offered jointly with the University of Kentucky.

General Program Areas. Applied Music, Composition, Music Education, Music History, Music Theory, Musicology, Piano Pedagogy, Voice Pedagogy.

Instruments Taught. Bass, Bassoon, Clarinet, Euphonium, Flute, Guitar, Harp, Harpsichord, Horn, Oboe, Organ, Percussion, Piano, Saxophone, Trombone, Trumpet, Tuba, Viola, Violin, Violoncello, Voice.

Musical Facilities

Practice Facilities. The School of Music Building contains 44 teaching studios and 76 practice rooms.

Concert Facilities. Recital Hall, seating 560.

Concerts/Musical Activities. Faculty groups include the Louisville String Quartet, the Louisville Woodwind Quintet, and the Louisville Brass Quintet; the Bach Society and the Speed Endowed Series offer frequent concerts; full schedule of performances by faculty, students, and the various student organizations.

Music Library. The Dwight Anderson Memorial Library consists of 45,000 titles and 20,000 uncatalogued items. Definitive editions of major composers, historical sets, and microtext materials are included, covering every area of music. The sound-recording collection includes 16,000 items. A special collection documents music in Kentucky, manuscripts of Kentucky composers, and Louisville imprints as represented in an extensive collection of early American sheet music. Other collections are Louisville Orchestra materials and the folksong collection of Jean Thomas.

Special Programs

Featured Programs. The Music Education Department of the School sponsors clinics for various instruments and summer institutes for both teachers and students.

The Suzuki Institute is held every summer on the campus.

Performance Groups. Orchestra, Band, Collegium Musicum, Opera Workshop, Chorus, Black Chorus, Pep Band, Marching Band, Concert Choir, Piano Ensemble, String Ensemble, Woodwind Ensemble, Brass Ensemble, Percussion Ensemble, Stage Band

Affiliated Programs. The Preparatory Music Department offers children a foundation for future growth in music. It offers students private instruction and classwork in music understanding, music literature, and ensemble.

Financial

Costs. Per academic year: Tuition in-state resident $1,340, out-of-state $3,820.

Financial Aid. Various types of music scholarships are available. Other sources of financial aid include grants, loans, and part-time employment. Financial aid/scholarship application due April 15.

Commentary

In 1985, the University awarded the first University of Louisville Grawemeyer Award in Music Composition to Witold Lutoslawski of Poland. The annual award, among the largest of its kind in the world, offers a prize of $150,000 in recognition of outstanding achievement by a composer in a large musical genre.

Morehead State University
Department of Music
Baird Music Hall
Morehead
Kentucky 40351

Telephone. (606) 783-2473
Chief Administrator. Christopher Gallaher, Chair.

Morehead State University traces its history to the establishment of the Morehead State Normal School in 1922. Through the years, facilities and offerings in varied disciplines, in addition to education, have been developed. The present name was adopted in 1966. The 820-acre campus comprises 42 buildings and is located in Morehead, midway between Lexington and Ashland, Kentucky.

The major goals of the Department of Music are the preparation of music teachers for the public schools at the elementary, middle school, and high school levels and the training of musicians for performance careers. The first music degree was awarded in 1937.

Accreditation. Southern Association of Colleges and Schools; National Association of Schools of Music.

Academic Information

Enrollment, Music Majors. Full-time 76 men, 46 women; part-time 4 men, 3 women. Foreign students 1.

Music Faculty. Full-time 22, part-time 2.

Term System. Semester. Academic year August 15 to May 15. Two 4-week summer sessions from June 1 to July 30.

Entrance Requirements. High school graduation; out-of-state students must rank in upper half of graduating class; ACT required. TOEFL examination required for foreign students. Advanced placement through CLEP and departmental examinations. An audition is essential for planning and counseling in the appropriate course of study.

Admission Procedure. Complete application form and submit all supporting transcripts and test scores.

Music Degrees Offered. Bachelor of Music; Bachelor of Music Education; Bachelor of Arts; Master of Music.

Music Degree Requirements. The Bachelor of Music degree is designed for students who are planning for professional careers in music either as performers or as private teachers. The program requires 45 hours of general education and 85 hours in music. Specialization is available in voice, piano, organ, harpsichord, strings, wind instruments, theory/composition, and jazz and studio music.

The Bachelor of Music Education degree requires the completion of 42 hours of professional education and 67 to 69 hours in music. The program is designed for students who are planning for careers as music teachers in the public schools. It includes the requirements for 12-grade music certificate with either the vocal or instrumental track. The emphasis in music education includes studies in music education, music research, music styles, applied music, and option to perform a Graduate Recital. The emphasis in performance includes studies in applied music, history and literature, research, and musical styles, plus the Graduate Recital.

The Bachelor of Arts degree with a major or minor in music provides for the study of music within a liberal arts curriculum. Emphasis is upon the study and performance of musical literature.

The Master of Music degree requires the completion of 30 hours. The program offers three options: one with a research orientation; one for elementary and secondary school teachers who retain a strong interest in performance; and one for elementary and secondary school teachers whose primary interest is the improvement of teaching skills at these levels. The flexibility within the various emphases also allows for a significant amount of work in conducting, composition, and other areas of particular interest to the student.

General Program Areas. Music Education, Performance.

Instruments Taught. Bass, Bassoon, Clarinet, Euphonium, Flute, Guitar, Harp, Harpsichord, Horn, Oboe, Organ, Percussion, Piano, Saxophone, Trombone, Trumpet, Tuba, Viola, Violin, Violoncello, Voice.

Musical Facilities

Practice Facilities. Special practice facilities for organists; Conn Custom organ, FX-20 Electone, Ward pipe organ, Hammond practice organ. Special practice facilities for percussionists. 39 piano practice rooms; 39 upright pianos (Yamaha, Wurlitzer, Hamilton); 4 grand pianos reserved for piano majors. Special computer studio; synthesizer studio.

Concert Facilities. The Duncan Recital Hall, seating 400, is located in Baird Music Hall. The University auditorium seats 1,400.

Concerts/Musical Activities. Weekly student recital series and junior/senior recitals. The members of the faculty are active in solo and chamber music performance.

Music Library. 10,000 musical scores; 3,000 books; 688 bound periodicals; 56 current periodical subscriptions; 9,000 phonograph recordings; 250 audiocassettes; 150 compact disks. Listening/Learning Center in music building has 16 listening stations.

Special Programs

Performance Groups. MSU Marching Band, Marching Band Fronts, Marching Percussion, Concert Band, Symphony Band, Jazz Ensemble, Orchestra, Chamber Singers, Concert Choir, University Chorus, Jazz Vocal Ensemble and Show Choir, Percussion Ensemble, Trombone Choir, Brass Choir.

Affiliated Programs. Phi Mu Alpha, Sigma Alpha Iota, OPUS (organization of keyboard students), Brotherhood of University Guitarists, Trumpet Guild, International Trombonist Association, Student Music Educators National Conference, Percussive Arts Society, National Association of Jazz Educators.

Financial

Costs. Per academic year: Tuition in-state resident $1,020, out-of-state $2,900. Fees $200. Room $920. Board $1,250. Off-campus housing approximately $400 per month.

Financial Aid. Financial aid is awarded on the basis of academic merit, financial need, musical ability. Institutional and state/federal aid available. 70 students receive financial aid; awards range from $300 to $3,000. Scholarship applications due March 15. Part-time employment (average earnings $2,000 per academic year) and College Work-Study program available.

Southern Baptist Theological Seminary School of Church Music
2825 Lexington Road
Louisville
Kentucky 40203

Telephone. (502) 897-4115

Chief Administrator. Dr. S. Milburn Price, Dean.

Southern Baptist Theological Seminary offers postbaccalaureate theological education designed to equip both men and women for leadership in all aspects of the Christian ministry. The campus is located in a residential area of Louisville.

The primary purpose of the School of Church Music is to offer graduate programs in church music to prepare students for the music ministry in local churches and other settings for which advanced training in church music is needed.

Accreditation. Southern Association of Schools and Colleges; National Association of Schools of Music; Association of Theological Schools in the United States and Canada.

Academic Information

Enrollment, Music Majors. 287.

Music Faculty. Full-time 14; adjunct 2.

Term System. Semester.

Entrance Requirements. Baccalaureate degree from a regionally accredited college.

Admission Procedure. Application with supporting documents to Office of Admissions.

Music Degrees Offered. Master of Church Music; Master of Divinity in Church Music; Doctor of Musical Arts; Doctor of Music Ministry.

Music Degree Requirements. The Master of Church Music degree is designed for college graduates with a major in music or its equivalent. All students have the first major in church music and the second major in theory/composition, music education, musicology, conducting, applied performance, applied pedagogy, or ministry. The Master of Divinity in Church Music degree program provides greater depth of preparation in Biblical, historical, and theological studies than that found in the Master of Church Music degree, while retaining a major portion of the musical requirements for the latter degree. The Doctor of Musical Arts degree program is designed as a continuation of the Master of Church Music or its equivalent. Emphases are offered in applied performance, research/performance, or ministry.

General Program Areas. Church Music, Composition, Conducting, Music Education, Music Theory, Musicology, Performance.

Instruments Taught. Brass, Organ, Percussion, Piano, Stringed Instruments, Voice, Woodwinds.

Musical Facilities

Practice Facilities. Cooke Hall houses the School of Church Music. Facilities include a 45-rank Schlicker pipe organ; Stein foretpiano (1773); Broadwood concert piano (1828); Challis and Sabathil harpsichords; student lounges; classrooms; audiovisual booth; organ teaching studios with Holtkamp, Moeller, Schlicker, and Steiner organs; electronic keyboard facilities; practice rooms; teaching studios; administrative offices.

Concert Facilities. Cooke Recital Hall, seating 230; Alumni Chapel, 1,400.

Concerts/Musical Activities. Student concerts and recitals; Faculty Concert Series; R. Inman Johnson Guest Recital Series.

Music Library. The Music Division of the seminary's Jame P. Boyce Centennial Library contains over 17,000 books, 37,000 scores, 8,000 phonodiscs, 98,000 anthems, 4,000 phonotapes, and subscriptions to 115 periodicals. Individual and multiple listening facilities are available for cassette and reel-to-reel tapes.

Special collections include: Converse Collection of Hymnology; Janet L. Ingersoll Collection of Gospel Music; part of Everett Helm Library.

Special Programs

Performance Groups. Oratorio Chorus, Seminary Choir, Male Chorale, Seminary Vocal Ensemble; Seminary Winds, Seminary Strings, String Quartet, Brass Quintet, Woodwind Quintet.

Financial

Costs. Per academic year: Registration fee $600. Private music instruction fee $120 or $240 (30 minutes or 1 hour). Dormitory room $80-$115 per month; apartment $135 to $270 per month.

Financial Aid. Since its inception in 1859, the Seminary has charged no tuition. A substantial portion of the instructional costs of educating its students is borne by the Southern Baptist Convention through the denomination's Cooperative Program of Financial Distribution. Student fees help to defray the costs of certain academic and student services.

Western Kentucky University
Department of Music
College Heights
Bowling Green
Kentucky 42101

Telephone. (502) 745-3751
Chief Administrator. Wayne Hobbs, Head.

Western Kentucky University is a publicly supported institution founded in 1906 as Western Kentucky Normal School. With the expansion of its programs and the addition of new colleges it was designated a university in 1966. The campus is located in College Heights overlooking the city of Bowling Green.

The Department of Music is committed to the training of professional musicians and teachers of music. Music may also be studied as a major within a diversified liberal arts program or as a minor. Opportunities are provided for the general university student to study privately and to participate in various instrumental and vocal performing groups.

Accreditation. Southern Association of Colleges and Schools; National Association of Schools of Music; National Council for Accreditation of Teacher Education.

Academic Information

Enrollment, Music Majors. (Total University) 9,918.
Music Faculty. 18.

Term System. Semester. One summer session.

Entrance Requirements. High school graduation; open enrollment for Kentucky residents; ACT required; placement examinations in music rudiments, sight reading, performance, and piano.

Admission Procedure. Application with supporting documents reviewed on a rolling admissions basis.

Music Degrees Offered. Bachelor of Music; Bachelor of Arts; Master of Music; Master of Arts.

Music Degree Requirements. The Bachelor of Music degree is offered with majors in performance and music education (instrumental, vocal, and combined options; double major in elementary education and elementary music). The Bachelor of Arts degree with a major in music is offered with a non-professional emphasis.

The Master of Music degree in performance provides professional training and courses in the area of music for those who seek a career in performance or in college and private applied teaching. The Master of Arts degree in education with a major in music offers a flexible schedule of education, music education, and music courses designed to broaden the public school teacher's background in all three areas.

General Program Areas. Applied Music, Composition, Music Education, Music History, Music Literature, Music Theory, Performance.

Instruments Taught. Bass, Clarinet, Cornet, Euphonium, Flute, Horn, Percussion, Piano, Saxophone, Trombone, Trumpet, Tuba, Viola, Violin, Violoncello.

Musical Facilities

Practice Facilities. The Ivan Wilson Center for Fine Arts houses the Department of Music.

Concert Facilities. Van Meter Auditorium; recital hall; theatre.

Concerts/Musical Activities. Student and faculty recitals and concerts.

Music Library. The Margie Helm Library and the Raymond L. Cravens Graduate Center and Library constitute the main library complex for undergraduate and graduate work at the University.

Special Programs

Performance Groups. Choral Union, University Choir, University Orchestra, Chamber Singers, Brass Choir, Marching Band, Concert Band, Percussion Ensemble, Jazz Ensemble, Opera Theatre, Piano Ensemble.

Financial

Costs. Per academic year: Tuition in-state resident $954, out-of-state $2,724. Music fee $100. Room and board $2,170.

Financial Aid. Financial aid is available in the form of scholarships, grants, loans, part-time employment, and a College Work-Study program. Financial aid/scholarship application due April 1.

LOUISIANA

Louisiana State University
School of Music
Baton Rouge
Louisiana 70803

Telephone. (504) 388-3261

Chief Administrator. Dr. Daniel P. Sher, Dean.

Louisiana State University had its origin in certain grants of land made by the U.S. government in 1806, 1811, and 1827 for the use of a seminary of learning in Pineville, Louisiana. In 1869, the destruction of the college building by fire caused a move to Baton Rouge where it has remained since. In 1870 the present name was adopted. In 1874, the Louisiana State Agricultural and Mechanical College was established and in 1877 merged with Louisiana State University under the legal title Louisiana State University and Agricultural and Mechanical College, a name it retains today. The University is located on a 1,944-acre tract of land in the southern part of the city. The University's more than 190 principal buildings are grouped on a 300-acre plateau that constitutes the main campus.

The School of Music seeks to help students develop their musical talents and make the musical arts a cultural asset in their lives. To attain these goals, the School offers programs in performance, education, composition, and church music. Graduate study through the doctoral level is offered.

Accreditation. Southern Association of Colleges and Schools; National Association of Schools of Music.

Academic Information

Enrollment, Music Majors. (Total University) 28,435.

Music Faculty. 42.

Term System. Semester. Summer session.

Entrance Requirements. High school graduation or GED; ACT. Foreign students must have the equivalent of a U.S. "B" grade and satisfactory English proficiency. Audition required (before faculty committee; held during registration or by appointment).

Admission Procedure. Application with $20 non-refundable fee due July 1 for Fall, December 1 for Spring, and May 1 for Summer.

Music Degrees Offered. Bachelor of Arts; Bachelor of Music; Bachelor of Music Education; Master of Arts; Master of Music; Master of Music Education; Doctor of Musical Arts; Doctor of Philosophy.

Music Degree Requirements. The Bachelor of Music degree is offered with majors in brass, composition, instrumental, organ, piano performance/studio teaching piano, sacred music (with options), string, voice, woodwind. Total credit hours required for the degree vary with curriculum followed. The Bachelor of Music Education degree program is designed to train students in vocal and instrumental teaching in the public schools where state certification is required. It is offered in conjunction with the College of Education. Students wishing a broader variety of subjects in addition to a basic foundation in music may follow one of the curricula leading to the Bachelor of Arts degree offered in conjunction with the College of Arts and Sciences. The first two years of a music therapy curriculum are provided.

The Graduate School offers the degrees Master of Music, Master of Music Education, Master of Arts with a major in music, Doctor of Musical Arts, and Doctor of Philosophy with a major in music.

General Program Areas. Applied Music, Composition, Music History, Music Theory, Performance, Sacred Music.

Instruments Taught. Brass, Organ, Percussion, Piano, Stringed Instruments, Voice, Woodwinds.

Musical Facilities

Practice Facilities. 60 practice rooms. 3 organs (Reuter, Holtkamp, Schlicker). 2 percussion-equipped practice rooms. 5 grand pianos reserved for piano majors. Electronic music studio.

Concert Facilities. 4 concert halls.

Concerts/Musical Activities. Recitals, concerts.

Music Library. A music reading room is located in the Music and Dramatic Arts Building. Listening facilities include 4 cassette systems and 16 playback units.

Special collections include: librettos printed in Louisiana in the mid-nineteenth century.

Special Programs

Featured Programs. Performing Arts Series; Festival of Contemporary Music.

Financial

Costs. Per academic year: Tuition in-state resident $1,-274, out-of-state $3,674. Room $1,250. Board $1,200.

Financial Aid. Scholarships and awards are available from the School of Music. These are awarded on the basis of academic achievement and musicianship. Scholarship applications due December 1.

Louisiana Tech University
Department of Music
Railroad Avenue
Ruston
Louisiana 71272

Telephone. (318) 257-4233

Chief Administrator. Raymond G. Young, Department Head.

Louisiana Tech was founded in 1894 as the Industrial Institute and College of Louisiana. Since that time, the institution's name, purpose, and functions have been modified as the needs of those whom it served have changed. In 1921, the school's name was changed to Louisiana Polytechnic Institute and in 1970, the present name was adopted. The 235-acre main campus is located in the city of Ruston in central Louisiana.

The primary purpose of the Department of Music is to provide its students with a well-rounded education, thus preparing them for a professional and/or teaching career in one of the many branches of music. The Department strives to combine high standards of performance, a scholarly approach to music, proficiency in pedagogical skills and educational research, and service to the University, local, and state communities.

Accreditation. Southern Association of Colleges and Schools; National Association of Schools of Music.

Academic Information

Term System. Quarter. (Credit is awarded in semester hours). 2 summer sessions.

Entrance Requirements. Accredited high school graduation or GED; ACT required; open admission policy; audition required; music theory placement examination.

Admission Procedure. Application with supporting documents and $5 nonrefundable fee due August 19.

Music Degrees Offered. Bachelor of Arts; Bachelor of Fine Arts; Master of Arts.

Music Degree Requirements. The Bachelor of Arts degree is offered with a major in music. The degree requires the completion of a distribution in music courses as well as the minor, the general education requirements, and electives for a total of 131 semester hours. The Bachelor of Fine Arts degree is designed for those who wish to stress the performing pedagogical aspects of their training in any major (voice, keyboard, or in some instrument of the symphonic orchestra or band). All majors are required to take a minimum of two quarters of a foreign language. Other academic electives are approved according to individual needs. The degree requires the completion of 129 semester hours.

In cooperation with the College of Education, the Bachelor of Arts and the Master of Arts degrees are offered in the music education curriculum.

General Program Areas. Applied Music, Music Education, Performance.

Instruments Taught. Bassoon, Clarinet, Euphonium, Flute, Harpsichord, Horn, Oboe, Organ, Percussion, Piano, Saxophone, Trombone, Trumpet, Tuba.

Musical Facilities

Practice Facilities. 3 practice rooms. Wickes organ. 20 pianos; 3 grand pianos reserved for piano majors.

Concert Facilities. Auditorium, Recital Hall.

Concerts/Musical Activities. Concerts and recitals.

Music Library. Recordings, tapes, and 5 listening stations (stereo).

Special Programs

Performance Groups. University Chorus, Concert Choir, Tech Chorale, Symphonic Band, Concert Band, Marching Band, Jazz Band, Instrumental and Percussion Ensemble, Ruston-Tech Civic Symphony Orchestra, String Ensembles, Piano Ensembles.

Foreign Programs. Six-week program in Rome, Italy.

Financial

Costs. Per academic year: Tuition in-state resident $1,-416, out-of-state $2,361. Room $1,080. Board $945.

Financial Aid. Financial aid is available in the form of scholarships, grants, loans, part-time employment, and a College Work-Study program.

Loyola University
College of Music
6383 St. Charles Avenue
New Orleans
Louisiana 70118

Telephone. (504) 865-3037

Chief Administrator. Dr. David Swanzy, Dean.

Loyola University is a Roman Catholic Jesuit university founded by the Society of Jesus in 1912. The University was authorized to grant degrees by The General Assembly of Louisiana in 1912. Loyola is a medium-size university with a total enrollment of 4,873 students, including 268 graduate and 701 law school students. The 19-acre campus is located in a residential area of New Orleans known as the University Section.

The College of Music, established in 1932, offers the opportunity to combine liberal arts studies with professional music courses in the only college of music administered by the Jesuit Fathers in the United States. Historically, New Orleans offers an abundance of cultural opportunities. The city supports an opera company, a major symphony orchestra, a symphony chorus, and numerous smaller professional organizations. Traditionally, students from Loyola have played an important role in the musical life of the city.

Accreditation. Southern Association of Colleges and Schools; National Association of Schools of Music; National Council for Accreditation of Teacher Education; National Association for Music Therapy.

Academic Information

Enrollment, Music Majors. 218.

Music Faculty. Full-time 20, part-time 25.

Term System. Semester. Academic year from August to May.

Entrance Requirements. Freshman admission is based on the credentials submitted by a student in the admissions portfolio; high school graduation; SAT or ACT; score at least 50 out of 10 on performance audition. Foreign students must have score of at least 500 on TOEFL.

Admission Procedure. Application with all supporting documents to Admissions Office.

Music Degrees Offered. Bachelor of Music; Bachelor of Music Education; Bachelor of Music Therapy; Master of Music; Master of Music Education; Master of Music Therapy.

Music Degree Requirements. The Bachelor of Music degree offers majors in performance, jazz studies, piano pedagogy, theory and composition, and music with secondary concentrations in business administration, communications, computer information processing, and drama. The Bachelor of Music Therapy degree curriculum leads to a professional degree designed for students who wish to work with the mentally ill, physically handicapped, and exceptional children. The Bachelor of Music Education degree is offered with concentrations in instrumental or keyboard applied area and keyboard or voice area; optional secondary concentrations are available in jazz studies and special music education. The bachelor's degrees require successful completion of from 131 to 147 semester hours.

The degree Master of Music in performance is offered with concentrations in instrumental, keyboard, and voice. The Master of Music Education degree may be pursued with concentrations in instrumental or vocal.

The Master of Music Therapy degree is also offered. The master's degrees require the completion of 30 to 36 semester hours, depending on concentration.

General Program Areas. Applied Music, Composition, Jazz Studies, Music Education, Music History, Music Theory, Music Therapy, Performance, Piano Pedagogy.

Instruments Taught. Bass, Bassoon, Flute, Guitar, Horn, Oboe, Organ, Percussion, Piano, Saxophone, Trombone, Trumpet, Tuba, Viola, Violin, Violoncello, Voice.

Musical Facilities

Practice Facilities. 35 practice rooms. 3 organs. Special practice facilities for percussionists. Electronic music and recording studio.

Concert Facilities. Concert Hall, seating 600.

Concerts/Musical Activities. Student/faculty recitals and concerts.

Music Library. 25,000 volumes; 6,300 scores; 65 current periodical subscriptions; 350 microforms; 6,800 phonograph recordings; 200 audiocassettes. 17 listening stations (stereo). The library of nearby Tulane University is also available to students.

Special Programs

Featured Programs. Student chapter of Music Educators National Conference.

Performance Groups. Loyola University Band, Loyola Chamber Orchestra, Loyola Symphony Orchestra, University Chorus, University Chorale, University Training Orchestra, Opera Ensemble, Chamber Singers, Brass Ensemble, Percussion Ensemble, String Ensemble, Woodwind Ensemble, Jazz Bands.

Financial

Costs. Per academic year: Tuition $5,420. Fees $125. Room $2,050. Board $1,630. Off-campus housing approximately $300 per month.

Financial Aid. The College of Music administers the Naomi Marie Adams Memorial Foundation Scholarship, a four-year full tuition award, and the Guy F. Bernard Memorial Scholarship, a four-year partial tuition award for keyboard performers. Additionally, the College of Music awards partial, tuition-remissive, University scholarships. These scholarships vary according to the recipient's performance competence and potential for continued musical and academic progress. They are strictly talent awards and not need-based.

Commentary

Loyola University benefits from the formidable jazz tradition of New Orleans' legendary French Quarter. The University's College of Music offers a jazz studies major supported by a distinguished faculty.

McNeese State University
Department of Music
4100 Ryan Street
Lake Charles
Louisiana 70609

Telephone. (318) 477-2520

Chief Administrator. Fred G. Sahlmann, Head.

McNeese State University was founded in 1939 as a division of Louisiana State University offering only the first two years of higher education. It advanced to a four-year status and became a separate entity in 1950. The 686-acre campus is located in the city of Lake Charles in southwestern Louisiana.

The Department of Music offers undergraduate and graduate programs. Each prospective music major must demonstrate proficiency on an instrument or voice in audition. Piano auditions and music theory placement examinations are also required.

Accreditation. Southern Association of Colleges and Schools; National Association of Schools of Music; National Council for Accreditation of Teacher Education.

Academic Information

Enrollment, Music Majors. (Total University) 7,981.

Music Faculty. 17.

Term System. Semester. One summer term.

Entrance Requirements. High school graduation or equivalent; open enrollment for Louisiana residents; placement examination and audition required. GRE required for graduate study.

Admission Procedure. Application and supporting documents with nonrefundable $5 fee to Office of Admissions.

Music Degrees Offered. Bachelor of Music; Bachelor of Music Education; Bachelor of Arts; Master of Music; Master of Music Education.

Music Degree Requirements. The Bachelor of Music degree is offered in performance (piano, organ, band, or orchestral instruments) or theory-composition with concentrations in piano pedagogy and jazz and commercial music (band or orchestral instruments). The Bachelor of Music Education degree is offered with curricula in vocal or instrumental school music. The Bachelor of Arts degree in performance or music theory is also available.

Graduate programs leading to the degrees Master of Music in applied music and Master of Music Education are available.

General Program Areas. Commercial Music, Composition, Jazz Studies, Music Education, Music Theory, Performance, Piano Pedagogy.

Instruments Taught. Brass, Guitar, Percussion, Piano, Stringed Instruments, Voice, Woodwinds.

Musical Facilities

Concerts/Musical Activities. Student/faculty recitals and concerts.

Music Library. The Lether E. Frazar Memorial Library houses over 300,000 volumes and supports the academic programs of the Department of Music.

Special Programs

Performance Groups. Trombone Choir, Wind Ensemble, Brass Choir, Percussion Ensemble, Orchestra, Band, Chamber Ensembles, University Chorus, A Cappella Choir, McNeese Madrigalians, Opera Workshop, Stage Band, Wind Ensemble, Orchestra, Band.

Financial

Costs. Per academic year: Tuition in-state resident $992, out-of-state $1,872. Room and board $1,600.

Financial Aid. Financial aid in the form of scholarships, grants, loans, part-time employment, and a College Work-Study program are available. Financial aid/scholarship application due May 1.

University of New Orleans
Department of Music
Lake Front
New Orleans
Louisiana 70148

Telephone. (504) 286-6381

Chief Administrator. Mary Ann Bulla, Chairperson.

The University of New Orleans was established in 1956 to bring publicly supported higher education to the citizens of the state's largest urban area. In 1974, the present name was adopted but the school remains a member of the Louisiana State University System. The University occupies a 195-acre campus on the southern shores of Lake Pontchartrain.

The Department of Music offers undergraduate and graduate programs for students interested in professional careers in performance or teaching, as well as courses for the general student.

Accreditation. Southern Association of Colleges and Schools; National Association of Schools of Music.

Academic Information

Enrollment, Music Majors. (Total University) 12,788.

Music Faculty. 13.

Term System. Semester. 7-week summer session.

Entrance Requirements. High school graduation; audition and placement examinations.

Admission Procedure. Application with supporting documents and nonrefundable $10 fee to Admissions Office.

Music Degrees Offered. Bachelor of Arts; Bachelor of Music Education; Master of Music.

Music Degree Requirements. The Bachelor of Arts degree curriculum includes majors in vocal or instrumental performance, music theory and composition, and music history. The Bachelor of Music Education degree is available with majors in vocal or instrumental music. A Master of Music degree program is also available.

General Program Areas. Composition, Music Education, Music History, Music Theory, Performance.

Instruments Taught. Baritone, Bass, Bassoon, Clarinet, Cornet, Flute, French Horn, Oboe, Percussion, Piano, Saxophone, Trombone, Trumpet, Tuba, Viola, Violin, Violoncello, Voice.

Musical Facilities

Practice Facilities. The Department of Music is housed in the Performing Arts Center; music rehearsal studios; electronically controlled piano laboratory; individual practice areas.

Concert Facilities. 2 theatres; recital hall.

Concerts/Musical Activities. Student/faculty recitals and concerts; visiting artists.

Music Library. The Earl K. Long Library houses over 1 million volumes and serves the academic programs of the Department of Music.

Special Programs

Performance Groups. Instrumental Ensembles, Jazz Band, University Band, Chorus, Chorale, Chamber Singers, Wind Ensemble, Orchestra, Opera Theatre.

Financial

Costs. Per academic year: Tuition in-state resident $984, out-of-state $2,294. Room $1,200. Board $1,300.

Financial Aid. Financial aid is awarded on the basis of academic merit and financial need. Both institutional and state/federal aid are available in the form of scholarships, grants, loans, and part-time employment. Financial aid/scholarship application due May 1.

Northeast Louisiana University
School of Music

700 University Avenue
Monroe
Louisiana 71209

Telephone. (318) 342-2120

Chief Administrator. Richard A. Worthington, Director.

Northeast Louisiana University opened in 1931 and functioned as a junior college until 1950 when it became a four-year institution governed by the Louisiana State Board of Education. The 216-acre campus is located in the eastern part of the city of Monroe.

The Department of Music offers undergraduate and graduate programs.

Accreditation. Southern Association of Colleges and Schools; National Association of Schools of Music.

Academic Information

Enrollment, Music Majors. (Total University) 9,856.

Music Faculty. 20.

Term System. Semester. Two summer terms.

Entrance Requirements. High school graduation; open enrollment policy for Louisiana residents; ACT required; audition and placement examinations. GRE required for graduate study.

Admission Procedure. Application with supporting documents to Office of Admissions; reviewed on a rolling admissions basis.

Music Degrees Offered. Bachelor of Music; Bachelor of Music Education; Bachelor of Arts; Master of Music; Master of Music Education.

Music Degree Requirements. The Bachelor of Music degree is offered with emphasis in instrumental or vocal performance, music history and literature, and music theory and composition. The Bachelor of Music Education degree is offered with emphases in instrumental, vocal, or combined instrumental-vocal music education. The Bachelor of Arts degree program in music is offered within the context of a liberal arts education.

Graduate programs leading to the degrees Master of Music in performance and Master of Education are also offered.

General Program Areas. Composition, Music Education, Music History, Music Literature, Music Theory, Performance.

Instruments Taught. Bass, Bassoon, Clarinet, Euphonium, Flute, French Horn, Guitar, Harpsichord, Oboe, Organ, Percussion, Piano, Recorder, Saxophone, Trombone, Trumpet, Tuba, Viola, Violin, Violoncello, Voice.

Musical Facilities

Practice Facilities. Biedenharn Hall houses the School of Music. Rehearsal rooms are located in the Band Building.

Concert Facilities. Brown Hall Auditorium; theatre.

Concerts/Musical Activities. Student/faculty recitals and concerts.

Music Library. Sandel Library serves the academic programs of the School of Music.

Special Programs

Performance Groups. Orchestra, Band, Madrigalians, Chorus, Concert Choir, Chamber Ensembles.

Financial

Costs. Per academic year: Tuition in-state resident $988, out-of-state $1,868. Room and board $1,782.

Financial Aid. Financial aid is awarded on the basis of academic merit and financial need. Scholarships, grants, loans, part-time employment, and a College Work-Study program are available. Financial aid/scholarship application due June 1.

Northwestern State University of Louisiana
Department of Music
School of Creative and Performing Arts
Natchitoches
Louisiana 71457

Telephone. (318) 357-4522
Chief Administrator. Richard E. Jennings, Head.
Northwestern State University was founded in 1884 as a two-year normal school and became a four-year institution in 1918. The 900-acre campus is located in the western part of Natchitoches, 58 miles northwest of Alexandria.

The Department of Music offers undergraduate and graduate programs.

Accreditation. Southern Association of Colleges and Schools; National Association of Schools of Music; National Council for Accreditation of Teacher Education.

Academic Information

Enrollment, Music Majors. (Total Enrollment) 4,382.
Music Faculty. 15.
Term System. Semester. One summer term.
Entrance Requirements. High school graduation; ACT required; audition and placement examinations.
Admission Procedure. Application with supporting documents reviewed on a rolling admissions basis.
Music Degrees Offered. Bachelor of Music; Bachelor of Arts; Master of Music.
Music Degree Requirements. The Bachelor of Music degree is offered with majors in performance and theory-composition. The Bachelor of Arts degree is offered in the context of a liberal arts program. A Bachelor of Music Education degree program is offered through the College of Education with concentrations in instrumental music and vocal music (voice and piano concentrations). The Master of Music degree can be earned with a major in music education. The Master of Music Education degree is also offered with a specified curriculum.
General Program Areas. Composition, Music Education, Music Theory, Performance.
Instruments Taught. Bass, Bassoon, Clarinet, Euphonium, Flute, French Horn, Harp, Harpsichord, Oboe, Organ, Percussion, Piano, Saxophone, Trombone, Trumpet, Tuba, Viola, Violin, Violoncello, Voice.

Special Programs

Performance Groups. Band, Chorale, Chamber Choir, Orchestra, String Ensemble, Jazz Ensemble, Opera Theater, Women's Chorus, Brass Ensemble, Percussion Ensemble, Woodwind Ensemble, Vocal Ensemble, University Choir.

Financial

Costs. Per academic year: Tuition in-state resident $1,085, out-of-state $2,135. Fees $219. Room $832. Board $1,040.
Financial Aid. Financial aid is awarded on the basis of academic merit and financial need. Scholarships, grants, loans, and part-time employment are available. Scholarship/financial aid application due May 1.

Southeastern Louisiana University
Department of Music
100 West Dakota Avenue
Hammond
Louisiana 70402

Telephone. (504) 549-2184
Chief Administrator. Dr. Robert Weatherly, Department Head.
Southeastern Louisiana University is a publicly supported institution established in 1925. It began its four-year curricula in 1937. The 375-acre campus is situated in the northwest section of the city of Hammond.

The objectives of the Department of Music are to: (1) provide preparation for many of the professions in music and related fields; (2) provide all University students with opportunities to learn about music in the context of a liberal arts education; (3) provide student, faculty, and visiting professional performances that are cultural assets to the university; and (4) serve as a leadership and resource center for elementary and secondary schools and for the community at large.

Accreditation. Southern Association of Colleges and Schools; National Association of Schools of Music; National Council for Accreditation of Teacher Education.

Academic Information

Enrollment, Music Majors. (Total University) 7,814.
Music Faculty. 13.
Term System. Semester. One summer session.
Entrance Requirements. High school graduation or equivalent; open enrollment policy for Louisiana residents; audition required.
Admission Procedure. Application with supporting documents and nonrefundable $5 fee to Office of Admissions.
Music Degrees Offered. Bachelor of Music; Bachelor of Arts; Master of Music.
Music Degree Requirements. The Bachelor of Music is a professional degree for students desiring to prepare for a career in performance, composition, private teaching, or church music; as background for graduate study; or as a terminal degree of a general education. Majors are offered in band or orchestral instruments and voice. The Bachelor of Arts degree is also offered with majors in voice or piano. The College of Education offers bac-

calaureate degree programs in music therapy and music education.

The Master of Music degree is granted in performance and music theory.

General Program Areas. Composition, Music Education, Music Theory, Performance.

Instruments Taught. Brass, Organ, Percussion, Piano, Stringed Instruments, Voice, Woodwinds.

Musical Facilities

Practice Facilities. The Department of Music is located in the Music Annex.

Concert Facilities. Recital hall.

Concerts/Musical Activities. Student/faculty concerts and recitals; visiting artists.

Music Library. A music score library is housed in the Music Building. The Linus A. Sims Memorial Library houses over 270,000 volumes and supports the academic program of the Department of Music.

Special Programs

Performance Groups. Music Theatre, Orchestra, Chamber Ensemble, Symphonic Band, Varsity Band, Chorus, Concert Choir.

Financial

Costs. Per academic year: Tuition in-state resident $1,-088, out-of-state $1,968. Room and board $1,520.

Financial Aid. Financial aid is awarded on the basis of academic merit and financial need. Institutional scholarships available. Other forms of financial aid include grants, loans, and part-time employment. Financial aid/scholarship application due May 1.

University of Southwestern Louisiana
School of Music
East University Avenue
Lafayette
Louisiana 70504

Telephone. (318) 231-6016
Chief Administrator. James Goodman, Director.

The University of Southwestern Louisiana is a comprehensive, public institution. It became a four-year senior college in 1921 and achieved university status in 1960. The 735-acre campus is located in Lafayette on the Vermillion River.

The School of Music offers curricula for those preparing to be private teachers, performers, composers, or instructors at the college level. It also offers a program in the liberal arts context and provides concerts for the community. A basic program in music education for those planning to teach music at the elementary and secondary level is offered by the College of Education.

Accreditation. Southern Association of Colleges and Schools; National Association of Schools of Music; National Council for Accreditation of Teacher Education.

Academic Information

Enrollment, Music Majors. (Total University) 14,339.
Music Faculty. 22.
Term System. Semester. One summer term.
Entrance Requirements. High school graduation; open enrollment policy for Louisiana residents; audition and placement examinations.
Admission Procedure. Application with supporting documents and nonrefundable $5 fee to Office of Admissions.
Music Degrees Offered. Bachelor of Music; Bachelor of Music Education; Bachelor of Arts; Master of Music; Master of Music Education.
Music Degree Requirements. The Bachelor of Music degree is offered with concentrations in theory-composition and performance. The Bachelor of Music Education degree is offered with vocal and instrumental emphases. The Bachelor of Arts degree program is offered with a major in music in the liberal arts context and also in music history-literature.

The Master of Music degree is designed for the professional musician and is offered with a concentration in performance. The program leading to the Master of Music Education degree is designed to provide the opportunity for advanced study and research in methods and techniques of teaching music in elementary schools, secondary schools, colleges, and universities.

General Program Areas. Music Education, Music History, Music Literature, Music Theory.

Instruments Taught. Baritone, Bass, Bassoon, Clarinet, Cornet, Flute, French Horn, Guitar, Harpsichord, Marimba, Oboe, Organ, Percussion, Piano, Saxophone, Trombone, Trumpet, Tuba, Vibraharp, Viola, Violin, Violoncello, Voice.

Musical Facilities

Concerts/Musical Activities. Student/faculty recitals and concerts; visiting artists.
Music Library. The Music Listening Room houses a collection of more than 4,500 recordings of music and drama, with modern listening equipment for individual use.

Special Programs

Performance Groups. Percussion Ensemble, Concert Band, Marching Band, Chamber Orchestra, University Orchestra, Universtiy Chorus, University Chorale, Men's Chorus, Women's Chorus, Singers Chorus, Piano Ensemble, Chamber Music Ensemble, Opera Ensemble, Jazz Ensemble, Woodwind Ensemble, Brass Ensemble.

Financial

Costs. Per academic year: Tuition in-state resident $804, out-of-state $1,584. Room and board $1,750.

Financial Aid. Scholarships, grants, loans, and part-time employment are available. Financial aid/scholarship application due March 31.

Tulane University
Newcomb College
Department of Music
1229 Broadway
New Orleans
Louisiana 70118

Telephone. (504) 865-5267

Chief Administrator. Francis L. Monachino, Chairman.

Tulane University was founded in 1834 and Newcomb College in 1886. Newcomb College is Tulane's liberal arts college for women, officially known as The H. Sophie Newcomb Memorial College for Women.

The Tulane/Newcomb Program in music gives students the opportunity to investigate many fields as either a music major or nonmajor. The student receives an intensive, specialized education as a performer, composer, conductor, historian, or teacher.

Accreditation. Southern Association of Colleges and Schools.

Academic Information

Enrollment, Music Majors. (Total University) 8,931.

Music Faculty. Full-time 13, adjunct 8. Artists-in-residence: First Monday Contemporary Chamber Ensemble, Louisiana Repertory Jazz Ensemble.

Term System. Semester. Academic year from late August to mid-May.

Entrance Requirements. High school graduation; completion of 16 units including 4 English, 4 mathematics, 2 foreign language, 2 science, 2 social science; SAT or ACT; audition required.

Admission Procedure. Application with supporting documents and $25 nonrefundable fee by February 1.

Music Degrees Offered. Bachelor of Arts; Bachelor of Fine Arts; Master of Arts; Master of Fine Arts.

Music Degree Requirements. The Bachelor of Arts degree in music provides a concentration in music literature, history, composition, or theory. It provides the preparation necessary for graduate work in musicology. The Bachelor of Fine Arts degree is a concentration in music performance. The baccalaureate degrees requires the completion of a minimum of 128 semester hours.

The Master of Arts program provides a concentration in musicology, theory, or composition. The Master of Fine Arts program provides a continuation of study in composition or performance in voice, instrument, or musical theater. The degrees are offered by arrangement with the Tulane University Graduate School.

General Program Areas. Applied Music, Composition, Music History, Music Literature, Music Theory, Musicology, Performance.

Instruments Taught. Brass, Percussion, Piano, Stringed Instruments, Voice, Woodwinds.

Musical Facilities

Practice Facilities. The Department of Music is located in the Brandt V. B. Dixon Performing Arts Center. Practice studios (most equipped with grand pianos); spacious teaching studios, band and orchestra rehearsal halls.

Concert Facilities. Dixon Auditorium, seating 1,000; Recital Hall, 200.

Concerts/Musical Activities. Shows, recitals, and concerts year-round; Downman Performance Series consists of three concerts and one fully staged opera or operetta; solo artists and chamber ensemble performances.

Music Library. The Maxwell Music Library contains 13,200 books, 13,500 musical scores, and 13,200 video and audio tapes and records. Special collections available to students include the William Ransom Hogan Jazz Archive and the Louisiana Collection. Students have access to the holdings of the Howard Tilton Memorial Library.

Special Programs

Performance Groups. Choral Ensemble, Instrumental Ensemble, Band, Opera Workshop, Orchestra, Jazz Ensemble, Summer Lyric Theatre.

Financial

Costs. Per academic year: Tuition $9,080. Applied music fee $150 for two half-hour lessons per week. Room $1,800 to $2,450. Board $1,560 to $1,720.

Financial Aid. Scholarships in voice, piano, and strings are available for qualified students. Other sources of financial aid include grants and loans.

MAINE

University of Maine
School of Performing Arts
Department of Music
123 Lord Hall
Orono
Maine 04469

Telephone. (207) 581-1240

Chief Administrator. Dr. Ludlow Hallman, Chairman.

The University of Maine is the land-grant university and sea-grant college of the state of Maine. It was originally established at Orono as the State College of Agriculture and the Mechanic Arts. It opened in 1868 with 12 students. The original name was changed to the University of Maine in 1897. The Orono campus is the largest of a statewide system that includes campuses at Augusta, Farmington, Fort Kent, Presque Isle, Machias, and Portland-Gorham. The Orono campus of over 3,200 acres borders the Stillwater River in a rural area eight miles from Bangor.

The Department of Music of the School of Performing Arts aims to provide music instruction of the highest quality to the students of the university community. It offers a program designed for the study of music within a strong liberal arts curriculum as well as to assist the gifted music student in preparation for a career in music performance.

Accreditation. New England Association of Schools and Colleges; National Association of Schools of Music.

Academic Information

Enrollment, Music Majors. Full-time 40 men, 42 women; part-time 1 man, 4 women. Foreign students 2.

Music Faculty. Full-time 15, part-time 9.

Term System. Semester. Academic year from Sept. to May. Summer session of 12 weeks from mid-June to late August.

Entrance Requirements. High school graduation; completion of 17 units including 4 English, 3 mathematics, 2 foreign language, 1 laboratory science, 1 social science, 6 electives; SAT and 1 Achievement test re-quired. Audition required (tape or in person); theory and piano placement examinations.

Admission Procedure. Application and supporting documents with $15 nonrefundable fee by December or April.

Music Degrees Offered. Bachelor of Arts; Bachelor of Music in Music Education; Bachelor of Music in Performance; Master of Music.

Music Degree Requirements. The Bachelor of Arts degree with a major in music requires completion of a total of 120 credits. It offers a broad coverage of the field of music with emphasis on the study of the history and theory of music. It furnishes an appropriate background for prospective candidates for advanced degrees who are preparing for non-performance centered careers. It does not qualify the graduate for certification as a public school music teacher. Candidates for the degree are expected to attain a level of performing ability equivalent to that required at the completion of the sophomore year in the Bachelor of Music program. A senior project is required in lieu of a recital. A total of 48 semester hours in music courses is required. The Bachelor of Music in Music Education is a four-year professional degree for students who intend to make music a career either as a public school teacher or supervisor of music. The degree provides for many professional opportunities and serves also as preparation for graduate study in music education. A total number of 120 semester hours including 81 in music is required for the degree. The Bachelor of Music in Performance places emphasis on performance, music theory, music history, and studies in the liberal arts. Graduation requirements include appropriate proficiency in playing or singing, excellent memory, substantial repertoire, and musicianship of a high order. A total number of 120 semester hours is required for the degree, including 87 in music.

The Master of Music degree is offered in Performance, Choral Conducting, Music Education. The degree requires the completion of 30 semester hours and fulfillment of all requirements as specified for the degree program.

General Program Areas. Composition, Music Education, Music History, Music Literature, Music Theory, Performance.

Instruments Taught. Baritone, Bass, Bassoon, Clarinet, Flute, French Horn, Guitar, Harpsichord, Oboe, Organ, Percussion, Piano, Saxophone, Trombone, Trumpet, Tuba, Viola, Violin, Violoncello, Voice.

Musical Facilities

Practice Facilities. Special practice facilities for organists; 2 organs (Hook, Boody). 2 practice rooms for percussionists. 16 practice rooms. 25 pianos (11 grands, 14 uprights); 6 grand pianos reserved for piano majors. Electronic piano lab; electronic music lab.

Concert Facilities. Recital Hall seating 145; Hauck Auditorium, 600; Hutchins Concert Hall, 1,600.

Concerts/Musical Activities. 28 recitals and 24 concerts performed on campus yearly.

Music Library. 9,977 volumes; 2,500 scores; 24 current periodical subscriptions; 4,000 audiovisual materials. 14 listening stations (stereo). Special collection on Maine music and musicians.

Special Programs

Performance Groups. University Singers, Oratorio Society, University Chorus, Marching Band, Concert Band, Pop Band, Symphonic Wind Ensemble, University Orchestra, Chamber Singers, Opera Workshop, Brass Ensemble, Trombone Ensemble, Twentieth Century Music Ensemble, Woodwind Ensemble, Horn Ensemble, String Ensemble, Karl Mellon Clarinet Choir.

Financial

Costs. Per academic year: Tuition in-state resident $1,509, out-of-state $4,560. Room and board $2,861 to $2,921.

Financial Aid. Financial aid is awarded on the basis of academic merit, financial need, musical ability. Institutional and state/federal aid available. 10 scholarship awards ranging from $100 to $700. Scholarship application due March 1. Part-time employment and College Work-Study program available.

Commentary

The Music Department was planning to move to a new location—the Maine Center for the Arts—as part of an effort to create a more visible state center for arts education. The University's Anthropology Museum has a collection of American Indian and African instruments.

MARYLAND

University of Maryland - Baltimore County
Department of Music
5401 Wilkens Avenue
Catonsville
Maryland 21228

Telephone. (301) 455-2942

Chief Administrator. Dr. Samuel Gordon, Chairman.

The University of Maryland - Baltimore County is one of the five campuses of the University of Maryland system. It was founded in 1963 and enrolls over 8,000 students each year. The 475-acre campus is located six miles from the city of Baltimore.

The study of music at UMBC stresses the interdependence of theory, history, and performance. The study of traditional western music is balanced with exploration of new music and music of other cultures.

Accreditation. Middle States Association of Colleges and Schools.

Academic Information

Enrollment, Music Majors. (Total University) 8,448.

Music Faculty. 9.

Term System. Semester. Two summer sessions.

Entrance Requirements. High school graduation or GED; SAT required; audition required. GRE required for graduate study.

Admission Procedure. Application with supporting documents and nonrefundable $15 fee to Office of Admissions.

Music Degrees Offered. Bachelor of Arts; Master of Arts; Doctor of Philosophy.

Music Degree Requirements. Students majoring in music receive a Bachelor of Arts degree in the visual and performing arts. The program prepares students for advanced study in applied music, theory, music history, ethnomusicology, or composition.

The Master of Arts and the Doctor of Philosophy degrees are offered in the field of ethnomusicology through the Graduate School.

General Program Areas. Composition, Ethnomusicology, Music History, Music Theory, Performance.

Instruments Taught. Brass, Guitar, Percussion, Piano, Stringed Instruments, Voice, Woodwinds.

Musical Facilities

Practice Facilities. The Department of Music is housed in the Fine Arts Building and has specialized studios and processing systems for research.

Concert Facilities. Recital Hall, seating 400 (2 Steinway Model D concert grand pianos and a Sabathil double manual harpsichord); Gallery, informal seating (Yamaha grand piano).

Concerts/Musical Activities. Student/faculty recitals and concerts.

Music Library. The Kuhn Library houses over 400,-000 monographs and books and maintains collections of musical scores, recordings, and tapes.

Special Programs

Performance Groups. Concert Choir, Camerata Chamber Choir, Community Symphony, Wind Ensemble, Gamelan Balinese/Javanese Ensemble, New Music Ensemble.

Financial

Costs. Per academic year: Tuition in-state resident $1,-640, out-of-state $4,516. Room $1,610. Board $1,440.

Financial Aid. The University assists students in meeting educational expenses by administering and coordinating a variety of federal, state, and institutional student aid programs including grants, scholarships, loans, and part-time employment. Financial aid/scholarship application due March 1.

University of Maryland - College Park
Department of Music
Division of Arts and Humanities
College Park
Maryland 20742

Telephone. (301) 454-2501
Chief Administrator. Dr. Paul P. Traver, Chairman.
The University of Maryland was founded in 1856. The campus in College Park is part of the University's five-campus system. Located between Baltimore and Washington, D.C., the 1,378-acre campus has 230 major buildings.

The objectives of the Department of Music are to: provide professional musical training based on a foundation in the liberal arts; help the general student develop sound critical judgment and discriminating taste in the performance and literature of music; prepare the student for graduate work in the field; and prepare the student to teach music in the public schools.

Accreditation. Middle States Association of Colleges and Schools; National Association of Schools of Music; National Council for Accreditation of Teacher Education.

Academic Information

Enrollment, Music Majors. (Total University) 38,679.
Music Faculty. 46.
Term System. Semester. Two summer sessions.
Entrance Requirements. High school graduation or GED; SAT required; audition before faculty committee. GRE required for graduate study.
Admission Procedure. Application with supporting documents and nonrefundable $15 fee to Admissions Office.
Music Degrees Offered. Bachelor of Music; Bachelor of Arts; Bachelor of Science.
Music Degree Requirements. The Bachelor of Music degree is designed for qualified students with extensive pre-college training and potential for successful careers in professional music. Majors are available in theory, composition, and performance. The Bachelor of Arts degree with a major in music is designed for students whose interests include broader career alternatives. The Bachelor of Science degree with a major in music education is offered in conjunction with the College of Education.

The Master of Music degree is offered with specializations in performance, musicology and ethnomusicology, and theory and composition. The Doctor of Musical Arts Degree is offered with specializations in composition and literature-performance.

Music education programs in cooperation with the College of Education lead to the Master of Arts, Master of Education, Doctor of Education, and Doctor of Philosophy degrees.

General Program Areas. Composition, Music Education, Music Theory, Performance.
Instruments Taught. Bass, Bassoon, Clarinet, Euphonium, Flute, Guitar, Harp, Historical Instruments, Horn, Oboe, Organ, Percussion, Piano, Saxophone, Trombone, Trumpet, Tuba, Viola, Violin, Violoncello, Voice.

Musical Facilities

Music Library. The Music Library contains such special collections as: Alfred Wallenstein Collection of musical scores; archival and research collections of the American Bandmasters Association; Music Educators National Conference; National Association of College Wind and Percussion Instructors; International Clarinet Society; International Piano Archives at Maryland; Jacob M. Coopersmith Collection; Andre Kostelanetz's working collection of orchestral scores and parts in manuscript. There were plans to publish a series of indexes to music periodicals from the late eighteenth to the early twentieth century. The Nonprint Media Services Department in the Hornbake Library has listening facilities for tapes and recordings. The International Piano Archives at Maryland has acquired Gary Graffman's private collection of materials relating to his career.

Special Programs

Performance Groups. University Bands, Orchestra, Chorale, Chorus, Jazz Ensemble, Instrumental Ensembles.

Financial

Costs. Per academic year: Tuition in-state resident $1,496, out-of-state $4,202. Room $1,842. Board $1,578.
Financial Aid. Scholarships, grants, loans, and part-time employment are available. Financial aid/scholarship application due February 15.

Commentary

Performance activities are an important aspect of university life on this campus. The University of Maryland has sponsored the annual University of Maryland Piano Festival and William Kapell Piano Competition for more than 15 years. In addition, the Guarneri String Quartet is in residence at the University.

Peabody Institute of The Johns Hopkins University
1 East Mt. Vernon Place
Baltimore
Maryland 21202

Telephone. (301) 659-8100
Chief Administrator. Robert O. Pierce, Director.

The Peabody Institute was founded in 1857 by George Peabody, a New Englander who moved to Baltimore where he eventually became a leading patron of education and the arts. The Institute was, in fact, the 19th-century equivalent of today's "cultural center." It had four divisions: a research and reference library; a collection of drawings, paintings, and sculptures; a series of lectures by accomplished scholars and scientists; and an academy of music, which quickly developed into a music conservatory in the best tradition of the Old World. Construction of the original conservatory building began in 1861 and was completed in 1866. The first classes of the Peabody Conservatory took place in 1868.

In accordance with an expanded sense of purpose and activity, the Conservatory in 1977 entered into an affiliation with The Johns Hopkins University, sharing curricular and extracurricular programs and facilities, and adopting its present name. In 1985, the Peabody Institute officially became a division of The Johns Hopkins University System, with several varieties of joint programs currently being developed between Peabody and other divisions of the University. All degrees earned at the Conservatory are granted by the University.

The Conservatory campus is a completely enclosed complex occupying a square block in a historic section of Baltimore.

Accreditation. Middle States Association of Colleges and Schools; National Association of Schools of Music.

Academic Information

Enrollment, Music Majors. Full-time 168 men, 147 women; part-time 53 men, 61 women. 62 foreign students.

Music Faculty. Full-time 52, part-time 63. Artists-in-residence: The American String Quartet.

Term System. Semester. One summer session.

Entrance Requirements. High school graduation from accredited school or GED; SAT required; audition required (live or taped, 15 to 30 minutes); placement tests in ear-training for Master of Music programs. Bachelor of Music degree or equivalent is a prerequisite for admission to graduate work.

Admission Procedure. Application with $40 non-refundable fee due January 1 or May 1.

Music Degrees Offered. Bachelor of Music; Master of Music; Doctor of Musical Arts; Artist Diploma; Performer's Certificate.

Music Degree Requirements. The Bachelor of Music degree is designed to prepare gifted students for careers in performance, composition, music education, recording arts, and related areas of professional activity. A minimum of 122 semester hours, excluding ensemble, is required. Residence in normally four years, during which time a student must maintain full-time status for at least four semesters, accumulating no fewer than 60 credits during those four semesters. The maximum number of semester hours taken during any year is 36. The general distribution of hours, depending on major field, includes 32 hours in the major, 8 in the minor, 88-96 in classroom subjects, and 6 semesters of ensembles. The major areas include performance, composition, music education (orchestral instruments, voice), and performance/recording arts and sciences.

The program leading to the degree of Master of Music provides for intensive development of performance skills, extensive knowledge of the literature in the major field of study, and achievement of a broadened knowledge of the art. The degree requires full-time attendence for a minimum of one year beyond receipt of the Bachelor of Music degree. The program components include music coursework, foreign languages, ensembles, recitals and compositions, and a master's essay. Major areas offered include performance, composition, music criticism, music education, and music history. The degree requires the completion of 34 to 36 credit hours plus ensembles.

The objective of the program leading to the degree of Doctor of Musical Arts is to provide a select number of qualified students with the highest level of professional development in the art of musical performance or the craft of musical composition, within a context of comprehensive understanding of the common body of theoretical and historical knowledge and of the literature specific to the applied major. The program of study normally requires an attendance of two years beyond receipt of the Master's degree for a total of 64 to 68 credits, depending on the major area of concentration. Major areas offered are conducting, performance, and composition.

In addition to degree programs, there is the Professional Studies alternative, with a minimum of academic requirements, for those not pursuing a degree.

General Program Areas. Composition, Conducting, Early Instruments, Electronic Music, Instrument Maintenance, Music Criticism, Music Education, Music History, Music Theory, Performance, Recording Arts.

Instruments Taught. Baritone, Bass, Bassoon, Clarinet, Flute, French Horn, Guitar, Harp, Harpsichord, Oboe, Organ, Percussion, Piano, Saxophone, Trombone, Trumpet, Tuba, Viola, Violin, Violoncello, Voice.

Musical Facilities

Practice Facilities. 75 practice rooms. 5 organs (1 Casavant Freres, 1 Malcker, 3 Hammerberger). 2 percussion-equipped practice rooms. 142 pianos (124 grands of which 65 are Steinway and others by Yamaha, Howard, Knabe, Mason & Hamlin, Baldwin; 5 uprights, 13 electrics). Electronic and computer music studio; recording studio.

Concert Facilities. Miriam A. Friedberg Concert Hall, seating 800; North Hall (recital); Leakin Hall (recital).

Concerts/Musical Activities. The concert calendar includes many faculty recitals, student recitals, and a concert series. Individual students and ensembles present over 300 concerts yearly; Tuesday Noon Recital Series.

Music Library. 50,000 volumes, including strong collections of performance materials, music reference materials, scholarly editions, and periodicals. The Record Library contains a collection of 15,000 recordings and corresponding listening facilities for discs, reel-to-reel tapes, and cassettes. Rare items include a collection of sixteenth century Venetian *laude;* the Enrico Caruso and John Charles Thomas collections of memorabilia; a small collection of early American sheet-music; and several early editions of scores and orchestral parts of Hector Berlioz. Other special collections include items from the personal library of Virgil Thomson; manuscripts and published works of George Boyle; Jacob Coopersmith materials.

Special Programs

Featured Programs. In 1984, Peabody hosted the first Peabody/Morgan Black Music Symposium, the topic of focus being Black Musical Theater, and hosted the national conference of the American Liszt Society.

The Yale Gordon Concerto Competition is held annually and rotates in the areas of strings, piano, and orchestral instruments. A cash prize, a performance with orchestra, and a solo appearance at Shriver Hall are awarded to the winner of this competition. Other competitions include the France Graage Performance Scholarships, the Sylvia L. Green Voice Competition, the Mieczyslaw Munz Piano Scholarship Competition, the William Marbury Prize, and the Dan Saslow Piano Competition.

Performance Groups. Orchestra, Wind Ensemble, Chorus, Concert Singers, Opera Theater, Opera Workshop, Chamber Ensemble, Jazz Ensemble, Baroque Performance Workshop.

Affiliated Programs. Cooperative cross-registration agreements with Loyola College and the Maryland Institute of Art in Baltimore. Peabody Conservatory is an affiliated division of The John Hopkins University.

Financial

Costs. Per academic year: Tuition $8,500. Room and board $3,530.

Financial Aid. Scholarships and grants-in-aid are awarded to full-time degree candidates on the basis of talent, needs of the student, and needs of the school. Auditions are held by the departmental faculties and by the Traveling Jury. All scholarships are for one year and are renewable annually depending on the progress of the student as indicated by examination and grade point average. Awards average $2,500 per annum. Scholarship applications due February 15. Other sources of financial aid include state/federal loans and grants, part-time employment, and a College Work-Study program.

Commentary

Among the more unusual undergraduate majors at Peabody are lute and recording arts and sciences. The graduate level features a music criticism program along with all the usual disciplines in an extremely well-balanced curriculum. In addition to the library resources at the Conservatory, the nearby Maryland Historical Society has a collection of eighteenth- and nineteenth-century American music imprints, and the Baltimore Museum of Arts, affiliated with The Johns Hopkins University, holds a collection of Western and ethnic instruments.

Towson State University
Department of Music
Towson
Maryland 21204

Telephone. (301) 321-2143

Chief Administrator. Dr. David Marchand, Chairperson.

Towson State University traces its history back to 1865. At that time the General Assembly of Maryland established a statewide public school system and authorized the Maryland State Normal School as the first state teacher training institution. It later became known as the State Teachers College at Towson, then in 1963 as Towson State College, and since 1976 as Towson State University. The University occupied three different locations in Baltimore before moving to its present suburban location in 1915. Towson State is committed to providing comprehensive opportunities for undergraduate and graduate education and offers a variety of programs in the traditional arts and sciences and in specialized professional fields.

The Department of Music, located in the Fine Arts Center, offers two major degree programs in music. Although there are many courses common to all degree programs and concentrations, each is designed with many of its own special requirements, especially in the junior and senior years. The Department also participates in the Elementary Education Program by offering a course in music fundamentals and a specific section of teaching music in the elementary school.

Accreditation. Middle States Association of Colleges and Schools; National Association of Schools of Music.

Academic Information

Enrollment, Music Majors. (Total University) 15,410.

Music Faculty. Full-time 32, part-time 30.

Term System. Semester. Academic year September to May. 5-week summer session.

Entrance Requirements. High school graduation; SAT 900; C+ average; audition; theory placement test. Foreign students must achieve a minimum score of 500 on

TOEFL; SAT, social security number, and financial certification form. Advanced placement in music theory only.

Admission Procedure. Students who wish to apply to the Department of Music must write to the chair of the Department as well as the Director of Admissions of the University. Applicants will receive information from both offices regarding the necessary entrance requirements and procedures. Admission to the university does not guarantee acceptance into the music major.

Music Degrees Offered. Bachelor of Arts; Bachelor of Science.

Music Degree Requirements. The Bachelor of Arts degree is offered with concentrations in vocal performance and music literature. The Bachelor of Science degree is offered with concentrations in instrumental music education, vocal-general music education, theory, instrumental performance, and jazz-commercial music. Students enrolled in the B.S. programs may, upon completion of the language requirement, receive a B.A. degree. Students pursuing the B.A. degree are required to complete the intermediate courses, or the equivalent, of a modern foreign language. A minimum of 120 credit hours is required for the bachelor's degree. Every music major must enroll for private lessons on instrument or in voice and all students (except those concentrating in theory and literature) are required to perform in recital. All students must reach a level of piano proficiency established for each degree and concentration. Ensemble participation is required and all students must attend 60 approved on-campus recitals/concerts before permission is granted to perform in senior recital. Of these 60, 15 must be faculty performances.

General Program Areas. Commercial Music, Jazz Studies, Music Education, Music Literature, Music Theory, Performance.

Instruments Taught. Brass, Organ, Percussion, Piano, Stringed Instruments, Voice, Woodwinds.

Musical Facilities

Practice Facilities. 32 practice rooms. 2 organs (Moeller). Special practice facilities for percussionists. 32 pianos (uprights and grands); 6 grand pianos reserved for piano majors. Recording studio.

Concert Facilities. 3 concert halls seating 750, 500, and 75, respectively.

Concerts/Musical Activities. 200 concerts/recitals per year by students, faculty, and guest artists.

Music Library. 12,000 volumes; 8,000 scores; 75 current periodical subscriptions; 100 microforms; 5,000 phonograph recordings. 20 listening stations. Special historic percussion collection.

Special Programs

Performance Groups. Band, Orchestra, Marching Band, Jazz Ensemble.

Financial

Costs. Per academic year: Tuition in-state resident $1,224, out-of-state $2,544. Music lesson fee $50 per credit. Room $3,582. Board $1,356.

Financial Aid. Financial aid is awarded on the basis of academic merit, financial need, and musical ability. Institutional and state/federal aid available. Financial aid/scholarship application due March 15. Part-time employment and College Work-Study program.

MASSACHUSETTS

Berklee College of Music
1140 Boylston Street
Boston
Massachusetts 02215

Telephone. (617) 266-1400

Chief Administrator. Lee Eliot Berk, President.

Berklee College of Music had its genesis in a Saturday afternoon music theory class—one teacher and three students, working together in a rented studio. The teacher was Lawrence Berk, an engineering graduate of the Massachusetts Institute of Technology. Berk, a former music student and club pianist, had studied with the legendary Joseph Schillinger, developer of the mathematically based music theory system bearing his name. Lawrence Berk was one of only a dozen authorized teachers of the Schillinger system. In 1945, Berk opened the school that was to become Berklee. Fewer than fifty students were enrolled in 1946, but returning servicemen quickly discovered the small school in Boston where they would waste no time connecting to the popular jazz styles of that period. Although quickly becoming known as a "jazz school," Berklee was much more than that, pioneering the then infant arts of electronic music and film scoring. Course offerings were expanded to match emerging trends in the world of professional music.

Founder Lawrence Berk's philosophy of emphasis on a broadly based, vocationally oriented curriculum has remained unchanged since Berklee's beginnings. The goal of the college remains to produce graduates who become multi-skilled music professionals capable of functioning effectively in an ever-changing musical landscape. The educational mission of Berklee College of Music is practical career preparation for the challenges facing today's music professional. This mission embodies the following principles: (1) To analyze the musical content and structure of the principal musical movements of our time so that student composers, arrangers, performers, producers, and teachers can be effective music professionals and make their own respective contributions to today's music; (2) to present musical learning experiences in the classrooms, concert and recital halls, and recording studios which simulate the challenges encountered by a contemporary music professional; (3) to keep abreast of today's music technology and the evolution of musical form and style; (4) to provide general education courses offering awareness of some of the basic fields of intellectual pursuit and which enable musicians to more effectively understand their place and time in the evolution of society; and (5) to provide a breadth of musical background so that areas of professional musicianship can be viewed in the larger context of significance to the music of past and present time.

Berklee offers a wide range of facilities which have been specifically designed to help the student realize the goal of becoming an effective music professional. These include facilities for the performer, facilities to maintain reference materials, and technical studio/laboratory/class facilities.

The college is situated in the heart of the culturally rich Back Bay section of Boston, close to Symphony Hall, the Museum of Fine Arts, the Gardner Museum, and the Boston Public Library.

Accreditation. New England Association of Schools and Colleges.

Academic Information

Enrollment, Music Majors. Total 2,292 men, 404 women. Foreign students 566.

Music Faculty. 204 full-time, 65 part-time.

Term System. Semester. Academic year September to May. Summer session of 12 weeks from June 1 to August 21.

Entrance Requirements. Successful completion of secondary school or equivalency diploma. At least 2 years of formal training on an approved principal instrument/voice or comparable experience; knowledge of basic music theory; ability to handle college work as determined by previous academic records; SAT or ACT.

Admission Procedure. Application and $50 fee; music reference; character reference; academic transcripts from high school and college. Rolling admissions.

Music Degrees Offered. Bachelor of Music. A four-year program leading to the Professional Diploma is also offered. In the degree program, music studies are combined with general education courses; the diploma program is devoted entirely to the study of music.

Music Degree Requirements. The Bachelor of Music degree requires completion of core courses (harmony, notation, arranging, ear training), music history (jazz or rock); concentrate courses; traditional studies courses; instrumental instruction; ensembles; general education courses; general electives. Minimum of 120 semester hours.

General Program Areas. Commercial Arranging, Composition, Film Scoring, Jazz Composition, Music Education, Music Production and Engineering, Music Synthesis, Performance, Professional Music, Songwriting.

Instruments Taught. Acoustic Bass, Alto Saxophone, Baritone Horn, Baritone Saxophone, Bassoon, Clarinet, Drumset, Electronic Bass, Flute, French Horn, Guitar, Mallets, Oboe, Piano, Tenor Saxophone, Trombone, Trumpet, Tuba, Viola, Violin, Violoncello, Voice.

Musical Facilities

Practice Facilities. Over 150 practice rooms; 40 ensemble and rehearsal rooms equipped with amplifiers and acoustic pianos; 75 private studios for individual instrumental lessons. Special studios include the Recording Complex with 6 studio/control room combinations; 5 music synthesis facilities; electronic piano rooms; film scoring laboratory.

Concert Facilities. Berklee Performance Center seats 1,224 in main hall; two recital halls with seating for 75 and 90, both equipped for both audio and video recording; Berklee Concert Pavilion with seating capacity of 130.

Concerts/Musical Activities. 550 concerts by students and faculty; over 75 professional shows; special seminars and clinics are held throughout the year.

Music Library. The Music Library contains 16,000 books, primarily in the field of music; recordings of over 5,000 jazz and pop LPs, 1,000 classical LPs, and 2,000 Berklee concerts and recitals. Library is equipped with 50 reel-to-reel tape decks. Score collection of over 14,-000. Music and general periodicals are received regularly. Materials are acquired to support the curriculum, as well as to address needs in the reference, independent study, and recreational reading and listening areas. The Berklee Ensemble Library contains works by noted professional arrangers as well as those by faculty members and outstanding students. All musical styles are represented.

Financial

Costs. Per academic year: Tuition for degree program, including all class, private, and ensemble instruction $5,-590. Professional Diploma program $5,190. Room and board $4,390. General facilities fee $100.

Financial Aid. Awarded on the basis of financial need and musical ability. Institutional and state/federal aid available. 70% of student body receives some form of financial aid. Scholarships average $1,000; need-based financial aid up to $4,000. Application for financial aid due March 31. College Work-Study Program and part-time employment available.

Commentary

The Berklee College of Music is one of the few institutions in the world specializing in jazz and commercial music, offering majors in such fields as commercial arranging and film scoring.

Boston Conservatory of Music
8 The Fenway
Boston
Massachusetts 02215

Telephone. (617) 536-6340

Chief Administrator. William A. Seymour, President.

The Boston Conservatory of Music was founded in 1867 by Julius Eichberg. The school was first incorporated under the laws of the Commonwealth of Massachusetts in 1896, with reorganizations in 1905 and 1914. The Boston Conservatory is committed to the belief that performance is fundamental to any career in the arts, and it is with this belief that the Conservatory seeks to develop performance skills in all students. It is the purpose of the Conservatory to provide professional training in the three performing arts (music, dance, and drama) reinforced by a sound general education that will make its graduates more resourceful as performers and teachers.

Accreditation. New England Association of Schools and Colleges; National Association of Schools of Music.

Academic Information

Enrollment, Music Majors. Full-time 111 men, 215 women, part-time 20 men, 31 women. 15 foreign students.

Music Faculty. Full-time 21, part-time 68.

Term System. Semester. One 6-week summer session.

Entrance Requirements. High school graduation or GED; 16 units including 4 English, 8 mathematics, laboratory science, foreign language, and social studies, and 4 elective; SAT required; audition required (in person preferred).

Admission Procedure. Applications with $45 non-refundable fee due April 15.

Music Degrees Offered. Bachelor of Music; Master of Music; Artist Diploma.

Music Degree Requirements. The Bachelor of Music degree is offered with majors in guitar, organ, piano, string and harp, voice, wind and percussion, opera, composition and theory, and music education. Each major has a definite curriculum plus a liberal arts core. The baccalaureate degree requires the completion of 130 to 144 credits, depending upon the major pursued.

The Graduate Division offers courses leading to Master of Music degrees with majors in applied music, choral conducting, composition, music education, and opera performance. Those who hold Bachelor of Music degrees or other equivalent baccalaureate degrees with major in music from a school of recognized standing are eligible to apply for admission. The minimum requirement for the degree is the completion of 32 credit hours of study, 26 of which must be earned in residence at the Conservatory. An overall average of B or better must be earned. Applied majors, or music education majors electing the recital option, are required to earn all of their applied music credits with the Boston Conservatory faculty.

The Artist Diploma requires the completion of 100 credit hours of prescribed courses.

General Program Areas. Applied Music, Chamber Music, Choral Conducting, Composition, Music Education, Music History, Music Literature, Opera.

Instruments Taught. Brass, Guitar, Harpsichord, Organ, Percussion, Piano, Stringed Instruments, Woodwinds.

Musical Facilities

Practice Facilities. 35 practice rooms. 4 organs. 4 percussion-equipped practice rooms. 8 grand pianos reserved for piano majors. Music education studio; opera studio; piano laboratory.

Concerts/Musical Activities. The Conservatory offers a full schedule of public performances. More than 250 such performances are offered throughout the academic year from faculty and student solo and chamber music recitals, senior dance projects, workshops, and major department performances by the Boston Conservatory Dance Theatre, the Boston Conservatory Theatre Company, the Opera Theatre, the Symphony Orchestra, and the Wind Ensemble. Faculty and guest artists appear frequently throughout the year. Ensembles in residence include the Boston Conservatory Dance Theatre and the Boston Chamber Music Society.

Music Library. The Albert Alphin Music Library houses a collection of 40,000 volumes; 1,700 volumes of urtext editions of *Gesamtausgaben;* 915 periodicals; 14,490 scores; 7,795 recordings. Listening facilities are housed in the Main Library and the Music Education Resource Center.

Special Programs

Performance Groups. Boston Conservatory Dance Theatre, Boston Conservatory Theatre Company, Opera Theatre, Sypmhony Orchestra, Wind Ensemble, Brass Ensemble, Contemporary Ensemble, Collegium Musicum, Guitar Ensemble, String Ensembles, Vocal Performance Class, Woodwind Ensembles, Jazz Ensemble.

Affiliated Programs. Member of Pro-Arts Consortium with Boston Architectural Center, The School of the Museum of Fine Arts, Massachusetts College of Art, and Emerson College.

Financial

Costs. Per academic year: Tuition $6,350. Room and board $3,200 to $3,550.

Financial Aid. A number of specific scholarship funds have been established in honor or in memory of various individuals who have been affiliated with the Conservatory. Scholarship applications due April 15. Other sources of financial aid include grants, loans, and a College Work-Study program.

Boston University
School of Music
855 Commonwealth Avenue
Boston
Massachusetts 02215

Telephone. (617) 353-3341

Chief Administrator. Dr. Robert Sirota, Director.

Boston University is an independent, nonsectarian university comprising sixteen schools and colleges with an enrollment of over 19,000 full-time students. The University traces its origins back to 1839 when a group of lay and ministerial delegates of the Methodist Episcopal Church began a school for the improvement of theological training. Boston University was incorporated by the Commonwealth of Massachusetts in 1869. Most of the University's schools and colleges line the south bank of the Charles River just west of downtown Boston.

The first Dean of Boston University's School of Music, Eben Tourjee, outlined its objectives in 1873: "A thorough preparation for the profession of music ... should embrace not only a comprehensive knowledge of the science of music and a good degree of skill as an executant upon some instrument or as a vocalist, but also a familiarity with two or three of the ancient or modern languages, mathematics, sciences, literature, and the fine arts. The knowledge and general intellectual culture acquired by such a course of study ... enable students to more intelligently interpret and perform the works of the masters, render their services as instructors more valuable, and qualify them to do far more towards elevating the art to its true position in the estimation of the public." Although time has modified some of its terms, the implications of this statement remain the guiding spirit of the School of Music. The School occupies space in the building housing the School for the Arts.

Accreditation. New England Association of Schools and Colleges; National Association of Schools of Music.

Academic Information

Enrollment, Music Majors. Full-time 400.

Music Faculty. Full-time 30, part-time 70. Artists in residence: Empire Brass Quintet; Muir String Quartet.

Term System. Semester. Academic year from September to May. Summer session of 8 weeks from mid-May to early August.

Entrance Requirements. High school graduation; SAT; audition required and arranged by appointment. The School seeks students with the highest standards and musical potential.

Admission Procedure. Application and supporting documents to Admissions Office. Contact School of Music for audition dates.

Music Degrees Offered. Bachelor of Music; Master of Music; Doctor of Musical Arts; Artist Diploma.

Music Degree Requirements. The Bachelor of Music degree requires the completion of 132 semester hours and a senior recital. Majors are available in performance (voice, piano, organ, string, woodwind, brass, percussion), history and literature of music, theory and composition of music or music education. Candidates for this degree take academic courses that vary according to the particular major concentration, in addition to professional training.

The Master of Music degree requires the completion of 32 credit hours plus 2 recitals. The degree Doctor of Musical Arts requires the completion of 48 credits plus 4 recitals and a dissertation.

General Program Areas. Accompanying, Applied Music, Church Music, Composition, Conducting, Music Education, Music History, Music Literature, Music Theory, Musicology, Opera, Performance.

Instruments Taught. Baritone, Bass, Bassoon, Clarinet, Flute, French Horn, Guitar, Harp, Harpsichord, Lute, Oboe, Organ, Percussion, Piano, Saxophone, Trombone, Trumpet, Tuba, Viola, Violin, Violoncello, Voice.

Musical Facilities

Practice Facilities. 300 practice rooms. 125 practice pianos (Baldwin); 40 grand pianos reserved for piano majors. Special practice facilities for organists. Electronic music studio.

Concert Facilities. Boston University Theatre, Marsh Chapel.

Concerts/Musical Activities. 300 student and faculty concerts per year.

Music Library. Located in the Mulgar Memorial Library (1,500,000 volumes). Listening facilities (stereo).

Special collections include: archives of the Boston Symphony Orchestra; manuscripts of works dedicated to the Boston Symphony Orchestra; archives of the Conservatoire de la Musique de Paris (from 1796 to early twentieth century); Liszt collection, Arthur Fiedler collection.

Special Programs

Performance Groups. Chorus, Women's Chorus, Opera Theatre, Orchestra, Chamber Ensemble, Vocal Ensemble, Piano Ensemble, Percussion Ensemble, Chapel Choir.

Financial

Costs. Per academic year: Tuition Undergraduate $11,800, graduate $6,800. Room and board $4,600.

Financial Aid. Financial aid is awarded on the basis of academic merit, financial need, and musical ability. Institutional and state/federal aid is received by 320 students. Application for aid due March 1. College Work-Study program available.

Brandeis University
Department of Music
415 South Street
Waltham
Massachusetts 02254

Telephone. (617) 647-2558

Chief Administrator. Dr. James D. Olesen, Chair, Undergraduate Studies; Dr. Robert L. Marshall, Chair, Graduate Faculty.

Brandeis University is a liberal arts and research institution founded in 1948 as a nonsectarian institution under Jewish sponsorship. The University enrolls over 4,000 students from every state in the union and more than forty foreign countries. The 250-acre campus in Waltham is ten miles west of Boston.

The Department of Music offers a program on concentration in music offering a broad perspective in keeping with the liberal arts philosophy of the University. Concentrators gain experience in history, theory, and performance. The four-semester survey of music history examines the styles, forms, and compositional techniques of Western music in its cultural and historical context and seeks to provide a close acquaintance with representative musical literature. The sequence of music history courses aims to provide training in basic musicianship necessary for all musical endeavors as well as the more specific skills necessary for musical analysis and composition.

Accreditation. New England Association of Schools and Colleges.

Academic Information

Enrollment, Music Majors. (Total University) Full-time 1,322 men, 1,453 women; part-time 32 men, 50 women.

Music Faculty. 16.

Term System. Semester. One summer session.

Entrance Requirements. High school graduation with high rank in graduating class; completion of 16 units including 4 English, 3 mathematics, 1 science, 3 foreign language, 1 social studies; SAT and 3 Achievment Tests required; audition not required but would be helpful (in person or tape); piano proficiency examination for placement purposes.

Admission Procedure. Application with nonrefundable $30 fee due February 1.

Music Degrees Offered. Bachelor of Arts; Master of Fine Arts; Doctor of Philosophy.

Music Degree Requirements. The Bachelor of Arts degree with a concentration in music requires the completion of courses in English composition, foreign language, University studies, physical education, and the concentration for a total of 32 semester courses.

The graduate program in music leading to the Master of Fine Arts and Doctor of Philosophy is designed to provide a command of the craft of composition and an understanding of the nature, structural basis, and historical development of music. The general fields of study offered are composition and musicology. Students must specialize in one of these areas, but composers are expected to undertake some work in music history and historians to acquire some competence in tonal writing. The Master of Fine Arts degree requires 12 half courses at the graduate level and must be completed within 5 years from the inception of study. The degree Doctor of Philosophy requires the completion of 16 courses and is ordinarily a minimum of 3 years of graduate study including a dissertation and final oral examination. The doctoral degree must be earned within 8 years from the inception of graduate study.

General Program Areas. Composition, Music History, Music Theory, Performance.

Instruments Taught. Early Instruments, Organ, Piano, Stringed Instruments, Voice.

Musical Facilities

Practice Facilities. 16 practice rooms. Noack pipe organ; electronic organ (plus three other electronic organs in the chapels). Percussion-equipped practice room. 14 pianos (10 grands, 4 uprights); 3 harpsichords. 2 electronic music studios.

Concert Facilities. Slosberg Recital Hall; recital hall in University Library; 2 theatres in Spingold Center.

Concerts/Musical Activities. Frequent concerts by student groups and by individuals; frequent professional concerts.

Music Library. 16,000 books; 14,000 scores; 83 periodical titles; 4,000 microforms; 14,500 recordings. Listening stations for 98 persons (72 for stereo). Main holdings in University Library; small separate collection of books, records, scores, and parts housed in Music Building. Special collections include: American sheet music (2,000 items); Victor Young Manuscript Collection; Medieval chant and theory; Renaissance music; collection of Heinrich Schutz; holographs and printed editions of Reginald De Koven.

Special Programs

Featured Programs. The Victor and Rita Young Music Foundation promotes the education of music students by enhancing departmental programs, providing for library acquisitions, supporting tutorials, and maintaining equipment.

Performance Groups. University Chorus, Early Music Ensembles, Concert Band, Orchestra.

Foreign Programs. Junior Year Abroad available to music concentrators.

Affiliated Programs. Brandeis students enjoy cross-registration privileges with the undergraduate schools of arts and sciences at Boston College, Boston University, Tufts University, and Wellesley College.

Financial

Costs. Per academic year: Tuition and required fees $11,275. Room $2,210. Board $2,550.

Financial Aid. Students receiving grant aid will usually be expected to assume loan and work obligations as part of a self-help package determined annually by the Committee of Admissions and Financial Aid. Scholarship applications due February 15. Part-time employment and a College Work-Study program available.

Harvard University Department of Music

Music Building
Cambridge
Massachusetts 02138

Telephone. (617) 495-2791

Chief Administrator. Dr. Christoph Wolff, Chairman.

Harvard University is a private, nonsectarian university established in 1636 by the General Court of the Colony of Massachusetts Bay. For more than 150 years after its founding, Harvard was a small school whose primary function—like that of its British counterparts, the Oxford and Cambridge colleges—was the training of ministers. As the nation industrialized, a traditional classical education no longer equipped students fully for life and work in an increasingly complex society. With the establishment of Harvard's professional schools—the Medical School in 1782, the Divinity School in 1816, the Law School in 1817, the Dental School in 1867, and the Graduate School of Arts and Sciences in 1872—Harvard College became the central unit of a large university.

The Department of Music seeks to train the student to be a thinking musician with discipline stemming from the study of music as one of the humanities. The graduate student chooses a field for specialization from composition, theory, musicology, or ethnomusicology.

Accreditation. New England Association of Schools and Colleges.

Academic Information

Enrollment, Music Majors. Undergraduate 35, graduate 50. Foreign students 5.

Music Faculty. Full-time 12, part-time 5.

Term System. Semester. 6-week summer session.

Entrance Requirements. High school graduation with 18 units (4 English, 4 mathematics, 3 laboratory science, 3 social studies, 3 foreign language, 1 fine arts); SAT; 3 Achievement Tests; basic training in music theory and musicianship. 14% of applicants accepted.

Admission Procedure. Application with nonrefundable $35 fee due January 1.

Music Degrees Offered. Bachelor of Arts; Doctor of Philosophy.

General Program Areas. Composition, Ethnomusicology, Music Theory, Musicology.

Instruments Taught. Brass, Organ, Piano, Stringed Instruments, Voice, Woodwinds.

Musical Facilities

Practice Facilities. 19 practice rooms. 18 practice pianos; 7 grands reserved for use by application only. Memorial Church organ built by Charles Fisk. Electronic music studio.

Concert Facilities. Paine Hall, seating 600; Sanders Theater, 1,200.

Concerts/Musical Activities. Concerts, recitals, music theater. The Radcliffe Grant-in-Aid Society and Harvard Gilbert and Sullivan Players, each producing two shows a year; annual Lowell House opera; numerous House musicals; Hasty Pudding Club's annual original musical with all-male cast; student-written revues and musical plays produced by The Harvard Premiere Society. The New World String Quartet presents the Blodgett Chamber Music Series as part of their residency at the university.

Music Library. Eda Kuhn Loeb Music Library has holdings of 100,000 volumes, 60,000 scores; 15,000 microforms; 40,000 records; 6,000 tapes. Listening facilities (16 cassette decks; 12 stereo turntables; 6 compact disc players. Several other facilities on the Harvard campus contain music and music-related materials. Special collections include: library of music critic Richard Aldrich; musical instrument collection; autograph manuscripts of many important composers of the 17th, 18th, 19th, and 20th centuries. In the Divinity School are hymn books and hymn texts from the 18th century to the present, concentrating upon 19th-century American materials.

Special Programs

Featured Programs. The Office for the Arts coordinates artistic activities at Harvard and Radcliffe. The Office runs a music teacher reference service, offers subsidies for music lessons, and sponsors "Learning from Performers." This program invites artists and performers visiting Boston to come to Harvard to speak with undergraduates in seminars, workshops, and master classes.

Performance Groups. Harvard-Radcliffe Orchestra, Bach Society, Mozart Society, Harvard Band, Marching Band, Wind Ensemble, Jazz Band, Harvard Glee Club, Radcliffe Choral Society, Collegium Musicum; small choral and close harmony groups including the Krokodiloes, the Pitches, the Opportunes, the Kuumba Singers, Undergraduate Chorale; informal musical groups including jazz and rock bands, chamber groups, madrigal societies; house musical societies which sponsor concerts by student soloists and groups.

Foreign Programs. The John Knowle Paine Fellowships are open to both graduate and undergraduate students for overseas study programs.

Financial

Costs. Per academic year: Tuition $11,390. Room, board, and fees $4,755.

Financial Aid. Depending on the amount of financial need, the Committee on Financial Aid will offer various packages of job, loan, and/or grant. Applications for aid due January 1. Part-time employment and College Work-Study program available.

Commentary

The Graduate Program of the Department of Music offers advanced training in the academic music disciplines leading only to the Ph.D. in Music. There is no admission to a separate A.M. program. Graduate students become Teaching Fellows during a part of their time at Harvard since teaching is considered an integral part of graduate training.

University of Lowell
College of Music
1 University Avenue
Lowell
Massachusetts 01854

Telephone. (617) 452-5000

Chief Administrator. Dr. Gerald J. Lloyd, Dean.

The University of Lowell was established as a result of the 1975 merger of Lowell Technological Institute and Lowell State College. It is one of three public universities in Massachusetts. Lowell Technological Institute was established in 1895 as Lowell Textile School and became part of the state higher education system. in 1918. Its name was changed to Lowell Textile Institute in 1920 and to Lowell Technological Institute in 1953. From 1950 until it became part of the University, the Institute engaged in a program of expansion and diversification in engineering, science, and business administration. Lowell State College was established in 1894 as the Massachusetts State Normal School at Lowell. The scope of the curriculum was expanded in 1912, and in 1932 the institution was made a four-year college with the right to confer the baccalaureate degree in both elementary and music education. In 1959, it began offering curricula in secondary education, and in the following year initiated programs in the liberal arts. The University is located 25 miles northwest of Boston at several sites, two of which were formerly the campuses of the merged institutions. In 1984, the University acquired a campus in the town of Chelmsford.

The College of Music, created in 1975, has the goals of training musicians, educating non-music majors, and contributing to the cultural and economic development of the region. Sound recording, music business, and music education are emphasized in the curriculum.

Accreditation. New England Association of Schools and Colleges; National Association of Schools of Music.

Academic Information

Enrollment, Music Majors. Undergraduate 249, graduate 46.

Music Faculty. Full-time 21, part-time 29.

Term System. Semester.

Entrance Requirements. High school graduation or GED; SAT required. Audition by invitation after academic credentials are accepted.

Admission Procedure. Application with $25 nonrefundable fee.

Music Degrees Offered. Bachelor of Music; Bachelor of Arts; Master of Music.

Music Degree Requirements. The Bachelor of Music and the Bachelor of Arts degrees require the completion of 134 to 151 semester hours, depending on area of concentration and including 30 to 33 hours of general studies and 90 to 105 hours of music and other courses outside music. The Master of Music degree requires the completion of 36 semester hours of study.

General Program Areas. Applied Music, Jazz Studies, Music Business, Music Composition, Music Education, Music Theory, Performance, Sound Recording.

Instruments Taught. Brass, Organ, Percussion, Piano, Stringed Instruments, Voice, Woodwinds.

Musical Facilities

Practice Facilities. 89 practice rooms. 1 Andover concert organ; 2 practice Andover. 12 percussion-equipped practice rooms. 100 pianos (80 uprights, 20 grands); 12 grand pianos reserved for piano majors. Electronic music studio.

Concert Facilities. 2 concert halls.

Concerts/Musical Activities. University-sponsored concert series; Cultural Activities series; Student Council series.

Music Library. 20,000 volumes; music education materials; performing ensemble libraries. Listening facilities (cassette, stereo). Special collection of early music instruments.

Special Programs

Performance Groups. Ensembles, orchestra.

Financial

Costs. Per academic year: Tuition in-state resident $1,180, out-of-state $3,636. Room $1,393. Applied music fee $328.

Financial Aid. 15 music scholarships ranging from $328 to $1,040 per year (average $500). Scholarship applications due June 1. College Work-Study program.

Commentary

In an effort to strengthen its performance emphasis and expand the graduate curriculum, Lowell University is awarding graduate assistantships with tuition waiver and generous stipends.

University of Massachusetts at Amherst Department of Music and Dance
Fine Arts Center
Amherst
Massachusetts 01003

Telephone. (413) 545-2227

Chief Administrator. Dr. Charles Bestor, Head of Department.

The University of Massachusetts at Amherst was established in 1863. The campus consists of 1,200 acres of land and 130 buildings.

The Music Department offers undergraduate programs leading to the baccalaureate degree. The programs are designed for students preparing for professional performance or teaching careers. Students not majoring in music may select nonspecialized courses in music appreciation, music history, and applied music and are eligible to participate in the various performing groups on campus. The University of Massachusetts is part of the five-college system which also includes Amherst, Hampshire, Mount Holyoke, and Smith Colleges.

Accreditation. New England Association of Schools and Colleges; National Association of Schools of Music.

Academic Information

Enrollment, Music Majors. (Total University) 27,156.

Music Faculty. 35.

Term System. Semester. Two summer terms.

Entrance Requirements. High school graduation with rank in upper three quarters of graduating class; completion of 16 college preparatory units including 4 English, 3 mathematics, 2 foreign language, 1 science, 1 social science; SAT required; audition required of all applicants.

Admission Procedure. Application with supporting documents and nonrefundable $10 fee ($40 for out-of-state) to Office of Admissions.

Music Degrees Offered. Bachelor of Music; Bachelor of Arts; Master of Music.

Music Degree Requirements. The Bachelor of Music degree may be earned with a concentration in performance, theory-composition, music education (vocal or instrumental), and Afro-American music and jazz (vocal or instrumental). The Bachelor of Arts degree with a major in music may be earned with a concentration in performance, theory-composition, or music history.

The Master of Music degree is offered with a concentration in music history, musicology, performance, theory, composition, jazz composition, arranging, music education (research, conducting, classroom, applied).

General Program Areas. Afro-American Music, Arranging, Composition, Jazz Studies, Music Education, Music History, Music Theory, Musicology, Performance.

Instruments Taught. Baritone, Bass, Bassoon, Clarinet, Flute, French Horn, Oboe, Organ, Percussion, Piano, Saxophone, Trombone, Trumpet, Tuba, Viola, Violin, Violoncello, Voice.

Musical Facilities

Practice Facilities. The Fine Arts Center houses the Music Department's rehearsal studios and practice rooms.

Concert Facilities. Concert Hall, seating 2,000; Frank Prentice Rand Theater; Bezanson Recital Hall.

Concerts/Musical Activities. Student/faculty recitals and concerts; the "Fine Arts Center Presents" series includes nationally and internationally recognized artists in the fields of music, dance, and theater, including major symphony orchestras, soloists, and jazz artists.

Music Library. The Music Library located in the Fine Arts Center contains all campus library materials relating to music. Special collections include: Philip Bezanson Collection; Harold Lebow Collection; manuscripts of Charles Fussell.

Special Programs

Performance Groups. University Chorale, Chamber Choir, Madrigals, University Orchestra, Five College Chamber Orchestra, Chamber Orchestra, Marching Band, Symphony Band, Wind Ensemble, Concert Band, Jazz Ensemble, Chamber Music, String Bass Ensemble, Chamber Jazz Ensemble, Percussion Ensemble, UMass Marimbas, Collegium Musicum, Vocal Jazz Ensemble.

Financial

Costs. Per academic year: Tuition in-state resident $1,296, out-of-state $4,320. Fees $894. Room $1,330. Board $1,132.

Financial Aid. Financial aid is available in the form of scholarships, grants, loans, and part-time employment. Scholarship/financial aid application due March 1.

Commentary

A Ph.D. program in theory and composition at the University of Massachusetts has been proposed.

Massachusetts Institute of Technology
Department of Music and Theater Arts
77 Massachusetts Avenue
Cambridge
Massachusetts 02139

Telephone. (617) 253-3210
Chief Administrator. Dr. John Harbinson.

The Massachusetts Institute of Technology (MIT) was established in 1861. The event marked the culmination of an effort by William Barton Rogers, MIT's founder, to create a new kind of educational institution relevant to the times and to the nation's need, where student would be educated in the application as well as the acquisition of knowledge. Today, education and related research continue to be MIT's central purpose. The institution is an independent, privately endowed university and is organized into five academic Schools. Within these Schools are the College and 22 academic departments. MIT enrolls over 9,500 students and has a total teaching staff of 1,900. The campus is in Cambridge on the north bank of the Charles River, facing the city of Boston.

Music began at Massachusetts Institute of Technology with vocal groups in 1883. Soon there were also instrumental groups, but it was all done informally. The Musical Theatre Guild, for example, remains a student-run group, which features a new student-written show each year. MIT began to hire music professors after World War II, and the Humanities Department (in which music is a "section") was founded in 1955-56. Today, the Music Section of the Humanities Department offers a broad range of opportunities to experience and explore the field of music. It seeks to offer a solid, basic training to composers and performers who also wish to pursue careers in scientific or technological fields. A great variety of subjects is given ranging from basic musicianship to computer music composition. They are arranged into five categories: introductory, history/literature, theory/composition, performance, and seminars/tutorials. Most students begin with introductory subjects, but anyone with musical training is encouraged to begin with history/literature or theory/composition subjects. Graduate credit is available for nearly all of the seminars and tutorials.

Accreditation. New England Association of Schools and Colleges.

Academic Information

Enrollment, Music Majors. Undergraduate 7.
Music Faculty. Full-time 14, part-time 16.
Term System. Semester.
Entrance Requirements. MIT expects that its applicants will have taken the broadest, most rigorous program available to them in high school; recommended units include 4 English, 2 or more history/social sciences, 4 mathematics, 3 laboratory science, foreign language; SAT; 3 Achievement Tests; audition not required. TOEFL for foreign students.
Admission Procedure. Applicants are encourage to write to MIT during their junior year for information regarding application procedure; candidates in their last year of high school must complete the application process by January 1 of the year of intended entrance; $40 nonrefundable application fee.
Music Degrees Offered. Bachelor of Science.
Music Degree Requirements. A full degree program in music is offered as well as joint majors for students interested in combining the study of engineering or science with humanities. The full major program includes four subjects in composition and three subjects in history and literature of music. The joint major includes two subjects in each of these areas. Students who declare music as their major must have demonstrated proficiency in instrumental or vocal performance and in harmony and counterpoint. Seniors in the full major participate in a tutorial program in preparation for a general examinations; those in the joint major take a senior music seminar. Especially qualified students may be permitted to substitute a thesis on an analytical or historical topic or an original composition for the general examination or seminar. The Bachelor of Science in Humanities, the Bachelor of Science in Humanities and Engineering, or the Bachelor of Science in Humanities and Science are the degrees awarded.
General Program Areas. Chamber Music, Composition, Computer Music, Music History, Music Literature, Music Theory, Musical Acoustics, Performance.

Musical Facilities

Practice Facilities. 2 organs (Holtkamps). 8 grand pianos (Steinway). Private music lessons are not offered by the faculty, but "chamber music" is offered as a course.
Concert Facilities. Kresge Auditorium, seating 1,200; Little Theater, 214; Elizabeth Parks Killian Hall, 150.
Concerts/Musical Activities. Chamber music groups, symphonic groups, and concert soloists appear each year as part of the Humanities Series entitled "Music at MIT;" student and faculty recitals and concerts.
Music Library. 9,893 books; 23,067 scores; 1,592 periodicals; 126 microfiche titles; 16,201 recordings, audio- and videotapes. Listening facilities include 3 cassette decks, 16 stereo turntables, 2 compact disc players. Spe-

cial collections include scores and recordings of composers associated with MIT; clipping file of MIT musical events.

Special Programs

Featured Programs. The Experimental Music Studio is located in the Arts Media Technology facility within the School of Architecture. The Media Lab of the facility brings together ten previously separate groups to establish an academic initiative called Media Arts and Sciences. The academic programs bring together the invention and creative use of modern media in general and electronic means, with special application to education, medicine, and the arts. The academic program includes concentrations in epistemology and learning, electronic media, and computer music.
Performance Groups. Symphony Orchestra, Concert Band, Chamber Music Society, Festival Jazz Ensemble, Concert Jazz Band, Gospel Choir, A Capella Choir, Logarthythms (all-male vocal club), Chorallaires, Choral Society.

Financial

Costs. Per academic year: Tuition $11,800. Room $1,930 to $2,552. Board $1,974 (maximum plan).
Financial Aid. The Student Financial Aid Office provides grants and loans based on the financial need of the individual student, as determined by analysis of a statement of family financial condition. Part-time employment and a College Work-Study program available.

New England Conservatory
290 Huntington Avenue
Boston
Massachusetts 02115

Telephone. (617) 262-1120
Chief Administrator. Laurence Lesser, President.

The conservatory system was first introduced to America by Dr. E. Tourjee in 1853 in the Musical Institute of Rhode Island, which later developed into the Providence Conservatory of Music. In 1867, the institution was moved to Boston and in 1870, by an act of the Massachusetts Legislature, incorporated as the New England Conservatory of Music. The school was modeled after Mendelssohn's Leipzig Conservatorium but with the added emphasis of the liberal arts in the form of an affiliation with the then new Boston University. This affiliation was terminated and another connection was established with Harvard University, enduring until the Conservatory began offering its own bachelor degree in 1925. The school currently offers a joint degree program with Tufts University.

The Conservatory is housed in three buildings on less than an acre in downtown Boston. Public transport by subway and bus is conveniently located. There is on-campus housing for 162 students in a coed residence hall.

Accreditation. New England Association of Schools and Colleges; National Association of Schools of Music; Association of Independent Conservatories of Music.

Academic Information

Enrollment, Music Majors. Full-time 345 men, 304 women; part-time 48 men, 41 women. 130 foreign students.

Music Faculty. 167.

Term System. Semester. Summer session offering courses in chamber music, studio, 20th century music, and music education.

Entrance Requirements. High school diploma or GED; SAT; audition in person or tape. Foreign students may audition by tape; TOEFL of at least 450.

Admission Procedure. Application due February 15th with $35 nonrefundable fee. Delayed admission with permission; mid-year admission on space-available basis.

Music Degrees Offered. Bachelor of Music; Master of Music; Artist Diploma; Post Master's; 3-year Certificate/Diploma.

Music Degree Requirements. The Bachelor of Music degree requires the completion of 120 credit hours including courses in studio, theory, history, ensemble, and liberal arts plus an annual evaluation and a senior recital. The Master of Music degree requires the completion of 36 credit hours. The Diploma requires the completion of 72 credit hours.

General Program Areas. Applied Music, Composition, Conducting, Early Music, Jazz Studies, Music Theory, Performance.

Instruments Taught. Baroque Instruments, Brass, Flute, Guitar, Lute, Oboe, Organ, Percussion, Piano, Recorder, Stringed Instruments, Viola da Gamba, Violin, Voice, Woodwinds.

Musical Facilities

Practice Facilities. 85 practice rooms. Organ practice facilities with Metzler, Noack, Hammerberg, Fisk, Flentrop kit organs. 6 percussion-equipped practice rooms. Pianos in all practice rooms; separate fee for use; none reserved for majors. 72 piano-teaching studios. Electronic music studio.

Concert Facilities. Jordan Hall; Brown Hall, Williams Hall; Keller Room.

Concerts/Musical Activities. Private organ teaching at Old West Church.

Music Library. 83,380 total volumes. 18,970 books; 40,672 scores; 21,450 recordings. Cassette and stereo listening facilities. Collection of 2,000 orchestrations; 1,435 chorus music titles.

Special collections include: autograph manuscript collection of music by New England composers, the "Boston School," and others; Elise Hall collection of saxophone music written by French and American composers; early Americana and other materials relating to Boston musical life; collection of autograph letters of over 50 distinguished 19th century musicians; Geraldine Farrar Collection of vocal scores; early jazz recordings; musical instrument collection.

Special Programs

Featured Programs. The Conservatory has programs in orchestral music, chamber music, jazz, voice, early music performance, and composition.

Performance Groups. Recitals/concerts.

Affiliated Programs. Joint degree 5-year program with Tufts University. Students may also take courses at Simmons, Northeastern, and Tufts with credit applicable to a New England Conservatory degree.

Financial

Costs. Per academic year: Tuition $7,550. Fees and expenses $270. Room $2,500. Board $1,350.

Financial Aid. 517 scholarships ranging from $1,000 to $7,500 (average $2,200). Scholarship application due March 1. Also available are loans, part-time employment, and a College Work-Study program.

Commentary

New England Conservatory's fortunate location, next to Boston's Symphony Hall, provides students with convenient access to one of the city's major cultural resources. The School's unique Sonic Analysis Laboratory explores recent advances in sound analysis technology of music.

Smith College
Department of Music
Northampton
Massachusetts 01063

Telephone. (413) 584-2700, Ext. 3150

Chief Administrator. Dr. Richard Sherr, Chairman, Department of Music.

Smith College was founded in 1871 and is a private, nonsectarian college for women. The College enrolls 2,550 students and has a faculty of over 300. The 125-acre campus includes 90 buildings in the city of Northampton (population 30,000), 8 miles north of Springfield in west-central Massachusetts.

The Department of Music provides for the study of music within the framework of a liberal arts curriculum. A student's program requires from 36 to 48 credits in music and 64 credits outside the Department.

Accreditation. New England Association of Schools and Colleges.

Academic Information

Enrollment, Music Majors. 729.
Music Faculty. 21.

Term System. Semester. No summer session.

Entrance Requirements. High school graduation or equivalent with high academic and personal promise; recommend completion of 16 units including 4 English, 3 mathematics, 3 foreign language, 2 laboratory science, 2 social studies); SAT or ACT; 3 Achievement Tests. Audition not required.

Admission Procedure. Application with $35 non-refundable fee due February 1.

Music Degrees Offered. Bachelor of Arts; Master of Arts.

Music Degree Requirements. The Bachelor of Arts degree with a major in music requires the completion of 128 semester hours. Classes are selected from courses in fundamentals, music history, theory, and performance. The Master of Arts degree requires the completion of 32 semester hours beyond the baccalaureate degree.

General Program Areas. Chamber Music, Choral Music, Performance.

Instruments Taught. Bass, Bassoon, Clarinet, Flute, Guitar, Harpsichord, Lute., Oboe, Organ, Percussion, Piano, Recorder, Trombone, Trumpet, Tuba, Viola, Viola da Gamba, Violin, Violoncello, Voice.

Musical Facilities

Practice Facilities. 20 practice rooms. 3 organs (Austin, 1910; Aeolian-Skinner, 1956; Andover, 1974). 19 pianos (17 grands, 2 uprights). Electronic music studio.

Concert Facilities. Sage Auditorium, seating 750; Hallie Flanagan Studio, 200.

Concerts/Musical Activities. Concerts and recitals; visiting artists.

Music Library. 26,479 books; 37,528 scores; 242 periodicals; 44,471 recordings. Listening facilities include 6 cassette units and 25 stereo units.

Special collections include: 15th and 16th century vocal music; 16th and 17th century instrumental music copied by Alfred Einstein; music collection of Henry S. and Sophie Drinker.

Special Programs

Featured Programs. The Five College Early Music Program seeks to provide educational and musical experience for those interested in the instrumental and vocal music of the Middle Ages, the Renaissance, and the Baroque.

Performance Groups. Five College Orchestra, Chamber Orchestra, Glee Club, College Choir, Smith Chorale, Chamber Singers.

Foreign Programs. Music students may spend their junior year overseas. Programs are offered in France, Germany, Switzerland, Italy, England, China, Japan, Spain, and Russia.

Affiliated Programs. Cross-registration with Amherst College, Mount Holyoke College, Hampshire College, and the University of Massachusetts.

Financial

Costs. Per academic year: Tuition $10,570. Practice room fee $30 per year for keyboard; $15 for other. Room and board $4,120.

Financial Aid. Each year the College awards scholarships equal to one-half the cost of lessons in practical music to students who have financial need and who are recommended by the Department of Music. Auditions are held for entering students after the opening of college. The Ernst Wallfisch Scholarship is a full-year music performance scholarship (vocal or instrumental) to be granted to a freshman, sophomore, or junior based on need and merit. Other sources of financial aid include state/federal grants and loans, part-time employment, and a College Work-Study program.

Commentary

Smith College, part of the five-college system also including the University of Massachusetts, and Amherst, Hampshire, and Mount Holyoke Colleges, has long had a fine music department with a strong choral tradition and a small but distinguished faculty.

MICHIGAN

Andrews University
Department of Music
1100 East Fifth Avenue
Berrien Springs
Michigan 49104

Telephone. (616) 471-3600

Chief Administrator. C. Warren Becker, Chair.

Andrews University had its beginning in 1874 when the Seventh-day Adventist denomination founded Battle Creek College. In a move to the campus of Emmanuel Missionary College in 1959, the college, the theological seminary, and the graduate school were united under the present name. The 1,573-acre campus is located in Berrien Springs, a small community in the southwestern part of the state.

The Department of Music offers four areas of concentration within the Bachelor of Music program and a major in music within the Bachelor of Arts curriculum. An elementary music education major is also offered. All majors must pass a piano proficiency examination or enroll for piano lessons at first registration. Students majoring in music must enroll in applied music in their major performance area and in a major ensemble each quarter in residence.

Accreditation. North Central Association of Colleges and Schools; National Association of Schools of Music; National Council for Accreditation of Teacher Education.

Academic Information

Enrollment, Music Majors. (Total University) 1,897.

Music Faculty. 10.

Term System. Quarter.

Entrance Requirements. High school graduation or equivalent; minimum of 10 units including English, mathematics, foreign language, science, social science; ACT required; audition required.

Admission Procedure. Application with supporting documents and nonrefundable $15 fee by September 15 to Director of Admissions and Records.

Music Degrees Offered. Bachelor of Arts; Bachelor of Music.

Music Degree Requirements. The Bachelor of Arts degree with a major in music requires the completion of 45 credits in the major. An elementary music education major is also offered and requires 55 credits in the major. The Bachelor of Music degree is offered in four areas: music education (emphasis in keyboard, vocal, or instrumental music), keyboard education, piano pedagogy, and performance. The baccalaureate degrees require the completion of a minimum of 190 quarter credits.

General Program Areas. Church Music, Conducting, Music Education, Music History, Music Literature, Music Theory, Piano Pedagogy.

Instruments Taught. Brass, Organ, Percussion, Piano, Stringed Instruments, Voice, Woodwinds.

Musical Facilities

Music Library. The James White Library collection supports the curriculum of the Department of Music.

Special Programs

Performance Groups. University Orchestra, University Band, University Chorale, Chamber Music Ensembles, Singing Men, Ladies Chorus, Wind Ensemble, University Singers, Piano Ensemble.

Financial

Costs. Per academic year: Tuition $5,985. Room and board $3,012.

Financial Aid. Music scholarships include the Andrews University Symphonic Band Scholarship, Beltz Church Music Scholarship, Mahlon and Irene Hamel Endowed Music Scholarships, Hamel Music Company Band Scholarship, Virginia Hamel Scholarship, Performance Scholarship (available to non-music students also), Presser Foundation Scholarships, and the Elaine Taylor Memorial Scholarship. Scholarship/financial aid application due June 1. Other sources of financial aid include state/federal grants and loans, part-time employment, and a College Work-Study program.

Central Michigan University
Department of Music
Powers Music Building
Mount Pleasant
Michigan 48859

Telephone. (517) 774-3281

Chief Administrator. Sue G. Gamble, Chairperson.

Central Michigan University opened for classes in 1892 as the Central Michigan Normal School and Business Institute. State-supported since 1897, the University is governed by an eight-member Board of Trustees appointed by the Governor of the State of Michigan with the consent of the Senate. The institution became known as Central State Teachers College in 1927, Central Michigan College of Education in 1941, and Central Michigan University in 1959. The 908-acre campus is located at the southern boundary of Mount Pleasant, a city of 23,-660.

The general objectives of the Department of Music are to provide an education for students aspiring to careers in music; to provide students who do not wish to pursue degrees in music with opportunities for exploring musical interests and developing musical skills; to serve the cultural needs of the University and the immediate community by presenting concerts and performances; and to provide professional assistance to schools and music programs in the state.

Accreditation. North Central Association of Colleges and Schools; National Association of Schools of Music; National Council for Accreditation of Teacher Education.

Academic Information

Enrollment, Music Majors. Undergraduate 185, graduate 20.

Music Faculty. Full-time 28, part-time 3.

Term System. Semester. Summer session.

Entrance Requirements. High school graduation with rank in top 50% of class; completion of 16 units including 4 English, 3 mathematics, 2 science, 2 foreign language, 3 social studies; ACT required. Audition required which may be different for each area (generally memorized piece, scales, sight reading).

Admission Procedure. Application to Admissions Office with supporting documents.

Music Degrees Offered. Bachelor of Music; Bachelor of Music Education; Bachelor of Arts; Bachelor of Applied Arts; Bachelor of Science.

Music Degree Requirements. The Bachelor of Music degree is offered with major concentration in orchestral instruments, piano, organ, voice, theory/composition, and church music. All students in this curriculum must complete the 30-hour University Program, the 28-hour core music program, and the major area of concentration for a total of 124 semester hours. The Bachelor of Music

Education degree program prepares students to teach music in elementary and secondary grades. A major and minor in music are required. Major concentrations are available in choral, instrumental, keyboard-choral, and keyboard-instrumental. The Bachelor of Arts, the Bachelor of Applied Arts, and the Bachelor of Science degree curricula are also offered. In order to be accepted as a major in the Department of Music it is necessary to meet certain departmental requirements which consist of an audition and an interview for placement in theory and piano.

General Program Areas. Applied Music, Church Music, Composition, Jazz Studies, Music Education, Music Literature, Music Theory, Pedagogy, Performance.

Instruments Taught. Brass, Organ, Percussion, Piano, Stringed Instruments, Woodwinds.

Musical Facilities

Practice Facilities. 2 organs. Percussion equipped practice room. 100 practice pianos (Yamaha and Hamilton uprights); 5 grand pianos reserved for piano majors. Listening laboratory; recording laboratory.

Concert Facilities. Concert Hall, seating 1,300.

Concerts/Musical Activities. Artists Series; student/faculty recitals and concerts.

Music Library. Music materials are located in the Charles V. Park Library.

Financial

Costs. Per academic year: Tuition in-state resident $1,-460, out-of-state $3,650. Room and board $2,220.

Financial Aid. The University, in conjunction with the federal and state governments and private and civic organizations, offers a variety of scholarship, grant, loan, and employment opportunities to assist students in financing their education.

Eastern Michigan University
Department of Music
Ypsilanti
Michigan 48197

Telephone. (313) 487-0244

Chief Administrator. Dr. James B. Hause, Head.

Eastern Michigan University is a state university consisting of five colleges: Arts and Sciences, Business, Education, Health and Human Services, and Technology; and the Graduate School. It was founded in 1849 as the sixth state normal school for teachers in the United States and the first west of the Allegheny Mountains. A Conservatory of Music was established in 1880 and was unified with "academic music" to become the Department of Music in 1946. A new music instruction facility was completed in 1981. The 457-acre campus has 36 buildings and is located on the north side of Ypsilanti near the Huron River. Ypsilanti is situated in southeastern Michigan, 30 miles west of Detroit and 8 miles from Ann Arbor.

The Department of Music believes that music is a humanizing force in an increasingly technological and impersonal world. Through its programs the Department strives to provide students with the knowledge and skills to meet the musical challenges of the twenty-first century. The Department seeks to create on campus and within the community an awareness that music is a living art, rich in historical tradition.

The individual programs present music in the context of a broad liberal education, prepare vocal and instrumental teachers for elementary and secondary schools, provide individual and group study in all performance media, offer cultural enrichment to students in all departments, and prepare students for graduate studies and college teaching. Basic training is given to those interested in professional careers as instrumentalists, singers and conductors, composers and arrangers, music scholars and librarians, and, in collaboration with other departments, work in dance, radio, television, and theater. A marketing minor is available to students who have interest in businesses related to music.

Accreditation. North Central Association of Colleges and Schools; National Association of Schools of Music; National Council for Accreditation of Teacher Education.

Academic Information

Enrollment, Music Majors. Undergraduate 204, graduate 84.

Music Faculty. Full-time 29, part-time 13.

Term System. Semester. Summer session (primarily a graduate program; some elective undergraduate courses).

Entrance Requirements. High school graduation or GED; SAT or ACT. Audition required; theory placement examination in musicianship.

Admission Procedure. Application with supporting documents and $20 nonrefundable fee. Students should write the director of music auditions and scholarships well in advance of intended registration date to arrange for audition and examination.

Music Degrees Offered. Bachelor of Music; Bachelor of Music Education; Bachelor of Music Therapy; Bachelor of Arts; Master of Arts.

Music Degree Requirements. The Bachelor of Music degree curriculum is available to voice, keyboard, and orchestral instruments. Students must complete all prescribed courses and have satisfied all basic studies, major, and minor requirements for the degree. The Bachelor of Music Education degree offers curricula for teachers of instrumental music and teachers of vocal music. The Bachelor of Music Therapy degree is awarded on completion of a curriculum either without teacher certification or with teacher certification in Music Education if additional requirements are fulfilled. The

Bachelor of Arts degree with a major in music requires the completion of 45 semester hours of music courses as well as the general education requirements for the degree.

The graduate program in music addresses itself primarily to serving the needs of musicians and educators in Michigan and the midwest. Curricula leading to the Master of Arts degree are offered in music education, choral music, music literature, theory-literature, performance, and piano pedagogy. All curricula are designed to expand musicianship, scholarship, and teaching skills; and to make available recent trends in music and music education. A total of 30 hours is required for the degree. Course offerings for the program are rotated so that part-time students can usually complete degree programs within two calendar years. Late afternoon and evening classes are offered in fall, winter, and spring sessions.

General Program Areas. Choral Conducting, Composition, Conducting, Music Education, Music History, Music Literature, Music Theory, Music Therapy, Performance.

Instruments Taught. Bass, Bassoon, Brass, Clarinet, Cornet, Euphonium, Flute, French Horn, Guitar, Harp, Oboe, Organ, Percussion, Piano, Saxophone, Trombone, Trumpet, Tuba, Viola, Violin, Violoncello, Voice.

Musical Facilities

Practice Facilities. Special practice facilities for organists; 4 organs (1 pneumatic-assisted Aeolian Skinner, 1 Gabriel Kney tracker, 1 Kuhn small tracker, 1 Rhuland tracker practice organ). 5 practice rooms for percussionists. 46 practice rooms. 23 pianos; 3 grand pianos reserved for piano majors. Electronic music studio. Choir, band, and orchestra have individual self-contained rehearsal facilities.

Concert Facilities. Pease Auditorium (dedicated in 1915 by Leopold Stokowski and the Philadelphia Orchestra) seating 1,700; Quirk Theatre, 380; Alexander Recital Hall, 146; Sponberg Theatre, 201.

Concerts/Musical Activities. Concerts and recitals presented by the Department; visiting artists.

Music Library. 10,000 titles maintained in the General Library.

Special Programs

Performance Groups. University Choir, Madrigal Ensemble, Opera Performance, University Orchestra, Collegium Musicum, University Symphonic Band, University Concert Winds, University Marching Band, Jazz Ensemble, Brass Ensemble, String Ensemble, University Women's Chorus, University Men's Chorus, Contemporary Chamber Ensemble, Opera Workshop.

Financial

Costs. Per academic year: Tuition in-state resident $1,489, out-of-state $3,600. Fees $42. Room and Board $2,698. Practice room fee $60 per semester.

Financial Aid. 104 music scholarships ranging from $100 to $2,200. Scholarship application due January 27. Part-time employment ($3.35 to $4.55 per hour) and College Work-Study program.

University of Michigan
School of Music
1100 Baits
Ann Arbor
Michigan 48109

Telephone. (313) 764-0583

Chief Administrator. Dr. Paul C. Boylan, Dean.

The University of Michigan was established in 1817 by an act of the Michigan Legislature, fostered by a group of public-spirited men in Detroit. The present name has been used since 1821. The original campus was formed at Ann Arbor on a 40-acre parcel of land given to the University as a gift. The campus has grown to 2,608 acres with 20 major buildings.

The School of Music at the University was founded in 1880.

Accreditation. North Central Association of Colleges and Schools; National Association of Schools of Music.

Academic Information

Enrollment, Music Majors. Full-time 374 men, 373 women. 25 foreign students.

Music Faculty. Full-time 83, part-time 19.

Term System. Semester.

Entrance Requirements. High school graduation with 20 units including 4 English, 3 mathematics, 3 laboratory science, 2 foreign language, 3 social studies, 5 electives (music, art, humanities); ACT or SAT; audition required on principal instrument before final action on application can be taken; in-person audition strongly recommended. Auditions are held each year beginning in December on the Ann Arbor campus. Foreign students must submit TOEFL score above 600; financial resource certification required.

Admission Procedure. Application with $20 non-refundable fee to Admissions Office.

Music Degrees Offered. Bachelor of Music; Bachelor of Musical Arts; Master of Arts; Master of Music; Master of Fine Arts; Master of Business Administration; Doctor of Musical Arts; Doctor of Philosophy; Specialist in Music.

Music Degree Requirements. Several curriculums are available leading to the degree Bachelor of Music. Though certain courses such as music theory, music history, and English composition and literature are common to all, a major part of each curriculum is designed to prepare the student in a specific field (arts administration, composition, conducting, performance, performance with teacher certification, music education). The degree requires the completion of a minimum of 120 semester hours. The Bachelor of Musical Arts degree program is designed to allow certain students greater flexibility in the choice of courses than is available through other curriculums, allowing students who qualify to design a larger part of their programs within stated guidelines and through consultation with a faculty adviser.

The Master of Fine Arts degree is offered in Musical Theatre for those who wish to work as performers in musical theatre, radio, television, and film. Master of Music and Master of Arts degree programs require a minimum of 30 hours of graduate credit with an average grade of B. A doctoral student must accumulate a total of at least 50 credit hours beyond the master's degree. If the master's degree is awarded through the Rackham School of Graduate Studies, a total of 68 credit hours is required.

The Doctor of Musical Arts degree is awarded in composition, conducting, and performance. The Doctor of Philosophy degree includes specialties in music education, music theory, and musicology. The Specialist in Music includes emphases in music education, string instruments, and wind and percussion instruments.

General Program Areas. Church Music, Composition, Conducting, Music Education, Music History, Music Theory, Musical Theatre, Musicology, Performance, Piano Pedagogy.

Instruments Taught. Bass, Bassoon, Clarinet, Euphonium, Flute, French Horn, Harp, Oboe, Organ, Percussion, Piano, Saxophone, Trombone, Trumpet, Tuba, Viola, Violin, Violoncello, Voice.

Musical Facilities

Practice Facilities. 155 practice rooms. 18 organs (Fisk, Aeolian-Skinner, Renter, Mohler). 123 pianos (100 Baldwin uprights, 23 Steinway and Baldwin grands); 23 grand pianos reserved for piano majors. 2 electronic music studios.

Concert Facilities. Hill Auditorium, seating 4,500; Power Center, 1,400; Rackham Auditorium, 1,200; Mendelssohn Theatre, 700; Trueblood Theatre, 300; Recital Hall, 244; McIntosh Theatre, 150.

Concerts/Musical Activities. 350 concerts per year; in addition, 60-70 professional concerts per year.

Music Library. 29,640 books; 37,760 scores; 3,300 microfiche; 22,000 recordings. Listening facilities (30 cassette, 11 stereo). Special collections include: Stearns Collection of Musical Instruments; Women's Music Collection; Stellfeld Collection (largely eighteenth century chamber music and operas); Michael Montgomery Collection of Popular Sheet Music; music of sons of J.S. Bach; manuscripts of big-band jazz arrangements; Jacob

Maurice Coopersmith Handel materials; Albert Luconi collection of woodwind ensemble music; Glenn Osser scores for radio and early television shows; letters of Arnold Schoenberg; seventeenth to nineteenth century Americana in Williams L. Clements Library.

Special Programs

Performance Groups. String Quartet, University Orchestra, Michigan Chamber Ensemble, Marching Band, University Band, Symphonic Choir, Women's Choir, Arts Chorale, Michigan Singers, Chamber Choir, Opera Chorus, Men's Glee Club, University Choral Union, Women's Glee Club, Early Music Ensemble, Jazz Band, Woodwind Ensemble, Small Brass Ensemble, Wind Chamber Music.

Affiliated Programs. A curriculum in arts administration is offered as a joint program with the School of Business Administration. It leads to two degrees, the Master of Business Administration and the Master of Music. The degree requires 60 hours, of which 15 hours may be applied to the Master of Music program.

Financial

Costs. Per academic year: Tuition undergraduate in-state resident $2,476 to $2,844, out-of-state $8,048 to $8,740; graduate in-state $4,180 to $4,280, out-of-state $8,748 to $8,740. Room and board $3,053. Married student housing $237 to $537 per month.

Financial Aid. 110 undergraduate music students receive scholarships ranging from $500 to $7,820 (average award $2,100). Scholarship applications due by March 1. Graduate student research and teaching assistantships also available. Other sources of financial aid include state/federal grants and loans, part-time employment, and a College Work-Study program.

Michigan State University
School of Music
East Lansing
Michigan 48824

Telephone. (517) 355-4583

Chief Administrator. Kenneth G. Bloomquist, Chairperson.

Michigan State University was founded in 1855 as an autonomous public institution of higher learning and was one of the earliest land-grant institutions in the United States. The University has evolved into an internationally-esteemed university, offering a comprehensive spectrum of programs and attracting gifted professors, staff members, and students. The yearly enrollment totals approximatley 42,700 including off-campus programs. The University occupies a contiguous parcel of land containing 5,248 acres in East Lansing.

Some student ensembles existed at Michigan State as far back as 1870. In 1896 private lessons and student ensembles were a part of the Department of Music program. The faculty grew in number through the early 1900s and in 1927 the School of Music had its formal beginning. The School's goals are to provide quality instruction in the undergraduate and graduate programs in music; to provide professional-level applied instruction and extensive performance experiences so that students are equipped to make a living as performers or teachers of performers; to provide specialized instruction in the scholarly areas; and to provide both classroom and clinical experience in music therapy.

Accreditation. North Central Association of Colleges and Schools; National Association of Schools of Music.

Academic Information

Enrollment, Music Majors. Full-time 175 men, 225 women. Foreign students 30.

Music Faculty. Full-time 51, part-time 3. Resident artist: Ralph Votapek.

Term System. Quarter. Academic year from mid-September to mid-June. Summer session of 5 weeks from late June to late July.

Entrance Requirements. Accredited high school graduation with completion of 16 units including 4 English; 3.0 GPA (4.0 scale); SAT or ACT required. Audition of prescribed repertoire. Foreign students must pass TOEFL; have graduated from high school or its equivalent; show proof of financial responsibility.

Admission Procedure. Application with supporting documents and $20 application fee.

Music Degrees Offered. Bachelor Music; Bachelor of Arts; Master of Music; Master of Arts; Doctor of Musical Arts; Doctor of Philosophy.

Music Degree Requirements. The Bachelor of Music degree is offered with majors in applied music, theory and composition, school music, and music therapy. The program requires the completion of 45 credits of general education plus the requirements of the specific curriculum chosen. A total of 180 quarter credits is required. The Bachelor of Music degree with a major in school music and a major in music therapy is a five-year program. The Bachelor of Arts degree with a major in music is a liberal arts program with a strong emphasis in music. *The Master of Music degree program offers concentration in the areas of applied music, music education, music theory, music composition, and music therapy. The degree requires the completion of 45 quarter hour credits to meet the curriculum chosen. The Master of Arts degree is offered with a major in musicology.*

The Doctor of Philosophy degree is offered with majors in music education, music theory, music composition, musicology, and applied music in combination with theory and music literature. Credits selected for the program are determined by orientation examination. The Doctor of Musical Arts degree is offered in applied music and conducting.

General Program Areas. Composition, Conducting, Music Education, Music Theory, Music Therapy, Musicology, Performance, Piano Pedagogy.

Instruments Taught. Brass, Electronic Music, Guitar, Organ, Percussion, Piano, Stringed Instruments, Woodwinds.

Musical Facilities

Practice Facilities. 130 practice rooms. Special practice facilities for organists and percussionists. 150 pianos (grands and uprights); 16 grand pianos reserved for piano majors. Electronic music studio; electronic/computer music studio; Music Therapy Clinic treatment rooms; reed-making room.

Concert Facilities. Wharton Center Great Hall seating 2,500; Festival Stage, 700; University Auditorium, 4,000; Fairchild Theatre, 700; Music Auditorium Recital Hall, 375; Kellogg Center Auditorium, 400; Hart Recital Hall, 100.

Community Facilities. Dart Auditorium seating 500; Civic Center, 5,000; various churches.

Concerts/Musical Activities. Solo and chamber music recitals; student ensemble concerts; faculty and students perform about 300-400 concerts/recitals on campus each year. The Wharton Center for the Performing Arts offers a full schedule of touring Broadway shows, leading dance troupes, world-famous soloists and ensembles, the Greater Lansing Symphony Orchestra, and the Opera Company of Mid-Michigan.

Music Library. 21,401 musical scores; over 100 current periodical subscriptions; 6,550 phonograph records. 17 listening stations (stereo). The University Main Library houses other music materials. Other library resources available to students include the University of Michigan at Ann Arbor, Wayne State University at Detroit, and Western Michigan University.

Special Programs

Performance Groups. University Chorale, State Singers, Collegiate Choir, Women's Glee Club, Singing Statesmen, University Symphony Orchestra, University Chamber Orchestra, Wind Symphony, Symphony Band, Concert Band, Repertory Band, Jazz Band, Jazz Ensemble, Spartan Marching Band, Spartan Brass.

Foreign Programs. A foreign string quartet is sponsored each year, usually from the Xian Conservatory of the Peoples Republic of China.

Financial

Costs. Per academic year: Tuition in-state resident $2,025, out-of-state $5,332. Fees $75. Room and board $2,538.

Financial Aid. Financial aid is awarded on the basis of musical ability. 215 music students receive financial aid (average award $1,000). Financial aid/scholarship application due February 15. Part-time employment and College Work-Study program available.

Oakland University
Department of Music, Theatre and Dance
Walton Boulevard and Squirrel Road
Rochester
Michigan 48063

Telephone. (313) 370-2030

Chief Administrator. Dr. David Daniels, Chairperson.

Oakland University, founded in 1957, is a state-assisted institution of approximately 12,500 students that offers a diverse set of academic programs, from baccalaureate to doctoral levels. Oakland University seeks both traditional and nontraditional students. While serving principally Michigan residents, it welcomes qualified applicants from other states and countries. A special effort is made to locate and admit disadvantaged students with strong potential for academic success and to provide the support needed to realize that potential.

Located between the cities of Pontiac and Rochester, Oakland University is easily accessible to Detroit metropolitan area residents. It is situated on a 1,500-acre campus, formerly the estate of the late Alfred G. and Matilda R. Wilson. On-campus dormitories are available as well as housing for married students.

The Department of Music, Theatre and Dance within the College of Arts and Sciences first granted the Bachelor of Arts with music major in 1964, the Bachelor of Science in music in 1975, the Bachelor of Music in 1981, and the Master of Music in 1978. Minors are offered in theatre, dance, and music, and a secondary teaching minor in music. In coordination with the Center for the Arts, the department offers student performance opportunities in dramatic productions, dance recitals, music ensembles and recitals, and music theater.

Accreditation. North Central Association of Colleges and Schools.

Academic Information

Enrollment, Music Majors. Undergraduate 112, graduate 27.

Music Faculty. Full-time 11, part-time 32.

Term System. Semester (4-1-4 plan). Summer session.

Entrance Requirements. Candidates for admission to undergraduate degree programs should have completed high school-level college preparatory work; GED is acceptable for students over 21 years of age and with a score of 55 or above; high school units should include 2 years history, 4 English, 3 mathematics, 3 natural science, 3 social science, 1 or 2 years of foreign language; ACT required; 2.5 grade point average. Graduate program requires a baccalaureate degree from an accredited college or university with a 3.0 grade point average; letters of recommendation and vitae of professional experience; entrance audition if electives will be in areas of performance or conducting, or a portfolio of compositions if concentration will be in composition.

Admission Procedure. Applications for undergraduate admissions should be submitted as early in the senior year as possible. Graduate degree program applicants must have official transcripts and letters of recommendation sent directly to the admissions office.

Music Degrees Offered. Bachelor of Arts with a music major; Bachelor of Music; Bachelor of Science with music education major; Master of Music.

Music Degree Requirements. The Bachelor of Arts degree with a music major requires, in addition to specific general university requirements, 48 credits in music; degree is intended for students who wish a broad general education without a high level of specialization in music. The Bachelor of Science degree with music education major is designed for students who wish to teach in the public schools and carries Michigan teaching certification. Bachelor of Music degree is intended for students who wish preprofessional and professional preparation in performance, early music, theory, composition, jazz, or commercial music. Ensemble requirements vary from one degree program to another.

The Master of Music degree is designed to prepare candidates for careers as practicing musicians in performance, conducting, composition, and arranging, and as teachers and administrators in private studios, public schools, and junior colleges; program also prepares candidates for further graduate work. Degree work consists of courses, independent study, and apprenticeships and includes a core program of 16 credits, a concentration of 16 credits, and a 4-credit elective; total of 36 hours and comprehensive examinations required; some concentrations require a successful recital.

General Program Areas. Choral Conducting, Commercial Music, Composition, Early Music, Instrumental Conducting, Instrumental Performance, Jazz Performance, Music Education, Orff Pedagogy, Organ Performance, Piano Pedagogy, Piano Performance, Sacred Music, Vocal Performance.

Instruments Taught. Bass, Bassoon, Clarinet, Flute, French Horn, Guitar, Harp, Harpsichord, Lute, Oboe, Organ, Percussion, Piano, Recorder, Renaissance Winds, Saxophone, Timpani, Trombone, Trumpet, Tuba, Viola, Viola da Gamba, Violin, Violoncello, Voice.

Musical Facilities

Practice Facilities. Tracker-action organ built by Casavant Freres Organ Company of Quebec, Canada. Two practice rooms for percussionists. 28 upright and 10 grand pianos. 21 practice rooms for pianists. Separate fee for organ practice room use ($10 per semester for small organ; $20 for Casavant organ). Special studios: recording, commercial music, early music.

Concert Facilities. Varner Recital Hall has 480-seat capacity.

Concerts/Musical Activities. Meadow Brook Music Festival, the summer home of the Detroit Symphony, was founded in 1967. Artists in residence: Lafayette String Quartet.

Music Library. The University Library and the Performing Arts Library house a music collection of 17,167 volumes; 10,538 scores; 6,629 music books; 56 current periodical subscriptions; 11 cassette decks; 6 stereo turntables; 1 compact disk player. Special collections include the *African Drum* collection; Orff instruments; authentic instruments for early music program.

Special Programs

Performance Groups. Music ensembles and recitals, music theater.

Financial

Costs. Per academic year: Tuition and fees state resident $2,775, nonresident $4,370.

Financial Aid. Music scholarships range from $200 to $2,500. Application due date April 1. Part-time employment available; range of earnings $3.35 to $4.50 per hour. College Work-Study program.

Wayne State University Department of Music
5980 Cass Avenue
Detroit
Michigan 48202

Telephone. (313) 577-1795

Chief Administrator. Robert F. Lawson, Chairperson.

Wayne State University has an enrollment exceeding 18,000 students. It is located in Detroit, a major industrial center of the United States.

The Department of Music offers programs providing professional training and for the general university student within a liberal arts context.

Accreditation. North Central Association of Colleges and Schools; National Association of Schools of Music.

Academic Information

Enrollment, Music Majors. (Total University) 18,637.

Music Faculty. 16 plus affiliated performance faculty.

Term System. Quarter.

Entrance Requirements. High school graduation with a B average; SAT or ACT; audition required. GRE required for graduate study.

Admission Procedure. Application with supporting documents and nonrefundable $15 fee to Office of Admissions.

Music Degrees Offered. Bachelor of Music; Bachelor of Arts; Master of Music; Master of Arts.

Music Degree Requirements. The Bachelor of Music degree is offered with a major in church music, composition, jazz studies and contemporary media, music education, music industry management, music therapy, performance, and theory. The Bachelor of Arts degree is offered with a major in music within the context of a liberal arts program.

The Master of Music degree is offered with a major in composition, choral conducting, theory, performance, and music education. The Master of Arts degree is offered with a major in music.

General Program Areas. Church Music, Composition, Jazz Studies, Music Education, Music History, Music Industry Management, Music Theory, Music Therapy, Performance.

Instruments Taught. Brass, Guitar, Harp, Organ, Percussion, Piano, Stringed Instruments, Voice, Woodwinds.

Musical Facilities

Practice Facilities. The Department of Music is located in the Music Wing of the Community Arts Center.

Concert Facilities. Community Arts Auditorium.

Concerts/Musical Activities. Student/faculty concerts and recitals; visiting artists.

Music Library. The University Library houses over 1,400,000 volumes and supports the academic programs of the Department of Music. It contains ethnomusicological, folklore, and sound recording collections.

Special Programs

Performance Groups. Marching Band, Symphony Band, Symphony Orchestra, Jazz Lab Band, Men's Glee Club, Choral Union, Chamber Singers, Opera Workshop, Women's Chorale.

Financial

Costs. Per academic year: Tuition in-state $1,680, out-of-state $3,780. Fees $80. Room $1,700.

Financial Aid. Scholarships, grants, loans, and College Work-Study employment are available. Financial aid/scholarship application due April 15.

Western Michigan University
School of Music
College of Fine Arts
Kalamazoo
Michigan 49008

Telephone. (616) 383-0910

Chief Administrator. Donald Bullock, Director.

Western Michigan University was founded in 1903 as Western State Normal School. It became Western State Teachers College in 1927 and Western Michigan College of Education in 1941. In 1955, the name was changed to Western Michigan College and the present name was adopted in 1957 when university status was achieved.

The University is located in Kalamazoo (pop. 79,146) midway between Chicago and Detroit. The East Campus consists of 70 acres; the West Campus, of more than 400 acres, is the location of current and anticipated University expansion.

The Music Department began offering courses in music in 1905 and the music degree program was initiated in 1945. As the School of Music in the College of Fine Arts, its goals are (1) to produce performers and composers; (2) to train teachers who will perpetuate viable musical traditions in the United States; (3) to train therapists who can use music to serve the health needs of others; (4) to prepare scholars who will disseminate historical and theoretical information concerning music; (5) to educate non-music majors in ways which will both enlighten them and allow them to develop constructive use of leisure time; and (6) to present concerts by student and faculty musicians for the cultural enrichment of the southwest Michigan community.

Accreditation. North Central Association of Colleges and Schools; National Council for Accreditation of Teacher Education; National Association of Schools of Music.

Academic Information

Enrollment, Music Majors. Full-time 113 men, 169 women. 5 foreign students.

Music Faculty. Full-time 39, part-time 1.

Term System. Semester. Academic year from early September to late April. 7-week summer session from July 2 to August 22.

Entrance Requirements. High school graduation or equivalent; ACT required; audition and music theory testing.

Admission Procedure. Application to Admissions Office with ACT score, official transcript; request audition packet from School of Music.

Music Degrees Offered. Bachelor of Music; Bachelor of Science; Bachelor of Arts; Master of Music.

Music Degree Requirements. The Bachelor of Music degree is offered with majors in music education (instrumental, vocal), performance (instrumental, vocal), teacher certification, music theory, composition, music history, and jazz studies. The Bachelor of Science degree is offered in elementary education-music through the College of Education. The baccalaureate degrees require the completion of 122 to 124 semester credit hours including general education, physical education, the major, and electives.

The Master of Music degree is offered with programs having a professional major focus. A total of 30 semester hours is required with 15 hours in the major, 12 hours in professional cognates, and electives. A final project (recital, thesis, paper) and oral examinations are required.

General Program Areas. Applied Music, Composition, Jazz Studies, Music Education, Music History, Music

Theory, Music Therapy, Performance.

Instruments Taught. Bass, Bassoon, Clarinet, Flute, French Horn, Oboe, Organ, Percussion, Piano, Saxophone, Trombone, Trumpet, Tuba, Viola, Violin, Violoncello, Voice.

Musical Facilities

Practice Facilities. 85 practice rooms. 5 organs (Schlicker, Moeller, Noack, Lauck, Felgemaker). Special practice facilities for percussionists. 75 pianos (17 grands, 58 uprights); 11 pianos reserved for piano majors. Electronic music studio; recording studio (24-track).

Concert Facilities. Auditorium, seating 3,500; Theatre, 550; Recital Halls, seating 450 and 110, respectively.

Concerts/Musical Activities. A wide variety of on-campus concerts offered each academic year; 373 such concerts in 1985-86.

Music Library. 12,500 volumes; 12,700 scores; 100 periodical subscriptions; 230 microform titles; 10,500 recordings; 200 audiocassettes. 26 listening stations (stereo). Special collection of 2,000 titles of popular American sheet music of early 20th century.

Special Programs

Performance Groups. Campus Choirs, Treble Choir, Collegiate Singers, Marching Band, Symphonic Band, University Orchestra, University Chorale, Grand Chorus, Concert Band, Wind Ensemble, Gold Company (jazz), Jazz Band, Jazz Orchestra, Chamber Music Ensembles (instrumental, vocal), Opera Workshop, New Music Ensemble, Collegium Musicum.

Financial

Costs. Per academic year: Tuition in-state resident $1,-477.50, out-of-state $3,697.50. Fees $213. Room and board $2,590.

Financial Aid. 117 music scholarships awarded; average award $875. Music scholarship deadline March 15th. Other sources of financial aid include institutional and state/federal grants and loans, part-time employment, and a College Work-Study program.

Commentary

Western Michigan University sponsors summer workshops in Alexander Technique, piano, and strings in Exeter, England. The University has a state-of-the-art Multi-Media Center and a 24-track recording studio.

MINNESOTA

Bemidji State University
Music Department
Bemidji
Minnesota 56601

Telephone. (218) 755-2915
Chief Administrator. Dr. Thomas L. Swanson, Chair.

Bemidji State University was established as a normal school in 1919. Today it offers a variety of undergraduate and graduate programs and enrolls over 3,800 students each year. The 83-acre campus is located on the west shore of Lake Bemidji near the headwaters of the Mississippi River.

The goal of the Department of Music is to provide all students an opportunity to develop their musical talents to the highest possible level. Performing groups, private lessons (applied music), and other selected courses are open to all students.

Accreditation. North Central Association of Colleges and Schools; National Council for Accreditation of Teacher Education.

Academic Information

Enrollment, Music Majors. 85.
Music Faculty. 12.
Term System. Quarter.
Entrance Requirements. High school graduation or equivalent; ACT, PSAT, or SAT; personal interview.
Admission Procedure. Application with supporting documents and nonrefundable $10 fee to Office of Admissions.
Music Degrees Offered. Bachelor of Science; Bachelor of Arts.
Music Degree Requirements. The Bachelor of Science (teacher licensure) degree is designed for students intent upon teaching in the elementary and secondary schools. It is a combination of courses in music and professional education which meets the State of Minnesota requirements. The four-year program leading to the Bachelor of Arts degree in music is for students who do not expect to teach in elementary or secondary schools. The curriculum features a core of courses in music theory and literature.
General Program Areas. Applied Music, Composition, Conducting, Jazz Studies, Music Education, Music History, Music Theory, Piano Pedagogy.
Instruments Taught. Brass, Organ, Percussion, Piano, Stringed Instruments, Voice, Woodwinds.

Musical Facilities

Practice Facilities. The Department of Music is housed in Bangsberg Hall.
Concert Facilities. Theatre, seating 300; Recital Hall, 250.
Concerts/Musical Activities. Student and faculty concerts and recitals; visiting artists.
Music Library. The A. C. Clark Library supports the academic programs of the Department of Music.

Special Programs

Performance Groups. Women's Glee Club, Varsity Choir, Bemidji Choir, Chamber Singers, Bemidji Chorale, Sweet Adelines, Barbershoppers, University Symphony Band, University Orchestra, Jazz Band, Instrumental Ensembles.

Financial

Costs. Per academic year: Tuition in-state resident $1,-462, out-of-state $2,352. Fees $210. Room and board $1,750.
Financial Aid. Scholarships, grants, part-time employment, and loans may be "packaged" or awarded individually to meet the student's documented needs.

Mankato State University
Department of Music
Mankato
Minnesota 56001

Telephone. (507) 389-1683
Chief Administrator. William R. Lecklider, Chairperson.

Mankato State University is a multipurpose institution which provides programs of general education and of specialization for professional and vocational goals. The campus of 380 acres has 16 buildings and is located in the city Mankato in southwestern Minnesota.

The Department of Music provides majors in education and performance. General courses and opportunities for participation in various musical ensembles are offered to nonmajors.

Accreditation. North Central Association of Colleges and Schools; National Association of Schools of Music; National Council for Accreditation of Teacher Education.

Academic Information

Enrollment, Music Majors. (Total University) 11,784.
Music Faculty. 14.
Term System. Quarter.
Entrance Requirements. High school graduation; SAT, PSAT, or ACT required; audition required. GRE required for graduate study.
Admission Procedure. Application with supporting documents and nonrefundable $10 fee to Office of Admissions.
Music Degrees Offered. Bachelor of Music; Bachelor of Science; Bachelor of Arts; Master of Music; Master of Science.
Music Degree Requirements. The Bachelor of Music degree includes performance majors in winds, strings, keyboard, and voice. The Bachelor of Arts degree in music is offered in the context of a liberal arts program. The Bachelor of Science degree in music (teacher licensure) is for the student who wishes to be licensed to teach in the public schools. The student majoring in this degree chooses one or more of the areas of specialization (band, orchestra, vocal/choral). A program is also available for students who are interest in a career in one of the many areas of the music industry including merchandising and management.

The Master of Music degree is offered with concentrations in applied music (instrumental, keyboard, voice), music theory, composition, and music education. A Master of Science degree in music is also available.

General Program Areas. Music Education, Music Management, Music Merchandising, Performance.
Instruments Taught. Brass, Organ, Percussion, Piano, Stringed Instruments, Voice, Woodwinds.

Musical Facilities

Practice Facilities. The Department of Music is located in the Performing Arts Building.
Concerts/Musical Activities. Student and faculty recitals and concerts; visiting artists.
Music Library. The Memorial Library has a branch Music Library which supports the programs of the Department of Music.

Special Programs

Performance Groups. Chorus, Symphonic Concert Band, Choral Ensemble, Concert Choir, Concert Wind Ensemble, University Orchestra, Opera Workshop, Service Bands, Pit Orchestra, Marching Band.

Financial

Costs. Per academic year: Tuition in-state $1,610, out-of-state $2,784. Room and board $1,715.
Financial Aid. Various forms of financial aid include scholarships, grants, loans, and part-time employment. Financial aid/scholarship application due April 22.

University of Minnesota - Duluth
Department of Music
School of Fine Arts
Duluth
Minnesota 55812

Telephone. (218) 726-8208
Chief Administrator. Dr. Robert E. Williams, Acting Department Head.

The University of Minnesota, Duluth became a coordinate campus of the University of Minnesota by legislative act in 1947. The campus, formerly named Duluth Teachers College, is administered by a chancellor who reports to the president of the University. The academic units of the campus are organized into six colleges and schools offering preprofessional and liberal arts programs. The 25-acre campus is located in Duluth, situated at the western end of Lake Superior. The city stretches nearly 25 miles along the 600-foot headlands of the lake.

The School of Fine Arts is a primary center in northern Minnesota for students seeking a comprehensive education in the visual and performing arts. The Department of Music became a part of the School in 1974. It offers curricula leading to the Bachelor of Music degree which prepares students for professional or teaching careers, and the Bachelor of Arts degree which includes the traditional liberal arts studies. The Graduate School offers the Master of Arts degree with a major in Education (Music Emphasis).

Accreditation. North Central Association of Colleges and Schools; National Association of Schools of Music; National Council for Accreditation of Teacher Education.

Academic Information

Enrollment, Music Majors. 35 men, 46 women. 1 foreign student.
Music Faculty. Full-time 13, part-time 17.
Term System. Quarter. 10-week summer session. Academic year from early September to late May.
Entrance Requirements. Students must have high school rank at 50th percentile or above or have test

scores at or above 50th percentile to be admitted to the School of Fine Arts; students not meeting this criteria may be admitted through the Supportive Services Program; audition required; PSAT required for freshman admission. TOEFL score of 500 required for foreign students. Advanced placement through CLEP.

Admission Procedure. Application to School of Fine Arts with nonrefundable fee of $20.

Music Degrees Offered. Bachelor of Music; Bachelor of Arts; Master of Arts in Education (Music Emphasis).

Music Degree Requirements. The Bachelor of Music degree is offered with emphases in performance (vocal, keyboard, band or orchestral instruments, instrumental jazz), theory-composition, or music education (band, orchestra, choral grades K-9; choral grades 5-12; piano pedagogy). A total of 194 quarter hours is required for the degree. The Bachelor of Arts degree program offers the study of music within a liberal arts curriculum. The Master of Arts degree requires the completion of 44 quarter hours in graduate courses with at least 27 credits in music education.

General Program Areas. Composition, Jazz Studies, Music Education, Music Theory, Performance, Piano Pedagogy.

Instruments Taught. Bass, Bassoon, Clarinet, Euphonium, Flute, Guitar, Harpsichord, Horn, Oboe, Organ, Percussion, Piano, Saxophone, Trombone, Trumpet, Tuba, Viola, Violin, Violoncello, Voice.

Musical Facilities

Practice Facilities. 26 practice rooms. 1 organ (Moeller). 2 Wenger modules for percussionists. 16 practice pianos; 8 grand pianos reserved for piano majors. Electronic music studio; piano laboratory.

Concert Facilities. Marshall Performing Arts Auditorium, seating 650; Bohannon Hall, 325.

Concerts/Musical Activities. 30 large ensemble performances per year; 8 faculty recitals; 5 visiting artists performances; 16 student (full) recitals; weekly student (individual) recitals.

Music Library. Music materials housed in main library. 4,262 volumes including scores; 29 current periodical subscriptions; 250 audiovisual titles; 100 microform titles; 4,500 phonograph recordings; 100 audiocassettes; 300 compact discs. Listening facilities (stereo). Additional scores housed in listening laboratory.

Special Programs

Performance Groups. University Singers, University Chorale, UMD-Community Oratorio Society, Freshman Chorus, Marching Band, Symphonic Wind Ensemble, Concert Band, Orchestra.

Financial

Costs. Tuition in-state resident $40.75 per credit, out-of-state $112.06 per credit. Fees $240. Room and board $2,600.

Financial Aid. Financial aid is awarded on the basis of academic merit, financial need, and musical ability. Both institutional and state/federal aid available. Scholarship/financial aid application due March 15 (priority date). Part-time employment and College Work-Study program available.

University of Minnesota - Twin Cities School of Music
Minneapolis
Minnesota 55455

Telephone. (612) 626-1616, 624-5740

Chief Administrator. Dr. Karen Wolff, Director.

The Twin Cities campus, the oldest of the University of Minnesota, has one of the largest enrollments of any campus in the country. It is located in two geographically distinct but nearby areas—one in Minneapolis and the other in St. Paul. Over 125 degrees are offered in 200 fields.

The School of Music has programs offering professional studies in performance, or in composition and theory and the major in music as part of a liberal arts curriculum. A cooperative program with the College of Education prepares students for careers in music education or music therapy.

Accreditation. North Central Association of Colleges and Schools; National Association of Schools of Music; National Council for Accreditation of Teacher Education.

Academic Information

Enrollment, Music Majors. (Total University) 42,568.

Music Faculty. 31; affiliated faculty 39.

Term System. Quarter.

Entrance Requirements. High school graduation or equivalent; admission based on high school rank percentile and aptitude test scores; ACT, PSAT, or SAT; audition required.

Admission Procedure. Application with supporting documents and nonrefundable $20 fee to Office of Admissions.

Music Degrees Offered. Bachelor of Music; Bachelor of Arts; Bachelor of Science; Master of Music; Master of Arts; Doctor of Musical Arts; Doctor of Philosophy.

Music Degree Requirements. The Bachelor of Music degree is offered with majors in performance, theory and composition, and jazz studies. The Bachelor of Arts degree program is designed for the student who wishes to major in music in the liberal arts context; it is recommended for students expecting to pursue major work in music history or musicology. The Bachelor of Science degree program requires the completion of core requirements in the School of Music and then a transfer to the College of Education for completion of the courses in music education or music therapy.

The Master of Music degree offers emphases in piano, harpsichord, organ, voice, violin, viola, cello, double bass, flute, oboe, clarinet, saxophone, bassoon, horn, trumpet, trombone, baritone, tuba, percussion, harp, guitar, choral conducting, and church music. The Master of Arts degree is offered with emphases in musicology, ethnomusicology, theory, composition, music education, and music therapy.

The program for the professional Doctor of Musical Arts degree has a performance-teaching orientation. Programs are offered in the areas of piano, voice, trumpet, clarinet, and organ. The Doctor of Philosophy degree is offered in musicology, ethnomusicology, theory and composition, and music education.

General Program Areas. Choral Conducting, Church Music, Composition, Ethnomusicology, Jazz Studies, Music Education, Music History, Music Theory, Music Therapy, Musicology, Performance.

Instruments Taught. Baritone, Bass, Bassoon, Clarinet, Flute, French Horn, Guitar, Harp, Harpsichord, Oboe, Organ, Percussion, Piano, Saxophone, Trombone, Trumpet, Tuba, Viola, Violin, Violoncello, Voice.

Musical Facilities

Concerts/Musical Activities. Student/faculty concerts and recitals; visiting artists.

Music Library. The University of Minnesota-Twin Cities Libraries have collections of more than 4 million catalogued volumes and support the academic programs of the School of Music.

Special collections include: Donald N. Ferguson Collection of rare books and scores; materials from Latin America; eighteenth and nineteenth century opera scores; large record library of operas and oratorios.

Special Programs

Performance Groups. Jazz Ensemble, Concert Band, Orchestra, Marching Band, Instrumental Ensembles, Brass Choir, University Chorus, Concert Choir, Women's Chorus, Men's Chorus, Opera Workshop, Chamber Singers, Collegium Musicum.

Financial

Costs. Per academic year: Tuition in-state resident $1,-633, out-of-state $4,493. Fees $273. Room and board $2,496.

Financial Aid. Student financial aid is provided in the form of grants, loans, scholarships, and employment. Financial aid/scholarship application due as soon as possible after January 1.

Moorhead State University
Music Department
Moorhead
Minnesota 56560

Telephone. (218) 236-2101
Chief Administrator. Dr. Robert Pattengale, Chair.

Established in 1885 as a Normal School, the institution began on six acres donated by State Senator Solomon G. Comstock. Major historical changes occurred in 1921 when it became Moorhead State Teachers College, authorized to offer the four-year degree of Bachelor of Science in Education. Other major changes occurred in 1946 when the Bachelor of Arts was added, in 1957 when the official name became Moorhead State College, and in 1975 when the school became Moorhead State University. It now has an enrollment of 7,600 students and a faculty of more than 300. The 104-acre campus includes 28 buildings. Moorhead, Minnesota and Fargo, North Dakota are on opposite sides of the Red River. The two cities support a symphony orchestra, community opera, community theatre, and several art galleries.

The Music Department was formed as a department in 1919. It offers traditional bachelor's degree programs, a special program combining music and business, and programs in arts management and mass communication. There are no private lesson fees for full-time music majors and minors. Non-music students may participate when space is available. Enrollment in the upper division, attained prior to presenting a senior recital, is achieved following a jury recommendation. Candidates for teaching licenses must hold baccalaureate degrees and complete the prescribed education requirements.

Accreditation. North Central Association of Colleges and Schools; National Association of Schools of Music; National Council for Accreditation of Teacher Education.

Academic Information

Enrollment, Music Majors. Full-time 60 men, 80 women. 5 foreign students.

Music Faculty. Full-time 15, part-time 3.

Term System. Quarter. Two 5-week summer sessions from early June to mid-July and mid-July to late August. Academic year from early September to late May.

Entrance Requirements. High school graduation or equivalent with rank in upper 50% of graduating class; ACT, PSAT, or SAT required; GRE required for graduate school. TOEFL and high school equivalent required of foreign students.

Admission Procedure. Applications accepted on a rolling basis.

Music Degrees Offered. Bachelor of Music; Bachelor of Arts; Bachelor of Science in Music Education; Master of Science in Music Education.

Music Degree Requirements. The Bachelor of Music degree is offered with performance concentrations in voice, keyboard, instrumental, and composition. A special program is offered in the music industry. The degree requires the completion of 192 quarter credits including 64 in liberal arts. The Bachelor of Arts degree in music education requires 70 credits in music; the degree Bachelor of Science in Music Education requires 96 credits in music.

The degree Master of Science in Music Education requires the completion of 45 quarter credits with thesis or 48 credits with project (lecture-recital, curriculum guide, or other acceptable project). The program should include, in addition to 9 hours of professional education, 27 hours of music with elective hours in the major or related areas.

General Program Areas. Applied Music, Arts Management, Composition, Mass Communications, Music Business, Music Education, Performance.

Instruments Taught. Bass, Clarinet, Flute, French Horn, Harpsichord, Oboe, Percussion, Piano, Saxophone, Trombone, Trumpet, Tuba, Viola, Violin, Violoncello, Voice.

Musical Facilities

Practice Facilities. 50 practice rooms. Special practice facilities for percussionists. 50 pianos (40 uprights, 10 grands); 3 grand pianos reserved for piano majors. Electronic music studio; synthesizer; recording studio.

Concert Facilities. Auditorium, seating 920; Thrust Stage, 300; Weld Auditorium, 400; Recital Hall, 120.

Concerts/Musical Activities. Artist Series (7 to 8 events annually); University ensembles (9 to 10 events annually); faculty recitals (3 to 6 annually).

Music Library. Music materials are housed in the Livingston Lord Library which has total holdings of over 300,000 volumes.

Special Programs

Featured Programs. Tri-College Percussion Ensemble in cooperation with Concordia College and North Dakota State University.

Performance Groups. Concert Band, Chamber Orchestra, Stage Band, Festival Choir, Snowfire, Symphonic Wind Ensemble, Opera Workshop, Concert Choir, Collegiate Chorale, Chamber Singers, Collegium Musicum, Women's Chorus; vocal and instrumental ensembles.

Affiliated Programs. Moorhead State University belongs to a cooperative arrangement with Concordia College (Moorhead) and North Dakota State University (Fargo) through which students may take courses at the other colleges without paying additional fees.

Financial

Costs. Per academic year: Tuition in-state resident $1,-596, out-of-state $2,770. Room and board $1,695.

Financial Aid. Financial aid is awarded on the basis of financial need. Approximately 5,000 students receive some form of financial aid (average award $1,500). Part-time employment and a College Work-Study program available.

St. Cloud State University
Department of Music
Performing Arts Center
St. Cloud
Minnesota 56301

Telephone. (612) 255-3223

Chief Administrator. Dr. Kenton Frohrip, Chairman.

St. Cloud State University first opened its doors as the Third State Normal School in 1869. Until 1898, St. Cloud Normal School was essentially a secondary school with a few students of college rank. Beginning in 1898, the school began offering a full junior college curriculum. In 1914, the high school portion of the program was terminated. In 1921, the institution was authorized by the State Legislature to adopt the name of St. Cloud State Teachers College. The word "teachers" was deleted in 1957. The current name was adopted in 1975. Although the University has been a teacher preparation institution during most of its history, students are now enrolled in many other programs available to them. Today the University is a multi-purpose and comprehensive institution offering a broad range of undergraduate and graduate programs of study. The 86-acre main campus contains 31 buildings in the city of St. Cloud, halfway between Minneapolis-St. Paul and northern Minnesota.

The functions of the Department of Music are to develop an awareness and perception within the student to the unique aesthetic experience of organized sound and its relationship to human senses and intellect; to prepare music teachers working in collegiate institutions, public schools, and private studios, as well as music performers, composers, and researchers; to contribute to the musical life of the university, community, state, and nation.

Accreditation. North Central Association of Colleges and Schools; National Association of Schools of Music.

Academic Information

Enrollment, Music Majors. Undergraduate 103, graduate 9.

Music Faculty. Full-time 16, part-time 4.

Term System. Quarter. Summer session (generally workshops).

Entrance Requirements. Graduation from high school in upper half of graduating class; ACT, PSAT, or SAT. GED accepted. GRE required for graduate students.

Admission Procedure. File Minnesota College Admission form, official transcripts, test scores and $10 non-refundable application fee.

Music Degrees Offered. Bachelor of Music; Bachelor of Arts; Bachelor of Science; Master of Science.

Music Degree Requirements. The Bachelor of Music degree program is primarily for those interested in professional performance and/or college or private studio teaching. Major emphasis may be in performance, piano pedagogy, piano performance, or sacred music. The Bachelor of Arts degree program is primarily for those interested in music as personal enrichment, as background for a career in the music industry, or preparation for further studies in music. The Bachelor of Science degree program is primarily for those interested in teaching music in the elementary and secondary schools. A minimum of 192 quarter hours is required for all baccalaureate degrees.

The Master of Science with a music education emphasis requires that the applicant for the degree must have completed an undergraduate teacher education program from an accredited teacher preparation institution and must have completed at least an undergraduate minor in music.

General Program Areas. Music Education, Music History, Music Theory, Performance, Piano Pedagogy.

Instruments Taught. Baritone, Bass, Bass Clarinet, Bassoon, Clarinet, English Horn, Flute, French Horn, Harpsichord, Oboe, Organ, Percussion, Piano, Piccolo, Saxophone, Trombone, Trumpet, Tuba, Viola, Violin, Violoncello, Voice.

Musical Facilities

Practice Facilities. 20 practice rooms. Special practice facilities for organists; 2 organs (Marrin and Phelps). Percussion-equipped practice room. 20 pianos (Wurlitzer); 2 grand pianos reserved for piano majors. Electronic music studio.

Concert Facilities. Stewart Hall seating 1,096; Recital Hall, 179.

Community Facilities. St. Mary's Cathedral is used for choral concerts.

Concerts/Musical Activities. Ensembles; student/faculty recitals.

Music Library. 1,900 music titles; 21 current periodicals; 2,250 phonograph records. Listening facilities in Learning Resource Center include 12 cassette decks; 3 stereo turntables; 3 compact disc players.

Special Programs

Performance Groups. Vocal Ensemble, Brass Ensemble, Woodwind Ensemble, Percussion Ensemble, Chamber Ensemble, Studio Jazz Band, Jazz Laboratory Band, Chamber Choir, University Chorus, Concert Choir, University Band, University Orchestra, Opera Theatre, Musical Theatre.

Financial

Costs. Per academic year: Tuition in-state resident $1,462, out-of-state $2,352. Room and board $1,850.

Financial Aid. Music scholarships available. College Work-Study program; non-work-study program, students hired by individual departments; average earnings $3.35 to $6.67 per hour.

St. Olaf College
Music Department
Northfield
Minnesota 55057

Telephone. (507) 663-3180

Chief Administrator. Dr. Melvin George, President.

A group of pioneer pastors, farmers, and businessmen in Rice, Dakota, and Goodhue counties in Minnesota laid the groundwork for the founding of the College in 1874. The purpose of the school, then as now, was to offer a program of liberal studies to students preparing for careers in business, politics, the clergy, and other professions. St. Olaf's was operated as an academy until 1886, when a college department was added. The name was changed to St. Olaf College in 1889 and the academy was discontinued in 1917. Throughout its history St. Olaf has been related to The American Lutheran Church, which will become part of the new Evangelical Lutheran Church in America in January, 1988. In 1900, the college department of the United Church Seminary was consolidated with St. Olaf, and in 1917 the college department of Red Wing Seminary was merged with St. Olaf.

The St. Olaf campus of 300 acres is located in Northfield, 40 miles south of Minneapolis/St. Paul. The community of 13,000 is situated in an area famous for its many dairy farms.

St. Olaf offers a diverse assortment of performance opportunities. All full-time students, including non-music majors, are encouraged to audition for the St. Olaf music ensembles. St. Olaf prides itself on the high quality of music majors as well as the musically talented non-majors who consistently contribute a great deal to the musical environment of the college. One-third of the student body is active in music at St. Olaf.

Accreditation. North Central Association of Colleges and Schools; National Council for Accreditation of Teacher Education; National Association of Schools of Music.

Academic Information

Enrollment, Music Majors. Total College enrollment 1,481 men, 1,692 women. Foreign students 57.

Music Faculty. Full-time 25, part-time 32.

Term System. Semester (4-1-4). Academic year from September to May. Two summer sessions from early

June to late August.

Entrance Requirements. Graduation from an accredited high school or equivalent with satisfactory completion of 15 units of credit or equivalent, including at least 3 units of English and 2 mathematics; 11 of 15 units must be academic subjects; satisfactory scores on SAT or ACT. Audition consists of a performance in the student's proposed major area of study in applied music, an optional secondary performing area, and a musicianship examination. Students with a score of 3 on the CEEB Advanced Placement Program may receive credit at the discretion of the department; scores of 4 or 5 will receive credit.

Admission Procedure. Application for Admission submitted together with high school transcript; SAT, ACT, or PSAT scores; two recommendations; medical report. Foreign student applications are reviewed by Foreign Student Admissions Committee which makes recommendations regarding admission and financial aid.

Music Degrees Offered. Bachelor of Music; Bachelor of Arts.

Music Degree Requirements. The Bachelor of Music degree is a professionally oriented program with approximately two-thirds of all coursework in music. Majors are offered in performance (keyboard instruments, voice, orchestral and band instruments, guitar), theory and composition, church music (organ or vocal performance), and music education (instrumental music—band/orchestra, K-12) or (vocal music—K-9, 5-12). A total of 35 courses, including the general education curriculum and departmental requirements, must be completed for the degree. The Bachelor of Arts degree with a major in music can be pursued with an emphasis in history and literature, theory and composition, or music education with teaching credentials.

General Program Areas. Church Music, Music Composition, Music Education, Music History, Music Literature, Music Theory, Performance.

Instruments Taught. Bass, Bassoon, Clarinet, Cornet, Euphonium, Flute, Guitar, Hardanger Fiddle, Harp, Harpsichord, Horn, Oboe, Organ, Percussion, Piano, Saxophone, Trombone, Trumpet, Tuba, Viola, Viola da Gamba, Violin, Violoncello, Voice.

Musical Facilities

Practice Facilities. Special practice facilities for organists; 9 organs (Schlicker, Dobson, Hendrickson, Flentrop). Practice facilities for percussionists. 40 piano practice rooms; 50 pianos (Steinway, Baldwin, Yamaha grand pianos; Mason and Hamlin, Everett, Hamilton uprights); 11 grand pianos reserved for piano majors. Electronic music studio; class piano studio.

Concert Facilities. Tormodsgaard-Bakken Recital Hall, seating 125; Urness Recital Hall, 400; Boe Memorial Chapel, 1,100. Opera and musical theater productions are performed in Kelsey Theater in the Speech-Theater Building.

Concerts/Musical Activities. Numerous concerts and recitals are held both on- and off-campus by the various performance groups. The St. Olaf Choir, the St. Olaf College Orchestra, and the St. Olaf Band tour nationally and internationally. The St. Olaf Christmas Festival concerts occur during the Advent-Christmas-Epiphany season. The Artist Series brings internationally renowned artists to the campus. Faculty recitals are held frequently throughout the academic year.

Music Library. Halvorsen Music Library is located in Christiansen Hall and houses 7,600 volumes; 10,800 musical scores; 7,000 phonograph recordings; 48 current periodicals. 22 listening stations. The resources of the Carleton College Library are available to students.

Special Programs

Featured Programs. The Minnesota Instrumental Conducting Symposium is a continuing education event sponsored by St. Olaf College and Phi Beta Mu, National Band Conducting Fraternity. In addition to conducting, all participants perform in the ensemble and attend lectures on score interpretation, repertoire, conducting technique, calisthenics, and reading and evaluation of new music.

The annual St. Olaf Summer Music Camp offers talented high school students the opportunity to make music with others from around the United States. All campers participate in large ensembles (band, choir, orchestra), private lessons (keyboard, voice, strings, woodwinds, brass, and percussion) and elective offerings (music theory, electronic music, beginning organ class, harp class, instrumental and vocal chamber music, musical theater, handbells, and conducting), recitals and concerts, and recreational activities.

The Annual Conference on Music and Worship brings 500 people to the campus for a summer week of study. Outstanding leaders in church music, organ, and conducting join with visiting theologians to provide a growing experience for all interested in the worship and music life of the local congregation. A unique dimension of this conference is the many choirs (children, handbell, chamber, and large mixed choir) which rehearse and sing during daily worship providing learning through doing opportunities for those in attendance.

Performance Groups. St. Olaf College Orchestra, St. Olaf Chamber Orchestra, Collegium Musicum, Opera/Music Theater, Chamber Music (piano, instrumental, vocal), Jazz Ensembles, Flute Choir, Chapel Choir, Nordic Strings, Clarinet Choir, Trombone Choir, Horn Club, Tuba-Euphonium Ensemble, Percussion Ensemble, St. Olaf Handbell Ensemble and Collegiate Ringers, Viking Chorus, Norseman Band, St. Olaf Cantorei, Wind Ensembles, Manitou Singers.

Financial

Costs. Per academic year: Comprehensive fee $10,750. Student activity fee $50.

Financial Aid. Financial aid is awarded on the basis of financial need. 52% of student body receives financial aid; average award $6,090 per student. Financial aid/scholarship application due March 1. College Work-Study program available.

Commentary

St. Olaf College is the home of WCAL, the oldest public radio station in the country. The year at St. Olaf is structured to include a January interim period for special projects.

MISSISSIPPI

Delta State University
Department of Music
School of Arts and Sciences
Cleveland
Mississippi 38733

Telephone. (601) 846-4615

Chief Administrator. Dr. William James Craig, Chairman.

Delta State University was created in 1924 as Delta State Teachers College. University status under the current name was acquired in 1974. The 263-acre campus is located in Cleveland, midway between Memphis and Vicksburg.

The Department of Music offers programs for the student who wishes to major in an individual performance area; for the student who desires to major in music with a broad cultural background; and for the student who seeks to teach in the public schools.

Accreditation. Southern Association of Colleges and Schools; National Association of Schools of Music.

Academic Information

Enrollment, Music Majors. (Total University) 4,004.

Music Faculty. Full-time 19, part-time 8.

Term System. Semester. Two summer sessions.

Entrance Requirements. High school graduation or GED; completion of 10 academic units including 4 English, 2 mathematics, 2 science, 2 social science; audition required.

Admission Procedure. Application with supporting documents to Office of Admissions.

Music Degrees Offered. Bachelor of Music; Bachelor of Music Education; Bachelor of Arts; Master of Music Education.

Music Degree Requirements. The Bachelor of Music degree is offered with majors in band or orchestra instruments, voice, or piano. The Bachelor of Music Education degree meets all requirements for state certification to teach in the public schools of Mississippi, as well as the requirements specified by various other accrediting agencies. The Bachelor of Arts degree with a major in music is offered in the context of a liberal arts program. The Master of Music Education degree provides study beyond the baccalaureate level in the areas of general, instrumental, and vocal music.

General Program Areas. Commercial Music, Music Education, Music Literature, Performance.

Instruments Taught. Bass, Bassoon, Clarinet, Euphonium, Flute, French Horn, Guitar, Harpsichord, Oboe, Organ, Percussion, Piano, Saxophone, Trombone, Trumpet, Tuba, Viola, Violin, Violoncello, Voice.

Musical Facilities

Practice Facilities. The William H. Zeigel Music Center houses the Department of Music. 15 practice rooms; 17 studio offices; music classrooms.

Concert Facilities. Rehearsal Hall, seating 200.

Concerts/Musical Activities. Student/faculty concerts and recitals; visiting artists.

Music Library. The W.B. Roberts Library houses the collections of the University and serves the academic programs of the Department of Music.

Special Programs

Performance Groups. Delta Chorale, Delta Singers, Delta Chamber Singers, Delta Choral Union, Band, Jazz Band, Instrumental Ensembles, Music Theatre Workshop.

Financial

Costs. Per academic year: Tuition in-state resident $1,675, out-of-state $2,857. Room and board $1,440.

Financial Aid. Music Department Artist Scholarships as well as others are available to deserving students. Other sources of financial aid include grants, loans, and part-time employment.

Jackson State University
Department of Music
School of Liberal Studies
14001 J.R. Lynch Street
Jackson
Mississippi 39217

Telephone. (601) 968-2141

Chief Administrator. Dr. Jimmie James, Jr., Chair.

Jackson State University was established in Natchez in 1877 as a private church school by the American Baptist Home Mission Society. It was moved to its present location in 1882 and became a teachers college of the state of Mississippi in 1940. Its present name was adopted in 1953. The 85-acre campus is located on in Jackson, the capital of the state.

The objectives of the Department of Music are to: offer curricula in music on various levels appropriate to the needs of the students; prepare effective teachers and proficient performers in music in general, vocal, keyboard, and instrumental areas; broaden the scope of study in emerging music styles, media, careers, and methodologies; provide opportunities for students majoring in fields other than music; and contribute to the cultural life of the University, area schools, and the community.

Accreditation. Southern Association of Colleges and Schools; National Association of Schools of Music.

Academic Information

Enrollment, Music Majors. (Total University) 5,418.

Music Faculty. 15.

Term System. Semester. Two summer sessions.

Entrance Requirements. High school graduation or GED; minimum C average and completion of 16 units; ACT required.

Admission Procedure. Application with supporting documents reviewed on a rolling admissions basis.

Music Degrees Offered. Bachelor of Music; Bachelor of Music Education; Master of Music Education.

Music Degree Requirements. The Bachelor of Music degree requires the completion of general education courses (language arts, social sciences, natural sciences) and major courses (including a music core, applied music, performance ensemble, and electives). The Bachelor of Music Education degree curriculum includes courses in general education, professional education, and the major area of concentration. A concentration in music is offered for elementary and special education majors.

The Master of Music Education degree is offered with concentrations in elementary school music education, secondary school music education (choral, general, instrumental), junior college music education (choral, instrumental), and comprehensive music education.

General Program Areas. Applied Music, Music Education, Music History, Music Literature, Music Theory.

Instruments Taught. Baritone, Bass, Bassoon, Clarinet, Flute, French Horn, Oboe, Organ, Percussion, Piano, Saxophone, Trombone, Trumpet, Tuba, Viola, Violin, Violoncello, Voice.

Musical Facilities

Practice Facilities. The Frederick Douglas Hall Music Center contains offices and classrooms for the Department of Music, practice rooms, and studios.

Concert Facilities. Douglas Recital Hall.

Concerts/Musical Activities. Student and faculty concerts and recitals; visiting artists.

Music Library. The Henry Thomas Sampson Library houses over 700,000 items and supports the academic programs of the Department of Music.

Special Programs

Performance Groups. Marching Band, Symphonic Wind Ensemble, Concert Band, Orchestra, Woodwind Ensemble, Brasswind Ensemble, Percussion Ensemble, Stage Band, ROTC Band, Jackson Municipal Band, Choir, Opera Workshop, Chorale, Chamber Singers, Opera South Chorus, JSU Singers.

Financial

Costs. Per academic year: Tuition in-state resident $1,472, out-of-state $2,648. Room $1,205. Board $1,015.

Financial Aid. Scholarships, grants, loans, and part-time employment are available. All financial aid is coordinated by the Office of Student Financial Aid.

University of Mississippi
Department of Music
University
Mississippi 38677

Telephone. (601) 232-7268

Chief Administrator. Dr. Ronald F. Vernon, Chairman.

The University of Mississippi, also known as "Ole Miss," was established in 1848. Closed during the Civil War, the University reopened in 1865, and became coeducational in 1882. The Graduate School was founded in 1927. The University consists of the College of Liberal Arts and professional schools in Education, Pharmacy, Law, Business, and Engineering. University, Mississippi is a part of Oxford, the seat of Lafayette County.

The Department of Music is in the College of Liberal Arts and is strongly supported by the College of Education in its teacher education programs. The undergraduate programs prepare students for music teaching, performance, or graduate study in many areas. Master's degrees further develop skills in teaching and performance. The doctorate prepares for college teaching in various disciplines.

Accreditation. Southern Association of Colleges and Schools; National Association of Schools of Music; National Council for Accreditation of Teacher Education.

Academic Information

Enrollment, Music Majors. Full-time 70 men, 75 women.

Music Faculty. Full-time 23, part-time 4.

Term System. Semester. Two 5-week summer sessions. Academic year from mid-August to mid-May.

Entrance Requirements. High school graduation or equivalent; ACT of 18; specific course requirements, but deficiencies may be made up or exempted with ACT of 24 or higher; performance audition. Foreign students must score 525 to 550 on TOEFL and have equivalent of high school diploma for undergraduates or baccalaureate degree for graduate students. Advanced placement through CLEP, faculty assessment for performance and theory placement. Graduate programs require a baccalaureate degree or equivalent from a recognized institution and an undergraduate program in which all required courses in the major field have been completed.

Admission Procedure. Application with supporting documents to Admissions Office.

Music Degrees Offered. Bachelor of Music; Bachelor of Arts; Master of Music; Master of Fine Arts; Music Specialist Degree in Music Education; Doctor of Arts.

Music Degree Requirements. The Bachelor of Music degree is available with emphases in applied music (performance), music education, and music theory-composition. All students enrolled in these curricula are required to take a major ensemble in their area of concentration every semester. The degree requires the completion of 126 to 140 semester hours depending on emphasis and including a liberal arts core curriculum plus professional requirements. The Bachelor of Arts degree with a major in music is also available.

The Master of Music degree is offered with emphases in piano performance, voice performance, instrumental performance, music theory, and music education. It requires a minimum of 30 semester hours of coursework, including a thesis where applicable. The major portion of the work on the thesis or the recital in the applied music program must be done while enrolled. The degree Master of Fine Arts in Musical Theatre is offered in cooperation with the Department of Theatre Arts and requires the completion of 60 semester hours in specified courses.

The Music Specialist degree in Music Education (M.Ed.S.) entitles a student to the AAA Teaching Certificate upon application to the State Department of Education. Prerequisites include a Master of Music degree, three years of successful teaching experience, and a minimum score of 430 on the GRE Test in Music. The degree requires the completion of 30 semester hours.

The Doctor of Arts degree is offered in the areas of music education, music theory, music history-literature, and applied music pedagogy (voice or piano). The degree requires 3 academic years of full-time study beyond the bachelor's degree and a minimum of 66 semester hours in various areas of music plus one other subject area.

General Program Areas. Applied Music, Composition, Music Education, Music Theory, Performance, Piano Pedagogy, Voice Pedagogy.

Instruments Taught. Brass, Organ, Percussion, Piano, Stringed Instruments, Voice, Woodwinds.

Musical Facilities

Practice Facilities. 28 practice rooms. 3 organs (Moeller, Casavant). 25 practice pianos (Steinway, Yamaha, Kawai, Baldwin uprights; 4 grands); 3 grand pianos reserved for piano majors. Special practice facilities for percussionists.

Concert Facilities. 2 concert halls, seating 917 and 231, respectively.

Community Facilities. Local area churches; recital hall in public library.

Concerts/Musical Activities. Concerts and solo recitals averaging 3 per week.

Music Library. 2,000 volumes; 4,500 scores; 5 music periodicals; 31 audiovisual items; 1,492 microforms; 5,707 phonograph recordings; 160 audiocassettes. 33 listening stations (stereo). Special collections include the Blues Archive; percussion instruments.

Special Programs

Performance Groups. Orchestra, Band, Choir, Chamber Music; various ensembles.

Financial

Costs. Per academic year: Tuition in-state resident $1,727, out-of-state $2,909. Room $1,200. Off-campus housing approximately $400 per month.

Financial Aid. Financial aid is awarded on the basis of academic merit, financial need, and musical ability. Both institutional and state/federal aid available as well as part-time employment and a College Work-Study program.

University of Southern Mississippi
School of Music
College of Fine Arts
Hattiesburg
Mississippi 39401

Telephone. (601) 266-5363

Chief Administrator. Ronald McCreery, Director.

The University of Southern Mississippi was founded in 1910 as the Mississippi Normal College in order to train teachers for the rural schools of the state. It became State Teachers College in 1924 and in 1940, was renamed

Mississippi Southern College. The institution did no grant degrees in its early years, but awarded certificates for the completion of certain specified courses of study. The first Bachelor of Arts degree was awarded in 1940. In the years since 1947, the University's graduate programs have been developed to meet the needs for professional competence beyond the baccalaureate degree. Upon achieving university status in 1962, the present name was adopted.

The primary purpose of the College of Fine Arts is to provide its students with a well-rounded preparation for professional and teaching careers in art, music, dance, or theater. In addition, it seeks to provide opportunities for all University students to participate in artistic activities and develop an awareness of cultural values. The School of Music offers two undergraduate majors (music and music education).

Accreditation. Southern Association of Colleges and Schools; National Association of Schools of Music; National Council for Accreditation of Teacher Education.

Academic Information

Enrollment, Music Majors. Full-time 139, part-time 109. 4 foreign students.

Music Faculty. Full-time 38.

Term System. Semester. Two summer sessions.

Entrance Requirements. Accredited high school graduation or equivalent; completion of 15 units; ACT score of 15 or over required; audition required (tape or live); theory placement test. GRE required for graduate study.

Music Degrees Offered. Bachelor of Music; Bachelor of Music Education; Master of Music; Master of Music Education; Doctor of Musical Arts; Doctor of Music Education; Doctor of Philosophy.

Music Degree Requirements. The Bachelor of Music degree is offered with emphases in voice, organ, strings, wind instruments, percussion, jazz, church music, composition, music history and literature, and music industry. The degree requires the completion of a total of 132 to 148 semester hours. The Bachelor of Music Education degree curricula are designed to prepare musicians who will teach in the public or private schools or teach privately. Emphases include instrumental, keyboard, vocal, guitar, and elementary music education.

The Master of Music degree is offered with emphases in performance, church music, conducting, music history and literature, theory and composition, and woodwind performance and pedagogy. The Master of Music Education degree is also offered. The master's degrees require the completion of 32 semester hours.

The doctoral degrees required the completion of 78 semester hours beyond the bachelor's degree. The degrees Doctor of Music Education, Doctor of Philosophy in Music Education, and Doctor of Musical Arts are offered by the School. The degree programs require regular admission procedures, qualifying examinations prior

to or during the first term, appointment of the major professor and graduate advisory committee, and completion of an approved course of studies designed jointly by the student and the entire graduate advisory committee.

General Program Areas. Church Music, Composition, Conducting, Jazz Studies, Music Education, Music History, Music Industry, Music Literature, Music Theory, Performance.

Instruments Taught. Bass, Bassoon, Clarinet, Euphonium, Flute, Guitar, Harpsichord, Horn, Oboe, Organ, Percussion, Piano, Saxophone, Trombone, Trumpet, Tuba, Viola, Violin, Violoncello, Voice.

Musical Facilities

Practice Facilities. 30 practice rooms. 3 organs. 2 percussion-equipped practice rooms. Recording studio; piano labs; computer lab.

Concert Facilities. 3 concert halls.

Concerts/Musical Activities. Student and faculty recitals and concerts.

Music Library. 10,200 volumes; 6,347 scores; 188 periodical titles; 5,523 LP recordings; 329 reel-to-reel tapes and cassettes. Listening facilities (cassette, stereo).

Special Programs

Performance Groups. Orchestra, Band, Chorus, Jazz Band, Collegium Musicum, Women's Chorus, Men's Chorus, University Singers, Chamber Singers.

Foreign Programs. British Studies program.

Affiliated Programs. Mokpo University (Korea).

Financial

Costs. Per academic year: Tuition in-state resident $1,400, out-of-state $2,582. Room $1,170. Board $900.

Financial Aid. Scholarships for music students average $250 per year. Other sources of financial aid include institutional and state/federal grants and loans, part-time employment, and a College Work-Study program.

William Carey College
Winters School of Music
Tuscan Avenue
Hattiesburg
Mississippi 39401

Telephone. (601) 582-5051, Ext. 229

Chief Administrator. Eugene Winters, Dean.

William Carey College, a private institution, was founded in 1906 and is affiliated with the Southern Baptist Convention. The campus of 64 acres is located in Hattiesburg, 70 miles north of Gulfport.

The general aim of music study at William Carey College is to help students discover and develop their musical capacities and interests on the undergraduate and graduate levels. The goals of the School of Music are to: acquaint each interested student with music as one area of general culture; give intensive professional training to students preparing for performance careers; prepare teachers and supervisors of music in state-approved curricula for elementary and secondary public or private schools; train for music leadership in Christian service; and prepare music majors for certification as registered music therapists.

Accreditation. Southern Association of Colleges and Schools; National Association of Schools of Music.

Academic Information

Enrollment, Music Majors. (Total University) 1,090.
Music Faculty. 8.
Term System. Semester. Two summer terms.
Entrance Requirements. High school graduation; completion of 16 units; ACT or SAT; placement testing.
Admission Procedure. Application with supporting documents and nonrefundable $10 fee to Office of Admissions.
Music Degrees Offered. Bachelor of Music; Bachelor of Arts; Master of Music; Master of Education.
Music Degree Requirements. The Bachelor of Music degree is offered with major areas of study in applied music, church music, music education, and music therapy. The Bachelor of Arts degree is a liberal arts program with a major in music.

Graduate programs lead to the the Master of Music degree (majors in church music, music education, music history and literature) and the Master of Education degree (music education).

General Program Areas. Applied Music, Church Music, Music Education, Music History, Music Literature, Music Theory, Music Therapy.

Instruments Taught. Baritone, Bass, Bassoon, Clarinet, Flute, French Horn, Oboe, Organ, Percussion, Piano, Piccolo, Saxophone, Trombone, Trumpet, Tuba, Viola, Violin, Violoncello, Voice.

Musical Facilities

Practice Facilities. The Fine Arts Center houses the complete facilities for the School of Music.
Concert Facilities. Smith Auditorium, seating 1,200.
Concerts/Musical Activities. Student and faculty concerts and recitals; visiting artists.
Music Library. The I.E. Rouse Library houses over 110,000 items, including books, bound periodicals, music scores, microtexts, phonodiscs, and other materials. The Clarence Dickinson Collection, centered around church music, contains 5,600 items.

Special Programs

Performance Groups. Chamber Ensemble, Carey Chapel Choir, Carey College Chorale, Madrigal Singers, Carpenter's Wood, Handbell Choir, Community Chorus

Financial

Costs. Per academic year: Tuition $3,170. Fees $100. Room and board $1,980.
Financial Aid. Financial aid in the form of scholarships, grants, loans, and part-time employment is available. Financial aid/scholarship application due February 1.

MISSOURI

Central Missouri State University
Department of Music
Warrensburg
Missouri 64093

Telephone. (816) 429-4530

Chief Administrator. Dr. Russell Coleman, Chair.

The Central Missouri State University was founded as the State Normal School for the Second Normal District of Missouri in 1871. It was accredited as a four-year teachers college in 1915 and became the Central State Teachers College in 1919. The present name was adopted in 1972. The University campus includes 70 buildings on 1,000 acres. It is located 50 miles southeast of Kansas City in Warrensburg, one of the oldest cities in the western prairie area.

The first graduates from the Department of Music were in the class of 1922. Since that time, 1,885 students have been awarded undergraduate degrees and 209 graduate degrees have been conferred. The first graduate degree was granted in the summer of 1954. The majority of graduates have entered the teaching profession; however, many are employed in the fields of performance, composition, and music technology. Many graduates successfully pursuing non-music careers have attributed their success to the discipline, organization, and creative skills they learned as music majors.

Accreditation. North Central Association of Colleges and Schools; National Association of Schools of Music; National Council for Accreditation of Teacher Education.

Academic Information

Enrollment, Music Majors. 150 majors and minors.

Music Faculty. Full-time 23.

Term System. Semester. Academic year begins last week in August, ends first week in May. 8- and 11-week summer sessions from May to August.

Entrance Requirements. Students from accredited high schools are considered for admission on the basis of class rank and academic preparation. Advanced placement available by departmental examination and CLEP. Placement evaluations are administered in music theory and applied performance.

Admission Procedure. Application and high school transcripts; ACT score.

Music Degrees Offered. Bachelor of Arts; Bachelor of Music; Bachelor of Music Education; Master of Arts; Master of Science in Education.

Music Degree Requirements. Bachelor degree requires 37-43 semester hours in general education; approved major or minor credit for a total of 124 semester hours. Master's degree requires 30 semester hours in approved graduate courses.

General Program Areas. Applied Performance, Commercial Music, Composition, Jazz, Music Education, Piano Pedagogy, Theory.

Instruments Taught. Bass, Bassoon, Clarinet, Electronic Bass, Euphonium, Flute, Guitar, Harpsichord, Horn, Oboe, Organ, Percussion, Piano, Saxophone, Trombone, Trumpet, Tuba, Viola, Violin, Violoncello.

Musical Facilities

Practice Facilities. Special practice facilities for organists; 3 organs (Charles McManis, Austin, Reuter). 32 piano practice rooms; 32 upright and grand pianos; 3 grand pianos reserved for piano majors. Electronic music studio with Moog synthesizer, Yamaha DX-7, and computer assisted composition.

Concert Facilities. Hendricks Hall with seating capacity of 1,200; Hart Recital Hall, 320; University Theater, 440.

Concerts/Musical Activities. Concerts, recitals, lectures by visiting professional musicians.

Music Library. 15,366 volumes; 836 musical scores; 84 periodical subscriptions; 4,000 phonograph records. 12 listening booths (stereo). Records and scores are housed in music building; research materials in main library. Essig Collection of Musical Instruments is a nationally ranked special collection.

Financial

Costs. Per academic year: Tuition $1,254. Room and board $2,070. Off-campus housing approximately $300 per month.

Financial Aid. Financial aid is awarded on the basis of academic merit, financial need, musical ability. Institutional and state/federal aid available. Part-time employment and College Work-Study program available.

University of Missouri - Columbia
Department of Music
College of Arts and Sciences
Columbia
Missouri 65211

Telephone. (314) 882-2604
Chief Administrator. Donald McGlothlin, Chairman.

The University of Missouri was established at Columbia in 1839 as the sole public university in Missouri. Located midway between Kansas City and St. Louis, it is now the largest of the four campuses of the University of Missouri system.

The Department of Music offers beginning or advanced professional training in music as well as instruction for those who wish to pursue music as an avocation. The Department also offers the opportunity for all students of the University to participate in various performing groups.

Accreditation. North Central Association of Colleges and Schools; National Association of Schools of Music; National Council for Accreditation of Teacher Education.

Academic Information

Enrollment, Music Majors. (Total University) 20,171.
Music Faculty. 26.
Term System. Semester. Two summer sessions.
Entrance Requirements. High school graduation or equivalent with completion of 14 units including 4 English, 3 mathematics, 1 laboratory science, 1-2 foreign language, 2 social studies; SAT or ACT required; audition required for performance majors.
Admission Procedure. Application with supporting documents and nonrefundable $20 fee to Office of Admissions.
Music Degrees Offered. Bachelor of Music; Bachelor of Arts; Master of Music; Master of Arts.
Music Degree Requirements. The Bachelor of Music degree is a professional degree and offers the maximum concentration in music. The student may emphasize instrumental, keyboard or vocal music, music theory, composition, music history, or music education. The Bachelor of Arts degree with a major in music is offered in a program of liberal arts.

The Master of Music degree is offered with concentrations in theory, composition, applied music (piano, piano accompanying, piano pedagogy, organ, strings, voice, wind, and percussion) or choral conducting. Educational degrees with a major in music education are offered in conjunction with the College of Education. The Master of Arts degree offers concentrations in music history and theory-composition.

General Program Areas. Accompanying, Applied Music, Choral Conducting, Composition, Music History, Music Theory, Performance, Piano Pedagogy.

Instruments Taught. Brass, Organ, Percussion, Piano, Stringed Instruments, Voice, Woodwinds.

Musical Facilities

Practice Facilities. The Department of Music is located in the Fine Arts Center; practice facilities available.

Concerts/Musical Activities. Student/faculty recitals and concerts; visiting artists.

Music Library. The University libraries have a collection of more than 2 million volumes and a musical instrument collection.

Special Programs

Performance Groups. University Philharmonic Orchestra, Marching Band, Symphonic Band, Concert Band, Choral Union, University Singers, Singsations, Collegium Musicum, Chamber Singers, Concert Chorale, Opera Workshop, Brass Choir, String Ensemble, Percussion Ensemble, Chamber Ensemble.

Financial

Costs. Per academic year: Tuition in-state resident $1,410, out-of-state $4,230. Fees $78. Room and board $2,195.

Financial Aid. Financial aid is awarded on the basis of academic merit and financial need. Institutional and state/federal aid are available in the form of scholarships, loans, grants, and part-time employment. Financial aid/scholarship application due February 26.

University of Missouri - Kansas City
Conservatory of Music
Center for the Performing Arts
4949 Cherry
Kansas City
Missouri 64110

Telephone. (816) 363-4300
Chief Administrator. Lindsey Merrill, Dean.

The Kansas City campus of the University of Missouri has been one of the four campuses of the University system since 1963. Prior to that date, the institution was known as the University of Kansas City, a privately endowed school founded in 1933. The University now enrolls over 6,000 full-time and 5,700 part-time students.

The Conservatory of Music traces its lineage to two early Kansas City conservatories, The Kansas City Conservatory of Music founded in 1906 and the Horner Institute of Fine Arts founded in 1914. These institutions merged in 1924 and the Horner Conservatory of Music was formed. It became the Conservatory of Kansas City in 1934. A second merger occurred in 1958 when the Horner Conservatory merged with the University of Kansas City. Four years later when the private University of Kansas City became part of the state university system, the Conservatory became a component college. It provides professional training in the performance and teaching of music, music therapy, church music ministry, theory, composition, conducting, and musicology. A wide variety of experiences in solo and ensemble performance is available. The Conservatory also seeks to help students to acquire a greater musical appreciation and critical judgment through courses in music history and literature, music theory, music composition, music performance, and ensemble, and attendance at various musical functions.

Accreditation. North Central Association of Colleges and Schools; National Association of Schools of Music; National Association for Music Therapy; National Council for Accreditation of Teacher Education.

Academic Information

Enrollment, Music Majors. Undergraduate 358, graduate 219.

Music Faculty. 57.

Term System. Semester. One summer session.

Entrance Requirements. High school graduation or equivalent; SAT, ACT, or SCAT required; admission based on combination of class rank and test scores; audition required; theory placement examination. Foreign students must submit test score on TOEFL; statement of financial solvency.

Admission Procedure. Applications accepted on a rolling basis; applicant should contact Conservatory for audition schedule.

Music Degrees Offered. Bachelor of Music; Bachelor of Arts; Master of Music; Master of Arts; Doctor of Musical Arts.

Music Degree Requirements. The Bachelor of Music degree is offered with major areas in performance (piano, organ, orchestral instruments, voice), music theory, and composition. The Bachelor of Music Education degree is offered leading to fulfillment of the minimum requirements to teach music in grades K-12 in either Missouri or Kansas. A music therapy curriculum leads to certification-registration by the National Association for Music Therapy as well as certification to teach in Missouri or Kansas. The Bachelor of Arts degree in music offers flexibility in designing a program which emphasizes musical strengths as well as abilities in other fields. The baccalaureate degrees require the completion of a minimum of 120 semester hours.

Graduate programs are offered leading to the degree Master of Music in performance, music theory, composition, conducting, and music history and literature. The Master of Music Education degree is also available. The master's degrees require the completion of a minimum of 30 semester hours.

The Doctor of Musical Arts degree is offered in performance, conducting, music history and literature, theory, composition, and music education. The degree requires the completion of 75 to 90 semester hours beyond the bachelor's degree.

General Program Areas. Applied Music, Composition, Conducting, Music Education, Music History, Music Literature, Music Theory, Music Therapy, Performance.

Instruments Taught. Accordion, Baritone, Bass, Bassoon, Clarinet, Flute, Guitar, Harpsichord, Horn, Oboe, Organ, Percussion, Piano, Saxophone, Trombone, Trumpet, Tuba, Viola, Violin, Violoncello, Voice.

Musical Facilities

Practice Facilities. Practice rooms, 3 major rehearsal rooms, teaching studios. Electronic music studio; recording studios.

Concert Facilities. Russell Stover Memorial Auditorium; Raymond White Recital Hall, seating 665; theater, 775.

Concerts/Musical Activities. Concerts and recitals held throughout the year.

Music Library. 120,000 books, scores, periodicals, tapes and disc recordings, microcards, microfiche, and microfilm. Listening facilities (stereo). Special collection of American music including movie scores from Leith Stevens (Hollywood film composer).

Special Programs

Featured Programs. The UMKC Conservatory's Institute for Studies in American Music was founded in 1967 to stimulate interest in American music and encourage performances of works by American composers. Courses are offered in this area and special library collections have been assembled. Symposia, lectures, and recitals are scheduled regularly to present the different facets of the American musical culture.

Performance Groups. Orchestra, Conservatory Wind Ensemble, Jazz Band, Conservatory Contemporary Chamber Ensemble, University Percussion Ensemble, Civic String Orchestra, Conservatory Chamber Percussion Ensemble, Heritage Chorale, University Singers, Conservatory Chamber Singers, Civic Chorus, Conservatory Opera Workshop, University Choir, Civic Orchestra, Renaissance Players, Accordion Orchestra, Conservatory Choraliers, Chamber Orchestra.

Affiliated Programs. Student exchange program with Rockhurst College and William Jewell College. Students may take one course per term at these institutions without additional fees.

Financial

Costs. Per academic year: Tuition undergraduate in-state $1,460, out-of-state $3,948; graduate in-state $1,908, out-of-state $4,788. Room and board $2,523.

Financial Aid. Conservatory scholarships are awarded on the basis of ability demonstrated at the audition, academic standing, and need. They are awarded for one year but are renewable annually. Conservatory scholarship applications are included with the application packet. Other forms of financial aid include state/federal grants and loans, part-time employment, and a College Work-Study program.

Northeast Missouri State University
Division of Fine Arts
Franklin Street
Kirksville
Missouri 63501

Telephone. (816) 785-4417
Chief Administrator. Dr. Dale A. Jorgenson, Division Head.

Northeast Missouri State University began in 1867 with the opening of the North Missouri Normal School and Commercial College. In 1870, it became the First District Normal School by act of the Missouri General Assembly. In 1919, the Normal School became known as Northeast Missouri State Teachers College and later as Northeast Missouri State College. The present name was adopted when university status was achieved in 1972. The University, where more than 6,900 students are enrolled each year, offers 140 undergraduate and graduate areas of study in 13 academic divisions. The University was named Premier State Liberal Arts Institution for the State of Missouri in 1986. The 120-acre campus has 39 buildings in the city of Kirksville in northeastern Missouri.

The programs in art and music education in the Division of Fine Arts prepare the student for a career in teaching or professional performance. The liberal arts program in Music Business is designed to provide students with a dual preparation in basic music and business courses leading to professional careers in music merchandising.

Accreditation. North Central Association of Colleges and Schools; National Association of Schools of Music; National Council for Accreditation of Teacher Education.

Academic Information

Enrollment, Music Majors. Undergraduate 191, graduate 12. Foreign students 1.
Music Faculty. Full-time 17, part-time 12.
Term System. Semester. Two 5-week summer terms.

Entrance Requirements. High school graduation or GED; ACT required (minimum score 18); audition required after acceptance.

Admission Procedure. Submit application and supporting documents to Admissions Office.

Music Degrees Offered. Bachelor of Music; Bachelor of Arts; Bachelor of Music Education; Master of Arts.

Music Degree Requirements. The Bachelor of Music degree requires the completion of 132 semester hours of which 44-46 are general education requirements and the remainder in music courses. The Bachelor of Arts degree is also offered with options in music and music business. The programs require the completion of 132 semester hours. The Bachelor of Music Education degree program qualifies the student for a career in teaching in the secondary or elementary schools, as well as for professional performance. Options are available in elementary music, instrumental emphasis, instrument emphasis with piano concentration, vocal emphasis with voice concentration, and vocal emphasis with piano concentration. The degree requires the completion of 129 to 142 semester hours depending on option pursued and including general education requirements.

The Master of Arts degree requires the completion of 32 semester hours of study.

General Program Areas. Music Business, Music Education, Music Literature, Music Theory, Performance.

Instruments Taught. Brass, Percussion, Piano, Stringed Instruments, Voice, Woodwinds.

Musical Facilities

Practice Facilities. 16 practice rooms. 3 percussion-equipped practice rooms. 16 practice pianos; 2 grand pianos reserved for piano majors. Electronic music studio; theory laboratory.

Concert Facilities. University Auditorium, seating 1,400.

Music Library. Music materials are housed in the Music Library Room of the Pickler Memorial Library. 2,741 scores; 4,721 recordings. Listening facilities include 6 cassette decks and 4 stereo turntables.

Financial

Costs. Per academic year: Tuition (16 hours per semester) in-state resident $770, out-of-state $1,540. Room and board $1,670.

Financial Aid. 16 music scholarships ranging from $200 to $1,000. Applications due February 1. Grants, loans, and student employment are other sources of financial aid.

Saint Louis Conservatory of Music
560 Trinity Avenue
St. Louis
Missouri 63130

Telephone. (314) 863-3033

Chief Administrator. Dr. Theodore C. Hansen, Dean.

The primary goal of the Saint Louis Conservatory of Music is to provide instruction to aspiring professionals. All program options, both baccalaureate and graduate, are performance oriented. The solfege, music theory, and music history courses provide a framework for the student's applied study.

The parent organization of the Conservatory, The Saint Louis Conservatory and Schools for the Arts, were formed by the merger in 1974 of two long-established institutions, the Saint Louis Institute of Music and the Community Music School.

Accreditation. National Association of School of Music.

Academic Information

Enrollment, Music Majors. Full-time 52 men, 47 women; part-time 3 men, 9 women. 18 foreign students.

Music Faculty. Full-time 16, part-time 41.

Term System. Semester. Academic year September to May.

Entrance Requirements. High school graduation; audition.

Admission Procedure. Application accepted on a rolling admissions basis.

Music Degrees Offered. Bachelor of Music; Master of Music; Diploma in Music Performance; Graduate Diploma in Music Performance.

Music Degree Requirements. The Bachelor of Music degree is offered with majors in string, woodwind, brass, piano, guitar, percussion, voice, and composition. The degree requires the completion of 133 to 138 semester hours (depending on the major) including 87 core curriculum credits.

The graduate curriculum leading to the Master of Music degree provides the widest possible artistic and intellectual foundation for the advanced student seeking to enter the professional world of music. The program, which can be completed in one year but is normally completed in two, has three phases: performance studies, classroom studies, and the culminating recital and comprehensive examinations. A total of 30 credits are required for the degree.

The Diploma in Music Performance curriculum is the same as that of the Bachelor of Music degree, except that all non-music academic courses are omitted from the requirements. The Graduate Diploma in Music Performance is designed for students who have already earned master's degrees and others whose only wish is to pursue studies in their major field without entering a degree program. This diploma is awarded upon completion of 24 credits, 8 of which must be in the major applied area and 4 of which must be earned as ensemble credits and forum.

General Program Areas. Composition, Music History, Music Literature, Music Theory, Performance.

Instruments Taught. Bass, Bassoon, Clarinet, English Horn, Flute, French Horn, Guitar, Harp, Harpsichord, Lute, Oboe, Organ, Percussion, Piano, Trombone, Trumpet, Tuba, Viola, Violin, Violoncello, Voice.

Musical Facilities

Practice Facilities. 26 practice rooms. Special practice suite for percussionists. 46 practice pianos (24 uprights, 22 grands); 6 grand pianos reserved for piano majors. Recording studio; videotape equipment.

Concert Facilities. Main Auditorium, seating 1,300; Concert Hall, 400; Recital Hall, 80.

Concerts/Musical Activities. Over 120 concerts per year (orchestra, opera, chamber music); Great Artist Series; Mae M. Whitaker International Competition.

Music Library. 2,400 volumes; 6,400 scores; 6,100 phonograph recordings; 2,101 audiocassettes. 8 listening stations (stereo).

Special Programs

Featured Programs. Master Classes permit students to work with artists, discuss performance techniques, and acquaint themselves with divergent musical ideas.

Performance Groups. Conservatory Orchestra; Conservatory String Ensemble, Percussion Ensemble, Early Music Ensemble, New Music Ensemble, Conservatory Opera Workshop, and Opera Studio.

Affiliated Programs. Degree credit can be earned in chamber music by summer studies through the Johannesen International School of the Arts in Victoria, British Columbia; through Kneisel Hall in Blue Hill, Maine; and the Franz Schubert Institute, Vienna, Austria.

Financial

Costs. Per academic year: Tuition $6,750. No on-campus housing.

Financial Aid. Financial aid is awarded on the basis of financial need and musical ability. Both institutional and state/federal aid available. 105 students receive some form of financial aid; average award $3,500. National scholarship auditions are held in Phoenix, San Francisco, San Antonio, New York, Interlochen, Atlanta, and Denver. Saint Louis auditions are arranged for individual students according to their major applied area. Scholarship applications accepted on a rolling basis. Part-time employment and College Work-Study program available.

Southeast Missouri State University
Department of Music
900 Normal Street
Cape Girardeau
Missouri 63701

Telephone. (314) 651-2141

Chief Administrator. Dr. Doyle A. Dumas, Chairman.

Southeast Missouri State University was established in 1873 as the Southeast Missouri Normal School. By legislative enactment in 1919, the institution became the Southeast Missouri State Teachers College. In 1946, the word "Teachers" was dropped from the name. University status was achieved in 1972 and the current name was adopted. The campus is located in Cape Girardeau overlooking the Mississippi River. Cape Girardeau is one of the oldest cities in Missouri.

The Department of Music has as its goals: to prepare teachers of vocal, and/or instrumental music at the elementary or secondary level; to provide professional preparation in applied music; to offer courses and music participation to students whose major is not music; and to enrich the musical life of the University and the community.

Accreditation. North Central Association of Colleges and Schools; National Association of Schools of Music; National Council for Accreditation of Teacher Education.

Academic Information

Enrollment, Music Majors. Full-time 60 men, 40 women; part-time 2 women.

Music Faculty. Full-time 17, part-time 1. Doctorate 11, master's 6.

Term System. Semester. 8-week summer session from mid-June to mid-August. Academic year from late August to mid-May.

Entrance Requirements. High school graduation or equivalent with rank in upper two-thirds of class; ACT.

Admission Procedure. Application with supporting documents and $10 nonrefundable fee to Admissions Office.

Music Degrees Offered. Bachelor of Music; Bachelor of Arts; Master of Music Education.

Music Degree Requirements. The Bachelor of Music degree is offered with emphases in performance, theory and composition, and music education. The Bachelor of Arts degree is offered with the music major within the broad framework of a liberal arts curriculum. The baccalaureate degrees require the completion of a minimum of 124 semester hours.

The graduate program in music education is designed to provide students with opportunities to improve their basic musicianship through performance and analysis of music literature, to increase their professional preparation for teaching at the elementary and/or secondary

levels, and to provide for scholastic growth in areas of special interest. The degree Master of Music Education requires the completion of 30 semester hours of study.

General Program Areas. Composition, Music Education, Music Theory, Performance.

Instruments Taught. Baritone, Bass, Bassoon, Clarinet, Flute, Guitar, Harpsichord, Horn, Oboe, Organ, Percussion, Piano, Saxophone, Trombone, Trumpet, Tuba, Viola, Violin, Violoncello, Voice.

Musical Facilities

Practice Facilities. 28 practice rooms. 1 organ (Casavant). Special practice facilities for percussionists. 32 pianos (30 uprights, 2 grands); 2 grands reserved for piano majors. Electronic music studio.

Concert Facilities. Academic auditorium, seating 1,500.

Community Facilities. Local churches.

Concerts/Musical Activities. Student recitals; small and large ensembles; 50 to 70 performances per year.

Special Programs

Performance Groups. Symphonic Wind Ensemble, Concert Band, University Symphony, Camerata String Orchestra, University Choir, Choral Union, Chamber Choir, Swing Choir, Opera Workshop, Percussion Ensemble, Low Brass Ensemble, Guitar Ensemble, Jazz Bands, Golden Eagles Marching Band.

Financial

Costs. Per academic year: Tuition undergraduate in-state resident $1,500, out-of-state $2,150; graduate in-state $1,115, out-of-state $2,180. Room and board $1,875.

Financial Aid. Institutional and state/federal grants and loans, student employment, and a College Work-Study plan are available. Scholarships and graduate assistantships are also offered.

Washington University
Department of Music
Campus Box 1032
One Brookings Drive
St. Louis
Missouri 63130

Telephone. (314) 889-5566

Chief Administrator. Dr. Jeffrey Kurtzman, Chairman.

Washington University is a private, independent university established in 1853 under the name of Eliot Seminary. Later, as the educational program developed, the present name was adopted. The University enrolls over 10,000 full- and part-time students. The 176-acre campus is comprised of 49 buildings and is located in St.

Louis, a major industrial and transportation center of the central United States.

The Department of Music was founded in 1947 and provides undergraduate education for music majors and non-majors with a variety of performing ensembles for both. Graduate education is offered in musicology, theory, composition, and performance. The Department stresses an integrated musical education, combining performance and composition with historical and theoretical studies.

Accreditation. North Central Association of Colleges and Schools; National Association of Schools of Music.

Academic Information

Enrollment, Music Majors. Undergraduate 18, graduate 55.

Music Faculty. Full-time 16, part-time 24.

Term System. Semester. Summer session offers courses in applied music, general music topics, and graduate seminars.

Entrance Requirements. High school graduation with 4 units English, 3-4 mathematics, 3-4 laboratory science, 3 social studies, 2 foreign language; SAT or ACT required. GRE required for graduate school. Audition required.

Admission Procedure. Application due January 15 with nonrefundable $30 fee.

Music Degrees Offered. Bachelor of Arts; Bachelor of Music; Master of Arts; Master of Music; Doctor of Philosophy.

Music Degree Requirements. The Bachelor of Arts degree with a major in music requires the completion of 54 credit hours in music courses, a minimum of one year study of piano for non-pianists, keyboard proficiency, and regular participation in Department of Music performing activities. The Bachelor of Music degree may be pursued with emphasis in composition, music history and literature, performance, or theory. Course requirements vary according to emphasis; specific requirements vary with program followed.

The Master of Music program offers emphasis in piano, voice, organ, woodwinds, brass, strings, choral conducting, and electronic music. The degree requires the completion of 33 credit hours of which 6 credit hours must be in music theory and 6 credit hours in music history; a reading knowledge of one language, normally French or German; keyboard proficiency; two semesters of group performance; recital; and a final oral examination. The Master of Arts degree is offered in Theory, Musicology, and Composition, each with specific requirements.

The Doctor of Philosophy degree is offered in Theory; Musicology; Performance Practices (Piano, Voice, Choral Conducting); and Composition. Each requires the completion of 72 credit hours of coursework plus other specific requirements.

General Program Areas. Choral Conducting, Composition, Music History, Music Theory, Musicology, Performance.

Instruments Taught. Brass, Harpsichord, Organ, Percussion, Piano, Stringed Instruments, Voice, Woodwinds.

Musical Facilities

Practice Facilities. Special practice facilities for organists; 2 organs. 1 practice room for percussionists. 22 practice rooms. 45 practice pianos (17 grand); 7 grand pianos reserved for piano majors. Electronic music laboratory; recording studio.

Concert Facilities. Graham Chapel seating 900; Steinberg Auditorium, 299.

Community Facilities. St. Louis Art Museum Auditorium and the Elliot Unitarian Chapel are local facilities used by the Department.

Concerts/Musical Activities. Numerous student/faculty ensembles and recitals.

Music Library. 70,000 books, scores, and bound periodicals; 17,500 records and tapes. Listening facilities in lower level of Music Library include 6 cassette decks, 11 stereo turntables, 2 compact disc players. The Krick Collection of classical guitar music includes 6,000 items of sheet music from before 1880 and 50,000 items from 1880-1985. Resources of the St. Louis Public Library are available to students.

Special collections include: scores of vocal music with first and early editions from eighteenth and nineteenth centuries; first editions and manuscripts of Paul A. Pisk; Ernest C. Kron's musicological library; George C. Krick Collection for classical guitar.

Financial

Costs. Per academic year: Tuition $10,500. Room and board $4,000.

Financial Aid. Financial aid in the form of scholarships and loans. 10 music scholarships available; application due date January 15.

Commentary

There has been discussion at Washington University about inaugurating new doctorates; a Ph.D. in Theory and a new design for a Ph.D. in Composition may be added to the existing doctoral programs.

Webster University
Department of Music
470 East Lockwood Avenue
St. Louis
Missouri 63119

Telephone. (314) 968-6900, Ext. 7032

Chief Administrator. Dr. Allen C. Larson, Chairman.

Founded in 1915 as a Catholic women's college, Webster University is one of several schools established by the teaching order of the Sisters of Loretto. Webster became an independent, coeducational institution in 1967, and in 1983 adopted its present name upon attaining university status. The main 32-acre campus is located in Webster Groves, a suburban area 10 miles from downtown St. Louis.

Professional training within a liberal arts setting is the focus of the Department of Music. The Department offers music courses to all university students and also a state-approved curricula for the preparation of teachers of music in the elementary and secondary schools.

Accreditation. North Central Association of Colleges and Schools; National Association of Schools of Music.

Academic Information

Enrollment, Music Majors. 64.

Music Faculty. 36.

Term System. Semester. Summer session.

Entrance Requirements. High school graduate or equivalent with rank in upper 60% of graduating class; completion of 16 units including 4 English, 2 mathematics, 2 foreign language, 1 laboratory science, 3 social science, 4 electives; SAT or ACT; audition required (play-sing for appropriate professor and others). Graduate students must have a baccalaureate degree with a major in music from an accredited institution.

Admission Procedure. Application with $20 nonrefundable fee due June for Fall enrollment.

Music Degrees Offered. Bachelor of Music; Bachelor of Music Education; Bachelor of Arts; Master of Music.

Music Degree Requirements. The Bachelor of Music degree is offered with emphases in performance (orchestral instruments, piano, piano pedagogy, voice), jazz studies, jazz studies with an emphasis in commercial music, and theory/composition. The Bachelor of Music Education degree is offered with emphasis in choral music and instrumental music. The Bachelor of Arts degree with a major in music is also available. A total of 128 semester hours is required for the degree, including general education and departmental requirements.

The Master of Music degree is offered with concentrations in composition, conducting, performance and pedagogy, and jazz studies. A total of 32 to 34 semester hours, depending on the area of concentration, is required for the degree.

General Program Areas. Choral Music, Commercial Music, Conducting, Jazz Studies, Music Composition, Music Theory, Performance, Piano Pedagogy.

Instruments Taught. Brass, Guitar, Organ, Percussion, Piano, Stringed Instruments, Voice, Woodwinds.

Musical Facilities

Practice Facilities. 18 practice rooms. 2 organs. Percussion-equipped practice room. 24 pianos (22 uprights, 2 grands); 2 grands reserved for piano majors. Electronic music studio.

Concert Facilities. 3 concert halls (including Winifred Moore Auditorium, seating 252).

Concerts/Musical Activities. Student and faculty concerts and recitals.

Music Library. Reference materials, books, and periodicals are housed in the Eden-Webster Library; records, scores, and collected editions are located in the music building. Listening facilities (cassette, stereo). Recordings of graduate recitals are collected in the music library for reference.

Special Programs

Performance Groups. Camerata Singers, Choral Union, Webster Symphony Orchestra, Chamber Music, Jazz Ensembles.

Foreign Programs. Webster University has campuses in Vienna, Austria; Leiden, Netherlands; Geneva, Switzerland; and London, England.

Financial

Costs. Per academic year: Tuition $5,100. Room $1,100 to $1,260. Board $1,350 to $1,590. Applied music fee $240 for 15 30-minute private lessons per semester; $480 for 15 60-minute private lessons per semester.

Financial Aid. The Joseph Alan Shepard Jazz Scholarship Fund was established in 1985 to provide financial assistance for outstanding jazz studies students of sophomore standing or above with a "B" or better grade point average. Grants, loans, part-time employment, and a College Work-Study program are other sources of financial aid.

Commentary

The Alyce St. Clair Billington Scholarship Fund was created specifically to assist women pursuing graduate studies in conducting.

MONTANA

University of Montana
Department of Music
Missoula
Montana 59801

Telephone. (406) 243-6880
Chief Administrator. Dr. Donald Simmons, Chairman.

The University of Montana was chartered in 1893. It enrolls 9,000 students each year. The 117-acre campus is located in Missoula in the western part of the state.

The Department of Music offers students either professional training or general music instruction. Complete sequences of courses are given to prepare a student for a career as a teacher or supervisor of music in the public schools; a career in composition, private teaching, or performance; or a thorough training in music within the structure of a liberal arts curriculum.

Accreditation. Northwest Association of Schools and Colleges; National Association of Schools of Music; National Council for Accreditation of Teacher Education.

Academic Information

Enrollment, Music Majors. (Total University) 8,989.
Music Faculty. 28.
Term System. Quarter.
Entrance Requirements. High school graduation or equivalent; open enrollment for Montana residents; rank in upper half of graduating class for nonresident students; ACT or SAT required; audition required. GRE required for graduate study.
Admission Procedure. Application with supporting documents and nonrefundable $20 fee to Office of Admissions.
Music Degrees Offered. Bachelor of Music; Bachelor of Music Education; Bachelor of Arts; Master of Music; Master of Music Education; Master of Arts.
Music Degree Requirements. The Bachelor of Music degree is offered with majors in performance (including emphasis in piano pedagogy), composition, and theory. The Bachelor of Music Education degree meets the state requirements for certification for public school teaching. The Bachelor of Arts degree with a major in music is offered in the context of a liberal arts program.

The graduate degree programs offered by the Department of Music are the only graduate programs in music approved by the Board of Regents for the state institutions in Montana. The programs lead to the Master of Music degree with a major in performance or composition; the Master of Music Education degree with an emphasis in elementary or secondary school music; and the Master of Arts degree in music and literature.

General Program Areas. Applied Music, Choral Conducting, Composition, Music Education, Music History, Music Literature, Music Theory, Performance.
Instruments Taught. Brass, Organ, Percussion, Piano, Stringed Instruments, Voice, Woodwinds.

Musical Facilities

Concert Facilities. Recital hall.
Concerts/Musical Activities. Vocal and instrumental concerts and recitals; visiting artists.
Music Library. Music scores and music reference works are located in the Instructional Materials Service, a centralized audiovisual library.

Special Programs

Performance Groups. University Choir, Collegiate Chorale, Orchestra, Marching Band, University Band, Jazz Band, Opera Workshop, Wind Ensemble, Renaissance Ensemble.

Financial

Costs. Per academic year: Tuition in-state resident $1,231; out-of-state $3,050. Room $1,152. Board $1,328.
Financial Aid. Scholarships, fellowships, grants, loans, and part-time employment are available. Financial aid/scholarship application due March 1.

Commentary

The Entire M.M.Ed. program at the University of Montana is offered during the summer to accommodate working teachers.

Montana State University
Department of Music
Bozeman
Montana 59717

Telephone. (406) 994-3561

Chief Administrator. W.J. Rost, Head of Department.

Montana State University was established in 1935 and enrolls over 10,000 students each year. The campus is located in Bozeman in southeastern Montana.

The Department of Music offers preparation for public and private teaching careers at all levels. In addition, music classes are offered to students from all departments of the University.

Accreditation. Northwest Association of Schools and Colleges; National Association of Schools of Music; National Council for Accreditation of Teacher Education.

Academic Information

Enrollment, Music Majors. (Total University) 10,710.

Music Faculty. 18.

Term System. Quarter.

Entrance Requirements. High school graduation or equivalent; ACT or SAT required.

Admission Procedure. Application with supporting documents and nonrefundable $20 fee to Admissions Office.

Music Degrees Offered. Bachelor of Music.

Music Degree Requirements. Three options are avaialable which lead to the Bachelor of Music degree: the school music K-12 broadfield option, the music industry option, and the studio teaching option. The latter option is designed for preparation for a career in private teaching and does not lead to certification to teach in the public schools. A music option is also provided in the Department of Elementary Education.

General Program Areas. Applied Music, Music Education.

Instruments Taught. Brass, Percussion, Piano, Stringed Instruments, Voice, Woodwinds.

Musical Facilities

Practice Facilities. Howard Hall, part of the Creative Arts Complex, contains practice rooms, rehearsal rooms, studios, a listening center, and electronic music studio.

Concert Facilities. Recital hall.

Concerts/Musical Activities. Concerts and recitals by musical organizations, advanced students, faculty, and guest artists.

Music Library. The Renne Library of the University supports the academic programs of the Department of Music.

Special Programs

Performance Groups. Marching Band, Pep Band, Symphonic Band, Campus Band, Jazz Band, Chorale, Montanans, Chamber Choir, University Choir, Chamber Orchestra, Opera Workshop.

Financial

Costs. Per academic year: Tuition in-state resident $1,064, out-of-state $2,882. Music fee, per course per quarter $12. Room $1,053. Board $1,713.

Financial Aid. The Office of Financial Aid Services administers several federal, state, and institutional aid programs. Financial aid/scholarship application due March 1.

NEBRASKA

University of Nebraska - Lincoln
School of Music
120 Westbrook Music Building
Lincoln
Nebraska 68588

Telephone. (402) 472-2503
Chief Administrator. Kerry S. Grant, Director.

The University of Nebraska was chartered by the Legislature in 1869 as the state's public university and land-grant institution. Founded in Lincoln, the University was expanded in 1968 into a state educational system. Other campuses of the system include the University of Nebraska at Omaha and the University of Nebraska Medical Center, also in Omaha. The Lincoln campus has a student enrollment of over 24,000 students.

The School of Music offers a variety of courses and programs to students on the University campus. For those registered in the College of Arts and Sciences, three major programs are available. Students who wish to include a substantial program of music study in their baccalaureate degree may pursue a major requiring about three years of study. Students wishing to take a course of study in music that will prepare them for graduate study and eventually a professional career in music theory, musicology, composition, or performance are offered the Bachelor of Music degree program. Those who plan to perform professionally in summer stock, repertory theatres, dinner theatres, or on Broadway are offered a program leading to the Bachelor of Fine Arts in Music Theatre. A program in music education is offered through the Teachers College of the University.

Accreditation. North Central Association of Colleges and Schools; National Association of Schools of Music; National Council for Accreditation of Teacher Education.

Academic Information

Music Faculty. Full-time 35, part-time 3.
Term System. Semester. Two 5-week summer sessions plus one 3-week pre-session.

Entrance Requirements. High school graduation or equivalent; open enrollment for state residents; out-of-state applicants must rank in upper half of graduating class; completion of 16 units required; SAT or ACT; audition required; musicianship examination for placement in comprehensive musicianship program (includes keyboard proficiency placement test). GRE required for graduate students.

Admission Procedure. Application with $10 application fee ($25 for non-residents) due August 15 for Fall semester.

Music Degrees Offered. Bachelor of Music; Bachelor of Arts; Bachelor of Science; Bachelor of Music Education; Bachelor of Fine Arts; Master of Music; Doctor of Musical Arts.

Music Degree Requirements. A three-year sequence of courses called Comprehensive Musicianship lies at the heart of the School of Music curriculum for majors and minors. Music theory, history, and ear training are covered in one basic course each semester. Students learn primarily through composing, performing, and listening to music, as well as through conducting and editing (or arranging). These activities are based on a repertoire centered on, but not confined to, Western art music. The degrees Bachelor of Music, Bachelor of Arts, and Bachelor of Fine Arts in Music Theatre are offered with varying requirements, depending on emphasis.

The Master of Music degree is offered with three options: performance, composition, and a program with a major in music and minor in education for students with certification as school teachers.

The Doctor of Musical Arts degree is offered in performance and composition. Performance majors must complete four recitals and a doctoral document in addition to other coursework, and composition majors must complete compositions and a doctoral document in addition to coursework.

General Program Areas. Applied Music, Church Music, Composition, Music Education, Music History, Music Literature, Music Theory, Musicology, Performance.

Instruments Taught. Baritone Horn, Bass, Bassoon, Clarinet, Flute, French Horn, Harp, Harpsichord, Oboe,

Organ, Percussion, Piano, Saxophone, Trombone, Trumpet, Tuba, Viola, Violin, Violoncello, Voice.

Musical Facilities

Practice Facilities. 75 practice rooms. 4 organs (Reuter). 2 percussion-equipped practice rooms. 70 pianos (generally Steinway, Yamaha and Baldwin grands, Baldwin and Yamaha uprights); 20 grand pianos reserved for piano majors. Electronic music studio.

Concert Facilities. 3 concert halls.

Concerts/Musical Activities. Concert/performance series offered each year through the School of Music; student/faculty recitals.

Music Library. 22,000 volumes and scores; 9,000 recordings; 145 periodicals. 28 listening booths (stereo). Special collections in historical jazz; 78 rpm recordings.

Special Programs

Performance Groups. Madrigal Singers, Oratorio Chorus, University Chorus-East, Varsity Glee Club, University Singers, University Chorale, Orchestra, Concert Band, Marching Band, Chamber Ensemble, Brass Choir, Brass Ensemble, Jazz Ensemble, Clarinet Choir, Flute Ensemble, Keyboard Ensemble, Scarlet and Cream Singers, Percussion Ensemble, Saxophone Ensemble, New Music Consort.

Financial

Costs. Per academic year: Tuition undergraduate in-state resident $1,313, out-of-state $3,570; graduate in-state $1,628, out-of-state $3,885. Room and board $2,035.

Financial Aid. Music scholarships range from $100 to $1,000 (average award $250 to $300 per semester). Other sources of financial aid include institutional and state/federal grants and loans, student employment, and a College Work-Study program.

Commentary

Training in the Alexander Technique is provided at the University of Nebraska's Lincoln campus.

University of Nebraska - Omaha
Department of Music
60th and Dodge Streets
Omaha
Nebraska 68182

Telephone. (402) 554-2251

Chief Administrator. Dr. Roger E. Foltz, Chairman.

Formerly the Municipal University of Omaha, an institution founded in 1908, the University came under the direction of the University of Nebraska Board of Regents in 1968. The 73-acre campus is located in east central Nebraska bordering on the Iowa border in the city of Omaha. The city is a cultural center of the region and its resources enhance the instructional programs of the University.

The Department of Music provides intensive training for music majors and offers performance experience for all students. The majority of graduates enter public school teaching careers or go on to graduate school as performance majors.

Accreditation. North Central Association of Colleges and Schools; National Association of Schools of Music.

Academic Information

Enrollment, Music Majors. Undergraduate 120, graduate 21. Foreign student 1.

Music Faculty. Full-time 15, part-time 20.

Term System. Semester. Summer session (applied music courses, workshops for senior/graduate students, early entry programs for talented and gifted high school seniors).

Entrance Requirements. Graduation from an accredited high school or equivalent; open enrollment policy; completion of 4 units English, 2 mathematics (1 algebra), 2 sciences, 2 social sciences; ACT or SAT. Audition required during first week of semester for undergraduates.

Admission Procedure. Application due August 1 with $10 fee ($25 for nonresident).

Music Degrees Offered. Bachelor of Music; Bachelor of Science; Master of Music.

Music Degree Requirements. The Bachelor of Music degree requires the completion of 130 semester hours including general education and departmental requirements. Departmental requirements include 15 hours in music theory, 4 hours ear training and sight singing, 6 hours music history, 8 hours ensemble performance, 10 hours applied music instruction for music education majors and 16 hours for music performance majors, 8 semesters of recital attendance.

General Program Areas. Applied Music, Music Education, Music History, Music Merchandising, Music Theory, Performance.

Instruments Taught. Bass, Bassoon, Clarinet, Euphonium, Flute, French Horn, Guitar, Harp, Oboe, Organ, Percussion, Piano, Saxophone, Trombone, Trumpet, Tuba, Viola, Violin, Violoncello, Voice.

Musical Facilities

Practice Facilities. 24 practice rooms. 1 Casavant pipe organ and 1 Allan electronic organ. 4 percussion-equipped practice rooms. 9 practice pianos (2 baby grands, 7 consoles); 2 grand pianos reserved for piano majors.

Concert Facilities. Recital Hall, seating 527.

Concerts/Musical Activities. Recitals/concerts.

Music Library. 9,050 volumes; 350 scores; 66 music periodicals; 7,023 recordings. Listening facilities (8 cassette decks, 4 stereo turntables, 1 compact disc player).

Listening scores and tapes are located in the Music Building; books, periodicals, and microfiche are in the University Library.

Special Programs

Performance Groups. Band, Choral Ensemble, Chamber Ensemble, Orchestra.

Foreign Programs. London Semester program.

Financial

Costs. Per academic year: Tuition in-state resident $1,265, out-of-state $3,050. Room $2,250. Board $3,515.

Financial Aid. Scholarships, grants, and loans (institutional and state/federal) are available. 52 music scholarships ranging from $100 to $800 per year. Scholarship application due March 1. Part-time employment and College Work-Study program available.

NEVADA

University of Nevada, Las Vegas
Department of Music
4505 Maryland Parkway
Las Vegas
Nevada 89154

Telephone. (702) 739-3332
Chief Administrator. James Stivers, Chairman.

The University of Nevada, Las Vegas was founded in 1957 as a southern regional division of the University of Nevada. It was named the Nevada Southern University in 1965 and in 1968 the University was granted autonomy under the state's higher education system, giving it status equal to that of the University of Nevada, Reno. The University has a faculty of more than 350 and offers 50 undergraduate and 30 graduate degree programs to a student population of more than 12,000. The 335-acre campus is located in metropolitan Las Vegas, a city of contrasts. Despite the common perception of Las Vegas as a resort city and an entertainment capital, there is a rapidly growing community of 600,000 residents. It claims to have more churches per capita than any other city in the world.

The Department of Music offers courses in music for the cultural benefit of all university students and for the training of those seeking a professional music career in the fields of teaching, performance, and composition.

Accreditation. Northwest Association of Schools and Colleges; National Association of Schools of Music; National Council for Accreditation of Teacher Education.

Academic Information

Enrollment, Music Majors. Full-time 20 men, 30 women; part-time 40 men, 40 women. 3 foreign students.

Music Faculty. Full-time 17, part-time 25.

Term System. Semester. Academic year from early September to mid-May. Two 5-week summer sessions from early June to mid-August.

Entrance Requirements. High school graduation; SAT or ACT; audition and theory placement test. GRE required for graduate study.

Admission Procedure. Application with transcripts, test scores to Office of Admissions.

Music Degrees Offered. Bachelor of Music; Bachelor of Arts; Master of Music.

Music Degree Requirements. The Bachelor of Music degree is offered with three areas of interest: applied music, theory-composition, and music education. The degree requires the completion of 124 credits including 90 credits in music. The Bachelor of Arts degree requires the completion of 124 credits with 50 to 54 credits in music courses, thus permitting the breadth of course distribution traditional for a liberal arts degree.

The Master of Music degree is offered with programs in applied music, music education, and theory/composition. The minimum number of credits required varies with the program pursued (30 to 38 credits).

General Program Areas. Applied Music, Composition, Conducting, Music Education, Music History, Music Literature, Music Theory.

Instruments Taught. Baritone, Bass, Bassoon, Clarinet, Flute, French Horn, Guitar, Harp, Oboe, Organ, Percussion, Piano, Saxophone, Trombone, Trumpet, Tuba, Viola, Violin, Violoncello, Voice.

Musical Facilities

Practice Facilities. 20 practice rooms. 1 organ. 70 pianos (25 grands); 6 grand pianos reserved for piano majors. Electronic music studio; recording studio.

Concert Facilities. Concert Hall, seating 2,000; small concert hall, 550; recital hall, 70.

Concerts/Musical Activities. 100 concerts per year.

Music Library. 8,000 volumes; 4,000 scores; 200 audiovisual materials; 4,500 recordings; 300 audiocassettes. 12 listening stations. Most holdings in main library; performance collection in Department of Music.

Special Programs

Performance Groups. University Chorus, Chamber Chorale, Oratorio Chorus, Vocal Jazz/Pop Ensemble, Marching Band, Symphony Band, Concert Band, Pep Band, Orchestra, Jazz Ensemble, Opera Workshop, Collegium Musicum, Chamber Players.

Financial

Costs. Per academic year: Tuition in-state $1,200, out-of-state $2,200. Music lesson fee $300. Practice room fee $70. Room and board $2,540.

Financial Aid. Financial aid is awarded on the basis of academic merit, financial need, and musical ability. Over 80 music students receive financial aid (average award $500). Financial aid/scholarship applications due April 1 for Fall semester, December 1 for Spring semester. Part-time employment and a College Work-Study program available.

University of Nevada, Reno
Department of Music
Ninth and Center Streets
Reno
Nevada 89557

Telephone. (702) 784-6145

Chief Administrator. Dr. Michael Cleveland, Chairman.

Established in 1864, the University of Nevada actually began in 1874 in Elko as one of the few schools of higher education in the region. In 1886, it moved to Reno near the center of the state's population. The 200-acre campus is located north of Reno's main business district.

The Department of Music offers curricula designed for the professional preparation of performing musicians and music teachers.

Accreditation. Northwest Association of Schools and Colleges; National Association of Schools of Music; National Council for Accreditation of Teacher Education.

Academic Information

Enrollment, Music Majors. (Total University) 9,817.

Music Faculty. 10.

Term System. Semester. Two summer terms.

Entrance Requirements. High school graduation; SAT or ACT; audition in applied performance area required.

Admission Procedure. Application with supporting documents and nonrefundable $20 fee to Admissions Office.

Music Degrees Offered. Bachelor of Music; Bachelor of Arts; Master of Music; Master of Arts.

Music Degree Requirements. The Bachelor of Music degree with a major in music education is a professional degree which meets present state of Nevada music certification requirements. The Bachelor of Music degree in applied music is offered to students approved by the entire faculty as showing professional promise in their applied performance areas. The Bachelor of Arts degree with a concentration in music is also offered. Courses in the areas of music theory, music history, applied music, and methods of music teaching are offered for cultural benefit and for professional preparation of performing musicians and music teachers.

The Master of Arts and Master of Music degrees are also offered and require the completion of a minimum of 30 credits. Comprehensive, oral, and piano proficiency examinations are required.

General Program Areas. Applied Music, Music Education, Music History, Music Theory, Performance.

Instruments Taught. Brass, Organ, Percussion, Piano, Stringed Instruments, Voice, Woodwinds.

Musical Facilities

Music Library. The Noble H. Getchell Library houses over 764,000 volumes and supports the academic programs of the Department of Music.

Special Programs

Performance Groups. University Band, Concert Choir, Symphonic Choir, Opera Theater, University-Community Symphony, Chamber Ensembles, Concert Jazz Band.

Financial

Costs. Per academic year: Tuition in-state resident $1,152, out-of-state $3,352. Room $1,300. Board $1,100.

Financial Aid. Financial aid is awarded on the basis of academic merit and financial need. Institutional and state/federal aid is available in the form of scholarships, grants, loans, and part-time employment. Financial aid/scholarship application due February 15.

NEW HAMPSHIRE

University of New Hampshire
Department of Music
Durham
New Hampshire 03824

Telephone. (603) 862-2404
Chief Administrator. Keith Polk, Chairperson.

The University of New Hampshire is a state institution founded in 1866 as the New Hampshire College of Agriculture and the Mechanic Arts, as part of Dartmouth College. In 1893, it moved to its present site and in 1923, was chartered under its present name. The 156-acre campus is located in southwestern New Hampshire in the city of Durham.

The Department of Music offers a Bachelor of Music program in performance, composition, or music education. A Bachelor of Arts program with a major in music is also available.

Accreditation. New England Association of Schools and Colleges; National Association of Schools of Music; National Council for Accreditation of Teacher Education.

Academic Information

Enrollment, Music Majors. (Total University) 13,602.
Music Faculty. 20.
Term System. Semester. 3 summer sessions.
Entrance Requirements. High school graduation with rank in upper 40 percent of graduating class; completion of 16 units including 4 English, 2 mathematics, 2 foreign language, 1 science, 2 social science; SAT and Achievement Test required; out-of-state admission is limited and very selective; audition required.
Admission Procedure. Application with supporting documents and nonrefundable $10 fee to Office of Admissions.
Music Degrees Offered. Bachelor of Music; Bachelor of Arts; Master of Arts; Master of Science.
Music Degree Requirements. The Bachelor of Music degree is offered with concentration in performance, composition, or music education. The program is recom-

mended to those considering graduate study. A public performance is required during the senior year (for performance majors this must be a full recital; for theory majors, a lecture, lecture-recital, or a recital including at least one original composition; for history majors, a lecture or a lecture-recital; for music education majors, a half recital is a minimum). The Bachelor of Arts program is intended for those who wish to pursue serious study of music and to acquire a broad general education.

The Master of Arts degree provides graduate study in music theory, literature, and performance/practice. The goal of the Master of Science in music education degree is to develop a broad knowledge at the graduate level in the fields of music education, performance, history, theory, and independent study.

General Program Areas. Composition, Music Education, Music History, Music Literature, Music Theory, Performance.
Instruments Taught. Bass, Brass, Harp, Harpsichord, Organ, Percussion, Piano, Viola, Violin, Violoncello, Voice, Woodwinds.

Musical Facilities

Practice Facilities. The Department of Music is located in the Paul Creative Arts Center.
Concert Facilities. Two theaters.
Concerts/Musical Activities. Well-known artists perform regularly on the Johnson Theater stage in two series presented annually—the September Arts Festival and the UNH Celebrity Series. Student/faculty concerts and recitals.
Music Library. The University Library houses over 825,000 volumes, 7,560 tapes and recordings, and 2,073 cassettes.

Special Programs

Performance Groups. Concert Choir, Chamber Chorus, Women's Chorus, The Newhampshiremen, Opera Workshop, UNH Training Orchestra, Symphonic Wind Ensemble, University Band, Marching Band, Piano Ensemble, String Ensemble, Woodwind Ensemble, Brass Ensemble, Percussion Ensemble, Jazz Ensemble, Vocal Ensemble.

Financial

Costs. Per academic year: Tuition in-state resident $2,-180, out-of-state $6,050. Fees $320. Room $1,446. Board $1,168.

Financial Aid. Aid is available in the form of grants, scholarships, loans, and part-time employment. Scholarship/financial aid application due February 15.

Commentary

The University of New Hampshire takes a leadership role in training music teachers in the state.

NEW JERSEY

Glassboro State College
Department of Music
School of Fine and Performing Arts
Glassboro
New Jersey 08028

Telephone. (609) 445-6041

Chief Administrator. Veda Zuponcic, Chair.

Glassboro State College opened its doors in 1923. It is part of the New Jersey statewide system of public higher education. Beginning as a two-year normal school, Glassboro became a four-year baccalaureate degree-granting teachers college in 1935. In 1966, the college added liberal arts majors and today it has four major academic schools: business administration, liberal arts and sciences, fine and performing arts, and professional studies. Located 20 miles southeast of Philadelphia, the college enjoys a small town atmosphere and the metropolitan area's cultural advantages.

The Department of Music provides three distinct program options: general music, music education, and applied performance (including jazz studies). The general curriculum is a liberal arts program with a music major and is designed for students who wish to acquire a thorough academic background with musical training providing the necessary background for further study in music history, musicology, and music criticism. The music education curriculum combines broad study in music with required courses in general education, providing the necessary background for a career as a public school teacher. The applied performance curricula combines in-depth study of music with required courses in general education, providing the initial preparation for careers as performers, composers, scholars, and college teachers. The three curricula offer specialization in voice, piano, organ, classical guitar, accordion, theory and composition, and all orchestral instruments.

Accreditation. Middle States Association of Colleges and Schools; National Association of Schools of Music; National Council for Accreditation of Teacher Education.

Academic Information

Enrollment, Music Majors. (Total College) 3,502 men, 5,160 women.

Term System. Semester. Two 5-week summer sessions.

Entrance Requirements. High school graduation with rank in upper 60%; completion of 12 academic units including 4 English, 2 mathematics, 1 laboratory science, 2 social sciences; SAT or ACT required; audition required; theory and piano placement tests.

Admission Procedure. Application with $25 non-refundable fee to Admissions Office by May 1.

Music Degrees Offered. Bachelor of Arts; Master of Arts.

Music Degree Requirements. The degree Bachelor of Arts in Music is a general music curriculum in the liberal arts and requires the completion of a total of 120 semester hours. The degree is also offered in a music education curriculum requiring the completion of 143 semester hours. Emphasis in the applied performance curriculum requires the completion of 128 semester hours.

The degree Master of Arts in Music Education is also offered and requires a total of 33 semester hours.

General Program Areas. Applied Music, Composition, Jazz Studies, Music Education, Music History, Music Theory, Musicology, Performance.

Instruments Taught. Accordion, Brass, Guitar, Organ, Percussion, Piano, Stringed Instruments, Voice, Woodwinds.

Musical Facilities

Practice Facilities. 80 practice rooms. 1 organ (Wicks). 8 percussion-equipped practice rooms. 5 grand pianos reserved for piano majors. Electronic music studio.

Concert Facilities. Auditorium, seating 1,000; recital hall.

Concerts/Musical Activities. Student/faculty concerts and recitals.

Music Library. The Music Library is located in the Harold Wilson Music Building. Listening facilities (cassette, stereo).

Special Programs

Performance Groups. Chamber Choir, Choral Union, College-Community Orchestra, College-Community Opera Company, Concert Choir, Contemporary Music Ensemble, Inspirational Gospel Choir, Lab Band, Jazz Ensemble, Percussion Ensemble, Piano Forum, Vocal Forum, Wind Ensemble, Vocal Jazz Ensemble, Collegium Musicum.

Financial

Costs. Per academic year: Tuition in-state $1,110, out-of-state $1,710. Fees $306. Room and Board $3,255.

Financial Aid. Scholarships, institution and state/federal grants and loans, part-time employment, and a College Work-Study program are available.

Jersey City State College
Music Department
2039 Kennedy Boulevard
Jersey City
New Jersey 07305

Telephone. (201) 547-3151

Chief Administrator. Dr. Richard D. Scott, Chairperson.

Jersey City State College was founded in 1929. The 14-acre campus is located two miles south of Journal Square, the center of Jersey City.

The Music Department offers eight major programs of specialization. The programs provide a general curriculum in music as well as professional preparation for music careers. In addition, these programs are designed to prepare students for graduate study in music.

Accreditation. Middle States Association of Colleges and Schools; National Association of Schools of Music.

Academic Information

Enrollment, Music Majors. (Total University) 7,450.
Music Faculty. 23.
Term System. Semester. Two summer terms.
Entrance Requirements. High school graduation or equivalent; completion of 4 units English, 2 mathematics, 1 laboratory science, 2 social science; SAT or ACT required; audition and examinations required.
Admission Procedure. Application with supporting documents and nonrefundable $10 fee to Admissions Office.
Music Degrees Offered. Bachelor of Arts; Master of Arts.
Music Degree Requirements. The Bachelor of Arts degree is offered with programs of specialization in music education (with certification), performance, jazz studies-commercial music, theory-composition, music-business administration, ethnomusicology, and sacred music.

The Master of Arts degree in music educaiton requires a minimum of 32 semester hours.

General Program Areas. Commercial Music, Composition, Ethnomusicology, Jazz Studies, Music Business, Music Education, Music Theory, Performance, Sacred Music.

Instruments Taught. Bass, Bassoon, Clarinet, Euphonium, Flute, French Horn, Guitar, Harp, Harpsichord, Oboe, Organ, Percussion, Piano, Saxophone, Trombone, Trumpet, Tuba, Viola, Violin, Violoncello, Voice.

Musical Facilities

Practice Facilities. Rossey Hall houses the Music Department; rehearsal rooms, classroom, laboratories.

Concert Facilities. Elizabeth Ingalls Recital Hall.

Concerts/Musical Activities. Student/faculty recitals and concerts.

Music Library. The Irwin Library houses over 250,000 volumes and supports the academic programs of the Department of Music, Dance, and Theatre.

Special Programs

Performance Groups. College Choir, Concert Choir, Women's Choir, Men's Choir, JCSC Community Orchestra, Symphonic Band, Wind Ensemble, Madrigal Singers, Opera Ensemble, Jazz-Show Ensemble, String Orchestra, Chamber Orchestra, Theatre Orchestra, Chamber Ensembles, Early Music Ensembles, Brass Choir, Percussion Ensemble, Double Bass Ensemble, Piano Ensemble, Guitar Ensemble, Jazz Combos.

Financial

Costs. Per academic year: Tuition in-state resident $1,395, out-of-state $1,995. Room $1,250.

Financial Aid. Financial aid is awarded on the basis of academic merit and financial need. Both institutional and state/federal aid are available in the form of scholarships, grants, loans, and part-time employment.

Montclair State College
Department of Music
School of Fine and Performing Arts
Upper Montclair
New Jersey 07043

Telephone. (201) 893-5227

Chief Administrator. Barbara L. Wheeler, Chairperson.

Montclair State College was founded in 1908 as a Normal School and became a State Teachers College in 1932. Its present name was adopted in 1958 and in 1966 the liberal arts programs were instituted. The 220-acre campus has 40 buildings and is located in the township of Montclair (population 40,000), a residential suburb 14 miles west of New York City and 6 miles northwest of

Newark.

In 1978, the State of New Jersey designated the College as a center for the fine and performing arts. The Department of Music offers both a professional and liberal arts curricula. At the undergraduate level, professional training is offered in performance, music education, theory and composition, music therapy, and music history. Graduate programs leading to the Master of Arts are offered with concentrations in music education, theory and composition, and performance.

Accreditation. Middle States Association of Colleges and Schools; National Association of Schools of Music; National Association for Music Therapy.

Academic Information

Enrollment, Music Majors. Undergraduate 150, graduate 150. Foreign students 5.

Music Faculty. Full-time 18, part-time 30.

Term System. Semester. Limited courses are offered during summer session.

Entrance Requirements. High school graduation or GED with 16 units (4 English, 3 mathematics, 2 laboratory science, 2 social studies, 2 foreign language, 3 other (must be from English, math, science, social studies, foreign language); SAT. Foreign students admitted with acceptable academic credentials and TOEFL. Audition required, held on scheduled days; includes primary instrument performance, music reading, interview, and placement tests.

Admission Procedure. Application with $10 nonrefundable fee due March 1.

Music Degrees Offered. Bachelor of Music; Bachelor of Arts; Master of Arts.

Music Degree Requirements. The Bachelor of Music degree requires the completion of 128 semester hours including core, major, and general requirements. The Bachelor of Arts degree with a music concentration requires 137 to 148 semester hours. The Master of Arts degree requires the completion of 32 semester hours.

General Program Areas. Composition, Music Education, Music History, Music Theory, Music Therapy, Performance.

Instruments Taught. Brass, Guitar, Harpsichord, Organ, Percussion, Piano, Stringed Instruments, Voice, Woodwinds.

Musical Facilities

Practice Facilities. 30 practice rooms. 65 pianos (practice uprights; a few Steinway grands for practice). Electronic music studio; recording studio.

Concert Facilities. Memorial Auditorium, seating 1,000; McEachern Recital Hall, 150.

Concerts/Musical Activities. Concerts; recitals.

Music Library. 8,873 books; 8,629 scores; 83 music periodicals; 3,505 microfiche; 6,000 recordings. Listening facilities include 16 cassette decks, 4 stereo turntables (additional facilities in main library).

Special Programs

Featured Programs. The Music Therapy training program of Montclair features closely supervised clinical work each semester, an on-campus Music Therapy Clinic, a Music Therapy Training Group, Phase I training for Guided Imagery and Music, and specialized courses for the music therapist in piano accompanying and clinical improvisation. In addition, the faculty involve students in on-going clinical research.

Performance Groups. Chamber Ensemble, College Choir, Chamber Choir, College Orchestra, Collegium Musicum, Concert Band, Opera Workshop, Madrigal Singers.

Financial

Costs. Per academic year: Tuition in-state resident $1,280, out-of-state $2,400. Fees $344. Room $2,368. Board $1,088.

Financial Aid. Scholarships range from $300 to $500. Scholarship application due May 15. Other financial aid in the form of loans, part-time employment, and College Work-Study program available.

Princeton University
Department of Music
Princeton
New Jersey 08544

Telephone. (609) 452-4241

Chief Administrator. Dr. Margaret Bent, Chairperson.

Princeton University was established in 1746 as the College of New Jersey. The original trustees of the college were leaders in the evangelical wing of the Presbyterian Church. The campus consists of eight adjoining tracts of land with a total area of 2,325 acres. Princeton is 50 miles southwest of New York City and 45 miles northeast of Philadelphia.

The Department of Music offers a program of study with a major in music leading to the baccalaureate degree, and a Ph.D. program in composition and historical musicology.

Accreditation. Middle States Association of Colleges and Schools.

Academic Information

Enrollment, Music Majors. (Total University) 6,293.

Music Faculty. 15.

Term System. Semester.

Entrance Requirements. Recommended completion of 16 units including 4 English, 4 mathematics, 4 of one foreign language, 2 laboratory science, 2 social science; SAT and 3 Achievement Tests required; admission highly selective.

Admission Procedure. Application and supporting documents with nonrefundable $40 fee to Office of Admissions.

Music Degrees Offered. Bachelor of Arts; Doctor of Philosophy.

Music Degree Requirements. The Bachelor of Arts degree in music is offered in a liberal arts program. Departmental concentrators are encouraged to pursue some kind of performance study.

The Doctor of Philosophy degree is offered with concentrations in composition and musicology. Music theory and ethnomusicology are available by special arrangement.

General Program Areas. Composition, Musicology.

Instruments Taught. Brass, Organ, Percussion, Piano, Stringed Instruments, Voice, Woodwinds.

Musical Facilities

Practice Facilities. The Department of Music is housed in the Woolworth Center of Musical Studies. Electronic sound-generating facilities.

Concert Facilities. McCarter Theatre.

Music Library. Within the Firestone Library is a separate music collection containing the Scheide Archive, which consists of the photographic collection of primary sources of J.S. Bach's works. Eighteenth century manuscripts, eighteenth century printed editions of G.F. Handel, and liturgical resources can be found in the Department of Rare Books and Special Collections in Firestone Library. A phonograph record library is housed in the Woolworth Center of Musical Studies.

Special Programs

Featured Programs. The Department of Music manages a noncredit extracurricular program for the private study of vocal and instrumental performance. Students wishing to participate in this program must audition for the relevant teachers in the program.

Performance Groups. University Chapel Choir; Glee Club, Freshman Singer, Chamber Chorus, University Orchestra, University Opera Theatre, Musica Alta, Jazz Ensemble, Marching Band.

Affiliated Programs. Special arrangements for instruction at Westminster Choir College can be made for a limited number of students through an interinstitutional exchange agreement.

Financial

Costs. Per academic year: Tuition $11,780. Room $1,895. Board $2,305.

Financial Aid. Financial aid is awarded on the basis of financial need. Institutional and state/federal aid is available in the form of scholarships, grants, loans, and part-time employment.

Rutgers, The State University of New Jersey
Department of Music

Mason Gross School of the Arts
New Brunswick
New Jersey 08903

Telephone. (201) 932-9302

Chief Administrator. James C. Scott, Chairman.

Rutgers, The State University of New Jersey, with over 47,000 students on campuses in Camden, Newark, and New Brunswick, is one of the major state university systems in the nation. The University is comprised of twenty-four degree-granting division: twelve undergraduate colleges, eleven graduate schools, and one school offering both undergraduate and graduate degrees. Four are located in Camden, seven in Newark, and thirteen in New Brunswick. Chartered in 1766 as Queen's College, the eighth institution to be founded in the colonies, the school opened its doors in New Brunswick in 1771. During this early period the college developed as a classic liberal arts institution. In 1825, the name of the college was changed to Rutgers to honor a former trustee and revolutionary war veteran, Colonel Henry Rutgers. The college assumed university status in 1924 and legislative acts in 1945 and 1956 designated all of its divisions as the State University of New Jersey.

The Department of Music of the Mason Gross School of the Arts (established in 1976) offers professional programs in performance, jazz studies, and music education, each leading to the Bachelor of Music degree. The curricula reflect the Department's concern for training in the areas of music history and theory/composition as well as the areas involving professional skills. The graduate program embraces the range of Western music, with particular strengths in the Renaissance, Baroque, and contemporary periods. The Department of Music is located on the Douglass College campus and is housed in the Music Building, Music House, and the fine arts complex consisting of Rehearsal Hall, Music Annex, and the Nicholas Music Center.

Master classes in recent years have been given by Loren Hollander, Samuel Baron, Phyllis Curtin, Ann Schein, Arminda Canteros, Bernard Goldberg, Philip Smith, Berton Coffice, and Stanley Drucker. Jazz workshops and concerts with student ensembles have included such artists as George Coleman, Curtis Fuller, James Moody, Dizzy Gillespie, Philly Joe Jones, the Machito Orchestra, Terri Quaye, Slide Hampton, Sonny Stitt, Sonny Fortune, and many others.

Accreditation. Middle States Association of Colleges and Schools; National Association of Schools of Music.

Academic Information

Enrollment, Music Majors. Full-time 60 men, 43 women; part-time 15 men, 12 women.

Music Faculty. Full-time 35, part-time 20. Artists-in-residence: St. Luke's Ensemble.

Term System. Semester. Academic year from early September to mid-May.

Entrance Requirements. High school graduation with 4 units English, 3 mathematics, 2 foreign language recommended; 9 additional units from natural and social sciences and electives; audition required; music aptitude test. Foreign students must have TOEFL and guarantee of financial support.

Admission Procedure. Application to Office of Admissions.

Music Degrees Offered. Bachelor of Music; Bachelor of Arts; Master of Music; Master of Arts; Doctor of Philosophy; Doctor of Musical Arts.

Music Degree Requirements. The Bachelor of Music degree in performance requires the completion of 120 credits; the jazz and music education curricula require the completion of 124 credits. All students, regardless of the area of concentration, must complete liberal arts requirements and a core curriculum in music. The Bachelor of Arts in music with a broad liberal arts program is also offered by Douglass College, Rutgers College, Livingston College, and University College-New Brunswick.

The Master of Music program is intended for emerging professional performing musicians wishing to broaden and intensify their abilities and knowledge in the total field of music study, while developing a performing artistry commensurate with the demands of the profession. The program utilizes the resources of a performance faculty, and through the Graduate School-New Brunswick, receives the benefits of a strong program in musicology, theory, and composition. The program requires two years for completion and consists of 36 credits of specific courses.

The Master of Arts degree from the Graduate School-New Brunswick requires the completion of ten one-term courses and a reading knowledge of one foreign language, usually German. All candidates must pass written comprehensive examinations. For the M.A. in history and theory, an essay must be submitted; for the M.A. in theory and composition, an original chamber work is required. The Master of Arts in theology majoring in music is offered through the New Brunswick Theological Seminary. The Doctor of Philosophy degree requires the completion of six one-term courses, including notation and the history of theory, in addition to a minimum of 24 credits in individual research.

General Program Areas. Applied Music, Baroque Music, Composition, Jazz Studies, Music Education, Music History, Music Literature, Music Theory, Musicology, Performance, Renaissance Music.

Instruments Taught. Bass, Bassoon, Clarinet, Flute, French Horn, Harpsichord, Jazz Drums, Jazz Guitar, Oboe, Organ, Percussion, Piano, Saxophone, Trombone, Trumpet, Viola, Violin, Violoncello, Voice.

Musical Facilities

Practice Facilities. 53 practice rooms. 2 concert organs (Schuke, Aeolian-Skinner), 4 practice organs. 68 pianos (upright studios: Kawai, Sohmer, Yamaha, Steinway; grands: Steinway, Chickering, Kawai, Knabe, Sohmer; 15 pianos reserved for piano majors. Synclavier studio; electronic music studio.

Concert Facilities. Nicholas Music Center, seating 800; Rehearsal Hall, 200; Music Building Auditorium, 200; Voorhees Chapel, 900; Kirkpatrick Chapel, 600.

Concerts/Musical Activities. Over 80 performances a year, including faculty, students, University concert series, guest artists, and 11 student performing organizations.

Music Library. 51,852 volumes; 320 current periodical subscriptions; 902 microform titles; 5,800 phonograph recordings (includes 700 tapes). Listening facilities include 10 reel-to-reel stereo decks, 9 turntables, and 2 VCR monitors (remote). Special collections include eighteenth century editions and manuscripts of G.F. Handel. Rare books, manuscripts, and early sheet music housed in special collections at Alexander Library. Libraries of Princeton University, Westminster Choir College in Princeton, the Jazz Institute at Rutgers-Newark campus, and music libraries in New York City are available to students.

Special collections include: Rutgers Institute of Jazz Studies library; library of Kurt Sachs; 18th century prints and Handel manuscripts, chiefly copies of anthems.

Special Programs

Performance Groups. Orchestra, Wind Ensemble, Jazz Ensemble, Opera Workshop, Collegium Musicum, University Choir, Musica Sacra, Voorhees Choir, Queen's Chorale, Kirkpatrick Choir, Glee Club, Band.

Foreign Programs. Bachelor of Arts students may participate in the University Junior Year Abroad program in France, Germany, and Italy.

Financial

Costs. Per academic year: Tuition undergraduate in-state resident $1,852, out-of-state $3,704; graduate in-state $2,638, out-of-state $3,800. Room $1,649. Board $1,266.

Financial Aid. Financial aid is awarded on the basis of academic merit, financial need, and musical ability. 67 music students receive some form of financial aid (average award $1,383). Application for aid/scholarship due March 15.

Commentary

Rutgers University has established a new D.M.A. program with a unique feature: there is a concert agency to find work for program participants, with the philosophy that, just as there is an internship for young doctors, so should there be the equivalent for musicians. An impressive faculty including cellist Bernard Greenhouse and pianist Theodore Lettvin has been assembled to attract gifted performers.

Trenton State College
Music Department
Pennington Road
Box 940, Hillwood Lakes
Trenton
New Jersey 08625

Telephone. (609) 771-2551
Chief Administrator. Dr. Robert J. Rittenhouse, Chair.

Trenton State College is a professional and liberal arts college established in 1855. The campus is located on 225 acres in the Hillwood Lakes district of suburban Ewing Township.

The Music Department has offered programs for the study of music since 1916. The Department offers curricula providing professional preparation for work in a variety of music careers.

Accreditation. Middle States Association of Colleges and Schools; National Association of Schools of Music.

Academic Information

Enrollment, Music Majors. (Total University) 8,652.
Music Faculty. 21.
Term System. Semester. One 6-week summer session.
Entrance Requirements. High school graduation or equivalency certificate; completion of 16 units including 4 English, 2 mathematics, 1 laboratory science, 2 social science; SAT or ACT required; audition and placement examinations. GRE required for graduate study.
Admission Procedure. Application with supporting documents and nonrefundable $10 fee to Office of Admissions.
Music Degrees Offered. Bachelor of Arts; Master of Arts; Master of Education.
Music Degree Requirements. The Bachelor of Arts degree is offered with concentrations in performance, music history-literature, music theory-composition, and music education. A minimum of 128 semester hours is required for graduation.

The Master of Arts and the Master of Education in music degrees require the completion of a minimum of 30 semester hours.

General Program Areas. Composition, Music History, Music Literature, Music Theory, Performance.

Instruments Taught. Brass, Percussion, Piano, Stringed Instruments, Voice, Woodwinds.

Musical Facilities

Practice Facilities. Bray Hall is the music center of the College; individual practice rooms; rehearsal hall.
Concert Facilities. Recital hall.
Concerts/Musical Activities. Student/faculty concerts and recitals; visiting artists.
Music Library. The Music Library is located in Bray Hall; record listening room.

Special Programs

Performance Groups. College Chorus, College Choir, Wind Symphony, Show Band, College Orchestra, Wind Ensemble, Collegium Musicum, Clarinet Choir, Jazz Lab, Percussion Ensemble, Brass Ensemble, String Ensemble.

Financial

Costs. Per academic year: Tuition in-state resident $1,184, out-of-state $1,824. Room and board $3,265.
Financial Aid. Financial aid is awarded on the basis of academic merit and financial need. Institutional and state/federal aid are available in the form of scholarships, grants, loans, and part-time employment. Financial aid/scholarship application due March 15.

Westminster Choir College
Hamilton Avenue at Walnut Lane
Princeton
New Jersey 08540

Telephone. (609) 921-7100
Chief Administrator. Dr. Ray E. Robinson, President.

Westminster Choir College is a privately supported college of music founded in 1926. The College began as the outgrowth of a choir begun by John Finley Williamson in the Westminster Presbyterian Church of Dayton, Ohio in 1920. In 1929 the College moved and became associated with what is now Ithaca College, and moved to its present location of Princeton in 1932. It maintains its status today as an interdenominational and international college of music. The 23-acre campus is centrally located in Princeton (population 12,311), 50 miles southwest of New York City and 45 miles northeast of Philadelphia.

The College, with its strong choral emphasis, is a college of music that educates men and women at the undergraduate and graduate levels for careers in church music, teaching, and performance. Professional training in musical skills with emphasis on performance is complemented by studies in the liberal arts in an atmosphere which encourages individuals in their personal and musical growth. Originally a pioneer in establishing high standards in church music and choral performance,

Westminster maintains the same commitment in its expanded program.

Accreditation. Middle States Association of Colleges and Schools; National Association of Schools of Music.

Academic Information

Enrollment, Music Majors. Full-time 324, part-time 60. Foreign students 25.

Music Faculty. Full-time 41, part-time 27.

Term System. Semester. One summer session (regular undergraduate and graduate offerings plus one-week festivals and workshops).

Entrance Requirements. Accredited high school graduation or equivalent; SAT required; ability to demonstrate some facility in singing and in playing an instrument or exceptional musical aptitude in pitch and rhythmic sense; entrance examination and audition in person or by tapes required.

Admission Procedure. Rolling admissions policy; application and nonrefundable $25 fee. Foreign students are required to present certification of funds and TOEFL scores.

Music Degrees Offered. Bachelor of Music; Master of Music.

Music Degree Requirements. The Bachelor of Music degree requires 124 or more semester hours; recital; piano and theory proficiency examinations; English reading and writing proficiency; keyboard majors must pass voice level examinations I and II; 8 semesters of choir; cumulative grade point average of at least 2.0 (2.5 for music education).

The Master of Music degree requires the completion of 32 semester hours.

General Program Areas. Composition, Conducting, Performance, Piano Pedagogy.

Instruments Taught. Organ, Piano, Voice.

Musical Facilities

Practice Facilities. Special practice facilities for organists; 28 organs, including: Aeolian-Skinner, Casavant, Fisk, Von Beckerath, Flentrop, Holtkamp, Moller, Noach, Phelps, Schantz. 61 practice rooms. 87 practice pianos. Synthesizer located in computer lab.

Concert Facilities. Bristol Chapel, Playhouse, Williamson Hall.

Community Facilities. The College arranges for fieldwork in area churches and schools. Graduate piano pedagogy and performance majors do additional work at the New School in Kingston, New Jersey.

Concerts/Musical Activities. Student, faculty, and guest recitals or concerts are held throughout each week both on- and off-campus. All students sing in one of Westminster's choirs.

Music Library. 45,600 volumes; 18,600 scores; 137 current periodical subscriptions; 6,300 phonograph recordings. Listening facilities (cassette and stereo equipment). The Performance Collection contains 4,100 titles of choral works totaling more than 250,000 copies of music. Other special collections include the Archival Collection of the Organ Historical Society and the Raitley Collection of books and hymnals. Princeton University's Firestone Library and the libraries of Rider College and Trenton State College are available to students.

Special collections include: Leopold Stokowski conducting score collection.

Special Programs

Performance Groups. Various choral and ensemble groups.

Affiliated Programs. Students may take classes at Rider College and Princeton University.

Financial

Costs. Per academic year: Tuition $6,330. Student fees and expenses $1,495. Room $1,345. Board $1,680. Practice room fee $37 to $47 per semester.

Financial Aid. 275 students receive some form of financial aid. Scholarships range from $100 to $10,850. Scholarship applications due May 1. Part-time employment and College Work-Study program.

Commentary

Westminster Choir College is one of the country's leading institutions for training choir directors.

William Paterson College
Department of Music

School of the Arts and Communication
300 Pompton Road
Wayne
New Jersey 07470

Telephone. (201) 595-2315

Chief Administrator. Dr. Stephen Marcone, Chair.

William Paterson College, founded in 1855, is a multipurpose institution of higher education. It is one of nine colleges in the New Jersey state college system. The College moved from its original location in Paterson to the Wayne campus, 20 miles from New York City, in 1951. Today 34 undergraduate and 13 graduate degree programs are offered in the College's seven schools.

The Department of Music offers programs that are structured to reflect the multifaceted demands on late twentieth century musicians. All degree curricula include courses teaching innovative ideas in contemporary music as well as those providing a solid background in traditional music. A performance audition is required of all applicants to the baccalaureate programs. The evaluation by the audition jury consists of performance and an evaluation of the applicant's ability in theory, keyboard, and aural skills.

Accreditation. Middle States Association of Colleges and Schools; National Association of Schools of Music.

Academic Information

Enrollment, Music Majors. Full-time 83 men, 67 women; part-time 19 men, 24 women.

Music Faculty. Full-time 19, part-time 35.

Term System. Semester. Academic year from September to May. 6-week summer session from late June to early August.

Entrance Requirements. High school graduation; completion of 16 units including 4 English, 2 mathematics, 1 science, 2 social science; high school class rank equal to or greater than the 50th percentile and a combined SAT score of 700 to 840; ACT score of 16 required; audition required.

Admission Procedure. Application and $10 nonrefundable fee to Admissions Office.

Music Degrees Offered. Bachelor of Music; Bachelor of Arts.

Music Degree Requirements. The Bachelor of Music degree is offered in classical performance, music management/classical performance, jazz studies/performance, and music management/jazz performance. The Bachelor of Arts degree is designed for students who desire a liberal education with emphasis on music while obtaining a diversified education in the liberal arts. The Bachelor of Science degree program in music education offers two concentrations: vocal and instrumental. The degree fulfills certification requirements for public school music teaching in New Jersey, grades K-12. The baccalaureate degrees require the completion of a minimum of 128 semester hour credits.

General Program Areas. Composition, Jazz Studies, Music Education, Music History, Music Literature, Music Management, Music Theory, Performance.

Instruments Taught. Brass, Clarinet, Flute, Guitar, Organ, Percussion, Piano, Stringed Instruments, Trumpet, Violin, Voice, Woodwinds.

Musical Facilities

Practice Facilities. 5 practice rooms. 2 organs. 25 upright pianos; 5 grand pianos reserved for piano majors. Special practice facilities for percussionists. Electronic music laboratory; 16-track recording studio.

Concert Facilities. Shea Performing Arts Center, seating 980; Wayne Recital Hall, 200.

Concerts/Musical Activities. Over 100 concerts per year; New Music Series; Midday Artists Series; Wayne Chamber Orchestra; Jazz Room Series; student ensembles and recitals.

Music Library. Listening facilities (stereo).

Special Programs

Performance Groups. Gospel Choir, Concert Choir, College Chorus, Chamber Singers, Concert Band, College Community Orchestra, Brass Ensemble, Brass Quintet, Woodwind Ensembles, Percussion Ensembles, Jazz Ensemble, Chamber Jazz Ensemble, Trombone Ensemble, Classical Guitar Ensemble, Twentieth Century Chamber Ensemble, Latin Jazz Ensemble, New Jazz Ensemble.

Financial

Costs. Per academic year: Tuition and fees in-state resident $1,297, out-of-state $2,080. Room and board $3,200.

Financial Aid. Financial aid is awarded on the basis of academic merit, financial need, musical ability. Institutional and state/federal aid plus part-time employment and a College Work-Study program are available.

NEW MEXICO

Eastern New Mexico University
School of Music
College of Fine Arts
Portales
New Mexico 88130

Telephone. (505) 562-2376

Chief Administrator. Paul K. Formo, Director.

Eastern Mexico University is a multicampus state university with a wide variety of undergraduate and graduate programs in the liberal arts and sciences, education, business, fine arts, and selected vocational/technical areas. The University is the youngest state university in New Mexico. It opened its doors in Portales in 1934 as a two-year college and became a four-year institution in 1940. A campus at Roswell was established in 1958 and has occupied the former Walker Air Force Base since 1967. A third campus at Clovis was established in 1971 on the site of the former Clovis Community College.

The School of Music provides professional preparation for its music majors and educational and cultural experiences for the university community, and the region it serves. Students are prepared for careers in performance, school or studio teaching, music therapy, music business, and music theory and composition. Many courses are available to the non-music major, from those covering styles on traditional Western European art music to jazz and ethnic music. Students pursuing a music education program can qualify for state certification in elementary education (grades K-8) with an endorsement in elementary music education or in grades K-12 with the endorsement in either vocal or instrumental music.

Accreditation. North Central Association of Colleges and Schools; National Association of Schools of Music.

Academic Information

Enrollment, Music Majors. (Total university) Full-time 1,393 men, 1,379 women, part-time 356 men, 582 women.

Music Faculty. 15.

Term System. Semester. 8-week summer session.

Entrance Requirements. High school graduation or GED; ACT for placement; open enrollment policy; music theory placement examination.

Admission Procedure. Application with $10 nonrefundable fee due July 1.

Music Degrees Offered. Bachelor of Music; Bachelor of Science; Bachelor of Music Education; Master of Music.

Music Degree Requirements. The Bachelor of Music degree is offered with majors in music therapy, theory/composition, and performance (emphases in piano performance and pedagogy, vocal performance and pedagogy, strings, winds, and percussion). The Bachelor of Science degree with majors in music or a composite of music with elective studies in business is also offered. The Bachelor of Music Education is available with emphases in strings, winds, percussion, choral music, and elementary music and elementary education. The bachelor's degrees require the completion of general education courses, electives, and a prescribed curriculum for the major for a minimum total of 128 semester hours.

General Program Areas. Choral Music, Composition, Music Business, Music Education, Music Theory, Music Therapy, Performance, Piano Pedagogy, Vocal Music.

Instruments Taught. Brass, Percussion, Piano, Stringed Instruments, Voice, Woodwinds.

Musical Facilities

Practice Facilities. 22 practice rooms. 1 percussion-equipped practice room. 12 practice pianos (uprights); 6 pianos reserved for piano majors.

Concert Facilities. Concert hall.

Concerts/Musical Activities. Ensemble performances, recitals, concerts; Associated Student Concert series.

Music Library. 4,150 volumes; 4,325 scores; 4,150 books; 44 periodicals; 6,882 phonograph recordings; 4,428 cassettes. Listening stations (cassette, stereo).

Special Programs

Performance Groups. 2 Bands, 3 Choirs, Symphony Orchestra, 2 Jazz Ensembles, Chamber Groups.

Foreign Programs. Student Exchange Program with institutions in Japan, Canada, Mexico, and England.

Financial

Costs. Per academic year: Tuition in-state resident $743, out-of-state $2,298. Room $760. Board (3-meal plan) $960.

Financial Aid. Scholarships, grants, loans, and a College Work-Study program are available. Application for financial aid due April 1.

University of New Mexico
Department of Music
College of Fine Arts
Albuquerque
New Mexico 87111

Telephone. (505) 277-2126

Chief Administrator. Dr. Peter L. Ciurczak, Chairperson.

The University of New Mexico was founded as an academy in 1889, twenty-five years before New Mexico became a state. As it approaches its centennial celebration, the University consists of fourteen schools and colleges and offers more than 4,000 courses in more than 125 fields of study. The 600-acre campus includes 180 buildings in the city of Albuquerque, situated on the banks of the historic Rio Grande.

The Department of Music provides programs and curricula that give students the opportunity to study music according to their interests and needs. A general curriculum leads to the Bachelor of Arts in Fine Arts and includes a thorough preparation in music theory and a limited amount of applied music. This program is designed for students who want a broad understanding of music in relation to other academic disciplines. A curriculum in music education certifies graduates to teach music in grades 1 through 12 in the state of New Mexico. A preprofessional curriculum is also offered with programs in music performance and composition/theory.

Accreditation. North Central Association of Schools and Colleges; National Association of Schools of Music; National Council for Accreditation of Teacher Education.

Academic Information

Enrollment, Music Majors. Undergraduate 300, graduate 50.

Music Faculty. Full-time 28, part-time 4.

Term System. Semester. 8-week summer session.

Entrance Requirements. High school graduation with completion of 13 units including 4 English, 3 mathematics, 2 laboratory science, 2 social studies; ACT required; live audition required.

Admission Procedure. Application with $15 nonrefundable fee due August 1.

Music Degrees Offered. Bachelor of Music; Bachelor of Music Education; Bachelor of Arts in Fine Arts; Master of Music; Master of Music Education.

Music Degree Requirements. The baccalaureate degrees require the completion of 128 semester hours. Specific curricula have been designed for the Bachelor of Music Education program and include instrumental and vocal tracks.

The Master of Music is offered with concentrations in music history and literature, composition or theory, performance, choral conducting, and piano accompanying. The Master of Music Education is offered in two plans (with or without thesis). The master's degrees require the completion of 32 semester hours.

General Program Areas. Accompanying, Applied Music, Choral Conducting, Composition, Music Education, Music History, Music Literature, Music Theory, Performance.

Instruments Taught. Brass, Guitar, Harpsichord, Organ, Percussion, Piano, Stringed Instruments, Voice, Woodwinds.

Musical Facilities

Practice Facilities. 57 practice rooms. 3 organs (Holtkamp, Reuter, Allan). 5 percussion-equipped practice rooms. 55 pianos (36 acoustic, 19 electronic); 6 grand pianos reserved for piano majors. Electronic music studio; recording studio; computer-assisted instruction laboratory.

Concert Facilities. Popejoy Hall, seating 2,094; Keller Recital Hall, 336.

Concerts/Musical Activities. Recitals; concerts; visiting artists.

Music Library. The Fine Arts Library encompasses materials from the areas of architecture, art, music, and photography. The music collection contains 20,000 books; 30,000 scores; 252 music periodicals; 4,600 microforms; 20,000 sound recordings. 50 listening stations (4 cassette decks, 12 stereo turntables, 2 compact disc players).

Special collections include: John Donald Robb Archive of Southwestern Music (sound recordings); Everett Helm Opera Collection of scores, with concentration on 19th-century French opera and art songs; G. Giaante Annotated Orchestral Score Collection; Zarzuela Collection.

Special Programs

Performance Groups. University Chorus, Opera Studio, Chamber Singers, Early Music Ensemble, Symphony Orchestra, Jazz Band, Collegiate Singers, Jazz Improvisation, University Band, Chorale.

Financial

Costs. Per academic year: Tuition in-state resident $818, out-of-state $1,784. Room and board $2,004 to $2,175.

Financial Aid. Scholarships, grants, loans, part-time employment, a College Work-Study program are available. The Department of Music has an endowment fund to used at their discretion in awarding scholarships.

Commentary

The University of New Mexico, with its campus architecture in a distinctive Hispanic and Pueblo Indian style, has the most extensive music curricula of the state's higher education institutions. A new degree, the B.F.A. in music theater, has been proposed.

New Mexico State University
Department of Music
Las Cruces
New Mexico 88003

Telephone. (505) 646-2421

Chief Administrator. Dr. Lee Richards, Department Head.

New Mexico State University was originally founded in 1888 as Las Cruces College. The University was established the next year as a land-grant college. The 6,250-acre campus is among the largest in the world. Las Cruces is located 40 miles from the Mexican border in Dona Ana County.

The Department of Music offers programs providing students with preparation for professional performance careers and private studio teaching as well as certification for public school teaching.

Accreditation. North Central Association of Colleges and Schools; National Association of Schools of Music; National Council for Accreditation of Teacher Education.

Academic Information

Enrollment, Music Majors. (Total University) 12,613.

Music Faculty. 14.

Term System. Semester. Two summer sessions.

Entrance Requirements. High school graduation or equivalent with a C grade average or better; completion of 15 units including 3 English, 2 mathematics, 1 science, 1 social science; SAT or ACT required; audition and placement examinations.

Admission Procedure. Application with supporting documents and nonrefundable $10 fee to Director of Admissions.

Music Degrees Offered. Bachelor of Music; Bachelor of Music Education; Master of Music.

Music Degree Requirements. The Bachelor of Music degree is offered with majors in applied music (piano, instrumental, or vocal performance), composition and theory, and piano (emphasis in pedagogy or piano accompanying/ensembles). The Bachelor of Music Education degree is offered in a diversified four-to-five year program in teaching, performance, and specialized studies in music. It qualifies the student for certification to teach music in the public schools, and serves as a foundation for advanced study. Majors are available in elementary and/or secondary teaching with vocal or instrumental emphasis.

The Master of Music degree is offered in the fields of applied music (performance and piano pedagogy), music theory/composition, music history/literature, music education, and conducting. A minimum of 32 semester hours is required for graduation.

General Program Areas. Accompanying, Composition, Conducting, Music Education, Music History, Music Literature, Music Theory, Performance, Piano Pedagogy.

Instruments Taught. Brass, Guitar, Percussion, Piano, Stringed Instruments, Voice, Woodwinds.

Musical Facilities

Music Library. The University Library houses over 750,000 volumes, and supports the academic programs of the Department of Music.

Special Programs

Performance Groups. Las Cruces Symphony at NMSU, Chamber Orchestra, University Singers, Women's Chorale, Men's Chorale, Jazz Ensembles, Chamber Ensembles, NMSU Shojazz, Pride Revue, Symphonic Winds, Concert Band, Marching Band, Percussion Ensemble, String Ensemble, Brass Ensemble, Woodwind Ensemble, Guitar Ensemble, Collegium Musicum.

Financial

Costs. Per academic year: Tuition in-state resident $1,026, out-of-state $3,652. Room $1,070. Board $930.

Financial Aid. A limited number of orchestra scholarships, band grants, and other music scholarships ranging from $100 to full tuition are available to any full-time registered student. Awards are on a competitive basis through the Department and scholarship committee. Other sources of financial aid include state/federal grants, loans, and part-time employment. Scholarship/financial aid application due March 1.

NEW YORK

City University of New York - Brooklyn College
Conservatory of Music
Bedford Avenue and Avenue H
Brooklyn
New York 11210

Telephone. (718) 780-5286
Chief Administrator. Dorothy Klotzman, Director.
Brooklyn College was founded in 1930 and its now a unit of the City University of New York. It occupies its own campus in the Flatbush residential section of Brooklyn.

The Conservatory of Music offers undergraduate programs leading to the baccalaureate degree.

Accreditation. Middle States Association of Colleges and Schools; National Council for Accreditation of Teacher Education.

Academic Information

Enrollment, Music Majors. (Total College) 15,568.
Music Faculty. 24.
Term System. Semester. Two summer sessions.
Entrance Requirements. High school graduation; completion of college preparatory units; open enrollment for New York City residents; audition required.
Admission Procedure. Application with supporting documents and nonrefundable $25 fee to Office of Admissions.
Music Degrees Offered. Bachelor of Arts; Bachelor of Science; Master of Arts.
Music Degree Requirements. The Bachelor of Arts degree curriculum includes courses in ear training, harmonic and contrapuntal techniques, analysis, history, and performance. Students in the Bachelor of Science degree program also take these courses with additional concentration in either composition or performance.

The Conservatory offers a Master of Arts degree in music with concentrations in composition, musicology, performance, or performance practice. The Master of Arts in teaching music (K-12) is also available.

General Program Areas. Composition, Music History, Music Theory, Musicology, Performance.
Instruments Taught. Brass, Guitar, Harp, Harpsichord, Organ, Percussion, Piano, Stringed Instruments, Voice, Woodwinds.

Musical Facilities

Practice Facilities. Rehearsal and practice studios are located in the Center for Performing Arts.

The Center for Computer Music is a research and production facility that includes two systems especially adapted for music. In addition, the Center has a sound studio for recording sound into and out of the computer, a room for users of the computer terminals, and an audio engineer's workshop. The Center sponsors a composer-in-residence program.

Concert Facilities. George Gershwin Theater, seating 500; Walt Whitman Hall, 2,500; Sam Levenson Theater, 168; New Workshop Theater, 135.

Concerts/Musical Activities. More than 300 musical, theatrical and dance performances are presented annually; Great Artist Series features over 75 professional performances each year.

Music Library. The Walter W. Gerboth Music Library is located in LaGuardia Hall. The collection comprises scores, phonograph recordings, periodicals, and technical and specialized books about music. Subject strengths lie in American music and musicological Festschriften. Collected works and the literature of music, musical instruction, and study are resources used for master's level programs.

The Institute for Studies in American Music, part of the Conservatory of Music, is a research and information center established to encourage and support the study of American music of all periods and styles. Its publications include bibliographies, discographies, a series of monographs dealing with American music studies, and the *I.S.A.M. Newsletter,* published biannually. The Institute also supervises a series of music editions, *Recent Research in American Music,* and is the seat of the Charles Ives Society. The Charles Ives Society has published a new catalog of its publications. It is available free of charge from Theodore Presser Co., Bryn Mawr, PA 19010.

Special Programs

Featured Programs. The Brooklyn College Preparatory Center for the Performing Arts, established in 1978, is the precollege component of the Conservatory of Music. The Center offers a complete training program in music, theater, and dance for children seven to eighteen years of age. In addition, it offers training at the preschool level in Suzuki violin, music and movement, and creative dance for children ages two to seven.

Performance Groups. Opera Workshop, Chorus, Chamber Chorus, Percussion Ensemble, Collegium Musicum, Chamber Music, Contemporary Music Ensemble, Orchestra, String Orchestra, Theater Orchestra, Wind Ensemble, Non-Western Music Ensemble, Jazz Ensemble.

Financial

Costs. Per academic year: Tuition in-state resident $1,350, nonresident $2,550.

Financial Aid. Financial aid is awarded on the basis of academic merit, financial need. Institutional and state/ federal aid are available in the form of scholarships, grants, loans, and part-time employment. Financial aid/ scholarship application due June 15.

City University of New York - City College Department of Music
Division of the Arts
Convent Avenue at 138th Street
New York
New York 10031

Telephone. (212) 690-5411

Chief Administrator. Dr. Barbara Hanning, Chair.

City College was founded in 1847 and is the oldest college in the City University of New York system. The campus occupies 35 acres in upper Manhattan in the area known as St. Nicholas Heights.

The Department of Music offers major programs leading to the Bachelor of Arts and Bachelor of Fine Arts degrees.

Accreditation. Middle States Association of Colleges and Schools.

Academic Information

Enrollment, Music Majors. (Total College) 12,481.

Music Faculty. 24.

Term System. Semester. One summer term.

Entrance Requirements. Academic average of 80 or better; graduation in top third of high school class; combined SAT score of 900.

Admission Procedure. Application with supporting documents to Office of Admissions.

Music Degrees Offered. Bachelor of Arts; Bachelor of Fine Arts.

Music Degree Requirements. The Bachelor of Arts degree is offered with concentrations in classical, jazz, and popular music in performance; music history, theory, and composition. Preprofessional training in classical, jazz, and popular performance leads to the Bachelor of Fine Arts degree.

General Program Areas. Composition, Jazz Studies, Music History, Music Theory, Performance.

Instruments Taught. Brass, Guitar, Percussion, Piano, Stringed Instruments, Voice, Woodwinds.

Musical Facilities

Practice Facilities. Aaron Davis Hall of the Davis Center for the Arts houses three performance areas. The Electronic Studio contains equipment for use by composition students and is used for class demonstration.

Concert Facilities. Shepard Recital Hall; Aaron Davis Hall.

Concerts/Musical Activities. Faculty members, students, and visiting performers present concerts twice weekly. Performances are also given at the CUNY Graduate Center.

Music Library. The Music Library is located in Shepard Hall and has a collection of over 11,000 recordings, 14,000 scores, and 8,000 books. All areas of music are present including Western art music, non-Western music, folk and ethnic music, jazz, blues, and popular music.

Special Programs

Featured Programs. Friends of Music is an organization open to all students. Its purpose is to promote and stimulate the performance of live music.

Performance Groups. Studio Orchestra, Orchestra, Chorus, Band, Jazz Ensemble, Instrumental Chamber Music Ensemble, Vocal Ensemble, Collegium Musicum, Latin Ensemble, Gospel Choir, World Folk Music Workshop.

Financial

Costs. Per academic year: Tuition in-state resident $1,250, nonresident $2,550. Fees $70.

Financial Aid. Various music scholarships and awards are available. Other forms of financial aid include grants, loans, and part-time employment. Financial aid/scholarship application due May 20.

City University of New York - Graduate School and University Center
Doctoral Program in Music
33 West 42nd Street
New York
New York 10036

Telephone. (212) 642-2301

Chief Administrator. Dr. Barry S. Brook, Executive Officer.

The Graduate School of The City University of New York, drawing its faculty from the several campuses of the University, offers the doctorate in 31 fields and has a current enrollment of over 3,500 students. The Graduate Center is located in the heart of Manhattan, directly across from the New York Public Library and within walking distance of many of the cultural and educational institutions of New York, among them the Library of the Performing Arts at Lincoln Center which houses one of the finest music collections in the country.

The CUNY Ph.D. Program in Music prepares students in the fields of music history, theory, and composition. Students in the program receive a thorough general background in the discipline. At the same time, the flexibility of the program and the varied interests of the faculty allow students a degree of latitude in pursuing their special interests. The new Doctor of Musical Arts in Performance program is geared toward providing performers with a solid, comprehensive, historical background in music.

Accreditation. Middle States Association of Colleges and Schools.

Academic Information

Enrollment, Music Majors. 90. 10 foreign students.

Music Faculty. 43.

Term System. Semester.

Entrance Requirements. Students must have the Bachelor of Arts or Master of Arts; GRE required.

Admission Procedure. Application to Admissions Office by February 15; two letters of recommendation; official transcript from each college or university attended; GRE scores for verbal and quantitative tests.

Music Degrees Offered. Doctor of Philosophy; Doctor of Musical Arts.

Music Degree Requirements. Students who enter the program with the B.A. must complete a total of 60 credits from courses in musicology, theory, and composition. A First Examination is required on reaching 30 credits; this serves as a qualifying examination for the final 30 credits and entitles the student to the "en route" M.A., which is awarded at 45 credits.

Students who enter with the M.A. must complete a total of 30 credits from courses in musicology, theory, and composition. All students must pass two language examinations (usually German and French) and pass the Second Examination on completion of all coursework. All students must submit a dissertation, which for composers consists of both a large-scale composition and a written essay.

General Program Areas. Composition, Music Theory, Musicology, Performance.

Musical Facilities

Music Library. The library at the Graduate Center maintains a music division with its own librarian. It contains original source materials on microfilm, mainly of medieval period and the 18th century. Students also have access to the libraries at Queens College, City College, Hunter College, and Brooklyn College, as well as the music division of the New York Public Library at Lincoln Center.

Special Programs

Featured Programs. The Ph.D. Program in Music serves as a home for a number of national and international musicological projects and publications: RILM (Répertoire International de Littérature Musicale); RCMI (Research Center for Musical Iconography); MLM (Music in the Life of Man: A World History); Pergolesi Research Center; International Alban Berg Society; Traditional Japanese Music Society. *Theory and Practice;* Garland Press Symphony Project; Pendragon Press French Opera Project.

Affiliated Programs. The Program has a close working relationship with the Institute for Studies in American Music at the Brooklyn College campus and the Music Instrument Collection of the Metropolitan Museum of Art.

Financial

Costs. Per academic year: Tuition in-state $950, out-of-state $1,600. Room and Board $3,900. The D.M.A. in Performance: tuition in-state $1,500, out-of-state and foreign $2,500.

Financial Aid. Financial aid is awarded on the basis of academic merit, financial need, musical ability. Institutional and state/federal aid available. Approximately 50 percent of the students receive financial aid (average award $3,000). Financial aid/scholarship application due February 1. For the D.M.A. program, financial aid is available in amounts up to $5,800 per year for highly qualified students.

Commentary

The recently-inaugurated D.M.A. Program in Performance provides candidates for the degree with a thorough historical background as well as advanced training in performance. The Graduate School offers unusual courses in iconography, the depiction of musical instruments in the visual arts, and organology, the classification of instruments, in association with the Music Instrument Collection of the Metropolitan Museum of

Art.

City University of New York - Hunter College
Department of Music
695 Park Avenue
New York
New York 10021

Telephone. (212) 772-5020
Chief Administrator. L. Michael Griffel, Chair.

Hunter College is a liberal arts college and a unit of the City University of New York. It was established in 1870 as a teacher training institution for young women and became coeducational in 1964. The College is located in midtown Manhattan.

The Department of Music offers a wide variety of music courses and music degree programs tailored to the needs of students with different professional objectives. Course offerings include a large selection of topics for both majors and nonmajors in music performance, theory, history, and literature. Most degrees can be completed by matriculation in evening courses.

Accreditation. Middle States Association of Colleges and Schools; National Council for Accreditation of Teacher Education.

Academic Information

Enrollment, Music Majors. (Total College) 18,606.
Music Faculty. 15.
Term System. Semester. One summer term.
Entrance Requirements. High school graduation or equivalent; 80 percent grade average or rank in top one-third of class; audition required.
Admission Procedure. Application with supporting documents reviewed on a rolling admissions basis.
Music Degrees Offered. Bachelor of Music; Bachelor of Arts; Bachelor of Science; Master of Arts.
Music Degree Requirements. The Bachelor of Music degree is designed for students planning to pursue careers as professional performers of music or as teachers of music performance. It provides intensive instruction in the student's instrument or voice, as well as solid training in music history and theory. The Bachelor of Arts degree is designed for students planning to pursue professional careers in music. It provides basic training and serves as a foundation for graduate study. This degree program is also offered for students wishing to study music in the context of a liberal arts program. The Bachelor of Science degree, designed for prospective music teachers, provides automatic provisional certification for teaching pre-school curricula and in elementary through secondary schools in New York State.

The Department offers the Master of Arts in music with concentrations in music history, ethnomusicology, composition, performance, or teacher education.

General Program Areas. Composition, Ethnomusicology, Music Education, Music History, Music Theory, Performance.
Instruments Taught. Brass, Percussion, Piano, Stringed Instruments, Voice, Woodwinds.

Musical Facilities

Music Library. The Jacqueline Grennan Wexler Library houses over 500,000 volumes and supports the academic programs of the Department of Music.

Special Programs

Performance Groups. College Choir, Hunter Symphony, Jazz Workshop, Collegium Musicum, Chamber Music Workshop.
Affiliated Programs. Hunter College music students are permitted to take elective courses at the Mannes College of Music under a consortium arrangement created to increase the variety of music courses available to the students of both schools.

Financial

Costs. Per academic year: Tuition in-state resident $1,250, nonresident $2,550.
Financial Aid. Financial aid is awarded on the basis of academic merit and financial need. Institutional and state/federal aid are available in the form of scholarships, grants, loans, and part-time employment. Financial aid/scholarship application due May 20.

City University of New York - Queens College
The Aaron Copland School of Music
65-30 Kissena Boulevard
Flushing
New York 11367

Telephone. (718) 520-7340
Chief Administrator. Dr. Rufus E. Hallmark, Jr., Director.

Queens College is a publicly supported liberal arts college and is part of the City University of New York. It enrolls over 10,000 men and women full-time and over 4,500 part-time. The 76-acre campus is located in a residential section of the Borough of Queens, a metropolitan area on the western end of Long Island.

The Aaron Copland School of Music began in 1937 as the Queens College Department of Music. By action of the Board of Trustees of the City University, in 1981 it was designated a School of Music and named after America's distinguished composer on the occasion of his eightieth birthday. The Aaron Copland School attracts students from all over the U.S.A. and from abroad. The School combines the advantages of a conservatory with the resources of a liberal arts college.

The goal of the School is to educate musicians. The undergraduate curriculum is structured to develop skills in performing, hearing, and understanding music in an organized and comprehensive way over a period of four years. Courses are interdependent and reinforce the all-around development of the student-musician. In 1988-89, the School will occupy a new building tailored to the needs of the music program.

Accreditation. Middle States Association of Colleges and Schools.

Academic Information

Enrollment, Music Majors. Full-time undergraduate 120 men, 130 women; full-time graduate 45, part-time 56. Foreign students 40.

Music Faculty. Full-time 31, part-time 67.

Term System. Semester. Academic year September 2 to May 18. Summer session of 6 weeks from July 1 to August 11.

Entrance Requirements. High school academic average of 80, or score over 900 on SAT combined, or top third of graduating class. Exceptional performers may be accepted in the Bachelor of Music program on audition alone. For liberal arts music majors, placement into the music major sequence is on the basis of a placement examination in theory and musical skills, including performance. For Bachelor of Music performance major, admission is by competitive audition. No audition required for Bachelor of Arts program.

Admission Procedure. Applicant files standard City University of New York application and transcripts. The Bachelor of Arts major in music is accepted on the basis of academic record; the Bachelor of Music applicant files an audition request with The Aaron Copland School in addition to the CUNY application and auditions on the major instrument. If performance applicant is not accepted into the Bachelor of Music program, applicant may enter the liberal arts program if academically acceptable. Foreign students must have a minimum score of 500 on TOEFL, or British "O" level in English; tape acceptable for conditional acceptance of overseas students.

Music Degrees Offered. Bachelor of Music; Bachelor of Arts; Master of Arts; Master of Science in Music Education.

Music Degree Requirements. The Bachelor of Music degree is designed for the gifted and advanced student who has potential for a successful performing career. The program requires the completion of 48 credits of general education curriculum; completion of music course sequence (7 semesters); listening examinations yearly; comprehensive senior examination; public recital for performance majors. The Bachelor of Arts degree with a music major student receives a comprehensive musical education, embracing music literature and history, performance (orchestra, choir, chamber music, and

other groups), music theory (including written and keyboard harmony, counterpoint, and analysis), ear training and sight singing, orchestration, conducting, and composition. Students take the College core curriculum of liberal arts courses.

The Master of Arts degree program is available in performance, composition, theory, or music history. It requires the completion of 30 credits of required courses and electives for non-performers; plus thesis or six credits of additional coursework. The program for performance majors (vocal, instrumental, conducting) requires the completion of 33 credits plus recital and paper. The Master of Science in Music Education degree is offered in cooperation with the School of Education. It requires the completion of 33 credits of prescribed courses.

General Program Areas. Conducting, Music Composition, Music Education, Music History, Music Theory, Performance.

Instruments Taught. Brass, Early Instruments, Guitar, Organ, Percussion, Piano, Stringed Instruments, Voice, Woodwinds.

Musical Facilities

Practice Facilities. Schlicker baroque organ. Special practice facilities for percussionists. 12 piano practice rooms; 22 Steinway studio uprights, 2 Hamilton (Baldwin) studio uprights; classroom grand pianos used primarily in teaching. Electronic music studio with both analog and digital capabilities; recording facilities.

Concert Facilities. Colden Center Auditorium, seating 2,143; Queens College Theater (opera, musical theatre), 476 plus 12 wheelchair; Rathaus Recital Hall, 150.

Concerts/Musical Activities. Orchestral concerts, chamber ensembles, choral concerts; 3 to 5 recitals per week during academic year.

Music Library. 23,438 volumes; 25,293 musical scores; 330 current periodical subscriptions; 8,400 microforms; 12,598 phonograph recordings. 38 listening stations. Special collections include: performance collections (orchestral and choral); Schola Cantorum choral collection; Karol Rathaus Archives; musical instrument collection. Elementary Music Education collection housed in Education Division of Paul Klapper Library. The Music Collection of the New York Public Library at Lincoln Center, the CUNY Graduate School Library, and the Brooklyn Public Library are available to students.

Special Programs

Featured Programs. The School offers master classes in various area of performance, which have recently been led by artists such as violinists Yehudi Menuhin and Ani Kavafian, and vocal coach/accompanist Martin Katz.

Performance Groups. Baroque and Renaissance Ensembles, *Nota Bene* Chamber Ensemble, Choral and Orchestral Societies, Opera Workshop, *Cappella Reginae* Vocal Ensemble, Brass Ensemble, Jazz Ensemble, Japanese Music Groups, Queens String Quartet.

Affiliated Programs. Joint Master's program in conjunciton with The Mannes College of Music.

Financial

Costs. Per academic year: Tuition undergraduate in-state resident $1,250, out-of-state $2,550; graduate in-state $1,900, out-of-state $3,200. Undergraduate fees $182, graduate $104. Off-campus housing approximately $400 per month.

Financial Aid. Financial aid is awarded on the basis of academic merit, financial need, and musical ability. 20 graduate students receive assistantship/orchestral stipends; 14 graduate students and 15 undergraduates receive scholarship assistance from the School of Music.

Columbia University Department of Music

703 Dodge Hall
New York
New York 10027

Telephone. (212) 280-3825
Chief Administrator. Dr. Leeman L. Perkins, Chairman.

Columbia University was founded in 1754 when a group of New York citizens were granted a charter by George II for the founding of King's College. In 1847, Columbia College moved to 49th Street and Madison Avenue and remained at that location until 1897 when it moved to Morningside Heights. Columbia's status as a university was established in 1912.

The Department of Music offers a major in music to students of Columbia College pursuing a liberal arts degree. On the graduate level, it trains professionals in their specialization and in the context of a major research university.

Accreditation. Middle States Association of Colleges and Schools.

Academic Information

Enrollment, Music Majors. Approximately 600 men and 400 women take courses in the Department in any given year. 92 graduate students. 9 foreign students.

Music Faculty. Full-time 27, part-time 24. Artists-in-residence: Composers String Quartet; Speculum Musicae.

Term System. Semester. Academic year from early September to mid-May. Two 6-week summer sessions from late May to mid-August.

Entrance Requirements. High school graduation required for undergraduate programs; recommended college-preparatory courses should include 4 English, 3 to 4 mathematics, 3 to 4 foreign language, 3 to 4 social sciences, 2 to 3 laboratory science; SAT and three Achievement Tests. Graduate students should have bac-

calaureate degree and a strong foundation in history and theory of Western music. TOEFL required of all students whose native language is not English.

Admission Procedure. Application to Office of Admissions of appropriate division: Columbia College, School of General Studies, or Graduate School of Arts and Sciences.

Music Degrees Offered. Bachelor of Arts; Master of Arts; Master of Philosophy; Doctor of Philosophy; Doctor of Musical Arts.

Music Degree Requirements. The Bachelor of Arts degree with a major in music is offered to undergraduate students in various colleges within the University. The degree requires the completion of 124 points of credit, satisfying distribution requirements. The Master of Arts degree in music is offered with concentrations in composition, ethnomusicology, historical musicology, and theory. This degree requires the completion of 30 points of "E" credit, languages, a thesis or essay(s). The Master of Philosophy degree requires 30 points of credit beyond the Master of Arts degree. Concentrations in historical musicology, ethnomusicology, ethnomusicology with a specialization in music theory, and in theory are available. The Doctor of Philosophy degree in historical musicology, ethnomusicology, or theory requires the completion of 30 points of "E" credit beyond the Master of Philosophy degree. It also requires one or two additional languages, a dissertation and defense. The Doctor of Musical Arts degree in composition is offered by the School of the Arts.

General Program Areas. Composition, Ethnomusicology, Historical Musicology, Music Theory, Performance..

Instruments Taught. Baroque Instruments, Brass, Harpsichord, Organ, Percussion, Piano, Renaissance Instruments, Stringed Instruments, Woodwinds.

Musical Facilities

Practice Facilities. 7 practice rooms. 2 organs (Aeolian, Skinner). 10 pianos (4 uprights, 4 baby grands, 2 electronic). Columbia-Princeton Electronic Music Center used primarily by graduate students in composition.

Concert Facilities. Kathryn Bache Miller Theater, seating 700; several smaller halls around campus (200-400 capacity).

Concerts/Musical Activities. Recitals and concerts by students and faculty.

Music Library. 32,000 books and serials; 26,000 musical scores; 100 periodical subscriptions; 6,000 microforms; 17,500 recordings. 12 listening stations. Special collections include: eighteenth and nineteenth century materials, including first editions (especially nineteenth century operas); Laura Boulton Collection of Traditional and Liturgical Music. Other libraries of the University contain: Berlioz materials; George A. Plimpton Manuscript Collection; Bela Bartok materials; autograph scores; microfilms of Beethoven materials; late eighteenth century and early nineteenth century opera scores; Judah A. Joffe record collection.

Students have access to all other university and college music collections in New York City as well as the music division of the New York Public Library at Lincoln Center. The Department of Music's Center for Studies in Ethnomusicology, which is world wide in scope, houses a collection of 35,000 sound and video recordings and a laboratory.

Special Programs

Performance Groups. University Orchestra, Barnard-Columbia Chorus, Jazz Band, Glee Club, Marching Band, Collegium Musicum.

Financial

Costs. Per academic year: Tuition $11,444. Room and board $630 per month.

Financial Aid. Financial aid is awarded on the basis of academic merit, financial need, musical ability. Institutional and state/federal aid available as well as part-time employment and a College Work-Study program. Financial aid/scholarships application due January 15th.

Cornell University
Department of Music
Lincoln Hall
Ithaca
New York 14853

Telephone. (607) 255-4097

Chief Administrator. Professor Thomas A. Sokol, Chairman.

Cornell University is a private institution founded in 1856. The university's activities are mainly centered in Ithaca, New York, on a campus comprising more than 90 major buildings on 730 acres. There is a medical college and a nursing school in New York City. The university operates the New York State Agricultural Experiment Station in Geneva, New York and an Ionsopheric Observatory in Puerto Rico. The city of Ithaca is located at the southern tip of Cayuga Lake in central New York.

The Department of Music at Cornell provides opportunities for the study and performance of music as part of a liberal arts education. The program is designed to increase an understanding of music that may already be familiar and to explore other less-known music. Any qualified student, regardless of his or her major, may enroll in courses in music history, theory, composition, and performance. Introductory courses, which have no prerequisites, are offered regularly, as is applied music instruction (for academic credit or not) in voice, keyboard, strings, brass, and winds. There are two options available to those majoring in music at Cornell. One is

selected by students who might not intend to pursue a career in music but who do want to take advantage of offerings to emphasize the study of music within a humanities setting. The other, more intensive, option provides a solid foundation for a professional career in music as a performer, composer, teacher, scholar, or librarian. There is no fixed program as such for graduate students at Cornell. The program of each student is determined by his or her Special Committee. Concentrations are offered in musicology, composition, ethnomusicology, and performance.

Accreditation. Middle States Association of Colleges and Schools.

Academic Information

Enrollment, Music Majors. (Total university) 10,440 men, 7,740 women.

Music Faculty. Full-time 19, part-time 2.

Term System. Semester. Academic year from late August to late May. 6-week summer session from late June to late May.

Entrance Requirements. Accredited high school graduation and completion of 16 college preparatory units (4 English, 3 mathematics, 3 of 1 foreign language, units of laboratory science and social studies; ACT or SAT with 3 Achievement Tests; GRE required for graduate programs.

Admission Procedure. Application with supporting documents and $20 nonrefundable application fee no later than January 1 of year of enrollment.

Music Degrees Offered. Bachelor of Arts; Master of Arts; Doctor of Musical Arts; Doctor of Philosophy.

Music Degree Requirements. A new Doctor of Musical Arts in historical performance of eighteenth century instrumental music is offered. This program takes advantage of Cornell University's community of performers and scholars specializing in the instrumental music of the eighteenth century. The program is designed primarily for professional and near-professional performers who wish to study this music in conjunction with the musical thought of the period.

General Program Areas. Applied Music, Composition, Eighteenth Century Music, Ethnomusicology, Music Theory, Musicology, Performance.

Instruments Taught. Brass, Organ, Percussion, Piano, Stringed Instruments, Voice, Woodwinds.

Musical Facilities

Practice Facilities. Aeolian-Skinner organ in Sage Chapel, Schlicker organ in Barnes Hall, Hellmuth Wolff tracker in Anabel Taylor Chapel. A small Challis harpsichord and clavichord are available for practice. A 1784 Stein fortepiano, an 1826 Graf fortepiano, and a Bösendorfer Imperial concert grand are reserved for advanced students and concerts. Electronic music studio.

Concert Facilities. Barnes Hall Auditorium, seating 280; Alice Statler Auditiorium, 900; Bailey Hall, 2,000.

Concerts/Musical Activities. More than 100 concerts and lectures on campus each year, given by faculty members, students, and distinguished visiting artists.

Music Library. 90,000 books and scores; 15,000 records. Special collections of early opera scores, librettos, and recordings from all periods; twentieth century scores and records; large microfilm collection of Renaissance sources, both theoretical and musical; materials on Ralph Vaughan Williams; eighteenth and nineteenth century German Protestant hymnals. The Department of Rare Books in Olin Library houses a collection of early printed books on music and musical manuscripts. The Verne S. Swan Collection of 30 musical instruments is especially rich in old stringed instruments, several of which have been restored to their original proportions.

Special Programs

Featured Programs. The Center for Eighteenth Century Music functions within the Department of Music as the focus for its various activities in this area including the D.M.A. program, several performing organizations that concentrate on recreating eighteenth century performing conditions, viola da gamba and fortepiano summer workshops, and M.A. and Ph.D. degrees in historical musicology with concentration in eighteenth century studies, visiting fellows in performance and research, and symposia and workshops devoted to research and performance.

Performance Groups. Collegium Musicum, Cornell Chamber Ensemble, Cornell Chamber Orchestra, Cornell Chorale, Cornell Chorus, Cornell Gamelan Ensemble, Cornell Glee Club, Cornell Jazz Ensemble, Cornell Symphonic Band, Sage Chapel Choir.

Financial

Costs. Per academic year: Tuition $11,500. Room $1,782 to $2,810. Board $670 to $1,655.

Financial Aid. Financial aid is awarded on the basis of academic merit and financial need. Institutional and state/federal aid available as well as a College Work-Study program.

Hofstra University
Department of Music
Hempstead
New York 11550

Telephone. (516) 560-5490

Chief Administrator. Dr. Edgar E. Dittemore, Chairperson.

Hofstra University is a privately supported, nonsectarian, liberal arts university. It was established in 1935. The colleges and schools of the University include Hofstra College of Liberal Arts and Sciences, School of Business, School of Education, New College of Hofstra, School of Law, Alumni College, and University College for Continuing Education. Enrollment exceeds 12,000 students. The 238-acre campus contains 80 buildings in the Long Island community of Hempstead, 25 miles east of Manhattan.

The Department of Music seeks to train musicians and music teachers with emphasis on performance and theoretical study.

Accreditation. Middle States Association of Colleges and Schools; National Council for Accreditation of Teacher Education.

Academic Information

Enrollment, Music Majors. Undergraduate 90. Foreign students 3.

Music Faculty. Full-time 6, part-time 10.

Term System. Semester. Summer sessions (Orff workshop, music instrument repair, piano pedagogy).

Entrance Requirements. High school graduation with 16 units (4 English, 3 mathematics, 2 laboratory science, 3 social studies, 2 foreign language); SAT combined score of 1000 or above; top one-third of graduating class. Audition required; sight-reading; 2 pieces in different styles; music theory placement test.

Admission Procedure. Complete application; transcripts of all previous work; application fee $100 (refundable); due by February 15.

Music Degrees Offered. Bachelor of Arts; Bachelor of Science.

Music Degree Requirements. The Bachelor of Arts degree with specialization in music requires the completion of 128 semester hours and a cumulative grade point average of 2.0 in work completed. Concentrations are offered in performance, theory/composition, history/literature, music merchandising, jazz and commercial music. Each concentration has specific requirements. The Bachelor of Science degree in education with specialization in music education leads to certification in the elementary and secondary schools of the State of New York. The aim of the program is to provide students with a basic understanding and comprehensive knowledge of music, which, together with fundamental courses in education, will lead to effective public school teaching. The degree requires the completion of 128 semester hours in a specified curriculum.

General Program Areas. Commercial Music, Composition, Ethnomusicology, Jazz, Music Education, Music History, Music Literature, Music Merchandising, Music Theory.

Instruments Taught. Baritone, Bass, Bassoon, Clarinet, Flute, French Horn, Guitar, Harp, Harpsichord, Oboe, Organ, Percussion, Piano, Piccolo, Saxophone, Trombone, Trumpet, Tuba, Viola, Violin, Violoncello, Voice.

Musical Facilities

Practice Facilities. 10 practice rooms. Percussion-equipped practice room. 10 pianos (studio uprights); 3 grand pianos reserved for piano majors. Electronic music studio; recording studio.

Concert Facilities. Concert Hall seating 1,100; 2 other halls seating 100 and 75 respectively.

Community Facilities. Organ classes are taught at Garden City Cathedral.

Concerts/Musical Activities. The Institute of the Arts provides broad cultural programs for the benefit of University and community audiences. The Institute supports interdisciplinary programs that relate to and serve the creative and performing arts.

Music Library. Major music holdings are in the main library. Music listening room in Emily Lowe Hall has a collection of 4,000 cataloged recordings.

Special Programs

Performance Groups. Concert Band, University Orchestra, Mixed Chorus, Collegium Musicum, Opera Theater, Jazz Repertory Company, New Music Ensemble, Flute Ensemble, String Ensemble, Brass Ensemble, Percussion Ensemble, Hofstra Singers.

Financial

Costs. Per academic year: Tuition $6,400. University fee $300. Room $1,500 to $2,000. Board $1,200 to $1,-900.

Financial Aid. Hofstra makes financial aid available to many students in the form of scholarships, grants, loans, and jobs. Approximately 45 music scholarships awarded ranging from $200 to $2,000. Part-time employment and College Work-Study program available.

Ithaca College
School of Music
Danby Road
Ithaca
New York 14850

Telephone. (607) 274-3171

Chief Administrator. Dr. Arthur E. Ostrander, Dean.

Ithaca College is a private, nondenominational institution offering a broadly diversified program of professional and liberal arts studies. Originally founded in 1892 as a Conservatory of Music, it became a nonprofit, private college in 1931. During the early decades of this century, the academic program was expanded to include other professional fields and at mid-century the institution began developing curricula in the liberal arts which have gradually evolved into the School of Humanities and Sciences. In the 1960s, the College moved from scattered buildings in downtown Ithaca to its modern campus on South Hill overlooking the city of Ithaca and Cayuga Lake.

The School of Music seeks to graduate students of professional competence in teaching, writing, and performance. Intensive intellectual and technical discipline in the major field is supported by general courses in the student's total program. All classes, ensembles, and lessons from the music degree programs are open to all qualified students regardless of major so long as space is available. In addition, certain courses of study which require no prior musical training have been developed primarily for the nonmajor.

Accreditation. Middle States Association of Colleges and Schools; National Association of Schools of Music.

Academic Information

Enrollment, Music Majors. Full-time 148 men, 171 women; part-time 8 men, 7 women.

Music Faculty. Full-time 49, part-time 16.

Term System. Semester. 2 summer sessions.

Entrance Requirements. High school graduation. All applicants to the School of Music must audition on their principal instrument or voice and pass a sightsinging test. Auditions are conducted on the Ithaca campus and in several off-campus locations.

Admission Procedure. Application with nonrefundable $25 fee by March 1 (preferred).

Music Degrees Offered. Bachelor of Music; Bachelor of Arts; Bachelor of Fine Arts; Master of Music.

Music Degree Requirements. The Bachelor of Music degree program is offered with major concentrations in music education, performance, performance/music education, theory, composition, and music in combination with an outside field. The Bachelor of Arts degree program with a major in music provides the opportunity for students to major in music and to pursue substantive studies in the liberal arts. The Bachelor of Fine Arts degree program is offered with major concentrations in music and related arts, jazz studies, and musical theatre. The Bachelor of Music degree in music education leads to provisional certification in grades K-12 for the State of New York and allows students to select from various special study options. A vocal/instrumental crossover major is available for students who want to have a teaching experience in the vocal or instrumental area opposite to that of their major performance field. Performance credits remain in the original major with curricular adjustments. Total credits for all baccalaureate degrees range from 124 to 129 semester hours. *The Master of Music degree requires the completion of 30 to 36 semester hours.*

General Program Areas. Composition, Jazz Studies, Music Education, Music History, Music Literature, Music Theory, Musical Theatre, Performance.

Instruments Taught. Bassoon, Clarinet, English Horn, Euphonium, Flute, French Horn, Oboe, Organ, Percussion, Piano, Saxophone, Trombone, Trumpet, Tuba, Viola, Violin, Violoncello, Voice.

Musical Facilities

Practice Facilities. 90 practice rooms. Special practice facilities for organists; 1 Schlicker, 3 practice organs. 2 practice rooms for percussionists. 100 practice pianos (including grands and uprights); 14 grand pianos reserved for piano majors. 2 electronic music studios.

Concert Facilities. Concert Hall, Recital Hall.

Concerts/Musical Activities. Numerous concerts and recitals each week.

Music Library. The main library houses over 300,000 volumes of which 6,000 are in music; 10,500 scores; 13,000 phonograph recordings. The Music Special Collections consist of the Gustav Haenschen and Donald Voorhees broadcast music libraries and Roberta Peters memorabilia. Pulitzer Prize-winning composer Karel Husa has recently designated the library as the repository for the complete collection of recordings and scores of all his music.

Special Programs

Performance Groups. Wind Ensemble, Concert Band, Symphonic Band, Orchestra, Women's Chorale, Chorus, Choir, Guitar Ensemble, Piano Ensemble, Vocal Jazz Ensemble.

Foreign Programs. Ithaca College has an extensive program in London, England.

Affiliated Programs. Tuition exchange program with Cornell University.

Financial

Costs. Per academic year: Tuition $7,646. Room $1,648. Board $1,748.

Financial Aid. Ithaca College subscribes to guidelines established by the College Scholarship Service which directs that financial assistance be based upon need, and that it be distributed as equitably as possible among eligible recipients. All applicants for admission to Ithaca College are eligible to apply for financial aid in the form of scholarship, work, or loans.

The Juilliard School

Lincoln Center Plaza
New York
New York 10023

Telephone. (212) 799-5000

Chief Administrator. Joseph W. Polisi, President.

The Juilliard School was established in 1905 as the Institute of Musical Art. A bequest of merchant Augustus D. Juilliard established the Juilliard Graduate School in 1924. In 1926, the Graduate School and the Institute merged under one president and Board of Trustees, but kept separate deans and identities. The amalgamation of the schools was gradual. The president of the schools, William Schuman, helped complete the process in 1946, forming The Juilliard School. Since 1969, The Juilliard School has been part of Lincoln Center for the Performing Arts.

The oldest and largest component of The Juilliard School is the Music Division. Major study is offered in all orchestral and keyboard instruments, piano accompanying (on the graduate level only), voice, composition, and conducting (both choral and orchestral). Training is rooted in private study with a major teacher. The major study is complemented by courses in music theory, music history, ear training, and other subjects, and by a great variety of performance activities.

Accreditation. Middle States Association of Colleges and Schools.

Academic Information

Enrollment, Music Majors. (Music Division) 750.

Music Faculty. 122. Artists-in-residence: Juilliard String Quartet; American Brass Quintet.

Term System. Semester.

Entrance Requirements. High school graduation or equivalent; completion of 16 units; entrance examination and audition required; admission for fall semester only; January 15 deadline for entrance examinations to be given in March (entrance examinations also given in Chicago and Los Angeles); March 15 deadline for May auditions; July 1 deadline for late August auditions.

Admission Procedure. Application with supporting documents and nonrefundable $60 fee to Office of Admissions.

Music Degrees Offered. Bachelor of Music; Master of Music; Doctor of Musical Arts; Diploma.

Music Degree Requirements. The Bachelor of Music degree is offered as the principal undergraduate program in music. Major studies can be pursued in composition, conducting (choral, orchestral), keyboard instruments, orchestral instruments, and voice.

The Master of Music degree is offered as an advanced course of study for musicians who hold the bachelor's degree and who seek graduate musical training and classroom learning to prepare more fully for careers as professional musicians. A concentration in accompanying is offered.

In 1988-89 the Diploma program will become the Certificate program.

General Program Areas. Accompanying, Applied Music, Composition, Conducting, Performance.

Instruments Taught. Bass, Bassoon, Clarinet, English Horn, Flute, Harp, Horn, Oboe, Organ, Percussion, Piano, Trombone, Trumpet, Tuba, Viola, Violin, Violoncello, Voice.

Musical Facilities

Practice Facilities. Orchestra and chorus rehearsal room; 15 two-story studios; 3 organ studios; 84 practice rooms; 27 classrooms; 35 private teaching studios; scenery and costume workshops; 200 pianos.

Concert Facilities. Four performance halls. Alice Tully Hall, the largest of the halls, seats 1,096; it is used for orchestra concerts and chamber, choral, and solo recital performances, and houses a 4,192-pipe organ by Kuhn. The Juilliard Theater seats 933. The C. Michael Paul Recital Hall, which seats 278, contains a 44-rank Holtkamp pipe organ.

Concerts/Musical Activities. Both students and faculty present public evening recitals throughout the year in C. Michael Paul Recital Hall; solo and chamber concerts are presented each Wednesday in Alice Tully Hall; Focus! is an annual week-long festival of twentieth-century music; master classes and performances by guest artists.

Music Library. The Lila Acheson Wallace Library houses a collection of over 19,000 volumes; 17,000 music performance and study scores; and 14,000 phonograph, cassette tape, and reel-to-reel tape recordings. Among these are rare scores, first edition and limited edition books, and manuscripts and scholarly editions of the complete sets of works by many composers. The library includes music and record stacks, reading and study areas, and listening rooms equipped with 28 phonographs, 4 cassette players, and 4 reel-to-reel tape decks.

The School's orchestral library has a complete collection of the standard repertoire in full scores and performing parts. The orchestral library also houses the School's collection of some 100 instruments ranging from contrabassoons and piccolos to strings and percussion. Rare violins, violas, and cellos are loaned at the discretion of the major teachers for important competitions, recitals, and solo engagements.

Other special collections include: 19th and 20th century opera piano-vocal scores and chamber music parts; 19th century opera librettos; early editions of Liszt; papers of Ernest Newman.

Special Programs

Featured Programs. Music study for elementary and secondary school students is offered through the Pre-College Division, and for adults and older students who are not matriculated at the School through the Extension Division.

Performance Groups. Juilliard Orchestra, Juilliard Symphony, Contemporary Ensemble, Chamber Orchestra, Conductors' Orchestra, Juilliard Chorus, Small Ensembles.

Affiliated Programs. The Juilliard American Opera Center has a program for advanced singers who wish to refine their skills through intensive training while acquiring performing experience in appropriate repertoire. The Center presents three operas every year.

Financial

Costs. Per academic year: Tuition $7,200. Fees $150.
Financial Aid. Among the types of financial aid available at Juilliard are scholarships, state and federally funded grants, loans, fellowships, and support earned by students in the College Work-Study program. Scholarships are awarded in all fields of major study. Scholarship/financial aid application due April 15.

Commentary

Chamber music has recently become a more structured aspect of the Juilliard education. Other changes have been instituted: the School has hired the American Brass Quintet as an ensemble-in-residence, dormitories are being built for the first time, the student newspaper has become an important institution of Juilliard life, the School is setting up its first archival and preservation program, and student ensembles are touring in various parts of the world. Joseph Polisi, the School's new President, is the moving spirit behind these innovative changes.

Long Island University - C.W. Post Campus
Music Department
Greenvale
New York 11548

Telephone. (516) 299-2474
Chief Administrator. Dr. Raoul Pleskow, Chairman.
The C.W. Post Campus of Long Island University enrolls over 9,500 students each year. The former home of Marjorie Merriweather Post is the site of the campus that contains 40 buildings on 350 acres.

The Music Department offers an undergraduate curricula in music for students desiring preparation for professional performance and teaching and for students who wish a strong music program which provides the opportunity for a well-rounded liberal arts background.

Accreditation. Middle States Association of Colleges and Schools.

Academic Information

Enrollment, Music Majors. (Total Campus) 9,670.
Term System. Semester. 3 summer terms.
Entrance Requirements. High school graduation with rank in upper 50 percent of graduating class; completion of 16 units including 4 English, 2 mathematics, 2 foreign language, 3 social studies; SAT; audition required.
Admission Procedure. Application with supporting documents and nonrefundable $20 fee to Office of Admissions.
Music Degrees Offered. Bachelor of Arts; Bachelor of Fine Arts; Bachelor of Science; Master of Arts; Master of Science.
Music Degree Requirements. The Bachelor of Arts degree with a major in music is offered in the context of a broad liberal arts program. The Bachelor of Science is offered with a music education concentration. The Bachelor of Fine Arts degree in music is also available. The Bachelor of Arts degree in music therapy provides

training for students who wish to use their creative and performing skills in a variety of health care facilities. The program emphasizes concentration in music and psychology.

The Department of Music offers courses leading toward the Master of Arts degree with concentrations in music theory and composition and in music history. The Master of Science degree is offered with a concentration in Music Education. New York University offers a Doctor of Philosophy program in music with the cooperation of the LIU/C.W. Post Music Department.

General Program Areas. Composition, Conducting, Music Education, Music History, Music Theory, Music Therapy, Performance.

Instruments Taught. Brass, Organ, Piano, Stringed Instruments, Voice, Woodwinds.

Musical Facilities

Practice Facilities. Music Building.

Concert Facilities. Bush-Brown Concert Theater, seating 2,200.

Concerts/Musical Activities. Student/faculty recitals and concerts.

Music Library. The B. Davis Schwartz Memorial Library houses the major collections of the campus including more than 700,000 books and periodicals.

Special Programs

Performance Groups. College Community Chorus, C.W. Post Chamber Singers, Madrigal Singers, College Band, Jazz Ensemble, Merriweather Consort, Chamber Orchestra.

Financial

Costs. Per academic year: Tuition $6,020. Fees $390. Room $1,800. Board $1,274.

Financial Aid. Financial aid is awarded on the basis of academic merit and financial need. Institutional and state/federal aid are available in the form of scholarships, grants, loans, and part-time employment. Financial aid/scholarship application due March 1.

Manhattan School of Music
120 Claremont Avenue
New York
New York 10027

Telephone. (212) 749-2802

Chief Administrator. Dr. Gideon Waldrop, President.

The Neighborhood Music School was founded in 1917 by Janet D. Schenck on the upper East Side of New York. In 1928, Helen Fahnstock Hubbard donated funds to erect a new building for the school, which in 1938 was renamed the Manhattan School of Music. In 1948 the institution was given a charter amendment to grant the Bachelor of Music degree; two subsequent amendments

authorized the school to grant the Master's degree (1947) and the Doctor of Musical Arts degree (1974). In 1956, Dr. Schenck retired and was followed by John Brownlee as Director, and later, President. George Schick became President in 1969, and in the same year the school moved to its new home on Claremont Avenue, the previous location of The Juilliard School. In 1976, John Crosby was appointed President and in 1986 Gideon Waldrop succeeded him in the position.

The Manhattan School of Music seeks to create well-rounded, thinking professional musicians. Students are provided with instruction from professors drawn from the New York professional community. The school strives to keep an open and friendly atmosphere which it believes will be more conducive to the study of music. There is a particular emphasis on the study and performance of contemporary music.

Accreditation. Middle States Association of Colleges and Schools.

Academic Information

Enrollment, Music Majors. Full-time 342 men, 272 women; part-time 39 men, 34 women. 119 foreign students.

Music Faculty. Full-time 15, part-time 174.

Term System. Semester. Two summer sessions.

Entrance Requirements. Audition for departmental faculty of the prospective student's major, and theoretical and music history placement tests. High school graduation not required as the High School Equivalency is granted by the state of New York upon successful completion of 24 college credits. Foreign students need proper visa and financial support documentation and TOEFL scores.

Admission Procedure. Application deadlines are March 15, April 15, July 15, November 15.

Music Degrees Offered. Bachelor of Music; Master of Music; Doctor of Musical Arts; Diploma; Post-Graduate Diploma.

Music Degree Requirements. The Bachelor of Music degree requires the completion of 122 semester hours, including performance and academic requirements. The Master of Music requires the completion of 30 semester hours, and the Doctor of Musical Arts, 58 semester hours. The Diploma requires 90 semester hours.

General Program Areas. Applied Music, Composition, Conducting, Music Theory, Performance.

Instruments Taught. Brass, Harpsichord, Percussion, Piano, Stringed Instruments, Voice, Woodwinds.

Musical Facilities

Practice Facilities. 50 practice rooms. 5 percussion-equipped practice rooms. 1 organ in recital hall; much of the organ teaching takes place at private studios outside of the school. 90 practice pianos (80 grands, 10 uprights). Electronic music studio.

Concert Facilities. Hubbard Recital Hall; Borden Hall.

Concerts/Musical Activities. Approximately 300 student performances are given each year, including opera, orchestral concerts, and recitals.

Music Library. 25,600 books; 55,000 scores; 70 current periodical titles; 18,300 records. Listening facilities include 2 cassette stations, 1 reel-to-reel tape station, and 17 stereo stations. Special collections include: record collection of Virgil Thomson. Students have reading privileges at Barnard College, Union Theological Seminary, Jewish Theological Seminary, Teachers College, and the New York Public Library at Lincoln Center.

Special Programs

Featured Programs. In fall 1988, a joint program of Manhattan School of Music and Union Theological Seminary will present two new graduate degrees: (1) Master of Music in Church Music and (2) Doctor of Musical Arts in Church Music. The program's Chair, Dr. Alec Wyton, is currently Director of Music, St. James Church, New York City. He was, for twenty years, Director of Music at the Cathedral of St. John the Divine in New York City. The carefully-formed curricula of the new program will include choral techniques and repertoire, conducting, church history, organ history and design, organ study, contemporary trends in church music, ecclesiology, theology, theory and pedagogy seminars, liturgy, church music history, and individually assigned fieldwork in churches and chapels throughout the area.

Currently open to organ majors only, the program may be expanded in the future to include additional disciplines. Auditions must demonstrate that the applicant is an organist of advanced accomplishment. Required pre-examinations include music theory, music history, theology, and church music. The candidate for the D.M.A. degree must have had at least two years of experience as a church organist-choir director, and must possess skill in choral conducting techniques.

Performance Groups. Ensembles and other performance groups.

Affiliated Programs. Students are permitted to take academic courses at Barnard College of Columbia University.

Financial

Costs. Per academic year: Tuition $6,100. Fees $1,810. Room $3,375. Board $2,565.

Financial Aid. 185 students receive some form of financial aid (22 freshmen). Scholarships available ranging from $1,000 to $6,100 (average amount $2,860). Scholarship application deadline March 1. Part-time employment and College Work-Study program available.

Commentary

The Manhattan School of Music is one of the leading conservatories of the Northeast. The opera department has become particularly active in recent years.

Mannes College of Music
150 West 85th Street
New York
New York 10024

Telephone. (212) 580-0210

Chief Administrator. Dr. Charles Kaufman, President.

The Mannes College of Music was founded by David and Clara Mannes, who were active in the early 1900s as a violin and piano duo. In addition, Mr. Mannes was Director of the Music School Settlement at East Third Street in New York City and Concertmaster of the New York Symphony Orchestra conducted by Walter Damrosch. In 1916, Mr. and Mrs. Mannes established the David Mannes Music School, which in 1933, was granted a charter from the University of the State of New York. In 1953, the School was authorized to grant the Bachelor of Science degree and the present name of the institution was adopted. In February 1984, the College moved to new quarters on Manhattan's Upper West Side.

In addition to degree programs, the College serves the musical needs of the community. The Preparatory Division offers instruction in all instruments, musicianship and theory, ensemble performance, as well as pre-instrumental instruction for pupils between 4 and 18 years of age. The Extension Division serves two constitutencies: adults who do not intend to pursue a career in music, and professionals who seek to refine their musical skills or add new ones. The program encompasses classical music and jazz studies and includes a curriculum leading to the award of a Diploma. Many Extension Division performance activities are open to College-division students with the Dean's permission.

Accreditation. Middle States Association of Colleges and Schools.

Academic Information

Enrollment, Music Majors. Full-time 77 men, 84 women; part-time 5 men, 4 women.

Music Faculty. Full-time 12, part-time 120.

Term System. Semester. One summer session (generally basic courses in musicianship).

Entrance Requirements. High school graduation; completion of 16 units including 4 English, 2 mathematics, 2 foreign language, 1 science; entrance examination and audition required; SAT or ACT; evidence of good musical ear and competence; music theory. Graduate students must demonstrate competence in theory and musicianship including four-part diatonic and chromatic harmony, three-part species or Baroque counterpoint, and two-part dictation; audition with a full recital program comprising works representative of three different style periods.

Admission Procedure. Application with $50 non-refundable fee accepted on a rolling basis.

Music Degrees Offered. Bachelor of Music; Bachelor of Science; Master of Music; Diploma; Post-Graduate Diploma.

Music Degree Requirements. The Bachelor of Music degree program is offered with concentrations in piano, organ, harpsichord; orchestral instruments; guitar; voice and opera; composition; orchestral conducting; and choral conducting. The degree requires the completion of 131 to 139 credit hours, depending on concentration.

The Master of Music degree is offered in orchestral instruments, piano, organ, harpsichord, orchestral conducting, choral conducting, historical performance, voice, guitar, composition, and theory. It is a two-year program requiring the completion of 32 to 34 credit hours.

The Artist's Diploma is an advanced course of study in performance, composition, or theory. Course requirements are flexible. The Post-Graduate Diploma has a residency requirement of two years and requires the completion of 32 credit hours. The Professional Study Diploma is an advanced course of study designed to enhance professional performance or composition skills.

General Program Areas. Choral Conducting, Composition, Music Theory, Orchestral Conducting, Performance.

Instruments Taught. Baroque Instruments, Brass, Guitar, Organ, Percussion, Piano, Renaissance Instruments, Stringed Instruments, Voice, Woodwinds.

Musical Facilities

Practice Facilities. 18 practice rooms. 2 organs (Baroque, Baldwin). Special practice facility for percussionists. Electronic music studio; audio studio.

Concert Facilities. Concert hall, seating 300; recital hall, 70.

Concerts/Musical Activities. 4 yearly orchestra concerts; 4 chamber orchestra concerts; student concerts and ensembles; 2 chorus concerts; 30 noonday concerts.

Music Library. 5,546 books; 21,266 scores; 50 periodical subscriptions; 4,000 recordings. Listening facilities (cassette, stereo). Carlos Salzedo Collection of harp music. Students have access to the music division of the New York Public Library's Library of the Performing Arts at Lincoln Center.

Special Programs

Performance Groups. Mannes Orchestra, Repertory Orchestra, Mannes Chorus, Wind Ensemble, Brass Repertory, Percussion Ensemble, Piano Ensemble, Guitar Ensemble, Contemporary Music Ensemble, Chamber Ensemble, Mannes Camerata, Baroque Chamber Ensemble, Renaissance Band.

Foreign Programs. Member of a consortium with the Fontainebleau Conservatory in France (summer program).

Affiliated Programs. Joint programs with Hunter College, Queens College, and Marymount Manhattan College.

Financial

Costs. Per academic year: Tuition $6,500 (degree course); $6,250 (diploma and post-graduate diploma courses).

Financial Aid. Each year more than one-third of Mannes students receive scholarship support directly from the College in recognition of outstanding talent, ability, and achievement. The general scholarship fund is supported by more than 170 individuals and organizations. Other sources of financial aid include grants, loans, part-time employment, and a College Work-Study program.

Commentary

Situated in an attractive building on Manhattan's Upper West Side, Mannes College of Music manages to retain a homey, friendly atmosphere despite its location in a big, sometimes impersonal, city. The large faculty, many of whom are part-time instructors, includes a number of very distinguished musicians.

New York University - College of Arts and Sciences
Department of Music
268 Waverly Building
Washington Square
New York
New York 10003

Telephone. (212) 998-8300

Chief Administrator. Dr. Edward Roesner, Chairman.

New York University is a private institution founded in 1831. The University enrolls students from all 50 states and 110 foreign countries. There are 21 schools and colleges at six major centers in Manhattan. The principal center for undergraduate and graduate study is at Washington Square in Manhattan's Greenwich Village.

The Department of Music of the College of Arts and Sciences offers a wide range of opportunities for studying and performing music. Areas of specialization in music history and theory include medieval, Renaissance, baroque, classical, and nineteenth and twentieth centuries. Courses are available for students with no previous musical experience, as well as for those with some background in the areas of music history, theory, composition and orchestration, ethnomusicology, and the history of musical instruments.

Accreditation. Middle States Association of Colleges and Schools; National Association of Schools of Music.

Academic Information

Enrollment, Music Majors. (Total University) 32,666.
Music Faculty. 11.
Term System. Semester.
Entrance Requirements. High school graduation or equivalent; completion of 16 units including 4 English, 3 mathematics, 2 or 3 laboratory science, 3 or 4 social studies; SAT and three Achievement Tests; audition required.
Admission Procedure. Application with supporting documents and nonrefundable $25 fee to Office of Admissions.
Music Degrees Offered. Bachelor of Arts; Master of Arts; Doctor of Philosophy.
Music Degree Requirements. The Bachelor of Arts degree requires the completion of 48 credits in music including a core of eight courses for a total of 128 semester hours. The Master of Arts and Doctor of Philosophy degrees are offered with a curriculum in musicology, including the areas of music history, literature, theory, and ethnomusicology. In addition to seminars in the music of specific historical periods and cultural areas, courses in research methods, style analysis, musical paleography, and performance practice are taught each year. Special programs lead to the Master of Arts with a concentration in urban ethnomusicology, and to the Certificate in Early Music.
General Program Areas. Ethnomusicology, Music History, Music Literature, Music Theory, Musicology, Performance.

Musical Facilities

Music Library. The Bobst Library houses the archives of the American Institute for Verdi Studies; a collection of microfilm resources; Gustave Reese collection of Medieval and Renaissance manuscripts; thematic catalogs of eighteenth century symphonies and concertos; New York Pro Musica instrument collection; numerous books and manuscripts. Students may use the research library at Lincoln Center.

Special Programs

Featured Programs. The Center for Early Music is devoted to research into problems of performance practice for music before c. 1630. The majority of courses offered by the center are at the graduate level; undergraduate students may audition to work with the Collegium Musicum, the performing ensemble of the center, using the Noah Greenberg Collection of Musical Instruments (formerly the performing collection of the New York Pro Musica Antigua).
Performance Groups. Washington Square Chorus, New York University Orchestra, Collegium Musicum.

Financial

Costs. Per academic year: Tuition $9,850. Room and board $5,015.
Financial Aid. Prizes awarded every year to students in the Department include the Elaine R. Brody Prize, the Hanna van Vollenhollen Memorial Prize, and the Isidore and Helen Sacks Memorial Prize in Music. Financial aid awards are based on academic achievement, financial need, and the availability of funds. Sources of aid include institutional and state/federal scholarships, grants, loans, and part-time employment. The Department of Music offers graduate fellowships, assistantships, and tuition remission to qualified students matriculated in its degree and certificate programs. Financial aid/scholarship application due February 15 for the Fall term or by December 1 for the Spring term.

New York University - School of Education, Health, Nursing, and Arts Professions
Department of Music and Music Education
777 Education Building
35 West 4th Street
New York
New York 10003

Telephone. (212) 998-5424
Chief Administrator. Dr. John V. Gilbert, Chairperson.

New York University is a private institution founded in 1831. The University enrolls students from all 50 states and 110 foreign countries. There are 21 schools and colleges at six major centers in Manhattan. The chief center for graduate and undergraduate study is at Washington Square in Manhattan's Greenwich Village.

The Department of Music and Music Education was established in 1925. The Department offers programs for teacher preparation in elementary and secondary schools and a program with specialization for music and business or music and technology. The New York College of Music program is offered in musical theater. Advisement is done on an individual basis with a recognition of accommodating individual differences and needs. Graduate offerings include a master's program, the sixth-year certificate, and doctoral level curricula for teachers, professors, administrators of school music programs, professional performers and composers, professionals in musical theater, and music therapists.

Accreditation. Middle States Association of Colleges and Schools; National Association of Schools of Music; National Association for Music Therapy; National Council for Accreditation of Teacher Education.

Academic Information

Enrollment, Music Majors. Full-time 300, part-time 300. 45 foreign students.

Music Faculty. Full-time 12, part-time 130.

Term System. Semester. Three 3-week summer sessions.

Entrance Requirements. High school graduation or equivalent; completion of 16 units including 4 years English, 3 mathematics, 2 or 3 laboratory science, 3 or 4 social studies; SAT; three Achievement Tests; audition required; theory placement examination. GRE required for doctoral programs. TOEFL required for foreign students.

Admission Procedure. Application with $25 non-refundable fee accepted on a rolling basis.

Music Degrees Offered. Bachelor of Music; Bachelor of Science; Master of Arts; Doctor of Arts; Doctor of Philosophy; Doctor of Education.

Music Degree Requirements. Majors offered by the Department include piano, voice, instrument, theory, and composition in the standard, contemporary, electronic, and jazz repertoires. The baccalaureate degrees require the completion of 130 to 136 semester hours, the master's degree 34 semester hours, and the doctorates 50 to 51 semester hours.

General Program Areas. Applied Music, Composition, Conducting, Electronic Music, Jazz Studies, Music Business, Music Education, Music History, Music Literature, Music Technology, Music Theory, Music Therapy, Musical Theatre, Opera, Performance.

Instruments Taught. Brass, Organ, Percussion, Piano, Stringed Instruments, Voice, Woodwinds.

Musical Facilities

Practice Facilities. 24 practice rooms. 2 percussion-equipped practice rooms. 24 practice pianos (Yamaha uprights). Electronic, computer, and synthesizer studios.

Concerts/Musical Activities. Student/faculty recitals and concerts.

Music Library. The Bobst Library and Study Center houses materials supportive of the music and music education programs. Special collections include: archives of the American Institute for Verdi Studies, a collection of microfilm resources, plus numerous books and manuscripts; Gustav Reese collection of Medieval and Renaissance manuscripts; thematic catalogs of 18th century symphonies and concertos; New York Pro Musica instrument collection. Students may use the research library at Lincoln Center.

Special Programs

Featured Programs. The Avery Fisher Center is designed to provide students with access to audiovisual equipment and microcomputer software to complement the research materials housed in the Bobst Library. The Center's resources include a music collection, an exten-sive collection of music and spoken word recordings, and a video collection which is particularly strong in the performing arts and the history of the cinema.

Performance Groups. University Band, University Orchestra, Chamber Ensembles, Percussion Ensemble, University Choral Arts Society, Opera Studio, Musical Theatre

Foreign Programs. Summer in Italy.

Financial

Costs. Per academic year: Tuition $9,074. Room and board $9,160.

Financial Aid. Scholarships for music students range from $200 to $500 (average $350). Other sources of financial aid include institutional and state/federal grants and loans, student employment, and a College Work-Study program.

Commentary

The Department of Music and Music Education of New York University's School of Education, Health, Nursing, and Arts Professions grants a Ph.D. in composition and performance. The performance doctorate is unusual because it entails more rigorous research and dissertation requirements than does the D.M.A., the more common degree for performance.

University of Rochester
Eastman School of Music
26 Gibbs Street
Rochester
New York 14604

Telephone. (716) 275-3032

Chief Administrator. Dr. Robert Freeman, Director.

The University of Rochester is an independent, privately endowed university. Its goal is to prepare promising students for outstanding scholarly and professional achievement by educating them in the skills of a discipline and in the moral values of intellectual life. To this end, the University has been heavily endowed by many benefactors, including George Eastman, founder of Eastman Kodak Company; Joseph Wilson, founder of Xerox Corporation; and Charles F. Hutchison. Today, the University is one of the most highly endowed universities in the United States. It enrolls over 6,900 full-time and 1,900 part-time students and has a faculty of more than 1,200 members.

In 1918, George Eastman proposed the founding of a school of music within the University of Rochester. The Eastman School of Music was founded in 1921 as a separately endowed college, becoming the first undergraduate and graduate professional school within the University. The School was directed between 1924 and 1964 by Howard Hanson, and between 1964 and 1972 by

Walter Hendl. The School was completely renovated at a cost of more than $8 million during the 1970s. It is located near downtown Rochester, on a portion of the University's original campus, which it shares with the the University's Memorial Art Gallery. The School occupies a five-story building containing the offices, studios, practice rooms, and classrooms. It is a comprehensive professional school, with baccalaureate, master's, and doctoral programs in composition, performance, scholarship, and pedagogy. Eastman aspires to transform the musical life of the nation through graduates in a variety of professional disciplines who work hard towards the development of a broader audience for music in America.

Accreditation. Middle States Association of Colleges and Schools; National Association of Schools of Music.

Academic Information

Enrollment, Music Majors. Full-time 309 men, 284 women; part-time 57 men, 50 women.

Music Faculty. Full-time 82, part-time 35. Foreign students 81.

Term System. Semester. Summer session.

Entrance Requirements. High school graduation or GED. In-person audition preferred (in Rochester or regional audition center); self-prepared tape acceptable; theory examination. Foreign students must read, write, and speak English with fluency; preferred minimum TOEFL scores 500 for undergraduates, 550 for graduates. Admission to the Eastman School is dependent upon musical accomplishment and promise.

Admission Procedure. Application due February 20 with nonrefundable $35 fee.

Music Degrees Offered. Bachelor of Music; Bachelor of Arts; Master of Music; Master of Arts; Doctor of Musical Arts; Doctor of Philosophy.

Music Degree Requirements. The Bachelor degree requires the completion of 120 to 140 credit hours; Master's 30 to 34 credit hours; Doctorate 60 or over credit hours. At any degree level, students must meet all specified course and credit requirements and must satisfy the faculty in terms of musical and academic understanding and accomplishment.

General Program Areas. Composition, Music Education, Musicology Jazz, Performance, Theory.

Instruments Taught. Bass, Bassoon, Clarinet, Euphonium, Flute, Harp, Harpsichord, Horn, Oboe, Organ, Percussion, Piano, Saxophone, Trombone, Trumpet, Tuba, Viola, Violin, Violoncello, Voice.

Musical Facilities

Practice Facilities. Special practice facilities for organists; 2 concert instruments (van Daalen, Skinner), 2 studio organs (Holtkamp, Aeolian-Skinner), 12 practice organs: 4 mechanical-action (2 Flentrop, Andover, Wahl), 8 others, including Aeolian-Skinner, Holtkamp, Moller, Schlicker. 8 practice rooms for percussionists.

169 piano practice rooms; 26 grand pianos (14 Steinway; remainder Baldwin, Mason-Hamlin, Yamaha); 85 upright pianos; 22 grand pianos reserved for piano majors.

Concert Facilities. The Eastman Theatre, built in 1923 and restored to its original elegance in 1971, seats 3,094 and serves as the main performance facility for the orchestras and large ensembles, as the home of the Rochester Philharmonic Orchestra, and as the scene of performances by traveling orchestras, artists, and opera and dance companies. Its main function, however, is to provide Eastman students with a thoroughly professional performance environment.

Kilbourn Hall, seating 459, has been called one of the finest recital and chamber music halls in the world because of its pure, undistorted acoustics. The Kilian and Caroline Schmitt Organ Recital Hall, seating 100, houses a two-manual mechanical action organ designed by Jan van Daalen. The Howard Hanson Recital Hall, seating 65, is especially suited for student recitals. It was completed in 1976 and has the most modern "self-service" stage, lighting, and recording equipment. The Kresge Recording Studios are linked by audio and closed-circuit television lines to the School's performance and rehearsal facilities, and also are used for the production of commercial recordings by both faculty members and student ensembles.

Concerts/Musical Activities. In addition to the concert life which is central to the academic program, extracurricular concert activities are extensive and take place mainly in the student union. Over 800 concerts and recitals are given each year as part of both the academic and extracurricular programs.

Music Library. The Sibley Music Library houses the largest collection of music literature and source materials of any music school in the Western hemisphere. It includes 277,853 volumes; 42,319 recordings; and autograph scores of masters of the past as well as those of many contemporary composers. Listening facilities for cassette and stereo equipment. There is an extensive rare book collection. A new building is planned for completion in the Fall of 1988.

Strengths of the library include medieval codices; manuscript liturgical books and detached leaves; theoretical treatises and partbooks of Baroque and Renaissance; operas and librettos; church music; performance collection; Americana; Rochester music history. Selected holdings include rare Wagner scores; Jacques Gordon collection; significant autograph manuscripts of important composers; Berlioz letters; manuscripts of American composers.

Special Programs

Performance Groups. Eastman Philharmonia, Eastman Wind Ensemble, Musica Nova, InterMusica, Collegium Musicum, Eastman Chorale, Eastman-Rochester Chorus, Eastman School Symphony Orchestra, Eastman Jazz Ensemble, Eastman Studio Orchestra.

Foreign Programs. Since 1980, following a competition with other principal American music schools, the Eastman Philharmonia under David Effron has been the regular resident orchestra of the Heidelberg Castle Festival in West Germany. Participating students receive expenses and fees for the performance in Heidelberg of operatic, symphonic, and chamber repertories during late July and August.

Financial

Costs. Per academic year: Tuition $9,600. Practice room fee $135 to $322. Room and board $3,600.

Financial Aid. Scholarships available ranging from $500 to $9,600; average award $3,750. Scholarship applications due March 1. GSL/NDSL loans range from $500 to $3,500; average loan $3,100.

Commentary

Eastman School of Music has a richly varied curriculum supported by an impressive faculty. Innovative programs inaugurated during the tenure of the current director, Robert Freeman, include the graduate quartet competition, in which a promising student group is chosen annually to coach with the resident Cleveland Quartet, and the Eastman Philharmonia's annual summer residency at the Heidelberg Castle Festival in West Germany.

State University of New York at Binghamton
Department of Music
Division of Humanities, Harpur College
Vestal Parkway East
Binghamton
New York 13901

Telephone. (607) 777-2591, 777-2592
Chief Administrator. Sam Chianis, Chairman.

The State University of New York at Binghamton is one of the four university centers of the SUNY system. The 606-acre campus is located in the town of Vestal, one mile west of Binghamton.

The Department of Music prescribes a core of ten courses as the basis for a liberal arts program in music. Since the development of comprehensive musicianship is one of the chief goals of the Department, music majors are required to participate for at least four semesters in any of the varied music-making activities provided by the department, such as the vocal and instrumental ensembles, opera workshop, accompanying, or keyboard training.

Accreditation. Middle States Association of Colleges and Schools.

Academic Information

Enrollment, Music Majors. (Total University) 12,191.
Music Faculty. 37.
Term System. Semester. Two summer terms.
Entrance Requirements. High school graduation or equivalent; completion of 4 units English, 2-3 mathematics, 2 science, 3 foreign language, 2 social studies; SAT or ACT required.
Admission Procedure. Application with supporting documents and nonrefundable $15 fee to Office of Admissions.
Music Degrees Offered. Bachelor of Arts; Master of Music; Master of Arts.
Music Degree Requirements. The Bachelor of Arts degree with a major in music is offered in a liberal arts program. The program requires the completion of 126 semester credits. The Department also offers courses to all interested students.

The Department of Music offers graduate studies leading to the Master of Arts and the Master of Music degrees. For the Master of Arts degree, the field of specialization may be composition, ethnomusicology, music history and literature, or music theory. For the Master of Music degree, the field of specialization may be composition, performance, or conducting. A special degree, Master of Music in Opera, is offered in conjunction with the Tri-Cities Opera Company, a regional opera company.

General Program Areas. Composition, Ethnomusicology, Music History, Music Literature, Music Theory, Performance.
Instruments Taught. Brass, Harpsichord, Organ, Percussion, Piano, Stringed Instruments, Woodwinds.

Musical Facilities

Practice Facilities. Facilities for fine and performing arts students include music listening and practice rooms in the Anderson Center for the Performing Arts.
Concert Facilities. Jean Casadesus Recital Hall.
Concerts/Musical Activities. Student/faculty recitals and concerts; visiting artists.
Music Library. The Fine Arts and Music Library serves the academic programs in the performing arts. Special collections include: recorded vocal and operatic repertory; Archive for Greek and Cypriot Ethnomusicological Studies (personal collection of Sam Chianis).

Special Programs

Performance Groups. Harpur Chorale, Women's Chorus, University Chorus, Opera Workshop, Orchestra, Concert Band, Woodwind Ensemble, Brass Ensemble, Percussion Ensemble, String Ensemble, Jazz Ensemble, Chamber Ensemble, Early Music Players, Chamber Orchestra, Greek Folk Music and Dance.

Financial

Costs. Per academic year: Tuition in-state resident $1,-350, out-of-state $3,200. Fees $150. Room $1,690. Board $1,286.

Financial Aid. Financial aid is awarded on the basis of academic merit and financial need. State/federal aid is available in the form of scholarships, grants, loans, and part-time employment. Financial aid/scholarship application due April 1.

Commentary

A new Bachelor of Music program in performance will be instituted during the 1988-89 academic year.

State University of New York at Buffalo
Department of Music
222 Baird Hall
North Campus
Buffalo
New York 14260

Telephone. (716) 636-2765
Chief Administrator. Jan Williams, Chair.

The State University of New York at Buffalo was founded in 1846 as the University of Buffalo and is today the largest single unit of the SUNY system. Academic facilities are divided between two campuses. The Main Street Campus is located on the northeast edge of the city of Buffalo, while the North Campus is located on a 1,-200-acre site in the town of Amherst.

The Department of Music provides students with a comprehensive knowledge of music theory, music history, and performance practice. New and experimental music play an important role in the activity of the Department. Private instruction is offered on all standard orchestral instruments, piano, organ, harpsichord, classical guitar, and voice.

Accreditation. Middle States Association of Colleges and Schools; National Association of Schools of Music.

Academic Information

Enrollment, Music Majors. (Total University) 22,896.
Music Faculty. 54.
Term System. Semester. Three summer sessions.
Entrance Requirements. High school graduation with rank in upper 20 percent; SAT required; evaluation audition required.
Admission Procedure. Application with supporting documents and nonrefundable $10 fee to Office of Admissions.
Music Degrees Offered. Bachelor of Arts; Bachelor of Fine Arts; Master of Music; Master of Arts; Doctor of Philosophy.
Music Degree Requirements. The Bachelor of Arts degree is offered with a major in music in a liberal arts curriculum. The degree requires the completion of 128 semester credits. The Bachelor of Fine Arts with major in music education (K-12) requires the completion of 128 to 162 semester credits of a required core, a required music education sequence, general education courses, and electives. The major in performance requires the completion of a total of 128 semester credits.

The Master of Music degree is offered with concentrations in music education and performance. The Master of Arts degree is offered with concentrations in music education, composition, music history, and music theory. The Doctor of Philosophy degree may be pursued with emphasis in composition, music history, music theory, or music education.

General Program Areas. Composition, Music Education, Music History, Music Theory, Performance.

Instruments Taught. Brass, Organ, Percussion, Piano, Stringed Instruments, Voice, Woodwinds.

Musical Facilities

Practice Facilities. The Department of Music is housed in the Baird Music Building which consists of classrooms, offices, a band complex, choral/recital hall, practice rooms, organ rooms, teaching studios, and the Music Library. The Frederick and Alice Slee Hall contains a 700-seat auditorium, recording studio, orchestra complex, artist and rehearsal rooms, a concert office, a complete electronic music studio, and classrooms.

Concerts/Musical Activities. Student/faculty recitals and concerts; visiting artists.

Music Library. The Music Library has a bound volume collection of over 75,000 volumes in addition to sound recordings and tapes. Listening stations offer high-quality electronic sound equipment.

Special collections include: Archive of the Center for the Creative and Performing Arts; Archive of Folklore, Traditional Music, and Oral History: Center for Studies in American Culture.

Special Programs

Performance Groups. University Chorus, Symphony Band, Wind Ensemble, University Philharmonia, Brass Ensemble, Keyboard Ensemble, Percussion Ensemble, Woodwind Ensemble, String Ensemble, Contemporary Music Ensemble, Vocal Chamber Music Ensemble, Collegium Musicum, Jazz Ensemble.

Financial

Costs. Per academic year: Tuition in-state resident $1,-350, out-of-state $3,200. Fees $240. Room $1,550. Board $1,430.

Financial Aid. The Department of Music offers numerous scholarships to qualified students. Scholarship decisions are made by the Undergraduate Committee based on recommendations and data compiled at the time of audition. Undergraduate Performance Awards, which carry a stipend of $1,000 per year, are made available through the Office of the Vice President of Academic Affairs to exceptionally gifted musicians. These and other departmental awards are renewable for up to four years. Other sources of financial aid include grants, loans, and part-time employment. Financial aid/scholarship application due March 15.

Commentary

The Slee Professorship, an endowed chair bringing an eminent composer each year for a residency, and the Buffalo-Slee Beethoven cycle, in which a different quartet is engaged annually to perform the complete Beethoven Quartets, have greatly enriched the life on campus at SUNY Buffalo. The Center for New Music has inherited the commitment to the avant-garde which began with the unique Center for the Creative and Performing Arts, active on campus in the 1960s and 1970s.

State University of New York at Stony Brook
Department of Music
Stony Brook
New York 11794

Telephone. (516) 246-5673
Chief Administrator. Dr. Billy Jim Layton, Chairperson.

The State University of New York at Stony Brook is one of the four university centers of the SUNY system. The 1,117-acre campus has 95 buildings in a suburban area on the north shore of Long Island, 60 miles east of New York City.

The Department of Music offers graduate and undergraduate programs. The undergraduate major in music is designed as a balanced educational program that serves as preparation for professional careers and advanced training in performance, composition, and teaching. Graduate programs are offered with emphases in composition, music history, music theory, and performance.

Accreditation. Middle States Association of Colleges and Schools.

Academic Information

Enrollment, Music Majors. (Total University) 14,360.
Music Faculty. 19; teaching assistants 58.
Term System. Semester.
Entrance Requirements. High school graduation or equivalent; completion of 4 units English; 3 mathematics, 3 foreign language, 3 science; SAT required; theory placement examination and audition required. GRE required for graduate study.
Admission Procedure. Application with supporting documents and nonrefundable $10 fee to Office of Admissions.

Music Degrees Offered. Bachelor of Arts; Master of Arts; Master of Music; Doctor of Musical Arts; Doctor of Philosophy.

Music Degree Requirements. The Bachelor of Arts degree is offered with majors in performance, composition, music theory, and music history and literature.

The Department offers programs leading to the Master of Arts degree and the Doctor of Philosophy degree in music with studies in music history, music theory, and composition. Also offered are programs leading to the Master of Music degree and the Doctor of Musical Arts degree in music performance. A special emphasis in each of these programs is the music of the twentieth century.

General Program Areas. Composition, Music History, Music Literature, Music Theory, Performance, Twentieth Century Music..

Instruments Taught. Bass, Bassoon, Clarinet, Flute, Guitar, Horn, Oboe, Percussion, Piano, Trombone, Trumpet, Tuba, Viola, Violin, Violoncello, Voice.

Musical Facilities

Practice Facilities. The Department of Music is housed in the Fine Arts Center. The Music Building contains a full range of rehearsal and teaching facilities, over 70 practice rooms and studios and more than 40 Steinway grand pianos. A fully equipped Electronic Music Studio complex provides advanced facilities for electronic music composition.

Concert Facilities. Main Theatre, seating 1,100; Recital Hall, 400; Student Union Auditorium, 365.

Concerts/Musical Activities. The Fine Arts Center schedules more than 50 major events during the year in addition to the more than 200 recitals and concerts by visiting artists, students, and faculty.

Music Library. The Music Library contains an extensive research collection of books, periodicals, scores, microfilms, and recordings. Listening facilities are available.

Special Programs

Featured Programs. The Bach Aria Festival and Institute supports forty young professional musicians on fellowships who study and perform the music of J.S. Bach with the members of the Bach Aria Group.

Performance Groups. University Orchestra, University Chorus, Wind Ensemble, Collegium Musicum, Chamber Chorus, Chamber Symphony, Concert Band, Gospel Choir.

Financial

Costs. Per academic year: Tuition in-state resident $1,350, out-of-state $3,200. Fees $127. Room $1,750. Board $1,360.

Financial Aid. Financial aid is awarded on the basis of academic merit and financial need. Forms of aid include scholarships, grants, loans, and part-time employment. Tuition waivers and graduate stipends are awarded to performance majors forming resident chamber ensembles. Scholarship/financial aid application due March 15.

State University of New York College at Fredonia
School of Music
Mason Hall
Fredonia
New York 14063

Telephone. (716) 673-3151

Chief Administrator. Dr. Patrick T. McMullen, Director.

The State University of New York College at Fredonia began as the Fredonia Academy in 1826 and became one of the new State Normal Schools in 1867. In 1948, when the State University of New York was established, Fredonia was designated as one of the eleven teacher colleges within the University. Its sole purpose was to prepare elementary school and music teachers. In 1961, the present name was adopted and the status of the institution reflected its expanded mission of serving the needs of the region and state in a variety of undergraduate and master's level graduate programs. The campus is located 45 miles from Buffalo in the community of Fredonia (population 11,000).

The School of Music is a multi-purpose education unit which offers professional and liberal arts programs plus instruction for music minors and the non-music major. All qualified students are admitted directly to the music program. However, since many first-year students have not yet decided on a specific major in music, the program of study in the first year is essentially the same for all students.

Accreditation. Middle States Association of Colleges and Schools; National Association of Schools of Music.

Academic Information

Enrollment, Music Majors. 400.

Music Faculty. Full-time 37, part-time 8.

Term System. Semester. Academic year from late August to mid-May. Two 6-week summer sessions from mid-May to early August.

Entrance Requirements. Each applicant's credentials are reviewed on an individual basis by Admissions Committee; they consider academic preparation, performance, special talents, and potential for success. Admission is competitive and determined by an evaluation of academic credentials, the music audition, and the number of spaces available in the program.

Admission Procedure. Application with supporting documents to Director of Admissions.

Music Degrees Offered. Bachelor of Arts; Bachelor of Fine Arts; Bachelor of Music; Bachelor of Science.

Music Degree Requirements. The Bachelor of Arts degree is offered with majors in applied music, theory/composition, and history of music. The Bachelor of Fine Arts degree is offered in musical theatre. The Bachelor of Music degree is offered with majors in performance and music education with certification to teach in the public schools. Concentrations for the music education major include general choral and instrumental. The Bachelor of Science degree is offered with majors in sound recording and music therapy. All baccalaureate programs have a prescribed curriculum including the general education and freshman music program requirements.

General Program Areas. Applied Music, Composition, Music Business, Music Education, Music History, Music Theory, Music Therapy, Musical Theatre, Performance, Sound Recording Technology.

Instruments Taught. Bass, Bassoon, Clarinet, Euphonium, Flute, French Horn, Guitar, Harp, Oboe, Organ, Percussion, Piano, Saxophone, Trombone, Trumpet, Tuba, Viola, Violin, Violoncello, Voice.

Musical Facilities

Practice Facilities. 130 practice rooms. 5 Schlicker organs. Special practice facilities for percussionists. 220 pianos (uprights, studio and concert grands); 6 grand pianos reserved for piano majors. Electronic music studio; 2 electronic piano laboratories.

Concert Facilities. Diers Recital Hall, seating 250; King Concert Hall, 1,100; Marvel Theatre, 400; Bartlett Theatre, 200.

Concerts/Musical Activities. 90 student recitals, ensemble concerts, 20 faculty recitals, guest artists, workshops; opera, musical theatre productions.

Music Library. 20,000 volumes; 40,000 musical scores; 60 audiovisual materials (titles); 150 microform titles; 20,000 phonograph records; 800 audiocassettes. 28 listening stations (stereo). Orchestra Library, Music Education Materials, and Choral Library housed in Music Building Library.

Special Programs

Featured Programs. The Sound Recording Technology program is modeled after the Tonmeister programs developed in Germany and England and is adapted to American recording industry practices and commercial expectations. The program is designed to provide undergraduate students with academic and professional preparation necessary for careers in music sound recording, and related professions in technical, artistic, and management positions.

Performance Groups. Symphony Orchestra, Wind Ensemble, Symphonic Band, All-College Band, Fredonia Chamber Singers, College Choir, Piano Ensemble, Percussion Ensemble, Festival Chorus, Saxophone Ensemble, Lyric Theatre Workshop, Opera Theatre, Jazz Workshop.

Foreign Programs. Semester of study in Vienna, Austria; students with good background in German language may qualify for a year of study at a German university.

Financial

Costs. Per academic year: Tuition in-state $1,350, out-of-state $3,200. Room $1,550. Board $650 to $1,340.

Financial Aid. Music scholarships are awarded to qualified new and returning students. Factors considered in awarding scholarships are financial need, music talent, academic achievement, and service to the School of Music. Other sources of financial aid include institutional and state/federal grants and loans, part-time employment, and a College Work-Study program.

State University of New York College at New Paltz
Department of Music
New Paltz
New York 12561

Telephone. (914) 257-2404
Chief Administrator. Dr. Peter Alexander, Chair.

The College at New Paltz was established in 1828 and is now a unit of the SUNY system. The College is located in the mid-Hudson region of New York, 95 miles north of New York City.

The Department of Music encourages flexibility in the planning of individual programs, both for those who wish to major in music and for those who may wish to acquaint themselves with this facet of our culture. Most music courses reflect an integrated approach to the study of music.

Accreditation. Middle States Association of Colleges and Schools; National Association of Schools of Music; National Association for Music Therapy.

Academic Information

Enrollment, Music Majors. (Total University) 7,392.
Music Faculty. 17.
Term System. Semester.
Entrance Requirements. Freshman applicants should have taken a strong scholastic program, including work in English, social studies, mathematics, laboratory science, and foreign language; SAT or ACT required; audition required (two solos on the major instrument, scales, and sight reading); interview with the chair; placement test.
Admission Procedure. Application with supporting documents and nonrefundable $15 fee to Office of Admissions.
Music Degrees Offered. Bachelor of Arts; Bachelor of Science.

Music Degree Requirements. The Bachelor of Arts degree is offered with concentrations in applied music, music history and literature, and music theory and composition. The Bachelor of Science degree in music therapy, with a separate set of requirements, is also available. The Department of Music does not have a program leading toward a graduate degree in music. However, the Department offers graduate courses appropriate to graduate degrees in other departments.

General Program Areas. Applied Music, Composition, Music History, Music Literature, Music Theory, Music Therapy.

Instruments Taught. Brass, Guitar, Organ, Percussion, Piano, Stringed Instruments, Trumpet, Voice, Woodwinds.

Musical Facilities

Concert Facilities. McKenna Theatre, seating 374; Parker Theatre, 199; Old Main Auditorium, 710.

Concerts/Musical Activities. Over 100 performances are presented yearly in the College's theatres including an extensive schedule of music and theatre during the summer season; student/faculty concerts and recitals.

Music Library. The Sojourner Truth Library supports the educational programs of the College with a collection of more than 350,000 books and 250,000 microeditions.

Special Programs

Performance Groups. College-Community Chorale, Symphonic Band, Concert Choir, Collegium Musicum, Chamber Singers, Jazz Ensemble, Instrumental Chamber Ensemble.

Financial

Costs. Per academic year: Tuition in-state resident $1,350, out-of-state $3,200. Fees $145. Room $1,640. Board $1,240.

Financial Aid. Financial aid is awarded on the basis of academic merit and financial need. State/federal aid is available in the form of scholarships, grants, loans, and part-time employment. Financial aid/scholarship application due February 15.

State University of New York College at Potsdam
Crane School of Music
Pierrepont Avenue
Potsdam
New York 13676

Telephone. (315) 267-2413, 267-2415
Chief Administrator. Dr. Thomas Tyra, Dean.

The SUNY College at Potsdam was founded in 1816 as St. Lawrence Academy. It became the Potsdam Normal School in 1867, the Potsdam State Teachers College in 1942, and part of the State University of New York in 1948. In 1962, the institution became the State University College of Arts and Sciences at Potsdam. The 250-acre campus is located in the city of Potsdam in the state's "North Country" in the St. Lawrence Valley.

The Crane Institute of Music, the first music school in the United States to prepare teachers for the public schools, became a major division of the College in 1926. The school is named for Julia E. Crane who began the program to prepare well-rounded musicians. Undergraduate programs are offered with majors in music education and performance. A Business of Music minor is available which is designed as a flexible course of study leading participants into career interest areas in the music business including arts administration, the recording industry, music publishing, music criticism, broadcast industry, unions and guilds, and music merchandising. The Crane School also offers programs leading to the Master of Music in composition, music education, music history and literature, performance, and theory. These programs are designed to meet students' interests, needs, and requirements within a framework that provides opportunities to pursue a balance of academic and professionally oriented courses.

Accreditation. Middle States Association of Colleges and Schools; National Association of Schools of Music.

Academic Information

Enrollment, Music Majors. Full-time 146 men, 182 women. 2 foreign students.

Music Faculty. Full-time 36, part-time 6.

Term System. Semester. One summer session.

Entrance Requirements. High school graduation or equivalent with rank in upper 40 percent; completion of 16 units; SAT or ACT required; personal interview and audition required.

Admission Procedure. Application and $15 nonrefundable fee accepted on a rolling basis.

Music Degrees Offered. Bachelor of Music; Bachelor of Arts; Master of Music.

Music Degree Requirements. The baccalaureate degrees require the completion of a total of 124 to 128 semester hours. Specific curricula are offered in the various major concentrations. The Master of Music degree requires the completion of 30 semester hours of study.

General Program Areas. Composition, Music Business, Music Education, Music History, Music Literature, Music Theory, Performance.

Instruments Taught. Bass, Bassoon, Clarinet, Euphonium, Flute, Guitar, Harpsichord, Horn, Oboe, Organ, Percussion, Piano, Trumpet, Tuba, Violin, Violoncello, Voice.

Musical Facilities

Practice Facilities. 70 practice rooms. 4 organs (Schlicker, Moeller, Shantz, Wicks). 10 percussion-equipped practice rooms. 40 practice pianos (33 uprights, 7 grands); 8 grand pianos reserved for piano majors. 3 recording studios; electronic music studio; music education laboratory; 2 electronic piano classrooms; computer laboratory in Piano Pedagogy Library.

Concert Facilities. Hosmer Hall, seating 1,400; Snell Music Theater, 450.

Concerts/Musical Activities. Over 260 concerts and recitals are performed each year.

Music Library. 21,500 volumes; 11,500 scores; 1,900 bound periodicals; 1,500 microfiche; 13,600 recordings; 140 current periodical titles. Listening facilities (37 turntables, 5 tape decks). Special collections include the Crane School of Music Archives.

Special Programs

Performance Groups. Band, Brass Choir, Brass Quintet, Choirs, Clarinet Choir, Contemporary Music Ensemble, Flute Ensemble, Guitar Ensemble, Horn Ensemble, Jazz Ensemble, Opera Ensemble, Orchestra, Percussion Ensemble, Saxophone Ensemble, Saxophone Quartets, String Quartets, Trombone Ensemble, Trombone Octet, Wind Ensemble, Woodwind Quintet.

Financial

Costs. Per academic year: Tuition in-state resident $1,350, out-of-state $3,200. Room $1,500. Board $1,300.

Financial Aid. Scholarships, grants, loans, part-time employment, and a College Work-Study program are available. Financial aid/scholarship application due March 1.

Commentary

The Crane School of Music has long enjoyed a reputation as a strong training ground for public school music teachers.

State University of New York College at Purchase
Division of Music

Lincoln Avenue
Purchase
New York 10577

Telephone. (914) 253-5031

Chief Administrator. Alvin Brehm, Dean.

The State University of New York College at Purchase began classes in 1971. The campus is located in the town of Purchase, 30 miles north of New York City.

The Division of Music offers a comprehensive musical education for a limited number of gifted students who wish to pursue the art of music at a professional level. Performance and composition are the basis of the curriculum. In exceptional cases, an interdisciplinary or divided major may be devised. The program provides thorough grounding in musicianship, theory, and ear training as the solid foundation for a professional career in music.

Accreditation. Middle States Association of Colleges and Schools.

Academic Information

Enrollment, Music Majors. (Total College) 3,875.
Music Faculty. 27.
Term System. Semester. One summer session.
Entrance Requirements. High school graduation or equivalent; SAT or ACT; audition required.
Admission Procedure. Application with supporting documents and nonrefundable $15 fee to Office of Admissions.
Music Degrees Offered. Bachelor of Arts.
Music Degree Requirements. The Bachelor of Arts curriculum is basically the same for all students throughout the four years and focuses primarily on performance. Actual study is in most instances either private or in small groups, allowing for flexibility of approach and for varying levels of advancement. The four principal areas of study are musicianship, performance, composition, and history-musicology.
General Program Areas. Composition, Conducting, Music History, Music Theory, Musicology, Performance.
Instruments Taught. Bass, Bassoon, Clarinet, Flute, Guitar, Harp, Harpsichord, Horn, Oboe, Organ, Percussion, Piano, Trombone, Trumpet, Tuba, Viola, Violin, Violoncello, Voice.

Musical Facilities

Practice Facilities. The Music Building provides large, acoustically isolated spaces for practice and teaching. A variety of rehearsal halls for chamber ensembles and large ensembles are available as well as a recital hall and an opera studio. The Building also houses several electronic music studios and recording facilities.
Concert Facilities. Performing Arts Center consists of four theater-concert halls.
Concerts/Musical Activities. Student/faculty recitals and concerts; visiting artists.
Music Library. The Library collection includes over 190,000 volumes. Collections of slides and sound recordings are available. Special collections include: Collection of New York Pro Musica; unpublished music by American composers (donated by Oliver Daniel).

Special Programs

Performance Groups. Orchestra, Woodwind Ensemble, Purchase Jazz Ensemble, Percussion Ensemble, Guitar Ensemble, Chamber Ensemble.

Financial

Costs. Per academic year: Tuition in-state resident $1,350, out-of-state $3,200. Fees $174. Room $1,822. Board $1,255.

Financial Aid. Financial aid is awarded on the basis of academic merit and financial need. State/federal aid is available in the form of scholarships, grants, loans, and part-time employment. Financial aid/scholarship application due March 15.

Syracuse University
School of Music
College of Visual and Performing Arts
Syracuse
New York 13244

Telephone. (315) 423-2191
Chief Administrator. Dr. George Pappastavrou, Director.

Syracuse University is a private institution with an enrollment of 12,000 undergraduates and 4,000 graduate students. The University is organized into 21 major academic units. It was founded in 1870. The 230-acre campus is located in a residential section at the southeastern edge of Syracuse in central New York.

The School of Music offers programs in performance, composition, music education, and music industry. The music education program is a dual program offered in conjunction with the School of Education. All students take a core program for the first two years to establish a firm foundation in basic musicianship. The final two years are devoted to a heavy concentration in the area of choice. The performance program stresses the development of technical skills, repertory, poise, and overall musicianship. The program in composition offers the opportunity to develop a wide range of musical skills, including a broad musical background, solid performance skills on at least one instrument, thorough training in music theory and music history, and a working knowledge of instrumentation and orchestration. The dual program with the School of Education prepares the student to teach music in the public schools of New York and other reciprocating states. The music industry program focuses on developing a high level of musical competency and to become knowledgeable about the theoretical and practical activities of the industry.

Accreditation. Middle States Association of Colleges and Schools; National Association of Schools of Music; National Council for Accreditation of Teacher Education.

Academic Information

Enrollment, Music Majors. Full-time 55 men, 65 women; part-time 5 men, 10 women. 5 foreign students.
Music Faculty. Full-time 20, part-time 35.
Term System. Semester. Academic year from September 1 to May 15. Two 6-week summer sessions from mid-May to early August.

Entrance Requirements. High school graduation; completion of 16 units; 2.5 minimum GPA; 1100 combined score on SAT; proficiency in a performance area; musical sensitivity; discriminating ear; audition required.

Admission Procedure. Application with supporting documents to Office of Admissions.

Music Degrees Offered. Bachelor of Music; Master of Music.

Music Degree Requirements. The Bachelor of Music degree is offered with concentrations in performance, composition, music education, and music industry. The degree requires the completion of 32 credits in the major area, 8 credits in the minor area, 46 credits in music theory and music history, 30 credits of academic subjects, and 12 elective credits for a total of 128 credits. The Bachelor of Arts degree with a major in music is offered for students in the context of a liberal arts program. The Master of Music degree requires the completion of 8 credits in the major, 3 credits in research, 18 credits in music history and music theory, and 6 credits in academic electives for a total of 35 credits.

General Program Areas. Composition, Music Education, Music History, Music Industry, Music Theory, Performance.

Instruments Taught. Bassoon, Clarinet, Euphonium, Flute, French Horn, Guitar, Harpsichord, Oboe, Organ, Percussion, Piano, Trumpet, Tuba, Viola, Violin, Violoncello.

Musical Facilities

Practice Facilities. 26 practice rooms. 3 organs (3,816-pipe Holtkamp organ is located in Crouse Auditorium). Percussion-equipped practice facilities. 30 pianos; 9 grand pianos reserved for piano majors. Electronic music studio (digital).

Concert Facilities. Crouse College Auditorium, seating 700; Goldstein Auditorium, 1,800.

Community Facilities. Civic Center; Crouse-Hinds Auditorium; Carrier Theatre.

Concerts/Musical Activities. The Crouse Concerts, held each Sunday afternoon during the academic year and on many evenings, comprise one of the oldest series of its kind in the United States. Faculty recitals performed weekly; daily student recitals; performing organizations present 2 to 3 concerts per semester.

Music Library. Most music materials housed in main library. 24,000 volumes; 28,500 musical scores; 20,000 audiovisual items; 8,000 phonograph recordings; 2,000 audiocassettes. 54 listening stations. Special collections include: family of viols; extensive collection of Renaissance and early Baroque instruments; four harpsichords; re-recording library converting obsolete forms of sound recordings; 17th century central European music. Choral library and orchestral library housed in the School of Music. Individual faculty collections; Belfer Archives.

Special Programs

Performance Groups. Ensembles, orchestra, band, choral groups.

Foreign Programs. The School of Music offers a three-week summer program in Vevey, Switzerland, called L'Ecole Hindemith. Classes are held at the Conservatoire de Vevy. Institut de Ribaupierre Concerts given by faculty, students, and guest artists are presented in the twelfth-century church of St. Legier-La Chiesaz.

Financial

Costs. Per academic year: Tuition $8,710. Fees $260. Room $2,150. Board $2,120.

Financial Aid. Financial aid is awarded on the basis of academic merit, financial need, musical ability. 100 music students receive some form of financial aid; average award $5,000. Institutional and state/federal aid and a College Work-Study program are available. Financial aid/scholarship application due January 31.

Commentary

Syracuse University's String Fellowship Program arranges for string students to play concerts with members of the Syracuse Symphony Orchestra while receiving lessons from the orchestra's principal players.

Teachers College of Columbia University
Department of Music and Music Education
525 West 120th Street
New York
New York 10027

Telephone. (212) 678-3283

Chief Administrator. Dr. Robert Pace, Program Coordinator.

Teachers College of Columbia University, a graduate professional school of education, was founded in 1887. It became formally affiliated with Columbia University in 1898 and all degrees are granted through the University. The main group of ten Teachers College buildings is situated on Morningside Heights, adjoining the main campus of the University.

The faculty in Music and Music Education strives to offer flexible and individualized programs for the preparation of music educators. Since the program's beginning as a department of Vocal Music in 1888, two basic areas of music education have been emphasized: the development of musicianship and skill in theory/composition and history/literature combined with artistry and proficiency in performance; and the advancement of knowledge, ideas, and skills concerning the nature of education, its social application, and the teacher-learner process. Analytical, philosophical, and historical methodologies and research-based practice are offered for the investigation of the origins and directions of educational policy as it pertains to the teaching and learning of music.

Accreditation. Middle States Association of Colleges and Schools; National Council for Accreditation of Teacher Education.

Academic Information

Enrollment, Music Majors. (Total College) 4,155.

Term System. Semester. Two summer sessions.

Entrance Requirements. Bachelor's degree or equivalent; GRE; advisory examination in theory, literature, and performance.

Admission Procedure. Application with supporting documents and nonrefundable $25 fee reviewed on a rolling admissions basis; apply to Teachers College Office of Admissions.

Music Degrees Offered. Master of Arts, Master of Education; Doctor of Education.

Music Degree Requirements. The graduate programs are designed to prepare students for teaching and supervision of music in elementary and secondary schools; teaching and administration of music in colleges and universities; as teachers of music in private schools and private studios; for research and practice of music in institutions of higher learning; and for positions in the interdisciplinary areas of arts and humanities, music and special education, and adult education.

The Master of Arts degree provides studies in the student's music specialization with a balance among performance, literature, theory, and pedagogy. The Master of Education degree is designed to prepare students as music educators in elementary schools, secondary schools, and colleges, emphasizing instructional skills, curriculum development, and administration and supervision of music programs.

The Doctor of Education degree is for students who desire to teach or administer music education, research, theory, and practice in schools and in higher education. The Doctor of Education degree in college teaching of an academic subject is an advanced degree offering students with high-level performance and composition skills the opportunity of writing a dissertation directly related to a recital, lecture-demonstration, or performance of an original composition.

A new arts-in-education Certificate program strives to train arts professionals to share their knowledge with students in the format of school arts residencies.

General Program Areas. Conducting, Music History, Music Literature, Pedagogy, Performance.

Instruments Taught. Baritone, Bass, Bassoon, Clarinet, Flute, French Horn, Guitar, Harp, Harpsichord, Oboe, Organ, Percussion, Piano, Recorder, Renaissance Instruments, Saxophone, Trombone, Trumpet, Tuba, Viola, Violin, Violoncello, Voice.

Musical Facilities

Music Library. The Milbank Memorial Library is housed in Russell Hall and contains the largest and richest collection of education materials in the world.

Special Programs

Featured Programs. The Department of Music and Arts in Education brings together faculty in the visual, performing, and literary arts who share a common concern for the centrality of the arts in education and throughout the life span. Teacher education programs in music, art, and dance are coordinated with teacher education programs in the Department of Curriculum and Teaching and other subject matter areas. Designed to prepare teachers for leadership roles in schools, this joint endeavor brings together students from various disciplines to study both the generic issues of schooling and the special problems facing other subject areas.

Financial

Costs. Per academic year: Tuition $6,560. Room $2,-650.

Financial Aid. A wide variety of financial resources are available to Teachers College students including state, federal, and institutional. Financial aid application due February 1.

NORTH CAROLINA

Appalachian State University
Department of Music
College of Arts and Sciences
Boone
North Carolina 28608

Telephone. (704) 262-3020

Chief Administrator. B.G. McCloud, Chairman.

Appalachian State University is part of the system of public higher education in the state of North Carolina. It evolved from Watauga Academy founded in 1899 and became part of the consolidated University of North Carolina in 1971. The 250-acre campus is located on the crest of the Blue Ridge Mountains in the city of Boone.

The objective of the Department of Music is the development of those elements which relate to the teaching, creation, business, and appreciation of music.

Accreditation. Southern Association of Colleges and Schools; National Association of Schools of Music; National Council for Accreditation of Teacher Education.

Academic Information

Enrollment, Music Majors. (Total University) 8,894.

Music Faculty. 23.

Term System. Semester. Two summer sessions.

Entrance Requirements. High school graduation or equivalent; presentation of a satisfactory combination of secondary school class rank and SAT or ACT; 4 units English, 3 mathematics, 2 social studies, 3 science; satisfactory health record; audition required.

Admission Procedure. Application with supporting documents to Office of Admissions.

Music Degrees Offered. Bachelor of Music; Bachelor of Arts; Bachelor of Science; Master of Music.

Music Degree Requirements. The Bachelor of Music degree is offered in performance with the following tracks: church music, theory/composition, piano pedagogy, vocal and instrumental. The degree is also offered in music education. All students in this program are required to meet certification as set by the North Carolina State Department of Public Instruction. The Bachelor of Arts degree in music is offered as a liberal arts program. The Bachelor of Science degree with a major in music merchandising is also available.

The Department offers two degree programs under the Master of Music degree: the Master of Music in music teaching and supervision and the Master of Music in community/junior college teaching.

General Program Areas. Applied Music, Church Music, Composition, Music Education, Music Theory, Performance, Piano Pedagogy.

Instruments Taught. Brass, Organ, Percussion, Piano, Stringed Instruments, Voice, Woodwinds.

Musical Facilities

Practice Facilities. The Department of Music is located in the Broyhill Music Center.

Concerts/Musical Activities. Student and faculty concerts and recitals; visiting artists.

Music Library. The Music Library contains music reference, scores, recordings, and a collection of material about the South Appalachian region including recordings of authentic folk music, oral history tapes, printed ballads, shape-note tunebooks, and musical instruments. The William Leonard Eury Appalachian Collection also includes material dealing with the Southern Appalachian region. Listening facilities available.

Special Programs

Performance Groups. Marching Band, Symphonic Band, Wind Ensemble, Brass Choir, Stage Band, Appalachian Symphony Orchestra, Chamber Orchestra, Clarinet Ensemble, String Quartet, Baroque Ensemble, University Singers, Appalachian Chorale, Treble Choir, Glee Club, Chamber Singers, Opera Workshop, Piano Ensemble, Percussion Ensemble.

Financial

Costs. Per academic year: Tuition in-state resident $833, out-of-state $2,826. Applied music courses $18 per credit hour. Room and board $1,650.

Financial Aid. Scholarships, grants, loans, and part-time employment are available. Scholarship/financial aid application due March 15.

Duke University
Department of Music
Trinity College of Arts and Sciences
Durham
North Carolina 27706

Telephone. (919) 684-2534

Chief Administrator. Dr. Peter Frederic Williams, Chairman.

Duke University is a private institution founded in 1838. It was reorganized as Trinity College in 1859 and became Duke University in 1924. The 878-acre campus has 177 buildings in the city of Durham in central North Carolina.

The Department of Music of the Trinity College of Arts and Sciences offers the major in music. Within the curriculum, students have the major responsibility for designing and maintaining course programs appropriate to their backgrounds and goals. They are assisted by faculty advisers, departmental directors, and academic deans.

Accreditation. Southern Association of Colleges and Schools.

Academic Information

Enrollment, Music Majors. (Total University) 9,753.

Music Faculty. 24.

Term System. Semester.

Entrance Requirements. Completion of 15 college preparatory units; SAT and 3 Achievement Tests preferred.

Admission Procedure. Application with supporting documents and nonrefundable $20 fee to Admissions Office.

Music Degrees Offered. Bachelor of Arts; Bachelor of Science; Master of Arts; Doctor of Philosophy.

Music Degree Requirements. The Bachelor of Arts and Bachelor of Science degrees are available with emphasis in music theory/composition and performance. Thirty-two courses are required for graduation.

The Department offers graduate work leading to the Master of Arts degree in composition or musicology and the Doctor of Philosophy degree in musicology. Students may be admitted to the Program in Medieval and Renaissance Studies.

General Program Areas. Applied Music, Composition, Ethnomusicology, Music History, Music Literature, Music Theory, Musicology.

Instruments Taught. Brass, Harpsichord, Organ, Piano, Stringed Instruments, Voice, Woodwinds.

Musical Facilities

Concerts/Musical Activities. Student and faculty concerts and recitals; series by resident Ciompi Quartet; visiting artists.

Music Library. The Department of Music has a record collection separate from the university libraries with facilities for listening to records and tapes. The libraries contain a Confederate Imprints Collection.

Special Programs

Performance Groups. Symphony Orchestra, Wind Symphony, Marching Band, Jazz Ensemble, Chamber Music, Collegium Musicum, Opera Workshop, Chapel Choir, Chorale.

Financial

Costs. Per academic year: Tuition $9,180. Fees $288. Room $1,508. Board $2,080.

Financial Aid. Scholarships, loans, grants, and part-time employment are available. Scholarship/financial aid application due February 1.

Commentary

Duke University has distinguished programs in composition and musicology. Although the performance faculty includes the noted Ciompi Quartet, the music department's orientation is largely academic and embodied in its Ph.D. program in musicology.

East Carolina University
School of Music
East 10th Street
Greenville
North Carolina 27834

Telephone. (919) 757-6851

Chief Administrator. Dr. Charles E. Stevens, Dean.

East Carolina University was founded in 1907 as a state-supported normal school. It became a four-year college in 1920 and achieved university status in 1967. It now has a student population of over 14,000. The University is a comprehensive instiution of higher learning and is a constituent of the University of North Carolina System. The 400-acre campus is within the city of Greenville in the east central part of North Carolina.

The School of Music offers programs which foster the development of musicianship and help realize to the fullest all potential of its students. Each music major or minor is required to have a major performance medium in any of the following areas: piano, organ, voice, string, woodwind, brass, or percussion. Private instruction in the chosen medium is required throughout the four-year program of study.

Accreditation. Southern Association of Colleges and Schools; National Association of Schools of Music; National Association of Music Therapists.

Academic Information

Enrollment, Music Majors. Full-time 146 men, 164 women. 7 foreign students.

Music Faculty. Full-time 42, part-time 5.

Term System. Semester. Two summer sessions.

Entrance Requirements. High school graduation or equivalent; minimum age of 16 by date of intended registration; completion of 20 units including 4 English, 3 mathematics, 3 laboratory science, 2 foreign language, 2 social studies, 6 electives; SAT or ACT required; audition required (in person or tape evaluated by minimum of three faculty members). Miller Analogies Test or GRE required for graduate study.

Admission Procedure. Application with nonrefundable $15 fee accepted on a rolling basis.

Music Degrees Offered. Bachelor of Music; Bachelor of Arts; Master of Music.

Music Degree Requirements. The Bachelor of Music degree is offered with majors in performance, church music, theory-composition, piano pedagogy, voice pedagogy, music education, music therapy, and music with elective studies in business. Minimum requirements for the degree range from 127 to 132 semester hours including 44 semester hours in general education courses. The Bachelor of Arts degree with a major in music is offered within the context of a liberal arts program and requires the completion of 124 semester hours including the general education requirements.

The Master of Music degree is offered with majors in performance, church music, music education, composition, piano pedagogy, accompanying.

General Program Areas. Accompanying, Church Music, Composition, Conducting, Music Education, Music Theory, Music Therapy, Performance, Piano Pedagogy, Voice Pedagogy.

Instruments Taught. Baritone, Bass, Bassoon, Clarinet, English Horn, Flute, French Horn, Oboe, Organ, Percussion, Piano, Piccolo, Saxophone, Trombone, Trumpet, Tuba, Viola, Violin, Violoncello, Voice.

Musical Facilities

Practice Facilities. 70 practice rooms. 5 pipe organs (13-stop Tracker in Recital Hall, 11 rank studio instrument and 3 practice organs). 113 pianos (65 in practice rooms of which 6 are grand pianos reserved for piano majors). Electronic music studio; 2 class piano studios.

Concert Facilities. A.J. Fletcher Recital Hall; Hendrix Theater; Wright Auditorium.

Community Facilities. Local churches.

Concerts/Musical Activities. Artists Series, Chamber Music Series, faculty recital series, student recitals, concerts by performing organizations.

Music Library. 20,691 books, phonographs, and periodicals. 960 reels microfilm. Listening facilities (5 cassette players, 1 compact disc player, 2 open reel tape decks, 8 turntables).

Special Programs

Performance Groups. Concert Choir, University Chorale, Men's Glee Club, Women's Chorus, Women's Glee Club, Chamber Singers, Marching Band, Concert Band, Wind Ensemble, Symphony Orchestra, Symphonic Band, Opera Theatre, String Chamber Music, Woodwind Chamber Music, Percussion Chamber Music, Saxophone Chamber Music, Collegium Musicum, Jazz Ensemble, Brass Chamber Music, Keyboard Chamber Music, Contemporary Chamber Music, Vocal Chamber Music.

Foreign Programs. Summer program in Ferrara, Italy.

Financial

Costs. Per academic year: Tuition in-state resident $746, out-of-state $3,304. Fees $354. Room $890. Board $1,120.

Financial Aid. 106 music scholarships awarded ranging from $100 to $1,500 (average $311). Scholarship application due by audition date in April. Other sources of financial aid include institutional and state/federal grants and loans, part-time employment, and a College Work-Study program.

University of North Carolina at Chapel Hill Department of Music
Hill Hall 020A
Chapel Hill
North Carolina 27514

Telephone. (919) 933-1039

Chief Administrator. Thomas Warburton, Chair.

The University of North Carolina began classes in 1795. It was the first state university in the United States to award state university diplomas to students. The University enrolls over 21,000 students and has a faculty of 1,880. The campus is located in Chapel Hill, a community in the central part of the state.

The Department of Music was founded in 1919 and began with four courses and a Glee Club. In 1934, under the chairmanship of Glen Haydon, graduate programs were instituted. The Department offers three curricula for undergraduates. All of these include a basic core of music theory, history, and literature courses. Each curriculum also requires that students be involved in performance throughout all or most of their undergraduate residency, both through private instruction and practice and through participation in ensembles. Graduate programs lead to the Master of Music and Doctor of Philosophy degrees.

Accreditation. Southern Association of Colleges and Schools; National Council for Accreditation of Teacher Education.

Academic Information

Enrollment, Music Majors. Undergraduate 85, graduate 50.

Music Faculty. Full-time 28, part-time 5.

Term System. Semesters. 9-week summer session from June to August. Academic year from August to May.

Entrance Requirements. High school graduation; 16 units with 4 English, 3 mathematics, 1 laboratory science, 1 social studies. SAT; minimum verbal and math combined score 800 required; audition required for transfer students, advised for freshmen. TOEFL for foreign students. GRE required for graduate study.

Admission Procedure. Application with $25 non-refundable fee due October 15, December 1, or January 15.

Music Degrees Offered. Bachelor of Music; Bachelor of Arts; Bachelor of Music Education; Master of Music; Master of Arts.

Music Degree Requirements. The Bachelor of Music degree places emphasis on intensive training in music performance or composition, backed by music theory, history and literature, and balanced by as rich an an experience in the liberal arts as the program will allow. The Bachelor of Music Education degree (administered by the School of Education) emphasizes music teaching and qualifies the student for the North Carolina Class A teaching certificate while also providing the requisite background in music theory, history and literature, and performance. The Bachelor of Arts degree provides a broad education in the liberal arts as well as more specialized training in music theory, history and literature, and performance. The baccalaureate degrees require the completion of 124 to 126 semester hours.

Graduate work in the Department of Music offers programs of study to students who intend to specialize in musicology, music history and literature, composition, performance, and choral conducting. The Department offers the Master of Arts degree in music history and literature; the Master of Music degree in composition or performance, including choral conducting; and the Doctor of Philosophy degree in musicology.

General Program Areas. Choral Conducting, Composition, Music Education, Music History, Music Literature, Music Theory, Musicology, Performance.

Instruments Taught. Bass, Bassoon, Clarinet, Flute, French Horn, Guitar, Harp, Harpsichord, Oboe, Organ, Percussion, Piano, Recorder, Saxophone, Trumpet, Tuba, Viola, Violin, Violoncello, Voice.

Musical Facilities

Practice Facilities. 30 practice rooms. 4 organs (2 Moeller, Schlicker, Reuter). 3 percussion-equipped practice rooms. 25 practice pianos (20 uprights, 5 grands); 5 grand pianos reserved for piano majors. Recording studio; electronic music studio.

Concert Facilities. Hill Hall Auditorium, seating 750; Person Recital Hall, 200; Hanes Art Auditorium, 200.

Concerts/Musical Activities. Ensemble performances; student and faculty recitals; visiting artists.

Music Library. 33,617 books; 56,689 scores; 750 music periodicals; 24,499 records. Listening facilities (15 cassette decks, 20 stereo turntables, 1 compact disk player).

Special collections include: opera librettos; early sheet music; New Music Quarterly; Medieval and Renaissance sources on microfilm; a Southern historical collection; folk music archive with an emphasis on North Carolina; the library of cellist Luigi Silva; Renaissance and Baroque music theory; Southern Historical Collection has material on southern composers and musical performance; manuscripts and scores of North Carolina composers.

Special Programs

Performance Groups. University Symphony, Chamber Orchestra, University Wind Symphony, New Music Ensemble, Jazz Band, Brass Chamber Ensemble, Woodwind Chamber Ensemble, Mixed Chamber Ensemble, Piano Ensemble, Marching Band, Pep Band, Concert Band, Guitar Ensemble, Percussion Ensemble, Carolina Choir, University Mixed Chorus, University Chamber Singers, Men's Glee Club, Opera Theatre, Women's Glee Club, Collegium Musicum.

Financial

Costs. Per academic year: Tuition in-state resident $480, out-of-state $3,400. Fees $314. Room $1,156. Board $1,599.

Financial Aid. 20 music scholarships awarded ranging from $250 to $2,000. Scholarship application due January 15. Other sources of financial aid include grants, loans, part-time employment, and a College Work-Study program.

Commentary

The University of North Carolina at Chapel Hill has one of the most extensive music libraries in the region. The Knapp Collection, housed at the William Haves Ackland Memorial Art Center, has a square Clementi pianoforte built in London in 1839.

University of North Carolina at Greensboro
School of Music
1000 Spring Garden Street
Greensboro
North Carolina 27412

Telephone. (919) 379-5789

Chief Administrator. Dr. Arthur R. Tollefson, Dean.

The University of North Carolina at Greensboro was chartered in 1891 to provide higher education for women. Since its founding as one of the three original institutions of the University of North Carolina, it has fostered and maintained a liberal arts tradition. In 1963, it became a comprehensive, coeducational university. The 158-acre campus is located one mile west of the central business district of Greensboro.

The School of Music offers the only comprehensive music program from undergraduate through doctoral study in both performance and music education in North Carolina.

Accreditation. Southern Association of Colleges and Schools; National Association of Schools of Music; National Council for Accreditation of Teacher Education.

Academic Information

Enrollment, Music Majors. Undergraduate 209, graduate 99.

Music Faculty. Full-time 38, part-time 10.

Term System. Semester. Two 6-week summer sessions.

Entrance Requirements. High school graduation or equivalent; completion of 15 units including 4 English, 3 mathematics, 1 laboratory science, 2 foreign language, 2 social studies; SAT required; audition required; keyboard placement test; theory examination for advanced placement.

Admission Procedure. Application with nonrefundable $25 fee due August 10 for Fall semester, December 10 for Spring semester.

Music Degrees Offered. Bachelor of Music; Bachelor of Arts; Master of Music; Doctor of Musical Arts; Doctor of Education.

Music Degree Requirements. The Bachelor of Music degree with a performance major is a professional music degree which prepares students for future careers as performers, composers, and/or teachers. It requires students to spend approximately two-thirds of their time in music study. The Bachelor of Music degree with a music education major prepares students for positions as choral directors or teachers of general music (principal performance area, usually voice, piano, guitar, or organ) or for positions as instrumental directors (principal performance area in orchestral or band instruments) in public schools. This degree program requires students to spend approximately two-thirds of their time in music study. The Bachelor of Music is also offered with a jazz studies concentration and a composition major. The Bachelor of Arts degree with a music major is a liberal arts degree which provides undergraduate preparation for a variety of careers. It requires students to spend approximately one-third of their time in music study. The baccalaureate degrees require the completion of 122 to 132 semester hours depending on the major. All programs contain all-University liberal arts requirements comprising the humanities, natural science and mathematics, and social and behavioral sciences.

Graduate study in the School of Music may lead to the degree Master of Music, the Certificate of Advanced Study (Sixth-Year Program in music education), the Doctor of Education in Music Education degree, or the Doctor of Musical Arts degree. The majors offered under the Master of Music degree include applied music (performance, vocal pedagogy, accompanying, choral conducting, instrumental conducting, and woodwinds), composition, music education, and theory. The Doctor of Musical Arts degree is offered in performance.

General Program Areas. Accompanying, Applied Music, Choral Conducting, Composition, Instrumental Conducting, Jazz Studies, Music Education, Music History, Music Literature, Music Theory, Performance, String Instrument Pedagogy, Vocal Pedagogy.

Instruments Taught. Bass, Bassoon, Clarinet, Euphonium, Flute, Guitar, Horn, Oboe, Organ, Percussion, Piano, Saxophone, Trumpet, Tuba, Viola, Viola da Gamba, Violin, Violoncello, Voice.

Musical Facilities

Practice Facilities. 40 classrooms and ensemble rooms may be used for practice at unscheduled times. 5 organs (Wicks, Schlicker, Schantz, Moeller). 11 percussion-equipped practice rooms. 62 pianos (Everette, Story and Clark, Yamaha, Steinway uprights); 18 grand pianos reserved for piano majors. Electronic music studio; electronic piano laboratory; computer theory laboratory; music education laboratory.

Concert Facilities. Recital Hall; 2 large auditoriums shared with other departments.

Concerts/Musical Activities. University Concert/Lecture Series; 6 choral organization performances; opera; symphony orchestra; 4 instrumental ensembles; Collegium Musicum; numerous small instrumental ensembles; concerts and master classes by visiting artists.

Music Library. Music books housed in Jackson Library. 11,885 books; 16,000 scores; 210 periodicals; 2,100 microfiche; 8,000 recordings. Music Listening Center (9 cassette players; 20 stereo stations). Special collections include the Luigi Silva Collection of Violoncello Music. Other resources for music students include the Fine Arts Library at North Carolina School of the Arts (Winston-Salem); music holdings of Wake Forest University (Winston-Salem), Music Library at University of North Carolina (Chapel Hill); and the Music Library at Duke University (Durham).

Special Programs

Performance Groups. University Women's Choir, Men's Glee Club, University Chorale, Symphonic Chorus, Masterworks Chorus, Chamber Singers, University Symphony Orchestra, University Wind Ensemble, University Concert Band, Jazz Ensemble, Collegium Musicum, Honors Woodwind Quintet, New Music Ensemble, Opera Chorus, Show Choir.

Foreign Programs. Summer Study Abroad program.

Affiliated Programs. UNC-Greensboro is a member of the Greensboro Regional Consortium for Higher Education. Students may cross-register at Bennett, Greensboro, Guilford, and High Point Colleges and at the North Carolina Agricultural and Technical State University.

Financial

Costs. Per academic year: Tuition in-state $480, out-of-state $3,400. Fees $248. Room $1,140 to $1,710. Board $1,050 to $1,190.

Financial Aid. 74 music scholarships awarded ranging from $100 to $1,000 (average award $407). Application for competitive scholarships due January 1; March 1 priority date for all others. Other sources of financial aid include institutional and state/federal grants and loans, part-time employment, and a College Work-Study program.

North Carolina School of the Arts
School of Music
Winston-Salem
North Carolina 27107

Telephone. (919) 784-7170
Chief Administrator. Robert Hickok, Dean.

The North Carolina School of the Arts was established in 1963. It is open, by audition, to college, high school, and younger students who have exceptional talent in dance, drama, or music. Students enrolled at the college level are expected to pursue both academic and art studies leading to the baccalaureate degree. The School is located on a 30-acre campus immediately south of the Old Salem restoration area in Winston-Salem.

The program of study in the School of Music is designed to provide both an artistic sanctuary in which each student pursues personal musical development and a professional training ground where the student is actively and realistically involved in preparing for the practical aspects of earning a living as a musician. Central to the curriculum and constant at all stages of study are private instruction and experience in public performance. Other components, such as study of music fundamentals, studies in literature and style, and other courses have been designed to support and enhance performance skills.

Accreditation. Southern Association of Colleges and Schools.

Academic Information

Enrollment, Music Majors. (Total School) 482.
Music Faculty. 37.
Term System. Trimester. One summer term.
Entrance Requirements. High school graduation or equivalent; completion of 16 units including 4 English, 1 mathematics, 2 science, 2 social science; open enrollment policy; entrance audition required.

Admission Procedure. Application with supporting documents and nonrefundable $15 fee to Office of Admissions.

Music Degrees Offered. Bachelor of Music; Performance Diploma.

Music Degree Requirements. The program leading to the Bachelor of Music degree consists of three phases, all of which are concurrent with private lessons and extensive performance experience: basic musicianship; studies in style, repertoire, specialized skills courses, and electives; the final year.

General Program Areas. Applied Music, Composition, Music Literature, Music Theory, Performance.

Instruments Taught. Brass, Organ, Percussion, Piano, Stringed Instruments, Voice, Woodwinds.

Musical Facilities

Practice Facilities. The School of Music is located in the original building of the School of the Arts and in the Workplace. Both contain teaching studios, practice rooms, offices, rehearsal rooms, classrooms, and piano laboratories. Sarah Graham Kenan Organ designed by Charles Fisk; Dowd harpsichord; Hamburg Steinway; Baldwin concert grand (all in Crawford Hall).

Concert Facilities. Crawford Hall; recital hall; Roger L. Stevens Center for the Performing Arts in downtown Winston-Salem serves as a major performance center for School of Music performances; opera productions take place in the Agnes de Mille Theater.

Concerts/Musical Activities. Student and faculty concerts and recitals; guest artists; master classes.

Music Library. Special emphasis has been placed on the performing arts in developing the book collection of 72,000 volumes. The music collection includes 28,000 scores, including critical editions of the works of the great composers, and 29,000 recordings.

Special Programs

Featured Programs. The Community Music School offers music instruction to Winston-Salem and the surrounding region on all band and orchestra instruments, piano, voice, and guitar. Summer programs are designed to provide learning experiences in music for high school and college musicians in the context of specialized workshops and seminars.

Performance Groups. Symphony Orchestra, Wind Ensemble, Chamber Chorus, Jazz Ensemble, Percussion Ensemble, Chamber Ensembles, Opera Workshop, Cantata Singers, Brass Ensemble, Saxophone Ensemble.

Foreign Programs. The School of Music's International Music Program is a summer study and performance experience for talented young orchestral and chamber music performers. The Program begins with three weeks of preparation in the United States followed by six weeks of intensive concert touring abroad.

Affiliated Programs. Piedmont Opera Theatre, a professional opera company based in Winston-Salem, involves many personnel from the School of Music.

Financial

Costs. Per academic year: Tuition in-state resident $732, out-of-state $3,290. Room and board $2,188.

Financial Aid. Discretionary scholarships are awarded to students whose audition evaluations and other records show unusual talent, ability, and potential. Other scholarships, merit awards, grants, and loans are also available.

NORTH DAKOTA

University of North Dakota
Department of Music
College of Fine Arts
Box 8124 University Station
Grand Forks
North Dakota 58201

Telephone. (701) 777-2644

Chief Administrator. Dr. James Fry, Chair.

The University of North Dakota was founded in 1883 by the Dakota Territorial Assembly. Organized initially as a College of Arts and Sciences with a Normal School for the education of teachers, the University has evolved into a multi-purpose institution. With more than 11,000 students, it is the largest postsecondary institution in the four-state region of the Dakotas, Montana, and Wyoming. The campus is situated in Grand Forks, a city of 44,000 in the Red River Valley.

Through its curricula and performance opportunities, the Department of Music serves a broad consitutency of students. Regardless of the degree program selected, all music majors are evaluated regularly through applied music jury examinations. In addition, they must pass all levels of the Piano Proficiency Sequence prior to the semester of graduation or before student teaching in music.

Accreditation. North Central Association of Colleges and Schools; National Association of Schools of Music; National Council for Accreditation of Teacher Education.

Academic Information

Enrollment, Music Majors. (College of Fine Arts) Full-time 32 men, 42 women; part-time 1 man, 7 women.

Music Faculty. Full-time 14, part-time 5.

Term System. Semester. 1 summer session.

Entrance Requirements. High school graduation or GED; completion 14 units; SAT or ACT; audition required. GRE required for graduate study.

Admission Procedure. Application with supporting documents to Office of Admissions.

Music Degrees Offered. Bachelor of Music; Bachelor of Arts.

Music Degree Requirements. The Bachelor of Music degree program offers majors in performance and music education. The performance major is designed for the student who wishes to become a professional musician and who has the ability and commitment to achieve that goal. The music education major is designed for the student who wishes to become a music teacher in the elementary and secondary schools. It is intended to develop the requisite knowledge, performance, and teaching abilities needed to function as a professional music educator. The degree requires the completion of 132 semester hours including general education and a preprofessional core curriculum. The Bachelor of Arts degree in music is offered through the College of Arts and Sciences and is designed for the student who wishes a general liberal arts education with emphasis in music. The degree requires the completion of 125 semester hours. The primary music degree program in the Center for Teaching and Learning is in music and elementary education and leads to the Bachelor of Science in Education. Students graduating from this program are certified to teach regular elementary school subjects in Grades K-8 as well as general music for those grades.

General Program Areas. Composition, Conducting, Music Education, Music History, Music Literature, Music Theory, Performance.

Instruments Taught. Brass, Carillon, Organ, Percussion, Piano, Stringed Instruments, Voice, Woodwinds.

Musical Facilities

Practice Facilities. 16 practice rooms. 2 organs (Johnson, Fargo). 14 pianos (Steinway, Grand Steinway, Hamilton Studio, Baldwin Grand, Karvi). Recording studio.

Concert Facilities. Chester Fritz Auditorium, seating 2,300; Josephine Campbell Recital Hall, 200.

Community Facilities. Local junior and senior high schools.

Music Library. Music materials are housed in the branch library collection in the College of Fine Arts.

Special Programs

Performance Groups. Concert Choir, Varsity Bards, Women's Chorus, Wind Ensemble, University Band, Symphony Orchestra, University Chamber Chorale, Community Chorus, Jazz Choir, Marching Band, Instrumental Jazz Ensemble, University Chamber Orchestra, Collegium Musicum, Chamber Music Groups.

Financial

Costs. Per academic year: Tuition in-state resident $1,-266, Minnesota resident $1,632, other out-of-state $2,-460. Room and board $1,962.

Financial Aid. Most student aid is awarded on the basis of need. Four different types of aid are offered: employment, loans, scholarships, and grants. A College-Work Study program is available.

OHIO

University of Akron
Department of Music
College of Fine and Applied Arts
Guzzetta Hall
Akron
Ohio 44325

Telephone. (216) 375-6930
Chief Administrator. Richard Shirey, Department Head.

The University of Akron was founded in 1870 as Buchtel College. In 1913, it became the Municipal University of Akron and in 1967, officially became a state university. The 150-acre campus with 70 buildings is within walking distance of downtown Akron.

The purpose of the College of Fine and Applied Arts is to provide a program of undergraduate and graduate education in the artistic, technological, clinical and studio experience in speech, the dramatic arts, music, social welfare, the visual arts, and the family-life arts. The Department of Music offers programs leading to the Bachelor of Arts and Bachelor of Music degrees.

Accreditation. North Central Association of Colleges and Schools; National Association of Schools of Music.

Academic Information

Enrollment, Music Majors. Undergraduate 300, graduate 60. 4 foreign students.
Music Faculty. Full-time 36, part-time 20.
Term System. Semester. Limited summer classes and ensembles; summer workshops.
Entrance Requirements. High school graduation; SAT or ACT; open enrollment policy for Ohio residents; audition required; placement tests in performance, functional keyboard, theory.
Admission Procedure. Application with nonrefundable $25 fee accepted on a rolling basis.
Music Degrees Offered. Bachelor of Music; Bachelor of Arts; Master of Music.
Music Degree Requirements. The Bachelor of Music degree is offered with majors in music history and litera-

ture, music education, performance, theory and composition, and jazz studies. The degree requires the completion of 127 to 161 semester hours depending on the degree option pursued. The Bachelor of Arts degree with a major in music is intended as a cultural course or as a preparation for graduate study but not as professional preparation for a performance or teaching career. The degree requires the completion of 127 semester hours including the university core curriculum.

The Master of Music degree is offered with emphasis in music history and literature, music education, performance, theory, composition, and accompanying.

General Program Areas. Accompanying, Composition, Jazz Studies, Music Education, Music History, Music Literature, Music Theory, Performance.

Instruments Taught. Brass, Guitar, Organ, Percussion, Piano, Stringed Instruments, Voice, Woodwinds.

Musical Facilities

Practice Facilities. 41 practice rooms. 3 organs (1 49-rank Moeller, 2 small practice organs). 4 percussion-equipped practice rooms. 20 practice pianos (consoles, grands); 6 grand pianos reserved for piano majors. Electronic music laboratory; recording studio; electronic piano laboratory; computer music laboratory.

Concert Facilities. E.J. Thomas Performing Arts Hall, seating 3,000; Guzzetta Recital Hall, 280.

Concerts/Musical Activities. Student and faculty recitals; concerts; visiting artists.

Music Library. 4,400 books; 16,000 scores; 155 music periodicals; 10,000 records. Music Resource Center (tape recorders, video equipment, record players). Special collection of early jazz recordings. Departmental library located in Guzzetta Hall. Other library resources for music students include Kent State University, Baldwin Wallace College, Oberlin College Conservatory of Music, Case Western Reserve University, Cleveland State University, and Youngstown State University.

Special Programs

Performance Groups. Ensembles, orchestra, band, choral groups.

Financial

Costs. Per academic year: Tuition in-state $1,783, out-of-state $4,364. Room and board $2,652.

Financial Aid. Several endowed scholarship accounts were given to the University with the express limitation that they be restricted to music majors. Other sources of financial aid include institutional and state/federal scholarships, grants, loans, part-time employment, and a College Work-Study program.

Baldwin-Wallace College
Conservatory of Music
96 Front Street
Berea
Ohio 44017

Telephone. (216) 826-2362

Chief Administrator. Dr. William R. Carlson, Director.

Baldwin University and German Wallace College were united as Baldwin-Wallace College in 1913. The privately-supported, liberal arts college is affiliated with the United Methodist Church. The 52-acre campus is located in Berea, a suburban community of 20,000, situated 14 miles southwest of Cleveland, Ohio.

The Conservatory of Music, one of the seven divisions of the College, is a professional school offering study in four main areas: (1) the study of the theory, history, and literature of music and the application of these studies to the student's performing medium; (2) musical performance, in which the student is expected to develop a high level of proficiency; (3) specialized advanced study in music with consideration given to areas appropriate to the student's career goals; and (4) a balanced selection of courses in the liberal arts relevant to the student's needs.

Accreditation. North Central Association of Colleges and Schools; National Association of Schools of Music; National Council for Accreditatin of Teacher Education.

Academic Information

Enrollment, Music Majors. Full-time 60 men, 95 women; part-time 4 men, 2 women.

Music Faculty. Full-time 22, part-time 16.

Term System. Quarter. Academic year from late September to mid-June.

Entrance Requirements. High school graduation with rank in upper 50 percent of graduating class; completion of 4 units English, 3 mathematics, 2 foreign language, 2 science, 3 social sciences; SAT or ACT. Auditions required in major applied instrument and minor applied instrument; examinations in rudiments of music, piano proficiency, and aural cmprehension.

Admission Procedure. Application with $15 non-refundable fee to Office of Admissions.

Music Degrees Offered. Bachelor of Music; Bachelor of Arts; Bachelor of Music Education.

Music Degree Requirements. The Bachelor of Music degree is offered with majors in theory, history and literature, composition, music therapy, piano, voice, organ, guitar, harp, and all string, wind, and percussion instruments used in band and orchestra. The degree requires the completion of 197 to 206 quarter hour credits depending upon the major pursued. The Bachelor of Arts degree is offered in a liberal arts program for students who wish to begin or continue study in applied music, to understand the elements of music theory, to develop aural and sight-singing skills, and to gain an introductory knowledge of music history and literature. The Bachelor of Music Education degree is offered with majors in vocal and instrumental music and requires the completion of a total of 201 and 206 quarter hours respectively.

General Program Areas. Applied Music, Composition, Music Education, Music History, Music Literature, Music Theory, Music Therapy.

Instruments Taught. Bass, Bassoon, Clarinet, Cornet, Euphonium, Flute, French Horn, Guitar, Harp, Oboe, Organ, Percussion, Piano, Saxophone, Trumpet, Tuba, Viola, Violin, Violoncello, Voice.

Musical Facilities

Practice Facilities. 50 practice rooms. 6 organs (Holtkamp, Austin, Ruggles). 55 practice pianos; 12 grand pianos reserved for piano majors. Special practice facilities for percussionists. Electronic music studio.

Concert Facilities. Fanny Nast Gamble Auditorium, seating 650; Kulas Chamber Music hall, 98.

Concerts/Musical Activities. Solo recitals; chamber music concerts; large ensemble concerts; lecture recitals (180 performances per year).

Music Library. Ferne Patterson Jones Music Library houses 11,000 musical scores; 30 audiovisual materials; 3 microform titles; 7,300 recordings; 78 audiocassettes. 17 listening stations (stereo). Ritter Library (main) houses books and periodicals on music. Special collections include the Delbert M. Beswick Memorial Music Theory Curriculum Library Reference collection. The Mildred Martin Kirschner Music Education Curriculum Center is a part of the Jones Library. Housed here is the Reimenschneider Bach Institute Library.

Special Programs

Featured Programs. The Riemenschneider Bach Institute was founded in 1969 for the purpose of coordinating baroque research, performance, and publication. The Institute publishes a quarterly journal, *BACH*, sponsors two symposium concert series each year, and operates the world famous Riemenschneider Bach Library. It also serves as a resource center for the annual Bach Festival founded in 1933 by Albert and Selma Riemenschneider.

Performance Groups. Symphony Orchestra, Symphonic Wind Ensemble, College Choir, Motet Choir, Women's Choir, Brass Choir, Clarinet Choir, Jazz Band, Flute Ensemble, Percussion Ensemble, Piano Ensemble, Guitar Ensemble, Collegium Musicum, Chamber Music Ensembles.

Financial

Costs. Per academic year: Tuition $7,104. Fees $336. Room $1,407. Board $1,575

Financial Aid. Baldwin-Wallace has a number of special scholarships made possible by alumni, friends, churches, civic organizations, corporations, foundations, and other friends of the College. As is the case with all College financial aid, these named scholarships are processed through the Financial Aid Office and do not require separate applications. Other forms of financial aid include grants, state/federal loans, part-time employment, and a College Work-Study program.

Bowling Green State University
College of Musical Arts
Bowling Green
Ohio 43403

Telephone. (419) 372-2181

Chief Administrator. Robert W. Thayer, Dean.

Established in 1910 as a teacher-training institution, Bowling Green held its first classes in 1914. In 1929, the functions of the University were expanded to provide four-year degree programs. The University offers more than 150 undergraduate degree programs, as well as 60 master's programs, 9 doctoral programs, four specialist's programs, and 17 associate degree programs. More than 16,000 students, including about 2,000 graduate students, attend classes on the main campus. The University enrolls an additional 3,000 students at the Firelands College and various off-campus centers. At the center of the University's academic community are the 725 faculty members, who are engaged in teaching, research, and scholarship activities.

The College of Musical Arts had its beginnings in 1914 as a Department of Music, formed for the express purpose of educating music teachers. In 1961 its name was changed to the School of Music in the College of Education. In 1975 the School gained its present autonomy as the College of Musical Arts and in 1979 a move was made into the present $9 million facility known as Moore Musical Arts Center. The primary objectives of the College are to educate talented musicians for professional careers in teaching, performance, composition, and musical scholarship; and to serve the University community by contributing to the general education program. The College also strives through its division of public mission to enhance the cultural climate of the entire campus and the community and to serve as a cultural resource for northwest Ohio.

Accreditation. North Central Association of Colleges and Schools; National Association of Schools of Music.

Academic Information

Enrollment, Music Majors. Total 434.

Music Faculty. Full-time 53, part-time 8. Artist groups in residence: BG String Quartet; BG Brass Quintet; BG Woodwind Quintet *(Venti Da Camera).*

Term System. Semester. Academic year from late August to mid-May. Summer session of 8-10 weeks from mid-June to mid-August.

Entrance Requirements. Graduation from an accredited high school or GED; ACT or SAT. Music majors must successfully complete an audition before the faculty of the College of Musical Arts. The audition consists of a performance audition with members of the applied music faculty; a placement examination in general musicianship, including music reading, elementary music theory, and aural skills; and an interview. Graduate applicants must possess a baccalaureate degree from an accredited college or university; Graduate Record Examination; placement examinations in music history and music theory. Students electing performance and conducting options must audition for area faculty for acceptance. Foreign students whose native language is not English are required to take an English proficiency test, either the TOEFL or the official Michigan Test.

Admission Procedure. High school students are encouraged to apply for admission beginning August 1 between their junior and senior years. Application form; submission transcripts of high school and all college and/or university work attempted; results of ACT or SAT; nonrefundable $25 application fee.

Music Degrees Offered. The Bachelor of Music provides undergraduate preparation for a professional career and a background for graduate study. To insure not only technical skills but a broad understanding of the social and cultural environment in which the art of music is practiced, breadth as well as depth are stressed in the curricular programs for each of these majors. An emphasis in instrumental specialist is offered for those who wish to develop a proficiency on more than one instrument. A minor in jazz is available to Bachelor of Music degree candidates. The Master of Music is available with emphasis in Performance, Basic Music Education, Music Education - Conducting, Composition, Music History, and Music Theory.

Music Degree Requirements. The Bachelor of Music degree requires the completion of 127 to 138 units of credit depending upon the degree program pursued. Recital attendance is required of all students (15 per term) and all music majors are required to pass level IV of aural skills prior to graduation. The Master of Music degree requires the completion 34 to 40 units of credit depending upon the emphasis selected.

General Program Areas. Composition, Conducting, Instrumental Specialist, Music Education, Music History, Music Literature, Performance, Theory.

Instruments Taught. Balinese Gamelan, Bass, Bassoon, Clarinet, Euphonium, Flute, Guitar, Harpsichord, Horn, Oboe, Organ, Percussion, Piano, Renaissance Instruments, Saxophone, Trombone, Trumpet, Tuba, Viola, Violin, Violoncello, Voice.

Musical Facilities

Practice Facilities. Special practice facilities for organists; organs available: 2 Beckerath, 1 Richland, 1 Casavant, 1 Schantz, 1 Moller. Special practice facilities for percussionists. 78 piano practice rooms available (12 reserved for piano majors); 82 upright pianos, 36 grand pianos. Special studios: Electronic, class piano, piano repair and maintenance, instrument repair.

Concert Facilities. Kobacker Hall seats 850; Bryan Recital Hall seats 250.

Music Library. The Jerome Library houses a collection of more than 756,000 volumes of which 9,000 are in the field of music. The Library maintains over 14,000 musical scores; 145 periodicals; 388,000 popular phonograph records; 48 listening booths. A special collection of popular music is housed at the Sound Recording Archives. The music holdings of the University of Michigan and Oberlin Conservatory are available to students of the College of Musical Arts.

Special Programs

Performance Groups. A Cappella Choir, Men's Chorus, Women's Chorus, Collegiate Chorale, Concert Band, Marching Band, Symphonic Band, Symphony Orchestra, Chamber Orchestra, Jazz Lab Band, Renaissance Ensemble, Balinese Gamelan Ensemble, New Music Ensemble.

Foreign Programs. Informal, ad hoc arrangements with Xian Conservatory, China.

Financial

Costs. Per academic year: Tuition, fees, room and board undergraduate full-time in-state resident $4,046, out-of-state $6,446; tuition and fees graduate full-time in-state resident $2,632, out-of-state $5,032.

Financial Aid. Financial aid is awarded on the basis of academic merit, financial need, musical ability. Institutional and state/federal aid available. 160 undergraduate and graduate students receive financial aid; average award per student $740. Financial aid/scholarship application due date generally at the beginning of each semester. Part-time employment available; average earnings range from $1,200 to $1,500 per student per year. College Work-Study program.

Case Western Reserve University
Department of Music
Haydn Hall
11118 Bellflower Road
Cleveland
Ohio 44106

Telephone. (216) 368-2400

Chief Administrator. Dr. Peter R. Webster, Chairman.

Case Western Reserve University was created in 1967 by action of the trustees of Case Institute of Technology and Western Reserve University. Before this formal alliance, the two schools had coexisted on adjacent campuses for nearly a century. The University offers undergraduate, graduate, and professional education in more than 60 fields.

The Department of Music is committed to creating educational opportunities and professional programs in music that balance humanistic knowledge of music with excellence in performance. Individual professional interests are encouraged and promoted. To foster this aim, the Department has established major degree programs in music and music education and has collaborated with the Cleveland Institute of Music in a Joint Music Program. This integrated music program at both the undergraduate and graduate levels offers students at either institution the benefit of pursuing studies at both schools. Both institutions share a campus setting in University Circle.

Accreditation. North Central Association of Colleges and Schools; National Association of Schools of Music.

Academic Information

Enrollment, Music Majors. Full-time 40 men, 20 women. 5 foreign students.

Music Faculty. Full-time 7, part-time 10.

Term System. Semester. 7-week summer session from June to August. Academic year from August to May.

Entrance Requirements. High school graduation with 16 units of solid academic subjects including 4 English, 3 mathematics, 1-2 years of laboratory science; SAT or ACT; audition required; music theory test; evidence of musical achievement.

Admission Procedure. Application with $20 non-refundable fee to Admissions Office.

Music Degrees Offered. Bachelor of Arts; Bachelor of Science; Master of Arts; Doctor of Philosophy.

Music Degree Requirements. The Bachelor of Arts degree with a major in music is offered within the context of liberal arts. It is also offered with a major in music history and literature, early music performance practices, and music education. The Bachelor of Science degree is offered with majors in music education and music therapy. The degrees require the completion of 120 credit hours. Students interested in these programs should apply to the University with the understanding that courses in music performance, music theory, and related studies will be taken at the Cleveland Institute of Music.

The Master of Arts degree is offered in music education, early music practices, and music history and literature. The degree requires the completion of 30 credit hours. The Doctor of Philosophy degree is offered in music education, early music performance practices, and musicology. The degree requires the completion of 60 credit hours.

General Program Areas. Early Music Practices, Music Education, Music History, Music Literature, Music Therapy, Musicology.

Instruments Taught. Baroque Instruments, Brass, Early Instruments, Guitar, Harpsichord, Organ, Percussion, Piano, Recorder, Renaissance Instruments, Stringed Instruments, Voice, Woodwinds.

Musical Facilities

Practice Facilities. 10 practice rooms. 2 organs. 15 practice pianos (13 uprights, 2 grands); 2 grand pianos reserved for piano majors. Computer music laboratory.

Concert Facilities. 3 concert/recital halls.

Community Facilities. Cleveland Music School Settlement, Museum of Art, Cleveland Institute of Music.

Concerts/Musical Activities. Ensembles; concerts.

Music Library. Kulas Music Library houses 28,000 volumes; 5,000 musical scores; 500 periodical subscriptions; 400 microforms; 2,000 phonograph recordings. 6 listening stations (stereo). Special collections include the Kulas Collection of Historical Instruments.

Special Programs

Performance Groups. Harp Ensemble, String Ensemble, Chamber Ensemble, Contemporary Music Ensemble, Collegium Musicum, Renaissance Instrument and Vocal Ensemble, Early Music Singers, Baroque Orchestra, Symphony Orchestra, Chamber Orchestra, University Circle Chorale, University Circle Chamber Choir, Cleveland Orchestra Chorus, Jazz Ensemble, Symphonic Wind Ensemble, Concert Band, University Circle Chamber Orchestra.

Affiliated Programs. The Joint Music Program with the Cleveland Institute of Music includes programs concentrating on the education of students whose professional interests include performance, composition, eurhythmics, music theory, piano accompanying, electronic music composition, and audio recording.

Financial

Costs. Per academic year: Tuition $9,100. Fees $696. Room and board $3,810.

Financial Aid. Financial aid is awarded on the basis of academic merit, financial need, musical ability. Both institutional and state/federal aid available. Financial aid/scholarship application due February 1. Part-time employment and a College Work-Study program are also available.

University of Cincinnati
College-Conservatory of Music
Campus Station
Cincinnati
Ohio 45221

Telephone. (515) 475-3737
Chief Administrator. Robert J. Werner, Dean.

The Cincinnati Conservatory of Music was founded by Clara Baur in 1867. Another institution, the College of Music of Cincinnati, was founded in 1878 by George Ward Nichols and Reuben R. Springer. Both charter members of the National Association of Schools of Music, the two schools combined in 1955 to become known as the College-Conservatory of Music of Cincinnati. In 1962, the Conservatory merged with the University of Cincinnati and is now one of the seventeen colleges of the University.

The major goal of the College-Conservatory is the education of musicians for professional careers in performance and teaching. The College-Conservatory offers programs in the performing arts, music, dance, and theater as well as a program in broadcasting (television and audio production).

Accreditation. North Central Association of Colleges and Schools; National Association of Schools of Music.

Academic Information

Enrollment, Music Majors. Full-time 423 men, 392 women; part-time 89 men, 61 women. 72 foreign students.

Music Faculty. Full-time 63, part-time 40.

Term System. Quarter. 10-week summer session from mid-June to late August. Academic year from late September to mid-June.

Entrance Requirements. High school graduation with academic distribution to include 4 units English, 3 mathematics, 2 science, 2 social studies, 2 foreign language, 1 fine arts, 2 additional units; top one-third of high school class; SAT or ACT; all students must audition in Cincinnati or at one of the national sites; international students may send tapes. Foreign students must submit TOEFL score; translated transcripts; bank statement, plus regular admissions process.

Admission Procedure. Application with transcripts, test results, and letters of recommendation. After audition, admissions committee reaches decision and notifies applicant.

Music Degrees Offered. Bachelor of Music; Bachelor of Arts; Master of Music; Doctor of Musical Arts; Doctor of Music Education; Artist Diploma.

Music Degree Requirements. All students admitted to Bachelor of Music degree programs follow a basic core curriculum during the freshman year. Majors are offered in performance areas and music education. Each major has general and specific requirements unique to that particular program. Credit requirements range from 194 to 212 quarter hours. The Bachelor of Arts degree with a major in music is offered jointly by the College-Conservatory of Music and the McMicken College of Arts and Sciences. This degree has been designed for those who wish to pursue a more liberal program of studies while maintaining their concentration in the professional areas of performance and general musicianship. The minimum requirements for this degree are 186 quarter credit hours.

The Master of Music degree is offered with majors in voice, piano, woodwinds, classical guitar, composition, music history, theory, music education, orchestral conducting, choral conducting, wind conducting, and accompanying. Credit requirements for the degree vary from 51 to 66 quarter hour credits depending upon the major area of concentration.

The degrees Doctor of Musical Arts, Doctor of Music Education, and Doctor of Philosophy in Music are offered in cooperation with the Division of Graduate Studies and Research. The Doctor of Musical Arts is a professional degree, confined mainly to the fields of performance, performance practices, and composition. The Doctor of Music Education degree emphasizes studies related to the music teaching-learning process applied to instructional settings. The Doctor of Philosophy degree program follows closely the traditional academic guidelines for the scholarly, research-oriented degree. At least one year of full-time study is required for doctoral degrees.

The Artist Diploma programs are also offered with emphases in opera performance, piano and harpsichord, and instrumental music performance. The two-year programs provide specialized training in the particular areas. Entrance into the programs is quite competitive and limited to a small number of graduate students.

General Program Areas. Accompanying, Choral Conducting, Composition, Jazz Studies, Music Education, Music History, Music Theory, Musicology, Opera, Orchestral Conducting, Performance, Wind Conducting.

Instruments Taught. Bass, Bassoon, Cello, Clarinet, Euphonium, Flute, French Horn, Guitar, Harp, Harpsichord, Oboe, Organ, Percussion, Piano, Saxophone, Trombone, Trumpet, Tuba, Viola, Violin, Voice.

Musical Facilities

Practice Facilities. 100 practice rooms. 14 organs (Casavant, 2 Moeller, 2 Steiner, McManis, Schlicker, Holtkamp, Walker; concert organs include Casavant, Harrison & Harrison, Balcolm and Vaughan). Special practice facilities for percussionists. 75 practice pianos (65 Baldwin studio uprights, 10 Baldwin grands); 16 grand pianos reserved for piano majors. Electronic music studio; electronic music laboratory.

Concert Facilities. Corbett Auditorium, seating 747; Patricia Corbett Theater, 400; Watson Recital Hall, 140; Baur Drawing Room, 75; Emery Recital Hall, 75.

Community Facilities. Local churches occasionally used for organ recitals and choral concerts.

Concerts/Musical Activities. Approximately 900 events per year (student ensembles, degree recitals, faculty recitals, guest recitals, faculty and guest master classes and lectures; nonrequired student recitals; professional society student recitals; major productions; workshop productions).

Music Library. 23,000 volumes; 30,000 musical scores; 250 current periodical subscriptions; 5,400 microforms; 23,200 phonograph recordings. 48 listening stations. Special collections include: Harline Collection of Film Music; Helm Collection of Rare Music; first and early editions of eighteenth and nineteenth century French music; Wurlitzer Collection of rare eighteenth and nineteenth century chamber music.

Special Programs

Performance Groups. Philharmonia Orchestra, Concert Orchestra, Instrumental Chamber Ensemble, Wind Ensemble, Symphonic Band, Bearcat Band (Marching), Varsity Band, Jazz Band, Contemporary Music Ensemble, Baroque Music Ensemble, Classical Guitar Ensemble, Brass Choir, Percussion Ensemble, Woodwind Ensemble, Double Bass Ensemble, Chamber Music Ensemble, Small Woodwind and Brass Ensemble, Harmonie Winds, Motet Choir, Chamber Choir, Chorale, University Singers, Chamber Singers, Renaissance Consort.

Financial

Costs. Per academic year: Tuition undergraduate in-state $2,091, out-of-state $4,989; graduate in-state $3,254, out-of-state $6,400. Room and board $3,189. Off-campus housing approximately $300 per month.

Financial Aid. All music applicants to the College-Conservatory of Music are automatically considered for a talent scholarship based solely on ability as demonstrated at the admissions audition/interview. Scholarships are awarded for one year and are renewable subject to certain conditions. Application for academic scholarship due January 15. Other sources of financial aid include institutional and state/federal grants and loans, part-time employment, and a College Work-Study program.

Cleveland Institute of Music
11021 East Boulevard
Cleveland
Ohio 44106

Telephone. (216) 791-5165
Chief Administrator. David Cerone, President.

The Cleveland Institute of Music was founded in 1920. It offers undergraduate and graduate programs which focus on classical training with intense concentration on practice, performance, and professionalism.

The Institute is located in University Circle, a cultural, educational, and scientific enclave within the city of Cleveland.

Accreditation. North Central Association of Colleges and Schools; National Association of Schools of Music.

Academic Information

Enrollment, Music Majors. 250 (plus 100 students from Case Western Reserve University).

Music Faculty. 135 (full- and part-time).

Term System. Semester.

Entrance Requirements. High school graduation or equivalent; completion of 16 units including 4 English, 3 mathematics, 3 foreign language, 3 social science; SAT; candidates for performance must pass entrance audition in their major area.

Admission Procedure. Application with supporting documents and nonrefundable $35 fee to Office of Admissions; applications reviewed on a rolling admissions basis.

Music Degrees Offered. Bachelor of Music; Bachelor of Arts; Bachelor of Science; Master of Music; Master of Arts; Doctor of Musical Arts; Doctor of Philosophy.

Music Degree Requirements. The Bachelor of Music is offered with majors in performance (piano, organ, classical guitar, violin, viola, violoncello, double bass, harp, woodwinds, brass, percussion, voice), eurhythmics, theory, and composition. The Bachelor of Arts degree in music, offered by Case Western Reserve University and the Institute as part of the Joint Music Program, permits students to emphasize music history and literature, music theory, early music performance practices, performance, general musicianship, or audio recording technology. The Bachelor of Science in music education curriculum prepares the student for the Ohio Special Certificate in Music (K-12). The Master of Music is offered in performance and Suzuki pedagogy.

Graduate programs are offered under the Joint Music Program with Case Western Reserve University and include concentrations in music history, music education, musicology, and performance.

General Program Areas. Audio Recording, Composition, Eurhythmics, Music Education, Music History, Music Literature, Music Theory, Musicology, Performance, Suzuki Pedagogy.

Instruments Taught. Bass, Brass, Guitar, Harp, Organ, Percussion, Piano, Viola, Violin, Violoncello, Voice, Woodwinds.

Musical Facilities

Practice Facilities. In addition to classrooms, the CIM Building has teaching studios, practice rooms, a specially-designed eurhythmics studio, and an opera theater workshop and studio. There are two concert and recital halls. Kulas Hall, the concert auditorium, houses two Steinway concert grand pianos and a Holtkamp 3-manu-

al tracker organ. Le Pavillon, annexed to the main building, contains a recital hall with two Steinway grand pianos, additional classrooms, the electronic music studios, library, and performer's lounge. All studios and practice rooms are equipped with Steinway grand pianos, with two in every piano teaching studio. There are two Dowd French double harpsichords, a clavichord, several concert harps, and comprehensive percussion equipment.

Concerts/Musical Activities. The Institute presents an annual series of concerts by guest artists. Students have the privilege of attending, at no charge, the rehearsals of The Cleveland Orchestra. Students and faculty present concerts and recitals throughout the year.

Music Library. The CIM Library provides materials for study, performance, and listening. The collection contains 45,400 books and scores (including 37,000 volumes). The sound recording collection numbers 11,400 items (with 7,500 records and 1,700 tapes), and includes the Jean Bassett Loesser Tape Library. The resources of the Case Western Reserve University libraries, especially those of the Kulas Music Library, provide extensive additional resource materials for CIM students.

Special Programs

Featured Programs. The biennial Robert Casadesus International Piano Competition is sponsored by the Institute.

Performance Groups. Harp Ensemble, Horn Ensemble, Percussion Ensemble, Wind Ensemble, Brass Ensemble, String Ensemble, Contemporary Music Ensemble, Collegium Musicum, Symphony Orchestra, Chamber Orchestra, University Circle Chorale, University Circle Chamber Choir, Cleveland Orchestra Chorus, Band, Symphonic Wind Ensemble, Spartan Marching Band, Concert Band, Opera Ensemble.

Affiliated Programs. The Institute cooperates in a joint program at both the undergraduate and graduate levels with adjacent Case Western Reserve University. This formal, cooperative plan for degree study by music students enrolled at either institution permits the Institute a concentration on the education and training of professionals skilled in the arts of performance, composition, and related musical disciplines, while the University pursues and develops studies in the fields of music history, musicology, and music education.

Financial

Costs. Per academic year: Tuition $7,500. Fees $448. Room $1,830. Board $1,870.

Financial Aid. Various institutional scholarships, fellowships, and assistantships are available. State- and federally-funded programs include grants, loans, and part-time employment. Financial aid/scholarship application due April 1.

Cleveland State University
Department of Music
1983 East 24th Street
Cleveland
Ohio 44115

Telephone. (216) 687-2033

Chief Administrator. Howie Smith, Chairman.

Established as a state-assisted university in 1964, Cleveland State University inherited the buildings, faculty, staff, and programs of Fenn College, a private college of 2,500 students. In 1969 it merged with the Cleveland-Marshall College of Law. The University offers bachelor's degrees in 60 major fields, 26 master's degrees, 5 Ph.D. and post-master's programs, and 2 law degrees. The expanding CSU campus currently consists of more than 50 acres, with 23 buildings used for teaching, research, housing, and recreation.

The Department of Music offers training for music majors in the areas of music education, music history, theory-composition, applied music, and music therapy. The urban setting of the University makes available applied instruction from members of the Cleveland Orchestra as well as opportunities in music education and performance. A new state-of-the-art music facility is planned.

Accreditation. North Central Association of Colleges and Schools; National Council for Accreditation of Teacher Education.

Academic Information

Enrollment, Music Majors. Full-time 57 men, 64 women, part-time 23 men, 14 women.

Music Faculty. Full-time 15, part-time 21.

Term System. Quarter. Academic year late September to mid-June. 11-week summer session from late June to early September.

Entrance Requirements. High school graduation; performance proficiency (audition required). Advanced placement through departmental examinations and faculty assessment.

Admission Procedure. Application with supporting documents to Admissions Office.

Music Degrees Offered. Bachelor of Music; Bachelor of Arts; Master of Music.

Music Degree Requirements. The Bachelor of Music degree is for the student who seeks primarily professional training and is offered with concentration in composition, music history, applied music, music education, and music therapy. The programs require the completion of 195 quarter hours including specific curriculum requirements and core courses. The Bachelor of Arts with a major in music requires the completion of 18 credits each in the three areas of music history, theory-composition, and applied music and/or ensemble. Beyond these credits, students specialize in an area of music of their choice

and pursue electives outside of music as well as the requirements of the University. A total of 195 quarter hours is required.

The Master of Music program offers concentration in composition, music education, music history, or performance. Cross-disciplinary programs between these concentrations are also encouraged. A diversity of courses and seminars offers students ample opportunity for an education in music aligned with their particular interests and needs. This program permits in-depth pursuit of such career objectives as teaching and supervising music in the public schools, teaching music at the college or university level, teaching applied music, or careers in composition, arranging, conducting, electronic music, musicology, criticism, performance, or other related fields. The master's degree requires the completion of 16 quarter hours in core curriculum, 16 in area requirements, and 16 in electives, for a total of 148 quarter hours.

General Program Areas. Applied Music, Composition, Music Education, Music History, Music Theory, Music Therapy.

Instruments Taught. Bass, Bassoon, Clarinet, Flute, Guitar, Harp, Harpsichord, Horn, Jazz Drums, Oboe, Organ, Percussion, Piano, Saxophone, Trombone, Trumpet, Tuba, Viola, Violin, Violoncello, Voice.

Musical Facilities

Practice Facilities. 31 practice rooms. 1 organ (Holtcamp). Special practice facilities for percussionists. 27 practice pianos (8 grands, 19 studio uprights); 20 Baldwin electric pianos; 5 grand pianos reserved for piano majors. 2 electronic music studios.

Concert Facilities. Concert hall, seating 450.

Concerts/Musical Activities. 50 concerts/recitals per year.

Music Library. 14,000 volumes; 6,000 scores; 18 current periodical subscriptions; 7,600 recordings; 1,350 audiocassettes. 22 listening stations (stereo). The music library maintains the Herbert Elwell Archives and the Contemporary Polish Music Collection.

Special Programs

Performance Groups. Band, Orchestra, Jazz Ensemble, Choral Ensemble, Chamber Music.

Affiliated Programs. Music therapy courses taught in consortium with four other institutions.

Financial

Costs. Per academic year: Tuition $2,037. Applied music fees $570. Room $1,350. Board $1,140.

Financial Aid. Financial aid is awarded on the basis of academic merit, financial need, and musical ability. 35% of student body receive institutional or state/federal aid (average award $1,200 per year). Financial aid application due August 21. Part-time employment and College Work-Study program available.

Kent State University
School of Music
Kent
Ohio 44242

Telephone. (216) 672-2172

Chief Administrator. Dr. Walter Watson, Director.

Kent State University is a medium-sized, public university with nationally recognized programs at the undergraduate and graduate levels. Established in 1910, it has grown steadily and now offers more than 170 fields of study. Eight separate northeastern Ohio campuses comprise the University system. The Kent campus is the largest and grants all the baccalaureate and graduate degrees. The seven regional campuses offer the associate degree in both technical and general programs. The Kent campus covers 1,200 acres and is a residential campus with facilities for more than 6,000 students in the residence halls. The city of Kent has a population of 30,000 and is 11 miles east of Akron and 45 miles south of Cleveland.

Music has been valued at Kent State since the opening of Kent State Normal School in 1910. The School of Music was created in 1941 as part of the College of Liberal Arts. In 1959, it became part of the College of Fine and Professional Arts. The purpose of the School of Music is to provide quality music instruction for students who wish to pursue music as a career and for those who wish to enrich their lives through non-career oriented study and/or performance. The School of Music is committed to conducting and promoting scholarly research and creative musical inquiry and activity. Through the presentation of diverse musical programs the School contributes to the cultural vitality of the University and community.

Accreditation. North Central Association of Colleges and Schools; National Association of Schools of Music; National Council for Accreditation of Teacher Education.

Academic Information

Enrollment, Music Majors. Full-time 126 men, 153 women. Foreign students 20.

Music Faculty. Full-time 36, part-time 10.

Term System. Semester. Academic year from August to May. Summer sessions of 3, 5, and 8 weeks.

Entrance Requirements. Completion of a college-preparatory program in high school with at least a 2.0 GPA including 4 units English, 3 mathematics, 3 science, 3 social studies, 3 foreign language; or having both a 2.5 GPA in high school and a 19 ACT composite score (or 900 SAT combined score). Audition required; theory placement evaluation; piano placement evaluation.

Admission Procedure. Submit application with official transcript, ACT or SAT scores, and $25 nonrefundable fee. Application deadlines July 1 for fall semester, December 15 for spring, June 1 for summer. Foreign students submit special application with all certificates of educational training; financial statement accompanied by an official affidavit of support; official TOEFL score.

Music Degrees Offered. Bachelor of Music; Bachelor of Arts; Master of Music; Master of Arts; Doctor of Philosophy.

Music Degree Requirements. The Bachelor of Music degree provides the most intensive specialization of the several degrees for music students. It requires special maturity and musicianship, and each candidate must pass an achievement examination at the end of the sophomore year in order to enter upper-division study. Concentrations are offered in piano, voice, organ, instrumental, theory, and composition. A total of 128 hours is required for the degree, including specified courses. The curriculum for the Bachelor of Music degree in Music Education leads to the Ohio Special Certificate in Music. Students expecting to teach music in the public schools, grades K-12, are encouraged to pursue this degree although they may elect the Bachelor of Science in Education in the College of Education. The two curricular concentrations are choral-general and instrumental. The degree requires the completion of 130 or 133 hours, depending on the concentration. The Bachelor of Arts degree with a major in music requires the completion of 129 hours, including specified music courses. Major ensemble required each semester for all programs.

The Master of Music and Master of Arts degrees require the completion of 32 hours beyond the baccalaureate degree plus a thesis or essay with oral examination. Coursework option is available in music education.

The Doctor of Philosophy degree requires the completion of 60-72 hours beyond the master's degree. The program is designed individually for each student based on diagnostic examinations. A candidacy examination, dissertation, and final oral examination are required.

General Program Areas. Conducting, Ethnomusicology, Music Education, Music Theory, Musicology, Performance, Piano Pedagogy.

Instruments Taught. African Instruments, Asian Instruments, Bass, Bassoon, Clarinet, Euphonium, Flute, French Horn, Guitar, Oboe, Organ, Percussion, Piano, Saxophone, Trombone, Trumpet, Tuba, Viola, Violin, Violoncello, Voice.

Musical Facilities

Practice Facilities. Special practice facilities for organists; 2 Shantz organs. Practice facilities for percussionists. 25 practice rooms. 20 pianos (Baldwin, Steinway, Tedashi, Seilor); all piano studios have 2 grands; 3 grand pianos reserved for piano majors. Electronic music studio; recording facility; piano laboratory.

Concert Facilities. Ludwig Recital Hall, seating 400; Stemp Theatre, 550; Ballroom, 600.

Community Facilities. United Church of Christ (Holt-kamp organ) and classroom space.

Concerts/Musical Activities. 200 concerts and recitals yearly (solo, large and small ensembles, ethno, jazz); guest artists.

Music Library. 12,400 volumes; 19,100 musical scores; 150 current periodical subscriptions; 494 microforms; 21,600 phonograph recordings. Listening stations (stereo). Special collection of Asian and African instruments; several complete works of composers. Other library resources available to students include the Cleveland Public Library, Oberlin Conservatory of Music, Akron University, Cleveland State University, and Youngstown University.

Special Programs

Performance Groups. Sinfonia Ensemble, Wind Ensemble, Symphony Band, KSU Chorale, University Chorus, Kent Chorus, Marching Band.

Foreign Programs. Fall semester in Florence, Italy for voice and piano majors (junior or above).

Affiliated Programs. The Blossom Festival School was established jointly by The Cleveland Orchestra and Kent State University in 1968 to provide an environment for the close interaction of academic and professional experiences in the visual and performing arts. It serves as an educational counterpart to the cultural programming of nearby Blossom Music Center. Programs in instrumental chamber music, vocal chamber music (including opera), and vocal accompanying duplicate the professional environment under the close guidance of visiting artists, members of The Cleveland Orchestra, and resident faculty of the University.

Financial

Costs. Per academic year: Tuition in-state resident $2,-104, out-of-state $6,950. Room and board $2,396.

Financial Aid. Financial aid is awarded on the basis of academic merit, financial need, musical ability. Scholarships available to music majors include KSU Orchestra Society Scholarships, the Kappa Kappa Psi Scholarship, Jonah Lipsom Scholarships, and the Marching Band Scholarship. Early application suggested. Part-time employment and College Work-Study program available.

Miami University
Department of Music
Oxford
Ohio 45056

Telephone. (513) 529-3014

Chief Administrator. Dr. John Heard, Chair.

Miami University was founded by legislative act in 1809 and opened its doors for instruction in 1824. It has a current enrollment of 15,000 students. The campus consists of more than 1,100 acres with 99 major build-

ings. It is located in the town of Oxford (population 8,500), 35 miles north of Cincinnati and 46 miles southwest of Dayton.

The Department of Music was established as part of the School of Fine Arts in 1929. The Department is committed to serving and furthering music in the cultural life of the University, community, and society at large. It offers a highly personalized mode of instruction within the framework of a university noted for its strong liberal arts tradition.

Accreditation. North Central Association of Colleges and Schools; National Association of Schools of Music.

Academic Information

Enrollment, Music Majors. Full-time 47 men, 55 women; part-time 7 men, 11 women.

Music Faculty. Full-time 29, part-time 4.

Term System. Semester. Academic year from last week in August to first week in May. Summer session of 14 weeks from third week in May to third week in August.

Entrance Requirements. Undergraduate admission based on high school record (class rank, grade point average, curriculum, ACT and/or SAT scores); required scores vary according to the number of application s each year. Graduate admission based on college record, minimum 2.5 GPA. Performance audition (including scales, sight reading, and two compositions of contrasting styles). Undergraduate foreign students must have completed 12 years of elementary and secondary school and possess a diploma, leaving certificate, or matriculation certificate; graduate foreign students must have earned baccalaureate degree or equivalent. TOEFL scores required.

Admission Procedure. Submit university application by March 1; no deadline for graduate admission; schedule audition through Department of Music. Advanced placement through CLEP, departmental examinations.

Music Degrees Offered. Bachelor of Music; Bachelor of Arts; Master of Music.

Music Degree Requirements. The Bachelor of Music degree is offered with concentrations in music education, performance, and theory/composition. Specific program areas are choral, instrumental, and general music education plus performance in various instruments. The Bachelor of Arts degree with a major in music is offered through the College of Arts and Science. The bachelor's degree programs offer preparation for careers in public school teaching, performance, music theory, composition, and for further study at the graduate level.

The degree Master of Music is offered in performance, music theory, composition, music education, and musicology. A diagnostic test is given early in the graduate program to confirm prerequisite competence in the following areas of music: music history, music theory, sight singing and dictation, and music education (for majors in that area). A keyboard proficiency examination for all graduate students in music is administered during the first semester of study. The content includes (1) figured bass, (2) harmonization of a simple melody, (3) open-score reading, (4) abstract chord progression in the keys of CM/m, GM/m, FM/m, (5) reading of a chorale and/or piece from *Microcosmos,* Vol. II, and (6) transposition to concert pitch of a melody written for a transposing instrument. An oral examination and a public performance are also required for graduation.

General Program Areas. Composition, Music Education, Music Theory, Musicology, Performance.

Instruments Taught. Bass, Bassoon, Clarinet, Euphonium, Flute, French Horn, Oboe, Organ, Percussion, Piano, Saxophone, Trombone, Trumpet, Tuba, Viola, Violin, Violoncello, Voice.

Musical Facilities

Practice Facilities. Special practice facilities for organists; 2 organs (Wicks, Moeller). Practice room for percussionists. 55 practice rooms. 27 upright and 10 grand pianos; 6 grand pianos reserved for piano majors. Two electronic music studios.

Concert Facilities. Souers Recital Hall, seating 150; Kelley Auditorium, 750; Hall Auditorium, 1,122; Gates-Abegglen Theater, 428; Millett Hall.

Concerts/Musical Activities. Approximately 125 concerts per year, ranging from visiting major symphony orchestras, ballet companies, chamber ensembles, and individual artists to frequent performances by students and student ensembles, faculty performances, and other guest artists.

Music Library. Amos Music Library contains 23,000 volumes including musical scores; 70 current periodical subscriptions; over 16,000 phonograph recordings. 40 listening stations (stereo). Special collections include: Archive of Ohio and International Folklore. Library resources of the College-Conservatory of Music at the University of Cincinnati are available to students.

Special Programs

Featured Programs. Miami's Department of Music is able to arrange auditions for qualified instrumentalists with several orchestras near Oxford. These include the Dayton Philharmonic Orchestra, the Whitewater Opera Orchestra, and the symphony orchestras of Hamilton, Middletown, and Richmond, Indiana. Compensation is paid directly to the student.

Performance Groups. University Symphony Orchestra, Marching Band, Symphonic Band, Collegiate Chorale (mixed voices), Choraliers (women), Men's Glee Club, Wind Ensemble, Jazz Ensemble, Percussion Ensemble, Brass Choir, Ensemble for New Music, various chamber music groups.

Foreign Programs. Miami University maintains a campus in Luxembourg.

Affiliated Programs. Full-time students may enroll in courses available through the Greater Cincinnati Consortium and the Dayton-Miami Valley Consortium.

Financial

Costs. Per academic year: Tuition undergraduate in-state resident $2,060, out-of-state $4,934; graduate in-state $2,210, out-of-state $5,084. General fee $524. Music lesson fee $120 to $190. Room $1,126. Board $1,300.

Financial Aid. Financial aid is awarded on the basis of academic merit, financial need, musical ability. Institutional and state/federal aid available. 107 department scholarships and assistantships; average award $1,150. Financial aid/scholarship application due February 1. Part-time employment and College Work-Study program available.

Oberlin College
Conservatory of Music
77 West College Street
Oberlin
Ohio 44074

Telephone. (216) 775-8200

Chief Administrator. David Boe, Dean.

Oberlin College was founded in 1833 and was the first college to grant undergraduate degrees to women. The private, liberal arts college comprises two divisions: The College of Arts and Sciences and the Conservatory of Music. The campus is located 35 miles southwest of Cleveland.

The Conservatory of Music was founded in 1865 as a private music school and two years later became part of Oberlin College. It has an annual enrollment of some 500 students. Since 1964, the Conservatory has utilized a complex of buildings designed by Minoru Yamasaki. The Conservatory of Music provides flexible programs to prepare students as professional musicians and teachers of music. In particular, it seeks talented musicians with considerable potential for further growth and development; performance is central, although some students focus on the related areas of music history, theory, composition, education, technology, or therapy.

Accreditation. North Central Association of Colleges and Schools; National Association of Schools of Music.

Academic Information

Enrollment, Music Majors. Full-time 500 men and women.

Music Faculty. Full-time 60, part-time 14.

Term System. Semester. Academic year August to May. Summer session of 6 weeks from mid-June to end of July.

Entrance Requirements. High school graduation with 15 academic units expected to include courses in English, foreign language, mathematics, laboratory science, social science. Applicant should have a clearly defined talent in a performing medium; single most important factor is the performance audition.

Admission Procedure. Prospective students submit application form, high school records, SAT or ACT scores. Live audition at Oberlin or regional sites preferred; tapes accepted. Tapes and academic material reviewed by admissions office and faculty member of appropriate department. Foreign students must submit results of TOEFL and Foreign Student Financial Aid and Declaration form. Advanced placement based on College Board's Advanced Placement examination; department decides amount of credit allowed.

Music Degrees Offered. Bachelor of Music; double degree (Bachelor of Music and Bachelor of Arts); Master of Music; Master of Music Education; Master of Music in Teaching.

Music Degree Requirements. The Bachelor of Music degree requires the completion of 124 credit hours with specific majors in performance, composition, music education, music therapy, and music history. For the performance major, the principal applied study may be piano, organ, voice, strings (violin, viola, cello, bass), woodwinds (flute, oboe, clarinet, bassoon), brass (French horn, trumpet, trombone, tuba), percussion, harp, or early instruments (harpsichord, recorder, lute, Baroque flute, Baroque oboe, Baroque violin, Baroque cello, viola da gamba). For the music education major the emphasis may be in vocal or instrumental music. In addition, majors in jazz studies, music theory, and technology in music and related arts are offered as part of a double major program, together with a second major in performance, composition, music education, music therapy, or music history.

The degree Bachelor of Fine Arts in Music requires completion of 124 credit hours. The program of study will have a major emphasis substantially different from that of the majors which lead to the Bachelor of Music degree. Proposals for an individual major must be approved by the Conservatory Individual Majors Committee. A student may not earn both the Bachelor of Music and Bachelor of Fine Arts degrees. A double degree program leads to a B.A. degree from the College of Arts and Sciences and a Bachelor of Music degree from the Conservatory of Music. This is a five-year program.

The College of Arts and Sciences offers a music major as well as an individual major (a component of which may be a concentration in music) leading to the B.A. degree. These majors programs meet the needs of students who wish to study music at Oberlin without the professional orientation of Conservatory majors.

The major emphasis in the Master of Music degree may be in conducting integrated with an Oberlin Bachelor of Music degree with a major in performance, composition, music education, music therapy, or music history; or may be in opera theater integrated with an Oberlin

Bachelor of Music degree with a major in voice performance. The major emphasis for the Master of Music Education degree is integration with a Bachelor of Music degree with a major in music education, either instrumental or vocal emphasis. The Master of Music Teaching degree emphasis is integration with an Oberlin Bachelor of Music degree with a major in performance.

The Artist Diploma is awarded upon completion of specified course and non-course requirements; 36 hours of course credits; 3 semesters of residence. The Performance Diploma is awarded upon completion of specified course and non-course requirements; 96 semester hours of course credits, 48 of which must be earned in Oberlin or in Oberlin College programs, 76 of which must be earned in Oberlin Conservatory courses or in music courses completed elsewhere for which earned transfer credit has been awarded; the residence requirement; winter term requirement.

General Program Areas. Composition, Early Instruments, Jazz Studies, Music Education, Music History, Music Theory, Music Therapy, Opera Theater, Performance, Technology in Music.

Instruments Taught. Baroque Cello, Baroque Flute, Baroque Oboe, Baroque Violin, Bass, Bassoon, Clarinet, Flute, French Horn, Harp, Harpsichord, Lute, Oboe, Organ, Percussion, Piano, Recorder, Trombone, Trumpet, Tuba, Viola, Viola da Gamba, Violin, Violoncello, Voice.

Musical Facilities

Practice Facilities. Special practice facilities for organists: Kulas Organ Center contains 16 practice rooms equipped with new organs, both mechanical action and electro-pneumatic; 6 Flentrops, 1 Brombaugh, 2 Noacks, 6 Holtkamps, 1 Moeller; teaching studios contain 4 Flentrops. Special practice facilities for percussionists. 182 practice rooms. 240 pianos: 180 grand pianos, including four Model D Steinways; each piano studio equipped with 2 Steinway grands. Five special studios including two for fundamentals, synthesizers, microcomputers, multi-tracking, Ridge 32; studio for experimental projects. On a revolving basis, violins, violas, cellos, and bows made by Gold-Medal winners of Violin Society of America Competitions will be housed at Oberlin, and will be available to students for performance and to others for observation.

Concert Facilities. Finney Chapel, seating 1,400; Warner Concert Hall, 700; Kulas Recital Hall, 150; Fairchild Chapel, 150.

Concerts/Musical Activities. Over 350 concerts sponsored by the Conservatory are offered each year. The Oberlin Artist Recital Series, the oldest such series in the country, brings internationally acclaimed artists and major orchestras to the campus. The Contemporary Focus Series includes campus visits by distinguished composers and performers.

Music Library. Shelved within the Conservatory as a separate collection; 28,000 volumes; 57,000 musical scores; 200 current periodical subscriptions; 500 audiovisual titles; 2,000 microform titles; 30,000 phonograph recordings. 25 listening stations; compact disk and stereo equipment available.

Special collections include: C.W. Best collection of autographs, letters, and photographs of over 100 composers and performers; holograph of Stravisnky's *Threni;* private library of Gustave Langenus, with emphasis on clarinet methods, solos, and etudes.

The Violin Society of America has chosen Oberlin College to house a jointly-owned library of unique and historic publications from around the world on the subject of stringed instrument making, playing, and teaching. Called the VSA-Goodkind Collection, these books are available to Oberlin students and to others for perusal and research.

Special Programs

Featured Programs. The Oberlin Conservatory of Music was one of the first schools in the United States to appreciate the importance of the performance of early music on historically based instruments and as a result has long been recognized as a pioneering center of early music activity.

In June, 1987, with the help of the Violin Society of America, Oberlin College gave its first six-week course in violin restoration and repair under the leadership of master violin maker Vahakn Nigogosian. Eventually the course may become a full-time two-year program.

Performance Groups. Baroque Ensemble, Collegium Musicum, Viola da Gamba Consort, Lute Consort, Woodwind Quintet.

Affiliated Programs. The Conservatory has close ties with the Aspen Summer Music School (Colorado).

Financial

Costs. Per academic year: Tuition $10,700. Fees $311. Room $1,805. Board $1,950.

Financial Aid. Financial aid is awarded on basis of academic merit, financial need, music ability. Institutional and state/federal aid available. 60% of music students receive financial aid; average award $5,385. Financial aid/scholarship application due February 15. Part-time employment (average earnings $350 to $1,100 per academic year) and College Work-Study program available.

The Ohio State University
School of Music
College of the Arts
1866 College Road
Columbus
Ohio 43210

Telephone. (614) 422-6571

Chief Administrator. Dr. David L. Meeker, Director.

The Ohio State University was founded in 1870. It now includes 17 colleges and a graduate school, and is the major center for graduate and professional education in Ohio. The campus has 380 buildings on 3,255 acres in the city of Columbus, the capital of the state.

The School of Music offers comprehensive curricula at both the graduate and undergraduate levels in performance, music education, music history, music theory and composition, and church music. Undergraduate majors are also available in jazz studies, audio recording, and music theatre.

Accreditation. North Central Association of Colleges and Schools; National Association of Schools of Music; National Council for Accreditation of Teacher Education.

Academic Information

Enrollment, Music Majors. Full-time 85 men, 94 women.

Music Faculty. Full-time 62, part-time 8.

Term System. Quarter. Two summer sessions.

Entrance Requirements. Open enrollment for Ohio residents; high school graduation or equivalent; recommend completion of 4 English, 3 mathematics, 2 science, 2 social science, 2 foreign language, 1 visual or performing arts, and 1 additional unit from any of the foregoing; performance audition music achievement test.

Admission Procedure. Application with supporting documents including autobiographical statement, 3 personal reference letters, and nonrefundable $10 fee to Office of Admissions.

Music Degrees Offered. Bachelor of Music; Bachelor of Music Education; Bachelor of Arts; Bachelor of Science; Bachelor of Fine Arts; Master of Music; Master of Arts; Doctor of Musical Arts; Doctor of Philosophy.

Music Degree Requirements. The Bachelor of Music degree is designed as preparation for professional careers in performance and composition. The major emphasis for the degree may be in audio recording, church music, jazz studies, music history, music theory, composition, orchestral instruments, organ, piano, or voice. A minimum of 196 quarter hours is required in this curriculum. The Bachelor of Music Education degree is offered jointly by the College of the Arts and the College of Education for preparation of teachers of general classroom, instrumental, and choral music. Graduates of the program are eligible for the Ohio Four-Year Provisional

Special Certificate, valid for teaching music in grades K-12. The Bachelor of Arts degree with a major in music offers a broad cultural education. The Bachelor of Science degree in audio recording is designed in conjunction with the Department of Electrical Engineering as preparation for a professional career in sound recording. The Bachelor of Fine Arts degree in musical theatre is also available.

Graduate programs include the Master of Arts degree in music education, theory, history, vocal and individual instruments pedagogy; Master of Music degree in conducting (instrumental/choral), composition, vocal and individual instruments performance; the Doctor of Philosophy degree in music education, theory, and history; and the Doctor of Musical Arts degree in composition and vocal and individual instruments performance.

General Program Areas. Audio Recording, Choral Music, Church Music, Composition, Conducting, Jazz Studies, Music Education, Music History, Music Theory, Performance.

Instruments Taught. Brass, Harpsichord, Organ, Percussion, Piano, Stringed Instruments, Voice, Woodwinds.

Musical Facilities

Practice Facilities. Special practice facilities for organists and percussionists.

Concert Facilities. Hughes Hall, seating 400; Weigel Hall, 700; Mershon Auditorium, 3,000.

Concerts/Musical Activities. More than 300 performances are presented annually by students, faculty, and visiting artists.

Music Library. The Music Library in Sullivant Hall is staffed by three full-time professional librarians. The library houses over 41,000 books and musical scores and 15,000 recordings; 575 current periodicals and serials are received.

Special collections include: Music Library of the American Broadcasting Company (Chicago); archive of published primitive, ethnic, and folk music.

Special Programs

Featured Programs. Careers in Music Day is designed to acquaint high school students with the careers available to musicians. Special clinics in vocal and instrumental music are offered during the academic year and summer session.

Performance Groups. University Chorus, University Symphonic Choir, University Chorale, Women's Glee Club, Men's Glee Club, University Symphony Orchestra, Chamber Orchestra, University Marching Band, Military Band, Concert Band, Buckeye Bands, Opera Theater, Percussion Ensemble, Jazz Ensembles, Scarlet and Gray Show.

Financial

Costs. Per academic year: Tuition in-state $1,890, out-of-state $4,602. Room and board $2,815.

Financial Aid. Financial aid is awarded on the basis of academic merit, financial need, musical ability. 87 students receive aid (average award $1,265). Financial aid/scholarship application due March 15. Part-time employment and a College Work-Study program available.

Ohio University
School of Music
College of Fine Arts
Athens
Ohio 45701

Telephone. (614) 594-5588

Chief Administrator. James Stewart, Director.

Ohio University was founded in 1804. It is a state-supported university with an enrollment of over 14,000 students. The 600-acre campus has 100 buildings in the city of Athens, 75 miles southeast of Columbus.

The curricula of the School of Music are designed to prepare students for careers in teaching, music therapy, performance, or music business. The School makes provision for individual study in all branches of vocal and instrumental music and offers a wide range of courses in the fields of theory or composition, music history and literature, music education, and music therapy. Students who specialize in music education may elect either instrumental or choral emphasis. Upon completion of the music education program, which includes the requirements of the State Board of Education, the student receives the Ohio Special Certificate to teach music.

Accreditation. North Central Association of Colleges and Schools; National Association of Schools of Music; National Council for Accreditation of Teacher Education.

Academic Information

Music Faculty. Full-time 29, part-time 6.

Term System. Quarter. Two 5-week summer terms.

Entrance Requirements. High school graduation or equivalent; recommend completion of 16 academic units including 4 English, 3 mathematics, 3 laboratory science, 2 foreign language, 3 social studies, 1 visual and performing arts; open enrollment policy for Ohio residents; out-of-state students must be in upper 50 percent of graduating class; SAT or ACT required; audition required. GRE required for graduate study.

Admission Procedure. Application with nonrefundable $25 fee due by June 15.

Music Degrees Offered. Bachelor of Music; Master of Music.

Music Degree Requirements. The Bachelor of Music degree is offered with majors in performance, music education, music history and literature, music theory, composition, music education, and music therapy. The degree requires the completion of 192 quarter hours of prescribed and general education courses. The major in music with a business emphasis is also available.

The Master of Music degree requires the completion of 48 quarter hours of study.

General Program Areas. Composition, Music Business, Music Education, Music History, Music Literature, Music Theory, Music Therapy, Performance.

Instruments Taught. Brass, Organ, Percussion, Piano, Stringed Instruments, Voice, Woodwinds.

Musical Facilities

Practice Facilities. 65 practice rooms. 3 organs (Moeller). 55 pianos, 8 grand pianos reserved for piano majors. Electronic music laboratory; 2 piano laboratories.

Concert Facilities. 1 concert hall.

Concerts/Musical Activities. Recitals, concerts, ensemble performances.

Music Library. 15,000 books; 16,000 scores; 118 periodicals; 1,900 microfiche; 10,500 recordings. Listening facilities (cassette, stereo).

Special Programs

Featured Programs. The Athens Community Music School, a unit within the School of Music, provides instruction for pre-college age students, University students who are not music majors, and other adults. Private instruction is offered in all instruments and voice.

Performance Groups. University Singers, Choral Union, University Orchestra, Band, Opera Theater, Jazz Ensembles, Chamber Ensembles.

Financial

Costs. Comprehensive fee per quarter: in-state resident $690, out-of-state $1,390. Room $1,509. Board $1,407.

Financial Aid. Scholarship application due February 15. Sources of financial aid include institutional and state/federal grants and loans, part-time employment, and a College Work-Study program.

Ohio Wesleyan University
Department of Music
Elizabeth Street
Delaware
Ohio 43015

Telephone. (614) 369-4431, Ext. 700

Chief Administrator. Robert A. Griffith, Chairman.

Ohio Wesleyan University was founded in 1842 and since that time has maintained its connection with the United Methodist Church. The 200-acre campus is located 20 miles north of Columbus.

The Department of Music offers undergraduate experience for those students majoring in music performance and music education. Courses are also offered to the non-music major to develop understanding and appreciation of music as one of the fine arts of a liberal education. In 1980-82, all of the music facilities on campus were renovated and Presser Hall and a band/orchestra rehearsal room were added to Sanborn Hall.

Accreditation. North Central Association of Colleges and Schools; National Association of Schools of Music.

Academic Information

Enrollment, Music Majors. (Total University) 810 men, 815 women.

Music Faculty. Full-time 6, part-time 12.

Term System. Semester. Academic year from August 20 to May 5. 5-week summer session from mid-May to late June.

Entrance Requirements. High school graduation with rank in upper 50 percent of graduating class; completion of 16 units including 4 English, 3-4 mathematics, 2-4 foreign language, 3-4 science, 3-4 social studies; SAT or ACT; audition required.

Admission Procedure. Application with test scores, counselor recommendation, teacher reference, and essay to Office of Admissions.

Music Degrees Offered. Bachelor of Music; Bachelor of Arts.

Music Degree Requirements. The Bachelor of Music degree curricula are designed for students who wish to prepare for professional work in music. The major in music performance is offered in piano, voice, organ, an orchestral or band instrument, or church music. The major in music education is offered in either a choral or instrumental major. A total of 34 graduation units is required for the degree. The curriculum for a music education major with a pre-music therapy emphasis is a four-year program with additional work in summer school. The student then matriculates in a music therapy program which normally consists of one year of professional training and an internship resulting in a certificate to practice music therapy. The Bachelor of Arts degree is offered with majors in applied music, history and literature, and theory.

General Program Areas. Applied Music, Church Music, Music History, Music Literature, Music Theory, Music Therapy, Performance.

Instruments Taught. Baritone, Bass, Bassoon, Clarinet, Flute, French Horn, Oboe, Organ, Percussion, Piano, Saxophone, Trombone, Trumpet, Tuba, Viola, Violin, Violoncello, Voice.

Musical Facilities

Practice Facilities. 25 practice rooms. 5 organs (Byrens, 2 Moeller, Blanchard, Klais). Special practice facilities for percussionists. 15 practice pianos (1 A.B. Chase, 2 Grinnell Brothers, 1 Kimball, 3 Hamilton, 1 Ivers and

Pond); 3 Steinway grands reserved for piano majors. Electric keyboard (piano) laboratory.

Concert Facilities. Jemison Auditorium, seating 229; Gray Chapel, 1,100.

Concerts/Musical Activities. Choral and instrumental organizations present performances each semester; Central Ohio Symphony Orchestra (college-community) presents 5 concerts per season; senior and junior student recitals, general student recitals, faculty recitals, and guest recitals as scheduled (usually at least one concert/ recital every week of the academic year); Performing Arts-Lecture Series includes 4 music events throughout the year.

Music Library. 4,820 volumes; 39 current periodical subscriptions; 3,111 recordings. 12 listening stations (stereo). Special collections include the archives of the Organ Historical Society. Interlibrary loan participant with Methodist Theological School and Ohio State University.

Special Programs

Performance Groups. String Ensemble, Brass Ensemble, Woodwind Ensemble, Percussion Ensemble, Chamber Singers, Opera Workshop, Choral Art Society, Symphonic Wind Ensemble, Jazz Band, Bishop Band, Central Ohio Symphony Orchestra.

Financial

Costs. Per academic year: Tuition $9,207. Room $1,-852. Board $1,809.

Financial Aid. Music merit scholarships were the first non-need-based awards at Ohio Wesleyan. Scholarship application due March 15. Other sources of financial aid include institutional and state/federal grants and loans, part-time employment, and a College Work-Study program.

Wright State University
Department of Music
3640 Colonel Glenn Highway
Dayton
Ohio 45435

Telephone. (513) 873-2346

Chief Administrator. Dr. Richard Knab, Chairman.

Wright State University is a state-assisted institution founded in 1964 as the Dayton Campus of the Miami and the Ohio State Universities. In 1967, it became autonomous and adopted its present name. The majority of students are undergraduates from southwestern Ohio. The campus of 639 acres has 19 buildings.

The Department of Music, established in 1966, prepares the music professional, contributes to the balanced education of students in non-music degree programs, and offers cultural and artistic events to the University and community.

Accreditation. North Central Association of Colleges and Schools; National Association of Schools of Music.

Academic Information

Enrollment, Music Majors. Undergraduate 92, graduate 11.

Music Faculty. Full-time 14, part-time 22.

Term System. Quarter. Two 5-week summer sessions, or one 10-week session.

Entrance Requirements. High school graduation with 16 units (4 English, 3 mathematics including algebra I and II, 3 laboratory science, 3 social studies, 1 visual or performing arts, 2 foreign language); SAT or ACT not required for admission but either one must be on file before students can register for classes. Audition required.

Admission Procedure. Recommended application due date for students needing housing by mid-December with $25 nonrefundable fee.

Music Degrees Offered. Bachelor of Music; Bachelor of Arts; Master of Music.

Music Degree Requirements. The Bachelor of Music degree is offered with majors in applied music, music education, music theory, music history and literature, and music composition. The Bachelor of Arts degree is offered with a major in music. The bachelor degrees require the completion of 183 quarter hours of credit including general education requirements; cumulative 2.0 or better GPA. Keyboard proficiency and recital and concert attendance is required for all programs.

The Master of Music degree with a major in music education is also offered and requires the completion of 45 to 48 quarter hours.

General Program Areas. Applied Music, Composition, Music Education, Music History, Music Listening, Music Literature, Music Theory, Performance.

Instruments Taught. Bass, Bassoon, Clarinet, Flute, Harpsichord, Horn, Oboe, Organ, Percussion, Piano, Saxophone, Trombone, Trumpet, Tuba, Viola, Violin, Violoncello, Voice.

Musical Facilities

Practice Facilities. 9 practice rooms. 2 organs (Allyn electric practice, Casavant 22-rank pipe). 1 percussion-equipped practice room. 16 practice pianos (9 uprights, 7 grands). 7 grand pianos reserved for piano majors. Electronic studio; recording studio.

Concert Facilities. Concert Hall, seating 383; Recital Hall, seating 123.

Concerts/Musical Activities. Recitals and concerts.

Music Library. 12,700 volumes; 7,360 scores; 3,550 music books; 67 musical periodicals; 4,251 recordings. Listening facility in the Department (Creative Arts Center) with cassette decks and stereo turntables.

Special Programs

Featured Programs. The Department of Music encourages students who have demonstrated superior academic ability to participate in the music honors program. Entrance to this program requires that the student be a junior or senior with a 3.0 cumulative GPA and a 3.5 GPA in music.

Performance Groups. Symphony Band, Concert Band, Brass Choir, Collegium Musicum, Jazz Ensemble, University Chorus, Chamber Singers, Orchestra.

Financial

Costs. Per academic year: Tuition in-state resident $1,-752, out-of-state $3,504. Room and board $2,841. Applied music fee $48 for 1 half-hour lesson per week (per quarter); $94 for 1 one-hour lesson per week (per quarter).

Financial Aid. Scholarships, loans, and student employment available. Scholarship application due February 1 for entering students, April 1 for continuing students, April 15 for transfer students.

Youngstown State University
Dana School of Music
410 Wick Avenue
Youngstown
Ohio 44555

Telephone. (216) 742-3636

Chief Administrator. Dr. Donald W. Byo, Director.

Youngstown State University was founded in 1908 and was sponsored by the Young Men's Christian Association as the School of Law of the Youngstown Association School. Over the years the name was changed to the Youngstown Institute of Technology, Youngstown College, the Youngstown University, and finally, in 1967, to Youngstown State University. Youngstown is locate in northeastern Ohio, five miles from the Pennsylvania border 65 miles northwest of Pittsburgh.

The Dana School of Music began in 1869 as Dana's Musical Institute in Warren, Ohio. It was merged with Youngstown College in 1941. The purpose of the school is to complement the general objectives of the University by providing professional training in music and to provide an opportunity for the non-music major to develop a background of musical knowledge.

The curriculum is divided into four components: music education, theory, performance, and liberal arts.

The School is one of three departmental units in the College of Fine and Performing Arts, which is housed in Bliss Hall.

Accreditation. North Central Association of Colleges and Schools; National Association of Schools of Music; National Council for Accreditation of Teacher Education.

Academic Information

Enrollment, Music Majors. Total university: 9,600.

Music Faculty. Total university: 470.

Term System. Quarter. Two summer sessions.

Entrance Requirements. High school graduation with 16 units including 3 English, 2 mathematics, 1 laboratory science, 2 foreign language, 1 social studies, 7 electives; ACT or SAT. It is anticipated that the applicant will have developed a certain proficiency in one or more branches of applied music before entering the University. Audition and theory examination required. GRE required for graduate students.

Admission Procedure. Application and supporting documents with $25 nonrefundable fee due June 1.

Music Degrees Offered. Bachelor of Arts; Bachelor of Music; Master of Music.

Music Degree Requirements. The Bachelor of Music degree is offered with a major in piano, organ, voice, standard string or wind instrument, percussion, theory, composition, or music education. In addition, it is possible to obtain the degree of Bachelor of Arts with majors in music history, theory, and applied music. All degree programs have specific core requirements. In cooperation with the School of Education, the School of Music prepares students for certification as music teachers in the public schools and offers other courses necessary for general elementary teaching certificates. Music education students have a variety of opportunities for observation and practice teaching through cooperation between the University and all area schools.

The Master of Music requires the completion of 48 quarter hours. Requirements vary depending on concentration pursued.

General Program Areas. Applied Music, Composition, Conducting, Jazz Studies, Music Education, Music History, Music Literature, Music Theory, Performance.

Instruments Taught. Baritone Horn, Bassoon, Clarinet, Flute, French Horn, Guitar, Harpsichord, Oboe, Organ, Percussion, Piano, Saxophone, String Bass, Trombone, Trumpet, Tuba, Viola, Violin, Violoncello, Voice.

Musical Facilities

Practice Facilities. Special practice facilities for organists; 5 organs (2 Schlicker, 3 Flentrop). 3 practice rooms for percussionists. 72 practice rooms. 100 pianos (32 Steinway, 68 other pianos); 10 grand pianos reserved for piano majors. Electronic music studio contains synthesizer and recording/audio equipment.

Concert Facilities. Recital hall seating 237; Stambaugh Auditorium; Powers Auditorium.

Concerts/Musical Activities. The Dana School of Music supplements the concerts of the Monday Musical Club and the Youngstown Symphony Orchestra with the Dana Concert Series; graduation recitals and student recitals.

Music Library. The library of band, orchestral, and choral music is extensive and representative of musical periods from the Renaissance to the present. The Materials Center and the Maag Library contain books and music for study by students in music literature, music education, and theory classes. There is an extensive collection of records and scores in the Materials Center of Bliss Hall where listening equipment is available for general use.

Special Programs

Performance Groups. Dana Chorale, University Chorus, Wind Ensemble, Concert Band, Marching Band, Dana Symphony Orchestra, Chamber Ensemble, Opera Workshop, Madrigal Singers, Women's Chorus, Men's Chorus, Jazz Ensemble, Woodwind Ensemble, Brass Ensemble, Percussion Ensemble, String Ensemble, Chamber Orchestra.

Financial

Costs. Per academic year: Tuition in-state resident $1,200, out-of-state $2,200. Fees $250. Room and board $1,000.

Financial Aid. 140 music students receive some form of financial aid. 40 scholarships ranging from $200 to $1,500. Scholarship applications due April 1.

OKLAHOMA

Central State University
Department of Music
100 North University Drive
Edmond
Oklahoma 73060

Telephone. (405) 341-2980, Ext. 2751
Chief Administrator. Dr. Clarence E. Garder, Chairman.

Central State University, classified by the Oklahoma Regents for Higher Education as a "regional university," was established in 1891 and is the oldest state educational institution in Oklahoma. The 200-acre campus is located in Edmond, 12 miles north of Oklahoma City.

The Department of Music offers programs in the College of Liberal Arts which prepare students to teach instrumental music or vocal music in grades 1-12. The major in performance with instrumental, piano, and voice options is also available.

Accreditation. North Central Association of Colleges and Schools.

Academic Information

Enrollment, Music Majors. (Total University) 13,412.
Term System. Semester. Academic year from late August to early May.
Entrance Requirements. High school graduation with rank in upper two thirds of graduating class; ACT; audition required.
Admission Procedure. Application with supporting documents to Office of Admissions.
Music Degrees Offered. Bachelor of Music; Bachelor of Music Education; Master of Music Education.
Music Degree Requirements. The baccalaureate degrees require the completion of 124 semester hours of courses in general education, music, and electives. The Master of Music Education degree program requires the completion of 32 hours of study plus a thesis, recital, lecture-recital, composition, or other approved project.
General Program Areas. Composition, Music Education, Music Theory, Performance.

Instruments Taught. Brass, Percussion, Piano, Stringed Instruments, Voice, Woodwinds.

Special Programs

Featured Programs. The Music Festival is held annually on the campus. It is open to all Oklahoma High School Students. Music students compete in band, orchestra, mixed chorus, glee club, instrumental and vocal ensembles, as well as being soloists in instrumental music and voice.
Performance Groups. Choir, Orchestra, Band, Stage Band, Brass Ensemble, String Ensemble, Woodwind Quintet, Male Quartet, Chamber Music Ensembles, Horn Quartet.

Financial

Costs. Per academic year: Tuition in-state resident $639, out-of-state $1,714.
Financial Aid. Two music awards are given each year, one in instrumental music and one in vocal music to senior music students who show the most promise as musicians and who have contributed most to the University. Other sources of financial aid include grants, loans, part-time employment, and a College Work-Study program.

University of Oklahoma
School of Music
100 Asp Avenue
Norman
Oklahoma 73019

Telephone. (405) 325-2081
Chief Administrator. Allan Ross, Director.

The University of Oklahoma was established in 1890. The campus is located in the city of Norman, near the center of the state.

The School of Music offers curricula for those who choose to pursue professional careers in music, and courses for all University students who may wish to acquaint themselves with music as listeners or participants. The School stresses scholarship, research, and the fundamentals of music, and provides opportunities for students to develop their powers of personal expression through performance, composition, historical, analytical, and pedagogical disciplines.

Accreditation. North Central Association of Colleges and Schools; National Association of Schools of Music; National Council for Accreditation of Teacher Education.

Academic Information

Enrollment, Music Majors. (Total University) 18,899. *Music Faculty.* 39.

Term System. Semester. One summer session.

Entrance Requirements. High school graduation with composite score of 17 or above on ACT or average grade of B in four years of high school study; audition required.

Admission Procedure. Application with supporting documents to Office of Admissions; $10 application fee for out-of-state students.

Music Degrees Offered. Bachelor of Music; Bachelor of Musical Arts; Bachelor of Fine Arts; Bachelor of Music Education; Master of Music; Master of Music Education; Doctor of Musical Arts; Doctor of Philosophy in Music Education.

Music Degree Requirements. The Bachelor of Music degree is offered with concentrations in composition, music history, performance (organ, piano, voice, wind, percussion, strings), piano pedagogy, and music theory. The Bachelor of Music Education degree is offered with specialization in instrumental, vocal, instrumental with vocal endorsement, or vocal with instrumental endorsement. The degrees Bachelor of Fine Arts with a music emphasis and Bachelor of Musical Arts are also available. All baccalaureate degrees require the completion of a minimum of 124 credit hours.

The Master of Music degree is awarded upon completion of an approved program of study in performance, choral conducting, composition, music history, or music theory. The Master of Music Education degree is awarded upon completion of an approved program of study designed to develop competence as a musician-teacher and allows emphasis in general, choral, or instrumental music, piano pedagogy, and elementary or secondary school administration. The Master of Music Education degree with emphasis in the Kodaly Concept is offered in cooperation with Silver Lake College, Manitowoc, Wisconsin. The degree program is comprised of twelve hours of Kodaly methodology and folk song research at Silver Lake and twenty hours of study in music and music education at the University of Oklahoma.

The Doctor of Musical Arts degree is awarded upon completion of an approved program of study in performance, composition, or choral conducting. The objectives of the program include the development of the artist-teacher and musician-scholar for professional ca-

reers in higher education. The Doctor of Philosophy degree in music education is awarded upon completion of an approved program encompassing study in music education, music history, music theory, and applied music. The objectives of the program include the development of a high level of competence as a musician-teacher and the ability to contribute to the solution of professional problems through scholarly or developmental research.

General Program Areas. Applied Music, Choral Conducting, Composition, Music Education, Music History, Music Theory, Performance, Piano Pedagogy.

Instruments Taught. Bass, Brass, Organ, Percussion, Piano, Viola, Violin, Violoncello, Voice, Woodwinds.

Musical Facilities

Practice Facilities. The School of Music is housed in four buildings: Stanley B. Catlett, Sr. Music Center, Holmberg Hall, Carpenter Hall, and Jacobson Hall. These facilities contain offices and studios for faculty and graduate assistants, practice rooms, classrooms, rehearsal rooms, a music library and listening area, and a large auditorium. A new laboratory for electronic music and mixed media is located in Holmberg Hall. More than one hundred grand and upright pianos and several pipe organs are available. Included in the inventory of practice pipe organs are three Moellers, a Reuter, and two Holtkamps. The auditorium in Holmberg Hall contains a three-manual organ for both recitals and teaching. Four harpsichords, one of which is a two-manual Rutkowski, are available for student and faculty performances.

Concerts/Musical Activities. Student and faculty recitals and concerts; visiting artists.

Music Library. The Music Library, located in the Catlett Music Center, houses collections of books, scores, recordings, periodicals, microfilms, ethnic instruments, and the complete works of many important composers. The University has recently become the base for the *Journal of Music Theory Pedagogy.*

Special Programs

Performance Groups. University Symphony Orchestra, Opera and Music Theater, Collegium Musicum, University Choir, University Chorale, University Chorus, Symphonic Band, Concert Band, Marching Band, Trombone Choir, Jazz Ensemble, Percussion Ensemble, Clarinet Choir, Brass Choir, Flute Choir, Woodwind Quintet, Brass Quintet, String Quartet.

Financial

Costs. Per academic year: Tuition in-state resident $700, out-of-state $2,257. Fees $130. Room and board $2,545.

Financial Aid. A number of scholarships and music awards are available to qualified music students. Several special awards are given annually to outstanding students. Other sources of financial aid include institutional scholarships and state/federal grants, loans, and part-time employment. Financial aid/scholarship application due March 1.

Oklahoma Baptist University
Department of Music
College of Fine Arts
500 West University
Shawnee
Oklahoma 74801

Telephone. (405) 275-2850, Ext. 2305

Chief Administrator. Paul Hammond, Dean, College of Fine Arts.

Oklahoma Baptist University was founded in 1910 and is supported by the Baptist General Convention of Oklahoma. The city of Shawnee contributed the original 60-acre campus. Shawnee is located 40 miles from Oklahoma City.

The Department of Music offers programs to prepare performers, public school teachers, and church musicians to function effectively in their chosen fields within the context of a liberal arts curriculum.

Accreditation. North Central Association of Colleges and Schools; National Association of Schools of Music; National Council for Accreditation of Teacher Education.

Academic Information

Enrollment, Music Majors. Full-time 81 men, 58 women. 5 foreign students.

Music Faculty. Full-time 31, part-time 4.

Term System. Semester. Academic year from late August to late May. 8-week summer session from early June to late July.

Entrance Requirements. High school graduation or equivalent; rank in upper half of graduating class; recommend completion of 4 units English, 2 mathematics, 2 science, 2 foreign language, 2 social studies; ACT minimum score of 16 or SAT of 720; theory placement examination; audition not required.

Admission Procedure. Application with $25 non-refundable fee accepted on a rolling basis.

Music Degrees Offered. Bachelor of Music; Bachelor of Music Education.

Music Degree Requirements. The Bachelor of Music degree is offered with majors in church music and theory and composition. The degree requires the completion of a unified studies core, degree core, major, minor, and electives. A total of 128 to 132 hours is required for the degree depending upon major pursued. The Bachelor of Music Education degree is offered in several plans with certification in various areas (vocal K-12, instrumental K-12, instrumental certificate/vocal endorsement K-12). The degree requires the completion of 137 to 138 hours.

General Program Areas. Church Music, Composition, Conducting, Music Education, Music Theory, Performance.

Instruments Taught. Brass, Clarinet, Harp, Horn, Organ, Percussion, Piano, Stringed Instruments, Trombone, Trumpet, Tuba, Voice.

Musical Facilities

Practice Facilities. 35 practice rooms. 6 organs (5 Reuter practice organs, 66-rank Reuter concert organ). 25 practice pianos (Sohmer uprights); 1 grand piano reserved for piano majors. Electronic music laboratory.

Concert Facilities. Potter Auditorium, seating 1,800; Yarborough Auditorium, 400.

Concerts/Musical Activities. Student recitals; guest artists; ensemble concerts weekly.

Music Library. 3,000 volumes; 2,000 musical scores; 27 periodical subscriptions; 5,500 phonograph recordings; 500 audiocassettes. 20 listening stations (stereo).

Special Programs

Performance Groups. Chapel Choir, Yahnseh Band, Stage Band, Bison Glee Club (men), Bisonette Glee Club (women), University Chorale, Brass Ensemble, Woodwind Ensemble, Laboratory Choir, University Ringers.

Financial

Costs. Per academic year: Tuition $3,040. Fees $40. Room $940. Board $1,250. Off-campus housing approximately $250 per month.

Financial Aid. Financial aid application due April 15, October 15, or March 1. Music talentships of $200 to $600 per year are awarded to outstanding students who demonstrate a high degree of musical competence in selected fields. The awards are made on an annual audition basis. Other sources of financial aid include institutional and state/federal grants and loans, institutional scholarships, part-time employment, and a College Work-Study program.

Oklahoma City University
School of Music and Performing Arts
N.W. 23rd and Blackwelder
Oklahoma City
Oklahoma 73106

Telephone. (405) 521-5315

Chief Administrator. Richard E. Thurston, Dean.

Oklahoma City University is a private institution founded in 1901 by the Methodist Episcopal Church, South in cooperation with the Oklahoma City Chamber of Commerce. Since the merger of three main branches of Methodism, the University has been owned and controlled by the United Methodist Church. The 64-acre campus is located in the northwest section of Oklahoma

City.

The School provides instruction for those interested in careers in performance, teaching, and church music. A thorough theoretical and performance foundation is available for students planning graduate work.

Accreditation. North Central Association of Colleges and Schools; National Association of Schools of Music.

Academic Information

Enrollment, Music Majors. (Total University) 2,293. *Music Faculty.* 44.

Term System. Semester. Two summer terms.

Entrance Requirements. High school graduation; recommend 4 units English, 3 mathematics, 2 foreign language, 2 laboratory science, 3 social science; SAT or ACT; audition required.

Admission Procedure. Application with supporting documents and nonrefundable $20 fee to Admissions Office.

Music Degrees Offered. Bachelor of Music; Bachelor of Arts; Master of Music.

Music Degree Requirements. The Bachelor of Music degree is offered with a major in guitar, performance (pedagogy, piano, organ, voice, orchestral instruments), musical theatre, composition, and music education (vocal, instrumental). The degree is also offered with an emphasis on arts administration and management. The Bachelor of Arts degree is designed to give the student a smaller amount of specialization in music than is required for the Bachelor of Music degree. It is awarded by the College of Arts and Sciences.

The School offers programs of private study, courses, and research leading to the degree of Master of Music. The degree is offered in instrumental performance (piano, organ, orchestral instruments), general vocal performance, and in opera performance.

General Program Areas. Applied Music, Composition, Music Education, Music Management, Music Theory, Musical Theatre, Opera, Pedagogy, Performance.

Instruments Taught. Brass, Organ, Percussion, Piano, Stringed Instruments, Voice, Woodwinds.

Musical Facilities

Practice Facilities. The Fine Arts Building contains fifteen studios with electronic equipment; twenty-five practice rooms; instrumental rehearsal room; two auditoriums; and classrooms. The sixty pianos in the music school include a Steinway and two Baldwin concert grands. A seventy-rank Holtkamp organ in the Bishop W. Angie Smith Chapel is used for organ study. There are also two modern practice organs. The choral rehearsal room is located in the chapel.

Concert Facilities. Kilpatrick Theatre, seating 1,100.

Concerts/Musical Activities. Student and faculty recitals and concerts; four music theatre events are presented each year.

Music Library. The Music Library contains over 5,000 books, thousands of musical scores, and an extensive record and tape collection. Listening carrels are available.

Special Programs

Performance Groups. University Singers, Choral Union, Chamber Choir, Surrey Singers, University Band, University Orchestra, Jazz Ensemble, Keshena Kids, Pep Band, Vocal Ensembles, Instrumental Ensembles.

Financial

Costs. Per academic year: Tuition $3,726. Fees $60. Room $1,176. Board $1,520.

Financial Aid. Financial aid is available in the form of scholarships, grants-in-aid, federal grants and loans, and part-time campus employment. Financial aid/scholarship application due March 1.

Southeastern Oklahoma State University Department of Music
Durant
Oklahoma 74701

Telephone. (405) 924-0121, Ext. 244

Chief Administrator. Dr. Paul Mansur, Chairman.

Southeastern Oklahoma State University opened its doors in 1909 as Southeastern State Normal School. Its original purpose was the education of teachers for the public schools of Oklahoma. In 1921, the institution became a four-year college and changed its name to Southeastern State Teachers College. University status was awarded in 1974 and the present name was adopted. The 110-acre campus is located in Durant within a ten minute drive of Lake Texoma.

The Department of Music offers programs serving the needs and interests of students majoring in music. Music performance and enrichment opportunities are provided to all other students in the University. The degree plans offered by the Department are designed to prepare graduates for a diversity of career opportunities. Besides placement in schools, graduates go directly into graduate study, enter the music therapy profession, open private teaching studios, become ministers of music and educational directors for churches, enter the college teaching profession, or become involved with some aspect of the music business.

Accreditation. North Central Association of Colleges and Schools; National Association of Schools of Music; National Council for Accreditation of Teacher Education.

Academic Information

Enrollment, Music Majors. Full-time 39 men, 33 women.

Music Faculty. Full-time 11.

Term System. Semester. 8-week summer session from early June to late July. Academic year from August to May.

Entrance Requirements. High school graduation with grade point average of 2.8; ACT score of 14; audition required. Foreign students must have TOEFL score of 500; maintain course load of at least 12 hours per semester.

Admission Procedure. Application with supporting documents to University Enrollment Center.

Music Degrees Offered. Bachelor of Arts; Bachelor of Music Education; Master of Education.

Music Degree Requirements. The Bachelor of Arts degree in applied music requires the completion of a minimum of 124 semester hours. Emphases are offered in applied music, sacred music, music theory, and composition. The Bachelor of Music Education degree is offered with emphases in instrumental, vocal, or instrumental/vocal combined. Graduates of this program receive teacher certification and most enter the teaching profession as choral music directors, band and orchestra directors, or elementary school music specialists. The Master of Education degree is offered with specialization in applied music or composition/theory.

General Program Areas. Composition, Music Education, Music Theory, Performance, Sacred Music.

Instruments Taught. Bassoon, Clarinet, Euphonium, Flute, Guitar, Marimba, Oboe, Organ, Percussion, Piano, Piccolo, Saxophone, Trombone, Trumpet, Tuba, Voice.

Musical Facilities

Practice Facilities. 9 practice rooms. 9 pianos (uprights); 3 grand pianos reserved for piano majors (2 Bosendorfer and 1 Kawai).

Concert Facilities. Montgomery Auditorium, seating 1,200; Fine Arts Recital Hall, 200.

Community Facilities. Organ students take their lessons at First Baptist Church of Durant.

Concerts/Musical Activities. Large ensemble, small ensemble, and solo recitals (average of 1 performance per week).

Music Library. 1,550 volumes; 22 current periodical subscriptions; 2,600 recordings. Books are housed in main campus library; recordings are maintained in the Fine Arts Building. 4 listening stations (stereo).

Special Programs

Performance Groups. Choral Union, University Chorale, Chorvettes, Chamber Singers, Opera Workshop, Marching Band, Concert Band, Stage Band, Instrumental Ensemble.

Financial

Costs. Per academic year: Tuition in-state resident $731, out-of-state $2,060. Applied music fee $28 per semester hour. Room $800. Board $944 to $1,320.

Financial Aid. Financial aid is awarded on the basis of academic merit, financial need, musical ability. Financial aid/scholarship application due March 1. Part-time employment and a College Work-study program available.

Southwestern Oklahoma State University Department of Music
100 Campus Drive
Weatherford
Oklahoma 73096

Telephone. (405) 772-6611, Ext. 4305

Chief Administrator. Dr. Charles Chapman, Chair.

Southwestern Oklahoma State University was established in 1901 as the Southwest Normal School. In 1920, the preparatory courses were eliminated and two additional years of college work were added. The name was changed to Southwestern State Teachers College and the first baccalaureate degrees were awarded in 1921. In 1971, the institution achieved university status and the present name was adopted. The 73-acre campus overlooks the city of Weatherford, 65 miles west of Oklahoma City.

The objectives of the Department of Music are to: (1) enrich the student's understanding of music through the study of literature, history, and theory; (2) provide the student with the necessary knowledge, skills, and material to teach music; (3) provide the student with performance experience; and (4) offer cultural enrichment to the student body.

Accreditation. North Central Association of Colleges and Schools; National Association of Schools of Music; National Association for Music Therapy.

Academic Information

Enrollment, Music Majors. (Total University) 5,000.

Music Faculty. Full-time 14, part-time 3.

Term System. Semester. 8-week summer session. Academic year from mid-August to early May.

Entrance Requirements. High school graduation with 18 units including 4 English, 1 mathematics, 1 laboratory science, 1 social science; rank in upper 70 percent of graduating class; score of 15 or above on ACT; audition and recommendation of high school director; graduate students must take entrance examination and audition. Foreign students must demonstrate proficiency in English with score of 500 or higher on TOEFL; financial certificate; grade average of 2.0 on 4.0 scale; ACT.

Admission Procedure. Application with supporting documents to Office of Admissions.

Music Degrees Offered. Bachelor of Arts; Bachelor of Music Education; Master of Music.

Music Degree Requirements. The Bachelor of Arts degree in music is offered with emphasis in applied music, sacred music, theory and composition, and music merchandising. The degree requires the completion of 125 semester hours of study. The Bachelor of Music Education degree is offered with specializations in instrumental, voice/piano/organ, combined vocal/instrumental, and music therapy.

The Master of Music degree program is designed to meet graduate education needs of individuals who wish to specialize in music performance, music teaching, church music, and related areas. The degree requires the completion of 32 hours.

General Program Areas. Applied Music, Church Music, Composition, Music Merchandising, Music Theory, Performance.

Instruments Taught. Brass, Guitar, Harpsichord, Organ, Percussion, Piano, Stringed Instruments, Voice, Woodwinds.

Musical Facilities

Practice Facilities. 27 practice rooms. 3 organs (Wicks, Austin, Moeller). 27 practice pianos (Baldwin, Hamilton studio spinets; 2 Baldwin grands); 2 grand pianos reserved for piano majors.

Concert Facilities. Fine Arts Auditorium, seating 1,-600; Old Science Auditorium, 300; Fine Arts Recital Hall, 150; Music Department Recital Hall, 75.

Concerts/Musical Activities. Performance organizations present 4 concerts per year; spring recitals presented 3 or 4 times per week.

Music Library. Music materials are housed in the main library; records and scores maintained in Department of Music. 7 listening stations (stereo).

Special Programs

Performance Groups. Mixed Chorus, Southwestern Singers, Show and Chamber Choir, Women's Glee Club, Men's Glee Club, Marching Band, Symphonic Band, Wind Symphony, Wind Ensemble, Jazz Ensemble, Woodwind Ensemble, Vocal Ensemble, Brass Ensemble, Small Instrumental Ensembles, Percussion Ensemble, Orchestra.

Financial

Costs. Per academic year: Tuition in-state resident $600, out-of-state $1,800. Private music lessons $18 per semester hour (one 25-minute period per week). Room $340 to $390. Board $770 to $810.

Financial Aid. The financial aid at Southwestern Oklahoma State University includes employment, loans, scholarships, tuition waivers, and grants from institutional, private, commercial, state, and federal agencies and programs. Financial aid/scholarship application due February 1.

University of Tulsa
Faculty of Music
600 South College Avenue
Tulsa
Oklahoma 74104

Telephone. (918) 592-6000, Ext. 2262
Chief Administrator. Judith Auer, Chair.

The forerunner of the University of Tulsa was the Henry Kendall College, founded at Muskogee, Indian Territory, in 1894 by the Presbyterian Board of Home Missions. The college moved to its permanent campus in 1907 and its present name was adopted in 1920.

The Faculty of Music offers undergraduate and graduate programs.

Accreditation. North Central Association of Colleges and Schools; National Association of Schools of Music.

Academic Information

Enrollment, Music Majors. (Total University) 4,437.
Music Faculty. 12.
Term System. Semester. Two summer sessions.
Entrance Requirements. High school graduation; completion of 15 college preparatory units including 4 English, 2 mathematics, 2 science, 2 social science; SAT or ACT required; audition required.
Admission Procedure. Application with supporting documents and nonrefundable $25 fee to Admissions Office.
Music Degrees Offered. Bachelor of Music; Bachelor of Music Education; Bachelor of Arts; Master of Music.
Music Degree Requirements. The Bachelor of Music degree is offered with majors in instrumental, piano, voice, and composition. The Bachelor of Music Education degree is offered with emphases in instrumental, piano and vocal, vocal, vocal and instrumental, and education. The Bachelor of Arts degree is offered with a major in music in a liberal arts program.

The Faculty of Music offers programs leading to the Master of Music degree which encompass major studies in composition, theory, or applied music history and theory.

General Program Areas. Applied Music, Composition, Music Education, Music History, Music Theory.

Instruments Taught. Baritone, Bass, Bassoon, Clarinet, Flute, French Horn, Guitar, Oboe, Organ, Percussion, Piano, Saxophone, Trombone, Trumpet, Tuba, Viola, Violin, Violoncello, Voice.

Musical Facilities

Practice Facilities. The Faculty of Music is housed in Tyrell Hall.

Concerts/Musical Activities. Student and faculty concerts and recitals; visiting artists.

Music Library. The University libraries contain more than a million items and support the programs of the

Faculty of Music.

Special Programs

Performance Groups. University Band, Wind Ensemble, Symphonic Band, Golden Hurricane Band, University Orchestra, University Chorale, Modern Choir, Jazz Workshop, Chamber Music Ensembles, Opera Theatre, String Orchestra.

Financial

Costs. Per academic year: Tuition $5,200. Fees $70. Room $1,170. Board $1,430.

Financial Aid. Financial aid is awarded on the basis of academic merit and financial need. Institutional and state/federal aid are available in the form of scholarships, grants, loans, and part-time employment. Financial aid/scholarship application due March 1.

OREGON

Lewis and Clark College
Music Department
0615 S.W. Palatine Hill Road
Portland
Oregon 97219

Telephone. (503) 293-2724
Chief Administrator. Dr. Lee Garrett, Chair.

Lewis and Clark College is a private institution founded in 1867. It is affiliated with the Presbyterian Church U.S.A. The campus occupies a country estate of 130 acres in the city of Portland, located at the juncture of the Willamette and Columbia Rivers.

The Music Department aims to enable students to achieve excellence in musical performance and scholarship and also, by deepening students' understanding and appreciation of the art, to establish music as an enriching element in their lives. The Department offers programs to prepare professionally oriented students for careers in music and to help majors and nonmajors integrate musical studies into a liberal arts education. The curriculum covers a wide range of musical activity and thought from technical studies and performance to history and literature, from theory and composition to research methods and music education. The interaction of theoretical concepts and practical performance is stressed. A number of courses deal with the relationship between music and society.

Accreditation. Northwest Association of Schools and Colleges; National Association of Schools of Music.

Academic Information

Enrollment, Music Majors. (Total College) 2,160.
Music Faculty. 25 (full- and part-time).
Term System. Quarter.
Entrance Requirements. High school graduation with rank in upper 20 percent of graduating class; SAT required; audition required.
Admission Procedure. Application with supporting documents and nonrefundable $20 fee to Office of Admissions.

Music Degrees Offered. Bachelor of Arts.
Music Degree Requirements. The Bachelor of Arts degree is offered with the major in music as part of a liberal arts program. Students are urged to declare their major interest in the freshman year. To qualify for honors candidacy, students must show outstanding promise as performers, scholars, composers, or teachers.
General Program Areas. Composition, Music Education, Music History, Music Literature, Music Theory, Performance.
Instruments Taught. Brass, Gamelan, Guitar, Percussion, Piano, Recorder, Stringed Instruments, Voice, Woodwinds.

Musical Facilities

Practice Facilities. The musical life of the College centers in Evans Music Building. Rehearsal rooms, 22 practice rooms, faculty offices and teaching studios, classrooms, and administrative offices are located here. 43 pianos including concert grands, 2 harpsichords, and a Baroque organ; 85-rank Casavant organ available in the Agnes Flanagan Chapel.
Concert Facilities. Evans Auditorium, seating 400; Agnes Flanagan Chapel; Fir Acres Theatre.
Concerts/Musical Activities. Student/faculty concerts and recitals; visiting artists.
Music Library. The Music Department makes use of an extensive collection of more than 4,000 recordings, tapes, and cassettes housed in the Aubrey Watzek Library. A fully equipped listening center is available.

Special Programs

Performance Groups. Chamber Music Ensembles, Concert Choir, Jazz Ensemble, Lewis and Clark Chamber Orchestra, Lewis and Clark Community Chorale, Opera Workshop, Palatine Hill Symphony Orchestra, Symphonic Wind Ensemble, Gamelan Ensemble.

Financial

Costs. Per academic year: Tuition $8,159. Fees $435. Room $1,560. Board $1,920.

Financial Aid. Financial aid is awarded primarily on the basis of need through scholarships, grants, loans, and part-time employment. The College also offers awards without regard to need to students selected as Presidential Scholars and to students demonstrating outstanding talent in music and forensics. Financial aid/scholarship application due February 15.

Commentary

Lewis and Clark College is affiliated with a number of study programs in different parts of the world. Students at the College are encouraged to take advantage of opportunities to travel and study abroad at some point during their four years of undergraduate work.

University of Oregon
School of Music
Eugene
Oregon 97403

Telephone. (503) 686-3761

Chief Administrator. Dr. Morrette Rider, Dean.

The University of Oregon began classes in 1876. Today it comprises the College of Arts and Sciences and seven professional schools and colleges. More than 900 full-time faculty members and several hundred adjunct professors and graduate teaching and research assistants serve the 16,000 undergraduate and graduate students. The 250-acre campus is located in Eugene, 60 miles east of the Pacific Ocean and 60 miles west of the Cascade Mountains.

The School of Music began as the Department of Music in 1886. It became the School of Music in 1900. The primary aims of the school are to help students prepare for a variety of professions in music, to provide nonmajors with elective studies that can enhance their understanding and enjoyment of music, and to provide the community with a rich diversity of musical experience. The School of Music is housed in a complex of five units, two completed in 1978.

Accreditation. Western Association of Schools and Colleges; National Association of Schools of Music.

Academic Information

Enrollment, Music Majors. Full-time 200 men, 250 women; part-time 50 men, 50 women. 30 foreign students.

Music Faculty. Full-time 37, part-time 30.

Term System. Quarter. 3 summer sessions (mostly specialized workshops).

Entrance Requirements. High school graduation or GED; Oregon graduates must have a minimum 2.75 GPA in all high school subjects; completion of 14 units including 4 English, 3 mathematics, 2 laboratory science, 3 social studies, 2 foreign language, performing arts, or computer studies; SAT or ACT; audition required, to include works from three periods; diagnostic musicianship examination.

Admission Procedure. Applications and $25 nonrefundable fee accepted on a rolling basis.

Music Degrees Offered. Bachelor of Music; Bachelor of Arts; Bachelor of Science; Master of Arts; Master of Music; Doctor of Musical Arts; Doctor of Philosophy; Doctor of Education.

Music Degree Requirements. The Bachelor of Arts degree in music is primarily for students wanting a broad liberal arts education while majoring in music. The Bachelor of Science degree in music is appropriate for students wanting a broad education in the sciences or social sciences while majoring in music. The degree requires the completion of core courses in music, general education, and other specific degree requirements. The Bachelor of Music degree is offered with majors in composition, education, education: choral-general, education: choral-instrumental, education: instrumental, music merchandising, performance (instrumental, keyboard, percussion, voice), and music theory. The baccalaureate degrees require the completion of 144 to 148 hours depending on major and program pursued.

The Master of Arts degree is offered with emphasis in music history, music theory, and music education. The Master of Music degree is offered with ares of focus in choral conducting, composition, music education (choral-general, choral-instrumental, instrumental); performance (instrumental, keyboard, percussion, voice), and piano pedagogy. Requirements for the master's degrees vary according to focus.

The Doctor of Musical Arts degree is offered in music composition, music education (choral-general, choral-instrumental, instrumental), music history, performance (instrumental, keyboard, percussion, voice), and music theory. The Doctor of Education or the Doctor of Philosophy degrees are offered in music education (choral-general, choral-instrumental, instrumental). A supporting area is offered in choral conducting.

General Program Areas. Choral Conducting, Composition, Music Education, Music History, Music Theory, Performance.

Instruments Taught. Baritone, Bass, Bassoon, Clarinet, Clavichord, Flute, Fortepiano, French Horn, Guitar, Harp, Harpsichord, Oboe, Organ, Piano, Recorder, Saxophone, Trombone, Trumpet, Tuba, Viola, Violin, Violoncello, Voice.

Musical Facilities

Practice Facilities. 65 practice rooms. 7 organs (concert instrument is baroque by Jurgend Ahrend). 5 percussion-equipped practice rooms. 100 practice pianos (Steinway); 7 grand pianos reserved for piano majors. Electronic music studio; ethnic instruments laboratory; reed-making studio.

Concert Facilities. Beall Hall, seating 700; Choral Hall, 200; Silva Hall, 2,600; Soreng Theater, 700.

Concerts/Musical Activities. 250 on-campus concerts annually plus 250 more in community chamber concert series; Bach Festival (30 concerts); opera, ballet, symphony.

Music Library. 11,000 books; 15,000 scores; 175 periodicals; 500 microfiche; 30,000 recordings. Listening facilities (stereo, cassette). Special collections include: folk songs; ethnic instruments; early instruments; jazz; extensive complete editions; American sheet music; American popular music of Henry J. Beau.

Special Programs

Featured Programs. The School of Music has conducted the annual Oregon Bach Festival during a two-week period in late June and early July for the past 17 years.

Performance Groups. University Singers, University Chorale, Chamber Choir, Contemporary Chorus, Oregon Wind Ensemble, University Percussion Ensemble, Marching Band, Symphonic Band, Pep Band, Symphony Orchestra, Sinfonietta, Brass Choir, Jazz Ensembles, Jazz Laboratory Bands, Vocal Jazz Ensembles, Opera Workshop, Collegium Musicum, Small Chamber Ensembles.

Foreign Programs. One-year advanced program in international music education for upper division graduate students in England and Germany.

Financial

Costs. Per academic year: Tuition in-state resident $990, out-of-state $2,793. Room and board $2,385.

Financial Aid. Financial aid in the form of scholarships, grants, loans, and employment is available to eligible students. 60 music scholarships awarded ranging from $500 to $3,000 (average award $2,000). Scholarship/financial aid application due February 1.

Commentary

The record collection at the University of Oregon Library is strong in music by women composers and has an impressive collection of 78 RPM recordings.

Oregon State University
Department of Music
Benton Hall
Corvallis
Oregon 97331

Telephone. (503) 754-4061

Chief Administrator. Dr. David Eiseman, Chair.

Oregon State University provides diverse educational opportunities through the undergraduate and graduate programs of its 12 colleges and schools. The University began as Corvallis College in 1858. It has been known as Oregon Agricultural College and State Agricultural College, after the state took control in 1885; as Oregon State College from the 1920s; and as Oregon State University since 1961. The University is now home for more than 16,000 undergraduate and graduate students, representing 75 countries and every state. The 400-acre campus is located in the city of Corvallis in the heart of the Willamette Valley between the Cascade Mountains on the east and the Coast Range on the west. Corvallis is 80 miles south of Portland.

The Department of Music was established in 1922 and is part of the College of Liberal Arts. It offers courses leading to the Bachelor of Arts and Bachelor of Science degrees in music or music education. A master's degree program is also offered. A wide diversity of courses, for which no background in music is required, is offered for the nonmajor.

Accreditation. Northwest Association of Schools and Colleges; National Association of Schools of Music; National Council for Accreditation of Teacher Education.

Academic Information

Term System. Quarter.

Entrance Requirements. High school graduation or equivalent; minimum 2.5 GPA in all high school subjects (2.75 for out-of-state students); SAT.

Admission Procedure. Application with supporting documents and $25 nonrefundable application fee.

Music Degrees Offered. Bachelor of Arts; Bachelor of Science; Master of Arts in Interdisciplinary Studies.

Music Degree Requirements. Through a basic core curriculum in the College of Liberal Arts, students can major in music while concurrently preparing for a career in business, medicine, law, dentistry, or a variety of technological fields. Through an expanded curriculum, music majors may concentrate on career preparation in music or music education alone. Music education majors have several areas of emphasis available including public school teaching with state certification in music at the elementary, junior, and senior high school levels (K-12 certificate); state certification in music in combination with preparation for elementary classroom teaching (K-9 certificate); or preparation for independent music teaching.

The Department of Music participates in the Master of Arts in Interdisciplinary Studies degree program and offers a graduate minor. Areas of specialization include music history and literature, theory and composition, performance, conducting, pedagogy, and world, folk, and jazz traditions.

General Program Areas. Composition, Conducting, Folk Music, Jazz Studies, Music History, Music Literature, Music Theory, Performance.

Instruments Taught. Brass, Percussion, Piano, Stringed Instruments, Voice, Woodwinds.

Musical Facilities

Practice Facilities. 16 practice rooms. Special practice facilities for percussionists. Electronic music studio houses high quality sound recording, duplicating, and playback equipment, and a custom-designed electronic music synthesizer.

Concert Facilities. Stewart Center Performance Auditorium, Corvallis Arts Center.

Concerts/Musical Activities. Student and faculty concerts and recitals; Corvallis and OSU Music Association and the Friends of Chamber Music bring artists of international fame to the campus for concerts and recitals.

Music Library. In addition to books and printed music in Kerr Library, phonograph records, printed music, modern listening facilities, and electronic and computerized learning aids are available in the Music Learning Center in Benton Hall.

Special Programs

Performance Groups. University Choir, University Singers, Vocal Jazz Ensemble, Men's Glee Club, Madrigal Singers, Vocal Ensemble, Symphonic Band, Concert Band, Jazz Band, Marching Band, University Symphony Orchestra, Chamber Orchestra, Woodwind Ensemble, Brass Ensemble, Percussion Ensemble, String Ensemble.

Financial

Costs. Per academic year: Tuition undergraduate residents $1,410, nonresidents $4,050; graduate residents $2,073, nonresidents $3,321. Practice room fee $10 per term for 1 hour per day.

Financial Aid. The music tuition scholarship program contributes toward tuition each term of a music major's four years in college. Auditions and interviews normally take place in February, March, and April each year. Selection is based on academic and musical achievement. Grants, loans, student employment, and a College Work-Study program are also sources of financial aid.

Portland State University
Department of Music

P.O. Box 751
Portland
Oregon 97207

Telephone. (503) 229-3011

Chief Administrator. Wilma F. Sheridan, Department Head.

Although Portland State is now a major university with nearly 15,000 students, its roots go back to 1946 when the State Board of Higher Education opened a small extension center in Portland. The Vanport Extension Center moved to its present downtown location in 1952, and in 1955 it became an independent, four-year, degree-granting institution. Its present name was adopted by student referendum. Occupying 28 buildings in a 28-block area, the campus is built around the Park Blocks, a greenway area reserved for pedestrians and bicyclists.

The Department of Music seeks to serve the needs of its students, both majors and nonmajors, through a curriculum designed to help them learn about music through performance and study. Experience gained in solo or group performance is enriched through knowledge of the structure and history of music. The Department offers graduate work in music education leading to the degrees of Master of Arts in Teaching and Master of Science in Teaching and toward recommendation for standard certificates (fifth year). The curriculum differentiates between specialists in vocal music and instrumental music, but candidates in both areas complete a core of required courses.

Accreditation. Northwest Association of Schools and Colleges; National Association of Schools of Music; National Council for Accreditation of Teacher Education.

Academic Information

Enrollment, Music Majors. Full-time 100 men, 84 women; part-time 35 men, 41 women. 8 foreign students.

Music Faculty. Full-time 12, part-time 10.

Term System. Quarter. A regular 8-week summer session covers the work of 1 quarter; a 3-week session offers concentrated courses.

Entrance Requirements. High school graduation or GED; minimum 2.25 GPA on all high school grades; out-of-state applicants must have 2.75 GPA; completion of 4 units English, 3 mathematics, 1 laboratory science, 2 social studies; audition required for placement; ability to read rhythm and pitch notation. GRE required for graduate study.

Admission Procedure. Application with $25 non-refundable fee due 6 weeks before admission.

Music Degrees Offered. Bachelor of Arts; Bachelor of Science; Master of Arts; Master of Science.

Music Degree Requirements. The Bachelor of Arts and the Bachelor of Science degrees are offered with a major in music requiring the completion of 186 quarter hours which include the core music curriculum. The term "music major" should be understood in its practical sense to designate students earning departmental degrees and also those earning music teaching certificates, whether their degrees are departmental or in general studies (arts and letters). Students who complete departmental majors in music and who wish to teach music in elementary and secondary schools must be accepted into the program in the School of Education and complete specific requirements in music and education. Students who major in general studies and who wish to teach must also be accepted into the School of Education program and complete specific requirements in music and education.

The Master of Arts in Teaching and the Master of

Science in Teaching degrees are offered with majors in theory/composition, history/literature, conducting, and performance. The program also requires a minimum of 9 to a maximum of 15 credits in education for a total of 45 quarter hours. All degree candidates take a final written examination which covers the areas of education, music theory, and music history. A final oral examination also may be required.

General Program Areas. Composition, Conducting, Music Education, Music History, Music Literature, Music Theory, Performance.

Instruments Taught. Brass, Guitar, Harpsichord, Organ, Percussion, Piano, Stringed Instruments, Voice, Woodwinds.

Musical Facilities

Practice Facilities. 23 practice rooms. 1 organ (Conn); a Moeller, Wicks, Casavant, and others including a tracker organ are in churches within a three-block radius of the campus. 43 practice pianos (22 upright, 14 Baldwin electronic, 6 grands); 6 grand pianos reserved for piano majors. Percussion-equipped practice room. Piano laboratory.

Concert Facilities. Concert Hall, Recital Hall.

Community Facilities. Local churches.

Concerts/Musical Activities. Twice weekly noon concerts; piano recital series; guitar recital series; student recitals and ensemble performances.

Music Library. 5,200 volumes; 5,000 scores; 35 periodicals; 580 microfiche; 4,200 recordings. Listening facilities (15 cassette players, 16 stereo). Other library resources for music students include the Multnomah County Library, the Art Museum, and the Oregon Historical Society.

Special Programs

Performance Groups. Chamber Ensembles, Band, Orchestra, Chorus, Jazz Lab Band.

Foreign Programs. Portland State is a member of the Northwest Interinstitutional Council on Study Abroad, a consortium of northwest universities whose faculty teach in Avignon, France, Reading, England, Cologne, West Germany, and Guadalajara, Mexico.

Financial

Costs. Per academic year: Tuition in-state resident $1,476, out-of-state $4,179.

Financial Aid. 10 music scholarships awarded ranging from $300 to $1,200 (average award $400). Scholarship application due February 28. Other sources of financial aid include institutional and state/federal grants and loans, student employment, and a College Work-Study program.

Willamette University
Department of Music
900 State Street
Salem
Oregon 97301

Telephone. (503) 370-6255

Chief Administrator. Dr. Martin Behnke, Chair.

Willamette University is an independent university founded in 1842 and has a historic relationship with the United Methodist Church. Its charter is nondenominational. The campus has 34 buildings on 57 acres in the city of Salem, Oregon's third largest city.

The purpose of the Music Department (the College of Music from 1900 to 1978) is to educate students for careers of musical leadership in musical education, musical performance, and musical therapy within the broad spectrum of a liberal arts education. It also affords the general student an opportunity to study the literature of music with an approach designed to develop basic musicianship, the ability to perform the literature well, and a set of principles and terms that lead to a fuller intellectual grasp of the art.

Accreditation. Northwest Association of Schools and Colleges; National Association of Schools of Music.

Academic Information

Enrollment, Music Majors. (Total University) 1,850.

Music Faculty. Full-time 10, part-time 12.

Term System. Semester.

Entrance Requirements. High school graduation or GED; rank in upper third of graduating class; completion of 16 units of college preparatory courses including 4 English, 3 mathematics, 2 foreign language, 2 science, 3 social science; SAT; audition required.

Admission Procedure. Application with $25 nonrefundable fee due March 1.

Music Degrees Offered. Bachelor of Music; Bachelor of Music Education; Bachelor of Arts; Bachelor of Science.

Music Degree Requirements. The Bachelor of Music degree in Performance is a professional program for those students who are preparing for careers as performers, scholars, private teachers, and as teachers at the college level. Majors are offered in voice, piano, organ, strings, woodwinds, brass, and percussion instruments. The Bachelor of Music Education degree is the basic professional program for students who plan to teach music at the elementary or secondary level. This degree satisfies all the requirements for teacher certification with the Basic Norm in Music for the state of Oregon. The degree Bachelor of Music in Music Therapy is a professional program for students who are working with children and adults needing special services because of emotional, learning, or physical disabilities. The degrees Bachelor of Arts and Bachelor of Science in Music are offered in the liberal arts programs. All baccalaureate music majors must satisfy a set of basic music requirements as well as the general education requirements and those specific to each degree program. The baccalaureate degrees require the completion of 31 credits of which no more than two may be earned in the major or professional internships.

General Program Areas. Music Education, Music History, Music Therapy, Performance.

Instruments Taught. Brass, Organ, Percussion, Piano, Stringed Instruments, Voice, Woodwinds.

Musical Facilities

Practice Facilities. 43 practice rooms. 2 practice organs. Percussion-equipped practice room. 38 pianos (grands and uprights); 5 grand pianos reserved for piano majors.

Concert Facilities. G. Herbert Smith Auditorium, seating 1,250; 2 recital halls.

Community Facilities. Local churches.

Concerts/Musical Activities. The Music Department presents a regular series of concerts and recitals by university ensembles, students, and faculty. It also offers a Distinguished Artists Series of guest artists who perform and present master classes on campus. Weekly student recitals are also performed.

Music Library. The Music Library contains a comprehensive and up-to-date collection of musical scores, books, microfilm, and recordings. Listening facilities (cassette, stereo).

Special Programs

Performance Groups. Willamette Singers, University-Community Choir, Willamette Chamber Orchestra, Chamber Music Ensembles, Willamette Opera Theatre, Willamette Symphonic Band, University Jazz Ensemble, Willamette-Community Orchestra.

Financial

Costs. Per academic year: Tuition $7,560. Room and board $3,200.

Financial Aid. A number of music scholarships, as well as institutional financial aid, are awarded to entering students. Student employment opportunities under the Federal Work-Study program also are available to music students; these include accompanying work in the Music Library, and various secretarial and clerical jobs. State/federal grants and loans are another source of financial aid.

PENNSYLVANIA

The Academy of Vocal Arts
1920 Spruce Street
Philadelphia
Pennsylvania 19103

Telephone. (215) 735-1685

Chief Administrator. K. James McDowell, Director.

The Academy of Vocal Arts (AVA) is a nonprofit organization which devotes all of its resources to the complete training of exceptionally talented singers. AVA was founded in October 1934 by the late Helen Corning Warden, with the purpose of "making available to talented and deserving young men and women opportunities for vocal instruction and to assist and supervise their work." The Academy is supported by its endowment funds and contributions from corporations, foundations, and individual patrons.

The objective of The Academy of Vocal Arts is to provide talented young men and women with tuition-free training in vocal instruction and other disciplines in order to prepare them for operatic and concert careers. The Academy accepts students exclusively on a full-tuition scholarship basis so that they can receive the professional training they need without bearing the prohibitive costs involved. Students are responsible for their own daily living expenses and for securing their own living quarters.

The full course at the Academy is four years. The curriculum is structured in two sections. In theory, the first two years are devoted to the teaching of basic studies. The next two years are involved with a fully professional-level performance experience.

Academic Information

Enrollment, Music Majors. 25 students only are admitted each year.

Music Faculty. 20.

Term System. Semester.

Entrance Requirements. Applicants should have at least two years, preferably four, of college training or its equivalent in private study; women applicants should be no older than 28 and men no older than 30. Audition required; applicants should be prepared to sing one aria of their own choice, and one selected by the auditions committee, from a list of five contrasting opera arias to be submitted by the applicant at the time of the audition.

Admission Procedure. Application with $20 fee by March 7.

Music Degrees Offered. Certificate of Merit.

General Program Areas. Music History, Music Theory, Opera, Solfege, Theater History, Voice Science.

Instruments Taught. Voice.

Musical Facilities

Concert Facilities. The Helen Corning Warden Theater.

Concerts/Musical Activities. Operatic productions are performed throughout the year.

Music Library. The AVA Library is a selective collection comprised primarily of opera vocal scores, song and aria collections; a limited number of light opera, musical comedy, and choral scores; and a small opera-oriented reference collection. Of special interest is the Baron Maximilian de Schauensee Collection of Recorded Vocal Music. The collection numbers more than 5,000 discs and is available for study in the Academy's Thomas Herndon Memorial Listening Room. The Academy's original record collection of approximately 400 discs is also available for listening.

Financial

Costs. No tuition; all students are granted a scholarship.

Financial Aid. Qualified students are helped financially and professionally by the AVA Concert Bureau which arranges auditions with opera companies, conductors, and agents, and provides opportunities to perform in outside, professional-level concerts.

Carnegie-Mellon University
Department of Music
College of Fine Arts
5000 Forbes Avenue
Pittsburgh
Pennsylvania 15213

Telephone. (412) 268-2372

Chief Administrator. Professor Joel Thome, Head, Department of Music.

Carnegie-Mellon University was founded in 1900 by steel industrialist Andrew Carnegie. The Carnegie Technical School evolved into an engineering college and in 1911 the College of Fine Arts was established. Carnegie Institute of Technology and the Mellon Institute merged in 1967 to form the present University. The 90-acre campus is located four miles from downtown Pittsburgh.

The Department of Music offers a comprehensive curriculum. Students receive individualized advising from faculty members in planning their programs, which provide preparation for careers in performance, composition, or teaching.

Accreditation. Middle States Association of Colleges and Schools; National Association of Schools of Music.

Academic Information

Enrollment, Music Majors. (Total University) 6,621.

Music Faculty. Full-time 13, adjunct 27.

Term System. Semester. Two summer sessions.

Entrance Requirements. High school graduation; completion of 16 college preparatory units; SAT or ACT and three Achievement Tests required; personal interview recommended.

Admission Procedure. Application and supporting documents with nonrefundable $30 fee to Office of Admissions.

Music Degrees Offered. Bachelor of Fine Arts; Master of Fine Arts.

Music Degree Requirements. The Bachelor of Fine Arts degree is offered with a major in performance (instrumental, keyboard, guitar, voice, music theatre voice, composition, music education with teacher certification). Within these options students may elect specializations in the areas of composer librettist, Dalcroze Eurhythmics Certification, and piano pedagogy.

The Department offers two-year programs leading to a Master of Fine Arts degree in the areas of applied music (performance), conducting, composition, and music education.

General Program Areas. Composition, Conducting, Eurhythmics, Music Education, Performance, Piano Pedagogy.

Instruments Taught. Brass, Guitar, Organ, Percussion, Piano, Stringed Instruments, Voice, Woodwinds.

Musical Facilities

Practice Facilities. The facilities of the Department of Music are located on the main floor and mezzanine of the College of Fine Arts and on the first floor of Margaret Morrison Hall. Facilities include practice rooms, listening rooms, audiovisual aids, teaching studios, an electronic and computer music studio, solfege laboratory, computer music research laboratory, and concert hall.

Concert Facilities. Mellon Institute; Carnegie Music Hall; Alumni Concert Hall; Kresge Theatre.

Concerts/Musical Activities. The Department of Music sponsors special performances, master classes, and lectures by national and international guest artists; student and faculty recitals and concerts.

Music Library. Music materials including books, records, and scores are housed on the fourth floor of Hunt Library. These include printed scores, either first editions or have inscriptions, by Beethoven, Schubert, and Wagner. Adjacent to the University are Carnegie Public Library and Music Hall.

Special Programs

Performance Groups. Carnegie-Mellon Symphony Orchestra, Wind Ensemble, Jazz Ensemble, Cameron Choir, Chamber Choir, Jazz Choir, Contemporary Ensemble.

Financial

Costs. Per academic year: Tuition $10,250. Fees $60. Room $2,230. Board $1,510.

Financial Aid. Financial aid is available in the form of scholarships, graduate assistantships, grants, loans, and part-time employment. Financial aid/scholarship application due February 15.

Combs College of Music
7500 Germantown Avenue
Philadelphia
Pennsylvania 19119

Telephone. (215) 248-1330

Chief Administrator. Dr. Frank A. DiBussolo, President.

The College was founded in 1885 as the Combs Broad Street Conservatory of Music. The present name was adopted in 1933. In 1986, the College entered into an arrangement with Spring Garden College, moving from Bryn Mawr to the Mt. Airy-Chestnut Hill section of Philadelphia.

Accreditation. Middle States Association of Colleges and Schools; Pennsylvania Department of Education.

Academic Information

Enrollment, Music Majors. Full-time 45 men, 24 women; part-time 16.

Music Faculty. Full-time 12, part-time 17.

Term System. Semester. One summer term.

Entrance Requirements. High school graduation with rank in upper 50 percent of class; completion of 15 units including 3 English, 1 mathematics, 2 foreign language, 1 science, 2 social science, 3 music; college entrance examination and audition required.

Admission Procedure. Application with supporting documents and nonrefundable $35 fee ($45 for graduate students) to Director of Admissions.

Music Degrees Offered. Bachelor of Music; Master of Music; Doctor of Musical Arts.

Music Degree Requirements. The Bachelor of Music degree is offered with programs in music education, performance, and music therapy. The program in music education prepares the student for a career in teaching at the elementary and secondary levels. It requires a minimum of 128 semester hours, including a full semester of supervised practice teaching. The program in music performance prepares the student for an active performance career in piano, organ, voice, guitar, jazz studies, orchestral instruments, and music composition. This program is flexible in choice of courses; the student is eligible for graduation upon the completion of 128 semester hours. The curriculum in music therapy prepares the student for a career as a music therapist in both clinical settings and private practice. With the completion of the required 133 semester hours, the student must complete an additional six months of full-time supervised internship in order to qualify for certification as a Registered Music Therapist by the National Association for Music Therapy. The baccalaureate degree programs require the completion of a liberal arts core. These courses are taught by Spring Garden College faculty.

The Master of Music degree requires the completion of minimum of 36 semester hours. Specializations are available in music education, performance, conducting, sacred music, and composition. The Doctor of Musical Arts degree requires the completion of 90 semester hour credits beyond the baccalaureate degree.

General Program Areas. Afro-American Music, Composition, Conducting, Jazz Studies, Music Education, Music History, Music Theory, Music Therapy, Performance, Sacred Music, World Music.

Instruments Taught. Brass, Guitar, Harpsichord, Organ, Percussion, Piano, Stringed Instruments, Voice, Woodwinds.

Musical Facilities

Practice Facilities. The Combs College of Music shares facilities on Spring Garden College's 33-acre campus.

Concerts/Musical Activities. Student/faculty recitals and concerts.

Music Library. The Combs College musical books, recordings, and scores are housed in the Spring Garden College Library.

Special Programs

Featured Programs. The College has been granted Program Approval in Music by the Pennsylvania Department of Education. This authorizes the College to recommend for state certification (Instructional I) those candidates who have successfully completed the College's approval program for the preparation of public school teachers of music.

Performance Groups. Chorus, Chamber Ensemble, Jazz Improvisation, Vocal Orchestra, Chamber Orchestra, Jazz Ensemble.

Financial

Costs. Per academic year: Tuition $5,075. Fees $200. Room $2,150. Board $1,400.

Financial Aid. Financial aid is awarded on the basis of academic merit and financial need. Institutional and state/federal aid are available in the form of scholarships, grants, loans, and part-time employment. Financial aid/scholarship application due June 1.

The Curtis Institute of Music
1726 Locust Street
Philadelphia
Pennsylvania 19103

Telephone. (215) 893-5252

Chief Administrator. Gary Graffman, Director.

The Curtis Institute of Music was founded in 1924 by Mary Louise Curtis Bok. The Institute's declared purpose is "to train exceptionally gifted young musicians for careers as performing artists on the highest professional level." Since 1928, it has been a full scholarship school, assuring talented young people the opportunity they deserve regardless of their financial situation.

Accreditation. Middle States Association of Colleges and Schools; National Association of Schools of Music.

Academic Information

Enrollment, Music Majors. Full-time 99 men, 83 women.

Music Faculty. Full-time 5, part-time 66.

Term System. Semester. No summer session.

Entrance Requirements. Sole requirements for admission are that the student shall demonstrate a native gift of music, a special aptitude for a chosen instrument, and personal characteristics that indicate the possibility of continuous further development to achieve a career on the highest professional level. To meet the compulsory educational requirements of the Commonwealth of Pennsylvania, the Institute offers its younger students an academic program of subjects leading to a secondary school diploma. Students are selected only after an audition or, for composition, after examination by the Composition Department of original compositions submitted.

Admission Procedure. Application with physician's certificate, one or two concert programs in which the applicant has participated, confidential statement from two musicians who are qualified to judge the applicant's personal and musical talents, and the most current transcript from high school or college, nonrefundable $25 fee.

Music Degrees Offered. Bachelor of Music; Master of Music in Opera; Diploma.

Music Degree Requirements. The Bachelor of Music degree is given upon completion of 124 semester hours including 48 hours in applied music, 26 hours in theory, 4 hours in techniques of 20th century music, 12 hours in solfège, 4 hours in music history, and 30 hours in academic subjects. Majors are offered in strings, woodwind, brass, percussion, piano, accompanying, and voice.

The Master of Music in Opera degree is given upon completion of 30 semester hours including 12 hours in voice lessons, 12 hours of participation in the opera program, and 6 hours in electives. Participation in the opera program includes not only opera department rehearsals and performances but also attendance at the opera history seminar. English diction class and other diction or vocal coachings are pursued as recommended by the director of the opera program. A two-year residency is expected.

The Diploma is given upon completion of 68 semester hours including 36 hours in applied music, 20 hours in theory, 8 hours in solfège, and 4 hours in music history. A minimum two-year residency is required for the diploma.

General Program Areas. Accompanying, Chamber Music, Conducting, Music History, Music Theory, Opera.

Instruments Taught. Bass, Bassoon, Clarinet, Flute, Harp, Horn, Oboe, Organ, Percussion, Piano, Trombone, Trumpet, Tuba, Viola, Violin, Violoncello, Voice.

Musical Facilities

Practice Facilities. 25 practice rooms. 2 Moeller organs; five-manual Aeolian-Skinner with 110 ranks of pipes in Curtis Hall. 2 percussion-equipped practice rooms. 72 Steinway grand pianos; each piano student receives a Steinway piano on loan in his room.

Concert Facilities. Curtis Hall, rehearsal hall.

Community Facilities. Public auditoriums are used for Symphony Orchestra and opera presentations.

Concerts/Musical Activities. Students perform three nights a week at the Institute plus conductor's orchestra, the Symphony Orchestra, and Opera Orchestra.

Music Library. The Library has 40,000 volumes and houses a special collection of rare music manuscripts, letters, and early editions. The orchestral library houses the complete Leopold Stokowski music collection which

includes his large personal library and his collection of percussion instruments. It also houses an instrument collection and a listening room. Further holdings include: autograph manuscripts of Mozart, Liszt, Schubert, Schumann; Burrell Collection; Charles Jarvis Collection of 18th and 19th century printed music.

Special Programs

Performance Groups. Symphony Orchestra, Opera Orchestra, ensembles.

Financial

Costs. Per academic year: Students are accepted on a scholarship basis exclusively and pay no tuition fees. All students are required to pay an annual $125 fee at the time of registration (high school fee $25). It is the responsibility of the student to provide for living accommodations.

Financial Aid. The Institute participates in government sponsored student assistance programs (Pell Grant, College Work-Study, Guaranteed Student Loan).

Commentary

Although an education at the Curtis Institute of Music is free, students must find their own living accommodations. Pianists receive a free loan of a Steinway grand piano for the duration of study at the Institute.

Duquesne University School of Music
600 Forbes Avenue
Pittsburgh
Pennsylvania 15282

Telephone. (412) 434-6080

Chief Administrator. Michael Kumer, Dean.

Duquesne University first opened its doors in 1878 as the Pittsburgh Catholic College of the Holy Ghost. By 1911, the school had achieved university status at which time the name Duquesne University of the Holy Ghost was adopted. Today, the University has over 6,000 students in its eight schools. The 39-acre hilltop campus is located adjacent to downtown Pittsburgh.

The School of Music was established in 1926. The objectives of the School are to educate promising students who are seeking professional training in the fields of performance, education, music therapy, and church music.

Accreditation. Middle States Association of Colleges and Schools; National Association of Schools of Music; National Association for Music Therapy.

Academic Information

Enrollment, Music Majors. 288. 11 foreign students.

Music Faculty. Full-time 23, part-time 63.

Term System. Semester. One 6-week summer session in addition to numerous special workshops.

Entrance Requirements. High school graduation or GED; completion of 16 units; SAT required; performance audition; theory and musicianship tests; interviews are required for music therapy and music education candidates.

Admission Procedure. Application with $20 non-refundable fee due July 1.

Music Degrees Offered. Bachelor of Music; Bachelor of Science; Master of Music.

Music Degree Requirements. The Bachelor of Music degree may be earned with a major in piano, organ, voice, orchestral instruments, jazz, and in sacred music with a major in organ or voice. The programs are intended for students interested primarily in performance careers in concert, television, radio, symphony orchestra, opera, or teaching in colleges and private studios and for those interested in pursuing careers as church musicians. The Bachelor of Science degree is offered in music education and music therapy. The music education program is designed to meet certification requirements for teaching in elementary and secondary schools; the program in music therapy leads to certification as a registered music therapist. All music therapy students are required to take a prescribed number and sequence of courses and give evidence of competency in the field. The program includes a six-month internship. All baccalaureate degrees require the completion of a minimum of 128 semester hours.

Master's degree programs are also available and required the completion of 36 semester hours of study.

General Program Areas. Composition, Conducting, Eurhythmics, Jazz Studies, Music Education, Music History, Music Literature, Music Theory, Music Therapy, Performance, Sacred Music.

Instruments Taught. Bass, Bassoon, Clarinet, Euphonium, Flute, Guitar, Harp, Horn, Oboe, Organ, Piano, Saxophone, Trombone, Trumpet, Tuba, Viola, Violin, Violoncello, Voice.

Musical Facilities

Practice Facilities. 40 practice rooms. 11 organs (2 Moeller and 1 Fisher practice organs, 3 manual Moeller and 1 Fuhrer tracker pipe organ, 2 pipe organs by Kilgen and Tellers, 1 Rodgers electronic theater organ. 5 percussion-equipped practice rooms. 73 pianos (Steinway uprights in practice rooms); 4 grand pianos reserved for piano majors. Computer laboratory with several microcomputers, keyboards, and related software.

Concert Facilities. Recital Hall, seating 315.

Concerts/Musical Activities. Over 150 performances are offered on campus each year. Duquesne University is located a few blocks from Heinz Hall, home of the Pittsburgh Symphony Orchestra and the Pittsburgh Opera.

Music Library. Most music books are housed in the main library. Record library is housed in the Music School Building. Listening facilities (10 cassette decks; 10 stereo turntables). Folk artifacts are housed in the Tamburitzan Cultural Center which also includes works devoted to East European Folk Arts as well as material relating to folk cultures of Eastern Europe and their immigrant communities in America. Special collections include manuscripts of Joseph W. Jenkins.

Special Programs

Featured Programs. The Duquesne University Tamburitzans were founded in 1937 at the University and were the first university-based performing folk ensemble in the United States. The group takes its name from the Tamburitza family of stringed instruments indigenous to the folk cultures of southeastern Europe. The group exists for the dual purpose of preserving and perpetuating the Eastern European cultural heritage in the United States and offering scholarship opportunities to deserving students.

Performance Groups. Brass Ensemble, Guitar Ensemble, Jazz Ensemble, Percussion Ensemble, String Orchestra, Tamburitza Ensemble, Woodwind Ensemble, Opera Workshop, Chamber Ensembles, Choral Ensembles, Band, Orchestra.

Affiliated Programs. Students may cross-register for courses offered by other institutions participating in the Pittsburgh Council on Higher Education.

Financial

Costs. Per academic year: Tuition $6,825. Room and board $3,250.

Financial Aid. Financial aid in the form of scholarships, grants, loans, part-time employment, and College Work-Study is available through the Financial Aid Office.

Commentary

The University's Tambritzans Institute of Folk Arts features courses in ethnomusicology and the study of Eastern European Folk instruments.

Indiana University of Pennsylvania Department of Music
Indiana
Pennsylvania 15705

Telephone. (412) 357-2390

Chief Administrator. Calvin E. Weber, Chairperson.

Indiana University of Pennsylvania began as a normal school in 1875. In 1920, control and ownership of the institution passed to the Commonwealth of Pennsylvania. It operated as a state college until 1965 when it was redesignated as a university. The 185-acre campus is located in the foothills of the Allegheny Mountains in western Pennsylvania.

The Department of Music has a three-fold mission: (1) professional preparation of music educators and performers, (2) general education for the University, and (3) programs of music for the community.

Accreditation. Middle States Association of Colleges and Schools; National Association of Schools of Music; National Council for Accreditation of Teacher Education.

Academic Information

Enrollment, Music Majors. (Total University) 12,938.

Music Faculty. 31.

Term System. Semester. Three summer sessions.

Entrance Requirements. High school graduation with rank in upper 30 to 40 percent; SAT or ACT required; audition required. GRE required for graduate study.

Admission Procedure. Application with supporting documents and nonrefundable $10 fee to Admissions Office.

Music Degrees Offered. Bachelor of Fine Arts; Bachelor of Arts; Master of Arts; Master of Education.

Music Degree Requirements. The program leading to the Bachelor of Fine Arts degree in music is a special program with a major in one of 21 areas of performance. The student in this program prepares to pursue a career as a professional performing musician. The program leading to the Bachelor of Arts degree in music has been designed to give the student a general experience in music. The student seeking this degree has the choice of four concentrations: music history/literature, music theory/composition, performance, and jazz studies.

Graduate programs are offered leading to the degrees Master of Arts in music and Master of Education in music education. These programs provide the student with opportunities to improve skills as teacher, performer, or scholar beyond the baccalaureate degree.

General Program Areas. Composition, Jazz Studies, Music History, Music Literature, Music Theory, Performance.

Instruments Taught. Brass, Guitar, Percussion, Piano, Stringed Instruments, Voice, Woodwinds.

Musical Facilities

Concerts/Musical Activities. The University Concert Committee presents major popular concerts throughout the year.

Music Library. The University Library houses over 540,000 volumes and supports the academic programs of the Department of Music.

Special Programs

Performance Groups. Brass Ensemble, Chamber Singers, University Chorale, Symphony Band, Glee Club, Marching Band, Music Theater, Percussion Ensemble, University Chamber Orchestra, University Symphony Orchestra, String Ensemble, University Wind Ensemble, Women's Chorus, Woodwind Ensemble, University Chorus, Jazz Ensemble, Mellowmen.

Financial

Costs. Per academic year: Tuition in-state $1,600, out-of-state $2,868. Fees $224. Room and board $2,110.

Financial Aid. The types of financial assistance offered by the Financial Aid Office include student employment, loans, grants, and scholarships. Financial aid/scholarship application due May 1.

Mansfield University
Department of Music
Mansfield
Pennsylvania 16933

Telephone. (717) 662-4710

Chief Administrator. Donald Stanley, Chairperson.

Mansfield University dates back to 1857 when the Mansfield Classical Seminary opened with 105 students. In 1862, the institution was designated a State Normal School for the training of teachers. In 1927, it was renamed the Mansfield State Teachers College; in 1960, the Mansfield State College, in 1983, university status was achieved and the present name was adopted. Today there are 76 undergraduate programs and 9 master's degree programs offered to over 2,800 students. The campus is located in Mansfield, a community of 4,000 population in the north central part of Pennsylvania.

The Department of Music has the goal of providing the requisite musical knowledge and skills for the graduate to begin a professional career.

Accreditation. Middle States Association of Colleges and Schools; National Association of Schools of Music.

Academic Information

Enrollment, Music Majors. Full-time 105 men, 85 women; part-time 5 men, 5 women. 2 foreign students.

Music Faculty. Full-time 22, part-time 3.

Term System. Semester. Academic year from late August to mid-May. 5- and 6-week summer sessions from June to August.

Entrance Requirements. High school graduation or equivalent with rank in the upper 60 percent of graduating class; SAT or ACT required; completion of 16 units including 3 English, 2 mathematics, 2 science, 2 foreign language, 2 social studies; above-average ability on major applied voice/instrument; satisfactory music aptitude score in voice audition. All students take musical aptitude tests in theory and literature; audition in voice (vocal/musical aptitude); piano; intended applied major (instrument or voice). Foreign students must score 700 or above on TOEFL and present letter of financial support.

Admission Procedure. Application with $15 nonrefundable fee to Admissions Office.

Music Degrees Offered. Bachelor of Music; Bachelor of Arts; Master of Education; Master of Arts.

Music Degree Requirements. The Bachelor of Music degree is offered with emphases in music history/literature, performance (instrumental, keyboard, voice), theory-composition, and music therapy. The Bachelor of Arts degree is offered with a major in music and is designed for students planning to teach on the college/university level or in private music schools, music library work, and other job opportunities similar to those of any student graduating with the liberal arts degree. A program in music merchandising is also offered and is designed for students interested in careers in instrument sales, sheet music, management of a music store, recording, arts management, instrument repair, entertainment manager, music engineer for stage productions, public relations for musical groups, and manager for musical tours. The baccalaureate degrees require the completion of 128 semester hours including the major and general education core.

The degrees Master of Education in music and Master of Arts in music are also offered. Most graduate courses are offered in the evenings and summer sessions at times convenient for professionals.

General Program Areas. Applied Music, Composition, Music History, Music Literature, Music Merchandising, Music Theory, Music Therapy, Performance.

Instruments Taught. Bass, Bassoon, Clarinet, Euphonium, Flute, Guitar, Harpsichord, Horn, Organ, Percussion, Piano, Saxophone, Trombone, Trumpet, Tuba, Viola, Violin, Violoncello, Voice.

Musical Facilities

Practice Facilities. 50 practice rooms. 4 organs (Moeller, Austin; Zinner and Moeller practice organs). Percussion-equipped practice facilities. 50 practice pianos (mostly Mason and Hamlin studio uprights); 6 grand pianos reserved for piano majors.

Concert Facilities. Steadman Theatre, seating 500; Strauch Auditorium, 1,300.

Concerts/Musical Activities. Over 100 concerts per year: solo, chamber, various large ensembles, opera scenes, music theatre.

Music Library. 6,700 volumes; 7,500 scores; 52 periodical subscriptions; 378 audiovisual items; 200 microform titles; 9,000 phonograph recordings and cassettes. 15 listening stations (stereo). All music materials housed in Butler Music Center.

Special Programs

Performance Groups. Band, Chorus, Piano Ensemble, Percussion Ensemble, Opera Workshop, Woodwind Ensemble, Brass Ensemble, Mansfieldians, Concert Jazz Band, String Ensemble, Chamber Singers, Small Jazz and Commercial Ensembles, Vocal Ensemble.

Financial

Costs. Per academic year: Tuition in-state resident $1,570, out-of-state $2,748. Fees $384. Room and Board $1,988. Off-campus housing approximately $200 per month.

Financial Aid. Financial aid is awarded on the basis of academic merit, financial need, musical ability. Both institutional and state/federal aid available. Financial aid/scholarship application due April 1. Part-time employment and a College Work-Study program available.

Marywood College
Music Department
2300 Adams Avenue
Scranton
Pennsylvania 18509

Telephone. (717) 348-6268

Chief Administrator. Sister Joan Paskert, Chairperson.

Marywood College was founded in 1917 by the Congregation of the Sisters, Servants of the Immaculate Heart of Mary. Begun as an undergraduate college for women, Marywood continues to give special attention to the undergraduate education of women but also responds to the needs of men and women by offering baccalaureate and master's degrees. The 180-acre campus is located in Scranton in northeastern Pennsylvania.

The programs in music are designed to provide the students with multiple learning experiences in liberal arts as well as professional education. In addition to specific careers appropriate to the programs outlined below, students also are prepared to pursue careers as music librarians, music arrangers, consultants to publishing companies, music journalists, arts managers, and in fields within the music industry and musical theater.

Accreditation. Middle States Association of Colleges and Schools; National Association of Schools of Music; National Association for Music Therapy; National Council for Accreditation of Teacher Education.

Academic Information

Enrollment, Music Majors. Full-time 20 men, 42 women; part-time 5 men, 10 women.

Music Faculty. Full-time 11, part-time 5.

Term System. Semester. Two summer sessions.

Entrance Requirements. High school graduation or equivalent; rank in upper 50 percent of graduating class; completion of 16 units including 4 English, 2 mathematics, 1 science, 3 social science; SAT required; audition required; placement theory and sight singing examination (undergraduate); performance on major instrument/voice (graduate).

Admission Procedure. Application with $20 non-refundable fee accepted on a rolling basis.

Music Degrees Offered. Bachelor of Music; Bachelor of Arts; Master of Arts.

Music Degree Requirements. The Bachelor of Music degree is offered with programs in music education, performance, church music, and music therapy. In general, the programs require the completion of a core music curriculum, prescribed courses in the major, and liberal arts courses for a minimum of 126 semester hours. The music therapy candidate must complete 146 hours of assigned clinical experience concurrent with academic studies. An internship of six months (1,040 hours) in a program approved by the National Association for Music Therapy is also required. The Bachelor of Arts degree is offered in the performing arts (concentration in music) and arts administration (primary concentration music, secondary concentration art or theatre).

The Master of Arts degree is offered with concentrations in music education, musicology, and church music. The degree requires the completion of 36 semester hours.

General Program Areas. Church Music, Music Education, Music Therapy, Musicology, Performance.

Instruments Taught. Accordion, Bass, Bassoon, Clarinet, Flute, French Horn, Guitar, Harp, Harpsichord, Oboe, Organ, Percussion, Piano, Saxophone, Trombone, Trumpet, Tuba, Viola, Violin, Violoncello, Voice.

Musical Facilities

Practice Facilities. 14 practice rooms. 2 organs (Moeller, Wurlitzer). 2 percussion-equipped practice rooms. 14 practice pianos; 10 studio pianos reserved for piano majors; Electronic piano laboratory; harp studio; harpsichord studio; Susuki studio.

Concert Facilities. Performing Arts Center Theatre, seating 1,050; Performing Arts Studio, 125.

Community Facilities. Local institutions (schools, nursing home, hospitals, handicapped center, churches) used for field work and clinical experience for music education, music therapy, and church music programs.

Concerts/Musical Activities. Major ensemble performances; Sacred Choral Concert; small ensemble concerts; Jazz Ensemble Festival; visiting artists.

Music Library. Books, scores, and recordings housed in the College Library. Listening room in Music Department.

Special Programs

Performance Groups. Chamber Choir, Campus Choir, Singers, Woodwind Ensemble, Piano Ensemble, Percussion Ensemble, Wind Ensemble, Jazz Ensemble, Orchestra, String Quartet, Guitar Ensemble, Brass Ensemble, Opera Workshop, Flute Ensemble.

Financial

Costs. Per academic year: Tuition undergraduate $4,480, graduate $2,610 to $3,000. Room and board $2,600.

Financial Aid. Talent scholarships are awarded to students majoring in music. Students should arrange an audition with the Chairperson of the Music Department. Other sources of financial aid include institutional scholarships and grants, federal and state programs, part-time employment, and a College Work-Study program.

University of Pennsylvania Department of Music

201 South 34th Street
Philadelphia
Pennsylvania 19104

Telephone. (215) 898-7544

Chief Administrator. Dr. Gary Tomlinson, Chairman.

The University of Pennsylvania is a private, independent institution founded in 1740, and a member of the Ivy League. It is privately endowed and gift supported, though it is allowed to share in the educational appropriations of the Commonwealth of Pennsylvania. Over 23,000 are enrolled each academic year and there is a faculty of 2,500.

The Department of Music provides an undergraduate program stressing the study of music as a liberal art. It is particularly designed to prepare students for graduate study in theory, composition, or the history of music. Exceptionally talented undergraduates in composition are allowed to study composition privately after fulfilling the theory requirements, and advanced students in history and theory may submatriculate into courses in the graduate program. The programs integrate performing activities into the academic discipline, in the hope that students may use their skills in performance as a means of learning about music composition. In the applied music program, music majors and minors may study for credit with instructors in the Philadelphia area.

Graduate study is offered in composition, history of music, and theory of music. The programs in composition aim primarily to develop the student's compositional craft and knowledge of contemporary repertory, but they also include substantial components of theory and analysis, designed to prepare students to teach these subjects at the university level. The programs in the history of music and theory of music are closely interconnected. Students uncertain in which of these two areas they may wish to concentrate may opt for one or the other as late as the end of their first year of study without delaying their progress toward the Ph.D. degree. Ethnomusicology courses are taught in the Southeast Asian Studies Department.

Accreditation. Middle States Association of Colleges and Schools; National Association of Schools of Music.

Academic Information

Enrollment, Music Majors. Undergraduate 10, graduate 40.

Music Faculty. Full-time 14, part-time 14.

Term System. Semester. Summer sessions.

Entrance Requirements. High school graduation with high rank in graduating class; completion of college preparatory program with recommended courses of 4 English, 3 mathematics, 3 foreign language, 3 laboratory science, 3 social science, SAT and 3 Achievement Tests required. GRE required for graduate students. Audition not required.

Admission Procedure. Application with all supporting documents to Admissions Office.

Music Degrees Offered. Bachelor of Arts; Master of Arts; Doctor of Philosophy.

Music Degree Requirements. The Bachelor of Arts degree is designed for the undergraduate who wishes to concentrate in music as a liberal art or who aspires to graduate training in composition or musicology with a thorough introduction to the history and theory of music.

The Master of Arts in composition requires the completion of 12 course units; comprehensive examination in analysis, style identification, and repertory identification; portfolio of compositions, and a public performance.

The Doctor of Philosophy degree in composition requires 8 course units beyond the 12 required for the master's; a major composition; an article-length essay on an analytical, historical, or theoretical subject.

General Program Areas. Applied Music, Composition, Music History, Music Theory.

Instruments Taught. Brass, Organ, Piano, Viola, Violin, Violoncello, Voice, Woodwinds.

Musical Facilities

Practice Facilities. 13 practice rooms. 1 organ. 13 practice pianos (Yamaha, Baldwin). 6 grand pianos reserved for piano majors.

Concert Facilities. Concert Hall, seating 750; small recital hall.

Concerts/Musical Activities. Concerts, recitals.

Music Library. The Otto E. Albrecht Music Library comprises more than 50,000 volumes and 30,000 discs and other sound recordings. The collection is especially strong in reference sources, critical editions, and literature on Western music history and theory. Other current collecting emphases include contemporary music, printed or recorded, and primary sources on microform. Extensive rare materials are found in the main library's Special Collections area. Archival holdings include the Alma Mahler Werfel Collection and the Marian Anderson Archives. Other special collections include an ethnomusicological sound recording collection and the papers of John Rowe Parker.

Special Programs

Featured Programs. Distinguished Artists Series.

Performance Groups. Collegium Musicum, Penn Contemporary Players, Penn Composers Guild, University Choir, University Choral Society, University Symphony Orchestra, University Wind Ensemble.

Foreign Programs. Study abroad program with University of Edinburgh. Faculty exchange with the Rubin Academy in Jerusalem.

Financial

Costs. Per academic year: Tuition undergraduate $11,200, graduate $11,734. Room $2,200.

Financial Aid. Scholarships, grants, loans and other forms of aid are awarded on the basis of financial need. College Work-Study program.

Pennsylvania State University School of Music
University Park
Pennsylvania 16802

Telephone. (814) 865-0431

Chief Administrator. Dr. Lyle Merriman, Director.

Pennsylvania State University, founded in 1855, comprises ten undergraduate colleges offering 125 majors. Graduate students may choose from 127 approved fields of study. The programs of the ten undergraduate colleges are distributed among the University Park campus, in central Pennsylvania, and the 21 branch campuses throughout the state.

The School of Music offers one general and two professional programs leading to baccalaureate degrees in music. Placement in any degree program is based partly on an audition, a placement examination, and an interview. Students in all programs take courses in theory, history, and their major instrument during their first four semesters. The School of Music also provides opportunities for the general student to participate in the wide range of musical activities. Graduate programs leading to the master's degree and the doctorate are also offered.

Accreditation. Middle States Association of Colleges and Schools; National Association of Schools of Music; National Council for Accreditation of Teacher Education.

Academic Information

Enrollment, Music Majors. (Total University) 35,028.

Term System. Semester.

Entrance Requirements. High school graduation; applicants are selected from those who have demonstrated by their secondary school records and SAT results that they are adequately prepared for classes in higher education; minimum 15 high school units; audition required.

Admission Procedure. Application with supporting documents and nonrefundable $20 fee to Office of Admissions.

Music Degrees Offered. Bachelor of Music; Bachelor of Arts; Bachelor of Science; Master of Music; Master of Education; Master of Arts; Doctor of Education.

Music Degree Requirements. The Bachelor of Music degree is intended to prepare students for careers in composition, history and literature, or performance. Completion of this program requires that the student achieve a high level of competence in order to begin professional work or pursue further studies at the graduate level. The degree requires the completion of 134 to 142 credits, depending upon the option pursued. The Bachelor of Arts degree in music combines a broad liberal education with a selection of courses in music. The degree is designed to develop basic musicianship, the ability to perform, and a set of principles that lead to a fuller intellectual grasp of the art. The three options offered are general, music history, and theory. A total of 130 credits is required for graduation. The Bachelor of Science degree in music education is a professional program preparing students for teaching in elementary and secondary schools. Graduates of this program receive the Pennsylvania Instrucitonal I certificate for teaching music K-12.

There are three options for emphasis available in the Master of Music degree program: performance, composition, and conducting. The degree requires the completion of 36 credits. The Master of Education degree can include emphasis in public school music teaching, music supervision, college teaching, administration, or research. The degree requires the completion of 30 credits. The Master of Arts degree, also requiring the completion of 30 credits, is directed toward musicological research.

The Doctor of Education in music education is designed to prepare teachers and researchers for positions in institutions of higher education, as well as positions of leadership in large city systems and state departments of education. The degree requires the completion of 90 credits beyond the baccalaureate degree.

General Program Areas. Composition, Music Education, Music History, Music Literature, Music Theory, Musicology, Performance.

Instruments Taught. Bass, Bassoon, Clarinet, Euphonium, Flute, French Horn, Guitar, Harpsichord, Oboe, Organ, Percussion, Piano, Saxophone, Trombone, Trumpet, Tuba, Viola, Violin, Violoncello, Voice.

Musical Facilities

Concerts/Musical Activities. Student/faculty concerts and recitals; visiting artists; master classes.

Music Library. The Arts Library supports the academic programs of the School of Music. Special collections include: field recordings of fiddlers' performances; materials of Charles Wakefield Cadman.

Special Programs

Performance Groups. Symphony Orchestra, Symphonic Wind Ensemble, Pep Band, Symphonic Blue Band, Marching Blue Band, Concert White Band, Nittany Lion Concert Band, Jazz Ensemble and Improvisation, Pop Choir, Percussion Ensemble, University Choir, Glee Club, Women's Chorus, Hi-Lo's/Keynotes, Penn State Singers, Concert Choir, Chamber Choir, Early Music Ensemble, Chapel Choir.

Financial

Costs. Per academic year: Tuition in-state resident $2,760, out-of-state $5,544. Room and board $2,750.

Financial Aid. Financial aid is available in the form of scholarships, grants, loans, and part-time employment. A College Work-Study program is also available. Scholarship/financial aid application due February 15.

Philadelphia College of the Performing Arts School of Music
250 South Broad Street
Philadelphia
Pennsylvania 19102

Telephone. (215) 875-2272, 875-2206

Chief Administrator. Dr. Donald Chittum, Director, School of Music.

The Philadelphia College of the Performing Arts is now part of the University of the Arts. The latter is successor to two century-old institutions: The Philadelphia College of Art and the Philadelphia College of the Performing Arts. The University of the Arts prepares students for more than one hundred professional career paths in the visual and performing arts and related fields. Although the Philadelphia College of the Performing Arts is still in the same buildings as before, it and the Philadelphia College of Art have merged together under the umbrella institution of a university.

The School of Music is dedicated to the preparation and training of students for a professional career, either as performer or as teacher. The curriculum combines the performance emphasis of a traditional conservatory approach, stressing individualized training, practice, and discipline, with a liberal arts education.

Accreditation. Middle States Association of Colleges and Schools; National Association of Schools of Music.

Academic Information

Enrollment, Music Majors. Full-time 177 men, 196 women; part-time 21 men, 19 women. 26 foreign students.

Music Faculty. Full-time 21, part-time 85.

Term System. Semester. One summer session.

Entrance Requirements. High school graduation or GED; SAT or ACT required; audition required.

Admission Procedure. Application with $30 fee (refundable through July 1) accepted on a rolling basis.

Music Degrees Offered. Bachelor of Music; Bachelor of Music Education; Master of Music; Certificate; Diploma.

Music Degree Requirements. The Performance Program is one that offers the music student concentrated studies and coaching in a major area. There is a strong emphasis on performance and the curriculum is designed to prepare for a full-time career in performance, composition, or music theory. It also prepares for graduate study, studio teaching, or further work in specialized disciplines in music. The Bachelor of Music degree is awarded. The Music Education Program offers a double degree: the Bachelor of Music and the Bachelor of Music Education. These programs overlap with music education courses beginning in the second year. The entire double-degree program is completed in ten semesters (5 years) with the tenth semester devoted to full-time internship in the Philadelphia/Delaware Valley area. The Opera Emphasis Program allows concentration in opera studies. Special courses start in the third year, with special courses in acting and staging, opera repertory, opera preparation and coaching, dance, and movement. The program includes regular performance in aria classes, stage performance of opera scenes, and full-length operas on the stage of the Shubert Theatre. The Jazz/Commercial Music Program is a four-year program that gives a basis for a career as a performer, arranger, or composer in jazz and/or commercial music.

The Diploma course is a four-year program designed primarily for foreign students who wish to take all portions of the undergraduate curriculum for their major area of study, except for the liberal arts academic courses.

A two-year program leading to a Master of Music Degree is offered with emphasis in performance or composition. Performance areas include orchestral instruments, piano, voice, and voice-opera.

The Graduate Diploma is a two-year advanced plan of study in performance. The curriculum is flexible in order to address the needs of the individual student.

General Program Areas. Commercial Music, Composition, Conducting, Jazz Studies, Music Theory, Opera, Performance.

Instruments Taught. Bass, Bassoon, Clarinet, Flute, French Horn, Guitar, Harp, Harpsichord, Oboe, Percussion, Piano, Saxophone, Trombone, Trumpet, Tuba, Viola, Violin, Violoncello, Voice.

Musical Facilities

Practice Facilities. 20 practice rooms. Percussion-equipped practice rooms. 10 pianos (baby grands). Electronic music laboratory; piano laboratory.

Concert Facilities. Shubert Theater, seating 1,700; Theater 200, 175; Black Box Theater, 200.

Concerts/Musical Activities. Concerts, recitals.

Music Library. 13,000 books; 5,000 scores; 120 periodicals; 14,000 recordings. Listening facilities (cassette, stereo). Other library resources for music students include the Presser Foundation, Curtis Institute, and the Philadelphia Orchestra Association.

Special Programs

Performance Groups. Symphony Orchestra, Symphonic Wind Ensemble, Jazz Ensembles, Mixed Chamber Ensembles, Guitar Ensemble, New Music Ensemble, Saxophone Ensemble, Trombone Choir, Chamber Ensembles, Chorus, Chamber Singers, Woodwind Ensembles, String Sectionals, Percussion Ensemble.

Financial

Costs. Per academic year: Tuition $6,500. Fees $400. Room and board $2,300.

Financial Aid. Scholarships range from $200 to $6,000 (average $1,250). Scholarship applications due April 1. Other sources of financial aid include institutional and state/federal grants and loans, part-time employment, and a College Work-Study program.

University of Pittsburgh Department of Music
4200 Fifth Avenue
Pittsburgh
Pennsylvania 15260

Telephone. (412) 624-4126

Chief Administrator. Robert Lord, Chairperson.

Established in 1787, the University of Pittsburgh is a state-related institution of the Commonwealth of Pennsylvania. The main campus is located on a 131-acre site in Oakland, a cultural center of Pittsburgh.

The Department of Music offers programs for both prospective musicians and students who wish to acquire knowledge about music for personal enrichment. A wide range of courses is available in Western art music, jazz, and the music of other cultures. Intensive training is provided in music history, theory, composition, and performance.

Accreditation. Middle States Association of Colleges and Schools.

Academic Information

Enrollment, Music Majors. (Total University) 28,710.

Music Faculty. 25.

Term System. Trimester.

Entrance Requirements. High school graduation with rank in upper 40 percent of graduating class; completion of 15 units including 4 English, 2 mathematics, 3 foreign language, 1 science, 1 history; SAT or ACT required; audition, ear test, and interview.

Admission Procedure. Application with supporting documents and nonrefundable $20 fee to Office of Admissions.

Music Degrees Offered. Bachelor of Arts; Master of Arts; Doctor of Philosophy.

Music Degree Requirements. The Bachelor of Arts degree in music is offered with concentrations in performance, composition, and music history. Students are encouraged to combine the study of music with another area of interest. A number of disciplines offered at the University can be related to music, such as business, computer science, communication, theater, history, psychology, and religion.

The Department of Music offers the Master of Arts and Doctor of Philosophy degrees in the areas of musicology, theory/composition, and ethnomusicology with emphasis in Afro-American, African, and East Asian music.

General Program Areas. African Music, Afro-American Music, Composition, East Asian Music, Ethnomusicology, Music History, Music Theory, Musicology, Performance.

Instruments Taught. Bass, Clarinet, Flute, Guitar, Harpsichord, Non-Western Instruments, Oboe, Organ, Percussion, Piano, Saxophone, Trombone, Trumpet, Viola, Violin, Violoncello, Voice.

Musical Facilities

Practice Facilities. The Music Building facilities include a computer and electronic music studio equipped with professional tape recorders, playback equipment; ARP Buchia, and Putney synthesizers; and a DEC LSI 11/23 computer for use by student composers. Eleven piano studios and a percussion room and organ studio are available for individual practice by music majors. The Department has a collection of instruments, including a set of African drums, Indian sitars, Chinese zithers, and modern reproductions of early strings, winds, brass, and keyboard instruments.

Concert Facilities. Recital hall; Heinz Chapel; Stephen Foster Memorial Theatre.

Concerts/Musical Activities. The Department of Music Concert Series of 50 to 75 concerts each year features both student and professional talent; Thursday noon series of student recitals and lecture/demonstrations by professional musicians and scholars.

Music Library. The Theodore M. Finney Music Library houses a sizable collection of books, scores, periodicals, and recordings. Special collections include: large collection of materials relating to the life and works of Stephen Collins Foster; manuscripts of Haydn; seventeenth century lute book; materials donated by William Steinberg: eighteenth century English and nineteenth century American popular music and sacred tunebooks. The Music Library of Carnegie Institute, one of the largest collections in the United States, is within short walking distance of the Music Building.

Special Programs

Performance Groups. Heinz Chapel Choir, Choral Society, Orchestra, Jazz Band, Concert Band, Opera Workshop, Guitar Ensemble, Percussion Ensemble, Piano Ensemble, Chamber Music, Non-Western Instruments, String Ensemble, Collegium Musicum, University Glee Clubs, Marching Band.

Financial

Costs. Per academic year: Tuition in-state resident $2,890, out-of-state $5,780. Fees $120. Room $1,698. Board $1,138.

Financial Aid. Financial aid is awarded on the basis of academic merit and financial need. Institutional and state/federal aid is available in the form of scholarships, graduate assistantships, grants, loans, and part-time employment. Financial aid/scholarship application due March 1.

Temple University
Esther Boyer College of Music
Thirteenth and Norris Streets
Philadelphia
Pennsylvania 19122

Telephone. (215) 787-8301

Chief Administrator. Helen Laird, Dean.

Temple University was founded in 1884 by Dr. Russell Conwell as an adjunct to his ministry of the Grace Baptist Church. The University is now an independent state-related institution with an enrollment of more than 30,000 students and 16 schools and colleges. The main 82-acre campus is located in the center of Philadelphia.

The music program at Temple University achieved College status in 1962. Due to a generous gift in 1985, the College of Music was changed to the Esther Boyer College of Music, offering a union of conservatory-type training with intense academically-oriented classroom teaching. In July of 1986, the New School of Music in Philadelphia merged with the Esther Boyer College of Music, becoming the New School Institute of Temple University. The Institute is now Temple University's center for ensemble and orchestral studies.

Accreditation. Middle States Association of Colleges and Schools; National Association of Schools of Music.

Academic Information

Enrollment, Music Majors. Full-time 191 men, 186 women; part-time 11 men, 14 women. 24 foreign students.

Music Faculty. Full-time 48, part-time 93. Artists-in-residence: Principal Winds, Philadelphia Orchestra; Chestnut Brass Company; Temple University Trio.

Term System. Semester. Two 6-week summer sessions from late May to mid-August. Academic year from September 1 to May 5.

Entrance Requirements. High school graduation; minimum SAT combined score 900; audition; basic musicianship test.

Admission Procedure. Application with all materials to Director of Music Admissions, Esther Boyer College of Music.

Music Degrees Offered. Bachelor of Music; Master of Music; Doctor of Musical Arts; Doctor of Philosophy.

Music Degree Requirements. The Bachelor of Music degree program is offered with majors in voice, piano, piano accompanying, piano pedagogy, organ, orchestral instruments, guitar, jazz/commercial music (emphases in performance, arranging/composition, commercial voice), theory, composition, music history, music education, and music therapy. The baccalaureate degree requires the completion of a minimum of 128 credit hours.

The Master of Music degree is offered in the areas of choral conducting, composition, music history, music education, music therapy, opera, organ, piano, piano pedagogy, piano accompanying and chamber music, stringed instruments, wind instruments, brass instruments, percussion instruments, voice, and music theory. The degree requires the completion of a minimum of 30 credit hours.

The Doctor of Musical Arts degree is available in performance, music education, and composition. The Doctor of Philosophy degree is offered in music education. The doctoral degrees require the completion of 42 to 60 credit hours beyond the master's degree.

General Program Areas. Accompanying, Chamber Music, Choral Conducting, Commercial Music, Composition, Jazz Studies, Music Education, Music History, Music Theory, Music Therapy, Opera, Performance, Piano Pedagogy.

Instruments Taught. Bass, Bassoon, Clarinet, Flute, French Horn, Guitar, Harp, Oboe, Organ, Percussion, Piano, Saxophone, Trombone, Trumpet, Tuba, Viola, Violin, Violoncello, Voice.

Musical Facilities

Practice Facilities. 54 practice rooms. Special practice facilities for organists and percussionists. 23 grand pianos reserved for piano majors. Computer/synthesizer laboratory; recording studio; keyboard laboratory.

Concert Facilities. Thomas Hall, seating 125; Tomlinson Theater, 550; Mitten Hall, 200; Rock Hall, 1,988; Klein Hall, 150.

Community Facilities. Academy of Music; local churches.

Concerts/Musical Activities. Over 225 recitals and concerts per season.

Music Library. Most music materials are housed in the Samuel Paley Library. 13,000 books; 11,000 scores; all major music periodicals. 20,000 phonograph recordings. 75 listening stations (stereo). Special collection of Renaissance instruments. 7,000 recordings and 1,000

scores housed in the College. The Fleischer Collection of the Philadelphia Public Library is available to music students.

Special Programs

Featured Programs. The Esther Boyer College of Music Preparatory and Extension Division offers the preteen, teenager, and adult an opportunity to pursue music studies with artist-teachers from the Philadelphia area. The Preparatory Division encourages the enrollment of young students who are interested in furthering their musical education through a combination of private instruction, theory, and aural skills classes. Programs are designed for elementary through high school students who are considering music as a career or as a serious avocation. The Extension Division is designed for adults who are interested in pursuing their musical interests through both private lessons and enrichment classes.

Performance Groups. Jazz Ensemble, Opera Theater, University Orchestra, Symphonic Band, Wind Ensemble, Marching Band, Wind Chamber Symphony, Percussion Ensemble, Collegium Musicum, Choral Groups.

Financial

Costs. Per academic year: Tuition in-state $3,300, out-of-state $5,796. Private lessons $200; theory lab fee $10. Room and board $3,296 (minimum).

Financial Aid. Financial aid is awarded on the basis of academic merit, financial need, musical ability. Both institutional and state/federal aid available. Financial aid/scholarship application due February 1. Part-time employment and a College Work-Study program available.

West Chester University of Pennsylvania School of Music
High Street
West Chester
Pennsylvania 19383

Telephone. (215) 436-2628

Chief Administrator. Dr. Malcolm J. Tait, Dean, School of Music.

West Chester University of Pennsylvania is a liberal arts institution. The 275-acre campus is located in southeastern Pennsylvania near Philadelphia.

The School of Music offers programs for students wishing to qualify for a Pennsylvania Instructional 1 Certificate to teach music in the public schools; for students majoring in music within the liberal arts curriculum; and for students interested in such areas as professional performance, studio teaching, and church music.

Accreditation. Middle States Association of Colleges and Schools; National Association of Schools of Music; National Council for Accreditation of Teacher Education.

Academic Information

Enrollment, Music Majors. (Total University) 9,953.
Music Faculty. 56.
Term System. Semester.
Entrance Requirements. High school graduation with rank in upper half of graduating class; SAT or ACT; audition and placement examinations. GRE required for graduate study.
Admission Procedure. Application with supporting documents and nonrefundable $15 fee to Office of Admissions.
Music Degrees Offered. Bachelor of Music; Bachelor of Arts; Bachelor of Science; Master of Music; Master of Arts; Master of Music Education.
Music Degree Requirements. The Bachelor of Music degree is offered with concentrations in theory, composition, music history, and performance. The Bachelor of Arts degree is offered with a major in music in the context of a liberal arts program. The Bachelor of Science degree in music education is offered in three teaching concentration programs—general, instrumental, and vocal-choral.

The School of Music offers programs leading to the Master of Arts degree in music history and literature and the Master of Music degree with concentrations in music education, performance, accompanying, music theory or composition, piano pedagogy, and Orff-Schulwerk. The Department of Music Education offers a program leading to the Master of Music Education. Options are available for a thesis or nonthesis basis.

General Program Areas. Accompanying, Composition, Music Education, Music History, Music Theory, Performance, Piano Pedagogy.

Instruments Taught. Baritone, Bass, Bassoon, Clarinet, Flute, French Horn, Guitar, Harp, Oboe, Organ, Percussion, Piano, Saxophone, Trombone, Trumpet, Tuba, Viola, Violin, Violoncello, Voice.

Musical Facilities

Concerts/Musical Activities. Student/faculty recitals and concerts.
Music Library. The Music Library in Swope Hall houses a collection of 23,000 scores (historical editions, collected works, opera, keyboard, vocal and instrumental music) and more than 21,000 recordings (classical, folk, non-western, popular). Listening facilities for 40 persons are available.

Special Programs

Performance Groups. Elementary Band, Concert Band, Marching Band, Symphonic Band, Elementary Orchestra, Chamber Orchestra, Studio/Pit Orchestra, Chamber Orchestra, Symphony Orchestra, Brass Ensemble, Percussion Ensemble, String Ensemble, Woodwind Ensemble, Jazz Ensemble, Freshman Chorus, Men's Chorus, Women's Chorus, Masterworks Chorus, Opera Chorus, Chamber Choir, Concert Choir.

Financial

Costs. Per academic year: Tuition in-state resident $1,-680, out-of-state $3,076. Room and board $2,168.
Financial Aid. Financial aid is awarded on the basis of academic merit and financial need. Institutional and state/federal aid are available in the form of scholarships, grants, loans, and part-time employment. Financial aid/scholarship application due May 1.

PUERTO RICO

Conservatory of Music of Puerto Rico

Box 41227
Minillas Station
Santurce
Puerto Rico 00940

Telephone. (809) 751-0160
Chief Administrator. Roberto Sierra, Acting Rector.
The Conservatory was founded in 1959.

Academic Information

Music Degrees Offered. Bachelor of Music.

Interamerican University
Music Department

San German
Puerto Rico 00753

Telephone. (809) 892-1095, Ext. 279
Chief Administrator. Salvador Rivera, Chairman.

Academic Information

Music Degrees Offered. Bachelor of Arts in Music;
Bachelor of Arts in Music Education.

Universidad de Puerto Rico
Department of Music

Rio Piedras
Puerto Rico 00931

Telephone. (809) 764-0000, Ext. 2293
Chief Administrator. Gustavo Batista, Chairman.
The music department grew out of the University's
fine arts and humanities faculties in the early 1960s. Two
former music department chairmen have been Francis
Schwartz and Donald Thompson.

Academic Information

Music Degrees Offered. Bachelor of Arts in Music;
Bachelor of Arts in Music Education.

Musical Facilities

Practice Facilities. The University houses the only academic electronic studio in Puerto Rico.
Concert Facilities. Concert hall (used for many years
as the performance venue for the Casals Festival.
Concerts/Musical Activities. Both the University
Chorus and Symphonic Band have had long performance traditions.

Special Programs

Affiliated Programs. The University is a center for
classical guitar study.

RHODE ISLAND

Brown University
Department of Music
Providence
Rhode Island 02912

Telephone. (401) 863-3234

Chief Administrator. Gerald M. Shapiro, Chairman.

Brown University was founded in 1764. Pembroke College, formerly an affiliated women's college, was completely merged with the University in 1970. The 52-acre campus with 100 buildings is located in Providence, the second largest city in New England.

The courses of study offered by the Department of Music permit areas of specialization in composition, musicology, and ethnomusicology. The Department seeks to cultivate in its students an approach to music that is both creative and scholarly, hence, the students are encouraged to devote a certain amount of time to both areas. Each student develops a program of study in consultation with a faculty advisor.

Accreditation. New England Association of Schools and Colleges.

Academic Information

Enrollment, Music Majors. (Total University) 7,198.

Music Faculty. 12.

Term System. Semester.

Entrance Requirements. High school graduation; completion of 16 units with a recommended 4 units English, 3 mathematics, 2 foreign language, 3 science, and 1 social science; SAT or ACT and three Achievement Tests required.

Admission Procedure. Application with supporting documents and nonrefundable $40 fee to Office of Admissions.

Music Degrees Offered. Bachelor of Arts; Master of Arts; Doctor of Philosophy.

Music Degree Requirements. The Bachelor of Arts degree is offered with a concentration in music as part of a liberal arts program. The program of study leading to the Master of Arts degree is offered with concentrations in either composition or ethnomusicology. The Doctor of Philosophy degree is offered with a concentration in ethnomusicology only. Specialties include topics in folk and popular music.

General Program Areas. Composition, Ethnomusicology, Musicology, Performance.

Instruments Taught. Brass, Percussion, Piano, Stringed Instruments, Voice, Woodwinds.

Musical Facilities

Music Library. The Brown University Library contains more than 3,900,000 items including books, periodicals, maps, microforms, videotapes, sheet music, phonograph records, and manuscripts. A Sheet Music Collection is housed in the John Hay Library on campus. The University has a large collection of non-classical American music. Other special collections include: Hamilton C. MacDougall Collection including eighteenth century Moravian and Shaker works; Harris Collection; twentieth century musical comedy orchestrations.

Special Programs

Performance Groups. Chorus, Orchestra, Wind Ensemble, Chamber Ensembles.

Financial

Costs. Per academic year: Tuition $11,690. Fees $342. Room $2,245. Board $1,635.

Financial Aid. Financial aid is awarded on the basis of financial need. Institutional and state/federal aid is available in the form of prizes, premiums, scholarships, grants, loans, and part-time employment. Financial aid/scholarship application due January 15.

University of Rhode Island
Department of Music
Kingston
Rhode Island 02881

Telephone. (401) 792-2431

Chief Administrator. Dr. Gene J. Pollart, Chairperson.

The University of Rhode Island was established as a state agricultural school in 1888. The School became the Rhode Island College of Agriculture and Mechanic Arts in 1892 and in 1909 the name was changed to Rhode Island State College. The institution achieved university status in 1951 and at that time adopted its present name. The University's campus is located in the village of Kingston, 30 miles south of Providence.

The Department of Music is basically a teacher training department but does offer a degree program in performance (instrumental or vocal).

Accreditation. New England Association of Schools and Colleges; National Association of Schools of Music.

Academic Information

Enrollment, Music Majors. (Total University) 5,942 men, 5,482 women.

Music Faculty. 24.

Term System. Semester. Two 5-week summer sessions.

Entrance Requirements. High school graduation; completion of 16 units including 4 English, 2 mathematics, 1 science, 1 history; SAT required; audition required. GRE required for graduate study.

Admission Procedure. Application with $15 nonrefundable fee due April 15.

Music Degrees Offered. Bachelor of Arts; Bachelor of Music; Master of Music.

Music Degree Requirements. The Bachelor of Music degree is offered with majors in classical guitar, voice, piano or organ, orchestral instruments, music history and literature, music theory and composition, and music education. All students must take the piano proficiency examination at the conclusion of one year of study or by the end of the second semester of the sophomore year. A total of 125 credits (126 for music education) is required for graduation. The Bachelor of Arts degree with a major in music requires the completion of 120 credits of which 42 must be in upper division courses.

The Master of Music degree is offered with specializations in performance and music education. The degree requires the completion of a minimum of 30 credits.

General Program Areas. Composition, Music Education, Music History, Music Literature, Music Theory, Orchestral Instruments.

Instruments Taught. Baritone, Bass, Bassoon, Clarinet, Flute, French Horn, Guitar, Harp, Harpsichord, Oboe, Organ, Percussion, Piano, Recorder, Saxophone, Trombone, Trumpet, Tuba, Viola, Violin, Violoncello, Voice.

Musical Facilities

Practice Facilities. 14 practice rooms. 1 organ. 2 percussion-equipped practice rooms. 2 grand pianos reserved for piano majors. Electronic music studio.

Concert Facilities. Recital Hall, seating 500.

Concerts/Musical Activities. Student/faculty recitals and concerts; visiting artists.

Music Library. 500 books; 1,000 scores. Listening laboratory in Music Building.

Special Programs

Performance Groups. University Symphony Orchestra, University Marching Band, Concert Band, University Chorus, Symphonic Wind Ensemble, Concert Choir, Jazz and Studio Ensemble, University Chamber Orchestra, Keyboard Ensemble, String Ensemble, Woodwind Ensemble, Brass Ensemble, Percussion Ensemble, Madrigal Singers, Guitar Ensemble, Saxophone Ensemble, Jazz Combo.

Financial

Costs. Per academic year: Tuition in-state resident $1,574, out-of-state $5,260. Room and board $3,530.

Financial Aid. Scholarships range from $150 to $1,500 (average $1,000). Scholarship application due April 15. Other sources of financial aid include institutional and state/federal grants and loans, part-time employment, and a College Work-Study program.

SOUTH CAROLINA

Bob Jones University
Division of Music
School of Fine Arts
1700 Wade Hampton Boulevard
Greenville
South Carolina 29614

Telephone. (803) 242-5100, Ext. 2716

Chief Administrator. Dr. Edward Dunbar, Chairman.

Bob Jones University is a privately controlled Protestant fundementalist school founded in 1927 as Bob Jones College at College Point, Florida. It moved to Cleveland, Tennessee in 1933 and then to the new Greenville campus in 1948. The University is a Christian liberal arts institution with a University-wide emphasis on the fine arts. The 200-acre campus is located just within the city limits of Greenville.

Music degrees have been offered at the University since 1936. In 1983 the Division of Music expanded its curriculum from the Bachelor of Arts and Masters of Arts programs to full, conservatory-level Bachelor of Music and Master of Music programs. All private and class instruction in the performance fields is offered to non-majors without additional charge above the regular academic tuition.

Academic Information

Enrollment, Music Majors. Full-time 79 men, 106 women; part-time 4 men, 7 women.

Music Faculty. Full-time 29, part-time 15.

Term System. Semester. Three 4-week summer sessions (May to July). Academic year begins Wednesday before Labor Day and ends first Saturday in May.

Entrance Requirements. High school graduation with rank in top 70% of high school class; recommend completion of 16 units including 3 English, 2 mathematics, 2 foreign language, 1 science, and 2 social science; ACT required; demonstrated natural talent and precollege study in music sufficient to meet the demands of the particular major program (voice, keyboard, instrument) on the college level; audition required. TOEFL required for students from non-English speaking countries; one-year minimum commitment required. Advanced placement available by departmental examinations in some areas. For graduate work, applicant must have a bachelor's degree with a major concentration in music.

Admission Procedure. Apply to Director of Admissions. Auditions are held (after academic acceptance) during opening registration; platform tests at the end of the freshman and sophomore years determine final eligibility for the specific music major being pursued.

Music Degrees Offered. Bachelor of Music; Bachelor of Science; Master of Music.

Music Degree Requirements. The Bachelor of Music degree is offered in voice, piano, piano pedagogy, organ, church music, or one of the standard orchestral instruments. A liberal arts core of English, history, speech, psychology or philosophy, and two years of a foreign language is required in addition to the major requirements for a total of 130 semester hours. The Bachelor of Science degree in music education is offered through the School of Education and requires a minimum of 51 hours in music plus general education courses and professional education courses for a total of 135 to 141 credit hours.

The Master of Music degree is offered with emphases in church music, organ, piano, voice, choral conducting, or orchestral instruments. A total of 32 semester hours is required.

General Program Areas. Choral Conducting, Church Music, Music Education, Music History, Music Literature, Music Theory, Performance, Piano Pedagogy, Vocal Music.

Instruments Taught. Bassoon, Clarinet, Cornet, Euphonium, French Horn, Oboe, Organ, Percussion, Piano, Piccolo, Stringed Instruments, Trombone, Trumpet, Tuba, Voice.

Musical Facilities

Practice Facilities. 90 practice rooms (35 for majors, 55 for non-majors). 3 organs (57-rank Zimmer pipe organ, 1967; 90-rank Allen electronic organ, 1973; 4-rank Zimmer pipe organ, 1965). Special practice facilities for percussionists. 45 practice pianos (32 uprights, 13 grands); most are newer Yamaha or Kawai; 13 grand pianos reserved for piano majors.

Concert Facilities. War Memorial Chapel, seating 450; Concert Center, 880; Rodeheaver Auditorium, 2,600; Founder's Memorial Amphitorium, 7,000.

Concerts/Musical Activities. A seven-program Concert, Opera, and Drama Series plus 20 to 30 student, faculty, and University music group recitals each semester.

Music Library. General titles and research materials are in the main library; all records and scores are in the music building. 3,290 scores; 132 audiovisual items; 8,400 recordings; 400 audiocassettes. 22 listening stations. Special collections include an extensive hymnology collection. The holdings of Furman University and the Greenville County Library are also available to students.

Special Programs

Performance Groups. Symphonic Band, University Chorale, Laboratory Chorus, University Choir, Flute Choir, Orchestra, vocal and instrumental ensembles.

Financial

Costs. Per academic year: Tuition $2,520. Fees $202. Practice room fee $50. Room and board $2,640.

Financial Aid. Financial aid is awarded on the basis of financial need. Institutional funding available. Approximately 35% of total University enrollment receives financial aid. Average award $150 per month (work scholarship). Part-time employment and a College Work-Study program available.

Converse College
School of Music
Spartanburg
South Carolina 29301

Telephone. (803) 596-9021

Chief Administrator. Dr. Henry Janiec, Dean.

Converse College is an independent liberal arts institution, with a professional School of Music, devoted primarily to the education of women. The College was was founded in 1889. It was the site of the Atlantic Music Festival from the turn of the century to the mid-1930s. The 70-acre campus is located in downtown Spartanburg, a city near the Blue Ridge Mountains and the Great Smokies.

The School of Music is a separate administrative unit within the College and enrolls both men and women at the undergraduate and graduate levels for the Bachelor of Music and Master of Music programs. Inasmuch as the College of Arts and Sciences serves only female students, the Bachelor of Arts in music and the double major, of which music is one component, is open only to female students. The School offers a broad curriculum of studies for the serious student of music, as well as a variety of courses for the nonmajor.

Accreditation. Southern Association of Colleges and Schools; National Association of Schools of Music.

Academic Information

Enrollment, Music Majors. Full-time 10 men, 105 women; part-time 2 men, 4 women. Foreign students 4.

Music Faculty. Full-time 21, part-time 4.

Term System. Semester. 7-week Winter Term. Summer session.

Entrance Requirements. High school graduation or GED; SAT; placement tests in music theory and history; audition. GRE required for graduate applicants.

Admission Procedure. Application with $20 nonrefundable fee due May 1. 85% of applicants accepted.

Music Degrees Offered. Bachelor of Music; Bachelor of Arts; Master of Music.

Music Degree Requirements. The Bachelor of Music degree program draws approximately 30 percent of its courses from the liberal arts area and 70 percent from the area of music. The distribution of coursework depends on the student's high school background and choice of major. Concentrations are offered in performance, music education, piano pedagogy, music theory, composition, and music history and literature. The degree requires the completion of 125 semester hours. The Bachelor of Arts degree with a major in music is offered through the College of Liberal Arts.

The Master of Music degree requires the completion of 30 semester hours with emphases in instrumental music, vocal music, music education, piano pedagogy, theory, composition, musicology.

General Program Areas. Applied Music, Composition, Music Education, Music History, Music Literature, Music Theory, Musicology, Performance, Piano Pedagogy, Vocal Music.

Instruments Taught. Brass, Organ, Percussion, Piano, Stringed Instruments, Voice, Woodwinds.

Musical Facilities

Practice Facilities. 52 practice rooms. 5 organs (Schantz). 23 practice pianos. Piano classroom with 12 pianos.

Concert Facilities. Twitchell Auditorium, seating 1,600; Daniel Recital Hall, 340; Carlisle House.

Concerts/Musical Activities. Guest artist series; recital series; visiting orchestras; annual festival (Baroque, contemporary); Spring Festival; 3 opera productions annually.

Music Library. 3,000 volumes; 8,000 scores; 6,500 phonograph recordings. Listening facilities include 15 cassette stations and 25 stereo turntables. The Spartanburg Public Library is near the School of Music and available to students.

Special Programs

Featured Programs. The Converse College School of Music offers musical training for the young people and adults in the area through its Department of Pre-College and Adult Music and Dance.

Performance Groups. Chamber Ensemble, Wind Ensemble, Symphony Chorus, Symphony Orchestra, Opera Workshop, Chorale, Piano Ensemble.

Affiliated Programs. Brevard Music Center, a summer festival with over 50 concert events during the seven-week season.

Financial

Costs. Per academic year: Comprehensive fee $9,250.

Financial Aid. Scholarship awards range from $1,000 to $5,000 (average amount $2,500). Application due May 1. Part-time employment and a College Work-Study program available.

University of South Carolina
School of Music
Columbia
South Carolina 29208

Telephone. (803) 777-4280

Chief Administrator. William Moody, Director.

The University was founded in 1801 as South Carolina College. It was chartered as the University of South Carolina in 1906. The 1970s were an important growth period during which graduate schools were expanded and the medical school was established. Situated downtown in the state capital, the 242-acre campus is well maintained and close to the principal governmental and shopping areas of Columbia. The city is located in the central part of the state and has many parks, an art museum, a Music Festival, and Choral Society.

The School of Music strives to improve students' awareness of the importance of quality in all areas of music. A new building for the School of Music adjacent to a new Fine Arts Center is planned.

Accreditation. Southern Association of Colleges and Schools; National Association of Schools of Music.

Academic Information

Enrollment, Music Majors. College of Humanities and Social Sciences: Full-time 1,396 men, 1,845 women.

Music Faculty. 42.

Term System. Semester. One 7-week and two 5-week summer sessions.

Entrance Requirements. High school graduation or GED; SAT. Foreign students must have TOEFL, financial statement, and sponsorship. GRE required for all graduate students. Audition required.

Admission Procedure. Application with $25 non-refundable fee due April 1.

Music Degrees Offered. Bachelor of Arts; Bachelor of Music; Master of Arts; Master of Music; Doctor of Philosophy; Doctor of Musical Arts.

Music Degree Requirements. All students majoring in music are enrolled in the College of Humanities and Social Sciences and are required to audition upon entrance to the School of Music prior to applied study. The audition is used to determine hours of credit and teacher assignment. If a scholarship audition is not taken, the audition will be given at the beginning of the first semester of study. All students must complete courses in music theory, music history, music literature, applied music and music ensembles, recital class, keyboard proficiency, and general education.

The Bachelor of Arts degree with a major in music requires the completion of 120 academic hours. Normally the student will perform in an ensemble each semester. Major ensemble participation of keyboard and guitar major will usually be in a choral ensemble. The Bachelor of Music degree with emphasis in performance, piano pedagogy, or theory/composition requires the completion of specified courses, both major and general education, for a minimum of 120 academic hours. The Bachelor of Music degree in theory/composition may be pursued with a jazz/commercial music emphasis. There are also two programs leading to the degree Bachelor of Music with emphasis in music education. Those students desiring to teach music in the elementary school or choral music in the middle school or high school follow the Choral Program. Those students interested in the band or orchestra emphasis will follow the Instrumental Program. Completion of either program will assure teacher certification in South Carolina.

The Master's degree programs require the completion of 30 academic hours and the Doctoral degree programs, 60 academic hours.

General Program Areas. Applied Music, Commercial Music, Composition, Conducting, Jazz Studies, Music Education, Music History, Music Literature, Music Theory, Performance, Piano Pedagogy, Vocal Studies.

Instruments Taught. Brass, Guitar, Percussion, Piano, Stringed Instruments, Voice, Woodwinds.

Musical Facilities

Practice Facilities. Special practice facilities for organists. Percussion-equipped practice rooms. Electronic music studio.

Concert Facilities. 2 concert halls.

Community Facilities. Local auditorium.

Concerts/Musical Activities. Recitals, concerts.

Music Library. Special collections include: South Carolina holdings.

Special Programs

Performance Groups. Concert Choir, University Chorus, Symphonic Band, Marching Band, Opera Workshop.

Financial

Costs. Per academic year: Tuition undergraduate in-state resident $2,030, out-of-state $4,250; graduate $2,028. Room and board $2,450.

Financial Aid. Scholarships, grants, and loans available. Part-time employment and College Work-Study program.

Commentary

The University of South Carolina has the largest and most cosmopolitan music division in the state. The University's School of Music offers a wide variety of music courses, from recording studio techniques and music for broadcast, film, and television, to the psychology of music.

Winthrop College
School of Music
701 Oakland Avenue
Rock Hill
South Carolina 29733

Telephone. (803) 323-2255
Chief Administrator. Dr. Jess Casey, Dean.

Winthrop College was founded in Columbia, South Carolina in 1886 by Dr. David Bancroft Johnson with support from the Peabody Education Fund to establish a training school for teachers. The institution was named for the President of the Board of Trustees of the Fund, the Honorable Robert C. Winthrop. In 1891, the College became a state-supported college, then called the South Carolina Industrial and Winthrop Normal College. In 1893, the name was changed to Winthrop Normal and Industrial College of South Carolina, and again in 1920 to Winthrop College, the South Carolina College for Women. The present name was adopted in 1974 when men were admitted as students. The 94-acre campus has 34 buildings and since 1895 has been located in Rock Hill, an industrial community located in the north central part of South Carolina in the center of the Piedmont Carolinas.

The School of Music has the goal of training musicians for a wide variety of positions within the profession. The academic programs are structured to achieve two fundamental aims: the fullest possible educational development of each student and the preparation of students for professional careers.

Accreditation. Southern Association of Colleges and Schools; National Association of Schools of Music.

Academic Information

Enrollment, Music Majors. Full-time 59 men, 75 women; part-time 5 men, 15 women. 1 foreign student.
Music Faculty. Full-time 15, part-time 12.

Term System. Semester. Summer session.
Entrance Requirements. High school graduation or GED with 16 units (4 English, 3 mathematics, 2 laboratory science, 2 foreign language, 3 social studies, 1 physical education/health); SAT; audition; music theory test.
Admission Procedure. Applications accepted on a rolling basis. Submit application with supporting documents and $15 nonrefundable fee.
Music Degrees Offered. Bachelor of Arts; Bachelor of Music; Bachelor of Music Education; Master of Music; Master of Music Education.
Music Degree Requirements. The degrees Bachelor of Arts in Music, Bachelor of Music in Church Music, Bachelor of Music Education, and Bachelor of Music in Music Performance require 124 to 138 semester hours of credit.

The degrees Master of Music in Music Performance and Master of Music Education each require the completion of 32 semester hours.
General Program Areas. Applied Music, Church Music, Music Education, Music History, Music Theory, Performance, Piano Pedagogy, Vocal Pedagogy.
Instruments Taught. Brass, Organ, Percussion, Piano, Stringed Instruments, Voice, Woodwinds.

Musical Facilities

Practice Facilities. 26 practice rooms. 4 organs (4-manual 70-rank Aeolian-Skinner; 2-manual 10-stop tracker by Kney; 5-stop tracker by Angerstein; 3-stop Moeller). 2 percussion-equipped practice rooms. 26 pianos (23 uprights, 3 grands); 3 grands reserved for piano majors. Music education laboratory; 16-station electronic piano laboratory.
Concert Facilities. Byrnes Auditorium, seating 3,500; Recital Hall, 216.
Concerts/Musical Activities. Approximately 95 musical programs scheduled each year.
Music Library. 6,869 volumes; 3,134 scores; 3 music periodicals; 3,562 phonograph recordings. Listening facilities include 8 cassette stations and 8 stereo turntables.

Financial

Costs. Per academic year: Tuition in-state resident $1,380, out-of-state $2,278. Room $1,240. Board 812.
Financial Aid. Scholarships, grants, loans, and student employment available. Financial aid applications due February 1.

SOUTH DAKOTA

University of South Dakota
Music Department
Vermillion
South Dakota 57069

Telephone. (605) 677-5274
Chief Administrator. Dr. Harold A. Popp, Chairperson.

The University of South Dakota was founded in 1862. The 113-acre campus is located in the city of Vermillion in the extreme southeastern part of the state.

The Department of Music offers undergraduate and graduate programs in the areas of performance and music education.

Accreditation. North Central Association of Colleges and Schools; National Association of Schools of Music.

Academic Information

Enrollment, Music Majors. (Total University) 5,214.
Music Faculty. 17.
Term System. Semester. Two summer sessions.
Entrance Requirements. High school graduation or equivalent; rank in upper two-thirds of graduating class; completion of 16 units; audition required.
Admission Procedure. Application with supporting documents and nonrefundable $15 fee to Admissions Office.
Music Degrees Offered. Bachelor of Music; Master of Music.
Music Degree Requirements. The Bachelor of Music degree is offered with emphases in applied music and music education. The music education concentration is offered with an emphasis in vocal and instrumental and requires a minimum of 128 semester hours.

The Master of Music degree is offered with concentrations in applied music, music literature, history of musical instruments, and music education. Orff-Schulwerk certification is possible.
General Program Areas. Applied Music, Music Education, Music Literature.

Instruments Taught. Baritone, Bass, Bassoon, Clarinet, Flute, Guitar, Harpsichord, Horn, Oboe, Organ, Percussion, Piano, Saxophone, Trombone, Trumpet, Tuba, Violin, Violoncello, Voice.

Musical Facilities

Practice Facilities. Warren M. Lee Center for the Fine Arts.
Concert Facilities. Theatre I; Arena Theatre.
Concerts/Musical Activities. A full program of concerts and recitals is offered each year.
Music Library. The Arne B. Larson Collection of Musical Instruments and Library consists of more than 2,500 musical instruments, plus an extensive library of books, music, and related materials. It is operated by the Center for Study of the History of Musical Instruments.

Special Programs

Performance Groups. University Choir, Women's Chorus, Men's Chorus, Orchestra, Marching Band, Symphonic Band, Varsity Band, Golden Age Band, Wind Ensemble, Chamber Singers, Opera Workshop, String Ensemble, Woodwind Ensemble, Guitar Ensemble, Brass Choir, Percussion Ensemble, Stage Band, Madrigal Singers.
Affiliated Programs. The Shrine to Music Museum and Center for the Study of the History of Musical Instruments, established in 1973, is one of the major institutions of its kind in the world. The Museum was designated a landmark of American music by the National Music Council in 1976.

Financial

Costs. Per academic year: Tuition in-state resident $1,032, out-of-state $2,352. Fees $539. Room and board $1,826.
Financial Aid. Financial aid is awarded on the basis of academic merit and financial need. Institutional and state/federal aid are available in the form of scholarships, grants, loans, and part-time employment. Financial aid/scholarship application due February 15.

TENNESSEE

Austin Peay State University
Department of Music
College Street
Clarksville
Tennessee 37044

Telephone. (615) 648-7818

Chief Administrator. Solie Fott, Chairman.

Austin Peay State University began as Austin Peay Normal School when it was created as a two-year junior college and teacher-training institute in 1927. It became a four-year college in 1943 and achieved university status in 1967. The 77-acre campus has 45 buildings and is located in the community of Clarksville, 50 miles northwest of Nashville.

The purposes of the Department of Music are: (1) to meet the need for music teachers in the state and surrounding territory; (2) to provide training for students preparing for careers in music performance; (3) to provide resources and experiences to all those who wish to include music in a humanistic education; (4) to provide music training for students majoring in elementary education; and (5) to make music important in the lives of students and in the community by providing a rich program of artistic and cultural events.

Accreditation. Southern Association of Colleges and Schools; National Association of Schools of Music; National Council for Accreditation of Teacher Education.

Academic Information

Enrollment, Music Majors. Full-time 50 men, 50 women; part-time 3 men, 2 women.

Music Faculty. Full-time 16, part-time 5.

Term System. Semester. 8-week summer from mid-June to early August. Academic year from mid-September to late May.

Entrance Requirements. ACT of 16 or high school GPA of 2.65. Audition required only for music scholarship. Foreign students must submit proof of proficiency in English (score of 500 on TOEFL) and proof of sufficient financial resources.

Admission Procedure. Application with supporting documents accepted on a rolling basis.

Music Degrees Offered. Bachelor of Arts; Bachelor of Science; Master of Music.

Music Degree Requirements. The Bachelor of Arts and Bachelor of Science degrees are offered with options in music performance and music education. The student who plans to teach music follows a concentration in the music education option. Students not intending to seek certification to teach music may elect a concentration in either the music performance option or the liberal arts music option.

The Master of Music degree is offered with a concentration in performance or music education.

General Program Areas. Applied Music, Music Education, Performance.

Instruments Taught. Baritone, Bass, Bassoon, Clarinet, Flute, French Horn, Guitar, Oboe, Organ, Percussion, Piano, Saxophone, Trombone, Trumpet, Tuba, Viola, Violin, Violoncello, Voice.

Musical Facilities

Practice Facilities. 34 practice rooms. Special practice facilities for percussionists. 35 pianos (32 uprights, 3 grands); 3 grand pianos reserved for piano majors. Piano laboratory.

Concert Facilities. Clement Auditorium, seating 600; Trahern Hall, 200.

Concerts/Musical Activities. Approximately 100 concerts each academic year.

Music Library. 4,000 volumes; 4,000 musical scores; 100 periodical subscriptions; 4,000 recordings. Listening facilities (stereo). Music materials housed in main library.

Special Programs

Performance Groups. Orchestra, Choir, Band, Pep Band, Chamber Ensemble, Woodwind Ensemble, Vocal Ensemble, Brass Choir, Jazz Band, Opera Workshop, Percussion Ensemble, Guitar Ensemble.

Financial

Costs. Per academic year: Tuition in-state resident $996, out-of-state $3,423. Fees $108. Room $900 to $1,100. Board $900.

Financial Aid. Financial aid is awarded on the basis of academic merit, financial need, musical ability. Sources of aid include scholarships, grants, loans, part-time employment, and a College Work-Study program.

Memphis State University
Music Department
College of Communication and Fine Arts
Memphis
Tennessee 38152

Telephone. (901) 454-3763

Chief Administrator. Dr. David Russell Williams, Chairman.

The roots of Memphis State University date back to 1912 with the establishment and opening of the West Tennessee State Normal School. Training of primary and secondary education teachers was provided. The school became the West Tennessee State Teachers College in 1925 and in 1941 the name was changed to Memphis State College. In 1957, university status was achieved and the current name adopted.

The Music Department's first and central purpose is to educate students to enter the professional and educational fields of music in all of its forms. The Department also exists to serve the musical educational needs of those students whose major areas of study are not in music. The Department is also a service department, providing music of high calibre for entertainment and enrichment at University and community functions. Through its own recording label, the Department presents important educational and archival recordings to the state of Tennessee. This is part of its more general mission to advance scholarly research in all genres of American and European music. The Department also offers strong programs in commercial music, jazz and studio music, and regional studies programs.

Accreditation. Southern Association of Colleges and Schools; National Association of Schools of Music; National Council for Accreditation of Teacher Education.

Academic Information

Enrollment, Music Majors. Full-time 90 men, 110 women; part-time 35 men, 40 women. 10 foreign students.

Music Faculty. Full-time 45, part-time 16.

Term System. Semester. Two 6-week summer sessions.

Entrance Requirements. High school graduation or GED; 19 units (4 English, 2 mathematics, 2 laboratory science, 1 social studies, 1 physical education, 9 electives); ACT minimum score 18. Audition required

before divisional committee; piano and theory placement examinations. TOEFL required for foreign students. GRE required for doctoral study.

Admission Procedure. Application with $5 nonrefundable fee by August 1.

Music Degrees Offered. Bachelor of Music; Bachelor of Fine Arts; Master of Arts; Master of Music; Doctor of Musical Arts; Doctor of Philosophy.

Music Degree Requirements. The Bachelor of Music is a professional degree, the requirements for which provide the student with an opportunity for specialization in the traditional disciplines of music and music education. Concentrations are available in performance, sacred music, composition, music theory, music history, school music (instrumental or choral emphasis). The degree requires the completion of a specified curriculum for a total of 132 to 134 semester hours. The Bachelor of Music with a major in commercial music is designed for students whose interests and abilities give strong evidence of potential for significant achievement in the areas of musical performance or composition/arranging in commercial music. The degree requires a minimum of 142 semester hours.

The Bachelor of Fine Arts degree in commercial music is designed for students whose interest and abilities indicate a strong potential for significant achievement in the business or recording areas of the music industry. Concentrations are offered in music business and recording/engineering. The intent of the program is to train individuals for entry and middle level positions in these areas of the music industry. A total of 138 semester hours is required for the degree.

The Master of Music and the Master of Arts degrees require the completion of 30 to 33 semester hours of study. The Doctor of Musical Arts and the Doctor of Philosophy degrees require the completion of 60 to 66 semester hours of study.

General Program Areas. Applied Music, Commercial Music, Composition, Jazz Studies, Music Business, Music Education, Music History, Music Theory, Orchestral Instruments, Performance, Sacred Music, School Music.

Instruments Taught. Brass, Guitar, Harpsichord, Organ, Percussion, Piano, Saxophone, Stringed Instruments, Viola da Gamba, Voice, Woodwinds.

Musical Facilities

Practice Facilities. 34 practice rooms. 3 organs (Moller). 6 percussion-equipped practice rooms. 24 pianos (8 grands, 16 uprights); 8 grand pianos reserved for piano majors. Electronic music studio; recording studio; Orff studio; class piano studio.

Concert Facilities. Concert Hall.

Concerts/Musical Activities. Concerts, recitals. New Music Festivals, held annually since 1972.

Music Library. 17,000 scores; 11,500 books; 10,000 recordings. Listening facilities include 5 stations for cassette, 15 for stereo.

Special collections include: Southern Music Archives (records, field recordings, jazz orchestrations); Plough Collection of Pop Records; Mississippi Valley Collection; materials concerning jazz and blues of Memphis area; Southern hymnals; oral history tapes; manuscripts of composer Johannes Smit.

Special Programs

Featured Programs. Suzuki piano and string programs are offered.

Performance Groups. University Concert Band, Varsity Band, Marching Band, University Gospel Choir, Women's Chorus, Men's Chorus, University Wind Ensemble, University Orchestra, University Singers, Opera Chorus, Oratorio Chorus, University Jazz Ensemble, Recording Ensemble for Studio Singers, Recording Orchestra for Instrumental Performance.

Affiliated Programs. The Orff-Schulwerk program relates to the use of the Orff techniques in the Memphis City Schools.

Financial

Costs. Per academic year: Tuition in-state resident $926, out-of-state $2,894. Fees $21. Room $830 to $1,510. Board $1,316.

Financial Aid. Scholarships available ranging from $50 to $1,500 (average $400). Scholarship application due April 1. Part-time jobs and College Work-Study program available.

Commentary

Memphis State University is the only Tennessee institution offering the doctorate in music. The Ph.D. in Regional Studies, the study of a topic relating to Southern regional music, is unique to this university.

Middle Tennessee State University
Department of Music
Box 47
Murfreesboro
Tennessee 37132

Telephone. (615) 898-2469
Chief Administrator. Dr. Tom L. Naylor, Chairman.

Middle Tennessee State University opened in 1911 as a normal school with a two-year program for training teachers. It became a four-year college in 1943 and was advanced to university status in 1965. The campus of over 500 acres is located in Murfreesboro, a city of 30,000 situated 32 miles southeast of Nashville.

The purposes of the Department of Music are to prepare teachers of music for elementary and secondary schools; to prepare professional musicians; to prepare individuals for careers in music-related business and industry; to offer music courses and musical participation

to students whose studies are concentrated in fields other than music; and to participate in the musical life of the area by providing advisory services and enriching the musical life of the University and community.

Accreditation. Southern Association of Colleges and Schools; National Association of Schools of Music; National Council for Accreditation of Teacher Education.

Academic Information

Enrollment, Music Majors. (Total University) 11,000.
Music Faculty. 13.
Term System. Semester. Three summer sessions.
Entrance Requirements. High school graduation or GED; minimum ACT score of 16 required; completion of 4 units English, 3 mathematics, 2 laboratory science, 1 social studies; audition required.
Admission Procedure. Application with $5 nonrefundable fee accepted on a rolling basis.
Music Degrees Offered. Bachelor of Music; Master of Arts.
Music Degree Requirements. The Bachelor of Music degree is offered with emphases in certification in instrumental music education, certification in school music education, voice performance, instrumental performance, music industry, and theory-composition. All majors are required certain participation in ensembles maintained by the department. A senior recital is required of all majors, and attendance at recitals and concerts is likewise a requirement.

The Master of Arts degree is offered as well as a Master of Arts in Teaching degree with a major in music. The Master of Arts degree has a thesis and a non-thesis option. The non-thesis option requires a minimum of 36 semester hours; the graduate recital is considered an alternative to the thesis. The thesis option requires the completion of 30 semester hours.

General Program Areas. Composition, Music Education, Music Industry, Music Theory, Performance.
Instruments Taught. Baritone, Bass, Bassoon, Clarinet, English Horn, Euphonium, Flute, French Horn, Guitar, Oboe, Organ, Percussion, Piano, Piccolo, Saxophone, Trombone, Trumpet, Tuba, Viola, Violin, Violoncello, Voice.

Musical Facilities

Practice Facilities. 4 organs (Casavant, 2 Moeller, Rodgers). 4 percussion-equipped practice rooms. 35 pianos; 4 grand pianos reserved for piano majors. Electronic music studio.
Concert Facilities. Charles M. Murphy Center.
Concerts/Musical Activities. Student/faculty concerts and recitals; visiting artists.
Music Library. All circulating books and reference works are housed in the Andrew L. Todd Library. 5,000 volumes; 4,000 scores; 35 periodicals; 2,000 recordings. Listening facilities (cassette, stereo).

Special Programs

Performance Groups. Piano Ensemble, Chorus, Chamber Choir, Opera Workshop, Orchestra, Band, Percussion Ensemble, Jazz Ensemble.

Financial

Costs. Per academic year: Tuition in-state resident $1,036, out-of-state $3,466. Room $1,054. Board $628.

Financial Aid. Financial aid is available through state, federal, and institutional programs including grants, loans, scholarships, and part-time employment.

University of Tennessee at Chattanooga
Cadek Department of Music
615 McCallie Avenue
Chattanooga
Tennessee 37402

Telephone. (615) 755-4601

Chief Administrator. Peter Edwin Gerschefski, Head.

Founded in 1886, the University of Chattanooga merged in 1969 with the Chattanooga City College to become part of the University of Tennessee. The 31-acre campus has 30 buildings and is located near downtown Chattanooga.

The Cadek Department of Music offers undergraduate and graduate programs in professional performance and teaching.

Accreditation. Southern Association of Colleges and Schools; National Association of Schools of Music.

Academic Information

Enrollment, Music Majors. (Total University) 6,356.

Music Faculty. 20.

Term System. Quarter.

Entrance Requirements. High school graduation; SAT or ACT; audition required. GRE required for graduate study.

Admission Procedure. Application with supporting documents and nonrefundable $15 fee to Office of Admissions.

Music Degrees Offered. Bachelor of Music; Bachelor of Arts; Bachelor of Science.

Music Degree Requirements. The Bachelor of Music degree provides four concentrations for the major: instrumental performance, vocal performance, sacred music, and theory/composition. The Bachelor of Arts degree with a major in music is offered to students who desire a strong liberal arts background. Elective hours outside the Department permit considerable study in other academic areas. The Bachelor of Science degree is appropriate for students who plan a career teaching public school music. Successful completion of the program leads to public school teaching certification.

General Program Areas. Composition, Music Education, Music Theory, Sacred Music.

Instruments Taught. Brass, Organ, Percussion, Piano, Stringed Instruments, Voice, Woodwinds.

Musical Facilities

Concerts/Musical Activities. Student/faculty recitals and concerts; visiting artists.

Music Library. The University's library holdings exceed 1,000,000 items of which more than 330,000 are books and periodicals.

Special Programs

Performance Groups. Chattanooga Singers, Chamber Singers, Choral Union, Singing Mocs, Marching Band, Concert Band, Wind Ensemble, Jazz Band, Opera Workshop, Opera Theatre, University Orchestra, Chamber Orchestra, Cadek Adult Orchestra.

Affiliated Programs. Functioning as an auxiliary of the Cadek Department of Music, the Cadek Conservatory of Music has as its goal the education of music students of all ages who are not enrolled at the University level. The Conservatory offers applied music courses in virtually all instruments and voice in a curriculum that includes theory, chamber music, and other ensemble activity. This comprehensive curriculum has special courses for young children including the Suzuki method of teaching in flute, harp, violin, and piano; Kinder-Keyboard; and Music and Movement. There is also a course of study designed to give precollege preparation to the student intending to pursue music as a major at the university level.

Financial

Costs. Per academic year: Tuition in-state resident $1,098, out-of-state $3,530. Room $1,260.

Financial Aid. Financial aid is available in the form of institutional and state/federal scholarships, grants, loans, and part-time employment. Financial aid/scholarship application due March 1.

University of Tennessee at Knoxville
Department of Music
Knoxville
Tennessee 37996

Telephone. (615) 974-3241

Chief Administrator. J.J. Meacham, Head.

The University of Tennessee was founded in 1794. The campus is located on a tract known as "The Hill" in Knoxville, a major business center in eastern Tennessee.

The Department of Music offers curricula designed to prepare students for graduate study and for professional music careers. A comprehensive liberal studies program is offered for students with an interest in music as a major. Graduate programs lead to the Master of Music and Master of Arts degrees.

Accreditation. Southern Association of Colleges and Schools; National Association of Schools of Music; National Council for Accreditation of Teacher Education.

Academic Information

Enrollment, Music Majors. (Total University) 22,572.
Music Faculty. 32.
Term System. Quarter.
Entrance Requirements. High school graduation or equivalent; in-state applicants are admitted if they meet one of the following: GPA of 2.75 or above; GPA of 2.40 or above and ACT of 15 or above; GPA of 2.00 or above and ACT of 10 or above; completion of 16 units including 3 English, 2 mathematics, 2 foreign languages; audition required. GRE required for graduate study.

Admission Procedure. Application with supporting documents and nonrefundable $10 fee to Office of Admissions.

Music Degrees Offered. Bachelor of Music; Bachelor of Arts; Bachelor of Science; Master of Music; Master of Arts.

Music Degree Requirements. The Bachelor of Music degree is offered with concentrations in applied music and music history/literature. The Bachelor of Arts degree is offered with a major in music in a liberal arts program. The Bachelor of Science in music education is designed for preparation for institutional teaching and is administered by the Department of Music Education.

The Department of Music offers the Master of Music degree in performance, composition, music theory, choral conducting, instrumental conducting, string pedagogy. The Master of Arts degree is offered in musicology and music theory.

General Program Areas. Applied Music, Composition, Conducting, Music Education, Music History, Music Literature, Music Theory, Musicology, Performance.

Instruments Taught. Baritone, Bass, Bassoon, Clarinet, Flute, Guitar, Harpsichord, Horn, Oboe, Organ, Percussion, Piano, Saxophone, Trombone, Trumpet, Tuba, Viola, Violin, Violoncello, Voice.

Musical Facilities

Practice Facilities. The music activities of the Department are centered in the Music Building.

Concerts/Musical Activities. Student/faculty recitals and concerts; visiting artists.

Music Library. The Music Library serves the academic programs of the Department of Music with a collection of books, scores, recordings, and tapes. Listening facilities are available. An affiliated university museum has a collection of historic American instruments. Other collections include: materials on Busoni and Galston; late nineteenth century Tennessee tunebooks and songsters.

Special Programs

Performance Groups. Chamber Music Ensemble, Woodwind Choir, Brass Choir, Jazz Ensemble, Studio Orchestra, Trombone Choir, Tuba Ensemble, Percussion Ensemble, Marimba Choir, Baroque Ensemble, UT Singers, Chamber Singers, Collegium Musicum, Saxophone Choir, Opera Theatre, Opera Workshop, Concert Band, Campus Band, Varsity Band, Laboratory Band, Marching Band, Symphony Orchestra, Chamber Orchestra, Concert Choir, University Chorus, Women's Chorale.

Financial

Costs. Per academic year: Tuition in-state resident $957, out-of-state $3,111. Fees $168. Room $1,170. Board $1,200.

Financial Aid. Financial aid is awarded on the basis of academic merit and financial need. Institutional and state/federal aid are available in the form of scholarships, grants, loans, and part-time employment. Financial aid/scholarship application due March 1.

TEXAS

Baylor University
School of Music
CSB Mail Room, Box 376
Waco
Texas 76798

Telephone. (817) 755-1161

Chief Administrator. Dr. Robert L. Blocker, Dean.

Baylor University was chartered in 1845 and is affiliated with the Baptist General Convention of Texas. As a Christian institution, the University strives to integrate the essence of the Christian faith in its whole process of education. There are 7 colleges and schools located in Waco and Dallas offering a program of liberal arts and professional education. The main campus of 350 acres is situated in Waco (population 100,000).

The original music department was reorganized into the School of Music in 1921. The bachelor's and master's degree programs are designed for professional preparation in performance, theory, and composition and as preparation for a teaching career in the public schools of Texas. The Bachelor of Arts degree with music as a major area offers music performance or academic areas while pursuing a liberal arts education. A low student/teacher ratio permits all students, both undergraduate and graduate, access to principal teachers. Ensembles of the School of Music have been invited to perform at conventions and festivals throughout the U.S.A.

Accreditation. Southern Association of Colleges and Schools; National Association of Schools of Music; Texas Association of Music Schools.

Academic Information

Enrollment, Music Majors. Full-time 336. 5 foreign students.

Music Faculty. Full-time 47, part-time 5.

Term System. Semester. Academic year September to May. Summer session June to Aug.

Entrance Requirements. Accredited high school graduation with rank in upper quarter of graduating class; ACT and/or SAT scores within certain limits; music audition; acceptance by School of Music subject to admission by University. Audition/recommendation by committee and Dean of School of Music.

Admission Procedure. Application to University with $20 nonrefundable fee and all supporting documents. Foreign students must have TOEFL score of 540 minimum for undergraduate and 550 minimum for graduate; confirmation of financial resources completed by parent or sponsor; confirmation from financial institution that funds are on deposit and available for support of student for each year of study. Advanced placement through CLEP; theory department placement test (keyboard, instrumental, and vocal assessment).

Music Degrees Offered. Bachelor of Music; Bachelor of Music Education; Bachelor of Arts; Master of Music.

Music Degree Requirements. The degrees Bachelor of Music, Bachelor of Music Education, and Bachelor of Arts with a major in either performance or an academic area require the completion of 125 to 151 semester hours. The Master of Music degree is offered with emphases in composition, music history and literature, theory, church music, choral conducting, woodwind instruments, piano pedagogy and performance, instrumental performance, and music education. The degree requires 25 to 36 semester hours of study.

General Program Areas. Choral Conducting, Church Music, Composition, Music Education, Music History, Music Literature, Music Theory, Performance, Piano Pedagogy.

Instruments Taught. Bass, Bassoon, Clarinet, Collegium Instruments, Euphonium, Flute, Guitar, Handbells, Harp, Harpsichord, Horn, Oboe, Organ, Percussion, Piano, Saxophone, Trumpet, Tuba, Viola, Violin, Violoncello, Voice.

Musical Facilities

Practice Facilities. 55 practice rooms. 5 practice rooms with organs (2 Ruffati, 1 Miller Chapel pipe, 1 studio organ); 5 practice organs (Redman, Wicks, Rodgers). 1 practice room with harp. 49 piano practice rooms (uprights and grands); 27 grand pianos reserved for piano majors. Recording studio; theory lab; electronic music studio; opera rehearsal facility. String division housed in Educational Building.

Concert Facilities. Roxy Grove Hall, seating 480; Recital Hall II, 120; Jones Theater, 380.

Community Facilities. Hippodrome Theater; Indian Springs Park; Waco Hall, seating 2,250.

Concerts/Musical Activities. Approximately 100 concerts per semester including faculty, student, Convocation, Symphony, choral, opera, ShowTime, visiting distinguished artists; master classes/recitals.

Music Library. 15,000 volumes; 54,500 musical scores; 200 current periodicals; 23 video cassettes; 200 microform titles; 25,000 phonograph records; 300 audiocassettes; 700 compact discs. 167 listening stations. Special collections include: Frances G. Spencer Collection of old American printed sheet music; O'Neil collection of rare instruments; 2,000 rare books; early American songbooks. Individual divisions of the School of Music house scores; academic materials and audio/video materials are in the main University Library (Moody Library).

Special Programs

Foreign Programs. Baylor in England; Baylor in Vienna. No actual participation with foreign schools.

Financial

Costs. Per academic year: $4,000 to $5,000. Room $1,300. Board $1,600. Off-campus housing $200 to $400 per month.

Financial Aid. Financial aid is awarded on the basis of academic merit, financial need, and musical ability. Institutional and state/federal aid available. Part-time employment and College Work-Study program available.

Commentary

Baylor University's resources include eighteenth and nineteenth century English church music and theory method books, as well as numerous eighteenth century editions of chamber music.

East Texas State University
Department of Music
Commerce
Texas 75428

Telephone. (214) 886-5303, 886-5304
Chief Administrator. Dr. Robert E. Houston, Head.
East Texas State University, which began as East Texas Normal College in 1889 in Cooper, Texas, moved to the city of Commerce, 60 miles northeast of Dallas, in 1894. In 1917, the college was taken over by the state of Texas and the name became East Texas State Normal College. This name changed in 1923 to East Texas State Teachers College, and the word "Teachers" was dropped in 1957. University status was achieved in 1965. The

University offers more than 100 major fields of study through 32 academic departments. The campus covers 1,883 acres of land in and near Commerce. The main 140-acre campus is located eight blocks southwest of Commerce's business center.

The Department of Music offers three undergraduate degrees to prepare students for teaching music in elementary and/or secondary schools (BME, BA, BS), and one undergraduate degree emphasizing performance or theory/composition (BMus). The teaching curricula emphasize: (1) vocal music—preparation for teaching music in the elementary grades, organizing and directing choral organizations, teaching courses in theory and music literature, and a general acquaintance with the instrumental music problems; (2) instrumental music—preparation for teaching individually and in groups the various band and orchestral instruments, organizing and directing bands and orchestras, teaching courses in theory and music literature, and a general acquaintance with vocal music problems. A vocal-instrumental combination may be elected if desired. The BS or the BA degrees also may be planned with a music history concentration and/or theory courses replacing teacher certification courses. The Bachelor of Music degree designates an emphasis upon performance or theory/composition. Master of Music and Master of Science degree programs are also offered.

Accreditation. Southern Association of Colleges and Schools; National Association of Schools of Music; National Council for Accreditation of Teacher Education; Texas Association of Music Schools.

Academic Information

Music Faculty. 18.
Term System. Semester. Summer session of 2 six-week terms.
Entrance Requirements. High school graduation; SAT score 800 or ACT score 18; audition by tape or personal visit; diagnostic tests required during first week of classes. Foreign students must complete admission requirements 3 months prior to enrollment; TOEFL minimum score 500; must subscribe to group hospitalization insurance program.
Admission Procedure. Application with $25 non-refundable fee due at least 3 weeks prior to classes.
Music Degrees Offered. Bachelor of Music; Bachelor of Arts; Bachelor of Science; Bachelor of Music Education; Master of Music; Master of Science.
Music Degree Requirements. The bachelor degrees requires the completion of 120 to 130 credit hours of a prescribed course with 56 to 60 hours in the major emphasis, 18 to 25 in the minor or certification area, and 60 in general studies. The Master of Music and Master of Science degrees require the completion of 36 credit hours. Music majors must enroll each semester in a major ensemble. All persons who register for student teaching should be on campus as full-time music majors either

two full semesters or one semester and a full summer session prior to registering for student teaching. Undergraduate music majors will be required to register each semester for recital attendance.

General Program Areas. Composition, Conducting, Music Education, Music History, Music Theory, Musicology, Performance.

Instruments Taught. Brass, Organ, Percussion, Piano, Stringed Instruments, Voice, Woodwinds.

Musical Facilities

Practice Facilities. 32 practice rooms. 2 practice rooms for organists. 9 percussion-equipped practice rooms. Various types of grands and studio uprights located in practice rooms and classrooms; 4 grand pianos reserved for piano majors. Electronic/recording studio used for instruction and research in composition, theory, and multi-track recording. Electronic piano laboratory contains 18 Fender Electronic Student Pianos equipped with individual headphones and metronomes.

Concert Facilities. Auditorium, seating 2,000; Concert Hall, 600 (planned).

Concerts/Musical Activities. At least 5 major cultural events are sponsored by the University each year; student recitals/concerts.

Music Library. Music materials are part of the main library which houses over 1 million volumes; 680 scores; 2,700 phonograph recordings. Listening facilities (cassette, stereo). Interlibrary loan through North Texas Federation (Texas Women's University, North Texas State).

Special Programs

Performance Groups. Orchestra, Band, Choir, Chorale, Chamber Singers, Jazz Ensemble, Marching Band.

Financial

Costs. Per academic year: Tuition resident $870, nonresident $3,900. Applied music fee $5 per semester hour; practice room fee $6 for 3 semester hours. Room and board approximately $1,100.

Financial Aid. Scholarships, grants, and loans available.

Hardin-Simmons University
School of Music
2200 Hickory
Abilene
Texas 79698

Telephone. (915) 677-7281, Ext. 426
Chief Administrator. Dr. Wesley Coffman, Dean.

Hardin-Simmons University, known originally as Abilene Baptist College, was founded in 1891. It was renamed Simmons College in honor of the first major donor, Dr. James B. Simmons, a Baptist minister of New York City, and in 1934 again renamed Hardin-Simmons University in recognition of gifts by Mr. and Mrs. John G. Hardin of Burkburnett, Texas. Control of the university passed to the Baptist General Convention of Texas in 1941. The 40-acre campus consists of 31 buildings and is located in Abilene (population 10,000), 150 miles west of Fort Worth. On-campus dormitories and married-student units are available.

The purpose of the School of Music is to prepare musicians for professions in music education, music ministry, performance, and theory/composition. In addition, the School serves as a cultural center for the university community. The School comprises the Departments of Applied Music, Music Education and Church Music, Music History and Literature, and Music Theory and Composition.

Accreditation. Southern Association of Colleges and Schools; National Association of Schools of Music.

Academic Information

Enrollment, Music Majors. Total university: full-time 647 men, 656 women; part-time 265 men, 266 women. Foreign students 19.

Music Faculty. Total university: full-time 98, part-time 22.

Term System. Semester. Two summer sessions.

Entrance Requirements. High school diploma or GED; SAT or ACT; audition for placement. Foreign students must submit two personal references; notarized statement indicating ability to assume all financial responsibilities while residing in the U.S.A.; current health forms; TOEFL, SAT, or ACT scores; $1,500 deposit toward payment of student expenses. GRE required for graduate school.

Admission Procedure. Applications accepted on a rolling admissions basis; $25 nonrefundable application fee. 87% of applicants are accepted and 90% of students applying for graduate degrees are admitted.

Music Degrees Offered. Bachelor of Music; Bachelor of Arts; Master of Music; Master of Arts.

Music Degree Requirements. The Bachelor's degree requires the completion of 124 credit hours. Undergraduate courses are offered in applied music, music education, church music, music history and literature, and theory and composition leading to the Bachelor of Music degree. Graduate study leading to the degree Master of Music is offered in music education, theory and composition, and applied music literature. The degree requires the completion of 36 credit hours. All music majors (B.M. degree) must pass the piano proficiency requirement and are required to attend an average of 16 recitals per semester for each semester in residence up to eight.

General Program Areas. Applied Music, Church Music, Music Composition, Music Education, Music Literature, Music Theory.

Instruments Taught. Brass, Conducting, Guitar, Organ, Percussion, Piano, Stringed Instruments, Voice, Woodwinds.

Musical Facilities

Practice Facilities. Special practice facilities for organists; 1 Skinner, 1 Visser Rowland. Practice room for percussionists. 35 practice rooms. 27 upright studio pianos, 5 grands; 3 grand pianos reserved for piano majors. Electronic music studio.

Concert Facilities. Woodward-Dellis Recital Hall.

Community Facilities. First Baptist Church is used by organ students.

Concerts/Musical Activities. The School of Music offers about 60 concerts (solo and ensemble by faculty and students) each year. The University sponsors several concerts during the school year through the Student Foundation.

Music Library. The Smith Music Library in Caldwell Hall contains study scores, collected works of various composers, recordings, and certain basic music books and reference materials. Listening equipment is provided, and the library houses all of the taped concerts and recitals of the School of Music. The Sims Hymnal Collection is also maintaned here.

Financial

Costs. Per academic year: Tuition $3,210. Fees: $216. Room $930. Board $1,320.

Financial Aid. 45% of students received some form of financial aid. Scholarships range from $250 to $5,000. Scholarship application due date July 1. Part-time employment and College Work-Study program available.

Commentary

Hardin-Simmons University plans to add a new degree program in music business.

University of Houston
School of Music
4800 Calhoun
Houston
Texas 77004

Telephone. (713) 749-1116

Chief Administrator. Dr. David Tomatz, Director.

The University of Houston is a publicly supported university founded as a four-year institution in 1934. The 384-acre campus contains 85 buildings. The Houston metropolitan area has a population of over 2,300,000.

Although virtually no details are known concerning the origins of music in the curriculum of the University of Houston, it is apparent that music has been present since the inception of the institution as a junior college in 1927. No formal organization of a music department

took place until 1940, six years after the junior college became the University of Houston. Degree programs were instituted the following year. By 1950, the department had begun to grow and new faculty added. In 1972, the School of Music moved into a new Fine Arts Building.

In 1977, the University of Houston joined with the Houston Grand Opera to create the Houston Opera Studio, a program of continued study and performing experience for young professional singers. Since then the program has expanded to include young coach-accompanists, stage directors, lighting designers, composers, and librettists.

Accreditation. Southern Association of Colleges and Schools; National Association of Schools of Music.

Academic Information

Enrollment, Music Majors. 358.

Music Faculty. Full-time 34, part-time 20.

Term System. Semester. Academic year August 31 to May 14. Summer sessions of 6-weeks from June to August.

Entrance Requirements. Freshmen and transfer students with less than 15 hours: minimum SAT score 800-1100 (depending on high school rank; minimum 400 verbal for all); or minimum ACT score of 17-26 with English usage minimum of 17 for all. Transfer students with 15-29 hours: minimum 2.5 GPA; with 30 or more hours: 2.0 GPA. Entering undergraduate students must pass a music theory placement test and an audition on major instrument or voice; graduate students must also pass a music history examination; graduate students must also have earned a Bachelor of Music or have at least 60 hours in music and take the GRE general examination and music subject examination. Advanced placement is available for most non-advanced, non-music courses.

Admission Procedure. Apply for admission through the main Admissions office; after being accepted to the University, students may take the theory examination and audition. Foreign students should request an International Students application from the School of Music; undergraduate foreign students should send all admission materials directly to the International Admissions Office; graduate foreign students to the Director of Graduate Studies at the School of Music.

Music Degrees Offered. Bachelor of Music; Bachelor of Arts; Master of Music.

Music Degree Requirements. The Bachelor of Music degree is offered with emphasis in performance (all orchestra and band instruments, piano, organ, harpsichord, voice), music theory, music composition, and music education. The degree requires the completion of 122 semester hours of courses including those required for the major area of emphasis. The Bachelor of Arts degree program has the same requirements as above with the addition of pedagogy, accompanying, and chamber music (piano), music literature, and music composition.

The Master of Music degree requires the completion of a minimum of 30 semester hours in advanced and graduate courses in applied music, composition, music literature. A Master of Music Education degree program was instituted in 1987.

General Program Areas. Applied Music, Composition, Music Literature, Music Theory, Opera, Performance.

Instruments Taught. Brass, Organ, Percussion, Piano, Stringed Instruments, Voice, Woodwinds.

Musical Facilities

Practice Facilities. Special practice facilities for organists; four 2-rank Wicks unified and extended direct-electric pipe organs, one 52-rank von Beckerath mechanical-action pipe organ, one 5-rank Hammer Reuter mechanical-action pipe organ. 53 piano practice rooms; 122 pianos (Yamaha, Steinway); 12 grand pianos reserved for piano majors. Electronic music studio; electronic piano classrooms.

Concert Facilities. Dudley Recital Hall, seating 288; Organ Hall, 200; Cullen Auditorium, 1,700; Wortham Theatre, 566.

Concerts/Musical Activities. Orchestra, Band, Woodwind Ensemble, and Chamber Music concerts; solo recitals.

Music Library. 10,987 volumes; 16,383 musical scores; 140 periodical subscriptions; 13,750 phonograph recordings. 43 listening stations. Music collections at Rice University, St. Thomas University, Houston Baptist University, and the Houston Public Library are available to students.

Special Programs

Performance Groups. Cougar Marching Band, Wind Ensembles, Symphony Orchestra, University Chorus, Concert Chorale, Houston Opera Studio, Chamber Music (brass, woodwind, string), Chamber Orchestra, Collegium Musicum, Cougar Brass, Jazz Ensemble, New Music Workshop, Opera Workshop, Percussion Ensemble, Today's Generation, Vocal Chamber Ensemble. Faculty Ensembles-in-Residence: Lyric Art Quintet, Fine Arts Brass Quintet, Western Arts Trio, Woodwinds of Houston.

Affiliated Programs. The Houston Opera Studio is a joint program of the Houston Grand Opera and the University of Houston. Singers must demonstrate major operatic potential and thorough musical and theatrical training. Preliminary auditions are held in Houston, Los Angeles, Chicago, and New York. All auditionees must prepare 5 selections, at least one each in Italian, French, German, and English.

Financial

Costs. Per academic year: Tuition in-state resident $384, out-of-state $1,440. Student service fee and building use fee $180. Private lesson fee (one-time fee—not a weekly fee) $72 for 1-hour per week lesson; $36 for½ hour lesson. Room and board approximately $2,000.

Financial Aid. Financial aid is awarded on the basis of academic merit, financial need, and musical ability. 102 students receive financial aid; average award $150 per semester. Nonresidents receiving a competitive scholarship of $200 or more per academic year pay in-state tuition. Part-time employment and College Work-Study program available.

Lamar University
Department of Music
Beaumont
Texas 77710

Telephone. (409) 880-8144

Chief Administrator. James M. Simmons, Department Head.

Lamar University is a liberal arts and technical institution established in 1923 as the South Park Junior College. It became a four-year state supported college in 1951 and was designated a university in 1960. The 200-acre campus is located in the center of industrial southeast Texas.

The Department of Music offers programs in applied music and music education.

Accreditation. Southern Association of Colleges and Schools; National Association of Schools of Music; National Council for Accreditation of Teacher Education.

Academic Information

Enrollment, Music Majors. (Total University) 14,151.

Music Faculty. 22.

Term System. Semester. Two summer sessions.

Entrance Requirements. High school graduation; recommend 4 units English, 2 laboratory sciences, 2 algebra, 1 geometry, 2½ social sciences; SAT or ACT required; audition required for junior level standing in the performance major.

Admission Procedure. Application with supporting documents to Admissions and Records Office due February 1 for Fall semester, October 1 for Spring semester.

Music Degrees Offered. Bachelor of Music; Master of Music; Master of Music Education.

Music Degree Requirements. The Bachelor of Music degree is offered with concentrations in composition, performance, and music education. The performance concentration may be in instrumental (strings, wind, or percussion), keyboard, or vocal music. The music education concentration (band, orchestra, vocal/choir) qualifies the graduate for teacher certification in music at all levels.

The degrees Master of Music in performance and Master of Music Education are designed to help performers and music educators improve skills and develop new concepts which may be applied to their particular fields of endeavor.

General Program Areas. Applied Music, Composition, Music Education, Music Literature, Music Theory, Performance.

Instruments Taught. Baritone, Bass, Bassoon, Clarinet, Cornet, Flute, French Horn, Oboe, Organ, Percussion, Piano, Saxophone, Trombone, Trumpet, Tuba, Viola, Violin, Violoncello, Voice.

Musical Facilities

Practice Facilities. The Music Building houses the Department of Music.

Concerts/Musical Activities. Student/faculty recitals and concerts; visiting artists.

Music Library. The Mary and John Gray Library houses over 800,000 volumes. The Library supports the academic programs of the Department of Music.

Special Programs

Performance Groups. Jazz Combo, Dance Band, Steel Band, Percussion Ensemble, Orchestra, Marching Band, Symphonic Band, A Cappella Choir, Cardinal Singers, Grand Chorus, Cardinal Moods, Cardinal Reflections, Opera Workshop, Chamber Music Ensemble.

Financial

Costs. Per academic year: Tuition in-state resident $360, out-of-state $3,600. Fees $400. Room and board $3,000.

Financial Aid. Financial aid is awarded on the basis of academic merit and financial need. Aid is available in the form of state/federal scholarships, grants, loans, and part-time employment. Financial aid/scholarship application due April 1.

North Texas State University
School of Music
Denton
Texas 76203

Telephone. (817) 565-2791
Chief Administrator. Dr. Marceau Myers, Dean.

North Texas State University was established in 1890 as a normal college and became a four-year institution in 1949. University status was achieved in 1961. The campus of 412 acres is located in southwest Denton, 30 miles north of Dallas.

The School of Music was created in 1945 based on the reorganization of the Music Department. Programs are offered for: (1) music majors in performance (applied music), music education, composition, theory, jazz studies, music history and literature, and musicology; (2) private teachers; (3) elementary education majors; and (4) university students desiring a cultural background in music.

Accreditation. Southern Association of Colleges and Schools; National Association of Schools of Music; National Council for Accreditation of Teacher Education.

Academic Information

Enrollment, Music Majors. 1,350. 50 foreign students.
Music Faculty. Full-time 78, part-time 9.
Term System. Semester. Two 5-week summer terms.
Entrance Requirements. High school graduation; SAT or ACT; audition tape (cassette preferred) of at least 10 minutes (no special repertoire is required but standard solo work should be represented).

Admission Procedure. Application accepted on a rolling admissions basis.

Music Degrees Offered. Bachelor of Music; Bachelor of Arts; Master of Music; Master of Music Education; Master of Arts; Doctor of Musical Arts; Doctor of Philosophy.

Music Degree Requirements. The Bachelor of Music degree may be earned with a major in performance, music education, composition, music theory, jazz studies, or music history and literature. The major in performance includes piano (performance), piano (pedagogy), organ, voice, or an orchestral instrument, including harp and classical guitar. The major in music education is designed to develop music teacher talent and emphasizes public school teacher expectations. The program includes training in elementary and secondary general music, secondary vocal-choral music and elementary-secondary instrumental music, leading to Texas teacher certification. The Bachelor of Arts degree with a major in music is offered through the College of Arts and Sciences.

The School of Music offers a diversity of graduate programs in all aspects of the musical arts to performers, composers, scholars, and music educators. The various programs lead to the degrees Master of Music, Master of Music Education, Master of Arts with a major in music, Doctor of Musical Arts, and Doctor of Philosophy. It is the purpose of these programs to develop and nurture the artistry, creativity, scholarship, and professional competence which will provide musical leadership and standards of excellence.

General Program Areas. Composition, Jazz Studies, Music Education, Music History, Music Literature, Music Theory, Musicology, Performance.

Instruments Taught. Bass, Bassoon, Clarinet, Euphonium, Flute, French Horn, Guitar, Harp, Harpsichord, Oboe, Organ, Percussion, Piano, Saxophone, Trombone, Trumpet, Tuba, Viola, Violin, Violoncello, Voice.

Musical Facilities

Practice Facilities. 350 practice rooms. Piano, instrumental, organ, and percussion practice rooms are located in the main Music Building and 2 separate practice buildings. 241 pianos (229 uprights, 12 grands). 5 electronic and recording studios.

Concert Facilities. Concert Hall, seating 250; Recital Hall, 250; Organ Recital Hall, 100; Stan Kenton Jazz Hall, 100; Main Auditorium, 2,200.

Concerts/Musical Activities. 600 concerts are performed each year.

Music Library. The Music Library holds more than 120,000 items of music books, periodicals, scores, parts, and microforms. It also owns complete works of more than 200 composers and over 100 historical collections. Special collections include: the manuscripts and letters of Arnold Schoenberg; the library of Lloyd Hibberd, distinguished North Texas musicologist, containing 10,-000 volumes especially strong in French baroque first editions and manuscripts; 1,000 Duke Ellington discs; Stan Kenton Collection of 1,600 original scores and parts. The Audio Center is adjacent to the Music Library and contains more than 96,000 musical recordings. The University has a cooperative agreement with West Texas State University for exchanging library resources.

Special Programs

Performance Groups. A Capella Choir, Chapel Choir, Men's Chorus, Women's Chorus, Grand Chorus, Symphony Orchestra, Symphonic Wind Ensemble, Concert Band, Marching Band, University Band, Jazz Lab Band, Harp Ensemble, Brass Choir, Brass Quintet, Trumpet Choir, Horn Choir, Trombone Choir, Tuba-Euphonium Ensemble, Wind Ensemble, Chamber Orchestra, Percussion Ensemble, Marimba Ensemble, Steel Drum Band, Flute Choir, Cello Choir, Chamber Choir, Jazz Singers, Woodwind Ensemble, Saxophone Ensemble, Opera Theatre, Collegium Musicum.

Financial

Costs. Per academic year: Tuition in-state resident $896, out-of-state $4,016. Room and board $2,494 (minimum).

Financial Aid. Music Scholarships and Service Awards are available. Other sources of financial aid include institutional and state/federal grants and loans, part-time employment, and a College Work-Study program.

Commentary

North Texas State University offers a comprehensive and well-balanced music curriculum. The instrumental and practice facilities are outstanding. NTSU is well-known for the scope and quality of its jazz program.

Rice University
Shepherd School of Music
6100 Main Street
Houston
Texas 77005

Telephone. (713) 527-4854

Chief Administrator. Dr. Michael Hammond, Dean.

Rice University, a private, independent, nonsectarian institution, was originally founded in 1891 as the William Marsh Institute, was renamed the Rice Institute in 1912, and was again renamed the William Marsh Rice University in 1960. It includes among its academic divisions both undergraduate and graduate studies in humanities, social sciences, natural sciences, engineering, architecture, administrative sciences, and music. About 60 percent of Rice's 2,500 undergraduate students live on campus in the eight residential colleges. Graduate students live off-campus in the University-owned Graduate House. The Rice campus of 300 acres is located 3 miles from downtown Houston.

The Shepherd School of Music was founded in 1973 and the first music degree programs were offered in 1975. The School offers both professional training and a broad liberal arts curriculum at the undergraduate level. At the graduate level, it provides professional music training for qualified students in a variety of programs. Undergraduate curricula include core music courses, applied music, other required music courses, chamber music and large ensembles, nonmusic courses as specified by the university, and electives. Music majors are entitled to one hour of private lessons each week each semester that they are enrolled as music majors.

Accreditation. Southern Association of Colleges and Schools.

Academic Information

Enrollment, Music Majors. Full-time 103 men, 113 women; part-time 10 men, 8 women. 22 foreign students.

Music Faculty. Full-time 22, part-time 24, adjunct 2.

Term System. Semester. 6-week summer sessions (music seldom included).

Entrance Requirements. High school graduation with 14 units (4 English, 3 mathematics, 1 laboratory science, 2 foreign language, 2 social studies, 2 electives); SAT; 3 CEEB Achievement Tests (English composition and 2 others). Audition required (live or tape); theory test (plus history for graduate applicants).

Admission Procedure. Application due February 1 (accepted on a rolling basis for School of Music).

Music Degrees Offered. Bachelor of Arts; Bachelor of Music; Master of Music; Doctor of Musical Arts.

Music Degree Requirements. The Bachelor degrees require a music core of 5 semesters each of theory, music history, and aural skills; minimum of 120 semester hours; participation in orchestra and two degree recitals.

The Master's degree requires the completion of 30 semester hours. The Doctor of Music Arts degree requires the completion of 90 semester hours beyond the Bachelor's degree.

General Program Areas. Composition, Conducting, Music History, Music Theory, Musicology, Performance.

Instruments Taught. Bass, Bassoon, Clarinet, Flute, Harp, Horn, Oboe, Organ, Percussion, Piano, Trombone, Trumpet, Tuba, Viola, Violin, Violoncello, Voice.

Musical Facilities

Practice Facilities. 30 practice rooms. 2 organs (Moller, Fisk); additional instruments used include Fisk, Rieger, Schantz, and Aeolian-Skinner. 2 percussion-equipped practice rooms; percussion studio. 14 practice pianos (12 Kawai grand, 4 uprights); 12 grand pianos reserved for piano majors. Opera studio. Electronic music laboratory.

Concert Facilities. Hamman Hall, Milford House Recital Hall, Shepherd School of Music Rehearsal Hall (recitals), University Chapel.

Concerts/Musical Activities. Diverse roster of recitals, showcase events, ensemble concerts, opera performances, chamber music recitals, and special events such as the Madrigal Dinner and Schubertiad.

Music Library. 11,100 scores; 9,300 books; 1,310 bound periodicals; 141 current periodical subscriptions; 15,677 phonograph recordings. Listening facilities (6 cassette players, 5 turntables, 7 reel-to-reel tape players). Special collections include: Richard Lert Conducting Archive; Henry L. Bartlett Beethoven Collection; Wilfred Batchelder double bass music collection; nineteenth century and early twentieth century sheet music. Music collections are also available at Houston Public Library and the University of Houston. Music librarians at these institutions have formed a cooperative organization to facilitate availability of collections where appropriate.

Special Programs

Performance Groups. Orchestra, Chamber Music, Shepherd Singers, Collegium Musicum.

Foreign Programs. Participation in Institute of European Studies; Beaver College Center for Education Abroad; exchange program with Trinity College, Cambridge (England).

Affiliated Programs. Rice-Swarthmore Exchange Program; dual degree program with Texas Southern University.

Financial

Costs. Per academic year: Tuition $4,100. Fees $213. Room and board $3,650.

Financial Aid. Scholarships, grants, and loans available. Application due April 1.

Commentary

Rice University's Shepherd School of Music is one of the foremost music institutions in the Southwest. The performance program is enhanced by a superior resident faculty.

Sam Houston State University Department of Music
Huntsville
Texas 77341

Telephone. (409) 294-1360

Chief Administrator. Dr. Herbert L. Koerselman, Chair.

Sam Houston State University was founded in 1879. It is a liberal arts and teacher training institution offering undergraduate and graduate programs. The 1,186-acre campus has 110 buildings in Huntsville, 70 miles north of Houston.

The Department of Music offers programs leading to baccalaureate and master's degrees in music education, performance, and music therapy.

Accreditation. Southern Association of Colleges and Schools; National Association of Schools of Music.

Academic Information

Enrollment, Music Majors. (Total University) 9,002.

Music Faculty. 29.

Term System. Semester.

Entrance Requirements. High school graduation; completion of 15 units including 3 English, 2 mathematics, 2 science; ACT or SAT required; audition required.

Admission Procedure. Application with supporting documents to Admissions Office.

Music Degrees Offered. Bachelor of Music; Bachelor of Music Education; Master of Music; Master of Education.

Music Degree Requirements. The Bachelor of Music degree is offered with concentrations in theory/composition, music literature, performance, and music therapy. The Bachelor of Music Education degree is offered with programs in instrumental, vocal, and elementary music (K-7).

The Master of Music degree is offered with major areas of study in conducting, the Kodaly Method of pedagogy, musicology, performance and literature, and theory/composition. The Master of Education degree program emphasizes music education in the secondary school.

General Program Areas. Composition, Conducting, Kodaly Pedagogy, Music Education, Music Literature, Music Theory, Music Therapy, Musicology, Performance.

Instruments Taught. Brass, Organ, Percussion, Piano, Stringed Instruments, Voice, Woodwinds.

Musical Facilities

Concerts/Musical Activities. Student/faculty recitals and concerts; visiting artists.

Music Library. The Newton Gresham Library serves the academic programs of the Department of Music. It houses over 850,000 books, bound journals and documents, 600,000 microforms, 8,000 phonograph records, and 4,500 periodical titles.

Special Programs

Performance Groups. Jazz Ensemble, Orchestra, Chamber Music, A Cappella Choir, Band, Men's Choir, Women's Choir, Brass Choir, Woodwind Choir, Opera Workshop, Wind Ensemble.

Financial

Costs. Per academic year: Tuition in-state resident $360, out-of-state $3,600. Fees $400. Room $1,000. Board $1,400.

Financial Aid. Financial aid is awarded on the basis of academic merit and financial need. State/federal aid is available in the form of scholarships, grants, loans, and part-time employment. Financial aid/scholarship application due July 15.

Southern Methodist University Meadows School of the Arts
Division of Music
Owen Arts Center
Dallas
Texas 75275

Telephone. (214) 692-2587

Chief Administrator. Dr. James A. Ode, Chairman, Division of Music.

Southern Methodist University is a private university founded in 1911 and affiliated with the United Methodist Church. The Owen Art Center, completed in 1968, houses instruction, performance, and exhibition in art, music, drama, dance, television, and film. This center also serves the public as a cultural center for Dallas and the surrounding region.

The Meadows School of the Arts is a professional school within the University. Through exposure to performance and a variety of courses, students may decide to combine careers in related areas such as arts administration, business (music retailing, publishing), law (copyright, management), music and medicine, as well as in performance and pedagogy. In addition to the core music curriculum, all freshmen are a part of Dedman College which offers a liberal arts curriculum.

Accreditation. Southern Association of Colleges and Schools; National Association of Schools of Music; National Association of Music Therapy.

Academic Information

Enrollment, Music Majors. Full-time 122 men, 162 women; part-time 18 men, 29 women. Foreign students 15.

Music Faculty. Full-time 35, part-time 34. Artists in residence: Tedd Joselson, Erick Friedman, Warren Benson.

Term System. Semester. Academic year August to May. Two 4-week summer sessions from early June to early August.

Entrance Requirements. High school graduation; SAT or ACT scores; recommendations; performance audition. Graduate admission is determined by a review of the applicant's undergraduate record, letters of reference, and the results of the performance audition or portfolio review in the case of composition candidates. Foreign students must have certification of financial responsibility and TOEFL.

Admission Procedure. Submit SMU application with supporting documents.

Music Degrees Offered. Bachelor of Music; Master of Music.

Music Degree Requirements. The Bachelor of Music degree is offered in performance, music education, music therapy, and theory/composition. The degree program in music education is designed to train musician/teachers. The curriculum integrates performance, conducting, rehearsal techniques, and methodology. Extensive observations in the schools are required early in the program. Students develop their philosophy of music education and demonstrate quality teaching techniques before beginning their supervised student teaching internship in the senior year. The curriculum in music therapy is competency-based, with strong elements in both clinical research areas. The program has affiliations with 26 allied health facilities in the Dallas area for clinical practicum experiences. The Bachelor of Music degree in performance is offered in orchestral instruments, piano, voice, and organ. The degree in theory/composition is awarded with a concentration in either theory or composition.

The Master of Music degree is offered in performance, music education, music therapy, theory, composition, conducting, music history/literature, and piano pedagogy. The Master of Sacred Music program is jointly sponsored by the Perkins School of Theology and the Meadows School of the Arts. Designed for the preparation of professional leadership in the church as well as the community, priority is placed on the conducting of ensembles as well as theology, literature, performance practice, and performance skills.

General Program Areas. Choral Conducting, Composition, Music Education, Music History, Music Literature, Music Theory, Music Therapy, Performance, Piano Pedagogy, Sacred Music.

Instruments Taught. Bass, Bassoon, Clarinet, Guitar, Harp, Harpsichord, Horn, Organ, Percussion, Piano, Saxophone, Trombone, Trumpet, Tuba, Viola, Violin, Violoncello, Voice.

Musical Facilities

Practice Facilities. Special practice facilities for organists; 1 Aeolian-Skinner pipe organ, 3 manual Holtkamp, 7 practice organs including a 7-stop organ built by Kern, and a 4-stop Positive. Practice facilities for percussionists. 75 practice rooms. 10 grand pianos and 26 upright (Steinway, Kawai, Mason & Hamlin, Baldwin, Grinell); 10 grand pianos in practice rooms and 25 grand pianos in classrooms and studios. 3 harpsichords (two-manual by Schuetze, two-manual by William Down, single-manual by Martin). Electronic music studio; computer-assisted learning lab with 10 Apple IIe and 2 Apple MacIntosh computers.

Concert Facilities. Caruth Auditorium, seating 521; Bob Hope Theatre, 390; McFarlin Auditorium, 2,800.

Concerts/Musical Activities. 8 symphony concerts, 8 choral concerts, 5 wind ensemble concerts, 5 new music concerts, 2 jazz ensembles, 2 percussion ensembles, 1 opera production, several composer forums, student and faculty recitals; guest artists, lecturers, student performers.

Music Library. 31,000 volumes; 17,000 musical scores; 125 current periodical subscriptions; 300 microforms; 13,300 phonograph recordings; 200 audiocassettes. 16 listening stations (stereo). Rare Books (including the Paul van Katwijk collection, manuscripts, and autographed letters of musical significance comprise a special collection. Nearby libraries include the Dallas Public Library, North Texas State University, and Texas Christian University.

Special Programs

Featured Programs. The SMU Conservatory is an annual summer program for serious music students of all ages and young professionals offering intensive training and performance opportunities for all orchestral instruments and keyboard.

Performance Groups. University Choral Union, University Choir, Mustang Chorale, Chapel Choir, SMU Symphony Orchestra, Symphonic Band, Wind Ensemble, Opera Theatre, SMU Jazz Ensemble, Perspectives Ensemble.

Financial

Costs. Per academic year: Tuition $6,987. Fees $892. Room $1,884. Board $2,106. Off-campus housing approximately $400 per month for 1-bedroom apartment.

Financial Aid. Financial aid is awarded on the basis of academic merit, financial need, musical ability. Institutional and state/federal aid available. 200 students receive financial aid; average award $4,000. Financial aid/scholarship application due March 1. Part-time employment (average earnings $2,00 per year) and College Work-Study program available.

Southwest Texas State University Department of Music
LBJ Drive and Pleasant Street
San Marcos
Texas 78666

Telephone. (512) 245-2651

Chief Administrator. Dr. Manny Brand, Chairman.

Southwest Texas State University was founded in 1903 as the Southwest Texas State Normal School. The Graduate School was added in 1935 and the present name was adopted in 1969. The 155-acre campus has 121 buildings in the city of San Marcos, 30 miles from Austin and 50 miles from San Antonio.

Music instruction was given at the University when it first opened in 1903 and an official Department of Music was created in 1941. The Department's goals are to prepare musicians for professional careers in music and music education; to guide the general student to an understanding and appreciation of the music of Western and other cultures; to provide experience and develop educational opportunities in music for all university students through music classes, lessons, and performance ensembles.

Accreditation. Southern Association of Colleges and Schools; National Association of Schools of Music; National Council for Accreditation of Teacher Education.

Academic Information

Enrollment, Music Majors. Full-time 82 men, 71 women; part-time 4 men. 4 foreign students.

Music Faculty. Full-time 24, part-time 9.

Term System. Semester. Two 5-week summer sessions. Academic year from early September to mid-May.

Entrance Requirements. High school graduation; SAT or ACT; audition required; theory diagnostic test; piano placement examination. Foreign students must have TOEFL score of 550 or above; official, certified, and translated transcripts of all work; foreign students must pay $50 to $100 for evaluation services.

Admission Procedure. Application with supporting documents; complete residence verification card; participate in orientation.

Music Degrees Offered. Bachelor of Music; Master of Music.

Music Degree Requirements. The Bachelor of Music degree is offered with concentrations in education (all levels or secondary), performance, and piano pedagogy. The emphasis in music education requires the completion of 168 semester hours including student teaching and senior recital. The emphasis in performance requires the completion of 147 semester hours including junior and senior recitals. The piano pedagogy major requires the completion of 153 semester hours including a senior recital and supervised teaching.

The Master of Music degree is offered with emphasis in music education, performance, and theory/composition. It is a non-thesis program and requires the completion of 36 semester hours plus an oral examination.

General Program Areas. Composition, Conducting, Electronic Music, Music Education, Music History, Music Literature, Music Theory, Musicology, Performance, Piano Pedagogy, Suzuki Training.

Instruments Taught. Brass, Flute, Guitar, Harpsichord, Organ, Percussion, Piano, Stringed Instruments, Voice, Woodwinds.

Musical Facilities

Practice Facilities. 32 practice rooms. 3 organs (2 Otto Hoffman, 1 Ed Swearingen). 20 practice pianos; 4 grand pianos reserved for piano majors. Electronic music studio; opera laboratory; piano laboratory.

Concert Facilities. Recital Hall, seating 150; University Performing Arts Center, 390; Evans Auditorium, 930.

Community Facilities. Local community churches are used for some performances.

Concerts/Musical Activities. 120 concerts per year (solo, faculty, students); opera productions; chamber music.

Music Library. 5,644 scores; 40 periodical subscriptions; 85 audiovisual materials; 20 microform titles; 2,-800 phonograph recordings. 31 listening stations (stereo). Books on music are housed in the main library.

Special Programs

Featured Programs. A Keyboard Workshop is held in early June and is open to junior high school and senior high school students and teachers who wish to spend a week in concentrated study on piano and organ. In addition to private lessons and master classes, special sessions will be held on piano technique, organ study for the pianist, accompanying, and sight reading. For organists, there are sessions on church repertoire and organ technique.

The Hill Country Choral Camp is a 4-day annual event for high school choir students. It is a concentrated study of the Texas All-State Choir Music and is held in the music facility of the University campus. There is also a Choral Adjudicators' Workshop for choir directors.

The Band Camp is for band students who will be in the seventh grade or above. Separate weeks of camp are for students in grades 7-8 and grades 9-12. Students participate in concert band or jazz ensemble and instrumental methods in addition to choosing elective courses from a curriculum of chamber ensemble, music theory, music appreciation, rhythm techniques, jazz/rock styles, and jazz improvisation. Auxiliary instruction is also available for color guards (flag and/or rifle instruction), drum majors, and twirlers.

Performance Groups. Concert Band, Jazz Ensemble, Choir, Chamber Ensemble, Orchestra.

Financial

Costs. Per academic year: Tuition in-state resident $512, out-of-state $3,840. Room and board $2,475.

Financial Aid. There are a number of music scholarships available. Some are restricted to an area of emphasis or geographical area while others are basic departmental scholarships. Applications due April 15. Part-time employment and College Work-Study program available.

Southwestern Baptist Theological Seminary School of Church Music
2001 West Seminary Drive
Fort Worth
Texas 76122

Telephone. (817) 923-1921
Chief Administrator. Dr. James C. McKinney, Dean.
Southwestern Baptist Theological Seminary was originally the theological department of Baylor University, established in 1901. In 1905, the department became Baylor Theological Seminary, was chartered as a separate institution in 1908, and moved to Fort Worth in 1910. The operation of the Seminary was assumed by the Southern Baptist Convention in 1925. The 175-acre campus includes 12 main buildings and is situated in an area known as Seminary Hill.

The Department of Gospel Music was created in 1915 and headed by I.E. Reynolds. Six years later, the school was named the School of Sacred Music and in 1957 underwent another title change when the present School of Sacred Music title was adopted.

The purpose of the School of Church Music is to provide graduate professional education for men and women preparing for the Christian ministry in church music. It seeks to provide competent music leadership for churches, colleges, denominational agencies, and mission fields. Specialized church music courses and general music instruction are made available for students in the Schools of Religious Education and Theology.

Accreditation. Southern Association of Colleges and Schools; Association of Theological Schools in the United States and Canada; National Association of Schools of Music.

Academic Information

Enrollment, Music Majors. 400.
Music Faculty. 25.
Term System. Semester. Academic year September to May. Summer session from late May to mid-July.

Entrance Requirements. Baccalaureate degree in music from an accredited college or university; placement audition prior to registering; placement examinations; piano and voice proficiency; conducting proficiency, Aptitude Test and Advanced Music Test of the Graduate Record Examination for Master's and Doctoral programs.

Admission Procedure. Application for School of Church Music accompanied by transcripts in duplicate to Registrar.

Music Degrees Offered. Master of Music; Doctor of Musical Arts; Associate in Church Music.

Music Degree Requirements. The Master of Music degree program is designed to give the basic skills needed in the ministry of church music and to bring the graduate student to an advanced level of performance and scholarship in church music. It normally requires four semesters for completion. Although church music is the major, students choose an area of concentration from the fields of composition, conducting, music history, music ministry, music theory, orchestral instrument, organ, piano, or voice. This is equivalent to a second major.

The Doctor of Musical Arts degree is designed to bring the doctoral candidate to the highest levels of development in church music; the emphasis is on creative scholarship and performance. Concentrations are available in composition, conducting, music ministry, musicology, music theory, organ performance, piano performance, voice pedagogy/literature, and voice performance. Each student's course of study consists of 20 hours of core courses and 20 hours in the concentration (including the dissertation) for a total of 40 hours beyond the Master of Music degree.

The Associate degree in Church Music program is provided for the student who is ineligible for a graduate degree program and who has not completed a baccalaureate degree. It is designed to bring the student to the highest level in church music that his/her ability will permit. The minimum age level for enrollment is thirty years.

General Program Areas. Accompanying, Choral Conducting, Church Music, Composition, Music History, Music Literature, Music Ministry, Music Theory, Performance.

Instruments Taught. Brass, Handbell, Organ, Percussion, Piano, Stringed Instruments, Voice, Woodwinds.

Musical Facilities

Practice Facilities. 20 practice rooms. 3 organs. 18 pianos; 2 grand pianos reserved for piano majors.

Concert Facilities. Truitt Auditorium, seating 1,220; studios and performance areas.

Concerts/Musical Activities. Recitals and concerts are held frequently.

Music Library. Located in Cowden Hall, near the studios and performance areas, the Music Library contains a well-rounded collection of books, scores, collections, ovations, as well as record albums, tape recordings, and anthems. Emphasis is placed upon church music, although all serious music, from the great masters of the past to modern avant-garde compositions, can also be found. Among the resources are the complete works of such composers as Bach, Brahms, Schubert, and Palestrina, the standard anthologies, collections of church music, and many other holdings. More than 341 music periodical titles are available. Special collection of hymnals and books on hymnology; choral octavos; early tunebooks; psalters; ethnic music materials. Special holdings in Baptist history. 145 listening stations.

Special Programs

Featured Programs. Weekly performance laboratory clinics are scheduled for the purpose of experience in public performance, listening experience on the part of the auditors, and an opportunity for the music faculty to evaluate the performance and progress of the participants. The Church Music Workshop is held early in the spring semester each year.

Performance Groups. Collegium Musicum, Chapel Choir, Men's Chorus, Opera Workshop, Southwestern Singers, Seminary Choir, Consort Singers, Handbell Choir, Men's Chorus, String Ensemble, Wind Ensemble, Brass Choir, Zimrah (service club), Oratorio Chorus.

Affiliated Programs. Student chapter of the Music Educators National Conference.

Financial

Costs. Per academic year: Matriculation fee $600, non-Southern Baptist $1,200; music fees $30 to $120; practice fees $5 to $60. Residence halls $75 to $120 per month. Seminary housing for married students $195 to $340 per month.

Financial Aid. Financial aid is awarded on the basis of need. Scholarships, awards, and part-time employment are available.

Stephen F. Austin State University
Department of Music
School of Fine Arts
SFA Station, Box 6078
Nacogdoches
Texas 75962

Telephone. (713) 568-4602

Chief Administrator. Robert W. Miller, Chairman.

Founded in 1921, Stephen F. Austin State University, an institution with a basic arts and sciences curriculum, offers preparation for teaching and administrative work in public schools and colleges. Specialized undergraduate and graduate work is also provided in a variety of other fields.

The Department of Music provides coursework for students wishing to enter careers in music as teachers or performers. The program stresses the development of musicianship and a broad background in liberal arts. Music activities and courses are made available to the general student as well as to those majoring in music.

Accreditation. Southern Association of Colleges and Schools; National Association of Schools of Music; National Council for Accreditation of Teacher Education.

Academic Information

Enrollment, Music Majors. (Total University) 11,420. *Music Faculty.* 21.

Term System. Semester. Two summer sessions. The Westbrook Quartet is an ensemble in residence.

Entrance Requirements. High school graduation; score of 20 or above on ACT or 900 or above on SAT or rank in upper half of graduating class; theory placement test; audition required.

Admission Procedure. Application with supporting documents to Office of Admissions.

Music Degrees Offered. Bachelor of Music; Bachelor of Music Education; Master of Arts.

Music Degree Requirements. The Bachelor of Music degree is offered with curriculum patterns in composition and applied keyboard, orchestral instruments, and voice performance. A total of 130 semester hours is required for graduation. The Bachelor of Music Education is offered with curriculum patterns in music education leading to either Provisional Secondary Certificate (grades 6-12) with concentration options in instrumental or choral/keyboard or an All-Level Certificate (grades K-12) with concentration options in instrumental, choral/keyboard, or elementary. The degree consists of 74-77 credit hours of music depending on the curriculum pattern chosen. A minimum of 130 hours is required for the degree.

Graduate programs in music lead to the Master of Arts degree and are intended to further the development of professional competency and intellectual maturity.

General Program Areas. Applied Music, Composition, Music Education, Music History, Music Literature, Music Theory, Performance.

Instruments Taught. Bass, Bassoon, Clarinet, Euphonium, Flute, Guitar, Harpsichord, Horn, Oboe, Organ, Percussion, Piano, Saxophone, Trombone, Trumpet, Tuba, Viola, Violin, Violoncello, Voice.

Musical Facilities

Concerts/Musical Activities. Students, faculty members, and guest artists are presented in recitals throughout the year.

Music Library. The Academic Assistance and Resource Center manages music recordings (discs and tapes), music scores, films, and filmstrips. A variety of listening and viewing equipment is available for student use in the Center. The Ralph W. Steen Library houses the main collection of over 335,000 catalogued books and serves the academic programs of the Department of Music.

Special Programs

Performance Groups. Opera Workshop, A Cappella Choir, Choral Union, University Symphony Orchestra, Symphonic Band, Concert Band, Wind Ensemble, Marching Band, Lab Band, Madrigals, Cabaret Singers, Trombone Choir, Brass Choir, String Ensemble, Brass Ensemble, Percussion Ensemble, Woodwind Ensemble, Keyboard Ensemble, Vocal Ensemble.

Financial

Costs. Per academic year: Tuition in-state resident $520, out-of-state $3,900. Fees $370. Room and board $2,570.

Financial Aid. Financial aid is awarded on the basis of academic merit and financial need. State/federal aid is available in the form of scholarships, grants, loans, and part-time employment. Graduate assistantships are awarded each year in the Department of Music to qualified students. Financial aid/scholarship application due April 1.

University of Texas at Arlington
Department of Music

101 Fine Arts Building
P.O. Box 19105
Arlington
Texas 76019

Telephone. (817) 273-2011

Chief Administrator. Dr. Gary L. Ebensberger, Chairman.

The University of Texas at Arlington is a comprehensive university located on a 345-acre campus. It was founded in 1895 as Arlington College, a private liberal arts institution. After a succession of names, ownerships, and missions, it was elevated to senior college rank in 1959, and in 1965, was transferred from the Texas A&M System to the University of Texas System. In 1967, the present name was adopted. Arlington is in the heart of the Dallas/Fort Worth metroplex.

The Department of Music offers programs in music education, performance, performance/pedagogy, theory and composition, and jazz studies.

Accreditation. Southern Association of Colleges and Schools; National Association of Schools of Music.

Academic Information

Enrollment, Music Majors. (Total University) 19,275. *Music Faculty.* 21.

Term System. Semester.

Entrance Requirements. Accredited high school graduation; completion of 15 units including 3 English, 2 mathematics, 1 science, 2 social science; SAT or ACT. GRE required for graduate programs.

Admission Procedure. Application with supporting documents to Director of Admissions.

Music Degrees Offered. Bachelor of Music.

Music Degree Requirements. The Bachelor of Music degree is offered with emphases in (1) teacher certification (all-level, secondary choral, secondary instrumental); (2) performance (brass, guitar, organ, percussion, piano, strings, voice, woodwinds); performance/pedagogy (guitar, piano, voice) or performance/accompanying (piano); (3) theory/composition; and (4) jazz studies. The graduate course offerings in music are provided to support other graduate degree programs and to meet the needs of students. No program leading to a graduate degree in music exists at this time.

General Program Areas. Accompanying, Choral Conducting, Composition, Instrumental Conducting, Jazz Studies, Music Education, Music Theory, Performance, Piano Pedagogy.

Instruments Taught. Brass, Guitar, Organ, Percussion, Piano, Stringed Instruments, Voice, Woodwinds.

Musical Facilities

Concerts/Musical Activities. Ensemble groups; visiting artists.

Music Library. The University of Texas at Arlington Library contains a collection of more than 970,000 books, journals, documents and technical reports. It subscribes to 4,000 periodicals and newspapers and maintains a collection of microfilm, microfiche, motion pictures, sound recordings, video tapes, filmstrips, and slides.

Special Programs

Performance Groups. University Singers, A Cappella Choir, Chamber Singers, Marching Band, Concert Band, Wind Ensemble, Jazz Orchestra, Opera Workshop, Orchestra.

Financial

Costs. Per academic year: Tuition $1,028 resident; $4,030 out-of-state. Room and board $2,300.

Financial Aid. Scholarships, fellowships, grants, and loans are available.

University of Texas at Austin
Department of Music
College of Fine Arts
26th and East Campus Drive
Austin
Texas 78712

Telephone. (512) 471-7764

Chief Administrator. Dr. Gerard Béhague, Chairman.

The Act of the Legislature providing for the organization of the University of Texas was passed in 1881. The main campus at Austin was established in 1883. The University is located on a 300-acre campus with 110 buildings in Austin (population 370,000), the capital of Texas.

The goals of the Department of Music are to help each student attain the skills and proficiencies of an artist and at the same time, a broad general education; to develop talent to the highest degree of artistic capability; to train teachers of the arts; and to help students acquire discriminating taste and sound critical judgment through coursework, concerts, plays, and through their association with distinguished artists and teachers.

Accreditation. Southern Association of Colleges and Schools; National Association of Schools of Music.

Academic Information

Enrollment, Music Majors. 654.

Music Faculty. Full-time 66, part-time 113.

Term System. Semester. Two 6-week summer sessions; one 9-week session; one 12-week session.

Entrance Requirements. High school graduation or GED; completion of 15.5 units including 4 English, 3 mathematics, 2 laboratory science, 2 foreign language, 3 social studies, 1.5 electives; SAT combined verbal and math of at least 1100; ACT accepted; 3 Achievement Tests (mathematics, English composition, foreign language); audition required (auditions are regularly scheduled throughout the year on campus; auditions by tape recording can be arranged if necessary); applicant must pass music theory diagnostic examination before registering for courses.

Admission Procedure. Application due March 1 for fall semester, October 1 for spring semester.

Music Degrees Offered. Bachelor of Music; Bachelor of Arts; Master of Music; Doctor of Musical Arts; Doctor of Philosophy.

Music Degree Requirements. The Bachelor of Music degree is offered with majors in applied music, music literature, music theory, composition, and music education. The baccalaureate in music education program leads to public school teaching certification in music in the state of Texas. The student may choose between programs leading to either secondary school certification or all-level i.e., elementary and secondary school, certification. Baccalaureate degrees required the completion of a prescribed curriculum for a total of 120 to 140 semester hours. The Bachelor of Arts degree with a major in music is offered in the context of a liberal arts program.

The Master of Music degree is offered with majors in performance (including conducting and opera performance), composition, theory, musicology (including ethnomusicology), music education, and literature and pedagogy. The degree requires the completion of 30 to 33 semester hours.

The Doctor of Musical Arts degree is offered with majors in performance or performance/literature (including conducting and opera), composition, and music education. The Doctor of Philosophy degree is offered with majors in music theory, musicology (including ethnomusicology), and music education. The degrees require the completion of 54 to 62 semester hours beyond the baccalaureate degree.

General Program Areas. Applied Music, Composition, Conducting, Ethnomusicology, Jazz Studies, Music Education, Music Literature, Musicology, Opera, Pedagogy, Performance.

Instruments Taught. Brass, Harp, Harpsichord, Organ, Percussion, Piano, Stringed Instruments, Voice, Woodwinds.

Musical Facilities

Practice Facilities. 150 practice modules. 4 organs (Visser-Wowland tracker, 3 other). 300 pianos (110 Steinway grands, 3 Hamburg Steinways); 50 grand pianos reserved for piano majors. Special practice facilities for percussionists. 5 electronic music studios; chamber music rooms; harp studio; Early Music Room; jazz rehearsal room; music education curriculum laboratory; 3 piano laboratories.

Concert Facilities. Bates Recital Hall, seating 700; Jesson Hall; Performing Arts Center, 3,000; Opera Lab Theater, 400; Music Recital Hall.

Concerts/Musical Activities. Student/faculty recitals and concerts; visiting artists.

Music Library. The Fine Arts Library houses over 1 million volumes of which the music collection is a part. 24,000 titles in the Performance Library. Special collections include a Medieval and Renaissance Instrument Collection; the Asian Collection; the Middle East Collection; and the Latin American Library. Listening facilities (cassette, stereo). Listening rooms are also in the undergraduate library on the University of Texas campus. Other local resources for music students include The Eugene C. Barker Texas History Library which contains manuscripts and recordings of Texas composers; The Harry Ransom Center on the University of Texas campus contains rare books related to 20th century composers; and the Austin Public Library.

Special Programs

Performance Groups. Jazz Orchestra, Symphony Band, Symphony Orchestra, Wind Ensemble, Longhorn Band, Choral Union, University Chorus, Women's Concert Choir, Chamber Singers, Concert Chorale, Pop Choral Ensemble, Small Instrument Ensembles, Collegium Musicum.

Financial

Costs. Per academic year: Tuition in-state resident $316, out-of-state $3,168. Fees $300. Room $1,430. Board $1,860.

Financial Aid. Department of Music Scholarships are available. Other sources of financial aid include institutional and state/federal grants and loans, part-time employment, and a College Work-Study program.

Commentary

The University of Texas at Austin has a music department well-balanced in its strengths. Noteworthy aspects include the performance faculty, the curricula of musicology (including ethnomusicology), and music education. The University recently announced a new cello competition under its sponsorship in memory of the eminent cellist, Emmanuel Feuermann.

University of Texas at El Paso
Music Department
El Paso
Texas 79968

Telephone. (915) 747-5606

Chief Administrator. Dr. Marcia T. Fountain, Chairperson.

The Texas Legislature created this institution in 1913 as the Texas School of Mines and Metallurgy. It became a branch of the University of Texas in 1919. In 1949 the name was changed to Texas Western College in recognition of the broadening of the college program. The present name was adopted in 1967.

The University campus of 75 acres is located in the foothills of a southern spur of the Rocky Mountains across the Rio Grande River from the Mexican border town of Juarez.

The Music Department was established in 1927. It offers programs leading to the Bachelor of Music degree in three major fields: performance, theory and composition, music education.

Accreditation. Southern Association of Colleges and Schools; National Association of Schools of Music.

Academic Information

Enrollment, Music Majors. 146 undergraduate; 19 graduate.

Music Faculty. Full-time 22, part-time 8.

Term System. Semester. Summer session.

Entrance Requirements. High school graduation or GED; SAT or ACT; GRE required for graduate programs. Audition; theory placement test.

Admission Procedure. Application due July 1.

Music Degrees Offered. Bachelor of Music.

Music Degree Requirements. The Bachelor of Music degree requires a minimum of 123 credit hours. The major in performance may select among orchestra/band instruments, keyboard instruments, voice, or ballet as an option within the major. The major in theory and composition may select among voice, orchestra, or keyboard as the major instrument. The Bachelor of Music degree may be combined with All-Levels certification in Music by completing a specified program for a minimum total of 140 semester hours including 30 advanced hours. Students may select either an instrument or a choral plan in the area of specialization. There are general and optional requirements for all major programs.

General Program Areas. Music Education, Music Theory, Performance.

Instruments Taught. Bass, Bassoon, Clarinet, Flute, Guitar, Harp, Horn, Oboe, Organ, Percussion, Piano, Trombone, Trumpet, Tuba, Viola, Violin, Violoncello.

Musical Facilities

Practice Facilities. 64 practice rooms. Special practice facilities for organists; 2 organs. 5 percussion-equipped practice rooms. 50 practice pianos; 5 grand pianos reserved for piano majors. Electronic music studio. Recording booth in Recital Hall and in Magoffin Auditorium.

Concert Facilities. Recital Hall, seating 452; Magoffin Auditorium, 1,300.

Concerts/Musical Activities. Ensembles, recitals, concerts.

Music Library. 5,000 scores; 10,936 books; 51 periodical titles; 50 microfiche titles; 18,079 phonograph recordings. Listening facilities (15 cassette decks; 15 stereo turntables).

Financial

Costs. Per academic year: Tuition (15 hours per semester) resident $666, nonresident $3,900. Housing (9 months) $2,400 to $3,000.

Financial Aid. Scholarships, grants, and loans available. College Work-Study program.

University of Texas at San Antonio
Division of Music
Loop 1604 at Babcock
San Antonio
Texas 78244

Telephone. (512) 691-4354 (5)

Chief Administrator. Dr. Donald A. Hodges, Director.

The University of Texas at San Antonio opened a four-year undergraduate program in 1966. A graduate division was established in the summer of 1973.

The primary objective of the Division of Music is to offer programs in the areas of music education, performance, theory-composition, and music marketing to students who seek training for a professional life in music.

Accreditation. Southern Association of Colleges and Schools; National Association of Schools of Music.

Academic Information

Enrollment, Music Majors. Undergraduate 188, graduate 63. 3 foreign students.

Music Faculty. Full-time 15, part-time 29.

Term System. Semester. Summer session; regular courses for majors and nonmajors; special one-week institutes.

Entrance Requirements. High school graduation or equivalent; recommend completion of 22 units including 4 English, 3 mathematics, 2 laboratory science, 2 social studies, 2 foreign language, 1 fine arts; SAT or ACT; audition required. GRE required for graduate study.

Admission Procedure. Application deadlines are August 1 for fall, May 1 for summer, December 1 for spring.

Music Degrees Offered. Bachelor of Music; Bachelor of Music Education; Master of Music.

Music Degree Requirements. The Bachelor of Music degree is offered with emphases in music performance, theory-composition, and music marketing. The degree requires the completion of 128 semester hours (music marketing requires 135 hours). The Bachelor of Music Education degree is offered with emphases in secondary choral (grades 6-12), all-level choral (grades K-12), and all-level instrumental (grades K-12). The minimum number of semester hours required for this degree, including the general education requirements and the Texas Education Agency Certification requirements, is 133.

The Master of Music degree is offered with emphases in performance (including conducting) or music education (including piano pedagogy). The degree requires the completion of 30 to 36 semester hours.

General Program Areas. Composition, Conducting, Music Education, Music Marketing, Music Theory, Performance, Piano Pedagogy.

Instruments Taught. Brass, Guitar, Harpsichord, Organ, Percussion, Piano, Stringed Instruments, Voice, Woodwinds.

Musical Facilities

Practice Facilities. 17 practice rooms. Casavant organ. Percussion-equipped practice room. 50 pianos (7 grands, 43 uprights); 7 grand pianos reserved for piano majors. Electronic music studio; recording booth.

Concert Facilities. Recital Hall, seating 500.

Concerts/Musical Activities. Concerts, recitals, ensemble performances; visiting artists.

Music Library. Music holdings are housed in the main library. 4,094 scores; 5,438 books; 3,901 microfiche; 2,631 recordings. Listening facilities (11 cassette decks, 3 stereo turntables, 1 compact disc player).

Special Programs

Performance Groups. Wind Ensemble, Symphonic Band, Orchestra, Jazz Ensemble, Roadrunner Band, Opera Workshop, Chorus, Concert Choir, Madrigal Singers.

Foreign Programs. Special programs are periodically arranged to be taught overseas.

Financial

Costs. Per academic year: Tuition in-state undergraduate resident $480, out-of-state $3,600; graduate in-state resident $288, out-of-state $2,160. Room $1,980.

Financial Aid. Funds from the Keyboard Endowment are used for piano and organ scholarships; funds from the Andrew Gurwitz Endowment are used for music scholarships. Other sources of financial aid include institutional and state/federal grants and loans, part-time employment, and a College Work-Study program.

Texas Christian University
Music Department
Box 32887
Fort Worth
Texas 76129

Telephone. (817) 921-7602
Chief Administrator. Dr. Peter J. Hodgson, Chair.

Texas Christian University is a private institution that had its beginning as the AddRan Male and Female College at Thorp Spring, Texas, in 1873. It became affiliated with the Christian Churches (Disciples of Christ) in 1889 and moved to its present location in 1911. The campus is situated on a 243-acre campus in the southwestern residential district of Fort Worth.

The Music Department offers music education in the context of a liberal arts program.

Accreditation. Southern Association of Colleges and Schools; National Association of Schools of Music.

Academic Information

Term System. Semester. Evening term; miniterm.

Entrance Requirements. High school graduation with 17 units (4 English, 3 mathematics, 3 laboratory science, 2 foreign language, 3 social studies, 2 electives); ACT or SAT required; GRE for graduate programs. Audition required either in person or by tape recording.

Admission Procedure. Application with $25 nonrefundable fee due prior to March 1.

Music Degrees Offered. Bachelor of Arts; Bachelor of Science; Bachelor of Fine Arts; Bachelor of Music; Master of Arts; Master of Fine Arts; Master of Music.

Music Degree Requirements. The bachelor degrees require the completion of 124 to 135 credit hours; the master's degrees 30 to 36 credit hours. Core requirements.

General Program Areas. Composition, Music History, Music Theory, Performance.

Instruments Taught. Baritone, Bass, Bassoon, Clarinet, Euphonium, Flute, French Horn, Harp, Harpsichord, Oboe, Organ, Percussion, Piano, Saxophone, Trombone, Trumpet, Tuba, Viola, Viola da Gamba, Violin, Violoncello, Voice.

Musical Facilities

Practice Facilities. 25 practice rooms. Special practice facilities for organists; 5 organs (2 Moellers, 1 Reuter, 1 Sipe, 1 Rossking). 2 percussion-equipped practice rooms. 30 pianos (20 uprights, 10 grands); 10 grands reserved for piano majors.

Concert Facilities. Concert Hall.

Concerts/Musical Activities. Program Council plans concerts and other activities.

Music Library. 20,776 scores; 12,660 books; 72 periodicals; 135 microfiche titles; 8,125 phonograph recordings. Listening facilities (cassette, stereo).

Financial

Costs. Per academic year: $3,238 including tuition, room, board, fees, and student expenses.

Financial Aid. Scholarships, grants, and loans available. Scholarship application due June 1 (need-based), January 1 (other).

Commentary

Texas Christian University has plans to build a 400-seat recital hall, practice rooms, and rehearsal facilities.

Texas Southern University
Department of Music
College of Arts and Sciences
3100 Cleburne Avenue
Houston
Texas 77004

Telephone. (713) 527-7537
Chief Administrator. Dr. Joseph B. Schmoll, Professor of Music.

Texas Southern University was established in 1947. It is located on a 70-acre campus with 27 buildings in the city of Houston in southeastern Texas.

The objectives of the Department of Music are: to acquaint all students with the discipline of music as an important aspect of the liberal arts curriculum and of general culture; to prepare students for careers as teachers, performers, scholars, and composers.

Accreditation. Southern Association of Colleges and Schools; National Council for Accreditation of Teacher Education.

Academic Information

Enrollment, Music Majors. (Total University) 8,654.

Music Faculty. 14.

Term System. Semester. Two summer sessions.

Entrance Requirements. High school graduation; completion of 15 college preparatory units; ACT required.

Admission Procedure. Application with supporting documents to Office of Admissions.

Music Degrees Offered. Bachelor of Music; Master of Music Education; Master of Arts.

Music Degree Requirements. The Bachelor of Music degree is offered with majors in composition, keyboard, orchestral instruments, and voice. The Bachelor of Music Education degree may be pursued in general supervision with choral, piano, instrumental emphasis and secondary certification, or emphasis in all-level certification in piano/voice or orchestral/band instruments.

Graduate study provides students an opportunity to increase skills in performance, theory/composition, and pedagogy. The Master of Music Education degree for teachers of music requires the completion of a minimum of 36 semester hours. The Master of Arts degree may be earned with a concentration in applied music, or in composition and advanced theory. This degree requires the completion of 30 semester hours.

General Program Areas. Composition, Music Education, Performance.

Instruments Taught. Brass, Guitar, Organ, Percussion, Piano, Stringed Instruments, Voice, Woodwinds.

Musical Facilities

Concerts/Musical Activities. Student/faculty recitals and concerts; visiting artists.

Music Library. The Central University Library supports the academic programs of the Department of Music.

Special Programs

Performance Groups. University Choir, Concert Choir, Men's Glee Club, Opera Workshop, Women's Glee Club, University Band, University Orchestra, Piano Ensemble, Jazz Ensemble.

Financial

Costs. Per academic year: Tuition in-state resident $476; out-of-state $1,336. Room $1,150. Board $1,188.

Financial Aid. Financial aid is awarded on the basis of need. The Office of Financial aid is responsible for aid awards in the form of scholarships, state/federal grants, loans, and part-time employment. Application deadline for all aid programs is April 15.

Texas Tech University
Department of Music

P.O. Box 4239
Lubbock
Texas 79413

Telephone. (806) 742-2270

Chief Administrator. Dr. Harold T. Luce, Chairperson.

Texas Tech University, a publicly supported institution, was established as the Texas Technological College

by legislation in 1923. In 1969, the institution adopted its present name. More than 23,000 students attend classes in Lubbock. The campus, 1,839 acres in one contiguous tract, is one of the largest in the United States. Lubbock (population 187,000) is located in the South Plains area of Texas, 320 miles west of Dallas and 320 miles southeast of Albuquerque, New Mexico.

The Department of Music first offered classes in 1925 and the first music major program in 1933. The Department's goal is to educate professional performers and teachers and to provide music instruction to nonmajors. The Department offers degree programs in performance, music history and literature, music theory, composition, and music education. Non-music majors may elect class or private instruction in voice or in any instrument, subject to the availability of faculty.

Accreditation. Southern Association of Colleges and Schools; National Association of Schools of Music; National Council for Accreditation of Teacher Education.

Academic Information

Enrollment, Music Majors. Undergraduate 318, graduate 57.

Music Faculty. Full-time 40, part-time 6.

Term System. Semester. Summer session (graduate courses, performance, music theatre).

Entrance Requirements. Accredited high school graduation; completion of 15 college preparatory units including 4 English, 3 mathematics, 2 science, 2 social science; combined SAT score of at least 900; out-of-state applicants must rank in top half of graduating class; GRE required for graduate students. Live audition on campus if possible (tape recording may be accepted); placement test in music theory.

Admission Procedure. Application and supporting documents by August 15.

Music Degrees Offered. Bachelor of Music; Bachelor of Arts; Bachelor of Music Education; Master of Music, Master of Music Education, Doctor of Philosophy.

Music Degree Requirements. The Bachelor of Music degree in performance is offered with curricula in piano, organ, voice, wind instrument or percussion, or stringed instrument. Other programs offer curricula in music composition, music music history and literature, and music theory. The degree requires the completion of 126 to 136 semester hours including specified courses for the program pursued. The Bachelor of Music Education degree is designed for the student who expects to teach or direct vocal or instrumental music in the public schools. It requires 132 to 138 semester hours including 18 hours in professional education and student teaching. Vocal music education majors must participate in chorus for eight semesters. Wind and percussion music education majors must participate in marching band for four semesters and concert band for four semesters; wind and percussion performance majors must play in a large ensemble for eight semesters and in a small ensemble for four semesters. String music education majors must participate in orchestra for eight semesters; string performance majors must participate in orchestra for eight semesters and chamber music for six semesters. Guitar music education majors must participate in guitar ensemble for four semesters and in a large ensemble (band, choir, or orchestra) for four semesters. Guitar performance majors participate in guitar ensemble for six semesters, in chamber music for six semesters, and in a large ensemble for two semesters. The Bachelor of Arts with a music concentration requires the completion of 124 semester hours.

The Master of Music and Master of Music Education degrees require the completion of 30 to 36 semester hours; the Doctor of Philosophy degree, 61 to 100 semester hours.

General Program Areas. Composition, Music Education, Music History, Music Literature, Music Theory, Performance.

Instruments Taught. Brass, Guitar, Harp, Harpsichord, Organ, Percussion, Piano, Stringed Instruments, Voice, Woodwinds.

Musical Facilities

Practice Facilities. Special practice facilities for organists; 1 81-rank Holtkamp, 2 Moeller practice organs. 3 practice rooms for percussionists. 45 practice rooms. 6 grand pianos reserved for piano majors. Electronic music studio.

Concert Facilities. Two concert halls seating 603 and 1,000 respectively.

Community Facilities. The Municipal Auditorium-Coliseum, located on the north edge of the campus, is operated by the City of Lubbock. The Auditorium has seating for 3,200.

Concerts/Musical Activities. Concerts, ensembles, and student/faculty recitals. A repertory season of musical plays is presented each summer.

Music Library. 18,000 volumes; 6,000 scores; 176 current periodical subscriptions; 5,300 phonograph recordings. Listening stations (cassette decks, stereo turntables, compact disc players). Musical instrument collection.

Special Programs

Performance Groups. University Choir, Symphonic Band, Marching Band, Jazz Ensemble, Music Theatre, Symphony Orchestra, University Singers, Collegiate Singers, Madrigal Singers, Men's Chorus, Women's Chorale, Court Jesters, Brass Band, Concert Bands, Chamber Orchestra, Jazz Bands and Combos, Brass Choir, Woodwind Ensemble, Guitar Ensemble, Viola Ensemble, Harp Ensemble, Flute Ensemble, Clarinet Ensemble, Oboe Ensemble, Saxophone Ensemble, Trumpet Ensemble, French Horn Ensemble, Trombone Ensemble, Tuba Ensemble, Percussion Ensemble, New Music Ensemble.

Financial

Costs. Per academic year: Tuition in-state resident $480, out-of-state $3,600. Fees $700. Room and Board $2,700.

Financial Aid. 55% of music majors receive financial aid. Scholarships range from $100 to $1,500. Scholarship application due March 1. College Work-Study program available.

Commentary

The graduate school of Texas Tech University encourages interdisciplinary study and research. The University museum has a collection of ethnic instruments, including some from the Yaqui Indian tribe.

Texas Woman's University
Department of Music and Drama
College of Humanities and Fine Arts
TWU Station, Box 23925
Denton
Texas 76204

Telephone. (817) 383-3586
Chief Administrator. Richard W. Rodean, Chairman.

Texas Woman's University is a multipurpose institution offering liberal arts programs and specialized or professional study. It was the first institution of higher education in Texas to offer a degree in music. The 270-acre campus is 35 miles northwest of Dallas.

The Music Division of the Department of Music and Drama offers undergraduate and graduate programs leading to the baccalaureate and master's degrees in music therapy, music education, and performance.

Accreditation. Southern Association of Colleges and Schools; National Association of Schools of Music.

Academic Information

Enrollment, Music Majors. (Total University) 5,588.
Music Faculty. 14.
Term System. Semester. Three summer sessions.
Entrance Requirements. High school graduation; completion of 15 units including 3 English, 2 mathematics, 2 science, 2 social science; ACT or SAT required; audition required for placement.

Admission Procedure. Application with supporting documents and nonrefundable $25 fee to Admissions Office.

Music Degrees Offered. Bachelor of Science; Master of Arts.

Music Degree Requirements. The Bachelor of Science degree is offered with concentrations in music education vocal music (all-level Teaching Certificate) or instrumental music (all-level Teaching Certificate), music therapy, and studio performance.

The Master of Arts degree in music is offered with

emphasis in applied music, music education, or music pedagogy (piano, violin, voice). A program in music therapy is also available.

General Program Areas. Instrumental Music, Music Education, Music Therapy, Performance, Vocal Music.

Instruments Taught. Brass, Percussion, Piano, Stringed Instruments, Voice, Woodwinds.

Musical Facilities

Practice Facilities. The Department of Music and Drama is housed in the Music Building.

Concerts/Musical Activities. Student/faculty recitals and concerts; visiting artists.

Music Library. The Library and Media Center houses a collection of over 750,000 items including books, cassettes, recordings, and films.

Special Programs

Performance Groups. University Chorus, Orchestra, Concert Choir, Chamber Music, Music Theater Workshop, Choraliers, Serenaders.

Financial

Costs. Per academic year: Tuition in-state resident $384, out-of-state $3,840. Room and Board $2,465.

Financial Aid. Financial aid programs include scholarships, grants, loans, and part-time employment. Financial aid/scholarship application due April 1.

West Texas State University
Department of Music
School of Fine Arts
Canyon
Texas 79016

Telephone. (806) 656-2016

Chief Administrator. Harry H. Haines, Department Head.

West Texas State University is a liberal arts and teachers college founded in 1910. The present name was adopted in 1963. The 92-acre campus is located in Canyon (population 11,000), an urban area 17 miles south of Amarillo in the Texas Panhandle.

The music programs offered by the Department of Music are designed to serve the respective needs of students whose primary interests or goals fall into one of the following categories: (1) general music education techniques, including methods and materials for classroom teaching in the public schools; (2) organization, training, and development of major vocal and instrumental organizations; (3) studio teaching and/or professional or semi-professional performance, and specialization in church ministry of music; (4) professional training in the area of music therapy designed to prepare registered music therapists for positions in treatment, rehabilita-

tion, and therapy settings; and (5) avocational and cultural advantages to be gained through limited coursework, studio training in keyboard, vocal, or instrumental performance, and/or active participation in one or more of the University's major musical organizations and associated activities, regardless of the student's major subject area.

Accreditation. Southern Association of Colleges and Schools; National Association of Schools of Music; National Council for Accreditation of Teacher Education.

Academic Information

Enrollment, Music Majors. Undergraduate 260, graduate 35. 7 foreign students.

Music Faculty. Full-time 24, part-time 4.

Term System. Semester. Summer session.

Entrance Requirements. High school graduation or GED; SAT or ACT; audition required. GRE required for graduate study.

Admission Procedure. Application accepted on a rolling admissions basis.

Music Degrees Offered. Bachelor of Music; Bachelor of Music Education; Master of Music; Master of Arts.

Music Degree Requirements. The Bachelor of Music degree is offered with majors in performance, pedagogy, music education, music business, and music therapy. A minimum of 128 semester hours is required for the degree. The Bachelor of Music Education degree requires the completion of 128 semester hours including the requirements for academic foundations and professional development for the secondary and all-level provisional certificates. Students majoring in music education are encouraged to attend at least one summer school session.

The Master of Music degree and the Master of Arts degree in music education are offered through the Graduate School. The degree requires the completion of 36 semester hours.

General Program Areas. Church Music, Conducting, Music Business, Music Education, Music Therapy, Performance.

Instruments Taught. Brass, Organ, Percussion, Piano, Stringed Instruments, Voice, Woodwinds.

Musical Facilities

Practice Facilities. 38 practice rooms. 7 organs (1 concert, 6 practice). 20 practice pianos; 4 grand pianos reserved for piano majors.

Concert Facilities. Recital Hall, seating 740; Theatre, 350.

Concerts/Musical Activities. Concerts and recitals; visiting artists.

Music Library. Music materials are housed in the Cornette Library. The University has a cooperative agreement with North Texas State University for exchanging library resources.

Special Programs

Performance Groups. Band, Orchestra, Chorale, Collegiate Choir, Chorus, Summer Band.

Financial

Costs. Per academic year: Tuition undergraduate in-state resident $470, out-of-state $1,550; graduate in-state $442, out-of-state $1,522. Room $1,038.

Financial Aid. The University provides a comprehensive program of scholarships, loans, grants, and work opportunities to assist students in their academic pursuits.

UTAH

Brigham Young University
Department of Music
Provo
Utah 84602

Telephone. (801) 378-1211, Ext. 3083

Chief Administrator. K. Newell Dayley, Chairman.

Brigham Young University began as an academy of the Church of Jesus Christ of Latter-Day Saints in 1875 and became a university in 1903. It is comprised of colleges of biological and agricultural sciences, business, education, family, home and social sciences, fine arts and communications, humanities, engineering sciences and technology, nursing, physical and mathematical sciences, physical education, religious instruction, and graduate studies. The 530-acre campus has 310 buildings and is located in Provo, 45 miles from Salt Lake City.

The Department of Music offers the bachelor's, master's, and doctoral degrees following the requirement guidelines of the National Association of Schools of Music. Religion courses are required on the undergraduate level.

Accreditation. Northwest Association of Schools and Colleges; National Association of Schools of Music.

Academic Information

Enrollment, Music Majors. Undergraduate full-time 111 men, 253 women; part-time 20 men, 31 women. 13 foreign students.

Music Faculty. Full-time 42, part-time 57.

Term System. Semester. Two summer sessions.

Entrance Requirements. High school graduation or equivalent; 4 units of English, 2 mathematics beyond algebra, 2 laboratory science, 1 advanced foreign language, 2 social studies, 2 humanities, 1 computer science; ACT (minimum score 24); audition not required; first semester enrollment is prospective music major only, major status awarded on merit. TOEFL test results required for foreign students. GRE required for graduate students.

Admission Procedure. Application due April 30 with $15 nonrefundable fee.

Music Degrees Offered. Bachelor of Music; Bachelor of Arts; Bachelor of Fine Arts (musical theatre); Master of Music; Master of Arts; Doctor of Musical Arts; Doctor of Philosophy.

Music Degree Requirements. The bachelor's degrees require the completion of a minimum of 128 semester hours in core curriculum, general education, religion, and major concentration requirements. The Master of Music and Master of Arts degrees are offered with concentrations in music education, theory, composition, and musicology. The master's degrees required the completion of 32 semester hours of study. The degrees Doctor of Philosophy in musicology and Doctor of Musical Arts in composition are also granted. Each requires the completion of 60 semester hours.

General Program Areas. Composition, Music Education, Music History, Music Theatre, Music Theory, Musicology, Performance.

Instruments Taught. Brass, Organ, Percussion, Piano, Stringed Instruments, Voice, Woodwinds.

Musical Facilities

Practice Facilities. 65 practice rooms. 18 organs by various builders. 4 percussion-equipped practice rooms. 65 pianos (studio and grand); 10 grand pianos reserved for piano majors. Electronic music studio; 24-track recording studio; group piano studio; synthesizer and organ laboratories.

Concert Facilities. Concert Hall, seating 1,440; Recital Hall, 420.

Concerts/Musical Activities. Performing Arts Series; Popular Concerts Series; extensive Music Department concerts and recitals.

Music Library. 18,000 scores; 18,000 books; 500 microfiche titles; 20,400 recordings. Complete listening facilities (tape, video, phonograph, cassette, compact disc) located in Learning Resources Center in library. Portable sound systems in offices and classrooms.

Special collections include: Van Buren Instrument Collection; Capitol Records Archive (manuscript collection); Josef Bonime Collection; Radio-Keith-Orpheum (RKO) Keith Music Library; William Primrose International Viola Archive; Serly Papers; Sam and Rosalie Pratt Harp Library Archive. Performance Library for ensemble parts and scores housed in Music Building. The Marriott Library of the University of Utah is also available for student access.

Special Programs

Performance Groups. Ensembles; Orchestra; Choral Groups.

Foreign Programs. Study abroad may be pursued in Vienna, London, Paris, and Jerusalem.

Financial

Costs. Per academic year: Tuition $1,550. Fees $280. Room and board $2,400.

Financial Aid. 206 music scholarships ranging from $120 to $880 (average $200). Scholarship applications due February 15. Other sources of financial aid include institution and state/federal aid, part-time employment, and College Work-Study program.

Commentary

Brigham Young University has one of the country's most important film music archives. Holdings include the personal papers, recordings, and works of Academy Award winning film composers Max Steiner and Hugo Friedhofer, and Republic Pictures Music Archives consisting of the entire studio archives from the period 1936-1957.

University of Utah
Department of Music
204 David Gardner Hall
Salt Lake City
Utah 84112

Telephone. (801) 581-6765

Chief Administrator. Dr. Edgar J. Thompson, Chairman.

The University of Utah, founded in 1850, is the oldest state university in the West. It is a comprehensive state-assisted institution of higher learning offering majors in 65 undergraduate subjects as well as more than 50 teaching majors and minors. Graduate degrees are available in 95 disciplines. Nearly 25,000 students represent all 50 states and many foreign countries. A teaching faculty of approximately 1,700 is supplemented by 1,800 clinical, adjunct, research, and visiting faculty. The 1,500-acre campus is centered in 210 buildings in the northeastern edge of Salt Lake City in the foothills of the Wasatch Mountains.

The Department of Music offers a wide variety of programs. Student performance opportunities abound, and there is regular contact with professional musicians outside the faculty. Departmental performing organizations make regular campus, local, and statewide appearances as well as U.S. and occasional international tours. Music is one of five departments comprising the College of Fine Arts.

The Department of Music provides training for solo and ensemble performance, historical and theoretical studies, and elective courses giving each student a balanced approach to musical understanding and musicianship.

Accreditation. Northwest Association of Schools and Colleges; National Association of Schools of Music.

Academic Information

Enrollment, Music Majors. 300.

Music Faculty. Full-time 26, part-time 60. Artist-in-residence: Vladimir Ussachevsky (electronic music).

Term System. Quarter. Summer session from late June to late August. Academic year from late September to early June.

Entrance Requirements. High school graduation with 4 units of English; ACT; audition required. Foreign students need score of 500 or better on TOEFL; ACT or SAT; statement of health by a licensed physician.

Admission Procedure. Apply to Admission Office.

Music Degrees Offered. Bachelor of Music; Master of Music; Master of Arts; Doctor of Philosophy.

Music Degree Requirements. The Bachelor of Music degree is offered with emphasis in performance, theory/composition, history, music education, and piano pedagogy. Students must satisfy the core curriculum in theory, history, and keyboard proficiency. The degree requires the successful completion of 183 credit hours including 35 to 45 hours of specific liberal education coursework.

The Master of Music degree is offered in performance, history, theory/composition, music education, and conducting. The degree requires a minimum of 45 hours of credit. The Master of Arts degree with emphasis in music history is also available. The degree Doctor of Philosophy with emphases in composition and music education is offered.

General Program Areas. Composition, Electronic Music, Jazz Studies, Music Education, Music History, Music Theory, Performance, Piano Pedagogy.

Instruments Taught. Brass, Harpsichord, Percussion, Piano, Stringed Instruments, Voice, Woodwinds.

Musical Facilities

Practice Facilities. 37 practice rooms. Special practice facilities for percussionists. 3 grand pianos reserved for piano majors. Digital and analog electronic studios and 2 special electronic practice rooms/orchestration studios.

Concert Facilities. Recital Hall, seating 80; Concert Hall, 300; Kingsbury Hall, 1,800.

Community Facilities. Assembly Hall in Temple Square, seating 1,500; Symphony Hall, 1,800.

Concerts/Musical Activities. 80 student chamber ensembles and individual recitals per year; major ensembles (orchestra, wind symphony, choral) present 2 major concerts each quarter; 10 faculty concerts per year.

Music Library. In addition to the music holdings in the Marriott Library, the Music Department maintains a small independent library in Gardner Hall. 9,000 volumes; 15,500 scores (includes sheet music and major scores); all major periodicals; 5,000 phonograph recordings. 20 listening stations of which 9 are equipped with cassette and disc player; an additional 5 stations are equipped with computer facilities which consist of 5 Mac Plus PCs and 5 DX7 or DX27 synthesizers. Special collections include the Arthur Shephard Collection; Leroy Robertson Collection; Hugo Leichetentritt Collection; Evans Sisters Collection. The library resources of Brigham Young University in Provo are also available for student access.

Special Programs

Performance Groups. Orchestra, Wind Symphony, Choral Ensembles, Chamber Music Ensembles, Marching Band.

Financial

Costs. Per academic year: Tuition in-state resident $1,272, out-of-state $3,630. Private study fee $210 for ½ hour lesson per week; $420 for 1 hour lesson per week; practice room fee $35. Room $1,100 to $1,600. Board $1,000 to $1,600. Off-campus housing $200 to $400 per month (single residency).

Financial Aid. Financial aid is awarded on the basis of academic merit, financial need, and musical ability. Both institutional and state/federal aid available. 85 music students receive financial aid (not including Marching Band members); awards range from $75 per quarter for certain band scholarships to full tuition. Scholarship/financial aid application due March 1. Part-time employment and a College Work-Study program available.

VERMONT

Bennington College
Music Department
Bennington
Vermont 05201

Telephone. (802) 442-5401

Chief Administrator. Jeffrey Levine, Chair.

Bennington College is a private institution founded in 1932 as a four-year undergraduate college for women. The College became coeducational in 1968. It makes available to students individually planned programs of study leading to the Bachelor of Arts degree. The 550-acre campus is located in the southwest corner of Vermont, four miles from the village of Bennington.

The music program requires students to do work in performance, composition, and improvisation. Classes are small and every piece written by a Bennington student is performed either by faculty or students. Buildings are never closed and practice rooms are available twenty-four hours per day during the term. The Music Building is open all day and night for student use.

Accreditation. New England Association of of Schools and Colleges.

Academic Information

Enrollment, Music Majors. (Total College) Full-time 200 men, 400 women. 50 foreign students.

Music Faculty. Full-time 6, part-time 8.

Term System. Semester. Work-study term from January 3 to March 1. Academic year September to June. No summer session.

Entrance Requirements. High school graduation or equivalent; SAT; essays. The major in music requires only a genuine interest and willingness to learn; no audition required.

Admission Procedure. Applications to Admissions office with supporting documents and $25 fee by February 1 for Fall term.

Music Degrees Offered. Bachelor of Arts; Master of Fine Arts.

Music Degree Requirements. The Bachelor of Arts in music requires the completion of 8 academic terms with four courses per term plus 4 work-study terms; significant work in major field. The Master of Fine Arts in music requires a two-year residency and 2 recitals.

General Program Areas. Chamber Music, Composition, Electronic Music, Improvisation, Instrument Building, Performance.

Instruments Taught. Brass, Percussion, Piano, Stringed Instruments, Voice, Woodwinds.

Musical Facilities

Practice Facilities. 20 practice rooms. 18 practice pianos (uprights and grands). Electronic music studio.

Concert Facilities. 2 concert halls, seating a total of 800.

Concerts/Musical Activities. Concerts held weekly.

Music Library. Music materials are housed in main library and include scores and parts for performance; 5,000 phonograph recordings. Listening facilities (cassette, stereo). Some books, periodicals, and general interest material available at Williams College (Massachusetts).

Special Programs

Featured Programs. Student musicians receive credit for performing in the local orchestra.

Financial

Costs. Per academic year: Comprehensive fee $17,900.

Financial Aid. Financial aid is awarded on the basis of financial need. Both institutional and state/federal aid available. Approximately 50% of student body receive some form of financial aid. Part-time employment and College Work-Study program available.

Commentary

Bennington College, which strongly encourages individual creativity in its approach to the arts, has a ten-week winter term during which students leave campus to work in jobs related to their major subjects. Music majors accordingly find work in music or arts administration. The College's lovely geographical setting, in the foothills of the White Mountains, masks a slightly less appealing characteristic: it is one of the most expensive institutions of higher education in the United States.

University of Vermont
Department of Music
1490 South Prospect Street
Burlington
Vermont 05405

Telephone. (802) 656-3040

Chief Administrator. Dr. James G. Chapman, Chairman.

The University of Vermont was chartered in 1791 and is one of the twenty oldest institutions of higher learning in the United States. The campus is located in Burlington, Vermont's largest city.

The Department of Music offers undergraduate programs for students who wish to pursue careers in music as performers, scholars, or private teachers.

Accreditation. New England Association of Schools and Colleges; National Association of Schools of Music.

Academic Information

Enrollment, Music Majors. (Total University) 10,908.

Music Faculty. 20.

Term System. Semester. Eight summer sessions.

Entrance Requirements. High school graduation or equivalent; rank in upper 40 percent of graduating class; completion of 16 units including 4 English, 3 mathematics, 2 foreign language, 2 science, 3 social studies; SAT required; audition required.

Admission Procedure. Application with supporting documents and nonrefundable $30 fee to Office of Admissions.

Music Degrees Offered. Bachelor of Music; Bachelor of Science.

Music Degree Requirements. The Bachelor of Music degree is offered with a concentration in performance or theory. The Bachelor of Science degree in music education prepares students for positions as instructors and supervisors of music in the public schools.

General Program Areas. Composition, Music Education, Music Theory, Performance.

Instruments Taught. Brass, Harpsichord, Organ, Percussion, Piano, Stringed Instruments, Voice, Woodwinds.

Musical Facilities

Practice Facilities. The Music Department is located in the Music Building which includes a recital hall housing a G.B. Fisk organ.

Concerts/Musical Activities. Major ensemble concerts, faculty recitals, and formal student recitals are presented frequently throughout the year; the George Bishop Lane Artists Series.

Music Library. The Bailey/Howe Library is the main unit of the University libraries and supports the academic programs of the Department of Music.

Special Programs

Performance Groups. Band, Choir, Choral Union, Orchestra, Vermont Wind Ensemble, Brass Ensemble, Contemporary Ensemble, Madrigal Choir, Opera Workshop, Percussion Ensemble, Stage Band, Trombone Choir.

Financial

Costs. Per academic year: Tuition in-state $2,914, out-of-state $8,184. Fees $258. Music lesson fee $140 per credit. Room $2,094. Board $1,062.

Financial Aid. Financial aid is awarded on the basis of academic merit and financial need. Institutional and state/federal aid are available in the form of scholarships, grants, loans, and part-time employment. Financial aid/scholarship application due March 1.

VIRGINIA

George Mason University
Department of Performing Arts - Music Division

4400 University Drive
Fairfax
Virginia 22030

Telephone. (703) 425-3900
Chief Administrator. Arnald D. Gabriel, Chairman.

George Mason University was first established in the mid-1950s as a two-year branch of the University of Virginia. It became independent in 1972 and is now the state university in northern Virginia. It offers graduate and undergraduate degree programs in more than 90 fields at the main campus in Fairfax and the 10-acre campus in Arlington. The 571-acre main campus is located in suburban Fairfax County, 16 miles from Washington, D.C.

The Department of Peforming Arts includes the music, theater, and dance divisions. A new complex housing the Department opened in 1986.

Accreditation. Southern Association of Colleges and Schools.

Academic Information

Enrollment, Music Majors. 110. Foreign students 5.

Music Faculty. Full-time 10, part-time 30. Faculty is strong in applied music with members from the National Symphony Orchestra, U.S. Air Force Band, and U.S. Army Band.

Term System. Semester. Academic year from late August to early May. Summer session from early June to early August.

Entrance Requirements. Undergraduate requirements: graduate of an accredited secondary or preparatory school based on no fewer than 15 units in an appropriate distribution; rank in upper 50% of graduation class; satisfactory scores on SAT or equivalent; evidence of academic achievement and promise; audition before a faculty committee; placement examinations in sight singing and ear training, keyboard harmony, and piano as a secondary instrument; credit by examination and advanced placement options available. Graduate requirements: baccalaureate degree from an accredited institution of higher education; 2.75 or better GPA (on a 4.0 scale) in last two years of undergraduate study; undergraduate preparation for the chosen field; GRE and GRE Advanced Test in Music; audition.

Admission Procedure. Application with all supporting documents to Admissions Office.

Music Degrees Offered. Bachelor of Music; Bachelor of Arts in Music; Master of Arts; Doctor of Arts in Education with music concentration.

Music Degree Requirements. The Bachelor of Music degree requires the completion of 130 credit hours with a distribution of 32 hours in general education, 58 hours in basic musicianship, 18 hours in music concentration, and 22 hours of free electives. The degree program is designed to provide a basic musical background upon which students may build special competence in one of the following concentrations: performance, composition, music education, accompanying, and music history and literature. The Bachelor of Arts degree with a major in music requires the completion of 120 credit hours with a distribution of 62 credits in general education, 42 hours in music, and 16 hours of electives. The curriculum for this degree program is designed to prepare graduates for a career in music or for advanced study of music at the graduate level.

The Master of Arts degree with a major in music requires the successful completion of 30 hours of credit in graduate music courses. Concentrations are available in music education, composition, conducting, performance, and accompanying. The degree Doctor of Arts in Education with a music concentration is offered through the Department of Education.

General Program Areas. Accompanying, Applied Music, Composition, Conducting, Music Education, Music History, Music Theory, Orchestral Instruments, Performance, Vocal Music.

Instruments Taught. Bass, Bassoon, Brass, Clarinet, Euphonium, Flute, Guitar, Harp, Horn, Koto, Oboe, Organ, Percussion, Piano, Saxophone, Trombone,

Trumpet, Viola, Viola da Gamba, Violin, Violoncello, Voice.

Musical Facilities

Practice Facilities. 15 practice rooms (includes 6 studios). 18 pianos (12 uprights, 4 grands, 2 concert grands). Percussion-equipped practice room.

Concert Facilities. Theater, seating 500; recital hall, 300. A 2,000 seat concert hall is planned.

Concerts/Musical Activities. Professional concert series on campus; numerous professional concerts in metropolitan area (John F. Kennedy Center, Wolf Trap Farm Park).

Music Library. Music collection is part of main library and contains 8,000 volumes; 2,800 scores; 75 current periodical subscriptions; 5,000 phonograph recordings; 1,000 compact discs. 21 listening stations. Special collections include the American Symphony Orchestra League Archives; Sophocles Pappas Guitar Music Collection; Wolftrap Archives; Federal Theater Project Archives; Country Music Collection (phonograph discs). Students have access to the library resources of the Washington metropolitan area, including the Library of Congress and the Smithsonian Institution.

Special Programs

Performance Groups. Chamber Orchestra, Jazz Ensemble, Symphonic Winds, Chamber Ensembles, University Chorale, Northern Virginia Symphonic Chorus, Gloriana Singers.

Financial

Costs. Per academic year: Tuition in-state residents $1,824, out-of-state $3,648. Room from $2,450 to $3,300. Board from $1,216 to $1,568. Off-campus housing from $350 per month.

Financial Aid. Financial aid is awarded on the basis of financial need and musical ability. Institutional and state/federal aid available. The Jean Carrington Cook Piano Scholarships are awarded by audition to incoming freshmen and transfer students who show promise as piano majors. Application due January 1. Part-time employment and College Work-Study program available.

James Madison University
Department of Music
Harrisonburg
Virginia 22807

Telephone. (703) 568-6197

Chief Administrator. Dr. Joseph J. Estock, Head.

James Madison University was established by the Virginia General Assembly in 1908 as the State Normal and Industrial School for Women at Harrisonburg. In 1914, the name of the University was changed to the State Normal School for Women at Harrisonburg, in 1924 became the State Teachers College at Harrisonburg, and in 1938 was named Madison College in honor of the fourth president of the United States. In 1966, the University became a coeducational institution and in 1977, the current name was adopted.

The campus is located in Harrisonburg, a city of 25,000 in the heart of the Shenandoah Valley of Virginia. The area is flanked by the Blue Ridge Mountains on the East and the Alleghenies on the west. The 334-acre campus faces on Main Street and extends in an eastward direction past Interstate 81.

The Department of Music offers specific programs leading to professional careers in music and provides opportunities for students to study music for personal enrichment. The Department has stated the following objectives: (1) to prepare students to teach vocal and/or instrumental music in public and private schools; (2) to provide a specialization for students who wish to pursue music as a profession in performance, composition, sacred music, or higher education; (3) to prepare students for opportunities and careers in music-business; and (4) to provide for all students basic music study and opportunities for further musical growth, including preparation for graduate study.

Accreditation. Southern Association of Colleges and Schools; National Association of Schools of Music; National Council for Accreditation of Teacher Education.

Academic Information

Enrollment, Music Majors. Undergraduate 249, graduate 20.

Music Faculty. Full-time 33, part-time 14.

Term System. Semester. 4-, 6-, and 8-week summer sessions.

Entrance Requirements. The Admissions Committee is most interested in the quality of the applicant's high school program of study; the applicant with solid achievement in four or five academic courses each year of the four years of high school will have a distinct advantage; SAT; recomendations; special talents and abilities indicating leadership, organizational and problem-solving skills are also important in the decision process. Foreign students will be considered after evidence of English proficiency and financial sufficiency has been presented. On-campus audition including 15-minute prepared piece(s), sight reading, theory entrance examination, piano placement examination, interview.

Admission Procedure. Application with $15 nonrefundable fee due February 1 for fall semester.

Music Degrees Offered. Bachelor of Music; Bachelor of Music Education; Master of Music.

Music Degree Requirements. All baccalaureate-level music majors must complete the 43-hour general studies program, 2 to 5 semester hours of elective credits, and a 26-credit-hour core program of music courses. The remaining hours (for a total of 128 to 132 hours) are specified for the various concentrations. The Bachelor of

Music degree is designed for students in four specialized areas: performance, for students who possess exceptional talent in applied music; sacred music; theory and composition; and music management. Concentrations in performance or in theory and composition are intended for students who desire to continue their musical training in graduate programs which will prepare them for a professional career in performance, composition, and/or teaching at the college level. The sacred music concentration will prepare students for employment as professional full-time church musicians, for further work at the graduate level either in performance or sacred music, or as private teachers. Those who elect the concentration in music management will be prepared for positions in a broad area of music-business occupations and for admission to a graduate professional school of business.

The Bachelor of Music Education degree is designed primarily for those preparing to teach instrumental or vocal music in the public schools. At the end of the common first year of study, students will have the opportunity to apply for admission into the program and will be evaluated in regard to their musical potential. In addition to qualifying students for certification in the public schools of Virginia and most other states, the broad background of the degree is also applicable to church music, private music teaching, work in the music industry, and graduate music study.

The Master of Music degree is offered by the Department and requires the completion of specified courses in an approved program.

General Program Areas. Applied Music, Choral Conducting, Composition, Music Education, Music Management, Music Theory, Orchestra Conducting, Performance, Piano Pedagogy, Sacred Music, Vocal Studies.

Instruments Taught. Bass, Bassoon, Clarinet, Euphonium, Flute, Guitar, Harpsichord, Horn, Oboe, Organ, Percussion, Piano, Saxophone, Trombone, Trumpet, Tuba, Viola, Violin, Violoncello, Voice.

Musical Facilities

Practice Facilities. 35 practice rooms. 4 practice studios for organists. 6 percussion-equipped practice rooms. 65 practice pianos (50 uprights, 15 grands); 8 grand pianos reserved for piano majors. Electronic composition studio; recording studio; electronic piano laboratory.

Concert Facilities. Wilson Hall, seating 1,372; Anthony-Seeger Hall, 228; Latimer-Shaeffer Auditorium, 344; Grafton-Stovall, 630.

Community Facilities. Local church.

Concerts/Musical Activities. Concerts, recitals.

Music Library. Listening facilities (cassette, stereo). Music librarian on staff of main library.

Special Programs

Performance Groups. Chamber Orchestra, University Orchestra, Marching Band, Concert Band, Wind Ensemble, Jazz Ensemble, Jazz Band, Jazz Rock Ensemble, String Ensemble, Woodwind Ensemble, Brass Ensemble, Guitar Ensemble, Percussion Ensemble, Chorus, Women's Concert Choir, Chorale, Madison Singers (Chamber Choir), Madisonians - Vocal Jazz and Show Choir, Opera Theater.

Foreign Programs. Semester Abroad program in London, Paris, Florence; specially designed courses for elective and/or transfer.

Financial

Costs. Per academic year: Tuition in-state resident $2,-392, out-of-state $4,222. Room and board $2,828. Music lessons (2 per week per semester) $80; 1 to 15 lessons per semester each $4.

Financial Aid. The Department of Music awards scholarships to qualified undergraduate and graduate students. Determined primarily on performing ability and department needs, stipends are awarded to keyboard, voice, wind, string, percussion, and composition students, and are assigned on either a one-time or continuing basis. For new students, scholarships are awarded on the basis of evaluations determined at entrance auditions.

Norfolk State University
Department of Music
2401 Corprew Avenue
Norfolk
Virginia 23504

Telephone. (804) 623-8544

Chief Administrator. Dr. Carl G. Harris, Jr., Department Head.

Norfolk State University was founded in 1935 as a junior college unit of Virginia Union University. In 1942, it was chartered as Norfolk Polytechnic College and became the Norfolk Division of Virginia State College in 1944. In 1956, the institution became a four-year college; the name was changed to Norfolk State College in 1969. The present name was adopted in 1979 upon achieving university status. The 105-acre campus with 22 buildings is two miles east of downtown Norfolk.

The Department of Music is located in a wing of the Fine Arts Building. It offers programs leading to the bachelor and master's degrees. The Music Media Program was one of the first such programs offered in the United States.

Accreditation. Southern Association of Colleges and Schools; National Association of Schools of Music.

Academic Information

Enrollment, Music Majors. Undergraduate 137, graduate 20.

Music Faculty. Full-time 23, part-time 3.

Term System. Semester. Summer session.

Entrance Requirements. High school graduation or GED; completion of 16 units including 4 English, 2 mathematics, 1 social studies, 1 laboratory science; SAT. Audition required; held by areas (vocal, keyboard, instrumental); theory placement test.

Admission Procedure. Application to Admissions Office; orientation period; advisement and counsel in department.

Music Degrees Offered. Bachelor of Music; Bachelor of Science; Master of Music.

Music Degree Requirements. The Bachelor of Music degree requires the completion of 126 semester hours of a core curriculum, major area, and general education requirements. A program in Music Media is offered. The Bachelor of Science with a major in public school music is also available. Non-majors must have proficiency on an instrument in order to take further study. The Master of Music degree is offered with concentrations in performance, music education, and theory-composition. The master's degree requires the successful completion of 30 semester hours.

General Program Areas. Composition, Music Education, Music Media, Music Theory, Performance.

Instruments Taught. Baritone, Bass, Bassoon, Clarinet, Flute, Oboe, Organ, Piano, Saxophone, Trombone, Trumpet, Tuba, Viola, Violin, Voice.

Musical Facilities

Practice Facilities. 17 practice rooms. 1 organ (Walcher). 2 percussion-equipped practice rooms. 17 pianos (Everett, Yamaha); 1 grand piano reserved for piano majors. Electronic music studio; recording studio; music media library-laboratory.

Concert Facilities. Brown Hall (theatre), seating 500; Fine Arts Hall, 200.

Community Facilities. Local churches used for organ lessons.

Concerts/Musical Activities. Student and faculty concerts/recitals; visiting artists concerts.

Music Library. 2,700 volumes; 4,000 scores; 21 music periodicals; 75 microfiche titles; 1,000 recordings. Listening facilities (cassette decks, stereo turntables, compact disc players). The holdings of the Norfolk Public Library, Chrysler Museum, and Old Dominion University libraries are also available to students.

Special Programs

Featured Programs. Junior Music Summer Program.

Performance Groups. Ensembles, Orchestra, Choral Groups.

Financial

Costs. Per academic year: Tuition in-state resident $1,-308, out-of-state $2,420. Room and board $1,140.

Financial Aid. 80 music scholarships ranging from $200 to full tuition. Scholarship application due by June 1 or October 1. Other sources of financial aid include grants, loans, part-time employment, and College Work-Study program.

Radford University
Department of Music

College of Visual and Performing Arts
East Norwood Street
Radford
Virginia 24142

Telephone. (703) 731-5177

Chief Administrator. Dr. Eugene C. Fellin, Chairperson.

Radford University was founded in 1910 as a state normal and industrial school for women. In 1924 it became the Radford State Teachers College; in 1944 the women's division of Virginia Polytechnic Institute, and in 1964 Radford College. University status was attained in 1979. This state-supported institution has an enrollment of 7,600 students. The 128-acre campus is situated in a residential section of Radford, approximately 45 miles southwest of Roanoke.

The objectives of the Department of Music are to prepare students for careers in music or for advanced professional study, provide training and experiences in music for non-majors, and provide leadership in the musical activities of the University and community. The choral program at Radford includes five different ensembles covering the entire spectrum of choral music. At the focal point of the program are the two most prestigious groups, the Radford Singers and the Madrigal Singers. The former group tours annually; the latter group presents the annual Madrigal Dinner which is a highlight of the Christmas season for the University and community. The University Chorus, open to all students, the Chorale, Highlander Band, Wind Ensemble, and the Jazz Ensemble are a few of the opportunities for student participation.

The Department of Music is located in Powell Hall of the Silverman Fine Arts Center.

Accreditation. Southern Association of Colleges and Schools; National Association of Schools of Music.

Academic Information

Enrollment, Music Majors. Full-time 25 men, 76 women; part-time 2 men, 17 women. Foreign students 4.

Music Faculty. Full-time 17, part-time 5.

Term System. Semester. Two 6-week summer sessions.

Entrance Requirements. High school graduation with rank in upper half of graduating class; completion of 16 units including 4 English, 2 mathematics, 1 laboratory science, 2 social studies including American history; SAT required. Foreign students must submit TOEFL score and evidence of financial responsibility.

Admission Procedure. Application form and supporting transcripts; $15 nonrefundable application fee. Music majors are required to have placement audition and music fundamentals test.

Music Degrees Offered. Bachelor of Arts; Bachelor of Science; Bachelor of Music; Bachelor of Music Therapy; Master of Arts; Master of Science.

Music Degree Requirements. The Department of Music offers four undergraduate degrees in music: Bachelor of Music with concentrations in music education, music business, piano performance, or composition; Bachelor of Music Therapy; Bachelor of Arts; Bachelor of Science. All degree candidates are required to take 45 semester hours of general education courses with the exception of those earning a Bachelor of Music Therapy degree (46 semester hours). The music core and other specified curricular requirements vary depending on program pursued.

Two graduate degrees are offered in music: the Master of Arts with concentrations in music or music therapy (30 semester hours) and the Master of Science with concentrations in music education or music therapy (33 semester hours). The objective of the Master of Arts degree program in music is to provide advanced study for musicians, music scholars, and music therapists in preparation for professional careers or doctoral study; for the Master of Science degree program the objective is to provide advanced study for music therapists and school music educators.

General Program Areas. Church Music, Composition, Conducting, Jazz Studies, Music Business, Music Education, Music Theory, Music Therapy, Performance.

Instruments Taught. Brass, Guitar, Organ, Percussion, Piano, Violin, Violoncello, Voice, Woodwinds.

Musical Facilities

Practice Facilities. Special practice facilities for organists; 1 M*oaller, 2 Wicks. 2 practice rooms for percussionists. 20 practice rooms. 15 pianos (Yamaha, Everett); 2 grand pianos reserved for piano majors. Music education laboratory; 12-position Baldwin piano laboratory; an Alpha-Syntari-equipped electronic music laboratory; computer-equipped music theory laboratory; tiered choral rehearsal room.

Concert Facilities. Porterfield Theater seating 500; Preston Auditorium, 1,500; 2 recital halls, 150 each.

Concerts/Musical Activities. Over 40 professional, faculty, and student recitals/concerts are offered annually.

Music Library. The main library includes music materials; 300,000 volumes. Listening facilities available.

Special Programs

Featured Programs. The University sponsors a concert series; master classes offered by Radford faculty and other artists in the area.

Performance Groups. Radford Singers, Madrigal Singers, University Chorus, Chorale, Highlander Band, Wind Ensemble, University Jazz Ensemble.

Financial

Costs. Per academic year: Tuition in-state resident $1,796, out-of-state $2,546. Room and board $3,050.

Financial Aid. Financial aid is awarded on the basis of academic merit, financial need, musical ability. Institutional and state/federal aid available. 62% of students receive some form of financial aid. Scholarships range from $500 to $4,000 per academic year. Scholarship application due February 1.

Shenandoah College and Conservatory
Winchester
Virginia 22625

Telephone. (703) 667-8714
Chief Administrator. Dr. Charlotte A. Collins, Dean.

Shenandoah College and Conservatory is located in Winchester, Virginia, 72 miles west of Washington, D.C. It was founded in 1875 in Dayton, Virginia, and moved to its current location in 1960. The College is privately supported and affiliated with the United Methodist Church. Nearly 50 programs of study are offered leading to the Bachelor and Master's degrees. The campus has six modern buildings for instruction, performance, and recreation, along with the century-old John Kerr Building in downtown Winchester. The campus has five dormitories.

The Conservatory offers nine degree programs in 20 concentrations, including such specialized fields as music therapy, arts management, and piano technology.

Accreditation. Southern Association of Colleges and Schools; National Association of Schools of Music.

Academic Information

Enrollment, Music Majors. 385.
Music Faculty. Full-time 40, part-time 23.
Term System. Semester. Academic year begins last week of August. Summer session of 8 weeks from mid-June to mid-August.

Entrance Requirements. Decision is based on high school record, recommendations, scores on SAT or ACT; audition. Foreign students must submit TOEFL score.

Admission Procedure. Application with supporting documents to Admissions office; schedule visit and audition.

Music Degrees Offered. Bachelor of Music; Bachelor of Science; Bachelor of Music Education; Master of Music; Master of Music Education; Associate of Arts.

Music Degree Requirements. The Bachelor degrees require the completion of 120 hours of study with a 2.0 GPA. Concentrations are offered in arts management, woodwind study, brass and percussion study, music composition, church music, piano technology, string study, voice study, music pedagogy, piano accompanying, performance, jazz studies and commercial music, and keyboard study. The Bachelor of Music Education degree curriculum is designed to guide students toward a successful career in teaching. Instrumental, vocal, or combined concentration is offered. Successful completion of all requirements will result in eligibility for certification and development of the ability to teach music at the elementary and secondary levels. The Bachelor of Music Therapy degree program is designed to train music therapists in the theoretical aspect of music therapy while simultaneously providing extensive practical experience.

The Master of Music Education degree curriculum is designed to meet the needs of experienced teachers seeking to enhance existing skills and enrichment opportunities as well as for the inexperienced teacher seeking in-depth preparation for teaching. Students may concentrate in the areas of music education, applied music and conducting, and music history and theory. The Master of Music degree is also offered. The Master's programs require the completion of a prescribed curriculum for a total of 30 hours with a 3.0 GPA.

General Program Areas. Accompanying, Applied Music, Arts Management, Church Music, Commercial Music, Composition, Conducting, Jazz Studies, Music Education, Music Pedagogy, Music Theory, Music Therapy, Performance, Piano Technology, Vocal Studies.

Instruments Taught. Bass, Brass, Guitar, Harp, Lute, Organ, Percussion, Piano, Stringed Instruments, Viola, Violin, Violoncello, Voice, Woodwinds.

Musical Facilities

Practice Facilities. 750 practice sites. 6 pipe organs (Moeller, Wicks). 135 pianos (46 grands); 12 grand pianos reserved for piano majors. Electronic music laboratory; theory laboratory; piano technology laboratory.

Concert Facilities. Armstrong Auditorium, seating 700; Theatre studio, 150; Goodson Chapel/Recital Hall, 250.

Community Facilities. Local auditoriums. Seven outstanding organs of varying types are located in the Winchester area and are available for student use.

Concerts/Musical Activities. 300 concerts, recitals, clinics, master classes, musical and operatic productions.

Music Library. 10,000 music scores; 7,000 recordings. Additional performance scores housed in Conservatory libraries.

Special Programs

Featured Programs. Composers' Forum, Performance Forum.

Performance Groups. Orchestra, Wind Ensemble, Band, Conservatory Choir, Theater Ensemble, Chamber Music, Jazz Ensemble.

Affiliated Programs. Residential camp programs for high school juniors and seniors in instrumental and voice music and music theatre. Summer program for selected high school juniors enables prospective students to study with professionals and earn college credit to Shenandoah after their high school graduation.

Financial

Costs. Per academic year: Tuition $6,600 (Virginia residents pay $5,550 after receiving a Virginia Tuition Assistance Grant, available to all state residents). Private lessons and class piano approximately $1,050. Room and board $2,800.

Financial Aid. About three-fourths of all students receive financial aid; average award $4,700.

University of Virginia
McIntire Department of Music
College of Arts and Sciences
112 Old Cabell Hall
Charlottesville
Virginia 22903

Telephone. (804) 924-3052

Chief Administrator. Dr. Donald G. Loach, Chair.

Chartered by the General Assembly in 1819 under the sponsorship of Thomas Jefferson, the University officially opened in 1825. Located on 1,800 acres, the campus has 240 major buildings in Charlottesville, a town situated in the foothills of the Blue Ridge Mountains, 100 miles southwest of Washington, D.C.

The Department of Music offers a program that presents the study of music as a part of a liberal arts education. The study develops both a command of the musical language through analysis and exercises in writing music as well as an understanding of significant musical styles. The Department of Music enjoys a particularly attractive position on campus. Occupying one of the University's oldest buildings, Cabell Hall, the Department directly faces Thomas Jefferson's famous rotunda across the University's Lawn.

Accreditation. Southern Association of Colleges and Schools; National Association of Schools of Music; National Council for Accreditation of Music Education.

Academic Information

Enrollment, Music Majors. (Total University) 18,518.

Music Faculty. 14.

Term System. Semester. One summer session.

Entrance Requirements. High school graduation with rank in top 30 percent of high school class; completion of 16 units including 4 English, 3 mathematics, 2 foreign language, 1 science, 1 social science; SAT and three Achievement Tests. GRE required for graduate programs.

Admission Procedure. Application with supporting documents and nonrefundable $20 fee to Office of Admissions.

Music Degrees Offered. Bachelor of Arts; Master of Arts; Master of Arts in Teaching.

Music Degree Requirements. The Bachelor of Arts degree is offered with a major in music. The degree requires the completion of 28 credits in the major with a total of 120 semester hour credits. The Master of Arts degree is offered with fields of study including music history, music theory, and composition. The Master of Arts in Teaching degree offers study in the fields of conducting, orchestration, choral and instrumental repertory, arranging and scoring, music theory, music analysis, composition, music history, and education.

General Program Areas. African Music, Composition, Conducting, Music Education, Music History, Music Literature, Music Theory, Orchestration, Performance.

Instruments Taught. Brass, Guitar, Harp, Harpsichord, Organ, Percussion, Piano, Stringed Instruments, Voice, Woodwinds.

Musical Facilities

Concerts/Musical Activities. Student/faculty recitals and concerts; visiting artists.

Music Library. The various libraries of the University house over 2.7 million books and 10 million manuscripts. The Music Library serves the academic programs of the McIntire Department of Music. Special collections include: Alfred Swan Collection of Russian Arts; nineteenth century American imprints; Thomas Jefferson Family Monticello Music Collection; English contemporary music, musicology, and history of chant.

Special Programs

Performance Groups. String Orchestra, Orchestra, Symphonic Band, Chamber Ensemble, Glee Club, University Singers, Women's Chorus, Collegium Musicum, New Music Ensemble, African Music Performance.

Financial

Costs. Per academic year: Tuition in-state resident $2,250, out-of-state $5,450. Room $1,200. Board $1,800.

Financial Aid. The University has a number of privately endowed, need-based scholarships. Financial aid applicants are automatically considered for any scholarships for which they qualify. Academic scholarships are not available. Other sources of financial aid include state/federal grants, loans, and part-time employment. Financial aid application due March 1.

Virginia Commonwealth University Department of Music

School of the Arts
910 West Franklin Street
Richmond
Virginia 23284

Telephone. (804) 257-1166, Ext. 6046

Chief Administrator. Richard Koehler, Chairman.

Virginia Commonwealth University was established in 1968 by combining the Richmond Professional Institute and the Medical College of Virginia. The 13-acre campus has 47 buildings and is located in a residential section near downtown Richmond, the state capital.

The Department of Music offers a comprehensive program designed to assist the student in acquiring skills and knowledge in various musical disciplines.

Accreditation. Southern Association of Colleges and Schools; National Association of Schools of Music; National Council for Accreditation of Teacher Education.

Academic Information

Enrollment, Music Majors. (Total University) 15,586.

Music Faculty. Full-time 27, part-time 34.

Term System. Semester. Seven summer sessions.

Entrance Requirements. High school graduation or equivalent; the School of the Arts does not have high school units requirements; degree applicants must complete an Art Administration Packet which is designed to measure the applicant's ability and aptitude for the arts; SAT required; audition and written general musicianship examination. GRE required for graduate study.

Admission Procedure. Application with supporting documents and nonrefundable $10 fee to Admissions Office.

Music Degrees Offered. Bachelor of Music Education; Master of Music.

Music Degree Requirements. The Department offers a program that leads to the Bachelor of Music Education degree. The program includes those requirements necessary to qualify for the Collegiate Professional Certificate issued by Virginia. The core of the instructional program is comprehensive musicianship. This is a competence-based course sequence which is fundamental to all major areas in the department. The core requires four semesters and deals with composing, conducting, performing, aural skills, elements of theory, orchestration, and music literature-history.

The Master of Music degree is offered with emphases

in applied music (solo performance and conducting), composition, music education, and piano pedagogy.

General Program Areas. Applied Music, Church Music, Composition, Conducting, Jazz Studies, Music Education, Music History, Music Literature, Music Theory, Orchestration, Performance, Piano Pedagogy.

Instruments Taught. Brass, Organ, Percussion, Piano, Stringed Instruments, Voice, Woodwinds.

Musical Facilities

Practice Facilities. The Department of Music is located in the Performing Arts Center.

Concert Facilities. Concert Hall, seating 502.

Concerts/Musical Activities. More than 150 public concerts by students and faculty are presented each year as well as studio and departmental recitals. Annual series of Terrace Concerts, a unique cooperative venture with the John F. Kennedy Center for the Performing Arts in Washington, D.C.

Music Library. The University Library Services supports the teaching, study, and research activities of the School of the Arts. Tapes of jazz, classical, and ethnic music form an extensive listening collection.

Special Programs

Performance Groups. New Music Ensemble, Madrigalists, Collegium Musicum, Opera Workshop, Vocal Ensemble, Piano Ensemble, Percussion Ensemble, Woodwind Ensemble, Brass Ensemble, Chamber Orchestra, String Ensemble, Guitar Ensemble, Jazz Ensemble, Jazz Orchestra.

Affiliated Programs. Pre-college, university, and adult students may receive private or class instruction through the Community School of the Performing Arts which is adjunct to the Department of Music.

Financial

Costs. Per academic year: Tuition in-state resident $1,680, out-of-state $4,300. Fees $452. Private music lessons $85 per semester for one credit, $170 for two credits, $230 for three credits. Room $1,570 to $2,250. Board $1,230 to $1,290.

Financial Aid. Financial aid is need-based and in the form of grants, loans, and work-study. Scholarships are awarded for superior personal and academic achievement. Financial aid/scholarship application due March 1.

Virginia Polytechnic Institute and State University
Department of Music

College of Arts and Sciences
256 Lane Hall
Blacksburg
Virginia 24061

Telephone. (703) 961-5685
Chief Administrator. Dr. John S. Husser, Jr., Chairman.

Virginia Tech was established as a land-grant college in 1872. The present name was adopted in 1970. Considered a primarily male and military college until the mid-sixties, now more than one-third of the 21,000 students are women, while about two percent of the student body is enrolled in the Corps of Cadets. Instruction is offered in more than 50 departments of the 7 academic colleges. The 2,600-acre campus with 100 major buildings is located in Blacksburg, 40 miles southwest of Roanoke.

The Department of Music of the College of Arts and Sciences offers the major in music, leading to the Bachelor of Arts degree. A music education major is offered at the undergraduate and graduate levels in cooperation with the College of Education.

Accreditation. Southern Association of Colleges and Schools; National Council for Accreditation of Teacher Education.

Academic Information

Enrollment, Music Majors. Full-time 35 men, 40 women. 5 foreign students.

Music Faculty. Full-time 21, part-time 5.

Term System. Semester. Academic year from late August to early May. Two 5-week summer sessions.

Entrance Requirements. High school graduation or equivalent; rank in upper 50 percent of graduating class; completion of 18 units including 4 English, 2 algebra, 1 geometry, 1 laboratory science; SAT and 2 Achievement Tests; audition required.

Admission Procedure. Application to Admissions Office as well as to the Department of Music.

Music Degrees Offered. Bachelor of Arts; Master of Arts; Doctor of Education.

Music Degree Requirements. The Bachelor of Arts degree with major in music is offered with emphases in performance, music history/literature, theory/composition, and music education. In addition to fulfilling the core curriculum requirements of the College of Arts and Sciences, the music major must pursue a concentration in one of the above areas of emphasis. The major consists of 50 semester hours of coursework within music and requires a minimum of 126 semester hours for graduation.

The Master of Arts and the Doctor of Education degrees are offered with concentration in music education.

General Program Areas. Composition, Music Education, Music History, Music Literature, Music Theory, Performance.

Instruments Taught. Bass, Bassoon, Clarinet, Flute, Horn, Oboe, Percussion, Piano, Saxophone, Trombone, Trumpet, Viola, Violin, Violoncello, Voice.

Musical Facilities

Practice Facilities. 24 practice rooms. Special practice facilities for percussionists. 20 pianos (Steinway and Kawai grands and uprights); 6 grand pianos reserved for piano majors. Electronic music studio.

Concert Facilities. Burruss Hall Auditorium, seating 3,003; Donaldson Brown Center, 600; Recital Salon, 225; Squires Auditorium, 450.

Concerts/Musical Activities. Concerts, recitals, visiting artists.

Music Library. Newman Library houses music materials. 500 audiovisual titles; 6,400 phonograph recordings; 1,000 audiocassettes. 45 listening stations (stereo).

Special Programs

Performance Groups. Choral Music Groups; Instrumental Ensembles.

Financial

Costs. Per academic year: Tuition in-state resident undergraduate $1,875, out-of-state $3,885; graduate in-state $2,187, out-of-state $2,430. Fees $144. Room and board $1,827.

Financial Aid. Virginia Tech awards aid to qualified students in the form of scholarships, grants, loans, and employment.

Virginia State University
Department of Music Education
School of Education
Petersburg
Virginia 23803

Telephone. (804) 520-5311

Chief Administrator. Margaret G. Dabney, Dean.

Virginia State University was founded in 1882. The 630-acre campus has 40 major buildings in Petersburg, 25 miles south of Richmond.

The objectives of the Department of Music Education are to provide students with a broad education and develop their performance and musicianship; to train them in teaching methods and materials, and provide practical teaching experience in choral and instrumental music for teaching in the elementary, junior, and senior high schools.

Accreditation. Southern Association of Colleges and Schools; National Association of Schools of Music; National Council for Accreditation of Teacher Education.

Academic Information

Enrollment, Music Majors. (Total University) 3,911.

Music Faculty. 15.

Term System. Semester. Two summer terms.

Entrance Requirements. High school graduation; completion of 12 units including 4 English, 2 mathematics, 2 foreign language, 2 science, 2 social science; SAT and Achievement Tests required; qualifying examination in music.

Admission Procedure. Application with supporting documents and nonrefundable $10 fee to Office of admissions.

Music Degrees Offered. Bachelor of Music Education; Bachelor of Music; Master of Science; Master of Education.

Music Degree Requirements. The Bachelor of Music Education degree is offered with curricula in choral music (voice major), choral music education (keyboard major), and instrumental music education (strings, brass, woodwind, percussion major). A program in applied music offered by the Division of Educational Leadership, Rehabilitative and Community Services leads to the Bachelor of Music degree. Areas of emphasis are strings, percussion, woodwinds, brass, piano, voice, and organ.

The Master of Science and the Master of Education degrees are also offered through the Graduate School.

General Program Areas. Applied Music, Choral Music, Instrumental Music, Music Education, Performance, Vocal Music.

Instruments Taught. Brass, Organ, Percussion, Piano, Stringed Instruments, Voice, Woodwinds.

Musical Facilities

Music Library. The Johnston Memorial Library, housing over 212,000 volumes, serves the academic programs of the University.

Special Programs

Performance Groups. Instrumental and vocal ensembles.

Financial

Costs. Per academic year: Tuition in-state resident $1,800, out-of-state $3,100. Room and board $2,200.

Financial Aid. Financial aid is awarded in the form of scholarships, loans, grants, and employment. Financial aid/scholarship application due April 1.

WASHINGTON

Central Washington University
Department of Music
Ellensburg
Washington 98926

Telephone. (509) 963-1216

Chief Administrator. Donald H. White, Chairman.

Central Washington University is a state-supported institution established in 1890. The University offers undergraduate programs in 101 subject areas and graduate programs in 35 subject areas. The 350-acre campus is located in Ellensburg, a small city in central Washington 106 miles east of Seattle.

The preparation of professional musicians for careers as performers, teachers, and scholars is a primary concern to the Department of Music, although the curriculum serves as part of the program of liberal education for all students. Training includes development of aural, analytical, and performance skills, and orientation in the historical aspects of music.

Accreditation. Northwest Association of Schools and Colleges; National Association of Schools of Music.

Academic Information

Enrollment, Music Majors. (Total University) 7,163.

Music Faculty. Full-time 19, part-time 1.

Term System. Quarter. Academic year from late September to mid-June. 9-week summer session from late June to mid-August.

Entrance Requirements. High school graduation with 2.5 GPA of 4.0 scale; prior college GPA of 2.0 on 4.0 scale; performance audition. Foreign students must submit official copies of all transcripts, 2 letters of recommendation, confidential financial statement, certificate of health, TOEFL score.

Admission Procedure. Application with $25 non-refundable fee and official transcripts (direct from the issuing institution).

Music Degrees Offered. Bachelor of Music; Bachelor of Arts; Bachelor of Science; Master of Music.

Music Degree Requirements. The Bachelor of Music degree is offered with majors in theory-composition, performance (percussion, string, keyboard, vocal, wind), and music education (broad area, elementary). The Bachelor of Arts and the Bachelor of Science degrees in music are offered within the context of a liberal arts and sciences program.

The Master of Music curriculum is designed to increase professional competence in teaching and performance, and to prepare for continued self-directed study or advanced graduate study. Major fields include music history and literature, theory, composition, conducting, performance, performance-pedagogy, and music education. All students must pass a comprehensive final examination, oral, or written and oral, based on the coursework and the thesis.

General Program Areas. Composition, Conducting, Music Education, Music History, Music Literature, Music Theory, Pedagogy, Performance, Suzuki Method.

Instruments Taught. Bass, Bassoon, Clarinet, Euphonium, Flute, Guitar, Harpsichord, Horn, Oboe, Organ, Percussion, Piano, Recorder, Saxophone, Trombone, Trumpet, Tuba, Viola, Violin, Violoncello, Voice.

Musical Facilities

Practice Facilities. 2 organs including 1 tracker by Coulter of Eugene, Oregon. 25 pianos (studio uprights and small grands). Percussion-equipped practice facilities. Electronic music studio.

Concert Facilities. Hertz Hall, seating 400; McConnell Auditorium, 1200.

Concerts/Musical Activities. Approximately 100 events per academic year (recitals, chamber music programs, large ensemble concerts, guest artists).

Music Library. Music holdings are housed in the main library; major performance libraries are housed in the Music Building. Listening facilities (stereo). Special collection of music education curriculum materials.

Special Programs

Featured Programs. The Department of Music offers a two-year program in Suzuki Pedagogy. This program is based on an enriched version of the Teacher-training guidelines as determined by the Suzuki Association of the Americas. Through this program, the university student is able to work with children from the community, first as an assistant and then as a teacher. Study beyond the two-year basic course is available through independent study.

Performance Groups. Vocal Jazz Choir, Brass Choir, Chamber Orchestra, Chamber Music Ensemble, Percussion Ensemble, Stage Band, Central Swingers, Madrigal Singers, Wind Ensemble, Chamber Choir, Orchestra, Marching Band, Concert Band, Women's Glee Club, Men's Glee Club, Pep Band.

Financial

Costs. Per academic year: Tuition undergraduate in-state resident $1,272, out-of-state $4,425; graduate in-state $1,797, out-of-state $5,361. Room and board $2,821.

Financial Aid. Financial aid is awarded on the basis of need. April 15 is deadline for first priority consideration for scholarship/financial aid. Aid is available in the form of institutional and state/federal grants, loans, part-time employment, and a College Work-Study program.

Eastern Washington University
Department of Music
Cheney
Washington 99004

Telephone. (509) 359-2241
Chief Administrator. William L. Maxson, Chair.

Eastern Washington University is a state-supported liberal arts institution founded in 1882. The campus is located in the city of Cheney, 16 miles from Spokane.

The Department of Music trains students who seek careers in music and provides music instruction and experience for the general university student. Five degree programs with a total of eleven options are offered for students who wish to become performers, composers, conductors, theorists, teachers, or scholars.

Accreditation. Northwest Association of Schools and Colleges; National Association of Schools of Music; National Council for Accreditation of Teacher Education.

Academic Information

Enrollment, Music Majors. (Total University) 8,102.
Music Faculty. 17.
Term System. Quarter.
Entrance Requirements. High school graduation; 4 years English, 3 college preparatory mathematics, 3 science, 2½ social science, 2 foreign language; audition

for placement in voice or instrumental lessons required.

Admission Procedure. Application with supporting documents and nonrefundable $25 fee to Office of Admissions.

Music Degrees Offered. Bachelor of Music; Bachelor of Arts in Education; Bachelor of Arts; Master of Music; Master of Arts.

Music Degree Requirements. In the program leading to the Bachelor of Music degree, the Department seeks to provide professional training. Options under this degree include majors in performance, theory, and composition. The degree Bachelor of Arts in Education with a major in music provides training for the student who wishes to teach music in elementary or secondary schools. In addition to the courses offered, practical and theoretical teacher training courses and classroom teaching experience are offered. The Bachelor of Arts degree with a major in music history and literature is designed for students who intend to enter college teaching, music librarianship, music journalism, music publishing, and some branches of the recording industry. A music merchandising option is available and is intended as an interdisciplinary approach to the modern world of music business utilizing the resources of the Department of Music and the School of Business.

The Master of Music degree is offered with concentrations in instrumental performance, vocal performance, conducting, music theory, and composition. The Master of Arts degree in music is offered with concentrations in music history/literature and music education.

General Program Areas. Composition, Conducting, Music Education, Music History, Music Literature, Music Merchandising, Music Theory, Performance.

Instruments Taught. Brass, Percussion, Piano, Stringed Instruments, Voice, Woodwinds.

Musical Facilities

Practice Facilities. The Department of Music facilities include a piano laboratory with 24 units, 32 practice rooms, an electronic music laboratory, and two large rehearsal rooms.

Concert Facilities. Recital Hall, seating 300.

Concerts/Musical Activities. Numerous public concerts and recitals are presented throughout the school year by faculty and students of the Department.

Music Library. The Music Library in the Music Building serves students and faculty with its collection of musical scores and recordings. Listening stations are provided.

Special Programs

Performance Groups. Band, Orchestra, Symphonic Choir, Music Theatre, Vocal Ensembles, Instrumental Ensembles.

Financial

Costs. Per academic year: Tuition in-state resident $1,212, out-of-state $4,206. Room and board $2,455.

Financial Aid. Financial assistance in the form of loans, grants, scholarships, and work/study employment is available. Scholarship/financial aid application due May 15.

Pacific Lutheran University
Department of Music

School of the Arts
Park Avenue and 121st Street
Tacoma
Washington 98447

Telephone. (206) 383-7601

Chief Administrator. David P. Robbins, Chair.

Pacific Lutheran University is a private institution affiliated with the American Lutheran Church. The University was founded in 1890. The 116-acre campus is located in Parkland, a suburb of Tacoma.

The Department of Music offers programs which prepare students for careers as conductors, composers, private teachers, classroom teachers, church organists and choir directors, music merchandising, performance, and concert management. Introductory music courses are offered to all students and are designed for exploration and self-fulfillment.

Accreditation. Northwest Association of Schools and Colleges; National Association of Schools of Music; National Council for Accreditation of Teacher Education.

Academic Information

Enrollment, Music Majors. (Total University) 3,758.

Music Faculty. 31.

Term System. Semester (4-1-4). Two summer sessions.

Entrance Requirements. High school graduation with rank in upper half of graduating class; recommended completion of 16 units including 4 English, 3 mathematics, 2 foreign language, 2 science, 2 social science; SAT or ACT required. GRE required for graduate study.

Admission Procedure. Application with supporting documents and nonrefundable $25 fee to Office of Admissions.

Music Degrees Offered. Bachelor of Music; Bachelor of Arts in Education; Bachelor of Arts; Bachelor of Fine Arts; Master of Music.

Music Degree Requirements. The Bachelor of Music degree is offered with emphases in performance (instrumental, organ, piano, vocal), theory and composition, and church music. The Bachelor of Arts in Education degree is offered with emphases in secondary choral, K-12 choral, elementary music specialist, secondary and elementary instrumental, and junior high school teaching. This degree is offered in cooperation with the School of Education. The Bachelor of Arts degree with a music major is offered within a liberal arts program. The Bachelor of Fine Arts degree in music is also available.

The Master of Music degree is is offered with concentrations in conducting, composition, music education, or performance.

General Program Areas. Church Music, Composition, Conducting, Music Theory, Performance.

Instruments Taught. Baritone, Bass, Bassoon, Clarinet, English Horn, Flute, French Horn, Guitar, Harp, Harpsichord, Oboe, Organ, Percussion, Piano, Saxophone, Trombone, Trumpet, Tuba, Viola, Violin, Violoncello.

Musical Facilities

Practice Facilities. Music facilities include space and instruments for individual practice and recital.

Concerts/Musical Activities. Student/faculty recitals and concerts; visiting artists.

Music Library. The Robert A.L. Mortvedt Library is the central multimedia learning resource center serving the entire University.

Special Programs

Performance Groups. Choir of the West, University Chorale, Opera Workshop, University Symphonic Band, University Jazz Ensemble, University Symphony Orchestra, Chamber Ensemble, Contemporary Directions Ensemble, Two-Piano Ensemble.

Financial

Costs. Per academic year: Tuition $7,155. Room $1,570. Board $1,640.

Financial Aid. Financial aid is available in the form of gift assistance (scholarships, talent awards, or grants), low interest deferred loans, or part-time employment. Financial aid/scholarship application due March 1.

University of Puget Sound
School of Music

1500 North Warner
Tacoma
Washington 98416

Telephone. (206) 756-3253, 756-3700

Chief Administrator. Dr. James Sorensen, Director.

In 1888, when Tacoma was only recently incorporated and Washington was still almost two years from statehood, a group of Methodist ministers and laymen secured a charter for the University of Puget Sound. In 1913, the school adopted a four-year college program and changed its name to the College of Puget Sound. In 1960, after several years of offering a full university curriculum, the college again became known as the University of Puget Sound. The 72-acre campus is located in

Tacoma's residential North End.

The School of Music, a member of the National Association of Schools of Music since 1947, offers courses leading to the Bachelor of Music and Bachelor of Arts degrees. University students with other majors may take music courses as electives. The School of Music contributes to the cultural climate of the campus and surrounding community through frequent recitals and appearances of performing groups.

Accreditation. Northwest Association of Schools and Colleges; National Association of Schools of Music.

Academic Information

Enrollment, Music Majors. (Total university) Full-time 1,074 men, 1,407 women; part-time 141 men, 203 women.

Music Faculty. 11; affiliate artist faculty 15.

Term System. Semester. Summer sessions include courses that are offered during the academic year; a tutorial course is offered for advanced high school juniors and seniors.

Entrance Requirements. High school graduate or GED; 14 units (4 in English, 3 mathematics, 2 laboratory science, 2 foreign language, 3 social studies). SAT or ACT; CEEB Achievement Test in English. 87% of applicants accepted. Foreign students must have TOEFL score of 550, financial statement showing sources of funds for education, and clear indication of academic ability.

Admission Procedure. Application with nonrefundable $20 fee due March 1. Audition required (special audition days or by appointment); placement examinations in music theory and music history for transfer students.

Music Degrees Offered. Bachelor of Music; Bachelor of Arts.

Music Degree Requirements. The Bachelor of Music is offered in performance (piano, voice, organ, guitar, and all orchestral instruments), music education, music business, and church music. Primary emphasis in the professional degrees is on the development of skills, concepts, and sensitivity essential to life as a professional musician. The Bachelor of Arts with a major in music is the traditional liberal arts degree. Emphasis is on a broad coverage of the field and on flexibility. Within the Bachelor of Arts program, the student can construct a program which will provide a background for the pursuit of advanced study in music theory, music history and musicology, composition, and music librarianship. The bachelor's degrees require the completion of 128 semester hours including the 40 semester hours of core requirements.

General Program Areas. Applied Music, Church Music, Conducting, Music Business, Music Education, Music History, Performance.

Instruments Taught. Brass, Guitar, Organ, Percussion, Piano, Stringed Instruments, Voice, Woodwinds.

Musical Facilities

Practice Facilities. 22 practice rooms. 4 organs (Schoenstein of San Francisco, Gebruder Spaeth of Germany, Herman Schlicker of Buffalo, Byard Dritts of Tacoma). 2 percussion-equipped practice rooms. 51 pianos (22 grands; 29 uprights); 10 pianos reserved for piano majors. Computer studio.

Concert Facilities. 2 concert halls.

Concerts/Musical Activities. Student recitals and concerts.

Music Library. 11,076 scores; 23,524 recorded compositions; 5,682 cassettes. Collections in jazz and composer biography. Listening facilities (cassette, stereo).

Special Programs

Performance Groups. Adelphian Concert Choir, University Wind Ensemble, University Symphony Orchestra, University Women's Chorus, Chamber Music, University Chorale, University Madrigal Singers, Jazz Band, Vocal Jazz Ensemble, University Band, Opera Workshop.

Affiliated Programs. Tacoma Symphony Orchestra, University of Puget Sound-Tacoma Civic Chorus.

Financial

Costs. Per academic year: Tuition $7,480. Room and board $3,240.

Financial Aid. A wide range of financial aid opportunities are available to Puget Sound students. College Work-Study program available.

Commentary

The University is currently raising funds for a new performing arts center.

University of Washington
School of Music
Seattle
Washington 98195

Telephone. (206) 543-1200

Chief Administrator. Daniel M. Neuman, Director.

The University of Washington, a state institution, was founded in 1861 in downtown Seattle. In 1895, it moved to its present 660-acre site on the shores of Lake Washington.

The School of Music prepares students for careers as composers, performers, teachers, or researchers. It also offers general courses to nonmajors designed to enhance the student's understanding of the art of music.

Accreditation. Northwest Association of Schools and Colleges; National Association of Schools of Music.

Academic Information

Enrollment, Music Majors. (Total University) 32,188.
Music Faculty. 59.

Term System. Quarter. Summer quarter is divided into two 4½ week terms.

Entrance Requirements. High school graduation or equivalent with completion of 14 units including 3 English, 3 mathematics, 1 laboratory science, 2 of a single foreign language, 2 social science; SAT, ACT, or Washington Pre-College Test required; combined test scores and GPA yield a competitive Admissions Index; audition required.

Admission Procedure. Application with $25 non-refundable fee due May 1.

Music Degrees Offered. Bachelor of Music; Bachelor of Arts; Master of Music; Master of Arts; Doctor of Musical Arts; Doctor of Philosophy.

Music Degree Requirements. The Bachelor of Music degree is designed for speciallly qualified students who wish to have professional training in performance or composition. A minimum of 180 credits is required. Major areas include applied music and composition. A concurrent Bachelor of Arts and Bachelor of Music degree program requires a minimum of 225 credits. Major areas available include composition, music history, piano, string instruments, voice, organ, orchestral instruments, music education, and systematic musicology. The double degree program requires five years of study. The Bachelor of Arts degree is offered with a major in music and requires the completion of 180 credits.

Graduate programs lead to the degrees of Master of Arts, Master of Music, Doctor of Musical Arts, and Doctor of Philosophy. Areas of specialization for the Master of Music and Doctor of Musical Arts degrees include performance (piano, organ, voice, strings, orchestral instruments), instrumental conducting, choral conducting, composition, opera production, and music education. The research-oriented programs lead to the Master of Arts and the Doctor of Philosophy degrees. Master's programs require the completion of 45 credits and the doctoral programs require 81 credits.

General Program Areas. Applied Music, Choral Conducting, Composition, Ethnomusicology, Instrumental Conducting, Music Education, Music History, Musicology, Opera, Performance.

Instruments Taught. Brass, Harp, Harpsichord, Organ, Percussion, Piano, Stringed Instruments, Voice.

Musical Facilities

Practice Facilities. 33 practice rooms. 3 organs. Percussion-equipped practice room. 32 pianos; 6 grand pianos reserved for piano majors. Electronic music studios.

Concert Facilities. 2 concert halls.

Concerts/Musical Activities. 700 concerts on campus sponsored by the Department of Music; visiting artists series.

Music Library. 16,552 books; 31,531 scores; 521 periodicals; 2,000 microfiche; 36,828 phonograph recordings. Listening facilities (cassette, stereo). Main library has an additional 5,000 music books; supplementary listening library. Special collections include: Americana; Massenet correspondence; Bartok letters; early records of Mozart vocal music.

Special Programs

Performance Groups. University Singers, University Symphony Orchestra, University Band, Vocal Jazz Ensemble, Opera Chorus, Woodwind Sinfonietta, Marching Band, Percussion Ensemble, University Oratorio Chorus, Studio Jazz Ensemble, University Chorale, Madrigal Singers, Piano Ensemble, Baroque Chamber Ensemble, Sinfonietta, Chamber Music, Opera Theater, Collegium Musicum.

Financial

Costs. Per academic year: Tuition undergraduate in-state resident $1,605, out-of-state $4,461; graduate resident $2,319, out-of-state $5,775. Private lesson fee $50 per quarter. Room and board $3,189.

Financial Aid. 57 music scholarships ranging from $200 to $3,300 (average $1,770). Scholarship application due February 15. Other sources of financial aid include state/federal grants and loans, part-time employment, and a College Work-Study program.

Commentary

The School of Music of the University of Washington plans to add a new wing to the music building, acquire a new concert organ, and provide a cohesive space for library facilities, currently divided among several locations.

Washington State University
Department of Music
School of Music and Fine Arts
Pullman
Washington 99164

Telephone. (509) 335-8524

Chief Administrator. H.O. Deming, Chairperson.

Since its founding in 1890, the state-supported University has been a multi-purpose public institution. It consists of seven colleges and a graduate school and offers more than 125 undergraduate major fields of study. The 415-acre campus is located in Pullman, nine miles west of the Idaho border in the southeastern part of Washington.

The chief objectives of the Music Department are to provide students with a foundation in the analysis and criticism of music and to guide them toward acquiring discriminating judgment in a progressive musical environment; to train teachers of music who can be effective in contemporary society; to assist the aspiring performer and composer in reaching his/her highest potential of artistic capacity; to contribute toward a varied humanistic education within the university community.

Accreditation. Northwest Association of Schools and Colleges; National Association of Schools of Music.

Academic Information

Enrollment, Music Majors. (Total University) full-time 14,530, part-time 906.

Music Faculty. 22.

Term System. Semester. 8-week summer session.

Entrance Requirements. High school graduation with 2.5 GPA or GED; recommend 4 units English, mathematics through geometry and trigonometry, 2 science, 1 laboratory science, 2 foreign language, 3 social studies; admission is based on an index system of GPA plus test scores; audition required. GRE required for graduate study.

Admission Procedure. Application with $25 non-refundable fee due May 1.

Music Degrees Offered. Bachelor of Music; Bachelor of Arts; Master of Arts.

Music Degree Requirements. The Bachelor of Music degree requires the completion of a minimum of 128 semester hours. It is a four-year program with options for specialization in performance, composition and theory, and music education. At least 42 of the 128 hours required must be upper-division courses. The Bachelor of Arts degree in music is designed to meet the needs of students wishing a broad liberal arts background. Of the total 120 hours required for a degree in this program, a minimum of 48 credits in music is required, 40 of which must be in upper-division courses. The Music Concentration may be in either theory-history or performance.

The Master of Arts degree in music requires the completion of a minimum of 30 semester hours.

General Program Areas. Composition, Music Education, Music History, Music Theory, Performance.

Instruments Taught. Baritone, Bass, Bassoon, Clarinet, Flute, Guitar, Horn, Oboe, Organ, Percussion, Piano, Saxophone, Trombone, Trumpet, Tuba, Viola, Violin, Violoncello, Voice.

Musical Facilities

Practice Facilities. 32 practice rooms. 2 pipe organs (Schauntz, Holtkamp). 3 percussion-equipped practice rooms. 25 pianos (11 grands, 14 uprights); 7 grand pianos reserved for piano majors.

Concert Facilities. 2 concert halls.

Concerts/Musical Activities. The Music Department presents a varied program of hundreds of concerts, recitals, workshops, and master classes each year. These presentations are given by faculty, students, and visiting artists.

Music Library. 9,000 books; 3,200 scores; 150 periodicals; 18,000 recordings; 3,500 tapes (open reel, cassette, video). Most books and reference materials housed in main library; listening library located in Music Building. 41 listening carrels; matrix switchboard connected to the carrels. Special collections include 10,000 titles of pop music (1880-present); 1,800 instrumental ensemble scores and parts; piano and vocal literature; software theory packages for use with microcomputers.

Special Programs

Performance Groups. Opera Workshop, Choir, University Singers, Ensemble Laboratory, Vocal Ensembles, Chamber Music, Concert Band, Jazz-Lab Band, Percussion Ensemble, Marching Band, Varsity Band, Symphony Orchestra, Wind Symphony, Chamber Orchestra.

Foreign Programs. Study abroad exchange programs in Wales, West Germany, Sweden, Japan, India, China, Scotland, and Denmark.

Financial

Costs. Per academic year: Tuition undergraduate in-state resident $1,606, out-of-state $4,462; graduate in-state $2,320, out-of-state $5,776. Room $1,100. Board $1,450.

Financial Aid. Scholarships range from $500 to $1,606 (average $1,000). Scholarship application due March 15. Other sources of financial aid include institutional and state/federal grants and loans, part-time employment, and a College Work-Study program.

Western Washington University Department of Music

College of Fine and Performing Arts
516 North High Street
Bellingham
Washington 98225

Telephone. (206) 676-3130

Chief Administrator. C. Bruce Pullan, Chair.

Western Washington University, a state institution, was established in 1893 as the New Whatcom State Normal School. From a normal school, the institution evolved into a degree-granting institution in 1933, College of Education in 1937, State College in 1961, and a university in 1977. The 224-acre campus is located in Belligham, a city of 46,000 in the northwestern corner of the state near the Canadian border.

The Department of Music, which was founded in 1947 and became part of the College of Fine and Performing Arts in 1976, provides music education within the context of a liberal arts institution. Music offerings are available to the general student population as well as the music major. The Department also strives to provide cultural enrichment for the surrounding local communities.

Accreditation. Northwest Association of of Schools and Colleges; National Association of Schools of Music; National Council for Accreditation of Teacher Education.

Academic Information

Enrollment, Music Majors. Undergraduate 184, graduate 19.

Music Faculty. Full-time 15, part-time 12.

Term System. Quarter. Six-week summer session; some workshops.

Entrance Requirements. High school graduation or equivalent with a 2.5 GPA or with rank in upper half of graduating class; 4 units English, 3 mathematics, 2 laboratory science, 3 social studies, 2 foreign language; Washington Pre-College Test is required for state residents, SAT or ACT for nonresidents; audition required (during "Western Preview" in April or during registration period. GRE required for graduate students; incoming graduate students and transfer students must take theory and history advisement/placement examinations.

Admission Procedure. Application with $25 non-refundable fee due September 1, December 1, and March 1.

Music Degrees Offered. Bachelor of Music; Bachelor of Arts; Master of Music.

Music Degree Requirements. Five undergraduate degree programs are offered by the Department of Music. The Bachelor of Music degree with majors in music performance, music history and literature, music composition, and jazz studies is offered for those who wish to continue advanced musical study in graduate school, enter private studio teaching, or launch a professional career in music. The Bachelor of Music degree with a music education major with concentrations in choral music, instrumental music, or elementary classroom music is offered for those who plan to teach in the public schools. The degree Bachelor of Arts in Education is offered with an elementary music major. State certification to teach is received concurrently with the granting of the degree. The baccalaureate requires the completion of a minimum of 180 quarter hours. The Master of Music degree requires the completion of 45 quarter hours.

General Program Areas. Composition, Jazz Studies, Music Education, Music History, Music Literature, Performance.

Instruments Taught. Brass, Guitar, Organ, Percussion, Piano, Stringed Instruments, Voice, Woodwinds.

Musical Facilities

Practice Facilities. 25 practice rooms. 6 organs (2 Moeller, Wilhelm, Pembroke, Martin Renshaw, Werner Bosch). Percussion-equipped practice room. 25 pianos (20 uprights, 5 grands); 5 grand pianos reserved for piano majors. Electronic music studio.

Concert Facilities. Concert Hall, seating 700; Auditorium, 1,200.

Community Facilities. Various local churches; Mount Baker Theatre; Birch Bay Grange Hall.

Concerts/Musical Activities. Student/faculty concerts and recitals; visiting artists.

Music Library. The Music Library is located in the Performing Arts Center and includes an extensive collection of scores, recordings, and books about music.

Special Programs

Featured Programs. Fairhaven College, a cluster college of the University, has a limited music program consisting mainly of popular music and music recording.

Performance Groups. University Choir, Concert Choir, Chamber Choirs, Symphonic Band, Wind Ensemble, Jazz Ensembles, University Symphony Orchestra, Chamber Music, Opera, Collegium Musicum, Small Ensembles.

Financial

Costs. Per academic year: Tuition in-state resident $1,200, out-of-state $4,194.

Financial Aid. 21 music scholarships ranging from $100 to $1,500. Other sources of financial aid include institutional scholarships, state/federal grants and loans, part-time employment, and a College Work-Study program.

WEST VIRGINIA

Marshall University
Department of Music
College of Fine Arts
Hal Greer Boulevard and 3rd Avenue
Huntington
West Virginia 25701

Telephone. (304) 696-3117
Chief Administrator. Dr. Donald R. Williams. Director.

Marshall University was established as Marshall Academy in 1838. Through the years it evolved from an academy to a teachers college and in 1961 achieved university status. The 86-acre campus is located near the center of Huntington on the Ohio River, close to the boundary of Ohio, Kentucky, and West Virginia.

The Department of Music goals are to educate and train students seeking professions in the Fine Arts, to support the University's general academic curriculum, to present regular varied programs for the enrichment of students and the community, and to provide leadership in the Fine Arts.

Accreditation. North Central Association of Colleges and Schools; National Association of Schools of Music.

Academic Information

Enrollment, Music Majors. (Total University) Full-time 6,825, part-time 4,493.
Music Faculty. 19.
Term System. Semester. Two 5-week summer sessions.
Entrance Requirements. High school graduation or equivalent; ACT required; placement audition in applicant's applied music area.
Admission Procedure. Application due 2 weeks before registration.
Music Degrees Offered. Bachelor of Fine Arts; Bachelor of Arts; Master of Arts.
Music Degree Requirements. The Bachelor of Fine Arts degree with a music option requires the completion of 82 credit hours of study in music. This is divided into the core curriculum of 49 credit hours and one of three concentrations of additional 33 credit hours of coursework. The concentrations include performance, music theory and composition, and music history and literature. The Bachelor of Arts degree with specialization in music teaching is offered through the College of Education. The baccalaureate degrees require a total of 128 credit hours.

The Master of Arts degree in music with a major in music education requires a minimum of 36 hours of coursework. In addition to this option, the Department offers graduate degrees with emphasis in applied music performance, music history and literature, and music theory and composition. The program for a major in these areas is 32 hours and must include 26 hours in major, cognate, and elective areas of music.

General Program Areas. Composition, Music Education, Music History, Music Literature, Music Theory, Performance.

Instruments Taught. Baritone, Bass, Bassoon, Clarinet, Flute, French Horn, Guitar, Oboe, Organ, Percussion, Piano, Saxophone, Trumpet, Tuba, Viola, Violin, Violoncello, Voice.

Musical Facilities

Practice Facilities. 35 practice rooms. 2 percussion-equipped practice rooms. 3 organs (Wicks and Rogers). 35 pianos (Yamaha, Steinway, Lester, Baldwin grands; 5 Yamaha, 22 Baldwin, 5 Mason/Hamlin uprights); 3 grand pianos reserved for piano majors. Electronic music studio; recording studio.

Concert Facilities. Smith Recital Hall; Old Main Auditorium.

Concerts/Musical Activities. Marshall Artists Series; concerts/recitals.

Music Library. 5,200 books; 5,500 scores; 50 periodicals; 7,500 recordings; 65 filmstrips; 1,950 reel-to-reel tapes. Listening facilities (3 cassette players, 2 reel-to-reel tape players; 6 stereo turntables). Music books and periodicals are housed in Main Library.

Special Programs

Performance Groups. Choral Union, University Chorus, Vocal Jazz Ensemble, Opera Workshop, Chamber Chorus, Marshall Community Symphony, Flute Ensemble, String Ensemble, Woodwind Ensemble, Percussion Ensemble, Brass Ensemble, Jazz Ensemble, Symphonic Band, Marching Band, Pep Band, Wind Symphony.

Financial

Costs. Per academic year: Tuition in-state resident $960, out-of-state $2,600. Room and board $2,578.

Financial Aid. Music scholarships range from $100 to $760. Scholarship application due one month before registration period. Other sources of financial aid include institutional scholarships, state/federal grants and loans, student employment, and a College Work-Study program.

West Virginia University
Division of Music
College of Creative Arts
P.O. Box 6111
Morgantown
West Virginia 26506

Telephone. (304) 293-4091

Chief Administrator. C.B. Wilson, Chair.

West Virginia University is a state institution established in 1867 as the Agricultural College of West Virginia. It achieved university status in 1895. Enrollment exceeds 19,000 students. The campuses cover over 800 acres with 89 buildings, including the downtown campus near the center of Morgantown.

The School of Music was founded at West Virginia University in 1895. It became the Division of Music of the College of Creative Arts in the early 1960s. In 1968, the Divisions of Music, Art, and Theatre moved to the new Creative Arts Center.

Accreditation. North Central Association of Colleges and Schools; National Association of Schools of Music; National Council for Accreditation of Teacher Education.

Academic Information

Enrollment, Music Majors. Full-time 250, part-time 50. 10 foreign students.

Music Faculty. Full-time 37, part-time 5.

Term System. Semester. Academic year from late August to early May. Two 6-week summer sessions from mid-May to mid-August.

Entrance Requirements. Admission is based on high school courses taken, GPA, and ACT. For residents of West Virginia a GPA of 2.0 or an ACT composite score of 16 or SAT 740 is required; nonresidents, 2.25 GPA

and ACT composite score of 18 or SAT 800; audition required in the principal performance area. Foreign students must have a TOEFL score of 550 and have appropriate academic credentials. Advanced placement by faculty assessment.

Admission Procedure. Application for admission to Office of Admissions and Records; apply for admission to Division of Music.

Music Degrees Offered. Bachelor of Music; Master of Music; Doctor of Musical Arts; Doctor of Philosophy.

Music Degree Requirements. The Bachelor of Music degree is offered with specialized programs in performance (applied music), theory-composition, music history-theory, and music education. Each of these curricula prepares the student for the added career option of private studio teaching in the principal performance area. Piano majors in performance may choose an alternative emphasis in pedagogy, accompanying, or jazz. Students who complete a curriculum in music education will have satisfied course requirements to teach both vocal and instrumental music, as well as general music, in the elementary and secondary schools, grades K-12. The degree requires the completion of 128 to 135 hours depending on curriculum pursued.

The Master of Music degree is offered in the same curricular areas as the baccalaureate programs. The degree requires the completion of 30 to 36 hours.

The Doctor of Musical Arts degree is offered with emphasis in composition, piano, voice, organ. The Doctor of Philosophy degree is offered in music education, theory, musicology. The doctoral degrees require comprehensive examinations and a complete dissertation (or equivalent).

General Program Areas. Composition, Music Education, Music History, Music Theory, Musicology, Performance.

Instruments Taught. Bass, Bassoon, Clarinet, Euphonium, Flute, Harpsichord, Horn, Oboe, Organ, Percussion, Piano, Saxophone, Trombone, Trumpet, Tuba, Viola, Violin, Violoncello, Voice.

Musical Facilities

Practice Facilities. 38 practice rooms. Special practice facilities for organists and percussionists. Electronic music studio.

Concert Facilities. Concert Theater, seating 1,400; Opera Theater, 200; Studio Theater, 200; Choral Recital Hall, 170.

Concerts/Musical Activities. 4 to 5 concerts/recitals per week.

Music Library. 25,000 volumes; 11,000 recordings. Listening facilities (stereo). Special collections include the Frey Jazz Collection.

Special Programs

Performance Groups. Glee Clubs, University Choir, Collegium Musicum, Marching Band, Concert Band, Wind Ensemble, University Choral Union, Opera Theater, Symphony Band, Mountaineer Marching Band, Varsity Band, Percussion Ensemble, Jazz Ensemble, Collegium Musicum, University-Community Symphony Orchestra.

Financial

Costs. Per academic year: Tuition in-state resident $1,-260, out-of-state $3,240. Room and board $3,041. Practice room fee $20.

Financial Aid. Division of Music scholarships are awarded independently of other University resources. Entering students are also encouraged to make application to the University Financial Aid Office which administers federal and state programs in the form of grants, loans, and work opportunities.

Commentary

West Virginia University is the only institution in Virginia or West Virginia which offers both the D.M.A. and Ph.D. in music. While there are ample resources for scholarly doctoral research, the D.M.A. performance options are limited to composition, piano, voice, and organ. Piano majors, in particular, have a diverse choice of curriculum emphases. Undergraduates may pursue a five-year double degree program in music education and applied music. An emphasis in jazz studies at the University has been proposed.

WISCONSIN

Lawrence University
Conservatory of Music
115 North Park Avenue
Appleton
Wisconsin 54912

Telephone. (414) 735-6614

Chief Administrator. Dr. Colin Murdoch, Dean of the Conservatory.

Amos A. Lawrence, a Boston merchant, pledged the initial sum of $10,000 to endow the school with a matching grant from the Methodists. The Lawrence Institute was granted a charter, a name that was changed to Lawrence University when classes first began in 1849. The University merged in 1964 with Milwaukee-Downer College for Women. Since this merger, the University has continued symbolically the separate identity of each institution by designating Lawrence College for Men and a Downer College for Women. Lawrence University is the second oldest coeducational institution in the country. It has an enrollment of over 1,000 students drawn from 40 states and 20 foreign countries.

The present campus, situated on 84 acres, contains 32 instructional, recreational, and administrative buildings. It is located in Appleton, a city of 60,000 in east-central Wisconsin, 90 miles north of Milwaukee.

The Conservatory of Music, initially founded in 1874, came into its own during the 30-year administration of Dr. Samuel Plantz commencing in 1894. The introduction of curricular offerings in public school music and music history, and the acquisition of a building devoted exclusively to music instruction, all combined to lay the groundwork for a full-fledged conservatory. Today, the Conservatory of Music affords students a blend of professional music training and liberal education, producing composers, performers, and music educators.

Accreditation. North Central Association of Colleges and Schools; National Association of Schools of Music.

Academic Information

Enrollment, Music Majors. Full-time men 500, women 550; part-time 15 men, 15 women. Foreign students 40.

Music Faculty. Full-time 108, part-time 6.

Term System. Trimester. No summer session.

Entrance Requirements. Lawrence admits students who can profit from what the University has to offer. It is recommended that high school students take at least 16 academic units from the areas of English, mathematics, history, social studies, physical sciences, and foreign languages; SAT or ACT. Candidates for the professional Bachelor of Music degree are judged on musicianship, musical background, performance potential, and teachers' recommendations, in addition to general academic ability.

Admission Procedure. In addition to the regular application forms, conservatory applicants must complete a Supplementary Music Blank, take a music theory examination, and audition in person or by recording. Application due March 1; nonrefundable application fee $25.

Music Degrees Offered. Bachelor of Arts in Music; Bachelor of Music in Music Education; Bachelor of Music in Theory-Composition.

Music Degree Requirements. Thirty-six term course credits (120 credits); six terms in residence; completion of requirements in the major in the category selected.

General Program Areas. Music Composition, Music Education, Music Theory, Performance.

Instruments Taught. Bass, Bassoon, Clarinet, Euphonium, Flute, Guitar, Harp, Harpsichord, Horn, Oboe, Organ, Percussion, Piano, Saxophone, Trombone, Trumpet, Tuba, Viola, Violin, Violoncello, Voice.

Musical Facilities

Practice Facilities. Practice facilities available for organists (Roderer-Evanston, Schlicker, Schantz organs). 3 practice rooms for percussionists. 80 practice pianos; 10 grand pianos reserved for piano majors; 33 piano practice rooms.

Concert Facilities. The Music-Drama Center houses teaching facilities for the Conservatory of Music and the Theatre Department and is the site of concerts, recitals, dramatic productions, films, and lectures. In the Peabody Wing of the Center are rehearsal rooms, studios, numerous practice rooms. Various recitals and the University's Chamber Music Series are held in the 250-seat William E. Harper Hall. The Lawrence Memorial Chapel, built in 1919 and refurbished in 1964, seats 1,249 and is used for the Lawrence Artist Series and ensemble concerts. Over the years, the Chapel has been host to such performing artists as Pablo Casals, the Juilliard String Quartet, Fritz Kreisler, and Isaac Stern. The Chapel contains music studios and a four-manual Schantz organ with an electronic carillon.

Concerts/Musical Activities. Weekly student and faculty recitals; frequent concerts performed by Lawrence choirs, the jazz ensemble, the symphony, and the wind ensemble.

Music Library. The Seeley G. Mudd Library contains a collection of over 260,000 volumes. The music collections include over 7,500 scores and 10,000 recordings.

Special Programs

Performance Groups. Lawrence Concert Choir, Downer Chorus, Lawrence Chamber Singers, Lawrence Choral Society, Vocal Jazz Ensemble, Opera Theatre, Wind Ensemble, Symphony Orchestra, Jazz Ensemble, Jazz Lab Band, Percussion Ensemble, Chamber Music Ensemble.

Foreign Programs. Comprehensive set of overseas programs including a London Center.

Financial

Costs. Comprehensive fee per three-term year: $11,826 ($9,252 for students not living in University halls).

Financial Aid. 55% of student body receives some form of financial aid; 50 scholarships ranging from $100 to $3,000. Part-time employment (earnings ranging from $200 to $1,400) and College Work-Study program available.

Commentary

The Lawrence Conservatory of Music offers a five-year B.M./B.A. combined degree program, utilizing the institution's dual identity as liberal arts college and music conservatory.

University of Wisconsin - Eau Claire
Department of Music
Eau Claire
Wisconsin 54701

Telephone. (715) 836-2284
Chief Administrator. Dr. Merton Johnson, Chairman.

The University of Wisconsin - Eau Claire was founded in 1916 as the Eau Claire State Normal School. Its present name was adopted when it gained university standing in 1964. The 333-acre campus is located on the banks of the Chippewa River in western Wisconsin.

All baccalaureate programs offered by the Department of Music emphasize the development of the skills and sensitivity required of the professional musician. Courses for the general university study are also available.

Accreditation. North Central Association of Colleges and Schools; National Association of Schools of Music; National Association for Music Therapy.

Academic Information

Enrollment, Music Majors. (Total University) Full-time 4,067 men, 5,277 women; part-time 423 men, 641 women.

Music Faculty. 36.

Term System. Semester. 8-week summer session.

Entrance Requirements. High school graduation or equivalent; recommend 16 units including 3 English, 2 mathematics, 1 laboratory science, 1 social studies, 9 academic electives; ACT preferred, SAT accepted; audition required on instrument; piano placement examination; theory and history placement examination for transfer students.

Admission Procedure. Application accepted on a rolling admissions basis.

Music Degrees Offered. Bachelor of Music; Bachelor of Music Education; Bachelor of Music Therapy; Bachelor of Arts; Bachelor of Science.

Music Degree Requirements. The Bachelor of Music is offered with majors in applied instrumental, applied voice, applied piano, applied organ, theory/composition, and music therapy. The degree requires the completion of a minimum of 128 semester hours of specific departmental requirements and the general education core curriculum. The Bachelor of Music Education is offered with concentrations in instrumental and general music teaching, choral and general music teaching (secondary emphasis), and choral and general music teaching (elementary emphasis). The degree requires the completion of 135 to 136 semester hours. The Bachelor of Arts and Bachelor of Science degrees in music are offered within the context of a liberal arts program.

General Program Areas. Applied Music, Composition, Music Education, Music Theory.

Instruments Taught. Baritone, Bass, Bassoon, Clarinet, Cornet, Flute, French Horn, Harp, Harpsichord, Oboe, Organ, Percussion, Piano, Saxophone, Trombone, Trumpet, Tuba, Viola, Violin, Violoncello, Voice.

Musical Facilities

Practice Facilities. 46 practice rooms. 3 organs (Skinner concert organ, 2 practice organs). 65 pianos (uprights); 5 grand pianos reserved for piano majors.

Electronic music studio.

Concert Facilities. Gantner Concert Hall, seating 650; Phillips Recital Hall, 200.

Concerts/Musical Activities. Student/faculty concerts and recitals; visiting artists.

Music Library. 2,200 recordings. Listening facilities (cassette, stereo).

Special Programs

Featured Programs. University Extension at Rice Lake offers Department of Music credit classes during the summer.

Performance Groups. Symphony Band, Concert Band, University Orchestra, Summer Band, Jazz Ensemble, Concert Choir, Summer Choir, Oratorio Society, Men's Glee Club (The Statesmen), Women's Chorus, Brass Ensemble, Woodwind Ensemble, Percussion Ensemble, Chamber Choir, Vocal Jazz Ensemble, Marimba Ensemble, Piano Ensemble.

Financial

Costs. Per academic year: Tuition in-state resident $1,447, out-of-state $4,250. Room $940 to $1,140. Board $1,100.

Financial Aid. Scholarships are available to a limited number of applicants who demonstrate superior musical ability. An application for the audition and placement constitutes an application for a Department of Music scholarship. Other sources of financial aid include state/federal grants and loans, part-time employment, and a College Work-Study program.

University of Wisconsin - La Crosse
Department of Music
1725 State Street
La Crosse
Wisconsin 54601

Telephone. (608) 785-8409

Chief Administrator. Dr. William V. Estes, Chairperson.

The University of Wisconsin - La Crosse is a multipurpose liberal arts university offering graduate and undergraduate programs. The 67-acre campus is located in a residential section of La Crosse, 170 miles northwest of Milwaukee.

The Department of Music offers preparation for careers in public school teaching or professional performance, as well as instruction for those students who major in music as part of a liberal arts education.

Accreditation. North Central Association of Colleges and Schools; National Association of Schools of Music; National Council for Accreditation of Teacher Education.

Academic Information

Enrollment, Music Majors. (Total University) 8,826.
Music Faculty. 14.

Term System. Semester. One summer session.

Entrance Requirements. High school graduation or equivalent with a C average; ACT required. GRE required for graduate study.

Admission Procedure. Application with supporting documents to Director of Admissions reviewed on a rolling admissions basis.

Music Degrees Offered. Bachelor of Arts; Bachelor of Science; Master of Science.

Music Degree Requirements. The Bachelor of Arts and the Bachelor of Science degrees are offered with emphases in performance, music history, and music theory. Programs are offered through the College of Arts, Letters, and Sciences and the School of Health and Human Services. A general music major program is offered through the College of Education leading to the Bachelor of Science degree. Emphases are available in elementary and secondary education, choral music (secondary education), and instrumental music (secondary education). A Master of Science degree in music education is also offered.

General Program Areas. Music Education, Music History, Music Theory, Performance.

Instruments Taught. Brass, Percussion, Piano, Stringed Instruments, Voice, Woodwinds.

Musical Facilities

Practice Facilities. The Department of Music is located in the Fine Arts Building; rehearsal and practice rooms.

Concert Facilities. Recital hall; theatre.

Concerts/Musical Activities. Student and faculty recitals and concerts; visiting artists.

Music Library. The Murphy Library houses over 480,000 volumes and serves the academic programs of the Department of Music.

Special Programs

Performance Groups. Band, University Singers, Orchestra, Mannerchoir, Women's Chorus, Concert Band, Choral Union, Opera Workshop, Instrumental Ensembles, Stage Band-Tribe, Stage Band-Council, Collegiates, Chamber Choir.

Financial

Costs. Per academic year: Tuition in-state resident $1,464, out-of-state $4,464. Room and board $1,615.

Financial Aid. Financial aid is available in the form of state/federal scholarships, grants, loans, and part-time employment. Financial aid/scholarship application due March 1.

University of Wisconsin - Madison
School of Music
455 North Park Street
Madison
Wisconsin 53706

Telephone. (608) 263-5972, 263-1900
Chief Administrator. Eudice Boardmann Meske, Director.

The University of Wisconsin - Madison, located in the state capital, is a public, land-grant institution, founded in 1849. It combines, on a single campus, nine schools and three colleges.

The School of Music offers a wide spectrum of degree programs which allow the individual student to attain a breadth of knowledge in the art of music and to acquire skills in a specific professional major. The curriculum is structured to prepare graduates for careers in composing, performing, teaching at all levels, music administration, music business, and/or promoting the arts as community leaders.

Accreditation. North Central Association of Colleges and Schools; National Association of Schools of Music.

Academic Information

Enrollment, Music Majors. (Total University) Full-time 36,836, part-time 7,382.

Music Faculty. 57.

Term System. Semester. One 8-week and two coinciding 4-week summer sessions.

Entrance Requirements. High school graduation; rank in upper 50 percent of graduating class; ACT or ACT accepted but not required; recommend completion of 16 units including 3 English, 2 mathematics, 4 from combination of foreign language, science, and social science, 3 additional academic subjects; audition required; performance and perception tests.

Admission Procedure. Application with $10 non-refundable fee due March 1.

Music Degrees Offered. Bachelor of Music; Bachelor of Arts; Bachelor of Science; Master of Music; Master of Arts; Doctor of Musical Arts; Doctor of Philosophy.

Music Degree Requirements. The Bachelor of Music degree is offered with concentration in piano, organ, brass instruments, percussion, woodwinds, strings, harp, voice, composition, jazz studies, and music theory. The degree requires the completion of a total of 130 credits. The Bachelor of Music in music education is offered with concentrations in general certification (grades K-12), instrumental certification (grades K-12), and choral certification (grades 7-12). The Bachelor of Arts and Bachelor of Science degrees with an emphasis in performance or music history make it possible for students to continue music study within the context of a liberal arts program. Either degree requires the completion of 120 semester credit.

The School of Music offers programs of study leading to the degrees Master of Music, Master of Arts in Music, Doctor of Musical Arts (A.Mus.D.), with concentration in voice, composition, performance in all orchestral instruments, piano, organ, and choral conducting, and Doctor of Philosophy with concentrations in music history, ethnomusicology, theory, or music education. These programs prepare students for teaching, administration, and scholarly research; for professional work in arranging, composing, conducting, and performing; and for positions in publishing, recording, or the dramatic arts.

General Program Areas. Composition, Conducting, Ethnomusicology, Jazz Studies, Music Education, Music History, Music Theory, Performance.

Instruments Taught. Bassoon, Brass, Clarinet, Euphonium, Flute, Harp, Horn, Oboe, Organ, Percussion, Piano, Saxophone, Trombone, Trumpet, Tuba, Viola, Violin, Violoncello, Voice, Woodwinds.

Musical Facilities

Practice Facilities. 150 practice rooms. 6 organ practice rooms. 5 percussion-equipped practice rooms. 84 pianos (52 uprights, 32 grands); 24 grand pianos reserved for piano majors. Electronic studio; composition studio; computer-assisted instruction studio.

Concert Facilities. Mills Hall, seating 800; Morphy Hall, 200; Eastman Recital Hall (primarily for organ recitals).

Concerts/Musical Activities. Student/faculty recitals and concerts; visiting artists.

Music Library. Mills Music Library is located in the lower floor of the Memorial Library. 40,000 books and periodicals; 60,000 scores; 100,000 recordings. Listening facilities (65 cassette decks, 11 stereo stations).

Special collections include: Band Library; Choral Library; Music Education Curriculum laboratory; pre-1900 imprints; music written by Wisconsin composers; materials of American musical theatre; film music and ethnomusicological sound recording collections; musical instrument collection.

Special Programs

Featured Programs. The Arts Outreach Program, funded by the Brittingham Trust and other gifts, provides opportunity for Wisconsin residents to enjoy the musical offerings of the University.

Performance Groups. Concert Choir, Chamber Singers, Master's Singers, Pro Musica, Women's Chorus, Choral Union, Wind Ensemble, Symphonic Band, Concert Band, University Band, Varsity Band, Marching Band, University Symphony, Opera Workshop, Jazz Ensemble, Black Music Ensemble, Collegium Musicum, Percussion Ensemble, two Gamelan Ensembles, Brass Quintet, Horn Choir.

Foreign Programs. Music students may practice teach in England.

Affiliated Programs. For over 50 years, the University of Wisconsin has provided enrichment opportunities for junior and senior high school students during Summer Music Clinic. A variety of experiences may be elected by students in applied study, chamber and large ensembles, and other courses designed to enhance musical understanding and musicianship.

Financial

Costs. Per academic year: Tuition in-state resident $1,570, out-of-state $4,914. Room and board $2,774.

Financial Aid. Limited funds are available for scholarships awarded by the School of Music to outstanding applicants. Other sources of financial aid include institutional scholarships, fellowships, and assistantships; state/federal grants and loans; part-time employment; College Work-Study program.

Commentary

The University of Wisconsin at Madison offers many options at the doctoral level for either the A.Mus.D. or Ph.D. Ethnomusicology and music history are particularly strong disciplines within the curriculum. Where no appropriate formal doctoral program exists, an interdisciplinary program may be proposed by the student.

University of Wisconsin - Milwaukee
Music Department
School of Fine Arts
Milwaukee
Wisconsin 53201

Telephone. (414) 963-4393

Chief Administrator. Dr. Gerard McKenna, Chairperson.

The University of Wisconsin - Milwaukee opened in 1885 as the Milwaukee State Normal School. In 1927, it became the Milwaukee State Teachers College and then the Wisconsin State College, Milwaukee in 1951. The present day institution was formally established in 1956 with the merger of the Wisconsin State College, Milwaukee and the University of Wisconsin's Extension Center in Milwaukee. The University is composed of 10 colleges and schools which provide liberal arts and science courses in the College of Letters and Science and professional education in various schools and colleges. The campus of 90 acres is located in a residential neighborhood several miles from downtown Milwaukee.

The Department of Music offers five undergraduate courses of study. Applied music studies in voice, keyboard, or other instruments prepare the student for both performance and studio teaching. The certification course by the State Department of Public Instruction prepares the student to teach and supervise public school music. A program in music literature studies prepare the

student for specialization in musicology and music criticism, and provide a strong background for subsequent graduate work in the fine arts. Studies in music theory and composition are offered to prepare the student for specialization in creative musical writing and related analytical skills. Music therapy studies prepare the student for certification by the National Association for Music Therapy as a Registered Music Therapist. Graduate curricula lead to the Master of Music or Master of Fine Arts degrees.

Accreditation. North Central Association of Colleges and Schools; National Association of Schools of Music; National Council for Accreditation of Teacher Education.

Academic Information

Enrollment, Music Majors. Full-time 103 men, 147 women.

Music Faculty. Full-time 34, part-time 1.

Term System. Semester. One summer session.

Entrance Requirements. Accredited high school graduation or equivalent with rank in upper 75% of class; completion of a minimum of 12 high school units from the academic areas of English, social studies, mathematics, science, and foreign languages; SAT or ACT for those high school graduates not in top three-quarters of class; audition required. GRE required for graduate programs.

Admission Procedure. Application accepted on a rolling basis.

Music Degrees Offered. Bachelor of Fine Arts; Master of Music; Master of Fine Arts.

Music Degree Requirements. The Bachelor of Fine Arts degree requires the completion of 130 credits, distributed among: music courses (as specified in each curriculum) 80 to 85 credits; core curriculum 45 credits; and 0 to 5 credits of general electives. Eight semesters of enrollment in a performing organization are required of all applied majors except piano; at least six semesters are required of all other departmental majors.

The Master of Music degree program permits concentration in applied music, conducting, music education, music history and literature, and theory and composition. The minimum degree requirement is 30 graduate credits. The Master of Fine Arts is offered through a cooperative program with the Department of Theatre and Dance. This program is designed to prepare the student for a professional career and includes two discipline areas: chamber music performance and composition.

General Program Areas. Applied Music, Chamber Music, Composition, Conducting, Music Education, Music History, Music Librarianship, Music Literature, Music Theory, Music Therapy, Musicology.

Instruments Taught. Baritone, Bassoon, Clarinet, Cornet, Flute, French Horn, Harp, Harpsichord, Oboe, Percussion, Piano, Saxophone, Trombone, Trumpet,

Tuba, Viola, Violin, Violoncello, Voice.

Musical Facilities

Practice Facilities. 50 practice rooms. 3 percussion-equipped practice rooms. 70 pianos (uprights and grands); 20 grand pianos reserved for piano majors. 3 electronic music studios.

Concert Facilities. The Fine Arts complex includes theatre and recital hall.

Concerts/Musical Activities. Ensembles; student/faculty recitals and concerts; visiting artists.

Music Library. The Golda Meir Library houses more than 1,350,000 volumes and serves the information requirements and research needs of the university community.

Special Programs

Featured Programs. The Institute of Chamber Music is a two-year program leading to a Certificate in Chamber Music Performance. In cooperation with the School of Library and Information Science, the Department of Music offers a Master of Music/Master of Library and Information Science program to prepare students for positions as music librarians.

Performance Groups. Concert Chorale, Choral Masterworks, Madrigal Singers, Vocal Jazz Ensemble, Symphony Band, Symphony Orchestra, University Band, Opera Theatre.

Financial

Costs. Per academic year: Tuition in-state resident $813.15, out-of-state $1,155.65. Room $1,461. Board $1,400.

Financial Aid. 44 music scholarships available ranging from $100 to $1,000 (average award $500). Scholarship application due on varying dates. Other sources of financial aid include student employment, a College Work-Study program, and state/federal loans.

Commentary

The University of Wisconsin - Milwaukee features an unusual approach to chamber music study. Students admitted to the Institute of Chamber Music receive a concentrated experience in chamber music as well as a carefully planned course load insuring sufficient practice time. The Fine Arts Quartet and Woodwind Arts Quintet comprise the Institute faculty.

University of Wisconsin - Oshkosh
Department of Music
Arts and Communication Center
800 Algoma Boulevard
Oshkosh
Wisconsin 54901

Telephone. (414) 424-4224
Chief Administrator. Bruce Wise, Chairperson.

The University of Wisconsin - Oshkosh originated as the Oshkosh Normal School in 1871. The school was designated Wisconsin State Teachers College in 1925. In 1949 it became known as Wisconsin State College, Oshkosh and assumed its present name in 1964 upon attaining university status. The 185-acre campus has 51 buildings in the city of Oshkosh on the west shore of Lake Winnebago, 70 miles northwest of Milwaukee.

The Department of Music offers programs in preparation for careers as professional performers, private and public school teachers, and music therapists.

Accreditation. North Central Association of Colleges and Schools; National Association of Schools of Music; National Council for Accreditation of Teacher Education.

Academic Information

Enrollment, Music Majors. (Total University) 9,875.
Music Faculty. 22.
Term System. Semester. One summer session.
Entrance Requirements. High school graduation or equivalent; rank in upper 75 percent of graduating class; 3 units English, 2 mathematics, 2 science, 2 social science, 8 electives (minimum of 4 academic units).
Admission Procedure. Application with supporting documents and nonrefundable $10 fee to Admissions Office.
Music Degrees Offered. Bachelor of Music; Bachelor of Arts; Bachelor of Science; Bachelor of Music Education; Master of Arts.
Music Degree Requirements. A major in music can lead to the degrees Bachelor of Arts, Bachelor of Science, or Bachelor of Music. A major in music therapy can lead to the Bachelor of Music degree and a major in music education can lead to the Bachelor of Music Education degree. Within the music major, the Department offers a choice of emphasis from among music merchandising, instrumental performance, keyboard performance, vocal performance, composition, and liberal arts. Within the music education major, the Department offers a choice of choral, general music, or instrumental emphasis. Students who complete a major in the Department may continue into the graduate program, offered in conjunction with English, Speech, and Art leading to the Master of Arts degree.
General Program Areas. Composition, Music Education, Music History, Music Literature, Music Merchan-

dising, Music Theory, Music Therapy, Performance.

Instruments Taught. Brass, Guitar, Harp, Organ, Percussion, Piano, Stringed Instruments, Voice, Woodwinds.

Musical Facilities

Practice Facilities. The Arts and Communication Center consists of two buildings. The West building on Algoma Boulevard houses the Frederic March Theatre and the Television Center. The North-South building houses the Departments of Speech, Art, Music, and Religion, as well as the Music Hall, the Allan Priebe Gallery, and the University radio station, WRST-FM.

Concerts/Musical Activities. The Department of Music sponsors an annual chamber arts series of four programs; visiting artists; faculty and student concerts and recitals.

Music Library. The University libraries and learning resources center provide reference and traditional service for all academic programs.

Special Programs

Performance Groups. Jazz Choir, University Opera Theater, University Wind Ensemble, Symphonic/Concert Band, Jazz Lab Ensemble, Percussion Ensemble, University Choir, University Symphony, University Women's Chorus, Chamber Ensemble, Opera Theatre, Titan Band.

Financial

Costs. Per academic year: Tuition in-state resident $1,-464, out-of-state $4,464. Room and board $1,880.

Financial Aid. Institutional and state/federal scholarships, grants, loans, and part-time employment constitute the financial aid available. Scholarship/financial aid application due as soon as possible after January 1 for consideration for the following academic year.

University of Wisconsin - Stevens Point
Department of Music
College of Fine Arts
100 Main Street
Stevens Point
Wisconsin 54481

Telephone. (715) 346-3107.

Chief Administrator. Donald E. Greene, Chair.

Originally Stevens Point Normal School, the University of Wisconsin - Stevens Point was founded in 1891. The original 5-acre campus has expanded to over 248 acres in Stevens Point, located in the center of the state.

The Department of Music offers programs which prepare students for careers in professional performance and public school/private teaching.

Accreditation. North Central Association of Colleges and Schools; National Association of Schools of Music.

Academic Information

Enrollment, Music Majors. (Total University) 8,482. *Music Faculty.* 27.

Term System. Semester. Summer session from mid-May to mid-August.

Entrance Requirements. High school graduation or equivalent with completion of 16 college preparatory courses; recommend 4 English, 2 foreign language, 3 mathematics, 2 natural, 5 speech, 2 social studies; ACT required; audition required for applied music.

Admission Procedure. Application with supporting documents to Director of Admissions.

Music Degrees Offered. Bachelor of Music; Master of Music Education.

Music Degree Requirements. The Bachelor of Music degree is offered with concentrations in applied music (piano, organ, voice, string instruments, wind instruments, percussion, jazz instruments, classical guitar), theory/composition, music literature, and music education (instrumental K-12, choral 7-12, general K-12).

The Master of Music Education degree is offered with instrumental, vocal/choral, Suzuki talent education, jazz education, and studio pedagogy emphases. The degree prepares students for a full range of classroom, performance, and administrative responsibilities as members of the music teaching discipline. The curriculum incorporates philosophy, methodology, literature, and applied musical experience, and presents recent trends and innovations in music education.

General Program Areas. Applied Music, Jazz Studies, Music Education.

Instruments Taught. Baritone, Bass, Bassoon, Clarinet, Flute, Guitar, Harp, Horn, Oboe, Organ, Percussion, Piano, Saxophone, Trombone, Trumpet, Tuba, Viola, Violin, Violoncello, Voice.

Musical Facilities

Practice Facilities. The Department of Music is housed in the College of Fine Arts Building; music studios, practice rooms, and rehearsal rooms.

Concert Facilities. Peter J. Michelsen Concert Hall; Warren Gard Jenkins Theatre.

Concerts/Musical Activities. Student/faculty concerts and recitals; visiting artists.

Music Library. The James H. Albertson Center for Learning Resources serves the academic programs of the University.

Special Programs

Performance Groups. Vocal Ensemble, String Ensemble, Flute Ensemble, Clarinet Ensemble, Saxophone Ensemble, Mixed Woodwind Ensemble, Low Brass Ensemble, Mixed Brass Ensemble, Percussion Ensemble, Jazz Band, Choir, Orchestra, Band, Vocal Jazz Ensemble, Instrumental Jazz Ensemble.

Financial

Costs. Per academic year: Tuition in-state resident $1,-464, out-of-state $4,464. Room and board $2,010.

Financial Aid. Special scholarships are available to high school seniors with outstanding talent in musical performance. These scholarships are awarded each spring on the basis of special auditions held before members of the music faculty. Other forms of financial aid include state/federal grants, loans, and part-time employment. Financial aid/scholarship application due March 15.

University of Wisconsin - Whitewater
Department of Music

College of the Arts
800 Main Street
Whitewater
Wisconsin 53190

Telephone. (414) 472-1310

Chief Administrator. Dr. Howard G. Inglefield, Chairman.

This institution began as the Whitewater Normal School in 1868 and in 1925 the name was changed to Whitewater State Teachers College. The present name was adopted in 1971 when it became a part of the University of Wisconsin system. The 385-acre campus is located in Whitewater (population 12,000), 45 miles southeast of Madison and 51 miles southwest of Milwaukee.

The Department of Music prepares students for careers in music as a teacher or performer or in a variety of related fields in the music industry and for graduate study in the areas of performance, theory, music education, and musicology. Music education focuses on skills needed in today's schools and emphasizes the music educator's role in the broader aspects of the educational process. A wide variety of performing experiences is available.

Accreditation. North Central Association of Colleges and Schools; National Association of Schools of Music.

Academic Information

Enrollment, Music Majors. Undergraduate 100, graduate 25.

Music Faculty. Full-time 18, part-time 4, adjunct 5.

Term System. Semester. Summer session (mostly graduate and general studies courses).

Entrance Requirements. Accredited high school graduation or equivalent with rank in upper 75% of class; completion of a minimum of 12 high school units from the academic areas of English, social studies, mathematics, science, and foreign languages; SAT or ACT for those high school graduates not in top three-quarters of class; audition required.

Admission Procedure. Application with supporting documents to Admissions Office; contact Department of Music for audition upon acceptance for admission to University.

Music Degrees Offered. Bachelor of Music; Bachelor of Arts.

Music Degree Requirements. The Bachelor of Music is offered with emphases in performance, music education, and music theory/history. The Bachelor of Arts in music requires completion of general studies, the major, minor, and electives. All baccalaureate degrees require the completion of a minimum of 120 credits. All music majors are required to appear in a minimum number of student recitals and to present a Senior Recital in their primary performance area. Attendance is also required at the weekly convocations and seminars of the Department of Music.

General Program Areas. Music Education, Music History, Music Theory, Performance.

Instruments Taught. Brass, Organ, Percussion, Piano, Stringed Instruments, Voice, Woodwinds.

Musical Facilities

Practice Facilities. 35 practice rooms. 1 organ (Wickes). 4 percussion-equipped practice rooms. 35 pianos; 3 grand pianos reserved for piano majors. Electronic music studio; recording studio.

Concert Facilities. Recital Hall, seating 350; Hyer Auditorium, 800.

Concerts/Musical Activities. Student/faculty recitals; ensemble performances; concerts; visiting artists.

Music Library. 7,500 volumes; 3,100 scores; 42 music-related periodicals; 2,500 recordings. Listening facilities in the Center for the Arts include 25 cassette decks and 6 stereo turntables.

Special Programs

Performance Groups. Symphonic Band, Concert Band, Warhawk Show Band, Jazz Laboratory Band, Concert Choir, University-Community Chorus, Swing Choir.

Financial

Costs. Per academic year: Tuition in-state resident $1,-450, out-of-state $4,253 (includes rental of textbooks).

Financial Aid. Financial aid is available in the form of scholarships, state/federal loans, student employment, and a College Work-Study program.

WYOMING

University of Wyoming
Music Department

Box 3037
University Station
Laramie
Wyoming 82071

Telephone. (307) 766-5243, 766-5242

Chief Administrator. Dr. James Cook, Chair.

The University of Wyoming was founded 1886 and is a land-grant institution. It is Wyoming's only four-year institution of higher learning and enrolls over 10,000 students annually. The university is made up of six undergraduate colleges and a graduate school. The 735-acre campus is located a few blocks from the center of Laramie. The city was named for Jacques LaRamie, an early trapper for the American Fur Company and was established in 1868. It is situated between the Snowy Range to the west and the Laramie Range to the east in the Medicine Bow National Forest.

The Music Department seeks to produce the best possible graduates with the best marketable skills in performance, music education, and arts management. It is located in the Music Wing of the Fine Arts Building.

Accreditation. North Central Association of Colleges and Schools; National Association of Schools of Music.

Academic Information

Enrollment, Music Majors. 237.

Music Faculty. Full-time 18, part-time 13.

Term System. Semester. 8-week summer session.

Entrance Requirements. High school graduation or equivalent; open enrollment policy for state residents; ACT; audition required (tape or in person).

Admission Procedure. Application due 2 months before enrollment.

Music Degrees Offered. Bachelor of Music; Bachelor of Music Education; Bachelor of Arts; Master of Arts; Master of Music.

Music Degree Requirements. The bachelor's degrees require the successful completion of all courses in the major, required courses in English, Wyoming history, physical education, and general education for a total of 120 to 140 semester hours, depending on the area of concentration. The major requirement includes 45 to 65 hours in music theory, applied lessons, ensembles, conducting, and methods.

The master's degrees require the successful completion of 30 semester hours of courses in theory, history, research, methods, applied lessons, plus either a "B" paper or thesis.

General Program Areas. Applied Music, Composition, Conducting, History, Music Theory, Performance.

Instruments Taught. Bass, Bassoon, Clarinet, Flute, French Horn, Harpsichord, Oboe, Organ, Percussion, Piano, Saxophone, Trombone, Trumpet, Tuba, Viola, Violin, Violoncello.

Musical Facilities

Practice Facilities. 25 practice rooms. 3 organs (1 Walcker concert organ, 2 Walcker Tracker). Percussion-equipped practice room. 20 pianos (6 uprights, 24 grands); 2 grand pianos reserved for piano majors. Electronic/computer music studio.

Concert Facilities. 2 concert halls.

Concerts/Musical Activities. Popular music concerts; concert series with a variety of serious artists; ensembles; faculty recitals; student concert groups and recitals.

Music Library. 5,075 books; 8,000 scores; 56 periodicals; 12 microfiche titles; 3,500 recordings. Listening facilities (6 cassette, 12 stereo). All texts, magazines, and scores are housed in the University Coe Library.

Special Programs

Performance Groups. Ensembles, Band, Orchestra, Choral Groups.

Financial

Costs. Per academic year: Tuition in-state resident $778, out-of-state $2,442. Room and board $2,622.

Financial Aid. Scholarships include full tuition and fees for in-state and out-of-state students. Other sources of financial aid include grants, loans, part-time employment, and College Work-Study program.

Commentary

The Music Department supplies concerts by students and faculty to every corner of the state through the University Cultural Outreach program. This program gives ample performing opportunities to faculty and students.

INTERNATIONAL

ALBANIA

**Instituti i Lartë i Arteve
(Institute of Fine Arts)**
Faculty of Music
Tiranë
Albania

The Institute was founded in 1966.

ALGERIA

**Conservatoire de Musique et de Déclamation
- Algiers**
2 Boulevard Ché Guévara
Algiers
Algeria

The Conservatory was founded in 1920.

Academic Information

Enrollment, Music Majors. 2,000.
Music Faculty. 80.

**Conservatoire Municipal de Musique et de
Déclamation - Oran**
5 Rue d'Igli
Oran
Algeria

Chief Administrator. Gilles Achache, Director.
The Conservatory was founded in 1932. It offers studies in music, dance, and drama.

Academic Information

Enrollment, Music Majors. 500.
Music Faculty. 20.

ARGENTINA

**Consejo Gral. de Educación
Escuela de Música**
Avenida 9 de Julio 321
3500 Resistencia
Provincia del Chaco
Argentina

Telephone. 609

Academic Information

Music Degree Requirements. Professional titles awarded upon completion of the course of study.

Conservatorio de Música de Chascomús
Lavalle 281
Chascomús
Provincia de Buenos Aires
Argentina

The Conservatorio de Música de Chascomús was founded in 1963 as a state institution under the jurisdiction of the Ministry of Education of Buenos Aires.

Academic Information

Enrollment, Music Majors. 160.
Term System. Trimester. Academic year April to November.
Entrance Requirements. Secondary school certificate; entrance examination.
Music Degrees Offered. Teaching Qualification.
Music Degree Requirements. Teaching Qualification after a three-year course; Instrument course covers seven to ten years.

Financial

Costs. No tuition.

Conservatorio de Música de Morón
San Martin 370
1708 Morón
Provincia de Buenos Aires
Argentina

Telephone. 629-3173

Academic Information

Music Degree Requirements. Professional titles awarded upon completion of the course of study.

Conservatorio de Música "Julián Aquirre"
Gral. Rodriguez 7672
Banfield
Provincia de Buenos Aires
Argentina

Academic Information

Music Degree Requirements. Professional titles awarded upon completion of the course of study.

Conservatorio Municipal de Música "Manuel de Falla"
Sarmiento 1551
1042 Buenos Aires
Argentina

Telephone. 40-5898
Chief Administrator. Augusto B. Rattenbach, Director.
The Conservatory has a school of instrument making.

Academic Information

Music Degrees Offered. Professional titles.
Music Degree Requirements. Professional titles awarded upon completion of the course of study.
General Program Areas. Instrument Making.

Conservatorio Nacional de Música "Carlos López Buchardo"
Callao 1521
1024 Buenos Aires
Argentina

Telephone. 44-4505
Chief Administrator. Maria Magdelena García Robson de Moreira, Director.

The Conservatorio Nacional de Música Carlos López Buchardo was founded in 1924.

Academic Information

Music Degrees Offered. Professional titles.
Music Degree Requirements. Professional titles awarded upon completion of the course of study.

Musical Facilities

Music Library. 1,000 volumes; 12,000 musical scores.

Conservatorio Provincial de Música - Buenos Aires
25 de Mayo y San Luis
7600 Mar del Plata
Provincia de Buenos Aires
Argentina

Telephone. 48520

Academic Information

Music Degree Requirements. Professional titles awarded upon completion of the course of study.

Conservatorio Provincial de Música de Bahía Blanca
Belgrano 446
8000 Bahía Blanca
Provincia de Buenos Aires
Argentina

Telephone. 27290
Chief Administrator. Héctor Clemente Valdovino, Director.
The Conservatorio Provincial de Música de Bahía Blanca was founded in 1957. It is a state institution under the jurisdiction of the Ministry of Education and the Province of Buenos Aires.

Academic Information

Term System. Trimester. Academic year April to November.
Entrance Requirements. Secondary school certificate; entrance examination.
Music Degrees Offered. Professional titles.
Music Degree Requirements. Professional titles awarded upon completion of the course of study.

Financial

Costs. No tuition.

Conservatorio Provincial de Música de Chivilcoy

Calle Frías 37
6620 Chivilcoy
Provincia de Buenos Aires
Argentina

Telephone. 2455

Academic Information

Music Degree Requirements. Professional titles awarded upon completion of the course of study.

Conservatorio Provincial Gilardo Gilardi

Calle 49 e/6v7
1900 La Plata
Provincia de Buenos Aires
Argentina

Telephone. 31668

Academic Information

Music Degree Requirements. Professional titles awarded upon completion of the course of study.

Instituto Santa Ana
Department of Music

Avenida del Libertador 6115/95
Buenos Aires
Argentina

Instituto Santa Ana is a private institution founded in 1960.

Academic Information

Term System. Academic year of four terms: March to May; May to July; August to September; September to December.
Music Degrees Offered. Professional titles; Teaching Qualification.
Music Degree Requirements. Professional titles are earned after a four- to seven-year course of study. Teaching Qualification can also be earned as part of the study. AIRES'

Pontificia Universidad Católica Argentina 'Santa María de los Buenos Aires' (Pontifical Catholic University of Argentina)

Faculty of Arts and Music
Juncal 1912
Buenos Aires 1116
Argentina

Telephone. 44-1035, 44-4224
The University's Faculty of Arts and Music was founded by Alberto Ginastera in the late 1950s. The first doctorate in music was awarded in 1967. The Departments include composition, musicology and criticism, sacred music, and music education.

Academic Information

Term System. Academic year from March to December.
Music Degrees Offered. Licenciado (five-year course); Doctorate.

Universidad Nacional de Cuyo
Escuela Superior de Música

Lavalle 373
5500 Mendoza (Provincia de Mendoza)
Argentina

Telephone. 25-7179

Academic Information

Music Degree Requirements. Professional titles awarded upon completion of the course of study.

AUSTRALIA

University of Adelaide
Elder Conservatorium of Music

G.P.O. Box 498
Adelaide, SA 5001
Australia

Telephone. (082) 223-4333
The Elder Conservatorium of Music was established in 1898.

Academic Information

Music Degrees Offered. Bachelor of Music; Bachelor of Music (Performance); Master of Music in Composition, Musicology, Performance; Doctor of Music awarded for an "original and substantial contribution of distinguished merit to some branch of music."

Music Degree Requirements. The Doctor of Music degree requires five years of study beyond the Bachelor's degree.

General Program Areas. Composition, Music Theory, Musicology, Performance.

Musical Facilities

Music Library. 16,000 scores; 20 manuscripts; 450 tapes; 5 films; 5,000 phonograph recordings. Centre for Aboriginal Studies in Music.

Canberra School of Music
GPO 804
Canberra 2601
Australia

Telephone. 46-7811

Chief Administrator. John Painter, Director.

The Canberra School of Music was founded in 1965. It occupies new, spacious facilities including many practice rooms, pianos, and modern well-equipped teaching studios.

Academic Information

Music Degrees Offered. Bachelor of Music; Diploma in Music (three years); Diploma in Jazz Studies (three years); Graduate Diploma Course (one year).

Musical Facilities

Music Library. 12,000 scores; 3,500 monographs; 150 journals; 4,000 records. Library telephone 46 7833.

University of Melbourne
Faculty of Music
Parkville
Victoria 3052
Australia

Telephone. (03) 344 4000

Chief Administrator. Professor R. Farren-Price, Head, Faculty of Music.

The Conservatorium of Music was established in 1911. There is a Percy Grainger Museum affiliated with the University.

Academic Information

Music Degrees Offered. Bachelor of Music (Composition, Musicology, Music Therapy, Performance); Bachelor of Music Education; Master of Music; Doctor of Music (Composition, Theory, History, and Aesthetics of Music).

Music Degree Requirements. The Doctor of Music degree requires five years of study beyond the Bachelor's degree.

General Program Areas. Aesthetics of Music, Composition, Music History, Music Theory, Music Therapy, Musicology, Performance.

Musical Facilities

Music Library. 18,277 volumes.

New South Wales State Conservatorium of Music
Macquarie Street
Sydney NSW 2000
Australia

Telephone. 02 230-1230

Chief Administrator. Dr. Ronald Smart, Director.

The Conservatorium was established in 1916 and is one of the oldest music schools in Australia. It occupies buildings that were once Government House stables, designed by the distinguished colonial architect Francis Greenway and built between 1817 and 1821. The Conservatorium is located adjacent to the Royal Botanic Gardens.

Academic Information

Enrollment, Music Majors. Full-time 191 men, 229 women; total part-time 801. 9 foreign students from Hong Kong, Malaysia, Indonesia, New Zealand.

Music Faculty. Full-time 57, part-time 135.

Term System. Semester. 2 18-week terms. Summer session.

Entrance Requirements. Secondary school diploma required for certain courses; audition and admission tests according to chosen degree/diploma program; aural theory tests for certain courses.

Admission Procedure. Application due first Monday in November.

Music Degrees Offered. Bachelor of Music; Bachelor of Music Education; Diploma in Operatic Art and Music Theatre; Graduate Diploma; Diploma of the State Conservatorium of Music (D.S.C.M); Associate Diploma; Certificate in Piano Tuning and Technology.

Music Degree Requirements. The Bachelor of Music is offered in Practical Studies (Performance), Composition, Musicology, and General Studies. The Bachelor of Music Education curriculum consists of three major study areas: practical music, musicology and composition, and education. The Graduate Diploma is offered in opera and music theatre, repetiteur studies, and accompaniment and chamber music. This diploma course requires one year of full-time or two years of part-time study. The Associate Diploma, a two-year full-time or four-year part-time course, is offered in church music, jazz studies, and music teaching.

General Program Areas. Composition, Jazz Studies, Music Theory, Opera, Performance, Vocal Music.

Instruments Taught. Bass, French Horn, Guitar, Harp, Harpsichord, Organ, Percussion, Piano, Timpani, Trombone, Trumpet, Tuba, Viola, Violin, Violoncello, Voice, Woodwinds.

Musical Facilities

Practice Facilities. 45 teaching studios available for practice when not in use. 65 pianos; 46 grand pianos reserved for piano majors. Special practice room for percussionists. 3 organs (Pogson, Finchman pipe organs; Muster pedal organ). Electronic Music Centre, Music Research Centre, Piano Tuning School, Audio Laboratory. Through combined projects of the Conservatorium's Opera School and the Australian Film and Television School, opera students have been able to study their own performances on video, and learn about television techniques.

Concert Facilities. Verbrugghen Hall, seating 900; Joseph Post Auditorium, 250.

Community Facilities. A number of church organs in the metropolitan area are available for student practice.

Concerts/Musical Activities. Recitals, master classes, ensemble and orchestral concerts held throughout each semester.

Music Library. 127,564 scores; 16,074 books; 376 music journal titles; 40 microfiche; 16,929 phonograph recordings. 14 listening stations (cassette, stereo). Bellhouse Collection of Asian Musical Instruments.

Special Programs

Featured Programs. The Sydney String Quartet and the Sydney Wind Quintet are ensembles-in-residence at the Conservatorium.

Financial

Costs. Per academic year: Foreign students $3,250 (Australian).

Financial Aid. Scholarships available to Australian students average $458 (Australian) per semester. Scholarship application due first Monday in November.

Newcastle Conservatorium of Music
Auckland Street
Newcastle, NSW 2300
Australia

Telephone. (049) 23961, 23967.

Chief Administrator. Michael Dudman, Principal.

The Newcastle Conservatorium was established in 1952 as a branch of the New South Wales Conservatorium of Music. Until 1980, the Conservatorium occupied the top floor of the Newcastle War Memorial Cultural Centre in Laman Street. That year, the N.S.W. State Government purchased new premises for the Conservatorium on Auckland Street, formerly known as the People's Palace. The school moved there in 1981, using the adjacent Mackie Building as a venue for concerts.

The Conservatorium has a strong commitment to community service and to the development of the musical life of the region through concerts by staff, students, and visiting artists and lecturers. Every year the school collaborates with the Australian Broadcasting Corporation in visiting major centres throughout the Hunter Valley, offering encouragement and guidance to young musicians, teachers, and schools.

Academic Information

Enrollment, Music Majors. 500.

Special Programs

Performance Groups. Chamber Choir, Chamber Orchestra, Children's Orchestra, Brass Ensemble, Wind Quintet, String Quartet, Jazz Band.

University of Queensland
Faculty of Music
St. Lucia, Queensland 4067
Australia

Telephone. (07) 377 1111

Chief Administrator. Professor W.A. Bebbington, Dean, Faculty of Music.

The University of Queensland was founded in 1910, and the Faculty of Music was established in 1967. The University campus is located in St. Lucia, about seven km. from the center of the city of Brisbane, the capital of the state of Queensland.

Academic Information

Music Faculty. 14.

Music Degrees Offered. Bachelor of Arts (Honors); Bachelor of Music; Master of Music; Doctor of Music.

Music Degree Requirements. The degrees Bachelor of Arts (Honors) in Music and Bachelor of Music are awarded after completion of four-year programs. The Master of Music degree is awarded after completion of two to three years of full-time study beyond the bachelor's degree. The Doctor of Music degree is awarded after five to seven years of study beyond the bachelor's degree.

Musical Facilities

Music Library. 13,000 scores; 6,400 phonograph recordings.

Queensland Conservatorium of Music

259 Vulture Street
South Brisbane 4101
Australia

Musical Facilities

Music Library. 7,000 scores; 2,300 monographs; 57 journals; 2,800 records; 400 tapes. Library address: Gardens Point, George Street, Brisbane 400 (P.O. Box 28 North Quay 4000). Telephone: 229 2650

University of Sydney
Department of Music

Sydney, NSW 2006
Australia

Telephone. (02) 692-2222
Chief Administrator. Professor P. Platt, Head, Department of Music.

Established in 1850, the University of Sydney is the oldest university in Australia. The Department of Music is housed in the Seymour Theatre Center of the University.

Academic Information

Music Degrees Offered. Bachelor of Music; Bachelor of Arts in Music; Master of Music; Doctor of Music; Diploma in Music Composition.

Music Degree Requirements. The Doctor of Music degree is awarded after five years of study beyond the Bachelor's degree.

General Program Areas. Composition, Music Theory, Performance.

Tasmanian Conservatorium of Music

G.P.O. Box 252 C
Hobart, Tasmania 7001
Australia

Telephone. (02) 20 3314
Chief Administrator. Professor David Cubbin, Director.

The Conservatorium was established in 1965. It offers comprehensive vocational preparation in instrumental and vocal performance, composition, and music education. It is located 10 minutes from the center of Hobart. A new building was planned for completion in 1988.

Academic Information

Enrollment, Music Majors. Full-time 49 men, 56 women; part-time 7 men, 12 women. 2 foreign students from China.

Music Faculty. Full-time 18, part-time 14.

Term System. Trimester. Teaching weeks of terms are 9, 8, and 13 weeks, respectively.

Entrance Requirements. Secondary school diploma required; comprehensive examination; practical audition of 20 minutes; 1½ hours written harmony test;½ hour aural test.

Admission Procedure. Application due by November 30.

Music Degrees Offered. Bachelor of Music; Master of Music; Graduate Diploma of Music; Diploma of Music; Associate Diploma of Music.

General Program Areas. Composition, Music Theory, Performance.

Instruments Taught. Brass, Organ, Percussion, Piano, Stringed Instruments, Woodwinds.

Musical Facilities

Practice Facilities. 12 practice rooms (4 piano, 8 instrumental). 1 percussion-equipped practice room. 4 practice pianos; six grand pianos reserved for piano majors. Special practice rooms for organists. Two hours of practice time per student per day. Electronic and audiovisual studios.

Concert Facilities. 2 theatres.

Community Facilities. Hobart Town Hall, City Cathedral, and State Libraries are used.

Concerts/Musical Activities. Approximately 120 concerts are presented by the Conservatorium each year.

Music Library. Music materials are housed with the University's general collection. 700 scores; 2,800 monographs; 39 music periodicals; 12,000 phonograph recordings; 150 tapes; 30 films. The library telephone is 20 3133.

Commentary

The Tasmanian Conservatorium of Music sponsors the Hobart String Summer School for a ten-day period each January. The course of the String Summer School, under the directorship of Jan Sedivka, focuses essentially on the development of individual professional string players.

University of Western Australia
Department of Music

Nedlands, WA 6009
Australia

Telephone. (09) 380-3838
Chief Administrator. D.E. Tunley, Head, Department of Music.

Academic Information

Music Degrees Offered. Bachelor of Music; Bachelor of Music Education; Master of Music (Composition, Performance); Master of Music Education; Doctor of Music.

General Program Areas. Composition, Music Education, Music History, Music Theory, Performance.

Wollongong Conservatorium "Gleniffer Brae"

Murphies Road
Wollongong, NSW 2500
Australia

Telephone. (042) 28 1122, 281431
Chief Administrator. James Powell, Principal.

The Wollongong branch of the New South Wales State Conservatorium was established in 1972. In 1984, the Conservatorium became affiliated with the University of Wollongong and continues its educational and artistic activities coordinated by a Board of Management with membership from various community organizations.

AUSTRIA

Hochschule für Musik und Darstellande Kunst "Mozarteum" Salzburg (College of Music and Dramatic Art "Mozarteum")

Mirabellplatz 1
5020 Salzburg
Austria

Telephone. (662) 75 5 34

The Hochschule was founded in 1841, transferred to the Mozarteum Foundation in 1881, and became a conservatory in 1914. It became a state institution in 1921, an Academy in 1953, and a university Hochschule in 1970.

Academic Information

Term System. Semesters. October to February; February to June.
Music Degrees Offered. Diploma and teaching qualifications are awarded.
Instruments Taught. Harpsichord, Orchestral Instruments, Organ, Piano.

Musical Facilities

Music Library. 43,000 volumes.

Commentary

Since 1914, Salzburg's Hochschule, also known as the Mozarteum, has been headquarters for the International Mozart Foundation. The Mozarteum building contains a Mozart archive featuring the composer's letters and musical autographs, as well as letters of his father Leopold. In the garden next to the school stands the restored house, which was brought here from its original location in Vienna, where Mozart is said to have composed his opera Zauberflöte (The Magic Flute). The Salzburg Orff Institute, attached to the Mozarteum, has gained recognition for its work in training music teachers for the elementary school level.

Hochschule für Musik und Darstellende Kunst Graz

Leonhardstr, 15
A-8010 Graz
Austria

Telephone. (316) 32053/4
Chief Administrator. Rektoratsdirecktor Dr. Hermann Becke.

Hochschule für Musik und darstellende Kunst in Graz was the first conservatory founded in Austria, in 1815. It has held the status of university since 1970. The institution is situated in several *palais* and old buildings in Graz.

Member of the Assocation Européenne des Conservatoires de Musique, Académies de Musique, et Musikhochschulen.

Academic Information

Enrollment, Music Majors. Full-time 970, part-time 206. 185 foreign students from various countries worldwide.
Music Faculty. Full-time 174, part-time 72.
Term System. Semester. October 1 to January 31; March 1 to June 30.
Entrance Requirements. Admission test required.
Music Degrees Offered. Magister Artium.
Music Degree Requirements. Four to eight years are required for the degree Magister Artium.
Instruments Taught. Harpsichord, Orchestral Instruments, Organ, Piano.

Musical Facilities

Practice Facilities. 5 organs (Walcker, Rieger); 1 percussion practice room. Special electronic music studio.
Concerts/Musical Activities. Events are held approximately 100 evenings in the academic year.
Music Library. 37,000 volumes; collections of Friedrich Bischoff and Heinrich E.J. Lannoy. Audiocassette and stereo equipment available.

Special Programs

Featured Programs. The school offers jazz education on the university level.

Financial

Costs. Per academic year: öS 4,000.

Financial Aid. Scholarship available for foreign students. Application due March 15.

Hochschule für Musik und Darstellende Kunst Wien

(College of Music and Dramatic Art)

Lothringerstrasse 18
1030 Wien
Austria

Telephone. (222) 56 16 85/87

Chief Administrator. Gottfried Scholz, Rector.

The Hoschschule für Musik und Darstellende Kunst in Vienna was founded as a choral society in 1812 and five years later became a singing school under the direction of Antonio Salieri. Rapidly growing in stature, the school enlarged in 1819 to include a violin class, and by 1821 provided instruction for all the instruments. The institution continued to expand, adding an opera school four years later. The Hochschule, which has been a state school since 1908, gained university status in 1970. Such historic musical figures as Gustav Mahler, Arthur Nikisch, and Fritz Kreisler have been educated at this venerable institution.

Member of the Assocation Européenne des Conservatoires de Musique, Académies de Musique, et Musikhochschulen.

Academic Information

Term System. Semester. October to February; March to June.

Music Degrees Offered. A Diploma is received after a four- to eight-year course.

Instruments Taught. Harpsichord, Orchestral Instruments, Organ, Piano.

Musical Facilities

Music Library. 90,000 volumes; 1,700 records; 700 tapes.

Commentary

The conducting course at the Hochschule is internationally renowned, attracting students from all over the world.

BELGIUM

Conservatoire Royal de Musique de Bruxelles

30 rue de la Régence
1000 Bruxelles
Belgium

Telephone. (02) 512-23-69

Chief Administrator. E. Feldbusch, Director, French-speaking Section.

See Koninklijk Muziekconservatorium.

Conservatoire Royal de Musique de Liège

14, Rue Forgeur
B-4000 Liège
Belgium

Telephone. (41) 22 03 06

Chief Administrator. Henri Pousseur, Directeur.

The Conservatoire Royal de Musique was founded in 1826. It is located between Boulevard Piercot and Rue Forgeur. The institution offers programs of study in all areas of music, with a particular emphasis in contemporary music.

Academic Information

Enrollment, Music Majors. Full-time 600. Foreign students 60.

Music Faculty. Full-time 120.

Term System. Trimester. October through July.

Entrance Requirements. Variable. Audition required.

Admission Procedure. Apply by September 10.

Music Degrees Offered. Premier Prix, Diplomes Supérieurs, Certificats d'Aptitude.

Musical Facilities

Practice Facilities. 3 studios for organists; 2 studios for percussionists; electronic music studio.

Concert Facilities. Theatre; concert hall (seats 1,000); 3 recital halls.

Community Facilities. Concert Hall seating 1,000 (home of l'Orchestre Philharmonique de Liege).

Music Library. 130,000 items. Collections of Grétry, L. Terry, and Debroux. The library telephone number is (041) 23 52 23.

A museum has been created in memory of the Belgian violinist-composer Eugène Ysaÿe (1858-1931). The library telephone number is (041) 23 52 23.

Conservatoire Royal de Musique de Mons
Rue de Nimy 7
7000 Mons
Belgium

Telephone. (065) 34 73 77
Chief Administrator. J. Baily, Director.
The Conservatoire was founded in 1926.

Musical Facilities

Music Library. 10,000 items. Bouilliot Collection of old instruments, scores, and furniture. Library phone (065) 3 27 28, 3 35 75.

Member of the Assocation Européenne des Conservatoires de Musique, Académies de Musique, et Musikhochschulen.

Koninklijk Beiaardschool Jef Denyn
F. de Mersdestraat 63
2800 Mechelen
Belgium

Telephone. 32-015-20-47-32
Chief Administrator. Jo Haazen, Director; Albert Torfs, Secretary.

Koninklijke Beiaardschool was founded in 1922 by Jef Denyn and was the first school in the world established exclusively to train students on the carillon. The school's home, a building called the "Court of Busleyden" with clock tower, is located near the Grand Market of Mechelen. A branch of the school is located in the city of Leuven (address: Vlamingenstraat 83, 3000 Leuven, Belgium). Classes are taught in Dutch, French, English, German, and Esperanto.

Accreditation. Ministry of Education (Belgium).

Academic Information

Enrollment, Music Majors. Part-time 36 men, 16 women. Foreign students 11 (representing 5 nationalities).

Term System. Late September to early July.

Entrance Requirements. Students must have sufficient musical background *(solfege)*.

Admission Procedure. Application due September with nonrefundable fee of 500 Belgian Francs.

Music Degrees Offered. Diploma, First Prize.

Music Degree Requirements. Diploma: L.D. requires completion of four courses (one year); M.D. requires completion of six courses (two years); H.D. requires completion of ten courses (two years). First Prize: H.D. plus First Prize *solfege* and harmony.

General Program Areas. Tower Instruments.

Instruments Taught. Carillon.

Musical Facilities

Practice Facilities. Students are assigned a practice room 1 hour daily; 8 practice rooms available. 2 practice pianos (Schimmel, Braunschwing). Mechelen location has 4 practice keyboards and access to 7 tower carillons; Leuven location has 7 practice keyboards and access to 3 tower carillons.

Concert Facilities. Concerts are held in Antwerp, Brussels, Mechelen.

Community Facilities. Tower instruments in the center of the city.

Music Library. 1,025 books; over 500 scores; 20 periodicals; 450 documentation maps; 85 recordings. The Beiaard Museum is located near the school and houses a collection of old carillon keyboards.

Financial

Costs. Per academic year: Tuition $2,000 (US).

Financial Aid. Foreign students are eligible for financial aid. Students may give carillon concerts during the summer.

Commentary

Mechelen is the world center for carilloneurs, or "bellringers." The Koninklijke Beiaardschool Jef Denyn trains amateur as well as professional players of the carillon. The school is currently re-defining the carillon art on a more professional performance level, which will lead to the institution of carillon concerts and the concept of the carillon as a viable performance medium.

Koninklijk Muziekconservatorium van Brussel
Regentschapstraat 30
1000 Brussels
Belgium

Telephone. (02) 513-45-87
Chief Administrator. Kamiel D'Hooghe, Director, Flemish-speaking Section.

Koninlijk Muziekconservatorium van Brussel and The Royal Conservatory of Brussels were created in 1832 upon the reorganization of the Royal Music School that had been founded prior to the independence of Belgium in 1830. Francois Joseph Fétis and August Gevaert, both famous musicologists and the first and second directors, gave the institute an international reputation. Many famous musicians have studied and taught here—Charles de Bériot, Henri Vieuxtemps, Don Albeniz, Henry Wieniawsky, Eugène Ysaÿe, Cesar Tompson, Alfred Dubois, Arthur Grumiaux, Adrien Francois Servais, Arthur de Greef, Edouardo del Puey—as well as the inventor of the saxophone, Adolphe Sax.

The Conservatory is located in the center of the city of Brussels, near the Royal Palace and Park, the Egmond

Palace, and the Court of Justice. The main building and annex date from 1877.

The major goal of the Conservatory is the training of orchestra members, teachers, and soloists.

Member of the Assocation Européenne des Conservatoires de Musique, Académies de Musique, et Musikhochschulen.

Academic Information

Enrollment, Music Majors. Full-time 720 French-speaking Section, 540 Flemish-speaking Section. 67 foreign students (representing 18 nationalities).

Music Faculty. 160 French Section, 150 Flemish Section.

Term System. School year from July 15 to October 1.

Entrance Requirements. Entrance examination and *numerus clausus.*

Admission Procedure. Applications due Sept. 10. $25 (US) for Belgian students; $667 (US) for foreign students. Foreign students must possess an authorization for provisional stay in Belgium (not applicable to students of an E.E.C. country); all candidates will be enrolled as regular students, i.e., they will be obliged to follow all the parallel courses of the instrument. Foreign students who at their enrollment can provide a certificate (diploma and/or results of solfege, harmony, history of music, chamber music, etc.) declaring that they have finished their full music education, will be enrolled as free students after director's agreement; when finishing school at the Royal Conservatory a certificate will be granted.

Music Degrees Offered. Higher Diploma.

Music Degree Requirements. Diploma (harmony, history of music, chamber music, instrumental performance).

Instruments Taught. Brass, Organ, Piano, Saxophone, Stringed Instruments, Woodwinds.

Musical Facilities

Practice Facilities. 2 practice rooms for organists; 2 organs. 1 practice room for percussionists. 30 practice pianos; 9 grand pianos reserved for piano students; 50 piano practice rooms.

Concert Facilities. 3 concert halls.

Community Facilities. Local churches.

Music Library. 360,000 volumes. Special museum of musical instruments and various collections of music from different periods; the Wagener collection has many manuscripts and copies from Telemann, C.P.E. Bach, Scarlatti. Collections of Ste. Gudule, Ste. Elisabeth de Mons, Marchot. The Royal Library is located nearby.

Special Programs

Performance Groups. Ensembles, Symphonic Orchestra, Harmony Orchestra, Brass Bands, Choirs.

Financial

Costs. Per academic year: Foreign students fee 40,000 Belgian francs; Belgian students 1,500 Belgian francs; partial exemption available under certain conditions. Housing $100 (US) per month.

Financial Aid. Scholarships available for foreign students; 10 students are currently receiving financial aid. Scholarship application due October 1.

Commentary

It is very important for a prospective student to know in which of the Conservatory's two autonomous sections a particular teacher or course of studies is located. For example, viola da gamba, one of the more internationally-recognized departments, is located on the Flemish-speaking side of the Conservatory, about which the French-speaking secretariat would be unlikely to furnish information.

Studies on viola da gamba and baroque flute in the Flemish-speaking section of the Conservatory are major strengths in the curriculum. The French-speaking section of the Conservatory is known as the Conservatoire Royal de Musique de Bruxelles.

Koninklijk Muziekconservatorium van Ghent
Hoogpoort 50
9000 Ghent
Belgium

Telephone. (091) 25 15 15
Chief Administrator. J. Huys, Director.
The Conservatorium was founded in 1879.

Musical Facilities

Music Library. 75,000 items (strong in nineteenth century chamber music).

Koninklijk Vlaams Conservatorium van Antwerpen
(Royal Flemish School of Music)
Desguinlei 25
2018 Antwerp
Belgium

Telephone. (03) 37 79 70
Chief Administrator. Kamiel Cooremans, Director.
The Conservatorium was founded in 1898. Its older building is at St. Jacobsmarkt 11 in Antwerp. Member of the Assocation Européenne des Conservatoires de Musique, Académies de Musique, et Musikhochschulen.

Academic Information

Enrollment, Music Majors. 560.
Music Faculty. 180.

Musical Facilities

Music Library. 150,000 music prints; 6,500 manuscripts; autographs of Flemish composers; 60,000 additional uncatalogued items.

BOLIVIA

Conservatorio Nacional de Musica - La Paz (National Conservatory of Music - La Paz)

St. 6 de Agosto No. 2092
La Paz
Bolivia

Telephone. 373297
Chief Administrator. Antonio Roberto Borda, Director.

The National Conservatory was founded in August 1907 and is currently under the jurisdiction of the Bolivian Institute of Culture. Since 1961 the Conservatory has occupied its own premises. From the beginning, there was an orchestra which eventually became the National Orquesta Sinfonica. There is also a chamber orchestra, two choral groups (one of children), and chamber groups (including percussion, clarinet, and brass quintet). Courses taught include harmony, counterpoint, acoustics, organology, choir, chamber music, orchestra, and orchestra composition. The Conservatory also has a preparatory division that offers a basic level of training in theory and solfege for children from nine to fourteen years of age.

Academic Information

Enrollment, Music Majors. 270. 6 foreign students from Peru, Chile, Argentina.
Music Faculty. 25.
Admission Procedure. For the Superior level, applicant must have passed preparatory courses in theory and solfege plus instrument, or take an admission test in these subjects.
Music Degrees Offered. Technical Superior in Music.
General Program Areas. Bolivian Music History, Chamber Music, Composition, Latin American Music History, Music History, Music Theory, Performance, Solfege, World Music History.
Instruments Taught. Bass, Bassoon, Clarinet, Flute, French Horn, Guitar, Oboe, Percussion, Soprano Recorder, Viola, Violin, Violoncello.

Musical Facilities

Practice Facilities. 12 pianos (5 grands). 1 percussion-equipped practice room.
Concert Facilities. 1 concert hall, seating 80.
Music Library. 300 books; 4,000 scores; 500 phonograph recordings; 600 periodicals. Listening facilities (phonograph).

Special Programs

Performance Groups. Chamber orchestra, 2 choral groups, percussion ensemble, clarinet ensemble, brass quintet, chamber groups.

Commentary

The National Conservatory is planning to construct a new building that would vastly increase the space of the current premises. The Conservatory considers chamber music to be one of its most important programs.

BRAZIL

Conservatorio Brasileiro de Música

Ave. Graça Aranha 57, No. 12
20,000 Rio de Janeiro
Brazil

Chief Administrator. Professora Amalia Fernandez Conde, Director.

The Conservatory was founded in 1936.

Conservatorio Dramático e Musical de São Paulo

Ave. São João 269
São Paulo
Brazil

The Conservatory was established in 1906.

Musical Facilities

Music Library. 30,000 volumes.

Escola de Música - Minas Gerais

Rua Santa Catarina 466
30,000 Belo Horizonte
Minas Gerais
Brazil

The Escola de Música was founded in 1954 under the auspices of Fundação Universidade Mineira de Arte.

Academic Information

Term System. Semester. March to June; August to December.

Entrance Requirements. Secondary school certificate.

Music Degrees Offered. Bacharel de Música (Bachelor of Music).

Escola de Música de Brasília

Brasília, D.F.
Brazil

Chief Administrator. Carlos Galvão, Director.

This school, supported by the city of Brasília, emphasizes the teaching of popular music idioms and traditional Brazilian instruments. Its 1,100 students are mainly of precollege age.

Escola de Música e Belas Artes do Paraná

Rua Emiliano Perneta 179
80,000 Curitiba
Paraná
Brazil

The Escola de Música e Belas Artes do Paraná was established in 1948. It is under the jurisdiction of the Secretariat for Education and Culture of the State of Paraná and supported by both the state and federal governments.

Academic Information

Term System. Semester. March to June; August to December.

Entrance Requirements. Secondary school certificate.

Music Degrees Offered. Professional titles are awarded in the following order: Pintor, Escultor, Cantor (four-year course of study); Instrumentista (seven-year course of study); Professor de Canto, Professor de Educação Musical (eight-year course of study); Professor de Música e Instrumentos (twelve-year course of study); Compositor, Maestro (thirteen-year course of study).

Faculdade de Música Mãe de Deus

Ave. São Paulo 651
CP106
86100 Londrina, Paraná
Brazil

Chief Administrator. Professora Theodolinda Gertrudes Moro, Director.

The Faculty of Music was established in 1965.

Musical Facilities

Music Library. 2,600 volumes.

Faculdade de Música "Sagrado Coracão de Jesus"

Rua Caraibas 882
CP 8383, Villa Pompéia
São Paulo
Brazil

Chief Administrator. Irmã Charitas Cavalli, Directora.

The Faculdade de Música was founded in 1948. It offers undergraduate and graduate studies as well as special courses.

Faculdade Santa Marcelina

Rua Dr. Emilio Ribas 89
Perdizes
05006 São Paulo
Brazil

Telephone. 826-9718

Chief Administrator. Angela Rivero, Director.

The Faculdade was created in 1929. There are Departments of Musical Instruments, Singing, Composition, Art Education, Visual Arts, and Design.

Academic Information

General Program Areas. Composition, Musical Instruments, Vocal Music.

Musical Facilities

Music Library. 22,000 volumes.

Fundação Universidade de Brasília (University of Brasília)

Institute of Arts and Communication
Campus Universitário, Asa Norte
70910 Brasília, D.F.
Brazil

Telephone. (061) 274-0022

The Universidade was founded in 1961.

Academic Information

Music Degrees Offered. Bacharel in Music; Licenciado in Music.

Instituto de Letras a Artes
Rua Marechal Floriano 179
96100 Pelotas RS
Brazil

Chief Administrator. Myriam Souza Anselma, Director.

The Instituto was founded in 1969. There are degree courses in music and art and a postgraduate course in the history of the arts.

Instituto de Música da Bahia
Rua Direito de Piedade 2
Salvador
Bahia
Brazil

Chief Administrator. Maria Carmelita Santos Anguiar, Secretary.

The Instituto was founded in 1897.

UNESP - Universidade Estadual Júlio de Mesquita Filho
Instituto do Artes do Planalto
Department of Music
Rua Dom Luís Lasagna No. 400
São Paulo
Brazil

Telephone. (011) 327171/79

The Universidade was founded in 1976.

The Department of Music of this institution focuses on the academic music disciplines. One research interest is historical musicology as it relates to Brazilian music.

The Sociedade Brasileira de Musicologia held its first Congress (January 27 - February 1, 1987) at this institution.

Academic Information

Term System. Semester. February to June; August to December.

Music Degrees Offered. Licenciado in Music; Professional Titles in Piano Studies.

Music Degree Requirements. The institution offers a four-year course in music.

Financial

Costs. No tuition.

Universidade do Rio de Janeiro
Letters and Arts Center - Music Course
Avenida Pasteur 296
22290 Rio de Janeiro
Brazil

Telephone. (021) 295-25-48, 295-02-43
Chief Administrator. José Maria Neves, Coordinator.

In 1942, a School for Music Teachers was organized by Heitor Villa-Lobos. The School is now a part of the University of Rio de Janeiro, offering curricula for music teachers and instrumentalists as well as courses in composition and conducting. The Department seeks to prepare musicians of high competence for teaching and performance.

Academic Information

Enrollment, Music Majors. 309. 3 foreign students from Argentina and Chile.

Music Faculty. 30.

Term System. Semester.

Entrance Requirements. Secondary school certificate; admission examination; audition tests, dictation, theory, and instrumental performance or voice singing.

Music Degrees Offered. Bachelor of Arts in teaching, instrument or voice singing, composition, conducting.

Music Degree Requirements. Fulfillment of all credits required for the degree pursued.

General Program Areas. Brazilian Music History, Composition, Conducting, Music Education, Music History, Music Theory, Performance.

Instruments Taught. Bass, Bassoon, Clarinet, Flute, French Horn, Oboe, Piano, Violin, Violoncello, Voice.

Musical Facilities

Practice Facilities. 10 practice rooms. 16 pianos (3 grands). 1 percussion-equipped practice room. Electronic music studio.

Concert Facilities. 2 concert halls, seating 150 and 300 respectively.

Community Facilities. The Sala Vera Janacopulos concert hall near the campus is used.

Music Library. 20,000 books; 6,600 scores; 1,700 phonograph recordings; 24 periodical titles. Listening facilities: 10 stations (phonographs).

Commentary

The University of Rio de Janeiro music course emphasizes the importance of all aspects of Brazilian music in its programs.

Universidade do São Paulo
Department of Music

Cidade Universitária
Butantã
05508 São Paulo
Brazil

Telephone. 2102122 R. 683
Chief Administrator. Olivier Toni, Director.
The Department of Music, founded in 1970 by the current director, was annexed to the School of Communication and Arts at the University of São Paulo. All orchestral instruments are taught plus theory, solfege, history of art, sociology of art, and psychology of art.

Academic Information

Enrollment, Music Majors. 120. 2 foreign students from Chile and Peru.
Entrance Requirements. Entrance examination; audition.
Music Degrees Offered. Bachelor of Music.
General Program Areas. Art (Psychology of), Art (Sociology of), Composition, Music Theory, Musicology, Performance, Solfege.
Instruments Taught. Brass, Percussion, Piano, Stringed Instruments, Woodwinds.

Musical Facilities

Practice Facilities. 16 pianos (2 grand pianos). 1 percussion-equipped practice room.
Concert Facilities. Small concert hall.
Music Library. 20,000 books; 5,000 scores; 5,000 phonograph recordings; 500 periodicals. Listening facilities (10 phonographs). Special collection: Archive of Música Colonial Brasileira.

Universidade Federal da Paraíba
(Federal University of Paraíba)

Department of Music, Cidade Universitária
58,000 João Pessôa
Paraíba
Brazil

Telephone. (9091) 224-7200
Chief Administrator. Ilza Nogueira, Directora, Department of Music.

Academic Information

Music Degrees Offered. Bacherel (Bachelor's degree) in Music.

Universidade Federal de Bahia
Escola de Música

Rua Augusto Viana s/n
40,000 Salvador
Bahia
Brazil

Telephone. (071) 245-2811
Chief Administrator. Paulo Lauro Nascimento Dourado, Director.
New Music composition and performance is emphasized in the school's curriculum.

Academic Information

Music Degrees Offered. Licenciado in Music; Profesional titles in performance (instruments or voice) and composition.

Universidade Federal de Minas Gerais
Escola de Música

Avenida Antônio Carlos 6627
Pampulha, 30,000 Belo Horizonte
Minas Gerais
Brazil

Telephone. 441-8077
Chief Administrator. Professor Sandra Loureiro de Freitas Reif, Directora.

Academic Information

Music Degrees Offered. Professional titles in Music are granted upon completion of a four-year course.

Universidade Federal do Rio de Janeiro
Escola de Música

Rua do Passeio 98
Rio de Janeiro
Brazil

Telephone. (021) 260-7491
Chief Administrator. Andrely Quintella de Paola, Director.
The Escola was founded in 1848 as Conservatório Imperial de Música. The name was changed to Instituto Nacional de Música and later to the present name.

Musical Facilities

Music Library. 280,000 volumes. Special collection of antique instruments.

Special Programs

Affiliated Programs. Centro de Pesquisas Folcloricas was established in 1943 and maintains collections of indigenous music on records. The Director of the Center is Sra. Dulce Lamas.

BULGARIA

Bulgarian State Conservatoire
11 Klement Gotvald Boulevard
Sofia 1505
Bulgaria

Telephone. (359-2) 44 21 97
Chief Administrator. Dimitre Rouskov, Rector.
The Conservatoire was founded in 1921 as the State Musical Academy. In 1954, the Academy acquired its present name and now has three departments: Vocal Department, Instrumental Department, and Department for Theory, Composition, and Conducting. A Training Opera Theatre is attached to the Vocal Department in which students are instructed in the interpretation of opera music and in stage movement. The Conservatoire also has an Academic Symphony Orchestra. Classes are taught in Bulgarian.
Member of the Assocation Européenne des Conservatoires de Musique, Académies de Musique, et Musikhochschulen.

Academic Information

Enrollment, Music Majors. Full-time 763; part-time 200. 80 foreign students from Brazil, Greece, France, Vietnam, Iraq, and Laos.
Music Faculty. Academic staff 250.
Term System. Academic year September to May.
Entrance Requirements. Secondary school certificate and entrance examination; special competitive examinations in the desired specialty, elementary theory of music, solfege, harmony, piano, and general cultural questions.
Admission Procedure. Secondary school certificate and entrance examination.
Music Degrees Offered. Diploma for teaching and professional qualification.
Music Degree Requirements. Course of study is 4 years plus 2 years of specialization.
General Program Areas. Composition, Conducting, Instrumental Music, Music History, Music Theory, Vocal Music.
Instruments Taught. Bass, Clarinet, Flute, Harp, Oboe, Organ, Percussion, Piano, Trumpet, Viola, Violin, Violoncello.

Musical Facilities

Practice Facilities. 64 pianos (7 grand). 1 organ. 3 percussion-equipped practice rooms.
Concert Facilities. 3 concert halls seating 200, 100, and 40, respectively.

Music Library. 17,500 books; 48,000 scores; 8,500 phonograph recordings; 900 periodicals. Listening facilities available.

Financial

Costs. Per academic year: No tuition.

Viss Musikalno-Pedagogiceski
U1. Todor Samodumov 2
Plovdiv 4025
Bulgaria

Telephone. 2-83-10/11
Chief Administrator. Georgy Atanassov, Rector; Ilya Dimov Matev, Director.
The Institute of Music was founded in 1964 as a branch of the Bulgarian State Conservatory in Sofia. The Institute became independent in 1972 and is governed by a General Assembly. The language of instruction is Bulgarian.

Academic Information

Enrollment, Music Majors. Full-time 435, part-time 166.
Music Faculty. Full-time 83, part-time 74.
Term System. Semester. September to December; February to May.
Entrance Requirements. Secondary school certificate; entrance examination.
Music Degrees Offered. Teaching and professional qualification.
Music Degree Requirements. Completion of 4-year course plus 2 years of specialization.

Special Programs

Foreign Programs. Exchange and cooperative agreements with Franz Liszt College of Music in Weimar, German Democratic Republic, and State College of Music in Gdansk, Poland.

BURMA

Institute of Fine Arts
Faculty of Music
Godwin Road
Dagon Post Office
Rangoon
Burma

Chief Administrator. U Mya Oo, Principal.
This Institute was established about forty years ago and functions under the auspices of Burma's Ministry of Culture.
For further information, write to Deputy Minister,

Ministry of Culture and Information, Minister's Office, Rangoon, Burma.

Academic Information

Instruments Taught. Burmese Harp and Orchestra, Oboe, Piano, Stringed Instruments, Voice, Xylophone.

Mandalay School of Music, Dance, Painting, and Sculpture
Mandalay

Burma

Chief Administrator. U Kan Nyunt, Principal.

The School, founded in 1953, operates under the country's Ministry of Culture.

For further information, write to Deputy Minister, Ministry of Culture and Information, Minister's Office, Rangoon, Burma.

Academic Information

Instruments Taught. Burmese Harp and Orchestra, Oboe, Piano, Stringed Instruments, Voice, Xylophone.

CANADA

Acadia University
School of Music
Wolfville, Nova Scotia

Canada B0P 1X0

Telephone. (902) 542-2201

Chief Administrator. Dr. Peter Riddle, Dean.

In 1838, the Nova Scotia Baptist Educational Society founded a liberal arts institution under the corporate name of "The Trustees, Governors, Fellows of Queen's College." Regular instruction began in January 1839. In 1841, the Act of Incorporation was amended and the corporate name was changed to Acadia College. In 1891, the institution became known as Acadia University. The campus is located in the Annapolis Valley town of Wolfville, 100 kilometers northwest of Halifax.

The School of Music provides modern facilities and equipment for students who wish to further their education in music. Programs of study are offered in performance, music education, and composition.

Accreditation. Association of Universities and Colleges of Canada.

Academic Information

Enrollment, Music Majors. (Total University) 3,300.

Music Faculty. 17.

Term System. Semester. Two summer sessions.

Entrance Requirements. High school graduation with 16 academic units; SAT; recommendation by school principal or guidance officer.

Admission Procedure. Application with supporting documents due July 1 for Fall semester.

Music Degrees Offered. Bachelor of Music; Bachelor of Arts; Bachelor of Music Education.

Music Degree Requirements. The Bachelor of Music degree is offered with major concentrations in instrumental music, voice, theory-composition, and music education (winds and percussion, strings, general and classroom music). The Bachelor of Arts degree in music is offered in the context of a liberal arts program.

General Program Areas. Applied Music, Composition, Music Education, Music Theory.

Instruments Taught. Bass, Bassoon, Clarinet, Euphonium, Flute, French Horn, Guitar, Harpsichord, Oboe, Organ, Percussion, Piano, Saxophone, Trombone, Trumpet, Tuba, Viola, Violin, Violoncello, Voice.

Musical Facilities

Concerts/Musical Activities. Student/faculty recitals and concerts; visiting artists.

Music Library. The Harold Campbell Vaughan Memorial Library houses over 500,000 volumes and serves the academic programs of the School of Music.

Special Programs

Performance Groups. University Band, University Chorus, University Orchestra, Brass Ensemble, Jazz Band, Piano Ensemble, New Music Ensemble, Percussion Ensemble, String Ensemble, Chamber Ensemble, Vocal Ensemble, Woodwind Ensemble.

Financial

Costs. Per academic year: Tuition $1,460. Room and board $3,178 to $3,435.

Financial Aid. Scholarships, bursaries, loans, and alumni awards are available. All financial aid programs are administered by the Office of Admissions and Student Assistance.

University of Alberta
Department of Music
Edmonton, Alberta

Canada T6G 2C9

Telephone. (403) 432-3263

Chief Administrator. Dr. Alfred Fisher, Chairman.

The University of Alberta ia a publicly supported institution established in 1906. The University's main campus of 154 acres is two miles from the business center of Edmonton.

The Department of Music offers programs for students interested in careers as professional performers, scholars, and teachers.

Accreditation. Association of Universities and Colleges of Canada; Association of Commonwealth Universities.

Academic Information

Enrollment, Music Majors. (Total University) 21,831.
Music Faculty. (Total University) 1,640.

Term System. Year. Academic year September to April.

Entrance Requirements. High school graduation; completion of college preparatory program including 3 units of English. GRE required for graduate study.

Admission Procedure. Application with supporting documents and nonrefundable $20 fee to Office of Admissions.

Music Degrees Offered. Bachelor of Arts; Bachelor of Arts (Honors); Bachelor of Music; Bachelor of Music (Honors); Master of Music; Doctor of Music.

Music Degree Requirements. The Bachelor of Arts degree in music is offered with emphasis in music history or theory. The Bachelor of Music provides a general music curriculum while the the Bachelor of Music (Honors) degree is offered with concentration in performance, music history and literature, or theory and composition.

The Master of Music degree is offered with concentrations in applied music (keyboard instruments, orchestral instruments, voice), composition, musicology, and music theory. Although ethnomusicology is not offered as a major, an ethnomusicology thesis may be submitted for the musicology degree. The Doctor of Music degree is offered only in performance (piano or organ).

General Program Areas. Composition, Ethnomusicology, Music History, Music Literature, Music Theory, Musicology, Performance.

Instruments Taught. Brass, Organ, Percussion, Piano, Stringed Instruments, Voice, Woodwinds.

Musical Facilities

Concerts/Musical Activities. Student/faculty concerts and recitals; visiting artists.

Music Library. The University Library houses more than two million volumes and serves the academic programs of the Department of Music. The Music Resources Centre is located on the campus.

Special Programs

Performance Groups. Instrument Ensembles, Vocal Ensembles, Orchestra, Choral Groups.

Affiliated Programs. The Western Board of Music was founded in 1935 in order to conduct examinations of a high standard in music. The Board includes the Universities of Alberta, Manitoba, and Saskatchewan. The central office is located at the University of Alberta and is funded by the prairie universities, and from revenue derived from examination fees. The Board awards the diplomas of Associate in Music and Licentiate in Music for the second highest and highest grades, respectively, in its examinations. Theoretical and practical examinations are held four times each year.

Financial

Costs. Per academic year: Tuition $800. Fees $246. Room and board $2,000.

Financial Aid. Bursaries, grants, and loans are available. Graduate students in music are eligible to compete for the general graduate awards.

Brandon University
School of Music
Brandon, Manitoba
Canada R7A 6A9

Telephone. (204) 727-9631

Chief Administrator. Dr. Lawrence Jones, Dean.

Brandon University was established as Brandon College in 1899 by the Baptist Union of Canada and became an affiliate of McMaster University in 1910. The Church withdrew its support in 1938, after which Brandon was incorporated as a nondenominational college of the University of Manitoba. In 1967 the University became an independent institution.

A School of Music was first established in 1906. The new music building was dedicated by Queen Elizabeth II in 1984 and named in her honor. The major goals are to develop the musical potential of each student; to produce music teachers for the public schools; to train professional performers; and to raise the level of musical awareness and appreciation in the Brandon community served by the University.

Accreditation. Association of Universities and Colleges of Canada; Association of Commonwealth Universities.

Academic Information

Enrollment, Music Majors. Undergraduate 150, graduate 40.

Music Faculty. Full-time 20, part-time 20. Artists-in-residence: Brandon University Trio.

Term System. Semester. Academic year September to April. 6-week summer session from early July to mid-August.

Entrance Requirements. High school graduation or GED; open enrollment; audition required; theory test. TOEFL for non-English speaking students.

Admission Procedure. Application with supporting documents to Admissions Office; $17.50 fee for out-of-province students; $60 fee for international students.

Music Degrees Offered. Bachelor of Music; Master of Music.

Music Degree Requirements. The Bachelor of Music degree is offered in an applied music or general program, each of which requires four years of study. The program in music education requires three or four years for completion plus two years for certification. The Master of Music degree is offered in performance and literature (strings and piano only). This degree requires one year plus a summer of study.

General Program Areas. Music Education, Music Literature, Performance.

Instruments Taught. Baroque Instruments, Brass, Harpsichord, Organ, Percussion, Piano, Stringed Instruments, Voice, Woodwinds.

Musical Facilities

Practice Facilities. 30 practice rooms; 30 pianos (6 grands, 24 uprights), 5 grand pianos reserved for piano majors; Allen and Gabriel Kney organs. Baldwin electronic piano laboratory with 1 teacher console and 6 student modules.

Concert Facilities. Queen Elizabeth II Music Building Recital Hall, seating 208.

Community Facilities. Western Manitoba Centennial Auditorium.

Concerts/Musical Activities. Annual concert series of international guest artists (3 to 5 per year); other visiting guest artists; student and faculty concerts and recitals (100 per year).

Music Library. 4,000 volumes; 7,000 scores; 100 periodical subscriptions; 200 microform titles; 5,000 phonograph recordings; 3,000 audiocassettes. 9 listening stations. Special collection on the musical theatre. Students have access to Large Ensemble Library.

Special Programs

Performance Groups. Concert Band, Jazz Band, Wind Ensemble, Chorale, Chorus, Orchestra.

Financial

Costs. Per academic year: Tuition $1,999.50 per 30 credit hours (new student); $1,189.50 (returning student). Room $1,282. Board $1,747.

Financial Aid. Financial aid is awarded on the basis of financial need and musical ability. Institutional awards average $100 to $300 per year. Financial aid/scholarship application due April 1.

Commentary

Brandon University's music education program offers special courses incorporating the teaching methods of Orff, Kodaly, Martenot, and Suzuki.

University of British Columbia
School of Music
6361 Memorial Road
Vancouver, British Columbia
Canada V6T 1W5

Telephone. (604) 228-3113
Chief Administrator. Dr. William E. Benjamin, Director.

The University of British Columbia is located on a 990-acre campus with over 400 buildings. On-campus housing is available in dormitories and fraternity/sorority houses. Housing is also available for married students. The School of Music offers undergraduate and graduate degrees in a broad range of music disciplines.

Academic Information

Enrollment, Music Majors. Full-time 128 men, 152 women; part-time 3 men, 4 women. Foreign students 4.

Music Faculty. Full-time 29, part-time (adjunct) 48.

Term System. Winter session September to April with two terms, registration only in September; Spring session May-July (evenings); Summer session July-August (days).

Entrance Requirements. High school graduation or entrance as mature student; if English is not native language, successful results required in TOEFL examination. Interview, music theory examination for undergraduates; examples of academic work for graduates.

Admission Procedure. Admission is by audition only; admission to performance majors by second audition only; live or tape audition. Application due April 30.

Music Degrees Offered. Bachelor of Music; Bachelor of Arts in Music; Master of Music; Master of Arts; Doctor of Musical Arts; Doctor of Philosophy.

Music Degree Requirements. The B.M. is offered in general studies, music education; the M.M. in performance, composition, opera; the M.A. in musicology, ethnomusicology, theory; the D.M.A. in composition, performance; the Ph.D. in musicology with either a historical musicology or theory emphasis. Baccalaureate degree requires 60-65 units; Master's 15-20 units; Doctorate 15-22 units. General requirements for baccalaureate degree: 3 years theory, 2 years history, 4 years performance study, 4 years non-music electives (including 2 literature courses), 4 years large ensemble, 2-4 years small ensemble, various music electives. Performance major requires 3rd and 4th year recitals, repertoire courses; composition major requires 4th year recital.

General Program Areas. Composition, Performance, Theory.

Instruments Taught. Bassoon, Cello, Chinese Instruments, Clarinet, Cornet, Double Bass, English Horn, Flute, French Horn, Guitar, Harp, Harpsichord, Historical Instruments, Oboe, Organ, Percussion, Piano, Piccolo, Saxophone, Trombone, Trumpet, Tuba, Viola, Violin, Voice.

Musical Facilities

Practice Facilities. Special practice facilities for organists; Casavant-Freres 64-rank organ, 1 practice organ. 3 practice rooms for percussionists. 125 upright and grand pianos; 32 piano practice rooms and 13 soundproof practice modules. Electronic music studio, electronic class piano studio, recording booth.

Concert Facilities. Recital Hall seating 289; Old Auditorium seating 607.

Concerts/Musical Activities. 150 student concerts are held per academic year.

Music Library. The music library has holdings of 60,-000 volumes; 10,000 recordings; 150 periodicals; 4,000 microfiche. There is a special collection of the works of Brahms, including many first editions.

Special Programs

Featured Programs. Ethnomusicology program taught in Asian Centre.

Financial

Costs. Per academic year: Tuition for Canadian and Washington (U.S.A.) students $1,500; non-Canadian $4,262. Room $1,510. Board $1,467.

Financial Aid. 80 students receive some form of financial aid. 36 scholarships ranging from $125 to $1,500. 44 loans; average student loan $3,900.

Commentary

The University has the Centre for Studies in Nineteenth Century Music/Centre International de recherche sur la presse musicale. This center was established in 1981 under the auspices of the International Musicological Society and the National Association of Music Libraries. It coordinates work on an international scale dealing with the nineteenth century press as a documentary resource for the music historian. In addition, the center maintains an archives, publishes a journal *(Periodica Musical),* and oversees the publicaton of *Le Repertoire International de la Presse Musicale.* The University also has a collection of historical and Asian instruments, of which the Northwest Indian items are of particular interest.

University of Calgary
Department of Music
2500 University Drive, N.W.
Calgary, Alberta
Canada T2N 1N4

Telephone. (403) 220-5376

Chief Administrator. Dr. Eugene C. Cramer, Head.

The University of Calgary had its origin in 1945 when the former Normal School became a branch of the Faculty of Education of the University of Alberta in Edmonton. A year later, the education faculty was moved to the present campus of the Southern Alberta Institute of Technology and courses in arts and sciences were offered to education students. In 1947, the first two years of a four-year Bachelor of Education program was offered, and in 1951, a branch of the Faculty of Arts and Science

was established in Calgary. In 1960, the University moved to its present campus in the northwest area of the city; in 1964, it gained autonomy in academic matters and in 1966, it gained full autonomy.

The 314-acre campus, located in the northwest section of Calgary, includes 25 buildings and housing for 1,000 students. Calgary has a population of over half a million people and is Canada's fifth largest city.

The goal of the Department of Music is to provide the qualified and talented young musician with a solid foundation in both performance and the academic areas of history and theory so that he/she may either enter the music profession directly or pursue an advanced degree according to ability and desire.

Accreditation. Member of Association of Universities of the British Commonwealth; Association of Universities and Colleges of Canada; International Association of Universities.

Academic Information

Enrollment, Music Majors. Full-time 59 men, 102 women; part-time 1 man, 6 women. Foreign students 2.

Music Faculty. Full-time 23, part-time 24.

Term System. Fall semester of 13 weeks, Winter semester of 13 weeks, Spring term of 6 weeks. Summer term of 6 weeks.

Entrance Requirements. High school graduation with 20 academic units required; SAT and 3 Achievement tests required of applicants from the United States; GRE for graduate students. Audition required (15 minutes, 2 works of different styles, sight reading); theory placement test; piano proficiency examination.

Admission Procedure. Application and $20 nonrefundable fee due June 1.

Music Degrees Offered. Bachelor of Music; Master of Arts; Master of Music; Diplomas.

Music Degree Requirements. Diploma requires completion of 4.5 full-course-equivalents, Bachelor degree 21 full-course-equivalents, Master's degree 35-45 full course equivalents. General requirements for baccalaureate degree: 3 years applied study, 3 years music theory, 3 years music history for Bachelor of Music. Master of Arts requires 4 years maximum; Master of Music, 5 years maximum. 3 summers of study for Diplomas, which are offered only in summers, and granted in Kodaly Concept, Wind Ensemble Literature, and Conducting.

General Program Areas. Composition, Music History, Performance, School Music, Theory.

Instruments Taught. Guitar, Harpsichord, Organ, Percussion, Piano, Stringed Instruments, Voice, Woodwinds.

Musical Facilities

Practice Facilities. Practice facilities available for organists (Walcker organ). 2 practice rooms for percussionists. 19 upright and grand pianos; 3 grand pianos reserved for piano majors; 19 practice rooms. Special studios for electronic music lab and class piano.

Concert Facilities. Recital Hall seating 200; Theatre seating 550.

Concerts/Musical Activities. Weekly recitals by students; concert season.

Music Library. Music Library houses over 48,000 volumes; 20,000 scores; 200 periodicals; 13,000 recordings. 11 stations for listening (stereo). A departmental listening room and resource center for music students. Special collections include the Morris Surdin Collection of scores and scripts relating to the CBC drama series, the Calgary Philharmonic Society Collection, and a manuscript collection of contemporary Canadian composers. A regional office of the Canadian Music Centre is housed in the Music Library.

Financial

Costs. Per academic year: Tuition undergraduate $808, graduate $1,011. Fee nonresident undergraduate $404, graduate $506.

Financial Aid. Financial aid is available.

Dalhousie University
Department of Music
Halifax, Nova Scotia
Canada B3H 3J5

Telephone. (902) 424-2418

Chief Administrator. Carol Van Feggelen, Chairperson.

Dalhousie University is a private university founded by the Earl of Dalhousie in 1818. The University is closely associated with the University of King's College with which a joint Faculty of Arts and Science is maintained. The 60-acre campus is located in southwest Halifax.

The Department of Music attempts to provide a thorough training to those whose demonstrated talent and specific pre-university studies qualify them for specialization in one of the music disciplines. Programs are offered leading to careers as professional performer, composer, theorist, historian, critic, or teacher.

Accreditation. Association of Universities and Colleges of Canada.

Academic Information

Enrollment, Music Majors. (Total University) 10,240.
Music Faculty. 19.

Term System. Academic year September to May.

Entrance Requirements. High school graduation; applicants from the United States must have completed 30 credit hours at a recognized university; supplementary application form from the Department of Music.

Admission Procedure. Application with supporting documents to Office of the Registrar.

Music Degrees Offered. Bachelor of Music; Bachelor of Music Education; Bachelor of Arts.

Music Degree Requirements. The Bachelor of Music degree is a four-year program mainly comprised of classes in music. Students may choose to concentrate in performance, music history and literature, or composition. The Bachelor of Music Education degree programs combine instrumental or vocal instruction, aural and keyboard skills, historical knowledge, and the methods and repertoires needed by the music teacher in the elementary and/or secondary school classroom. Observation and field experience in classroom settings constitute an important part of the programs. The Bachelor of Arts degree with a major in music is a three-year course offered in the context of a liberal arts program.

General Program Areas. Composition, Music Education, Music History, Music Literature, Music Theory, Performance.

Instruments Taught. Brass, Guitar, Lute, Organ, Percussion, Piano, Recorder, Stringed Instruments, Voice, Woodwinds.

Musical Facilities

Concert Facilities. Rebecca Cohn Auditorium.

Concerts/Musical Activities. Student/faculty concerts and recitals; visiting artists.

Music Library. The Dalhousie University Library System has a collection of over 615,000 volumes and serves the programs of all Faculties and Departments. There is a special collection of the papers of pianist Ellen Ballon.

Special Programs

Performance Groups. Chorale, Chamber Choir, Symphonic Wind Ensemble, Chamber Orchestra, Jazz Band, Brass Ensemble, Dalhousie Musica Antiqua, Percussion Ensemble, Opera Workshop, Guitar Ensemble, Nova Scotia Youth Orchestra, Chebucto Orchestra.

Financial

Costs. Per academic year: Tuition $1,570. Room $1,776 to $3,380. Board $1,450.

Financial Aid. Scholarships, bursaries, grants, and loans are available.

University of Manitoba
School of Music
65 Dafoe Road
Winnipeg, Manitoba
Canada R3T 2N2

Telephone. (204) 474-9310

Chief Administrator. Dr. T. Herman Keahey, Director.

The University of Manitoba was established in 1877 and was western Canada's first university. It is a corporate and associative institutional hybrid comprising a medical school, college of pharmacy, agricultural college, arts and science college, the Mennonite Bible College, St. Andrew's College for Ukranian and Greek Orthodox ministers, St. John's for Anglican ordinations, health sciences center, and French-speaking St. Boniface College. The student population is over 19,000.

The University of Manitoba Music Department began in 1944 and became the School of Music in 1964 with a 3-year Bachelor of Music program. A new building for the School was occupied in 1974. The goal of the School of Music is to prepare students for careers in music, especially music education and performance, and postgraduate study. The School has a strong outreach to the community and there is close contact between students and staff.

Academic Information

Enrollment, Music Majors. Full-time men 53, women 67; part-time men 2, women 3.

Music Faculty. Full-time 14, part-time 32. Foreign students 8.

Term System. Semester. Intersession, summer session.

Entrance Requirements. High school graduation with 20 academic units; high school graduates with C average are accepted. TOEFL required for students whose native language is not English; foreign students must comply with Immigration Department regulations. Audition required; 10-12 minutes (out-of-city applicants may submit a tape); theory examination; sight reading; keyboard skills.

Admission Procedure. Application due July 1. 40% of applicants accepted.

Music Degrees Offered. Bachelor of Music; Bachelor of Music/Bachelor of Education.

Music Degree Requirements. 138 credit hours; history, theory, major practical instrument and ensembles required each year; 2.0 grade point average; every music course requires 60% grade for credit. 5 years required for the integrated degree Bachelor of Music/Bachelor of Education.

General Program Areas. Composition, Music Education, Music History, Performance.

Instruments Taught. Organ, Percussion, Piano, Stringed Instruments, Voice, Woodwinds.

Musical Facilities

Practice Facilities. Special practice facilities for organists; 2 Cassavant organs, Beckerath practice organ. 2 practice rooms for percussionists. 16 practice rooms for piano students; 12 practice pianos including Yamaha, Grobrian, Steinway, Heintzmann, Baldwin; 6 grand pianos reserved for piano majors. Electronic music studio.

Concert Facilities. Eva Clare Hall.

Music Library. The University Library houses over 1,200,000 titles of which over 45,000 are in the field of music. A special collection of contemporary Canadian music is maintained.

Financial

Costs. Per academic year: Tuition provincial resident $700, nonresident $1,020. Student fees $100. Room and board $1,958.

Financial Aid. Scholarships available ($100 to $1,000).

Commentary

The University of Manitoba is a member of the Western Board of Music, which provides a graded syllabus for theoretical and practical examinations in music at the high school level.

McGill University
Faculty of Music
555 Sherbrooke Street West
Montreal, Québec
Canada H3A 1E3

Telephone. (514) 398-4535

Chief Administrator. John Rea, Dean.

McGill University was founded in 182 and teaching began in the Faculty of Medicine in 1829, and Faculty of Arts in 1843. In 1885 the name McGill University was formally adopted. The campus is situated in Montreal, the second largest French-speaking city in the world. Despite its location, the general language of instruction at McGill is English.

The Conservatorium of Music was established in 1904 and became the Faculty of Music in 1920. Formerly housed in various buildings belonging to the University, the Faculty moved in 1972 to one location, the Strathcona Music Building, previously the main section of the Royal Victoria College. The goals of the Faculty are to educate professional musicians and research scholars in music and to provide general musical education for nonspecialists.

Accreditation. Association of Universities and Colleges of Canada.

Academic Information

Enrollment, Music Majors. 650.

Music Faculty. Full-time 36, part-time 77.

Term System. Two terms of 13 weeks each; two summer sessions.

Entrance Requirements. High School graduation with a B average or better; 16 academic units including 4 English; SAT and three Achievement Tests; audition required (15 minutes, live or taped).

Admission Procedure. Application with supporting documents and $15 nonrefundable fee to Admissions Office by March 1.

Music Degrees Offered. Bachelor of Music; Master of Music; Master of Arts; Doctor of Music; Concert Diploma; Licentiate in Music.

Music Degree Requirements. The Bachelor of Music degree may be obtained in the fields of composition, music history, performance, early music performance, jazz performance, school music, and theory. The degree programs normally require three years of study following completion of the Québec Diploma of Collegial Studies or four years of study following completion of secondary school elsewhere. The Licentiate in Music is offered in performance and is designed for advanced instrumentalists and singers who wish to concentrate on their practical subject while limiting their theoretical studies to basic areas in history, theory, and ear training. This program normally requires three years of study. The Concert Diploma is available only to highly-gifted instrumentalists and singers who demonstrate the talent and capacity for a professional performance career. This program normally requires two years of study following the completion of the Licentiate in Music.

The Master of Arts degree may be obtained in the fields of musicology, school music, and theory. The Master of Music degree is offered in the fields of composition, performance, and sound recording. The master's programs required two years of study. The Doctor of Music degree is available in composition and requires a minimum of two years of study following the completion of the Master of Music degree in composition.

General Program Areas. Composition, Music Education, Music History, Music Theory, Musicology, Performance, Sound Recording.

Instruments Taught. Brass, Harpsichord, Organ, Percussion, Piano, Stringed Instruments, Voice, Woodwinds.

Musical Facilities

Practice Facilities. The Strathcona Music Building has 64 practice rooms; 5 percussion-equipped practice rooms. 5 organs (Wolff, Casavant, Tsuji, Brunzema). 29 pianos (Yamaha uprights and Wagner grands); 8 grand pianos reserved for piano majors. 4 electronic music studios; 2 recording studios.

Concert Facilities. Pollack Concert Hall, seating 600; Redpath Hall, 350; Recital Hall, 100.

Concerts/Musical Activities. Over 300 concerts and other public events are presented annually.

Music Library. The Music Library houses a collection of over 37,000 monograph-volumes, bound journals, and scores; 17,000 recordings and texts on microform. The Performance Library has over 4,000 titles. Special collections include the manuscripts of the Viennese composer Julius Schloss; several Alban Berg autographs; scores of Canadian composer Kelsey Jones.

Special Programs

Performance Groups. Symphony Orchestra, Faculty Choirs, Bands, Chamber Ensembles, Jazz Bands, Opera Studio.

Affiliated Programs. The McGill Conservatory of Music offers instruction in all instruments, voice, theory, and ear training from the elementary level up to and including Collegial II.

Financial

Costs. Per academic year: Tuition $800; non-Canadians $6,030.

Financial Aid. A limited number of music entrance scholarships in certain instruments and in male voices are awarded to incoming students on the basis of auditions. Also, the University Scholarships Committee makes a number of awards each year to undergraduates based on a student's academic standing. Scholarship application due March 1.

McMaster University
Department of Music
1280 Main Street West
Hamilton, Ontario
Canada L8S 4M2

Telephone. (416) 525-9140

Chief Administrator. Dr. Hugh Hartwell, Chairman.

McMaster University is a publicly supported institution. It was established in 1887 in Toronto by Baptists. McMaster moved to Hamilton in 1930 and became nonsectarian in 1957. The campus is located in Hamilton's west end adjacent to the Royal Botanical Gardens on the shore of Lake Ontario.

The Department of Music offers programs of study leading to baccalaureate degrees with concentrations in performance, music education, and history and theory, and the master's degree with an emphasis of music criticism.

Accreditation. Association of Universities and Colleges of Canada.

Academic Information

Enrollment, Music Majors. (Total University) 15,000.
Music Faculty. Full-time 11, part-time 26.
Term System. Year. Two summer sessions.
Entrance Requirements. High school graduation with prescribed academic units; United States high school graduates with an A average or one year of college work accepted.
Admission Procedure. Application with supporting documents to Office of Admissions.
Music Degrees Offered. Bachelor of Music; Bachelor of Arts; Master of Arts.

Music Degree Requirements. The Bachelor of Music degree is offered with concentrations in music history and theory, music education, and performance. The Bachelor of Arts degree in music is a general program in the liberal arts context. The Master of Arts is offered in music criticism. As a part of this master's program, distinguished music critics have come to McMaster University to participate in residencies and international symposia.

General Program Areas. Music Education, Music History, Music Theory, Performance.

Instruments Taught. Brass, Percussion, Piano, Stringed Instruments, Voice, Woodwinds.

Musical Facilities

Concerts/Musical Activities. Student/faculty recitals and concerts; visiting artists.

Music Library. The collection of the University Library contains over 1,395,000 volumes. Music materials are housed in the Mills Memorial Library. Special collections include first editions of Mahler and Wagner; eighteenth century musical treatises; papers of Klaus Pringsheim, Sir Robert Mayer, and Eric Walter White.

Special Programs

Performance Groups. Orchestra, Choir, Concert Band, Jazz Ensemble, Chamber Ensembles.

Financial

Costs. Per academic year: Tuition and fees $1,327, non-Canadian students $4,273. Room and board $2,500.

Financial Aid. Financial aid to help students meet the costs of postsecondary education is available from the federal and provincial governments through the Ontario Student Assistance Programme. Forms of aid include grants, loans, bursaries, and work-study.

Queen's University
School of Music
Kingston, Ontario
Canada K7L 3N6

Telephone. (613) 545-2066

Chief Administrator. Dr. F.R.C. Clarke, Director.

Queen's University was founded in 1841 on a Royal Charter from H.R.M. Queen Victoria. The Music Department within the Faculty of Arts and Science was established by in 1935. Programs are offered for students interested in professional careers as orchestral, band, choir, and studio musicians; arrangers and composers; radio and television personnel; music teachers in schools and studios; and arts administrators.

Accreditation. Association of Universities and Colleges of Canada.

Academic Information

Enrollment, Music Majors. Full-time 54 men, 109 women; part-time 5 women.

Music Faculty. Full-time 15, part-time 35. Master's 15. Artists-in-residence: Vaghy String Quartet.

Term System. Semester. Academic year from September to April. 6-week summer session from early July to mid-August.

Entrance Requirements. Ontario grade 13 or equivalent; musical entrance requires Grade 9 (Royal Conservatory of Music) voice or instrument, Grade 6 piano, grade 2 theory; audition required (performance, ear test, and interview; students living more than 500 km. from Kingston may send certified tape).

Admission Procedure. Application to Faculty of Arts and Science at Queen's University.

Music Degrees Offered. Bachelor of Music; Bachelor of Arts; Bachelor of Arts (Honours).

Music Degree Requirements. The Bachelor of Music degree is offered with concentrations in performance, music education, theory/composition, and music history/literature. Queen's University also offers a four-year Bachelor of Arts (Honours) program with a major concentration in music history, a Medial Concentration (seven courses), and a three-year Bachelor of Arts degree with a minor concentration (five courses) in music.

General Program Areas. Chamber Music, Composition, Conducting, Ethnomusicology, Eurhythmics, Music Education, Music History, Music Theory, Performance.

Instruments Taught. Accordion, Bass, Bassoon, Clarinet, Euphonium, Flute, French Horn, Guitar, Harpsichord, Lute, Oboe, Organ, Percussion, Piano, Saxophone, Trombone, Trumpet, Tuba, Viola, Violin, Violoncello, Voice.

Musical Facilities

Practice Facilities. The Harrison-LeCaine Hall houses classrooms, teaching and practice studios, rehearsal halls, staff offices, the music library, electronic and computer music studios, and an eletronic piano laboratory. 3 pipe organs; 1 two-manual harpsichord; collection of orchestral and band instruments.

Concert Facilities. Concert halls in Dunning Hall and Grant Hall on campus.

Concerts/Musical Activities. Student/faculty concerts and recitals; visiting artists.

Music Library. The Music Library houses 12,000 musical scores; 35 videocassettes; 2,000 microforms; 12,-000 recordings; 400 audiocassettes and compact discs. 1,000 pieces of Canadian sheet music housed in Douglas Library Special Collections; collection of Canadian concert programs. Performance Library of scores also available.

Special Programs

Performance Groups. Choral Ensemble, Chamber Singers, Collegium Musicum, Wind Ensemble, Symphonic Band Orchestra, New Music Group, Jazz Ensemble, Clarinet Choir, Percussion Ensemble, Pro Arte Singers, Kingston Choral Society.

Affiliated Programs. During the summer months, the School of Music is host to a number of organizations, among them the National Youth Orchestra of Canada and the Suzuki Summer Institute.

Financial

Costs. Per academic year: Tuition $1,700. Room and board $3,000.

Financial Aid. Financial aid is awarded on the basis of academic merit, financial need, and musical ability. All applicants for admission are considered for a number of general proficiency entrance awards. In addition, scholarships are open to competition among students.

Commentary

The School of Music has proposed plans to add a two-year Licenciate (Diploma) program in performance and a master's degree curriculum.

University of Regina
Department of Music
Regina, Saskatchewan
Canada S4S 0A2

Telephone. (306) 584-4832

Chief Administrator. William B. Moore, Chairman.

The University of Regina is a state-supported institution. It was established by the provincial legislature in 1907 as Regina College and was joined until 1974 with the University of Saskatchewan. The campus is located in Regina, the provincial capital.

The Department of Music offers programs for students desiring careers as composers, performers, and teachers.

Accreditation. Association of Universities and Colleges of Canada.

Academic Information

Enrollment, Music Majors. (Total University) 9,158.
Music Faculty. 13.
Term System. Semester.
Entrance Requirements. High school graduation; audition required; music placement test in theory; interview.

Admission Procedure. Application with supporting documents and nonrefundable $25 fee to Office of Admissions.

Music Degrees Offered. Bachelor of Music; Bachelor of Arts; Bachelor of Music Education; Master of Music.

Music Degree Requirements. The Bachelor of Music degree is offered with concentrations in performance, composition, and music history. The first four semesters are common to all concentrations. The Bachelor of Arts degree is a general curriculum offered with a major in music. The Bachelor of Music Education degree is a four-year program offered jointly with the Faculty of Education. This program allows the student to select as a major area of interest one of the following: choral, instrumental, or general music education.

The Master of Music degree is offered with concentrations in performance (voice, piano, harpsichord, violin, viola, violoncello, clarinet, bassoon, trumpet, trombone), composition, and choral conducting.

General Program Areas. Choral Conducting, Composition, Music Education, Music Theory, Performance.

Instruments Taught. Baritone, Bass, Bassoon, Clarinet, Flute, Harpsichord, Horn, Oboe, Organ, Percussion, Piano, Saxophone, Trombone, Trumpet, Tuba, Viola, Violin, Violoncello, Voice.

Musical Facilities

Concerts/Musical Activities. Student/faculty recitals and concerts; visiting artists.

Music Library. The libraries on the University of Regina campus house a book collection of over 660,000 volumes.

Special Programs

Featured Programs. At the University's Bilingual Center, music courses are offered to students in French.

Performance Groups. Concert Band, Jazz Ensemble, Opera Ensemble, Concert Choir, Chamber Singers, Collegium Musicum, Chamber Orchestra, Piano Ensemble, Small Instrumental Ensembles.

Financial

Costs. Tuition $141 per 4-credit hour class. Room and board $1,302.

Financial Aid. Financial aid is available in the form of scholarships, bursaries, grants, loans, and part-time employment.

University of Saskatchewan
Department of Music
Saskatoon, Saskatchewan
Canada S7N 0W0

Telephone. (306) 966-6169

Chief Administrator. Richard B. Wedgewood, Department Head.

The act establishing the University of Saskatchewan was passed by the legislative assembly of the province in 1907, and the University began offering classes in 1909. The 350-acre main campus is located in Saskatoon, a city known as the "City of Bridges" in the south central part of the province.

The goal of the Department of Music is to prepare students for careers in music education, performance, conducting, composition, theory, and history by providing the requisite methods, materials, and experiences.

Accreditation. Association of Universities and Colleges of Canada.

Academic Information

Enrollment, Music Majors. 113.

Music Faculty. Full-time 14, part-time 16.

Term System. Year. Two 6-week summer terms.

Entrance Requirements. High school graduation; audition required; interview; theory examination for placement.

Admission Procedure. Application with $20 fee due August 1.

Music Degrees Offered. Bachelor of Music; Bachelor of Arts; Master of Education, Master of Arts.

Music Degree Requirements. The Bachelor of Music degree is a four-year program and is offered with concentrations in theory-composition, history-literature, or performance. The degree requires the completion of 132 credit units. The Bachelor of Music in music education is a four-year program requiring the completion of 153 credit units, offered through the College of Education. The Bachelor of Arts degree with a major in music is offered in both a three-year and a four-year program.

The Master of Education degree is also offered through the School of Education. The Bachelor of Arts and Master of Arts degrees are offered through the College of Arts and Sciences.

General Program Areas. Composition, Music Education, Music History, Music Literature, Music Theory, Performance.

Instruments Taught. Accordion, Baritone, Bass, Bassoon, Clarinet, Flute, French Horn, Guitar, Harpsichord, Oboe, Organ, Percussion, Piano, Recorder, Saxophone, Trombone, Trumpet, Tuba, Viola, Violin, Violoncello, Voice.

Musical Facilities

Practice Facilities. 17 practice rooms. 2 percussion-equipped practice rooms. 16 pianos (uprights); 3 grand pianos reserved for piano majors. Electronic music studio.

Concert Facilities. Centennial Auditorium.

Concerts/Musical Activities. Many concerts and recitals are presented each year by visiting artists; Celebrity Series; Faculty Series; Student Recital Series.

Music Library. 11,716 books; 5,524 scores; 88 music periodicals; 4,637 recordings.

Special Programs

Performance Groups. Quance Chorus, Collegium Musicum, Graystone Singers, University Chorus, Concert Band, Wind Ensemble, Jazz Ensembles, Percussion Ensemble, Music Theatre, Contemporary Ensemble, Chamber Orchestra, Brass Ensemble, Woodwind Ensemble, Recorder Ensemble, Vocal Ensemble, String Ensemble, Keyboard Ensemble.

Financial

Costs. $240 per six-credit course, $120 per three-credit course. Room and board $1,034.

Financial Aid. Music prizes, scholarships, graduate assistantships, and bursaries are available to music students.

University of Toronto
Faculty of Music
Edward Johnson Building
80 Queen's Park Crescent East
Toronto, Ontario
Canada M5S 1A1

Telephone. (416) 978-3750

Chief Administrator. Carl Morey, Dean.

The University of Toronto was founded in 1827 as King's College at York. The several campuses are located at various locations throughout the Toronto area with the main campus near in the midtown section of the city.

The first Bachelor of Music degree was granted in 1846 and the present Faculty of Music was established in 1918, the first faculty at a Canadian university created for the scholarly and professional study of music. Programs are offered to prepare students for careers as composers, scholars, performers, and teachers.

Accreditation. Association of Universities and Colleges of Canada.

Academic Information

Enrollment, Music Majors. 475.

Music Faculty. Full-time 34, part-time 80. Artists-in-residence: The Orford String Quartet.

Term System. Year. Academic year from September to May.

Entrance Requirements. Ontario high school graduation certificate or equivalent; audition required.

Admission Procedure. Application with supporting documents to Admissions Office, Faculty of Music; $15 application/audition fee.

Music Degrees Offered. Bachelor of Music; Artist Diploma; Licentiate Diploma; Diploma in Operatic Performance; Master of Music; Master of Arts; Doctor of Music; Doctor of Philosophy.

Music Degree Requirements. The Bachelor of Music degree is offered with concentrations in composition, conducting, history and literature, theory, music education and performance. The Artist Diploma program is designed to prepare performing artists; the Licentiate Diploma program is designed to prepare teachers of piano. To complete these three-year programs, students must obtain satisfactory standing in the courses specified at a rate of between 10 and 20 units per year. The Diploma in Operatic Performance is an advanced diploma requiring two or three years of full-time residence. It is designed to prepare students through vocal and operatic experiences for professional operatic careers.

The Master of Music is offered with concentrations in composition, music education, and performance. A graduate program in musicology leads to the Master of Arts and Doctor of Philosophy degrees. The Doctor of Music degree is offered with concentration in composition.

General Program Areas. Composition, Conducting, Music Education, Music History, Music Literature, Musicology, Opera Performance, Theory.

Instruments Taught. Accordion, Bass, Bassoon, Clarinet, French Horn, Guitar, Harp, Harpsichord, Lute, Oboe, Percussion, Piano, Recorder, Saxophone, Trombone, Trumpet, Tuba, Viola, Violin, Violoncello, Voice.

Musical Facilities

Practice Facilities. The Edward Johnson Building is the home of the Faculty of Music. 30 practice rooms; 30 pianos; electronic music studio.

Concert Facilities. MacMillan Theatre, a fully-equipped opera house, seating 800; Walter Hall, 500.

Concerts/Musical Activities. Over 250 presentations are given annually by students, faculty, and guest artists.

Music Library. The Edward Johnson Music Library is a comprehensive reference and research library with particular strengths in scholarly editions, medieval and renaissance music history, violin recordings, and reprint editions. Special collections include French opera and early twentieth century music. The Sniderman Recording Archives of the Music Library include holdings of the Hart House String Quartet, Kathleen Parlow, and Edward Johnson. The Rare Book Room houses a large collection.

Special Programs

Performance Groups. String Ensemble, Folk Music Ensemble, Contemporary Music Ensemble, Guitar Orchestra, Early Music Ensemble, Jazz Ensemble, Concert Band, String Quartet, Woodwind Quintet, Piano Trios, Percussion Ensemble, Concert Choir, Symphony Orchestra, Opera Chorus, University Singers, Wind Symphony, Collegium Musicum.

Financial

Costs. Per academic year: Tuition $1,215. Fees $164.

Financial Aid. Bursaries usually range from $100 to $500. Loans, scholarships, and prizes are also available.

Université de Montréal
Faculty of Music
2900 Boulevard Edouard-Montpetit
Montréal, Québec
Canada H3C 3J7

Telephone. (514) 343-6427

Chief Administrator. Pierre Rolland, Dean.

The Université de Montréal was established in 1878 as a branch of Laval University but became autonomous under a papal constitution of 1919 and an act of the legislature of Québec in 1920. In the 1960s it became an independent institution of the Roman Catholic Church and is now a provincial university. The campus is located on the northern side of Mount Royal Park.

The Faculty of Music offers extensive courses in composition, theory, musicology, ethnomusicology, early instruments and music, contemporary music, chamber music, electronic music composition, and performance areas.

Accreditation. Association of Universities and Colleges of Canada.

Academic Information

Enrollment, Music Majors. (Total University) Full-time 14,000.

Music Faculty. 28.

Term System. Year.

Entrance Requirements. High school graduation; Collegiate Studies diploma for Québec students; fluency in French.

Admission Procedure. Application with supporting documents to Office of Admissions.

Music Degrees Offered. Bachelor of Music; Master of Arts; Master of Music; Doctor of Music; Doctor of Philosophy.

Music Degree Requirements. The Bachelor of Music degree is offered with concentrations in general music studies, performance (voice, organ, piano, percussion, classical guitar, orchestral instruments, jazz), composition, musicology, and theory. The Bachelor of Arts in music has been available but is not currently operative. The Master of Music is offered in composition, theory, and performance. The Master of Arts is available with a concentration in musicology. The Doctor of Music is offered with a concentration in composition or performance and the Doctor of Philosophy is available with a concentration in musicology.

General Program Areas. Composition, Ethnomusicology, Jazz Studies, Music Theory, Musicology, Performance.

Instruments Taught. Accordion, Bass, Bassoon, Clarinet, Flute, Guitar, Harp, Lute, Oboe, Organ, Piano, Saxophone, Trombone, Trumpet, Tuba, Viola, Violin, Violoncello, Voice.

Musical Facilities

Concerts/Musical Activities. Student and faculty recitals and concerts; visiting artists.

Music Library. The University Library maintains a collection of over 1,500,000 volumes.

Special Programs

Performance Groups. Vocal Ensemble, Contemporary Music Ensemble, Guitar Ensemble, Chorale, Orchestra, Small Ensembles, Baroque Ensemble.

Financial

Costs. Per academic year: Tuition $740; non-Canadian $4,350. Room and board $3,000.

Financial Aid. Financial aid in the form of scholarships, bursaries, grants, loans, and part-time employment is available.

Université Laval
Ecole de Musique
Pavillon Louis-Jacques-Cassault
Ste. Foy, Québec
Canada G1K 7P4

Telephone. (418) 656-7061

Chief Administrator. Dr. Pierre Thibault, Director.

Université Laval owes its origin to the Seminary of Québec, founded in 1663 by Francois de Montmorency Laval, the first bishop of Québec. In December 1852, Queen Victoria signed a royal charter granting the Seminary the rights and privileges of a university and in December 1970, the national assembly of Québec granted a new charter to Université Laval. Since 1964, Université Laval has gradually occupied the new Cité Universitaire, one square mile in the western outskirts of Québec. The present buildings were erected between 1948 and 1980.

Academic Information

Enrollment, Music Majors. Full-time 400, part-time 50.

Music Faculty. Full-time 40, part-time (adjunct) 60.

Term System. Semester.

Entrance Requirements. Diplome d'études collegiales; United States students are required one year of college. Performance programs require audition; two-year specialized college program required (Cegep).

Admission Procedure. Application with $15 nonrefundable fee due May 1.

Music Degrees Offered. Bachelor of Music; Bachelor of Music Education; Master of Music; Doctor of Music.

Music Degree Requirements. The Master of Music is offered in musicology, music education, composition, performance; the Doctor of Music in music education, musicology. Bachelor's degree requires three years, Master's two years, Doctorate three years.

General Program Areas. Jazz, Music Education, Music History, Opera, Performance.

Instruments Taught. Organ, Percussion, Piano, Stringed Instruments, Woodwinds.

Musical Facilities

Practice Facilities. Special practice facilities for organists; 4 organs available. 40 piano practice rooms; 35 concert, 14 grand, and 120 upright pianos; 4 grand pianos reserved for piano majors. Electronic and computer studios.

Concert Facilities. Two.

Concerts/Musical Activities. 150 student concerts per year.

Music Library. The university library houses over 1,300,000 volumes. There is a special emphasis in Roman Catholic church music, French music, and historical and contemporary Canadian compositions. Special collections include eighteenth century and early nineteenth century orchestral and chamber music parts; clippings on musicians of Québec province.

Financial

Costs. Per academic year: Tuition provincial resident $600, nonresident $1,200. Fees $300.

Financial Aid. 60% of students receive some form of financial aid.

University of Victoria
School of Music
Victoria, British Columbia
Canada V8W 2Y2

Telephone. (604) 721-7903

Chief Administrator. Paul Kling, Director.

The University of Victoria came into being in 1963, but it had enjoyed a prior tradition as Victoria College. The campus in Victoria covers 340 acres with over 30 major buildings.

Begun as a Department of Music in 1968, it became the School of Music in 1978 to coincide with its move into a new music building. The School seeks to educate musicians to their fullest capabilities both in academic subjects and performance disciplines. Programs are offered in musicology, performance, and composition.

Accreditation. Canadian Association of University Schools of Music.

Academic Information

Enrollment, Music Majors. Full-time 83 men, 111 women; part-time 5 men, 2 women.

Music Faculty. Full-time 21, part-time 17.

Term System. Year.

Entrance Requirements. High school graduation; audition required (taped auditions may earn preliminary acceptance).

Admission Procedure. Application and supporting documents with nonrefundable $15 fee ($35 for those whose transcripts, in whole or in part, originate outside of British Columbia) to Admissions Office by May 15.

Music Degrees Offered. Bachelor of Music; Master of Music; Master of Arts; Doctor of Philosophy.

Music Degree Requirements. The Bachelor of Music degree is offered with majors in composition and theory, history and literature, performance, and music education (secondary-instrumental, secondary-choral, elementary). A general program is also offered.

The Master of Music degree is offered with majors in composition or performance. The Master of Arts and Doctor of Philosophy degrees are offered with concentration in the area of musicology.

General Program Areas. Composition, Music Education, Music History, Music Literature, Music Theory, Musicology, Performance.

Instruments Taught. Brass, Harp, Harpsichord, Organ, Percussion, Piano, Stringed Instruments, Voice, Woodwinds.

Musical Facilities

Practice Facilities. Special practice facilities for organists and percussionists. 40 practice rooms; 3 rehearsal halls; electronic music studio.

Concert Facilities. Concert Hall, seating 1,300; Recital Hall, 202.

Concerts/Musical Activities. Student/faculty concerts and recitals; visiting artists.

Music Library. The McPherson Library contains over one million volumes. The music collection includes 18,-000 books, 14,000 scores, and more than 30,000 records and tapes. Special collections include a collection of modern reproductions of medieval and Renaissance instruments; Hofmann Collection (ethnic artifacts); Shakespeare Music Collection; Salon Orchestra Collection.

Special Programs

Performance Groups. University Orchestra, University Wind Symphony, University Chorus, University Chamber Singers, Collegium Musicum, New Music Ensemble, Opera Ensemble, Jazz Ensemble.

Foreign Programs. The School of Music has an affiliation with the Utrechts Conservatorium in the Netherlands.

Financial

Costs. Per academic year: Tuition provincial students $1,300, out-of-province $2,275. Fees $400. Room and board $2,692 to $3,043.

Financial Aid. Scholarships range in award from $100 to $8,500 (average $400). Graduate fellowships available. Other sources of financial aid include bursaries, loans, and part-time employment.

University of Western Ontario
Faculty of Music
London, Ontario
Canada N6A 3K7

Telephone. (519) 661-2043

Chief Administrator. Dr. Jeffrey Stokes, Dean.

The University of Western Ontario received its charter from the Ontario Legislature in 1878. Since that time, it has grown into a prominent liberal arts university. The 400-acre campus in located in the city of London, eighty miles west of Hamilton.

The Faculty of Music offers three- and four-year baccalaureate programs leading to degrees in music education and performance. A general program in the liberal arts with a major in music is also offered.

Accreditation. Association of Universities and Colleges of Canada.

Academic Information

Music Faculty. 79.

Term System. Semester.

Entrance Requirements. High school graduation; United States students of high academic standing or one year of college accepted; audition required.

Admission Procedure. Application with supporting documents to Admissions Office; applicants should apply in writing to the Faculty of Music for an audition in performance no later than three weeks prior to the commencement of the period of enrollment.

Music Degrees Offered. Bachelor of Music; Bachelor of Musical Arts; Bachelor of Arts; Artist Diploma; Master of Music; Master of Arts.

Music Degree Requirements. The Bachelor of Music with Honors degree is offered with concentrations in music education, music history, performance (any standard orchestral or band instrument, piano, organ, harpsichord, harp, or voice), and theory and composition. The degree is a four-year program; three-year programs lead to the degrees Bachelor of Musical Arts and Bachelor of Arts in Music.

The Artist Diploma in performance is a one-year program offered to students holding the Bachelor of Musical Arts degree in performance or its equivalent.

The Master of Music degree is offered with emphases in music theory, composition, music education, music literature, and performance. The Master of Arts degree is offered with emphasis in musicology.

General Program Areas. Composition, Music Education, Music History, Music Literature, Music Theory, Musicology, Performance.

Instruments Taught. Brass, Harp, Harpsichord, Organ, Percussion, Piano, Stringed Instruments, Voice, Woodwinds.

Musical Facilities

Concerts/Musical Activities. Student/faculty concerts and recitals; visiting artists.

Music Library. The Library has a special collection of printed and manuscript opera scores covering the years 1600-1900.

Special Programs

Performance Groups. Orchestra, Band, Chorus, New Music Ensemble, Collegium Musicum, Opera Workshop.

Financial

Costs. Per academic year: Tuition $1,345, non-Canadian $4,278. Room and board $2,925.

Financial Aid. Numerous scholarships and professional awards are available for music students. Other forms of financial aid include bursaries, grants, loans, and part-time employment.

Wilfrid Laurier University
Faculty of Music
75 University Avenue West
Waterloo, Ontario
Canada N2L 3C5

Telephone. (519) 884-1970

Chief Administrator. Dr. Gordon K. Greene, Dean.

In 1910, the Canada Synod and the Synod of Central Canada of the Lutheran Church entered into an agreement to establish the Evangelical and Lutheran Seminary of Canada. Facilities for pretheological education were established in 1914. In 1925 the Faculty of Arts of Waterloo College became affiliated with the University of Western Ontario but this connection ended in 1960 when a revised charter changed the name of Waterloo College to Waterloo Lutheran University. In 1973, the University became a provincially assisted, nondenominational institution with the new name of Wilfrid Laurier University. The 40-acre campus has 20 major buildings.

The goal of the Faculty of Music is to train music students to be professional performers with a strong background in music theory and history.

Accreditation. Association of Universities and Colleges of Canada; Association of Commonwealth Universities.

Academic Information

Enrollment, Music Majors. Full-time 62 men, 120 women; part-time 21 men, 66 women.

Music Faculty. Full-time 14, part-time 39.

Term System. Trimester. 6-week summer session.

Entrance Requirements. High school graduation with 30 units. Approximately 30 percent of applicants accepted; audition required (live performance of a minimum of two pieces of a contrasting style); theory placement test for basic rudiments.

Admission Procedure. Application with supporting documents to Office of the Registrar by April 30.

Music Degrees Offered. Bachelor of Music; Bachelor of Music Therapy; Bachelor of Arts; Diploma in Opera.

Music Degree Requirements. The Bachelor of Music degree program is intended for students who plan to become professional musicians, composers, church organists, performers, teachers, musicologists, and music librarians. The core of required courses in performance, theory, music history, and conducting, together with participation in choir and/or orchestra and chamber music is designed to ensure that every student completing the program has a sound knowledge of music history and theory and is a competent performer. A comprehensive program is available that allows the student to choose a maximum number of music elective courses in order to design a course of study in accordance with the student's own musical interests. Other Bachelor of Music programs are offered in music education (elementary, secondary), Baroque and early music, church music, composition, history, theory, and performance. The Bachelor of Music Therapy degree is a four-year program beyond Ontario grade 13 or equivalent standing. It prepares for professional work in music therapy. A six months internship beyond the degree is required of graduates for accreditation by the Canadian Association of Music Therapy. The Bachelor of Arts degree with a major in music offers the student a liberal arts background with some specialization in music.

The Opera Diploma program is intended for singers who have completed an undergraduate degree in music and who wish to continue their studies in voice and opera.

General Program Areas. Baroque Music, Church Music, Composition, Conducting, Medieval Music, Music Education, Music History, Music Theory, Music Therapy, Opera, Performance, Renaissance Music.

Instruments Taught. Bass, Bassoon, Clarinet, Flute, French Horn, Guitar, Oboe, Organ, Percussion, Piano, Recorder, Saxophone, Trombone, Trumpet, Tuba, Viola, Violin, Violoncello, Voice.

Musical Facilities

Practice Facilities. 20 practice rooms; 20 pianos (2 grand pianos reserved for piano majors). Special practice rooms for organists and percussionists. 4 organs. Electronic music studio; piano laboratory.

Concert Facilities. Theatre-Auditorium, seating 600.

Concerts/Musical Activities. Student/faculty concerts and recitals; visiting artists.

Music Library. The University Library houses a collection of over one million items and serves the academic programs of the Faculty of Music. Students have direct borrowing privileges from the neighboring University of

Waterloo, Brock University, the University of Guelph, the University of Western Ontario, the University of Windsor, and York University.

Special Programs

Performance Groups. New Music Ensemble, Baroque Ensemble, Chapel Choir, WLU Choir, Laurier Singers, Opera Ensemble, Orchestra, Wind Ensemble, Jazz Ensemble, String Ensemble, Brass Ensemble, Percussion Ensemble.

Financial

Costs. Per academic year: Tuition provincial students $1,264, non-Canadian students $4,450. Room $1,700. Board $1,800.

Financial Aid. Bursaries, grants, loans, and part-time employment are available. Scholarships range from $100 to $1,100. Applications for awards are accepted up to March 15 of the current academic year.

University of Windsor
School of Music
Sunset Avenue
Windsor, Ontario
Canada N9B 3P4

Telephone. (519) 253-4232, Ext. 2780
Chief Administrator. E. Gregory Butler, Director.

The University of Windsor was founded in 1857 as Assumption College. It assumed its present name in 1963. The campus is located in Windsor, Ontario, across the Detroit River from Detroit, Michigan.

The Department of Music was formed in 1967 and became a School of Music in 1976. The School prepares students for careers as professional performers and teachers.

Accreditation. Association of Universities and Colleges of Canada; Association of Commonwealth Universities.

Academic Information

Music Faculty. Full-time 12, part-time 13.
Term System. Semester. One summer session.
Entrance Requirements. High school graduation with 33 credits; audition required; theory and listening skills evaluation test.
Admission Procedure. Application with supporting documents and nonrefundable $9 fee due May 1.
Music Degrees Offered. Bachelor of Music; Bachelor of Arts (combined honors in music and a second subject); Bachelor of Musical Arts; Bachelor of Fine Arts; Church Music Diploma.
Music Degree Requirements. The Bachelor of Music degree is offered in four program areas: history and literature, school music, performance, and individual pro-

grams. The Bachelor of Musical Arts degree is an academic program and requires the completion of a total of thirty-two courses. A program in music theatre leads to the Bachelor of Fine Arts degree.

General Program Areas. Church Music, Music Education, Music History, Music Theatre, Music Theory, Pedagogy, Performance.

Instruments Taught. Bass, Bassoon, Clarinet, Euphonium, Flute, French Horn, Guitar, Harp, Harpsichord, Oboe, Organ, Percussion, Piano, Saxophone, Trombone, Trumpet, Tuba, Viola, Violin, Violoncello, Voice.

Musical Facilities

Practice Facilities. 13 practice rooms. 2 organs (Gabriel Kney, Karl Wilhelm). Special practice facilities for percussionists. 14 pianos (Baldwin uprights). Electronic music studio.

Concert Facilities. Student Union.

Community Facilities. Local churches are used for organ lessons and recitals.

Concerts/Musical Activities. Student/faculty concerts and recitals; visiting artists.

Music Library. The University Library contains over one million volumes and serves the academic programs of the School of Music. 10 listening stations (cassette, stereo). A collection of 3,100 recordings is housed in the School of Music.

Special Programs

Performance Groups. Community Choir, University Singers, Wind Ensemble, Orchestra, Jazz Ensemble, Chamber Choir, Small Ensembles.

Affiliated Programs. Assumption University, Holy Redeemer College, Canterbury College, and Iona College are affiliated with the University of Windsor.

Financial

Costs. Per academic year: Tuition Canadian students $1,214, non-Canadian students $4,584. Fees $125. Room $1,700. Board $1,600.

Financial Aid. Scholarships, bursaries, grants, loans, and part-time employment are available. Scholarships range from $50 to $1,000 (average $400). Scholarship application due March 31.

York University
Department of Music
McLaughlin College, Room 043
4700 Keele Street
North York, Ontario
Canada M3J 1P3

Telephone. (416) 736-5186

Chief Administrator. James R. McKay, Chairman.

The Department of Music at York University was founded in 1970. The aim of the Department is to develop musicians with the broad range of abilities required to perform, invent, experience, and conduct research in music. The Department provides qualified students with a choice among several programs of study, combining performance, composition, theory, music history, and ehtnomusicology. The general objective of the curriculum is to provide a broad foundation of musicianship, integrating music making of many different kinds with the development of mind and imagination. The Department gives particular emphasis to musical creativity, defined in relation to contemporary concerns and practices. Special prominence is also given to performance programs in chamber music, jazz, South Indian music, and to ethnomusicological studies.

Accreditation. Association of Universities and Colleges of Canada.

Academic Information

Enrollment, Music Majors. Full-time 180, part-time 40. Foreign students 30.

Music Faculty. Full-time 14, part-time 32. Doctorate 10, master's 4, baccalaureate 32. Artists-in-residence: Canadian Piano Trio.

Term System. Year. Academic year from September to April. 6- and 12-week summer sessions from June to August.

Entrance Requirements. Ontario high school graduation (Grade XIII); musical requirement equivalent to Grade VIII Royal Conservatory of Music; audition and interview required.

Admission Procedure. Application with supporting documents to Office of Admissions.

Music Degrees Offered. Bachelor of Arts (Honours); Bachelor of Fine Arts (Honours); Bachelor of Education; Master of Music.

Music Degree Requirements. The Bachelor of Arts (Honours) degree is offered with areas of study in theory/composition/musicianship, history and area studies, and performance. This degree requires eight courses in music out of a total of twenty courses. The Bachelor of Fine Arts (Honours) degree requires ten courses in music, also out of a total of twenty courses. Co-registration with the Faculty of Education is possible for those students who wish to teach music in elementary schools. The program leads to the Bachelor of Education degree.

The Master of Music degree is offered in the fields of musicology and ethnomusicology.

General Program Areas. Composition, Ethnomusicology, Music History, Music Theory, Musicology, Performance, South Indian Music.

Instruments Taught. Bass, Brass, Guitar, Percussion, Piano, Viola, Violin, Violoncello, Voice, Woodwinds.

Musical Facilities

Practice Facilities. 20 practice rooms. Special practice facilities for percussionists. 26 pianos (24 uprights, 2 grands); 4 pianos reserved for piano majors. Electronic music studio; acoustic research laboratory.

Concert Facilities. McLaughlin Hall, seating 250; Burton Auditorium, 650.

Concerts/Musical Activities. Over 100 concerts and recitals are performed each year.

Music Library. 20,000 volumes; 10,000 musical scores; 20 current periodical subscriptions. 18 listening stations. The holdings of the Library have an emphasis in folk and popular music. Special collections include the Performance Library and an instrument collection containing a number of modern reproductions of Renaissance wind instruments as well as some reproductions of stringed instruments.

Special Programs

Performance Groups. Jazz Orchestra, Contemporary Ensembles, Toronto Community Orchestra, University Choir, Wind Symphony, York University Choir, Philippine Kolintang Ensemble

Financial

Costs. Per academic year: Tuition $1,479. Lab fees $75 to $135. Room $2,680. Board $2,900.

Financial Aid. Financial aid is awarded on the basis of academic merit, financial need, musical ability. Both institutional and province/commonwealth aid available. Music students receive some form of financial aid ranging from $150 to $1,000. Part-time employment available.

CHILE

Pontificia Universidad Católica de Chile
Faculty of Architecture and Fine Arts
Alameda 340
Casilla 114-D
Santiago
Chile

Telephone. 222 4516

Chief Administrator. Renato Parada B., Dean.

This institution was founded in 1888 by decree of the Archbishop of Santiago.

Academic Information

Term System. Semester. March to July; August to December.

Music Degrees Offered. Licenciado in Music after completion of a five-year course.

Universidad Católica de Valparaíso
Conservatory of Music
Avenida Brasil 2950
Valparaíso
Chile

Telephone. 251024

Chief Administrator. Juan Enrique Froemel, Rector of University.

The University was founded in 1928 and recognized as a Catholic university by the Holy See in 1961.

Academic Information

Term System. Semester. March to August; August to December.

Music Degree Requirements. Professional titles awarded upon completion of the course of study.

Universidad de Concepción
Departamento de Arte
Barros Arana
Concepción
Chile

Telephone. (56) 41 24985

Chief Administrator. Enrique Ordóñez, Director.

The Departamento de Arte was originally founded in 1963 as a School of Music. It became a department of the Institute of Arts in 1971 and in 1980 became the Department of Arts of the University. The Department offers training for secondary school music teachers.

Academic Information

Enrollment, Music Majors. Full-time 70 men, 65 women.

Music Faculty. Full-time 14, part-time 8.

Term System. Academic year March to December.

Entrance Requirements. Secondary school diploma; scholastic aptitude test.

Admission Procedure. Application due March for national students; December for foreign students.

Music Degrees Offered. Licenciado in Musical Education.

General Program Areas. Music Education.

Instruments Taught. Guitar, Piano, Recorder.

Musical Facilities

Practice Facilities. 8 practice rooms. 8 pianos (uprights). Choir conducting is taught at the University Choir Building.

Concert Facilities. University Concert Hall.

Community Facilities. Local churches used for recitals.

Music Library. 4,000 volumes. 3,555 scores; 131 books; 175 periodicals; 165 recordings. Listening facilities (cassette, stereo).

CHINA

Central Conservatory of Music
43 Bao Jia Street, Western District
Beijing
People's Republic of China

Telephone. 66 7120

Chief Administrator. Wu Zu Qiang, Director.

Preparations for the establishment of the Central Conservatory of Music began in 1949 and the school was formally set up in Tianjin in 1950. The Conservatory was formed from a number of other music departments. At first the school had only four departments (composition, vocal music, piano, and orchestral instruments). The move to Beijing took place in 1958. Musicology and conducting departments were added. For the development of Chinese national music, the national instrumental and vocal departments were formed and the National Music Research Institute was placed under the leadership of the Conservatory. In early 1964, the department of national instrumental music, the department of national vocal music, and the research institute combined with the music department of the former Beijing Arts College to become the Chinese Musical Academy. During the 10 years of political turmoil during the Cultural Revolution, the Conservatory suffered serious disruption and was faced with complete distintegration. However, in late 1977, the Ministry of Culture restored the name and organizational system of the Central Conservatory of Music.

The Conservatory has affiliated middle and primary music schools. The Writing and Research Department is responsible for writing articles on music, scientific research, translation and publication of foreign musical material. A public musical education department and a school factory have also been established.

Academic Information

Enrollment, Music Majors. Undergraduate 223; graduate 6; special students 113.

Music Faculty. Full-time 359.

Term System. Two semesters: September to January, February to March.

Music Degree Requirements. The Departments of National Musical Instruments, Piano, and Orchestral Instruments offer programs requiring completion of four years of study; the Departments of Composition, Musicology, Conducting, Vocal Music, and Opera require the completion of five years of study. From 1979 until the present, graduate students have been admitted for a study of two years. The Conservatory is currently enrolling graduate students working toward master's and doctorate degrees in three-year programs. A special three-year advanced study program for teachers and working people has also been organized.

General Program Areas. Conducting, Music History, Music Theory, Musicology, Opera, Performance, Vocal Music.

Instruments Taught. Brass, Chinese National Instruments, Percussion, Piano, Stringed Instruments, Woodwinds.

Musical Facilities

Music Library. 200,000 items of which 130,000 are scores and books; 140,000 Chinese and foreign phonograph recordings. Publications compiled and edited by the Conservatory are *The Journal of the Central Conservatory of Music* and *Reference Material of Foreign Music.*

Special Programs

Foreign Programs. The Conservatory has intensified the exchange of music culture with foreign countries. Internationally known teachers have been invited and Chinese teachers have been sent abroad. Relations with music academies of some countries have been established for the exchange of musical material and information.

Commentary

As the music school of Beijing, the capital of the People's Republic of China, the Central Conservatory of Music is the most famous of the Chinese conservatories. Many of its students participate in international competitions and the government often selects this institution for foreign exchange projects. A new library and an apartment building for foreign students and specialists has recently been constructed.

Conservatory of Chinese Music
17 Qian Hai Xi Jie
Beijing
People's Republic of China

Telephone. 664120
Chief Administrator. Li Xi An, Dean.
The institution was founded in the 1950s to provide education in the study of Chinese music. During the Cultural Revolution, it was merged with the Central Conservatory of Beijing, but in the 1970s it returned to its independent stature. The Conservatory is housed in a former noble family's palace. The building is well known as the home described in the Chinese 3-volume epic literary work, *Dream of the Red Mansions.* The Conservatory specializes in the performance practices of Chinese traditional music. Other conservatories in China have departments of Chinese music but this is the only national conservatory set up specifically for the teaching of traditional music. Most graduates become performers and teachers of Chinese instruments.

Academic Information

Enrollment, Music Majors. 500.
General Program Areas. Chinese Traditional Music, Performance.

Guangzhou Conservatory of Music
Guangzhou
Guangdong Province
People's Republic of China

Chief Administrator. Liang Han-guang, President.
The Conservatory was founded in 1960. Western and Chinese instruments are taught. A four-year course of study is offered to earn the equivalent of a Bachelor of Music degree.

Commentary

In Guangzhou there is an instrument factory run by violin maker Xu Fu who has been lauded internationally for his fine instruments. Plans are being made for a new conservatory course in violin making in which students would study the craft at this local factory.

Harbin Normal University
Department of Music
Harbin
Heilong Jiang Province
People's Republic of China

The University specializes in training teachers. The Department of Music was founded in 1983 and both Western and Chinese instruments are taught. A four-year course leads to a Bachelor of Music Education degree.

Academic Information

Music Degrees Offered. Bachelor of Music Education.

Northwest Teacher's College
Department of Music
Lanzhou
Gansu Province
People's Republic of China

Chief Administrator. Dr. Li Bin-De, Director.
The goals of the College, which was founded in 1939, are to train music teachers for different educational levels and to prepare musicians for orchestral careers.

Academic Information

Enrollment, Music Majors. 116.
Music Faculty. 31.

Music Degrees Offered. Bachelor of Music; Bachelor of Arts; Master of Arts; Doctor of Philosophy.

Commentary

This college is typical of a group of about thirty Chinese teacher's colleges which have music departments. The primary mission of these institutions is to train music educators for the primary and secondary school levels.

Shandong Academy of Arts
Music Division
Shandong Province
People's Republic of China

The Academy was founded in 1958.

Academic Information

Enrollment, Music Majors. 200.
Music Faculty. 109.

Commentary

This school is representative of a category of arts institutions in the People's Republic of China including Guangxi Academy of Arts (Guangxi Autonomous Region), Hubei Academy of Arts (Hubei Province), Nanjing Academy of Arts (Jiangsu Province), Hunan Academy of Arts (Hunan Province), and Tianjin Academy of Arts (Tianjin Municipality).

Shanghai Conservatory of Music
20 Fen Yang Road
Shanghai
People's Republic of China

Telephone. 370137
Chief Administrator. Sang Tong, President; Chang Shouzhong, Director.

The Conservatory was founded in 1927 and is responsible to the Ministry of Culture. The institution consists of the College, Primary School, and Research Institute. Chamber music is emphasized in the curriculum, resulting in the formation of such groups as the Shanghai Quartet, which has studied and performed both in the People's Republic of China and abroad.

The Conservatory publishes *Art of Music* quarterly.

Academic Information

Enrollment, Music Majors. 450. Foreign students 11.
Music Faculty. 425.
Term System. Semester. September to January; March to July.
Music Degrees Offered. Bachelor of Arts (four-year course); Master of Arts (three years beyond the bachelor's degree); Doctorate (three years beyond the master's degree).

General Program Areas. Chamber Music, Composition, Music Theory, Performance.
Instruments Taught. Piano, Stringed Instruments.

Musical Facilities

Music Library. Special reference library containing exclusively foreign materials. Audiovisual materials; records library; recording rooms.

Special Programs

Featured Programs. The Shanghai Ladies Quartet, a faculty quartet (all female) in residence, is one of the only string quartets in the People's Republic of China.
Foreign Programs. There are dormitories for students from outside Shanghai. Run-Shan Chao is the head of the Foreign Affairs Section. As Shanghai and San Francisco are "sister cities," cultural exchanges between the conservatories of these cities have been arranged in the past.

Shanxi University
Department of Music
Taiyuan Province
People's Republic of China

Chief Administrator. Chen Shun-Li, President.

The University was founded in 1902. This is the only university in China which has a music department for training professional musicians with a performance orientation. Western and Chinese instruments are taught. The Department offers a four-year course of study leading to the Bachelor of Music degree.

Academic Information

Enrollment, Music Majors. 50.
Music Faculty. 54.
Music Degrees Offered. Bachelor of Music.

Shengyang Conservatory of Music
Shengyang, Liaoning Province
People's Republic of China

Telephone. 482223, 482165
Chief Administrator. Ding Ming, Director.

The Shengyang Conservatory, located in the northeast region of China, was founded in 1938. It began as a music department of an arts school and in 1948 it became a conservatory. In 1953 it was granted status as an independent institution and in 1958 adopted its current name. Shengyang is an important transportation center of the northeastern Liaoning Province. The Conservatory is situated on a 162-acre campus. There are Departments of Theory, Composition, Chinese Instruments, Chinese Singing, Strings, Winds, Brass, Conducting, Vocal, Piano, Instrument Making and Repair, Teachers College, and Music Research Institute. The language of instruction is Mandarin.

Academic Information

Enrollment, Music Majors. 700.

Music Faculty. 30 professors and associate professors; 140 lecturers.

Term System. Semester. September to January; March to July.

Music Degrees Offered. Bachelor's degree awarded after five-year program; Master's degree after two- to three-year program; Diploma awarded after two-year program. Teachers' College offers a four-year program.

General Program Areas. Chinese Instruments, Chinese Singing, Composition, Conducting, Instrument Making, Instrument Repair, Music Education, Music History, Music Research, Music Theory, Musicology, Performance, Vocal Music.

Instruments Taught. Brass, Chinese Instruments, Piano, Stringed Instruments, Voice, Woodwinds.

Musical Facilities

Practice Facilities. 300 practice rooms. 400 pianos. 700 Chinese and Western instruments. Sound and video equipment.

Concert Facilities. Concert Hall for school and public performances.

Music Library. 160,000 volumes; 70,000 scores; 25,000 phonograph recordings and tapes.

Special Programs

Foreign Programs. Projects concerning Chinese music history and instruments are undertaken by foreign students.

Commentary

Conservatory students who come from areas outside of Liaoning Province are provided with living facilities, practice rooms, instruments, medical care, and living expenses. In the Conservatory curriculum, theory and composition and instrument-making are considered the institution's specialities.

Sichuan Conservatory of Music
Chengdu, Sichuan
People's Republic of China

The Sichuan Conservatory of Music, founded in 1953, is the only higher institute of music in southwest China. The institution was originally called the Southwest Musical Academy. In 1959, the current name was adopted. The predecessor of the school was the Sichuan Provincial Experimental Academy of Drama and Music established in 1939 and followed by the Chengdu Art Academy.

The Conservatory is located near the Jingjiang River in the south of Chengdu, a culturally and historically important city in southwest China. The 15-acre campus of the institution is surrounded by statues, fountains, flowers and plants, and pavilions. The tombstone of Mr. Wang Guangqi, the first man in China to receive a Ph.D. in musicology, is preserved as a historical monument on the campus.

The Conservatory consists of a College, affiliated Middle School, and organizations for research. There are departments of musical composition, wind and string instruments, piano, vocal, Chinese traditional instruments, accordion, and musical education.

The Conservatory publishes the academic journal *Explorations in Music* quarterly.

Academic Information

Enrollment, Music Majors. 500. The majority of students come from the provinces of Yunnan, Guizhou, Sichuan, and the Tibet Autonomous Region.

Music Faculty. 300.

Music Degrees Offered. Diploma; Bachelor of Arts; Master of Arts.

Music Degree Requirements. Undergraduates receive diplomas upon graduation; the best among them receive Bachelor of Arts degrees; postgraduates are awarded Master of Arts degrees. All courses of study are for four years except composition, theory, conducting (five years); teachers training (two years); graduate study (three years). After graduation, all students are offered jobs by the State.

General Program Areas. Chinese Instruments, Composition, Conducting, Music Education, Music Theory, Musicology, Performance, Vocal Music.

Instruments Taught. Accordion, Chinese Instruments, Chinese Singing, Piano, Stringed Instruments, Voice, Wind Instruments.

Musical Facilities

Practice Facilities. 350 pianos; 1 concert grand Steinway. 1,000 string and wind instruments. Electronic music studio.

Concert Facilities. Concert Hall, seating 1,000.

Music Library. 200,000 books and music scores; 42,-000-piece listening library (recordings, cassette tapes, videotapes). Special collection of scores for the Chinese Guqin.

Special Programs

Foreign Programs. Since 1980, musicians and professors from over 30 countries have visited to present concerts and lectures. The Conservatory welcomes cultural and musical exchanges with other countries and encourages those interested in such activities to contact the President's Office at the above address.

Xi'an Music Conservatory
Shaanxi Province
People's Republic of China

Chief Administrator. Liu Heng-Zhi, Director.

The Conservatory was founded in 1948 as the Northwest Academy of the Arts. In 1960, it became the Xi'an Music Conservatory. Western and Chinese instruments are taught. The four-year course of study leads to the Bachelor of Music degree.

Academic Information

Enrollment, Music Majors. 331.
Music Faculty. 132.
Music Degrees Offered. Bachelor of Music.

COLOMBIA

Conservatorio de Música del Ibagué
Calle 9, No. 1-18
Ibagué, Tolima
Colombia

Chief Administrator. Pilar Jaramillo Lozano, Director.

The Conservatorio was founded in 1906.

Musical Facilities

Music Library. 1,800 volumes.

Conservatorio Nacional de Música
Departamento de Música
Facultad de Artes
Universidad Nacional
Bogatá
Colombia

Chief Administrator. Siegfried Miklin, Director.

The Conservatory was founded in 1882 as Academia Nacional de Música and received its current name in 1910.

Academic Information

Enrollment, Music Majors. 900.
Music Faculty. 60.

Musical Facilities

Music Library. 11,000 books, scores, and recordings.

Corporación Universitaria Adventista
Department of Music
Carrera 84 No. 33A
A-1 Medellín
Colombia

Telephone. 432269
Chief Administrator. Leonardo Suescún F., Rector.

This institution, privately administered by the Seventh Day Adventist Church, was founded in 1937 as the Instituto Colombo Venezolano.

Academic Information

Term System. Semester. February to June; July to November.

Music Degree Requirements. Licenciado is awarded at the completion of a four-year course of study.

Instituto Musical de Cartagena
Apdo Aéreo No. 17-67
Cartagena, Bolívar
Colombia

Chief Administrator. Professor Jiri Pitro, Director.

The Instituto Musical was founded in 1890.

Musical Facilities

Music Library. 1,500 volumes.

Universidad de Antioquía
Facultad de Artes, Departamento de Música
Apartado aéreo 1226
Medellín
Colombia

Telephone. 231249, 230599
Chief Administrator. Mario Yepes Londoño, Dean.

The present Department was founded as a Conservatory of Music in 1969. In 1980, when the Faculty of Arts was created, it became the Department of Music. The campus is located on the outskirts of Medellín. The school's goal is to prepare competent musicians in order to increase the number of orchestras and chamber music groups in Colombia, as well as to improve the quality of existing groups.

Academic Information

Enrollment, Music Majors. Full-time 42 men, 38 women; part-time 23 men, 9 women.

Music Faculty. Full-time 27, part-time 13.

Term System. Semester. February to June; August to December.

Entrance Requirements. sixth grade study certificate; twelve years of age; audition for students who have musical study background; musical aptitude test for students who will begin their musical formation.

Admission Procedure. Application due December 15.

Music Degrees Offered. Diploma (Musical Performer).

Music Degree Requirements. Completion of all courses in the program (52 courses for 203 credits); presentation and approval of recital.

General Program Areas. Composition, Conducting, Music Theory, Performance.

Instruments Taught. Bassoon, Clarinet, Flute, Guitar, Oboe, Piano, Violin, Violoncello.

Musical Facilities

Practice Facilities. 25 practice rooms. 1 percussion-equipped practice room. 8 pianos (7 Baldwin uprights, 1 Steinway grand).

Concert Facilities. The University Theatre is used for concerts and recitals.

Music Library. 2,500 scores; 100 books; 399 phonograph recordings. Listening facilities (cassette, stereo). More musical material can be found in the University General Library.

Financial

Costs. Tuition based on individual economic circumstances.

Universidad de Nariño
Escuela de Música
Calle 21, No. 23-90
Pasto, Nariño
Colombia

Telephone. 5652

Chief Administrator. Fausto Martinez, Director.

Universidad de Nariño was founded in 1689 as a college and became a university in 1905.

Academic Information

Music Degrees Offered. Professional Titles.

Music Degree Requirements. "Experto" in Music after completion of a five-year course.

Universidad del Atlántico
Conservatorio de Música (School of Music)
Carrera 43 Nos. 50-53, Apartado Nacional
148
Aéreo 1890
Barranquilla
Colombia

Telephone. 315313

Chief Administrator. Esteban Páez Polo, Rector; Prof. Gunter Renz, Director.

This institution was founded in 1941 as Museo del Atlántico. It acquired its present structure and university status in 1946. The Universidad is recognized by the State and functions under the jurisdiction of the Ministry of Education.

Academic Information

Term System. Semester. January to June; July to December.

Music Degree Requirements. Licenciado and Professional titles are earned after four- and five-year courses of study, respectively.

COSTA RICA

Escuela de Música - Heredia
Universidad Nacional
Apartado 86
Heredia
Costa Rica

Telephone. (506) 37-40-60

Chief Administrator. Carmen Mendez, Director.

In 1974, the School of Fine Arts was formed from four departments. An attempt was made in 1977 to create an Arts Center with faculty status. In 1979, each department became a separate school under the Faculty of Arts and Letters (Music, Dance, Theater, Plastic Arts), and in 1984, an Arts Center (CIDEA) was formed. The main curriculum changes occurred in 1978 during the directorship of Roger Wesby.

Academic Information

Enrollment, Music Majors. Full-time 125, part-time 50. 5 foreign students from Guatemala, Nicaragua, El Salvador, Honduras, Panamá.

Music Faculty. Full-time 10, part-time 13.

Term System. Semester. Academic year from March to November.

Entrance Requirements. Secondary school diploma not a requirement for admission but is required for graduation; aptitude test for new students (melodic and rhythmic memory and coordination; audition required if student has previous musical studies (committee determines future course level). Applicants should have aural capabilities and must successfully complete a two-week screening period during which the basics of music reading and dictation are evaluated.

Admission Procedure. Application due December.

Music Degrees Offered. Bachelor of Music in Music Education; Diploma in Community Service and Performance (instrumental or vocal).

Music Degree Requirements. Student must meet University requirements which include general studies and introductory courses; four years of music reading/harmony courses; four years ensemble; seven semesters piano; eight semesters history/analysis; other courses in major area.

General Program Areas. Choral Music, Jazz Studies, Music Education, Music Theory, Performance.

Instruments Taught. Brass, Guitar, Percussion, Piano, Voice, Woodwinds.

Musical Facilities

Practice Facilities. 8 practice rooms. 7 pianos (6 uprights, 1 grand). 3 percussion-equipped practice rooms. Jazz rehearsal room.

Concert Facilities. Small multi-purpose auditorium.

Music Library. Very small quantity of scores, books, and cassettes has accumulated through private donations. The University has a general library. The National Symphony Orchestra sometimes shares materials with the Music School.

CUBA

Instituto Superior de Arte
Facultad de Música
Calle 120 No. 1110
Cubanacán
Playa
Cuba

Telephone. 218650

Chief Administrator. Dr. Hilda Mellis Grass, Dean; Aracelys Maffes Carbonell, Secretaria Docente.

The Music Faculty of The Instituto Superior de Arte (ISA) is the only university-level music institution in Cuba. There are five courses within the musicology discipline: ethnomusicology, aesthetics and historiography, musical pedagogical training, musical psychology and sociology, and economics and technology of music.

ISA is located in Cubanacán, on the outskirts of Havana, in a complex of buildings which was once a country club and hotel. The Institute is surrounded by an attractive campus. Because the main building was previously a hotel, each room has bathroom facilities and there is a swimming pool on the premises. There are more concert halls than in most conservatories; these spaces are simply converted ballrooms, lounges, and lecture facilities from the former country club era.

Academic Information

Enrollment, Music Majors. 400. 10-12 foreign students from Mexico, Spain, East European countries.

Music Faculty. 110.

Entrance Requirements. Students enter directly from the secondary-level music schools, also called "Escuelas Nivel Medio," of which there are five in Cuba: the Escuela Nacional de Música, located on the same campus as ISA, and the Conservatorio Amadeo Roldán, both in Havana; the Escuela de Música in Santiago de Cuba; the Escuela de Música in Camagüey; and the Escuela de Música in Holguin. Audition required; cultural conversation to determine general level; composer's work is judged by jury; musicology examination.

Admission Procedure. Application due February or May.

Music Degrees Offered. Diploma.

Music Degree Requirements. Completion of a five-year course.

General Program Areas. Composition, Conducting, Ethnomusicology, Music Theory, Musicology, Performance.

Instruments Taught. Brass, Cuban Percussion Instruments, Guitar, Harpsichord, Organ, Percussion, Piano, Saxophone, Stringed Instruments, Voice, Woodwinds.

Musical Facilities

Practice Facilities. 40 practice rooms. 70 pianos (Steinway, Yamaha, Rancola—50 uprights, 20 grands). 3 percussion-equipped practice rooms. 1 harpsichord, 1 electric organ. Electronic music studio. Sound recording studio.

Concert Facilities. 10 halls of various sizes; largest has seating for 450, smallest for 30.

Music Library. Scores, recordings (2,000). Listening facilities (turntables, cassettes). These listening facilities can be connected to classrooms by an intercom system.

Special Programs

Foreign Programs. Exchange programs with Mexico, Spain, Brazil, East European countries.

Financial

Costs. No tuition.

Commentary

There are plans to expand the curricula of ISA by adding a course for sound engineers, a division for studying the harp, and a new doctoral program. An adult education program in music is offered in the evenings to accommodate working people. The strongest aspects of the curriculum are the departments of percussion—offering training in both traditional Cuban and standard orchestral instruments, guitar, and composition.

CZECHOSLOVAKIA

Janáčkova Akademie Mûzickŷch Umeni (Janáček's Academy of Music and Dramatic Arts)

Komenskeho nam. 6
Brno 66215
Czechoslovakia

Telephone. 26842
Chief Administrator. Jaroslav Jankovych, Director.
The Janáček Academy of Music and Dramatic Art was founded in 1947 as a state institution. The language of instruction is Czech.

Academic Information

Enrollment, Music Majors. Full-time 160, plus 43 external students.
Music Faculty. Full-time 49, part-time 30.
Term System. Semester. September to December; February to June.
Music Degrees Offered. Diploma.
Music Degree Requirements. Completion of 4- to 5-year course.

Musical Facilities

Music Library. 72,000 volumes.

Special Programs

Foreign Programs. Program of exchange and cooperation with the State Conservatories of Gdansk, Poland and Novosibirsk, U.S.S.R.

Financial

Costs. No tuition.

Konzervatoř v Praze (State Conservatory Prague)

Na Rejdišti 1
Praha 110 00
Czechoslovakia

Telephone. 231 91 02
Chief Administrator. Professor František Martiník
The Prague Conservatory was founded in 1811 as the first institution of its type in Middle Europe. Among the professors of the conservatory were J. Kocián; O. Sevčík, professor of J. Kubelík; V. Kurz, professor of R. Firkušný. One of the directors was Antonín Dvořák. Students of the Conservatory have been awarded prizes in international competitions, and they frequently give concerts in European music centers and festivals. Programs offered include training for music school teachers and performers. There is a popular music department and a

theatre department for actors.

Academic Information

Enrollment, Music Majors. 600. 7-10 foreign students enroll each year (Sweden, Denmark, Finland, Korea, Vietnam).
Music Faculty. 25.
Music Degrees Offered. Diploma (after four years).
General Program Areas. Conducting, Folk Music, Music Education, Music Theory, Performance, Popular Music, Solfege, Theater.
Instruments Taught. Brass, Organ, Percussion, Piano, Stringed Instruments, Voice, Woodwinds.

Musical Facilities

Practice Facilities. 92 pianos (5 grands); 4 organs. 4 percussion-equipped practice rooms.
Concert Facilities. 4 concert halls, seating 150, 200, 250, and 1,500 respectively.
Music Library. 5,200 books; 30,000 periodicals; 57,800 scores; 16,800 recordings. Listening facilities include 69 record players. Special collection of 162 historical instruments.

Financial

Costs. No tuition.

Commentary

The State Conservatory of Prague, like the other conservatories in Czechoslovakia, is a secondary school within the country's music education system. A graduate of one of the state conservatories may go on to receive a university education in music at the Akademie of Music and Dramatic Arts in Prague, Janáček's Academy of Music and Dramatic Arts in Brno, or the College of Music and Dramatic Arts in Bratislava.

Konzervatorium - Bratislava

Tolstého 11
Bratislava 811 06
Czechoslovakia

Telephone. 335341
Chief Administrator. Dr. Zdenko Nováček, Director.
The Konzervatorium was founded in 1919 as the first music school for Slovakia. In 1928, the Ministry of Education granted the establishment public rights and agreed to the title of The Bratislava Academy of Music and Drama. The Academy did not become a state institution until 1941 when it was given the new title of State Conservatoire. It eventually became known as the Bratislava Conservatoire.

The two youngest departments of the Konzervatorium are Folk Instruments and Ballet. The Konzervatorium regards its current task to be: (1) making sure that there is no departure from the high artistic standard of the preceding decades and (2) supplementing that high standard with new conceptions.

Member of the Assocation Européenne des Conservatoires de Musique, Académies de Musique, et Musikhochschulen.

Academic Information

Enrollment, Music Majors. 450.
Music Faculty. 88 internal; 51 external.
Entrance Requirements. Completion of basic school; 14 years of age; a certain degree of ability in playing the instrument elected; good musical ear; basic knowledge of music theory.
Music Degrees Offered. "Graduate."
General Program Areas. Composition, Conducting, Music Theory, Opera, Slovakian Music.
Instruments Taught. Brass, Organ, Percussion, Piano, Stringed Instruments, Voice, Woodwinds.

Musical Facilities

Practice Facilities. 2 organs. 1 percussion-equipped practice room. 92 pianos (61 grand pianos).
Concert Facilities. 2 concert halls seating 240 and 70, respectively.
Music Library. 5,000 books; 40,000 scores; 7,000 phonograph recordings; 800 tapes. Listening facilities.

Financial

Costs. No tuition.

Commentary

The Konservatorium of Bratislava is one of the secondary schools within Czechoslovakia's music education system. *See* commentary for Konzervatoř v Praze.

Vysoká Skola Mûzických Umeni v Bratislave
(Academy of Music and Dramtic Arts Bratislava)
Jiráskova 3
Bratislava
Czechoslovakia

Telephone. 336141
Chief Administrator. Professor Miloš Jurkovič, Rector; Miloš Starosta, Dean, Faculty of Music.

The College of Music was founded in 1949 as a state institution.

Academic Information

Enrollment, Music Majors. 150.
Music Faculty. 130.
Term System. Semester. October to January; February to September.

Entrance Requirements. Secondary school certificate.
Music Degrees Offered. Diploma.
Music Degree Requirements. Completion of a five-year course of study.

Musical Facilities

Practice Facilities. Research and Recording Centre.

Financial

Costs. No tuition.

Vysoká Skola Mûzických Umeni v Praha
Academy of Music and Dramatic Arts
Dům umělců
Alsovo nábřeží 12
1101 00 Prague 1
Czechoslovakia

Telephone. 231 93 59 (Dean), 231 94 96 (Secretary of the Faculty), 231 68 12 Central Office, House of Artists)
Chief Administrator. Dr. Václav Felix, Dean.

The Music Faculty began its teaching activity in 1947. Up until this date there was no music school at the university level in Czechoslovakia, although the Conservatory of Prague had existed since 1811. Here pupils studied after finishing their basic education for a period of 4 to 7 years. In 1919, a senior school was founded to extend the education of the best graduates of the Conservatory. Only the major subjects were taught and the graduates had no certification or the qualification degree of university graduates. The founding of the Academy of Music and Dramatic Arts in 1946 granted the status and rights to a college-educated musician equal to that of university graduates and graduates of the Polytechnic Institution. The Music Faculty was founded with the aim of educating composers, conductors, opera directors, singers and performers on the following instruments: piano, organ, violin, viola, violoncello, bass, harp, flute, oboe, clarinet, bassoon, French horn; and in chamber music. Later, trumpet and trombone were added, and later still, harpsichord and guitar. Recently music theory and composing has been given particular emphasis in the curriculum. Two years of post-graduate studies in music theory are available. The Faculty of Music is part of a larger educational unit encompassing the dramatic arts, film, and television as well.

Member of the Assocation Européenne des Conservatoires de Musique, Académies de Musique, et Musikhochschulen.

Academic Information

Enrollment, Music Majors. Full-time 179, plus 79 external students, 20 research students. 30-35 students are admitted every year. 10 full-time foreign students from Poland, Yugoslavia, Korea, and Cyprus.

Entrance Requirements. High school graduation; audition and entrance examination (music history, music theory, social science).

Music Degrees Offered. Graduates receive no special degrees but may be named as graduates in the respective subject completed, and have the same rights as graduates of all other colleges and universities in Czechoslovakia.

General Program Areas. Chamber Music, Composition, Conducting, Instrumental Music, Music Education, Music History, Music Theory, Opera, Opera Direction, Vocal Music.

Instruments Taught. Bass, Bassoon, Clarinet, Flute, French Horn, Guitar, Harp, Harpsichord, Oboe, Organ, Piano, Trombone, Trumpet, Viola, Violin, Violoncello, Voice.

Musical Facilities

Practice Facilities. 4 organs. 61 pianos (45 grand). Electronic music studio for recording, acoustical analysis, and for production of electroacoustic music.

Concert Facilities. Auditorium seating 273. Opera Theatre.

Community Facilities. Local auditoriums are available for concerts.

Music Library. 130,000 total volumes; 8,700 books; 29,654 scores; 30 periodical titles; 15,000 phonograph recordings. Listening facilities (20 phonographs; 40 tape recorders).

Financial

Costs. No tuition.

DENMARK

Det Fynske Musikkonservatorium
(The Funen Academy of Music)
Islandsgade 2
5000 Odense C
Denmark

Telephone. (09) 11 06 63

Chief Administrator. Sven Erik Werner, Rektor.

This institution, founded in 1929, is affiliated with the Royal Danish Academy of Music in Copenhagen.

Member of the Assocation Européenne des Conservatoires de Musique, Académies de Musique, et Musikhochschulen.

Academic Information

Term System. Semester. Academic year September to December; January to June.

Music Degrees Offered. Diplomas are earned after three- and six-year courses.

Det Jydske Musikkonservatorium
(Royal Academy of Music, Aarhus)
Fuglesangs Allé 26
8210 Aarhus V
Denmark

Telephone. (06) 15 53 88

Chief Administrator. Professor Elisabeth Sigurdsson, Principal.

This Academy, affiliated with the Royal Academy in Copenhagen, was founded as a private school in 1927, becoming a state institution in 1963.

Member of the Assocation Européenne des Conservatoires de Musique, Académies de Musique, et Musikhochschulen.

Academic Information

Term System. Semester. Academic year September to December; January to June.

Music Degrees Offered. Diploma awarded after three- and six-year courses; Professional qualification after six- and nine-year courses.

Musical Facilities

Music Library. 13,000 volumes; 4,000 phonograph recordings.

Det Kongelige Danske Musikkonservatorium
(The Royal Danish Academy of Music)
Niels Brocks Gade 7
1574 Købebhavn V
Denmark

Telephone. (01) 12 42 74

Chief Administrator. Anker Blyme, Rector.

The Musikkonservatorium was first founded in 1867 as a private institution. It received its current status as a state institution in 1948.

Member of the Assocation Européenne des Conservatoires de Musique, Académies de Musique, et Musikhochschulen.

Academic Information

Term System. Semester. Academic year September to December; January to June.

Music Degrees Offered. Diploma (requires five years); Teaching qualification (six years); Soloist qualification (nine years).

Musical Facilities

Music Library. 50,000 volumes.

Nordjysk Musikkonservatorium
(North Jutland Academy of Music)
Ryesgade 52
9000 Aalborg
Denmark

Telephone. (08) 12 77 44
Chief Administrator. Erik Bach, Rektor.
The Musikkonservatorium, founded in 1930 as a private institution, became a state school in 1972.
Member of the Assocation Européenne des Conservatoires de Musique, Académies de Musique, et Musikhochschulen.

Academic Information

Term System. Semester. Academic year September to December; January to June.
Music Degrees Offered. Diplomas are earned after three- and six-year courses.

Special Programs

Affiliated Programs. There is an exchange program with the National Academy of Music in Oslo, Norway and the Birmingham School of Music in the United Kingdom.

Vestjysk Musikkonservatorium
(West Jutland Academy of Music)
Islandsgade 50
6700 Esbjerg
Denmark

Telephone. (05) 12 61 00
Chief Administrator. Anette Faaborg, Rektor.
The Musikkonservatorium was established in 1946.
Member of the Assocation Européenne des Conservatoires de Musique, Académies de Musique, et Musikhochschulen.

Academic Information

Term System. Semester. Academic year September to December; January to June.
Music Degrees Offered. Diplomas are earned after three- and six-year courses.

DOMINICAN REPUBLIC

Conservatorio Nacional de Música - Santo Domingo
Cesar Nicolas Penson
Santo Domingo
Dominican Republic

Telephone. (809) 688-8917

The Conservatory, under the auspices of the Department of Education, offers seminars such as the History of Opera to adults, as well as the general music curriculum.

Commentary

Additional informaiton about the music institutions of the Dominican Republic can be obtained from the following agencies:
Professor Licinio Mancebo, Director del Archivo National de Musica, Palacio de Bellas Artes, Santo Domingo, Republica Dominica
Professora Florencia Pierret, Directora General de Bellas Artes, Palacio de Bellas Artes, Santo Domingo, Republica Dominica
From the United States and Canada, any telephone number for a cultural institution in the Dominican Republic or other Caribbean location (except Haiti and Cuba) can be obtained from telephone information at (809) 555-1212.

EAST GERMANY

Evangelische Kirchenmusikschule der Kirchenprovinz Sachsen
(Evangelical Church Music School of the Church Province Saxony)
E. - Abderhalden - Str. 10
DDR-4020 Halle (Saale)
German Democratic Republic

Telephone. 21327
Chief Administrator. Helmut Gleim, Director.
The goal of this institution is to train instrumentalists, singers, and conductors for church-related music vocations.

Academic Information

Music Degrees Offered. Professional titles are conferred upon graduates.
General Program Areas. Choral Conducting, Liturgy, Music History, Music Theory, Orchestral Conducting, Vocal Music.
Instruments Taught. Brass, Harpsichord, Organ, Piano, Voice.

Commentary

Other church music schools in the German Democratic Republic are located in the cities of Dresden and Rostock.

Hochschule für Music Franz Liszt
Platz der Demokratie 2/3
DDR 5300 Weimar
German Democratic Republic

Telephone. 5241

Chief Administrator. Professor Dr. Diethelm Müller-Nilsson, Rector; Gert Frischmuth, Prorector.

The Hochschule für Music Franz Liszt was founded as the Duncal Orchestral School in 1872 by Karl Müller-Hartung and became a state institution in 1930. The Hochschule also has a Division for Dance and Light Music and an Institute for Folk Music Research. Residential facilities are available for students.

Member of the Assocation Européenne des Conservatoires de Musique, Académies de Musique, et Musikhochschulen.

Academic Information

Enrollment, Music Majors. 650 to 700 students.

Term System. Semester. September to January; February to June.

Entrance Requirements. Secondary school certificate (Reifezeugnis).

Music Degrees Offered. State Diploma.

Music Degree Requirements. Completion of four- to five-year course.

General Program Areas. Chamber Music, Composition, Conducting, Music Education, Music Theory.

Instruments Taught. Accordion, Brass, Guitar, Organ, Piano, Stringed Instruments, Voice, Woodwinds.

Musical Facilities

Music Library. 65,000 volumes. 45,000 tapes; 300 manuscripts. Special collection of Franz Liszt materials. The Goethe-Schiller-Archiv (Bibliothek, Am Burgplatz 4, DDR-53 Weimar), located very near the Hochschule, has the collection of Goethe's music library. The Goethe-National-Museum (Bibliothek, Goethes Wohnhaus, Frauenplan 1-2, DDR-53 Weimar) administers the collection of Liszt-Haus. The Zentrakbibliothek (Platz der Demokratie 1, DDR-53 Weimar, telephone 35 52), also in close proximity to the Hochschule, has a Liszt collection of first editions as well as manuscripts composed by Friedrich Nietzsche.

Special Programs

Featured Programs. Division for Dance and Light Music; Institute for Folk Music Research.

Foreign Programs. Program of cooperation and exchange with the Viss Muzikalno-Pedagogiceski Institut in Plovdiv, Bulgaria.

Financial

Costs. No tuition.

Commentary

The Hochschule für Music Franz Liszt is well known for its instrumental summer master classes which draw students from many countries.

Hochschule für Musik Carl Maria von Weber
Blochmannstrasse 2/4
DDR 8010 Dresden
German Democratic Republic

Telephone. 4590213

Chief Administrator. Professor Dr. Gerd Schönfelder, Rector.

The Hochschule für Musik Carl Maria von Weber was founded in 1856 as a private school and became a state institution in 1945. From 1946 to 1951 the Rektor was Fidelio F. Finke. In 1952, the school was given university status under the Rektorship of musicologist Karl Laux, and in 1959 was named after Weber. Composer and musicologist Siegfried Kohler was appointed Rector in 1968, and six years later, in 1974, the Department of Musicology was founded under Gerd Schönfelder. Student housing is available.

Member of the Assocation Européenne des Conservatoires de Musique, Académies de Musique, et Musikhochschulen.

Academic Information

Term System. Semester. September to January; February to July.

Entrance Requirements. Secondary school certificate (Reifezeugnis).

Music Degrees Offered. State diploma.

Music Degree Requirements. Completion of a 4- to 5-year course.

Instruments Taught. Brass, Organ, Piano, Stringed Instruments, Voice, Woodwinds.

Musical Facilities

Music Library. 32,000 volumes and music works; 2,000 phonograph recordings; 180 archival tapes. A collection of musical instruments is maintained. Record players available. The school publishes *Schriftenreihe.* Library telephone: 63 592, 63 544.

Financial

Costs. No tuition.

Hochschule für Musik Felix Mendelssohn-Bartholdy

Grassistrasse 8
7010 Leipzig
German Democratic Republic

Telephone. 311402
Chief Administrator. Professor Gustav Schmahl, Rector.

The Hochschule für Musik Felix Mendelssohn-Bartholdy was founded in 1843 by the composer for whom it is named. In 1876, it was designated a royal institution and eleven years later, in 1887, it moved to a new building designed by Hugo Licht, where it is presently located. After World War II, Rudolph Fischer was Rektor, and he was succeeded in the position by violinist Gustav Schmahl in 1974. Over the years teachers at the Hochschule have included R. Schumann, Ignaz Mosceles, and Max Reger, while among the illustrious graduates are Edvard Grieg, Adrian Boult, and Frederick Delius. The school has a Division for Dance and Light Music.

Member of the Assocation Européenne des Conservatoires de Musique, Académies de Musique, et Musikhochschulen.

Academic Information

Term System. Semester. September to January; February to July.
Entrance Requirements. Secondary school certificate (Reifezeugnis).
Music Degrees Offered. State Diploma.
Music Degree Requirements. Completion of a four- to five-year course of study.
General Program Areas. Composition, Music Theory.
Instruments Taught. Brass, Organ, Percussion, Piano, Stringed Instruments, Voice, Woodwinds.

Musical Facilities

Music Library. 7,500 books; 52,000 music works, including some from before 1800; 2,000 records. Library telephone 3 32 11.

Financial

Costs. No tuition.

Commentary

Over the years, a great number of Gewandhaus Orchestra members have been trained at the Hochschule für Musik Felix Mendelssohn-Bartholdy. This venerable institution is located in the old Gewandhaus Quarter of Leipzig, near the old Gewandhaus which unfortunately did not survive World War II. The world-famous collection of musical instruments in Leipzig is located in the Grassi Museum, administered under the auspices of the Karl Marx University.

Hoschschule für Music Hans Eisler

Otto-Grotewohl-Strasse 19
DDR Berlin 1080
German Democratic Republic

Telephone. 2202626
Chief Administrator. Professor Dieter Zechlin, Director.

The Hochschule für Music Hans Eisler was founded in 1950. The first director, until 1959, was Georg Knepler, who was succeeded by Eberhard Rebling. Some housing facilities are available in hostels.

Member of the Assocation Européenne des Conservatoires de Musique, Académies de Musique, et Musikhochschulen.

Academic Information

Enrollment, Music Majors. 540.
Music Faculty. 100.
Term System. Semester. September to February; February to July.
Entrance Requirements. Secondary school certificate (Reifezeugnis) or certificate from a State school of music.
Music Degrees Offered. State Diploma.
Music Degree Requirements. Completion of four- to five-year course.
General Program Areas. Composition, Conducting, Music Theory, Musical Stage Direction.
Instruments Taught. Accordion, Brass, Guitar, Stringed Instruments, Voice, Woodwinds.

Musical Facilities

Music Library. 42,000 volumes; 28,000 music works. Listening facilities. The Deutsche Staatsbibliothek (Musikabteilung, Unter den Linden 8, DDR-108 Berlin, telephone: 22 808 357) has important holdings including 350,000 music works, 60,000 manuscripts, and collections of records and musicians' portraits.

Special Programs

Featured Programs. The College has a Division of Evening and Correspondence Courses.

Financial

Costs. No tuition.

ECUADOR

Conservatorio Nacional de Música - Quito

Carrión 514 y Reina Victoria
Quito
Ecuador

Telephone. (5932) 21 10 22

Chief Administrator. Professor Gerardo Guevara, Rector.

The Conservatorio was founded in 1900. It is the main national conservatory in Ecuador with affiliated music schools in Loja, Cuenca, and Guayaquil.

Academic Information

Music Degrees Offered. Licenciado de Musica.

EGYPT

Cairo Conservatory of Music
Academy of Arts
Avenue of the Pyramids
Giza
Egypt

Telephone. 853451
Chief Administrator. Dr. Ekram Matar, Dean; Dr. Samha El-Kholy, Head of Academy of Arts.

The Cairo Conservatory of Music was the first of the cultural organizations belonging to the Academy of Arts to be founded. In the early years after the 1952 revolution, the state designated an Arts Council and within that, a music committee. The founding of a conservatory to train Egyptian musicians was recommended and in August 1959, President Nasser issued the official decree for its creation. The goal of the Conservatory is to give each student a thorough knowledge of Western music without threatening his/her sense of spiritual belonging to the Egyptian culture.

The first site for the school was a villa by the Nile River on Zamalek Island. In September 1962, the conservatory moved to a new seven-story building with an adjoining concert hall (Sayed Darwish). At that time the school had a student body of 70, divided between a Secondary School and the Conservatory. In 1968, a third part—a children's music school—was added.

The other schools which make up the structure of the Academy—Drama, Ballet, Cinema, Arab Music, Art Appreciation—joined the existing Music Conservatory in 1969.

Academic Information

Enrollment, Music Majors. 350.
Music Faculty. 108. From the school's beginnings, a multinational staff was hired, a characteristic it still retains.
Music Degrees Offered. Diploma.
Music Degree Requirements. The Diploma is earned after four years of undergraduate courses. Each student is required to take a course in traditional Arab music. Solfege and ear-training majors study both Oriental and Western harmonies. All graduating singers and instrumentalists must include an Arabic Egyptian work in

their final recitals.

EL SALVADOR

Centro Nacional de Artes "CENAR"
Calles Delgado
Edificio Bendeck 524
San Salvador
El Salvador

The Centro Nacional de Artes can supply information about the cultural institutions in El Salvador.

Conservatorio Nacional de Música
1a A.N. no. 821
San Salvador
El Salvador

ETHIOPIA

Yared National Institute of Music
c/o Ministry of Culture
P.O. Box 1902
Addis Ababa
Ethiopia

Telephone. 44-6338
Chief Administrator. Commissioner Girma Yilma, Head, Ministry of Culture.

The National School of Music was established in 1963 and funded by the old Ministry of Education and Fine Arts. Administratively, it operated under the Assistant Minister of Fine Arts. From 1963-65 the National School of Music was housed in a six-room structure within the compounds of Haile Selassie I University at Sidist Kilo. With the leadership of Ashenafi Kebede (currently Professor of Ethnomusicology at Florida State University) and the patronage of Emperor Haile Selassie, the million (Ethiopian) dollar building complex, which had been contributed by the Bulgarian government, was completed in June, 1965. The complex consisted of three buildings: administration and classrooms; practice rooms; and an 800-seat Concert Hall, rehearsal rooms, and a recreation veranda with a cafe. Coinciding with this new structure and expansion, the school was renamed after Saint Yared, an Ethiopian ecclesiastic scholar-musician who lived during the reign of King Gebre Meskel (476-571 A.D.).

Dr. Kebede wrote the syllabus for the Yared School of Music and served as its first Director. The Yared School had the continued patronage of the Emperor until 1970 and became the residence of the Ethiopian National Music Committee and a member of UNESCO's International Music Council (IMC). In the late 1960s, the instructors and students at the Institute performed at the Shiraz Festival in Iran and the Zagreb Bienale in Yugoslavia. In addition, they have performed traditional Ethiopian music in Paris and Berlin, sponsored by the International Music Council and International Institute for Comparative Music Studies (Berlin).

Academic Information

Music Degrees Offered. Elementary Teaching Certificates are awarded upon completion of the four-year course; Performance Diplomas are awarded to students who successfully complete a five-year course.

Music Degree Requirements. The programs of the Yared School emphasize traditional musical education. Students are required to be familiar with the following subjects: Ethiopian Orthodox Music Education system, an approach followed by Saint Yared and modified by Professor Kebede; performance on the traditional secular musical instruments, such as the *masinko* (fiddle), *krar* (lyre), and *washint* (flute); Ethiopian poetry and verse; and traditional secular music and dances. The concepts of "bi-musicality" are encouraged in the third year, after the student demonstrates satisfactory knowledge of his/her own music culture. In the third and fourth years, students are permitted to study Western music and musical instruments—such as solfege, history, composition, and jazz.

General Program Areas. Composition, Ethiopian Instruments, Jazz Studies, Music History.

Instruments Taught. Krar, Masinko, Washint.

Commentary

Further information about the Yared Institute of Music can be obtained from:

Ministry of Information and National Guidance
Commissioner Felike Gidle-Giorgis
P.O. Box 1020
Addis Ababa
Ethiopia
Telephone: 11124

FINLAND

The East Helsinki Music Institute
Roihuvuorentie 28
SF-00820 Helsinki
Finland

Telephone. (90) 755-3165
Chief Administrator. Géza Szilvay, Director.

The East Helsinki Music Institute prepares students for university studies. It was founded in 1965 and follows the Kodaly philosophy of educating musicians. The language of instruction is Finnish; Swedish when required. The pupils are usually from the East Helsinki area.

Accreditation. Member of the Finnish Association of Music Institutes.

Academic Information

Enrollment, Music Majors. Full-time 562 men, 985 women.

Term System. Autumn term August 15 to December 31; Spring term January 1 to May 31. Two-week summer music campus.

Entrance Requirements. General musicality. Audition required (singing and playing).

Admission Procedure. Application due May.

Music Degrees Offered. Certification for studying at the University and the Music Academy.

Music Degree Requirements. Stringed instruments are emphasized; courses for string teachers are given in the Colour Strings Method.

General Program Areas. Colour Strings Method.

Instruments Taught. Orchestral Instruments.

Musical Facilities

Concerts/Musical Activities. LP records are made by the Helsinki Junior and Children Strings.

Commentary

The music institutes in Finland provide pre-college-level music education. They are, however, an integral part of the Finnish music education system directly connected to the Sibelius Academy of Music. Music education majors from the Academy visit the East Helsinki Institute to observe the string teaching method used there.

Kuopion Konservatorio
Kuopionlahdenkatu 23 C.
70100 Kuopio
Finland

Telephone. (71) 117-122
Chief Administrator. Heikki Halme, Director.

Education activities began at the Kuopion Konservatorio in 1954 and the educational programs for professionals commenced in 1974. The major goal of the school is to educate music school teachers. The future direction of the school will aim to decrease part-time education of children and increase the full-time programs for professionals.

The conservatory and the church music branch of Sibelius Academy which share some of the same faculty, are both located in the Kuopio Music Center (1985) in the center of Kuopio. After conservatory students complete their studies, they have the possibility of continuing with the Sibelius Academy.

Accreditation. Member of Music School and Conservatory System in Finland (SML).

Academic Information

Enrollment, Music Majors. Full-time 21 men, 30 women; part-time 323 men, 490 women.

Music Faculty. Full-time 42, part-time 66.

Term System. Semester. August to December, January to May. Two-week summer orchestra camp.

Entrance Requirements. Solo instrument course (about nine years of study), music theory I, solfege I, music knowledge I; usually age eighteen. Audition required; compulsory and elective pieces of about 15 minutes; *prima vista* piece.

Admission Procedure. Application due April 30.

Music Degrees Offered. Diploma for music school teachers and orchestral musicians.

Music Degree Requirements. 175 weeks required to complete the program.

General Program Areas. Chamber Music, Counterpoint, Harmony, Music History, Pedagogics, Piano, Solfege, Structure Analysis.

Instruments Taught. Brass, Flute, Guitar, Harpsichord, Organ, Percussion, Piano, Stringed Instruments, Trumpet, Voice, Woodwinds.

Musical Facilities

Practice Facilities. 10 full-time practice rooms, 20 part-time rooms. Practice rooms available for organists; 2 organs (Heinrichs and Kangasala). 2 practice rooms for percussionists. 10 practice rooms for pianists (20 available part-time); 10 upright pianos; 10 grand pianos reserved for piano majors. Students assigned practice rooms for about 15 hours per week. Special studios for jazz and dance.

Concert Facilities. Concert hall seating 1,064; chamber music hall, 240; examination hall, 100.

Concerts/Musical Activities. Student concerts as organized by the conservatory.

Music Library. 7,692 volumes; 7,167 scores; 525 books; 8 periodicals; 230 records. Listening facilities for both audiocassette and stereo equipment.

Financial

Costs. National and foreign students $100 per year. Estimated housing expenses $60 per month.

Financial Aid. Financial aid available in the form of loans from banks and the state. Average loan $2,000.

Commentary

The dance teacher education program has recently been added to The Konservatorio curriculum. This institution plans to decrease the part-time curriculum for children and increase the full-time programs for professional musicians.

Pohjois-Kymen Musiikkiopisto (North Kymi Music Institute)
Varuskuntakatu 11
45100 Kouvola
Finland

Telephone. (951) 14334 (office), 17818 (Principal)

Chief Administrator. Pentti Koto, Principal.

The North Kymi Music Institute was established in 1971, evolving from an already existing institution, the Kouvola Music School, founded in 1950. In 1972, it became a state school; in 1982, a modern, well-equipped building was completed. The goal of the Institute is to educate well-balanced youths with good skills and knowledge of music and to give a good basis for further studies at a conservatory, academy, or university. A major offering of the Institute is the training in flute and piano. Pupils are mainly school children. Departments include the Music Institute, Music School, Department for Adults, Preliminary Instruction, and Music Play School. Instruction is offered in 16 locations and is given in all classical instruments and the kantele (Finnish national instrument). Students are not housed at the Institute.

Accreditation. Member of Finnish Music Institutes Union.

Academic Information

Enrollment, Music Majors. Music Institute 47, Music School 514, Department for Adults 62, Preliminary Instruction 87, Music Play 240.

Term System. Academic year from mid-August to late May (38 weeks per year). Summer music camp for 1 week (70 pupils).

Entrance Requirements. Musical tests are required (not in Music School department); secondary school diploma and comprehensive examination required for Music Institute department). Audition involves a tape test to measure capacity for hearing musical elements, pitch, melody, rhythm, etc.

Admission Procedure. Application due in April.

Music Degrees Offered. Diploma.

Music Degree Requirements. Examination of Music School and Music Institute; 25 main subjects (instruments or song) plus general subjects; hours dependent on pupil; in general, the examination of the Music School department must be completed by the age of sixteen after which there are four years in the Music Institute; requirements are determined by the examination results.

General Program Areas. Folk Music, Jazz Studies, Music Theory, Organ.

Instruments Taught. Brass, Kantele, Organ, Percussion, Piano, Stringed Instruments, Woodwinds.

Musical Facilities

Practice Facilities. 25 practice rooms; percussion-equipped percussion practice room. 38 pianos; 3 grand pianos reserved for piano majors.

Concert Facilities. 2 concert halls.

Concerts/Musical Activities. About 50 student recitals/concerts per year.

Music Library. 2,330 volumes; 150 scores; 6 periodicals; 500 phonograph records. Listening facilities for 10 students; 3 cassette recorders and 7 record players.

Financial

Costs. Fees dependent upon departments and subjects.

Financial Aid. Scholarship application due September. 12% of students receive financial aid.

Commentary

This institution sponsors studies which are unusual in Finland on the institute level: a jazz-pop music section, lied seminars, and the Suzuki method of teaching in piano and violin. Music institutes are preparatory schools for the university or academy education, although in Finland they are part of the overall Sibelius Academy of Music system.

Sibelius Academy of Music

Töölönkatu 28
SF-00260 Helsinki 26
Finland

Telephone. (90) 408-166

Chief Administrator. Ellen Urho, Principal.

Sibelius Academy of Music, the only university-level music institution in Finland, was a private music college until August 1, 1980 when it became a state institution. It was established as the Helsinki Institute of Music in 1882 and its first director was Martin Wegelius. In 1924, the Institute changed its name to the Helsinki Conservatory, and the current name was adopted in 1939.

The Sibelius Academy is officially bilingual providing all instruction in both Finnish and Swedish.

Member of the Assocation Européenne des Conservatoires de Musique, Académies de Musique, et Musikhochschulen; the Nordisk Konservatorierd.

Academic Information

Enrollment, Music Majors. 911 students.

Music Faculty. 163 full-time teachers.

Music Degrees Offered. Candidate of Music, Licentiate; Doctor of Music.

Music Degree Requirements. The Candidate of Music course, a 180-week or a 5½ year period, is available in composition and theory, orchestral and choral conducting, performance (instrumental or vocal), music education, church music for organists and other church musicians, jazz studies, folk music. Postgraduate courses are offered in research, pedagogics, church music, composition, performance.

General Program Areas. Church Music, Conducting, Folk Music, Jazz, Music Composition, Music Education, Music Theory, Opera, Organ, Performance.

Musical Facilities

Concerts/Musical Activities. The Academy publishes both recordings and literary publications. Recordings are chiefly of compositions by teachers and students at the Academy. The Yearbook contains scientific articles. The Maj Lind Piano Competition for young Finnish pianists is held here every three years. Also offered is the Helmi Vesa competition for pianists.

Music Library. 43,000 volumes of music; 54,000 books; 3,000 phonorecords. The music library comprises a reading room, a record and tape section, music book and printed music sections. There are about 9,000 recordings, 9,500 books, and 64,000 items of printed music. The goal is eventually to develop the library into a central national music library. Special holdings: Evert Katela's library of 1,000 volumes owned by Association of Musicians in Finland. Library telephone: (90) 44 49 99 or 49 24 44.

Special Programs

Foreign Programs. The Sibelius Academy regularly organizes exchanges with about 20 European music academies. Participation in the Nordic biennale for young Nordic soloists (every other year) is offered to students.

Commentary

As the only music academy in Finland, the Sibelius Academy is responsible for all advanced music education throughout the country. The other institutions, including the konservatorios (conservatories), music colleges, and music institutes (music schools) are part of the comprehensive academy network. Ellen Urho, Principal of the Sibelius Academy, has stated a basic mission of the institution: "One of the primary goals of cultural policy in the 1980s is the promotion of international cooperation. This is absolutely vital in a small country such as Finland." Opera training has flourished at the Academy in recent years.

Sibeliusmuseum
Musikvetenskapliga Institutionen vid Åbo Akademi

(Musicological Institution at Åbo Academy)
Biskopsgatan 17 20500
Åbo 50
Finland

Telephone. (921) 335 133, 137 28
Chief Administrator. Ilpo Tolvas, Curator.

The Sibeliusmuseum is a musicological institute which holds collections including the Sibelius Collection, the library of Professor Otto Andersson, Finnish music and records, and a number of documents and musical instruments. The institution was founded in 1926.

Tampereen Konservatorio
Lundelininpolku 2
33230 Tampere
Finland

Telephone. (31) 35244
Chief Administrator. Pentti Suojanen, Director.

The goal of the Tampereen Konservatorio is to educate professional musicians of high quality, and in particular, music teachers. It was founded in 1931 as a Music School and became a Conservatory in 1978. The institution occupies a building in the center of Tampere.

Accreditation. Member of the Finnish Music School Union.

Academic Information

Enrollment, Music Majors. Full-time 46 men, 54 women; part-time 280 men, 491 women.
Music Faculty. Full-time 52, part-time 51. Foreign students 1 (U.S.A.).
Term System. Semester. Academic year August to December; January to June. Summer session offers only theoretical subjects.
Entrance Requirements. Comprehensive examination required; admission tests are given yearly in April.
Music Degrees Offered. Diploma.
Music Degree Requirements. 13 courses required.
Instruments Taught. Brass, Organ, Percussion, Stringed Instruments, Woodwinds.

Musical Facilities

Practice Facilities. 2 practice rooms for percussionists. 2 organs (Kangasalan Urkutehdas). 57 practice pianos; 2 grand pianos reserved for piano majors.
Concert Facilities. Concert Hall, seating 318; auditorium, 100.
Music Library. 2,517 books; 8,972 scores; 790 phonograph recordings. Listening facilities include 10 record players and 3 magnetophones. Instrument collection includes 5 krummhorns, 1 zink. The Tampere City Library is also a nearby resource for students.

Financial

Financial Aid. Scholarship applications accepted April 1-30. 102 students receive scholarship aid.

Commentary

In addition to the Kuopion Konservatorio and the Tampereen Konservatorio listed in this section, there are other schools of the same category all over Finland. They are: (1) Helsingen Konservatorio, Fredrikinkatu 34B, 00100 Helsinki 10; (2) JyvÄskylÄ Konservatorio, Gummeruksen Katu 6, 40100 JyvÄskylÄ 10; (3) Oulu Konservatorio Lintulammentie 1, 91040 Oulu 14; (4) Turku Konservatorio, Linnankatu 43, 20100 Turku 70; as well as the conservatories of Lahti and Pietarsaari.

FRANCE

Conservatoire National de Région, Bordeaux
Bordeaux
France

A new Conservatoire building was constructed in the early 1980s and the facilities are extremely modern. The Conservatoire has one of the finest departments for the study of saxophone in the world. The professor of saxophone attracting an international class of students is Jean-Marie Londeix.

Special Programs

Performance Groups. Special ensemble: L'Ensemble International de Saxophones de Bordeaux.

Conservatoire National de Région, Marseille
2 Place Carli
13001 Marseilles
France

Telephone. (91) 553574; Library 487673, 474008
Chief Administrator. Pierre Barbizet, Director.
The curriculum at the Conservatoire includes electronic music.

Musical Facilities

Practice Facilities. Electronic music studio.
Music Library. 2,000 volumes. Special collections include seventeenth century cantata manuscripts and additional seventeenth-eighteenth century vocal literature.

Conservatoire National de Région, Strasbourg
2, avenue de la Marseillaise
67000 Strasbourg
France

Telephone. (88) 36 55 02
Chief Administrator. Jean-Paul Baumgartner, Director.

The Conservatoire was founded in 1855.

Member of the Assocation Européenne des Conservatoires de Musique, Académies de Musique, et Musikhochschulen.

Musical Facilities

Music Library. Library telephone: 35 49 84.

Conservatoire National Supérieur de Musique

14, rue de Madrid
75008 Paris
France

Telephone. (1) 42 92 15 20

Chief Administrator. Raymond Gallois Montbrun, Director.

A free school of music was established by the Convention Nationale on August 3, 1795 and Bernard Sarrette was appointed president of the newly incorporated conservatoire de musique on rue de Madrid. The organization of the school was later modified by Napoleon Bonaparte in March 1800 and it was again reorganized on October 15, 1812. In 1814, Sarrette was dismissed, but reinstated in 1815. His retirement came later that year. The school closed until April 1816 and later reopened under the name Ecole Royale de Musique—with François Louis Perne as Inspector General. Luigi Cherubini succeeded him in 1822 and remained in that position for 20 years. He was replaced by Daniel Auber, and future directors of the conservatoire included Ambroise Thomas, Theodore Dubois, Gabriel Fauré, and Henri Rabaud.

Member of the Assocation Européenne des Conservatoires de Musique, Académies de Musique, et Musikhochschulen.

Academic Information

Term System. Three terms. October to December; January to March; April to June.

Music Degrees Offered. Diploma.

Music Degree Requirements. Awarded after one to four years, depending on course.

Musical Facilities

Music Library. 100,000 volumes. Museum of Music Instruments. All rare materials are located at 2 rue Louvois. Library telephone: 522 29 30.

Commentary

Early music, and the study of Baroque violin in particular, have recently attracted much student interest at the Paris Conservatoire.

Conservatoire National Supérieur de Musique de Lyon

3, rue de l'Angile
69005 Lyon
France

Telephone. (7) 839 63 40

Chief Administrator. Gilbert Amy, Director.

The Conservatoire was established in 1979. Its goal is to educate students in all areas of music and to equip them for professional careers.

Member of the Assocation Européenne des Conservatoires de Musique, Académies de Musique, et Musikhochschulen.

Accreditation. Association Internationale des Bibliothèques Musicales.

Academic Information

Enrollment, Music Majors. Full-time 128 men, 83 women.

Music Faculty. Full-time 78, part-time 10. 8 foreign students representing 6 nationalities (American, English, Chinese, Spanish, Iranian, Italian).

Term System. Trimester.

Entrance Requirements. Audition required.

Admission Procedure. Application due September 14.

Music Degrees Offered. Diploma.

Music Degree Requirements. Completion of prescribed courses; four years.

Musical Facilities

Practice Facilities. 17 practice rooms. 3 percussion-equipped practice rooms. 19 Kawai pianos. 2 grand pianos reserved for piano majors.

Community Facilities. Local churches used for public concerts and recitals. Organ classes are held in Toulouse.

Music Library. 25,000 scores; 6,000 books; 600 phonograph recordings; 17 videocassettes; 500 microfiche; 40 periodicals; 500 manuscripts. Collection of Nadia Boulanger.

GHANA

Advanced Teacher Training College - Winneba
Music Department

P.O. Box 129
Winneba
Ghana

Telephone. 139

This institution is a branch of the University of Cape Coast and trains music teachers.

Academic Information

Music Degrees Offered. Associate.
Music Degree Requirements. The degree is awarded after completion of a two-year course.

University of Cape Coast
Department of Music
Cape Coast
Ghana

Telephone. 2440-9, 2480-9
Chief Administrator. Eric Akrofi, Head, Department of Music.

The University offers a four-year course in music and trains music teachers. An Overseas Office is located in London, U.K. at the following address: Universities of Ghana Office, 321 City Road, London EC1V 1LJ, U.K. Telephone (01) 278-7413 (4,5).

Academic Information

Music Degrees Offered. Bachelor of Music Education.

University of Ghana
School of Performing Arts
P.O. Box 25
Legon
Ghana

Telephone. Accra 75381
An Overseas Office is located in London, U.K. at the following address: Universities of Ghana Office, 321 City Road, London EC1V 1LJ, U.K. Telephone (01) 278-7413 (4,5).

Academic Information

Music Degrees Offered. Bachelor of Music; Diploma.
Music Degree Requirements. The Degree is awarded at the completion of a three-year course. The Diploma in African music is awarded at the end of a two-year course; the Music diploma, after a three-year course.

GREECE

Hellenic Odeion - Athens
(Greek Conservatory)
Athens
Greece

This Conservatory was founded in 1919. There are several smaller music schools throughout Greece which are affiliated with the Hellenic Conservatory.

Academic Information

Music Degrees Offered. Diploma.
Music Degree Requirements. The Diploma is awarded after completion of studies.

Kratikon Odeion Thessaloniki
(State Conservatory of Music)
Odos Olympiou Diamanti 7
Thessaloniki
Greece

Telephone. 510551
Chief Administrator. Dr. Dimitrios Themelis, Director.

The Conservatory was founded in 1914. It offers studies in instrumental, vocal, and theoretical subjects.

Academic Information

Music Degrees Offered. Diploma.
Music Degree Requirements. The Diploma is received after completion of the studies.
General Program Areas. Composition, Music Theory, Performance, Vocal Music.

Musical Facilities

Music Library. 6,000 volumes. Special collection in Braille.

Nikos Skalkotas Conservatory
Agias Lavras 78
Ano Patisia
Athens 11141
Greece

Telephone. (1) 223 23 39
Chief Administrator. George Pazaitis, Director; John Iaannidis, Artistic Director.

The Conservatory was founded in 1981 in the memory of the distinguished Greek composer and violinist, Nikos Skalkotas (1904-1949). It was established to create an institution offering a complete musical education in all levels. Specialized and individual attention is given to each student's educational and musical needs. Since 1985, the Conservatory has been the examination center in Greece, representing Trinity College of London. The Conservatory sponsors seminars with master classes given by artists of international reputation.

Academic Information

Enrollment, Music Majors. 2,000. Foreign students 15 (Israel, Japan, France, Germany, Italy, Netherlands).
Music Faculty. 126.
Entrance Requirements. Requirements are established by the Ministry of Culture depending on age and level

of musical ability.

Music Degrees Offered. Performance degree; Music Education degree; degrees in theory, harmony and composition.

General Program Areas. Music History, Orchestration, Organology, Performance, Solfege.

Instruments Taught. Brass, Guitar, Organ, Percussion, Piano, Stringed Instruments, Woodwinds.

Musical Facilities

Practice Facilities. 50 pianos (2 concert grands); 15 organs.

Concert Facilities. 3 concert halls, seating 120 to 1,500.

Community Facilities. Access to several halls within the city of Athens.

Music Library. Audio and video library including records, video cassettes, record players. Several complete collections of scores for classical guitar; collection of the complete works of J.S. Bach; many first editions for strings; collection of unusual editions of chamber music for string instruments.

Odeion Athenon
(Conservatory of Athens)
Odos Rigillis and Vassileos Georgiou 17/19
Athens
Greece

Chief Administrator. M.G. Pallandios, Director.

The Odeon was established in 1871. It is the oldest and historically the most important of the Greek conservatories. Artists such as Maria Callas and Dimitri Mitropolous studied here.

Academic Information

Enrollment, Music Majors. 1,200.
Music Degrees Offered. Diploma.
Music Degree Requirements. The Diploma is received after completing the studies.
General Program Areas. Byzantine Church Music, Composition, Military Music, Music Theory.

Odeion Ethnikon - Athens
(National Conservatory)
Odos Maizonos 8
108 Athens
Greece

Chief Administrator. Krino Kalomiri, Leonidas Zoras, Directors.

This institution was founded in 1926 by Monolis Kolomiris, a man who was extremely influential to the history of Greek music in the twentieth century. The Conservatory specializes in vocal studies. Maria Callas

and other important Greek singers received their training at Odeion Ethnikon.

Academic Information

Music Degrees Offered. Diploma.
Music Degree Requirements. The Diploma is awarded after completion of studies.

GUATEMALA

Conservatorio Nacional de Música -
Guatemala City
3a Avenida 4-61
Zona 1
Guatemala City
Guatemala

Telephone. (502) (2) 28726

The Conservatorio Nacional de Música was founded on June 29, 1873. It was first housed in the former convent of Santo Domingo and then moved to its current location in the mid-twentieth century. The first director of the conservatory was Juan Aberle, an Italian opera conductor.

HAITI

Academy Promusica - Port-au-Prince
Angle Rue M et Jean-Claude Duvalier
B.P. 454
Port-au-Prince
Haiti

Telephone. (5091) 50939
Chief Administrator. Fritz Benjamin, Señora Michelene Laudun Denis, Directors.

The Academy Promusica, a privately supported institution, is one of the few functioning music schools in Haiti. Haiti's Conservatoire National de Musique has been closed.

École de Musique Ste. Trinité
P.O. Box 857
Port-au-Prince
Haiti

Chief Administrator. Ernest Delva, Director.

HONDURAS

Escuela Nacional de Música

Callejon la Moncada No. 901
Tegucigalpa, D.C.
Honduras

Telephone. (504) 222170
Chief Administrator. Profesora Nelia Chavarria Pineda, Directora.

HONG KONG

Chinese University of Hong Kong
Faculty of Music

Shatin
New Territories
Hong Kong

Telephone. (0) 6352111
Chief Administrator. Professor D. Gwilt, Head, Faculty of Music.

The University was established in 1963. Chinese and English are both languages of instruction.

Academic Information

Music Degrees Offered. Bachelor of Arts in music; Master of Philosophy in music.

University of Hong Kong
Faculty of Music

Pokfulam Road
Hong Kong

Telephone. 5-8592111
Chief Administrator. Anne E. Boyd, Head, Faculty of Music.

The University was established in 1911.

Academic Information

Music Degrees Offered. Bachelor of Arts in music.

Musical Facilities

Music Library. The Music Library houses approximately 4,000 volumes.

The Hong Kong Academy for Performing Arts
School of Music

1 Gloucester Road
Wanchai
Hong Kong

Telephone. 5-282662, 5-8231500
Chief Administrator. Dr. Basil Deane, Director; Angus Watson, Dean of Music.

The Hong Kong Academy for the Performing Arts was established in 1984. It is comprised of the School of Dance, School of Drama, School of Music, and School of Technical Arts. The institution consists of three main buildings: the Academy Block, the Theatre Block, and the Administrative Block. These triangular structures are connected by a glass-covered atrium which houses the foyer areas. The sophisticated performance venues can be altered for multiple purposes with movable ceiling and walls.

The School of Music provides comprehensive training for students who aspire to become professional performers or teachers of music. The School accommodates up to 40 students each year.

Academic Information

Music Faculty. Full-time 13, part-time 37.

Admission Procedure. Application forms can be obtained from the Academy's enquiry counter or by mail; applications must be submitted **in person** before May 16; a nonrefundable fee of $20 should be paid into the bank account of the Academy at any branch office of the Standard Chartered Band before submission of the application.

Music Degree Requirements. The Foundation Course (one year) aims to provide intensive study of the students' major interests, as well as supporting technical work in musical literacy, sight reading, and aural training. The Diploma Course (three years), is more extensive but regulated carefully to allow the student sufficient practice time. The major study can be a Chinese instrument, a Western instrument, including all orchestral instruments, guitar, organ, voice, or composition. In the case of advanced students, occasionally the foundation year preceding the three-year Diploma Course is waived. There are also short-term training courses for professionals and amateurs.

Instruments Taught. Brass, Chinese Instruments, Organ, Percussion, Piano, Stringed Instruments, Voice, Woodwinds.

Musical Facilities

Practice Facilities. 20 practice rooms; 41-stop pipe organ in Orchestral Hall; television studio; audiovisual facilities with video and computer resources.

Concert Facilities. Lyric Theatre, seating 1,188 (can be reduced to 884); Open Air Theatre, 500; Drama Theatre, 416; Recital Hall, 100.

Music Library. 7,000 books and scores; 2,000 records; 1,000 orchestral scores and parts. Leathlean Collection of 533 records. Interlibrary loan service is available.

Financial

Costs. Per academic year: Tuition for Foundation and Diploma Course HK$6,800; Certificate courses HK$5,100.

Financial Aid. Student grants and loans are available to full-time students who have resided in Hong Kong continuously for three years immediately prior to their applications for financial assistance. The level of grants and loans offered will be commensurate with the student's family financial circumstances.

HUNGARY

Ferenc Liszt Academy of Music
Liszt Ferenc tér. 8
Budapest VI
Hungary

Telephone. 224-827, 224-448

Chief Administrator. József Ujfalussy, Rector.

The Liszt Academy opened its doors in 1875. Franz (Ferenc) Liszt was the first and founding president. Only piano and composition were taught in the early years of the Academy. The first building was in Hal-ter (Fish Square)—a structure rented by the Academy. During the 1879-1880 academic year, the school moved to the Liszt House which had an apartment where Liszt lived at No. 67 Sugár út., now Népköztársaság útja. In 1907 the present building was completed and became the new home of the Academy.

In 1951, Bence Szabolcsi founded the department of musicology, unusual for a European conservatory as this subject was normally part of the university structure. In the Academy of today, there is an endeavor to form a close link between musicological research and the musical artistry of performance activities.

Distinguished graduates of the Academy include Béla Bartók, Zoltán Kodály, Antal Dorati, Jenö Hubay, Ernö Dohnányi, George Solti, Eugene Ormandy, Janos Starker, and Gabor Rejto. Additional telephone number: 224-448.

Member of the Assocation Européenne des Conservatoires de Musique, Académies de Musique, et Musikhochschulen.

Academic Information

Enrollment, Music Majors. 450; 60-70 foreign students.

Music Faculty. 150 full-time, 150 part-time.

Entrance Requirements. All students at the Academy must swim once a week for the duration of the program; it is a prerequisite for graduation.

Music Degrees Offered. Diploma.

Music Degree Requirements. Completion of a five-year course of study.

General Program Areas. Accompanying, Chamber Music, Choral Conducting, Composition, Folk Music, Music Education, Music History, Music Theory, Musicology.

Instruments Taught. Brass, Harp, Organ, Piano, Stringed Instruments, Voice, Woodwinds.

Musical Facilities

Practice Facilities. 2 organs and a fortepiano in the concert halls. 50 teaching studios equipped with 50 grand pianos. Pianists must find their own place to practice as there are no practice rooms in the Academy. Electronic music studio is in another building located at Voorsmarty tér.

Concert Facilities. Great Hall, seating 1,000; Little Hall, 400; special hall for chamber music is located in another building at Pesti Vigado, Budapest, V, Vigado tér.

Community Facilities. Chamber concerts are held in the reconstructed Liszt Museum.

Music Library. 50,000 books; 250 periodical titles; 80 recent periodical issues; 250,000 scores; 7,000 phonograph recordings; 300 tapes. The Academy library is the largest music library in Hungary. Listening facilties (cassette, phonograph). Other resources in Budapest include a library in Buddha Castle. The Szechenyi Library music division holds autographs and manuscripts of Joseph Haydn and Haydn's contemporaries. The first building belonging to the Academy, the Liszt House, has become the Liszt Museum. The authentic furnishings and decor reflect the period of 1880. The Liszt collections of the Academy are housed here.

Special Programs

Featured Programs. There are many visiting guest lecturers. Master classes are given at the Academy throughout the year. Kodály seminars are held each year to provide information on Hungarian music education.

Foreign Programs. Student and teacher exchange programs and joint concerts with the academies of Vienna, Helsinki, Moscow, Prague, and Wiemar. Dormitory located at Students Hostel, Budapest, VII, Gorkij fasor 33 (telephone 421-581) houses 80 Hungarian students; others must find their own accommodations.

Országos Pedagogiai Intézet
Gorkij Fasor 17-21 II.e. 212
Budapest VI
Hungary

Telephone. 211-200

Chief Administrator. Dr. Szabolcsi Miklós, Coordinator; Mária Pataki, Head of Music Research.

The Pedagogical Institute serves as a liaison between the Ministry of Culture and Education of Hungary and the primary schools for music throughout the country. It functions as an advisory body to the Ministry of Culture and Education by making recommendations about teaching methodology and materials on 37 different instruments and theoretical subjects. The recommendations guide the curricula of 155 state music schools where 65,000 children are taught music subjects.

There are 37 working groups at the Institute, one for each discipline. These groups help the coordinator decide details about how each musical subject should be taught at the various age levels. Through team work, educational materials are composed in the Institute. Every ten years the curriculum for each subject is revised.

The Institute shares a building with advisory boards dealing with all aspects of education. The structure is owned by the church and rented by the state.

Zeneiskolai Tanárkepző Intézet
(Music Teachers Training Institute of the Liszt Academy of Music)
V. Semmelweis 12
Budapest 1052
Hungary

Telephone. 182-044

Chief Administrator. János Králik, Director.

The Music Teachers Training Institute is the Department of Teaching Music and Singing of the Liszt Academy of Music. There are six sections of the Institute: one in Budapest at the above address and five others throughout Hungary (Debrecen, Györ, Miskoc, Pécs, and Szeged).

The Institute was founded in 1966 and occupies a 146-year old building.

Academic Information

Enrollment, Music Majors. 600 (170 in Budapest, 430 in the five affiliated institutes outside Budapest). 10 foreign students (Budapest).

Music Faculty. 70 (in Budapest).

Term System. Semester. Summer courses given in Debrecen in new Institute building.

Admission Procedure. Foreign students interested in applying must write to the Cultural Ministry in Hungary which then contacts the school.

Music Degrees Offered. Diploma.

Music Degree Requirements. Completion of a three-year course; diploma entitles the holder to teach instrumental and solfeggio beginners courses plus singing in elementary school (primary level).

General Program Areas. Folk Music, Music History, Music Theory, Solfege.

Instruments Taught. Brass, Guitar, Percussion, Piano, Stringed Instruments, Woodwinds.

Musical Facilities

Concert Facilities. Small recital hall seating 100 on second floor of building.

Music Library. 1,500 volumes, books, and scores are housed on first floor of building. Tapes, listening facilities, video equipment.

Financial

Costs. Per academic year: Foreign students must pay approximately $1,600. No tuition for Hungarian students; stipends given.

Commentary

The Director of the Music Teachers Training Institute would like to see the present curriculum expanded to four years.

Zenetudományi Intézet
(Musicological Institute)
Táncsics u.
Budapest 1014
Hungary

Telephone. 757-449

Chief Administrator. Zoltán Falvy, Director.

The Musicological Institute is a part of the Hungarian Academy of Sciences and is unique in Europe. It is an archive, an examining body, and publisher of scholarly works. The Institute began as an archive-institute to preserve and study Hungarian folk music collections. Tunes were heard on tape, transcribed, and published in three volumes: Volume I, children's songs; Volume II, songs of the big events in life; and Volume III, wedding songs. Altogether, 150,000 folk works were collected. In 1961, the Musicological Institute was created and incorporated the Bartók Archives established by Professor Bence Szabolcsi. In 1969, the present name was adopted and in 1974, the different institutes were combined.

Various projects of the Institute include the publication of folk music, Hungarian music history (five volumes), critical editions for study and performance, and yearly compilation of articles. The *Musicalia Danubiana Series* is a series of volumes of source publications appearing under the auspices of the Institute. The series covers written sources from the Middle Ages to the early nineteenth century, and strives to encourage rather than to summarize the research being done. Another series published by the Institute is the *Gypsy Folk Music of Europe*.

Other pedagogical activities include a museum, temporary exhibitions, permanent instruments exhibition, archive of folk music collected by Béla Bartók and Zoltán Kodály. There is no teaching or regular lectures; however, a few Institute members teach at the Liszt Academy on the Faculty of Philosophy. There is also a post-graduate course for music librarians.

Academic Information

Music Faculty. 40 researchers.

Music Degrees Offered. Diploma; Ph.D.; Candidate; Doctor in Musicology.

Music Degree Requirements. There are four categories in the degree process: (1) five years at the Ferenc Liszt Academy and completion of the dissertation; the musicology major there receives a diploma in musicology; (2) three or more years and another dissertation; a Ph.D. is awarded; (3) the third dissertation is approved; the student becomes a candidate; (4) the fourth dissertation is approved; the special title of Doctor in Musicology is conferred.

ICELAND

Tonlistarskolinn i Reykjavik

Skipholti 33
105 Reykjavik
Iceland

Telephone. (1) 30625
Chief Administrator. Jon Nordal, Director.

Academic Information

Enrollment, Music Majors. 270.

General Program Areas. Composition, Music Education, Music History, Music Theory, Performance.

Instruments Taught. Harpsichord, Orchestral Instruments, Organ, Piano, Voice.

INDIA

Akhil Bharatiya Gandharva Mahavidyalaya Mandal

Gandharva Niketan
Brahmanpuri, Miraj 416410
India

Telephone. 2526 Miraj
Chief Administrator. Shri. Vinaychandra Maudgalya, President.

Pt. Vishnu Digambar Paluskar, in an effort to improve music education and raise the status of the musician in society, established a music institution named Gardharva Mahavidyalaya in Lahore in 1901. After his death in 1931, his disciples, who had opened other institutions throughout India, founded Akhil Bharatiya Gandharva Mahavidyalaya Mandal in memory of their late Guru. The institution was subsequently registered in 1946 and again in 1957 (adding the words "Akhil Bharatiya") under the Societies Registration Act and the Bombay Public Trusts Act. The Mandal has its own building and office at Miraj and has proposed to have one at Bombay in the future.

The Mandal is not an autonomous university. There are 283 music institutions from all over India that are affiliated for the purpose of utilizing the examinations conducted by the Mandal.

The Mandal administers the following courses of study for Hindustani Music (including vocal, instrumental, dance) and South Music: Praveshika (Matriculation), two years; Madhyama (Intermediate), two years; Visharad (Bachelor of Music), two years; Alankar (Master of Music), two years; Praveen (Doctor of Music), two years; Sangeet Shikshak Sanad (S.T.C. of Music), after passing Madhyma; Sangeet Shiksha Visharad (Bachelor of Music Education), after pasing Visharad; Sangeet Shiksha Parangat (Master of Music Education), after passing Alankar. These examinations are held twice a year, in April and November, at about 300 centers throughout India. Most of India's universities have recognized the Mandal's examinations as equivalent to theirs.

The school publishes a magazine entitled *Sangeet Kala Vihar* (official Journal of the Mandal) monthly in two languages: Hindi and Marathi. It deals with all aspects of music including topics in composition and theory. The Mandal also publishes biographies and textbooks.

Academic Information

Music Degrees Offered. Praveshika (Matriculation), two years; Madhyama (Intermediate), two years; Visharad (Bachelor of Music), two years; Alankar (Master of Music), two years; Praveen (Doctor of Music), two years; Sangeet Shikshak Sanad (S.T.C. of Music), after passing Madhyma; Sangeet Shiksha Visharad (Bachelor of Music Education), after passing Visharad; Sangeet Shiksha Parangat (Master of Music Education), after passing Alankar.

Musical Facilities

Music Library. The Mandal's objective is to maintain an up-to-date library of books on Hindustani, Carnatic, and Western music. Listening facilities. Special collections include documentary films such as one about Pt. Vishnu Digambar Paluskar.

Special Programs

Affiliated Programs. The Mandal has created a music techers association called "Akhil Bharatiya Sangeet Shikshak Parishad" which holds conferences and organizes activities to help music teachers solve problems related to music education.

Commentary

This institution is an accrediting body which administers examinations and awards diplomas, following the example of the United Kingdom's Royal Boards of Music.

Banaras Hindu University
Varanasi
Uttar Pradesh 221005
India

Telephone. 54291
The University has Departments of Instrumental and Vocal Music.

Academic Information

Music Degrees Offered. Bachelor of Music; Master of Music in instrumental music, musicology, vocal music; Doctor of Music; Diploma in instrumental music, vocal music, and Karnatak (South Indian classical style).
General Program Areas. Composition, Instrumental Music, Music Theory, Musicology, Performance, Vocal Music.

Commentary

The Department of Music at Banaras Hindu University combines performance and musicology in the context of a religious institution.

Bhavan's Bharatiya Sangeet and Nartan Skikshapeeth
(Academy of Music and Dance)
Chaupatty Road
Bombay 4000007
India

Telephone. 351461/2/3/4/5
Chief Administrator. Pandit Dinkar Kaikini, Director.
The Academy was founded in 1946. It is a department of the Bharatiya Vidya Bhavan for teaching and conducting Hindustani music courses and is affiliated with the Bhatkhande Sangeet Vidyapeeth, Lucknow. The Shikshapeeth is recognized by the government of Maharashtra. At present a classical music wing conducts classes in vocal Hindustani music, sitar, and tabla. There is also a light music wing in which Sugum Sangeet, harmonium, and electric guitar are taught.

The school is situated in central Bombay near the seaside. It occupies the second floor of a large building of Bharatiya Vidya Bhavan, head office of a cultural and educational body that has 18 centers in different parts of India, London, and the U.S.A. The Academy seeks to inculcate the Indian culture among young people through Indian traditional music (Raagsangeet) and dance and to bring about a uniform system and method of imparting musical knowledge along with Indian philosophy.

Academic Information

Music Degrees Offered. Prathma Certificate awarded after 2½ years of study; Madhyama Diploma awarded after 3 years of study; Visharad Pt. I and II degree awarded after 2 years of study.
General Program Areas. Hindustani Music, Indian Traditional Music.
Instruments Taught. Electric Guitar, Harmonium, Sitar, Tabla, Voice.

Musical Facilities

Music Library. Existing masters in the vocal and instrumental music are invited to give performances for the students.

Commentary

The focus of study at this Academy is in Hindustani (North Indian) music.

Indira Kala Sangit Vishwavidyalaya
(University of Music and Fine Arts)
Khairagarth
Madhya Pradesh 491881
India

Telephone. Khairagarth 32
Chief Administrator. Dr. A.C. Choubey, Dean, Faculty of Music; Mohammed Shariff, Dean, Faculty of Folk Music.
The University was founded in 1956. This institution, in the innovative structure of an arts university, teaches both the North (Hindustani) and South (Karnak) Classical styles of India. It has departments of Dance, English, Folk Music and Art, Hindi, History of Indian Art and Culture, Instrumental Music, Musicology and Aesthetics, Painting, Physics of Sound, Sanskrit, and Vocal Music.

Academic Information

Music Degrees Offered. Bachelor of Music; Bachelor of Arts in folk music, instrumental music, vocal music; Master of Music; Doctor of Music; Diploma in light vocal music (Geetanjali), stringed instrument repairing, folk music (Loksangeet); Chhattisgarhi folk music, music appreciation.

General Program Areas. Indian Folk Music, Instrumental Music, Musicology, Physics of Sound, Stringed Instrument Repair, Vocal Music.

Instruments Taught. Sitar, Tabla, Violin.

Musical Facilities

Music Library. 30,000 volumes; 264 periodical titles.

Commentary

This institution is unique in India, as it is devoted exclusively to the arts. Although Indian music institutions usually concentrate on teaching only one of the classical forms—North Indian (Hindustani) or South Indian (Karnatak)—the Indira Kala Sangit Vishwavidalaya teaches both.

Kalakshetra
Tiruvanmiyur
Madras 600041
India

Telephone. 411836

The Kalakshetra was founded in 1936 and is a center for education in classical music, dancing, theatrical art, painting, and various handicrafts.

Karnatak University
College of Music
Dharwad
Kharnataka 580003
India

Telephone. (Dharwad) 8194
Chief Administrator. Sharada Hangal, Principal.

The College of Music offers programs leading to the Bachelor of Music, Master of Music, Master of Arts in Music, and the Music Certificate.

Commentary

The College of Music at Karnatak University concentrates on the study of South Indian (Karnatak) music.

University of Madras
Department of Indian Music
University Centenary Building
Chepauk, Triplicane P.O., Tamil Nadu
Madras 600005
India

Telephone. 568778

The University's Department of Indian Music is performance-oriented in its approach to the study of Indian music.

Academic Information

General Program Areas. Indian Music.

Commentary

Most of the music students at the University of Madras are women. One explanation for this phenomenon may be that in the context of the society, studying music is one way for women to obtain a university education. Men, on the other hand, may choose to study an instrument with a known mentor outside the university structure. In Indian culture, it is more important with whom one studies than where the study has taken place.

The Music Academy, Madras
Teachers' College of Music
306, T.T.K. Road
Madras 600 014
India

Telephone. 475619
Chief Administrator. B. Rajam Iyer, Principal.

The Music Academy of Madras operates the Teachers' College of Music. The College, founded in 1927, is recognized by the government and trains students to appear for the governmental examination. Those who pass the examination are given a diploma and become eligible to be appointed as music teachers in schools. The course is for one year but for those who are not "up to the mark," there is a pre-certificate course for one year. Those who pass the pre-certificate course are admitted to the certificate course. There is also a junior class for beginners.

Apart from the Teachers' College of Music, the Academy, which is a music society, operates a one year course for advanced training in music. Students of this class are trained to become concert artists and upon completion of the course are given a diploma conferring the title of Sangita Ratna. The Academy also trains students in veena playing.

Academic Information

Enrollment, Music Majors. 183.
Term System. Academic year June to April.
Music Degrees Offered. Diploma.
General Program Areas. Music Education, Performance.

Prayag Sangit Samiti
12-C, Kamla Nehru Road
Alfred Park
Allahabad 211001
India

Telephone. 52447
Chief Administrator. Shri Lalji Srivastava, Head.

The school was founded in 1926 with the aim of popularizing the cause of classical music in India. The founders sought to give an honorable status to music and musicians in Indian society. In the past, trained musicians were the exclusive preserve of privileged noblemen. Through the efforts of Prayag Sangit Samiti, there has been a change in the public attitude towards music and musicians. The institution is dedicated to popularizing and propagating the cause of classical music in its 3 branches: vocal, instrumental, and dance.

The school has two buildings, one situated in the center of the city of South Malaka and the other in Alfred Park. The Central Government and the general public contributed to the cost of the new Mehta Auditorium.

Academic Information

Enrollment, Music Majors. 1,000.
Music Faculty. 40.
Music Degrees Offered. The Samiti has affiliated more than 1,352 examination centers (following the example of Britain's Royal Schools of Music Examinations) scattered throughout India. The Samiti awards the Junior Diploma after a course of 2 years; Senior Diploma after a course of 4 years; Sangeet Prabhakar after a course of 6 years; Sangeet Pravin after a course of 8 years; Sangit Acharya (research degree).
General Program Areas. Music Theory, Performance.
Instruments Taught. Flute, Guitar, Sitar, Tabla, Violin.

Musical Facilities

Practice Facilities. 25 percussion-equipped practice rooms.
Concert Facilities. Mehta Auditorium, seating 3,000; Muktangan (open stage).
Music Library. 1,500 rare books; 150 recordings. Listening facilities (phonographs, tape recorders, cassette players).

Special Programs

Featured Programs. After completion of 6- and 8-year courses, Pryag Sangit Samiti awards degrees to successful candidates; most of them are currently top artists in India. These students appear on the national media and are popular in concerts organized in India and abroad. They also become professors and lecturers at colleges and universities.

Affiliated Programs. The All India Music Conference takes place each year as does the All India Music Competition.

Commentary

The Prayag Sangit Samiti is essentially an accrediting body which administers examinations and awards certificates, using as its role model the United Kingdom's Royal Schools of Music Examinations.

Sangeet Natak Akademi
(National Academy of Music, Dance, and Drama)
Rabindra Bhavan
Feroze Shah Road
New Delhi 110001
India

Telephone. 387246
The Academy is a research institute that sponsors research and data collection about the arts in India. It also offers a continuing education curriculum and publishes the journal *Sangeet Natak.*

Commentary

A note about music institutions in India: The establishment of conservatories during the last one hundred years in India has made music more accessible to the middle classes. Although music schools here are not responsible for training a next generation of musicians, they do have an important role in the society by increasing the number of people who can benefit from a musical education. The master-disciple relationship integral in Indian teaching has to some degree been incorporated into the conservatory structure.

From an official perspective, a foreigner studying in India is often required to have a visa, which can be obtained only when sponsored by an institution, even if most of the actual studies takes place outside the institution.

Tamil University
Faculty of Music
Palace Buildings
Thanjavur
Tamil Nadu 613001
India

Telephone. Thanjavur 1901-1906
Chief Administrator. Professor D.A. Thanapandian, Dean of Arts.

The University was inaugurated in September 1981 by the Governor of Tamil Nadu. It is exclusively a graduate institution. A video facility on campus is used to document performances in Thanjavur.

Visva-Bharati
Sangit-Bhavana (College of Music and Dance)
P.O. Santiniketan
District Birbhum
West Bengal 731235
India

Telephone. 451-456
Chief Administrator. Nilima Sen, Principal, Sangit-Bhavana.

The Sangit-Bhavana is a college of music and dance founded in 1934.

Academic Information

Music Degrees Offered. Bachelor of Music in Hindustani classical music or Rabindra-Sangit (vocal or instrumental); Master of Music in Hindustani classical music (vocal or instrumental) or Rabinda-Sangit; Diploma (Tabla performance); Certificate.
Music Degree Requirements. The Bachelor of Music requires 4 years of study; there is a special two-year Bachelor of Music.
General Program Areas. Hindustani Classical Music.
Instruments Taught. Sitar, Tabla.

Commentary

Visva-Bharati concentrates on the study of North Indian vocal and instrumental classical forms.

INDONESIA

Academi Seni Tari Indonesia
J1. Buahbatu 212
Bandung
Indonesia

Telephone. 421532
Chief Administrator. Dr. Ma'mur Danasasmita, Director.

The Academy was founded in 1970. Tatung Suryana is Head of the Department of Music.

Academic Information

Enrollment, Music Majors. 342.
Music Faculty. 74.
Music Degrees Offered. Degrees are awarded in traditional music and dance.

Musical Facilities

Music Library. 5,113 volumes.

Academy Seni Karawitan Indonesia
Kampus ASKI
Kentingan
Jebres
Solo Jawa Tengah
Indonesia

Telephone. (0271) 7658
Chief Administrator. Sri Hastanto, Head of Music Department.

The Academy of Traditional Music, Theatre, and Dance was founded in 1964.

Academic Information

Enrollment, Music Majors. 606.
Music Faculty. 167.
Music Degrees Offered. Diploma; First Degree (Bachelor's); Master's.

Musical Facilities

Music Library. 15,000 volumes.

Commentary

The Academy Seni Karawitan Indonesia (Academy of Traditional Music, Theatre, and Dance), campus ASKI in Kentingan, Jebres (an old court city of central Java) is considered the most important of the Indonesian music schools. First-rate performers teach here and there is a particular focus at this institution on experimentation of new works. Some members of the ASKI faculty—gifted in teaching as well as performing—have been guest professors in such American universities as the University of Wisconsin at Madison. The enrollment of students at ASKI has increased significantly over the past decade.

Over a period of time, the cultural life of Indonesian society has been quite affected by the existence of national music academies. First of all, they have added a new legitimacy to traditional music, and secondly, a new forum has been provided for experimentation in the writing of both traditional and avant-garde pieces.

Academy Seni Karawitan Indonesia Padang Panjang
Jl. Puti Bungsu 35
Sumatera Barat
Indonesia

Telephone. 77
Chief Administrator. Professor Mardjani Martamin, Director.

The Academy for Traditional Music and Dance was founded in 1966. Dr. Djaruddin Amar is the Head of the Traditional Music Department. Dirwan Wakidi heads the Department of School Music.

Academic Information

Enrollment, Music Majors. 428.
Music Faculty. 62.
Music Degrees Offered. Diploma.

Musical Facilities

Music Library. 6,196 volumes.

Commentary

Akademi Seni Karawitan Indonesia Padang Panjang has had a controversial history. After completing traditional Western musical education in Belgium, the Indonesian violist Bustanil Arifin became the director of this academy. He wanted to Westernize the school's approach to music education, including changing such fundamental indigenous elements as the tuning system. Apparently, none of this was too popular and the school was in a state of confusion for years afterward.

Institut Kesenian Jakarta
Taman Ismial Marzuki
Jalan Cikini
Jakarta
Indonesia

The Institute has been granting degrees since the early 1980s and is quite Western in its orientation. Located in Jakarta's National Arts Center, the school has departments in film, drama, graphic arts, and Western performance and composition. The Institute was recently recognized by the state as an Arts Academy.

Institut Seni Indonesia
Yogyakarta
Indonesia

This research institute for the arts combines the disciplines of visual arts, dance, Javanese music, and Western music. In the future, the Institute will have the authority to grant degrees at the doctoral level.

Academic Information

General Program Areas. Javanese Music.

IRAN

Dâeshgâhé Farabi
(Farabi University)
Department of Music
Tehran
Iran

The University was founded in 1975.

Academic Information

Music Degrees Offered. Bachelor of Arts; Master of Arts; Doctorate.

Commentary

No recent information has been received from the Iranian institutions listed in this *Guide*. Therefore, changes in the schools' structure and curriculum may have occurred of which the author is unaware.

National Conservatory of Music - Tehran
South Palestine Avenue
Tehran
Iran

The Conservatory was founded in 1949 and offers courses in composition and instrumental performance.

University of Teheran
Department of Music
Avenue Enghelab
Tehran
Iran

Telephone. 6111
In the past, the Department of Music sponsored studies in both Persian and Western music. The Persian music studies, a strong element of the Department, reflect a conservative approach to preserving the tradition and avoiding the modernization of the national music.

Academic Information

General Program Areas. Persian Music.

IRAQ

Jami 'at Baghdad
(University of Baghdad)
Academy of Fine Arts
Jadyriya
Baghdad
Iraq

Telephone. 93091
Chief Administrator. Taha T. Al-Naimi, President of the University.

The Academy of Fine Arts sponsors a curriculum in the making of traditional Iraqi instruments and the art of performance on these instruments. Students learn to make instruments from master craftsmen. The instruments used in Iraqi traditional music are the santur (hammer dulcimer), 'ud (Arabic lute), nay (reed flute), and jawzah (fiddle).

Ministry of Information
Music Division
Baghdad
Iraq

Telephone. 5370091
Chief Administrator. Munir Bashir, Director of Music.

The Ministry of Information sponsors a music section with music archives, music library, collection of instruments, practice rooms, and recording studio. The Ministry, under the guidance of Munir Bashir, has plans to establish a Maqam Institute to teach "maqam," the classical music tradition of Baghdad.

IRELAND

Royal Irish Academy of Music
36-38 Westland Row
Dublin 2
Ireland

Telephone. 764412/3
Chief Administrator. James Callery, Principal Officer/ Secretary.

The Royal Academy of Music in Dublin was founded in 1856 and is the senior institute in Ireland for the teaching of music in all its forms. The Academy occupies a renovated townhouse formerly belonging to Lord Conyngham. Classes are given in singing, all orchestral instruments, harmony, composition, speech, and drama.

Academic Information

Enrollment, Music Majors. 3,000.
Music Degrees Offered. Associate in teaching; Licentiate in teaching or performing.
General Program Areas. Composition, Drama, Harmony, Speech, Vocal Music.
Instruments Taught. Keyboard Instruments, Orchestral Instruments.

Special Programs

Featured Programs. In addition to the regular conservatory program, there is a two-week summer school available to students over the age of sixteen.

ISRAEL

The Jerusalem Rubin Academy of Music and Dance
Givat-Ram Campus
Jerusalem
Israel

Telephone. (02) 636232-9
Chief Administrator. Mendi Rodan, Director.

The Jerusalem Rubin Academy strives to train performers and music teachers at the highest possible level. It is hoped that the graduates will become active participants within the musical life of the country. The Academy is located on the Givat-Ram campus of the Hebrew University.
Accreditation. Council of Higher Education.

Academic Information

Enrollment, Music Majors. Full-time 313, part-time 16.
Music Faculty. Full-time 26, part-time 42. Foreign students from U.S.A., France, South America, Scandinavia.
Term System. Trimester. Special seminars and summer courses.
Entrance Requirements. High school diploma; comprehensive examination; theory solfege examination; audition preferred (tape accepted).
Admission Procedure. Application with nonrefundable $25 fee due April, July, September.
Music Degrees Offered. Artist Diploma; Bachelor of Arts; Bachelor of Music Education; Master of Arts.
Music Degree Requirements. The baccalaureate degrees require the successful completion of four years of study. The Bachelor of Arts in music and the Master of Arts in music are offered in cooperation with Hebrew University.
General Program Areas. Music Education.
Instruments Taught. Brass, Guitar, Harpsichord, Organ, Percussion, Piano, Stringed Instruments, Voice,

Woodwinds.

Musical Facilities

Practice Facilities. 37 teaching/practice rooms. 2 percussion-equipped practice rooms; 1 practice room for organists. 37 pianos (uprights); 8 grand pianos reserved for piano majors. Practice rooms assigned by appointment. Electronic studio.

Music Library. 11,000 books; 120 periodicals; 5,000 phonograph records; 1,200 cassettes. Special collection of 500 original manuscripts of Jewish music. Listening facilities (cassette, stereo). The Academy has the Amli Music library, which includes a special collection of Jewish and Israeli music. The Hebrew University, with which the Academy is now affiliated, has the E. Gerson-Kiwi Collection of Jewish and Oriental Music Folklore Research Centre housed in the city's Terra Sancta Building. Hebrew University also has an exceptional National Sound Archives and Jewish Research Center.

Financial

Costs. Per academic year: Tuition $1,000.
Financial Aid. 60% of students receive some form of scholarship assistance.

Levinsky Teachers College
Music Teachers Seminary

15 Shoshana Persitz Street North
P.O. Box 48130
Tel-Aviv
Israel

Telephone. (03) 426162
Chief Administrator. Ovadia Tuvia, Principal.

The Music Teachers Seminary was founded in 1945. It first offered a two-year program. From 1972, it offered a three-year program granting the Senior Music Teacher degree and a four-year program granting the degree Bachelor of Music in Education. The Seminary trains teachers in music eurhythmics for kindergarden, public schools, high schools, and for retarded special education. The Seminary occupies a new building in North Tel-Aviv containing all types of classrooms, library, concert hall, tools for eurythmics instruction, and is also equipped with sport facilities.

Accreditation. Council of Higher Education.

Academic Information

Enrollment, Music Majors. Full-time 20 men, 140 women; part-time 4 men, 11 women. Foreign students from Canada, U.S.A., France, Argentina, United Kingdom, Russia.

Term System. Yearly programs. 4-week summer session.

Entrance Requirements. High school graduation; comprehensive examination; admission tests in theory, solfege, harmony. Audition preferred; tape accepted.

Admission Procedure. Application with $25 non-refundable fee accepted January-June.

Music Degrees Offered. Senior Music Teacher; Bachelor of Music Education.

Music Degree Requirements. Four-year program (25 hours weekly plus 20 hours practical class work) for Bachelor of Music Education; three-year program for Senior Music Teacher.

General Program Areas. Choral Conducting, Music Education, Music Therapy.

Instruments Taught. Accordion, Flute, Guitar, Piano.

Musical Facilities

Practice Facilities. 14 practice rooms. 10 piano practice rooms (4 with grand pianos); 14 pianos (4 grand, 10 upright). Eurythmics and Orff practice rooms. Room assigned by appointment.

Concert Facilities. Concert halls available.

Community Facilities. Practical class work is accomplished at public schools.

Music Library. 12,000 volumes; 4,000 scores; 5,000 phonograph records. Listening facilities (cassette, stereo).

Special Programs

Affiliated Programs. Non-formal connection with Department of Musicology at Tel-Aviv University.

Financial

Costs. Per academic year: Tuition $670.

Rimon School of Jazz and Contemporary Music

Rehov Shmuel Hanagid
Morasha
Ramat Hasharon
Israel

The Rimon School of Jazz and Contemporary Music was founded in 1985 by Guri Agmon, Gil Dor, Yehuda Eder, and Ilan Mochiach. These musicians felt the need for Israel to have its own formal school for training jazz and popular musicians. The school is a "practical" school for musicians with a goal of preparing students for the "real world" of popular music, jazz, and recording. There is a classical music division as well, including the study of contemporary music. The Rimon School is located in a suburb of Tel Aviv.

Academic Information

Enrollment, Music Majors. 120.
General Program Areas. Contemporary Music, Jazz Studies.

Samuel Rubin Conservatory of Music
9 Haparsim Street
Haifa
Israel

Telephone. (4) 521530
Chief Administrator. Yigal Cohen, Director.

The Rubin Conservatory of Music in Haifa, like the conservatories of the same name in Jerusalem and Beersheva, train students at the elementary and secondary school levels in performance, theory, and history of music. What is unusual about the conservatory in Haifa is that for a short time in the early 1970s it had a small Arab music wing which focused on the study of traditional Arab music. The Arab music section had evolved from a music club founded by Hikmat Shaheen in the late 1950s which became the Arab Music Conservatory in 1963. In 1971, for about a year, this school was incorporated into the Conservatory curriculum. Now performance and study of Arab music in Haifa takes place at Beit Hagefen, a musical club in the city.

Tel Aviv University
Faculty of Fine Arts
Rubin Academy of Music
Ramat-Aviv
Tel-Aviv
Israel

Telephone. (03) 420415
Chief Administrator. Joseph Dorfman, Director.

The major goal of the Rubin Academy of Music is to train performers, conductors, and composers. It was founded in 1945 and became part of Tel-Aviv University in 1966. In 1972, the Academy became part of the Faculty of Fine Arts. The Academy occupies a building completed with a substantial donation by Samuel Rubin.
Accreditation. Council of Higher Education.

Academic Information

Enrollment, Music Majors. Full-time 100 men, 150 women. 10 foreign students (Finland, United Kingdom, Japan, Singapore, Costa Rica, U.S.A.).
Term System. Yearly courses.
Entrance Requirements. Graduation from secondary school; comprehensive examination; applied and theory tests. Audition in person preferred; tapes accepted.
Admission Procedure. Application with $25 fee due February-March.

Music Degrees Offered. Artist Diploma; Bachelor of Arts; Bachelor of Music; Master of Arts in Music.
Music Degree Requirements. Four-year course of study.
General Program Areas. Composition, Conducting, Music History, Music Theory, Performance.
Instruments Taught. Brass, Guitar, Harp, Harpsichord, Percussion, Piano, Stringed Instruments, Voice, Woodwinds.

Musical Facilities

Practice Facilities. Special practice rooms for organists (one) and percussionists (two). 15 practice pianos; 15 grand pianos reserved for piano majors. Practice rooms assigned by appointment.
Concert Facilities. Concert halls available.
Concerts/Musical Activities. Weekly concerts, workshops, and competitions.
Music Library. 50,000 scores; 400 volumes (in main library); 3 current periodicals; 6,000 phonograph recordings. Listening facilities (cassette, stereo). The Mark L. Grinstein Music Library of the Rubin Academy of Music, Tel Aviv University, has holdings of approximately 50,000 items.

Financial

Costs. Per academic year: Tuition $1,000.
Financial Aid. Scholarship applications accepted through first semester.

ITALY

Conservatorio di Musica "A. Vivaldi"
Via Parma 1
Allessandria
Italy

Telephone. (0131) 5 33 63

Conservatorio di Musica "Arrigo Boito"
Via del Conservatorio 27
43100 Parma
Italy

Telephone. (0521) 2 23 20
Chief Administrator. P. Guarino, Director.

The Conservatory at Parma, established in 1825, is housed in an old Carmelite convent and contains a four-foot organ built at the end of the sixteenth century. Arturo Toscanini received his training here.

Musical Facilities

Music Library. The Conservatory's library contains fourteenth century manuscripts, treatises, and manuscripts of more than 400 Scarlatti sonatas.

Conservatorio di Musica "Benedetto Marcello"
Palazzo Pisani
San Marco 2809
30124 Venice
Italy

Telephone. (041) 2 56 04
Chief Administrator. Ugo Amendola, Director.
The Conservatory was founded in 1877. It has Venetian eighteenth century manuscripts, items from the Venetian school of sacred music and opera, and a museum of instruments.

Conservatorio di Musica "Cesare Pollini"
Via Eremitani 6
Padua
Italy

Telephone. 2 09 28
The conservatory was founded in 1875.

Conservatorio di Musica "Claudio Monteverdi"
Piazza Domenicani, 19
I-39100 Bolzano
Italy

Telephone. (0471) 97 87 64
Chief Administrator. Giuseppe Mattivi, Director of Secretariat; Professor Dr. Hubert Stuppner, Director.
The Conservatory, founded in 1939, occupies an old monastery building in the historic city of Bolzano. It offers training for music teachers, composers, and orchestra performers. The languages of instruction are Italian and German, reflecting its proximity to the Italian-Austrian border.

Academic Information

Enrollment, Music Majors. 166 men, 197 women. 2 foreign students (from Germany).
Term System. Semester. One summer session in June.
Entrance Requirements. Secondary school diploma required; comprehensive examination; audition required (test on instruments).
Admission Procedure. Application due May 15.
Music Degrees Offered. Diploma.

Music Degree Requirements. Completion of 21 courses.
General Program Areas. Music Composition.
Instruments Taught. Brass, Organ, Percussion, Piano, Stringed Instruments, Woodwinds.

Musical Facilities

Practice Facilities. 31 practice rooms. Special practice rooms for organists; 3 organs (Roverato of Padua, Mascioni of Varese, Tamburini of Cremona). 15 practice pianos; 10 grand pianos reserved for piano majors.
Concert Facilities. Concert hall.
Music Library. 11,514 scores and books about music; 12 periodical subscriptions; 359 phonograph recordings. Listening facilities (stereo). First editions of works published 1800-1810.

Commentary

The Conservatory "Claudio Monteverdi" identifies its own particular strengths as composition, organ study, and the study of stringed instruments. The International Busoni Piano Competition is held at the Conservatory annually.

Conservatorio di Musica "Francesco Morlacchi"
Via Fratti 14
Perugia
Italy

Telephone. 6 63 13

Musical Facilities

Music Library. The library contains a collection of autographed manuscripts of Morlacchi; also various manuscripts.

Conservatorio di Musica "G. Frescobaldi"
Via Previati 22
L'Aquila
Italy

Telephone. 2 17 28

Conservatorio di Musica "G. Tartini" e Scuola Media Statale Annessa
Via Carlo Ghega 12
34132 Trieste
Italy

Telephone. (040) 63 00 87
There is a small preparatory school (lower school) attached to the conservatory. The director has the option

of acccepting exceptionally gifted students into the conservatory who do not have previous records from a recognized school of music.

Academic Information

Enrollment, Music Majors. 135.
Music Faculty. 53.

Conservatorio di Musica "Giocchino Rossini"

Piazza Olivieri 5
61100 Pesaro
Italy

Telephone. (0721) 3 36 70
Chief Administrator. M. Marvulli, Director.

The Conservatory was founded in 1882. There are Rossini manuscripts housed in the Archives and Rossini Museum as well as vocal manuscripts of Donizetti, Morlacchi, and Paisiello. There is also a collection of musical instruments in the Sezione di Strumenti Musicali Esotici of the conservatory library. Also housed is an important collection of string quartet parts from the early eighteenth century and opera arias published by Marescalchi and Barberis.

Musical Facilities

Music Library. Contains vocal manuscripts of Rossini, Donizetti, Pergolesi, and others, and early string quartet parts by Haydn, Mozart, and Beethoven.

Conservatorio di Musica "Giuseppe Verdi"

Via del Conservatorio 12
20122 Milan
Italy

Telephone. (02) 70 17 55
Chief Administrator. Marcello Abbado, Director.

Founded in 1808, the conservatory possesses a number of rare collections, among which are various manuscripts, autographs, fifteenth century French and Italian songs, and opera scores.

Conservatorio di Musica "Niccolo Paganini"

Villa Bombrini
Via Albaro
Genoa
Italy

Telephone. 16 07 47

The conservatory was founded in 1829 as a free school of vocal studies. A bronze statue of Paganini, a Genoan by birth, by sculptor Guido Gallo is in the conservatory's main hall. Paganini's violin is kept in a glass case at the Palazzo Tursi, near the mayor's office. Each year a known violinist is invited to come and play it.

Musical Facilities

Music Library. The conservatory library contains memorabilia of Paganini.

Conservatorio di Musica "Niccolo Piccinni"

Via Brigata Bari 26
70124 Bari
Italy

Telephone. (080) 34 79 62
Chief Administrator. G. Rota, Director.

The conservatory was founded in 1925 by Giovanni Capaldi.

Conservatorio di Musica "San Pietro a Majella"

Via San Pietro a Majella 35
80138 Naples
Italy

Telephone. (081) 45 92 55
Chief Administrator. Dr. A. Collucci, Director.

The conservatory is the successor of four older conservatories, all dating from the sixteenth century. The present conservatory has been housed in the buildings of San Pietro a Majella since 1826.

Musical Facilities

Music Library. The library of the conservatory contains sixteenth century editions, treatises, opera autographs, opera libretti, and rare sets of madrigals.

Conservatorio di Musica "Santa Cecilia"

Via dei Greci 18
00187 Rome
Italy

Telephone. (06) 68 45 52
Chief Administrator. Giorgio Cambissa, Director.

The conservatory was founded under the name Congregazione di Maestri e Professori di Musica in Roma. In 1839, the institution was granted the title of Academy. In 1877, a Liceo Musicale opened in the building of the former Ursulines nunnery, given to the Academy by the Italian state. In 1919, the conservatory became a state school of music.

Academic Information

Admission Procedure. Initial inquiries concerning admission to Italian conservatories should be made through Italian embassies and consulates. For further information, contact the Dirizioni di Corsi Superiori di Studi Musicali per Stranieri at the address above.

Music Degrees Offered. Diploma.

General Program Areas. Choir Music, Composition, Conducting, Polyphonic Vocal Composition.

Instruments Taught. Bass, Bassoon, Clarinet, Harp, Horn, Oboe, Organ, Piano, Trombone, Trumpet, Viola, Violin, Violoncello, Voice.

Musical Facilities

Music Library. The conservatory library contains libretti, a collection of French, Spanish, and Italian tragedies and comedies of the sixteenth to eighteenth centuries, and since 1879 all copies of music printed in Italy.

Special Programs

Featured Programs. Supplementary courses are offered in solfeggio, harmony, chamber music, acting, singing, history, aesthetics, Italian, history and geography, literature, religion, physical education.

Conservatorio di Musica "Vincenzo Bellini"

Via Squarcialupo 45
90133 Palermo (Sicily)
Italy

Telephone. (091) 21 18 03, 24 02 41
Chief Administrator. V. Mannino, Director.

Musical Facilities

Music Library. The conservatorio library contains seventeenth and eighteenth century manuscripts and sixteenth century editions of treatises.

Conservatorio Statale di Musica "G. Pierluigi da Palestrina"

Via Bacaredda
09100 Cagliari
Italy

Telephone. 49 40 48
Chief Administrator. Nino Bonavolontá, Director.

The conservatory was founded in 1921. The Instituzione dei Concerti del Conservatorio organizes and sponsors concerts throughout the year.

Musical Facilities

Music Library. The Conservatory library contains a collection of autographs of contemporary Italian and foreign composers.

Conservatorio Statale di Musica "Giovanni Battista Martini"

Piazza Rossini 2
(Entrance at Via Zamboni 33)
40126 Bologna
Italy

Telephone. (051) 22 14 83, 23 21 88

The Liceo Filarmonico was organized in 1804 with the purpose of unifying the musical life of Bologna. It was renamed the Liceo Musicale G.B. Martini in 1963 and at the same time became state-supported with the status of a national conservatory.

Conservatorio Statale di Musica "Giuseppe Verdi" e Scuola Media Annessa

Via Mazzini 11
Piazza Bodoni
10123 Turin
Italy

Telephone. (011) 53 07 87
Chief Administrator. Giorgio Ferrari, Director.

The conservatory was founded in 1867. A lower (preparatory) school is connected to the institution.

Musical Facilities

Music Library. Among the Conservatory's holdings is a collection of autographs of operas, manuscripts, and printed works by Turin composers.

Instituto Professionale Artigianato Liutario e del Legno
Palazzo dell'Arte

Via Bell'Aspa 3
(Scuola Internazionale di Liuteria)
Cremona
Italy

Telephone. 2 71 76

This school, also called the Stradivari School of String Instrument Making, is government sponsored and supported. It issues diplomas to violin makers.

Academic Information

General Program Areas. String Instrument Making.

Pontifical Institute of Sacred Music
Via di Torre Rossa 21
I - 00165 Roma
Italy

Telephone. (06) 620 173; 540 422 (Concert Hall)

Chief Administrator. Rt. Rev. Mons. Dr. Johannes Overath, President.

The Pontifical Institute of Sacred Music, founded in 1910, is affiliated with the Roman Catholic Church. It is part of the Pontifical Universities at Rome and is subject to the Congregation for Catholic Education. The Torre Rossa location is a former abbey of S. Girolamo. The concert hall is located on Piazza S. Agostino 20/A, near Piazza Navona. The languages of instruction are Italian, Spanish, English, Latin, French, German, and Portuguese.

Academic Information

Enrollment, Music Majors. Full-time 45, part-time 16. Foreign students representing 15 nationalities.

Music Faculty. Full-time 13, part-time 2.

Term System. Semester.

Entrance Requirements. High school diploma; admissions tests; audition required; examination (theory).

Admission Procedure. Apply by October 1 with non-refundable $90 fee.

Music Degrees Offered. Baccalaureate; Licentiate; Master's; Doctorate.

Music Degree Requirements. Completion of specific requirements for each degree program.

General Program Areas. Music Theory, Performance.

Instruments Taught. Organ, Piano.

Musical Facilities

Practice Facilities. 20 practice rooms. Special practice rooms for organists; 8 organs (4 Mascioni, 2 Balbiani, 1 Rieger, 1 Klais). 11 practice pianos; 4 grand pianos for piano majors. Practice rooms assigned daily 1 hour per student from October 15 to May 15.

Concert Facilities. Church and concert hall (aula magna Gregorio XVI).

Concerts/Musical Activities. "Saggi" (public recital) required of all students twice a year.

Music Library. 35,000 volumes. Listening facilities (stereo). Specialized library of church music.

Special Programs

Affiliated Programs. Optional attendance at Roman Pontifical Universities or the Academia di S. Cecilia is possible.

Financial

Costs. Per academic year: Tuition $105 first year, $60 thereafter.

Commentary

The Pontifical Institute of Sacred Music considers its strongest disciplines to be the theory and practice of Gregorian chant, liturgy, musicology, ethnomusicology, and organ study.

Universita degli Studi
Facolta di Lettere e Filosofia
Instituto di Storia della Musica
Via Maqueda 172
Palermo (Sicily)
Italy

Telephone. 22 37 14

The Universita degli Studi is one of the few universities in Italy with a musicological institute that gives courses and offers music degrees.

IVORY COAST

Institute of Beaux Arts - Abidjan
Department of Music
Abidjan
Republic of Ivory Coast

Telephone. (331) 442673/4/5, 442031

JAMAICA

Cultural Training Center - Kingston
School of Music
1 Arthur Wint Drive
Kingston 5
Jamaica

Telephone. (809) 9292351

Chief Administrator. Pamela O'Gorman, Director; Kay Anderson, Acting Dean-Registrar of the CTC.

The School of Music of the Cultural Training Center was founded as the Jamaica School of Music on September 25, 1961. In 1976, the government constructed a new building and brought all of the schools (music, art, dance, and drama) together to form the Center (CTC). The building, considered a work of art in itself, is an avant-garde circular structure created around a Roman amphitheatre. Each of the four schools has been given its own special design and character. The building is the work of the Jamaican architect Patrick Stanigar.

The Cultural Training Center has been accredited by the Organization of American States. Through the OAS, Scholarships to the school can be obtained by citizens of member countries.

JAPAN

Elizabeth University of Music
4-15 Nobori-cho
Naka-ku
Hiroshima 730
Japan

Telephone. (0822) 21-0918
Chief Administrator. J.M. Benitez, President; Y. Mizushima, Dean of Academic Affairs.

The institution was founded in 1948 and became a junior college in 1952. It achieved university status in 1963 and is affiliated with the Pontifico Instituto di Musica Sacra in Rome. The University specializes in the study of sacred music. Organ and voice are emphasized in the curriculum.

Academic Information

Music Degrees Offered. Bachelor of Sacred Music.
Music Degree Requirements. The course of study covers a four-year period.
General Program Areas. Sacred Music, Vocal Music.
Instruments Taught. Organ, Voice.

Musical Facilities

Music Library. 5,000 modern volumes. The Library also has holdings for the Institute of Oriental Religious Music.

Kunitachi College of Music
5-5-1 Kashiwa-cho
Tachikawa-shi
Tokyo 190
Japan

Telephone. (0425) 36-0326
Chief Administrator. Professor B. Ebisawa, President.
The Kunitachi College of Music was established in 1950.

Academic Information

Enrollment, Music Majors. 4,000.

Musical Facilities

Music Library. 35,000 volumes on music literature, 35,000 other; 70,000 scores; 20,000 phonograph recordings; 2,500 microfilm reels; 250 periodicals; 26 reels of 16mm film. The Library is the headquarters for the Japan Music Library Association. Special collections include 1,000 slides and 2,000 picture postcards on musical subjects and a collection of early editions including eighteenth and nineteenth century European and Japanese books and scores.

Commentary

Three major instrument collections in Japan are at the Kunitachi College of Music, the Musashino College of Music, and the Osaka College of Music.

Musashino Ongaku Daigaku (Musashino College of Music)
Hazawa 1-13
Nerima-ku
Tokyo 176
Japan

Telephone. (03) 992 1121
Chief Administrator. Naotaka Fukui, President.
The College was founded in 1929 and recognized by the government in 1932. It received university status in 1949.

Although Japanese music history is taught, the emphasis of the curriculum is on Western composition and instruments.

Academic Information

Music Degrees Offered. Bachelor of Fine Arts (four years); Master of Arts (two years beyond the B.F.A.); teaching qualifications.

Musical Facilities

Music Library. Musashino Ongaku Daigaku Gakki-Hakubutsukan: The College has an Instrument Museum with a large collection.

Ochanomizu Joshi Daigaku (Ochanomizu Woman's University)
Faculty of Music
2-1-1 Otsuka
Bunkyo-ku
Tokyo 112
Japan

Telephone. (03) 943 3151/9
This institution was founded in 1874 and became a national university in 1949. The Faculty of Music is academic in its orientation.

Academic Information

Term System. Academic year of two semesters: April to October, October to March.

Music Degrees Offered. Bachelor's; Master's.

Osaka Ongaku Daigaku (Osaka College of Music)

1-1-8 Saiwaimachi, Shonai
Toyonaka
Osaka 561
Japan

Telephone. (06) 334-2131
Chief Administrator. Fujimaro Kubota, Director.

The Osaka College of Music seeks to endow students with a firm foundation in the fundamental studies of music and to foster personal growth as a musician and member of society. It was founded in 1915 as the Osaka Music School. The Osaka Junior College of Music was formed in 1951 and it became the Osaka College of Music in 1958. A postgraduate master's course was inaugurated in 1968.

The College, which comprises thirteen school buildings and one dormitory, is a short walk from the Shonai Station on the Hankya (Takarazuka) Line.

Academic Information

Enrollment, Music Majors. Full-time 184 men, 2,214 women. 27 foreign students from North Korea, South Korea, China, Taiwan.

Music Faculty. Full-time 147, part-time 400.

Term System. Semester. April to September; October to March.

Entrance Requirements. Secondary school diploma; audition in major and test in oral and written Japanese.

Admission Procedure. Application due January 17 or October 17.

Music Degrees Offered. Bachelor of Fine Arts; Diploma of Graduation; Master of Fine Arts.

Music Degree Requirements. The bachelor's degree requires the completion of 128 credit hours (24 in liberal arts, 12 music fundamentals, 4 gymnastics, 76 professional studies). The Diploma requires the completion of 62 credit hours (18 liberal arts, 6 foreign languages, 2 gymnastics, 36 professional studies). The Master's degree requires the completion of 36 credit hours (36 in professional studies plus a master's composition; performance or thesis).

General Program Areas. Composition, Music History, Music Research, Music Theory, Musicology, Performance, Puppet Theater Music.

Instruments Taught. Brass, Japanese Music, Koto, Opera, Organ, Percussion, Piano, Stringed Instruments, Voice, Woodwinds.

Musical Facilities

Practice Facilities. 67 practice rooms. 2 organs (Emil Hammer II type-19, August Laukhuff). 2 percussion-equipped practice rooms. 82 practice pianos (Yamaha, Kawai, Miki); 70 grand pianos reserved for piano majors. Opera studio; recording studio.

Concert Facilities. Concert Hall.

Concerts/Musical Activities. Student concerts (chorus, brass, early music, Japanese music).

Music Library. 20,000 scores (modern editions); 51,000 books; 600 periodicals; 800 microfiche; 20,000 records. Listening facilities (cassette, stereo). The Mizukawa Memorial Building houses the Museum of Musical Instruments, a collection of 250 Japanese instruments from the seventeenth and eighteenth centuries, 150 other Asian instruments, 100 European instruments from the seventeenth, eighteenth, and nineteenth centuries including an early nineteenth century Broadwood piano.

Financial

Costs. Per academic year: Tuition $3,388 to $3,755. Estimated housing cost $718 per month.

Financial Aid. Scholarship aid available. Application due April.

Commentary

Osaka College of Music offers the study of music for the puppet theatre (bunraku). The College has a research division focusing its work on the sociology of music and the study of listening habits of Japanese people.

Soai Women's College (Soai Joshi Daigaku) Faculty of Music

27 Banchi, 4-chome
Higashi-ku, Osaka-shi
Osaka 541
Japan

Telephone. (06) 262-0621

The College was founded in 1906 as a conservatory and received its current standing in 1958.

Academic Information

Enrollment, Music Majors. 1,500.
Music Degrees Offered. Bachelor of Science in Music.

Musical Facilities

Music Library. 35,000 volumes.

Toho Gakuen School of Music

1-41-1, Wakaba-cho
Chofu-shi
Tokyo
Japan

Telephone. (81) 03 307-4101

Chief Administrator. Akira Miyoshi, President.

This institution comprises the Toho Gakuen College of Music, founded in 1961, and the Toho Gakuen Music High School. It is located in Sengawa, a suburb of Tokyo. The two-building campus is 40 minutes by train from the center of Tokyo and is a five minute walk from the Sengawa station of Kero Railroad.

Academic Information

Enrollment, Music Majors. College: full-time 118 men, 722 women; part-time 55 men, 84 women. High School: full-time 32 men, 295 women. 9 foreign students from West Germany, Canada, Brazil, China, Korea, Taiwan, U.S.A.

Music Faculty. Full-time 105, part-time 31.

Term System. Semester.

Entrance Requirements. Secondary school diploma; comprehensive examination; audition in performance before examiners; other requirements include music theory, solfege, harmony, melody; piano audition (except for piano majors); composition essay in Japanese, English, German, or French; interview.

Admission Procedure. Application due February 6.

Music Degrees Offered. High School Certificate; Bachelor of Arts (Music).

Music Degree Requirements. The High School Certificate requires the completion of 88 units; the Bachelor of Art requires 124 units.

General Program Areas. Composition, Music History, Music Theory, Performance.

Instruments Taught. Bassoon, Cembalo, Clarinet, Flute, Harp, Oboe, Percussion, Piano, Recorder, Saxophone, Trombone, Trumpet, Tuba, Viola, Viola da Gamba, Violin, Violoncello.

Musical Facilities

Practice Facilities. 53 practice rooms. 1 percussion-equipped practice room. 125 pianos (102 grands, 23 uprights). 102 grand pianos reserved for piano majors. If practice rooms are not being used, students may use them at any time from 5:00 P.M. until 10:00 P.M. in one-hour units. Electronic music studio.

Concerts/Musical Activities. Concerts and recitals; approximately 30 concerts are held outside the school; ensemble groups; orchestra.

Music Library. 10,000 modern books and scores; 6,705 periodicals; 160 microfiche; 16,852 recordings. Listening facilities (cassette, stereo).

Special Programs

Performance Groups. The Toho Gakuen Orchestra has taken overseas concert tours in 1964, 1970, and 1974.

Foreign Programs. A special free audit course is available for foreign students wishing to study instrumental music.

Financial

Costs. Per academic year: Tuition for High School $2,686; College $3,571.

Financial Aid. Scholarship aid available. Application due January 31 for applicants who want to enter Toho; May 31 for current Toho students.

Commentary

In the string curriculum at the Toho Gakuen School of Music, all violinists are required to study viola. The institution's conducting course is based on a unique method established by the late Professor Hideo Saito. Among the distinguished graduates is Seiji Ozawa.

The Tokyo College of Music

3-4-5 Minami-Ikebukuro
Toshima-ku
Tokyo 171
Japan

Telephone. 81-03-982-3186

Chief Administrator. Akira Ifukube, President.

The Tokyo College of Music provides both general and music education for the preparation of professional musicians and music teachers at the secondary school level. The four-building institution is located in the center of Tokyo, a short walk from both the Ikebukuro Station and Mejiro Station of the National Railroad. The College was founded in 1907 and is the oldest private music institution in Japan. It became a four-year music college in 1963. The language of instruction is Japanese.

Academic Information

Enrollment, Music Majors. Full-time 189 men, 1,333 women; part-time 2 men, 9 women.

Music Faculty. Full-time 32, part-time 39. Foreign students 4 (U.S.A., Republic of Korea, North Korea, People's Republic of China).

Term System. Term from April to February.

Entrance Requirements. Secondary school diploma required; Japanese and English tests; audition; (comprehensive test in chorbungen, sight reading, listening comprehension, musical grammar, piano).

Admission Procedure. Application and $140 nonrefundable fee due January 25 to February 6.

Music Degrees Offered. Bachelor of Arts.

Music Degree Requirements. The Bachelor of Arts degree requires the completion of 146 acceptable credits.

General Program Areas. Music Composition, Music Theory, Performance.

Instruments Taught. Brass, Harpsichord, Japanese Traditional Instruments, Organ, Percussion, Piano, Stringed Instruments.

Musical Facilities

Practice Facilities. Special practice room for organists; 2 organs. 4 practice rooms for percussionists. 120 practice rooms for piano students; 100 upright pianos; 100 grand pianos reserved for piano majors. Recording studio and synthesizer-equipped practice room.

Concert Facilities. Concert hall seating 740.

Concerts/Musical Activities. Many concerts available both on- and off-campus.

Music Library. 38,500 books; 36,700 scores; 629 periodicals; 22,000 recordings. 34 listening stations (stereo).

Financial

Costs. Per academic year: Tuition $3,600. Estimated housing expenses $700; other student expenses including practice facilities $4,700.

Financial Aid. Scholarship application due July 25 to July 30. 18 students receive scholarship aid; average amount $2,208 per year. 192 students receive loans; average amount $130 per month.

Tokyo Daigaku (University of Tokyo)
Faculty of Musicology
7-3-1 Hongo
Bungyo-ku
Tokyo 113
Japan

Telephone. (03) 812 2111

The University was founded in 1877 as Tokyo Daigaku, and later was renamed Imperial University and then Tokyo Imperial University. In 1949 the institution was reorganized again under its current name.

Students undertake research of topics in both Japanese and Western music.

Academic Information

Term System. Academic year of two semesters: April to July, September to March.

Music Degrees Offered. Bachelor's; Master's; Doctorate.

Tokyo Geijutsu Daigaku (Tokyo University of Fine Arts and Music)
Faculty of Music
Ueno Koen 12-8
Taito-ku
Tokyo 110
Japan

Telephone. (03) 828 6111

The University was founded in 1949 as a result of merging the Tokyo School of Fine Arts with the Tokyo School of Music. This is the only institution in Japan that offers a degree specifically in the study of traditional Japanese instruments such as the koto or shamisen.

Academic Information

Term System. Academic year of two semesters: April to September, October to March.

Entrance Requirements. Graduation from high school; entrance examination.

Music Degrees Offered. Bachelor of Fine Arts; Master of Fine Arts; Doctor of Science.

Ueno Gakuen College
24-12, Higashi Ueno 4-chome
Taitō-ku
Tokyo 110
Japan

Telephone. (81) 3 842-1021

Chief Administrator. Shōichi Onishi, Director.

Ueno Gakuen College was founded in 1958 by the Educational Foundation, Ueno Gakuen, which was founded in 1904. The College is for women only and provides undergraduate courses in musicology, instrumental and vocal music, and a one-year postgraduate course. The College is located in central Tokyo.

Academic Information

Enrollment, Music Majors. Full-time 492 women. 1 student from Korea.

Music Faculty. Full-time 35, part-time 73.

Term System. Semester. April to September; October to March.

Entrance Requirements. High school graduate or 12 years of education in Japan or abroad; comprehensive examination; live audition; other requirements in solfege and music theory.

Admission Procedure. Application due January 10 to February 1.

Music Degrees Offered. Bachelor of Arts.

Music Degree Requirements. The degree requires completion of 4 years of study for 134 prescribed credits.

General Program Areas. Composition, Instrumental Music, Japanese Music, Music Theory, Musicology, Performance, Vocal Music.

Instruments Taught. Brass, Guitar, Harp, Harpsichord, Lute, Organ, Percussion, Piano, Recorder, Stringed Instruments, Viola da Gamba, Voice, Woodwinds.

Musical Facilities

Practice Facilities. 40 practice rooms. Special practice rooms for organists; 1 grand organ (Johannes Klais) and 1 positive organ (Walker). 2 percussion-equipped practice rooms. 80 pianos (70 grands, 10 uprights); 40 grand pianos reserved for piano majors. Electronic music studio.

Concert Facilities. Ishibashi Memorial Hall, seating 700; Aeolian Hall, 150.

Concerts/Musical Activities. Each student must perform at an open concert once in the junior year and once in the senior year before graduation.

Music Library. 22,792 scores; 37,318 books; 2,655 periodicals; 1,067 microfiche; 8,661 records. Listening facilities (cassette, stereo). Special collection of manuscripts of Japanese composers including Yoritsune Matsudaira; early editions of many 17th to 19th century composers including Rameau, Purcell, and Beethoven. The College, besides having the general music library with standard Western reference works, has a separate, outstanding library with materials pertaining only to Japanese traditional music. The Tokyo Metropolitan Festival Hall Library is also available to students.

Financial

Costs. Per academic year: Tuition $3,100. Estimated housing costs $1,184.

Financial Aid. Scholarship aid available.

Commentary

Ueno Gakuen College, in addition to having a general music library with standard Western reference works, has a separate library with materials pertaining only to Japanese traditional music, the Research Archives for Japanese Music.

The course for early music and the instruction of instruments such as viola da gamba and lute is an unusual aspect of the institution.

KAMPUCHEA

Université des Beaux-Arts
Faculty of Music
Boulevard U.R.S.S.
Phnom Penh
Kampuchea

The University, a state institution under the Ministry of Culture, was founded in 1965 by the merger of the existing schools of art and music.

Academic Information

Music Degrees Offered. Bachelor of Arts; Diploma.

Commentary

No recent information has been received from Kampuchea. The above entry is based on research undertaken in the early 1980s.

KENYA

Kenya Conservatoire of Music
P.O.B. 41343
Nairobi
Kenya

Telephone. Nairobi 22933
Chief Administrator. Kevin P. Allen, Director.

The Conservatoire was founded in 1944 as one of the first "non-racial" institutions in East Africa. It is an independent, non-subsidized organization, administered by the Director. Students are prepared for the Theory and Practial examinations of the Associated Board of the Royal Schools of Music, London, from Grade one up to L.R.S.M. In general, pupils are not accepted under the age of seven. Lessons of 30 minutes, 45 minutes, and 1 hour are given and can be taken once or twice a week. Theory correspondence courses are also available. A teacher's certificate course in Recorder is offered.

Academic Information

Enrollment, Music Majors. 600.
Music Faculty. 25.
Music Degrees Offered. LRSM; Teacher's Certificate.
Music Degree Requirements. The LRSM is offered for Overseas Diplomas. The Teacher's Certificate is in Recorder.

General Program Areas. Music Theory, Performance.

Instruments Taught. Clarinet, Flute, Guitar, Organ, Piano, Recorder, Violin, Violoncello, Voice.

Musical Facilities

Practice Facilities. 1 organ. 15 pianos (3 grands).
Concerts/Musical Activities. The Conservatoire administers regular concerts at the Kenya National Theatre and elsewhere, often in collaboration with foreign cultural institutions.

Music Library. Extensive library of musical scores (approximately 2,000). Small collection of records. Listening facilities (stereo).

KOREA (DPR)

College of Music and Dance - Pyongyang
Pyongyang
North Korea

The College of Music and Dance was founded in 1948.

Academic Information

Music Degrees Offered. Diploma.
Music Degree Requirements. A Diploma is earned after a four- to five-year course of study.

KOREA

Baejae College
Department of Music
439-6 Doma-dong
Joong-gu, Taejon City
Choongnam 30001
South Korea

Telephone. 45-0035/9
Baejae College, a private institution, was founded as a school in 1885. It became a junior college in 1978 and achieved university status in 1981.

Academic Information

Term System. Semester. March to August; September to February.
Music Degrees Offered. Bachelor of Arts in Music.
Music Degree Requirements. The Bachelor of Arts requires the completion of a four-year course of study.

Commentary

There is no independent conservatory in the Republic of Korea, but a number of colleges and universities—such as Baejae College—have music divisions which offer at least four years of formal education and training in music.

Ewha Women's University
College of Music
11-1 Taehyun-dong
Sodaemun-gu
Seoul 120
South Korea

Telephone. 362-6151
Chief Administrator. Eun-Soo Kwak, Dean, College of Music
The University is a private institution founded in 1886 by the Methodist missionary, Mary Scranton. It became

a college in 1910 and achieved university status in 1945.

Academic Information

Term System. Semester. March to July; September to February.
Music Degrees Offered. Bachelor of Music; Master of Music.
Music Degree Requirements. The Bachelor of Music requires the completion of a four-year course; the Master of Music is awarded after an additional two years of study.

Hanyang University
College of Music
17 Haengdang-dong
Songdong-gu
Seoul 133
South Korea

Telephone. 292-2111
Chief Administrator. Yun-Taik Hong, Dean, College of Music.

The University is a private institution and was founded in 1939 as Dong-Ah Polytechnic Academy. It was reorganized in 1945 and 1948 and achieved university status under its current name in 1956.

Academic Information

Term System. Semester. March to June; September to December.
Music Degrees Offered. Bachelor of Music; Master of Music.
Music Degree Requirements. The Bachelor of Music requires the completion of a four-year course; the Master of Music is awarded after an additional two years of study.

Hoseo College
Department of Music
Mt. 120-1, Anseo-dong
Cheonan
Choongnam Province 330
South Korea

Telephone. (0417) 3-1811/9
Chief Administrator. Yoo-sun Lee, Chairman, Department of Music.

Hoseo College is a private institution founded as a junior college in 1978. It achieved its current status in 1980.

Academic Information

Term System. Semester. March to August; September to February.

Music Degrees Offered. Bachelor of Music.

Music Degree Requirements. The Bachelor of Music requires the completion of a four-year course of study.

Kangreung National University
Department of Music and Fine Arts

1 Chibyo-Dong
Kangreung 210
Gang-weon
South Korea

Telephone. 3-2076/80

The University, a state institution, was established in 1969 as a teacher training college. It achieved university status in 1979.

Academic Information

Term System. Semester. March to August; September to February.

Music Degrees Offered. Bachelor of Arts in Music.

Music Degree Requirements. The Bachelor of Arts requires the completion of a four-year course of study.

Keimyung University
College of Music

2139 Daemyeong-dong
Nam-gu
Taegu
South Korea

Telephone. 67-1321/30

The University began as a small liberal arts college in 1954 supported by the Korean Presbyterian Church. It received a government charter in 1956.

Academic Information

Term System. Semester. March to August; September to February.

Music Degrees Offered. Bachelor of Music.

Music Degree Requirements. The Bachelor of Music requires completion of a four-year course of study.

Kongju National Teachers' College
Department of Music

9-6 Shinkwan-li
Changgi-myon, Kongju-kun
Chung Nam 301
South Korea

Telephone. (2) 2151-7

This teacher training college was founded in 1948 and achieved its present status in 1954. It functions under the aegis of the Ministry of Education.

Academic Information

Term System. Semester. March to August; September to February.

Music Degrees Offered. Bachelor of Music.

Music Degree Requirements. The Bachelor of Music requires the completion of a four-year course of study.

Korean Union College
Department of Music

Cheongryang
P.O. Box 18
Seoul
South Korea

Telephone. (972) 3606

The College was founded as a Seventh-day Adventist Denominational Training School in 1906. It became a college in 1961 and adopted its present name in 1966.

Academic Information

Term System. Semester. March to July; August to September.

Music Degrees Offered. Bachelor of Arts in Music.

Music Degree Requirements. The Bachelor of Arts requires the completion of a four-year course of study.

Kyung Hee University
College of Music

1 Hoegi-dong
Tongadaemun-gu
Seoul 131
South Korea

Telephone. 966-0061

The University is a private institution established in 1949 as Shin Hung College. It achieved university status in 1951.

Academic Information

Term System. Semester. March to July; September to December.

Music Degrees Offered. Bachelor of Music; Master of Music.

Music Degree Requirements. The Bachelor of Music requires the completion of a four-year course of study; the Master of Music requres an additional two and one-half years of study.

Kyungpook National University
College of Music and Visual Arts
1370 San Kyung-dong
Puk ku
Taegu 635
South Korea

Telephone. (053) 94-5001/45

Chief Administrator. Jin-Gyun Kim, Dean, College of Music and Visual Arts.

The University was founded in 1952 upon the merger of five existing colleges. It operates under the jurisdiction of the Ministry of Education.

Academic Information

Term System. Semester. March to June; September to December.

Music Degrees Offered. Bachelor of Music.

Music Degree Requirements. The Bachelor of Music degree requires the completion of a four-year course of study.

Sang-Myeong Women's College of Education
Department of Music
Jongro-gu
Seoul
South Korea

Telephone. (73) 0291/5

The College is a private institution founded in 1938. It acquired its current status in 1955.

Academic Information

Term System. Semester. March to August; September to December.

Music Degrees Offered. Bachelor of Arts.

Music Degree Requirements. The Bachelor of Arts requires the completion of a four-year course of study.

Seoul National University
College of Music
San 56-1, Shinrim-dong
Kwanak-gu
Seoul 151
South Korea

Telephone. 877-0101/9

Chief Administrator. Sung-Jae Lee, Dean, College of Music.

The University is a state institution responsible to the Ministry of Education. It was founded in 1946 as successor to the former Keijo Imperial University and was restructured in 1975.

Academic Information

Term System. Semester. March to June; September to December.

Music Degrees Offered. Bachelor of Music; Master of Music.

Music Degree Requirements. The Bachelor of Music requires completion of a four-year course; the Master of Music is awarded after an additional two years of study.

Sookmyung Women's University
College of Music
San Z-1, Chungpa-dong
Yongsan-gu
Seoul
South Korea

Telephone. 43-5161/7

The University is a private institution founded in 1938 as a college, achieving university status in 1955.

Academic Information

Term System. Semester. March to July; September to December.

Music Degrees Offered. Bachelor of Arts in Music; Master of Arts in Music.

Music Degree Requirements. The Bachelor of Arts requires the completion of a four-year course of study; the Master of Arts is awarded after an additional two years of study.

Yeungnam University
College of Music
Gyongsan-gun
Gyeong-Bug 632
South Korea

Telephone. (053) 82-5111

Chief Administrator. Bang-Song Song, Dean, College of Music.

The University is privately supported and was established in 1967 with the merger of two existing institutions, Taego College and Chonggu College.

Academic Information

Term System. Semester. March to August; September to February.

Music Degrees Offered. Bachelor of Music; Master of Music.

Music Degree Requirements. The Bachelor of Music requires the completion of a four-year course of study; the Master of Music is awarded after an additional two years of study.

Yongsei University
College of Music
134 Shinchon-dong
Sodaemun-gu
Seoul 120
South Korea

Telephone. 33-0131/0141

The institution was first established in 1885 as a Severance Union Medical Clinic and merged with Chosun Christian College to form Yongsei University in 1957. The University receives some financial support from the government.

Academic Information

Term System. Semester. March to August; August to December.

Music Degrees Offered. Bachelor of Music; Master of Music.

Music Degree Requirements. The Bachelor of Music requires the completion of a four-year course of study; the Master of Music is awarded after an additional two years of study.

KUWAIT

Higher Institute of Music and Performing Arts - Safat
c/o Undersecretary
Minister of Information
P.O. Box 193
Safat 133002
Kuwait

The Instiute offers the study of Middle Eastern music. Telex number: 46151.

Academic Information

Music Degrees Offered. Certificate.

Music Degree Requirements. Certificate (equivalent to the Bachelor's degree) awarded after completion of a three- to four-year course of study.

General Program Areas. Middle Eastern Music.

LEBANON

University of the Holy Ghost
Institute of Musicology and School of Music
Kaslik
Jounieh
Lebanon

Chief Administrator. Louis Hage, Dean, Institute of Musicology; Jacques Badwi, Director, School of Music.

The University of the Holy Ghost is a private institution founded in 1949 by the Lebanese Maronite Order.

Academic Information

Music Degrees Offered. Licentiate Diploma.

Music Degree Requirements. The Licentiate diploma is earned after a four- to five-year course of study.

Commentary

No recent information has been received from Lebanon. The information about the institutions of Lebanon included in the *Guide* is based on research undertaken in the early 1980s.

Lebanese Academy of Fine Arts
Beirut
Lebanon

This institution was founded in 1937. Afif Bolus, the distinguished musician and author of a book on Arabic music, was once a teacher at the Academy.

Lebanese National Conservatory
Eastern Section
Beirut
Lebanon

Western music theory and solfege, and piano studies are the preparation for studies in this conservatory, devoted solely to the study of Arabic instruments and vocal music.

Academic Information

General Program Areas. Arabic Instruments.

LIBERIA

Cuttington University College
Box 277
Monrovia
Liberia

Although the mailing address for this institution is Monrovia, the school is actually located in Suakoko, about 90 miles outside the city, in the bush. Music courses in both African and Western music are offered. The university has a choir and performance troupes of traditional music and dance.

Academic Information

Music Degrees Offered. Bachelor of Arts.
General Program Areas. African Traditional Music.

University of Liberia
Department of Music
Monrovia
Liberia

LUXEMBOURG

Conservatoire de Musique de la Ville de Luxembourg
33 Rue Charles Martel
2134 Luxembourg City
Luxembourg

Telephone. 4796-2950
Chief Administrator. Josy Hamer, Director.
The Conservatory was founded in 1906.
Member of the Assocation Européenne des Conservatoires de Musique, Académies de Musique, et Musikhochschulen.

Academic Information

Music Faculty. 100.

Conservatoire de Musique d'Esch-sur-Alzette
10 Rue de l'Eglise
BP 145
4002 Esch-sur-Alzette
Luxembourg

Telephone. 547383-490
The Conservatory is under the administration of Esch-sur-Alzette.
Member of the Assocation Européenne des Conservatoires de Musique, Académies de Musique, et Musik-

hochschulen.

MEXICO

Conservatorio de Las Rosas
Jardin Las Rosas 347
Morelia, Michoacán
Mexico

Conservatorio Nacional de México
Avenida Presidente Masaryk 582
Mexico City 5, D.F.
Mexico

Chief Administrator. Maestro Leopoldo Tellez, Director.
The Conservatory was founded in 1866.

Academic Information

Enrollment, Music Majors. 170.

Musical Facilities

Music Library. 48,000 volumes.

Escuela Nacional de Música
Universidad Nacional Autónoma de México
Xicotencatl 126
Coyoacán
Mexico City, D.F. 04100
Mexico

Telephone. 688 13 95, 688 33 08, 688 03 58
Chief Administrator. Jorge Suárez, Director.
The School of Music was founded in 1929 when the University of México became autonomous. This new School planned music teaching on the principle of the teacher's creative freedom in the presentation of a given program *("Libertad de cátedra")* and on the musical needs of the country. The School reorganized and updated its programs in 1939, 1967, 1968, and most recently in 1984.

Academic Information

Enrollment, Music Majors. Children, 900; Preparatory Course, 599; Bachelor of Music level, 171; Extension Courses, 100. Foreign students, 15 (South American 13, European 2).
Music Faculty. 238.
Entrance Requirements. Applicants must have finished high school and a six-semester preparatory course (given at the School).

Music Degrees Offered. Bachelor of Music; "Propedéutico" awarded for preparatory course.

General Program Areas. Ear Training, Ethnomusicology, Instrument Making, Music Computing, Music Education, Music History of Mexico, Music Theory, Solfege, World Music History.

Instruments Taught. Accordion, Bass, Bassoon, Clarinet, English Horn, Flute, French Horn, Harp, Harpsichord, Oboe, Organ, Percussion, Piano, Recorder, Saxophone, Trombone, Trumpet, Tuba, Viola, Violin, Violoncello, Voice.

Musical Facilities

Practice Facilities. 80 pianos (9 grands); 2 organs. 2 percussion-equipped practice rooms.

Concert Facilities. 2 concert halls seating 350 and 120.

Concerts/Musical Activities. Community Concerts.

Music Library. 6,000 books; 13,000 scores; 4,000 records; 110 periodical titles. 7 record players. Special collection of Mexican music (printed and manuscript).

Special Programs

Featured Programs. The School has a Centro de Iniciación Musical for children, beginning at age six.

MONACO

Académie de Musique Prince Rainier III de Monaco
17 Rue Princesse Florestine
Monaco
Monaco

The school was founded in 1934.

MOROCCO

Conservatoire de Musique - Marrakesh
Marrakesh
Morocco

This school is part of a national network of regional conservatories throughout the country.

Conservatoire de Tanger
Tanger
Morocco

This school is part of a national network of regional conservatories throughout the country.

Conservatoire National de Musique, de Danse, et d'Art Dramatique - Ribad
Ribad
Morocco

Chief Administrator. Ahmed Awatef, Director.

The Conservatoire trains students in Western, Eastern, and Moroccan music. The students are divided into three different ensembles: classical, Eastern music, and traditional Andalusian orchestras. One of the three principal Andalusian orchestras in Morocco is in Ribad.

Academic Information

General Program Areas. Andalusian Music, Moroccan Music.

Commentary

Morocco's three national conservatories are in Ribad, Fez, and Tetouan. When small music schools were established in the 1930s, they served mainly as meeting places for musicians. In the mid to late 1960s, French and Egyptian trained teachers brought solfege with them to Morocco. French pedagogical material, which uses Western scales, was soon required for students in the conservatories. It had little to do with the Andalusian music taught at the conservatories and played by Moroccan musicians.

As time has progressed, conservatories have helped to spread the traditional music to people outside of Moroccan cities. Not only can it be heard on radio but in live performances as well, all the while educating an increasing number of listeners.

École Nationale de Musique - Casablanca
133 Ave. Ziraoui
Casablanca
Morocco

Chief Administrator. Oulhadj Brahim, Director.

This school is part of a national network of regional conservatories throughout the country.

École Nationale de Musique - Meknes
22 Rue Marrakchia
Kaa Ouarda
Meknes
Morocco

Chief Administrator. Abdelaziz Benabdeljalil, Director.

This school is part of a national network of regional conservatories throughout the country.

Institut National de Musique et de Danse - Kenitra

Ave. Mohamed V
Kenitra
Morocco

Chief Administrator. Abbes Alkhayyati, Director.
This school is part of a national network of regional conservatories throughout the country.

National Conservatoire Dan Adyel

Fez
Morocco

This Conservatory is near one of the country's three principal Andalusian orchestras.

National Conservatoire of Tetouan

Tetouan
Morocco

This Conservatory is near one of the country's three principal Andalusian orchestras. The institution's instrument collection includes approximately 30 European and Arabic instruments.

NETHERLANDS

Akademie voor Musiek

Koninginneweg 25
Hilversum Postkode 1217 KR
Netherlands

Telephone. 035-47548
Chief Administrator. Martin Kamminga, Director.
The Academy occupies six buildings in Koninginneweg. Dutch, English, and German are the languages of instruction.

Academic Information

Enrollment, Music Majors. Full-time 380 men, 80 women; part-time 90 men, 60 women. 50 foreign students representing 4 nationalities.
Term System. Academic year September to June.
Entrance Requirements. Secondary school diploma; comprehensive examination; audition.
Admission Procedure. Application due May 1.
Music Degrees Offered. Diploma (performer, teacher).
General Program Areas. Jazz Studies, Light Music.
Instruments Taught. Brass, Organ, Percussion, Piano, Stringed Instruments, Woodwinds.

Musical Facilities

Practice Facilities. 60 practice rooms. Organ practice in local churches and cathedrals. 2 percussion-equipped practice rooms. 6 grand pianos reserved for piano majors. Electronic music studio.
Concert Facilities. 3 concert halls.
Concerts/Musical Activities. Many concerts and recitals.
Music Library. 250 scores; 7,500 books; 20 periodicals; 350 phonograph recordings. Listening facilities (stereo).

Financial

Financial Aid. Scholarship aid and loans (government) available. Application due January 31.

Commentary

The Akademie considers its strongest department to be jazz/light music, which includes the study of all popular contemporary musical forms.

Conservatorium voor Muziek-Nederland

Bonnefanten 15
6211 KL Maastricht
Netherlands

Chief Administrator. Hans Besselink, Director.
The Conservatorium was founded in 1957.
Member of the Assocation Européenne des Conservatoires de Musique, Académies de Musique, et Musikhochschulen.

Musical Facilities

Music Library. 23,000 volumes.

Koninklijk Conservatorium voor Muziek en Dans
(Royal Conservatory of Music and Dance)

1 Juliana van Stolberglaan
2595 CA The Hague
Netherlands

Telephone. (070) 63 99 25, 81 42 51
Chief Administrator. Frans de Ruiter, Director.
The Conservatorium was founded in 1826 and is the oldest conservatory in Holland. Some scholarships are awarded by the Dutch government to foreign students. Additional telephone number: (070) 81 42 51.
Member of the Assocation Européenne des Conservatoires de Musique, Académies de Musique, et Musikhochschulen.

Academic Information

Enrollment, Music Majors. 850.
Music Faculty. 200.

Musical Facilities

Music Library. 20,000 volumes.

Commentary

Early music and instruction on viola da gamba in particular, as well as chamber music, are emphasized in the curriculum of The Hague's Koninklijk Conservatorium.

Nederlands Instituut voor Kerkmuziek
Plompeforengracht 3
NL-3512 CA
Utrecht
Netherlands

Telephone. (30) 314092
Chief Administrator. Frans Brouwer, Director.
The Institute was originally founded as a private Roman Catholic school for church music. Since 1980, it has been ecumenical and partly supported by the state. It is the only school for specialization in church music in Holland. The language of instruction is Dutch. The Institute occupies an eighteenth century building in the center of Utrecht.

Academic Information

Enrollment, Music Majors. Full-time 13 men, 9 women; part-time 2 men, 1 woman. 1 foreign student.
Term System. Academic year September to July.
Entrance Requirements. Secondary school diploma required; at least 3 years musical education with attainment in organ and piano; audition (a committee of 5 professors makes the admission decision).
Admission Procedure. Application due June 1.
Music Degrees Offered. Diploma Kerkmusicus.
Music Degree Requirements. Five- to seven-year programs.
General Program Areas. Choral Conducting, Performance.
Instruments Taught. Harpsichord, Organ, Piano.

Musical Facilities

Practice Facilities. 6 practice rooms. 4 organs (2 Flentrop, 1 Pels, 1 19th century). 8 practice pianos; 5 grand pianos reserved for piano majors.
Concert Facilities. 1 concert hall for organ, grand piano, and choir concerts/recitals.
Community Facilities. Local church organ used for practice.
Music Library. 300 scores; 600 books; 40 periodicals; 200 phonograph recordings. Listening facilities (cassette, stereo).

Special Programs

Performance Groups. Every student plays in a church.

Financial

Costs. Per academic year: Tuition HFL 700.
Financial Aid. Scholarship applications due January 15. 15 students receive scholarship aid.

Commentary

The Instituut plans to change its seven-year program to a four-year curriculum in the future. Choir direction and organ are the disciplines considered to be the strongest by the school's administration.

Rotterdams Conservatorium
Pieter de Hoochweg 122
3024 BJ Rotterdam
Netherlands

Chief Administrator. John Floore, Director.
The Conservatorium was founded in 1971.
Member of the Assocation Européenne des Conservatoires de Musique, Académies de Musique, et Musikhochschulen.

Stedelijke Muziekpedagogische Akademie
Eewal 56-58
Leeuwarden
Netherlands

Telephone. (058) 120275
Chief Administrator. W.D. van Ligtenberg, Director.
The main purpose of the Academy is the training of music teachers and conductors of bands and choirs. There is an emphasis in the curriculum on music theory and education. The Academy was founded in 1965 as a professional institution, and in 1973 it became a Training College for Musicians. The Academy occupies three buildings in the center of Leeuwarden.

Academic Information

Enrollment, Music Majors. Full-time 160 men, 90 women; part-time 40 men, 30 women.
Music Faculty. Full-time 23, part-time 42.
Term System. Semester.
Entrance Requirements. Secondary school diploma required. Audition in studied repertory and a new piece. Other requirements depending on course chosen, instrumental/vocal.
Admission Procedure. Application due May 1 with $5 nonrefundable application fee.
Music Degrees Offered. Diploma.

Music Degree Requirements. 5-year program full-time. General requirements include music theory, aural training, and history.

General Program Areas. Conducting, Music History, Music Theory, Performance, School Music.

Instruments Taught. Brass, Organ, Percussion, Piano, Stringed Instruments, Voice, Woodwinds.

Musical Facilities

Practice Facilities. 3 practice rooms for percussion. 2 organs (Muller, 1723; Bakker and Timminga, 1966). 20 pianos (upright); 12 grand pianos reserved for piano majors. Pop music studio.

Community Facilities. Two local churces are used for organ lessons; local concert hall for concerts.

Concerts/Musical Activities. Concerts are organized by the Institute.

Music Library. 350 scores; 1,900 books; 45 periodicals; 425 phonograph recordings. Listening facilities (cassette, stereo).

Financial

Costs. Per academic year: Tuition $350. Estimated housing expenses $4,000.

Financial Aid. Scholarship applications due May 1. 160 students receive scholarship aid.

Commentary

Brass instruments, percussion, and organ study are emphasized in the curriculum of the Akademie.

Stichting Sweelinck Conservatorium Amsterdam
Van Baerlestraat 27
1071 AN Amsterdam
Netherlands

Telephone. (020) 647641
Chief Administrator. Ms. H.J. Lyre, Director.
The Conservatorium was founded in 1975.
Member of the Assocation Européenne des Conservatoires de Musique, Académies de Musique, et Musikhochschulen.

Academic Information

Enrollment, Music Majors. 800.
Music Faculty. 200.

Musical Facilities

Music Library. 30,000 volumes.

Utrechts Conservatorium
Mariaplaats 28
3511 LL Utrecht
Netherlands

Chief Administrator. Ton Hartsuiker, Director.
The Conservatorium was founded in 1947.
Member of the Assocation Européenne des Conservatoires de Musique, Académies de Musique, et Musikhochschulen.

Musical Facilities

Music Library. 14,000 volumes.

NEW CALEDONIA

Conservatoire National des Artes et Métiers
BP 3562
French Overseas Territories
Nouméa Cedex
New Caledonia

Telephone. 28 37 07
Chief Administrator. Bernard Schall, Director.
The Conservatory is located in the French Overseas Territory of New Caledonia. It was established in 1971 and is attached to the Conservatoire National des Arts et Métiers in Paris.

Academic Information

Enrollment, Music Majors. 500.

NEW ZEALAND

University of Auckland
Faculty of Music
Private Bag
Auckland
New Zealand

Telephone. 737999
Chief Administrator. G.W.J. Drake, Dean, Faculty of Music.

The University was originally established in 1882 as Auckland University College. In 1957, it became the University of Auckland and in 1961, by further act of the legislature, became an autonomous degree-granting university.

Academic Information

Music Degrees Offered. Bachelor of Music; Diploma of Music; Master of Arts, Master of Music; Doctor of Music.

Music Degree Requirements. The Bachelor of Music program in performance is a 4-year course. The Bachelor of Music in other disciplines is a 3-year course. The Master of Arts in Music requires an additional course of 1 to 2 years of study beyond the bachelor's degree. The Master of Music in composition or practical performance requires 1 year of full-time study beyond the bachelor's degree. The Doctor of Music is awarded after 5 years of study beyond the bachelor's degree. The Diploma of Music program requires completion of a 3-year course.

Musical Facilities

Music Library. 10,000 volumes; 2,500 phonograph records. Listening facilities available. Loan collection of phonograph records and cassette tapes.

Commentary

The Center for Continuing Education at the University of Auckland sponsors the Cambridge Music School, a ten-day summer school held annually under university auspices, but open to the public. Further information about the school can be obtained from:

Mr. Ronald Dellow, Director
Cambridge Music School
Centre for Continuing Education
University of Auckland
Private Bag
Auckland, New Zealand

University of Canterbury
Faculty of Music
Christchurch 1
New Zealand

Telephone. 488-489
Chief Administrator. Professor M.A. Till, Dean of Music and Fine Arts

The institution was established as Canterbury College in 1873. It became a university in 1957 and was granted full degree-granting status in 1961.

Academic Information

Music Degrees Offered. Bachelor of Music; Bachelor of Music (Honors); Master of Arts in Music; Ph.D.; Doctor of Music; Diploma.

Music Degree Requirements. The Bachelor of Music program is a 3-year course; the Bachelor of Music (Honors) requires a minimum of 1 year after the Bachelor of Music in Composition, Music Education, Musicology, and Performance. The Master of Arts in Music requires 1 year of study after the Bachelor's program. The Doctor of Philosophy degree requires 2 years beyond the Bachelor of Music (Honors). The Doctor of Music requires 5 years of study beyond the Bachelor degree program in musical composition. The Diploma of Music is a 3-year

course of study.

Musical Facilities

Music Library. The music collection is part of the main library. Listening facilties are available. Library's telephone number is 65-819.

University of Otago
Arts and Music
P.O. Box 56
Dunedin
New Zealand

Telephone. 771-640
Chief Administrator. J.D.S. McKenzie, Dean, Arts and Music.

The University of Otago, New Zealand's oldest university, was founded in 1869. The first classes were held in 1871, at which time the University had the power to grant degrees in arts, medicine, law, and music. In 1874, the University affiliated with the University of New Zealand. In 1967, when the University of New Zealand was disestablished, the power to confer degrees was restored to the University of Otago.

Academic Information

Music Degrees Offered. Bachelor of Music; Bachelor of Music (Honors); Master of Music; Master of Arts in Music; Doctor of Music; Diploma.

Music Degree Requirements. The Bachelor of Music requires the completion of a 3-year course; the Bachelor of Music (Honors), 4 years. The Master of Music requires 1 year of full-time study after the Bachelor of Music (Honors); the Master of Arts in Music, 1 year after the Bachelor of Music. The Doctor of Music requires the completion of 5 years of study beyond the Bachelor of Music. The Diploma in Music is a 1-year course of study.

Musical Facilities

Music Library. 10,000 volumes of music works; 300 records. Listening facilities. Special collections in Renaissance and avant-garde music. The music collection is part of the main library (telephone 79-664).

Victoria University of Wellington
Faculty of Music
Private Bag
Wellington 1
New Zealand

Telephone. 721-000
Chief Administrator. P.G. Walls, Head, Faculty of Music.

The University was orginally established as Victoria University College in 1897 and became affiliated with the University of New Zealand in 1899. The Victoria University of Wellington became an autonomous institution in 1962.

Academic Information

Music Degrees Offered. Bachelor of Music; Bachelor of Music (Honors); Master of Music; Doctor of Music.

Music Degree Requirements. The Bachelor of Music requires the completion of a 3-year course (may be granted also through extramural studies at Massey University); the Bachelor of Music (Honors) is a four-year course. The Master of Music requires an additional 1 year of study beyond the Bachelor of Music (Honors) and is awarded in history and literature of music and composition. The Doctor of Music requires 5 years of study beyond the Bachelor of Music.

Musical Facilities

Music Library. 10,000 music works; 1,000 records. Listening facilities. Special collection of Douglas Lilburn scores. The music collection is part of the main library.

NICARAGUA

Escuela Nacional de Música - Managua
c/o Ministry of Culture
Antigua Hacienda el Retiro
Managua
Nicaragua

Telephone. (5052) 27831
Chief Administrator. Pablo Antonio Buitrago, Director.

NIGERIA

University of Ife
Department of Music
Ile-Ife
Nigeria

Telephone. Ile-Ife 2291
Chief Administrator. A.M. Adegbite, Acting Head, Department of Music.
The University was founded in 1961.

Academic Information

Music Faculty. 7.
Term System. Semester.
Music Degrees Offered. Bachelor of Arts; Associate Certificate.

Music Degree Requirements. The Bachelor of Arts in music is awarded after completion of a three-year course. The Associate Certificate in music is awarded after completion of a one-year course.

University of Lagos
Department of Music
Lagos
Nigeria

Telephone. Lagos 821 111
Chief Administrator. N.Z. Nayo, Acting Head, Department of Music.

The University was founded in 1962. The Center of Cultural Studies was established in 1975 to coordinate cultural activities in the University and produce a balanced academic program in the arts, with emphasis on Nigerian traditional culture and experimental works. The Center has plans to establish a museum and archives for the arts.

Academic Information

Music Faculty. 4.
Music Degrees Offered. Bachelor of Arts in Music.

University of Nigeria
Department of Music
Nsukka, Anambra State
Nigeria

Telephone. 6251
Chief Administrator. A.O. Ifionu, Acting Head, Department of Music.
The University was founded in 1960.

Academic Information

Music Faculty. 7.
Music Degrees Offered. Bachelor of Arts; Diploma.

Music Degree Requirements. The Bachelor of Arts in music is awarded after completion of a four-year program. The Diploma in Music Education is awarded after completion of a three-year program.

NORWAY

Norges Musikkhøgskole
(The Norwegian State Academy of Music)
Nordahl Brunsgt. 8
Postboks 6877 St. Olavs Pl.
N-0130 Oslo 1
Norway

Telephone. (02) 20 70 19

Chief Administrator. Gunnar Nessing, Senior Managing Officer.

The Academy was established in 1973 with the Department of Advanced Studies at the Music Conservatory of Oslo as a nucleus. Its goal is to qualify music performers, composers, conductors, and teachers; it is the only state institution at this level. The Academy occupies three buildings in the center of Oslo and was scheduled to move into a new building in 1988.

Member of the Assocation Européenne des Conservatoires de Musique, Académies de Musique, et Musikhochschulen.

Academic Information

Enrollment, Music Majors. Full-time 171 men, 136 women; part-time 9 men, 11 women. Foreign students 39, representing 9 nationalities.

Music Faculty. Full-time 58, part-time 121.

Term System. Semester (Spring and Autumn).

Entrance Requirements. Secondary school diploma required; comprehensive examination (general studies up to university level). Audition required; set pieces to be performed in ninth week; test in music theory and aural training. Foreign students must meet same requirements.

Admission Procedure. Application due by December 15.

General Program Areas. Composition, Conducting, Music Education, Music Theory, Performance.

Instruments Taught. Brass, Guitar, Lute, Percussion, Piano, Stringed Instruments, Viola da Gamba, Voice, Woodwinds.

Musical Facilities

Practice Facilities. 61 practice rooms. 2 organs. 4 percussion-equipped rooms. 47 practice pianos; 15 grand pianos reserved for piano majors. 2 special studios.

Community Facilities. Organ facilities in Oslo churches.

Music Library. 33,700 scores; 4,500 books; 146 periodicals; 5,100 phonograph recordings. Listening facilities (cassette, compact disc players, phonographs, tape recorders, amplifiers). Special collection of historical instruments located outside the Main Music Library.

Financial

Costs. Per academic year: Student fee $70. Estimated housing expenses $1,000.

Financial Aid. The Academy does not offer scholarships. Norwegian students may receive state loans of $3,500 per year.

Rogaland Musikkonservatorium
Bjergsted
N-4000 Stavanger
Norway

Telephone. (47) 4 533480

Chief Administrator. Odd Leren, Director.

The Conservatory educates teachers and performers to obtain a qualified background in music and music education. It is a small institution striving for high standards. The Conservatory moved into a new building in 1979, designed especially for it and the Stavanger Symphony Orchestra. The school was founded in 1971.

Member of the Assocation Européenne des Conservatoires de Musique, Académies de Musique, et Musikhochschulen.

Academic Information

Enrollment, Music Majors. Full-time 28 men, 44 women; part-time 3 men, 2 women. 2 foreign students (Denmark, Sweden).

Term System. Semester. September to December; January to June.

Entrance Requirements. Secondary school diploma; admission tests in general education and music; audition required (playing the main instrument, auditive tests, piano playing, and singing on an elementary level).

Admission Procedure. Application due February 1.

Music Degrees Offered. Diploma (Music Teacher, Church Musician, Performer).

Music Degree Requirements. Completion of two- to three-year programs.

General Program Areas. Music Education, Performance.

Instruments Taught. Brass, Harpsichord, Organ, Percussion, Piano, Stringed Instruments, Voice, Woodwinds.

Musical Facilities

Practice Facilities. 20 practice rooms. 3 practice rooms for organists; 3 organs (Magnusson, Jørgensen, Bruhn). 2 percussion-equipped practice rooms. 15 practice pianos; 11 grand pianos reserved for piano majors. Recording studio.

Concert Facilities. 2 concert halls.

Community Facilities. Local churches; Stavanger Concert Hall.

Concerts/Musical Activities. "Home" concerts; regional concerts; concerts in various social institutions.

Music Library. 11,181 volumes; 950 scores; 2,870 books; 1,941 phonograph recordings. Separate listening room (compact disc equipment).

Special Programs

Featured Programs. Practice teaching is required in primary and secondary schools.

Affiliated Programs. Various student services available at the regional college in Stavanger.

Financial

Costs. Per academic year: No tuition. Students provide sheet music, books, utensils for instruments. Estimated housing expenses $200 monthly.

Financial Aid. No scholarships. Norwegian students eligible for government loans. Application due February 1.

Statens Operahøgskole
(National College of Operatic Art)
Tjuvholmen, bygning B
0250 Oslo 2
Norway

Telephone. (02) 42 52 74
Chief Administrator. Kresimir Sipusch, Director.
The College was founded in 1964 under the supervision of the Ministry of Cultural and Scientific Affairs.

Academic Information

Term System. Semester. September to December; January to May.
Music Degrees Offered. Diploma.
Music Degree Requirements. Completion of three-year course.

Musical Facilities

Music Library. Collection of operatic literature.

OMAN

Oman Center for Traditional Music
P.O. Box 2000
Seeb
Muscat
Oman

Telephone. 601317
This institution is a research center and archives of Omani traditional music. Included in the archives is a collection of examples of music from each region of the country; e.g., sailor songs from the seacoast and puppet performance materials from Bedouin areas of the country. The Center's archival collections are based on videotapes.

Sultan Qaboos University
Al Khoudh
Muscat
Oman

This is a new university offering the Bachelor of Arts, Bachelor of Science, and Bachelor of Medical Science. The first students were admitted in 1986. A music division within the university structure has been planned for the future.

PANAMA

Escuela Nacional de Música - Panama City
Apartado 1414
Panama City
Panama

Chief Administrator. Jaime Ingram, Director.
The Escuela Nacional de Música was founded in 1941 and is affiliated with the Instituto Nacional de Cultura.

Academic Information

Enrollment, Music Majors. 400.
Music Faculty. 41.

PARAGUAY

Conservatorio Municipal de Música
Mcal Estigarribia
E-Pai Perez y Curupayty
Asunción
Paraguay

Telephone. (021) 203468
The Conservatorio offers a comprehensive curriculum in music studies.

Direccion de Institutos Artisticos
Municipales
Colón 1038
Asunción
Paraguay

Telephone. (021) 46744
This is an institution that administers three municipal art schools: Escuela Municipal de Canto, Escuela Municipal de Danse, and Escuela Municipal de Arte Scenico.

Escuela Municipal de Canto

Dr. Eduardo Victor Haedo 682
Asunción
Paraguay

Telephone. (021) 49697
The Escuela Municipal de Canto offers only vocal studies.

PERU

Conservatorio Nacional de Música
(National Conservatory of Music)

Ave. Emancipatión 180
Lima 1
Peru

Telephone. 274066
Chief Administrator. Armando Sánchez Málaga, Director.

The Conservatorio was founded in 1908 as the Academia Nacional de Música Alcedo. It acquired its present name in 1946 and has been an autonomous institution since 1966. Students at the Conservatory are sent to participate in international musical events.

Academic Information

Enrollment, Music Majors. 500. One foreign student (U.S.A.)
General Program Areas. Aural Training, Choral Conducting, Composition, Conducting, Latin American Music, Music Education, Music Theory, Musicology, Peruvian Traditional Music, Vocal Music.
Instruments Taught. Brass, Guitar, Percussion, Piano, Stringed Instruments, Voice, Woodwinds.

Musical Facilities

Practice Facilities. One electric organ; 9 pianos (2 Steinways).
Concert Facilities. One Concert hall.
Music Library. 4,500 volumes. 488 scores, 2,000 records, 2,500 periodicals. Listening facilities include 2 record players. Archive of Peruvian music.

Special Programs

Featured Programs. Pre-conservatory program for adolescents.

Universidad Nacional de "San Agustín"
(National University of "San Agustín")

Music Department
Santa Catalina 117
Arequipa, Casilla Postal 23
Peru

Telephone. 229922
The University, located in a picturesque city in southern Peru, was established as an academy in 1825 and acquired university status in 1928.

PHILIPPINES

Colegio del Sagrado Corazón de Jesus
Department of Music

P.O. Box 211
General Hughes Street
Iloilo City
The Philippines

Telephone. 7-46-54
The College was founded in 1917.

Academic Information

Term System. Academic year of two semesters: June to October, November to March.
Music Degrees Offered. Bachelor of Music.

Lourdes College
Department of Music

Capistrano Street
Cagayan de Oro City
The Philippines

Telephone. 38-34
Lourdes College, a private institution, was established in 1928 as an elementary school and achieved university status in 1947.

Academic Information

Term System. Academic year of two semesters: June to October, November to March.
Music Degrees Offered. Bachelor of Music.

Pamantasang Centro Escolar
(Centro Escolar University)
College of Music
9 Meniola Street
San Miguel, Manila
The Philippines

Telephone. 741-09-15

The University was founded in 1907 as a private institution.

Academic Information

Term System. Academic year of two semesters: June to October, November to March.

Music Degrees Offered. Bachelor of Music; Master of Music; Associate in Music; Music Teacher's Diploma.

University of the Philippines
College of Music
Abelardo Hall
Diliman
Quezon City
The Philippines

Telephone. 97-69-63

Chief Administrator. Dr. Ramon P. Santos, Dean.

The College of Music was established in 1916 as a Conservatory of Music and was elevated to its current status as a college in 1970. It is located on the Diliman campus of the University of the Philippines. The College seeks to provide quality and professional instruction in the diverse areas of specialization in music. It offers a balanced orientation in Western music, Asian music, and contemporary thought.

Academic Information

Enrollment, Music Majors. Full-time 143 men, 160 women. 19 foreign students from China, Indonesia, Thailand, U.S.A., Korea, Hong Kong.

Music Faculty. Full-time 35, part-time 21.

Term System. Semester. 6-week summer session.

Entrance Requirements. Secondary school diploma; National College Entrance Examination; audition (sight reading, performance); theory placement examination.

Admission Procedure. Application due May.

Music Degrees Offered. Diploma; Bachelor of Music; Master of Music.

Music Degree Requirements. The Diploma requires the completion of 60 courses (150 hours); the Bachelor of Music requires the completion of 72 courses (190 hours); the Master of Music requires the completion of 36 hours. Recitals, theses, and comprehensive examinations are also required for graduation.

General Program Areas. Asian Music, Choral Conducting, Composition, Ethnomusicology, Music History, Music Theory, Performance.

Instruments Taught. Brass, Gamelan, Kalinga, Kulintang, P'hipad, Percussion, Piano, Pipa, Sitar, Stringed Instruments, Woodwinds.

Musical Facilities

Practice Facilities. 10 practice rooms. 2 percussion-equipped practice rooms. 33 practice pianos (30 uprights, 3 baby grands); 6 grand pianos reserved for piano majors. Sound control room.

Concert Facilities. Recital Hall, seating 530 (with orchestral pit). Sound control room.

Concerts/Musical Activities. An average of 80 recitals, concerts, and special events are held each year.

Music Library. 13,336 scores; 2,821 books; 67 periodical titles; 2,803 phonograph recordings; 946 tapes. Listening facilities (cassette, stereo). Collection of Asian and African instruments.

Financial

Financial Aid. Scholarship aid available in the form of tuition grants. Application due May.

Commentary

The University of the Philippines College of Music maintains an extensive archive of Asian traditional music materials. The College administration considers its strongest disciplines to be piano, composition, ethnomusicology, and choral conducting.

Sacred Heart College
Department of Music
1 Merchant Street
Lucena City
The Philippines

Telephone. 38-88

Sacred Heart College was established in 1884 as a school by the Daughters of Charity of Saint Vincent de Paul. It acquired university status in 1947.

Academic Information

Term System. Academic year of two semesters: June to October, October to March.

Music Degrees Offered. Bachelor of Music (four-year program); Associate in Music (two-year program; Diploma of Junior Music Teacher (one-year program).

St. Paul College
College of Music
680 Pedro Gil Street
Malate
Manila
The Philippines

Telephone. 50-66-26
The College was founded in 1911 by the Sisters of St. Paul of Chartres and attained university status in 1940.

Academic Information

Term System. Academic year of two semesters: June to October, November to March.
Music Degrees Offered. Bachelor of Music.

St. Scholastica's College
School of Music
2560 Leon Guinto Sr. Street
Malate
Manila
The Philippines

Chief Administrator. Mary Placid Abejo, Dean, School of Music.
St. Scholastica's College, a private institution, was established in 1906 by Benedictine Sisters. It became a college in 1957.

Academic Information

Term System. Academic year of two semesters: June to October, November to March.
Music Degrees Offered. Bachelor of Music; Bachelor of Music Education.

University of San Augustín
Conservatory of Music
General Luna Street
Iloilo City 5901
The Philippines

Telephone. 7-4841/2
The University was established in 1904 by the Augustinian Fathers and attained university status in 1953.

Academic Information

Term System. Academic year of two semesters: June to October, October to March.
Music Degrees Offered. Bachelor of Music.

University of Santo Tomas
Conservatory of Music
España
Manila
The Philippines

Telephone. 731-40-22
Chief Administrator. Dr. Alejandra C. Atabug, Dean, Conservatory of Music.

The Conservatory of Music was founded in 1946, offering the Music Teacher's Certificate and the Bachelor of Music course in the different branches of musical art, i.e., piano, violin, voice, composition, conducting, and musical sciences. Later, the Artist Diploma was introduced. More recently, the Music Education Course was added to its curricula in order to meet the demand for trained teachers in both public and private elementary and high schools. The University is a Roman Catholic Pontifical University. The Conservatory's goal is to prepare students for careers in performance and teaching. The language of instruction is English. The Conservatory is located on the third and fifth floors of the Albertus Magnus (Education) Building.

Academic Information

Enrollment, Music Majors. Full-time 123 men, 238 women; part-time 6 men, 11 women. 7 foreign students representing 4 nationalities.
Music Faculty. Full-time 16, part-time 22.
Term System. Semester.
Entrance Requirements. Secondary school diploma; fluency in English; intelligence and aptitude tests; audition before a jury of 2 or 3 teachers.
Music Degrees Offered. Teacher's Certificate; Performance Certificate; Artist Diploma; Bachelor of Music.
Music Degree Requirements. 150 to 166 hours (25 courses) required for the Bachelor of Music. The Artist Diploma requires the completion of 103 to 108 hours.
General Program Areas. Composition, Music Education, Music Theory, Performance.
Instruments Taught. Bass, Brass, Flute, Guitar, Percussion, Piano, Viola, Violin, Woodwinds.

Musical Facilities

Practice Facilities. One percussion-equipped practice room. 22 upright pianos; 3 grand pianos reserved for piano majors. Studios used for practice when not in use for classes. Organ lessons given off-campus.
Concert Facilities. Albertus Magnus Auditorium; Audiovisual Room. Concerts sometimes given in the University Chapel and in the lobby of the Main Building.
Concerts/Musical Activities. Students are required to attend student recitals which are held once a month.
Music Library. 2,265 scores; 1,876 books; 150 periodicals; 1,382 recordings. Listening facilities available. Special collection of indigenous instruments.

Financial

Financial Aid. Scholarship aid available. Application due end of second semester (March).

Commentary

The Conservatory administration considers its strongest disciplines to be piano, voice, brass and woodwind instruments, music education, and composition. Future plans at the Conservatory include adding additional lecture rooms and studios, and establishing a program for liturgical music.

POLAND

Akademia Muzyczna im. Feliksa Nowowiejskiego w Bydgoszczy
(F. Nowowiejski Academy of Music of Bydgoszczy)

Ul. J. Słowackiego 7
85-008 Bydgoszcz
Poland

Telephone. 21 11 42
Chief Administrator. Dr. Roman Suchecki, Rector.
This Academy is the youngest of Poland's music institutions.

Akademia Muzyczna im. Stanisław Moniuszko w Gdańsku
(S. Moniuszko Academy of Music of Gdańsk)

Łagiewniki 3
80-847 Gdańsk
Poland

Telephone. 31 77 15
Chief Administrator. Dr. Antoni Poszowski, Rector.
This state institution, under the jurisdiction of the Ministry of Culture, was founded in 1947. Faculties of composition and theory, instrumentation, singing, music education, institute of music theory, music teaching (in Koszalin).

Academic Information

Term System. Semester. October to February; February to June.
Music Degrees Offered. Magister sztuki; Doctorate.
Music Degree Requirements. The Magister sztuki requires five years of study; the Doctorate at least two additional years.

Musical Facilities

Music Library. 50,000 volumes.

Akademia Muzyczna Poznaniu
(State College of Music of Poznań)

Ul. Czerwonej Armii 87
61-808 Poznań
Poland

Telephone. 55132, 53502
Chief Administrator. Dr. Waldemar Andrzejewski, Rector.
This state institution was founded in 1920. The art of instrument-making is taught here and the Academy serves as a center for this skill in Poland. Faculties of composition, theory, conducting, instruments, voice, music teaching.

Academic Information

Enrollment, Music Majors. Semester. October to January; February to June.
Music Degrees Offered. Magister sztuki.
Music Degree Requirements. Completion of a four- to six-year course.

Musical Facilities

Music Library. 11,000 volumes.

Akademia Muzyczna w Krakowie

Ul. Bohaterów Stalingradu 3
31-038 Kraków
Poland

Telephone. 22 32 50, 22 04 55
Chief Administrator. Krzysztof Penderecki, Rector; Prorectors: Doc. Janusz Zathey, Professor Krystyna Moszumańska-Nazar.

The Academy was founded in 1888 as a private music institution. After World War II, it became a state college and in 1979 it became the Academy in its present form. The Academy occupies a building belonging to a convent but plans for a new home are being made. There are living facilities for 130 students.

The Academy has four faculties: Faculty of Composition, Conducting, Theory of Music; Instrumental Faculty (keyboard, strings, brass, harp, guitar, lute); Vocal Theatrical Faculty; Faculty of Music Education. Additional telephone number: 22 78 44.

Member of the Assocation Européenne des Conservatoires de Musique, Académies de Musique, et Musikhochschulen.

Academic Information

Enrollment, Music Majors. 400. Foreign students 10.
Music Degrees Offered. Bachelor; Master of Arts; Diploma; Doctorate in Music Theory.

Music Degree Requirements. Completion of prescribed course. Postgraduate studies include the High Professional Studies of Music Editing, a three-year program, which is a special course for graduates holding a Master of Arts degree from a music academy or university.

General Program Areas. Composition, Conducting, Music Editing, Music Theory, Performance.

Instruments Taught. Accordion, Bass, Bassoon, Clarinet, Flute, French Horn, Guitar, Harp, Harpsichord, Lute, Oboe, Organ, Percussion, Piano, Saxophone, Trombone, Trumpet, Tuba, Viola, Viola da Gamba, Violin, Violoncello.

Musical Facilities

Practice Facilities. 69 practice rooms. 49 pianos. 4 harpsichords. 1 percussion-equipped practice room. Electronic music studio.

Concert Facilities. Small concert hall, seating 100.

Community Facilities. Concert Hall, seating 200, at Barstoca, Krakow.

Music Library. 7,000 books; 33,000 scores; 5,000 phonograph recordings; 900 reel-to-reel tapes. Listening facilities (cassette, phonograph).

Special Programs

Featured Programs. The section for Music Edition, Transcription, and Notation is offered only in Krakow. The head of the Polish Music Edition (PME), Janusz Zathey, is a professor in this section.

Foreign Programs. There are exchange programs with schools in Gratz, Florence, Helsinki, and Nürenberg.

Akademia Muzyczna w Lódź
(Academy of Music of Lódź)
Ul. Gdańska 32
90-716 Lódź
Poland

Telephone. 32 67 40
Chief Administrator. Zygmunt Gzella, Rector.

In 1922, a Conservatorium in Lodz was founded by Helena Kijerirka, who was rector from 1922 to 1939. During World War II, the Germans found a building which has been erected in 1900—the former Palace of a wealthy businessman—and created a conservatory for German children. After the war, this building was reclaimed as the Lódź Conservatory of Music and regular teaching resumed in March 1945 under the direction of the new Rector, Kazimeirz Wilkomerski. After the war, Lódź and Kraków were the only cultural centers intact in Poland, as Warsaw had been badly damaged.

The Academy has 4 departments: Composition, Music History, Music Theory; Instrumental; Vocal; and Music Education. Student housing accommodates 80 students.

Academic Information

Enrollment, Music Majors. 425.
Music Faculty. Full-time 156, part-time 34, other 16.
Term System. Semester.
Music Degrees Offered. Diploma; Master of Arts.
Music Degree Requirements. Completion of prescribed course of study; after completion, students must go to the Academy in Warsaw for a more advanced degree.

General Program Areas. Chamber Music, Composition, Early Music, Eurythmics, Music Education, Music History, Music Theory, Performance.

Instruments Taught. Brass, Organ, Percussion, Piano, Stringed Instruments, Voice, Woodwinds.

Musical Facilities

Practice Facilities. 83 practice rooms. 2 percussion-equipped rooms; 50 upright pianos, 6 Steinway grands. 1 organ. Recording studio. Computer studio. Workshops for music education in grammar school. Equipment for music education includes a blackboard with musical notes which ring when touched. Film apparatus; eurythmics rooms.

Concert Facilities. Chamber Hall, seating 150; Rococo Salle, 80; Baciewitz Salle, 80.

Concerts/Musical Activities. A competition in chamber music is sponsored by the Academy. Students come from all the other academies of music.

Music Library. 50,000 books and scores; 70 periodicals (2 Polish titles); 8,000 phonograph recordings; 1,000 tapes. Special collection of old instruments including viola da gamba, lute, and guitar.

Special Programs

Featured Programs. String players must take a course about the physiology of playing stringed instruments. Wind players must take a course in how to make reeds and conserve them. All students must study the interpretation of modern music. There is a Music Moderna Concert Series.

Performance Groups. Each student must play in public each semester. There is a special series in which students play "Monday Evening Concerts."

Foreign Programs. The Lódź Academy exchanges students with the Sweelincks Conservatory in Amsterdam. In the future, the Academy hopes to inaugurate such a program with the music schools of Riga, U.S.S.R. and Glasgow, Scotland.

Akademia Muzyczna Wroclawiu
(Academy of Music in Wrocław)
Ul. Powstańców Śląskich 204
53-140 Wrocław
Poland

Telephone. 67 60 12
Chief Administrator. Dr. Zygmunt Herembeszta, Rector.

This state institution was founded in 1948. Music therapy is taught at this Academy which serves as a center for the discipline in Poland.

Academic Information

Term System. Semester. October to February; February to June.
Music Degrees Offered. Magister sztuki.
Music Degree Requirements. Completion of a four- to six-year course.

Musical Facilities

Music Library. 40,000 volumes.

Akademia Muzycznaj im. Fryderyka Chopina w Warzawie
(Frederic Chopin Academy of Music of Warsaw)
Ul. Okólnik 2
00-368 Warsaw
Poland

Telephone. 278 303
Chief Administrator. Professor Andrej Rakowski, Rector.

The Chopin Academy of Music is the oldest and largest music school of Poland. Originally founded as the School of Drama to train opera singers and performers in 1810, it was expanded in 1816 with the addition of piano classes. In 1821, the main School of Music was set up as an independent conservatory under Josef Elsner. The rapid expansion of the school came to an abrupt halt at the time of the 1830/31 uprising. In 1861, Apolinary Katski obtained permission from the czarist occupation authorities to found the Institute of Music which later became the State Music Conservatory (1919-1939). After World War II the school was reestablished and granted the status of State High School of Music. In 1962, the school acquired full recognition as an academic university with the right to issue Master of Arts diploma in all domains of music. Construction of a new building, replete with concert hall, was begun in 1959 and completed in 1966. In the 1979/80 academic year, as the result of persistent efforts by its rectors, the school was renamed the Frederic Chopin Academy of Music.

The Academy's activities are organized into seven departments: Composition, Conducting, Theory of Music; Piano, Harpsichord, Organ; Orchestral Instruments; Vocal; Music Education; Sound Recording; Music Pedagogy.

Member of the Assocation Européenne des Conservatoires de Musique, Académies de Musique, et Musikhochschulen.

Academic Information

Enrollment, Music Majors. 900. 40 foreign students representing countries from every continent.
Music Faculty. 231.
Term System. Semester. Master classes are organized during summers.
Music Degrees Offered. Graduates receive the Master of Arts degree, Doctorate, Adjunct (reader), and Docent (Assistant Professor).
Music Degree Requirements. Completion of prescribed course of study. Postgraduate studies include a two-year course in methodology of music education at the Institute for Research in Music Education for teachers in primary and secondary music schools; one-year course in the Department of Piano, Harpsichord, and Organ for those preparing to take part in international competitions; two-year doctoral course in the Department of Composition, Conducting, and Theory of Music to prepare candidates for a Ph.D. in music theory.
General Program Areas. Composition, Conducting, Music Education, Music Theory.
Instruments Taught. Brass, Harpsichord, Organ, Percussion, Piano, Stringed Instruments, Voice, Woodwinds.

Special Programs

Foreign Programs. Exchange programs with foreign conservatories include close and long-term cooperative agreements with music institutions in Berlin, Budapest, Ereven, Helsinki, Copenhagen, Moscow, and Prague. These activities include exchange of joint meetings, lectures, concerts, and opera performances.

Commentary

The Frederic Chopin Academy of Music offers innovative programs at the graduate level. In addition to performance studies, the course in music education at the Institute for Research in Music Education and the Ph.D. program in music theory are particularly important aspects of the curriculum.

Karol Szymanowski Academy of Music of Katowice
Ul. Zacisze 3
Katowice
Poland

Telephone. 51 54 21
Chief Administrator. Doc. Jan Wicenty Hawel, Rector.

The Academy of Music in Katowice, the oldest college in Silesia, was founded in 1929 as the State Conservatory of Music. The first director of the school was Witold Friemann. In 1934 the Academy was given the name of Silesian Conservatory of Music. It was changed again in 1945 to the State Music College and in 1979 to its present name. In the years 1945-1979, the College qualified 1,194 graduates as Masters of Arts in various specialties.

The Academy occupies three buildings and there are living accommodations are available for 120 students. The curriculum includes a five-year program for strings, piano, theory, and conducting; a six-year program for vocalists including dramatic training for opera; and a four-year program for wind instruments.

Academic Information

Enrollment, Music Majors. 417.
Music Faculty. Full-time 111, part-time 40-50, professors emeriti 20-30.
Music Degrees Offered. Diploma; Master of Arts.
Music Degree Requirements. After 5 years, a diploma is granted; as the student's career develops, the following categories are attained: Assistant, Master Assistant, Adjunct, Docent, Professor.
General Program Areas. Chamber Music, Conducting, Jazz Studies, Music Theory, Opera.
Instruments Taught. Brass, Piano, Stringed Instruments, Voice, Woodwinds.

Musical Facilities

Practice Facilities. The Katowice Academy uses three buildings: one building for administration and two buildings for playing, teaching, and practice rooms.
Concert Facilities. Concert Hall, seating 184; Recital Hall, 60; both halls have organs. Recording studio is in the same building as the library, through whose auspices concerts, exams, and master classes are recorded; 2 percussion studios.
Music Library. 25,300 books; 46,400 scores; 5,000 records; 630 tapes; 500 periodical titles. Listening facilities (cassette, phonograph). Since 1945, the Music Library has been collecting, preparing, and rendering accessible much historical material about the rich culture of the Silesian region. Collections have been divided into three main departments: literature on music, printed music, and recordings. A reading room, music room, and lending and reference library were introduced after 1960. The Archives of Silesian Music Culture were founded within the Library in 1968. The Department of Literature possesses the largest collection of music books in Poland. The iconography collection includes original graphic art, drawings, and oil paintings containing original portraits of composers, as well as a collection of Polish and foreign stamps on the subject of music. The library collects all documentation of the Silesian music culture, including programs, posters, and leaflets. Publishing activities began in 1959 and continue with the production of bibliographies and music histories. Special collections: 1,300 manuscripts; 500 ex libres (book emblems); 300 Polish stamps with musical subjects. Collection of Silesian culture—old music and modern Silesian music. The Archives of Silesian Music Culture pursue their own research activities and arrange concerts to help popularize Silesian music.

Special Programs

Foreign Programs. Exchange and cooperation with Hochschule für Musik "Franz Liszt" in Weimar, German Democratic Republic, and Academy of Fine Arts, Prague, Czechoslovakia.

Commentary

The instruction for woodwind instruments and jazz is a strong facet of the Academy's curriculum. Indeed, the Katowice Academy's wind class is considered the best in Poland. Composition, violin, piano, and chamber music sections are also strong departments.

The Archives of Silesian Musical Culture and the Academy library, in general, are valued resources in Poland.

The Academy plans to build a new chamber music hall and enlarge the faculty, while keeping the size of the student body the same.

PORTUGAL

Conservatório Municipal - Oporto
87 Travassa do Carregal
Oporto
Portugal

Telephone. (02) 3 37 19

Musical Facilities

Music Library. 5,000 musical works; 2,500 books. The library receives copies of all musical works and recordings published in Portugal.

Conservatório Nacional - Lisbon
Rua dos Caetanos 29
Lisbon 2
Portugal

Telephone. 3 35 41
Chief Administrator. Manuel de Ascencao Antunes, Secretary.

The Conservatorio was founded in 1835. The first director was João Domingos Bomtempo.

Musical Facilities

Music Library. 50,000 items. Eighteenth and nineteenth Portuguese religious manuscripts; writings on Hindu music by R. Tagore. The library receives copies of all musical compositions and recordings published in Portugal. The Museum of Musical Instruments has more than 500 art music and folk instruments and a special collection of stringed instruments, harps, and clavichords made in Portugal during the period of the seventeenth to twentieth centuries.

QATAR

Folklore Center - Qatar
Doha
Qatar

This research center is particularly important because it collects folklore from the entire Persian Gulf region as a joint project of the Gulf states.

ROMANIA

Conservatorul de Musică George Dima
(Conservatory of Music)
Str. 23 August 25
3400 Cluj-Napoca
Romania

Telephone. 2 59 73
Chief Administrator. Dr. Rodica Pop, Director.
The Conservatory was founded in 1819 and reorganized in 1919. It is the main cultural center of Transylvania. The first director was Edmund Farkas. George Dima, for whom the school is now named, was a high authority in the music culture of Transylvania and became director after Farkas. At the time of its founding, the language of instruction at the school was Hungarian. Publications of the conservatory include *Lucrari de Muzicologie,* issued annually.

Academic Information

Enrollment, Music Majors. 250.
Music Faculty. 86.
General Program Areas. Composition, Counterpoint, Harmony, Instrumental Music, Musicology, Vocal Music.

Musical Facilities

Music Library. 130,000 volumes.

Conservatorul de Muzică Ciprian Porumbescu
(Conservatory of Music)
Str. Stirbei Vodă 33
70732 Bucharest
Romania

Telephone. 14 63 41
Chief Administrator. Nicolae Călinoiu, Petre Brincusi, Rectors.
This institution in the major cultural center of Romania was founded in 1864. Eduard Wachmann was the first director, followed by D. Dinica. Among the early faculty, Carl Flesch taught violin during the period 1879-1901. In 1906, the composition chair of the Conservatory was especially created for George Enescu. A chair in music education was established in 1927. The composition, counterpoint, harmony, and conducting courses have been strongly emphasized in traditional Romanian music education.

Member of the Assocation Européenne des Conservatoires de Musique, Académies de Musique, et Musikhochschulen.

Academic Information

Enrollment, Music Majors. 339.
Music Faculty. 107.
General Program Areas. Composition, Conducting, Counterpoint, Harmony, Instrumental Music, Musicology, Pedagogy, Vocal Music.

Musical Facilities

Music Library. 207,000 musical works.

Conservatorul Georges Enescu
(Conservatory of Music)
Cuza Vodă 29
6600 Iasi
Romania

Telephone. (981) 11 2 37
Chief Administrator. Professor Dan Hatmanu, Rector.
The Conservatory, in the capital of Moldavia, was established in 1860 and adopted its present name in 1960. The first director was Eduard Candella.

Academic Information

Enrollment, Music Majors. 130.
Music Faculty. 60.
General Program Areas. Composition, Counterpoint, Harmony, Instrumental Music, Vocal Music.

Musical Facilities

Music Library. 97,000 volumes.

SAUDI ARABIA

King Saud University
Riyadh Conservatory
P.O. Box 2454
Riyadh 11451
Saudi Arabia

Chief Administrator. Tariq AbdelHakim, Dean.

The music school teaches contemporary (Egyptian-based) Arabic music. The purpose of the conservatory is to give basic music training and to teach composition skills needed to produce nationalistic music. The Dean and chief administrator of the school, Tariq Abdel-Hakim, has had a career as a popular Saudi singer.

SENEGAL

Conservatoire National de Musique, de
**   Danse, et d'Art Dramatique**
(National Conservatory of Music, Dance,
**   and Dramatic Art)**
B.P. 3111
Dakar
Senegal

Telephone. 212511

The Conservatoire was founded in 1948 as a school and received its current status and title in 1978.

Academic Information

Enrollment, Music Majors. 300.
Music Faculty. 50 plus part-time staff.
Music Degrees Offered. Certificat.

SOUTH AFRICA

University of Cape Town
Faculty of Music
Private Bag, Rondebosch 7700
Cape Town
Republic of South Africa

Telephone. 21 655-006
Chief Administrator. Professor Gerrit Bon, Director.

The Faculty of Music was established in 1910 under the name South African College of Music and was incorporated into the University of Capetown in 1923. The University has a College of Music, School of Opera, and School of Ballet.

Academic Information

Enrollment, Music Majors. Full-time 175, part-time 100.

Term System. Semester. February to June; July to December.

Music Degrees Offered. Bachelor of Music; Master of Music; Doctor of Music; Diplomas in Performance, Education; Postgraduate Diploma in Music Therapy.

Music Degree Requirements. Completion of prescribed curriculum; three- to five-year course.

General Program Areas. Composition, Music Education, Music Therapy, Musicology, Performance.

Musical Facilities

Music Library. Separate library facilities are available within the Faculty of Music. The music library has approximately 9,000 music books, 37,000 items of printed music, 9,000 records, and a collection of South African music.

Special Programs

Featured Programs. In the Republic of South Africa, the Postgraduate Diploma program in music therapy is unique to the University of Capetown.

Commentary

The University of Capetown is one of five South African universities with a department or faculty of music offering advanced degrees. These five institutions, all listed in the *Guide,* are considered to have the most important university-level music programs in the Republic of South Africa. However, the following nine universities also have music departments offering both performance and musicology degrees: Potchefstroom University of Christian Higher Education, University of South Africa, University of Natal, University of Port Elizabeth, Rhodes University, University of the Western Cape, University of Fort Hare, University of Zululand, and University of Durban-Westville.

University of Orange Free State
Department of Music
P.O. Box 339
9300 Bloemfontein
Republic of South Africa

Telephone. (27) 51 70711
Chief Administrator. Professor Johan Potgieter, Director.

The Department of Music was established in 1946.

Academic Information

Enrollment, Music Majors. Full-time 120, part-time 100.

Music Degrees Offered. Bachelor of Music; Master of Music; Doctor of Music.

General Program Areas. Composition, Music Education, Musicology, Performance.

Special Programs

Featured Programs. The Bachelor of Music in Orchestral Performance is offered at this university.

University of Pretoria
Department of Music
002 Pretoria
Republic of South Africa

Telephone. (27) 12 436051
The Department of Music was founded in 1960.

Academic Information

Enrollment, Music Majors. Full-time 150.

Music Degrees Offered. Bachelor of Music; Master of Music; Doctor of Music; Diploma.

General Program Areas. Church Music, Composition, Music Education, Musicology, Performance.

Special Programs

Featured Programs. The Diploma in Church Music program is a unique course of study offered at this university.

University of Stellenbosch
Department of Music (Conservatoire)
7600 Stellenbosch
Republic of South Africa

Telephone. (27) 2231 71140
Chief Administrator. Professor Richard Behrens, Director.

The Music Department was founded under the name South Africa Conservatorium of Music in 1905. It is the oldest conservatory in the Republic of South Africa.

Academic Information

Enrollment, Music Majors. Full-time 180, part-time 150.

Music Degrees Offered. Bachelor of Music; Master of Music; Doctor of Music.

General Program Areas. Composition, Music Education, Musicology, Performance.

Special Programs

Featured Programs. At this University, the Bachelor of Music in Orchestral Performance is offered.

University of the Witwatersrand
Wits School of Music
Jan Smuts Avenue
2001 Johannesburg
Republic of South Africa

Telephone. (27) 11 716879
Chief Administrator. Professor Walter Mony, Director.

The Wits School of Music was founded in 1922 as part of the University.

Academic Information

Enrollment, Music Majors. Full-time 100, part-time 120.

Music Degrees Offered. Bachelor of Music; Master of Music; Doctor of Music.

General Program Areas. Composition, Music Education, Musicology, Performance.

Special Programs

Featured Programs. The Bachelor of Music in Light Music is offered at this university.

SPAIN

Conservatorio Superior de Música de Barcelona
Calle Bruch 112
Barcelona 9
Spain

Telephone. (005) 257 6077
Chief Administrator. Marcal Gols, Director.

The Conservatorio was founded in 1838. It now incorporates the Conservatorio Superior Municipal de Musica and the Conservatorio de Musica del Liceo.

Musical Facilities

Music Library. 9,000 volumes; 6,000 records. Special collections: instrument collection in the Museo Municipal de Musica. Museo telephone: 258 15 38.

Conservatorio Superior de Música y Escuela de Arte Dramatico y Danza
Calle Angel de Saavedra 1
Cordoba
Spain

Chief Administrator. Rafael Quero Castro, Director.
The Conservatory was founded in 1962.

Musical Facilities

Music Library. 12,500 volumes.

Conservatorio Superior de Música y Escuela de Arte Dramatico
Calle Jesus del Gran Poder 49
41002 Seville
Spain

Telephone. (954) 381009
Chief Administrator. Mariano Perez Gutierrez, Director.
The Conservatory was founded in 1935.
Member of the Assocation Européenne des Conservatoires de Musique, Académies de Musique, et Musikhochschulen.

Musical Facilities

Music Library. 7,000 volumes; 13,000 scores. DE VALENCIA

Conservatorio Superior de Música y Escuela de Arte Dramatico y Danza de Valencia
Plaza San Esteban 3
Valencia
Spain

Telephone. (960) 31 92 21
Chief Administrator. Salvador Segui Perez, Director.
The Conservatory was founded in 1879.

Musical Facilities

Music Library. 11,000 volumes. Library telephone: 31 92 94.

Escuela Superior de Pedagogia Musical
(Higher School of Music Teaching)
Juan A. Mendizabal 65, 3rd level
28008 Madrid
Spain

Telephone. (91) 241-31
Chief Administrator. Rafael Martinez, Director.

The School was founded in 1925.

Musical Facilities

Music Library. 10,000 volumes; 3,000 phonograph recordings.

Real Conservatorio Superior de Música de Madrid
(Royal Academy of Music)
Plaza de Isabel II
Madrid 13
Spain

Telephone. (91) 241 4381, 247 4173
Chief Administrator. Encarnacion Lopez de Arenosa, Acting Director.

The Conservatorio was founded in 1830 by Queen Maria Cristina de Bourbon, and is situated directly across the plaza from the main concert hall of Madrid. The library of the Conservatorio was created in 1872.

Academic Information

Entrance Requirements. The instruction is divided into three levels: elementary, middle, and upper. The elementary level requires a student to be eight years of age; the middle level, thirteen years of age with completion of the elementary level; and the upper level, sixteen years of age with completion of the middle level.

General Program Areas. Accompanying, Acoustics, Choral Music, Composition, Folklore, Music Education, Music History, Music Theory, Orchestration.

Instruments Taught. Brass, Guitar, Harp, Lute, Organ, Percussion, Piano, Viola, Violin, Violoncello, Voice.

Musical Facilities

Music Library. 50,000 volumes. Collection of manuscripts of opera, tonadillas, and other Spanish vocal music from the eighteenth and nineteenth centuries; early printed works of Beethoven and others. The library receives copies of all Spanish music and books on music. Library telephone: 248 4202.

SRI LANKA

Institute of Aesthetic Studies
21 Albert Crescent
Colombo 7
Sri Lanka

Telephone. (5) 96971, 96972, 91483
Chief Administrator. Professor Tissa Kariyawasam, Director.

The Government College of Fine Arts, the predecessor of the Institute, was established in 1952. The Institute of Aesthetic Studies was founded in 1974 and granted the first B.F.A. degree in 1982. It is located in Colombo near the Museum with a branch at Horana, 22 miles from the city. The languages of instruction are Sinhala, English, and Hindi. It is the only Institute in Sri Lanka under the jurisdiction of the Ministry of Higher Education.

Academic Information

Enrollment, Music Majors. Full-time 34 men, 171 women. 2 foreign students from the U.S.A.

Term System. Trimester. 3 terms of 15 weeks each.

Entrance Requirements. Advanced level of G.C.E.; interview; audition (vocal and instrumental).

Admission Procedure. Application due July 31.

Music Degrees Offered. Bachelor of Fine Arts.

Music Degree Requirements. The Bachelor of Fine Arts requires the completion of four academic years of study.

General Program Areas. Composition, Music Education, Music Theory, Performance.

Instruments Taught. Drums, Esraj, Flute, Sitar, Tabla, Violin.

Musical Facilities

Practice Facilities. 13 practice rooms.

Concert Facilities. Concert hall.

Community Facilities. Some classes given at the National Museum.

Concerts/Musical Activities. Student concerts are given once per term.

Music Library. 12,500 volumes; 6 periodicals. Listening facilities (cassette, stereo). Special collection of Sri Lankan Arts.

Financial

Costs. No tuition for national students.

Financial Aid. Scholarship aid available. Application due July 31.

Commentary

There are plans to add an ethnomusicology curriculum and a postgraduate research program during the next few years.

SUDAN

Institute of Music and Drama
Khartoum
The Sudan

In 1978 Professor Ashenafi Kebede was appointed UNESCO expert to the government of Sudan and wrote, in collaboration with Sudanese music educators, the current syllabus used at the Institute. The emphasis of study is on traditional Sudanese music.

Institute of Music and Drama - Omdurman
P.O. Box 80
El Mourada
Omdurman
The Sudan

Chief Administrator. El Mahi Ismail, Dean.

The Institute of Music and Drama was founded in 1969 as an Institute of Music, Drama, and Folklore, and acquired its present title in 1976. In 1978, Professor Ashenafi Kedebe was appointed as a UNESCO Expert to the Government of Sudan, and authored, with the assistance of Sudanese music educators, the current syllabus and system of music education for the Institute. The emphasis is on traditional music: Kedebe's method stresses mastery of one's own musical language before attempting to learn a foreign idiom. His system of education in Africa has similarities to the Kodaly system in Hungary and to the Orff method in Germany. The Institue of Music and Drama is a state institution under the authority of the Ministry of Culture and Information. The language of instruction is Arabic.

Academic Information

Enrollment, Music Majors. Total 174. Foreign students 2.

Term System. Semester. January to April; July to November.

Entrance Requirements. Secondary school certificate; entrance audition required.

Music Degrees Offered. Diploma; Certificate.

Music Degree Requirements. The Diploma in Music is awarded upon completion of a five-year course; the Certificate in Music, after a four-year course.

Financial

Costs. No tuition.

SWEDEN

Musicdramatiska Skolan i Stockholm (Music Drama School)
Strandvägen 82
115 27 Stockholm
Sweden

Telephone. (08) 62 61 81

The school was founded in the eighteenth century and acquired its current title and staus in 1968. This small state institution functions under the supervision of the National Board of Universities and Colleges. The minimum age for admission is twenty.

Academic Information

Term System. Semester. September to December; January to June.
Music Degrees Offered. Diploma.
Music Degree Requirements. Completion of three-year course.

Musikhögskolan i Göteberg
Dicksonsg 10
412 56 Göteberg
Sweden

Chief Administrator. Gunnar Sjöström, President; Gösta Ohlin, Dean.
The College was founded in 1971.
Member of the Assocation Européenne des Conservatoires de Musique, Académies de Musique, et Musikhochschulen.

Academic Information

Enrollment, Music Majors. 330.
Music Faculty. 135.

Musikhögskolan i Stockholm
National College of Music
Valhallavägen 103-109
115 31 Stockholm
Sweden

Telephone. (08) 631190
Chief Administrator. Professor Ingemar Gabrielsson, Principal.
The Musikhögskolan was founded in 1771 as a part of the Royal Academy of Music. It is now an independent school (university college) belonging to the Swedish University System. Only fifty students a year are accepted into the Musician Department, seventy in the School Music Department, ten in Church Music, and twenty in additional studies for future soloists. The school occupies two buildings in central Stockholm.
Member of the Assocation Européenne des Conservatoires de Musique, Académies de Musique, et Musikhochschulen.

Academic Information

Enrollment, Music Majors. Full-time 350 men, 250 women; part-time 10 men, 10 women. 20 foreign students, mostly from Scandinavian countries.
Music Faculty. Full-time 110, part-time 110.
Term System. Semester. August 20 to December 20; January 1 to June 1.
Entrance Requirements. Secondary school diploma; entrance examinations without exception.

Admission Procedure. Application due December 15.
Music Degrees Offered. Master of Fine Arts in music, church music, school music.
Music Degree Requirements. Completion of 4 years of studies.
General Program Areas. Church Music, Conducting, Music Education, Performance.
Instruments Taught. Brass, Guitar, Percussion, Piano, Stringed Instruments, Voice, Woodwinds.

Musical Facilities

Practice Facilities. 45 practice rooms. 5 organs (small Swedish with 8-20 stops). 5 percussion-equipped practice rooms. 45 practice pianos. Electronic music studio.
Concert Facilities. 2 concert halls.
Community Facilities. Organ lessons given in local churches.
Concerts/Musical Activities. 50 concerts per year.
Music Library. Students have access to the library of the Royal Academy of Music.

Financial

Financial Aid. Scholarships are given only to students of excellence and mostly without application. 150 students receive scholarship aid.

Commentary

The College considers its strongest disciplines to be singing, violin, woodwind instruments, and choir conducting.

Musikhögskolan och Teaterhögskolan i Malmö
Ystadvägen 25
Box 13515
S-200 44 Malmö
Sweden

Chief Administrator. Häkan Lundström, Rector.
The College was founded in 1907.
Member of the Assocation Européenne des Conservatoires de Musique, Académies de Musique, et Musikhochschulen.

Academic Information

Enrollment, Music Majors. 400.
Music Faculty. 150.

SWITZERLAND

Conservatoire de Musique de Genève
Place Neuve
1204 Genève
Switzerland

Telephone. (22) 21 76 33; Library 25 00 71, 26 31 20.
Chief Administrator. M. Claude Viala, Director.

The conservatory was founded in 1835 and has a central location in the city of Genève. The language of instruction is French.

Member of the Assocation Européenne des Conservatoires de Musique, Académies de Musique, et Musikhochschulen.

Academic Information

Enrollment, Music Majors. 200 men, 300 women. 180 foreign students from Europe, Egypt, Israel, Japan, Korea, China, Australia, U.S.A., Central and South America.

Term System. Academic year from September 20 to June 25. Summer session in August of even years; three weeks (piano, violin, cello, voice).

Entrance Requirements. Audition required. Foreign students admitted by competition.

Admission Procedure. Application due June 30 with $25 nonrefundable fee.

Musical Facilities

Practice Facilities. Special practice rooms for organists; 3 organs. 3 percussion-equipped practice rooms. Electronic music studio.

Concert Facilities. 2 concert halls.

Music Library. 300,000 documents. Listening facilities in the University located near the Conservatory. Collection of 20,000 items: strong in eighteenth century works such as manuscripts of Italian opera arias and compositions of the Russian school of composers.

Conservatoire de Musique de La Chaux-de-Fonds - Le Locle
Avenue Léopold-Robert 34
2300 La Chaux-de-Fonds
Switzerland

Telephone. (039) 23 43 13
Chief Administrator. Cyril J. Squire, Director.

The Conservatory was founded in 1927, and is connected with the Conservatoire de Neuelitel. The language of instruction is French.

Academic Information

Term System. Semester.

Entrance Requirements. Secondary school diploma not required; age limits for those preparing for a diploma or certificate.

Admission Procedure. Application due mid-August.

Music Degrees Offered. Diploma (professional); Teacher's Diploma.

Music Degree Requirements. Students must first obtain a 1st certificate; completion of prescribed courses.

Instruments Taught. Brass, Percussion, Piano, Stringed Instruments, Woodwinds.

Financial

Costs. Per academic year: Tuition 1200 Swiss francs.

Conservatoire de Musique de Lausanne
6 Rue du Midi
1000 Lausanne
Switzerland

Telephone. (021) 22 26 08
Chief Administrator. Jean-Jacques Rapin, Director.

The Conservatoire was established in 1861 under the auspices of the State and the City of Lausanne. The library was founded in 1942 after a successful appeal for public support.

Member of the Assocation Européenne des Conservatoires de Musique, Académies de Musique, et Musikhochschulen.

Musical Facilities

Music Library. 10,000 volumes.

Conservatoire de Musique de Neuchâtel
106 Faubourg Hôpital
2000 Neuchâtel
Switzerland

Telephone. (038) 25 20 53
Chief Administrator. R. Boss, Director.

Academic Information

Music Degrees Offered. Professional or Teaching Diplomas.

Conservatoire et Académie de Musique - Fribourg
228-A Rue Pierre Aeby
1700 Fribourg
Switzerland

Chief Administrator. J.M. Hayoz, Director.

Konservatorium für Musik und Theater
Spitalgasse 26
CH-3011 Berne
Switzerland

Telephone. (031) 22 62 21
Chief Administrator. Agnes Schneiter.

The Conservatory was founded in 1927 and is located in the center of the city of Berne. The language of instruction is German.

Member of the Assocation Européenne des Conservatoires de Musique, Académies de Musique, et Musikhochschulen.

Academic Information

Enrollment, Music Majors. 110 men, 125 women. 53 foreign students representing 11 nationalities.
Music Faculty. 48.
Term System. Semester. April to September, October to March.
Entrance Requirements. Audition required (three pieces of three epochs).
Admission Procedure. Application with $35 nonrefundable application fee due February 15th or August 15.
Music Degrees Offered. Diploma (pedagogical); postgraduate diploma; soloist diploma.
Music Degree Requirements. Pedagogical diploma requires seven to nine semesters; others seven to twelve semesters.
Instruments Taught. Guitar, Orchestral Instruments, Organ, Piano, Voice.

Musical Facilities

Practice Facilities. 20 practice rooms. Special practice rooms for organists; 4 organs (3 Kuhn, 1 Gohl). 1 percussion-equipped practice room. 20 pianos (Steinway).
Concerts/Musical Activities. Concerts for advanced students once per year.
Music Library. 23,000 scores; 5,000 books; 20 periodicals; 2,000 phonograph recordings. Listening facilities (cassette, stereo). Collection of 7,500 items: programs of Bernische Musikgesellschaft (founded in 1815); records of Musikschule (founded in 1858) and Conservatory (founded in 1927).

Financial

Financial Aid. Scholarship application due date March 15 or September 15. 12 students receive scholarship aid.

Commentary

Violin studies and the postgraduate program are emphasized within the Konservatorium's curriculum.

Konservatorium und Musikhochschule - Zürich
Birchstrasse 95
8050 Zürich
Switzerland

Telephone. (01) 312 20 70
Chief Administrator. Hans Ulrich Lehmann, Director.

This insitution was established in 1876. It offers music courses for teachers, performers, composers, and conductors. There is also a department for children and amateur musicians.

Member of the Assocation Européenne des Conservatoires de Musique, Académies de Musique, et Musikhochschulen.

Academic Information

Enrollment, Music Majors. 2,400.
Music Faculty. 150.
Music Degrees Offered. State Diploma.
General Program Areas. Composition, Conducting, Music Education, Music Theory, Performance.

Musical Facilities

Music Library. 2,000 items. Performing editions of instrumental and vocal repertoire; orchestral library exchanges with Radio Zürich and other Swiss conservatories.

Musik-Akademie der Stadt Basel
Schola Cantorum Basiliensis
(Lehr- und Forschungsinstitut für alte Musik)
Leonhardsstrasse 4
CH-4051 Basel
Switzerland

Telephone. (061) 25 57 22
Chief Administrator. Dr. Peter Reidemeister, Head of Department.

The Schola Cantorum was founded in 1933 by Dr. Paul Sacher. Since 1954 it has been a part of the Musik-Akademie der Stadt Basel. The school offers training on early wind, string, and plucked instruments; praxis of medieval music; any form of ensemble playing; and theory classes. The school is located in the center of the city of Basel.

Member of the Assocation Européenne des Conservatoires de Musique, Académies de Musique, et Musikhochschulen.

Academic Information

Enrollment, Music Majors. Full-time 35 men, 55 women; part-time 25 men, 35 women. Foreign students from Germany, France, Italy, Sweden, U.S.A., Japan, Australia.

Music Faculty. Full-time 30, part-time 40.

Term System. Semester. Winter (October to February); Summer (March to July).

Entrance Requirements. Entrance exam (practical, theoretical, and general); audition of three pieces in different styles; ear test; dictation; sight reading; improvisation; keyboard instrument; four-part choral-prima vista.

Admission Procedure. Application due July 31.

Music Degrees Offered. Diplom fúr alte Musik; Blockflóten-Lehrdiplom.

Music Degree Requirements. Completion of four-year course; 16-20 lessons per week; major examination and public concert; nine minor exams; thesis; pedagogical examination.

General Program Areas. Medieval Instruments, Medieval Music, Renaissance Instruments.

Instruments Taught. Clavichord, Early Fortepiano, Harpsichord, Spinet, Voice.

Musical Facilities

Practice Facilities. Gottfried Andreas Silbermann (18th century) organ. Practice rooms each contain harpsichord, spinet, clavichord, or early fortepiano. 5 grand harpsichords.

Concert Facilities. 2 concert halls seating 350 and 100, respectively.

Community Facilities. Local churches used for organ practice.

Concerts/Musical Activities. Many student concerts within the school; official concerts of the school.

Music Library. 5,000 scores; 10,000 books; 35 periodicals; 2,000 microfiche; 1,000 phonograph recordings. Listening facilities (cassette, stereo). Special collection of early instruments available for loan to students. Libraries of the University and the Musicological Institute are available to students.

Special Programs

Affiliated Programs. Cooperation with the Musicological Institute of the University of Basel.

Financial

Financial Aid. Scholarship application due November 1.

Commentary

The Schola Cantorum Basiliensis is a major European center for the study of early music. The primary goals of the school are to teach its students that style is not less important than technique; to broaden the repertory; and to undertake research while maintaining the spontaneity of performance.

Musik-Akademie der Stadt Basel (Konservatorium)
Konservatorium (Musikhochschule)
Leonhardsstrasse 6
CH-4051
Basel
Switzerland

Telephone. 061 25 57 22

Chief Administrator. Gerhard Hildenbrand, Head of Department.

The Konservatorium (Musikhochschule) is a Department of the Musik-Akademie der Stadt Basel and offers professional education in all disciplines of classical music. It was founded in 1905 and has been part of the Musik-Akademie since 1954. The school is located in the center of the city of Basel.

Member of the Assocation Européenne des Conservatoires de Musique, Académies de Musique, et Musikhochschulen.

Academic Information

Enrollment, Music Majors. 340. Most of the students are Swiss or German.

Term System. Semester. Winter (October to February); Summer (March to July).

Entrance Requirements. Theoretical and practical entrance examinations; audition of 20 minutes' playing time before a jury.

Admission Procedure. Application due by end of June.

Music Degrees Offered. Diplomas: music-teacher, chamber-music, orchestra, soloist, opera, conducting, composition.

Music Degree Requirements. Completion of four- to seven-year programs. Minimum of four years of study; major examination with public concert; several minor examinations also required.

General Program Areas. Chamber Music, Composition, Conducting, Music Education, Music Theory, Opera, Performance.

Instruments Taught. Brass, Harpsichord, Organ, Percussion, Piano, Stringed Instruments, Voice, Woodwinds.

Musical Facilities

Practice Facilities. Practice rooms open from 7:30 A.M. to 10:00 P.M. 2 percussion-equipped practice rooms. 4 organs. 8 grand pianos reserved for piano majors. Electronic studio.

Concert Facilities. 2 concert halls.

Community Facilities. Various churches and concert rooms in the city of Basel.

Concerts/Musical Activities. Student concerts within the school; participation in official concerts of the school.

Music Library. 60,000 scores; 30,000 books; 35 periodicals; 5,000 phonograph recordings. Listening facilities (cassette, stereo). Students have access to the libraries of the University and the Musicological Institute.

Special Programs

Affiliated Programs. Cooperation with the Musicological Institute of the University of Basel.

Financial

Financial Aid. Scholarship application due October.

Commentary

The unususal aspects of the Musik-Akademie are the study of non-European music and the emphasis on contemporary music in the curriculum.

Musikschule und Konservatorium
Schaffhausen
Rosengasse 16
CH-8200
Schaffhausen
Switzerland

Telephone. (053) 5 34 03
Chief Administrator. Klaus Cornell, Director.
The Conservatory was founded in 1978. The main goal of the school is to train music teachers. Master classes are offered for violoncello, piano, and oboe. The languages of instruction are German, French, and English.

Academic Information

Enrollment, Music Majors. Students from Switzerland, Austria, France, Germany, Italy, Yugoslavia, Spain, United States.
Music Faculty. Full-time 44, part-time 23.
Term System. Semester.
Entrance Requirements. Secondary school diploma; comprehensive examination; practical and theoretical examination.
Admission Procedure. Application due February 15th.
Music Degrees Offered. Teaching Diploma; Concert Artist Diploma; Soloist Diploma.
Music Degree Requirements. Completion of courses of study from two- to four-years.
General Program Areas. Composition, Music Theory, Vocal Music.
Instruments Taught. Brass, Oboe, Percussion, Piano, Stringed Instruments, Violoncello, Voice, Woodwinds.

Musical Facilities

Practice Facilities. 10 practice rooms. 1 percussion-equipped practice room. 22 practice pianos; 10 grand pianos reserved for piano majors. Electronic music studio. Organ taught at outside facilities.

Concert Facilities. 5 concert/recital halls.
Community Facilities. Municipal theatre; municipal hall; local churches.
Concerts/Musical Activities. Frequent concerts throughout the year.
Music Library. 6,000 volumes. Listening stations (cassette, stereo).

Musikschule und Konservatorium
Winterthur
Tössertobelstrasse 1
CH-8400 Winterthur
Switzerland Fritz Năf, Director.

The Conservatory was founded in 1873.
Member of the Assocation Européenne des Conservatoires de Musique, Académies de Musique, et Musikhochschulen.

SYRIA

Aleppo Institute of Music
Aleppo
Syria

The Institute was founded in 1955. It has Departments of Eastern and Western Music.

Commentary

Aleppo has had a rich cultural history, and is still known as a center for making fine Arab traditional instruments such as the 'Ud.

National Conservatory of Music - Damascus
Damascus
Syria

Performance of traditional Arabic instruments is emphasized in the curriculum.
For more information concerning the conservatories of Syria, contact:
Office of the Minister of Culture
Dr. Najah Attar
Al-Roudah
Damascus
Syria
Telephone: 37467, 38632

TAIWAN

National Institute of the Arts
Music Department
172 Chung Cheng Road
Ru Chow
Taipei County
Taiwan (Republic of China)

Telephone. (02) 2821331-5, 2818475

Chief Administrator. Professor Ma Shui-Long, Chairman.

The Institute was founded in 1982. In 1988 it will move to a new location and offer an expanded curriculum, including a master's program. Training in Chinese music is emphasized.

Academic Information

Enrollment, Music Majors. 185. 3 foreign students (Malyasia, Hong Kong).

Music Faculty. Full-time 20, part-time 65.

Term System. Semester. End of September to end of January; February to June. String master classes sometimes offered during the summer months.

Music Degrees Offered. Bachelor of Music.

Music Degree Requirements. Each student must have 2 years of intensive study of a traditional Chinese instrument (one out of twenty instruments offered). The Bachelor of Music is awarded after completion of a 5-year course.

General Program Areas. Chinese Music, Composition, Conducting, Performance, Vocal Music.

Instruments Taught. Bass, Bassoon, Brass, Chinese Instruments, Clarinet, Flute, Harp, Harpsichord, Horn, Oboe, Percussion, Piano, Stringed Instruments, Trombone, Trumpet, Tuba, Viola, Violin, Violoncello, Voice, Woodwinds.

Musical Facilities

Practice Facilities. 50 practice rooms. 2 percussion-equipped practice rooms. 45 pianos (30 grand pianos); 2 harpsichords. (Note: new expanded quarters scheduled for 1988 include 100 practice rooms, choir room, 10 rehearsal studios for ensembles, 4 percussion rooms, large percussion practice room, percussion ensemble room.)

Concert Facilities. 2 recital halls, seating 500 and 250 respectively.

Music Library. 6,000 records. Music library will be expanded in new facility and will have listening stations for 50 students.

National Taiwan Academy of Arts
59, Sec. I, Ta Kuan Road
Pan-Chiao Park
Taipei County
Taiwan (Republic of China)

Telephone. 9616136/9

Chief Administrator. T.L. Chang, President.

The National Taiwan Academy of Arts is a state institution and was founded as the Art School in 1956. It received its current status and name in 1960. There are three departments for music: Department of Western Music, Department of Chinese Music (including Chinese Opera), and Department of Chinese Folk Music. The other disciplines offered at the Academy include cinema, drama, radio, television, fine arts, painting, graphic arts, and industrial arts.

The Academy publishes the *Seminar of Arts* twice per year.

Academic Information

Enrollment, Music Majors. 2,000.

Music Faculty. 120.

Term System. Semester. September to February; March to July.

Entrance Requirements. Graduation from high school; entrance examination.

Music Degrees Offered. Diploma.

Music Degree Requirements. Diplomas are earned after completing a three- to five-year course of study.

General Program Areas. Chinese Folk Music, Chinese Music.

Musical Facilities

Music Library. 53,000 volumes.

TANZANIA

University of Dar es Salaam
P.O. Box 35091
Dar es Salaam
Tanzania

Telephone. 49192

Chief Administrator. D. Mbilinyi, Contact Person.

The University offers music degree programs through the Department of Art, Music, and Theatre. The language of instruction is English.

Academic Information

Music Degrees Offered. Bachelor of Arts in Music; Master of Arts in Music.

THAILAND

Institute of Technology and Vocational Education
Faculty of Drama and Music
339 Samsen Roak
Bankok 10300
Thailand

Telephone. 2823847
Chief Administrator. Prakob Larpkesorn, Dean, Faculty of Drama and Music.

The Institute was established in 1975. The language of instruction is Thai.

Academic Information

Term System. Semester. June to October; November to March.
Music Degrees Offered. Bachelor of Arts; Vocational Certificate.

Special Programs

Foreign Programs. There is a cooperative agreement with Oklahoma State University, Sunderland Polytechnic University, Huddersfield Polytechnic University, and the University of Tubingen.

TUNISIA

Conservatoire de Musique
5 rue Zarkoun
Tunis
Tunisia

The Conservatoire teaches Tunisian art music theory, the basics of Western theory, and Arabic and Western instruments. In addition, a teaching diploma is offered at this institution. Graduates become music teachers in the country's schools and cultural houses.

Institut Supérieure de Musique - Tunis
20 Avenue de Paris
Tunis
Tunisia

The Institute, formerly called the Conservatoire National de Musique, has a strong curriculum in Tunisian art music theory—the study of the complex rhythmic and melodic modes which define the traditional music. Arabic and Western instruments and the basics of Western music theory are also taught.

Commentary

In addition to the two major conservatories in Tunis, there are a number of cultural houses in areas outside the capital. These are community centers where numerous activities in theater, dance, and music take place, such as the rehearsals and performances of the Malouf—traditional Tunisian—orchestras.

TURKEY

Ege Üniversitesi
(Aegean University)
Izmir State Conservatory of Turkish Music
Bornova, Izmir
Turkey

Telephone. 180110
Chief Administrator. Sermet Akgün, Rektor of University; Refet Saygili, Director of Conservatory.

The Izmir State Conservatory, founded in 1975, became affiliated with the Aegean University in 1982.

Academic Information

Music Degrees Offered. Master's; Diploma.

Hacettepe Üniversitesi
(Hacettepe University)
School of Music (Ankara State Conservatory)
Hacetlepe Parki
Ankara
Turkey

Telephone. 11 94 42
Chief Administrator. A. Yüksel Bozer, Rector of the University; Ersin Onay, Director, Ankara State Conservatory.

The Ankara State Conservatory was established in 1936 by order of the Turkish leader Atatürk Mustafa Kenal. Paul Hindemith, who was in Turkey when the Conservatory was founded, helped to organize its Western music education curriculum. Now part of Hacettepe University, the Conservatory functions under the jurisdiction of the Ministry of Education. All of the conservatories of Turkey—which were formerly responsible to the Minister of Culture—are now the music faculties of major Turkish universities. The current director of the Conservatory, Ersin Onay, is a well known pianist.

Academic Information

Music Faculty. 104.
Music Degrees Offered. Master's; Diploma.

Musical Facilities

Music Library. There is a small collection of folk instruments in the Folklor Arşivi of the Conservatory, which was assembled by the late Professor Muzaffer Sarisözen.

Special Programs

Featured Programs. The Ethnomusicology Department was founded by Ahmet Yürür.

Istanbul Teknik Üniversitesi
(Istanbul Technical University)
Turkish Music Conservatory
Ayazağa
Istanbul
Turkey

Telephone. 176-17-29
Chief Administrator. Kemal Kafali, Rector.
Unlike the other two conservatories in Instanbul which teach mainly Western music, the Turkish Conservatory teaches primarily Eastern and Turkish music: voice, Turkish instruments, and composition. There is also a Western music education department. The Conservatory, which was founded in 1975, teaches the art of making both Turkish and Western instruments.

Academic Information

Music Degrees Offered. Bachelor's and Master's.

Special Programs

Performance Groups. Turkish Folk Music Chorus and Folk Dance Ensemble; Turkish Classical Music Chorus; both have performed at the Istanbul Festival.

Commentary

Ayhan Turan, a violin teacher at the Conservatory, has established an innovative violin teaching method, producing a very successful class of students. He and his students have been invited abroad to perform for distinguished colleagues such as violinist Yehudi Menuhin.

Istanbul Üniversitesi
(University of Istanbul)
Municipal Conservatory of Istanbul
Beyazit
Istanbul
Turkey

Telephone. 5 22 14 87
Chief Administrator. Cem'i Demiroğu, Rektor of University.

The Municipal Conservatory of Istanbul, established in 1923, is the oldest conservatory in Turkey. Its origins date back to the period of the Ottoman Empire, at which time there was popular support among political leaders for Western music education. The House of Tunes—a music club—was created to present concerts of prominent musicians such as Franz Liszt. Eventually this organization became the Municipal Conservatory, whose curriculum was based on the French system of music education. Cenal Resit Rey, distinguished pianist, composer, and conductor, was an important advisor to the school and conductor of its orchestra. In 1986 the Conservatory became affiliated with Istanbul University. There are Departments of Western Music, Drama, and Dance and a Turkish Music Division.

Academic Information

Music Degrees Offered. Bachelor's; Master's.
General Program Areas. Turkish Music.

Commentary

The Turkish music division of the Municipal Conservatory is small and casually structured, focusing on the singing and playing of folk music and traditional Turkish music by amateur musicians.

Mimar Sinan Üniversitesi
(Mimar Sinan University)
Istanbul State Conservatory of Music
Findikli
Istanbul
Turkey

Telephone. 145 87 60, 145 00 00
Chief Administrator. Muhteşem Giray, Rektor; Özer Sezgin, Director of State Conservatory.

The Istanbul State Conservatory of Music, established in 1971, is now part of Mimar Sinan University, an institution devoted exclusively to education in the fine arts. The current director, Özer Sezgin, is a viola teacher and performer. There are departments of Turkish music, Western music, dance, drama, and a special program in musicology.

Academic Information

Music Faculty. 68.
Music Degrees Offered. Diploma; Master's; Doctorate in Performance.

UGANDA

Makerere University
Department of Music, Dance, and Drama
P.O. 7064
Kampala
Uganda

Telephone. 42471

The Department was founded by Dr. S. Mbabi-Katana. The emphasis of the curricula is on the integrated study of the traditional arts. All students must study in each of the three disciplines of music, dance, and drama.

UNITED KINGDOM

Birmingham School of Music
City of Birmingham Polytechnic
Paradise Circus
Birmingham B3 3HG
United Kingdom

Telephone. (021) 359-6721
Chief Administrator. Louis Carus, Head.

Member of the Assocation Européenne des Conservatoires de Musique, Académies de Musique, et Musikhochschulen.

Academic Information

Music Degrees Offered. Bachelor of Arts (Honours) in Music; GBSM (Graduate of the Birmingham School of Music); ABSM (Associate of the Birmingham School of Music).

Musical Facilities

Music Library. The library of the School of Music can be reached at (021) 359-6721, extension 282. The University Music Library of the Barber Institute of Fine Arts is located in close proximity to the Birmingham School of Music.

City of Leeds College of Music
Cookridge Street
Leeds LS2 8BH
United Kingdom

Telephone. (0532) 452069
Chief Administrator. Joseph Stones, Director.

The College of Music was founded in 1961 as a Music Centre offering part-time courses. In 1966, full-time programs were added and in 1971, the present name was adopted. The College, housed in two adjacent Victorian buildings, is situated in the Leeds City Center.

Member of the Assocation Européenne des Conservatoires de Musique, Académies de Musique, et Musikhochschulen.

Academic Information

Enrollment, Music Majors. Full-time 175 men, 74 women; part-time 1,244 men, 1,179 women. Foreign students from Austria, Norway, China, Australia, Germany, South Africa, U.S.A., Spain, France, New Zealand.
Music Faculty. Full-time 46, part-time 55.
Term System. Semester. 3 terms.
Entrance Requirements. Minimum age of eighteen; a standard on the First Study equivalent to Grade VIII Associated Board; GCE passes including English language; audition (performance, written paper, aural tests). Foreign students must submit documentary evidence and cassette of performance and need required general admission qualifications, provisional place offered and is conditional on arrival.
Admission Procedure. Apply as early as possible in the academic year with $10 nonrefundable application fee.
Music Degrees Offered. Graduate Diploma in Jazz and Contemporary Music; College Diploma in Music; Certificate in Musical Instrument Technology; Foundation Certificate.
Music Degree Requirements. The Graduate Diploma in Jazz and Contemporary Music program emphasizes the wide range of activities practiced in the field of jazz, contemporary and popular styles of music with consideration of the musical and technical demands. The course requires the completion of three years of study. The three-year course leading to the College Diploma in Music trains performers who wish to teach and instrumental teachers who wish to perform. The Certificate in Musical Instrument Technology course, a two-year program, provides a general training for those seeking a career in instrument repair and also lays a foundation on which more specialized training in instrument making and technology can be built. The Foundation Certificate course gives students a firm foundation of musical skill and knowledge, preparing them for entry to an advanced course (Performer Graduate) at a College of Music, University or Polytechnic, or at a College of Higher Education. This course requires two or three years according to age and ability.
General Program Areas. Composition, Instrument Repair, Jazz Studies, Music Education, Music Theory.
Instruments Taught. Brass, Guitar, Harmonium, Organ, Percussion, Piano, Saxophone, Sitar, Stringed Instruments, Tabla, Voice, Woodwinds.

Musical Facilities

Practice Facilities. 12 practice rooms plus practice in studios when not in use for classes; practice rooms booked in advance, studios as available. Special practice rooms for organists; 4 organs (2 pipe, 2 electronic). 27

pianos (20 upright, 7 grand); 4 grand pianos reserved for piano majors. 4 percussion-equipped practice rooms. 2 aural labs; record studio; audiovisual studio; electronic music studio.

Concert Facilities. Small concert hall.

Community Facilities. Some concerts given in Leeds Town Hall, Civic Theatre, and local churches.

Concerts/Musical Activities. Weekly lunchtime recitals; at least one evening concert per week; the College produces about 175 concerts each year, including 2 festivals and an opera week.

Music Library. Large orchestral, band, and choral sections; 3,500 books; 50 periodical titles (4,000 back issues); 5,000 phonograph recordings. Listening facilities (disc, cassette). Special collection of Jazz records; Jones Collection of Cello and String Chamber Music.

Special Programs

Performance Groups. Symphony Orchestra, Choral Society, Opera Group, Chamber Orchestra, Wind Ensemble.

Foreign Programs. The City of Leeds is "twinned" with Dortmund, Lille, and Seigen and the College has musical exchanges with these European cities.

Affiliated Programs. Leeds University provides moderators for course examinations and also sends some of its students to the College for instrumental training.

Financial

Costs. Per academic year: Tuition over 18 years and advanced $625, non-advanced $386; foreign students advanced $3,975, non-advanced $2,187.

Commentary

The College plans to develop the college diploma and musical instruments technology courses into graduate-level programs, as well as establish a curriculum for teaching Eastern Music.

Guildhall School of Music and Drama
Barbican
London EC2Y 8DT
United Kingdom

Telephone. (01) 628-2571

Chief Administrator. John Hosier, Principal.

The School forms part of the Barbican Centre, the largest complex of arts facilities in Western Europe, located in the heart of the city of London. The School was founded by the City of London in 1880 and moved into its current premises in 1977. The School prepares students for a professional life in music, particularly in performance, but also in conducting, composing, music therapy, and teaching. The School is the only conservatory in the United Kingdom with an advanced Jazz and Rock course. Performers receive training in the com-

munication skills necessary to bring music to wider and more unfamiliar audiences. Groups from the school visit hospitals, hospices, inner city schools, centers for the aged and handicapped, and prisons.

Member of the Assocation Européenne des Conservatoires de Musique, Académies de Musique, et Musikhochschulen.

Accreditation. British Department of Education and Science. Member of: Association of British Music Colleges.

Academic Information

Enrollment, Music Majors. Full-time 722, part-time 625.

Music Faculty. Full-time 5, part-time 285.

Term System. Trimester.

Entrance Requirements. Secondary school diploma (depends on course); graduate course requires some school examination passes; audition in person or by cassette; aural tests and musical perception tests for undergraduate and conducting courses.

Admission Procedure. Application accepted anytime with $40 nonrefundable application fee.

Music Degrees Offered. GGSM; AGSM; Diploma in Music Therapy (York University).

Music Degree Requirements. Completion of three or four years of continuous study.

General Program Areas. Composition, Conducting, Music Education, Music Theory, Music Therapy, Performance.

Instruments Taught. Brass, Organ, Percussion, Piano, Stringed Instruments, Voice, Woodwinds.

Musical Facilities

Practice Facilities. 70 practice rooms, allocated by the Hall Keeper in rotation; students may have as many hours daily as facilities permit. Special practice room for organists; 1 organ; 2 percussion-equipped rooms; 80 pianos; 14 grand pianos reserved for piano majors. Recording studio.

Concert Facilities. Music Hall; lecture recital room.

Community Facilities. Regular concerts in Barbican Hall (seating 2,000), St. Giles, Cripplegate, and other City halls.

Concerts/Musical Activities. Concert halls in and around London offer students complimentary tickets (Royal Opera House, Covent Garden, ENO, Coliseum).

Music Library. 50,000 books and scores; 4,000 phonograph recordings. Listening facilities (6 cassette players, 8 phonograph record players, 2 FM receivers).

Special Programs

Featured Programs. The School provides instrumental teaching for students registered at the City University and some of the third year graduate students attend classes at the University.

Affiliated Programs. By special arrangement, students in the fourth year at the University will take all of their fourth year studies at the Guildhall School. From September 1986, the one-year post graduate/diploma course in Music Therapy will be validated by the University of York. The course will lead to the qualification of Diploma in Music Therapy at the University of York (Dip.M.Th., GSMD-York).

Financial

Costs. Per academic year: Tuition national residents $5,400; foreign students $8,840. Estimated housing expenses $5,000 per year.

Financial Aid. Scholarship applications due June 28. Variable number available from year to year (average $2,765).

Royal Academy of Music
Marylebone Road
London NW1 5HT
United Kingdom

Telephone. (01) 935-5461
Chief Administrator. David Lumsden, Principal.

The Royal Academy of Music, the oldest institution for advanced musical training in England, was founded in 1822 through the efforts of John Fane, Lord Burghersh (later 11th Earl of Westmoreland), and began its work in March 1823 under the direct patronage of King George IV, with William Crotch as principal. The RAM was granted a Royal Charter in 1830, although the institution had years of financial turmoil until 1968. In 1912, the school moved to more spacious premises on Marylebone Road. A small theatre and lecture hall were added in 1926 and a new library was opened in 1968. Since 1972, a large plan of renovation has been undertaken. Thus far, the Sir Jack Lyons Theatre and a new small Concert Room have been completed.

Member of the Association Européenne des Conservatoires de Musique, Académies de Musique, et Musikhochschulen.

The aim of the Academy is to provide the highest possible professional training in all aspects of performance. This involves the continuous study of technique and interpretation, both solo and ensemble, in chamber music, orchestral and choral music, and in opera.

Academic Information

Music Degrees Offered. GRSM Diploma; Professional Certificate; Performer's Course (LRAM Diploma); Bachelor of Music (with University of London); Master of Music (with University of London).

General Program Areas. Aural Studies and Musicianship, Chamber Music, Composition, Conducting, Early Music, Music History, Music Theory, Opera.

Instruments Taught. Brass, Harpsichord, Organ, Percussion, Piano, Stringed Instruments, Voice, Woodwinds.

Musical Facilities

Practice Facilities. Students' Club (with bar) provides a meeting place for students.

Music Library. 50,000 volumes. Many orchestral and choral scores and parts, including Sir Henry Wood library of orchestral music. G.D. Cunningham collection of organ music, autographs, and rare eighteenth century instrumental music. Libraries of English Bach Society, Angelina Goetz (full scores), A. Kalische (vocal scores), G. Kimpton (orchestral music), H. Prendergast (church music), Ferdinand Ries, Royal Philharmonic Society (printed scores and parts), and Earl of Westmoreland. The emphasis of the library collection is on performance material for borrowing, with appropriate background material for all courses and general music study. The Library includes a reading room and listening facilities. Interlibrary loan operated through the British Library gives access to further resources.

Special Programs

Featured Programs. Westmoreland Concerts on the South Bank offer concert opportunities to former students of the Academy. These concerts, six of which are given each year at the Purcell Room, are available to former students by audition.

Foreign Programs. Student Exchange, funded by the LSO American Foundation, with the Juilliard School in New York City.

Financial

Costs. Fees (1985/86): UK and EEC students, 1,308 English pounds; overseas students, 4,086 pounds.

Royal College of Music
Prince Consort Road
London, SW7 2BS
United Kingdom

Telephone. (01) 589-3643
Chief Administrator. Michael Gough Matthews, Director.

The Royal College of Music was founded by the Prince of Wales (later to be King Edward VII) in 1883, and incorporated by Royal Charter. The President of the College has always been a member of the Royal Family. This position has been held since 1952 by Her Majesty The Queen Mother. Her Majesty The Queen is a Patron of the College. The main building, located in South Kensington, was erected in 1894 through the generosity of Mr. Samson Fox on a site which had been granted by the Royal Commissioners of the Exhibition of 1851. The New Building was completed in 1964 and the Britten

Opera Theatre is now being completed.

Member of the Association Européenne des Conservatoires de Musique, Académies de Musique, et Musik-hochschulen.

The College provides training for those who wish to perform or teach, or prepare for another career in music. Practical and academic tuition is offered to instrumentalists, singers, conductors, and composers. The College also caters to potential teachers who, in preference to a course at a College of Education, seek musical training where greater emphasis is placed on developing performance skills than on academic subjects.

Academic Information

Enrollment, Music Majors. 600.

Music Faculty. 170.

Music Degrees Offered. Closing date for applications is early October; overseas applicants by early November.

Music Degree Requirements. Performers' Course (four years) leads to DipRCM (Performer); GRSM (Honours) Course (three years) leads to the GRSM diploma, carrying the status of an Honours degree; Bachelor of Music (Honours) Course (three years) leads to the University of London Bachelor of Music degree with Honours. Postgraduate courses include Advanced Study Course, Opera Training Course, Repetiteurs' Course, Conductors' Course, Early Music Course, Master of Music for composers.

General Program Areas. Alexander Technique, Aural Studies and Musicianship, Composition, Conducting, Early Music, Electronic Music, Music History, Opera.

Instruments Taught. Brass, Organ, Percussion, Piano, Stringed Instruments, Voice, Woodwinds.

Musical Facilities

Practice Facilities. 3 practice rooms with organ, 2 with harpsichord; 30 practice rooms with piano and teaching rooms are available for practice when not in use; Students' Common Room (including a bar) which was opened in 1983.

Concert Facilities. Concert Hall (built in 1903); Recital Hall in the New Building; Parry Opera Theater, seating 300; Britten Opera Theatre. Electronics studio.

Music Library. 10,000 volumes. The Library opened in 1985, combining extensive lending, reference, and listening facilities with a large reading room for quiet study. It also houses the College's large collection of early printed music and manuscripts, to which students and visitors may apply for access. Museum of Historical Instruments contains an extensive collection of early and rare instruments. The Department of Portraits is responsible for the collection of musical portraits, various categories of related material, and the College archives.

Special Programs

Featured Programs. A few places are available for students who for some reason are ineligible for other courses. For these students a Special Course is offered with a curriculum created to suit each student's individual needs.

Financial

Costs. Annual fees (1985/86): students from the United Kingdom and EEC countries 1,308 English pounds. Overseas students: Opera Training Course 4,833 pounds; Advanced Study Course 1-1/2 hours individual tuition weekly 3,225 pounds; 2 hours individual tuition weekly 4,089 pounds; all other courses 4,089 pounds.

Royal Northern College of Music
124 Oxford Road
Manchester M13 9RD
United Kingdom

Telephone. (061) 273 6283

Chief Administrator. John Manduell, Principal.

The Royal Northern College of Music was founded in 1973 as a result of the merger between two existing institutions, the Royal Manchester College of Music and the Northern School of Music, both of which had been functioning for nearly 100 years. It is situated in a modern, centrally-located structure with teaching and practice rooms, concert hall, and opera theater. A separate hall of residence accommodates 176 students.

Member of the Assocation Européenne des Conservatoires de Musique, Académies de Musique, et Musik-hochschulen.

Academic Information

Enrollment, Music Majors. 218 men, 279 women. 29 foreign students from Denmark, Norway, France, West Germany, Hong Kong, Iceland, India, Ireland, Japan, Korea, Netherlands, Poland, South Africa, U.S.A.

Music Faculty. Full-time 48, part-time 77.

Term System. Trimester. September to December (Autumn); January to March (Spring); April to June (Summer). Academic year of 34 weeks.

Entrance Requirements. Admission is solely on merit and audition.

Music Degrees Offered. Diploma; Bachelor of Music.

Music Degree Requirements. Normally a four-year course for undergraduates; one- or two-year course for postgraduate students.

General Program Areas. Baroque Music, Composition, Music Theory, Opera, Performance, Renaissance Music.

Instruments Taught. Brass, Percussion, Piano, Stringed Instruments, Voice, Woodwinds.

Musical Facilities

Practice Facilities. 60 practice rooms (including teaching rooms). 2 percussion-equipped practice rooms. 3-manual tracker action organ (Hradetzky) in main concert hall. 37 grand pianos; separate fee for practice room use of grand piano (Steinway).

Concert Facilities. Main Concert Hall, Opera Theatre.

Concerts/Musical Activities. Demanding program of student concerts is a vital part of the courses at the College.

Music Library. 49,391 books; 11,000 phonograph recordings. Listening facilities (2 cassette decks, 17 stereo decks).

Special Programs

Foreign Programs. The College has exchange arrangements for performances with music colleges in Europe; the student orchestras frequently tour.

Affiliated Programs. Undergraduate students may study concurrently for a Bachelor of Music degree at the University of Manchester and a Diploma at the College. Postgraduate students may study at the College for a University of Manchester master's degree in performance or composition.

Financial

Costs. Per academic year: Tuition national residents undergraduate $729, postgraduate $2,288; foreign students $3,450. Overseas students should allow $4,185 for living expenses.

Financial Aid. Overseas students are eligible to compete for college scholarships and exhibitions which are awarded annually to about 34 students; normal award value between $279 and $1,674.

Commentary

Since its establishment in 1973, the Royal Northern College of Music has consistently attracted a distinguished faculty of internationally recognized artists. The College is particularly proud of its opera training program.

Royal Scottish Academy of Music and Drama

58 St. George's Place
Glasgow G2 1BS
United Kingdom

Telephone. (041) 332 4101

Chief Administrator. Philip Ledger, Principal.

The Royal Scottish Academy was founded as the Glasgow Athenaeum in 1847. It became the Scottish National Academy of Music in 1928 and adopted the present name in 1951. It is currently housed in Victorian buildings in the center of Glasgow. A new structure, also in the center of Glasgow, was due to be completed in 1988 at 100 Renfrew Street, Glasgow G2 3DD.

Member of the Association Européenne des Conservatoires de Musique, Académies de Musique, et Musikhochschulen.

Academic Information

Enrollment, Music Majors. Full-time 94 men, 139 women; part-time 47 men, 88 women.

Term System. Trimester. 3 terms (one 12-week term and two 11-week terms).

Entrance Requirements. Secondary school diploma; comprehensive examination; practical and theory paper; audition required; sight reading; aural test.

Admission Procedure. Applications due January 31 with $25 nonrefundable application fee.

Music Degrees Offered. Bachelor of Arts in Music Performance, Music Education; Diploma (RSAMD).

Music Degree Requirements. Completion of three years of study; minimum degree requirements two "A" levels and three "0" levels; Grade eight Associated Board in first study instrument. (Degree courses are validated by the University of Glasgow.)

General Program Areas. Composition, Music Education, Music Theory, Opera, Performance.

Instruments Taught. Brass, Harpsichord, Organ, Piano, Stringed Instruments, Voice, Woodwinds.

Musical Facilities

Practice Facilities. 65 practice rooms. Special practice rooms for organists; 3 organs (Hill, Hradetsky, Allen). 4 percussion-equipped practice rooms. 90 pianos (Welmar Model "C"); 39 grand pianos reserved for piano majors. Practice rooms available 9 A.M. to 9 P.M. except when being used for teaching. Electronic music studio. Opera School located outside the Academy.

Concert Facilities. Concert Hall.

Community Facilities. Glasgow City Hall is used for major orchestral concerts.

Concerts/Musical Activities. Student concerts and visiting professionals' performances held every week; frequent recitals outside the Academy.

Music Library. 76,323 volumes; 4,860 books; 36 current periodicals; 29 microfiche; 5,608 discs; 200 tapes; 45 cassettes. Listening facilities (cassette, stereo). The Mitchell Public Library and the library of the University of Glasgow are available to students.

Financial

Costs. Per academic year: Tuition $627.50; foreign students $3,765. Estimated housing expenses $2,510.

Financial Aid. Scholarship application due January 31. 10 students receive scholarships ($2,000 and fees).

Trinity College of Music
11-13 Mandeville Place
London W1M 6AQ
United Kingdom

Telephone. (01) 935-5773

Chief Administrator. Meredith Davies, Principal.

The Trinity College of Music was founded in 1872 as a school for the study and practice of church music. It was incorporated by a special act of Parliament in 1875. It remains an independent college, governed by a corporation, but receiving an annual grant from the British government. The College has been a pioneer in many fields of musical education. In 1906, the Junior Exhibitions were inaugurated, giving a valuable early training for those still at school. In 1937, a Department of Sixteenth and Seventeenth Century Music was established, later becoming the Department of Renaissance and Baroque Music. A complete course of training is provided for teachers and performers in music. The school, comprising the main building and annex with practice rooms, is located in central London.

Member of the Assocation Européenne des Conservatoires de Musique, Académies de Musique, et Musikhochschulen.

Academic Information

Enrollment, Music Majors. Full-time 149 men, 261 women; part-time 14 men, 18 women. 29 foreign students representing the nationalities Malaysian, Japanese, Australian, German, American, Indian, Irish, Colombian, Thai, Polish, Singaporean, Finnish, Canadian, Chinese, Libyan, Danish, Sri Lankan, Venezuelean, Israeli.

Term System. Trimester. September to December (Michaelmas); January to March (Lent); April to June (Summer).

Entrance Requirements. GCE with five different passes, two of which must be "A" level; audition required; all applicants are called for a personal audition at which they must perform and give evidence of musicianship and general background; written examination in theory.

Admission Procedure. Applications due October or February with $42 nonrefundable application fee.

Music Degrees Offered. GTCL; LTCL; FTCL; Bachelor of Music.

Music Degree Requirements. Completion of specified requirements. The Bachelor of Music is offered through the University of London.

General Program Areas. Baroque Music, Choral Music, Composition, Music Theory, Renaissance Music.

Instruments Taught. Brass, Organ, Percussion, Piano, Stringed Instruments, Voice, Woodwinds.

Musical Facilities

Practice Facilities. 60 practice rooms. 3 practice rooms for organists; 3 organs (2 J.W. Walker; 1 Hill, Norman, and Beard). 62 pianos (52 grand, 10 upright). Electronic music studio.

Concert Facilities. Outside halls are used for performances.

Community Facilities. Major concerts are held at the Royal Albert Hall, Queen Elizabeth Hall, South Bank.

Concerts/Musical Activities. Recitals take place frequently in the college Lecture Hall.

Music Library. 2,000 books and scores; 17 periodicals; 1,310 phonograph recordings. Listening facilities (2 cassette decks; 6 stereo decks). Special collection of Renaissance and baroque instruments.

Special Programs

Affiliated Programs. Trinity College of Music is entitled to admit undergraduates for the University of London degree of Bachelor of Music. Admission requirements are those of the University of London.

Financial

Costs. Per academic year: Tuition national residents $2,640, foreign students $6,798.

Financial Aid. 30 students receive scholarship aid.

Welsh College of Music and Drama
Castle Grounds
Cathays Park
Cardiff, CF1 3ER
United Kingdom

Telephone. (0222) 42854

Chief Administrator. Peter Fletcher, Principal.

The Welsh College of Music and Drama was founded in 1949 in Cardiff Castle. It is presently situated in Cathays Park opposite the Cardiff Civic Centre and near the City Centre, St. David's Hall, and the Welsh National Opera, occupying a structure built in 1973-74. An opera theatre is currently under construction. The College achieved national conservatory status in 1984. The languages of instruction are English and Welsh.

Member of the Assocation Européenne des Conservatoires de Musique, Académies de Musique, et Musikhochschulen.

Academic Information

Enrollment, Music Majors. 160 men, 190 women. 5 foreign students (Hong Kong, Malaysia, Australia, Canada).

Music Faculty. 40.

Term System. Trimester. 3 terms of 12 weeks each.

Entrance Requirements. Secondary school diploma and comprehensive examination (depending on course);

audition required (performance of practical pieces); general musicianship paper and interview. Foreign students audition by tape and reference.

Admission Procedure. Applications accepted anytime.

Music Degrees Offered. Diploma in Performance; Advanced Certificate; Bachelor of Arts (University of Wales).

Music Degree Requirements. Completion of three years of full-time attendance; degree requires two "A" level passes for admission.

Instruments Taught. Brass, Harp, Organ, Percussion, Piano, Stringed Instruments, Voice, Woodwinds.

Musical Facilities

Practice Facilities. 40 practice rooms. Special practice rooms for organists; 2 electronic organs. 2 percussion-equipped practice rooms. 42 pianos (12 grand, 30 upright). No special practice room assignments; students may practice 4 hours per day. Electronic studio; broadcasting studio; television studio.

Concert Facilities. Theatre/Concert Hall; new Opera Theatre to be built.

Community Facilities. Plays are performed in city theatres; concerts in city Cathedrals, churches, and St. David's Hall.

Concerts/Musical Activities. Frequent recitals and concerts.

Music Library. 2,000 books; 4,000 phonograph records; 1,000 tapes. Listening facilities (cassette, stereo, video recorder).

Special Programs

Affiliated Programs. Degree course validated by the University of Wales.

Financial

Costs. Per academic year: Tuition for national residents $1,140, foreign students $6,620. Estimated housing expenses $3,600.

Financial Aid. Scholarship application due by autumn term. 10 students receive scholarship aid (approximately $200). Most students on British Government Higher Education Awards.

Commentary

The major goal of the College is to train drama and music students as performers. Several changes are anticipated during the next ten years, including new buildings, increase in student enrollment, establishment of a four-year Performer's Course, and inauguration of a dance program.

URUGUAY

Escuela Universitaria de Música - Montevideo
Paysandú 843
Montevideo
Uruguay

Telephone. 908415, 900612

Chief Administrator. Hector Tosar, Director.

The Escuela Universitaria de Música was founded in 1951 by the Ministry of Culture as a National Conservatory of Music. It became part of the Universidad de la República in 1957, and in 1974 was known as the Instituto de Musicologia de la Universidad República. The current name was adopted in 1986.

Academic Information

Enrollment, Music Majors. 240. 12 foreign students from Mexico, Chile, Argentina, Paraguay, Brazil.

Music Faculty. 52.

Entrance Requirements. Secondary school diploma; admission examination.

Music Degrees Offered. Licenciatura (Diploma) in musicology, voice, choral and orchestral conducting, composition, instruments.

General Program Areas. Acoustics, Aesthetics, Composition, Conducting, Folk Music, Music Education, Music History, Music History (Latin America), Music History (Uruguay), Music Theory, Orchestration, Performance, Solfege.

Instruments Taught. Bassoon, Clarinet, Cornet, Flute, Harp, Oboe, Organ, Percussion, Piano, Trombone, Viola, Violin, Violoncello.

Musical Facilities

Practice Facilities. 9 pianos (4 grands). 1 organ. 1 percussion-equipped practice room.

Concert Facilities. 1 concert hall, seating 50.

Music Library. 1,278 books; 11,892 scores; 3,509 phonograph recordings; 168 periodical titles. Listening facilities (6 phonographs). Special collection of records from UNESCO.

U.S.S.R.

Alma-Ata Kurmangazy State Conservatory
Kommunistichesky Pr. 90
480091 Alma-Ata 91, Kazahskaja SSR
U.S.S.R.

The Conservatory has Departments of Piano, Orchestral and Folk Instruments, Singing, Choral Conducting, Drama, and Composition. Post-graduate studies (aspirantura) are offered. Courses are taught in Russian and Mongolian Kasach.

Academic Information

Term System. Academic year September to July.
General Program Areas. Choral Conducting, Composition, Drama, Vocal Music.
Instruments Taught. Folk Instruments, Orchestral Instruments, Piano.

Musical Facilities

Music Library. 56,000 volumes.

Astrakhan State Conservatory
Sovetskaya Ul. 28
414000 Astrakhan, Rossiskaja SFSR
U.S.S.R.

The Conservatory offers specialization in conducting and orchestral instruments. Courses are taught in Russian and Mongolian.

Academic Information

Term System. Academic year September to July.
General Program Areas. Conducting.
Instruments Taught. Orchestral Instruments.

A.V. Nezhdanova Odessa Conservatory
Ul. Ostrovidova 63
270000 Odessa, Ukrainskaja SSR
U.S.S.R.

Chief Administrator. V.P. Pvozun, Rector.
The Conservatory in Odessa is one of the oldest higher institutions of musical instruction in the U.S.S.R. It was founded in 1913 from the Music School of the Russian Music Society. In 1950 it was named in honor of A.V. Nezhdanova. As of 1974, the Odessa Conservatory had Departments of Piano Theory (with divisions of piano, musicology, and composition), Orchestra (with divisions of string, folk, and wind instruments), Voice and Chorus (with divisions of vocal instruction and conducting).

Academic Information

Enrollment, Music Majors. 800.
Music Faculty. 140.
Term System. Academic year September to July.
General Program Areas. Choral Conducting, Composition, Music Theory, Musicology, Vocal Music.
Instruments Taught. Folk Instruments, Piano, Stringed Instruments, Voice, Wind Instruments.

Musical Facilities

Music Library. 100,000 volumes.

Azerbaijan S.S.R. U. Gajibekov State Conservatory
Ul. Dimitrova 98
370014 Baku, Azerbajdžanskaja SSR
U.S.S.R.

Chief Administrator. A.I. Gadzhiev, Rector.
The Conservatory was founded in 1920. There are Departments of Piano, Orchestral Instruments, Folk Instruments, Singing, Choral Conducting, and Composition. Courses are taught in Russian and Azerbayan.

Academic Information

Enrollment, Music Majors. 800.
Music Faculty. 180.
Term System. Academic year September to July.
General Program Areas. Choral Conducting, Composition, Vocal Music.
Instruments Taught. Folk Instruments, Orchestral Instruments, Piano.

Musical Facilities

Music Library. 200,000 volumes; 124,000 scores.

Byelorussian State Conservatory
Internationalnaya Ul. 30
220030 Minsk, Belorusskaja SSR
U.S.S.R.

Chief Administrator. V.V. Olovnikov, Rector.
The Conservatory was founded in 1932 in the Byelorussian city of Minsk. There are Departments of Piano, Orchestral and Folk Instruments, and Composition. Postgraduate studies (aspirantura) are offered. Courses are taught in Russian and Byelorussian.

Academic Information

Enrollment, Music Majors. 1,100.
Music Faculty. 150.
Term System. Academic year September to July.
General Program Areas. Composition.
Instruments Taught. Folk Instruments, Orchestral Instruments, Piano.

Musical Facilities

Music Library. 95,000 volumes.

Donetsk Musical-Pedagogical Institute
Ul. Artena 44
340086 Donetsk, Ukrainskaja SSR
U.S.S.R.

The Institute has Departments of Orchestral Instruments, Choral Conducting, and Singing. Courses are taught in Russian and Ukranian.

Academic Information

Term System. Academic year September to July.
General Program Areas. Choral Conducting, Vocal Music.
Instruments Taught. Orchestral Instruments.

Erevan Komitas State Conservatory
Ul. Sayatnovy 1a
375009 Erevan 9, Armjanskaja SSR
U.S.S.R.

The Conservatory was founded in 1926. There are Departments of Piano, Orchestral Instruments, Singing, Choral Conducting, and Composition. Postgraduate studies (aspirantura) are offered. Courses are taught in Russian and Armenian.

Academic Information

Term System. Academic year September to July.
General Program Areas. Choral Conducting, Composition, Vocal Music.
Instruments Taught. Orchestral Instruments, Piano.

Musical Facilities

Music Library. 43,000 volumes.

Far-Eastern Pedagogical Institute of the Arts
Ul. 1 Maya 3
690678 Vladivostok, Rossiskaja SFSR
U.S.S.R.

The Institute has Departments of Piano, Orchestral Instruments, Folk Instruments, Singing, Choral Conducting, and Drama.

Academic Information

Term System. Academic year September to July.
General Program Areas. Choral Conducting, Drama, Vocal Music.
Instruments Taught. Folk Instruments, Orchestral Instruments, Piano.

Gnessinsky State Musical and Pedagogical Institute
Ul. Vorovskogo 30/36
121069 Moscow G-69, Rossiskaja SFSR
U.S.S.R.

Chief Administrator. V.I. Minin, Rector.
The Institute was founded in 1944. There are Departments of Piano, Orchestral Instruments, Singing, Choral Conducting, Composition, and Musicology.

Academic Information

Enrollment, Music Majors. 1,250.
Music Faculty. 310.
Term System. Academic year September to July.
General Program Areas. Choral Conducting, Composition, Musicology, Vocal Music.
Instruments Taught. Orchestral Instruments, Piano.

Musical Facilities

Music Library. 190,000 volumes.

Gorky M.I. Glinka State Conservatory
Ul. Piskunova 40
603005 Gorky, Rossiskaja SFSR
U.S.S.R.

Chief Administrator. G.S. Dombayev, Rector.
The Conservatory was founded in 1946. There are Departments of Piano, Orchestra and Folk Instruments, Choral Conducting, Singing, and Composition.

Academic Information

Enrollment, Music Majors. 700.
Music Faculty. 90.
Term System. Academic year September to July.
General Program Areas. Choral Conducting, Composition, Vocal Music.
Instruments Taught. Folk Instruments, Orchestral Instruments, Piano.

Musical Facilities

Music Library. 61,000 volumes.

Kazan State Conservatory
Ul. B. Krasnaya 38
420015 Kazan 15, Rossiskaja SFSR
U.S.S.R.

Chief Administrator. N.G. Zhiganov, Rector.
The Conservatory was founded in the Tatar Soviet Socialist Republic in 1945. There are Departments of Piano, Orchestral and Folk Instruments, Voice, Chorus Training, and Composition. Courses are taught in Rus-

sian and Tatar.

Academic Information

Enrollment, Music Majors. 700.
Music Faculty. 120.
Term System. Academic year September to July.
General Program Areas. Chorus Training, Composition, Vocal Music.
Instruments Taught. Folk Instruments, Orchestral Instruments, Piano.

Musical Facilities

Music Library. 100,000 volumes.

Kharkov State Institute of Arts
Pl. Teveleva 11/13
310003 Kharkov
U.S.S.R. The Institute has Departments of Piano, Orchestral and Folk Instruments, Singing, Chorus Training, Composition, and Drama.

Academic Information

Term System. Academic year September to July.
General Program Areas. Chorus Training, Composition, Drama, Vocal Music.
Instruments Taught. Folk Instruments, Orchestral Instruments, Piano.

Musical Facilities

Music Library. 100,000 volumes.

Kiev P.I. Tchaikovsky Conservatory
Ul. K. Marxa 1-3/II
252001 Kiev, Ukrainskaja SSR
U.S.S.R.

Chief Administrator. I.F. Lyashenko, Rector.
The Conservatory in Kiev was founded in 1913. In Czarist times, the Conservatories of Kiev, Odessa, Saratov, St. Petersburg, and Moscow were under the jurisdiction of the Russian Musical Society. After the February 1917 Bolshevik Revolution, these five conservatories submitted a plan for autonomy to the Provisional Government, but no action was taken. There was a decree on July 12, 1918 concerning the nationalization of the conservatories.

The Conservatory has Faculties of Piano, History and Theory, Composing, Orchestra, Conducting, and Singing. The Kiev Conservatory is one of eight in the U.S.S.R. to offer postgraduate studies (aspirantura).

Academic Information

Enrollment, Music Majors. 950.
Music Faculty. 220.
Term System. Academic year September to July.
General Program Areas. Composition, Conducting, History of Music, Theory of Music, Vocal Music.
Instruments Taught. Orchestral Instruments, Piano.

Musical Facilities

Music Library. 200,000 volumes. R.P. Sabadash, Librarian.

Latvian S.S.R. Y. Vitol State Conservatory
Ul. Krishyana Barona 1
226050 Riga, Latvijskaja SSR
U.S.S.R.

Telephone. 22-86-84
Chief Administrator. Y. A. Ozolim, Rector.
The Conservatory was founded in Latvia in 1919. There are Departments of Piano, Orchestral and Folk Instruments, Singing, Choral Conducting, Composition, Drama, and Musical Comedy. Postgraduate studies (aspirantura) are offered. Courses are taught in Russian, Latvian, and German.

Academic Information

Enrollment, Music Majors. 520.
Music Faculty. 140.
Term System. Academic year September to July.
General Program Areas. Choral Conducting, Composition, Drama, Musical Comedy, Vocal Music.
Instruments Taught. Folk Instruments, Orchestral Instruments, Piano.

Musical Facilities

Music Library. 110,000 volumes.

Leningrad N.A. Rimsky-Korsakov State Conservatory
Teatralnaya Pl. 3
192041 Leningrad, Rossiskaja SFSR
U.S.S.R.

Chief Administrator. P.A. Sorebryakov, Rector.
The Conservatory in Leningrad, founded in 1862, is the oldest higher music institution in the U.S.S.R. It was founded by the Russian Music Society at the initiatve of A.G. Rubinstein and named after Rimsky-Korsakov in 1944. A.K. Glazunov was the Conservatory director from 1905-1928 and exerted an important influence. Among the school's alumni are P.I. Tchaikovsky, S. Prokofiev, D. Shostakovich, and A.S. Arenskii.

There are Departments of Theory, Composition,

Musicology, Conducting (Symphonic and Choral), Orchestral and Folk Instruments, Opera Workshop (since 1923), and Opera and Ballet Stage Management. While the curriculum is standardized for all conservatories in the country, the Leningrad Conservatory is permitted to experiment with curriculum. A new instructional plan for musicologists was introduced in 1962. The second year included a seminar in archival and bibliographical work; the third year included a seminar in music criticism (including reviewing books, music, concerts, operas); and the fourth year culminated in a history seminar. In addition, the student musicologists were taught the techniques of publishing under the guidance of an editor of the State Publishing House (MUZGIZ/ Leningrad). Postgraduate studies (aspirantura) are offered.

Academic Information

Enrollment, Music Majors. Over 1,500.
Music Faculty. 275.
Term System. Academic year September to July.
Music Degrees Offered. Diploma.
Music Degree Requirements. The four-year student leaves the Conservatory with a regular diploma. Outstanding musicology students are retained for a fifth year to undertake special research projects.
General Program Areas. Composition, Conducting, Music Theory, Musicology, Opera, Stage Management.
Instruments Taught. Brass, Folk Instruments, Organ, Percussion, Piano, Stringed Instruments, Woodwinds.

Musical Facilities

Music Library. 300,000 items, including more than 10,000 phonograph recordings.

Special Programs

Featured Programs. A system of music instruction for non-resident students, usually teachers, requires them to come to Leningrad for personal instruction for two months (January, June) per year, remaining on salary in their regular jobs. The other part of the year, they receive and return their lesson assignments by mail.

Lithuanian State Conservatory
Pr. Lenin 42
232001 Vilnius, Litovskaja SSR
U.S.S.R.

Telephone. 612691
Chief Administrator. Professor V. Laurusas, Rector.
The Conservatory was founded in Lithuania in 1933. There are Faculties of Piano, Theory of Music, Orchestral and Choral Conducting, Drama, Culture, and Education (in Klaipeda). Courses are taught in Russian and Lithuanian.

Academic Information

Enrollment, Music Majors. 2,100.
Music Faculty. 422.
Term System. Academic year September to July.
General Program Areas. Choral Conducting, Drama, Music Culture, Music Education, Music Theory, Orchestral Conducting.
Instruments Taught. Piano.

Musical Facilities

Music Library. 2 libraries (412,000 volumes); 2 record libraries (23,000 phonograph recordings, 8,700 tapes). Special laboratory of folk music research including a cataloged collection of 50,000 items.

Lvov M.V. Lysenko State Conservatory
Ul. Boyko 5
290005 Lvov, Ukrainskaja SSR
U.S.S.R.

Chief Administrator. Z.O. Dashak, Director.
The Conservatory was founded in the city of Boyko in the Ukraine in 1903. There are Departments of Piano, Orchestral and Folk Instruments, Choral Training, Composition, and Singing. Courses are taught in Russian and Ukranian.

Academic Information

Enrollment, Music Majors. 1,000.
Music Faculty. 156.
Term System. Academic year September to July.
General Program Areas. Choral Training, Composition, Vocal Music.
Instruments Taught. Folk Instruments, Orchestral Instruments, Piano.

Musical Facilities

Music Library. 113,000 volumes.

Moldavian S.S.R. G. Musichesku State Conservatory
Ul. Sadovaya 87
277014 Kishinev, Moldavskaja SSR
U.S.S.R.

Chief Administrator. A.K. Suslov, Rector.
The U.S.S.R. city of Kishinev was previously called Chisinau when this area was within Romanian borders. The Chisinau Conservatory was founded in 1919. The Romanian composer George Enescu was its honorary president. Under Soviet leadership, the new State Conservatory was founded in 1940. Courses are taught in Russian and Romanian (in cyrrilic letters). Anatoly Tushmalov, a reknowned violin teacher (now deceased),

attracted many fine violin students to study at this conservatory during his years on the faculty.

Academic Information

Enrollment, Music Majors. 1,050.
Music Faculty. 220.
Term System. Academic year September to July.
General Program Areas. Choral Conducting, Composition, Drama, Vocal Music.
Instruments Taught. Folk Instruments, Orchestral Instruments, Piano.

Musical Facilities

Music Library. 152,000 volumes.

Moscow P.I. Tchaikovsky State Conservatory

Ul. Gerzena 13
103009 Moscow K-9, Rossiskaja SFSR
U.S.S.R.

Telephone. 229 20 60
Chief Administrator. A.V. Sveshnikov and Prof. Boris I. Kulikov, Rectors.

The Moscow Conservatory was founded in 1866 by the Russian Musical Society on the initiative of N.G. Rubinstein. In 1940 it was named after Tchaikovsky and was awarded the Order of Lenin in 1946 and 1966. The school has graduated such students as S. Rachmaninoff, A. Scriabin, D. Kabalevsky, R. Gliere, M. Rostropovich, A. Kachaturian, and L. Kogan. The Conservatory occupies a building on Hertzen Street. It is rectangular in shape with a courtyard in the center. In this square is a statue of the school's namesake, P.I. Tchaikovsky. There are 60 classrooms, a library, an acoustical laboratory with recording equipment divided into three units: sound reproduction, sound recording, and acoustics research. The Ginlea Museum, once located here, has occupied its own building since 1965 on Georgievskii Pereulok.

The Departments of the Conservatory include Theory and Composition, Musicology, Vocal Music (Choral Conducting and Singing), Orchestra (sections of stringed instruments, operatic and symphonic conducting), Continuing Education (for instructors at higher musical education institutions). The Conservatory has a graduate division, a teaching assistantship program, 26 sub-departments, an opera studio (founded in 1934), a music school with a regular seven-year secondary academic program, and a central music school with a ten-year secondary academic program. The study of folk music was begun in 1937 under the direction of K.V. Kvitka.

Member of the Assocation Européenne des Conservatoires de Musique, Académies de Musique, et Musikhochschulen.

Academic Information

Enrollment, Music Majors. 1,100.
Music Faculty. 286.
Term System. Academic year September to July.
Music Degrees Offered. Candidate, Doctorate, Aspirantura (postgraduate).
General Program Areas. Composition, Conducting, Folk Music, Music Theory, Opera, Performance.
Instruments Taught. Organ, Percussion, Piano, Stringed Instruments, Voice, Wind Instruments, Woodwinds.

Musical Facilities

Concert Facilities. Two concert halls; one for chamber concerts (seats 300-400) and one for larger concerts (seats over 1,000). Both are equipped with recording facilities.
Music Library. 700,000 volumes; 13,000 phonograph recordings; 6,000 km. of tape recordings; most classrooms are equipped with speakers and connected by direct lines with a central "playback" room equipped with tape machines and turntables. The collection for the study of folk music contains 20,000 pieces of music.

Commentary

The Tchaikovsky State Conservatory in Moscow is probably the most famous music institution in the USSR. It is the venue for the highly publicized international Tchaikovsky Competition.

Novosibirsk M.I. Glinka State Conservatory

Ul. Sovetskaya 31
630099 Novosibirsk 99, Rossiskaja SFSR
U.S.S.R.

Chief Administrator. E.G. Gurenko, Rector.

The Conservatory was established in 1956. There are Departments of Piano, Orchestral and Folk Instruments, Choral Training, Voice, and Theory and Composition.

Academic Information

Term System. Academic year September to July.
General Program Areas. Choral Training, Composition, Music Theory.
Instruments Taught. Folk Instruments, Orchestral Instruments, Piano, Voice.

Musical Facilities

Music Library. 75,000 volumes.

Rostov State Institute of Pedagogics and Music
Budennovsky Pr. 23
344007 Rostov-on-Don, Rossiskaja SFSR
U.S.S.R.

Chief Administrator. E. Beloded, Rector.
The Institute was founded in 1967. There are Faculties of Orchestra, Theory, and Composition.

Academic Information

Enrollment, Music Majors. 527.
Music Faculty. 107.
Term System. Academic year September to July.
General Program Areas. Composition, Music Theory, Orchestral Music.

Musical Facilities

Music Library. 80,000 volumes.

Saratov L.V. Sobinov State Conservatory
Kirova Pr. 1
410000 Saratov, Rossiskaja SFSR
U.S.S.R.

The Conservatory has Departments of Piano, Orchestral Instruments, and Folk Instruments.

Academic Information

Term System. Academic year September to July.
Instruments Taught. Folk Instruments, Orchestral Instruments, Piano.

Musical Facilities

Music Library. 52,000 volumes.

Tallinn State Conservatory
Vabaduse Pst. 130
200015 Tallinn, Estonskaja SSR
U.S.S.R.

Chief Administrator. V.A. Alumyae, Rector.
The Conservatory was founded in the city of Tallinn in Estonia in 1919. The Departments include Singing, Orchestral Instruments, and Choral Conducting. Courses are taught in Russian, Estonian, and German.

Academic Information

Enrollment, Music Majors. 554.
Music Faculty. 134.
Term System. Academic year September to July.
General Program Areas. Choral Conducting, Vocal Music.

Instruments Taught. Orchestral Instruments.

Musical Facilities

Music Library. 60,000 volumes.

Tashkent State Conservatory
Pushkinskaya 31
700000 Tashkent, Uzbekskaja SSR
U.S.S.R.

The Conservatory in the Uzbek S.S.R. has Departments of Piano, Orchestral and Folk Instruments, Voice, Conducting (operatic, symphonic, choral), and Composition.

Academic Information

General Program Areas. Choral Conducting, Composition, Operatic Conducting, Symphonic Conducting, Vocal Music.
Instruments Taught. Folk Instruments, Orchestral Instruments, Piano.

Musical Facilities

Music Library. 92,000 volumes.

Tbilisi V. Sarajishvili State Conservatory
Ul. Griboedova 8
380004 Tbilisi 4, Gruzinskaja SSR
U.S.S.R.

Chief Administrator. S.F. Tsintsadze, Rector.
The Conservatory was founded in 1917 and has Departments of Piano, Singing, Conducting (operatic, symphonic, choral), Folk and Orchestral Instruments, and Chamber Ensembles. Postgraduate studies (aspirantura) are offered. Courses are taught in Russian and Georgian.

Academic Information

Enrollment, Music Majors. 1,300.
Music Faculty. 250.
Term System. Academic year September to July.
General Program Areas. Chamber Music, Choral Conducting, Operatic Conducting, Symphonic Conducting, Vocal Music.
Instruments Taught. Folk Instruments, Orchestral Instruments, Piano.

Musical Facilities

Music Library. 100,000 volumes.

Ufa State Institute of Fine Arts
Ul. Lenin 14
450025 Ufa, Bashkir ASSR
U.S.S.R.

The Institute, located in the Bashkir S.S.R., has Departments in Orchestral Instruments, Folk Music, Choral Conducting, Drama Production, Cinema and Film Acting, and Singing. Courses are taught in Russian and Bashkirian (a Mongolian language).

Academic Information

General Program Areas. Choral Conducting, Drama, Drama Production, Folk Music, Vocal Music.
Instruments Taught. Orchestral Instruments.

Urals M.P. Mussorgsky State Conservatory
Lenina Pr. 26
620014 Sverdlovsk, Rossiskaja SFSR
U.S.S.R.

The Conservatory has Departments of Piano, Orchestral and Folk Instruments, Singing, Choral Conducting, Composition, and Musical Comedy.

Academic Information

Term System. Academic year September to July.
General Program Areas. Choral Conducting, Composition, Musical Comedy, Vocal Music.
Instruments Taught. Folk Instruments, Orchestral Instruments, Piano.

Musical Facilities

Music Library. 83,000 volumes.

VENEZUELA

Academia de Música Fischer
(Fischer Academy of Music)
Edificio Léon de San Marco
Avenida Ciencias y Calle Risquez, Los
  Chaguaramos
Caracas
Venezuela

Chief Administrator. Carmen de Fischer, Director.

Centro para las Culturas Populares y Tradicionales (CCPYT)
c/o Consejo Nacional de la Cultura
  (CONAC)
Edf. Los Roques
Ave. Ppal. Urb. Chuao
Caracas 1060
Venezuela

Chief Administrator. Daria Hernandez, Directora.

The Centro Para Las Culturas Populares y Tradicionales (CCPYT) was recently established to investigate the areas of popular culture and ethnomusicology. This center has incorporated three pre-existing research institutions: (1) Instituto Nacional de Folklore (1947-1986); (2) Instituto Interamericano de Ethnomusicología y Folklore (1970-1986); and (3) Museo Nacional de Folklore (1972-1986).

The Center produces twenty-three publications. The "Lista de Publicaciones" can be obtained from the Consejo Nacional de la Cultura.

Consejo Nacional de la Cultura (CONAC)
Edf. Los Roques
Ave. Ppal. Urb. Chuao
Caracas 1060
Venezuela

For more information about any of the music schools in Venezuela, contact the Consejo Nacional de la Cultura at the above address.

Conservatorio Nacional de Música - Caracas Juan José Landaeta
Urbanización Campo Alegre
4a Avenida
Caracas
Venezuela

Telephone. (02) 331585

Escuela de Música Lino Gallardo
Avenida Principal de la Castellana
Entre 2a y 3a Transversales
Quinta Yudith
Caracas
Venezuela

Telephone. (02) 333275

Escuela de Música Prudencio Esás

Avenida Principal El Paraíso
Quinta Villa Helena
Caracas
Venezuela

Telephone. (02) 422122

Escuela Nacional de Música "José Ángel Lamas"

Veroes a Santa Capilla
Avenida Urdaneta
Caracas 1010
Venezuela

Telephone. (02) 819628, 831618
This institution is the oldest national music school in Venezuela, founded in 1887.

Escuela Nacional de Opera - Caracas
Dirección de Cultura y Bellas Artes del Ministerio de Educación

Este 2 con Sur 25
El Conde, Los Caobos
Caracas
Venezuela

Chief Administrator. Primo Casale, Director.

Universidad Cecilio Acosto
Facultad de Música

Cabimas
Venezuela

VIETNAM

Conservatoire of Hò Chí Minh City

112 Nguyêd Du Street
Hò Chí Minh City
Socialist Republic of Vietnam

Nhac Viên Hànôi
(Conservatoire of Hànôi)

Ô Cha Duà
Hànôi
Socialist Republic of Vietnam

Telephone. 54969

Chief Administrator. Nguyên Trong Bàng, Director.
The Conservatoire of Hànôi was founded in 1956. It is under the jurisdiction of the Ministry of Culture and Information. The language of instruction is Vietnamese.

Academic Information

Enrollment, Music Majors. 677.
Term System. Semester. September to January; February to June.
Entrance Requirements. Secondary school certificate.
Music Degrees Offered. Diploma.
Music Degree Requirements. The Diploma is awarded after the completion of a 5-year course of study.

WEST GERMANY

Fachakademie für Music - Augsburg
Leopold Mozart-Konservatorium der Stadt Augsburg

Maximilianstrasse 59
Augsberg
Federal Republic of Germany

Telephone. (0821) 3 24 28 91
Chief Administrator. Klaus Volk, Director.
The Academy offers seminars for music teachers and seminars in Catholic Church Music.

Academic Information

General Program Areas. Chamber Music, Music, Choral Conducting, Church Music (Catholic), Composition, Eurythmics, Harmony, Italian, Latin, Musicology, Opera, Orchestra Conducting, Orff Method, Rhythmic Education, Speech, Studio New Music, Studio Old Music, Vocal Music.
Instruments Taught. Harpsichord, Orchestral Instruments, Piano, Voice.

Fachakademie für Musik - München
Richard Strauss-Konservatorium der Stadt

München mit Sing-und Musikschule
Ismaningerstrasse 29
München 80
Federal Republic of Germany

Telephone. (089) 47 51 06
Chief Administrator. Peter Jona Korn, Director.

Academic Information

General Program Areas. Church Music (Catholic), Church Music (Protestant), Composition, Conducting, Early Music Education, Ensemble Playing, Eurythmics, Folk Music, Jazz, Music Education, Music Pedagogy, Music Theory, Old Music, Opera, Orchestra, Orff Method, Performance.

Instruments Taught. Orchestral Instruments, Piano.

Fachakademie für Musik - Nürnberg
Konservatorium der Stadt Nürnberg
Am Katharinenkloster 6
Nürnberg
Federal Republic of Germany

Telephone. (0911) 16 23 73
Chief Administrator. Dr. Wolfgang Graetschel, Director.

Academic Information

General Program Areas. Choral Conducting, Composition, Eurythmics, Instrumental Methods, Music Education, Music Theatre, Music Theory, Musicology, Performance, Vocal Music.

Instruments Taught. Harpsichord, Orchestral Instruments, Piano.

Hermann-Zilcher-Konservatorium
Hofstrasse 13
D-8700 Würzburg
Federal Republic of Germany

Telephone. (0931) 37 49 3
Chief Administrator. Martin Krüger, Director.

When the former Bayerisches Staatskonservatorium became a Hoschschule für Musik in 1975, the Conservatory was established. The school offers seminars for music teachers and for orchestral musicians.

Academic Information

Enrollment, Music Majors. Full-time 77 men, 94 women; part-time 23 men, 10 women. 2 foreign students from the U.S.A.

Music Faculty. Full-time 24, part-time 32.

Term System. Academic year October to July.

Entrance Requirements. Completion of middle school and advanced knowledge of an instrument; audition (must contain several compositions of various epochs).

Admission Procedure. Application due May 30.

Music Degree Requirements. Completion of prescribed courses (four years).

General Program Areas. Aural Training, Chamber Music, Choral Conducting, Church Music (Catholic), Early Music, Early Music Education, Eurythmics, Instrumental Conducting, Music Education, Music Theory, Musicology, Orff Method, Vocal Music.

Instruments Taught. Accordion, Bass, Clarinet, Flute, Guitar, Harpsichord, Horn, Lute, Mandolin, Oboe, Organ, Percussion, Recorder, Trumpet, Tuba, Viola, Viola da Gamba, Violin, Violoncello, Voice.

Musical Facilities

Practice Facilities. 7 practice rooms. 7 organs (W. Elenz/Würzburg). 1 percussion-equipped practice room. 30 pianos; 6 pianos reserved for piano majors.

Concert Facilities. 1 small concert hall.

Community Facilities. Organ courses are taught in local churches. Several halls throughout the city are used for recitals and concerts.

Concerts/Musical Activities. Concerts by students as soloists, choir, and orchestra.

Music Library. 200 scores; 800 books; 12 periodicals; 350 phonograph recordings. Listening facilities (cassette, stereo).

Financial

Costs. Per academic year: No tuition.

Financial Aid. Scholarship application due November.

Hochschule der Künste Berlin
Ernst-Reuter-Platz 10
1000 Berlin 10
Federal Republic of Germany

Telephone. (030) 3185-0
Chief Administrator. Ulrich Roloff-Momin, President.

The Hochschule was founded in 1696 as an academy and received its present title in 1975.

Member of the Assocation Européenne des Conservatoires de Musique, Académies de Musique, et Musikhochschulen.

Academic Information

Term System. Semester. October to February; April to July.

Music Degrees Offered. Diploma.

Music Degree Requirements. Completion of three- to five-year course.

General Program Areas. Chamber Music, Church Music, Composition, Conducting, Eurythmics, Film Music, Sound Engineer/Music Transmission, Structure and Ear Training.

Instruments Taught. Harpsichord, Orchestral Instruments, Piano, Saxophone.

Hochschule für Gestaltende Kunst und Musik
(State College for Creative Art and Music)
Department of Music
Am Wandrahm 23
2800 Bremen 1
Federal Republic of Germany

Telephone. (0421) 17 00 51

Chief Administrator. Karl-August Welp, Director.

The Academy was founded in 1873 as a School of Handicrafts and came under the jurisdiction of the State of Bremen. After incorporating the Conservatory of Bremen in 1979, it acquired its present name.

Academic Information

Term System. Semester. September to February; March to August.

Music Degrees Offered. Professional titles in music.

General Program Areas. Acoustics, Aural Training, Collective Improvisation, Composition, Conducting, Film Music, Gregorian Chant, Italian, Jazz Studies, Music Education, Music History, Music Theory, Musicology, Opera, Organ Building, Organology, Popular Music, Studio Early Music, Studio New Music.

Hochschule für Music und Darstellende Kunst Hamburg

Harvestehuder Weg 12
2000 Hamburg 13
Federal Republic of Germany

Telephone. (040) 44 19 55 80

Chief Administrator. Professor Dr. Hermann Rauhe, President.

The Hochschule, under jurisdiction of the State of Hamburg, was founded in 1950 and became an autonomous institution in 1967. The school has Departments of Music Theory, Instrumental Music, Performing Arts, Music Education, Church Music, Opera, and Stage Management.

Member of the Assocation Européenne des Conservatoires de Musique, Académies de Musique, et Musikhochschulen.

Academic Information

Term System. Semester. April to September; October to March.

Music Degrees Offered. Staatsexamen in Music Education; Diploma in Church Music.

Music Degree Requirements. Staatsexamen requires completion of four years of study; the Diploma in Church Music requires five years of study.

General Program Areas. Church Music, Composition, Instrumental Music, Music Education, Music Theory, Opera, Performance, Stage Management.

Instruments Taught. Baroque Violin, Harpsichord, Orchestral Instruments, Piano, Recorder, Viola da Gamba, Woodwinds.

Musical Facilities

Music Library. 9,385 volumes; 1,892 phonograph recordings.

Hochschule für Musik · München

Arcisstrasse 12
8000 München 2
Federal Republic of Germany

Telephone. (089) 55 91 587

Chief Administrator. Professor Diethard Hellmann, President.

The Hochschule was founded in 1867 as the Royal School of Music, and was financed by Ludwig II. Currently supported by the State of Bavaria, it acquired its present status in 1924.

Member of the Assocation Européenne des Conservatoires de Musique, Académies de Musique, et Musikhochschulen.

Academic Information

Music Degrees Offered. Diplomas (with professional titles); teaching qualifications.

General Program Areas. Acoustics, Art Song History, Art Songs (Interpretation of), Aural Training, Catholic Liturgy, Chamber Music, Choral Conducting, Church Music (Catholic), Church Music (Protestant), Composition, German Liturgical Singing, Gregorian Chant, Instrumental Conducting, Media Knowledge, Music Education, Music Theory, Musicology, Opera History, Organ Building, Organ Repertoire, Organology, Performance Rights, Piano Music History, Radio Seminar, TV Seminar.

Instruments Taught. Guitar, Keyboard, Lute, Orchestral Instruments, Organ.

Hochschule für Musik · Würzburg

Hofstallstrasse 6-8
D-8700 Würzburg
Federal Republic of Germany

Telephone. 0931 50641

Chief Administrator. Professor Franz Hennevogl, President.

The Hochschule was founded as a conservatory in 1804. It acquired its current status in 1973 and came under the jurisdiction of the State of Bavaria.

Member of the Assocation Européenne des Conservatoires de Musique, Académies de Musique, et Musikhochschulen.

Academic Information

Enrollment, Music Majors. Full-time 250 men, 250 women. 100 foreign students representing Korea, Greece, Italy, Japan, China, Brazil, Switzerland, and Austria.

Term System. Semester. October to March; April to September.

Entrance Requirements. Secondary school diploma (depending on course pursued); audition (15 minutes on main instrument); aural training test; history test.

Admission Procedure. Application due May 1.

Music Degrees Offered. Diploma; professional qualifications.

Music Degree Requirements. Completion of prescribed course.

General Program Areas. Acoustics, Art Song Accompaniment, Aural Training, Breath Control, Choral Conducting, Church Music (Catholic), Church Music (Protestant), Composition, Electronic Music, Eurythmics, Figured Bass, Historical Dance, Historical Instruments, Instrumentation, Italian, Jazz Studies, Music Education, Music History, Music Pedagogy, Music Theory, Musical Ornaments, New Music, Opera, Opera History, Orchestra Conducting, Organology, Performance, Speech Training, Structures Techniques, Vocal Music.

Instruments Taught. Brass, Percussion, Piano, Stringed Instruments, Woodwinds.

Musical Facilities

Practice Facilities. 10 practice rooms. 4 percussion-equipped practice rooms. 20 pianos (grand). Electronic music studio.

Concert Facilities. Concert Hall, seating 1,000; 2 recital halls, 150 each.

Concerts/Musical Activities. Student concerts and recitals. Special festivals for contemporary music and pre-classical music.

Music Library. 40,000 volumes. Listening facilities (cassette, stereo).

Hochschule für Musik und Darstellende Kunst Frankfurt am Main

Eschersheimer Landstrasse 29-39
6000 Frankfurt am Main 1
Federal Republic of Germany

Telephone. (069) 55 08 26/28

Chief Administrator. Professor Hans-Dieter Resch, Director.

The Hochschule, supported by the State of Hesse, was founded in 1938. There are Departments of Music Education, Performing Arts, Professional Training, and Church Music.

Member of the Assocation Européenne des Conservatoires de Musique, Académies de Musique, et Musikhochschulen.

Academic Information

Term System. Semester. April to September; October to March.

Music Degrees Offered. Diploma; Teaching Qualification.

Music Degree Requirements. The Diploma is awarded after completion of a four- or five-year course. The Teaching Qualification requires four years of study for the organist and choir director course and five to six years for the Konzertexamen course.

General Program Areas. Aural Training, Ballet, Chamber Music, Church Music, Composition, Conducting, Music Education, Opera, Performance, Speech, Studio New Music, Studio Old Music.

Instruments Taught. Guitar, Harpsichord, Lute, Orchestral Instruments, Piano.

Musical Facilities

Music Library. 20,000 volumes.

Hochschule für Musik und Theater Hannover

Emmichplatz 1
3000 Hannover 1
Federal Republic of Germany

Telephone. 511 31001

Chief Administrator. Professor Richard Jakoby, President.

The school was founded as a state-supported institution in 1973. It attained university status in 1977.

Member of the Assocation Européenne des Conservatoires de Musique, Académies de Musique, et Musikhochschulen.

Academic Information

Music Faculty. Full-time 101, part-time 90.

Term System. Semester. April to September; October to March.

Entrance Requirements. Secondary school diploma (depending on the course pursued). Audition on main instrument (piano in some courses); ear training; singing.

Admission Procedure. Application due May 31st.

Music Degrees Offered. M., M.E., M. Pedagogy; Ph.D.

Music Degree Requirements. Completion of prescribed course of study. The Ph.D. is offered in music history and music education.

General Program Areas. Art Songs (Interpretation of), Breath Control, Chamber Music, Choral Conducting, Church Music, Composition, Conducting, Dance, Dance History, Drama, Eurythmics, Fencing, Italian, Music Education, Music History, Music Pedagogy, Music Psychology, Music Theory, Musicology, Opera, Opera Choir, Philosophy, Psychology, Speech, Stage Management, Theater History, Theater Law, Vocal Music.

Instruments Taught. Brass, Organ, Percussion, Piano, Stringed Instruments, Voice, Woodwinds.

Musical Facilities

Practice Facilities. 60 practice rooms. Special practice rooms for organists; 6 organs (Beckerath, Hellebrandt, Off, Schúke). 3 percussion-equipped practice rooms. 50 pianos; 12 grand pianos reserved for piano majors. Practice rooms available to each student for four hours a day.

Concert Facilities. 2 concert halls.

Community Facilities. Local churches used by students of church music.

Music Library. 70,000 scores; 60,000 books; 60 periodicals; 3,000 phonograph recordings. Listening facilities (6 cassette decks, 6 stereo decks). The libraries of the University and the city are available to students.

Financial

Financial Aid. Scholarships and loans are available.

Commentary

The granting of a Ph.D. at Hochschule für Musik is unusual. Most often in the Federal Republic of Germany, the Ph.D. is specifically the domain of the university.

Musikhochschule des Saarlandes
Bismarckstrasse 1
6600 Saarbrücken 3
Federal Republic of Germany

Telephone. (0681) 624 08/9

Chief Administrator. Professor Dr. Werner Müller-Bech, Director.

The Musikhochschule, supported by the Ministry of Culture of the State of the Saar, was founded as a conservatory in 1947. It became a college in 1957. There are Faculties of Vocal Music, Instrumental Music, and Theory of Music.

Vocal Music Faculty courses: Singing and Art Song Interpretation, Vocal Physiology and Speech Training, Gregorian Chant, Liturgy, Dramatic Exercises, Ensemble and Study of Rôles, Italian, Fencing, Body Training.

Instrumental Music Faculty courses: All Orchestral Instruments, Piano, Organ, Harpsichord, Chamber Music, Old Music.

Music Theory Faculty courses: Musicology, Psychology, Music Theory and Composition, Didactics, Conducting.

There are Departments of School Music, Church Music, Interpretative Arts, Orchestral and Ensemble Music, Music Education.

Member of the Assocation Européenne des Conservatoires de Musique, Académies de Musique, et Musikhochschulen.

Academic Information

Term System. Semester. October to March; April to September.

Music Degrees Offered. Diploma.

Music Degree Requirements. Completion of three to six years of study.

General Program Areas. Body Training, Chamber Music, Church Music, Composition, Conducting, Ensemble Music, Fencing, Gregorian Chant, Instrumental Music, Interpretative Arts, Italian, Liturgy, Music Education, Music Theory, Musicology, Old Music, Orchestral Music, Psychology, School Music, Speech, Vocal Music.

Instruments Taught. Harpsichord, Orchestral Instruments, Organ, Piano.

Musical Facilities

Music Library. 40,000 volumes.

Musikhochschule Lübeck
Grosse Petersgrube 17-29
2400 Lübeck
Federal Republic of Germany

Telephone. (0451) 718 41-44

Chief Administrator. Professor Dr. Manfred Tessmer, President.

The Musickhochschule, under the jurisdiction of the State of Schleswig-Holstein, was founded in 1933 as a conservatory. It acquired its present status in 1973.

Member of the Assocation Européenne des Conservatoires de Musique, Académies de Musique, et Musikhochschulen.

Academic Information

Enrollment, Music Majors. 240.

Music Degrees Offered. Diplomas (with professional titles); teaching qualifications.

General Program Areas. Catholic Liturgy, Church Music, Eurythmics, Hymnology, Music Education, Organ Improvisation, Organology, Protestant Liturgy, Psychology, School Music, Theater History, Vocal Music.

Instruments Taught. Orchestral Instruments, Organ, Voice.

Staatliche Hochschule für Musik Freiburg
Schwarzwaldstrasse 141
D-7800 Freiburg i. Br.
Federal Republic of Germany

Telephone. (0761) 31 91 50

Chief Administrator. Professor Joh. Georg Schaarschmidt, Director.

485

The school was founded in 1946 as an institution of the city of Freiburg. Since 1962, it has been under the jurisdiction of the government of Baden-Württemberg. The school occupies a new building completed in 1983. The departments include: Keyboard Instruments and Plucked Instruments, Composition-Theory-Musicology, String Instruments, Wind Instruments and Percussion, Singing and Speech Training, Conducting, Eurythmics and Early Music Education, Church Music, Opera School.

Member of the Assocation Européenne des Conservatoires de Musique, Académies de Musique, et Musikhochschulen.

Academic Information

Enrollment, Music Majors. Full-time 312 men, 289 women; part-time (only for lessons) 29. Foreign students from Japan, Korea, Switzerland.

Term System. Semester. April to July (Summer term); October to February (Winter term).

Entrance Requirements. Admission test required; audition (instrument/voice), piano, theory.

Admission Procedure. Apply by July 15 or January 31.

Music Degrees Offered. Diploma; postgraduate degree.

Music Degree Requirements. The diploma program (teaching, orchestra, church music, secondary school) requires the completion of eight to ten terms; the postgraduate degree four terms.

General Program Areas. Church Music, Church Music, Composition, Conducting, Early Music Education, Eurythmics, Music Education, Music Theory, Musicology, Opera, Performance, Speech, Vocal Music.

Instruments Taught. Bass, Brass, Clavichord, Guitar, Harp, Harpsichord, Oboe d'Amore, Organ, Percussion, Piano, Viola, Viola d'Amore, Viola da Gamba, Violin, Violoncello, Voice, Woodwinds.

Musical Facilities

Practice Facilities. 35 practice rooms. 4 special practice rooms for organists; 5 organs; 1 percussion-equipped practice room. 40 pianos; 30 grand pianos reserved for piano majors. Special studios for rhythmics, new music, opera. Electronic studio.

Music Library. Staff of 3. University of Freiberg library and the city library are available to students.

Financial

Financial Aid. Scholarships are not available to foreign students.

Commentary

Because of this Hochschule's particularly distinguished and diverse faculty, unusual instruments such as the clavichord, oboe d'amore, and viola d'amore are offered. World-class performers including Heinz Holliger, Ursula Holliger, and Hermann Bauman teach at the school.

Staatliche Hochschule für Musik Heidelberg-Mannheim
Friedrich-Ebert-Anlage 62
Federal Republic of Germany

Telephone. (06221) 200 40

Chief Administrator. Professor Gerald Kegelmann, Director.

The Hochschule, under the jurisdiction of the State of Baden-Württemberg, was founded in 1971, incorporating all of the previously existing colleges of music and drama in Heidelberg. There are Departments of Music Education, Professional Training, and Orchestral Music.

Member of the Assocation Européenne des Conservatoires de Musique, Académies de Musique, et Musikhochschulen.

Academic Information

Term System. Semester. October to March; April to September.

Music Degrees Offered. Diplomas (corresponding to professional titles).

General Program Areas. Composition, Dance, Music Education, Music Theory, Musicology, Opera, Orchestral Music, Vocal Music.

Instruments Taught. Keyboards, Orchestral Insruments, Voice.

Staatliche Hochschule für Musik Karlsruhe
Weberstrasse 8
7500 Karlsruhe 1
Federal Republic of Germany

Telephone. (0721) 135-3294

The Hochschule, supported by the State of Baden-Württemburg, was founded in 1929. There are Departments of School Music, Music Education, Orchestral Music, Catholic Church Music, Conducting, Composition, Opera, Chamber Music, Orchestral Instruments, Musicology.

Member of the Assocation Européenne des Conservatoires de Musique, Académies de Musique, et Musikhochschulen.

Academic Information

Term System. Semester. October to February; April to July.

Music Degrees Offered. Diplomas (with professional titles); teaching qualifications.

General Program Areas. Chamber Music, Church Music, Composition, Conducting, Music Education, Musicology, Opera, Orchestral Music, School Music.

Instruments Taught. Lute, Orchestral Instruments, Saxophone.

Staatliche Hochschule für Musik Rheinland - Aachen
Grenzland-Institut Aachen
Theaterstrasse 2-4
Aachen
Federal Republic of Germany

Telephone. (0241) 45 53 78, 45 54 15

Chief Administrator. Professor H. Jochem Münstermann, Dean.

The Hochschule offers seminars for music education. Music Therapy is offered in cooperation with the hospital of the city of Herdecke.

Academic Information

General Program Areas. Aural Training, Ballet, Big Band, Chamber Music, Choral Conducting, Choral Music, Composition, Eurythmics, Italian, Jazz Studies, Music Education, Music History, Music Theory, Music Therapy, Opera, Psychology, Solfege, Speech, Vocal Music.

Instruments Taught. Guitar, Lute, Orchestral Instruments, Voice.

Staatliche Hochschule für Musik Rheinland - Düsseldorf
(State College of Music)
Robert-Schumann-Institute Düsseldorf
Fischerstrasse 110
D-4000 Düsseldorf
Federal Republic of Germany

Telephone. (0211) 48 40 38

Chief Administrator. Professor Dr. Helmut Kirchmeyer, Dean.

Academic Information

General Program Areas. College Choir, Composition, Conducting, Early Music, Electronic Music, Elementary Music, Fencing, Improvisation, Music Education, Music Pedagogy, Music Sociology, Musical Acoustics, Musicology, Old Music, Opera School, Organ Building, Organology, Pantomime, Popular Music, Rhythmics, Song Accompaniment.

Instruments Taught. Woodwinds.

Staatliche Hochschule für Musik Rheinland - Köln
Dagobertstrasse 38
D-5000 Köln 1
Federal Republic of Germany

Telephone. 221 12 40 33

Chief Administrator. Professor Dr. Franz Müller-Heuser, Director.

The Musckhochschule Köln was founded in 1858 and became a college in 1925. The college is under the jurisdiction of the State of North Rhine-Westphalia. The Staatliche Hochschule für Musick Rheinland also has institutions in Aachen, Düsseldorf, and Wuppertal.

Member of the Assocation Européenne des Conservatoires de Musique, Académies de Musique, et Musikhochschulen.

Academic Information

Enrollment, Music Majors. Full-time 713 men, 594 women. 189 foreign students representing 32 nationalities.

Music Faculty. Full-time 98, part-time 141.

Term System. Semester. October to March; April to September.

Entrance Requirements. Secondary school diploma required; comprehensive examination; audition.

Music Degrees Offered. Künstleriche Abschlussprüfung; Konzertexamen; Staatliche Prüfungen.

Music Degree Requirements. 8-12 semesters; 4 semesters for Augbaustudiengänge. Completion of prescribed program of studies.

General Program Areas. Art Song Accompaniment, Chamber Music, Church Music, Composition, Electronic Music, Music History, Music Theory, Opera, Performance.

Instruments Taught. Brass, Organ, Percussion, Piano, Saxophone, Stringed Instruments, Viola da Gamba, Voice, Woodwinds.

Musical Facilities

Practice Facilities. 146 practice rooms. Special practice rooms for organists; 6 organs (1 Beckerath, 1 Klais, 1 Chuke, 3 Herstellern). 3 percussion-equipped practice rooms. 157 pianos (25 upright, 132 grand); 30 grand pianos reserved for piano majors. Music theater; jazz seminar, rhythmic seminar. Electronic music studio.

Concert Facilities. Grosser Konzertssal, seating 800 to 1,000; Kammermusiksaal, 200; Ubehaus, 61.

Community Facilities. Choir and organ concerts are held in local churches.

Concerts/Musical Activities. Orchestra and choral concerts; ensemble recitals.

Music Library. 130,000 scores; 7,000 books; 48 periodicals; 4,000 phonograph recordings. Listening facilities (cassette, stereo). Special collection of 590 historical manuscripts.

Staatliche Hochschule für Musik Rheinland - Wuppertal
Institute Wuppertal
Friedrich-Ebert-Strasse 141
Wuppertal
Federal Republic of Germany

Telephone. (0202) 30 30 31
Chief Administrator. Professor Ingo Schmitt, Dean.

Academic Information

General Program Areas. Chamber Music, Composition, Conducting, Eurythmics, Italian, Music History, Music Pedagogy, Music Therapy, New Music, Opera, Performance, Psychology, Speech, Vocal Music.

Instruments Taught. Harpsichord, Mandolin, Orchestral Instruments, Organ, Piano, Voice.

Staatliche Hochschule für Musik Ruhr
Abtei 43
4300 Essen 16
Federal Republic of Germany

Telephone. (0201) 49030
Chief Administrator. Professor Werner Krotzinger, Head.

The Hochschule was founded as the Foldwangschule für Musik, Tanz, und Sprechen in 1927. It became a Staatliche Hochschule, supported by the State of North Rhine-Westphalia, in 1972.

Member of the Assocation Européenne des Conservatoires de Musique, Académies de Musique, et Musikhochschulen.

Academic Information

Term System. Semester. October to March; April to September.

Music Degrees Offered. Diploma; Staatsexamen; Konzertexamen.

Music Degree Requirements. The Diploma requires completion of a four- to five-year course; Staatsexamen requires the completion of a four-year course; Konzertexamen requires the completion of a one- to two-year course.

General Program Areas. Chamber Music, Composition, Conducting, Eurythmics, Music Education, Music Pedagogy, Music Theory, Musical Theater, Musicology, Vocal Music.

Instruments Taught. Harpsichord, Orchestral Instruments, Piano.

Musical Facilities

Music Library. 80,000 volumes.

Staatliche Hochschule für Musik Trossingen
Schultheiss-Koch-Platz 3
D-7218 Trossingen 1
Federal Republic of Germany

Telephone. 07425 6057
Chief Administrator. Professor Jürgen Weimer, Director.

The Hochschule was founded in 1944 and became a state high school of music in 1977. It is located in a park in Trossingen.

Member of the Assocation Européenne des Conservatoires de Musique, Académies de Musique, et Musikhochschulen.

Academic Information

Enrollment, Music Majors. Full-time 210 men, 222 women. 35 foreign students representing Japan, Korea, Switzerland, Spain, France, Sweden, Italy, Poland, Bulgaria, Taiwan, and Israel.

Term System. Semester. October to March; April to September.

Entrance Requirements. Secondary school diploma; if the candidate has not earned the diploma, an examination is necessary to prove the ability to follow courses. Audition required, playing or singing for 20 to 30 minutes; other requirements include theoretical examination in music notation, solfege, harmony.

Admission Procedure. Application due January 15th or July 15th.

Music Degrees Offered. Diploma; Kunstlerische Ausbildung (artistic further development).

Music Degree Requirements. Completion of required courses.

General Program Areas. Choral Conducting, Composition, Eurythmics, Instrumental Conducting, Music Education, Music History Musicology, Music Theory, Performance, Vocal Music.

Instruments Taught. Bass, Bassoon, Clarinet, Flute, Harpsichord, Horn, Oboe, Organ, Percussion, Piano, Recorder, Trombone, Trumpet, Viola, Violin, Violoncello, Voice.

Musical Facilities

Practice Facilities. 20 practice rooms. Practice rooms for organists; 7 organs. 2 percussion-equipped practice rooms. 16 pianos; 4 grand pianos reserved for piano majors. Practice rooms available to students for 3 hours a day. Electronic music studio.

Concert Facilities. Concert Hall, Aula (small recital hall).

Community Facilities. Student concerts are sometimes given in neighboring communities.

Concerts/Musical Activities. Concerts and recitals.

Financial

Costs. No tuition.
Financial Aid. Limited scholarship aid available to foreign students.

Staatliche Hochschule für Musik und Darstellende Kunst Stuttgart

Urbanplatz 2
7000 Stuttgart 1
Federal Republic of Germany

Telephone. (0711) 21248 40, 212 48 41
Chief Administrator. Professor Konrad Richter, Director.

The Hochschule was founded in 1922. There are Departments of Professional Training, Private Music, School of Opera, Electronic Studio, Seminar for Music Pedagogy.

Member of the Assocation Européenne des Conservatoires de Musique, Académies de Musique, et Musikhochschulen.

Academic Information

Enrollment, Music Majors. 630.
Music Degrees Offered. Diplomas (with professional titles).
General Program Areas. Church Music (Catholic), Church Music (Protestant), Drama, Electronic Music, Eurythmics, German Chorale, Gregorian Chant, Liturgy, Modern Music, Music Pedagogy, Opera, Organology, Rhythmic Education, School Music, Speech.

Staatliche Hochschule für Musik Westfalen-Lippe

Allee 22
4930 Detmold
Federal Republic of Germany

Telephone. (05231) 7407-0
Chief Administrator. Professor Friedrich Wilhelm Schnurr, Director.

The Hochschule, supported by the State of North Rhine-Westphalia, was founded as an academy in 1947. It became a Staatliche Hochschule in 1972 with institutes in Dortmund and Muenster. The School holds seminars for teachers at music schools and free-lance music teachers. It holds a seminar of musicology in cooperation with the University of Paderborn. There is a department for Sound Engineering.

Member of the Assocation Européenne des Conservatoires de Musique, Académies de Musique, et Musikhochschulen.

Academic Information

Term System. Semester. October to February; April to July.
Music Degrees Offered. Diplomas (with professional titles).
General Program Areas. Art Songs (Interpretation of), Chamber Music, Choral Conducting, Church Music, Composition, Conducting, Music Education, Music Theory, Opera, School Music, Sound Engineering, Speech, Vocal Music.
Instruments Taught. Harpsichord, Orchestral Instruments, Organ, Piano.

Staatliche Hochschule für Musik Westfalen-Lippe
Institut Dortmund

Hanastrasse 7
D-4600 Dortmund 1
Federal Republic of Germany

Telephone. (0231) 144230
Chief Administrator. Professor Wolfgang Benfer, Director.

The Institute was founded as private conservatory in 1901. It became a part of the Staatliche Hochschule für Music Westfalen-Lippe in 1972. The school has a studio for contemporary music, jazz seminars/jazz ensembles.

Academic Information

Enrollment, Music Majors. Semester.
Music Faculty. Full-time 192 men, 175 women; part-time 2 women. Foreign students 13.
Term System. Full-time 18, part-time 66.
Entrance Requirements. Secondary school diploma. Audition required.
Admission Procedure. Application due January.
Music Degrees Offered. Diploma.
Music Degree Requirements. Six to ten semesters.
General Program Areas. Art Songs (Interpretation of), Aural Training, Chamber Music, Church Music (Catholic), Church Music (Protestant), Composition, Contemporary Music, Eurythmics, Improvisation, Jazz Studies, Liturgy, Music History, Music Pedagogy, Music Theory, Musical Acoustics, Musical Analysis, Opera, Organology, Score Reading.
Instruments Taught. Brass, Harpsichord, Organ, Percussion, Piano, Stringed Instruments, Voice, Woodwinds.

Musical Facilities

Practice Facilities. 35 practice rooms. 3 practice rooms for organists. 16 practice pianos.
Concert Facilities. Concert hall; recital halls.
Community Facilities. Local music halls also used for concerts and recitals.

489

Concerts/Musical Activities. Recitals for soloists, organists, and orchestra.

Music Library. 36,249 scores; 2,774 books; 689 periodicals; 829 phonograph recordings. Listening facilities (cassette, stereo). FüR MUSIKERZIEHER E.V.

Wiesbadener Konservatorium und staatliche anerkannte private Fachschule für Musikerzieher e.V.
(Conservatory and Seminary for Music Education)
Bodenstedtstrasse 2
6200 Wiesbaden
Federal Republic of Germany

Telephone. (06121) 37 05 96

Chief Administrator. Dr. Richard Meissner, Director.

The Konservatorium was founded in 1888.

The structure of the institution includes a Seminar for Private Music Teachers, Instrumental Courses/Orchestra School, and Opera School.

Academic Information

Instruments Taught. Accordion, Bass, Clarinet, Flute, Guitar, Horn, Oboe, Organ, Percussion, Piano, Recorder, Trombone, Trumpet, Violin, Violoncello, Voice.

YEMEN

Military Institute of Music - Sana'a
Sana'a
Yemen Arab Republic

The Institute trains musicians to play in military bands which are comprised mainly of Western woodwind and brass instruments, and bagpipes.

Academic Information

General Program Areas. Bagpipes, Brass, Woodwinds.

Commentary

In addition to the two music institutes in the capital of Sana'a, there are local cultural centers in the cities of Hodeida and Taiz which sponsor music classes.

National Institute of Music - Sana'a
Sana'a
Yemen Arab Republic

This Institute was establsihed in the mid-1970s and is under the jurisdiction of the Minister of Information and Culture. Instruments offered for instruction are the Egyptian 'ud, violin, cello, piano, and percussion. Composition skills needed for the writing of nationalistic music are taught as well. The faculty has been trained mainly in Egypt and Eastern Europe.

Academic Information

General Program Areas. Composition, Yemen Nationalistic Music.

Instruments Taught. Egyptian 'Ud, Percussion, Piano, Violin, Violoncello.

Commentary

One of the paradoxes of having an Egyptian- and Eastern European-trained faculty at the National Institute is that teachers are not able to use music vocabulary learned elsewhere to give meaning to, or teach about, Yemenite traditional art music. Instead, a new genre of music has been created.

YUGOSLAVIA

Akademija za Glasbo
(Musical Academy)
Gosposka 8
YU-61000 Ljubljana
Yugoslavia

Telephone. (061) 221-268, 221-842

Chief Administrator. Professor Marian Gabrijelcic, Dean.

The Academy was founded in 1919. There are Departments of Composition, Conducting, Voice, Piano, Strings, Winds, and Brass. There is also a department for training music teachers. Additional telephone number: 221-842.

Member of the Assocation Européenne des Conservatoires de Musique, Académies de Musique, et Musikhochschulen.

Academic Information

Enrollment, Music Majors. 192.

Music Faculty. 29.

Music Degrees Offered. Bachelor of Music.

Music Degree Requirements. The equivalent of a Bachelor of Music is awarded after completion of a four-year course.

Musical Facilities

Music Library. 30,000 items including scores, sheet music, books, periodicals, and recordings.

Facultet za Muzička umetnost
(Faculty for Music and Arts)
Pita Guli 1
YU-91000 Skopje
Yugoslavia

Telephone. (091) 233-264
Chief Administrator. Professor Blagoje Nikolovski, Dean.

This is the music faculty of the University in Skopje.
Member of the Assocation Européenne des Conservatoires de Musique, Académies de Musique, et Musikhochschulen.

Academic Information

Music Degrees Offered. Bachelor of Music.
Music Degree Requirements. The equivalent of a Bachelor of Music is awarded after completion of a four-year course.

Muzička Akademija
Maršala tita 50
YU-11000 Belgrade
Yugoslavia

Telephone. (011) 642-414, 659-689
Chief Administrator. Professor Vladimir Markovic, Dean.

The Academy was founded in 1937.
Member of the Assocation Européenne des Conservatoires de Musique, Académies de Musique, et Musikhochschulen.

Academic Information

Enrollment, Music Majors. 539.
Music Faculty. 100.
Music Degrees Offered. Bachelor of Music.
Music Degree Requirements. The equivalent of a Bachelor of Music is awarded after completion of a four-year course.

Musical Facilities

Music Library. 20,000 books and periodicals; 45,000 scores; 6,000 phonograph recordings. Listening facilities available. There are also collections of the ethnomusicologist Vladimr R. Dordević, the composer Miloje Milojević, and the composer-violinist Petar Stojanović.

Muzička Akademija a Sarajevo
Svetozara Markovića I/II
YU-71000 Sarajevo
Yugoslavia

Telephone. (071) 23-112
Chief Administrator. Matusia Blum, Dean.

The Academy was established in 1955. There are Departments of Composition, Conducting, Singing, Piano, Strings and Winds, History and Folklore, and Theoretical Teaching.
Member of the Assocation Européenne des Conservatoires de Musique, Académies de Musique, et Musikhochschulen.

Academic Information

Music Degrees Offered. Bachelor of Music.
Music Degree Requirements. The equivalent of a Bachelor of Music is awarded after completion of a four-year course.

Musical Facilities

Music Library. 8,000 titles; 1,500 recordings. There is a rare 14th century translation of Kukuzel's treatise on notation.

Muzičke Akademije
Gundulićeva 6
YU-41000 Zagreb
Yugoslavia

Telephone. (041) 440-662
Chief Administrator. Professor Ruben Radica, Dean.

The Academy was founded in 1927 as part of Zagreb University. The Croatian Music Institute, which shares library space at the Academy, was established in 1827. The Academy's musicological institute was opened in June 1967 and devotes its activities to the study of Croatian music.

The Academy publishes *The International Review of the Aesthetics and Sociology of Music* (in English, French, German, Italian).

Member of the Assocation Européenne des Conservatoires de Musique, Académies de Musique, et Musikhochschulen.

Academic Information

Enrollment, Music Majors. 324.
Music Faculty. 63.
Music Degrees Offered. Bachelor of Music.
Music Degree Requirements. The equivalent of a Bachelor of Music is awarded after completion of a four-year course.

Musical Facilities

Music Library. The Academy's collection of 20,000 items includes standard research works, recordings, periodicals, and orchestral and choral scores and parts. The Hrvatski Glazbeni Zavod, Knjižnica (Croatian Music Institute), also housed in the library, has a collection of material dealing with 19th and 20th century Croatian music, as well as an anthology of 18th century Croatian church songs. There is also a collection of autographs by Croatian composers.

Muzikološki Institut Muzičke Akademije

Berislavićeva 16
YU-41000 Zagreb
Yugoslavia

Telephone. (041) 417-270
Chief Administrator. This address is the office for the administration of the Academy's Musicological Institute. One of the Institute's main goals is the cataloging of collections which have been inaccessible. Publications of the institute include a catalogue of twentieth century Croatian authors and a catalogue of Croatian chant.

Muzikološki Institut Srpske Akademije Nauka i Umetnosti
Musicological Institute of the Serbian Academy of Sciences and Arts

Knez Mihajlova 35/II
YU-1100 Belgrade
Yugoslavia

Telephone. (011) 633-252, Extension 28
The Institute was founded in 1948. This is not a teaching institution. The small research section of the library contains standard international refrence works, while the score collection mainly comprises works of such Serbian composers as Isidor Bojić, Petar Krstić, and Kosta Manojlović. Rare manuscripts, including Slavonic and Greek liturgical books, are kept on the first floor of the building. There is a collection of ethnomusicological material covering Serbia, Macedonia, and Montenegro.

Visoka Muzička Skola
(High School of Music)

Nas. Karpoš II bb
YU-91000 Skopje
Yugoslavia

Telephone. (091) 51-937
This school is a two-year institution of higher education. Its library was established in 1944 to serve as a practical circulating collection for students and faculty. The holdings include approximately 6,000 items, mainly music scores, and 1,000 recordings. The school has plans to move to a new cultural arts complex on Bulevar Goce Delčev.

Zavod Za Istraživanje Folklora Iff
(Folklore Research Department of the Institute for Philology and Folklore)

Socijalističke revolucije 17
YU-41000 Zagreb
Yugoslavia

Telephone. (041) 410-617
This Institute is not a teaching institution. The department has material on Croatian composers and a collection of written folk melodies and tapes of the Croatian folk tunes.

ZAIRE

Institut National des Arts - Kinshasa
Department of Music

B.P. 8332
Kinshasa
Zaire

The Institut became part of the Université Nationale du Zaire in 1971, and in 1981 became an autonomous institution. The school functions under the governing body of the Conseil d'administration. There are two departments: Dramatic Arts and Music.

ZAMBIA

Institute of African Studies

P.O. Box 50
Lusaka
Zambia

Chief Administrator. Mwesa Mapoma, Music Institute, Contact Person.
Research on traditional African music is undertaken at the Institute.

University of Zambia at Lusaka
Centre for Arts
P.O. Box 32379
Lusaka
Zambia

Telephone. (01) 219624-9
Chief Administrator. M.I. Mapoma, Director; G.O. Twerefoo, Senior Lecturer in Music.

The Centre for Arts, established in 1983, promotes and develops performing and fine arts through documentation and performance.

ZIMBABWE

Zimbabwe Academy of Music
Hillside Road Shore Grounds
P.O. Box 1678
Bulawayo
Zimbabwe

Telephone. (9) 60684, 67195

The Academy specializes in research on African music. Results are applied to music education at teacher-training and primary-education levels.

Zimbabwe College of Music
Civic Center
Rotten Row
Harare C3
Zimbabwe

Telephone. (0) 723803, 723862
The College of Music was founded in 1948.

INSTITUTION INDEX

The Aaron Copland School of Music
  See City University of New York -
  Queens College
Academi Seni Tari Indonesia
  Bandung, Indonesia
Academia de Música Fischer
  (Fischer Academy of Music)
  Caracas, Venezuela
Académie de Musique Prince Rainier III de
  Monaco
  Monaco, Monaco
The Academy of Vocal Arts
  Philadelphia, Pennsylvania
Academy Promusica - Port-au-Prince
  Port-au-Prince, Haiti
Academy Seni Karawitan Indonesia
  Kampus ASKI
  Solo Jawa Tengah, Indonesia
Academy Seni Karawitan Indonesia Padang
  Panjang
  Sumatera Barat, Indonesia
Acadia University
  School of Music
  Wolfville, Nova Scotia, Canada
University of Adelaide
  Elder Conservatorium of Music
  Adelaide, SA 5001, Australia
Advanced Teacher Training College -
  Winneba
  Music Department
  Winneba, Ghana
Akademia Muzyczna im. Feliksa
  Nowowiejskiego w Bydgoszczy
  (F. Nowowiejski Academy of Music of
  Bydgoszczy)
  85-008 Bydgoszcz, Poland
Akademia Muzyczna im. Stanisław
  Moniuszko w Gdańsku
  (S. Moniuszko Academy of Music of
  Gdańsk)
  80-847 Gdańsk, Poland
Akademia Muzyczna Poznaniu
  (State College of Music of Poznań)
  61-808 Poznań, Poland
Akademia Muzyczna w Krakowie
  31-038 Kraków, Poland
Akademia Muzyczna w Lódź
  (Academy of Music of Lódź)
  90-716 Lódź, Poland
Akademia Muzyczna Wroclawiu
  (Academy of Music in Wrocław)
  53-140 Wrocław, Poland
Akademia Muzycznaj im. Fryderyka
  Chopina w Warzawie
  (Frederic Chopin Academy of Music of
  Warsaw)

00-368 Warsaw, Poland
Akademie voor Musiek
  Hilversum Postkode 1217 KR, Netherlands
Akademija za Glasbo
  (Musical Academy)
  YU-61000 Ljubljana, Yugoslavia
Akhil Bharatiya Gandharva Mahavidyalaya
  Mandal
  Brahmanpuri, Miraj 416410, India
University of Akron
  Department of Music
  Akron, Ohio
University of Alabama
  School of Music
  University, Alabama
Alabama State University
  School of Music
  Montgomery, Alabama
University of Alaska
  Music Department
  Fairbanks, Alaska
University of Alberta
  Department of Music
  Edmonton, Alberta, Canada
Aleppo Institute of Music
  Aleppo, Syria
Alma-Ata Kurmangazy State Conservatory
  480091 Alma-Ata 91, Kazahskaja SSR,
  U.S.S.R.
American Conservatory of Music
  Chicago, Illinois
Andrews University
  Department of Music
  Berrien Springs, Michigan
Appalachian State University
  Department of Music
  Boone, North Carolina
University of Arizona
  School of Music
  Tucson, Arizona
Arizona State University
  School of Music
  Tempe, Arizona
University of Arkansas
  Department of Music
  Fayetteville, Arkansas
Arkansas State University
  Department of Music
  State University, Arkansas
Arkansas Tech University
  Department of Music
  Russellville, Arkansas
University of the Arts
  See Philadelphia College of the
  Performing Arts

Astrakhan State Conservatory
  414000 Astrakhan, Rossiskaja SFSR,
  U.S.S.R.
Auburn University
  Department of Music
  Auburn, Alabama
University of Auckland
  Faculty of Music
  Auckland, New Zealand
Austin Peay State University
  Department of Music
  Clarksville, Tennessee
A.V. Nezhdanova Odessa Conservatory
  270000 Odessa, Ukrainskaja SSR,
  U.S.S.R.
Azerbaijan S.S.R. U. Gajibekov State
  Conservatory
  370014 Baku, Azerbajdžanskaja SSR,
  U.S.S.R.
Azusa Pacific University
  School of Music
  Azusa, California
Baejae College
  Department of Music
  Choongnam 30001, South Korea
Baldwin-Wallace College
  Conservatory of Music
  Berea, Ohio
Ball State University
  School of Music
  Muncie, Indiana
Banaras Hindu University
  Uttar Pradesh 221005, India
Baylor University
  School of Music
  Waco, Texas
Bemidji State University
  Music Department
  Bemidji, Minnesota
Benjamin T. Rome School of Music
  See Catholic University of America
Bennington College
  Music Department
  Bennington, Vermont
Berklee College of Music
  Boston, Massachusetts
Bhavan's Bharatiya Sangeet and Nartan
  Skikshapeeth
  (Academy of Music and Dance)
  Bombay 4000007, India
Biola University
  Department of Music
  La Mirada, California
Birmingham School of Music
  City of Birmingham Polytechnic
  Birmingham B3 3HG, United Kingdom

495

Bob Jones University
  Division of Music
  Greenville, South Carolina
Boise State University
  Music Department
  Boise, Idaho
Boston Conservatory of Music
  Boston, Massachusetts
Boston University
  School of Music
  Boston, Massachusetts
Bowling Green State University
  College of Musical Arts
  Bowling Green, Ohio
Bradley University
  Division of Music and Theatre Arts
  Peoria, Illinois
Brandeis University
  Department of Music
  Waltham, Massachusetts
Brandon University
  School of Music
  Brandon, Manitoba, Canada
Brigham Young University
  Department of Music
  Provo, Utah
University of British Columbia
  School of Music
  Vancouver, British Columbia, Canada
Brooklyn College
  See City University of New York -
  Brooklyn College
Brown University
  Department of Music
  Providence, Rhode Island
Bulgarian State Conservatoire
  Sofia 1505, Bulgaria
Butler University
  Jordan College of Fine Arts
  Indianapolis, Indiana
Byelorussian State Conservatory
  220030 Minsk, Belorusskaja SSR,
  U.S.S.R.
Cairo Conservatory of Music
  Academy of Arts
  Giza, Egypt
University of Calgary
  Department of Music
  Calgary, Alberta, Canada
University of California, Berkeley
  Department of Music
  Berkeley, California
University of California, Davis
  Department of Music
  Davis, California
University of California, Irvine
  School of Fine Arts
  Irvine, California
University of California, Los Angeles
  Department of Music
  Los Angeles, California
University of California, Riverside
  Department of Music
  Riverside, California
University of California, San Diego
  Department of Music
  La Jolla, California
University of California, Santa Barbara
  Department of Music
  Santa Barbara, California
University of California, Santa Cruz
  Music Board, Division of the Arts
  Santa Cruz, California
California Institute of the Arts
  School of Music
  Valencia, California

California State University, Chico
  Department of Music
  Chico, California
California State University, Fresno
  Department of Music
  Fresno, California
California State University, Fullerton
  Department of Music
  Fullerton, California
California State University, Hayward
  Department of Music
  Hayward, California
California State University, Long Beach
  Department of Music
  Long Beach, California
California State University, Los Angeles
  Department of Music
  Los Angeles, California
California State University, Northridge
  Music Department
  Northridge, California
California State University, Sacramento
  Department of Music
  Sacramento, California
Canberra School of Music
  Canberra 2601, Australia
University of Canterbury
  Faculty of Music
  Christchurch 1, New Zealand
University of Cape Coast
  Department of Music
  Cape Coast, Ghana
University of Cape Town
  Faculty of Music
  Cape Town, Republic of South Africa
Carnegie-Mellon University
  Department of Music
  Pittsburgh, Pennsylvania
Case Western Reserve University
  Department of Music
  Cleveland, Ohio
The Catholic University of America
  The Benjamin T. Rome School of Music
  Washington, District of Columbia
University of Central Arkansas
  Department of Music
  Conway, Arkansas
Central Conservatory of Music
  Beijing, People's Republic of China
University of Central Florida
  Department of Music
  Orlando, Florida
Central Michigan University
  Department of Music
  Mount Pleasant, Michigan
Central Missouri State University
  Department of Music
  Warrensburg, Missouri
Central State University
  Department of Music
  Edmond, Oklahoma
Central Washington University
  Department of Music
  Ellensburg, Washington
Centro Nacional de Artes "CENAR"
  San Salvador, El Salvador
Centro para las Culturas Populares y
  Tradicionales (CCPYT)
  c/o Consejo Nacional de la Cultura
  (CONAC)
  Caracas 1060, Venezuela
University of Chicago
  Department of Music
  Chicago, Illinois

Chicago Musical College
  See Roosevelt University
Chinese University of Hong Kong
  Faculty of Music
  New Territories, Hong Kong
University of Cincinnati
  College-Conservatory of Music
  Cincinnati, Ohio
City College
  See City University of New York - City
  College
City of Leeds College of Music
  Leeds LS2 8BH, United Kingdom
City University of New York - Brooklyn
  College
  Conservatory of Music
  Brooklyn, New York
City University of New York - City College
  Department of Music
  New York, New York
City University of New York - Graduate
  School and University Center
  Doctoral Program in Music
  New York, New York
City University of New York - Hunter
  College
  Department of Music
  New York, New York
City University of New York - Queens
  College
  The Aaron Copland School of Music
  Flushing, New York
The Claremont Graduate School
  Music Department
  Claremont, California
Cleveland Institute of Music
  Cleveland, Ohio
Cleveland State University
  Department of Music
  Cleveland, Ohio
Colegio del Sagrado Corazon de Jesus
  Department of Music
  Iloilo City, The Philippines
College of Music and Dance - Pyongyang
  Pyongyang, North Korea
University of Colorado at Boulder
  College of Music
  Boulder, Colorado
University of Colorado at Denver
  College of Music
  Denver, Colorado
Colorado State University
  Department of Music, Theatre, and
  Dance
  Fort Collins, Colorado
Columbia University
  Department of Music
  New York, New York
Columbus College
  Department of Music
  Columbus, Georgia
Combs College of Music
  Philadelphia, Pennsylvania
University of Connecticut
  Department of Music
  Storrs, Connecticut
Consejo Gral. de Educación
  Escuela de Música
  Provincia del Chaco, Argentina
Consejo Nacional de la Cultura (CONAC)
  Caracas 1060, Venezuela
Conservatoire de Musique
  Tunis, Tunisia
Conservatoire de Musique - Marrakesh
  Marrakesh, Morocco

Conservatoire de Musique de Genève
1204 Genève, Switzerland

Conservatoire de Musique de La
Chaux-de-Fonds - Le Locle
2300 La Chaux-de-Fonds, Switzerland

Conservatoire de Musique de la Ville de
Luxembourg
2134 Luxembourg City, Luxembourg

Conservatoire de Musique de Lausanne
1000 Lausanne, Switzerland

Conservatoire de Musique de Neuchâtel
2000 Neuchâtel, Switzerland

Conservatoire de Musique
d'Esch-sur-Alzette
4002 Esch-sur-Alzette, Luxembourg

Conservatoire de Musique et de
Déclamation - Algiers
Algiers, Algeria

Conservatoire de Tanger
Tanger, Morocco

Conservatoire et Académie de Musique -
Fribourg
1700 Fribourg, Switzerland

Conservatoire Municipal de Musique et de
Déclamation - Oran
Oran, Algeria

Conservatoire National de Musique, de
Danse, et d'Art Dramatique
(National Conservatory of Music, Dance,
and Dramatic Art)
Dakar, Senegal

Conservatoire National de Musique, de
Danse, et d'Art Dramatique - Ribad
Ribad, Morocco

Conservatoire National de Région, Bordeaux
Bordeaux, France

Conservatoire National de Région, Marseille
13001 Marseilles, France

Conservatoire National de Région,
Strasbourg
67000 Strasbourg, France

Conservatoire National des Artes et Métiers
Nouméa Cedex, New Caledonia

Conservatoire National Supérieur de
Musique
75008 Paris, France

Conservatoire National Supérieur de
Musique de Lyon
69005 Lyon, France

Conservatoire of Hò Chí Minh City
*Hò Chí Minh City, Socialist Republic of
Vietnam*

Conservatoire Royal de Musique de
Bruxelles
1000 Bruxelles, Belgium

Conservatoire Royal de Musique de Liège
B-4000 Liège, Belgium

Conservatoire Royal de Musique de Mons
7000 Mons, Belgium

Conservatório Brasileiro de Música
20,000 Rio de Janeiro, Brazil

Conservatorio de Las Rosas
Jardin Las Rosas 347
Morelia, Michoacán, Mexico

Conservatorio de Música de Chascomús
Provincia de Buenos Aires, Argentina

Conservatorio de Música de Morón
Provincia de Buenos Aires, Argentina

Conservatorio de Música del Ibagué
Ibagué, Tolima, Colombia

Conservatorio de Música "Julián Aquirre"
Provincia de Buenos Aires, Argentina

Conservatorio di Musica "A. Vivaldi"
Allessandria, Italy

Conservatorio di Musica "Arrigo Boito"
43100 Parma, Italy

Conservatorio di Musica "Benedetto
Marcello"
30124 Venice, Italy

Conservatorio di Musica "Cesare Pollini"
Padua, Italy

Conservatorio di Musica "Claudio
Monteverdi"
I-39100 Bolzano, Italy

Conservatorio di Musica "Francesco
Morlacchi"
Perugia, Italy

Conservatorio di Musica "G. Frescobaldi"
L'Aquila, Italy

Conservatorio di Musica "G. Tartini" e
Scuola Media Statale Annessa
34132 Trieste, Italy

Conservatorio di Musica "Giocchino
Rossini"
61100 Pesaro, Italy

Conservatorio di Musica "Giuseppe Verdi"
20122 Milan, Italy

Conservatorio di Musica "Niccolo Paganini"
Genoa, Italy

Conservatorio di Musica "Niccolo Piccinni"
70124 Bari, Italy

Conservatorio di Musica "San Pietro a
Majella"
80138 Naples, Italy

Conservatorio di Musica "Santa Cecilia"
00187 Rome, Italy

Conservatorio di Musica "Vincenzo Bellini"
90133 Palermo (Sicily), Italy

Conservatorio Dramático e Musical de São
Paulo
São Paulo, Brazil

Conservatório Municipal - Oporto
Oporto, Portugal

Conservatorio Municipal de Música
Asunción, Paraguay

Conservatorio Municipal de Música
"Manuel de Falla"
1042 Buenos Aires, Argentina

Conservatório Nacional - Lisbon
Lisbon 2, Portugal

Conservatorio Nacional de México
Mexico City 5, D.F., Mexico

Conservatorio Nacional de Música
Departamento de Música
Bogatá, Colombia

Conservatorio Nacional de Música
(National Conservatory of Music)
Lima 1, Peru

Conservatorio Nacional de Música
1a A.N. no. 821
San Salvador, El Salvador

Conservatorio Nacional de Música - Caracas
Juan José Landaeta
Caracas, Venezuela

Conservatorio Nacional de Música -
Guatemala City
Guatemala City, Guatemala

Conservatorio Nacional de Musica - La Paz
(National Conservatory of Music - La
Paz)
La Paz, Bolivia

Conservatorio Nacional de Música - Quito
Quito, Ecuador

Conservatorio Nacional de Música - Santo
Domingo
Santo Domingo, Dominican Republic

Conservatorio Nacional de Música "Carlos
López Buchardo"
1024 Buenos Aires, Argentina

Conservatorio Provincial de Música -
Buenos Aires
Provincia de Buenos Aires, Argentina

Conservatorio Provincial de Música de
Bahía Blanca
Provincia de Buenos Aires, Argentina

Conservatorio Provincial de Música de
Chivilcoy
Provincia de Buenos Aires, Argentina

Conservatorio Provincial Gilardo Gilardi
Provincia de Buenos Aires, Argentina

Conservatorio Statale di Musica "G.
Pierluigi da Palestrina"
09100 Cagliari, Italy

Conservatorio Statale di Musica "Giovanni
Battista Martini"
40126 Bologna, Italy

Conservatorio Statale di Musica "Giuseppe
Verdi" e Scuola Media Annessa
10123 Turin, Italy

Conservatorio Superior de Música de
Barcelona
Barcelona 9, Spain

Conservatorio Superior de Música y Escuela
de Arte Dramatico y Danza
Cordoba, Spain

Conservatorio Superior de Música y Escuela
de Arte Dramatico
41002 Seville, Spain

Conservatorio Superior de Música y Escuela
de Arte Dramatico y Danza de Valencia
Valencia, Spain

Conservatorium voor Muziek-Nederland
6211 KL Maastricht, Netherlands

Conservatorul de Musică George Dima
(Conservatory of Music)
3400 Cluj-Napoca, Romania

Conservatorul de Muzică Ciprian
Porumbescu
(Conservatory of Music)
70732 Bucharest, Romania

Conservatorul Georges Enescu
(Conservatory of Music)
6600 Iasi, Romania

Conservatory of Chinese Music
Beijing, People's Republic of China

Conservatory of Music of Puerto Rico
Santurce, Puerto Rico

Converse College
School of Music
Spartanburg, South Carolina

Cornell University
Department of Music
Ithaca, New York

Corporación Universitaria Adventista
Department of Music
A-1 Medellín, Colombia

Crane School of Music
See State University of New York College
at Potsdam.

Cultural Training Center - Kingston
School of Music
Kingston 5, Jamaica

The Curtis Institute of Music
Philadelphia, Pennsylvania

Cuttington University College
Monrovia, Liberia

Dâeshgâhé Farabi
(Farabi University)
Tehran, Iran

Dalhousie University
Department of Music
Halifax, Nova Scotia, Canada

Dana School of Music
See Youngstown State University

University of Dar es Salaam
Dar es Salaam, Tanzania
University of Delaware
Department of Music
Newark, Delaware
Delta State University
Department of Music
Cleveland, Mississippi
University of Denver
Lamont School of Music
Denver, Colorado
DePaul University
School of Music
Chicago, Illinois
DePauw University
School of Music
Greencastle, Indiana
Det Fynske Musikkonservatorium
(The Funen Academy of Music)
5000 Odense C, Denmark
Det Jydske Musikkonservatorium
(Royal Academy of Music, Aarhus)
8210 Aarhus V, Denmark
Det Kongelige Danske
Musikkonservatorium
(The Royal Danish Academy of Music)
1574 København V, Denmark
Direccion de Institutos Artisticos
Municipales
Asunción, Paraguay
Donetsk Musical-Pedagogical Institute
*340086 Donetsk, Ukrainskaja SSR,
U.S.S.R.*
Drake University
Department of Music
Des Moines, Iowa
Duke University
Department of Music
Durham, North Carolina
Duquesne University
School of Music
Pittsburgh, Pennsylvania
East Carolina University
School of Music
Greenville, North Carolina
The East Helsinki Music Institute
SF-00820 Helsinki, Finland
East Texas State University
Department of Music
Commerce, Texas
Eastern Illinois University
Department of Music
Charleston, Illinois
Eastern Kentucky University
Department of Music
Richmond, Kentucky
Eastern Michigan University
Department of Music
Ypsilanti, Michigan
Eastern New Mexico University
School of Music
Portales, New Mexico
Eastern Washington University
Department of Music
Cheney, Washington
Eastman School of Music
See University of Rochester
École de Musique Ste. Trinité
Port-au-Prince, Haiti
École Nationale de Musique - Casablanca
Casablanca, Morocco
École Nationale de Musique - Meknes
Meknes, Morocco
Ege Üniversitesi
(Aegean University)
Bornova, Izmir, Turkey

Elder Conservatorium of Music
See University of Adelaide
Elizabeth University of Music
Hiroshima 730, Japan
Emporia State University
Division of Music
Emporia, Kansas
Erevan Komitas State Conservatory
*375009 Erevan 9, Armjanskaja SSR,
U.S.S.R.*
Escola de Música - Minas Gerais
Minas Gerais, Brazil
Escola de Música de Brasília
Brasília, D.F., Brazil
Escola de Música e Belas Artes do Paraná
Paraná, Brazil
Escuela de Música - Heredia
Universidad Nacional
Heredia, Costa Rica
Escuela de Música Lino Gallardo
Avenida Principal de la Castellana
Caracas, Venezuela
Escuela de Música Prudencio Esás
Caracas, Venezuela
Escuela Municipal de Canto
Asunción, Paraguay
Escuela Nacional de Música
Universidad Nacional Autónoma de
México
Mexico City, D.F. 04100, Mexico
Escuela Nacional de Música
Tegucigalpa, D.C., Honduras
Escuela Nacional de Música - Managua
c/o Ministry of Culture
Managua, Nicaragua
Escuela Nacional de Música - Panama City
Panama City, Panama
Escuela Nacional de Música "José Ángel
Lamas"
Caracas 1010, Venezuela
Escuela Nacional de Opera - Caracas
Dirección de Cultura y Bellas Artes del
Ministerio de Educación
Caracas, Venezuela
Escuela Superior de Pedagogia Musical
(Higher School of Music Teaching)
28008 Madrid, Spain
Escuela Universitaria de Música -
Montevideo
Montevideo, Uruguay
Esther Boyer College of Music
See Temple University
Evangelische Kirchenmusikschule der
Kirchenprovinz Sachsen
(Evangelical Church Music School of the
Church Province Saxony)
*DDR-4020 Halle (Saale), German
Democratic Republic*
University of Evansville
Music Department
Evansville, Indiana
Ewha Women's University
College of Music
Seoul 120, South Korea
Fachakademie für Music - Augsburg
Leopold Mozart-Konservatorium der
Stadt Augsburg
Augsberg, Federal Republic of Germany
Fachakademie für Musik - München
Richard Strauss-Konservatorium der
Stadt
*München 80, Federal Republic of
Germany*
Fachakademie für Musik - Nürnberg
Konservatorium der Stadt Nürnberg
Nürnberg, Federal Republic of Germany

Faculdade de Música Mãe de Deus
86100 Londrina, Paraná, Brazil
Faculdade de Música "Sagrado Coracão de
Jesus"
São Paulo, Brazil
Faculdade Santa Marcelina
05006 São Paulo, Brazil
Facultet za Muzička umetnost
(Faculty for Music and Arts)
YU-91000 Skopje, Yugoslavia
Far-Eastern Pedagogical Institute of the
Arts
*690678 Vladivostok, Rossiskaja SFSR,
U.S.S.R.*
Ferenc Liszt Academy of Music
Budapest VI, Hungary
University of Florida
Department of Music
Gainesville, Florida
Florida State University
School of Music
Tallahassee, Florida
Folklore Center - Qatar
Doha, Qatar
Fort Hays State University
Department of Music
Hays, Kansas
Fundação Universidade de Brasília
(University of Brasília)
70910 Brasília, D.F., Brazil
George Mason University
Department of Performing Arts - Music
Division
Fairfax, Virginia
University of Georgia
School of Music
Athens, Georgia
Georgia Southern College
Department of Music
Statesboro, Georgia
Georgia State University
School of Music
Atlanta, Georgia
University of Ghana
School of Performing Arts
Legon, Ghana
Glassboro State College
Department of Music
Glassboro, New Jersey
Gnessinsky State Musical and Pedagogical
Institute
*121069 Moscow G-69, Rossiskaja SFSR,
U.S.S.R.*
Gorky M.I. Glinka State Conservatory
603005 Gorky, Rossiskaja SFSR, U.S.S.R.
Guangzhou Conservatory of Music
*Guangdong Province, People's Republic of
China*
Guildhall School of Music and Drama
London EC2Y 8DT, United Kingdom
Hacettepe Üniversitesi
(Hacettepe University)
Ankara, Turkey
Hanyang University
College of Music
Seoul 133, South Korea
Harbin Normal University
Department of Music
*Heilong Jiang Province, People's Republic
of China*
Hardin-Simmons University
School of Music
Abilene, Texas
University of Hartford
Hartt School of Music
West Hartford, Connecticut

Hartt School of Music
  See University of Hartford
Harvard University
  Department of Music
  Cambridge, Massachusetts
University of Hawaii at Manoa
  Music Department
  Honolulu, Hawaii
Hellenic Odeion - Athens
  (Greek Conservatory)
  Athens, Greece
Henderson State University
  Department of Music
  Arkadelphia, Arkansas
Hermann-Zilcher-Konservatorium
  *D-8700 Würzburg, Federal Republic of
  Germany*
Higher Institute of Music and Performing
Arts - Safat
  c/o Undersecretary
  Safat 133002, Kuwait
Hochschule der Künste Berlin
  *1000 Berlin 10, Federal Republic of
  Germany*
Hochschule für Gestaltende Kunst und
Musik
  (State College for Creative Art and
  Music)
  *2800 Bremen 1, Federal Republic of
  Germany*
Hochschule für Music Franz Liszt
  *DDR 5300 Weimar, German Democratic
  Republic*
Hochschule für Music und Darstellende
Kunst Hamburg
  *2000 Hamburg 13, Federal Republic of
  Germany*
Hochschule für Musik - München
  *8000 München 2, Federal Republic of
  Germany*
Hochschule für Musik - Würzburg
  *D-8700 Würzburg, Federal Republic of
  Germany*
Hochschule für Musik Carl Maria von
Weber
  *DDR 8010 Dresden, German Democratic
  Republic*
Hochschule für Musik Felix
Mendelssohn-Bartholdy
  *7010 Leipzig, German Democratic
  Republic*
Hochschule für Musik und Darstellande
Kunst "Mozarteum" Salzburg
  (College of Music and Dramatic Art
  "Mozarteum")
  5020 Salzburg, Austria
Hochschule für Musik und Darstellende
Kunst Frankfurt am Main
  *6000 Frankfurt am Main 1, Federal
  Republic of Germany*
Hochschule für Musik und Darstellende
Kunst Graz
  A-8010 Graz, Austria
Hochschule für Musik und Darstellende
Kunst Wien
  (College of Music and Dramatic Art)
  1030 Wien, Austria
Hochschule für Musik und Theater
Hannover
  *3000 Hannover 1, Federal Republic of
  Germany*
Hofstra University
  Department of Music
  Hempstead, New York

University of the Holy Ghost
  Institute of Musicology and School of
  Music
  Jounieh, Lebanon
University of Hong Kong
  Faculty of Music, Hong Kong
The Hong Kong Academy for Performing
Arts
  School of Music
  Wanchai, Hong Kong
Hoschschule für Music Hans Eisler
  *DDR Berlin 1080, German Democratic
  Republic*
Hoseo College
  Department of Music
  Choongnam Province 330, South Korea
University of Houston
  School of Music
  Houston, Texas
Howard University
  Department of Music
  Washington, District of Columbia
Hunter College
  See City University of New York -
  Hunter College
University of Idaho
  School of Music
  Moscow, Idaho
University of Ife
  Department of Music
  Ile-Ife, Nigeria
University of Illinois
  School of Music
  Urbana, Illinois
Illinois State University
  Department of Music
  Normal, Illinois
Illinois Wesleyan University
  School of Music
  Bloomington, Illinois
Indiana State University
  Department of Music
  Terre Haute, Indiana
Indiana University - Bloomington
  School of Music
  Bloomington, Indiana
Indiana University of Pennsylvania
  Department of Music
  Indiana, Pennsylvania
Indira Kala Sangit Vishwavidyalaya
  (University of Music and Fine Arts)
  Madhya Pradesh 491881, India
Institut Kesenian Jakarta
  Taman Ismial Marzuki
  Jakarta, Indonesia
Institut National de Musique et de Danse -
Kenitra
  Kenitra, Morocco
Institut National des Arts - Kinshasa
  Department of Music
  Kinshasa, Zaire
Institut Seni Indonesia
  Yogyakarta, Indonesia
Institut Supérieure de Musique - Tunis
  Tunis, Tunisia
Institute of Aesthetic Studies
  Colombo 7, Sri Lanka
Institute of African Studies
  Lusaka, Zambia
Institute of Beaux Arts - Abidjan
  Department of Music
  Abidjan, Republic of Ivory Coast
Institute of Fine Arts
  Faculty of Music
  Rangoon, Burma

Institute of Music and Drama
  Khartoum, The Sudan
Institute of Music and Drama - Omdurman
  Omdurman, The Sudan
Institute of Technology and Vocational
Education
  Faculty of Drama and Music
  Bankok 10300, Thailand
Instituti i Lartë i Arteve
  (Institute of Fine Arts)
  Tiranë, Albania
Instituto de Letras a Artes
  96100 Pelotas RS, Brazil
Instituto de Música da Bahia
  Bahia, Brazil
Instituto Musical de Cartagena
  Cartagena, Bolívar, Colombia
Instituto Professionale Artigianato Liutario
e del Legno
  Palazzo dell'Arte
  Cremona, Italy
Instituto Santa Ana
  Department of Music
  Buenos Aires, Argentina
Instituto Superior de Arte
  Facultad de Música
  Playa, Cuba
Interamerican University
  Music Department
  San German, Puerto Rico
University of Iowa
  School of Music
  Iowa City, Iowa
Iowa State University
  Department of Music
  Ames, Iowa
Istanbul Teknik Üniversitesi
  (Istanbul Technical University)
  Istanbul, Turkey
Istanbul Üniversitesi
  (University of Istanbul)
  Istanbul, Turkey
Ithaca College
  School of Music
  Ithaca, New York
Jackson State University
  Department of Music
  Jackson, Mississippi
Jacksonville State University
  Department of Music
  Jacksonville, Alabama
James Madison University
  Department of Music
  Harrisonburg, Virginia
Jami 'at Baghdad
  (University of Baghdad)
  Baghdad, Iraq
Janáčkova Akademie
  (Janáček's Academy of Music and
  Dramatic Arts)
  Brno 66215, Czechoslovakia
Jersey City State College
  Music Department
  Jersey City, New Jersey
The Jerusalem Rubin Academy of Music
and Dance
  Jerusalem, Israel
Jordan College of Fine Arts
  See Butler University
The Juilliard School
  New York, New York
Kalakshetra
  Tiruvanmiyur
  Madras 600041, India

Kangreung National University
  Department of Music and Fine Arts
  Gang-weon, South Korea
University of Kansas
  School of Fine Arts
  Lawrence, Kansas
Kansas State University
  Department of Music
  Manhattan, Kansas
Karnatak University
  College of Music
  Kharnataka 580003, India
Karol Szymanowski Academy of Music of
  Katowice
  Katowice, Poland
Kazan State Conservatory
  420015 Kazan 15, Rossiskaja SFSR,
  U.S.S.R.
Keimyung University
  College of Music
  Taegu, South Korea
Kent State University
  School of Music
  Kent, Ohio
University of Kentucky
  School of Music
  Lexington, Kentucky
Kenya Conservatoire of Music
  Nairobi, Kenya
Kharkov State Institute of Arts
  310003 Kharkov, U.S.S.R.
Kiev P.I. Tchaikovsky Conservatory
  252001 Kiev, Ukrainskaja SSR, U.S.S.R.
King Saud University
  Riyadh Conservatory
  Riyadh 11451, Saudi Arabia
Kongju National Teachers' College
  Department of Music
  Chung Nam 301, South Korea
Koninklijk Beiaardschool Jef Denyn
  2800 Mechelen, Belgium
Koninklijk Conservatorium voor Muziek en
  Dans
  (Royal Conservatory of Music and
  Dance)
  2595 CA The Hague, Netherlands
Koninklijk Muziekconservatorium van
  Brussel
  1000 Brussels, Belgium
Koninklijk Muziekconservatorium van
  Ghent
  9000 Ghent, Belgium
Koninklijk Vlaams Conservatorium van
  Antwerpen
  (Royal Flemish School of Music)
  2018 Antwerp, Belgium
Konservatorium für Musik und Theater
  CH-3011 Berne, Switzerland
Konservatorium und Musikhochschule -
  Zürich
  8050 Zürich, Switzerland
Konzervatoř v Praze
  (State Conservatory Prague)
  Praha 110 00, Czechoslovakia
Konzervatorium - Bratislava
  Bratislava 811 06, Czechoslovakia
Korean Union College
  Department of Music
  Seoul, South Korea
Kratikon Odeion Thessaloniki
  (State Conservatory of Music)
  Thessaloniki, Greece
Kunitachi College of Music
  Tokyo 190, Japan

Kuopion Konservatorio
  70100 Kuopio, Finland
Kyung Hee University
  College of Music
  Seoul 131, South Korea
Kyungpook National University
  College of Music and Visual Arts
  Taegu 635, South Korea
University of Lagos
  Department of Music
  Lagos, Nigeria
Lamar University
  Department of Music
  Beaumont, Texas
Lamont School of Music
  See University of Denver
Latvian S.S.R. Y. Vitol State Conservatory
  226050 Riga, Latvijskaya SSR, U.S.S.R.
Lawrence University
  Conservatory of Music
  Appleton, Wisconsin
Lebanese Academy of Fine Arts
  Beirut, Lebanon
Lebanese National Conservatory
  Eastern Section
  Beirut, Lebanon
Leningrad N.A. Rimsky-Korsakov State
  Conservatory
  192041 Leningrad, Rossiskaja SFSR,
  U.S.S.R.
Levinsky Teachers College
  Music Teachers Seminary
  Tel-Aviv, Israel
Lewis and Clark College
  Music Department
  Portland, Oregon
University of Liberia
  Department of Music
  Monrovia, Liberia
Lithuanian State Conservatory
  232001 Vilnius, Litovskaja SSR, U.S.S.R.
Long Island University - C.W. Post Campus
  Music Department
  Greenvale, New York
Louisiana State University
  School of Music
  Baton Rouge, Louisiana
Louisiana Tech University
  Department of Music
  Ruston, Louisiana
University of Louisville
  School of Music
  Louisville, Kentucky
Lourdes College
  Department of Music
  Cagayan de Oro City, The Philippines
University of Lowell
  College of Music
  Lowell, Massachusetts
Loyola University
  College of Music
  New Orleans, Louisiana
Lvov M.V. Lysenko State Conservatory
  290005 Lvov, Ukrainskaja SSR, U.S.S.R.
University of Madras
  Department of Indian Music
  Madras 600005, India
University of Maine
  School of Performing Arts
  Orono, Maine
Makerere University
  Department of Music, Dance, and Drama
  Kampala, Uganda
Mandalay School of Music, Dance,
  Painting, and Sculpture
  Mandalay, Burma

Manhattan School of Music
  New York, New York
University of Manitoba
  School of Music
  Winnipeg, Manitoba, Canada
Mankato State University
  Department of Music
  Mankato, Minnesota
Mannes College of Music
  New York, New York
Mansfield University
  Department of Music
  Mansfield, Pennsylvania
Marshall University
  Department of Music
  Huntington, West Virginia
University of Maryland - Baltimore County
  Department of Music
  Catonsville, Maryland
University of Maryland - College Park
  Department of Music
  College Park, Maryland
Marywood College
  Music Department
  Scranton, Pennsylvania
Mason Gross School of the Arts
  See Rutgers, The State University of New
  Jersey
University of Massachusetts at Amherst
  Department of Music and Dance
  Amherst, Massachusetts
Massachusetts Institute of Technology
  Department of Music and Theater Arts
  Cambridge, Massachusetts
McGill University
  Faculty of Music
  Montreal, Québec, Canada
McMaster University
  Department of Music
  Hamilton, Ontario, Canada
McNeese State University
  Department of Music
  Lake Charles, Louisiana
Meadows School of the Arts
  See Southern Methodist University
University of Melbourne
  Faculty of Music
  Victoria 3052, Australia
Memphis State University
  Music Department
  Memphis, Tennessee
University of Miami
  School of Music
  Coral Gables, Florida
Miami University
  Department of Music
  Oxford, Ohio
University of Michigan
  School of Music
  Ann Arbor, Michigan
Michigan State University
  School of Music
  East Lansing, Michigan
Middle Tennessee State University
  Department of Music
  Murfreesboro, Tennessee
Military Institute of Music - Sana'a
  Sana'a, Yemen Arab Republic
Millikin University
  School of Music
  Decatur, Illinois
Mills College
  Music Department
  Oakland, California

Mimar Sinan Üniversitesi
(Mimar Sinan University)
Istanbul, Turkey
Ministry of Information
Music Division
Baghdad, Iraq
University of Minnesota - Duluth
Department of Music
Duluth, Minnesota
University of Minnesota - Twin Cities
School of Music
Minneapolis, Minnesota
University of Mississippi
Department of Music
University, Mississippi
University of Missouri - Columbia
Department of Music
Columbia, Missouri
University of Missouri - Kansas City
Conservatory of Music
Kansas City, Missouri
Moldavian S.S.R. G. Musichesku State
Conservatory
*277014 Kishinev, Moldavskaja SSR,
U.S.S.R.*
University of Montana
Department of Music
Missoula, Montana
Montana State University
Department of Music
Bozeman, Montana
Montclair State College
Department of Music
Upper Montclair, New Jersey
University of Montevallo
Department of Music
Montevallo, Alabama
Moorhead State University
Music Department
Moorhead, Minnesota
Morehead State University
Department of Music
Morehead, Kentucky
Moscow P.I. Tchaikovsky State
Conservatory
*103009 Moscow K-9, Rossiskaja SFSR,
U.S.S.R.*
Musashino Ongaku Daigaku
(Musashino College of Music)
Tokyo 176, Japan
The Music Academy, Madras
Teachers' College of Music
Madras 600 014, India
Musicdramatiska Skolan i Stockholm
(Music Drama School)
115 27 Stockholm, Sweden
Musik-Akademie der Stadt Basel
Schola Cantorum Basiliensis
CH-4051 Basel, Switzerland
Musik-Akademie der Stadt Basel
(Konservatorium)
Konservatorium (Musikhochschule)
Basel, Switzerland
Musikhochschule des Saarlandes
*6600 Saarbrücken 3, Federal Republic of
Germany*
Musikhochschule Lübeck
Grosse Petersgrube 17-29
*2400 Lübeck, Federal Republic of
Germany*
Musikhögskolan i Göteberg
412 56 Göteberg, Sweden
Musikhögskolan i Stockholm
National College of Music
115 31 Stockholm, Sweden

Musikhögskolan och Teaterhögskolan i
Malmö
S-200 44 Malmö, Sweden
Musikschule und Konservatorium
Schaffhausen
Schaffhausen, Switzerland
Musikschule und Konservatorium
Winterthur
CH-8400 Winterthur, Switzerland
Muzička Akademija
YU-11000 Belgrade, Yugoslavia
Muzička Akademija a Sarajevo
YU-71000 Sarajevo, Yugoslavia
Muzičke Akademije
YU-41000 Zagreb, Yugoslavia
Muzikološki Institut Muzičke Akademije
YU-41000 Zagreb, Yugoslavia
Muzikološki Institut Srpske Akademije
Nauka i Umetnosti
Musicological Institute of the Serbian
Academy of Sciences and Arts
YU-1100 Belgrade, Yugoslavia
National Conservatoire Dan Adyel
Fez, Morocco
National Conservatoire of Tetouan
Tetouan, Morocco
National Conservatory of Music - Damascus
Damascus, Syria
National Conservatory of Music - Tehran
Tehran, Iran
National Institute of Music - Sana'a
Sana'a, Yemen Arab Republic
National Institute of the Arts
Music Department
*Taipei County, Taiwan (Republic of
China)*
National Taiwan Academy of Arts
*Taipei County, Taiwan (Republic of
China)*
University of Nebraska - Lincoln
School of Music
Lincoln, Nebraska
University of Nebraska - Omaha
Department of Music
Omaha, Nebraska
Nederlands Instituut voor Kerkmuziek
Utrecht, Netherlands
University of Nevada, Las Vegas
Department of Music
Las Vegas, Nevada
University of Nevada, Reno
Department of Music
Reno, Nevada
New England Conservatory
Boston, Massachusetts
University of New Hampshire
Department of Music
Durham, New Hampshire
University of New Mexico
Department of Music
Albuquerque, New Mexico
New Mexico State University
Department of Music
Las Cruces, New Mexico
University of New Orleans
Department of Music
New Orleans, Louisiana
New School of Music
See Temple University
New South Wales State Conservatorium of
Music
Sydney NSW 2000, Australia
New York University - College of Arts and
Sciences
Department of Music
New York, New York

New York University - School of Education,
Health, Nursing, and Arts Professions
Department of Music and Music
Education
New York, New York
Newcastle Conservatorium of Music
Newcastle, NSW 2300, Australia
Newcomb College
See Tulane University
Nhac Viên Hànôi
(Conservatoire of Hànôi)
Hànôi, Socialist Republic of Vietnam
University of Nigeria
Department of Music
Nsukka, Anambra State, Nigeria
Nikos Skalkotas Conservatory
Athens 11141, Greece
Nordjysk Musikkonservatorium
(North Jutland Academy of Music)
9000 Aalborg, Denmark
Norfolk State University
Department of Music
Norfolk, Virginia
Norges Musikkhøgskole
(The Norwegian State Academy of Music)
N-0130 Oslo 1, Norway
University of North Carolina at Chapel Hill
Department of Music
Chapel Hill, North Carolina
University of North Carolina at Greensboro
School of Music
Greensboro, North Carolina
North Carolina School of the Arts
School of Music
Winston-Salem, North Carolina
University of North Dakota
Department of Music
Grand Forks, North Dakota
North Texas State University
School of Music
Denton, Texas
Northeast Louisiana University
School of Music
Monroe, Louisiana
Northeast Missouri State University
Division of Fine Arts
Kirksville, Missouri
Northeastern Illinois University
Department of Music
Chicago, Illinois
Northern Arizona University
Music Department
Flagstaff, Arizona
University of Northern Colorado
School of Music
Greeley, Colorado
Northern Illinois University
School of Music
DeKalb, Illinois
University of Northern Iowa
School of Music
Cedar Falls, Iowa
Northwest Teacher's College
Department of Music
*Gansu Province, People's Republic of
China*
Northwestern State University of Louisiana
Department of Music
Natchitoches, Louisiana
Northwestern University
School of Music
Evanston, Illinois
University of Notre Dame
Department of Music
Notre Dame, Indiana

Novosibirsk M.I. Glinka State Conservatory
630099 Novosibirsk 99, Rossiskaja SFSR, U.S.S.R.
Oakland University
Department of Music, Theatre and Dance
Rochester, Michigan
Oberlin College
Conservatory of Music
Oberlin, Ohio
Ochanomizu Joshi Daigaku (Ochanomizu Woman's University)
Faculty of Music
Tokyo 112, Japan
Odeion Athenon
(Conservatory of Athens)
Athens, Greece
Odeion Ethnikon - Athens
(National Conservatory)
108 Athens, Greece
The Ohio State University
School of Music
Columbus, Ohio
Ohio University
School of Music
Athens, Ohio
Ohio Wesleyan University
Department of Music
Delaware, Ohio
University of Oklahoma
School of Music
Norman, Oklahoma
Oklahoma Baptist University
Department of Music
Shawnee, Oklahoma
Oklahoma City University
School of Music and Performing Arts
Oklahoma City, Oklahoma
Oman Center for Traditional Music
Muscat, Oman
University of Orange Free State
Department of Music
9300 Bloemfontein, Republic of South Africa
University of Oregon
School of Music
Eugene, Oregon
Oregon State University
Department of Music
Corvallis, Oregon
Országos Pedagogiai Intézet
Budapest VI, Hungary
Osaka Ongaku Daigaku
(Osaka College of Music)
Osaka 561, Japan
University of Otago
Arts and Music
Dunedin, New Zealand
Ouachita Baptist University
School of Music
Arkadelphia, Arkansas
University of the Pacific
Conservatory of Music
Stockton, California
Pacific Lutheran University
Department of Music
Tacoma, Washington
Pamantasang Centro Escolar
(Centro Escolar University)
San Miguel, Manila, The Philippines
Peabody Institute of The Johns Hopkins University
Baltimore, Maryland
University of Pennsylvania
Department of Music
Philadelphia, Pennsylvania

Pennsylvania State University
School of Music
University Park, Pennsylvania
Philadelphia College of the Performing Arts
School of Music
Philadelphia, Pennsylvania
University of the Philippines
College of Music
Quezon City, The Philippines
Pittsburg State University
Department of Music
Pittsburg, Kansas
University of Pittsburgh
Department of Music
Pittsburgh, Pennsylvania
Pohjois-Kymen Musiikkiopisto
(North Kymi Music Institute)
45100 Kouvola, Finland
Pomona College
Music Department
Claremont, California
Pontifical Institute of Sacred Music
I - 00165 Roma, Italy
Pontificia Universidad Católica Argentina
'Santa María de los Buenos Aires'
(Pontifical Catholic University of Argentina)
Buenos Aires 1116, Argentina
Pontificia Universidad Católica de Chile
Faculty of Architecture and Fine Arts
Santiago, Chile
Portland State University
Department of Music
Portland, Oregon
Prayag Sangit Samiti
Allahabad 211001, India
University of Pretoria
Department of Music
002 Pretoria, Republic of South Africa
Princeton University
Department of Music
Princeton, New Jersey
University of Puget Sound
School of Music
Tacoma, Washington
Queen's University
School of Music
Kingston, Ontario, Canada
University of Queensland
Faculty of Music
St. Lucia, Queensland 4067, Australia
Queensland Conservatorium of Music
South Brisbane 4101, Australia
Radford University
Department of Music
Radford, Virginia
Real Conservatorio Superior de Música de Madrid
(Royal Academy of Music)
Madrid 13, Spain
University of Redlands
School of Music
Redlands, California
University of Regina
Department of Music
Regina, Saskatchewan, Canada
University of Rhode Island
Department of Music
Kingston, Rhode Island
Rice University
Shepherd School of Music
Houston, Texas
Rimon School of Jazz and Contemporary Music
Ramat Hasharon, Israel

Riyadh Conservatory
See King Saud University
University of Rochester
Eastman School of Music
Rochester, New York
Rogaland Musikkonservatorium
N-4000 Stavanger, Norway
Roosevelt University
Chicago Musical College
Chicago, Illinois
Rostov State Institute of Pedagogics and Music
344007 Rostov-on-Don, Rossiskaja SFSR, U.S.S.R.
Rotterdams Conservatorium
3024 BJ Rotterdam, Netherlands
Royal Academy of Music
London NW1 5HT, United Kingdom
Royal College of Music
London, SW7 2BS, United Kingdom
Royal Irish Academy of Music
Dublin 2, Ireland
Royal Northern College of Music
Manchester M13 9RD, United Kingdom
Royal Scottish Academy of Music and Drama
Glasgow G2 1BS, United Kingdom
Rubin Academy of Music
See Tel-Aviv University
Rutgers, The State University of New Jersey
Department of Music
New Brunswick, New Jersey
Sacred Heart College
Department of Music
Lucena City, The Philippines
St. Cloud State University
Department of Music
St. Cloud, Minnesota
Saint Louis Conservatory of Music
St. Louis, Missouri
St. Olaf College
Music Department
Northfield, Minnesota
St. Paul College
College of Music
Manila, The Philippines
St. Scholastica's College
School of Music
Manila, The Philippines
Sam Houston State University
Department of Music
Huntsville, Texas
Samford University
School of Music
Birmingham, Alabama
Samuel Rubin Conservatory of Music
Haifa, Israel
University of San Augustín
Conservatory of Music
Iloilo City 5901, The Philippines
San Diego State University
Music Department
San Diego, California
San Francisco Conservatory of Music
San Francisco, California
San Francisco State University
Department of Music
San Francisco, California
San Jose State University
Department of Music
San Jose, California
Sangeet Natak Akademi
(National Academy of Music, Dance, and Drama)
New Delhi 110001, India

Sang-Myeong Women's College of
Education
Department of Music
Seoul, South Korea
University of Santo Tomas
Conservatory of Music
Manila, The Philippines
Saratov L.V. Sobinov State Conservatory
410000 Saratov, Rossiskaja SFSR,
U.S.S.R.
University of Saskatchewan
Department of Music
Saskatoon, Saskatchewan, Canada
Seoul National University
College of Music
Seoul 151, South Korea
Shandong Academy of Arts
Music Division
Shandong Province, People's Republic of
China
Shanghai Conservatory of Music
Shanghai, People's Republic of China
Shanxi University
Department of Music
Taiyuan Province, People's Republic of
China
Shenandoah College and Conservatory
Winchester, Virginia
Shengyang Conservatory of Music
Shengyang, Liaoning Province, People's
Republic of China
Shepherd School of Music
See Rice University
Shorter College
Department of Music
Rome, Georgia
Sibelius Academy of Music
SF-00260 Helsinki 26, Finland
Sibeliusmuseum
Musikvetenskapliga Institutionen vid Åbo
Akademi
Åbo 50, Finland
Sichuan Conservatory of Music
Chengdu, Sichuan, People's Republic of
China
Smith College
Department of Music
Northampton, Massachusetts
Soai Women's College (Soai Joshi Daigaku)
Faculty of Music
Osaka 541, Japan
Sookmyung Women's University
College of Music
Seoul, South Korea
University of South Carolina
School of Music
Columbia, South Carolina
University of South Dakota
Music Department
Vermillion, South Dakota
University of South Florida
Department of Music
Tampa, Florida
Southeast Missouri State University
Department of Music
Cape Girardeau, Missouri
Southeastern Louisiana University
Department of Music
Hammond, Louisiana
Southeastern Oklahoma State University
Department of Music
Durant, Oklahoma
Southern Baptist Theological Seminary
School of Church Music
Louisville, Kentucky

University of Southern California
School of Music
Los Angeles, California
Southern Illinois University at Carbondale
School of Music
Carbondale, Illinois
Southern Illinois University at Edwardsville
Department of Music
Edwardsville, Illinois
Southern Methodist University
Meadows School of the Arts
Dallas, Texas
University of Southern Mississippi
School of Music
Hattiesburg, Mississippi
Southwest Texas State University
Department of Music
San Marcos, Texas
Southwestern Baptist Theological Seminary
School of Church Music
Fort Worth, Texas
University of Southwestern Louisiana
School of Music
Lafayette, Louisiana
Southwestern Oklahoma State University
Department of Music
Weatherford, Oklahoma
Staatliche Hochschule für Musik Freiburg
D-7800 Freiburg i. Br., Federal Republic
of Germany
Staatliche Hochschule für Musik
Heidelberg-Mannheim
Friedrich-Ebert-Anlage 62, Federal
Republic of Germany
Staatliche Hochschule für Musik Karlsruhe
7500 Karlsruhe 1, Federal Republic of
Germany
Staatliche Hochschule für Musik Rheinland
- Aachen
Grenzland-Institut Aachen
Aachen, Federal Republic of Germany
Staatliche Hochschule für Musik Rheinland
- Düsseldorf
(State College of Music)
D-4000 Düsseldorf, Federal Republic of
Germany
Staatliche Hochschule für Musik Rheinland
- Köln
D-5000 Köln 1, Federal Republic of
Germany
Staatliche Hochschule für Musik Rheinland
- Wuppertal
Institute Wuppertal
Wuppertal, Federal Republic of Germany
Staatliche Hochschule für Musik Ruhr
4300 Essen 16, Federal Republic of
Germany
Staatliche Hochschule für Musik Trossingen
D-7218 Trossingen 1, Federal Republic of
Germany
Staatliche Hochschule für Musik und
Darstellende Kunst Stuttgart
7000 Stuttgart 1, Federal Republic of
Germany
Staatliche Hochschule für Musik
Westfalen-Lippe
4930 Detmold, Federal Republic of
Germany
Staatliche Hochschule für Musik
Westfalen-Lippe
Institut Dortmund
D-4600 Dortmund 1, Federal Republic of
Germany
Stanford University
Department of Music
Stanford, California

State University of New York at
Binghamton
Department of Music
Binghamton, New York
State University of New York at Buffalo
Department of Music
Buffalo, New York
State University of New York at Stony
Brook
Department of Music
Stony Brook, New York
State University of New York College at
Fredonia
School of Music
Fredonia, New York
State University of New York College at
New Paltz
Department of Music
New Paltz, New York
State University of New York College at
Potsdam
Crane School of Music
Potsdam, New York
State University of New York College at
Purchase
Division of Music
Purchase, New York
Statens Operahøgskole
(National College of Operatic Art)
0250 Oslo 2, Norway
Stedelijke Muziekpedagogische Akademie
Leeuwarden, Netherlands
University of Stellenbosch
Department of Music (Conservatoire)
7600 Stellenbosch, Republic of South
Africa
Stephen F. Austin State University
Department of Music
Nacogdoches, Texas
Stetson University
School of Music
Deland, Florida
Stichting Sweelinck Conservatorium
Amsterdam
1071 AN Amsterdam, Netherlands
Sultan Qaboos University
Muscat, Oman
University of Sydney
Department of Music
Sydney, NSW 2006, Australia
Syracuse University
School of Music
Syracuse, New York
Tallinn State Conservatory
200015 Tallinn, Estonskaja SSR, U.S.S.R.
Tamil University
Faculty of Music
Tamil Nadu 613001, India
Tampereen Konservatorio
33230 Tampere, Finland
Tashkent State Conservatory
700000 Tashkent, Uzbekskaja SSR,
U.S.S.R.
Tasmanian Conservatorium of Music
Hobart, Tasmania 7001, Australia
Tbilisi V. Sarajishvili State Conservatory
380004 Tbilisi 4, Gruzinskaja SSR,
U.S.S.R.
Teachers College of Columbia University
Department of Music and Music
Education
New York, New York
University of Teheran
Department of Music
Tehran, Iran

Tel Aviv University
  Faculty of Fine Arts
  Tel-Aviv, Israel
Temple University
  Esther Boyer College of Music
  Philadelphia, Pennsylvania
University of Tennessee at Chattanooga
  Cadek Department of Music
  Chattanooga, Tennessee
University of Tennessee at Knoxville
  Department of Music
  Knoxville, Tennessee
University of Texas at Arlington
  Department of Music
  Arlington, Texas
University of Texas at Austin
  Department of Music
  Austin, Texas
University of Texas at El Paso
  Music Department
  El Paso, Texas
University of Texas at San Antonio
  Division of Music
  San Antonio, Texas
Texas Christian University
  Music Department
  Fort Worth, Texas
Texas Southern University
  Department of Music
  Houston, Texas
Texas Tech University
  Department of Music
  Lubbock, Texas
Texas Woman's University
  Department of Music and Drama
  Denton, Texas
Toho Gakuen School of Music
  Tokyo, Japan
The Tokyo College of Music
  Tokyo 171, Japan
Tokyo Daigaku (University of Tokyo)
  Faculty of Musicology
  Tokyo 113, Japan
Tokyo Geijutsu Daigaku (Tokyo University
  of Fine Arts and Music)
  Faculty of Music
  Tokyo 110, Japan
Tonlistarskolinn i Reykjavik
  105 Reykjavik, Iceland
University of Toronto
  Faculty of Music
  Toronto, Ontario, Canada
Towson State University
  Department of Music
  Towson, Maryland
Trenton State College
  Music Department
  Trenton, New Jersey
Trinity College of Music
  London W1M 6AQ, United Kingdom
Troy State University
  Department of Music
  Troy, Alabama
Tulane University
  Newcomb College
  New Orleans, Louisiana
University of Tulsa
  Faculty of Music
  Tulsa, Oklahoma
Ueno Gakuen College
  Tokyo 110, Japan
Ufa State Institute of Fine Arts
  450025 Ufa, Bashkir ASSR, U.S.S.R.
UNESP - Universidade Estadual Júlio de
  Mesquita Filho
  Instituto do Artes do Planalto

São Paulo, Brazil
Universidad Católica de Valparaíso
  Conservatory of Music
  Valparaíso, Chile
Universidad Cecilio Acosto
  Facultad de Música
  Cabimas, Venezuela
Universidad de Antioquía
  Facultad de Artes, Departamento de
  Música
  Medellín, Colombia
Universidad de Concepción
  Departamento de Arte
  Concepción, Chile
Universidad de Nariño
  Escuela de Música
  Pasto, Nariño, Colombia
Universidad de Puerto Rico
  Department of Music
  Rio Piedras, Puerto Rico
Universidad del Atlántico
  Conservatorio de Música (School of
  Music)
  Barranquilla, Colombia
Universidad Nacional de Cuyo
  Escuela Superior de Música
  *5500 Mendoza (Provincia de Mendoza),
  Argentina*
Universidad Nacional de "San Agustín"
  (National University of "San Agustín")
  Arequipa, Casilla Postal 23, Peru
Universidade do Rio de Janeiro
  Letters and Arts Center - Music Course
  22290 Rio de Janeiro, Brazil
Universidade do São Paulo
  Department of Music
  05508 São Paulo, Brazil
Universidade Federal da Paraíba
  (Federal University of Paraíba)
  Paraíba, Brazil
Universidade Federal de Bahia
  Escola de Música
  Bahia, Brazil
Universidade Federal de Minas Gerais
  Escola de Música
  Minas Gerais, Brazil
Universidade Federal do Rio de Janeiro
  Escola de Música
  Rio de Janeiro, Brazil
Universita degli Studi
  Facolta di Lettere e Filosofia
  Palermo (Sicily), Italy
Université de Montréal
  Faculty of Music
  Montréal, Québec, Canada
Université des Beaux-Arts
  Faculty of Music
  Phnom Penh, Kampuchea
Université Laval
  Ecole de Musique
  Ste. Foy, Québec, Canada
Urals M.P. Mussorgsky State Conservatory
  *620014 Sverdlovsk, Rossiskaja SFSR,
  U.S.S.R.*
University of Utah
  Department of Music
  Salt Lake City, Utah
Utrechts Conservatorium
  3511 LL Utrecht, Netherlands
Valdosta State College
  Department of Music
  Valdosta, Georgia
Valparaiso University
  Department of Music
  Valparaiso, Indiana

VanderCook College of Music
  Chicago, Illinois
University of Vermont
  Department of Music
  Burlington, Vermont
Vestjysk Musikkonservatorium
  (West Jutland Academy of Music)
  6700 Esbjerg, Denmark
University of Victoria
  School of Music
  Victoria, British Columbia, Canada
Victoria University of Wellington
  Faculty of Music
  Wellington 1, New Zealand
University of Virginia
  McIntire Department of Music
  Charlottesville, Virginia
Virginia Commonwealth University
  Department of Music
  Richmond, Virginia
Virginia Polytechnic Institute and State
  University
  Department of Music
  Blacksburg, Virginia
Virginia State University
  Department of Music Education
  Petersburg, Virginia
Visoka Muzička Skola
  (High School of Music)
  YU-91000 Skopje, Yugoslavia
Viss Musikalno-Pedagogiceski
  Plovdiv 4025, Bulgaria
Visva-Bharati
  Sangit-Bhavana (College of Music and
  Dance)
  West Bengal 731235, India
Vysoká Skola Mûzickych Umeni v
  Bratislave
  (Academy of Music and Dramtic Arts
  Bratislava)
  Bratislava, Czechoslovakia
Vysoká Skola Mûzickych Umeni v Praha
  Academy of Music and Dramatic Arts
  1101 00 Prague 1, Czechoslovakia
University of Washington
  School of Music
  Seattle, Washington
Washington State University
  Department of Music
  Pullman, Washington
Washington University
  Department of Music
  St. Louis, Missouri
Wayne State University
  Department of Music
  Detroit, Michigan
Webster University
  Department of Music
  St. Louis, Missouri
Welsh College of Music and Drama
  Cardiff, CF1 3ER, United Kingdom
Wesleyan University
  Department of Music
  Middletown, Connecticut
West Chester University of Pennsylvania
  School of Music
  West Chester, Pennsylvania
West Georgia College
  Department of Music
  Carrollton, Georgia
West Texas State University
  Department of Music
  Canyon, Texas
West Virginia University
  Division of Music
  Morgantown, West Virginia

University of Western Australia
  Department of Music
  Nedlands, WA 6009, Australia
Western Illinois University
  Department of Music
  Macomb, Illinois
Western Kentucky University
  Department of Music
  Bowling Green, Kentucky
Western Michigan University
  School of Music
  Kalamazoo, Michigan
University of Western Ontario
  Faculty of Music
  London, Ontario, Canada
Western Washington University
  Department of Music
  Bellingham, Washington
Westminster Choir College
  Princeton, New Jersey
Wheaton College
  Conservatory of Music
  Wheaton, Illinois
Wichita State University
  School of Music
  Wichita, Kansas
Wiesbadener Konservatorium und staatliche
  anerkannte private Fachschule für
  Musikerzieher e.V.
  (Conservatory and Seminary for Music
  Education)
  *6200 Wiesbaden, Federal Republic of
  Germany*
Wilfrid Laurier University
  Faculty of Music
  Waterloo, Ontario, Canada
Willamette University
  Department of Music
  Salem, Oregon
William Carey College
  Winters School of Music
  Hattiesburg, Mississippi
William Paterson College
  Department of Music
  Wayne, New Jersey
University of Windsor
  School of Music
  Windsor, Ontario, Canada
Winters School of Music
  See William Carey College
Winthrop College
  School of Music
  Rock Hill, South Carolina
University of Wisconsin - Eau Claire
  Department of Music
  Eau Claire, Wisconsin
University of Wisconsin - La Crosse
  Department of Music
  La Crosse, Wisconsin
University of Wisconsin - Madison
  School of Music
  Madison, Wisconsin
University of Wisconsin - Milwaukee
  Music Department
  Milwaukee, Wisconsin
University of Wisconsin - Oshkosh
  Department of Music
  Oshkosh, Wisconsin
University of Wisconsin - Stevens Point
  Department of Music
  Stevens Point, Wisconsin
University of Wisconsin - Whitewater
  Department of Music
  Whitewater, Wisconsin

Wits School of Music
  University of the Witwatersrand
University of the Witwatersrand
  Wits School of Music
  *2001 Johannesburg, Republic of South
  Africa*
Wollongong Conservatorium
  "Gleniffer Brae"
  Wollongong, NSW 2500, Australia
Wright State University
  Department of Music
  Dayton, Ohio
University of Wyoming
  Music Department
  Laramie, Wyoming
Xi'an Music Conservatory
  *Shaanxi Province, People's Republic of
  China*
Yale College (Yale University)
  Department of Music
  New Haven, Connecticut
Yale University
  School of Music
  New Haven, Connecticut
Yared National Institute of Music
  Addis Ababa, Ethiopia
Yeungnam University
  College of Music
  Gyeong-Bug 632, South Korea
Yongsei University
  College of Music
  Seoul 120, South Korea
York University
  Department of Music
  North York, Ontario, Canada
Youngstown State University
  Dana School of Music
  Youngstown, Ohio
University of Zambia at Lusaka
  Centre for Arts
  Lusaka, Zambia
Zavod Za Istraživanje Folklora Iff
  (Folklore Research Department of the
  Institute for Philology and Folklore)
  YU-41000 Zagreb, Yugoslavia
Zeneiskolai Tanárkepzó Intézet
  (Music Teachers Training Institute of the
  Liszt Academy of Music)
  Budapest 1052, Hungary
Zenetudományi Intézet
  (Musicological Institute)
  Budapest 1014, Hungary
Zimbabwe Academy of Music
  Bulawayo, Zimbabwe
Zimbabwe College of Music
  Harare C3, Zimbabwe

INDEX OF PROGRAM AREAS

ACCOMPANYING

University of Akron
   Department of Music
   Akron, Ohio
Boston University
   School of Music
   Boston, Massachusetts
Bradley University
   Division of Music and Theatre Arts
   Peoria, Illinois
California State University, Fullerton
   Department of Music
   Fullerton, California
University of Cincinnati
   College-Conservatory of Music
   Cincinnati, Ohio
The Curtis Institute of Music
   Philadelphia, Pennsylvania
East Carolina University
   School of Music
   Greenville, North Carolina
Ferenc Liszt Academy of Music
   Budapest VI, Hungary
George Mason University
   Department of Performing Arts - Music
   Division
   Fairfax, Virginia
Indiana University - Bloomington
   School of Music
   Bloomington, Indiana
The Juilliard School
   New York, New York
University of Miami
   School of Music
   Coral Gables, Florida
University of Missouri - Columbia
   Department of Music
   Columbia, Missouri
University of New Mexico
   Department of Music
   Albuquerque, New Mexico
New Mexico State University
   Department of Music
   Las Cruces, New Mexico
University of North Carolina at Greensboro
   School of Music
   Greensboro, North Carolina
Real Conservatorio Superior de Música de
Madrid
   (Royal Academy of Music)
   Madrid 13, Spain
San Francisco Conservatory of Music
   San Francisco, California
Shenandoah College and Conservatory
   Winchester, Virginia

University of Southern California
   School of Music
   Los Angeles, California
Southwestern Baptist Theological Seminary
   School of Church Music
   Fort Worth, Texas
Temple University
   Esther Boyer College of Music
   Philadelphia, Pennsylvania
University of Texas at Arlington
   Department of Music
   Arlington, Texas
West Chester University of Pennsylvania
   School of Music
   West Chester, Pennsylvania

ACOUSTICS

Escuela Universitaria de Música -
Montevideo
   Montevideo, Uruguay
Hochschule für Gestaltende Kunst und
Musik
   (State College for Creative Art and
   Music)
   *2800 Bremen 1, Federal Republic of
   Germany*
Hochschule für Musik - München
   *8000 München 2, Federal Republic of
   Germany*
Hochschule für Musik - Würzburg
   *D-8700 Würzburg, Federal Republic of
   Germany*
Real Conservatorio Superior de Música de
Madrid
   (Royal Academy of Music)
   Madrid 13, Spain

AESTHETICS

Escuela Universitaria de Música -
Montevideo
   Montevideo, Uruguay

University of Melbourne
   Faculty of Music
   Victoria 3052, Australia

AFRICAN MUSIC

University of Pittsburgh
   Department of Music
   Pittsburgh, Pennsylvania
University of Virginia
   McIntire Department of Music
   Charlottesville, Virginia

AFRICAN TRADITIONAL MUSIC

Cuttington University College
   Monrovia, Liberia

AFRO-AMERICAN MUSIC

Combs College of Music
   Philadelphia, Pennsylvania
Howard University
   Department of Music
   Washington, District of Columbia
University of Massachusetts at Amherst
   Department of Music and Dance
   Amherst, Massachusetts
University of Pittsburgh
   Department of Music
   Pittsburgh, Pennsylvania
Wesleyan University
   Department of Music
   Middletown, Connecticut

ALEXANDER TECHNIQUE

Royal College of Music
   London, SW7 2BS, United Kingdom

ANDALUSIAN MUSIC

Conservatoire National de Musique, de
Danse, et d'Art Dramatique - Ribad
   Ribad, Morocco

APPLIED MUSIC

Acadia University
   School of Music
   Wolfville, Nova Scotia, Canada
Appalachian State University
   Department of Music
   Boone, North Carolina
University of Arkansas
   Department of Music
   Fayetteville, Arkansas
Austin Peay State University
   Department of Music
   Clarksville, Tennessee
Azusa Pacific University
   School of Music
   Azusa, California
Baldwin-Wallace College
   Conservatory of Music
   Berea, Ohio
Ball State University
   School of Music
   Muncie, Indiana
Bemidji State University
   Music Department
   Bemidji, Minnesota

Boston Conservatory of Music
  Boston, Massachusetts
Boston University
  School of Music
  Boston, Massachusetts
Bradley University
  Division of Music and Theatre Arts
  Peoria, Illinois
Butler University
  Jordan College of Fine Arts
  Indianapolis, Indiana
University of California, Davis
  Department of Music
  Davis, California
University of Central Arkansas
  Department of Music
  Conway, Arkansas
University of Central Florida
  Department of Music
  Orlando, Florida
Central Michigan University
  Department of Music
  Mount Pleasant, Michigan
Cleveland State University
  Department of Music
  Cleveland, Ohio
University of Connecticut
  Department of Music
  Storrs, Connecticut
Converse College
  School of Music
  Spartanburg, South Carolina
Cornell University
  Department of Music
  Ithaca, New York
University of Delaware
  Department of Music
  Newark, Delaware
DePauw University
  School of Music
  Greencastle, Indiana
Drake University
  Department of Music
  Des Moines, Iowa
Duke University
  Department of Music
  Durham, North Carolina
Eastern Kentucky University
  Department of Music
  Richmond, Kentucky
George Mason University
  Department of Performing Arts - Music
  Division
  Fairfax, Virginia
Georgia Southern College
  Department of Music
  Statesboro, Georgia
Glassboro State College
  Department of Music
  Glassboro, New Jersey
Hardin-Simmons University
  School of Music
  Abilene, Texas
University of Hartford
  Hartt School of Music
  West Hartford, Connecticut
University of Houston
  School of Music
  Houston, Texas
Howard University
  Department of Music
  Washington, District of Columbia
University of Illinois
  School of Music
  Urbana, Illinois

Indiana University - Bloomington
  School of Music
  Bloomington, Indiana
University of Iowa
  School of Music
  Iowa City, Iowa
Jackson State University
  Department of Music
  Jackson, Mississippi
Jacksonville State University
  Department of Music
  Jacksonville, Alabama
James Madison University
  Department of Music
  Harrisonburg, Virginia
The Juilliard School
  New York, New York
Kansas State University
  Department of Music
  Manhattan, Kansas
University of Kentucky
  School of Music
  Lexington, Kentucky
Lamar University
  Department of Music
  Beaumont, Texas
Louisiana State University
  School of Music
  Baton Rouge, Louisiana
Louisiana Tech University
  Department of Music
  Ruston, Louisiana
University of Louisville
  School of Music
  Louisville, Kentucky
University of Lowell
  College of Music
  Lowell, Massachusetts
Loyola University
  College of Music
  New Orleans, Louisiana
Manhattan School of Music
  New York, New York
Mansfield University
  Department of Music
  Mansfield, Pennsylvania
Memphis State University
  Music Department
  Memphis, Tennessee
University of Miami
  School of Music
  Coral Gables, Florida
Millikin University
  School of Music
  Decatur, Illinois
University of Mississippi
  Department of Music
  University, Mississippi
University of Missouri - Columbia
  Department of Music
  Columbia, Missouri
University of Missouri - Kansas City
  Conservatory of Music
  Kansas City, Missouri
University of Montana
  Department of Music
  Missoula, Montana
Montana State University
  Department of Music
  Bozeman, Montana
Moorhead State University
  Music Department
  Moorhead, Minnesota
University of Nebraska - Lincoln
  School of Music
  Lincoln, Nebraska

University of Nebraska - Omaha
  Department of Music
  Omaha, Nebraska
University of Nevada, Las Vegas
  Department of Music
  Las Vegas, Nevada
University of Nevada, Reno
  Department of Music
  Reno, Nevada
New England Conservatory
  Boston, Massachusetts
University of New Mexico
  Department of Music
  Albuquerque, New Mexico
New York University - School of Education,
  Health, Nursing, and Arts Professions
  Department of Music and Music
  Education
  New York, New York
University of North Carolina at Greensboro
  School of Music
  Greensboro, North Carolina
North Carolina School of the Arts
  School of Music
  Winston-Salem, North Carolina
University of Northern Iowa
  School of Music
  Cedar Falls, Iowa
Ohio Wesleyan University
  Department of Music
  Delaware, Ohio
University of Oklahoma
  School of Music
  Norman, Oklahoma
Oklahoma City University
  School of Music and Performing Arts
  Oklahoma City, Oklahoma
Ouachita Baptist University
  School of Music
  Arkadelphia, Arkansas
University of Pennsylvania
  Department of Music
  Philadelphia, Pennsylvania
Pittsburg State University
  Department of Music
  Pittsburg, Kansas
University of Puget Sound
  School of Music
  Tacoma, Washington
Roosevelt University
  Chicago Musical College
  Chicago, Illinois
Rutgers, The State University of New Jersey
  Department of Music
  New Brunswick, New Jersey
San Francisco Conservatory of Music
  San Francisco, California
San Jose State University
  Department of Music
  San Jose, California
Shenandoah College and Conservatory
  Winchester, Virginia
Shorter College
  Department of Music
  Rome, Georgia
University of South Carolina
  School of Music
  Columbia, South Carolina
University of South Dakota
  Music Department
  Vermillion, South Dakota
University of South Florida
  Department of Music
  Tampa, Florida
Southern Illinois University at Carbondale
  School of Music

Carbondale, Illinois
Southern Illinois University at Edwardsville
Department of Music
Edwardsville, Illinois
Southwestern Oklahoma State University
Department of Music
Weatherford, Oklahoma
State University of New York College at
Fredonia
School of Music
Fredonia, New York
State University of New York College at
New Paltz
Department of Music
New Paltz, New York
Stephen F. Austin State University
Department of Music
Nacogdoches, Texas
Stetson University
School of Music
Deland, Florida
University of Tennessee at Knoxville
Department of Music
Knoxville, Tennessee
University of Texas at Austin
Department of Music
Austin, Texas
Tulane University
Newcomb College
New Orleans, Louisiana
University of Tulsa
Faculty of Music
Tulsa, Oklahoma
Virginia Commonwealth University
Department of Music
Richmond, Virginia
Virginia State University
Department of Music Education
Petersburg, Virginia
University of Washington
School of Music
Seattle, Washington
Western Illinois University
Department of Music
Macomb, Illinois
Western Kentucky University
Department of Music
Bowling Green, Kentucky
Western Michigan University
School of Music
Kalamazoo, Michigan
Wichita State University
School of Music
Wichita, Kansas
William Carey College
Winters School of Music
Hattiesburg, Mississippi
Winthrop College
School of Music
Rock Hill, South Carolina
University of Wisconsin - Eau Claire
Department of Music
Eau Claire, Wisconsin
University of Wisconsin - Milwaukee
Music Department
Milwaukee, Wisconsin
University of Wisconsin - Stevens Point
Department of Music
Stevens Point, Wisconsin
Wright State University
Department of Music
Dayton, Ohio
University of Wyoming
Music Department
Laramie, Wyoming

Youngstown State University
Dana School of Music
Youngstown, Ohio

APPLIED MUSIC PEDAGOGY

Northeastern Illinois University
Department of Music
Chicago, Illinois

APPLIED PERFORMANCE

Central Missouri State University
Department of Music
Warrensburg, Missouri

ARABIC INSTRUMENTS

Lebanese National Conservatory
Eastern Section
Beirut, Lebanon

ARCHIVAL AND MANUSCRIPT STUDIES

Yale College (Yale University)
Department of Music
New Haven, Connecticut

ARRANGING

University of Colorado at Denver
College of Music
Denver, Colorado
University of Massachusetts at Amherst
Department of Music and Dance
Amherst, Massachusetts

ART (PSYCHOLOGY OF)

Universidade do São Paulo
Department of Music
05508 São Paulo, Brazil

ART (SOCIOLOGY OF)

Universidade do São Paulo
Department of Music
05508 São Paulo, Brazil

ART SONG ACCOMPANIMENT

Hochschule für Musik - Würzburg
D-8700 Würzburg, Federal Republic of Germany
Staatliche Hochschule für Musik Rheinland - Köln
D-5000 Köln 1, Federal Republic of Germany

ART SONG HISTORY

Hochschule für Musik - München
8000 München 2, Federal Republic of Germany

ART SONGS (INTERPRETATION OF)

Hochschule für Musik - München
8000 München 2, Federal Republic of Germany
Hochschule für Musik und Theater Hannover
3000 Hannover 1, Federal Republic of Germany
Staatliche Hochschule für Musik Westfalen-Lippe
4930 Detmold, Federal Republic of Germany
Staatliche Hochschule für Musik Westfalen-Lippe
Institut Dortmund
D-4600 Dortmund 1, Federal Republic of Germany

ARTS ADMINISTRATION

Butler University
Jordan College of Fine Arts
Indianapolis, Indiana

ARTS MANAGEMENT

Moorhead State University
Music Department
Moorhead, Minnesota
Northern Arizona University
Music Department
Flagstaff, Arizona
Shenandoah College and Conservatory
Winchester, Virginia

ASIAN MUSIC

University of the Philippines
College of Music
Quezon City, The Philippines

AUDIO RECORDING

Cleveland Institute of Music
Cleveland, Ohio
The Ohio State University
School of Music
Columbus, Ohio

AUDIO RECORDING TECHNOLOGY

University of Northern Iowa
School of Music
Cedar Falls, Iowa

AURAL STUDIES AND MUSICIANSHIP

Royal Academy of Music
London NW1 5HT, United Kingdom
Royal College of Music
London, SW7 2BS, United Kingdom

AURAL TRAINING

Conservatorio Nacional de Música
(National Conservatory of Music)
Lima 1, Peru
Hermann-Zilcher-Konservatorium
D-8700 Würzburg, Federal Republic of Germany
Hochschule für Gestaltende Kunst und Musik
(State College for Creative Art and Music)
2800 Bremen 1, Federal Republic of Germany
Hochschule für Musik - München
8000 München 2, Federal Republic of Germany
Hochschule für Musik - Würzburg
D-8700 Würzburg, Federal Republic of Germany
Hochschule für Musik und Darstellende Kunst Frankfurt am Main
6000 Frankfurt am Main 1, Federal Republic of Germany
Staatliche Hochschule für Musik Rheinland - Aachen
Grenzland-Institut Aachen
Aachen, Federal Republic of Germany
Staatliche Hochschule für Musik Westfalen-Lippe
Institut Dortmund
D-4600 Dortmund 1, Federal Republic of Germany

BAGPIPES

Military Institute of Music - Sana'a
Sana'a, Yemen Arab Republic

BALINESE MUSIC

California Institute of the Arts
School of Music
Valencia, California

BALLET

Hochschule für Musik und Darstellende
Kunst Frankfurt am Main
*6000 Frankfurt am Main 1, Federal
Republic of Germany*
Staatliche Hochschule für Musik Rheinland
- Aachen
Grenzland-Institut Aachen
Aachen, Federal Republic of Germany

BAROQUE MUSIC

Mills College
Music Department
Oakland, California
Royal Northern College of Music
Manchester M13 9RD, United Kingdom
Rutgers, The State University of New Jersey
Department of Music
New Brunswick, New Jersey
San Francisco Conservatory of Music
San Francisco, California
Stanford University
Department of Music
Stanford, California
Trinity College of Music
London W1M 6AQ, United Kingdom
Wilfrid Laurier University
Faculty of Music
Waterloo, Ontario, Canada
Yale College (Yale University)
Department of Music
New Haven, Connecticut

BIG BAND

Staatliche Hochschule für Musik Rheinland
- Aachen
Grenzland-Institut Aachen
Aachen, Federal Republic of Germany

BODY TRAINING

Musikhochschule des Saarlandes
*6600 Saarbrücken 3, Federal Republic of
Germany*

BOLIVIAN MUSIC HISTORY

Conservatorio Nacional de Musica - La Paz
(National Conservatory of Music - La
Paz)
La Paz, Bolivia

BRAZILIAN MUSIC HISTORY

Universidade do Rio de Janeiro
Letters and Arts Center - Music Course
22290 Rio de Janeiro, Brazil

BREATH CONTROL

Hochschule für Musik - Würzburg
*D-8700 Würzburg, Federal Republic of
Germany*
Hochschule für Musik und Theater
Hannover

*3000 Hannover 1, Federal Republic of
Germany*

BYZANTINE CHURCH MUSIC

Odeion Athenon
(Conservatory of Athens)
Athens, Greece

CATHOLIC LITURGY

Hochschule für Musik - München
*8000 München 2, Federal Republic of
Germany*
Musikhochschule Lübeck
Grosse Petersgrube 17-29
*2400 Lübeck, Federal Republic of
Germany*

CHAMBER MUSIC

Akademia Muzyczna w Lódź
(Academy of Music of Lódź)
90-716 Lódź, Poland
Bennington College
Music Department
Bennington, Vermont
Boston Conservatory of Music
Boston, Massachusetts
The Catholic University of America
The Benjamin T. Rome School of Music
Washington, District of Columbia
Conservatorio Nacional de Musica - La Paz
(National Conservatory of Music - La
Paz)
La Paz, Bolivia
The Curtis Institute of Music
Philadelphia, Pennsylvania
Fachakademie für Music - Augsburg
Leopold Mozart-Konservatorium der
Stadt Augsburg
Augsberg, Federal Republic of Germany
Ferenc Liszt Academy of Music
Budapest VI, Hungary
Hermann-Zilcher-Konservatorium
*D-8700 Würzburg, Federal Republic of
Germany*
Hochschule der Künste Berlin
*1000 Berlin 10, Federal Republic of
Germany*
Hochschule für Music Franz Liszt
*DDR 5300 Weimar, German Democratic
Republic*
Hochschule für Musik - München
*8000 München 2, Federal Republic of
Germany*
Hochschule für Musik und Darstellende
Kunst Frankfurt am Main
*6000 Frankfurt am Main 1, Federal
Republic of Germany*
Hochschule für Musik und Theater
Hannover
*3000 Hannover 1, Federal Republic of
Germany*
Indiana University - Bloomington
School of Music
Bloomington, Indiana
Karol Szymanowski Academy of Music of
Katowice
Katowice, Poland
Kuopion Konservatorio
70100 Kuopio, Finland
Massachusetts Institute of Technology
Department of Music and Theater Arts
Cambridge, Massachusetts
Musik-Akademie der Stadt Basel
(Konservatorium)
Konservatorium (Musikhochschule)

Basel, Switzerland
Musikhochschule des Saarlandes
*6600 Saarbrücken 3, Federal Republic of
Germany*
Queen's University
School of Music
Kingston, Ontario, Canada
Royal Academy of Music
London NW1 5HT, United Kingdom
San Francisco Conservatory of Music
San Francisco, California
Shanghai Conservatory of Music
Shanghai, People's Republic of China
Smith College
Department of Music
Northampton, Massachusetts
Staatliche Hochschule für Musik Karlsruhe
*7500 Karlsruhe 1, Federal Republic of
Germany*
Staatliche Hochschule für Musik Rheinland
- Aachen
Grenzland-Institut Aachen
Aachen, Federal Republic of Germany
Staatliche Hochschule für Musik Rheinland
- Köln
*D-5000 Köln 1, Federal Republic of
Germany*
Staatliche Hochschule für Musik Rheinland
- Wuppertal
Institute Wuppertal
Wuppertal, Federal Republic of Germany
Staatliche Hochschule für Musik Ruhr
*4300 Essen 16, Federal Republic of
Germany*
Staatliche Hochschule für Musik
Westfalen-Lippe
*4930 Detmold, Federal Republic of
Germany*
Staatliche Hochschule für Musik
Westfalen-Lippe
Institut Dortmund
*D-4600 Dortmund 1, Federal Republic of
Germany*
Tbilisi V. Sarajishvili State Conservatory
*380004 Tbilisi 4, Gruzinskaja SSR,
U.S.S.R.*
Temple University
Esther Boyer College of Music
Philadelphia, Pennsylvania
Vysoká Skola Mûzickych Umeni v Praha
Academy of Music and Dramatic Arts
1101 00 Prague 1, Czechoslovakia
University of Wisconsin - Milwaukee
Music Department
Milwaukee, Wisconsin
Yale College (Yale University)
Department of Music
New Haven, Connecticut

CHINESE FOLK MUSIC

National Taiwan Academy of Arts
*Taipei County, Taiwan (Republic of
China)*

CHINESE INSTRUMENTS

Shengyang Conservatory of Music
*Shengyang, Liaoning Province, People's
Republic of China*
Sichuan Conservatory of Music
*Chengdu, Sichuan, People's Republic of
China*

CHINESE MUSIC

National Institute of the Arts
Music Department
Taipei County, Taiwan (Republic of China)
National Taiwan Academy of Arts
Taipei County, Taiwan (Republic of China)

CHINESE SINGING

Shengyang Conservatory of Music
Shengyang, Liaoning Province, People's Republic of China

CHINESE TRADITIONAL MUSIC

Conservatory of Chinese Music
Beijing, People's Republic of China

CHOIR MUSIC

Conservatorio di Musica "Santa Cecilia"
00187 Rome, Italy

CHORAL CONDUCTING

Alma-Ata Kurmangazy State Conservatory
480091 Alma-Ata 91, Kazahskaja SSR, U.S.S.R.
A.V. Nezhdanova Odessa Conservatory
270000 Odessa, Ukrainskaja SSR, U.S.S.R.
Azerbaijan S.S.R. U. Gajibekov State
Conservatory
370014 Baku, Azerbajdžanskaja SSR, U.S.S.R.
Baylor University
School of Music
Waco, Texas
Bob Jones University
Division of Music
Greenville, South Carolina
Boston Conservatory of Music
Boston, Massachusetts
California State University, Northridge
Music Department
Northridge, California
California State University, Sacramento
Department of Music
Sacramento, California
The Catholic University of America
The Benjamin T. Rome School of Music
Washington, District of Columbia
University of Central Arkansas
Department of Music
Conway, Arkansas
University of Cincinnati
College-Conservatory of Music
Cincinnati, Ohio
Colorado State University
Department of Music, Theatre, and
Dance
Fort Collins, Colorado
Conservatorio Nacional de Música
(National Conservatory of Music)
Lima 1, Peru
Donetsk Musical-Pedagogical Institute
340086 Donetsk, Ukrainskaja SSR, U.S.S.R.
Eastern Kentucky University
Department of Music
Richmond, Kentucky
Eastern Michigan University
Department of Music
Ypsilanti, Michigan
Erevan Komitas State Conservatory
375009 Erevan 9, Armjanskaja SSR, U.S.S.R.

Evangelische Kirchenmusikschule der
Kirchenprovinz Sachsen
(Evangelical Church Music School of the
Church Province Saxony)
*DDR-4020 Halle (Saale), German
Democratic Republic*
Fachakademie für Music - Augsburg
Leopold Mozart-Konservatorium der
Stadt Augsburg
Augsberg, Federal Republic of Germany
Fachakademie für Musik - Nürnberg
Konservatorium der Stadt Nürnberg
Nürnberg, Federal Republic of Germany
Far-Eastern Pedagogical Institute of the
Arts
690678 Vladivostok, Rossiskaja SFSR, U.S.S.R.
Ferenc Liszt Academy of Music
Budapest VI, Hungary
University of Georgia
School of Music
Athens, Georgia
Georgia State University
School of Music
Atlanta, Georgia
Gnessinsky State Musical and Pedagogical
Institute
121069 Moscow G-69, Rossiskaja SFSR, U.S.S.R.
Gorky M.I. Glinka State Conservatory
603005 Gorky, Rossiskaja SFSR, U.S.S.R.
Henderson State University
Department of Music
Arkadelphia, Arkansas
Hermann-Zilcher-Konservatorium
*D-8700 Würzburg, Federal Republic of
Germany*
Hochschule für Musik - München
*8000 München 2, Federal Republic of
Germany*
Hochschule für Musik - Würzburg
*D-8700 Würzburg, Federal Republic of
Germany*
Hochschule für Musik und Theater
Hannover
*3000 Hannover 1, Federal Republic of
Germany*
James Madison University
Department of Music
Harrisonburg, Virginia
Latvian S.S.R. Y. Vitol State Conservatory
226050 Riga, Latvijskaya SSR, U.S.S.R.
Levinsky Teachers College
Music Teachers Seminary
Tel-Aviv, Israel
Lithuanian State Conservatory
232001 Vilnius, Litovskaja SSR, U.S.S.R.
Mannes College of Music
New York, New York
University of Minnesota - Twin Cities
School of Music
Minneapolis, Minnesota
University of Missouri - Columbia
Department of Music
Columbia, Missouri
Moldavian S.S.R. G. Musichesku State
Conservatory
277014 Kishinev, Moldavskaja SSR, U.S.S.R.
University of Montana
Department of Music
Missoula, Montana
Nederlands Instituut voor Kerkmuziek
Utrecht, Netherlands
University of New Mexico
Department of Music

Albuquerque, New Mexico
University of North Carolina at Chapel Hill
Department of Music
Chapel Hill, North Carolina
University of North Carolina at Greensboro
School of Music
Greensboro, North Carolina
Oakland University
Department of Music, Theatre and
Dance
Rochester, Michigan
University of Oklahoma
School of Music
Norman, Oklahoma
University of Oregon
School of Music
Eugene, Oregon
University of the Philippines
College of Music
Quezon City, The Philippines
Pittsburg State University
Department of Music
Pittsburg, Kansas
University of Regina
Department of Music
Regina, Saskatchewan, Canada
Southern Methodist University
Meadows School of the Arts
Dallas, Texas
Southwestern Baptist Theological Seminary
School of Church Music
Fort Worth, Texas
Staatliche Hochschule für Musik Rheinland
- Aachen
Grenzland-Institut Aachen
Aachen, Federal Republic of Germany
Staatliche Hochschule für Musik Trossingen
*D-7218 Trossingen 1, Federal Republic of
Germany*
Staatliche Hochschule für Musik
Westfalen-Lippe
*4930 Detmold, Federal Republic of
Germany*
Tallinn State Conservatory
200015 Tallinn, Estonskaja SSR, U.S.S.R.
Tashkent State Conservatory
700000 Tashkent, Uzbekskaja SSR, U.S.S.R.
Tbilisi V. Sarajishvili State Conservatory
380004 Tbilisi 4, Gruzinskaja SSR, U.S.S.R.
Temple University
Esther Boyer College of Music
Philadelphia, Pennsylvania
University of Texas at Arlington
Department of Music
Arlington, Texas
Ufa State Institute of Fine Arts
450025 Ufa, Bashkir ASSR, U.S.S.R.
Urals M.P. Mussorgsky State Conservatory
620014 Sverdlovsk, Rossiskaja SFSR, U.S.S.R.
University of Washington
School of Music
Seattle, Washington
Washington University
Department of Music
St. Louis, Missouri
Yale University
School of Music
New Haven, Connecticut

511

CHORAL MUSIC

University of Alabama
    School of Music
    University, Alabama
Arizona State University
    School of Music
    Tempe, Arizona
California State University, Long Beach
    Department of Music
    Long Beach, California
University of Colorado at Boulder
    College of Music
    Boulder, Colorado
DePauw University
    School of Music
    Greencastle, Indiana
Eastern New Mexico University
    School of Music
    Portales, New Mexico
Escuela de Música - Heredia
    Universidad Nacional
    Heredia, Costa Rica
Henderson State University
    Department of Music
    Arkadelphia, Arkansas
University of Idaho
    School of Music
    Moscow, Idaho
University of Illinois
    School of Music
    Urbana, Illinois
Indiana State University
    Department of Music
    Terre Haute, Indiana
University of Montevallo
    Department of Music
    Montevallo, Alabama
The Ohio State University
    School of Music
    Columbus, Ohio
Real Conservatorio Superior de Música de Madrid
    (Royal Academy of Music)
    Madrid 13, Spain
Roosevelt University
    Chicago Musical College
    Chicago, Illinois
Smith College
    Department of Music
    Northampton, Massachusetts
University of Southern California
    School of Music
    Los Angeles, California
Staatliche Hochschule für Musik Rheinland - Aachen
    Grenzland-Institut Aachen
    Aachen, Federal Republic of Germany
Trinity College of Music
    London W1M 6AQ, United Kingdom
Virginia State University
    Department of Music Education
    Petersburg, Virginia
Webster University
    Department of Music
    St. Louis, Missouri
Wichita State University
    School of Music
    Wichita, Kansas

CHORAL MUSIC EDUCATION

The Catholic University of America
    The Benjamin T. Rome School of Music
    Washington, District of Columbia
Northern Arizona University
    Music Department
    Flagstaff, Arizona

CHORAL TEACHING

California State University, Los Angeles
    Department of Music
    Los Angeles, California

CHORAL TRAINING

Lvov M.V. Lysenko State Conservatory
    290005 Lvov, Ukrainskaja SSR, U.S.S.R.
Novosibirsk M.I. Glinka State Conservatory
    630099 Novosibirsk 99, Rossiskaja SFSR, U.S.S.R.

CHORUS TRAINING

Kazan State Conservatory
    420015 Kazan 15, Rossiskaja SFSR, U.S.S.R.
Kharkov State Institute of Arts
    310003 Kharkov, U.S.S.R.

CHURCH MUSIC

Andrews University
    Department of Music
    Berrien Springs, Michigan
Appalachian State University
    Department of Music
    Boone, North Carolina
Auburn University
    Department of Music
    Auburn, Alabama
Azusa Pacific University
    School of Music
    Azusa, California
Baylor University
    School of Music
    Waco, Texas
Biola University
    Department of Music
    La Mirada, California
Bob Jones University
    Division of Music
    Greenville, South Carolina
Boston University
    School of Music
    Boston, Massachusetts
Central Michigan University
    Department of Music
    Mount Pleasant, Michigan
University of Colorado at Boulder
    College of Music
    Boulder, Colorado
DePaul University
    School of Music
    Chicago, Illinois
DePauw University
    School of Music
    Greencastle, Indiana
Drake University
    Department of Music
    Des Moines, Iowa
East Carolina University
    School of Music
    Greenville, North Carolina
University of Evansville
    Music Department
    Evansville, Indiana
University of Florida
    Department of Music
    Gainesville, Florida
Florida State University
    School of Music
    Tallahassee, Florida
Georgia Southern College
    Department of Music
    Statesboro, Georgia
Hardin-Simmons University
    School of Music
    Abilene, Texas
Hochschule der Künste Berlin
    1000 Berlin 10, Federal Republic of Germany
Hochschule für Music und Darstellende Kunst Hamburg
    2000 Hamburg 13, Federal Republic of Germany
Hochschule für Musik und Darstellende Kunst Frankfurt am Main
    6000 Frankfurt am Main 1, Federal Republic of Germany
Hochschule für Musik und Theater Hannover
    3000 Hannover 1, Federal Republic of Germany
Illinois Wesleyan University
    School of Music
    Bloomington, Illinois
Indiana University - Bloomington
    School of Music
    Bloomington, Indiana
University of Kansas
    School of Fine Arts
    Lawrence, Kansas
Marywood College
    Music Department
    Scranton, Pennsylvania
University of Michigan
    School of Music
    Ann Arbor, Michigan
Millikin University
    School of Music
    Decatur, Illinois
University of Minnesota - Twin Cities
    School of Music
    Minneapolis, Minnesota
Musikhochschule des Saarlandes
    6600 Saarbrücken 3, Federal Republic of Germany
Musikhochschule Lübeck
    Grosse Petersgrube 17-29
    2400 Lübeck, Federal Republic of Germany
Musikhögskolan i Stockholm
    National College of Music
    115 31 Stockholm, Sweden
University of Nebraska - Lincoln
    School of Music
    Lincoln, Nebraska
Northwestern University
    School of Music
    Evanston, Illinois
The Ohio State University
    School of Music
    Columbus, Ohio
Ohio Wesleyan University
    Department of Music
    Delaware, Ohio
Oklahoma Baptist University
    Department of Music
    Shawnee, Oklahoma
Ouachita Baptist University
    School of Music
    Arkadelphia, Arkansas
Pacific Lutheran University
    Department of Music
    Tacoma, Washington
University of Pretoria
    Department of Music
    002 Pretoria, Republic of South Africa
University of Puget Sound
    School of Music

Tacoma, Washington
Radford University
  Department of Music
  Radford, Virginia
St. Olaf College
  Music Department
  Northfield, Minnesota
Samford University
  School of Music
  Birmingham, Alabama
Shenandoah College and Conservatory
  Winchester, Virginia
Shorter College
  Department of Music
  Rome, Georgia
Sibelius Academy of Music
  SF-00260 Helsinki 26, Finland
Southern Baptist Theological Seminary
  School of Church Music
  Louisville, Kentucky
University of Southern California
  School of Music
  Los Angeles, California
University of Southern Mississippi
  School of Music
  Hattiesburg, Mississippi
Southwestern Baptist Theological Seminary
  School of Church Music
  Fort Worth, Texas
Southwestern Oklahoma State University
  Department of Music
  Weatherford, Oklahoma
Staatliche Hochschule für Musik Freiburg
  D-7800 Freiburg i. Br., Federal Republic of Germany
Staatliche Hochschule für Musik Karlsruhe
  7500 Karlsruhe 1, Federal Republic of Germany
Staatliche Hochschule für Musik Rheinland - Köln
  D-5000 Köln 1, Federal Republic of Germany
Staatliche Hochschule für Musik Westfalen-Lippe
  4930 Detmold, Federal Republic of Germany
Stetson University
  School of Music
  Deland, Florida
Valparaiso University
  Department of Music
  Valparaiso, Indiana
Virginia Commonwealth University
  Department of Music
  Richmond, Virginia
Wayne State University
  Department of Music
  Detroit, Michigan
West Texas State University
  Department of Music
  Canyon, Texas
Wilfrid Laurier University
  Faculty of Music
  Waterloo, Ontario, Canada
William Carey College
  Winters School of Music
  Hattiesburg, Mississippi
University of Windsor
  School of Music
  Windsor, Ontario, Canada
Winthrop College
  School of Music
  Rock Hill, South Carolina

CHURCH MUSIC (CATHOLIC)

Fachakademie für Music - Augsburg
  Leopold Mozart-Konservatorium der Stadt Augsburg
  Augsberg, Federal Republic of Germany
Fachakademie für Musik - München
  Richard Strauss-Konservatorium der Stadt
  München 80, Federal Republic of Germany
Hermann-Zilcher-Konservatorium
  D-8700 Würzburg, Federal Republic of Germany
Hochschule für Musik - München
  8000 München 2, Federal Republic of Germany
Hochschule für Musik - Würzburg
  D-8700 Würzburg, Federal Republic of Germany
Staatliche Hochschule für Musik und Darstellende Kunst Stuttgart
  7000 Stuttgart 1, Federal Republic of Germany
Staatliche Hochschule für Musik Westfalen-Lippe
  Institut Dortmund
  D-4600 Dortmund 1, Federal Republic of Germany

CHURCH MUSIC (PROTESTANT)

Fachakademie für Musik - München
  Richard Strauss-Konservatorium der Stadt
  München 80, Federal Republic of Germany
Hochschule für Musik - München
  8000 München 2, Federal Republic of Germany
Hochschule für Musik - Würzburg
  D-8700 Würzburg, Federal Republic of Germany
Staatliche Hochschule für Musik und Darstellende Kunst Stuttgart
  7000 Stuttgart 1, Federal Republic of Germany
Staatliche Hochschule für Musik Westfalen-Lippe
  Institut Dortmund
  D-4600 Dortmund 1, Federal Republic of Germany

COLLECTIVE IMPROVISATION

Hochschule für Gestaltende Kunst und Musik
  (State College for Creative Art and Music)
  2800 Bremen 1, Federal Republic of Germany

COLLEGE CHOIR

Staatliche Hochschule für Musik Rheinland - Düsseldorf
  (State College of Music)
  D-4000 Düsseldorf, Federal Republic of Germany

COLOUR STRINGS METHOD

The East Helsinki Music Institute
  SF-00820 Helsinki, Finland

COMMERCIAL ARRANGING

Berklee College of Music
  Boston, Massachusetts

COMMERCIAL MUSIC

American Conservatory of Music
  Chicago, Illinois
California State University, Los Angeles
  Department of Music
  Los Angeles, California
Central Missouri State University
  Department of Music
  Warrensburg, Missouri
Delta State University
  Department of Music
  Cleveland, Mississippi
Hofstra University
  Department of Music
  Hempstead, New York
Jersey City State College
  Music Department
  Jersey City, New Jersey
McNeese State University
  Department of Music
  Lake Charles, Louisiana
Memphis State University
  Music Department
  Memphis, Tennessee
Oakland University
  Department of Music, Theatre and Dance
  Rochester, Michigan
Philadelphia College of the Performing Arts
  School of Music
  Philadelphia, Pennsylvania
Roosevelt University
  Chicago Musical College
  Chicago, Illinois
Shenandoah College and Conservatory
  Winchester, Virginia
University of South Carolina
  School of Music
  Columbia, South Carolina
Temple University
  Esther Boyer College of Music
  Philadelphia, Pennsylvania
Towson State University
  Department of Music
  Towson, Maryland
Webster University
  Department of Music
  St. Louis, Missouri

COMPOSITION

Acadia University
  School of Music
  Wolfville, Nova Scotia, Canada
University of Adelaide
  Elder Conservatorium of Music
  Adelaide, SA 5001, Australia
Akademia Muzyczna w Krakowie
  31-038 Kraków, Poland
Akademia Muzyczna w Lódź
  (Academy of Music of Lódź)
  90-716 Lódź, Poland
Akademia Muzycznaj im. Fryderyka Chopina w Warzawie
  (Frederic Chopin Academy of Music of Warsaw)
  00-368 Warsaw, Poland
University of Akron
  Department of Music
  Akron, Ohio
Alabama State University
  School of Music
  Montgomery, Alabama
University of Alberta
  Department of Music
  Edmonton, Alberta, Canada

Alma-Ata Kurmangazy State Conservatory
480091 Alma-Ata 91, Kazahskaja SSR,
U.S.S.R.
American Conservatory of Music
Chicago, Illinois
Appalachian State University
Department of Music
Boone, North Carolina
University of Arizona
School of Music
Tucson, Arizona
Arizona State University
School of Music
Tempe, Arizona
Arkansas State University
Department of Music
State University, Arkansas
Arkansas Tech University
Department of Music
Russellville, Arkansas
Auburn University
Department of Music
Auburn, Alabama
A.V. Nezhdanova Odessa Conservatory
270000 Odessa, Ukrainskaja SSR,
U.S.S.R.
Azerbaijan S.S.R. U. Gajibekov State
Conservatory
370014 Baku, Azerbajdžanskaja SSR,
U.S.S.R.
Baldwin-Wallace College
Conservatory of Music
Berea, Ohio
Ball State University
School of Music
Muncie, Indiana
Banaras Hindu University
Uttar Pradesh 221005, India
Baylor University
School of Music
Waco, Texas
Bemidji State University
Music Department
Bemidji, Minnesota
Bennington College
Music Department
Bennington, Vermont
Berklee College of Music
Boston, Massachusetts
Biola University
Department of Music
La Mirada, California
Boise State University
Music Department
Boise, Idaho
Boston Conservatory of Music
Boston, Massachusetts
Boston University
School of Music
Boston, Massachusetts
Bowling Green State University
College of Musical Arts
Bowling Green, Ohio
Bradley University
Division of Music and Theatre Arts
Peoria, Illinois
Brandeis University
Department of Music
Waltham, Massachusetts
Brigham Young University
Department of Music
Provo, Utah
University of British Columbia
School of Music
Vancouver, British Columbia, Canada

Brown University
Department of Music
Providence, Rhode Island
Bulgarian State Conservatoire
Sofia 1505, Bulgaria
Butler University
Jordan College of Fine Arts
Indianapolis, Indiana
Byelorussian State Conservatory
220030 Minsk, Belorusskaja SSR,
U.S.S.R.
University of Calgary
Department of Music
Calgary, Alberta, Canada
University of California, Berkeley
Department of Music
Berkeley, California
University of California, Los Angeles
Department of Music
Los Angeles, California
University of California, Riverside
Department of Music
Riverside, California
University of California, San Diego
Department of Music
La Jolla, California
University of California, Santa Barbara
Department of Music
Santa Barbara, California
California Institute of the Arts
School of Music
Valencia, California
California State University, Chico
Department of Music
Chico, California
California State University, Fresno
Department of Music
Fresno, California
California State University, Fullerton
Department of Music
Fullerton, California
California State University, Hayward
Department of Music
Hayward, California
California State University, Long Beach
Department of Music
Long Beach, California
California State University, Los Angeles
Department of Music
Los Angeles, California
California State University, Northridge
Music Department
Northridge, California
California State University, Sacramento
Department of Music
Sacramento, California
University of Cape Town
Faculty of Music
Cape Town, Republic of South Africa
Carnegie-Mellon University
Department of Music
Pittsburgh, Pennsylvania
Central Michigan University
Department of Music
Mount Pleasant, Michigan
Central Missouri State University
Department of Music
Warrensburg, Missouri
Central State University
Department of Music
Edmond, Oklahoma
Central Washington University
Department of Music
Ellensburg, Washington
University of Chicago
Department of Music

Chicago, Illinois
University of Cincinnati
College-Conservatory of Music
Cincinnati, Ohio
City of Leeds College of Music
Leeds LS2 8BH, United Kingdom
City University of New York - Brooklyn
College
Conservatory of Music
Brooklyn, New York
City University of New York - City College
Department of Music
New York, New York
City University of New York - Graduate
School and University Center
Doctoral Program in Music
New York, New York
City University of New York - Hunter
College
Department of Music
New York, New York
The Claremont Graduate School
Music Department
Claremont, California
Cleveland Institute of Music
Cleveland, Ohio
Cleveland State University
Department of Music
Cleveland, Ohio
University of Colorado at Boulder
College of Music
Boulder, Colorado
Columbia University
Department of Music
New York, New York
Combs College of Music
Philadelphia, Pennsylvania
University of Connecticut
Department of Music
Storrs, Connecticut
Conservatorio di Musica "Santa Cecilia"
00187 Rome, Italy
Conservatorio Nacional de Música
(National Conservatory of Music)
Lima 1, Peru
Conservatorio Nacional de Musica - La Paz
(National Conservatory of Music - La
Paz)
La Paz, Bolivia
Conservatorul de Musică George Dima
(Conservatory of Music)
3400 Cluj-Napoca, Romania
Conservatorul de Muzică Ciprian
Porumbescu
(Conservatory of Music)
70732 Bucharest, Romania
Conservatorul Georges Enescu
(Conservatory of Music)
6600 Iasi, Romania
Converse College
School of Music
Spartanburg, South Carolina
Cornell University
Department of Music
Ithaca, New York
Dalhousie University
Department of Music
Halifax, Nova Scotia, Canada
University of Delaware
Department of Music
Newark, Delaware
University of Denver
Lamont School of Music
Denver, Colorado
DePaul University
School of Music

Chicago, Illinois
DePauw University
  School of Music
  Greencastle, Indiana
Drake University
  Department of Music
  Des Moines, Iowa
Duke University
  Department of Music
  Durham, North Carolina
Duquesne University
  School of Music
  Pittsburgh, Pennsylvania
East Carolina University
  School of Music
  Greenville, North Carolina
East Texas State University
  Department of Music
  Commerce, Texas
Eastern Illinois University
  Department of Music
  Charleston, Illinois
Eastern Kentucky University
  Department of Music
  Richmond, Kentucky
Eastern Michigan University
  Department of Music
  Ypsilanti, Michigan
Eastern New Mexico University
  School of Music
  Portales, New Mexico
Eastern Washington University
  Department of Music
  Cheney, Washington
Emporia State University
  Division of Music
  Emporia, Kansas
Erevan Komitas State Conservatory
  375009 Erevan 9, Armjanskaja SSR,
  U.S.S.R.
Escuela Universitaria de Música -
  Montevideo
  Montevideo, Uruguay
Fachakademie für Music - Augsburg
  Leopold Mozart-Konservatorium der
  Stadt Augsburg
  Augsberg, Federal Republic of Germany
Fachakademie für Musik - München
  Richard Strauss-Konservatorium der
  Stadt
  München 80, Federal Republic of
  Germany
Fachakademie für Musik - Nürnberg
  Konservatorium der Stadt Nürnberg
  Nürnberg, Federal Republic of Germany
Faculdade Santa Marcelina
  05006 São Paulo, Brazil
Ferenc Liszt Academy of Music
  Budapest VI, Hungary
University of Florida
  Department of Music
  Gainesville, Florida
Fort Hays State University
  Department of Music
  Hays, Kansas
George Mason University
  Department of Performing Arts - Music
  Division
  Fairfax, Virginia
University of Georgia
  School of Music
  Athens, Georgia
Georgia Southern College
  Department of Music
  Statesboro, Georgia

Glassboro State College
  Department of Music
  Glassboro, New Jersey
Gnessinsky State Musical and Pedagogical
  Institute
  121069 Moscow G-69, Rossiskaja SFSR,
  U.S.S.R.
Gorky M.I. Glinka State Conservatory
  603005 Gorky, Rossiskaja SFSR, U.S.S.R.
Guildhall School of Music and Drama
  London EC2Y 8DT, United Kingdom
University of Hartford
  Hartt School of Music
  West Hartford, Connecticut
Harvard University
  Department of Music
  Cambridge, Massachusetts
University of Hawaii at Manoa
  Music Department
  Honolulu, Hawaii
Henderson State University
  Department of Music
  Arkadelphia, Arkansas
Hochschule der Künste Berlin
  1000 Berlin 10, Federal Republic of
  Germany
Hochschule für Gestaltende Kunst und
  Musik
  (State College for Creative Art and
  Music)
  2800 Bremen 1, Federal Republic of
  Germany
Hochschule für Music Franz Liszt
  DDR 5300 Weimar, German Democratic
  Republic
Hochschule für Music und Darstellende
  Kunst Hamburg
  2000 Hamburg 13, Federal Republic of
  Germany
Hochschule für Musik - München
  8000 München 2, Federal Republic of
  Germany
Hochschule für Musik - Würzburg
  D-8700 Würzburg, Federal Republic of
  Germany
Hochschule für Musik Felix
  Mendelssohn-Bartholdy
  7010 Leipzig, German Democratic
  Republic
Hochschule für Musik und Darstellende
  Kunst Frankfurt am Main
  6000 Frankfurt am Main 1, Federal
  Republic of Germany
Hochschule für Musik und Theater
  Hannover
  3000 Hannover 1, Federal Republic of
  Germany
Hofstra University
  Department of Music
  Hempstead, New York
Hoschschule für Music Hans Eisler
  DDR Berlin 1080, German Democratic
  Republic
University of Houston
  School of Music
  Houston, Texas
Howard University
  Department of Music
  Washington, District of Columbia
University of Idaho
  School of Music
  Moscow, Idaho
University of Illinois
  School of Music
  Urbana, Illinois

Illinois State University
  Department of Music
  Normal, Illinois
Illinois Wesleyan University
  School of Music
  Bloomington, Illinois
Indiana University - Bloomington
  School of Music
  Bloomington, Indiana
Indiana University of Pennsylvania
  Department of Music
  Indiana, Pennsylvania
Institute of Aesthetic Studies
  Colombo 7, Sri Lanka
Instituto Superior de Arte
  Facultad de Música
  Playa, Cuba
University of Iowa
  School of Music
  Iowa City, Iowa
Iowa State University
  Department of Music
  Ames, Iowa
Ithaca College
  School of Music
  Ithaca, New York
James Madison University
  Department of Music
  Harrisonburg, Virginia
Jersey City State College
  Music Department
  Jersey City, New Jersey
The Juilliard School
  New York, New York
University of Kansas
  School of Fine Arts
  Lawrence, Kansas
Kansas State University
  Department of Music
  Manhattan, Kansas
Kazan State Conservatory
  420015 Kazan 15, Rossiskaja SFSR,
  U.S.S.R.
University of Kentucky
  School of Music
  Lexington, Kentucky
Kharkov State Institute of Arts
  310003 Kharkov, U.S.S.R.
Kiev P.I. Tchaikovsky Conservatory
  252001 Kiev, Ukrainskaja SSR, U.S.S.R.
Konservatorium und Musikhochschule -
  Zürich
  8050 Zürich, Switzerland
Konzervatorium - Bratislava
  Bratislava 811 06, Czechoslovakia
Kratikon Odeion Thessaloniki
  (State Conservatory of Music)
  Thessaloniki, Greece
Lamar University
  Department of Music
  Beaumont, Texas
Latvian S.S.R. Y. Vitol State Conservatory
  226050 Riga, Latvijskaya SSR, U.S.S.R.
Leningrad N.A. Rimsky-Korsakov State
  Conservatory
  192041 Leningrad, Rossiskaja SFSR,
  U.S.S.R.
Lewis and Clark College
  Music Department
  Portland, Oregon
Long Island University - C.W. Post Campus
  Music Department
  Greenvale, New York
Louisiana State University
  School of Music
  Baton Rouge, Louisiana

University of Louisville
    School of Music
    Louisville, Kentucky
Loyola University
    College of Music
    New Orleans, Louisiana
Lvov M.V. Lysenko State Conservatory
    290005 Lvov, Ukrainskaja SSR, U.S.S.R.
University of Maine
    School of Performing Arts
    Orono, Maine
Manhattan School of Music
    New York, New York
University of Manitoba
    School of Music
    Winnipeg, Manitoba, Canada
Mannes College of Music
    New York, New York
Mansfield University
    Department of Music
    Mansfield, Pennsylvania
Marshall University
    Department of Music
    Huntington, West Virginia
University of Maryland - Baltimore County
    Department of Music
    Catonsville, Maryland
University of Maryland - College Park
    Department of Music
    College Park, Maryland
University of Massachusetts at Amherst
    Department of Music and Dance
    Amherst, Massachusetts
Massachusetts Institute of Technology
    Department of Music and Theater Arts
    Cambridge, Massachusetts
McGill University
    Faculty of Music
    Montreal, Québec, Canada
McNeese State University
    Department of Music
    Lake Charles, Louisiana
University of Melbourne
    Faculty of Music
    Victoria 3052, Australia
Memphis State University
    Music Department
    Memphis, Tennessee
University of Miami
    School of Music
    Coral Gables, Florida
Miami University
    Department of Music
    Oxford, Ohio
University of Michigan
    School of Music
    Ann Arbor, Michigan
Michigan State University
    School of Music
    East Lansing, Michigan
Middle Tennessee State University
    Department of Music
    Murfreesboro, Tennessee
Mills College
    Music Department
    Oakland, California
University of Minnesota - Duluth
    Department of Music
    Duluth, Minnesota
University of Minnesota - Twin Cities
    School of Music
    Minneapolis, Minnesota
University of Mississippi
    Department of Music
    University, Mississippi

University of Missouri - Columbia
    Department of Music
    Columbia, Missouri
University of Missouri - Kansas City
    Conservatory of Music
    Kansas City, Missouri
Moldavian S.S.R. G. Musichesku State
Conservatory
    *277014 Kishinev, Moldavskaja SSR,
    U.S.S.R.*
University of Montana
    Department of Music
    Missoula, Montana
Montclair State College
    Department of Music
    Upper Montclair, New Jersey
Moorhead State University
    Music Department
    Moorhead, Minnesota
Moscow P.I. Tchaikovsky State
Conservatory
    *103009 Moscow K-9, Rossiskaja SFSR,
    U.S.S.R.*
Musik-Akademie der Stadt Basel
(Konservatorium)
    Konservatorium (Musikhochschule)
    Basel, Switzerland
Musikhochschule des Saarlandes
    *6600 Saarbrücken 3, Federal Republic of
    Germany*
Musikschule und Konservatorium
Schaffhausen
    Schaffhausen, Switzerland
National Institute of Music - Sana'a
    Sana'a, Yemen Arab Republic
National Institute of the Arts
    Music Department
    *Taipei County, Taiwan (Republic of
    China)*
University of Nebraska - Lincoln
    School of Music
    Lincoln, Nebraska
University of Nevada, Las Vegas
    Department of Music
    Las Vegas, Nevada
New England Conservatory
    Boston, Massachusetts
University of New Hampshire
    Department of Music
    Durham, New Hampshire
University of New Mexico
    Department of Music
    Albuquerque, New Mexico
New Mexico State University
    Department of Music
    Las Cruces, New Mexico
University of New Orleans
    Department of Music
    New Orleans, Louisiana
New South Wales State Conservatorium of
Music
    Sydney NSW 2000, Australia
New York University - School of Education,
Health, Nursing, and Arts Professions
    Department of Music and Music
    Education
    New York, New York
Norfolk State University
    Department of Music
    Norfolk, Virginia
Norges Musikkhøgskole
    (The Norwegian State Academy of
    Music)
    N-0130 Oslo 1, Norway
University of North Carolina at Chapel Hill
    Department of Music

Chapel Hill, North Carolina
University of North Carolina at Greensboro
    School of Music
    Greensboro, North Carolina
North Carolina School of the Arts
    School of Music
    Winston-Salem, North Carolina
University of North Dakota
    Department of Music
    Grand Forks, North Dakota
North Texas State University
    School of Music
    Denton, Texas
Northern Illinois University
    School of Music
    DeKalb, Illinois
University of Northern Iowa
    School of Music
    Cedar Falls, Iowa
Northwestern State University of Louisiana
    Department of Music
    Natchitoches, Louisiana
Northwestern University
    School of Music
    Evanston, Illinois
Novosibirsk M.I. Glinka State Conservatory
    *630099 Novosibirsk 99, Rossiskaja SFSR,
    U.S.S.R.*
Oakland University
    Department of Music, Theatre and
    Dance
    Rochester, Michigan
Oberlin College
    Conservatory of Music
    Oberlin, Ohio
Odeion Athenon
    (Conservatory of Athens)
    Athens, Greece
The Ohio State University
    School of Music
    Columbus, Ohio
Ohio University
    School of Music
    Athens, Ohio
University of Oklahoma
    School of Music
    Norman, Oklahoma
Oklahoma Baptist University
    Department of Music
    Shawnee, Oklahoma
Oklahoma City University
    School of Music and Performing Arts
    Oklahoma City, Oklahoma
University of Orange Free State
    Department of Music
    *9300 Bloemfontein, Republic of South
    Africa*
University of Oregon
    School of Music
    Eugene, Oregon
Oregon State University
    Department of Music
    Corvallis, Oregon
Osaka Ongaku Daigaku
    (Osaka College of Music)
    Osaka 561, Japan
Ouachita Baptist University
    School of Music
    Arkadelphia, Arkansas
University of the Pacific
    Conservatory of Music
    Stockton, California
Pacific Lutheran University
    Department of Music
    Tacoma, Washington

Peabody Institute of The Johns Hopkins
University
Baltimore, Maryland
University of Pennsylvania
Department of Music
Philadelphia, Pennsylvania
Pennsylvania State University
School of Music
University Park, Pennsylvania
Philadelphia College of the Performing Arts
School of Music
Philadelphia, Pennsylvania
University of the Philippines
College of Music
Quezon City, The Philippines
Pittsburg State University
Department of Music
Pittsburg, Kansas
University of Pittsburgh
Department of Music
Pittsburgh, Pennsylvania
Portland State University
Department of Music
Portland, Oregon
University of Pretoria
Department of Music
002 Pretoria, Republic of South Africa
Princeton University
Department of Music
Princeton, New Jersey
Queen's University
School of Music
Kingston, Ontario, Canada
Radford University
Department of Music
Radford, Virginia
Real Conservatorio Superior de Música de
Madrid
(Royal Academy of Music)
Madrid 13, Spain
University of Redlands
School of Music
Redlands, California
University of Regina
Department of Music
Regina, Saskatchewan, Canada
University of Rhode Island
Department of Music
Kingston, Rhode Island
Rice University
Shepherd School of Music
Houston, Texas
University of Rochester
Eastman School of Music
Rochester, New York
Roosevelt University
Chicago Musical College
Chicago, Illinois
Rostov State Institute of Pedagogics and
Music
*344007 Rostov-on-Don, Rossiskaja SFSR,
U.S.S.R.*
Royal Academy of Music
London NW1 5HT, United Kingdom
Royal College of Music
London, SW7 2BS, United Kingdom
Royal Irish Academy of Music
Dublin 2, Ireland
Royal Northern College of Music
Manchester M13 9RD, United Kingdom
Royal Scottish Academy of Music and
Drama
Glasgow G2 1BS, United Kingdom
Rutgers, The State University of New Jersey
Department of Music
New Brunswick, New Jersey

Saint Louis Conservatory of Music
St. Louis, Missouri
Sam Houston State University
Department of Music
Huntsville, Texas
Samford University
School of Music
Birmingham, Alabama
San Diego State University
Music Department
San Diego, California
San Francisco Conservatory of Music
San Francisco, California
San Francisco State University
Department of Music
San Francisco, California
San Jose State University
Department of Music
San Jose, California
University of Santo Tomas
Conservatory of Music
Manila, The Philippines
University of Saskatchewan
Department of Music
Saskatoon, Saskatchewan, Canada
Shanghai Conservatory of Music
Shanghai, People's Republic of China
Shenandoah College and Conservatory
Winchester, Virginia
Shengyang Conservatory of Music
*Shengyang, Liaoning Province, People's
Republic of China*
Sichuan Conservatory of Music
*Chengdu, Sichuan, People's Republic of
China*
University of South Carolina
School of Music
Columbia, South Carolina
Southeast Missouri State University
Department of Music
Cape Girardeau, Missouri
Southeastern Louisiana University
Department of Music
Hammond, Louisiana
Southeastern Oklahoma State University
Department of Music
Durant, Oklahoma
Southern Baptist Theological Seminary
School of Church Music
Louisville, Kentucky
University of Southern California
School of Music
Los Angeles, California
Southern Illinois University at Carbondale
School of Music
Carbondale, Illinois
Southern Illinois University at Edwardsville
Department of Music
Edwardsville, Illinois
Southern Methodist University
Meadows School of the Arts
Dallas, Texas
University of Southern Mississippi
School of Music
Hattiesburg, Mississippi
Southwest Texas State University
Department of Music
San Marcos, Texas
Southwestern Baptist Theological Seminary
School of Church Music
Fort Worth, Texas
Southwestern Oklahoma State University
Department of Music
Weatherford, Oklahoma
Staatliche Hochschule für Musik Freiburg
D-7800 Freiburg i. Br., Federal Republic

of Germany
Staatliche Hochschule für Musik
Heidelberg-Mannheim
*Friedrich-Ebert-Anlage 62, Federal
Republic of Germany*
Staatliche Hochschule für Musik Karlsruhe
*7500 Karlsruhe 1, Federal Republic of
Germany*
Staatliche Hochschule für Musik Rheinland
- Aachen
Grenzland-Institut Aachen
Aachen, Federal Republic of Germany
Staatliche Hochschule für Musik Rheinland
- Düsseldorf
(State College of Music)
*D-4000 Düsseldorf, Federal Republic of
Germany*
Staatliche Hochschule für Musik Rheinland
- Köln
*D-5000 Köln 1, Federal Republic of
Germany*
Staatliche Hochschule für Musik Rheinland
- Wuppertal
Institute Wuppertal
Wuppertal, Federal Republic of Germany
Staatliche Hochschule für Musik Ruhr
*4300 Essen 16, Federal Republic of
Germany*
Staatliche Hochschule für Musik Trossingen
*D-7218 Trossingen 1, Federal Republic of
Germany*
Staatliche Hochschule für Musik
Westfalen-Lippe
*4930 Detmold, Federal Republic of
Germany*
Staatliche Hochschule für Musik
Westfalen-Lippe
Institut Dortmund
*D-4600 Dortmund 1, Federal Republic of
Germany*
Stanford University
Department of Music
Stanford, California
State University of New York at
Binghamton
Department of Music
Binghamton, New York
State University of New York at Buffalo
Department of Music
Buffalo, New York
State University of New York at Stony
Brook
Department of Music
Stony Brook, New York
State University of New York College at
Fredonia
School of Music
Fredonia, New York
State University of New York College at
New Paltz
Department of Music
New Paltz, New York
State University of New York College at
Potsdam
Crane School of Music
Potsdam, New York
State University of New York College at
Purchase
Division of Music
Purchase, New York
University of Stellenbosch
Department of Music (Conservatoire)
*7600 Stellenbosch, Republic of South
Africa*
Stephen F. Austin State University
Department of Music

Nacogdoches, Texas
University of Sydney
Department of Music
Sydney, NSW 2006, Australia
Syracuse University
School of Music
Syracuse, New York
Tashkent State Conservatory
700000 Tashkent, Uzbekskaja SSR,
U.S.S.R.
Tasmanian Conservatorium of Music
Hobart, Tasmania 7001, Australia
Tel Aviv University
Faculty of Fine Arts
Tel-Aviv, Israel
Temple University
Esther Boyer College of Music
Philadelphia, Pennsylvania
University of Tennessee at Chattanooga
Cadek Department of Music
Chattanooga, Tennessee
University of Tennessee at Knoxville
Department of Music
Knoxville, Tennessee
University of Texas at Arlington
Department of Music
Arlington, Texas
University of Texas at Austin
Department of Music
Austin, Texas
University of Texas at San Antonio
Division of Music
San Antonio, Texas
Texas Christian University
Music Department
Fort Worth, Texas
Texas Southern University
Department of Music
Houston, Texas
Texas Tech University
Department of Music
Lubbock, Texas
Toho Gakuen School of Music
Tokyo, Japan
Tonlistarskolinn i Reykjavik
105 Reykjavik, Iceland
University of Toronto
Faculty of Music
Toronto, Ontario, Canada
Trenton State College
Music Department
Trenton, New Jersey
Trinity College of Music
London W1M 6AQ, United Kingdom
Tulane University
Newcomb College
New Orleans, Louisiana
University of Tulsa
Faculty of Music
Tulsa, Oklahoma
Ueno Gakuen College
Tokyo 110, Japan
Universidad de Antioquía
Facultad de Artes, Departamento de
Música
Medellín, Colombia
Universidade do Rio de Janeiro
Letters and Arts Center - Music Course
22290 Rio de Janeiro, Brazil
Universidade do São Paulo
Department of Music
05508 São Paulo, Brazil
Université de Montréal
Faculty of Music
Montréal, Québec, Canada

Urals M.P. Mussorgsky State Conservatory
620014 Sverdlovsk, Rossiskaja SFSR,
U.S.S.R.
University of Utah
Department of Music
Salt Lake City, Utah
Valparaiso University
Department of Music
Valparaiso, Indiana
University of Vermont
Department of Music
Burlington, Vermont
University of Victoria
School of Music
Victoria, British Columbia, Canada
Virginia Commonwealth University
Department of Music
Richmond, Virginia
Virginia Polytechnic Institute and State
University
Department of Music
Blacksburg, Virginia
Vysoká Skola Mûzickych Umeni v Praha
Academy of Music and Dramatic Arts
1101 00 Prague 1, Czechoslovakia
University of Washington
School of Music
Seattle, Washington
Washington State University
Department of Music
Pullman, Washington
Washington University
Department of Music
St. Louis, Missouri
Wayne State University
Department of Music
Detroit, Michigan
Wesleyan University
Department of Music
Middletown, Connecticut
West Chester University of Pennsylvania
School of Music
West Chester, Pennsylvania
West Virginia University
Division of Music
Morgantown, West Virginia
University of Western Australia
Department of Music
Nedlands, WA 6009, Australia
Western Kentucky University
Department of Music
Bowling Green, Kentucky
Western Michigan University
School of Music
Kalamazoo, Michigan
University of Western Ontario
Faculty of Music
London, Ontario, Canada
Western Washington University
Department of Music
Bellingham, Washington
Westminster Choir College
Princeton, New Jersey
Wheaton College
Conservatory of Music
Wheaton, Illinois
Wichita State University
School of Music
Wichita, Kansas
Wilfrid Laurier University
Faculty of Music
Waterloo, Ontario, Canada
William Paterson College
Department of Music
Wayne, New Jersey

University of Wisconsin - Eau Claire
Department of Music
Eau Claire, Wisconsin
University of Wisconsin - Madison
School of Music
Madison, Wisconsin
University of Wisconsin - Milwaukee
Music Department
Milwaukee, Wisconsin
University of Wisconsin - Oshkosh
Department of Music
Oshkosh, Wisconsin
University of the Witwatersrand
Wits School of Music
2001 Johannesburg, Republic of South
Africa
Wright State University
Department of Music
Dayton, Ohio
University of Wyoming
Music Department
Laramie, Wyoming
Yale University
School of Music
New Haven, Connecticut
Yared National Institute of Music
Addis Ababa, Ethiopia
York University
Department of Music
North York, Ontario, Canada
Youngstown State University
Dana School of Music
Youngstown, Ohio

COMPUTER MUSIC

University of California, San Diego
Department of Music
La Jolla, California
Indiana University - Bloomington
School of Music
Bloomington, Indiana
Massachusetts Institute of Technology
Department of Music and Theater Arts
Cambridge, Massachusetts

COMPUTERS IN MUSIC

Florida State University
School of Music
Tallahassee, Florida

CONDUCTING

Akademia Muzyczna w Krakowie
31-038 Kraków, Poland
Akademia Muzycznaj im. Fryderyka
Chopina w Warzawie
(Frederic Chopin Academy of Music of
Warsaw)
00-368 Warsaw, Poland
University of Alabama
School of Music
University, Alabama
Andrews University
Department of Music
Berrien Springs, Michigan

Astrakhan State Conservatory
414000 Astrakhan, Rossiskaja SFSR,
U.S.S.R.
Azusa Pacific University
School of Music
Azusa, California
Bemidji State University
Music Department
Bemidji, Minnesota
Boston University
School of Music
Boston, Massachusetts
Bowling Green State University
College of Musical Arts
Bowling Green, Ohio
Bradley University
Division of Music and Theatre Arts
Peoria, Illinois
Bulgarian State Conservatoire
Sofia 1505, Bulgaria
Butler University
Jordan College of Fine Arts
Indianapolis, Indiana
University of California, Berkeley
Department of Music
Berkeley, California
University of California, Los Angeles
Department of Music
Los Angeles, California
California State University, Fullerton
Department of Music
Fullerton, California
Carnegie-Mellon University
Department of Music
Pittsburgh, Pennsylvania
Central Conservatory of Music
Beijing, People's Republic of China
Central Washington University
Department of Music
Ellensburg, Washington
City University of New York - Queens
College
The Aaron Copland School of Music
Flushing, New York
The Claremont Graduate School
Music Department
Claremont, California
University of Colorado at Boulder
College of Music
Boulder, Colorado
Combs College of Music
Philadelphia, Pennsylvania
University of Connecticut
Department of Music
Storrs, Connecticut
Conservatorio di Musica "Santa Cecilia"
00187 Rome, Italy
Conservatorio Nacional de Música
(National Conservatory of Music)
Lima 1, Peru
Conservatorul de Muzică Ciprian
Porumbescu
(Conservatory of Music)
70732 Bucharest, Romania
The Curtis Institute of Music
Philadelphia, Pennsylvania
University of Denver
Lamont School of Music
Denver, Colorado
Duquesne University
School of Music
Pittsburgh, Pennsylvania
East Carolina University
School of Music
Greenville, North Carolina

East Texas State University
Department of Music
Commerce, Texas
Eastern Michigan University
Department of Music
Ypsilanti, Michigan
Eastern Washington University
Department of Music
Cheney, Washington
Escuela Universitaria de Música -
Montevideo
Montevideo, Uruguay
Fachakademie für Musik - München
Richard Strauss-Konservatorium der
Stadt
München 80, Federal Republic of
Germany
University of Florida
Department of Music
Gainesville, Florida
George Mason University
Department of Performing Arts - Music
Division
Fairfax, Virginia
Guildhall School of Music and Drama
London EC2Y 8DT, United Kingdom
Hochschule der Künste Berlin
1000 Berlin 10, Federal Republic of
Germany
Hochschule für Gestaltende Kunst und
Musik
(State College for Creative Art and
Music)
2800 Bremen 1, Federal Republic of
Germany
Hochschule für Music Franz Liszt
DDR 5300 Weimar, German Democratic
Republic
Hochschule für Musik und Darstellende
Kunst Frankfurt am Main
6000 Frankfurt am Main 1, Federal
Republic of Germany
Hochschule für Musik und Theater
Hannover
3000 Hannover 1, Federal Republic of
Germany
Hoschschule für Music Hans Eisler
DDR Berlin 1080, German Democratic
Republic
University of Idaho
School of Music
Moscow, Idaho
Indiana University - Bloomington
School of Music
Bloomington, Indiana
Instituto Superior de Arte
Facultad de Música
Playa, Cuba
University of Iowa
School of Music
Iowa City, Iowa
Jacksonville State University
Department of Music
Jacksonville, Alabama
The Juilliard School
New York, New York
Karol Szymanowski Academy of Music of
Katowice
Katowice, Poland
Kent State University
School of Music
Kent, Ohio
University of Kentucky
School of Music
Lexington, Kentucky

Kiev P.I. Tchaikovsky Conservatory
252001 Kiev, Ukrainskaja SSR, U.S.S.R.
Konservatorium und Musikhochschule -
Zürich
8050 Zürich, Switzerland
Konzervatoř v Praze
(State Conservatory Prague)
Praha 110 00, Czechoslovakia
Konzervatorium - Bratislava
Bratislava 811 06, Czechoslovakia
Leningrad N.A. Rimsky-Korsakov State
Conservatory
192041 Leningrad, Rossiskaja SFSR,
U.S.S.R.
Long Island University - C.W. Post Campus
Music Department
Greenvale, New York
Manhattan School of Music
New York, New York
University of Miami
School of Music
Coral Gables, Florida
University of Michigan
School of Music
Ann Arbor, Michigan
Michigan State University
School of Music
East Lansing, Michigan
University of Missouri - Kansas City
Conservatory of Music
Kansas City, Missouri
Moscow P.I. Tchaikovsky State
Conservatory
103009 Moscow K-9, Rossiskaja SFSR,
U.S.S.R.
Musik-Akademie der Stadt Basel
(Konservatorium)
Konservatorium (Musikhochschule)
Basel, Switzerland
Musikhochschule des Saarlandes
6600 Saarbrücken 3, Federal Republic of
Germany
Musikhögskolan i Stockholm
National College of Music
115 31 Stockholm, Sweden
National Institute of the Arts
Music Department
Taipei County, Taiwan (Republic of
China)
University of Nevada, Las Vegas
Department of Music
Las Vegas, Nevada
New England Conservatory
Boston, Massachusetts
New Mexico State University
Department of Music
Las Cruces, New Mexico
New York University - School of Education,
Health, Nursing, and Arts Professions
Department of Music and Music
Education
New York, New York
Norges Musikkhøgskole
(The Norwegian State Academy of
Music)
N-0130 Oslo 1, Norway
University of North Dakota
Department of Music
Grand Forks, North Dakota
University of Northern Colorado
School of Music
Greeley, Colorado
University of Northern Iowa
School of Music
Cedar Falls, Iowa

Northwestern University
  School of Music
  Evanston, Illinois
The Ohio State University
  School of Music
  Columbus, Ohio
Oklahoma Baptist University
  Department of Music
  Shawnee, Oklahoma
Oregon State University
  Department of Music
  Corvallis, Oregon
Pacific Lutheran University
  Department of Music
  Tacoma, Washington
Peabody Institute of The Johns Hopkins
  University
  Baltimore, Maryland
Philadelphia College of the Performing Arts
  School of Music
  Philadelphia, Pennsylvania
Pomona College
  Music Department
  Claremont, California
Portland State University
  Department of Music
  Portland, Oregon
University of Puget Sound
  School of Music
  Tacoma, Washington
Queen's University
  School of Music
  Kingston, Ontario, Canada
Radford University
  Department of Music
  Radford, Virginia
University of Redlands
  School of Music
  Redlands, California
Rice University
  Shepherd School of Music
  Houston, Texas
Royal Academy of Music
  London NW1 5HT, United Kingdom
Royal College of Music
  London, SW7 2BS, United Kingdom
Sam Houston State University
  Department of Music
  Huntsville, Texas
Samford University
  School of Music
  Birmingham, Alabama
Shenandoah College and Conservatory
  Winchester, Virginia
Shengyang Conservatory of Music
  *Shengyang, Liaoning Province, People's
  Republic of China*
Sibelius Academy of Music
  SF-00260 Helsinki 26, Finland
Sichuan Conservatory of Music
  *Chengdu, Sichuan, People's Republic of
  China*
University of South Carolina
  School of Music
  Columbia, South Carolina
University of South Florida
  Department of Music
  Tampa, Florida
Southern Baptist Theological Seminary
  School of Church Music
  Louisville, Kentucky
University of Southern California
  School of Music
  Los Angeles, California
Southern Illinois University at Carbondale
  School of Music

Carbondale, Illinois
Southern Illinois University at Edwardsville
  Department of Music
  Edwardsville, Illinois
University of Southern Mississippi
  School of Music
  Hattiesburg, Mississippi
Southwest Texas State University
  Department of Music
  San Marcos, Texas
Staatliche Hochschule für Musik Freiburg
  *D-7800 Freiburg i. Br., Federal Republic
  of Germany*
Staatliche Hochschule für Musik Karlsruhe
  *7500 Karlsruhe 1, Federal Republic of
  Germany*
Staatliche Hochschule für Musik Rheinland
  - Düsseldorf
  (State College of Music)
  *D-4000 Düsseldorf, Federal Republic of
  Germany*
Staatliche Hochschule für Musik Rheinland
  - Wuppertal
  Institute Wuppertal
  Wuppertal, Federal Republic of Germany
Staatliche Hochschule für Musik Ruhr
  *4300 Essen 16, Federal Republic of
  Germany*
Staatliche Hochschule für Musik
  Westfalen-Lippe
  *4930 Detmold, Federal Republic of
  Germany*
Stanford University
  Department of Music
  Stanford, California
State University of New York College at
  Purchase
  Division of Music
  Purchase, New York
Stedelijke Muziekpedagogische Akademie
  Leeuwarden, Netherlands
Teachers College of Columbia University
  Department of Music and Music
  Education
  New York, New York
Tel Aviv University
  Faculty of Fine Arts
  Tel-Aviv, Israel
University of Tennessee at Knoxville
  Department of Music
  Knoxville, Tennessee
University of Texas at Austin
  Department of Music
  Austin, Texas
University of Texas at San Antonio
  Division of Music
  San Antonio, Texas
University of Toronto
  Faculty of Music
  Toronto, Ontario, Canada
Troy State University
  Department of Music
  Troy, Alabama
Universidad de Antioquía
  Facultad de Artes, Departamento de
  Música
  Medellín, Colombia
Universidade do Rio de Janeiro
  Letters and Arts Center - Music Course
  22290 Rio de Janeiro, Brazil
University of Virginia
  McIntire Department of Music
  Charlottesville, Virginia
Virginia Commonwealth University
  Department of Music
  Richmond, Virginia

Vysoká Skola Múzickych Umeni v Praha
  Academy of Music and Dramatic Arts
  1101 00 Prague 1, Czechoslovakia
Webster University
  Department of Music
  St. Louis, Missouri
West Texas State University
  Department of Music
  Canyon, Texas
Westminster Choir College
  Princeton, New Jersey
Wichita State University
  School of Music
  Wichita, Kansas
Wilfrid Laurier University
  Faculty of Music
  Waterloo, Ontario, Canada
University of Wisconsin - Madison
  School of Music
  Madison, Wisconsin
University of Wisconsin - Milwaukee
  Music Department
  Milwaukee, Wisconsin
University of Wyoming
  Music Department
  Laramie, Wyoming
Youngstown State University
  Dana School of Music
  Youngstown, Ohio

CONTEMPORARY MUSIC

Rimon School of Jazz and Contemporary
  Music
  Ramat Hasharon, Israel
Staatliche Hochschule für Musik
  Westfalen-Lippe
  Institut Dortmund
  *D-4600 Dortmund 1, Federal Republic of
  Germany*

COUNTERPOINT

Conservatorul de Musică George Dima
  (Conservatory of Music)
  3400 Cluj-Napoca, Romania
Conservatorul de Muzică Ciprian
  Porumbescu
  (Conservatory of Music)
  70732 Bucharest, Romania
Conservatorul Georges Enescu
  (Conservatory of Music)
  6600 Iasi, Romania
Kuopion Konservatorio
  70100 Kuopio, Finland

DANCE

Hochschule für Musik und Theater
  Hannover
  *3000 Hannover 1, Federal Republic of
  Germany*
Staatliche Hochschule für Musik
  Heidelberg-Mannheim
  *Friedrich-Ebert-Anlage 62, Federal
  Republic of Germany*

DANCE HISTORY

Hochschule für Musik und Theater
  Hannover
  *3000 Hannover 1, Federal Republic of
  Germany*

DRAMA

Alma-Ata Kurmangazy State Conservatory
  *480091 Alma-Ata 91, Kazahskaja SSR,
  U.S.S.R.*

Far-Eastern Pedagogical Institute of the
Arts
*690678 Vladivostok, Rossiskaja SFSR,
U.S.S.R.*
Hochschule für Musik und Theater
Hannover
*3000 Hannover 1, Federal Republic of
Germany*
Kharkov State Institute of Arts
310003 Kharkov, U.S.S.R.
Latvian S.S.R. Y. Vitol State Conservatory
226050 Riga, Latvijskaya SSR, U.S.S.R.
Lithuanian State Conservatory
232001 Vilnius, Litovskaja SSR, U.S.S.R.
Moldavian S.S.R. G. Musichesku State
Conservatory
*277014 Kishinev, Moldavskaja SSR,
U.S.S.R.*
Royal Irish Academy of Music
Dublin 2, Ireland
Staatliche Hochschule für Musik und
Darstellende Kunst Stuttgart
*7000 Stuttgart 1, Federal Republic of
Germany*
Ufa State Institute of Fine Arts
450025 Ufa, Bashkir ASSR, U.S.S.R.

DRAMA PRODUCTION

Ufa State Institute of Fine Arts
450025 Ufa, Bashkir ASSR, U.S.S.R.

EAR TRAINING

Escuela Nacional de Música
Universidad Nacional Autónoma de
México
Mexico City, D.F. 04100, Mexico

EARLY INSTRUMENTS

Oberlin College
Conservatory of Music
Oberlin, Ohio
Peabody Institute of The Johns Hopkins
University
Baltimore, Maryland

EARLY MUSIC

Akademia Muzyczna w Łódź
(Academy of Music of Łódź)
90-716 Łódź, Poland
Hermann-Zilcher-Konservatorium
*D-8700 Würzburg, Federal Republic of
Germany*
Indiana University - Bloomington
School of Music
Bloomington, Indiana
New England Conservatory
Boston, Massachusetts
Oakland University
Department of Music, Theatre and
Dance
Rochester, Michigan
Royal Academy of Music
London NW1 5HT, United Kingdom
Royal College of Music
London, SW7 2BS, United Kingdom
Staatliche Hochschule für Musik Rheinland
- Düsseldorf
(State College of Music)
*D-4000 Düsseldorf, Federal Republic of
Germany*

EARLY MUSIC EDUCATION

Fachakademie für Musik - München
Richard Strauss-Konservatorium der
Stadt

*München 80, Federal Republic of
Germany*
Hermann-Zilcher-Konservatorium
*D-8700 Würzburg, Federal Republic of
Germany*
Staatliche Hochschule für Musik Freiburg
*D-7800 Freiburg i. Br., Federal Republic
of Germany*

EARLY MUSIC PRACTICES

Case Western Reserve University
Department of Music
Cleveland, Ohio

EAST ASIAN MUSIC

University of Pittsburgh
Department of Music
Pittsburgh, Pennsylvania

EIGHTEENTH CENTURY MUSIC

Cornell University
Department of Music
Ithaca, New York

ELECTRO-ACOUSTIC COMPOSITION

California Institute of the Arts
School of Music
Valencia, California

ELECTRONIC MUSIC

Bennington College
Music Department
Bennington, Vermont
University of California, Davis
Department of Music
Davis, California
University of California, Santa Cruz
Music Board, Division of the Arts
Santa Cruz, California
Hochschule für Musik - Würzburg
*D-8700 Würzburg, Federal Republic of
Germany*
Indiana University - Bloomington
School of Music
Bloomington, Indiana
Mills College
Music Department
Oakland, California
New York University - School of Education,
Health, Nursing, and Arts Professions
Department of Music and Music
Education
New York, New York
Peabody Institute of The Johns Hopkins
University
Baltimore, Maryland
Royal College of Music
London, SW7 2BS, United Kingdom
Southwest Texas State University
Department of Music
San Marcos, Texas
Staatliche Hochschule für Musik Rheinland
- Düsseldorf
(State College of Music)
*D-4000 Düsseldorf, Federal Republic of
Germany*
Staatliche Hochschule für Musik Rheinland
- Köln
*D-5000 Köln 1, Federal Republic of
Germany*
Staatliche Hochschule für Musik und
Darstellende Kunst Stuttgart
*7000 Stuttgart 1, Federal Republic of
Germany*

University of Utah
Department of Music
Salt Lake City, Utah
Valparaiso University
Department of Music
Valparaiso, Indiana

ELEMENTARY MUSIC

Staatliche Hochschule für Musik Rheinland
- Düsseldorf
(State College of Music)
*D-4000 Düsseldorf, Federal Republic of
Germany*

ENSEMBLE

University of Arkansas
Department of Music
Fayetteville, Arkansas
University of Northern Colorado
School of Music
Greeley, Colorado

ENSEMBLE MUSIC

Jacksonville State University
Department of Music
Jacksonville, Alabama
Musikhochschule des Saarlandes
*6600 Saarbrücken 3, Federal Republic of
Germany*

ENSEMBLE PLAYING

Fachakademie für Musik - München
Richard Strauss-Konservatorium der
Stadt
*München 80, Federal Republic of
Germany*

ETHIOPIAN INSTRUMENTS

Yared National Institute of Music
Addis Ababa, Ethiopia

ETHNOMUSICOLOGY

University of Alaska
Music Department
Fairbanks, Alaska
University of Alberta
Department of Music
Edmonton, Alberta, Canada
Brown University
Department of Music
Providence, Rhode Island
University of California, Berkeley
Department of Music
Berkeley, California
University of California, Los Angeles
Department of Music
Los Angeles, California
University of California, Santa Cruz
Music Board, Division of the Arts
Santa Cruz, California
City University of New York - Hunter
College
Department of Music
New York, New York
Columbia University
Department of Music
New York, New York
Cornell University
Department of Music
Ithaca, New York
Duke University
Department of Music
Durham, North Carolina
Escuela Nacional de Música
Universidad Nacional Autónoma de

México
Mexico City, D.F. 04100, Mexico
Harvard University
Department of Music
Cambridge, Massachusetts
University of Hawaii at Manoa
Music Department
Honolulu, Hawaii
Hofstra University
Department of Music
Hempstead, New York
University of Illinois
School of Music
Urbana, Illinois
Indiana University - Bloomington
School of Music
Bloomington, Indiana
Instituto Superior de Arte
Facultad de Música
Playa, Cuba
Jersey City State College
Music Department
Jersey City, New Jersey
Kent State University
School of Music
Kent, Ohio
University of Maryland - Baltimore County
Department of Music
Catonsville, Maryland
Mills College
Music Department
Oakland, California
University of Minnesota - Twin Cities
School of Music
Minneapolis, Minnesota
New York University - College of Arts and
Sciences
Department of Music
New York, New York
University of the Philippines
College of Music
Quezon City, The Philippines
University of Pittsburgh
Department of Music
Pittsburgh, Pennsylvania
Queen's University
School of Music
Kingston, Ontario, Canada
San Diego State University
Music Department
San Diego, California
State University of New York at
Binghamton
Department of Music
Binghamton, New York
University of Texas at Austin
Department of Music
Austin, Texas
Université de Montréal
Faculty of Music
Montréal, Québec, Canada
University of Washington
School of Music
Seattle, Washington
Wesleyan University
Department of Music
Middletown, Connecticut
Wheaton College
Conservatory of Music
Wheaton, Illinois
University of Wisconsin - Madison
School of Music
Madison, Wisconsin
York University
Department of Music
North York, Ontario, Canada

EURAMERICAN PERFORMANCE

California Institute of the Arts
School of Music
Valencia, California

EURYTHMICS

Akademia Muzyczna w Lódź
(Academy of Music of Lódź)
90-716 Lódź, Poland
Carnegie-Mellon University
Department of Music
Pittsburgh, Pennsylvania
Cleveland Institute of Music
Cleveland, Ohio
Duquesne University
School of Music
Pittsburgh, Pennsylvania
Fachakademie für Music - Augsburg
Leopold Mozart-Konservatorium der
Stadt Augsburg
Augsberg, Federal Republic of Germany
Fachakademie für Musik - München
Richard Strauss-Konservatorium der
Stadt
München 80, Federal Republic of
Germany
Fachakademie für Musik - Nürnberg
Konservatorium der Stadt Nürnberg
Nürnberg, Federal Republic of Germany
Hermann-Zilcher-Konservatorium
D-8700 Würzburg, Federal Republic of
Germany
Hochschule der Künste Berlin
1000 Berlin 10, Federal Republic of
Germany
Hochschule für Musik - Würzburg
D-8700 Würzburg, Federal Republic of
Germany
Hochschule für Musik und Theater
Hannover
3000 Hannover 1, Federal Republic of
Germany
Musikhochschule Lübeck
Grosse Petersgrube 17-29
2400 Lübeck, Federal Republic of
Germany
Staatliche Hochschule für Musik Freiburg
D-7800 Freiburg i. Br., Federal Republic
of Germany
Staatliche Hochschule für Musik Rheinland
- Aachen
Grenzland-Institut Aachen
Aachen, Federal Republic of Germany
Staatliche Hochschule für Musik Rheinland
- Wuppertal
Institute Wuppertal
Wuppertal, Federal Republic of Germany
Staatliche Hochschule für Musik Ruhr
4300 Essen 16, Federal Republic of
Germany
Staatliche Hochschule für Musik Trossingen
D-7218 Trossingen 1, Federal Republic of
Germany
Staatliche Hochschule für Musik und
Darstellende Kunst Stuttgart
7000 Stuttgart 1, Federal Republic of
Germany
Staatliche Hochschule für Musik
Westfalen-Lippe
Institut Dortmund
D-4600 Dortmund 1, Federal Republic of
Germany

FENCING

Hochschule für Musik und Theater
Hannover
3000 Hannover 1, Federal Republic of
Germany
Musikhochschule des Saarlandes
6600 Saarbrücken 3, Federal Republic of
Germany
Staatliche Hochschule für Musik Rheinland
- Düsseldorf
(State College of Music)
D-4000 Düsseldorf, Federal Republic of
Germany

FIGURED BASS

Hochschule für Musik - Würzburg
D-8700 Würzburg, Federal Republic of
Germany

FILM MUSIC

Hochschule der Künste Berlin
1000 Berlin 10, Federal Republic of
Germany
Hochschule für Gestaltende Kunst und
Musik
(State College for Creative Art and
Music)
2800 Bremen 1, Federal Republic of
Germany

FILM SCORING

Berklee College of Music
Boston, Massachusetts

FOLK MUSIC

Escuela Universitaria de Música -
Montevideo
Montevideo, Uruguay
Fachakademie für Musik - München
Richard Strauss-Konservatorium der
Stadt
München 80, Federal Republic of
Germany
Ferenc Liszt Academy of Music
Budapest VI, Hungary
Konzervatoř v Praze
(State Conservatory Prague)
Praha 110 00, Czechoslovakia
Moscow P.I. Tchaikovsky State
Conservatory
103009 Moscow K-9, Rossiskaja SFSR,
U.S.S.R.
Oregon State University
Department of Music
Corvallis, Oregon
Pohjois-Kymen Musiikkiopisto
(North Kymi Music Institute)
45100 Kouvola, Finland
Sibelius Academy of Music
SF-00260 Helsinki 26, Finland
Ufa State Institute of Fine Arts
450025 Ufa, Bashkir ASSR, U.S.S.R.
Wesleyan University
Department of Music
Middletown, Connecticut
Zeneiskolai Tanárkepzó Intézet
(Music Teachers Training Institute of the
Liszt Academy of Music)
Budapest 1052, Hungary

FOLKLORE

Real Conservatorio Superior de Música de
Madrid
  (Royal Academy of Music)
  Madrid 13, Spain

GERMAN CHORALE

Staatliche Hochschule für Musik und
Darstellende Kunst Stuttgart
  *7000 Stuttgart 1, Federal Republic of
  Germany*

GERMAN LITURGICAL SINGING

Hochschule für Musik - München
  *8000 München 2, Federal Republic of
  Germany*

GREGORIAN CHANT

Hochschule für Gestaltende Kunst und
Musik
  (State College for Creative Art and
  Music)
  *2800 Bremen 1, Federal Republic of
  Germany*
Hochschule für Musik - München
  *8000 München 2, Federal Republic of
  Germany*
Musikhochschule des Saarlandes
  *6600 Saarbrücken 3, Federal Republic of
  Germany*
Staatliche Hochschule für Musik und
Darstellende Kunst Stuttgart
  *7000 Stuttgart 1, Federal Republic of
  Germany*

HARMONY

Conservatorul de Musică George Dima
  (Conservatory of Music)
  3400 Cluj-Napoca, Romania
Conservatorul de Muzică Ciprian
Porumbescu
  (Conservatory of Music)
  70732 Bucharest, Romania
Conservatorul Georges Enescu
  (Conservatory of Music)
  6600 Iasi, Romania
Fachakademie für Music - Augsburg
  Leopold Mozart-Konservatorium der
  Stadt Augsburg
  Augsberg, Federal Republic of Germany
Kuopion Konservatorio
  70100 Kuopio, Finland
Royal Irish Academy of Music
  Dublin 2, Ireland

HINDUSTANI CLASSICAL MUSIC

Visva-Bharati
  Sangit-Bhavana (College of Music and
  Dance)
  West Bengal 731235, India

HINDUSTANI MUSIC

Bhavan's Bharatiya Sangeet and Nartan
Skikshapeeth
  (Academy of Music and Dance)
  Bombay 4000007, India

HISTORICAL DANCE

Hochschule für Musik - Würzburg
  *D-8700 Würzburg, Federal Republic of
  Germany*

HISTORICAL INSTRUMENTS

Hochschule für Musik - Würzburg
  *D-8700 Würzburg, Federal Republic of
  Germany*

HISTORICAL MUSICOLOGY

Columbia University
  Department of Music
  New York, New York
Wesleyan University
  Department of Music
  Middletown, Connecticut

HISTORY

University of Wyoming
  Music Department
  Laramie, Wyoming

HISTORY OF MUSIC

Kiev P.I. Tchaikovsky Conservatory
  252001 Kiev, Ukrainskaja SSR, U.S.S.R.

HYMNOLOGY

Musikhochschule Lübeck
  Grosse Petersgrube 17-29
  *2400 Lübeck, Federal Republic of
  Germany*

IMPROVISATION

Bennington College
  Music Department
  Bennington, Vermont
Staatliche Hochschule für Musik Rheinland
- Düsseldorf
  (State College of Music)
  *D-4000 Düsseldorf, Federal Republic of
  Germany*
Staatliche Hochschule für Musik
Westfalen-Lippe
  Institut Dortmund
  *D-4600 Dortmund 1, Federal Republic of
  Germany*

INDIAN FOLK MUSIC

Indira Kala Sangit Vishwavidyalaya
  (University of Music and Fine Arts)
  Madhya Pradesh 491881, India

INDIAN MUSIC

University of Madras
  Department of Indian Music
  Madras 600005, India

INDIAN TRADITIONAL MUSIC

Bhavan's Bharatiya Sangeet and Nartan
Skikshapeeth
  (Academy of Music and Dance)
  Bombay 4000007, India

INSTRUMENT BUILDING

Bennington College
  Music Department
  Bennington, Vermont

INSTRUMENT MAINTENANCE

Peabody Institute of The Johns Hopkins
University
  Baltimore, Maryland

INSTRUMENT MAKING

Conservatorio Municipal de Música
"Manuel de Falla"
  1042 Buenos Aires, Argentina

Escuela Nacional de Música
  Universidad Nacional Autónoma de
  México
  Mexico City, D.F. 04100, Mexico
Shengyang Conservatory of Music
  *Shengyang, Liaoning Province, People's
  Republic of China*

INSTRUMENT REPAIR

City of Leeds College of Music
  Leeds LS2 8BH, United Kingdom
Shengyang Conservatory of Music
  *Shengyang, Liaoning Province, People's
  Republic of China*

INSTRUMENTAL CONDUCTING

California State University, Northridge
  Music Department
  Northridge, California
The Catholic University of America
  The Benjamin T. Rome School of Music
  Washington, District of Columbia
Hermann-Zilcher-Konservatorium
  *D-8700 Würzburg, Federal Republic of
  Germany*
Hochschule für Musik - München
  *8000 München 2, Federal Republic of
  Germany*
University of North Carolina at Greensboro
  School of Music
  Greensboro, North Carolina
Oakland University
  Department of Music, Theatre and
  Dance
  Rochester, Michigan
San Francisco Conservatory of Music
  San Francisco, California
Staatliche Hochschule für Musik Trossingen
  *D-7218 Trossingen 1, Federal Republic of
  Germany*
University of Texas at Arlington
  Department of Music
  Arlington, Texas
University of Washington
  School of Music
  Seattle, Washington

INSTRUMENTAL METHODS

Fachakademie für Musik - Nürnberg
  Konservatorium der Stadt Nürnberg
  Nürnberg, Federal Republic of Germany

INSTRUMENTAL MUSIC

Arizona State University
  School of Music
  Tempe, Arizona
Banaras Hindu University
  Uttar Pradesh 221005, India
Bulgarian State Conservatoire
  Sofia 1505, Bulgaria
California State University, Long Beach
  Department of Music
  Long Beach, California
Conservatorul de Musică George Dima
  (Conservatory of Music)
  3400 Cluj-Napoca, Romania
Conservatorul de Muzică Ciprian
Porumbescu
  (Conservatory of Music)
  70732 Bucharest, Romania
Conservatorul Georges Enescu
  (Conservatory of Music)
  6600 Iasi, Romania
Hochschule für Music und Darstellende
  Kunst Hamburg

2000 Hamburg 13, Federal Republic of
Germany
Indira Kala Sangit Vishwavidyalaya
(University of Music and Fine Arts)
Madhya Pradesh 491881, India
Musikhochschule des Saarlandes
6600 Saarbrücken 3, Federal Republic of
Germany
Texas Woman's University
Department of Music and Drama
Denton, Texas
Ueno Gakuen College
Tokyo 110, Japan
Virginia State University
Department of Music Education
Petersburg, Virginia
Vysoká Skola Mûzickych Umeni v Praha
Academy of Music and Dramatic Arts
1101 00 Prague 1, Czechoslovakia
Wichita State University
School of Music
Wichita, Kansas

INSTRUMENTAL MUSIC EDUCATION

The Catholic University of America
The Benjamin T. Rome School of Music
Washington, District of Columbia
Northern Arizona University
Music Department
Flagstaff, Arizona

INSTRUMENTAL PERFORMANCE

Oakland University
Department of Music, Theatre and
Dance
Rochester, Michigan

INSTRUMENTAL SPECIALIST

Bowling Green State University
College of Musical Arts
Bowling Green, Ohio

INSTRUMENTAL TEACHING

California State University, Los Angeles
Department of Music
Los Angeles, California

INSTRUMENTAL TECHNIQUES

University of Northern Colorado
School of Music
Greeley, Colorado

INSTRUMENTATION

Hochschule für Musik - Würzburg
D-8700 Würzburg, Federal Republic of
Germany

INTERPRETATIVE ARTS

Musikhochschule des Saarlandes
6600 Saarbrücken 3, Federal Republic of
Germany

ITALIAN

Fachakademie für Music - Augsburg
Leopold Mozart-Konservatorium der
Stadt Augsburg
Augsberg, Federal Republic of Germany
Hochschule für Gestaltende Kunst und
Musik
(State College for Creative Art and
Music)
2800 Bremen 1, Federal Republic of
Germany
Hochschule für Musik - Würzburg
D-8700 Würzburg, Federal Republic of

Germany
Hochschule für Musik und Theater
Hannover
3000 Hannover 1, Federal Republic of
Germany
Musikhochschule des Saarlandes
6600 Saarbrücken 3, Federal Republic of
Germany
Staatliche Hochschule für Musik Rheinland
- Aachen
Grenzland-Institut Aachen
Aachen, Federal Republic of Germany
Staatliche Hochschule für Musik Rheinland
- Wuppertal
Institute Wuppertal
Wuppertal, Federal Republic of Germany

JAPANESE MUSIC

Ueno Gakuen College
Tokyo 110, Japan

JAVANESE MUSIC

California Institute of the Arts
School of Music
Valencia, California
Institut Seni Indonesia
Yogyakarta, Indonesia
Wesleyan University
Department of Music
Middletown, Connecticut

JAZZ

Central Missouri State University
Department of Music
Warrensburg, Missouri
Fachakademie für Musik - München
Richard Strauss-Konservatorium der
Stadt
München 80, Federal Republic of
Germany
Hofstra University
Department of Music
Hempstead, New York
Sibelius Academy of Music
SF-00260 Helsinki 26, Finland
Université Laval
Ecole de Musique
Ste. Foy, Québec, Canada

JAZZ COMPOSITION

Berklee College of Music
Boston, Massachusetts
California Institute of the Arts
School of Music
Valencia, California

JAZZ PEDAGOGY

University of Miami
School of Music
Coral Gables, Florida

JAZZ PERFORMANCE

California Institute of the Arts
School of Music
Valencia, California
Oakland University
Department of Music, Theatre and
Dance
Rochester, Michigan
Southern Illinois University at Carbondale
School of Music
Carbondale, Illinois

JAZZ STUDIES

Akademie voor Musiek
Hilversum Postkode 1217 KR,
Netherlands
University of Akron
Department of Music
Akron, Ohio
American Conservatory of Music
Chicago, Illinois
University of Arizona
School of Music
Tucson, Arizona
Auburn University
Department of Music
Auburn, Alabama
Bemidji State University
Music Department
Bemidji, Minnesota
California State University, Hayward
Department of Music
Hayward, California
California State University, Los Angeles
Department of Music
Los Angeles, California
Central Michigan University
Department of Music
Mount Pleasant, Michigan
University of Cincinnati
College-Conservatory of Music
Cincinnati, Ohio
City of Leeds College of Music
Leeds LS2 8BH, United Kingdom
City University of New York - City College
Department of Music
New York, New York
Combs College of Music
Philadelphia, Pennsylvania
DePaul University
School of Music
Chicago, Illinois
Duquesne University
School of Music
Pittsburgh, Pennsylvania
Escuela de Música - Heredia
Universidad Nacional
Heredia, Costa Rica
Florida State University
School of Music
Tallahassee, Florida
University of Georgia
School of Music
Athens, Georgia
Georgia State University
School of Music
Atlanta, Georgia
Glassboro State College
Department of Music
Glassboro, New Jersey
University of Hartford
Hartt School of Music
West Hartford, Connecticut
Hochschule für Gestaltende Kunst und
Musik
(State College for Creative Art and
Music)
2800 Bremen 1, Federal Republic of
Germany
Hochschule für Musik - Würzburg
D-8700 Würzburg, Federal Republic of
Germany
Howard University
Department of Music
Washington, District of Columbia
Indiana University - Bloomington
School of Music

Bloomington, Indiana
Indiana University of Pennsylvania
  Department of Music
  Indiana, Pennsylvania
University of Iowa
  School of Music
  Iowa City, Iowa
Ithaca College
  School of Music
  Ithaca, New York
Jersey City State College
  Music Department
  Jersey City, New Jersey
University of Kansas
  School of Fine Arts
  Lawrence, Kansas
Karol Szymanowski Academy of Music of Katowice
  Katowice, Poland
University of Lowell
  College of Music
  Lowell, Massachusetts
Loyola University
  College of Music
  New Orleans, Louisiana
University of Massachusetts at Amherst
  Department of Music and Dance
  Amherst, Massachusetts
McNeese State University
  Department of Music
  Lake Charles, Louisiana
Memphis State University
  Music Department
  Memphis, Tennessee
University of Miami
  School of Music
  Coral Gables, Florida
Millikin University
  School of Music
  Decatur, Illinois
University of Minnesota - Duluth
  Department of Music
  Duluth, Minnesota
University of Minnesota - Twin Cities
  School of Music
  Minneapolis, Minnesota
New England Conservatory
  Boston, Massachusetts
New South Wales State Conservatorium of Music
  Sydney NSW 2000, Australia
New York University - School of Education, Health, Nursing, and Arts Professions
  Department of Music and Music Education
  New York, New York
University of North Carolina at Greensboro
  School of Music
  Greensboro, North Carolina
North Texas State University
  School of Music
  Denton, Texas
University of Northern Colorado
  School of Music
  Greeley, Colorado
University of Northern Iowa
  School of Music
  Cedar Falls, Iowa
Oberlin College
  Conservatory of Music
  Oberlin, Ohio
The Ohio State University
  School of Music
  Columbus, Ohio
Oregon State University
  Department of Music

Corvallis, Oregon
Philadelphia College of the Performing Arts
  School of Music
  Philadelphia, Pennsylvania
Pohjois-Kymen Musiikkiopisto
  (North Kymi Music Institute)
  45100 Kouvola, Finland
Radford University
  Department of Music
  Radford, Virginia
Rimon School of Jazz and Contemporary Music
  Ramat Hasharon, Israel
Roosevelt University
  Chicago Musical College
  Chicago, Illinois
Rutgers, The State University of New Jersey
  Department of Music
  New Brunswick, New Jersey
San Diego State University
  Music Department
  San Diego, California
San Jose State University
  Department of Music
  San Jose, California
Shenandoah College and Conservatory
  Winchester, Virginia
University of South Carolina
  School of Music
  Columbia, South Carolina
University of South Florida
  Department of Music
  Tampa, Florida
University of Southern California
  School of Music
  Los Angeles, California
Southern Illinois University at Edwardsville
  Department of Music
  Edwardsville, Illinois
University of Southern Mississippi
  School of Music
  Hattiesburg, Mississippi
Staatliche Hochschule für Musik Rheinland - Aachen
  Grenzland-Institut Aachen
  Aachen, Federal Republic of Germany
Staatliche Hochschule für Musik Westfalen-Lippe
  Institut Dortmund
  D-4600 Dortmund 1, Federal Republic of Germany
Temple University
  Esther Boyer College of Music
  Philadelphia, Pennsylvania
University of Texas at Arlington
  Department of Music
  Arlington, Texas
University of Texas at Austin
  Department of Music
  Austin, Texas
Towson State University
  Department of Music
  Towson, Maryland
Université de Montréal
  Faculty of Music
  Montréal, Québec, Canada
University of Utah
  Department of Music
  Salt Lake City, Utah
Virginia Commonwealth University
  Department of Music
  Richmond, Virginia
Wayne State University
  Department of Music
  Detroit, Michigan

Webster University
  Department of Music
  St. Louis, Missouri
Wesleyan University
  Department of Music
  Middletown, Connecticut
Western Michigan University
  School of Music
  Kalamazoo, Michigan
Western Washington University
  Department of Music
  Bellingham, Washington
William Paterson College
  Department of Music
  Wayne, New Jersey
University of Wisconsin - Madison
  School of Music
  Madison, Wisconsin
University of Wisconsin - Stevens Point
  Department of Music
  Stevens Point, Wisconsin
Yared National Institute of Music
  Addis Ababa, Ethiopia
Youngstown State University
  Dana School of Music
  Youngstown, Ohio

KODALY METHOD

The Catholic University of America
  The Benjamin T. Rome School of Music
  Washington, District of Columbia
University of Hartford
  Hartt School of Music
  West Hartford, Connecticut

KODALY PEDAGOGY

Sam Houston State University
  Department of Music
  Huntsville, Texas

LATIN

Fachakademie für Music - Augsburg
  Leopold Mozart-Konservatorium der Stadt Augsburg
  Augsberg, Federal Republic of Germany

LATIN AMERICAN MUSIC

Conservatorio Nacional de Música
  (National Conservatory of Music)
  Lima 1, Peru

LATIN AMERICAN MUSIC HISTORY

Conservatorio Nacional de Musica - La Paz
  (National Conservatory of Music - La Paz)
  La Paz, Bolivia

LIGHT MUSIC

Akademie voor Musiek
  Hilversum Postkode 1217 KR, Netherlands

LITURGICAL MUSIC

The Catholic University of America
  The Benjamin T. Rome School of Music
  Washington, District of Columbia
University of Notre Dame
  Department of Music
  Notre Dame, Indiana

LITURGY

Evangelische Kirchenmusikschule der Kirchenprovinz Sachsen
  (Evangelical Church Music School of the Church Province Saxony)

DDR-4020 Halle (Saale), German
  Democratic Republic
Musikhochschule des Saarlandes
  6600 Saarbrücken 3, Federal Republic of
  Germany
Staatliche Hochschule für Musik und
Darstellende Kunst Stuttgart
  7000 Stuttgart 1, Federal Republic of
  Germany
Staatliche Hochschule für Musik
Westfalen-Lippe
  Institut Dortmund
  D-4600 Dortmund 1, Federal Republic of
  Germany

MASS COMMUNICATIONS

Moorhead State University
  Music Department
  Moorhead, Minnesota

MEDIA KNOWLEDGE

Hochschule für Musik - München
  8000 München 2, Federal Republic of
  Germany

MEDIEVAL INSTRUMENTS

Musik-Akademie der Stadt Basel
  Schola Cantorum Basiliensis
  CH-4051 Basel, Switzerland

MEDIEVAL MUSIC

Musik-Akademie der Stadt Basel
  Schola Cantorum Basiliensis
  CH-4051 Basel, Switzerland
Wilfrid Laurier University
  Faculty of Music
  Waterloo, Ontario, Canada
Yale College (Yale University)
  Department of Music
  New Haven, Connecticut

MIDDLE EASTERN MUSIC

Higher Institute of Music and Performing
Arts - Safat
  c/o Undersecretary
  Safat 133002, Kuwait

MILITARY MUSIC

Odeion Athenon
  (Conservatory of Athens)
  Athens, Greece

MODERN MUSIC

Staatliche Hochschule für Musik und
Darstellende Kunst Stuttgart
  7000 Stuttgart 1, Federal Republic of
  Germany

MOROCCAN MUSIC

Conservatoire National de Musique, de
Danse, et d'Art Dramatique - Ribad
  Ribad, Morocco

MUSIC ADMINISTRATION

University of Alabama
  School of Music
  University, Alabama

MUSIC BUSINESS

Bradley University
  Division of Music and Theatre Arts
  Peoria, Illinois
DePauw University
  School of Music

Greencastle, Indiana
Eastern New Mexico University
  School of Music
  Portales, New Mexico
University of Evansville
  Music Department
  Evansville, Indiana
Jersey City State College
  Music Department
  Jersey City, New Jersey
University of Lowell
  College of Music
  Lowell, Massachusetts
Memphis State University
  Music Department
  Memphis, Tennessee
Millikin University
  School of Music
  Decatur, Illinois
Moorhead State University
  Music Department
  Moorhead, Minnesota
New York University - School of Education,
  Health, Nursing, and Arts Professions
  Department of Music and Music
  Education
  New York, New York
Northeast Missouri State University
  Division of Fine Arts
  Kirksville, Missouri
Ohio University
  School of Music
  Athens, Ohio
University of Puget Sound
  School of Music
  Tacoma, Washington
Radford University
  Department of Music
  Radford, Virginia
Roosevelt University
  Chicago Musical College
  Chicago, Illinois
Southern Illinois University at Carbondale
  School of Music
  Carbondale, Illinois
State University of New York College at
Fredonia
  School of Music
  Fredonia, New York
State University of New York College at
Potsdam
  Crane School of Music
  Potsdam, New York
Valparaiso University
  Department of Music
  Valparaiso, Indiana
West Texas State University
  Department of Music
  Canyon, Texas

MUSIC COMPOSITION

University of California, Irvine
  School of Fine Arts
  Irvine, California
City University of New York - Queens
College
  The Aaron Copland School of Music
  Flushing, New York
Conservatorio di Musica "Claudio
Monteverdi"
  I-39100 Bolzano, Italy
Hardin-Simmons University
  School of Music
  Abilene, Texas

Lawrence University
  Conservatory of Music
  Appleton, Wisconsin
University of Lowell
  College of Music
  Lowell, Massachusetts
University of Northern Colorado
  School of Music
  Greeley, Colorado
St. Olaf College
  Music Department
  Northfield, Minnesota
Sibelius Academy of Music
  SF-00260 Helsinki 26, Finland
The Tokyo College of Music
  Tokyo 171, Japan
Webster University
  Department of Music
  St. Louis, Missouri

MUSIC COMPUTING

Escuela Nacional de Música
  Universidad Nacional Autónoma de
  México
  Mexico City, D.F. 04100, Mexico

MUSIC CRITICISM

University of Florida
  Department of Music
  Gainesville, Florida
Peabody Institute of The Johns Hopkins
University
  Baltimore, Maryland

MUSIC CULTURE

Lithuanian State Conservatory
  232001 Vilnius, Litovskaja SSR, U.S.S.R.

MUSIC EDITING

Akademia Muzyczna w Krakowie
  31-038 Kraków, Poland

MUSIC EDUCATION

Acadia University
  School of Music
  Wolfville, Nova Scotia, Canada
Akademia Muzyczna w Lódź
  (Academy of Music of Lódź)
  90-716 Lódź, Poland
Akademia Muzycznaj im. Fryderyka
Chopina w Warzawie
  (Frederic Chopin Academy of Music of
  Warsaw)
  00-368 Warsaw, Poland
University of Akron
  Department of Music
  Akron, Ohio
University of Alabama
  School of Music
  University, Alabama
Alabama State University
  School of Music
  Montgomery, Alabama
University of Alaska
  Music Department
  Fairbanks, Alaska
American Conservatory of Music
  Chicago, Illinois
Andrews University
  Department of Music
  Berrien Springs, Michigan
Appalachian State University
  Department of Music
  Boone, North Carolina

University of Arizona
School of Music
Tucson, Arizona
University of Arkansas
Department of Music
Fayetteville, Arkansas
Arkansas State University
Department of Music
State University, Arkansas
Arkansas Tech University
Department of Music
Russellville, Arkansas
Auburn University
Department of Music
Auburn, Alabama
Austin Peay State University
Department of Music
Clarksville, Tennessee
Azusa Pacific University
School of Music
Azusa, California
Baldwin-Wallace College
Conservatory of Music
Berea, Ohio
Ball State University
School of Music
Muncie, Indiana
Baylor University
School of Music
Waco, Texas
Bemidji State University
Music Department
Bemidji, Minnesota
Berklee College of Music
Boston, Massachusetts
Biola University
Department of Music
La Mirada, California
Bob Jones University
Division of Music
Greenville, South Carolina
Boise State University
Music Department
Boise, Idaho
Boston Conservatory of Music
Boston, Massachusetts
Boston University
School of Music
Boston, Massachusetts
Bowling Green State University
College of Musical Arts
Bowling Green, Ohio
Brandon University
School of Music
Brandon, Manitoba, Canada
Brigham Young University
Department of Music
Provo, Utah
Butler University
Jordan College of Fine Arts
Indianapolis, Indiana
University of California, Los Angeles
Department of Music
Los Angeles, California
California State University, Chico
Department of Music
Chico, California
California State University, Fresno
Department of Music
Fresno, California
California State University, Fullerton
Department of Music
Fullerton, California
California State University, Hayward
Department of Music
Hayward, California

California State University, Los Angeles
Department of Music
Los Angeles, California
California State University, Northridge
Music Department
Northridge, California
California State University, Sacramento
Department of Music
Sacramento, California
University of Cape Town
Faculty of Music
Cape Town, Republic of South Africa
Carnegie-Mellon University
Department of Music
Pittsburgh, Pennsylvania
Case Western Reserve University
Department of Music
Cleveland, Ohio
University of Central Arkansas
Department of Music
Conway, Arkansas
University of Central Florida
Department of Music
Orlando, Florida
Central Michigan University
Department of Music
Mount Pleasant, Michigan
Central Missouri State University
Department of Music
Warrensburg, Missouri
Central State University
Department of Music
Edmond, Oklahoma
Central Washington University
Department of Music
Ellensburg, Washington
University of Cincinnati
College-Conservatory of Music
Cincinnati, Ohio
City of Leeds College of Music
Leeds LS2 8BH, United Kingdom
City University of New York - Hunter
College
Department of Music
New York, New York
City University of New York - Queens
College
The Aaron Copland School of Music
Flushing, New York
The Claremont Graduate School
Music Department
Claremont, California
Cleveland Institute of Music
Cleveland, Ohio
Cleveland State University
Department of Music
Cleveland, Ohio
University of Colorado at Boulder
College of Music
Boulder, Colorado
Colorado State University
Department of Music, Theatre, and
Dance
Fort Collins, Colorado
Columbus College
Department of Music
Columbus, Georgia
Combs College of Music
Philadelphia, Pennsylvania
University of Connecticut
Department of Music
Storrs, Connecticut
Conservatorio Nacional de Música
(National Conservatory of Music)
Lima 1, Peru

Converse College
School of Music
Spartanburg, South Carolina
Dalhousie University
Department of Music
Halifax, Nova Scotia, Canada
University of Delaware
Department of Music
Newark, Delaware
Delta State University
Department of Music
Cleveland, Mississippi
University of Denver
Lamont School of Music
Denver, Colorado
DePaul University
School of Music
Chicago, Illinois
DePauw University
School of Music
Greencastle, Indiana
Drake University
Department of Music
Des Moines, Iowa
Duquesne University
School of Music
Pittsburgh, Pennsylvania
East Carolina University
School of Music
Greenville, North Carolina
East Texas State University
Department of Music
Commerce, Texas
Eastern Illinois University
Department of Music
Charleston, Illinois
Eastern Kentucky University
Department of Music
Richmond, Kentucky
Eastern Michigan University
Department of Music
Ypsilanti, Michigan
Eastern New Mexico University
School of Music
Portales, New Mexico
Eastern Washington University
Department of Music
Cheney, Washington
Emporia State University
Division of Music
Emporia, Kansas
Escuela de Música - Heredia
Universidad Nacional
Heredia, Costa Rica
Escuela Nacional de Música
Universidad Nacional Autónoma de
México
México City, D.F. 04100, Mexico
Escuela Universitaria de Música -
Montevideo
Montevideo, Uruguay
University of Evansville
Music Department
Evansville, Indiana
Fachakademie für Musik - München
Richard Strauss-Konservatorium der
Stadt
*München 80, Federal Republic of
Germany*
Fachakademie für Musik - Nürnberg
Konservatorium der Stadt Nürnberg
Nürnberg, Federal Republic of Germany
Ferenc Liszt Academy of Music
Budapest VI, Hungary
University of Florida
Department of Music

Gainesville, Florida
Florida State University
    School of Music
    Tallahassee, Florida
Fort Hays State University
    Department of Music
    Hays, Kansas
George Mason University
    Department of Performing Arts - Music
    Division
    Fairfax, Virginia
University of Georgia
    School of Music
    Athens, Georgia
Georgia Southern College
    Department of Music
    Statesboro, Georgia
Georgia State University
    School of Music
    Atlanta, Georgia
Glassboro State College
    Department of Music
    Glassboro, New Jersey
Guildhall School of Music and Drama
    London EC2Y 8DT, United Kingdom
Hardin-Simmons University
    School of Music
    Abilene, Texas
University of Hartford
    Hartt School of Music
    West Hartford, Connecticut
Henderson State University
    Department of Music
    Arkadelphia, Arkansas
Hermann-Zilcher-Konservatorium
    D-8700 Würzburg, Federal Republic of
    Germany
Hochschule für Gestaltende Kunst und
Musik
    (State College for Creative Art and
    Music)
    2800 Bremen 1, Federal Republic of
    Germany
Hochschule für Music Franz Liszt
    DDR 5300 Weimar, German Democratic
    Republic
Hochschule für Music und Darstellende
Kunst Hamburg
    2000 Hamburg 13, Federal Republic of
    Germany
Hochschule für Musik - München
    8000 München 2, Federal Republic of
    Germany
Hochschule für Musik - Würzburg
    D-8700 Würzburg, Federal Republic of
    Germany
Hochschule für Musik und Darstellende
Kunst Frankfurt am Main
    6000 Frankfurt am Main 1, Federal
    Republic of Germany
Hochschule für Musik und Theater
Hannover
    3000 Hannover 1, Federal Republic of
    Germany
Hofstra University
    Department of Music
    Hempstead, New York
Howard University
    Department of Music
    Washington, District of Columbia
University of Idaho
    School of Music
    Moscow, Idaho
University of Illinois
    School of Music
    Urbana, Illinois

Illinois Wesleyan University
    School of Music
    Bloomington, Illinois
Indiana State University
    Department of Music
    Terre Haute, Indiana
Indiana University - Bloomington
    School of Music
    Bloomington, Indiana
Institute of Aesthetic Studies
    Colombo 7, Sri Lanka
University of Iowa
    School of Music
    Iowa City, Iowa
Iowa State University
    Department of Music
    Ames, Iowa
Ithaca College
    School of Music
    Ithaca, New York
Jackson State University
    Department of Music
    Jackson, Mississippi
Jacksonville State University
    Department of Music
    Jacksonville, Alabama
James Madison University
    Department of Music
    Harrisonburg, Virginia
Jersey City State College
    Music Department
    Jersey City, New Jersey
The Jerusalem Rubin Academy of Music
and Dance
    Jerusalem, Israel
University of Kansas
    School of Fine Arts
    Lawrence, Kansas
Kansas State University
    Department of Music
    Manhattan, Kansas
Kent State University
    School of Music
    Kent, Ohio
University of Kentucky
    School of Music
    Lexington, Kentucky
Konservatorium und Musikhochschule -
Zürich
    8050 Zürich, Switzerland
Konzervatoř v Praze
    (State Conservatory Prague)
    Praha 110 00, Czechoslovakia
Lamar University
    Department of Music
    Beaumont, Texas
Lawrence University
    Conservatory of Music
    Appleton, Wisconsin
Levinsky Teachers College
    Music Teachers Seminary
    Tel-Aviv, Israel
Lewis and Clark College
    Music Department
    Portland, Oregon
Lithuanian State Conservatory
    232001 Vilnius, Litovskaja SSR, U.S.S.R.
Long Island University - C.W. Post Campus
    Music Department
    Greenvale, New York
Louisiana Tech University
    Department of Music
    Ruston, Louisiana
University of Louisville
    School of Music
    Louisville, Kentucky

University of Lowell
    College of Music
    Lowell, Massachusetts
Loyola University
    College of Music
    New Orleans, Louisiana
University of Maine
    School of Performing Arts
    Orono, Maine
University of Manitoba
    School of Music
    Winnipeg, Manitoba, Canada
Mankato State University
    Department of Music
    Mankato, Minnesota
Marshall University
    Department of Music
    Huntington, West Virginia
University of Maryland - College Park
    Department of Music
    College Park, Maryland
Marywood College
    Music Department
    Scranton, Pennsylvania
University of Massachusetts at Amherst
    Department of Music and Dance
    Amherst, Massachusetts
McGill University
    Faculty of Music
    Montreal, Québec, Canada
McMaster University
    Department of Music
    Hamilton, Ontario, Canada
McNeese State University
    Department of Music
    Lake Charles, Louisiana
Memphis State University
    Music Department
    Memphis, Tennessee
University of Miami
    School of Music
    Coral Gables, Florida
Miami University
    Department of Music
    Oxford, Ohio
University of Michigan
    School of Music
    Ann Arbor, Michigan
Michigan State University
    School of Music
    East Lansing, Michigan
Middle Tennessee State University
    Department of Music
    Murfreesboro, Tennessee
Millikin University
    School of Music
    Decatur, Illinois
Mills College
    Music Department
    Oakland, California
University of Minnesota - Duluth
    Department of Music
    Duluth, Minnesota
University of Minnesota - Twin Cities
    School of Music
    Minneapolis, Minnesota
University of Mississippi
    Department of Music
    University, Mississippi
University of Missouri - Kansas City
    Conservatory of Music
    Kansas City, Missouri
University of Montana
    Department of Music
    Missoula, Montana

Montana State University
Department of Music
Bozeman, Montana
Montclair State College
Department of Music
Upper Montclair, New Jersey
University of Montevallo
Department of Music
Montevallo, Alabama
Moorhead State University
Music Department
Moorhead, Minnesota
Morehead State University
Department of Music
Morehead, Kentucky
The Music Academy, Madras
Teachers' College of Music
Madras 600 014, India
Musik-Akademie der Stadt Basel
(Konservatorium)
Konservatorium (Musikhochschule)
Basel, Switzerland
Musikhochschule des Saarlandes
*6600 Saarbrücken 3, Federal Republic of
Germany*
Musikhochschule Lübeck
Grosse Petersgrube 17-29
*2400 Lübeck, Federal Republic of
Germany*
Musikhögskolan i Stockholm
National College of Music
115 31 Stockholm, Sweden
University of Nebraska - Lincoln
School of Music
Lincoln, Nebraska
University of Nebraska - Omaha
Department of Music
Omaha, Nebraska
University of Nevada, Las Vegas
Department of Music
Las Vegas, Nevada
University of Nevada, Reno
Department of Music
Reno, Nevada
University of New Hampshire
Department of Music
Durham, New Hampshire
University of New Mexico
Department of Music
Albuquerque, New Mexico
New Mexico State University
Department of Music
Las Cruces, New Mexico
University of New Orleans
Department of Music
New Orleans, Louisiana
New York University - School of Education,
Health, Nursing, and Arts Professions
Department of Music and Music
Education
New York, New York
Norfolk State University
Department of Music
Norfolk, Virginia
Norges Musikkhøgskole
(The Norwegian State Academy of
Music)
N-0130 Oslo 1, Norway
University of North Carolina at Chapel Hill
Department of Music
Chapel Hill, North Carolina
University of North Carolina at Greensboro
School of Music
Greensboro, North Carolina
University of North Dakota
Department of Music

Grand Forks, North Dakota
North Texas State University
School of Music
Denton, Texas
Northeast Louisiana University
School of Music
Monroe, Louisiana
Northeast Missouri State University
Division of Fine Arts
Kirksville, Missouri
Northeastern Illinois University
Department of Music
Chicago, Illinois
Northern Arizona University
Music Department
Flagstaff, Arizona
University of Northern Colorado
School of Music
Greeley, Colorado
University of Northern Iowa
School of Music
Cedar Falls, Iowa
Northwestern State University of Louisiana
Department of Music
Natchitoches, Louisiana
Northwestern University
School of Music
Evanston, Illinois
Oakland University
Department of Music, Theatre and
Dance
Rochester, Michigan
Oberlin College
Conservatory of Music
Oberlin, Ohio
The Ohio State University
School of Music
Columbus, Ohio
Ohio University
School of Music
Athens, Ohio
University of Oklahoma
School of Music
Norman, Oklahoma
Oklahoma Baptist University
Department of Music
Shawnee, Oklahoma
Oklahoma City University
School of Music and Performing Arts
Oklahoma City, Oklahoma
University of Orange Free State
Department of Music
*9300 Bloemfontein, Republic of South
Africa*
University of Oregon
School of Music
Eugene, Oregon
Ouachita Baptist University
School of Music
Arkadelphia, Arkansas
University of the Pacific
Conservatory of Music
Stockton, California
Peabody Institute of The Johns Hopkins
University
Baltimore, Maryland
Pennsylvania State University
School of Music
University Park, Pennsylvania
Pittsburg State University
Department of Music
Pittsburg, Kansas
Portland State University
Department of Music
Portland, Oregon

University of Pretoria
Department of Music
002 Pretoria, Republic of South Africa
University of Puget Sound
School of Music
Tacoma, Washington
Queen's University
School of Music
Kingston, Ontario, Canada
Radford University
Department of Music
Radford, Virginia
Real Conservatorio Superior de Música de
Madrid
(Royal Academy of Music)
Madrid 13, Spain
University of Redlands
School of Music
Redlands, California
University of Regina
Department of Music
Regina, Saskatchewan, Canada
University of Rhode Island
Department of Music
Kingston, Rhode Island
University of Rochester
Eastman School of Music
Rochester, New York
Rogaland Musikkonservatorium
N-4000 Stavanger, Norway
Roosevelt University
Chicago Musical College
Chicago, Illinois
Royal Scottish Academy of Music and
Drama
Glasgow G2 1BS, United Kingdom
Rutgers, The State University of New Jersey
Department of Music
New Brunswick, New Jersey
St. Cloud State University
Department of Music
St. Cloud, Minnesota
St. Olaf College
Music Department
Northfield, Minnesota
Sam Houston State University
Department of Music
Huntsville, Texas
Samford University
School of Music
Birmingham, Alabama
San Diego State University
Music Department
San Diego, California
San Francisco State University
Department of Music
San Francisco, California
San Jose State University
Department of Music
San Jose, California
University of Santo Tomas
Conservatory of Music
Manila, The Philippines
University of Saskatchewan
Department of Music
Saskatoon, Saskatchewan, Canada
Shenandoah College and Conservatory
Winchester, Virginia
Shengyang Conservatory of Music
*Shengyang, Liaoning Province, People's
Republic of China*
Shorter College
Department of Music
Rome, Georgia
Sibelius Academy of Music
SF-00260 Helsinki 26, Finland

Sichuan Conservatory of Music
Chengdu, Sichuan, People's Republic of China
University of South Carolina
School of Music
Columbia, South Carolina
University of South Dakota
Music Department
Vermillion, South Dakota
University of South Florida
Department of Music
Tampa, Florida
Southeast Missouri State University
Department of Music
Cape Girardeau, Missouri
Southeastern Louisiana University
Department of Music
Hammond, Louisiana
Southeastern Oklahoma State University
Department of Music
Durant, Oklahoma
Southern Baptist Theological Seminary
School of Church Music
Louisville, Kentucky
University of Southern California
School of Music
Los Angeles, California
Southern Illinois University at Carbondale
School of Music
Carbondale, Illinois
Southern Illinois University at Edwardsville
Department of Music
Edwardsville, Illinois
Southern Methodist University
Meadows School of the Arts
Dallas, Texas
University of Southern Mississippi
School of Music
Hattiesburg, Mississippi
Southwest Texas State University
Department of Music
San Marcos, Texas
University of Southwestern Louisiana
School of Music
Lafayette, Louisiana
Staatliche Hochschule für Musik Freiburg
D-7800 Freiburg i. Br., Federal Republic of Germany
Staatliche Hochschule für Musik
Heidelberg-Mannheim
Friedrich-Ebert-Anlage 62, Federal Republic of Germany
Staatliche Hochschule für Musik Karlsruhe
7500 Karlsruhe 1, Federal Republic of Germany
Staatliche Hochschule für Musik Rheinland
- Aachen
Grenzland-Institut Aachen
Aachen, Federal Republic of Germany
Staatliche Hochschule für Musik Rheinland
- Düsseldorf
(State College of Music)
D-4000 Düsseldorf, Federal Republic of Germany
Staatliche Hochschule für Musik Ruhr
4300 Essen 16, Federal Republic of Germany
Staatliche Hochschule für Musik Trossingen
D-7218 Trossingen 1, Federal Republic of Germany
Staatliche Hochschule für Musik
Westfalen-Lippe
4930 Detmold, Federal Republic of Germany
State University of New York at Buffalo
Department of Music

Buffalo, New York
State University of New York College at Fredonia
School of Music
Fredonia, New York
State University of New York College at Potsdam
Crane School of Music
Potsdam, New York
University of Stellenbosch
Department of Music (Conservatoire)
7600 Stellenbosch, Republic of South Africa
Stephen F. Austin State University
Department of Music
Nacogdoches, Texas
Stetson University
School of Music
Deland, Florida
Syracuse University
School of Music
Syracuse, New York
Temple University
Esther Boyer College of Music
Philadelphia, Pennsylvania
University of Tennessee at Chattanooga
Cadek Department of Music
Chattanooga, Tennessee
University of Tennessee at Knoxville
Department of Music
Knoxville, Tennessee
University of Texas at Arlington
Department of Music
Arlington, Texas
University of Texas at Austin
Department of Music
Austin, Texas
University of Texas at El Paso
Music Department
El Paso, Texas
University of Texas at San Antonio
Division of Music
San Antonio, Texas
Texas Southern University
Department of Music
Houston, Texas
Texas Tech University
Department of Music
Lubbock, Texas
Texas Woman's University
Department of Music and Drama
Denton, Texas
Tonlistarskolinn i Reykjavik
105 Reykjavik, Iceland
University of Toronto
Faculty of Music
Toronto, Ontario, Canada
Towson State University
Department of Music
Towson, Maryland
Troy State University
Department of Music
Troy, Alabama
University of Tulsa
Faculty of Music
Tulsa, Oklahoma
Universidad de Concepción
Departamento de Arte
Concepción, Chile
Universidade do Rio de Janeiro
Letters and Arts Center - Music Course
22290 Rio de Janeiro, Brazil
Université Laval
Ecole de Musique
Ste. Foy, Québec, Canada

University of Utah
Department of Music
Salt Lake City, Utah
Valdosta State College
Department of Music
Valdosta, Georgia
Valparaiso University
Department of Music
Valparaiso, Indiana
VanderCook College of Music
Chicago, Illinois
University of Vermont
Department of Music
Burlington, Vermont
University of Victoria
School of Music
Victoria, British Columbia, Canada
University of Virginia
McIntire Department of Music
Charlottesville, Virginia
Virginia Commonwealth University
Department of Music
Richmond, Virginia
Virginia Polytechnic Institute and State University
Department of Music
Blacksburg, Virginia
Virginia State University
Department of Music Education
Petersburg, Virginia
Vysoká Skola Mûzickych Umeni v Praha
Academy of Music and Dramatic Arts
1101 00 Prague 1, Czechoslovakia
University of Washington
School of Music
Seattle, Washington
Washington State University
Department of Music
Pullman, Washington
Wayne State University
Department of Music
Detroit, Michigan
West Chester University of Pennsylvania
School of Music
West Chester, Pennsylvania
West Georgia College
Department of Music
Carrollton, Georgia
West Texas State University
Department of Music
Canyon, Texas
West Virginia University
Division of Music
Morgantown, West Virginia
University of Western Australia
Department of Music
Nedlands, WA 6009, Australia
Western Illinois University
Department of Music
Macomb, Illinois
Western Kentucky University
Department of Music
Bowling Green, Kentucky
Western Michigan University
School of Music
Kalamazoo, Michigan
University of Western Ontario
Faculty of Music
London, Ontario, Canada
Western Washington University
Department of Music
Bellingham, Washington
Wheaton College
Conservatory of Music
Wheaton, Illinois

Wichita State University
School of Music
Wichita, Kansas
Wilfrid Laurier University
Faculty of Music
Waterloo, Ontario, Canada
Willamette University
Department of Music
Salem, Oregon
William Carey College
Winters School of Music
Hattiesburg, Mississippi
William Paterson College
Department of Music
Wayne, New Jersey
University of Windsor
School of Music
Windsor, Ontario, Canada
Winthrop College
School of Music
Rock Hill, South Carolina
University of Wisconsin - Eau Claire
Department of Music
Eau Claire, Wisconsin
University of Wisconsin - La Crosse
Department of Music
La Crosse, Wisconsin
University of Wisconsin - Madison
School of Music
Madison, Wisconsin
University of Wisconsin - Milwaukee
Music Department
Milwaukee, Wisconsin
University of Wisconsin - Oshkosh
Department of Music
Oshkosh, Wisconsin
University of Wisconsin - Stevens Point
Department of Music
Stevens Point, Wisconsin
University of Wisconsin - Whitewater
Department of Music
Whitewater, Wisconsin
University of the Witwatersrand
Wits School of Music
*2001 Johannesburg, Republic of South
Africa*
Wright State University
Department of Music
Dayton, Ohio
Youngstown State University
Dana School of Music
Youngstown, Ohio

MUSIC ENGINEERING TECHNOLOGY

Ball State University
School of Music
Muncie, Indiana
University of Miami
School of Music
Coral Gables, Florida

MUSIC HISTORY

The Academy of Vocal Arts
Philadelphia, Pennsylvania
Akademia Muzyczna w Lódź
(Academy of Music of Lódź)
90-716 Lódź, Poland
University of Akron
Department of Music
Akron, Ohio
Alabama State University
School of Music
Montgomery, Alabama
University of Alaska
Music Department

Fairbanks, Alaska
University of Alberta
Department of Music
Edmonton, Alberta, Canada
American Conservatory of Music
Chicago, Illinois
Andrews University
Department of Music
Berrien Springs, Michigan
University of Arizona
School of Music
Tucson, Arizona
Arizona State University
School of Music
Tempe, Arizona
University of Arkansas
Department of Music
Fayetteville, Arkansas
Arkansas Tech University
Department of Music
Russellville, Arkansas
Azusa Pacific University
School of Music
Azusa, California
Baldwin-Wallace College
Conservatory of Music
Berea, Ohio
Ball State University
School of Music
Muncie, Indiana
Baylor University
School of Music
Waco, Texas
Bemidji State University
Music Department
Bemidji, Minnesota
Bob Jones University
Division of Music
Greenville, South Carolina
Boise State University
Music Department
Boise, Idaho
Boston Conservatory of Music
Boston, Massachusetts
Boston University
School of Music
Boston, Massachusetts
Bowling Green State University
College of Musical Arts
Bowling Green, Ohio
Brandeis University
Department of Music
Waltham, Massachusetts
Brigham Young University
Department of Music
Provo, Utah
Bulgarian State Conservatoire
Sofia 1505, Bulgaria
Butler University
Jordan College of Fine Arts
Indianapolis, Indiana
University of Calgary
Department of Music
Calgary, Alberta, Canada
University of California, Berkeley
Department of Music
Berkeley, California
University of California, Los Angeles
Department of Music
Los Angeles, California
University of California, Riverside
Department of Music
Riverside, California
University of California, Santa Barbara
Department of Music
Santa Barbara, California

University of California, Santa Cruz
Music Board, Division of the Arts
Santa Cruz, California
California State University, Chico
Department of Music
Chico, California
California State University, Fullerton
Department of Music
Fullerton, California
California State University, Hayward
Department of Music
Hayward, California
California State University, Long Beach
Department of Music
Long Beach, California
California State University, Los Angeles
Department of Music
Los Angeles, California
California State University, Northridge
Music Department
Northridge, California
California State University, Sacramento
Department of Music
Sacramento, California
Case Western Reserve University
Department of Music
Cleveland, Ohio
The Catholic University of America
The Benjamin T. Rome School of Music
Washington, District of Columbia
University of Central Arkansas
Department of Music
Conway, Arkansas
Central Conservatory of Music
Beijing, People's Republic of China
Central Washington University
Department of Music
Ellensburg, Washington
University of Chicago
Department of Music
Chicago, Illinois
University of Cincinnati
College-Conservatory of Music
Cincinnati, Ohio
City University of New York - Brooklyn
College
Conservatory of Music
Brooklyn, New York
City University of New York - City College
Department of Music
New York, New York
City University of New York - Hunter
College
Department of Music
New York, New York
City University of New York - Queens
College
The Aaron Copland School of Music
Flushing, New York
The Claremont Graduate School
Music Department
Claremont, California
Cleveland Institute of Music
Cleveland, Ohio
Cleveland State University
Department of Music
Cleveland, Ohio
University of Colorado at Boulder
College of Music
Boulder, Colorado
Colorado State University
Department of Music, Theatre, and
Dance
Fort Collins, Colorado
Columbus College
Department of Music

Columbus, Georgia
Combs College of Music
   Philadelphia, Pennsylvania
University of Connecticut
   Department of Music
   Storrs, Connecticut
Conservatorio Nacional de Musica - La Paz
   (National Conservatory of Music - La
   Paz)
   La Paz, Bolivia
Converse College
   School of Music
   Spartanburg, South Carolina
The Curtis Institute of Music
   Philadelphia, Pennsylvania
Dalhousie University
   Department of Music
   Halifax, Nova Scotia, Canada
University of Denver
   Lamont School of Music
   Denver, Colorado
DePauw University
   School of Music
   Greencastle, Indiana
Duke University
   Department of Music
   Durham, North Carolina
Duquesne University
   School of Music
   Pittsburgh, Pennsylvania
East Texas State University
   Department of Music
   Commerce, Texas
Eastern Kentucky University
   Department of Music
   Richmond, Kentucky
Eastern Michigan University
   Department of Music
   Ypsilanti, Michigan
Eastern Washington University
   Department of Music
   Cheney, Washington
Escuela Universitaria de Música -
   Montevideo
   Montevideo, Uruguay
Evangelische Kirchenmusikschule der
   Kirchenprovinz Sachsen
   (Evangelical Church Music School of the
   Church Province Saxony)
   DDR-4020 Halle (Saale), German
   Democratic Republic
University of Evansville
   Music Department
   Evansville, Indiana
Ferenc Liszt Academy of Music
   Budapest VI, Hungary
University of Florida
   Department of Music
   Gainesville, Florida
George Mason University
   Department of Performing Arts - Music
   Division
   Fairfax, Virginia
University of Georgia
   School of Music
   Athens, Georgia
Georgia Southern College
   Department of Music
   Statesboro, Georgia
Georgia State University
   School of Music
   Atlanta, Georgia
Glassboro State College
   Department of Music
   Glassboro, New Jersey

University of Hartford
   Hartt School of Music
   West Hartford, Connecticut
University of Hawaii at Manoa
   Music Department
   Honolulu, Hawaii
Henderson State University
   Department of Music
   Arkadelphia, Arkansas
Hochschule für Gestaltende Kunst und
Musik
   (State College for Creative Art and
   Music)
   2800 Bremen 1, Federal Republic of
   Germany
Hochschule für Musik - Würzburg
   D-8700 Würzburg, Federal Republic of
   Germany
Hochschule für Musik und Theater
Hannover
   3000 Hannover 1, Federal Republic of
   Germany
Hofstra University
   Department of Music
   Hempstead, New York
Howard University
   Department of Music
   Washington, District of Columbia
University of Idaho
   School of Music
   Moscow, Idaho
University of Illinois
   School of Music
   Urbana, Illinois
Illinois State University
   Department of Music
   Normal, Illinois
Indiana University - Bloomington
   School of Music
   Bloomington, Indiana
Indiana University of Pennsylvania
   Department of Music
   Indiana, Pennsylvania
University of Iowa
   School of Music
   Iowa City, Iowa
Iowa State University
   Department of Music
   Ames, Iowa
Ithaca College
   School of Music
   Ithaca, New York
Jackson State University
   Department of Music
   Jackson, Mississippi
Jacksonville State University
   Department of Music
   Jacksonville, Alabama
University of Kansas
   School of Fine Arts
   Lawrence, Kansas
Kansas State University
   Department of Music
   Manhattan, Kansas
University of Kentucky
   School of Music
   Lexington, Kentucky
Kuopion Konservatorio
   70100 Kuopio, Finland
Lewis and Clark College
   Music Department
   Portland, Oregon
Long Island University - C.W. Post Campus
   Music Department
   Greenvale, New York

Louisiana State University
   School of Music
   Baton Rouge, Louisiana
University of Louisville
   School of Music
   Louisville, Kentucky
Loyola University
   College of Music
   New Orleans, Louisiana
University of Maine
   School of Performing Arts
   Orono, Maine
University of Manitoba
   School of Music
   Winnipeg, Manitoba, Canada
Mansfield University
   Department of Music
   Mansfield, Pennsylvania
Marshall University
   Department of Music
   Huntington, West Virginia
University of Maryland - Baltimore County
   Department of Music
   Catonsville, Maryland
University of Massachusetts at Amherst
   Department of Music and Dance
   Amherst, Massachusetts
Massachusetts Institute of Technology
   Department of Music and Theater Arts
   Cambridge, Massachusetts
McGill University
   Faculty of Music
   Montreal, Québec, Canada
McMaster University
   Department of Music
   Hamilton, Ontario, Canada
University of Melbourne
   Faculty of Music
   Victoria 3052, Australia
Memphis State University
   Music Department
   Memphis, Tennessee
University of Michigan
   School of Music
   Ann Arbor, Michigan
Mills College
   Music Department
   Oakland, California
University of Minnesota - Twin Cities
   School of Music
   Minneapolis, Minnesota
University of Missouri - Columbia
   Department of Music
   Columbia, Missouri
University of Missouri - Kansas City
   Conservatory of Music
   Kansas City, Missouri
University of Montana
   Department of Music
   Missoula, Montana
Montclair State College
   Department of Music
   Upper Montclair, New Jersey
University of Nebraska - Lincoln
   School of Music
   Lincoln, Nebraska
University of Nebraska - Omaha
   Department of Music
   Omaha, Nebraska
University of Nevada, Las Vegas
   Department of Music
   Las Vegas, Nevada
University of Nevada, Reno
   Department of Music
   Reno, Nevada

University of New Hampshire
  Department of Music
  Durham, New Hampshire
University of New Mexico
  Department of Music
  Albuquerque, New Mexico
New Mexico State University
  Department of Music
  Las Cruces, New Mexico
University of New Orleans
  Department of Music
  New Orleans, Louisiana
New York University - College of Arts and Sciences
  Department of Music
  New York, New York
New York University - School of Education, Health, Nursing, and Arts Professions
  Department of Music and Music Education
  New York, New York
Nikos Skalkotas Conservatory
  Athens 11141, Greece
University of North Carolina at Chapel Hill
  Department of Music
  Chapel Hill, North Carolina
University of North Carolina at Greensboro
  School of Music
  Greensboro, North Carolina
University of North Dakota
  Department of Music
  Grand Forks, North Dakota
North Texas State University
  School of Music
  Denton, Texas
Northeast Louisiana University
  School of Music
  Monroe, Louisiana
Northeastern Illinois University
  Department of Music
  Chicago, Illinois
Northern Arizona University
  Music Department
  Flagstaff, Arizona
University of Northern Colorado
  School of Music
  Greeley, Colorado
Northern Illinois University
  School of Music
  DeKalb, Illinois
University of Northern Iowa
  School of Music
  Cedar Falls, Iowa
Northwestern University
  School of Music
  Evanston, Illinois
University of Notre Dame
  Department of Music
  Notre Dame, Indiana
Oberlin College
  Conservatory of Music
  Oberlin, Ohio
The Ohio State University
  School of Music
  Columbus, Ohio
Ohio University
  School of Music
  Athens, Ohio
Ohio Wesleyan University
  Department of Music
  Delaware, Ohio
University of Oklahoma
  School of Music
  Norman, Oklahoma
University of Oregon
  School of Music

Eugene, Oregon
Oregon State University
  Department of Music
  Corvallis, Oregon
Osaka Ongaku Daigaku
  (Osaka College of Music)
  Osaka 561, Japan
University of the Pacific
  Conservatory of Music
  Stockton, California
Peabody Institute of The Johns Hopkins University
  Baltimore, Maryland
University of Pennsylvania
  Department of Music
  Philadelphia, Pennsylvania
Pennsylvania State University
  School of Music
  University Park, Pennsylvania
University of the Philippines
  College of Music
  Quezon City, The Philippines
Pittsburg State University
  Department of Music
  Pittsburg, Kansas
University of Pittsburgh
  Department of Music
  Pittsburgh, Pennsylvania
Pomona College
  Music Department
  Claremont, California
Portland State University
  Department of Music
  Portland, Oregon
University of Puget Sound
  School of Music
  Tacoma, Washington
Queen's University
  School of Music
  Kingston, Ontario, Canada
Real Conservatorio Superior de Música de Madrid
  (Royal Academy of Music)
  Madrid 13, Spain
University of Rhode Island
  Department of Music
  Kingston, Rhode Island
Rice University
  Shepherd School of Music
  Houston, Texas
Roosevelt University
  Chicago Musical College
  Chicago, Illinois
Royal Academy of Music
  London NW1 5HT, United Kingdom
Royal College of Music
  London, SW7 2BS, United Kingdom
Rutgers, The State University of New Jersey
  Department of Music
  New Brunswick, New Jersey
St. Cloud State University
  Department of Music
  St. Cloud, Minnesota
Saint Louis Conservatory of Music
  St. Louis, Missouri
St. Olaf College
  Music Department
  Northfield, Minnesota
San Diego State University
  Music Department
  San Diego, California
San Francisco State University
  Department of Music
  San Francisco, California
San Jose State University
  Department of Music

San Jose, California
University of Saskatchewan
  Department of Music
  Saskatoon, Saskatchewan, Canada
Shengyang Conservatory of Music
  Shengyang, Liaoning Province, People's Republic of China
University of South Carolina
  School of Music
  Columbia, South Carolina
University of South Florida
  Department of Music
  Tampa, Florida
Southern Illinois University at Carbondale
  School of Music
  Carbondale, Illinois
Southern Illinois University at Edwardsville
  Department of Music
  Edwardsville, Illinois
Southern Methodist University
  Meadows School of the Arts
  Dallas, Texas
University of Southern Mississippi
  School of Music
  Hattiesburg, Mississippi
Southwest Texas State University
  Department of Music
  San Marcos, Texas
Southwestern Baptist Theological Seminary
  School of Church Music
  Fort Worth, Texas
University of Southwestern Louisiana
  School of Music
  Lafayette, Louisiana
Staatliche Hochschule für Musik Rheinland - Aachen
  Grenzland-Institut Aachen
  Aachen, Federal Republic of Germany
Staatliche Hochschule für Musik Rheinland - Köln
  D-5000 Köln 1, Federal Republic of Germany
Staatliche Hochschule für Musik Rheinland - Wuppertal
  Institute Wuppertal
  Wuppertal, Federal Republic of Germany
Staatliche Hochschule für Musik Westfalen-Lippe
  Institut Dortmund
  D-4600 Dortmund 1, Federal Republic of Germany
Stanford University
  Department of Music
  Stanford, California
State University of New York at Binghamton
  Department of Music
  Binghamton, New York
State University of New York at Buffalo
  Department of Music
  Buffalo, New York
State University of New York at Stony Brook
  Department of Music
  Stony Brook, New York
State University of New York College at Fredonia
  School of Music
  Fredonia, New York
State University of New York College at New Paltz
  Department of Music
  New Paltz, New York
State University of New York College at Potsdam
  Crane School of Music

Potsdam, New York
State University of New York College at
Purchase
Division of Music
Purchase, New York
Stedelijke Muziekpedagogische Akademie
Leeuwarden, Netherlands
Stephen F. Austin State University
Department of Music
Nacogdoches, Texas
Stetson University
School of Music
Deland, Florida
Syracuse University
School of Music
Syracuse, New York
Teachers College of Columbia University
Department of Music and Music
Education
New York, New York
Tel Aviv University
Faculty of Fine Arts
Tel-Aviv, Israel
Temple University
Esther Boyer College of Music
Philadelphia, Pennsylvania
University of Tennessee at Knoxville
Department of Music
Knoxville, Tennessee
Texas Christian University
Music Department
Fort Worth, Texas
Texas Tech University
Department of Music
Lubbock, Texas
Toho Gakuen School of Music
Tokyo, Japan
Tonlistarskolinn i Reykjavik
105 Reykjavik, Iceland
University of Toronto
Faculty of Music
Toronto, Ontario, Canada
Trenton State College
Music Department
Trenton, New Jersey
Troy State University
Department of Music
Troy, Alabama
Tulane University
Newcomb College
New Orleans, Louisiana
University of Tulsa
Faculty of Music
Tulsa, Oklahoma
Universidade do Rio de Janeiro
Letters and Arts Center - Music Course
22290 Rio de Janeiro, Brazil
Université Laval
Ecole de Musique
Ste. Foy, Québec, Canada
University of Utah
Department of Music
Salt Lake City, Utah
Valparaiso University
Department of Music
Valparaiso, Indiana
University of Victoria
School of Music
Victoria, British Columbia, Canada
University of Virginia
McIntire Department of Music
Charlottesville, Virginia
Virginia Commonwealth University
Department of Music
Richmond, Virginia

Virginia Polytechnic Institute and State
University
Department of Music
Blacksburg, Virginia
Vysoká Skola Mûzickych Umeni v Praha
Academy of Music and Dramatic Arts
1101 00 Prague 1, Czechoslovakia
University of Washington
School of Music
Seattle, Washington
Washington State University
Department of Music
Pullman, Washington
Washington University
Department of Music
St. Louis, Missouri
Wayne State University
Department of Music
Detroit, Michigan
West Chester University of Pennsylvania
School of Music
West Chester, Pennsylvania
West Virginia University
Division of Music
Morgantown, West Virginia
University of Western Australia
Department of Music
Nedlands, WA 6009, Australia
Western Kentucky University
Department of Music
Bowling Green, Kentucky
Western Michigan University
School of Music
Kalamazoo, Michigan
University of Western Ontario
Faculty of Music
London, Ontario, Canada
Western Washington University
Department of Music
Bellingham, Washington
Wheaton College
Conservatory of Music
Wheaton, Illinois
Wichita State University
School of Music
Wichita, Kansas
Wilfrid Laurier University
Faculty of Music
Waterloo, Ontario, Canada
Willamette University
Department of Music
Salem, Oregon
William Carey College
Winters School of Music
Hattiesburg, Mississippi
William Paterson College
Department of Music
Wayne, New Jersey
University of Windsor
School of Music
Windsor, Ontario, Canada
Winthrop College
School of Music
Rock Hill, South Carolina
University of Wisconsin - La Crosse
Department of Music
La Crosse, Wisconsin
University of Wisconsin - Madison
School of Music
Madison, Wisconsin
University of Wisconsin - Milwaukee
Music Department
Milwaukee, Wisconsin
University of Wisconsin - Oshkosh
Department of Music
Oshkosh, Wisconsin

University of Wisconsin - Whitewater
Department of Music
Whitewater, Wisconsin
Wright State University
Department of Music
Dayton, Ohio
Yale College (Yale University)
Department of Music
New Haven, Connecticut
Yared National Institute of Music
Addis Ababa, Ethiopia
York University
Department of Music
North York, Ontario, Canada
Youngstown State University
Dana School of Music
Youngstown, Ohio
Zeneiskolai Tanárkepzó Intézet
(Music Teachers Training Institute of the
Liszt Academy of Music)
Budapest 1052, Hungary

MUSIC HISTORY (LATIN AMERICA)

Escuela Universitaria de Música -
Montevideo
Montevideo, Uruguay

MUSIC HISTORY (URUGUAY)

Escuela Universitaria de Música -
Montevideo
Montevideo, Uruguay

MUSIC HISTORY MUSICOLOGY

Staatliche Hochschule für Musik Trossingen
D-7218 Trossingen 1, Federal Republic of
Germany

MUSIC HISTORY OF MEXICO

Escuela Nacional de Música
Universidad Nacional Autónoma de
México
Mexico City, D.F. 04100, Mexico

MUSIC INDUSTRY

Middle Tennessee State University
Department of Music
Murfreesboro, Tennessee
University of Southern Mississippi
School of Music
Hattiesburg, Mississippi
Syracuse University
School of Music
Syracuse, New York

MUSIC INDUSTRY MANAGEMENT

Wayne State University
Department of Music
Detroit, Michigan

MUSIC LIBRARIANSHIP

The Catholic University of America
The Benjamin T. Rome School of Music
Washington, District of Columbia
University of Miami
School of Music
Coral Gables, Florida
University of Wisconsin - Milwaukee
Music Department
Milwaukee, Wisconsin

MUSIC LISTENING

Wright State University
Department of Music
Dayton, Ohio

MUSIC LITERATURE

University of Akron
Department of Music
Akron, Ohio
Alabama State University
School of Music
Montgomery, Alabama
University of Alberta
Department of Music
Edmonton, Alberta, Canada
American Conservatory of Music
Chicago, Illinois
Andrews University
Department of Music
Berrien Springs, Michigan
Arizona State University
School of Music
Tempe, Arizona
University of Arkansas
Department of Music
Fayetteville, Arkansas
Azusa Pacific University
School of Music
Azusa, California
Baldwin-Wallace College
Conservatory of Music
Berea, Ohio
Baylor University
School of Music
Waco, Texas
Bob Jones University
Division of Music
Greenville, South Carolina
Boston Conservatory of Music
Boston, Massachusetts
Boston University
School of Music
Boston, Massachusetts
Bowling Green State University
College of Musical Arts
Bowling Green, Ohio
Brandon University
School of Music
Brandon, Manitoba, Canada
University of California, Berkeley
Department of Music
Berkeley, California
University of California, Los Angeles
Department of Music
Los Angeles, California
California State University, Hayward
Department of Music
Hayward, California
California State University, Long Beach
Department of Music
Long Beach, California
California State University, Los Angeles
Department of Music
Los Angeles, California
California State University, Northridge
Music Department
Northridge, California
California State University, Sacramento
Department of Music
Sacramento, California
Case Western Reserve University
Department of Music
Cleveland, Ohio
University of Central Arkansas
Department of Music
Conway, Arkansas
Central Michigan University
Department of Music
Mount Pleasant, Michigan

Central Washington University
Department of Music
Ellensburg, Washington
Cleveland Institute of Music
Cleveland, Ohio
University of Colorado at Boulder
College of Music
Boulder, Colorado
Colorado State University
Department of Music, Theatre, and
Dance
Fort Collins, Colorado
Converse College
School of Music
Spartanburg, South Carolina
Dalhousie University
Department of Music
Halifax, Nova Scotia, Canada
University of Delaware
Department of Music
Newark, Delaware
Delta State University
Department of Music
Cleveland, Mississippi
University of Denver
Lamont School of Music
Denver, Colorado
Duke University
Department of Music
Durham, North Carolina
Duquesne University
School of Music
Pittsburgh, Pennsylvania
Eastern Michigan University
Department of Music
Ypsilanti, Michigan
Eastern Washington University
Department of Music
Cheney, Washington
University of Evansville
Music Department
Evansville, Indiana
University of Florida
Department of Music
Gainesville, Florida
Fort Hays State University
Department of Music
Hays, Kansas
University of Georgia
School of Music
Athens, Georgia
Georgia State University
School of Music
Atlanta, Georgia
Hardin-Simmons University
School of Music
Abilene, Texas
University of Hawaii at Manoa
Music Department
Honolulu, Hawaii
Henderson State University
Department of Music
Arkadelphia, Arkansas
Hofstra University
Department of Music
Hempstead, New York
University of Houston
School of Music
Houston, Texas
Howard University
Department of Music
Washington, District of Columbia
University of Idaho
School of Music
Moscow, Idaho

University of Illinois
School of Music
Urbana, Illinois
Illinois State University
Department of Music
Normal, Illinois
Indiana University - Bloomington
School of Music
Bloomington, Indiana
Indiana University of Pennsylvania
Department of Music
Indiana, Pennsylvania
University of Iowa
School of Music
Iowa City, Iowa
Ithaca College
School of Music
Ithaca, New York
Jackson State University
Department of Music
Jackson, Mississippi
Kansas State University
Department of Music
Manhattan, Kansas
University of Kentucky
School of Music
Lexington, Kentucky
Lamar University
Department of Music
Beaumont, Texas
Lewis and Clark College
Music Department
Portland, Oregon
University of Maine
School of Performing Arts
Orono, Maine
Mansfield University
Department of Music
Mansfield, Pennsylvania
Marshall University
Department of Music
Huntington, West Virginia
Massachusetts Institute of Technology
Department of Music and Theater Arts
Cambridge, Massachusetts
Mills College
Music Department
Oakland, California
University of Missouri - Kansas City
Conservatory of Music
Kansas City, Missouri
University of Montana
Department of Music
Missoula, Montana
University of Nebraska - Lincoln
School of Music
Lincoln, Nebraska
University of Nevada, Las Vegas
Department of Music
Las Vegas, Nevada
University of New Hampshire
Department of Music
Durham, New Hampshire
University of New Mexico
Department of Music
Albuquerque, New Mexico
New Mexico State University
Department of Music
Las Cruces, New Mexico
New York University - College of Arts and
Sciences
Department of Music
New York, New York
New York University - School of Education,
Health, Nursing, and Arts Professions
Department of Music and Music

Education
New York, New York
University of North Carolina at Chapel Hill
Department of Music
Chapel Hill, North Carolina
University of North Carolina at Greensboro
School of Music
Greensboro, North Carolina
North Carolina School of the Arts
School of Music
Winston-Salem, North Carolina
University of North Dakota
Department of Music
Grand Forks, North Dakota
North Texas State University
School of Music
Denton, Texas
Northeast Louisiana University
School of Music
Monroe, Louisiana
Northeast Missouri State University
Division of Fine Arts
Kirksville, Missouri
Northern Arizona University
Music Department
Flagstaff, Arizona
University of Northern Colorado
School of Music
Greeley, Colorado
Northern Illinois University
School of Music
DeKalb, Illinois
University of Northern Iowa
School of Music
Cedar Falls, Iowa
Northwestern University
School of Music
Evanston, Illinois
Ohio University
School of Music
Athens, Ohio
Ohio Wesleyan University
Department of Music
Delaware, Ohio
Oregon State University
Department of Music
Corvallis, Oregon
Ouachita Baptist University
School of Music
Arkadelphia, Arkansas
Pennsylvania State University
School of Music
University Park, Pennsylvania
Portland State University
Department of Music
Portland, Oregon
University of Rhode Island
Department of Music
Kingston, Rhode Island
Roosevelt University
Chicago Musical College
Chicago, Illinois
Rutgers, The State University of New Jersey
Department of Music
New Brunswick, New Jersey
Saint Louis Conservatory of Music
St. Louis, Missouri
St. Olaf College
Music Department
Northfield, Minnesota
Sam Houston State University
Department of Music
Huntsville, Texas
San Diego State University
Music Department
San Diego, California

San Francisco State University
Department of Music
San Francisco, California
San Jose State University
Department of Music
San Jose, California
University of Saskatchewan
Department of Music
Saskatoon, Saskatchewan, Canada
University of South Carolina
School of Music
Columbia, South Carolina
University of South Dakota
Music Department
Vermillion, South Dakota
Southern Illinois University at Carbondale
School of Music
Carbondale, Illinois
Southern Illinois University at Edwardsville
Department of Music
Edwardsville, Illinois
Southern Methodist University
Meadows School of the Arts
Dallas, Texas
University of Southern Mississippi
School of Music
Hattiesburg, Mississippi
Southwest Texas State University
Department of Music
San Marcos, Texas
Southwestern Baptist Theological Seminary
School of Church Music
Fort Worth, Texas
University of Southwestern Louisiana
School of Music
Lafayette, Louisiana
State University of New York at
Binghamton
Department of Music
Binghamton, New York
State University of New York at Stony
Brook
Department of Music
Stony Brook, New York
State University of New York College at
New Paltz
Department of Music
New Paltz, New York
State University of New York College at
Potsdam
Crane School of Music
Potsdam, New York
Stephen F. Austin State University
Department of Music
Nacogdoches, Texas
Teachers College of Columbia University
Department of Music and Music
Education
New York, New York
University of Tennessee at Knoxville
Department of Music
Knoxville, Tennessee
University of Texas at Austin
Department of Music
Austin, Texas
Texas Tech University
Department of Music
Lubbock, Texas
University of Toronto
Faculty of Music
Toronto, Ontario, Canada
Towson State University
Department of Music
Towson, Maryland
Trenton State College
Music Department

Trenton, New Jersey
Tulane University
Newcomb College
New Orleans, Louisiana
University of Victoria
School of Music
Victoria, British Columbia, Canada
University of Virginia
McIntire Department of Music
Charlottesville, Virginia
Virginia Commonwealth University
Department of Music
Richmond, Virginia
Virginia Polytechnic Institute and State
University
Department of Music
Blacksburg, Virginia
Western Kentucky University
Department of Music
Bowling Green, Kentucky
University of Western Ontario
Faculty of Music
London, Ontario, Canada
Western Washington University
Department of Music
Bellingham, Washington
Wheaton College
Conservatory of Music
Wheaton, Illinois
Wichita State University
School of Music
Wichita, Kansas
William Carey College
Winters School of Music
Hattiesburg, Mississippi
William Paterson College
Department of Music
Wayne, New Jersey
University of Wisconsin - Milwaukee
Music Department
Milwaukee, Wisconsin
University of Wisconsin - Oshkosh
Department of Music
Oshkosh, Wisconsin
Wright State University
Department of Music
Dayton, Ohio
Youngstown State University
Dana School of Music
Youngstown, Ohio

MUSIC MANAGEMENT

University of Colorado at Denver
College of Music
Denver, Colorado
University of Hartford
Hartt School of Music
West Hartford, Connecticut
James Madison University
Department of Music
Harrisonburg, Virginia
Mankato State University
Department of Music
Mankato, Minnesota
Oklahoma City University
School of Music and Performing Arts
Oklahoma City, Oklahoma
University of the Pacific
Conservatory of Music
Stockton, California
William Paterson College
Department of Music
Wayne, New Jersey

MUSIC MARKETING

University of Texas at San Antonio
Division of Music
San Antonio, Texas

MUSIC MEDIA

Norfolk State University
Department of Music
Norfolk, Virginia

MUSIC MERCHANDISING

Drake University
Department of Music
Des Moines, Iowa
Eastern Kentucky University
Department of Music
Richmond, Kentucky
Eastern Washington University
Department of Music
Cheney, Washington
Emporia State University
Division of Music
Emporia, Kansas
Georgia Southern College
Department of Music
Statesboro, Georgia
Hofstra University
Department of Music
Hempstead, New York
Indiana State University
Department of Music
Terre Haute, Indiana
Mankato State University
Department of Music
Mankato, Minnesota
Mansfield University
Department of Music
Mansfield, Pennsylvania
University of Miami
School of Music
Coral Gables, Florida
University of Nebraska - Omaha
Department of Music
Omaha, Nebraska
Southern Illinois University at Edwardsville
Department of Music
Edwardsville, Illinois
Southwestern Oklahoma State University
Department of Music
Weatherford, Oklahoma
University of Wisconsin - Oshkosh
Department of Music
Oshkosh, Wisconsin

MUSIC MINISTRY

Southwestern Baptist Theological Seminary
School of Church Music
Fort Worth, Texas

MUSIC PEDAGOGY

Fachakademie für Musik - München
Richard Strauss-Konservatorium der
Stadt
*München 80, Federal Republic of
Germany*
Hochschule für Musik - Würzburg
*D-8700 Würzburg, Federal Republic of
Germany*
Hochschule für Musik und Theater
Hannover
*3000 Hannover 1, Federal Republic of
Germany*
Shenandoah College and Conservatory
Winchester, Virginia

Staatliche Hochschule für Musik Rheinland
- Düsseldorf
(State College of Music)
*D-4000 Düsseldorf, Federal Republic of
Germany*
Staatliche Hochschule für Musik Rheinland
- Wuppertal
Institute Wuppertal
Wuppertal, Federal Republic of Germany
Staatliche Hochschule für Musik Ruhr
*4300 Essen 16, Federal Republic of
Germany*
Staatliche Hochschule für Musik und
Darstellende Kunst Stuttgart
*7000 Stuttgart 1, Federal Republic of
Germany*
Staatliche Hochschule für Musik
Westfalen-Lippe
Institut Dortmund
*D-4600 Dortmund 1, Federal Republic of
Germany*

MUSIC PEDAGOGY AND TECHNIQUES

University of Arkansas
Department of Music
Fayetteville, Arkansas

MUSIC PRODUCTION AND ENGINEERING

Berklee College of Music
Boston, Massachusetts

MUSIC PSYCHOLOGY

Hochschule für Musik und Theater
Hannover
*3000 Hannover 1, Federal Republic of
Germany*

MUSIC RECORDING ARTS

California State University, Los Angeles
Department of Music
Los Angeles, California

MUSIC RECORDING INDUSTRY

San Francisco State University
Department of Music
San Francisco, California

MUSIC RESEARCH

Osaka Ongaku Daigaku
(Osaka College of Music)
Osaka 561, Japan
Shengyang Conservatory of Music
*Shengyang, Liaoning Province, People's
Republic of China*

MUSIC SOCIOLOGY

Staatliche Hochschule für Musik Rheinland
- Düsseldorf
(State College of Music)
*D-4000 Düsseldorf, Federal Republic of
Germany*

MUSIC SYNTHESIS

Berklee College of Music
Boston, Massachusetts

MUSIC TECHNOLOGY

New York University - School of Education,
Health, Nursing, and Arts Professions
Department of Music and Music
Education
New York, New York

MUSIC THEATRE

Brigham Young University
Department of Music
Provo, Utah
Fachakademie für Musik - Nürnberg
Konservatorium der Stadt Nürnberg
Nürnberg, Federal Republic of Germany
University of Northern Colorado
School of Music
Greeley, Colorado
University of Windsor
School of Music
Windsor, Ontario, Canada

MUSIC THEORY

The Academy of Vocal Arts
Philadelphia, Pennsylvania
Acadia University
School of Music
Wolfville, Nova Scotia, Canada
University of Adelaide
Elder Conservatorium of Music
Adelaide, SA 5001, Australia
Akademia Muzyczna w Krakowie
31-038 Kraków, Poland
Akademia Muzyczna w Lódź
(Academy of Music of Lódź)
90-716 Lódź, Poland
Akademia Muzycznaj im. Fryderyka
Chopina w Warzawie
(Frederic Chopin Academy of Music of
Warsaw)
00-368 Warsaw, Poland
University of Akron
Department of Music
Akron, Ohio
Alabama State University
School of Music
Montgomery, Alabama
University of Alaska
Music Department
Fairbanks, Alaska
University of Alberta
Department of Music
Edmonton, Alberta, Canada
American Conservatory of Music
Chicago, Illinois
Andrews University
Department of Music
Berrien Springs, Michigan
Appalachian State University
Department of Music
Boone, North Carolina
University of Arizona
School of Music
Tucson, Arizona
Arizona State University
School of Music
Tempe, Arizona
Arkansas State University
Department of Music
State University, Arkansas
Arkansas Tech University
Department of Music
Russellville, Arkansas
Auburn University
Department of Music
Auburn, Alabama
A.V. Nezhdanova Odessa Conservatory
*270000 Odessa, Ukrainskaja SSR,
U.S.S.R.*
Azusa Pacific University
School of Music
Azusa, California

Baldwin-Wallace College
Conservatory of Music
Berea, Ohio
Ball State University
School of Music
Muncie, Indiana
Banaras Hindu University
Uttar Pradesh 221005, India
Baylor University
School of Music
Waco, Texas
Bemidji State University
Music Department
Bemidji, Minnesota
Biola University
Department of Music
La Mirada, California
Bob Jones University
Division of Music
Greenville, South Carolina
Boise State University
Music Department
Boise, Idaho
Boston University
School of Music
Boston, Massachusetts
Bradley University
Division of Music and Theatre Arts
Peoria, Illinois
Brandeis University
Department of Music
Waltham, Massachusetts
Brigham Young University
Department of Music
Provo, Utah
Bulgarian State Conservatoire
Sofia 1505, Bulgaria
University of California, Irvine
School of Fine Arts
Irvine, California
University of California, Los Angeles
Department of Music
Los Angeles, California
University of California, Riverside
Department of Music
Riverside, California
University of California, San Diego
Department of Music
La Jolla, California
University of California, Santa Barbara
Department of Music
Santa Barbara, California
University of California, Santa Cruz
Music Board, Division of the Arts
Santa Cruz, California
California State University, Chico
Department of Music
Chico, California
California State University, Fullerton
Department of Music
Fullerton, California
California State University, Hayward
Department of Music
Hayward, California
California State University, Los Angeles
Department of Music
Los Angeles, California
California State University, Northridge
Music Department
Northridge, California
California State University, Sacramento
Department of Music
Sacramento, California
The Catholic University of America
The Benjamin T. Rome School of Music
Washington, District of Columbia

University of Central Arkansas
Department of Music
Conway, Arkansas
Central Conservatory of Music
Beijing, People's Republic of China
Central Michigan University
Department of Music
Mount Pleasant, Michigan
Central State University
Department of Music
Edmond, Oklahoma
Central Washington University
Department of Music
Ellensburg, Washington
University of Chicago
Department of Music
Chicago, Illinois
University of Cincinnati
College-Conservatory of Music
Cincinnati, Ohio
City of Leeds College of Music
Leeds LS2 8BH, United Kingdom
City University of New York - Brooklyn
College
Conservatory of Music
Brooklyn, New York
City University of New York - City College
Department of Music
New York, New York
City University of New York - Graduate
School and University Center
Doctoral Program in Music
New York, New York
City University of New York - Hunter
College
Department of Music
New York, New York
City University of New York - Queens
College
The Aaron Copland School of Music
Flushing, New York
Cleveland Institute of Music
Cleveland, Ohio
Cleveland State University
Department of Music
Cleveland, Ohio
University of Colorado at Boulder
College of Music
Boulder, Colorado
Colorado State University
Department of Music, Theatre, and
Dance
Fort Collins, Colorado
Columbia University
Department of Music
New York, New York
Columbus College
Department of Music
Columbus, Georgia
Combs College of Music
Philadelphia, Pennsylvania
University of Connecticut
Department of Music
Storrs, Connecticut
Conservatorio Nacional de Música
(National Conservatory of Music)
Lima 1, Peru
Conservatorio Nacional de Musica - La Paz
(National Conservatory of Music - La
Paz)
La Paz, Bolivia
Converse College
School of Music
Spartanburg, South Carolina
Cornell University
Department of Music

Ithaca, New York
The Curtis Institute of Music
Philadelphia, Pennsylvania
Dalhousie University
Department of Music
Halifax, Nova Scotia, Canada
University of Delaware
Department of Music
Newark, Delaware
University of Denver
Lamont School of Music
Denver, Colorado
DePaul University
School of Music
Chicago, Illinois
DePauw University
School of Music
Greencastle, Indiana
Duke University
Department of Music
Durham, North Carolina
Duquesne University
School of Music
Pittsburgh, Pennsylvania
East Carolina University
School of Music
Greenville, North Carolina
East Texas State University
Department of Music
Commerce, Texas
Eastern Illinois University
Department of Music
Charleston, Illinois
Eastern Kentucky University
Department of Music
Richmond, Kentucky
Eastern Michigan University
Department of Music
Ypsilanti, Michigan
Eastern New Mexico University
School of Music
Portales, New Mexico
Eastern Washington University
Department of Music
Cheney, Washington
Escuela de Música - Heredia
Universidad Nacional
Heredia, Costa Rica
Escuela Nacional de Música
Universidad Nacional Autónoma de
México
Mexico City, D.F. 04100, Mexico
Escuela Universitaria de Música -
Montevideo
Montevideo, Uruguay
Evangelische Kirchenmusikschule der
Kirchenprovinz Sachsen
(Evangelical Church Music School of the
Church Province Saxony)
*DDR-4020 Halle (Saale), German
Democratic Republic*
University of Evansville
Music Department
Evansville, Indiana
Fachakademie für Musik - München
Richard Strauss-Konservatorium der
Stadt
*München 80, Federal Republic of
Germany*
Fachakademie für Musik - Nürnberg
Konservatorium der Stadt Nürnberg
Nürnberg, Federal Republic of Germany
Ferenc Liszt Academy of Music
Budapest VI, Hungary
University of Florida
Department of Music

Gainesville, Florida
Fort Hays State University
Department of Music
Hays, Kansas
George Mason University
Department of Performing Arts - Music
Division
Fairfax, Virginia
Georgia Southern College
Department of Music
Statesboro, Georgia
Georgia State University
School of Music
Atlanta, Georgia
Glassboro State College
Department of Music
Glassboro, New Jersey
Guildhall School of Music and Drama
London EC2Y 8DT, United Kingdom
Hardin-Simmons University
School of Music
Abilene, Texas
University of Hartford
Hartt School of Music
West Hartford, Connecticut
Harvard University
Department of Music
Cambridge, Massachusetts
University of Hawaii at Manoa
Music Department
Honolulu, Hawaii
Henderson State University
Department of Music
Arkadelphia, Arkansas
Hermann-Zilcher-Konservatorium
*D-8700 Würzburg, Federal Republic of
Germany*
Hochschule für Gestaltende Kunst und
Musik
(State College for Creative Art and
Music)
*2800 Bremen 1, Federal Republic of
Germany*
Hochschule für Music Franz Liszt
*DDR 5300 Weimar, German Democratic
Republic*
Hochschule für Music und Darstellende
Kunst Hamburg
*2000 Hamburg 13, Federal Republic of
Germany*
Hochschule für Musik - München
*8000 München 2, Federal Republic of
Germany*
Hochschule für Musik - Würzburg
*D-8700 Würzburg, Federal Republic of
Germany*
Hochschule für Musik Felix
Mendelssohn-Bartholdy
*7010 Leipzig, German Democratic
Republic*
Hochschule für Musik und Theater
Hannover
*3000 Hannover 1, Federal Republic of
Germany*
Hofstra University
Department of Music
Hempstead, New York
Hoschschule für Music Hans Eisler
*DDR Berlin 1080, German Democratic
Republic*
University of Houston
School of Music
Houston, Texas
University of Idaho
School of Music
Moscow, Idaho

Illinois State University
Department of Music
Normal, Illinois
Indiana State University
Department of Music
Terre Haute, Indiana
Indiana University - Bloomington
School of Music
Bloomington, Indiana
Indiana University of Pennsylvania
Department of Music
Indiana, Pennsylvania
Institute of Aesthetic Studies
Colombo 7, Sri Lanka
Instituto Superior de Arte
Facultad de Música
Playa, Cuba
University of Iowa
School of Music
Iowa City, Iowa
Ithaca College
School of Music
Ithaca, New York
Jackson State University
Department of Music
Jackson, Mississippi
Jacksonville State University
Department of Music
Jacksonville, Alabama
James Madison University
Department of Music
Harrisonburg, Virginia
Jersey City State College
Music Department
Jersey City, New Jersey
University of Kansas
School of Fine Arts
Lawrence, Kansas
Kansas State University
Department of Music
Manhattan, Kansas
Karol Szymanowski Academy of Music of
Katowice
Katowice, Poland
Kent State University
School of Music
Kent, Ohio
University of Kentucky
School of Music
Lexington, Kentucky
Kenya Conservatoire of Music
Nairobi, Kenya
Konservatorium und Musikhochschule -
Zürich
8050 Zürich, Switzerland
Konzervatoř v Praze
(State Conservatory Prague)
Praha 110 00, Czechoslovakia
Konzervatorium - Bratislava
Bratislava 811 06, Czechoslovakia
Kratikon Odeion Thessaloniki
(State Conservatory of Music)
Thessaloniki, Greece
Lamar University
Department of Music
Beaumont, Texas
Lawrence University
Conservatory of Music
Appleton, Wisconsin
Leningrad N.A. Rimsky-Korsakov State
Conservatory
*192041 Leningrad, Rossiskaja SFSR,
U.S.S.R.*
Lewis and Clark College
Music Department
Portland, Oregon

Lithuanian State Conservatory
232001 Vilnius, Litovskaja SSR, U.S.S.R.
Long Island University - C.W. Post Campus
Music Department
Greenvale, New York
Louisiana State University
School of Music
Baton Rouge, Louisiana
University of Louisville
School of Music
Louisville, Kentucky
University of Lowell
College of Music
Lowell, Massachusetts
Loyola University
College of Music
New Orleans, Louisiana
University of Maine
School of Performing Arts
Orono, Maine
Manhattan School of Music
New York, New York
Mannes College of Music
New York, New York
Mansfield University
Department of Music
Mansfield, Pennsylvania
Marshall University
Department of Music
Huntington, West Virginia
University of Maryland - Baltimore County
Department of Music
Catonsville, Maryland
University of Maryland - College Park
Department of Music
College Park, Maryland
University of Massachusetts at Amherst
Department of Music and Dance
Amherst, Massachusetts
Massachusetts Institute of Technology
Department of Music and Theater Arts
Cambridge, Massachusetts
McGill University
Faculty of Music
Montreal, Québec, Canada
McMaster University
Department of Music
Hamilton, Ontario, Canada
McNeese State University
Department of Music
Lake Charles, Louisiana
University of Melbourne
Faculty of Music
Victoria 3052, Australia
Memphis State University
Music Department
Memphis, Tennessee
University of Miami
School of Music
Coral Gables, Florida
Miami University
Department of Music
Oxford, Ohio
University of Michigan
School of Music
Ann Arbor, Michigan
Michigan State University
School of Music
East Lansing, Michigan
Middle Tennessee State University
Department of Music
Murfreesboro, Tennessee
University of Minnesota - Duluth
Department of Music
Duluth, Minnesota

University of Minnesota - Twin Cities
School of Music
Minneapolis, Minnesota
University of Mississippi
Department of Music
University, Mississippi
University of Missouri - Columbia
Department of Music
Columbia, Missouri
University of Missouri - Kansas City
Conservatory of Music
Kansas City, Missouri
University of Montana
Department of Music
Missoula, Montana
Montclair State College
Department of Music
Upper Montclair, New Jersey
Moscow P.I. Tchaikovsky State
Conservatory
*103009 Moscow K-9, Rossiskaja SFSR,
U.S.S.R.*
Musik-Akademie der Stadt Basel
(Konservatorium)
Konservatorium (Musikhochschule)
Basel, Switzerland
Musikhochschule des Saarlandes
*6600 Saarbrücken 3, Federal Republic of
Germany*
Musikschule und Konservatorium
Schaffhausen
Schaffhausen, Switzerland
University of Nebraska - Lincoln
School of Music
Lincoln, Nebraska
University of Nebraska - Omaha
Department of Music
Omaha, Nebraska
University of Nevada, Las Vegas
Department of Music
Las Vegas, Nevada
University of Nevada, Reno
Department of Music
Reno, Nevada
New England Conservatory
Boston, Massachusetts
University of New Hampshire
Department of Music
Durham, New Hampshire
University of New Mexico
Department of Music
Albuquerque, New Mexico
New Mexico State University
Department of Music
Las Cruces, New Mexico
University of New Orleans
Department of Music
New Orleans, Louisiana
New South Wales State Conservatorium of
Music
Sydney NSW 2000, Australia
New York University - College of Arts and
Sciences
Department of Music
New York, New York
New York University - School of Education,
Health, Nursing, and Arts Professions
Department of Music and Music
Education
New York, New York
Norfolk State University
Department of Music
Norfolk, Virginia
Norges Musikkhøgskole
(The Norwegian State Academy of
Music)

N-0130 Oslo 1, Norway
University of North Carolina at Chapel Hill
Department of Music
Chapel Hill, North Carolina
University of North Carolina at Greensboro
School of Music
Greensboro, North Carolina
North Carolina School of the Arts
School of Music
Winston-Salem, North Carolina
University of North Dakota
Department of Music
Grand Forks, North Dakota
North Texas State University
School of Music
Denton, Texas
Northeast Louisiana University
School of Music
Monroe, Louisiana
Northeast Missouri State University
Division of Fine Arts
Kirksville, Missouri
Northeastern Illinois University
Department of Music
Chicago, Illinois
Northern Arizona University
Music Department
Flagstaff, Arizona
University of Northern Colorado
School of Music
Greeley, Colorado
Northern Illinois University
School of Music
DeKalb, Illinois
University of Northern Iowa
School of Music
Cedar Falls, Iowa
Northwestern State University of Louisiana
Department of Music
Natchitoches, Louisiana
Northwestern University
School of Music
Evanston, Illinois
University of Notre Dame
Department of Music
Notre Dame, Indiana
Novosibirsk M.I. Glinka State Conservatory
*630099 Novosibirsk 99, Rossiskaja SFSR,
U.S.S.R.*
Oberlin College
Conservatory of Music
Oberlin, Ohio
Odeion Athenon
(Conservatory of Athens)
Athens, Greece
The Ohio State University
School of Music
Columbus, Ohio
Ohio University
School of Music
Athens, Ohio
Ohio Wesleyan University
Department of Music
Delaware, Ohio
University of Oklahoma
School of Music
Norman, Oklahoma
Oklahoma Baptist University
Department of Music
Shawnee, Oklahoma
Oklahoma City University
School of Music and Performing Arts
Oklahoma City, Oklahoma
University of Oregon
School of Music
Eugene, Oregon

Oregon State University
Department of Music
Corvallis, Oregon
Osaka Ongaku Daigaku
(Osaka College of Music)
Osaka 561, Japan
Ouachita Baptist University
School of Music
Arkadelphia, Arkansas
Pacific Lutheran University
Department of Music
Tacoma, Washington
Peabody Institute of The Johns Hopkins
University
Baltimore, Maryland
University of Pennsylvania
Department of Music
Philadelphia, Pennsylvania
Pennsylvania State University
School of Music
University Park, Pennsylvania
Philadelphia College of the Performing Arts
School of Music
Philadelphia, Pennsylvania
University of the Philippines
College of Music
Quezon City, The Philippines
Pittsburg State University
Department of Music
Pittsburg, Kansas
University of Pittsburgh
Department of Music
Pittsburgh, Pennsylvania
Pohjois-Kymen Musiikkiopisto
(North Kymi Music Institute)
45100 Kouvola, Finland
Pomona College
Music Department
Claremont, California
Pontifical Institute of Sacred Music
I - 00165 Roma, Italy
Portland State University
Department of Music
Portland, Oregon
Prayag Sangit Samiti
Allahabad 211001, India
Queen's University
School of Music
Kingston, Ontario, Canada
Radford University
Department of Music
Radford, Virginia
Real Conservatorio Superior de Música de
Madrid
(Royal Academy of Music)
Madrid 13, Spain
University of Regina
Department of Music
Regina, Saskatchewan, Canada
University of Rhode Island
Department of Music
Kingston, Rhode Island
Rice University
Shepherd School of Music
Houston, Texas
Roosevelt University
Chicago Musical College
Chicago, Illinois
Rostov State Institute of Pedagogics and
Music
*344007 Rostov-on-Don, Rossiskaja SFSR,
U.S.S.R.*
Royal Academy of Music
London NW1 5HT, United Kingdom
Royal Northern College of Music
Manchester M13 9RD, United Kingdom

Royal Scottish Academy of Music and
 Drama
 Glasgow G2 1BS, United Kingdom
Rutgers, The State University of New Jersey
 Department of Music
 New Brunswick, New Jersey
St. Cloud State University
 Department of Music
 St. Cloud, Minnesota
Saint Louis Conservatory of Music
 St. Louis, Missouri
St. Olaf College
 Music Department
 Northfield, Minnesota
Sam Houston State University
 Department of Music
 Huntsville, Texas
Samford University
 School of Music
 Birmingham, Alabama
San Diego State University
 Music Department
 San Diego, California
San Francisco Conservatory of Music
 San Francisco, California
San Francisco State University
 Department of Music
 San Francisco, California
San Jose State University
 Department of Music
 San Jose, California
University of Santo Tomas
 Conservatory of Music
 Manila, The Philippines
University of Saskatchewan
 Department of Music
 Saskatoon, Saskatchewan, Canada
Shanghai Conservatory of Music
 Shanghai, People's Republic of China
Shenandoah College and Conservatory
 Winchester, Virginia
Shengyang Conservatory of Music
 *Shengyang, Liaoning Province, People's
 Republic of China*
Sibelius Academy of Music
 SF-00260 Helsinki 26, Finland
Sichuan Conservatory of Music
 *Chengdu, Sichuan, People's Republic of
 China*
University of South Carolina
 School of Music
 Columbia, South Carolina
University of South Florida
 Department of Music
 Tampa, Florida
Southeast Missouri State University
 Department of Music
 Cape Girardeau, Missouri
Southeastern Louisiana University
 Department of Music
 Hammond, Louisiana
Southeastern Oklahoma State University
 Department of Music
 Durant, Oklahoma
Southern Baptist Theological Seminary
 School of Church Music
 Louisville, Kentucky
University of Southern California
 School of Music
 Los Angeles, California
Southern Illinois University at Carbondale
 School of Music
 Carbondale, Illinois
Southern Illinois University at Edwardsville
 Department of Music
 Edwardsville, Illinois

Southern Methodist University
 Meadows School of the Arts
 Dallas, Texas
University of Southern Mississippi
 School of Music
 Hattiesburg, Mississippi
Southwest Texas State University
 Department of Music
 San Marcos, Texas
Southwestern Baptist Theological Seminary
 School of Church Music
 Fort Worth, Texas
University of Southwestern Louisiana
 School of Music
 Lafayette, Louisiana
Southwestern Oklahoma State University
 Department of Music
 Weatherford, Oklahoma
Staatliche Hochschule für Musik Freiburg
 *D-7800 Freiburg i. Br., Federal Republic
 of Germany*
Staatliche Hochschule für Musik
 Heidelberg-Mannheim
 *Friedrich-Ebert-Anlage 62, Federal
 Republic of Germany*
Staatliche Hochschule für Musik Rheinland
 - Aachen
  Grenzland-Institut Aachen
  Aachen, Federal Republic of Germany
Staatliche Hochschule für Musik Rheinland
 - Köln
  *D-5000 Köln 1, Federal Republic of
  Germany*
Staatliche Hochschule für Musik Ruhr
 *4300 Essen 16, Federal Republic of
 Germany*
Staatliche Hochschule für Musik Trossingen
 *D-7218 Trossingen 1, Federal Republic of
 Germany*
Staatliche Hochschule für Musik
 Westfalen-Lippe
 *4930 Detmold, Federal Republic of
 Germany*
Staatliche Hochschule für Musik
 Westfalen-Lippe
  Institut Dortmund
  *D-4600 Dortmund 1, Federal Republic of
  Germany*
Stanford University
 Department of Music
 Stanford, California
State University of New York at
 Binghamton
 Department of Music
 Binghamton, New York
State University of New York at Buffalo
 Department of Music
 Buffalo, New York
State University of New York at Stony
 Brook
 Department of Music
 Stony Brook, New York
State University of New York College at
 Fredonia
 School of Music
 Fredonia, New York
State University of New York College at
 New Paltz
 Department of Music
 New Paltz, New York
State University of New York College at
 Potsdam
 Crane School of Music
 Potsdam, New York
State University of New York College at
 Purchase

 Division of Music
 Purchase, New York
Stedelijke Muziekpedagogische Akademie
 Leeuwarden, Netherlands
Stephen F. Austin State University
 Department of Music
 Nacogdoches, Texas
Stetson University
 School of Music
 Deland, Florida
University of Sydney
 Department of Music
 Sydney, NSW 2006, Australia
Syracuse University
 School of Music
 Syracuse, New York
Tasmanian Conservatorium of Music
 Hobart, Tasmania 7001, Australia
Tel Aviv University
 Faculty of Fine Arts
 Tel-Aviv, Israel
Temple University
 Esther Boyer College of Music
 Philadelphia, Pennsylvania
University of Tennessee at Chattanooga
 Cadek Department of Music
 Chattanooga, Tennessee
University of Tennessee at Knoxville
 Department of Music
 Knoxville, Tennessee
University of Texas at Arlington
 Department of Music
 Arlington, Texas
University of Texas at El Paso
 Music Department
 El Paso, Texas
University of Texas at San Antonio
 Division of Music
 San Antonio, Texas
Texas Christian University
 Music Department
 Fort Worth, Texas
Texas Tech University
 Department of Music
 Lubbock, Texas
Toho Gakuen School of Music
 Tokyo, Japan
The Tokyo College of Music
 Tokyo 171, Japan
Tonlistarskolinn i Reykjavik
 105 Reykjavik, Iceland
Towson State University
 Department of Music
 Towson, Maryland
Trenton State College
 Music Department
 Trenton, New Jersey
Trinity College of Music
 London W1M 6AQ, United Kingdom
Troy State University
 Department of Music
 Troy, Alabama
Tulane University
 Newcomb College
 New Orleans, Louisiana
University of Tulsa
 Faculty of Music
 Tulsa, Oklahoma
Ueno Gakuen College
 Tokyo 110, Japan
Universidad de Antioquía
 Facultad de Artes, Departamento de
 Música
 Medellín, Colombia
Universidade do Rio de Janeiro
 Letters and Arts Center - Music Course

22290 Rio de Janeiro, Brazil
Universidade do São Paulo
  Department of Music
  05508 São Paulo, Brazil
Université de Montréal
  Faculty of Music
  Montréal, Québec, Canada
University of Utah
  Department of Music
  Salt Lake City, Utah
Valparaiso University
  Department of Music
  Valparaiso, Indiana
VanderCook College of Music
  Chicago, Illinois
University of Vermont
  Department of Music
  Burlington, Vermont
University of Victoria
  School of Music
  Victoria, British Columbia, Canada
University of Virginia
  McIntire Department of Music
  Charlottesville, Virginia
Virginia Commonwealth University
  Department of Music
  Richmond, Virginia
Virginia Polytechnic Institute and State
  University
  Department of Music
  Blacksburg, Virginia
Vysoká Skola Mûzickych Umeni v Praha
  Academy of Music and Dramatic Arts
  1101 00 Prague 1, Czechoslovakia
Washington State University
  Department of Music
  Pullman, Washington
Washington University
  Department of Music
  St. Louis, Missouri
Wayne State University
  Department of Music
  Detroit, Michigan
Webster University
  Department of Music
  St. Louis, Missouri
West Chester University of Pennsylvania
  School of Music
  West Chester, Pennsylvania
West Virginia University
  Division of Music
  Morgantown, West Virginia
University of Western Australia
  Department of Music
  Nedlands, WA 6009, Australia
Western Kentucky University
  Department of Music
  Bowling Green, Kentucky
Western Michigan University
  School of Music
  Kalamazoo, Michigan
University of Western Ontario
  Faculty of Music
  London, Ontario, Canada
Wichita State University
  School of Music
  Wichita, Kansas
Wilfrid Laurier University
  Faculty of Music
  Waterloo, Ontario, Canada
William Carey College
  Winters School of Music
  Hattiesburg, Mississippi
William Paterson College
  Department of Music
  Wayne, New Jersey

University of Windsor
  School of Music
  Windsor, Ontario, Canada
Winthrop College
  School of Music
  Rock Hill, South Carolina
University of Wisconsin - Eau Claire
  Department of Music
  Eau Claire, Wisconsin
University of Wisconsin - La Crosse
  Department of Music
  La Crosse, Wisconsin
University of Wisconsin - Madison
  School of Music
  Madison, Wisconsin
University of Wisconsin - Milwaukee
  Music Department
  Milwaukee, Wisconsin
University of Wisconsin - Oshkosh
  Department of Music
  Oshkosh, Wisconsin
University of Wisconsin - Whitewater
  Department of Music
  Whitewater, Wisconsin
Wright State University
  Department of Music
  Dayton, Ohio
University of Wyoming
  Music Department
  Laramie, Wyoming
Yale College (Yale University)
  Department of Music
  New Haven, Connecticut
York University
  Department of Music
  North York, Ontario, Canada
Youngstown State University
  Dana School of Music
  Youngstown, Ohio
Zeneiskolai Tanárkepzó Intézet
  (Music Teachers Training Institute of the
  Liszt Academy of Music)
  Budapest 1052, Hungary

MUSIC THERAPY

Arizona State University
  School of Music
  Tempe, Arizona
Baldwin-Wallace College
  Conservatory of Music
  Berea, Ohio
California State University, Long Beach
  Department of Music
  Long Beach, California
California State University, Northridge
  Music Department
  Northridge, California
University of Cape Town
  Faculty of Music
  Cape Town, Republic of South Africa
Case Western Reserve University
  Department of Music
  Cleveland, Ohio
The Catholic University of America
  The Benjamin T. Rome School of Music
  Washington, District of Columbia
Cleveland State University
  Department of Music
  Cleveland, Ohio
Colorado State University
  Department of Music, Theatre, and
  Dance
  Fort Collins, Colorado
Combs College of Music
  Philadelphia, Pennsylvania

DePaul University
  School of Music
  Chicago, Illinois
Duquesne University
  School of Music
  Pittsburgh, Pennsylvania
East Carolina University
  School of Music
  Greenville, North Carolina
Eastern Michigan University
  Department of Music
  Ypsilanti, Michigan
Eastern New Mexico University
  School of Music
  Portales, New Mexico
University of Evansville
  Music Department
  Evansville, Indiana
Florida State University
  School of Music
  Tallahassee, Florida
Guildhall School of Music and Drama
  London EC2Y 8DT, United Kingdom
Illinois State University
  Department of Music
  Normal, Illinois
University of Iowa
  School of Music
  Iowa City, Iowa
University of Kansas
  School of Fine Arts
  Lawrence, Kansas
Levinsky Teachers College
  Music Teachers Seminary
  Tel-Aviv, Israel
Long Island University - C.W. Post Campus
  Music Department
  Greenvale, New York
Loyola University
  College of Music
  New Orleans, Louisiana
Mansfield University
  Department of Music
  Mansfield, Pennsylvania
Marywood College
  Music Department
  Scranton, Pennsylvania
University of Melbourne
  Faculty of Music
  Victoria 3052, Australia
University of Miami
  School of Music
  Coral Gables, Florida
Michigan State University
  School of Music
  East Lansing, Michigan
University of Minnesota - Twin Cities
  School of Music
  Minneapolis, Minnesota
University of Missouri - Kansas City
  Conservatory of Music
  Kansas City, Missouri
Montclair State College
  Department of Music
  Upper Montclair, New Jersey
New York University - School of Education,
  Health, Nursing, and Arts Professions
  Department of Music and Music
  Education
  New York, New York
Oberlin College
  Conservatory of Music
  Oberlin, Ohio
Ohio University
  School of Music
  Athens, Ohio

Ohio Wesleyan University
Department of Music
Delaware, Ohio
Radford University
Department of Music
Radford, Virginia
Sam Houston State University
Department of Music
Huntsville, Texas
Shenandoah College and Conservatory
Winchester, Virginia
Southern Methodist University
Meadows School of the Arts
Dallas, Texas
Staatliche Hochschule für Musik Rheinland
- Aachen
Grenzland-Institut Aachen
Aachen, Federal Republic of Germany
Staatliche Hochschule für Musik Rheinland
- Wuppertal
Institute Wuppertal
Wuppertal, Federal Republic of Germany
State University of New York College at
Fredonia
School of Music
Fredonia, New York
State University of New York College at
New Paltz
Department of Music
New Paltz, New York
Temple University
Esther Boyer College of Music
Philadelphia, Pennsylvania
Texas Woman's University
Department of Music and Drama
Denton, Texas
Wayne State University
Department of Music
Detroit, Michigan
West Texas State University
Department of Music
Canyon, Texas
Western Illinois University
Department of Music
Macomb, Illinois
Western Michigan University
School of Music
Kalamazoo, Michigan
Wilfrid Laurier University
Faculty of Music
Waterloo, Ontario, Canada
Willamette University
Department of Music
Salem, Oregon
William Carey College
Winters School of Music
Hattiesburg, Mississippi
University of Wisconsin - Milwaukee
Music Department
Milwaukee, Wisconsin
University of Wisconsin - Oshkosh
Department of Music
Oshkosh, Wisconsin

MUSICAL ACOUSTICS

Massachusetts Institute of Technology
Department of Music and Theater Arts
Cambridge, Massachusetts
Staatliche Hochschule für Musik Rheinland
- Düsseldorf
(State College of Music)
*D-4000 Düsseldorf, Federal Republic of
Germany*
Staatliche Hochschule für Musik
Westfalen-Lippe

Institut Dortmund
*D-4600 Dortmund 1, Federal Republic of
Germany*

MUSICAL ANALYSIS

Staatliche Hochschule für Musik
Westfalen-Lippe
Institut Dortmund
*D-4600 Dortmund 1, Federal Republic of
Germany*

MUSICAL COMEDY

Latvian S.S.R. Y. Vitol State Conservatory
226050 Riga, Latvijskaya SSR, U.S.S.R.
Urals M.P. Mussorgsky State Conservatory
*620014 Sverdlovsk, Rossiskaja SFSR,
U.S.S.R.*

MUSICAL INSTRUMENTS

Faculdade Santa Marcelina
05006 São Paulo, Brazil

MUSICAL ORNAMENTS

Hochschule für Musik - Würzburg
*D-8700 Würzburg, Federal Republic of
Germany*

MUSICAL STAGE DIRECTION

Hoschschule für Music Hans Eisler
*DDR Berlin 1080, German Democratic
Republic*

MUSICAL THEATRE

University of Hartford
Hartt School of Music
West Hartford, Connecticut
Ithaca College
School of Music
Ithaca, New York
University of Miami
School of Music
Coral Gables, Florida
University of Michigan
School of Music
Ann Arbor, Michigan
New York University - School of Education,
Health, Nursing, and Arts Professions
Department of Music and Music
Education
New York, New York
Oklahoma City University
School of Music and Performing Arts
Oklahoma City, Oklahoma
State University of New York College at
Fredonia
School of Music
Fredonia, New York
Stetson University
School of Music
Deland, Florida

MUSICOLOGY

University of Adelaide
Elder Conservatorium of Music
Adelaide, SA 5001, Australia
University of Alberta
Department of Music

Edmonton, Alberta, Canada
American Conservatory of Music
Chicago, Illinois
A.V. Nezhdanova Odessa Conservatory
*270000 Odessa, Ukrainskaja SSR,
U.S.S.R.*
Ball State University
School of Music
Muncie, Indiana
Banaras Hindu University
Uttar Pradesh 221005, India
Boston University
School of Music
Boston, Massachusetts
Brigham Young University
Department of Music
Provo, Utah
Brown University
Department of Music
Providence, Rhode Island
University of California, Berkeley
Department of Music
Berkeley, California
University of California, Davis
Department of Music
Davis, California
University of California, Los Angeles
Department of Music
Los Angeles, California
University of California, Santa Barbara
Department of Music
Santa Barbara, California
California State University, Fresno
Department of Music
Fresno, California
California State University, Northridge
Music Department
Northridge, California
University of Cape Town
Faculty of Music
Cape Town, Republic of South Africa
Case Western Reserve University
Department of Music
Cleveland, Ohio
Central Conservatory of Music
Beijing, People's Republic of China
University of Cincinnati
College-Conservatory of Music
Cincinnati, Ohio
City University of New York - Brooklyn
College
Conservatory of Music
Brooklyn, New York
City University of New York - Graduate
School and University Center
Doctoral Program in Music
New York, New York
The Claremont Graduate School
Music Department
Claremont, California
Cleveland Institute of Music
Cleveland, Ohio
University of Colorado at Boulder
College of Music
Boulder, Colorado
Conservatorio Nacional de Música
(National Conservatory of Music)
Lima 1, Peru
Conservatorul de Musică George Dima
(Conservatory of Music)
3400 Cluj-Napoca, Romania
Conservatorul de Muzică Ciprian
Porumbescu
(Conservatory of Music)
70732 Bucharest, Romania

Converse College
School of Music
Spartanburg, South Carolina
Cornell University
Department of Music
Ithaca, New York
Duke University
Department of Music
Durham, North Carolina
East Texas State University
Department of Music
Commerce, Texas
Emporia State University
Division of Music
Emporia, Kansas
Fachakademie für Music - Augsburg
Leopold Mozart-Konservatorium der
Stadt Augsburg
Augsberg, Federal Republic of Germany
Fachakademie für Musik - Nürnberg
Konservatorium der Stadt Nürnberg
Nürnberg, Federal Republic of Germany
Ferenc Liszt Academy of Music
Budapest VI, Hungary
Glassboro State College
Department of Music
Glassboro, New Jersey
Gnessinsky State Musical and Pedagogical
Institute
*121069 Moscow G-69, Rossiskaja SFSR,
U.S.S.R.*
Harvard University
Department of Music
Cambridge, Massachusetts
University of Hawaii at Manoa
Music Department
Honolulu, Hawaii
Hermann-Zilcher-Konservatorium
*D-8700 Würzburg, Federal Republic of
Germany*
Hochschule für Gestaltende Kunst und
Musik
(State College for Creative Art and
Music)
*2800 Bremen 1, Federal Republic of
Germany*
Hochschule für Musik - München
*8000 München 2, Federal Republic of
Germany*
Hochschule für Musik und Theater
Hannover
*3000 Hannover 1, Federal Republic of
Germany*
Howard University
Department of Music
Washington, District of Columbia
University of Illinois
School of Music
Urbana, Illinois
Indiana University - Bloomington
School of Music
Bloomington, Indiana
Indira Kala Sangit Vishwavidyalaya
(University of Music and Fine Arts)
Madhya Pradesh 491881, India
Instituto Superior de Arte
Facultad de Música
Playa, Cuba
University of Iowa
School of Music
Iowa City, Iowa
Kent State University
School of Music
Kent, Ohio
University of Kentucky
School of Music

Lexington, Kentucky
Leningrad N.A. Rimsky-Korsakov State
Conservatory
*192041 Leningrad, Rossiskaja SFSR,
U.S.S.R.*
University of Louisville
School of Music
Louisville, Kentucky
Marywood College
Music Department
Scranton, Pennsylvania
University of Massachusetts at Amherst
Department of Music and Dance
Amherst, Massachusetts
McGill University
Faculty of Music
Montreal, Québec, Canada
University of Melbourne
Faculty of Music
Victoria 3052, Australia
University of Miami
School of Music
Coral Gables, Florida
Miami University
Department of Music
Oxford, Ohio
University of Michigan
School of Music
Ann Arbor, Michigan
Michigan State University
School of Music
East Lansing, Michigan
University of Minnesota - Twin Cities
School of Music
Minneapolis, Minnesota
Musikhochschule des Saarlandes
*6600 Saarbrücken 3, Federal Republic of
Germany*
University of Nebraska - Lincoln
School of Music
Lincoln, Nebraska
New York University - College of Arts and
Sciences
Department of Music
New York, New York
University of North Carolina at Chapel Hill
Department of Music
Chapel Hill, North Carolina
North Texas State University
School of Music
Denton, Texas
University of Notre Dame
Department of Music
Notre Dame, Indiana
University of Orange Free State
Department of Music
*9300 Bloemfontein, Republic of South
Africa*
Osaka Ongaku Daigaku
(Osaka College of Music)
Osaka 561, Japan
Pennsylvania State University
School of Music
University Park, Pennsylvania
University of Pittsburgh
Department of Music
Pittsburgh, Pennsylvania
University of Pretoria
Department of Music
002 Pretoria, Republic of South Africa
Princeton University
Department of Music
Princeton, New Jersey
Rice University
Shepherd School of Music
Houston, Texas

Roosevelt University
Chicago Musical College
Chicago, Illinois
Rutgers, The State University of New Jersey
Department of Music
New Brunswick, New Jersey
Sam Houston State University
Department of Music
Huntsville, Texas
Shengyang Conservatory of Music
*Shengyang, Liaoning Province, People's
Republic of China*
Sichuan Conservatory of Music
*Chengdu, Sichuan, People's Republic of
China*
Southern Baptist Theological Seminary
School of Church Music
Louisville, Kentucky
University of Southern California
School of Music
Los Angeles, California
Southwest Texas State University
Department of Music
San Marcos, Texas
Staatliche Hochschule für Musik Freiburg
*D-7800 Freiburg i. Br., Federal Republic
of Germany*
Staatliche Hochschule für Musik
Heidelberg-Mannheim
*Friedrich-Ebert-Anlage 62, Federal
Republic of Germany*
Staatliche Hochschule für Musik Karlsruhe
*7500 Karlsruhe 1, Federal Republic of
Germany*
Staatliche Hochschule für Musik Rheinland
- Düsseldorf
(State College of Music)
*D-4000 Düsseldorf, Federal Republic of
Germany*
Staatliche Hochschule für Musik Ruhr
*4300 Essen 16, Federal Republic of
Germany*
State University of New York College at
Purchase
Division of Music
Purchase, New York
University of Stellenbosch
Department of Music (Conservatoire)
*7600 Stellenbosch, Republic of South
Africa*
University of Tennessee at Knoxville
Department of Music
Knoxville, Tennessee
University of Texas at Austin
Department of Music
Austin, Texas
University of Toronto
Faculty of Music
Toronto, Ontario, Canada
Tulane University
Newcomb College
New Orleans, Louisiana
Ueno Gakuen College
Tokyo 110, Japan
Universidade do São Paulo
Department of Music
05508 São Paulo, Brazil
Université de Montréal
Faculty of Music
Montréal, Québec, Canada
University of Victoria
School of Music
Victoria, British Columbia, Canada
University of Washington
School of Music
Seattle, Washington

Washington University
Department of Music
St. Louis, Missouri
West Virginia University
Division of Music
Morgantown, West Virginia
University of Western Ontario
Faculty of Music
London, Ontario, Canada
Wheaton College
Conservatory of Music
Wheaton, Illinois
Wichita State University
School of Music
Wichita, Kansas
University of Wisconsin - Milwaukee
Music Department
Milwaukee, Wisconsin
University of the Witwatersrand
Wits School of Music
*2001 Johannesburg, Republic of South
Africa*
York University
Department of Music
North York, Ontario, Canada

MUSICOLOGY JAZZ

University of Rochester
Eastman School of Music
Rochester, New York

NEW MUSIC

Hochschule für Musik - Würzburg
*D-8700 Würzburg, Federal Republic of
Germany*
Staatliche Hochschule für Musik Rheinland
- Wuppertal
Institute Wuppertal
Wuppertal, Federal Republic of Germany

NINETEENTH CENTURY MUSIC

University of California, Davis
Department of Music
Davis, California

NON-WESTERN INSTRUMENTS

San Diego State University
Music Department
San Diego, California

NORTH INDIAN MUSIC

California Institute of the Arts
School of Music
Valencia, California

OLD MUSIC

Fachakademie für Musik - München
Richard Strauss-Konservatorium der
Stadt
*München 80, Federal Republic of
Germany*
Musikhochschule des Saarlandes
*6600 Saarbrücken 3, Federal Republic of
Germany*
Staatliche Hochschule für Musik Rheinland
- Düsseldorf
(State College of Music)
*D-4000 Düsseldorf, Federal Republic of
Germany*

OPERA

The Academy of Vocal Arts
Philadelphia, Pennsylvania
Boston Conservatory of Music
Boston, Massachusetts

Boston University
School of Music
Boston, Massachusetts
University of California, Los Angeles
Department of Music
Los Angeles, California
Central Conservatory of Music
Beijing, People's Republic of China
University of Cincinnati
College-Conservatory of Music
Cincinnati, Ohio
The Curtis Institute of Music
Philadelphia, Pennsylvania
Fachakademie für Music - Augsburg
Leopold Mozart-Konservatorium der
Stadt Augsburg
Augsberg, Federal Republic of Germany
Fachakademie für Musik - München
Richard Strauss-Konservatorium der
Stadt
*München 80, Federal Republic of
Germany*
University of Hartford
Hartt School of Music
West Hartford, Connecticut
Hochschule für Gestaltende Kunst und
Musik
(State College for Creative Art and
Music)
*2800 Bremen 1, Federal Republic of
Germany*
Hochschule für Music und Darstellende
Kunst Hamburg
*2000 Hamburg 13, Federal Republic of
Germany*
Hochschule für Musik - Würzburg
*D-8700 Würzburg, Federal Republic of
Germany*
Hochschule für Musik und Darstellende
Kunst Frankfurt am Main
*6000 Frankfurt am Main 1, Federal
Republic of Germany*
Hochschule für Musik und Theater
Hannover
*3000 Hannover 1, Federal Republic of
Germany*
University of Houston
School of Music
Houston, Texas
University of Iowa
School of Music
Iowa City, Iowa
Karol Szymanowski Academy of Music of
Katowice
Katowice, Poland
Konzervatorium - Bratislava
Bratislava 811 06, Czechoslovakia
Leningrad N.A. Rimsky-Korsakov State
Conservatory
*192041 Leningrad, Rossiskaja SFSR,
U.S.S.R.*
Moscow P.I. Tchaikovsky State
Conservatory
*103009 Moscow K-9, Rossiskaja SFSR,
U.S.S.R.*
Musik-Akademie der Stadt Basel
(Konzervatorium)
Konzervatorium (Musikhochschule)
Basel, Switzerland
New South Wales State Conservatorium of
Music
Sydney NSW 2000, Australia
New York University - School of Education,
Health, Nursing, and Arts Professions
Department of Music and Music
Education

New York, New York
Oklahoma City University
School of Music and Performing Arts
Oklahoma City, Oklahoma
Philadelphia College of the Performing Arts
School of Music
Philadelphia, Pennsylvania
Royal Academy of Music
London NW1 5HT, United Kingdom
Royal College of Music
London, SW7 2BS, United Kingdom
Royal Northern College of Music
Manchester M13 9RD, United Kingdom
Royal Scottish Academy of Music and
Drama
Glasgow G2 1BS, United Kingdom
Sibelius Academy of Music
SF-00260 Helsinki 26, Finland
Southern Illinois University at Carbondale
School of Music
Carbondale, Illinois
Staatliche Hochschule für Musik Freiburg
*D-7800 Freiburg i. Br., Federal Republic
of Germany*
Staatliche Hochschule für Musik
Heidelberg-Mannheim
*Friedrich-Ebert-Anlage 62, Federal
Republic of Germany*
Staatliche Hochschule für Musik Karlsruhe
*7500 Karlsruhe 1, Federal Republic of
Germany*
Staatliche Hochschule für Musik Rheinland
- Aachen
Grenzland-Institut Aachen
Aachen, Federal Republic of Germany
Staatliche Hochschule für Musik Rheinland
- Köln
*D-5000 Köln 1, Federal Republic of
Germany*
Staatliche Hochschule für Musik Rheinland
- Wuppertal
Institute Wuppertal
Wuppertal, Federal Republic of Germany
Staatliche Hochschule für Musik und
Darstellende Kunst Stuttgart
*7000 Stuttgart 1, Federal Republic of
Germany*
Staatliche Hochschule für Musik
Westfalen-Lippe
*4930 Detmold, Federal Republic of
Germany*
Staatliche Hochschule für Musik
Westfalen-Lippe
Institut Dortmund
*D-4600 Dortmund 1, Federal Republic of
Germany*
Temple University
Esther Boyer College of Music
Philadelphia, Pennsylvania
University of Texas at Austin
Department of Music
Austin, Texas
Université Laval
Ecole de Musique
Ste. Foy, Québec, Canada
Vysoká Skola Mûzickych Umeni v Praha
Academy of Music and Dramatic Arts
1101 00 Prague 1, Czechoslovakia
University of Washington
School of Music
Seattle, Washington
Wilfrid Laurier University
Faculty of Music
Waterloo, Ontario, Canada

OPERA CHOIR

Hochschule für Musik und Theater
Hannover
3000 Hannover 1, Federal Republic of Germany

OPERA COACHING

Indiana University - Bloomington
School of Music
Bloomington, Indiana

OPERA DIRECTION

Vysoká Skola Mûzickych Umeni v Praha
Academy of Music and Dramatic Arts
1101 00 Prague 1, Czechoslovakia

OPERA HISTORY

Hochschule für Musik - München
8000 München 2, Federal Republic of Germany
Hochschule für Musik - Würzburg
D-8700 Würzburg, Federal Republic of Germany

OPERA PERFORMANCE

University of Toronto
Faculty of Music
Toronto, Ontario, Canada

OPERA SCENIC TECHNIQUE

Indiana University - Bloomington
School of Music
Bloomington, Indiana

OPERA SCHOOL

Staatliche Hochschule für Musik Rheinland
- Düsseldorf
(State College of Music)
D-4000 Düsseldorf, Federal Republic of Germany

OPERA THEATER

Oberlin College
Conservatory of Music
Oberlin, Ohio

OPERATIC CONDUCTING

Tashkent State Conservatory
700000 Tashkent, Uzbekskaja SSR, U.S.S.R.
Tbilisi V. Sarajishvili State Conservatory
380004 Tbilisi 4, Gruzinskaja SSR, U.S.S.R.

ORCHESTRA

Fachakademie für Musik - München
Richard Strauss-Konservatorium der
Stadt
München 80, Federal Republic of Germany

ORCHESTRA CONDUCTING

Fachakademie für Music - Augsburg
Leopold Mozart-Konservatorium der
Stadt Augsburg
Augsberg, Federal Republic of Germany
Hochschule für Musik - Würzburg
D-8700 Würzburg, Federal Republic of Germany
James Madison University
Department of Music
Harrisonburg, Virginia

ORCHESTRAL CONDUCTING

University of Central Arkansas
Department of Music
Conway, Arkansas
University of Cincinnati
College-Conservatory of Music
Cincinnati, Ohio
Colorado State University
Department of Music, Theatre, and
Dance
Fort Collins, Colorado
Evangelische Kirchenmusikschule der
Kirchenprovinz Sachsen
(Evangelical Church Music School of the
Church Province Saxony)
DDR-4020 Halle (Saale), German Democratic Republic
Lithuanian State Conservatory
232001 Vilnius, Litovskaja SSR, U.S.S.R.
Mannes College of Music
New York, New York
Yale University
School of Music
New Haven, Connecticut

ORCHESTRAL INSTRUMENTS

The Catholic University of America
The Benjamin T. Rome School of Music
Washington, District of Columbia
George Mason University
Department of Performing Arts - Music
Division
Fairfax, Virginia
Memphis State University
Music Department
Memphis, Tennessee
University of Rhode Island
Department of Music
Kingston, Rhode Island

ORCHESTRAL MUSIC

Musikhochschule des Saarlandes
6600 Saarbrücken 3, Federal Republic of Germany
Rostov State Institute of Pedagogics and
Music
344007 Rostov-on-Don, Rossiskaja SFSR, U.S.S.R.
Staatliche Hochschule für Musik
Heidelberg-Mannheim
Friedrich-Ebert-Anlage 62, Federal Republic of Germany
Staatliche Hochschule für Musik Karlsruhe
7500 Karlsruhe 1, Federal Republic of Germany

ORCHESTRATION

Escuela Universitaria de Música -
Montevideo
Montevideo, Uruguay
Nikos Skalkotas Conservatory
Athens 11141, Greece
Real Conservatorio Superior de Música de
Madrid
(Royal Academy of Music)
Madrid 13, Spain
University of Virginia
McIntire Department of Music
Charlottesville, Virginia
Virginia Commonwealth University
Department of Music
Richmond, Virginia

ORFF METHOD

Fachakademie für Music - Augsburg
Leopold Mozart-Konservatorium der
Stadt Augsburg
Augsberg, Federal Republic of Germany
Fachakademie für Musik - München
Richard Strauss-Konservatorium der
Stadt
München 80, Federal Republic of Germany
Hermann-Zilcher-Konservatorium
D-8700 Würzburg, Federal Republic of Germany

ORFF PEDAGOGY

Oakland University
Department of Music, Theatre and
Dance
Rochester, Michigan

ORFF SCHULWERK

University of Denver
Lamont School of Music
Denver, Colorado

ORGAN

Pohjois-Kymen Musiikkiopisto
(North Kymi Music Institute)
45100 Kouvola, Finland
Sibelius Academy of Music
SF-00260 Helsinki 26, Finland

ORGAN BUILDING

Hochschule für Gestaltende Kunst und
Musik
(State College for Creative Art and
Music)
2800 Bremen 1, Federal Republic of Germany
Hochschule für Musik - München
8000 München 2, Federal Republic of Germany
Staatliche Hochschule für Musik Rheinland
- Düsseldorf
(State College of Music)
D-4000 Düsseldorf, Federal Republic of Germany

ORGAN IMPROVISATION

Musikhochschule Lübeck
Grosse Petersgrube 17-29
2400 Lübeck, Federal Republic of Germany

ORGAN PERFORMANCE

Oakland University
Department of Music, Theatre and
Dance
Rochester, Michigan

ORGAN REPERTOIRE

Hochschule für Musik - München
8000 München 2, Federal Republic of Germany

ORGANOLOGY

Hochschule für Gestaltende Kunst und
Musik
(State College for Creative Art and
Music)
2800 Bremen 1, Federal Republic of Germany
Hochschule für Musik - München
8000 München 2, Federal Republic of

Germany
Hochschule für Musik - Würzburg
  D-8700 Würzburg, Federal Republic of
  Germany
Musikhochschule Lübeck
  Grosse Petersgrube 17-29
  2400 Lübeck, Federal Republic of
  Germany
Nikos Skalkotas Conservatory
  Athens 11141, Greece
Staatliche Hochschule für Musik Rheinland
  - Düsseldorf
  (State College of Music)
  D-4000 Düsseldorf, Federal Republic of
  Germany
Staatliche Hochschule für Musik und
  Darstellende Kunst Stuttgart
  7000 Stuttgart 1, Federal Republic of
  Germany
Staatliche Hochschule für Musik
  Westfalen-Lippe
  Institut Dortmund
  D-4600 Dortmund 1, Federal Republic of
  Germany

PANTOMIME

Staatliche Hochschule für Musik Rheinland
  - Düsseldorf
  (State College of Music)
  D-4000 Düsseldorf, Federal Republic of
  Germany

PEDAGOGICS

Kuopion Konservatorio
  70100 Kuopio, Finland

PEDAGOGY

Bradley University
  Division of Music and Theatre Arts
  Peoria, Illinois
Central Michigan University
  Department of Music
  Mount Pleasant, Michigan
Central Washington University
  Department of Music
  Ellensburg, Washington
Conservatorul de Muzică Ciprian
  Porumbescu
  (Conservatory of Music)
  70732 Bucharest, Romania
University of Montevallo
  Department of Music
  Montevallo, Alabama
University of Northern Colorado
  School of Music
  Greeley, Colorado
Northwestern University
  School of Music
  Evanston, Illinois
Oklahoma City University
  School of Music and Performing Arts
  Oklahoma City, Oklahoma
Teachers College of Columbia University
  Department of Music and Music
  Education
  New York, New York
University of Texas at Austin
  Department of Music
  Austin, Texas
University of Windsor
  School of Music
  Windsor, Ontario, Canada

PERFORMANCE

University of Adelaide
  Elder Conservatorium of Music
  Adelaide, SA 5001, Australia
Akademia Muzyczna w Krakowie
  31-038 Kraków, Poland
Akademia Muzyczna w Lódź
  (Academy of Music of Lódź)
  90-716 Lódź, Poland
University of Akron
  Department of Music
  Akron, Ohio
University of Alabama
  School of Music
  University, Alabama
Alabama State University
  School of Music
  Montgomery, Alabama
University of Alaska
  Music Department
  Fairbanks, Alaska
University of Alberta
  Department of Music
  Edmonton, Alberta, Canada
American Conservatory of Music
  Chicago, Illinois
Appalachian State University
  Department of Music
  Boone, North Carolina
University of Arizona
  School of Music
  Tucson, Arizona
Arizona State University
  School of Music
  Tempe, Arizona
Arkansas State University
  Department of Music
  State University, Arkansas
Arkansas Tech University
  Department of Music
  Russellville, Arkansas
Auburn University
  Department of Music
  Auburn, Alabama
Austin Peay State University
  Department of Music
  Clarksville, Tennessee
Banaras Hindu University
  Uttar Pradesh 221005, India
Baylor University
  School of Music
  Waco, Texas
Bennington College
  Music Department
  Bennington, Vermont
Berklee College of Music
  Boston, Massachusetts
Biola University
  Department of Music
  La Mirada, California
Bob Jones University
  Division of Music
  Greenville, South Carolina
Boise State University
  Music Department
  Boise, Idaho
Boston University
  School of Music
  Boston, Massachusetts
Bowling Green State University
  College of Musical Arts
  Bowling Green, Ohio
Bradley University
  Division of Music and Theatre Arts
  Peoria, Illinois

Brandeis University
  Department of Music
  Waltham, Massachusetts
Brandon University
  School of Music
  Brandon, Manitoba, Canada
Brigham Young University
  Department of Music
  Provo, Utah
University of British Columbia
  School of Music
  Vancouver, British Columbia, Canada
Brown University
  Department of Music
  Providence, Rhode Island
Butler University
  Jordan College of Fine Arts
  Indianapolis, Indiana
University of Calgary
  Department of Music
  Calgary, Alberta, Canada
University of California, Berkeley
  Department of Music
  Berkeley, California
University of California, Davis
  Department of Music
  Davis, California
University of California, Irvine
  School of Fine Arts
  Irvine, California
University of California, Los Angeles
  Department of Music
  Los Angeles, California
University of California, Riverside
  Department of Music
  Riverside, California
University of California, San Diego
  Department of Music
  La Jolla, California
University of California, Santa Barbara
  Department of Music
  Santa Barbara, California
University of California, Santa Cruz
  Music Board, Division of the Arts
  Santa Cruz, California
California State University, Chico
  Department of Music
  Chico, California
California State University, Fresno
  Department of Music
  Fresno, California
California State University, Fullerton
  Department of Music
  Fullerton, California
California State University, Hayward
  Department of Music
  Hayward, California
California State University, Long Beach
  Department of Music
  Long Beach, California
California State University, Los Angeles
  Department of Music
  Los Angeles, California
California State University, Northridge
  Music Department
  Northridge, California
California State University, Sacramento
  Department of Music
  Sacramento, California
University of Cape Town
  Faculty of Music
  Cape Town, Republic of South Africa
Carnegie-Mellon University
  Department of Music
  Pittsburgh, Pennsylvania

The Catholic University of America
  The Benjamin T. Rome School of Music
  Washington, District of Columbia
University of Central Arkansas
  Department of Music
  Conway, Arkansas
Central Conservatory of Music
  Beijing, People's Republic of China
Central Michigan University
  Department of Music
  Mount Pleasant, Michigan
Central State University
  Department of Music
  Edmond, Oklahoma
Central Washington University
  Department of Music
  Ellensburg, Washington
University of Cincinnati
  College-Conservatory of Music
  Cincinnati, Ohio
City University of New York - Brooklyn
College
  Conservatory of Music
  Brooklyn, New York
City University of New York - City College
  Department of Music
  New York, New York
City University of New York - Graduate
School and University Center
  Doctoral Program in Music
  New York, New York
City University of New York - Hunter
College
  Department of Music
  New York, New York
City University of New York - Queens
College
  The Aaron Copland School of Music
  Flushing, New York
The Claremont Graduate School
  Music Department
  Claremont, California
Cleveland Institute of Music
  Cleveland, Ohio
University of Colorado at Boulder
  College of Music
  Boulder, Colorado
University of Colorado at Denver
  College of Music
  Denver, Colorado
Colorado State University
  Department of Music, Theatre, and
  Dance
  Fort Collins, Colorado
Columbus College
  Department of Music
  Columbus, Georgia
Combs College of Music
  Philadelphia, Pennsylvania
Conservatorio Nacional de Musica - La Paz
  (National Conservatory of Music - La
  Paz)
  La Paz, Bolivia
Conservatory of Chinese Music
  Beijing, People's Republic of China
Converse College
  School of Music
  Spartanburg, South Carolina
Cornell University
  Department of Music
  Ithaca, New York
Dalhousie University
  Department of Music
  Halifax, Nova Scotia, Canada
Delta State University
  Department of Music

Cleveland, Mississippi
University of Denver
  Lamont School of Music
  Denver, Colorado
DePaul University
  School of Music
  Chicago, Illinois
DePauw University
  School of Music
  Greencastle, Indiana
Duquesne University
  School of Music
  Pittsburgh, Pennsylvania
East Carolina University
  School of Music
  Greenville, North Carolina
East Texas State University
  Department of Music
  Commerce, Texas
Eastern Illinois University
  Department of Music
  Charleston, Illinois
Eastern Kentucky University
  Department of Music
  Richmond, Kentucky
Eastern Michigan University
  Department of Music
  Ypsilanti, Michigan
Eastern New Mexico University
  School of Music
  Portales, New Mexico
Eastern Washington University
  Department of Music
  Cheney, Washington
Emporia State University
  Division of Music
  Emporia, Kansas
Escuela de Música - Heredia
  Universidad Nacional
  Heredia, Costa Rica
Escuela Universitaria de Música -
Montevideo
  Montevideo, Uruguay
University of Evansville
  Music Department
  Evansville, Indiana
Fachakademie für Musik - München
  Richard Strauss-Konservatorium der
  Stadt
  *München 80, Federal Republic of
  Germany*
Fachakademie für Musik - Nürnberg
  Konservatorium der Stadt Nürnberg
  Nürnberg, Federal Republic of Germany
Florida State University
  School of Music
  Tallahassee, Florida
Fort Hays State University
  Department of Music
  Hays, Kansas
George Mason University
  Department of Performing Arts - Music
  Division
  Fairfax, Virginia
University of Georgia
  School of Music
  Athens, Georgia
Georgia Southern College
  Department of Music
  Statesboro, Georgia
Georgia State University
  School of Music
  Atlanta, Georgia
Glassboro State College
  Department of Music
  Glassboro, New Jersey

Guildhall School of Music and Drama
  London EC2Y 8DT, United Kingdom
University of Hawaii at Manoa
  Music Department
  Honolulu, Hawaii
Henderson State University
  Department of Music
  Arkadelphia, Arkansas
Hochschule für Music und Darstellende
Kunst Hamburg
  *2000 Hamburg 13, Federal Republic of
  Germany*
Hochschule für Musik - Würzburg
  *D-8700 Würzburg, Federal Republic of
  Germany*
Hochschule für Musik und Darstellende
Kunst Frankfurt am Main
  *6000 Frankfurt am Main 1, Federal
  Republic of Germany*
University of Houston
  School of Music
  Houston, Texas
University of Idaho
  School of Music
  Moscow, Idaho
University of Illinois
  School of Music
  Urbana, Illinois
Illinois Wesleyan University
  School of Music
  Bloomington, Illinois
Indiana State University
  Department of Music
  Terre Haute, Indiana
Indiana University - Bloomington
  School of Music
  Bloomington, Indiana
Indiana University of Pennsylvania
  Department of Music
  Indiana, Pennsylvania
Institute of Aesthetic Studies
  Colombo 7, Sri Lanka
Instituto Superior de Arte
  Facultad de Música
  Playa, Cuba
University of Iowa
  School of Music
  Iowa City, Iowa
Iowa State University
  Department of Music
  Ames, Iowa
Ithaca College
  School of Music
  Ithaca, New York
James Madison University
  Department of Music
  Harrisonburg, Virginia
Jersey City State College
  Music Department
  Jersey City, New Jersey
The Juilliard School
  New York, New York
University of Kansas
  School of Fine Arts
  Lawrence, Kansas
Kansas State University
  Department of Music
  Manhattan, Kansas
Kent State University
  School of Music
  Kent, Ohio
University of Kentucky
  School of Music
  Lexington, Kentucky
Kenya Conservatoire of Music
  Nairobi, Kenya

Konservatorium und Musikhochschule -
Zürich
8050 Zürich, Switzerland
Konzervatoř v Praze
(State Conservatory Prague)
Praha 110 00, Czechoslovakia
Kratikon Odeion Thessaloniki
(State Conservatory of Music)
Thessaloniki, Greece
Lamar University
Department of Music
Beaumont, Texas
Lawrence University
Conservatory of Music
Appleton, Wisconsin
Lewis and Clark College
Music Department
Portland, Oregon
Long Island University - C.W. Post Campus
Music Department
Greenvale, New York
Louisiana State University
School of Music
Baton Rouge, Louisiana
Louisiana Tech University
Department of Music
Ruston, Louisiana
University of Lowell
College of Music
Lowell, Massachusetts
Loyola University
College of Music
New Orleans, Louisiana
University of Maine
School of Performing Arts
Orono, Maine
Manhattan School of Music
New York, New York
University of Manitoba
School of Music
Winnipeg, Manitoba, Canada
Mankato State University
Department of Music
Mankato, Minnesota
Mannes College of Music
New York, New York
Mansfield University
Department of Music
Mansfield, Pennsylvania
Marshall University
Department of Music
Huntington, West Virginia
University of Maryland - Baltimore County
Department of Music
Catonsville, Maryland
University of Maryland - College Park
Department of Music
College Park, Maryland
Marywood College
Music Department
Scranton, Pennsylvania
University of Massachusetts at Amherst
Department of Music and Dance
Amherst, Massachusetts
Massachusetts Institute of Technology
Department of Music and Theater Arts
Cambridge, Massachusetts
McGill University
Faculty of Music
Montreal, Québec, Canada
McMaster University
Department of Music
Hamilton, Ontario, Canada
McNeese State University
Department of Music
Lake Charles, Louisiana

University of Melbourne
Faculty of Music
Victoria 3052, Australia
Memphis State University
Music Department
Memphis, Tennessee
University of Miami
School of Music
Coral Gables, Florida
Miami University
Department of Music
Oxford, Ohio
University of Michigan
School of Music
Ann Arbor, Michigan
Michigan State University
School of Music
East Lansing, Michigan
Middle Tennessee State University
Department of Music
Murfreesboro, Tennessee
Mills College
Music Department
Oakland, California
University of Minnesota - Duluth
Department of Music
Duluth, Minnesota
University of Minnesota - Twin Cities
School of Music
Minneapolis, Minnesota
University of Mississippi
Department of Music
University, Mississippi
University of Missouri - Columbia
Department of Music
Columbia, Missouri
University of Missouri - Kansas City
Conservatory of Music
Kansas City, Missouri
University of Montana
Department of Music
Missoula, Montana
Montclair State College
Department of Music
Upper Montclair, New Jersey
University of Montevallo
Department of Music
Montevallo, Alabama
Moorhead State University
Music Department
Moorhead, Minnesota
Morehead State University
Department of Music
Morehead, Kentucky
Moscow P.I. Tchaikovsky State
Conservatory
*103009 Moscow K-9, Rossiskaja SFSR,
U.S.S.R.*
The Music Academy, Madras
Teachers' College of Music
Madras 600 014, India
Musik-Akademie der Stadt Basel
(Konservatorium)
Konservatorium (Musikhochschule)
Basel, Switzerland
Musikhögskolan i Stockholm
National College of Music
115 31 Stockholm, Sweden
National Institute of the Arts
Music Department
*Taipei County, Taiwan (Republic of
China)*
University of Nebraska - Lincoln
School of Music
Lincoln, Nebraska

University of Nebraska - Omaha
Department of Music
Omaha, Nebraska
Nederlands Instituut voor Kerkmuziek
Utrecht, Netherlands
University of Nevada, Reno
Department of Music
Reno, Nevada
New England Conservatory
Boston, Massachusetts
University of New Hampshire
Department of Music
Durham, New Hampshire
University of New Mexico
Department of Music
Albuquerque, New Mexico
New Mexico State University
Department of Music
Las Cruces, New Mexico
University of New Orleans
Department of Music
New Orleans, Louisiana
New South Wales State Conservatorium of
Music
Sydney NSW 2000, Australia
New York University - College of Arts and
Sciences
Department of Music
New York, New York
New York University - School of Education,
Health, Nursing, and Arts Professions
Department of Music and Music
Education
New York, New York
Nikos Skalkotas Conservatory
Athens 11141, Greece
Norfolk State University
Department of Music
Norfolk, Virginia
Norges Musikkhøgskole
(The Norwegian State Academy of
Music)
N-0130 Oslo 1, Norway
University of North Carolina at Chapel Hill
Department of Music
Chapel Hill, North Carolina
University of North Carolina at Greensboro
School of Music
Greensboro, North Carolina
North Carolina School of the Arts
School of Music
Winston-Salem, North Carolina
University of North Dakota
Department of Music
Grand Forks, North Dakota
North Texas State University
School of Music
Denton, Texas
Northeast Louisiana University
School of Music
Monroe, Louisiana
Northeast Missouri State University
Division of Fine Arts
Kirksville, Missouri
Northeastern Illinois University
Department of Music
Chicago, Illinois
Northern Arizona University
Music Department
Flagstaff, Arizona
University of Northern Colorado
School of Music
Greeley, Colorado
Northern Illinois University
School of Music
DeKalb, Illinois

University of Northern Iowa
  School of Music
   Cedar Falls, Iowa
Northwestern State University of Louisiana
  Department of Music
   Natchitoches, Louisiana
Northwestern University
  School of Music
   Evanston, Illinois
University of Notre Dame
  Department of Music
   Notre Dame, Indiana
Oberlin College
  Conservatory of Music
   Oberlin, Ohio
The Ohio State University
  School of Music
   Columbus, Ohio
Ohio University
  School of Music
   Athens, Ohio
Ohio Wesleyan University
  Department of Music
   Delaware, Ohio
University of Oklahoma
  School of Music
   Norman, Oklahoma
Oklahoma Baptist University
  Department of Music
   Shawnee, Oklahoma
Oklahoma City University
  School of Music and Performing Arts
   Oklahoma City, Oklahoma
University of Orange Free State
  Department of Music
   9300 Bloemfontein, Republic of South Africa
University of Oregon
  School of Music
   Eugene, Oregon
Oregon State University
  Department of Music
   Corvallis, Oregon
Osaka Ongaku Daigaku
  (Osaka College of Music)
   Osaka 561, Japan
University of the Pacific
  Conservatory of Music
   Stockton, California
Pacific Lutheran University
  Department of Music
   Tacoma, Washington
Peabody Institute of The Johns Hopkins University
   Baltimore, Maryland
Pennsylvania State University
  School of Music
   University Park, Pennsylvania
Philadelphia College of the Performing Arts
  School of Music
   Philadelphia, Pennsylvania
University of the Philippines
  College of Music
   Quezon City, The Philippines
University of Pittsburgh
  Department of Music
   Pittsburgh, Pennsylvania
Pomona College
  Music Department
   Claremont, California
Pontifical Institute of Sacred Music
   I - 00165 Roma, Italy
Portland State University
  Department of Music
   Portland, Oregon

Prayag Sangit Samiti
   Allahabad 211001, India
University of Pretoria
  Department of Music
   002 Pretoria, Republic of South Africa
University of Puget Sound
  School of Music
   Tacoma, Washington
Queen's University
  School of Music
   Kingston, Ontario, Canada
Radford University
  Department of Music
   Radford, Virginia
University of Redlands
  School of Music
   Redlands, California
University of Regina
  Department of Music
   Regina, Saskatchewan, Canada
Rice University
  Shepherd School of Music
   Houston, Texas
University of Rochester
  Eastman School of Music
   Rochester, New York
Rogaland Musikkonservatorium
   N-4000 Stavanger, Norway
Royal Northern College of Music
   Manchester M13 9RD, United Kingdom
Royal Scottish Academy of Music and Drama
   Glasgow G2 1BS, United Kingdom
Rutgers, The State University of New Jersey
  Department of Music
   New Brunswick, New Jersey
St. Cloud State University
  Department of Music
   St. Cloud, Minnesota
Saint Louis Conservatory of Music
   St. Louis, Missouri
St. Olaf College
  Music Department
   Northfield, Minnesota
Sam Houston State University
  Department of Music
   Huntsville, Texas
Samford University
  School of Music
   Birmingham, Alabama
San Diego State University
  Music Department
   San Diego, California
San Francisco Conservatory of Music
   San Francisco, California
San Francisco State University
  Department of Music
   San Francisco, California
San Jose State University
  Department of Music
   San Jose, California
University of Santo Tomas
  Conservatory of Music
   Manila, The Philippines
University of Saskatchewan
  Department of Music
   Saskatoon, Saskatchewan, Canada
Shanghai Conservatory of Music
   Shanghai, People's Republic of China
Shenandoah College and Conservatory
   Winchester, Virginia
Shengyang Conservatory of Music
   Shengyang, Liaoning Province, People's Republic of China
Sibelius Academy of Music
   SF-00260 Helsinki 26, Finland

Sichuan Conservatory of Music
   Chengdu, Sichuan, People's Republic of China
Smith College
  Department of Music
   Northampton, Massachusetts
University of South Carolina
  School of Music
   Columbia, South Carolina
Southeast Missouri State University
  Department of Music
   Cape Girardeau, Missouri
Southeastern Louisiana University
  Department of Music
   Hammond, Louisiana
Southeastern Oklahoma State University
  Department of Music
   Durant, Oklahoma
Southern Baptist Theological Seminary
  School of Church Music
   Louisville, Kentucky
Southern Illinois University at Carbondale
  School of Music
   Carbondale, Illinois
Southern Illinois University at Edwardsville
  Department of Music
   Edwardsville, Illinois
Southern Methodist University
  Meadows School of the Arts
   Dallas, Texas
University of Southern Mississippi
  School of Music
   Hattiesburg, Mississippi
Southwest Texas State University
  Department of Music
   San Marcos, Texas
Southwestern Baptist Theological Seminary
  School of Church Music
   Fort Worth, Texas
Southwestern Oklahoma State University
  Department of Music
   Weatherford, Oklahoma
Staatliche Hochschule für Musik Freiburg
   D-7800 Freiburg i. Br., Federal Republic of Germany
Staatliche Hochschule für Musik Rheinland - Köln
   D-5000 Köln 1, Federal Republic of Germany
Staatliche Hochschule für Musik Rheinland - Wuppertal
  Institute Wuppertal
   Wuppertal, Federal Republic of Germany
Staatliche Hochschule für Musik Trossingen
   D-7218 Trossingen 1, Federal Republic of Germany
Stanford University
  Department of Music
   Stanford, California
State University of New York at Binghamton
  Department of Music
   Binghamton, New York
State University of New York at Buffalo
  Department of Music
   Buffalo, New York
State University of New York at Stony Brook
  Department of Music
   Stony Brook, New York
State University of New York College at Fredonia
  School of Music
   Fredonia, New York
State University of New York College at Potsdam

Crane School of Music
Potsdam, New York
State University of New York College at
Purchase
Division of Music
Purchase, New York
Stedelijke Muziekpedagogische Akademie
Leeuwarden, Netherlands
University of Stellenbosch
Department of Music (Conservatoire)
*7600 Stellenbosch, Republic of South
Africa*
Stephen F. Austin State University
Department of Music
Nacogdoches, Texas
University of Sydney
Department of Music
Sydney, NSW 2006, Australia
Syracuse University
School of Music
Syracuse, New York
Tasmanian Conservatorium of Music
Hobart, Tasmania 7001, Australia
Teachers College of Columbia University
Department of Music and Music
Education
New York, New York
Tel Aviv University
Faculty of Fine Arts
Tel-Aviv, Israel
Temple University
Esther Boyer College of Music
Philadelphia, Pennsylvania
University of Tennessee at Knoxville
Department of Music
Knoxville, Tennessee
University of Texas at Arlington
Department of Music
Arlington, Texas
University of Texas at Austin
Department of Music
Austin, Texas
University of Texas at El Paso
Music Department
El Paso, Texas
University of Texas at San Antonio
Division of Music
San Antonio, Texas
Texas Christian University
Music Department
Fort Worth, Texas
Texas Southern University
Department of Music
Houston, Texas
Texas Tech University
Department of Music
Lubbock, Texas
Texas Woman's University
Department of Music and Drama
Denton, Texas
Toho Gakuen School of Music
Tokyo, Japan
The Tokyo College of Music
Tokyo 171, Japan
Tonlistarskolinn i Reykjavik
105 Reykjavik, Iceland
Towson State University
Department of Music
Towson, Maryland
Trenton State College
Music Department
Trenton, New Jersey
Tulane University
Newcomb College
New Orleans, Louisiana

Ueno Gakuen College
Tokyo 110, Japan
Universidad de Antioquía
Facultad de Artes, Departamento de
Música
Medellín, Colombia
Universidade do Rio de Janeiro
Letters and Arts Center - Music Course
22290 Rio de Janeiro, Brazil
Universidade do São Paulo
Department of Music
05508 São Paulo, Brazil
Université de Montréal
Faculty of Music
Montréal, Québec, Canada
Université Laval
Ecole de Musique
Ste. Foy, Québec, Canada
University of Utah
Department of Music
Salt Lake City, Utah
Valdosta State College
Department of Music
Valdosta, Georgia
Valparaiso University
Department of Music
Valparaiso, Indiana
VanderCook College of Music
Chicago, Illinois
University of Vermont
Department of Music
Burlington, Vermont
University of Victoria
School of Music
Victoria, British Columbia, Canada
University of Virginia
McIntire Department of Music
Charlottesville, Virginia
Virginia Commonwealth University
Department of Music
Richmond, Virginia
Virginia Polytechnic Institute and State
University
Department of Music
Blacksburg, Virginia
Virginia State University
Department of Music Education
Petersburg, Virginia
University of Washington
School of Music
Seattle, Washington
Washington State University
Department of Music
Pullman, Washington
Washington University
Department of Music
St. Louis, Missouri
Wayne State University
Department of Music
Detroit, Michigan
Webster University
Department of Music
St. Louis, Missouri
Wesleyan University
Department of Music
Middletown, Connecticut
West Chester University of Pennsylvania
School of Music
West Chester, Pennsylvania
West Georgia College
Department of Music
Carrollton, Georgia
West Texas State University
Department of Music
Canyon, Texas

West Virginia University
Division of Music
Morgantown, West Virginia
University of Western Australia
Department of Music
Nedlands, WA 6009, Australia
Western Kentucky University
Department of Music
Bowling Green, Kentucky
Western Michigan University
School of Music
Kalamazoo, Michigan
University of Western Ontario
Faculty of Music
London, Ontario, Canada
Western Washington University
Department of Music
Bellingham, Washington
Westminster Choir College
Princeton, New Jersey
Wheaton College
Conservatory of Music
Wheaton, Illinois
Wichita State University
School of Music
Wichita, Kansas
Wilfrid Laurier University
Faculty of Music
Waterloo, Ontario, Canada
Willamette University
Department of Music
Salem, Oregon
William Paterson College
Department of Music
Wayne, New Jersey
University of Windsor
School of Music
Windsor, Ontario, Canada
Winthrop College
School of Music
Rock Hill, South Carolina
University of Wisconsin - La Crosse
Department of Music
La Crosse, Wisconsin
University of Wisconsin - Madison
School of Music
Madison, Wisconsin
University of Wisconsin - Oshkosh
Department of Music
Oshkosh, Wisconsin
University of Wisconsin - Whitewater
Department of Music
Whitewater, Wisconsin
University of the Witwatersrand
Wits School of Music
*2001 Johannesburg, Republic of South
Africa*
Wright State University
Department of Music
Dayton, Ohio
University of Wyoming
Music Department
Laramie, Wyoming
Yale College (Yale University)
Department of Music
New Haven, Connecticut
Yale University
School of Music
New Haven, Connecticut
York University
Department of Music
North York, Ontario, Canada
Youngstown State University
Dana School of Music
Youngstown, Ohio

PERFORMANCE PEDAGOGY

San Francisco Conservatory of Music
San Francisco, California

PERFORMANCE PRACTICES

Stanford University
Department of Music
Stanford, California

PERFORMANCE RIGHTS

Hochschule für Musik - München
8000 München 2, Federal Republic of Germany

PERSIAN MUSIC

University of Teheran
Department of Music
Tehran, Iran

PERUVIAN TRADITIONAL MUSIC

Conservatorio Nacional de Música
(National Conservatory of Music)
Lima 1, Peru

PHILOSOPHY

Hochschule für Musik und Theater
Hannover
3000 Hannover 1, Federal Republic of Germany

PHYSICS OF SOUND

Indira Kala Sangit Vishwavidyalaya
(University of Music and Fine Arts)
Madhya Pradesh 491881, India

PIANO

Kuopion Konservatorio
70100 Kuopio, Finland

PIANO MUSIC HISTORY

Hochschule für Musik - München
8000 München 2, Federal Republic of Germany

PIANO PEDAGOGY

American Conservatory of Music
Chicago, Illinois
Andrews University
Department of Music
Berrien Springs, Michigan
Appalachian State University
Department of Music
Boone, North Carolina
Auburn University
Department of Music
Auburn, Alabama
Baylor University
School of Music
Waco, Texas
Bemidji State University
Music Department
Bemidji, Minnesota
Bob Jones University
Division of Music
Greenville, South Carolina
Carnegie-Mellon University
Department of Music
Pittsburgh, Pennsylvania

The Catholic University of America
The Benjamin T. Rome School of Music
Washington, District of Columbia
University of Central Florida
Department of Music
Orlando, Florida
Central Missouri State University
Department of Music
Warrensburg, Missouri
University of Colorado at Boulder
College of Music
Boulder, Colorado
Columbus College
Department of Music
Columbus, Georgia
Converse College
School of Music
Spartanburg, South Carolina
University of Denver
Lamont School of Music
Denver, Colorado
Drake University
Department of Music
Des Moines, Iowa
East Carolina University
School of Music
Greenville, North Carolina
Eastern New Mexico University
School of Music
Portales, New Mexico
Florida State University
School of Music
Tallahassee, Florida
Georgia Southern College
Department of Music
Statesboro, Georgia
Georgia State University
School of Music
Atlanta, Georgia
University of Idaho
School of Music
Moscow, Idaho
Illinois Wesleyan University
School of Music
Bloomington, Illinois
James Madison University
Department of Music
Harrisonburg, Virginia
Kent State University
School of Music
Kent, Ohio
University of Louisville
School of Music
Louisville, Kentucky
Loyola University
College of Music
New Orleans, Louisiana
McNeese State University
Department of Music
Lake Charles, Louisiana
University of Michigan
School of Music
Ann Arbor, Michigan
Michigan State University
School of Music
East Lansing, Michigan
University of Minnesota - Duluth
Department of Music
Duluth, Minnesota
University of Mississippi
Department of Music
University, Mississippi
University of Missouri - Columbia
Department of Music
Columbia, Missouri

New Mexico State University
Department of Music
Las Cruces, New Mexico
Northeastern Illinois University
Department of Music
Chicago, Illinois
Oakland University
Department of Music, Theatre and Dance
Rochester, Michigan
University of Oklahoma
School of Music
Norman, Oklahoma
Roosevelt University
Chicago Musical College
Chicago, Illinois
St. Cloud State University
Department of Music
St. Cloud, Minnesota
Shorter College
Department of Music
Rome, Georgia
University of South Carolina
School of Music
Columbia, South Carolina
University of South Florida
Department of Music
Tampa, Florida
Southern Illinois University at Carbondale
School of Music
Carbondale, Illinois
Southern Methodist University
Meadows School of the Arts
Dallas, Texas
Southwest Texas State University
Department of Music
San Marcos, Texas
Temple University
Esther Boyer College of Music
Philadelphia, Pennsylvania
University of Texas at Arlington
Department of Music
Arlington, Texas
University of Texas at San Antonio
Division of Music
San Antonio, Texas
University of Utah
Department of Music
Salt Lake City, Utah
Virginia Commonwealth University
Department of Music
Richmond, Virginia
Webster University
Department of Music
St. Louis, Missouri
West Chester University of Pennsylvania
School of Music
West Chester, Pennsylvania
Westminster Choir College
Princeton, New Jersey
Wichita State University
School of Music
Wichita, Kansas
Winthrop College
School of Music
Rock Hill, South Carolina

PIANO PERFORMANCE

Oakland University
Department of Music, Theatre and Dance
Rochester, Michigan

PIANO TECHNICIAN

American Conservatory of Music
Chicago, Illinois

PIANO TECHNOLOGY

Florida State University
School of Music
Tallahassee, Florida
Shenandoah College and Conservatory
Winchester, Virginia

POLYPHONIC VOCAL COMPOSITION

Conservatorio di Musica "Santa Cecilia"
00187 Rome, Italy

POPULAR MUSIC

Hochschule für Gestaltende Kunst und
Musik
(State College for Creative Art and
Music)
*2800 Bremen 1, Federal Republic of
Germany*
Konzervatoř v Praze
(State Conservatory Prague)
Praha 110 00, Czechoslovakia
Staatliche Hochschule für Musik Rheinland
- Düsseldorf
(State College of Music)
*D-4000 Düsseldorf, Federal Republic of
Germany*

PROFESSIONAL MUSIC

Berklee College of Music
Boston, Massachusetts

PROTESTANT LITURGY

Musikhochschule Lübeck
Grosse Petersgrube 17-29
*2400 Lübeck, Federal Republic of
Germany*

PSYCHOLOGY

Hochschule für Musik und Theater
Hannover
*3000 Hannover 1, Federal Republic of
Germany*
Musikhochschule des Saarlandes
*6600 Saarbrücken 3, Federal Republic of
Germany*
Musikhochschule Lübeck
Grosse Petersgrube 17-29
*2400 Lübeck, Federal Republic of
Germany*
Staatliche Hochschule für Musik Rheinland
- Aachen
Grenzland-Institut Aachen
Aachen, Federal Republic of Germany
Staatliche Hochschule für Musik Rheinland
- Wuppertal
Institute Wuppertal
Wuppertal, Federal Republic of Germany

PSYCHOMUSICOLOGY

University of Connecticut
Department of Music
Storrs, Connecticut

PUPPET THEATER MUSIC

Osaka Ongaku Daigaku
(Osaka College of Music)
Osaka 561, Japan

RADIO SEMINAR

Hochschule für Musik - München
*8000 München 2, Federal Republic of
Germany*

RECORDING ARTS

Peabody Institute of The Johns Hopkins
University
Baltimore, Maryland

RECORDING INDUSTRY

University of Colorado at Denver
College of Music
Denver, Colorado

RECORDING MEDIA

Mills College
Music Department
Oakland, California

RENAISSANCE INSTRUMENTS

Musik-Akademie der Stadt Basel
Schola Cantorum Basiliensis
CH-4051 Basel, Switzerland

RENAISSANCE MUSIC

Royal Northern College of Music
Manchester M13 9RD, United Kingdom
Rutgers, The State University of New Jersey
Department of Music
New Brunswick, New Jersey
Stanford University
Department of Music
Stanford, California
Trinity College of Music
London W1M 6AQ, United Kingdom
Wilfrid Laurier University
Faculty of Music
Waterloo, Ontario, Canada
Yale College (Yale University)
Department of Music
New Haven, Connecticut

RHYTHMIC EDUCATION

Fachakademie für Music - Augsburg
Leopold Mozart-Konservatorium der
Stadt Augsburg
Augsberg, Federal Republic of Germany
Staatliche Hochschule für Musik und
Darstellende Kunst Stuttgart
*7000 Stuttgart 1, Federal Republic of
Germany*

RHYTHMICS

Staatliche Hochschule für Musik Rheinland
- Düsseldorf
(State College of Music)
*D-4000 Düsseldorf, Federal Republic of
Germany*

SACRED MUSIC

Arkansas State University
Department of Music
State University, Arkansas
Combs College of Music
Philadelphia, Pennsylvania
Duquesne University
School of Music
Pittsburgh, Pennsylvania
Elizabeth University of Music
Hiroshima 730, Japan
Georgia State University
School of Music
Atlanta, Georgia

University of Iowa
School of Music
Iowa City, Iowa
James Madison University
Department of Music
Harrisonburg, Virginia
Jersey City State College
Music Department
Jersey City, New Jersey
Louisiana State University
School of Music
Baton Rouge, Louisiana
Memphis State University
Music Department
Memphis, Tennessee
Oakland University
Department of Music, Theatre and
Dance
Rochester, Michigan
Southeastern Oklahoma State University
Department of Music
Durant, Oklahoma
Southern Methodist University
Meadows School of the Arts
Dallas, Texas
University of Tennessee at Chattanooga
Cadek Department of Music
Chattanooga, Tennessee

SCHOOL MUSIC

University of Calgary
Department of Music
Calgary, Alberta, Canada
Memphis State University
Music Department
Memphis, Tennessee
Musikhochschule des Saarlandes
*6600 Saarbrücken 3, Federal Republic of
Germany*
Musikhochschule Lübeck
Grosse Petersgrube 17-29
*2400 Lübeck, Federal Republic of
Germany*
Staatliche Hochschule für Musik Karlsruhe
*7500 Karlsruhe 1, Federal Republic of
Germany*
Staatliche Hochschule für Musik und
Darstellende Kunst Stuttgart
*7000 Stuttgart 1, Federal Republic of
Germany*
Staatliche Hochschule für Musik
Westfalen-Lippe
*4930 Detmold, Federal Republic of
Germany*
Stedelijke Muziekpedagogische Akademie
Leeuwarden, Netherlands

SCORE READING

Staatliche Hochschule für Musik
Westfalen-Lippe
Institut Dortmund
*D-4600 Dortmund 1, Federal Republic of
Germany*

SLOVAKIAN MUSIC

Konzervatorium - Bratislava
Bratislava 811 06, Czechoslovakia

SOLFEGE

The Academy of Vocal Arts
Philadelphia, Pennsylvania
Conservatorio Nacional de Musica - La Paz
(National Conservatory of Music - La
Paz)
La Paz, Bolivia

Escuela Nacional de Música
   Universidad Nacional Autónoma de
   México
   Mexico City, D.F. 04100, Mexico
Escuela Universitaria de Música -
   Montevideo
   Montevideo, Uruguay
Konzervatoř v Praze
   (State Conservatory Prague)
   Praha 110 00, Czechoslovakia
Kuopion Konservatorio
   70100 Kuopio, Finland
Nikos Skalkotas Conservatory
   Athens 11141, Greece
Staatliche Hochschule für Musik Rheinland
   - Aachen
   Grenzland-Institut Aachen
   Aachen, Federal Republic of Germany
Universidade do São Paulo
   Department of Music
   05508 São Paulo, Brazil
Zeneiskolai Tanárkepző Intézet
   (Music Teachers Training Institute of the
   Liszt Academy of Music)
   Budapest 1052, Hungary

SONG ACCOMPANIMENT

Staatliche Hochschule für Musik Rheinland
   - Düsseldorf
   (State College of Music)
   *D-4000 Düsseldorf, Federal Republic of
   Germany*

SONGWRITING

Berklee College of Music
   Boston, Massachusetts

SOUND ENGINEER/MUSIC TRANSMISSION

Hochschule der Künste Berlin
   *1000 Berlin 10, Federal Republic of
   Germany*

SOUND ENGINEERING

Staatliche Hochschule für Musik
   Westfalen-Lippe
   *4930 Detmold, Federal Republic of
   Germany*

SOUND RECORDING

University of Lowell
   College of Music
   Lowell, Massachusetts
McGill University
   Faculty of Music
   Montreal, Québec, Canada

SOUND RECORDING TECHNOLOGY

State University of New York College at
Fredonia
   School of Music
   Fredonia, New York

SOUND SYNTHESIS

University of Colorado at Denver
   College of Music
   Denver, Colorado

SOUTH INDIAN MUSIC

York University
   Department of Music
   North York, Ontario, Canada

SPEECH

Fachakademie für Music - Augsburg
   Leopold Mozart-Konservatorium der
   Stadt Augsburg
   Augsberg, Federal Republic of Germany
Hochschule für Musik und Darstellende
   Kunst Frankfurt am Main
   *6000 Frankfurt am Main 1, Federal
   Republic of Germany*
Hochschule für Musik und Theater
Hannover
   *3000 Hannover 1, Federal Republic of
   Germany*
Musikhochschule des Saarlandes
   *6600 Saarbrücken 3, Federal Republic of
   Germany*
Royal Irish Academy of Music
   Dublin 2, Ireland
Staatliche Hochschule für Musik Freiburg
   *D-7800 Freiburg i. Br., Federal Republic
   of Germany*
Staatliche Hochschule für Musik Rheinland
   - Aachen
   Grenzland-Institut Aachen
   Aachen, Federal Republic of Germany
Staatliche Hochschule für Musik Rheinland
   - Wuppertal
   Institute Wuppertal
   Wuppertal, Federal Republic of Germany
Staatliche Hochschule für Musik und
   Darstellende Kunst Stuttgart
   *7000 Stuttgart 1, Federal Republic of
   Germany*
Staatliche Hochschule für Musik
   Westfalen-Lippe
   *4930 Detmold, Federal Republic of
   Germany*

SPEECH TRAINING

Hochschule für Musik - Würzburg
   *D-8700 Würzburg, Federal Republic of
   Germany*

STAGE MANAGEMENT

Hochschule für Music und Darstellende
   Kunst Hamburg
   *2000 Hamburg 13, Federal Republic of
   Germany*
Hochschule für Musik und Theater
Hannover
   *3000 Hannover 1, Federal Republic of
   Germany*
Leningrad N.A. Rimsky-Korsakov State
Conservatory
   *192041 Leningrad, Rossiskaja SFSR,
   U.S.S.R.*

STRING INSTRUMENT MAKING

Instituto Professionale Artigianato Liutario
e del Legno
   Palazzo dell'Arte
   Cremona, Italy

STRING INSTRUMENT PEDAGOGY

University of North Carolina at Greensboro
   School of Music
   Greensboro, North Carolina

STRINGED INSTRUMENT REPAIR

Indira Kala Sangit Vishwavidyalaya
   (University of Music and Fine Arts)
   Madhya Pradesh 491881, India

STRUCTURE ANALYSIS

Kuopion Konservatorio
   70100 Kuopio, Finland

STRUCTURE AND EAR TRAINING

Hochschule der Künste Berlin
   *1000 Berlin 10, Federal Republic of
   Germany*

STRUCTURES TECHNIQUES

Hochschule für Musik - Würzburg
   *D-8700 Würzburg, Federal Republic of
   Germany*

STUDIO EARLY MUSIC

Hochschule für Gestaltende Kunst und
Musik
   (State College for Creative Art and
   Music)
   *2800 Bremen 1, Federal Republic of
   Germany*

STUDIO JAZZ WRITING

University of Miami
   School of Music
   Coral Gables, Florida

STUDIO MUSIC

Southern Illinois University at Edwardsville
   Department of Music
   Edwardsville, Illinois

STUDIO NEW MUSIC

Fachakademie für Music - Augsburg
   Leopold Mozart-Konservatorium der
   Stadt Augsburg
   Augsberg, Federal Republic of Germany
Hochschule für Gestaltende Kunst und
Musik
   (State College for Creative Art and
   Music)
   *2800 Bremen 1, Federal Republic of
   Germany*
Hochschule für Musik und Darstellende
   Kunst Frankfurt am Main
   *6000 Frankfurt am Main 1, Federal
   Republic of Germany*

STUDIO OLD MUSIC

Fachakademie für Music - Augsburg
   Leopold Mozart-Konservatorium der
   Stadt Augsburg
   Augsberg, Federal Republic of Germany
Hochschule für Musik und Darstellende
   Kunst Frankfurt am Main
   *6000 Frankfurt am Main 1, Federal
   Republic of Germany*

SUZUKI METHOD

Central Washington University
   Department of Music
   Ellensburg, Washington

SUZUKI PEDAGOGY

Cleveland Institute of Music
   Cleveland, Ohio
University of Denver
   Lamont School of Music
   Denver, Colorado

SUZUKI TRAINING

Southwest Texas State University
   Department of Music
   San Marcos, Texas

SYMPHONIC CONDUCTING

Tashkent State Conservatory
700000 Tashkent, Uzbekskaja SSR,
U.S.S.R.
Tbilisi V. Sarajishvili State Conservatory
380004 Tbilisi 4, Gruzinskaja SSR,
U.S.S.R.

TECHNOLOGY IN MUSIC

Oberlin College
    Conservatory of Music
    Oberlin, Ohio

THEATER

Konzervatoř v Praze
    (State Conservatory Prague)
    Praha 110 00, Czechoslovakia

THEATER HISTORY

The Academy of Vocal Arts
    Philadelphia, Pennsylvania
Hochschule für Musik und Theater
Hannover
    3000 Hannover 1, Federal Republic of
    Germany
Musikhochschule Lübeck
    Grosse Petersgrube 17-29
    2400 Lübeck, Federal Republic of
    Germany

THEATER LAW

Hochschule für Musik und Theater
Hannover
    3000 Hannover 1, Federal Republic of
    Germany

THEORY

University of Arkansas
    Department of Music
    Fayetteville, Arkansas
Bowling Green State University
    College of Musical Arts
    Bowling Green, Ohio
University of British Columbia
    School of Music
    Vancouver, British Columbia, Canada
Butler University
    Jordan College of Fine Arts
    Indianapolis, Indiana
University of Calgary
    Department of Music
    Calgary, Alberta, Canada
University of California, Berkeley
    Department of Music
    Berkeley, California
Central Missouri State University
    Department of Music
    Warrensburg, Missouri
University of the Pacific
    Conservatory of Music
    Stockton, California
University of Rochester
    Eastman School of Music
    Rochester, New York
University of Toronto
    Faculty of Music
    Toronto, Ontario, Canada

THEORY OF MUSIC

Kiev P.I. Tchaikovsky Conservatory
    252001 Kiev, Ukrainskaja SSR, U.S.S.R.

THEORY-COMPOSITION

West Georgia College
    Department of Music
    Carrollton, Georgia

TONAL MUSIC

Yale College (Yale University)
    Department of Music
    New Haven, Connecticut

TOWER INSTRUMENTS

Koninklijk Beiaardschool Jef Denyn
    2800 Mechelen, Belgium

TURKISH MUSIC

Istanbul Üniversitesi
    (University of Istanbul)
    Istanbul, Turkey

TV SEMINAR

Hochschule für Musik - München
    8000 München 2, Federal Republic of
    Germany

TWENTIETH CENTURY MUSIC

University of California, Davis
    Department of Music
    Davis, California
State University of New York at Stony
Brook
    Department of Music
    Stony Brook, New York

VOCAL ARTS

University of Southern California
    School of Music
    Los Angeles, California

VOCAL MUSIC

Alma-Ata Kurmangazy State Conservatory
    480091 Alma-Ata 91, Kazahskaja SSR,
    U.S.S.R.
A.V. Nezhdanova Odessa Conservatory
    270000 Odessa, Ukrainskaja SSR,
    U.S.S.R.
Azerbaijan S.S.R. U. Gajibekov State
Conservatory
    370014 Baku, Azerbajdžanskaja SSR,
    U.S.S.R.
Banaras Hindu University
    Uttar Pradesh 221005, India
Bob Jones University
    Division of Music
    Greenville, South Carolina
Bulgarian State Conservatoire
    Sofia 1505, Bulgaria
Central Conservatory of Music
    Beijing, People's Republic of China
Conservatorio Nacional de Música
    (National Conservatory of Music)
    Lima 1, Peru
Conservatorul de Musică George Dima
    (Conservatory of Music)
    3400 Cluj-Napoca, Romania
Conservatorul de Muzică Ciprian
Porumbescu
    (Conservatory of Music)
    70732 Bucharest, Romania
Conservatorul Georges Enescu
    (Conservatory of Music)
    6600 Iasi, Romania

Converse College
    School of Music
    Spartanburg, South Carolina
Donetsk Musical-Pedagogical Institute
    340086 Donetsk, Ukrainskaja SSR,
    U.S.S.R.
Eastern New Mexico University
    School of Music
    Portales, New Mexico
Elizabeth University of Music
    Hiroshima 730, Japan
Erevan Komitas State Conservatory
    375009 Erevan 9, Armjanskaja SSR,
    U.S.S.R.
Evangelische Kirchenmusikschule der
Kirchenprovinz Sachsen
    (Evangelical Church Music School of the
    Church Province Saxony)
    DDR-4020 Halle (Saale), German
    Democratic Republic
Fachakademie für Music - Augsburg
    Leopold Mozart-Konservatorium der
    Stadt Augsburg
    Augsberg, Federal Republic of Germany
Fachakademie für Musik - Nürnberg
    Konservatorium der Stadt Nürnberg
    Nürnberg, Federal Republic of Germany
Faculdade Santa Marcelina
    05006 São Paulo, Brazil
Far-Eastern Pedagogical Institute of the
Arts
    690678 Vladivostok, Rossiskaja SFSR,
    U.S.S.R.
George Mason University
    Department of Performing Arts - Music
    Division
    Fairfax, Virginia
Gnessinsky State Musical and Pedagogical
Institute
    121069 Moscow G-69, Rossiskaja SFSR,
    U.S.S.R.
Gorky M.I. Glinka State Conservatory
    603005 Gorky, Rossiskaja SFSR, U.S.S.R.
Hermann-Zilcher-Konservatorium
    D-8700 Würzburg, Federal Republic of
    Germany
Hochschule für Musik - Würzburg
    D-8700 Würzburg, Federal Republic of
    Germany
Hochschule für Musik und Theater
Hannover
    3000 Hannover 1, Federal Republic of
    Germany
Indira Kala Sangit Vishwavidyalaya
    (University of Music and Fine Arts)
    Madhya Pradesh 491881, India
Kazan State Conservatory
    420015 Kazan 15, Rossiskaja SFSR,
    U.S.S.R.
Kharkov State Institute of Arts
    310003 Kharkov, U.S.S.R.
Kiev P.I. Tchaikovsky Conservatory
    252001 Kiev, Ukrainskaja SSR, U.S.S.R.
Kratikon Odeion Thessaloniki
    (State Conservatory of Music)
    Thessaloniki, Greece
Latvian S.S.R. Y. Vitol State Conservatory
    226050 Riga, Latvijskaya SSR, U.S.S.R.
Lvov M.V. Lysenko State Conservatory
    290005 Lvov, Ukrainskaja SSR, U.S.S.R.
Moldavian S.S.R. G. Musichesku State
Conservatory
    277014 Kishinev, Moldavskaja SSR,
    U.S.S.R.
Musikhochschule des Saarlandes
    6600 Saarbrücken 3, Federal Republic of

Germany
Musikhochschule Lübeck
   Grosse Petersgrube 17-29
   *2400 Lübeck, Federal Republic of
   Germany*
Musikschule und Konservatorium
   Schaffhausen
   Schaffhausen, Switzerland
National Institute of the Arts
   Music Department
   *Taipei County, Taiwan (Republic of
   China)*
New South Wales State Conservatorium of
   Music
   Sydney NSW 2000, Australia
Royal Irish Academy of Music
   Dublin 2, Ireland
San Jose State University
   Department of Music
   San Jose, California
Shengyang Conservatory of Music
   *Shengyang, Liaoning Province, People's
   Republic of China*
Sichuan Conservatory of Music
   *Chengdu, Sichuan, People's Republic of
   China*
Staatliche Hochschule für Musik Freiburg
   *D-7800 Freiburg i. Br., Federal Republic
   of Germany*
Staatliche Hochschule für Musik
   Heidelberg-Mannheim
   *Friedrich-Ebert-Anlage 62, Federal
   Republic of Germany*
Staatliche Hochschule für Musik Rheinland
   - Aachen
   Grenzland-Institut Aachen
   Aachen, Federal Republic of Germany
Staatliche Hochschule für Musik Rheinland
   - Wuppertal
   Institute Wuppertal
   Wuppertal, Federal Republic of Germany
Staatliche Hochschule für Musik Ruhr
   *4300 Essen 16, Federal Republic of
   Germany*
Staatliche Hochschule für Musik Trossingen
   *D-7218 Trossingen 1, Federal Republic of
   Germany*
Staatliche Hochschule für Musik
   Westfalen-Lippe
   *4930 Detmold, Federal Republic of
   Germany*
Tallinn State Conservatory
   200015 Tallinn, Estonskaja SSR, U.S.S.R.
Tashkent State Conservatory
   *700000 Tashkent, Uzbekskaja SSR,
   U.S.S.R.*
Tbilisi V. Sarajishvili State Conservatory
   *380004 Tbilisi 4, Gruzinskaja SSR,
   U.S.S.R.*
Texas Woman's University
   Department of Music and Drama
   Denton, Texas
Ueno Gakuen College
   Tokyo 110, Japan
Ufa State Institute of Fine Arts
   450025 Ufa, Bashkir ASSR, U.S.S.R.
Urals M.P. Mussorgsky State Conservatory
   *620014 Sverdlovsk, Rossiskaja SFSR,
   U.S.S.R.*
Virginia State University
   Department of Music Education
   Petersburg, Virginia
Vysoká Skola Mûzickych Umeni v Praha
   Academy of Music and Dramatic Arts
   1101 00 Prague 1, Czechoslovakia

VOCAL PEDAGOGY

The Catholic University of America
   The Benjamin T. Rome School of Music
   Washington, District of Columbia
University of North Carolina at Greensboro
   School of Music
   Greensboro, North Carolina
Roosevelt University
   Chicago Musical College
   Chicago, Illinois
Winthrop College
   School of Music
   Rock Hill, South Carolina

VOCAL PERFORMANCE

Oakland University
   Department of Music, Theatre and
   Dance
   Rochester, Michigan

VOCAL STUDIES

James Madison University
   Department of Music
   Harrisonburg, Virginia
Shenandoah College and Conservatory
   Winchester, Virginia
University of South Carolina
   School of Music
   Columbia, South Carolina

VOICE PEDAGOGY

East Carolina University
   School of Music
   Greenville, North Carolina
University of Louisville
   School of Music
   Louisville, Kentucky
University of Mississippi
   Department of Music
   University, Mississippi

VOICE SCIENCE

The Academy of Vocal Arts
   Philadelphia, Pennsylvania

WEST AFRICAN MUSIC

California Institute of the Arts
   School of Music
   Valencia, California

WESTERN ART MUSIC

Wesleyan University
   Department of Music
   Middletown, Connecticut

WIND CONDUCTING

University of Cincinnati
   College-Conservatory of Music
   Cincinnati, Ohio

WOODWINDS

Military Institute of Music - Sana'a
   Sana'a, Yemen Arab Republic

WORLD MUSIC

Combs College of Music
   Philadelphia, Pennsylvania

WORLD MUSIC HISTORY

Conservatorio Nacional de Musica - La Paz
   (National Conservatory of Music - La
   Paz)
   La Paz, Bolivia

Escuela Nacional de Música
   Universidad Nacional Autónoma de
   México
   Mexico City, D.F. 04100, Mexico

WORLD MUSIC PERFORMANCE

California Snstitute of the Arts
   School of Music
   Valencia, California

YEMEN NATIONALISTIC MUSIC

National Institute of Music - Sana'a
   Sana'a, Yemen Arab Republic

INDEX OF INSTRUMENTS TAUGHT

ACCORDION

Akademia Muzyczna w Krakowie
31-038 Kraków, Poland
California State University, Long Beach
Department of Music
Long Beach, California
Escuela Nacional de Música
Universidad Nacional Autónoma de
México
Mexico City, D.F. 04100, Mexico
Glassboro State College
Department of Music
Glassboro, New Jersey
Hermann-Zilcher-Konservatorium
*D-8700 Würzburg, Federal Republic of
Germany*
Hochschule für Music Franz Liszt
*DDR 5300 Weimar, German Democratic
Republic*
Hoschschule für Music Hans Eisler
*DDR Berlin 1080, German Democratic
Republic*
Levinsky Teachers College
Music Teachers Seminary
Tel-Aviv, Israel
Marywood College
Music Department
Scranton, Pennsylvania
University of Missouri - Kansas City
Conservatory of Music
Kansas City, Missouri
Queen's University
School of Music
Kingston, Ontario, Canada
University of Saskatchewan
Department of Music
Saskatoon, Saskatchewan, Canada
Sichuan Conservatory of Music
*Chengdu, Sichuan, People's Republic of
China*
University of Toronto
Faculty of Music
Toronto, Ontario, Canada
Université de Montréal
Faculty of Music
Montréal, Québec, Canada
Wiesbadener Konservatorium und staatliche
anerkannte private Fachschule für
Musikerzieher e.V.
(Conservatory and Seminary for Music
Education)
*6200 Wiesbaden, Federal Republic of
Germany*

ACOUSTIC BASS

Berklee College of Music
Boston, Massachusetts

AFRICAN DRUM

California Institute of the Arts
School of Music
Valencia, California

AFRICAN INSTRUMENTS

Kent State University
School of Music
Kent, Ohio

ALTO SAXOPHONE

University of Arkansas
Department of Music
Fayetteville, Arkansas
Berklee College of Music
Boston, Massachusetts

ASIAN INSTRUMENTS

Kent State University
School of Music
Kent, Ohio

ASIAN PERCUSSION INSTRUMENTS

San Jose State University
Department of Music
San Jose, California

BALINESE GAMELAN

Bowling Green State University
College of Musical Arts
Bowling Green, Ohio

BARITONE

University of Arizona
School of Music
Tucson, Arizona
University of Arkansas
Department of Music
Fayetteville, Arkansas
Austin Peay State University
Department of Music
Clarksville, Tennessee
Boston University
School of Music
Boston, Massachusetts

California State University, Hayward
Department of Music
Hayward, California
University of Central Florida
Department of Music
Orlando, Florida
University of Denver
Lamont School of Music
Denver, Colorado
DePaul University
School of Music
Chicago, Illinois
Drake University
Department of Music
Des Moines, Iowa
East Carolina University
School of Music
Greenville, North Carolina
Eastern Illinois University
Department of Music
Charleston, Illinois
University of Hartford
Hartt School of Music
West Hartford, Connecticut
Hofstra University
Department of Music
Hempstead, New York
Howard University
Department of Music
Washington, District of Columbia
Illinois Wesleyan University
School of Music
Bloomington, Illinois
Indiana University - Bloomington
School of Music
Bloomington, Indiana
Jackson State University
Department of Music
Jackson, Mississippi
Kansas State University
Department of Music
Manhattan, Kansas
Lamar University
Department of Music
Beaumont, Texas
University of Maine
School of Performing Arts
Orono, Maine
Marshall University
Department of Music
Huntington, West Virginia
University of Massachusetts at Amherst
Department of Music and Dance
Amherst, Massachusetts
Middle Tennessee State University
Department of Music

Murfreesboro, Tennessee
University of Minnesota - Twin Cities
  School of Music
  Minneapolis, Minnesota
University of Missouri - Kansas City
  Conservatory of Music
  Kansas City, Missouri
University of Nevada, Las Vegas
  Department of Music
  Las Vegas, Nevada
University of New Orleans
  Department of Music
  New Orleans, Louisiana
Norfolk State University
  Department of Music
  Norfolk, Virginia
Ohio Wesleyan University
  Department of Music
  Delaware, Ohio
University of Oregon
  School of Music
  Eugene, Oregon
University of the Pacific
  Conservatory of Music
  Stockton, California
Pacific Lutheran University
  Department of Music
  Tacoma, Washington
Peabody Institute of The Johns Hopkins
  University
  Baltimore, Maryland
University of Regina
  Department of Music
  Regina, Saskatchewan, Canada
University of Rhode Island
  Department of Music
  Kingston, Rhode Island
St. Cloud State University
  Department of Music
  St. Cloud, Minnesota
Samford University
  School of Music
  Birmingham, Alabama
University of Saskatchewan
  Department of Music
  Saskatoon, Saskatchewan, Canada
University of South Dakota
  Music Department
  Vermillion, South Dakota
Southeast Missouri State University
  Department of Music
  Cape Girardeau, Missouri
Southern Illinois University at Carbondale
  School of Music
  Carbondale, Illinois
Southern Illinois University at Edwardsville
  Department of Music
  Edwardsville, Illinois
University of Southwestern Louisiana
  School of Music
  Lafayette, Louisiana
Teachers College of Columbia University
  Department of Music and Music
  Education
  New York, New York
University of Tennessee at Knoxville
  Department of Music
  Knoxville, Tennessee
Texas Christian University
  Music Department
  Fort Worth, Texas
University of Tulsa
  Faculty of Music
  Tulsa, Oklahoma
Valparaiso University
  Department of Music

Valparaiso, Indiana
VanderCook College of Music
  Chicago, Illinois
Washington State University
  Department of Music
  Pullman, Washington
West Chester University of Pennsylvania
  School of Music
  West Chester, Pennsylvania
William Carey College
  Winters School of Music
  Hattiesburg, Mississippi
University of Wisconsin - Eau Claire
  Department of Music
  Eau Claire, Wisconsin
University of Wisconsin - Milwaukee
  Music Department
  Milwaukee, Wisconsin
University of Wisconsin - Stevens Point
  Department of Music
  Stevens Point, Wisconsin

BARITONE HORN

Berklee College of Music
  Boston, Massachusetts
University of Miami
  School of Music
  Coral Gables, Florida
University of Nebraska - Lincoln
  School of Music
  Lincoln, Nebraska
Northern Arizona University
  Music Department
  Flagstaff, Arizona
San Diego State University
  Music Department
  San Diego, California
Youngstown State University
  Dana School of Music
  Youngstown, Ohio

BARITONE SAXOPHONE

Berklee College of Music
  Boston, Massachusetts

BAROQUE CELLO

Oberlin College
  Conservatory of Music
  Oberlin, Ohio

BAROQUE FLUTE

Oberlin College
  Conservatory of Music
  Oberlin, Ohio

BAROQUE INSTRUMENTS

Brandon University
  School of Music
  Brandon, Manitoba, Canada
Case Western Reserve University
  Department of Music
  Cleveland, Ohio
Columbia University
  Department of Music
  New York, New York
Indiana University - Bloomington
  School of Music
  Bloomington, Indiana
Mannes College of Music
  New York, New York
New England Conservatory
  Boston, Massachusetts
San Jose State University
  Department of Music
  San Jose, California

Stanford University
  Department of Music
  Stanford, California
Wesleyan University
  Department of Music
  Middletown, Connecticut

BAROQUE OBOE

Oberlin College
  Conservatory of Music
  Oberlin, Ohio

BAROQUE VIOLIN

Hochschule für Music und Darstellende
  Kunst Hamburg
  *2000 Hamburg 13, Federal Republic of
  Germany*
Oberlin College
  Conservatory of Music
  Oberlin, Ohio

BASS

Acadia University
  School of Music
  Wolfville, Nova Scotia, Canada
Akademia Muzyczna w Krakowie
  31-038 Kraków, Poland
University of Alabama
  School of Music
  University, Alabama
University of Alaska
  Music Department
  Fairbanks, Alaska
American Conservatory of Music
  Chicago, Illinois
University of Arizona
  School of Music
  Tucson, Arizona
University of Arkansas
  Department of Music
  Fayetteville, Arkansas
Arkansas Tech University
  Department of Music
  Russellville, Arkansas
Austin Peay State University
  Department of Music
  Clarksville, Tennessee
Baldwin-Wallace College
  Conservatory of Music
  Berea, Ohio
Baylor University
  School of Music
  Waco, Texas
Boise State University
  Music Department
  Boise, Idaho
Boston University
  School of Music
  Boston, Massachusetts
Bowling Green State University
  College of Musical Arts
  Bowling Green, Ohio
Bradley University
  Division of Music and Theatre Arts
  Peoria, Illinois
Bulgarian State Conservatoire
  Sofia 1505, Bulgaria
University of California, Irvine
  School of Fine Arts
  Irvine, California
University of California, Los Angeles
  Department of Music
  Los Angeles, California
University of California, Riverside
  Department of Music

Riverside, California
University of California, San Diego
   Department of Music
   La Jolla, California
University of California, Santa Barbara
   Department of Music
   Santa Barbara, California
University of California, Santa Cruz
   Music Board, Division of the Arts
   Santa Cruz, California
California State University, Hayward
   Department of Music
   Hayward, California
California State University, Sacramento
   Department of Music
   Sacramento, California
The Catholic University of America
   The Benjamin T. Rome School of Music
   Washington, District of Columbia
University of Central Florida
   Department of Music
   Orlando, Florida
Central Missouri State University
   Department of Music
   Warrensburg, Missouri
Central Washington University
   Department of Music
   Ellensburg, Washington
University of Cincinnati
   College-Conservatory of Music
   Cincinnati, Ohio
The Claremont Graduate School
   Music Department
   Claremont, California
Cleveland Institute of Music
   Cleveland, Ohio
Cleveland State University
   Department of Music
   Cleveland, Ohio
University of Colorado at Boulder
   College of Music
   Boulder, Colorado
Colorado State University
   Department of Music, Theatre, and
   Dance
   Fort Collins, Colorado
University of Connecticut
   Department of Music
   Storrs, Connecticut
Conservatorio di Musica "Santa Cecilia"
   00187 Rome, Italy
Conservatorio Nacional de Musica - La Paz
   (National Conservatory of Music - La
   Paz)
   La Paz, Bolivia
The Curtis Institute of Music
   Philadelphia, Pennsylvania
Delta State University
   Department of Music
   Cleveland, Mississippi
University of Denver
   Lamont School of Music
   Denver, Colorado
DePaul University
   School of Music
   Chicago, Illinois
DePauw University
   School of Music
   Greencastle, Indiana
Drake University
   Department of Music
   Des Moines, Iowa
Duquesne University
   School of Music
   Pittsburgh, Pennsylvania

East Carolina University
   School of Music
   Greenville, North Carolina
Eastern Illinois University
   Department of Music
   Charleston, Illinois
Eastern Michigan University
   Department of Music
   Ypsilanti, Michigan
Emporia State University
   Division of Music
   Emporia, Kansas
Escuela Nacional de Música
   Universidad Nacional Autónoma de
   México
   Mexico City, D.F. 04100, Mexico
University of Florida
   Department of Music
   Gainesville, Florida
Florida State University
   School of Music
   Tallahassee, Florida
George Mason University
   Department of Performing Arts - Music
   Division
   Fairfax, Virginia
University of Hartford
   Hartt School of Music
   West Hartford, Connecticut
University of Hawaii at Manoa
   Music Department
   Honolulu, Hawaii
Hermann-Zilcher-Konservatorium
   *D-8700 Würzburg, Federal Republic of
   Germany*
Hofstra University
   Department of Music
   Hempstead, New York
Howard University
   Department of Music
   Washington, District of Columbia
University of Idaho
   School of Music
   Moscow, Idaho
University of Illinois
   School of Music
   Urbana, Illinois
Illinois Wesleyan University
   School of Music
   Bloomington, Illinois
Indiana State University
   Department of Music
   Terre Haute, Indiana
Indiana University - Bloomington
   School of Music
   Bloomington, Indiana
University of Iowa
   School of Music
   Iowa City, Iowa
Iowa State University
   Department of Music
   Ames, Iowa
Jackson State University
   Department of Music
   Jackson, Mississippi
James Madison University
   Department of Music
   Harrisonburg, Virginia
Jersey City State College
   Music Department
   Jersey City, New Jersey
The Juilliard School
   New York, New York
Kansas State University
   Department of Music
   Manhattan, Kansas

Kent State University
   School of Music
   Kent, Ohio
University of Kentucky
   School of Music
   Lexington, Kentucky
Lamar University
   Department of Music
   Beaumont, Texas
Lawrence University
   Conservatory of Music
   Appleton, Wisconsin
University of Louisville
   School of Music
   Louisville, Kentucky
Loyola University
   College of Music
   New Orleans, Louisiana
University of Maine
   School of Performing Arts
   Orono, Maine
Mansfield University
   Department of Music
   Mansfield, Pennsylvania
Marshall University
   Department of Music
   Huntington, West Virginia
University of Maryland - College Park
   Department of Music
   College Park, Maryland
Marywood College
   Music Department
   Scranton, Pennsylvania
University of Massachusetts at Amherst
   Department of Music and Dance
   Amherst, Massachusetts
University of Miami
   School of Music
   Coral Gables, Florida
Miami University
   Department of Music
   Oxford, Ohio
University of Michigan
   School of Music
   Ann Arbor, Michigan
Middle Tennessee State University
   Department of Music
   Murfreesboro, Tennessee
Millikin University
   School of Music
   Decatur, Illinois
University of Minnesota - Duluth
   Department of Music
   Duluth, Minnesota
University of Minnesota - Twin Cities
   School of Music
   Minneapolis, Minnesota
University of Missouri - Kansas City
   Conservatory of Music
   Kansas City, Missouri
Moorhead State University
   Music Department
   Moorhead, Minnesota
Morehead State University
   Department of Music
   Morehead, Kentucky
National Institute of the Arts
   Music Department
   *Taipei County, Taiwan (Republic of
   China)*
University of Nebraska - Lincoln
   School of Music
   Lincoln, Nebraska
University of Nebraska - Omaha
   Department of Music
   Omaha, Nebraska

University of Nevada, Las Vegas
  Department of Music
  Las Vegas, Nevada
University of New Hampshire
  Department of Music
  Durham, New Hampshire
University of New Orleans
  Department of Music
  New Orleans, Louisiana
New South Wales State Conservatorium of
  Music
  Sydney NSW 2000, Australia
Norfolk State University
  Department of Music
  Norfolk, Virginia
University of North Carolina at Chapel Hill
  Department of Music
  Chapel Hill, North Carolina
University of North Carolina at Greensboro
  School of Music
  Greensboro, North Carolina
North Texas State University
  School of Music
  Denton, Texas
Northeast Louisiana University
  School of Music
  Monroe, Louisiana
Northern Arizona University
  Music Department
  Flagstaff, Arizona
University of Northern Iowa
  School of Music
  Cedar Falls, Iowa
Northwestern State University of Louisiana
  Department of Music
  Natchitoches, Louisiana
Oakland University
  Department of Music, Theatre and
  Dance
  Rochester, Michigan
Oberlin College
  Conservatory of Music
  Oberlin, Ohio
Ohio Wesleyan University
  Department of Music
  Delaware, Ohio
University of Oklahoma
  School of Music
  Norman, Oklahoma
University of Oregon
  School of Music
  Eugene, Oregon
University of the Pacific
  Conservatory of Music
  Stockton, California
Pacific Lutheran University
  Department of Music
  Tacoma, Washington
Peabody Institute of The Johns Hopkins
  University
  Baltimore, Maryland
Pennsylvania State University
  School of Music
  University Park, Pennsylvania
Philadelphia College of the Performing Arts
  School of Music
  Philadelphia, Pennsylvania
Pittsburg State University
  Department of Music
  Pittsburg, Kansas
University of Pittsburgh
  Department of Music
  Pittsburgh, Pennsylvania
Pomona College
  Music Department
  Claremont, California

Queen's University
  School of Music
  Kingston, Ontario, Canada
University of Redlands
  School of Music
  Redlands, California
University of Regina
  Department of Music
  Regina, Saskatchewan, Canada
University of Rhode Island
  Department of Music
  Kingston, Rhode Island
Rice University
  Shepherd School of Music
  Houston, Texas
University of Rochester
  Eastman School of Music
  Rochester, New York
Rutgers, The State University of New Jersey
  Department of Music
  New Brunswick, New Jersey
St. Cloud State University
  Department of Music
  St. Cloud, Minnesota
Saint Louis Conservatory of Music
  St. Louis, Missouri
St. Olaf College
  Music Department
  Northfield, Minnesota
Samford University
  School of Music
  Birmingham, Alabama
San Diego State University
  Music Department
  San Diego, California
San Francisco Conservatory of Music
  San Francisco, California
San Francisco State University
  Department of Music
  San Francisco, California
San Jose State University
  Department of Music
  San Jose, California
University of Santo Tomas
  Conservatory of Music
  Manila, The Philippines
University of Saskatchewan
  Department of Music
  Saskatoon, Saskatchewan, Canada
Shenandoah College and Conservatory
  Winchester, Virginia
Smith College
  Department of Music
  Northampton, Massachusetts
University of South Dakota
  Music Department
  Vermillion, South Dakota
University of South Florida
  Department of Music
  Tampa, Florida
Southeast Missouri State University
  Department of Music
  Cape Girardeau, Missouri
University of Southern California
  School of Music
  Los Angeles, California
Southern Illinois University at Carbondale
  School of Music
  Carbondale, Illinois
Southern Illinois University at Edwardsville
  Department of Music
  Edwardsville, Illinois
Southern Methodist University
  Meadows School of the Arts
  Dallas, Texas

University of Southern Mississippi
  School of Music
  Hattiesburg, Mississippi
University of Southwestern Louisiana
  School of Music
  Lafayette, Louisiana
Staatliche Hochschule für Musik Freiburg
  *D-7800 Freiburg i. Br., Federal Republic
  of Germany*
Staatliche Hochschule für Musik Trossingen
  *D-7218 Trossingen 1, Federal Republic of
  Germany*
State University of New York at Stony
  Brook
  Department of Music
  Stony Brook, New York
State University of New York College at
  Fredonia
  School of Music
  Fredonia, New York
State University of New York College at
  Potsdam
  Crane School of Music
  Potsdam, New York
State University of New York College at
  Purchase
  Division of Music
  Purchase, New York
Stephen F. Austin State University
  Department of Music
  Nacogdoches, Texas
Teachers College of Columbia University
  Department of Music and Music
  Education
  New York, New York
Temple University
  Esther Boyer College of Music
  Philadelphia, Pennsylvania
University of Tennessee at Knoxville
  Department of Music
  Knoxville, Tennessee
University of Texas at El Paso
  Music Department
  El Paso, Texas
Texas Christian University
  Music Department
  Fort Worth, Texas
University of Toronto
  Faculty of Music
  Toronto, Ontario, Canada
Troy State University
  Department of Music
  Troy, Alabama
University of Tulsa
  Faculty of Music
  Tulsa, Oklahoma
Universidade do Rio de Janeiro
  Letters and Arts Center - Music Course
  22290 Rio de Janeiro, Brazil
Université de Montréal
  Faculty of Music
  Montréal, Québec, Canada
Valparaiso University
  Department of Music
  Valparaiso, Indiana
VanderCook College of Music
  Chicago, Illinois
Virginia Polytechnic Institute and State
  University
  Department of Music
  Blacksburg, Virginia
Vysoká Skola Mûzickych Umeni v Praha
  Academy of Music and Dramatic Arts
  1101 00 Prague 1, Czechoslovakia
Washington State University
  Department of Music

Pullman, Washington
West Chester University of Pennsylvania
  School of Music
  West Chester, Pennsylvania
West Virginia University
  Division of Music
  Morgantown, West Virginia
Western Illinois University
  Department of Music
  Macomb, Illinois
Western Kentucky University
  Department of Music
  Bowling Green, Kentucky
Western Michigan University
  School of Music
  Kalamazoo, Michigan
Wichita State University
  School of Music
  Wichita, Kansas
Wiesbadener Konservatorium und staatliche
anerkannte private Fachschule für
Musikerzieher e.V.
  (Conservatory and Seminary for Music
  Education)
  *6200 Wiesbaden, Federal Republic of
  Germany*
Wilfrid Laurier University
  Faculty of Music
  Waterloo, Ontario, Canada
William Carey College
  Winters School of Music
  Hattiesburg, Mississippi
University of Windsor
  School of Music
  Windsor, Ontario, Canada
University of Wisconsin - Eau Claire
  Department of Music
  Eau Claire, Wisconsin
University of Wisconsin - Stevens Point
  Department of Music
  Stevens Point, Wisconsin
Wright State University
  Department of Music
  Dayton, Ohio
University of Wyoming
  Music Department
  Laramie, Wyoming
Yale University
  School of Music
  New Haven, Connecticut
York University
  Department of Music
  North York, Ontario, Canada

BASS CLARINET

St. Cloud State University
  Department of Music
  St. Cloud, Minnesota

BASSOON

Acadia University
  School of Music
  Wolfville, Nova Scotia, Canada
Akademia Muzyczna w Krakowie
  31-038 Kraków, Poland
University of Alabama
  School of Music
  University, Alabama
American Conservatory of Music
  Chicago, Illinois
University of Arizona
  School of Music
  Tucson, Arizona
University of Arkansas
  Department of Music

Fayetteville, Arkansas
Arkansas Tech University
  Department of Music
  Russellville, Arkansas
Austin Peay State University
  Department of Music
  Clarksville, Tennessee
Baldwin-Wallace College
  Conservatory of Music
  Berea, Ohio
Baylor University
  School of Music
  Waco, Texas
Berklee College of Music
  Boston, Massachusetts
Bob Jones University
  Division of Music
  Greenville, South Carolina
Boston University
  School of Music
  Boston, Massachusetts
Bowling Green State University
  College of Musical Arts
  Bowling Green, Ohio
Bradley University
  Division of Music and Theatre Arts
  Peoria, Illinois
University of British Columbia
  School of Music
  Vancouver, British Columbia, Canada
Butler University
  Jordan College of Fine Arts
  Indianapolis, Indiana
University of California, Irvine
  School of Fine Arts
  Irvine, California
University of California, Los Angeles
  Department of Music
  Los Angeles, California
University of California, Riverside
  Department of Music
  Riverside, California
University of California, San Diego
  Department of Music
  La Jolla, California
University of California, Santa Barbara
  Department of Music
  Santa Barbara, California
University of California, Santa Cruz
  Music Board, Division of the Arts
  Santa Cruz, California
California State University, Hayward
  Department of Music
  Hayward, California
The Catholic University of America
  The Benjamin T. Rome School of Music
  Washington, District of Columbia
University of Central Arkansas
  Department of Music
  Conway, Arkansas
University of Central Florida
  Department of Music
  Orlando, Florida
Central Missouri State University
  Department of Music
  Warrensburg, Missouri
Central Washington University
  Department of Music
  Ellensburg, Washington
University of Cincinnati
  College-Conservatory of Music
  Cincinnati, Ohio
The Claremont Graduate School
  Music Department
  Claremont, California

Cleveland State University
  Department of Music
  Cleveland, Ohio
University of Colorado at Boulder
  College of Music
  Boulder, Colorado
Colorado State University
  Department of Music, Theatre, and
  Dance
  Fort Collins, Colorado
University of Connecticut
  Department of Music
  Storrs, Connecticut
Conservatorio di Musica "Santa Cecilia"
  00187 Rome, Italy
Conservatorio Nacional de Musica - La Paz
  (National Conservatory of Music - La
  Paz)
  La Paz, Bolivia
The Curtis Institute of Music
  Philadelphia, Pennsylvania
Delta State University
  Department of Music
  Cleveland, Mississippi
University of Denver
  Lamont School of Music
  Denver, Colorado
DePaul University
  School of Music
  Chicago, Illinois
DePauw University
  School of Music
  Greencastle, Indiana
Drake University
  Department of Music
  Des Moines, Iowa
Duquesne University
  School of Music
  Pittsburgh, Pennsylvania
East Carolina University
  School of Music
  Greenville, North Carolina
Eastern Illinois University
  Department of Music
  Charleston, Illinois
Eastern Michigan University
  Department of Music
  Ypsilanti, Michigan
Emporia State University
  Division of Music
  Emporia, Kansas
Escuela Nacional de Música
  Universidad Nacional Autónoma de
  México
  Mexico City, D.F. 04100, Mexico
Escuela Universitaria de Música -
Montevideo
  Montevideo, Uruguay
University of Florida
  Department of Music
  Gainesville, Florida
Florida State University
  School of Music
  Tallahassee, Florida
George Mason University
  Department of Performing Arts - Music
  Division
  Fairfax, Virginia
University of Hawaii at Manoa
  Music Department
  Honolulu, Hawaii
Hofstra University
  Department of Music
  Hempstead, New York
Howard University
  Department of Music

Washington, District of Columbia
University of Idaho
School of Music
Moscow, Idaho
University of Illinois
School of Music
Urbana, Illinois
Illinois Wesleyan University
School of Music
Bloomington, Illinois
Indiana State University
Department of Music
Terre Haute, Indiana
Indiana University - Bloomington
School of Music
Bloomington, Indiana
University of Iowa
School of Music
Iowa City, Iowa
Iowa State University
Department of Music
Ames, Iowa
Ithaca College
School of Music
Ithaca, New York
Jackson State University
Department of Music
Jackson, Mississippi
Jacksonville State University
Department of Music
Jacksonville, Alabama
James Madison University
Department of Music
Harrisonburg, Virginia
Jersey City State College
Music Department
Jersey City, New Jersey
The Juilliard School
New York, New York
University of Kansas
School of Fine Arts
Lawrence, Kansas
Kansas State University
Department of Music
Manhattan, Kansas
Kent State University
School of Music
Kent, Ohio
University of Kentucky
School of Music
Lexington, Kentucky
Lamar University
Department of Music
Beaumont, Texas
Lawrence University
Conservatory of Music
Appleton, Wisconsin
Louisiana Tech University
Department of Music
Ruston, Louisiana
University of Louisville
School of Music
Louisville, Kentucky
Loyola University
College of Music
New Orleans, Louisiana
University of Maine
School of Performing Arts
Orono, Maine
Mansfield University
Department of Music
Mansfield, Pennsylvania
Marshall University
Department of Music
Huntington, West Virginia

University of Maryland - College Park
Department of Music
College Park, Maryland
Marywood College
Music Department
Scranton, Pennsylvania
University of Massachusetts at Amherst
Department of Music and Dance
Amherst, Massachusetts
Miami University
Department of Music
Oxford, Ohio
University of Michigan
School of Music
Ann Arbor, Michigan
Middle Tennessee State University
Department of Music
Murfreesboro, Tennessee
Millikin University
School of Music
Decatur, Illinois
Mills College
Music Department
Oakland, California
University of Minnesota - Duluth
Department of Music
Duluth, Minnesota
University of Minnesota - Twin Cities
School of Music
Minneapolis, Minnesota
University of Missouri - Kansas City
Conservatory of Music
Kansas City, Missouri
Morehead State University
Department of Music
Morehead, Kentucky
National Institute of the Arts
Music Department
Taipei County, Taiwan (Republic of China)
University of Nebraska - Lincoln
School of Music
Lincoln, Nebraska
University of Nebraska - Omaha
Department of Music
Omaha, Nebraska
University of Nevada, Las Vegas
Department of Music
Las Vegas, Nevada
University of New Orleans
Department of Music
New Orleans, Louisiana
Norfolk State University
Department of Music
Norfolk, Virginia
University of North Carolina at Chapel Hill
Department of Music
Chapel Hill, North Carolina
University of North Carolina at Greensboro
School of Music
Greensboro, North Carolina
North Texas State University
School of Music
Denton, Texas
Northeast Louisiana University
School of Music
Monroe, Louisiana
Northern Arizona University
Music Department
Flagstaff, Arizona
University of Northern Iowa
School of Music
Cedar Falls, Iowa
Northwestern State University of Louisiana
Department of Music
Natchitoches, Louisiana

Northwestern University
School of Music
Evanston, Illinois
Oakland University
Department of Music, Theatre and Dance
Rochester, Michigan
Oberlin College
Conservatory of Music
Oberlin, Ohio
Ohio Wesleyan University
Department of Music
Delaware, Ohio
University of Oregon
School of Music
Eugene, Oregon
University of the Pacific
Conservatory of Music
Stockton, California
Pacific Lutheran University
Department of Music
Tacoma, Washington
Peabody Institute of The Johns Hopkins University
Baltimore, Maryland
Pennsylvania State University
School of Music
University Park, Pennsylvania
Philadelphia College of the Performing Arts
School of Music
Philadelphia, Pennsylvania
Pittsburg State University
Department of Music
Pittsburg, Kansas
Pomona College
Music Department
Claremont, California
Queen's University
School of Music
Kingston, Ontario, Canada
University of Redlands
School of Music
Redlands, California
University of Regina
Department of Music
Regina, Saskatchewan, Canada
University of Rhode Island
Department of Music
Kingston, Rhode Island
Rice University
Shepherd School of Music
Houston, Texas
University of Rochester
Eastman School of Music
Rochester, New York
Rutgers, The State University of New Jersey
Department of Music
New Brunswick, New Jersey
St. Cloud State University
Department of Music
St. Cloud, Minnesota
Saint Louis Conservatory of Music
St. Louis, Missouri
St. Olaf College
Music Department
Northfield, Minnesota
San Diego State University
Music Department
San Diego, California
San Francisco Conservatory of Music
San Francisco, California
San Francisco State University
Department of Music
San Francisco, California
San Jose State University
Department of Music

San Jose, California
University of Saskatchewan
Department of Music
Saskatoon, Saskatchewan, Canada
Smith College
Department of Music
Northampton, Massachusetts
University of South Dakota
Music Department
Vermillion, South Dakota
University of South Florida
Department of Music
Tampa, Florida
Southeast Missouri State University
Department of Music
Cape Girardeau, Missouri
Southeastern Oklahoma State University
Department of Music
Durant, Oklahoma
Southern Illinois University at Carbondale
School of Music
Carbondale, Illinois
Southern Illinois University at Edwardsville
Department of Music
Edwardsville, Illinois
Southern Methodist University
Meadows School of the Arts
Dallas, Texas
University of Southern Mississippi
School of Music
Hattiesburg, Mississippi
University of Southwestern Louisiana
School of Music
Lafayette, Louisiana
Staatliche Hochschule für Musik Trossingen
D-7218 Trossingen 1, Federal Republic of Germany
State University of New York at Stony Brook
Department of Music
Stony Brook, New York
State University of New York College at Fredonia
School of Music
Fredonia, New York
State University of New York College at Potsdam
Crane School of Music
Potsdam, New York
State University of New York College at Purchase
Division of Music
Purchase, New York
Stephen F. Austin State University
Department of Music
Nacogdoches, Texas
Syracuse University
School of Music
Syracuse, New York
Teachers College of Columbia University
Department of Music and Music Education
New York, New York
Temple University
Esther Boyer College of Music
Philadelphia, Pennsylvania
University of Tennessee at Knoxville
Department of Music
Knoxville, Tennessee
University of Texas at El Paso
Music Department
El Paso, Texas
Texas Christian University
Music Department
Fort Worth, Texas

Toho Gakuen School of Music
Tokyo, Japan
University of Toronto
Faculty of Music
Toronto, Ontario, Canada
Troy State University
Department of Music
Troy, Alabama
University of Tulsa
Faculty of Music
Tulsa, Oklahoma
Universidad de Antioquía
Facultad de Artes, Departamento de Música
Medellín, Colombia
Universidade do Rio de Janeiro
Letters and Arts Center - Music Course
22290 Rio de Janeiro, Brazil
Université de Montréal
Faculty of Music
Montréal, Québec, Canada
Valparaiso University
Department of Music
Valparaiso, Indiana
VanderCook College of Music
Chicago, Illinois
Virginia Polytechnic Institute and State University
Department of Music
Blacksburg, Virginia
Vysoká Skola Mûzickych Umeni v Praha
Academy of Music and Dramatic Arts
1101 00 Prague 1, Czechoslovakia
Washington State University
Department of Music
Pullman, Washington
West Chester University of Pennsylvania
School of Music
West Chester, Pennsylvania
West Virginia University
Division of Music
Morgantown, West Virginia
Western Illinois University
Department of Music
Macomb, Illinois
Western Michigan University
School of Music
Kalamazoo, Michigan
Wichita State University
School of Music
Wichita, Kansas
Wilfrid Laurier University
Faculty of Music
Waterloo, Ontario, Canada
William Carey College
Winters School of Music
Hattiesburg, Mississippi
University of Windsor
School of Music
Windsor, Ontario, Canada
University of Wisconsin - Eau Claire
Department of Music
Eau Claire, Wisconsin
University of Wisconsin - Madison
School of Music
Madison, Wisconsin
University of Wisconsin - Milwaukee
Music Department
Milwaukee, Wisconsin
University of Wisconsin - Stevens Point
Department of Music
Stevens Point, Wisconsin
Wright State University
Department of Music
Dayton, Ohio

University of Wyoming
Music Department
Laramie, Wyoming
Yale College (Yale University)
Department of Music
New Haven, Connecticut
Yale University
School of Music
New Haven, Connecticut
Youngstown State University
Dana School of Music
Youngstown, Ohio

BONANG

Wesleyan University
Department of Music
Middletown, Connecticut

BRASS

Akademia Muzyczna w Lódź
(Academy of Music of Lódź)
90-716 Lódź, Poland
Akademia Muzycznaj im. Fryderyka Chopina w Warzawie
(Frederic Chopin Academy of Music of Warsaw)
00-368 Warsaw, Poland
Akademie voor Musiek
Hilversum Postkode 1217 KR, Netherlands
University of Akron
Department of Music
Akron, Ohio
Alabama State University
School of Music
Montgomery, Alabama
University of Alberta
Department of Music
Edmonton, Alberta, Canada
Andrews University
Department of Music
Berrien Springs, Michigan
Appalachian State University
Department of Music
Boone, North Carolina
Arizona State University
School of Music
Tempe, Arizona
Arkansas State University
Department of Music
State University, Arkansas
Auburn University
Department of Music
Auburn, Alabama
Azusa Pacific University
School of Music
Azusa, California
Ball State University
School of Music
Muncie, Indiana
Bemidji State University
Music Department
Bemidji, Minnesota
Bennington College
Music Department
Bennington, Vermont
Biola University
Department of Music
La Mirada, California
Boston Conservatory of Music
Boston, Massachusetts
Brandon University
School of Music
Brandon, Manitoba, Canada

Brigham Young University
Department of Music
Provo, Utah
Brown University
Department of Music
Providence, Rhode Island
University of California, Berkeley
Department of Music
Berkeley, California
University of California, Davis
Department of Music
Davis, California
California Institute of the Arts
School of Music
Valencia, California
California State University, Chico
Department of Music
Chico, California
California State University, Fresno
Department of Music
Fresno, California
California State University, Fullerton
Department of Music
Fullerton, California
California State University, Long Beach
Department of Music
Long Beach, California
California State University, Los Angeles
Department of Music
Los Angeles, California
California State University, Northridge
Music Department
Northridge, California
Carnegie-Mellon University
Department of Music
Pittsburgh, Pennsylvania
Case Western Reserve University
Department of Music
Cleveland, Ohio
Central Conservatory of Music
Beijing, People's Republic of China
Central Michigan University
Department of Music
Mount Pleasant, Michigan
Central State University
Department of Music
Edmond, Oklahoma
City of Leeds College of Music
Leeds LS2 8BH, United Kingdom
City University of New York - Brooklyn
College
Conservatory of Music
Brooklyn, New York
City University of New York - City College
Department of Music
New York, New York
City University of New York - Hunter
College
Department of Music
New York, New York
City University of New York - Queens
College
The Aaron Copland School of Music
Flushing, New York
Cleveland Institute of Music
Cleveland, Ohio
University of Colorado at Denver
College of Music
Denver, Colorado
Columbia University
Department of Music
New York, New York
Columbus College
Department of Music
Columbus, Georgia

Combs College of Music
Philadelphia, Pennsylvania
Conservatoire de Musique de La
Chaux-de-Fonds - Le Locle
2300 La Chaux-de-Fonds, Switzerland
Conservatorio di Musica "Claudio
Monteverdi"
I-39100 Bolzano, Italy
Conservatorio Nacional de Música
(National Conservatory of Music)
Lima 1, Peru
Converse College
School of Music
Spartanburg, South Carolina
Cornell University
Department of Music
Ithaca, New York
Dalhousie University
Department of Music
Halifax, Nova Scotia, Canada
University of Delaware
Department of Music
Newark, Delaware
Duke University
Department of Music
Durham, North Carolina
East Texas State University
Department of Music
Commerce, Texas
Eastern Kentucky University
Department of Music
Richmond, Kentucky
Eastern Michigan University
Department of Music
Ypsilanti, Michigan
Eastern New Mexico University
School of Music
Portales, New Mexico
Eastern Washington University
Department of Music
Cheney, Washington
Escuela de Música - Heredia
Universidad Nacional
Heredia, Costa Rica
Evangelische Kirchenmusikschule der
Kirchenprovinz Sachsen
(Evangelical Church Music School of the
Church Province Saxony)
*DDR-4020 Halle (Saale), German
Democratic Republic*
University of Evansville
Music Department
Evansville, Indiana
Ferenc Liszt Academy of Music
Budapest VI, Hungary
University of Florida
Department of Music
Gainesville, Florida
Fort Hays State University
Department of Music
Hays, Kansas
George Mason University
Department of Performing Arts - Music
Division
Fairfax, Virginia
University of Georgia
School of Music
Athens, Georgia
Georgia Southern College
Department of Music
Statesboro, Georgia
Georgia State University
School of Music
Atlanta, Georgia
Glassboro State College
Department of Music

Glassboro, New Jersey
Guildhall School of Music and Drama
London EC2Y 8DT, United Kingdom
Hardin-Simmons University
School of Music
Abilene, Texas
Harvard University
Department of Music
Cambridge, Massachusetts
Henderson State University
Department of Music
Arkadelphia, Arkansas
Hochschule für Music Franz Liszt
*DDR 5300 Weimar, German Democratic
Republic*
Hochschule für Musik - Würzburg
*D-8700 Würzburg, Federal Republic of
Germany*
Hochschule für Musik Carl Maria von
Weber
*DDR 8010 Dresden, German Democratic
Republic*
Hochschule für Musik Felix
Mendelssohn-Bartholdy
*7010 Leipzig, German Democratic
Republic*
Hochschule für Musik und Theater
Hannover
*3000 Hannover 1, Federal Republic of
Germany*
The Hong Kong Academy for Performing
Arts
School of Music
Wanchai, Hong Kong
Hoschschule für Music Hans Eisler
*DDR Berlin 1080, German Democratic
Republic*
University of Houston
School of Music
Houston, Texas
Illinois State University
Department of Music
Normal, Illinois
Indiana University of Pennsylvania
Department of Music
Indiana, Pennsylvania
Instituto Superior de Arte
Facultad de Música
Playa, Cuba
The Jerusalem Rubin Academy of Music
and Dance
Jerusalem, Israel
Karol Szymanowski Academy of Music of
Katowice
Katowice, Poland
Koninklijk Muziekconservatorium van
Brussel
1000 Brussels, Belgium
Konzervatoř v Praze
(State Conservatory Prague)
Praha 110 00, Czechoslovakia
Konzervatorium - Bratislava
Bratislava 811 06, Czechoslovakia
Kuopion Konservatorio
70100 Kuopio, Finland
Leningrad N.A. Rimsky-Korsakov State
Conservatory
*192041 Leningrad, Rossiskaja SFSR,
U.S.S.R.*
Lewis and Clark College
Music Department
Portland, Oregon
Long Island University - C.W. Post Campus
Music Department
Greenvale, New York

Louisiana State University
  School of Music
  Baton Rouge, Louisiana
University of Lowell
  College of Music
  Lowell, Massachusetts
Manhattan School of Music
  New York, New York
Mankato State University
  Department of Music
  Mankato, Minnesota
Mannes College of Music
  New York, New York
University of Maryland - Baltimore County
  Department of Music
  Catonsville, Maryland
McGill University
  Faculty of Music
  Montreal, Québec, Canada
McMaster University
  Department of Music
  Hamilton, Ontario, Canada
McNeese State University
  Department of Music
  Lake Charles, Louisiana
Memphis State University
  Music Department
  Memphis, Tennessee
Michigan State University
  School of Music
  East Lansing, Michigan
University of Mississippi
  Department of Music
  University, Mississippi
University of Missouri - Columbia
  Department of Music
  Columbia, Missouri
University of Montana
  Department of Music
  Missoula, Montana
Montana State University
  Department of Music
  Bozeman, Montana
Montclair State College
  Department of Music
  Upper Montclair, New Jersey
University of Montevallo
  Department of Music
  Montevallo, Alabama
Musik-Akademie der Stadt Basel
  (Konservatorium)
  Konservatorium (Musikhochschule)
  Basel, Switzerland
Musikhögskolan i Stockholm
  National College of Music
  115 31 Stockholm, Sweden
Musikschule und Konservatorium
  Schaffhausen
  Schaffhausen, Switzerland
National Institute of the Arts
  Music Department
  Taipei County, Taiwan (Republic of China)
University of Nevada, Reno
  Department of Music
  Reno, Nevada
New England Conservatory
  Boston, Massachusetts
University of New Hampshire
  Department of Music
  Durham, New Hampshire
University of New Mexico
  Department of Music
  Albuquerque, New Mexico
New Mexico State University
  Department of Music

Las Cruces, New Mexico
New York University - School of Education,
  Health, Nursing, and Arts Professions
  Department of Music and Music
  Education
  New York, New York
Nikos Skalkotas Conservatory
  Athens 11141, Greece
Norges Musikkhøgskole
  (The Norwegian State Academy of
  Music)
  N-0130 Oslo 1, Norway
North Carolina School of the Arts
  School of Music
  Winston-Salem, North Carolina
University of North Dakota
  Department of Music
  Grand Forks, North Dakota
Northeast Missouri State University
  Division of Fine Arts
  Kirksville, Missouri
Northeastern Illinois University
  Department of Music
  Chicago, Illinois
University of Northern Colorado
  School of Music
  Greeley, Colorado
Northern Illinois University
  School of Music
  DeKalb, Illinois
University of Notre Dame
  Department of Music
  Notre Dame, Indiana
The Ohio State University
  School of Music
  Columbus, Ohio
Ohio University
  School of Music
  Athens, Ohio
University of Oklahoma
  School of Music
  Norman, Oklahoma
Oklahoma Baptist University
  Department of Music
  Shawnee, Oklahoma
Oklahoma City University
  School of Music and Performing Arts
  Oklahoma City, Oklahoma
Oregon State University
  Department of Music
  Corvallis, Oregon
Osaka Ongaku Daigaku
  (Osaka College of Music)
  Osaka 561, Japan
Ouachita Baptist University
  School of Music
  Arkadelphia, Arkansas
University of Pennsylvania
  Department of Music
  Philadelphia, Pennsylvania
University of the Philippines
  College of Music
  Quezon City, The Philippines
Pohjois-Kymen Musiikkiopisto
  (North Kymi Music Institute)
  45100 Kouvola, Finland
Portland State University
  Department of Music
  Portland, Oregon
Princeton University
  Department of Music
  Princeton, New Jersey
University of Puget Sound
  School of Music
  Tacoma, Washington

Radford University
  Department of Music
  Radford, Virginia
Real Conservatorio Superior de Música de
  Madrid
  (Royal Academy of Music)
  Madrid 13, Spain
Rogaland Musikkonservatorium
  N-4000 Stavanger, Norway
Roosevelt University
  Chicago Musical College
  Chicago, Illinois
Royal Academy of Music
  London NW1 5HT, United Kingdom
Royal College of Music
  London, SW7 2BS, United Kingdom
Royal Northern College of Music
  Manchester M13 9RD, United Kingdom
Royal Scottish Academy of Music and
  Drama
  Glasgow G2 1BS, United Kingdom
Sam Houston State University
  Department of Music
  Huntsville, Texas
University of Santo Tomas
  Conservatory of Music
  Manila, The Philippines
Shenandoah College and Conservatory
  Winchester, Virginia
Shengyang Conservatory of Music
  *Shengyang, Liaoning Province, People's
  Republic of China*
University of South Carolina
  School of Music
  Columbia, South Carolina
Southeastern Louisiana University
  Department of Music
  Hammond, Louisiana
Southern Baptist Theological Seminary
  School of Church Music
  Louisville, Kentucky
University of Southern California
  School of Music
  Los Angeles, California
Southwest Texas State University
  Department of Music
  San Marcos, Texas
Southwestern Baptist Theological Seminary
  School of Church Music
  Fort Worth, Texas
Southwestern Oklahoma State University
  Department of Music
  Weatherford, Oklahoma
Staatliche Hochschule für Musik Freiburg
  *D-7800 Freiburg i. Br., Federal Republic
  of Germany*
Staatliche Hochschule für Musik Rheinland
  - Köln
  *D-5000 Köln 1, Federal Republic of
  Germany*
Staatliche Hochschule für Musik
  Westfalen-Lippe
  Institut Dortmund
  *D-4600 Dortmund 1, Federal Republic of
  Germany*
Stanford University
  Department of Music
  Stanford, California
State University of New York at
  Binghamton
  Department of Music
  Binghamton, New York
State University of New York at Buffalo
  Department of Music
  Buffalo, New York

State University of New York College at New Paltz
Department of Music
New Paltz, New York
Stedelijke Muziekpedagogische Akademie
Leeuwarden, Netherlands
Stetson University
School of Music
Deland, Florida
Tampereen Konservatorio
33230 Tampere, Finland
Tasmanian Conservatorium of Music
Hobart, Tasmania 7001, Australia
Tel Aviv University
Faculty of Fine Arts
Tel-Aviv, Israel
University of Tennessee at Chattanooga
Cadek Department of Music
Chattanooga, Tennessee
University of Texas at Arlington
Department of Music
Arlington, Texas
University of Texas at Austin
Department of Music
Austin, Texas
University of Texas at San Antonio
Division of Music
San Antonio, Texas
Texas Southern University
Department of Music
Houston, Texas
Texas Tech University
Department of Music
Lubbock, Texas
Texas Woman's University
Department of Music and Drama
Denton, Texas
The Tokyo College of Music
Tokyo 171, Japan
Towson State University
Department of Music
Towson, Maryland
Trenton State College
Music Department
Trenton, New Jersey
Trinity College of Music
London W1M 6AQ, United Kingdom
Tulane University
Newcomb College
New Orleans, Louisiana
Ueno Gakuen College
Tokyo 110, Japan
Universidade do São Paulo
Department of Music
05508 São Paulo, Brazil
University of Utah
Department of Music
Salt Lake City, Utah
Valdosta State College
Department of Music
Valdosta, Georgia
University of Vermont
Department of Music
Burlington, Vermont
University of Victoria
School of Music
Victoria, British Columbia, Canada
University of Virginia
McIntire Department of Music
Charlottesville, Virginia
Virginia Commonwealth University
Department of Music
Richmond, Virginia
Virginia State University
Department of Music Education
Petersburg, Virginia

University of Washington
School of Music
Seattle, Washington
Washington University
Department of Music
St. Louis, Missouri
Wayne State University
Department of Music
Detroit, Michigan
Webster University
Department of Music
St. Louis, Missouri
Welsh College of Music and Drama
Cardiff, CF1 3ER, United Kingdom
Wesleyan University
Department of Music
Middletown, Connecticut
West Georgia College
Department of Music
Carrollton, Georgia
West Texas State University
Department of Music
Canyon, Texas
University of Western Ontario
Faculty of Music
London, Ontario, Canada
Western Washington University
Department of Music
Bellingham, Washington
Wheaton College
Conservatory of Music
Wheaton, Illinois
Willamette University
Department of Music
Salem, Oregon
William Paterson College
Department of Music
Wayne, New Jersey
Winthrop College
School of Music
Rock Hill, South Carolina
University of Wisconsin - La Crosse
Department of Music
La Crosse, Wisconsin
University of Wisconsin - Madison
School of Music
Madison, Wisconsin
University of Wisconsin - Oshkosh
Department of Music
Oshkosh, Wisconsin
University of Wisconsin - Whitewater
Department of Music
Whitewater, Wisconsin
Yale College (Yale University)
Department of Music
New Haven, Connecticut
Yale University
School of Music
New Haven, Connecticut
York University
Department of Music
North York, Ontario, Canada
Zeneiskolai Tanárkepző Intézet
(Music Teachers Training Institute of the Liszt Academy of Music)
Budapest 1052, Hungary

BURMESE HARP AND ORCHESTRA

Institute of Fine Arts
Faculty of Music
Rangoon, Burma
Mandalay School of Music, Dance, Painting, and Sculpture
Mandalay, Burma

CARILLON

University of California, Riverside
Department of Music
Riverside, California
University of California, Santa Barbara
Department of Music
Santa Barbara, California
University of Florida
Department of Music
Gainesville, Florida
Indiana University - Bloomington
School of Music
Bloomington, Indiana
Iowa State University
Department of Music
Ames, Iowa
Koninklijk Beiaardschool Jef Denyn
2800 Mechelen, Belgium
University of North Dakota
Department of Music
Grand Forks, North Dakota
Samford University
School of Music
Birmingham, Alabama

CELLO

University of British Columbia
School of Music
Vancouver, British Columbia, Canada
Butler University
Jordan College of Fine Arts
Indianapolis, Indiana
University of Cincinnati
College-Conservatory of Music
Cincinnati, Ohio
Florida State University
School of Music
Tallahassee, Florida
University of the Pacific
Conservatory of Music
Stockton, California
San Diego State University
Music Department
San Diego, California

CEMBALO

Toho Gakuen School of Music
Tokyo, Japan

CHINESE INSTRUMENTS

University of British Columbia
School of Music
Vancouver, British Columbia, Canada
The Hong Kong Academy for Performing Arts
School of Music
Wanchai, Hong Kong
National Institute of the Arts
Music Department
Taipei County, Taiwan (Republic of China)
Shengyang Conservatory of Music
Shengyang, Liaoning Province, People's Republic of China
Sichuan Conservatory of Music
Chengdu, Sichuan, People's Republic of China

CHINESE NATIONAL INSTRUMENTS

Central Conservatory of Music
Beijing, People's Republic of China

CHINESE SINGING

Sichuan Conservatory of Music
Chengdu, Sichuan, People's Republic of China

CLARINET

Acadia University
School of Music
Wolfville, Nova Scotia, Canada
Akademia Muzyczna w Krakowie
31-038 Kraków, Poland
University of Alabama
School of Music
University, Alabama
University of Alaska
Music Department
Fairbanks, Alaska
American Conservatory of Music
Chicago, Illinois
University of Arizona
School of Music
Tucson, Arizona
University of Arkansas
Department of Music
Fayetteville, Arkansas
Arkansas Tech University
Department of Music
Russellville, Arkansas
Austin Peay State University
Department of Music
Clarksville, Tennessee
Baldwin-Wallace College
Conservatory of Music
Berea, Ohio
Baylor University
School of Music
Waco, Texas
Berklee College of Music
Boston, Massachusetts
Bob Jones University
Division of Music
Greenville, South Carolina
Boston University
School of Music
Boston, Massachusetts
Bowling Green State University
College of Musical Arts
Bowling Green, Ohio
Bradley University
Division of Music and Theatre Arts
Peoria, Illinois
University of British Columbia
School of Music
Vancouver, British Columbia, Canada
Bulgarian State Conservatoire
Sofia 1505, Bulgaria
Butler University
Jordan College of Fine Arts
Indianapolis, Indiana
University of California, Irvine
School of Fine Arts
Irvine, California
University of California, Los Angeles
Department of Music
Los Angeles, California
University of California, Riverside
Department of Music
Riverside, California
University of California, San Diego
Department of Music
La Jolla, California
University of California, Santa Barbara
Department of Music
Santa Barbara, California

University of California, Santa Cruz
Music Board, Division of the Arts
Santa Cruz, California
California State University, Hayward
Department of Music
Hayward, California
The Catholic University of America
The Benjamin T. Rome School of Music
Washington, District of Columbia
University of Central Arkansas
Department of Music
Conway, Arkansas
University of Central Florida
Department of Music
Orlando, Florida
Central Missouri State University
Department of Music
Warrensburg, Missouri
Central Washington University
Department of Music
Ellensburg, Washington
University of Cincinnati
College-Conservatory of Music
Cincinnati, Ohio
The Claremont Graduate School
Music Department
Claremont, California
Cleveland State University
Department of Music
Cleveland, Ohio
Colorado State University
Department of Music, Theatre, and Dance
Fort Collins, Colorado
Conservatorio di Musica "Santa Cecilia"
00187 Rome, Italy
Conservatorio Nacional de Musica - La Paz
(National Conservatory of Music - La Paz)
La Paz, Bolivia
The Curtis Institute of Music
Philadelphia, Pennsylvania
Delta State University
Department of Music
Cleveland, Mississippi
University of Denver
Lamont School of Music
Denver, Colorado
DePaul University
School of Music
Chicago, Illinois
DePauw University
School of Music
Greencastle, Indiana
Drake University
Department of Music
Des Moines, Iowa
Duquesne University
School of Music
Pittsburgh, Pennsylvania
East Carolina University
School of Music
Greenville, North Carolina
Eastern Illinois University
Department of Music
Charleston, Illinois
Eastern Michigan University
Department of Music
Ypsilanti, Michigan
Emporia State University
Division of Music
Emporia, Kansas
Escuela Nacional de Música
Universidad Nacional Autónoma de México
Mexico City, D.F. 04100, Mexico

Escuela Universitaria de Música - Montevideo
Montevideo, Uruguay
University of Florida
Department of Music
Gainesville, Florida
Florida State University
School of Music
Tallahassee, Florida
George Mason University
Department of Performing Arts - Music Division
Fairfax, Virginia
University of Hartford
Hartt School of Music
West Hartford, Connecticut
University of Hawaii at Manoa
Music Department
Honolulu, Hawaii
Hermann-Zilcher-Konservatorium
D-8700 Würzburg, Federal Republic of Germany
Hofstra University
Department of Music
Hempstead, New York
Howard University
Department of Music
Washington, District of Columbia
University of Idaho
School of Music
Moscow, Idaho
University of Illinois
School of Music
Urbana, Illinois
Illinois Wesleyan University
School of Music
Bloomington, Illinois
Indiana State University
Department of Music
Terre Haute, Indiana
Indiana University - Bloomington
School of Music
Bloomington, Indiana
University of Iowa
School of Music
Iowa City, Iowa
Iowa State University
Department of Music
Ames, Iowa
Ithaca College
School of Music
Ithaca, New York
Jackson State University
Department of Music
Jackson, Mississippi
Jacksonville State University
Department of Music
Jacksonville, Alabama
James Madison University
Department of Music
Harrisonburg, Virginia
Jersey City State College
Music Department
Jersey City, New Jersey
The Juilliard School
New York, New York
University of Kansas
School of Fine Arts
Lawrence, Kansas
Kansas State University
Department of Music
Manhattan, Kansas
Kent State University
School of Music
Kent, Ohio

University of Kentucky
  School of Music
  Lexington, Kentucky
Kenya Conservatoire of Music
  Nairobi, Kenya
Lamar University
  Department of Music
  Beaumont, Texas
Lawrence University
  Conservatory of Music
  Appleton, Wisconsin
Louisiana Tech University
  Department of Music
  Ruston, Louisiana
University of Louisville
  School of Music
  Louisville, Kentucky
University of Maine
  School of Performing Arts
  Orono, Maine
Mansfield University
  Department of Music
  Mansfield, Pennsylvania
Marshall University
  Department of Music
  Huntington, West Virginia
University of Maryland - College Park
  Department of Music
  College Park, Maryland
Marywood College
  Music Department
  Scranton, Pennsylvania
University of Massachusetts at Amherst
  Department of Music and Dance
  Amherst, Massachusetts
University of Miami
  School of Music
  Coral Gables, Florida
Miami University
  Department of Music
  Oxford, Ohio
University of Michigan
  School of Music
  Ann Arbor, Michigan
Middle Tennessee State University
  Department of Music
  Murfreesboro, Tennessee
Millikin University
  School of Music
  Decatur, Illinois
Mills College
  Music Department
  Oakland, California
University of Minnesota - Duluth
  Department of Music
  Duluth, Minnesota
University of Minnesota - Twin Cities
  School of Music
  Minneapolis, Minnesota
University of Missouri - Kansas City
  Conservatory of Music
  Kansas City, Missouri
Moorhead State University
  Music Department
  Moorhead, Minnesota
Morehead State University
  Department of Music
  Morehead, Kentucky
National Institute of the Arts
  Music Department
  Taipei County, Taiwan (Republic of China)
University of Nebraska - Lincoln
  School of Music
  Lincoln, Nebraska

University of Nebraska - Omaha
  Department of Music
  Omaha, Nebraska
University of Nevada, Las Vegas
  Department of Music
  Las Vegas, Nevada
University of New Orleans
  Department of Music
  New Orleans, Louisiana
Norfolk State University
  Department of Music
  Norfolk, Virginia
University of North Carolina at Chapel Hill
  Department of Music
  Chapel Hill, North Carolina
University of North Carolina at Greensboro
  School of Music
  Greensboro, North Carolina
North Texas State University
  School of Music
  Denton, Texas
Northeast Louisiana University
  School of Music
  Monroe, Louisiana
Northern Arizona University
  Music Department
  Flagstaff, Arizona
University of Northern Iowa
  School of Music
  Cedar Falls, Iowa
Northwestern State University of Louisiana
  Department of Music
  Natchitoches, Louisiana
Northwestern University
  School of Music
  Evanston, Illinois
Oakland University
  Department of Music, Theatre and Dance
  Rochester, Michigan
Oberlin College
  Conservatory of Music
  Oberlin, Ohio
Ohio Wesleyan University
  Department of Music
  Delaware, Ohio
Oklahoma Baptist University
  Department of Music
  Shawnee, Oklahoma
University of Oregon
  School of Music
  Eugene, Oregon
University of the Pacific
  Conservatory of Music
  Stockton, California
Pacific Lutheran University
  Department of Music
  Tacoma, Washington
Peabody Institute of The Johns Hopkins University
  Baltimore, Maryland
Pennsylvania State University
  School of Music
  University Park, Pennsylvania
Philadelphia College of the Performing Arts
  School of Music
  Philadelphia, Pennsylvania
Pittsburg State University
  Department of Music
  Pittsburg, Kansas
University of Pittsburgh
  Department of Music
  Pittsburgh, Pennsylvania
Pomona College
  Music Department
  Claremont, California

Queen's University
  School of Music
  Kingston, Ontario, Canada
University of Redlands
  School of Music
  Redlands, California
University of Regina
  Department of Music
  Regina, Saskatchewan, Canada
University of Rhode Island
  Department of Music
  Kingston, Rhode Island
Rice University
  Shepherd School of Music
  Houston, Texas
University of Rochester
  Eastman School of Music
  Rochester, New York
Rutgers, The State University of New Jersey
  Department of Music
  New Brunswick, New Jersey
St. Cloud State University
  Department of Music
  St. Cloud, Minnesota
Saint Louis Conservatory of Music
  St. Louis, Missouri
St. Olaf College
  Music Department
  Northfield, Minnesota
Samford University
  School of Music
  Birmingham, Alabama
San Diego State University
  Music Department
  San Diego, California
San Francisco Conservatory of Music
  San Francisco, California
San Francisco State University
  Department of Music
  San Francisco, California
San Jose State University
  Department of Music
  San Jose, California
University of Saskatchewan
  Department of Music
  Saskatoon, Saskatchewan, Canada
Smith College
  Department of Music
  Northampton, Massachusetts
University of South Dakota
  Music Department
  Vermillion, South Dakota
Southeast Missouri State University
  Department of Music
  Cape Girardeau, Missouri
Southeastern Oklahoma State University
  Department of Music
  Durant, Oklahoma
Southern Illinois University at Carbondale
  School of Music
  Carbondale, Illinois
Southern Illinois University at Edwardsville
  Department of Music
  Edwardsville, Illinois
Southern Methodist University
  Meadows School of the Arts
  Dallas, Texas
University of Southern Mississippi
  School of Music
  Hattiesburg, Mississippi
University of Southwestern Louisiana
  School of Music
  Lafayette, Louisiana
Staatliche Hochschule für Musik Trossingen
  D-7218 Trossingen 1, Federal Republic of Germany

State University of New York at Stony
Brook
  Department of Music
  Stony Brook, New York
State University of New York College at
Fredonia
  School of Music
  Fredonia, New York
State University of New York College at
Potsdam
  Crane School of Music
  Potsdam, New York
State University of New York College at
Purchase
  Division of Music
  Purchase, New York
Stephen F. Austin State University
  Department of Music
  Nacogdoches, Texas
Syracuse University
  School of Music
  Syracuse, New York
Teachers College of Columbia University
  Department of Music and Music
  Education
  New York, New York
Temple University
  Esther Boyer College of Music
  Philadelphia, Pennsylvania
University of Tennessee at Knoxville
  Department of Music
  Knoxville, Tennessee
University of Texas at El Paso
  Music Department
  El Paso, Texas
Texas Christian University
  Music Department
  Fort Worth, Texas
Toho Gakuen School of Music
  Tokyo, Japan
University of Toronto
  Faculty of Music
  Toronto, Ontario, Canada
Troy State University
  Department of Music
  Troy, Alabama
University of Tulsa
  Faculty of Music
  Tulsa, Oklahoma
Universidad de Antioquía
  Facultad de Artes, Departamento de
  Música
  Medellín, Colombia
Universidade do Rio de Janeiro
  Letters and Arts Center - Music Course
  22290 Rio de Janeiro, Brazil
Université de Montréal
  Faculty of Music
  Montréal, Québec, Canada
Valparaiso University
  Department of Music
  Valparaiso, Indiana
VanderCook College of Music
  Chicago, Illinois
Virginia Polytechnic Institute and State
University
  Department of Music
  Blacksburg, Virginia
Vysoká Skola Mûzickych Umeni v Praha
  Academy of Music and Dramatic Arts
  1101 00 Prague 1, Czechoslovakia
Washington State University
  Department of Music
  Pullman, Washington
West Chester University of Pennsylvania
  School of Music

West Chester, Pennsylvania
West Virginia University
  Division of Music
  Morgantown, West Virginia
Western Illinois University
  Department of Music
  Macomb, Illinois
Western Kentucky University
  Department of Music
  Bowling Green, Kentucky
Western Michigan University
  School of Music
  Kalamazoo, Michigan
Wichita State University
  School of Music
  Wichita, Kansas
Wiesbadener Konservatorium und staatliche
anerkannte private Fachschule für
Musikerzieher e.V.
  (Conservatory and Seminary for Music
  Education)
  *6200 Wiesbaden, Federal Republic of
  Germany*
Wilfrid Laurier University
  Faculty of Music
  Waterloo, Ontario, Canada
William Carey College
  Winters School of Music
  Hattiesburg, Mississippi
William Paterson College
  Department of Music
  Wayne, New Jersey
University of Windsor
  School of Music
  Windsor, Ontario, Canada
University of Wisconsin - Eau Claire
  Department of Music
  Eau Claire, Wisconsin
University of Wisconsin - Madison
  School of Music
  Madison, Wisconsin
University of Wisconsin - Milwaukee
  Music Department
  Milwaukee, Wisconsin
University of Wisconsin - Stevens Point
  Department of Music
  Stevens Point, Wisconsin
Wright State University
  Department of Music
  Dayton, Ohio
University of Wyoming
  Music Department
  Laramie, Wyoming
Yale College (Yale University)
  Department of Music
  New Haven, Connecticut
Yale University
  School of Music
  New Haven, Connecticut
Youngstown State University
  Dana School of Music
  Youngstown, Ohio

CLAVICHORD

Mills College
  Music Department
  Oakland, California
Musik-Akademie der Stadt Basel
  Schola Cantorum Basiliensis
  CH-4051 Basel, Switzerland
University of Oregon
  School of Music
  Eugene, Oregon
Staatliche Hochschule für Musik Freiburg
  D-7800 Freiburg i. Br., Federal Republic

of Germany

COLLEGIUM INSTRUMENTS

Baylor University
  School of Music
  Waco, Texas

CONDUCTING

Hardin-Simmons University
  School of Music
  Abilene, Texas

CONTRABASS

Butler University
  Jordan College of Fine Arts
  Indianapolis, Indiana

CORNET

University of Alaska
  Music Department
  Fairbanks, Alaska
University of Arkansas
  Department of Music
  Fayetteville, Arkansas
Baldwin-Wallace College
  Conservatory of Music
  Berea, Ohio
Bob Jones University
  Division of Music
  Greenville, South Carolina
University of British Columbia
  School of Music
  Vancouver, British Columbia, Canada
Eastern Michigan University
  Department of Music
  Ypsilanti, Michigan
Escuela Universitaria de Música -
Montevideo
  Montevideo, Uruguay
University of Illinois
  School of Music
  Urbana, Illinois
Indiana University - Bloomington
  School of Music
  Bloomington, Indiana
Iowa State University
  Department of Music
  Ames, Iowa
Lamar University
  Department of Music
  Beaumont, Texas
University of New Orleans
  Department of Music
  New Orleans, Louisiana
University of Northern Iowa
  School of Music
  Cedar Falls, Iowa
University of the Pacific
  Conservatory of Music
  Stockton, California
St. Olaf College
  Music Department
  Northfield, Minnesota
University of Southwestern Louisiana
  School of Music
  Lafayette, Louisiana
Western Kentucky University
  Department of Music
  Bowling Green, Kentucky
University of Wisconsin - Eau Claire
  Department of Music
  Eau Claire, Wisconsin
University of Wisconsin - Milwaukee
  Music Department
  Milwaukee, Wisconsin

CUBAN PERCUSSION INSTRUMENTS

Instituto Superior de Arte
Facultad de Música
Playa, Cuba

DOUBLE BASS

University of British Columbia
School of Music
Vancouver, British Columbia, Canada
University of Kansas
School of Fine Arts
Lawrence, Kansas

DRUMS

Institute of Aesthetic Studies
Colombo 7, Sri Lanka

DRUMSET

Berklee College of Music
Boston, Massachusetts

EARLY FORTEPIANO

Musik-Akademie der Stadt Basel
Schola Cantorum Basiliensis
CH-4051 Basel, Switzerland

EARLY INSTRUMENTS

Brandeis University
Department of Music
Waltham, Massachusetts
Case Western Reserve University
Department of Music
Cleveland, Ohio
City University of New York - Queens
College
The Aaron Copland School of Music
Flushing, New York
University of Kentucky
School of Music
Lexington, Kentucky
San Diego State University
Music Department
San Diego, California

EARLY WIND INSTRUMENTS

Kansas State University
Department of Music
Manhattan, Kansas

EGYPTIAN 'UD

National Institute of Music - Sana'a
Sana'a, Yemen Arab Republic

ELECTRIC GUITAR

Bhavan's Bharatiya Sangeet and Nartan
Skikshapeeth
(Academy of Music and Dance)
Bombay 4000007, India

ELECTRONIC BASS

Berklee College of Music
Boston, Massachusetts
Central Missouri State University
Department of Music
Warrensburg, Missouri

ELECTRONIC MUSIC

Michigan State University
School of Music
East Lansing, Michigan

ENGLISH HORN

University of British Columbia
School of Music
Vancouver, British Columbia, Canada
Butler University
Jordan College of Fine Arts
Indianapolis, Indiana
East Carolina University
School of Music
Greenville, North Carolina
Emporia State University
Division of Music
Emporia, Kansas
Escuela Nacional de Música
Universidad Nacional Autónoma de
México
Mexico City, D.F. 04100, Mexico
Indiana University - Bloomington
School of Music
Bloomington, Indiana
Ithaca College
School of Music
Ithaca, New York
The Juilliard School
New York, New York
University of Kentucky
School of Music
Lexington, Kentucky
Middle Tennessee State University
Department of Music
Murfreesboro, Tennessee
Pacific Lutheran University
Department of Music
Tacoma, Washington
University of Redlands
School of Music
Redlands, California
St. Cloud State University
Department of Music
St. Cloud, Minnesota
Saint Louis Conservatory of Music
St. Louis, Missouri

ESRAJ

Institute of Aesthetic Studies
Colombo 7, Sri Lanka

EUPHONIUM

Acadia University
School of Music
Wolfville, Nova Scotia, Canada
University of Alabama
School of Music
University, Alabama
Arkansas Tech University
Department of Music
Russellville, Arkansas
Baldwin-Wallace College
Conservatory of Music
Berea, Ohio
Baylor University
School of Music
Waco, Texas
Bob Jones University
Division of Music
Greenville, South Carolina
Bowling Green State University
College of Musical Arts
Bowling Green, Ohio
Butler University
Jordan College of Fine Arts
Indianapolis, Indiana
The Catholic University of America
The Benjamin T. Rome School of Music
Washington, District of Columbia

University of Central Arkansas
Department of Music
Conway, Arkansas
Central Missouri State University
Department of Music
Warrensburg, Missouri
Central Washington University
Department of Music
Ellensburg, Washington
University of Cincinnati
College-Conservatory of Music
Cincinnati, Ohio
University of Colorado at Boulder
College of Music
Boulder, Colorado
Colorado State University
Department of Music, Theatre, and
Dance
Fort Collins, Colorado
University of Connecticut
Department of Music
Storrs, Connecticut
Delta State University
Department of Music
Cleveland, Mississippi
Duquesne University
School of Music
Pittsburgh, Pennsylvania
Eastern Michigan University
Department of Music
Ypsilanti, Michigan
Emporia State University
Division of Music
Emporia, Kansas
University of Florida
Department of Music
Gainesville, Florida
Florida State University
School of Music
Tallahassee, Florida
George Mason University
Department of Performing Arts - Music
Division
Fairfax, Virginia
University of Hawaii at Manoa
Music Department
Honolulu, Hawaii
University of Illinois
School of Music
Urbana, Illinois
Indiana State University
Department of Music
Terre Haute, Indiana
Indiana University - Bloomington
School of Music
Bloomington, Indiana
University of Iowa
School of Music
Iowa City, Iowa
Iowa State University
Department of Music
Ames, Iowa
Ithaca College
School of Music
Ithaca, New York
James Madison University
Department of Music
Harrisonburg, Virginia
Jersey City State College
Music Department
Jersey City, New Jersey
University of Kansas
School of Fine Arts
Lawrence, Kansas
Kent State University
School of Music

Kent, Ohio
University of Kentucky
School of Music
Lexington, Kentucky
Lawrence University
Conservatory of Music
Appleton, Wisconsin
Louisiana Tech University
Department of Music
Ruston, Louisiana
University of Louisville
School of Music
Louisville, Kentucky
Mansfield University
Department of Music
Mansfield, Pennsylvania
University of Maryland - College Park
Department of Music
College Park, Maryland
Miami University
Department of Music
Oxford, Ohio
University of Michigan
School of Music
Ann Arbor, Michigan
Middle Tennessee State University
Department of Music
Murfreesboro, Tennessee
Millikin University
School of Music
Decatur, Illinois
University of Minnesota - Duluth
Department of Music
Duluth, Minnesota
Morehead State University
Department of Music
Morehead, Kentucky
University of Nebraska - Omaha
Department of Music
Omaha, Nebraska
University of North Carolina at Greensboro
School of Music
Greensboro, North Carolina
North Texas State University
School of Music
Denton, Texas
Northeast Louisiana University
School of Music
Monroe, Louisiana
University of Northern Iowa
School of Music
Cedar Falls, Iowa
Northwestern State University of Louisiana
Department of Music
Natchitoches, Louisiana
Pennsylvania State University
School of Music
University Park, Pennsylvania
Pittsburg State University
Department of Music
Pittsburg, Kansas
Queen's University
School of Music
Kingston, Ontario, Canada
University of Rochester
Eastman School of Music
Rochester, New York
St. Olaf College
Music Department
Northfield, Minnesota
University of South Florida
Department of Music
Tampa, Florida
Southeastern Oklahoma State University
Department of Music
Durant, Oklahoma

University of Southern Mississippi
School of Music
Hattiesburg, Mississippi
State University of New York College at Fredonia
School of Music
Fredonia, New York
State University of New York College at Potsdam
Crane School of Music
Potsdam, New York
Stephen F. Austin State University
Department of Music
Nacogdoches, Texas
Syracuse University
School of Music
Syracuse, New York
Texas Christian University
Music Department
Fort Worth, Texas
Troy State University
Department of Music
Troy, Alabama
West Virginia University
Division of Music
Morgantown, West Virginia
Western Illinois University
Department of Music
Macomb, Illinois
Western Kentucky University
Department of Music
Bowling Green, Kentucky
Wichita State University
School of Music
Wichita, Kansas
University of Windsor
School of Music
Windsor, Ontario, Canada
University of Wisconsin - Madison
School of Music
Madison, Wisconsin

FLUTE

Acadia University
School of Music
Wolfville, Nova Scotia, Canada
Akademia Muzyczna w Krakowie
31-038 Kraków, Poland
University of Alabama
School of Music
University, Alabama
University of Alaska
Music Department
Fairbanks, Alaska
American Conservatory of Music
Chicago, Illinois
University of Arizona
School of Music
Tucson, Arizona
University of Arkansas
Department of Music
Fayetteville, Arkansas
Arkansas Tech University
Department of Music
Russellville, Arkansas
Austin Peay State University
Department of Music
Clarksville, Tennessee
Baldwin-Wallace College
Conservatory of Music
Berea, Ohio
Baylor University
School of Music
Waco, Texas

Berklee College of Music
Boston, Massachusetts
Boston University
School of Music
Boston, Massachusetts
Bowling Green State University
College of Musical Arts
Bowling Green, Ohio
Bradley University
Division of Music and Theatre Arts
Peoria, Illinois
University of British Columbia
School of Music
Vancouver, British Columbia, Canada
Bulgarian State Conservatoire
Sofia 1505, Bulgaria
Butler University
Jordan College of Fine Arts
Indianapolis, Indiana
University of California, Irvine
School of Fine Arts
Irvine, California
University of California, Los Angeles
Department of Music
Los Angeles, California
University of California, Riverside
Department of Music
Riverside, California
University of California, San Diego
Department of Music
La Jolla, California
University of California, Santa Barbara
Department of Music
Santa Barbara, California
University of California, Santa Cruz
Music Board, Division of the Arts
Santa Cruz, California
California State University, Hayward
Department of Music
Hayward, California
California State University, Sacramento
Department of Music
Sacramento, California
The Catholic University of America
The Benjamin T. Rome School of Music
Washington, District of Columbia
University of Central Arkansas
Department of Music
Conway, Arkansas
University of Central Florida
Department of Music
Orlando, Florida
Central Missouri State University
Department of Music
Warrensburg, Missouri
Central Washington University
Department of Music
Ellensburg, Washington
University of Cincinnati
College-Conservatory of Music
Cincinnati, Ohio
The Claremont Graduate School
Music Department
Claremont, California
Cleveland State University
Department of Music
Cleveland, Ohio
University of Colorado at Boulder
College of Music
Boulder, Colorado
Colorado State University
Department of Music, Theatre, and Dance
Fort Collins, Colorado
University of Connecticut
Department of Music

Storrs, Connecticut

Conservatorio Nacional de Musica - La Paz (National Conservatory of Music - La Paz)
La Paz, Bolivia

The Curtis Institute of Music
Philadelphia, Pennsylvania

Delta State University
Department of Music
Cleveland, Mississippi

University of Denver
Lamont School of Music
Denver, Colorado

DePaul University
School of Music
Chicago, Illinois

DePauw University
School of Music
Greencastle, Indiana

Drake University
Department of Music
Des Moines, Iowa

Duquesne University
School of Music
Pittsburgh, Pennsylvania

East Carolina University
School of Music
Greenville, North Carolina

Eastern Illinois University
Department of Music
Charleston, Illinois

Eastern Michigan University
Department of Music
Ypsilanti, Michigan

Emporia State University
Division of Music
Emporia, Kansas

Escuela Nacional de Música
Universidad Nacional Autónoma de México
Mexico City, D.F. 04100, Mexico

Escuela Universitaria de Música - Montevideo
Montevideo, Uruguay

University of Florida
Department of Music
Gainesville, Florida

Florida State University
School of Music
Tallahassee, Florida

George Mason University
Department of Performing Arts - Music Division
Fairfax, Virginia

University of Hartford
Hartt School of Music
West Hartford, Connecticut

University of Hawaii at Manoa
Music Department
Honolulu, Hawaii

Hermann-Zilcher-Konservatorium
D-8700 Würzburg, Federal Republic of Germany

Hofstra University
Department of Music
Hempstead, New York

Howard University
Department of Music
Washington, District of Columbia

University of Idaho
School of Music
Moscow, Idaho

University of Illinois
School of Music
Urbana, Illinois

Illinois Wesleyan University
School of Music
Bloomington, Illinois

Indiana State University
Department of Music
Terre Haute, Indiana

Indiana University - Bloomington
School of Music
Bloomington, Indiana

Institute of Aesthetic Studies
Colombo 7, Sri Lanka

University of Iowa
School of Music
Iowa City, Iowa

Iowa State University
Department of Music
Ames, Iowa

Ithaca College
School of Music
Ithaca, New York

Jackson State University
Department of Music
Jackson, Mississippi

Jacksonville State University
Department of Music
Jacksonville, Alabama

James Madison University
Department of Music
Harrisonburg, Virginia

Jersey City State College
Music Department
Jersey City, New Jersey

The Juilliard School
New York, New York

University of Kansas
School of Fine Arts
Lawrence, Kansas

Kansas State University
Department of Music
Manhattan, Kansas

Kent State University
School of Music
Kent, Ohio

University of Kentucky
School of Music
Lexington, Kentucky

Kenya Conservatoire of Music
Nairobi, Kenya

Kuopion Konservatorio
70100 Kuopio, Finland

Lamar University
Department of Music
Beaumont, Texas

Lawrence University
Conservatory of Music
Appleton, Wisconsin

Levinsky Teachers College
Music Teachers Seminary
Tel-Aviv, Israel

Louisiana Tech University
Department of Music
Ruston, Louisiana

University of Louisville
School of Music
Louisville, Kentucky

Loyola University
College of Music
New Orleans, Louisiana

University of Maine
School of Performing Arts
Orono, Maine

Mansfield University
Department of Music
Mansfield, Pennsylvania

Marshall University
Department of Music

Huntington, West Virginia

University of Maryland - College Park
Department of Music
College Park, Maryland

Marywood College
Music Department
Scranton, Pennsylvania

University of Massachusetts at Amherst
Department of Music and Dance
Amherst, Massachusetts

University of Miami
School of Music
Coral Gables, Florida

Miami University
Department of Music
Oxford, Ohio

University of Michigan
School of Music
Ann Arbor, Michigan

Middle Tennessee State University
Department of Music
Murfreesboro, Tennessee

Millikin University
School of Music
Decatur, Illinois

Mills College
Music Department
Oakland, California

University of Minnesota - Duluth
Department of Music
Duluth, Minnesota

University of Minnesota - Twin Cities
School of Music
Minneapolis, Minnesota

University of Missouri - Kansas City
Conservatory of Music
Kansas City, Missouri

Moorhead State University
Music Department
Moorhead, Minnesota

Morehead State University
Department of Music
Morehead, Kentucky

National Institute of the Arts
Music Department
Taipei County, Taiwan (Republic of China)

University of Nebraska - Lincoln
School of Music
Lincoln, Nebraska

University of Nebraska - Omaha
Department of Music
Omaha, Nebraska

University of Nevada, Las Vegas
Department of Music
Las Vegas, Nevada

New England Conservatory
Boston, Massachusetts

University of New Orleans
Department of Music
New Orleans, Louisiana

Norfolk State University
Department of Music
Norfolk, Virginia

University of North Carolina at Chapel Hill
Department of Music
Chapel Hill, North Carolina

University of North Carolina at Greensboro
School of Music
Greensboro, North Carolina

North Texas State University
School of Music
Denton, Texas

Northeast Louisiana University
School of Music
Monroe, Louisiana

Northern Arizona University
  Music Department
  Flagstaff, Arizona
University of Northern Iowa
  School of Music
  Cedar Falls, Iowa
Northwestern State University of Louisiana
  Department of Music
  Natchitoches, Louisiana
Northwestern University
  School of Music
  Evanston, Illinois
Oakland University
  Department of Music, Theatre and
  Dance
  Rochester, Michigan
Oberlin College
  Conservatory of Music
  Oberlin, Ohio
Ohio Wesleyan University
  Department of Music
  Delaware, Ohio
University of Oregon
  School of Music
  Eugene, Oregon
University of the Pacific
  Conservatory of Music
  Stockton, California
Pacific Lutheran University
  Department of Music
  Tacoma, Washington
Peabody Institute of The Johns Hopkins
  University
  Baltimore, Maryland
Pennsylvania State University
  School of Music
  University Park, Pennsylvania
Philadelphia College of the Performing Arts
  School of Music
  Philadelphia, Pennsylvania
Pittsburg State University
  Department of Music
  Pittsburg, Kansas
University of Pittsburgh
  Department of Music
  Pittsburgh, Pennsylvania
Pomona College
  Music Department
  Claremont, California
Prayag Sangit Samiti
  Allahabad 211001, India
Queen's University
  School of Music
  Kingston, Ontario, Canada
University of Redlands
  School of Music
  Redlands, California
University of Regina
  Department of Music
  Regina, Saskatchewan, Canada
University of Rhode Island
  Department of Music
  Kingston, Rhode Island
Rice University
  Shepherd School of Music
  Houston, Texas
University of Rochester
  Eastman School of Music
  Rochester, New York
Rutgers, The State University of New Jersey
  Department of Music
  New Brunswick, New Jersey
St. Cloud State University
  Department of Music
  St. Cloud, Minnesota

Saint Louis Conservatory of Music
  St. Louis, Missouri
St. Olaf College
  Music Department
  Northfield, Minnesota
Samford University
  School of Music
  Birmingham, Alabama
San Diego State University
  Music Department
  San Diego, California
San Francisco Conservatory of Music
  San Francisco, California
San Francisco State University
  Department of Music
  San Francisco, California
San Jose State University
  Department of Music
  San Jose, California
University of Santo Tomas
  Conservatory of Music
  Manila, The Philippines
University of Saskatchewan
  Department of Music
  Saskatoon, Saskatchewan, Canada
Smith College
  Department of Music
  Northampton, Massachusetts
University of South Dakota
  Music Department
  Vermillion, South Dakota
University of South Florida
  Department of Music
  Tampa, Florida
Southeast Missouri State University
  Department of Music
  Cape Girardeau, Missouri
Southeastern Oklahoma State University
  Department of Music
  Durant, Oklahoma
Southern Illinois University at Carbondale
  School of Music
  Carbondale, Illinois
Southern Illinois University at Edwardsville
  Department of Music
  Edwardsville, Illinois
University of Southern Mississippi
  School of Music
  Hattiesburg, Mississippi
Southwest Texas State University
  Department of Music
  San Marcos, Texas
University of Southwestern Louisiana
  School of Music
  Lafayette, Louisiana
Staatliche Hochschule für Musik Trossingen
  *D-7218 Trossingen 1, Federal Republic of
  Germany*
State University of New York at Stony
  Brook
  Department of Music
  Stony Brook, New York
State University of New York College at
  Fredonia
  School of Music
  Fredonia, New York
State University of New York College at
  Potsdam
  Crane School of Music
  Potsdam, New York
State University of New York College at
  Purchase
  Division of Music
  Purchase, New York
Stephen F. Austin State University
  Department of Music

  Nacogdoches, Texas
Syracuse University
  School of Music
  Syracuse, New York
Teachers College of Columbia University
  Department of Music and Music
  Education
  New York, New York
Temple University
  Esther Boyer College of Music
  Philadelphia, Pennsylvania
University of Tennessee at Knoxville
  Department of Music
  Knoxville, Tennessee
University of Texas at El Paso
  Music Department
  El Paso, Texas
Texas Christian University
  Music Department
  Fort Worth, Texas
Toho Gakuen School of Music
  Tokyo, Japan
Troy State University
  Department of Music
  Troy, Alabama
University of Tulsa
  Faculty of Music
  Tulsa, Oklahoma
Universidad de Antioquía
  Facultad de Artes, Departamento de
  Música
  Medellín, Colombia
Universidade do Rio de Janeiro
  Letters and Arts Center - Music Course
  22290 Rio de Janeiro, Brazil
Université de Montréal
  Faculty of Music
  Montréal, Québec, Canada
Valparaiso University
  Department of Music
  Valparaiso, Indiana
VanderCook College of Music
  Chicago, Illinois
Virginia Polytechnic Institute and State
  University
  Department of Music
  Blacksburg, Virginia
Vysoká Skola Mûzickych Umeni v Praha
  Academy of Music and Dramatic Arts
  1101 00 Prague 1, Czechoslovakia
Washington State University
  Department of Music
  Pullman, Washington
West Chester University of Pennsylvania
  School of Music
  West Chester, Pennsylvania
West Virginia University
  Division of Music
  Morgantown, West Virginia
Western Illinois University
  Department of Music
  Macomb, Illinois
Western Kentucky University
  Department of Music
  Bowling Green, Kentucky
Western Michigan University
  School of Music
  Kalamazoo, Michigan
Wichita State University
  School of Music
  Wichita, Kansas
Wiesbadener Konservatorium und staatliche
  anerkannte private Fachschule für
  Musikerzieher e.V.
  (Conservatory and Seminary for Music
  Education)

6200 Wiesbaden, Federal Republic of
Germany
Wilfrid Laurier University
Faculty of Music
Waterloo, Ontario, Canada
William Carey College
Winters School of Music
Hattiesburg, Mississippi
William Paterson College
Department of Music
Wayne, New Jersey
University of Windsor
School of Music
Windsor, Ontario, Canada
University of Wisconsin - Eau Claire
Department of Music
Eau Claire, Wisconsin
University of Wisconsin - Madison
School of Music
Madison, Wisconsin
University of Wisconsin - Milwaukee
Music Department
Milwaukee, Wisconsin
University of Wisconsin - Stevens Point
Department of Music
Stevens Point, Wisconsin
Wright State University
Department of Music
Dayton, Ohio
University of Wyoming
Music Department
Laramie, Wyoming
Yale College (Yale University)
Department of Music
New Haven, Connecticut
Yale University
School of Music
New Haven, Connecticut
Youngstown State University
Dana School of Music
Youngstown, Ohio

FOLK INSTRUMENTS

Alma-Ata Kurmangazy State Conservatory
480091 Alma-Ata 91, Kazahskaja SSR,
U.S.S.R.
A.V. Nezhdanova Odessa Conservatory
270000 Odessa, Ukrainskaja SSR,
U.S.S.R.
Azerbaijan S.S.R. U. Gajibekov State
Conservatory
370014 Baku, Azerbajdžanskaja SSR,
U.S.S.R.
Byelorussian State Conservatory
220030 Minsk, Belorusskaja SSR,
U.S.S.R.
Far-Eastern Pedagogical Institute of the
Arts
690678 Vladivostok, Rossiskaja SFSR,
U.S.S.R.
Gorky M.I. Glinka State Conservatory
603005 Gorky, Rossiskaja SFSR, U.S.S.R.
Kazan State Conservatory
420015 Kazan 15, Rossiskaja SFSR,
U.S.S.R.
Kharkov State Institute of Arts
310003 Kharkov, U.S.S.R.
Latvian S.S.R. Y. Vitol State Conservatory
226050 Riga, Latvijskaya SSR, U.S.S.R.
Leningrad N.A. Rimsky-Korsakov State
Conservatory
192041 Leningrad, Rossiskaja SFSR,
U.S.S.R.
Lvov M.V. Lysenko State Conservatory
290005 Lvov, Ukrainskaja SSR, U.S.S.R.

Moldavian S.S.R. G. Musichesku State
Conservatory
277014 Kishinev, Moldavskaja SSR,
U.S.S.R.
Novosibirsk M.I. Glinka State Conservatory
630099 Novosibirsk 99, Rossiskaja SFSR,
U.S.S.R.
Saratov L.V. Sobinov State Conservatory
410000 Saratov, Rossiskaja SFSR,
U.S.S.R.
Tashkent State Conservatory
700000 Tashkent, Uzbekskaja SSR,
U.S.S.R.
Tbilisi V. Sarajishvili State Conservatory
380004 Tbilisi 4, Gruzinskaja SSR,
U.S.S.R.
Urals M.P. Mussorgsky State Conservatory
620014 Sverdlovsk, Rossiskaja SFSR,
U.S.S.R.

FORTEPIANO

University of Oregon
School of Music
Eugene, Oregon

FRENCH HORN

Acadia University
School of Music
Wolfville, Nova Scotia, Canada
Akademia Muzyczna w Krakowie
31-038 Kraków, Poland
University of Alabama
School of Music
University, Alabama
University of Alaska
Music Department
Fairbanks, Alaska
University of Arkansas
Department of Music
Fayetteville, Arkansas
Arkansas Tech University
Department of Music
Russellville, Arkansas
Austin Peay State University
Department of Music
Clarksville, Tennessee
Baldwin-Wallace College
Conservatory of Music
Berea, Ohio
Berklee College of Music
Boston, Massachusetts
Bob Jones University
Division of Music
Greenville, South Carolina
Boise State University
Music Department
Boise, Idaho
Boston University
School of Music
Boston, Massachusetts
Bradley University
Division of Music and Theatre Arts
Peoria, Illinois
University of British Columbia
School of Music
Vancouver, British Columbia, Canada
University of California, Irvine
School of Fine Arts
Irvine, California
University of California, Los Angeles
Department of Music
Los Angeles, California
University of California, Riverside
Department of Music
Riverside, California

University of California, San Diego
Department of Music
La Jolla, California
University of California, Santa Barbara
Department of Music
Santa Barbara, California
University of California, Santa Cruz
Music Board, Division of the Arts
Santa Cruz, California
California State University, Hayward
Department of Music
Hayward, California
California State University, Sacramento
Department of Music
Sacramento, California
University of Central Arkansas
Department of Music
Conway, Arkansas
University of Central Florida
Department of Music
Orlando, Florida
University of Cincinnati
College-Conservatory of Music
Cincinnati, Ohio
Colorado State University
Department of Music, Theatre, and
Dance
Fort Collins, Colorado
University of Connecticut
Department of Music
Storrs, Connecticut
Conservatorio Nacional de Musica - La Paz
(National Conservatory of Music - La
Paz)
La Paz, Bolivia
Delta State University
Department of Music
Cleveland, Mississippi
DePaul University
School of Music
Chicago, Illinois
DePauw University
School of Music
Greencastle, Indiana
Drake University
Department of Music
Des Moines, Iowa
East Carolina University
School of Music
Greenville, North Carolina
Eastern Michigan University
Department of Music
Ypsilanti, Michigan
Escuela Nacional de Música
Universidad Nacional Autónoma de
México
Mexico City, D.F. 04100, Mexico
University of Florida
Department of Music
Gainesville, Florida
University of Hartford
Hartt School of Music
West Hartford, Connecticut
University of Hawaii at Manoa
Music Department
Honolulu, Hawaii
Hofstra University
Department of Music
Hempstead, New York
Howard University
Department of Music
Washington, District of Columbia
University of Idaho
School of Music
Moscow, Idaho

University of Illinois
  School of Music
  Urbana, Illinois
Illinois Wesleyan University
  School of Music
  Bloomington, Illinois
Indiana University - Bloomington
  School of Music
  Bloomington, Indiana
Iowa State University
  Department of Music
  Ames, Iowa
Ithaca College
  School of Music
  Ithaca, New York
Jackson State University
  Department of Music
  Jackson, Mississippi
Jacksonville State University
  Department of Music
  Jacksonville, Alabama
Jersey City State College
  Music Department
  Jersey City, New Jersey
University of Kansas
  School of Fine Arts
  Lawrence, Kansas
Kent State University
  School of Music
  Kent, Ohio
University of Kentucky
  School of Music
  Lexington, Kentucky
Lamar University
  Department of Music
  Beaumont, Texas
University of Maine
  School of Performing Arts
  Orono, Maine
Marshall University
  Department of Music
  Huntington, West Virginia
Marywood College
  Music Department
  Scranton, Pennsylvania
University of Massachusetts at Amherst
  Department of Music and Dance
  Amherst, Massachusetts
University of Miami
  School of Music
  Coral Gables, Florida
Miami University
  Department of Music
  Oxford, Ohio
University of Michigan
  School of Music
  Ann Arbor, Michigan
Middle Tennessee State University
  Department of Music
  Murfreesboro, Tennessee
Millikin University
  School of Music
  Decatur, Illinois
University of Minnesota - Twin Cities
  School of Music
  Minneapolis, Minnesota
Moorhead State University
  Music Department
  Moorhead, Minnesota
University of Nebraska - Lincoln
  School of Music
  Lincoln, Nebraska
University of Nebraska - Omaha
  Department of Music
  Omaha, Nebraska

University of Nevada, Las Vegas
  Department of Music
  Las Vegas, Nevada
University of New Orleans
  Department of Music
  New Orleans, Louisiana
New South Wales State Conservatorium of
Music
  Sydney NSW 2000, Australia
University of North Carolina at Chapel Hill
  Department of Music
  Chapel Hill, North Carolina
North Texas State University
  School of Music
  Denton, Texas
Northeast Louisiana University
  School of Music
  Monroe, Louisiana
Northern Arizona University
  Music Department
  Flagstaff, Arizona
University of Northern Iowa
  School of Music
  Cedar Falls, Iowa
Northwestern State University of Louisiana
  Department of Music
  Natchitoches, Louisiana
Oakland University
  Department of Music, Theatre and
  Dance
  Rochester, Michigan
Oberlin College
  Conservatory of Music
  Oberlin, Ohio
Ohio Wesleyan University
  Department of Music
  Delaware, Ohio
University of Oregon
  School of Music
  Eugene, Oregon
University of the Pacific
  Conservatory of Music
  Stockton, California
Pacific Lutheran University
  Department of Music
  Tacoma, Washington
Peabody Institute of The Johns Hopkins
University
  Baltimore, Maryland
Pennsylvania State University
  School of Music
  University Park, Pennsylvania
Philadelphia College of the Performing Arts
  School of Music
  Philadelphia, Pennsylvania
Queen's University
  School of Music
  Kingston, Ontario, Canada
University of Rhode Island
  Department of Music
  Kingston, Rhode Island
Rutgers, The State University of New Jersey
  Department of Music
  New Brunswick, New Jersey
St. Cloud State University
  Department of Music
  St. Cloud, Minnesota
Saint Louis Conservatory of Music
  St. Louis, Missouri
Samford University
  School of Music
  Birmingham, Alabama
San Diego State University
  Music Department
  San Diego, California

San Francisco Conservatory of Music
  San Francisco, California
San Jose State University
  Department of Music
  San Jose, California
University of Saskatchewan
  Department of Music
  Saskatoon, Saskatchewan, Canada
Southern Illinois University at Edwardsville
  Department of Music
  Edwardsville, Illinois
University of Southwestern Louisiana
  School of Music
  Lafayette, Louisiana
State University of New York College at
Fredonia
  School of Music
  Fredonia, New York
Syracuse University
  School of Music
  Syracuse, New York
Teachers College of Columbia University
  Department of Music and Music
  Education
  New York, New York
Temple University
  Esther Boyer College of Music
  Philadelphia, Pennsylvania
Texas Christian University
  Music Department
  Fort Worth, Texas
University of Toronto
  Faculty of Music
  Toronto, Ontario, Canada
University of Tulsa
  Faculty of Music
  Tulsa, Oklahoma
Universidade do Rio de Janeiro
  Letters and Arts Center - Music Course
  22290 Rio de Janeiro, Brazil
Valparaiso University
  Department of Music
  Valparaiso, Indiana
VanderCook College of Music
  Chicago, Illinois
Vysoká Skola Mûzických Umeni v Praha
  Academy of Music and Dramatic Arts
  1101 00 Prague 1, Czechoslovakia
West Chester University of Pennsylvania
  School of Music
  West Chester, Pennsylvania
Western Michigan University
  School of Music
  Kalamazoo, Michigan
Wichita State University
  School of Music
  Wichita, Kansas
Wilfrid Laurier University
  Faculty of Music
  Waterloo, Ontario, Canada
William Carey College
  Winters School of Music
  Hattiesburg, Mississippi
University of Windsor
  School of Music
  Windsor, Ontario, Canada
University of Wisconsin - Eau Claire
  Department of Music
  Eau Claire, Wisconsin
University of Wisconsin - Milwaukee
  Music Department
  Milwaukee, Wisconsin
University of Wyoming
  Music Department
  Laramie, Wyoming

Yale College (Yale University)
  Department of Music
  New Haven, Connecticut
Yale University
  School of Music
  New Haven, Connecticut
Youngstown State University
  Dana School of Music
  Youngstown, Ohio

GAMELAN

California Institute of the Arts
  School of Music
  Valencia, California
Lewis and Clark College
  Music Department
  Portland, Oregon
Mills College
  Music Department
  Oakland, California
University of the Philippines
  College of Music
  Quezon City, The Philippines
Roosevelt University
  Chicago Musical College
  Chicago, Illinois

GUITAR

Acadia University
  School of Music
  Wolfville, Nova Scotia, Canada
Akademia Muzyczna w Krakowie
  31-038 Kraków, Poland
University of Akron
  Department of Music
  Akron, Ohio
University of Alaska
  Music Department
  Fairbanks, Alaska
American Conservatory of Music
  Chicago, Illinois
University of Arizona
  School of Music
  Tucson, Arizona
Austin Peay State University
  Department of Music
  Clarksville, Tennessee
Baldwin-Wallace College
  Conservatory of Music
  Berea, Ohio
Baylor University
  School of Music
  Waco, Texas
Berklee College of Music
  Boston, Massachusetts
Boise State University
  Music Department
  Boise, Idaho
Boston Conservatory of Music
  Boston, Massachusetts
Boston University
  School of Music
  Boston, Massachusetts
Bowling Green State University
  College of Musical Arts
  Bowling Green, Ohio
University of British Columbia
  School of Music
  Vancouver, British Columbia, Canada
University of Calgary
  Department of Music
  Calgary, Alberta, Canada
University of California, Irvine
  School of Fine Arts
  Irvine, California

University of California, Los Angeles
  Department of Music
  Los Angeles, California
University of California, Riverside
  Department of Music
  Riverside, California
University of California, Santa Barbara
  Department of Music
  Santa Barbara, California
University of California, Santa Cruz
  Music Board, Division of the Arts
  Santa Cruz, California
California State University, Hayward
  Department of Music
  Hayward, California
California State University, Long Beach
  Department of Music
  Long Beach, California
California State University, Northridge
  Music Department
  Northridge, California
California State University, Sacramento
  Department of Music
  Sacramento, California
Carnegie-Mellon University
  Department of Music
  Pittsburgh, Pennsylvania
Case Western Reserve University
  Department of Music
  Cleveland, Ohio
The Catholic University of America
  The Benjamin T. Rome School of Music
  Washington, District of Columbia
University of Central Arkansas
  Department of Music
  Conway, Arkansas
University of Central Florida
  Department of Music
  Orlando, Florida
Central Missouri State University
  Department of Music
  Warrensburg, Missouri
Central Washington University
  Department of Music
  Ellensburg, Washington
University of Cincinnati
  College-Conservatory of Music
  Cincinnati, Ohio
City of Leeds College of Music
  Leeds LS2 8BH, United Kingdom
City University of New York - Brooklyn
  College
  Conservatory of Music
  Brooklyn, New York
City University of New York - City College
  Department of Music
  New York, New York
City University of New York - Queens
  College
  The Aaron Copland School of Music
  Flushing, New York
The Claremont Graduate School
  Music Department
  Claremont, California
Cleveland Institute of Music
  Cleveland, Ohio
Cleveland State University
  Department of Music
  Cleveland, Ohio
University of Colorado at Boulder
  College of Music
  Boulder, Colorado
Colorado State University
  Department of Music, Theatre, and
  Dance
  Fort Collins, Colorado

Combs College of Music
  Philadelphia, Pennsylvania
University of Connecticut
  Department of Music
  Storrs, Connecticut
Conservatorio Nacional de Música
  (National Conservatory of Music)
  Lima 1, Peru
Conservatorio Nacional de Musica - La Paz
  (National Conservatory of Music - La
  Paz)
  La Paz, Bolivia
Dalhousie University
  Department of Music
  Halifax, Nova Scotia, Canada
Delta State University
  Department of Music
  Cleveland, Mississippi
University of Denver
  Lamont School of Music
  Denver, Colorado
DePaul University
  School of Music
  Chicago, Illinois
Duquesne University
  School of Music
  Pittsburgh, Pennsylvania
Eastern Kentucky University
  Department of Music
  Richmond, Kentucky
Eastern Michigan University
  Department of Music
  Ypsilanti, Michigan
Emporia State University
  Division of Music
  Emporia, Kansas
Escuela de Música - Heredia
  Universidad Nacional
  Heredia, Costa Rica
University of Evansville
  Music Department
  Evansville, Indiana
Florida State University
  School of Music
  Tallahassee, Florida
Fort Hays State University
  Department of Music
  Hays, Kansas
George Mason University
  Department of Performing Arts - Music
  Division
  Fairfax, Virginia
University of Georgia
  School of Music
  Athens, Georgia
Glassboro State College
  Department of Music
  Glassboro, New Jersey
Hardin-Simmons University
  School of Music
  Abilene, Texas
University of Hartford
  Hartt School of Music
  West Hartford, Connecticut
University of Hawaii at Manoa
  Music Department
  Honolulu, Hawaii
Hermann-Zilcher-Konservatorium
  *D-8700 Würzburg, Federal Republic of
  Germany*
Hochschule für Music Franz Liszt
  *DDR 5300 Weimar, German Democratic
  Republic*
Hochschule für Musik - München
  *8000 München 2, Federal Republic of
  Germany*

Hochschule für Musik und Darstellende
Kunst Frankfurt am Main
*6000 Frankfurt am Main 1, Federal
Republic of Germany*
Hofstra University
Department of Music
Hempstead, New York
Hoschschule für Music Hans Eisler
*DDR Berlin 1080, German Democratic
Republic*
Howard University
Department of Music
Washington, District of Columbia
Illinois State University
Department of Music
Normal, Illinois
Indiana University - Bloomington
School of Music
Bloomington, Indiana
Indiana University of Pennsylvania
Department of Music
Indiana, Pennsylvania
Instituto Superior de Arte
Facultad de Música
Playa, Cuba
Iowa State University
Department of Music
Ames, Iowa
James Madison University
Department of Music
Harrisonburg, Virginia
Jersey City State College
Music Department
Jersey City, New Jersey
The Jerusalem Rubin Academy of Music
and Dance
Jerusalem, Israel
Kent State University
School of Music
Kent, Ohio
University of Kentucky
School of Music
Lexington, Kentucky
Kenya Conservatoire of Music
Nairobi, Kenya
Konservatorium für Musik und Theater
CH-3011 Berne, Switzerland
Kuopion Konservatorio
70100 Kuopio, Finland
Lawrence University
Conservatory of Music
Appleton, Wisconsin
Levinsky Teachers College
Music Teachers Seminary
Tel-Aviv, Israel
Lewis and Clark College
Music Department
Portland, Oregon
University of Louisville
School of Music
Louisville, Kentucky
Loyola University
College of Music
New Orleans, Louisiana
University of Maine
School of Performing Arts
Orono, Maine
Mannes College of Music
New York, New York
Mansfield University
Department of Music
Mansfield, Pennsylvania
Marshall University
Department of Music
Huntington, West Virginia

University of Maryland - Baltimore County
Department of Music
Catonsville, Maryland
University of Maryland - College Park
Department of Music
College Park, Maryland
Marywood College
Music Department
Scranton, Pennsylvania
McNeese State University
Department of Music
Lake Charles, Louisiana
Memphis State University
Music Department
Memphis, Tennessee
University of Miami
School of Music
Coral Gables, Florida
Michigan State University
School of Music
East Lansing, Michigan
Middle Tennessee State University
Department of Music
Murfreesboro, Tennessee
Millikin University
School of Music
Decatur, Illinois
Mills College
Music Department
Oakland, California
University of Minnesota - Duluth
Department of Music
Duluth, Minnesota
University of Minnesota - Twin Cities
School of Music
Minneapolis, Minnesota
University of Missouri - Kansas City
Conservatory of Music
Kansas City, Missouri
Montclair State College
Department of Music
Upper Montclair, New Jersey
Morehead State University
Department of Music
Morehead, Kentucky
Musikhögskolan i Stockholm
National College of Music
115 31 Stockholm, Sweden
University of Nebraska - Omaha
Department of Music
Omaha, Nebraska
University of Nevada, Las Vegas
Department of Music
Las Vegas, Nevada
New England Conservatory
Boston, Massachusetts
University of New Mexico
Department of Music
Albuquerque, New Mexico
New Mexico State University
Department of Music
Las Cruces, New Mexico
New South Wales State Conservatorium of
Music
Sydney NSW 2000, Australia
Nikos Skalkotas Conservatory
Athens 11141, Greece
Norges Musikkhøgskole
(The Norwegian State Academy of
Music)
N-0130 Oslo 1, Norway
University of North Carolina at Chapel Hill
Department of Music
Chapel Hill, North Carolina
University of North Carolina at Greensboro
School of Music

Greensboro, North Carolina
North Texas State University
School of Music
Denton, Texas
Northeast Louisiana University
School of Music
Monroe, Louisiana
Northern Arizona University
Music Department
Flagstaff, Arizona
University of Northern Colorado
School of Music
Greeley, Colorado
Northern Illinois University
School of Music
DeKalb, Illinois
University of Northern Iowa
School of Music
Cedar Falls, Iowa
Northwestern University
School of Music
Evanston, Illinois
University of Notre Dame
Department of Music
Notre Dame, Indiana
Oakland University
Department of Music, Theatre and
Dance
Rochester, Michigan
University of Oregon
School of Music
Eugene, Oregon
University of the Pacific
Conservatory of Music
Stockton, California
Pacific Lutheran University
Department of Music
Tacoma, Washington
Peabody Institute of The Johns Hopkins
University
Baltimore, Maryland
Pennsylvania State University
School of Music
University Park, Pennsylvania
Philadelphia College of the Performing Arts
School of Music
Philadelphia, Pennsylvania
University of Pittsburgh
Department of Music
Pittsburgh, Pennsylvania
Portland State University
Department of Music
Portland, Oregon
Prayag Sangit Samiti
Allahabad 211001, India
University of Puget Sound
School of Music
Tacoma, Washington
Queen's University
School of Music
Kingston, Ontario, Canada
Radford University
Department of Music
Radford, Virginia
Real Conservatorio Superior de Música de
Madrid
(Royal Academy of Music)
Madrid 13, Spain
University of Redlands
School of Music
Redlands, California
University of Rhode Island
Department of Music
Kingston, Rhode Island
Roosevelt University
Chicago Musical College

Chicago, Illinois
Saint Louis Conservatory of Music
  St. Louis, Missouri
St. Olaf College
  Music Department
  Northfield, Minnesota
San Diego State University
  Music Department
  San Diego, California
San Francisco Conservatory of Music
  San Francisco, California
San Francisco State University
  Department of Music
  San Francisco, California
San Jose State University
  Department of Music
  San Jose, California
University of Santo Tomas
  Conservatory of Music
  Manila, The Philippines
University of Saskatchewan
  Department of Music
  Saskatoon, Saskatchewan, Canada
Shenandoah College and Conservatory
  Winchester, Virginia
Smith College
  Department of Music
  Northampton, Massachusetts
University of South Carolina
  School of Music
  Columbia, South Carolina
University of South Dakota
  Music Department
  Vermillion, South Dakota
University of South Florida
  Department of Music
  Tampa, Florida
Southeast Missouri State University
  Department of Music
  Cape Girardeau, Missouri
Southeastern Oklahoma State University
  Department of Music
  Durant, Oklahoma
University of Southern California
  School of Music
  Los Angeles, California
Southern Illinois University at Carbondale
  School of Music
  Carbondale, Illinois
Southern Illinois University at Edwardsville
  Department of Music
  Edwardsville, Illinois
Southern Methodist University
  Meadows School of the Arts
  Dallas, Texas
University of Southern Mississippi
  School of Music
  Hattiesburg, Mississippi
Southwest Texas State University
  Department of Music
  San Marcos, Texas
University of Southwestern Louisiana
  School of Music
  Lafayette, Louisiana
Southwestern Oklahoma State University
  Department of Music
  Weatherford, Oklahoma
Staatliche Hochschule für Musik Freiburg
  D-7800 Freiburg i. Br., Federal Republic
  of Germany
Staatliche Hochschule für Musik Rheinland
- Aachen
  Grenzland-Institut Aachen
  Aachen, Federal Republic of Germany
State University of New York at Stony
Brook

Department of Music
  Stony Brook, New York
State University of New York College at
Fredonia
  School of Music
  Fredonia, New York
State University of New York College at
New Paltz
  Department of Music
  New Paltz, New York
State University of New York College at
Potsdam
  Crane School of Music
  Potsdam, New York
State University of New York College at
Purchase
  Division of Music
  Purchase, New York
Stephen F. Austin State University
  Department of Music
  Nacogdoches, Texas
Stetson University
  School of Music
  Deland, Florida
Syracuse University
  School of Music
  Syracuse, New York
Teachers College of Columbia University
  Department of Music and Music
  Education
  New York, New York
Tel Aviv University
  Faculty of Fine Arts
  Tel-Aviv, Israel
Temple University
  Esther Boyer College of Music
  Philadelphia, Pennsylvania
University of Tennessee at Knoxville
  Department of Music
  Knoxville, Tennessee
University of Texas at Arlington
  Department of Music
  Arlington, Texas
University of Texas at El Paso
  Music Department
  El Paso, Texas
University of Texas at San Antonio
  Division of Music
  San Antonio, Texas
Texas Southern University
  Department of Music
  Houston, Texas
Texas Tech University
  Department of Music
  Lubbock, Texas
University of Toronto
  Faculty of Music
  Toronto, Ontario, Canada
University of Tulsa
  Faculty of Music
  Tulsa, Oklahoma
Ueno Gakuen College
  Tokyo 110, Japan
Universidad de Antioquía
  Facultad de Artes, Departamento de
  Música
  Medellín, Colombia
Universidad de Concepción
  Departamento de Arte
  Concepción, Chile
Université de Montréal
  Faculty of Music
  Montréal, Québec, Canada
Valparaiso University
  Department of Music
  Valparaiso, Indiana

VanderCook College of Music
  Chicago, Illinois
University of Virginia
  McIntire Department of Music
  Charlottesville, Virginia
Vysoká Skola Mûzickych Umeni v Praha
  Academy of Music and Dramatic Arts
  1101 00 Prague 1, Czechoslovakia
Washington State University
  Department of Music
  Pullman, Washington
Wayne State University
  Department of Music
  Detroit, Michigan
Webster University
  Department of Music
  St. Louis, Missouri
West Chester University of Pennsylvania
  School of Music
  West Chester, Pennsylvania
Western Illinois University
  Department of Music
  Macomb, Illinois
Western Washington University
  Department of Music
  Bellingham, Washington
Wheaton College
  Conservatory of Music
  Wheaton, Illinois
Wichita State University
  School of Music
  Wichita, Kansas
Wiesbadener Konservatorium und staatliche
anerkannte private Fachschule für
Musikerzieher e.V.
  (Conservatory and Seminary for Music
  Education)
  6200 Wiesbaden, Federal Republic of
  Germany
William Paterson College
  Department of Music
  Wayne, New Jersey
University of Windsor
  School of Music
  Windsor, Ontario, Canada
University of Wisconsin - Oshkosh
  Department of Music
  Oshkosh, Wisconsin
University of Wisconsin - Stevens Point
  Department of Music
  Stevens Point, Wisconsin
Yale College (Yale University)
  Department of Music
  New Haven, Connecticut
Yale University
  School of Music
  New Haven, Connecticut
York University
  Department of Music
  North York, Ontario, Canada
Youngstown State University
  Dana School of Music
  Youngstown, Ohio
Zeneiskolai Tanárkepzó Intézet
  (Music Teachers Training Institute of the
  Liszt Academy of Music)
  Budapest 1052, Hungary

HANDBELL

Baylor University
School of Music
Waco, Texas

Southwestern Baptist Theological Seminary
School of Church Music
Fort Worth, Texas

HARDANGER FIDDLE

St. Olaf College
Music Department
Northfield, Minnesota

HARMONIUM

Bhavan's Bharatiya Sangeet and Nartan
Skikshapeeth
(Academy of Music and Dance)
Bombay 4000007, India
City of Leeds College of Music
Leeds LS2 8BH, United Kingdom

HARP

Akademia Muzyczna w Krakowie
31-038 Kraków, Poland
American Conservatory of Music
Chicago, Illinois
University of Arizona
School of Music
Tucson, Arizona
Baldwin-Wallace College
Conservatory of Music
Berea, Ohio
Baylor University
School of Music
Waco, Texas
Boston University
School of Music
Boston, Massachusetts
University of British Columbia
School of Music
Vancouver, British Columbia, Canada
Bulgarian State Conservatoire
Sofia 1505, Bulgaria
Butler University
Jordan College of Fine Arts
Indianapolis, Indiana
University of California, Los Angeles
Department of Music
Los Angeles, California
University of California, San Diego
Department of Music
La Jolla, California
University of California, Santa Barbara
Department of Music
Santa Barbara, California
California Institute of the Arts
School of Music
Valencia, California
California State University, Fresno
Department of Music
Fresno, California
California State University, Hayward
Department of Music
Hayward, California
University of Central Florida
Department of Music
Orlando, Florida
University of Cincinnati
College-Conservatory of Music
Cincinnati, Ohio
City University of New York - Brooklyn
College
Conservatory of Music

Brooklyn, New York
The Claremont Graduate School
Music Department
Claremont, California
Cleveland Institute of Music
Cleveland, Ohio
Cleveland State University
Department of Music
Cleveland, Ohio
University of Colorado at Boulder
College of Music
Boulder, Colorado
Colorado State University
Department of Music, Theatre, and
Dance
Fort Collins, Colorado
University of Connecticut
Department of Music
Storrs, Connecticut
Conservatorio di Musica "Santa Cecilia"
00187 Rome, Italy
The Curtis Institute of Music
Philadelphia, Pennsylvania
University of Denver
Lamont School of Music
Denver, Colorado
DePaul University
School of Music
Chicago, Illinois
Duquesne University
School of Music
Pittsburgh, Pennsylvania
Eastern Michigan University
Department of Music
Ypsilanti, Michigan
Emporia State University
Division of Music
Emporia, Kansas
Escuela Nacional de Música
Universidad Nacional Autónoma de
México
Mexico City, D.F. 04100, Mexico
Escuela Universitaria de Música -
Montevideo
Montevideo, Uruguay
University of Evansville
Music Department
Evansville, Indiana
Ferenc Liszt Academy of Music
Budapest VI, Hungary
George Mason University
Department of Performing Arts - Music
Division
Fairfax, Virginia
University of Georgia
School of Music
Athens, Georgia
University of Hartford
Hartt School of Music
West Hartford, Connecticut
University of Hawaii at Manoa
Music Department
Honolulu, Hawaii
Hofstra University
Department of Music
Hempstead, New York
Howard University
Department of Music
Washington, District of Columbia
University of Illinois
School of Music
Urbana, Illinois
Indiana University - Bloomington
School of Music
Bloomington, Indiana

University of Iowa
School of Music
Iowa City, Iowa
Jersey City State College
Music Department
Jersey City, New Jersey
The Juilliard School
New York, New York
University of Kansas
School of Fine Arts
Lawrence, Kansas
University of Kentucky
School of Music
Lexington, Kentucky
Lawrence University
Conservatory of Music
Appleton, Wisconsin
University of Louisville
School of Music
Louisville, Kentucky
University of Maryland - College Park
Department of Music
College Park, Maryland
Marywood College
Music Department
Scranton, Pennsylvania
University of Miami
School of Music
Coral Gables, Florida
University of Michigan
School of Music
Ann Arbor, Michigan
Mills College
Music Department
Oakland, California
University of Minnesota - Twin Cities
School of Music
Minneapolis, Minnesota
Morehead State University
Department of Music
Morehead, Kentucky
National Institute of the Arts
Music Department
*Taipei County, Taiwan (Republic of
China)*
University of Nebraska - Lincoln
School of Music
Lincoln, Nebraska
University of Nebraska - Omaha
Department of Music
Omaha, Nebraska
University of Nevada, Las Vegas
Department of Music
Las Vegas, Nevada
University of New Hampshire
Department of Music
Durham, New Hampshire
New South Wales State Conservatorium of
Music
Sydney NSW 2000, Australia
University of North Carolina at Chapel Hill
Department of Music
Chapel Hill, North Carolina
North Texas State University
School of Music
Denton, Texas
Northern Arizona University
Music Department
Flagstaff, Arizona
University of Northern Colorado
School of Music
Greeley, Colorado
University of Northern Iowa
School of Music
Cedar Falls, Iowa

Northwestern State University of Louisiana
  Department of Music
  Natchitoches, Louisiana
Northwestern University
  School of Music
  Evanston, Illinois
Oakland University
  Department of Music, Theatre and
  Dance
  Rochester, Michigan
Oberlin College
  Conservatory of Music
  Oberlin, Ohio
Oklahoma Baptist University
  Department of Music
  Shawnee, Oklahoma
University of Oregon
  School of Music
  Eugene, Oregon
University of the Pacific
  Conservatory of Music
  Stockton, California
Pacific Lutheran University
  Department of Music
  Tacoma, Washington
Peabody Institute of The Johns Hopkins
  University
  Baltimore, Maryland
Philadelphia College of the Performing Arts
  School of Music
  Philadelphia, Pennsylvania
Real Conservatorio Superior de Música de
  Madrid
  (Royal Academy of Music)
  Madrid 13, Spain
University of Redlands
  School of Music
  Redlands, California
University of Rhode Island
  Department of Music
  Kingston, Rhode Island
Rice University
  Shepherd School of Music
  Houston, Texas
University of Rochester
  Eastman School of Music
  Rochester, New York
Saint Louis Conservatory of Music
  St. Louis, Missouri
St. Olaf College
  Music Department
  Northfield, Minnesota
San Diego State University
  Music Department
  San Diego, California
San Francisco Conservatory of Music
  San Francisco, California
San Francisco State University
  Department of Music
  San Francisco, California
Shenandoah College and Conservatory
  Winchester, Virginia
University of South Florida
  Department of Music
  Tampa, Florida
University of Southern California
  School of Music
  Los Angeles, California
Southern Illinois University at Edwardsville
  Department of Music
  Edwardsville, Illinois
Southern Methodist University
  Meadows School of the Arts
  Dallas, Texas
Staatliche Hochschule für Musik Freiburg
  D-7800 Freiburg i. Br., Federal Republic

of Germany
State University of New York College at
  Fredonia
  School of Music
  Fredonia, New York
State University of New York College at
  Purchase
  Division of Music
  Purchase, New York
Teachers College of Columbia University
  Department of Music and Music
  Education
  New York, New York
Tel Aviv University
  Faculty of Fine Arts
  Tel-Aviv, Israel
Temple University
  Esther Boyer College of Music
  Philadelphia, Pennsylvania
University of Texas at Austin
  Department of Music
  Austin, Texas
University of Texas at El Paso
  Music Department
  El Paso, Texas
Texas Christian University
  Music Department
  Fort Worth, Texas
Texas Tech University
  Department of Music
  Lubbock, Texas
Toho Gakuen School of Music
  Tokyo, Japan
University of Toronto
  Faculty of Music
  Toronto, Ontario, Canada
Ueno Gakuen College
  Tokyo 110, Japan
Université de Montréal
  Faculty of Music
  Montréal, Québec, Canada
Valparaiso University
  Department of Music
  Valparaiso, Indiana
University of Victoria
  School of Music
  Victoria, British Columbia, Canada
University of Virginia
  McIntire Department of Music
  Charlottesville, Virginia
Vysoká Skola MûzickŠch Umeni v Praha
  Academy of Music and Dramatic Arts
  1101 00 Prague 1, Czechoslovakia
University of Washington
  School of Music
  Seattle, Washington
Wayne State University
  Department of Music
  Detroit, Michigan
Welsh College of Music and Drama
  Cardiff, CF1 3ER, United Kingdom
West Chester University of Pennsylvania
  School of Music
  West Chester, Pennsylvania
University of Western Ontario
  Faculty of Music
  London, Ontario, Canada
Wheaton College
  Conservatory of Music
  Wheaton, Illinois
Wichita State University
  School of Music
  Wichita, Kansas
University of Windsor
  School of Music
  Windsor, Ontario, Canada

University of Wisconsin - Eau Claire
  Department of Music
  Eau Claire, Wisconsin
University of Wisconsin - Madison
  School of Music
  Madison, Wisconsin
University of Wisconsin - Milwaukee
  Music Department
  Milwaukee, Wisconsin
University of Wisconsin - Oshkosh
  Department of Music
  Oshkosh, Wisconsin
University of Wisconsin - Stevens Point
  Department of Music
  Stevens Point, Wisconsin
Yale College (Yale University)
  Department of Music
  New Haven, Connecticut
Yale University
  School of Music
  New Haven, Connecticut

HARPSICHORD

Acadia University
  School of Music
  Wolfville, Nova Scotia, Canada
Akademia Muzyczna w Krakowie
  31-038 Kraków, Poland
Akademia Muzycznaj im. Fryderyka
  Chopina w Warzawie
  (Frederic Chopin Academy of Music of
  Warsaw)
  00-368 Warsaw, Poland
University of Alabama
  School of Music
  University, Alabama
University of Arizona
  School of Music
  Tucson, Arizona
University of Arkansas
  Department of Music
  Fayetteville, Arkansas
Arkansas Tech University
  Department of Music
  Russellville, Arkansas
Baylor University
  School of Music
  Waco, Texas
Biola University
  Department of Music
  La Mirada, California
Boston Conservatory of Music
  Boston, Massachusetts
Boston University
  School of Music
  Boston, Massachusetts
Bowling Green State University
  College of Musical Arts
  Bowling Green, Ohio
Bradley University
  Division of Music and Theatre Arts
  Peoria, Illinois
Brandon University
  School of Music
  Brandon, Manitoba, Canada
University of British Columbia
  School of Music
  Vancouver, British Columbia, Canada
Butler University
  Jordan College of Fine Arts
  Indianapolis, Indiana
University of Calgary
  Department of Music
  Calgary, Alberta, Canada

University of California, Los Angeles
Department of Music
Los Angeles, California
University of California, Riverside
Department of Music
Riverside, California
University of California, Santa Barbara
Department of Music
Santa Barbara, California
University of California, Santa Cruz
Music Board, Division of the Arts
Santa Cruz, California
California State University, Chico
Department of Music
Chico, California
California State University, Hayward
Department of Music
Hayward, California
Case Western Reserve University
Department of Music
Cleveland, Ohio
The Catholic University of America
The Benjamin T. Rome School of Music
Washington, District of Columbia
Central Missouri State University
Department of Music
Warrensburg, Missouri
Central Washington University
Department of Music
Ellensburg, Washington
University of Cincinnati
College-Conservatory of Music
Cincinnati, Ohio
City University of New York - Brooklyn
College
Conservatory of Music
Brooklyn, New York
The Claremont Graduate School
Music Department
Claremont, California
Cleveland State University
Department of Music
Cleveland, Ohio
University of Colorado at Boulder
College of Music
Boulder, Colorado
Colorado State University
Department of Music, Theatre, and
Dance
Fort Collins, Colorado
Columbia University
Department of Music
New York, New York
Combs College of Music
Philadelphia, Pennsylvania
Delta State University
Department of Music
Cleveland, Mississippi
University of Denver
Lamont School of Music
Denver, Colorado
DePauw University
School of Music
Greencastle, Indiana
Drake University
Department of Music
Des Moines, Iowa
Duke University
Department of Music
Durham, North Carolina
Eastern Illinois University
Department of Music
Charleston, Illinois
Emporia State University
Division of Music
Emporia, Kansas

Escuela Nacional de Música
Universidad Nacional Autónoma de
México
Mexico City, D.F. 04100, Mexico
Evangelische Kirchenmusikschule der
Kirchenprovinz Sachsen
(Evangelical Church Music School of the
Church Province Saxony)
*DDR-4020 Halle (Saale), German
Democratic Republic*
University of Evansville
Music Department
Evansville, Indiana
Fachakademie für Music - Augsburg
Leopold Mozart-Konservatorium der
Stadt Augsburg
Augsberg, Federal Republic of Germany
Fachakademie für Musik - Nürnberg
Konservatorium der Stadt Nürnberg
Nürnberg, Federal Republic of Germany
University of Florida
Department of Music
Gainesville, Florida
Florida State University
School of Music
Tallahassee, Florida
University of Hartford
Hartt School of Music
West Hartford, Connecticut
Henderson State University
Department of Music
Arkadelphia, Arkansas
Hermann-Zilcher-Konservatorium
*D-8700 Würzburg, Federal Republic of
Germany*
Hochschule der Künste Berlin
*1000 Berlin 10, Federal Republic of
Germany*
Hochschule für Music und Darstellende
Kunst Hamburg
*2000 Hamburg 13, Federal Republic of
Germany*
Hochschule für Musik und Darstellande
Kunst "Mozarteum" Salzburg
(College of Music and Dramatic Art
"Mozarteum")
5020 Salzburg, Austria
Hochschule für Musik und Darstellende
Kunst Frankfurt am Main
*6000 Frankfurt am Main 1, Federal
Republic of Germany*
Hochschule für Musik und Darstellende
Kunst Graz
A-8010 Graz, Austria
Hochschule für Musik und Darstellende
Kunst Wien
(College of Music and Dramatic Art)
1030 Wien, Austria
Hofstra University
Department of Music
Hempstead, New York
University of Illinois
School of Music
Urbana, Illinois
Illinois State University
Department of Music
Normal, Illinois
Illinois Wesleyan University
School of Music
Bloomington, Illinois
Instituto Superior de Arte
Facultad de Música
Playa, Cuba
Iowa State University
Department of Music
Ames, Iowa

James Madison University
Department of Music
Harrisonburg, Virginia
Jersey City State College
Music Department
Jersey City, New Jersey
The Jerusalem Rubin Academy of Music
and Dance
Jerusalem, Israel
Kansas State University
Department of Music
Manhattan, Kansas
University of Kentucky
School of Music
Lexington, Kentucky
Kuopion Konservatorio
70100 Kuopio, Finland
Lawrence University
Conservatory of Music
Appleton, Wisconsin
Louisiana Tech University
Department of Music
Ruston, Louisiana
University of Louisville
School of Music
Louisville, Kentucky
University of Maine
School of Performing Arts
Orono, Maine
Manhattan School of Music
New York, New York
Mansfield University
Department of Music
Mansfield, Pennsylvania
Marywood College
Music Department
Scranton, Pennsylvania
McGill University
Faculty of Music
Montreal, Québec, Canada
Memphis State University
Music Department
Memphis, Tennessee
University of Miami
School of Music
Coral Gables, Florida
Mills College
Music Department
Oakland, California
University of Minnesota - Duluth
Department of Music
Duluth, Minnesota
University of Minnesota - Twin Cities
School of Music
Minneapolis, Minnesota
University of Missouri - Kansas City
Conservatory of Music
Kansas City, Missouri
Montclair State College
Department of Music
Upper Montclair, New Jersey
University of Montevallo
Department of Music
Montevallo, Alabama
Moorhead State University
Music Department
Moorhead, Minnesota
Morehead State University
Department of Music
Morehead, Kentucky
Musik-Akademie der Stadt Basel
Schola Cantorum Basiliensis
CH-4051 Basel, Switzerland
Musik-Akademie der Stadt Basel
(Konservatorium)
Konservatorium (Musikhochschule)

Basel, Switzerland
Musikhochschule des Saarlandes
  6600 Saarbrücken 3, Federal Republic of
  Germany
National Institute of the Arts
  Music Department
  Taipei County, Taiwan (Republic of
  China)
University of Nebraska - Lincoln
  School of Music
  Lincoln, Nebraska
Nederlands Instituut voor Kerkmuziek
  Utrecht, Netherlands
University of New Hampshire
  Department of Music
  Durham, New Hampshire
University of New Mexico
  Department of Music
  Albuquerque, New Mexico
New South Wales State Conservatorium of
Music
  Sydney NSW 2000, Australia
University of North Carolina at Chapel Hill
  Department of Music
  Chapel Hill, North Carolina
North Texas State University
  School of Music
  Denton, Texas
Northeast Louisiana University
  School of Music
  Monroe, Louisiana
University of Northern Colorado
  School of Music
  Greeley, Colorado
University of Northern Iowa
  School of Music
  Cedar Falls, Iowa
Northwestern State University of Louisiana
  Department of Music
  Natchitoches, Louisiana
Oakland University
  Department of Music, Theatre and
  Dance
  Rochester, Michigan
Oberlin College
  Conservatory of Music
  Oberlin, Ohio
The Ohio State University
  School of Music
  Columbus, Ohio
University of Oregon
  School of Music
  Eugene, Oregon
University of the Pacific
  Conservatory of Music
  Stockton, California
Pacific Lutheran University
  Department of Music
  Tacoma, Washington
Peabody Institute of The Johns Hopkins
University
  Baltimore, Maryland
Pennsylvania State University
  School of Music
  University Park, Pennsylvania
Philadelphia College of the Performing Arts
  School of Music
  Philadelphia, Pennsylvania
Pittsburg State University
  Department of Music
  Pittsburg, Kansas
University of Pittsburgh
  Department of Music
  Pittsburgh, Pennsylvania
Pomona College
  Music Department

Claremont, California
Portland State University
  Department of Music
  Portland, Oregon
Queen's University
  School of Music
  Kingston, Ontario, Canada
University of Redlands
  School of Music
  Redlands, California
University of Regina
  Department of Music
  Regina, Saskatchewan, Canada
University of Rhode Island
  Department of Music
  Kingston, Rhode Island
University of Rochester
  Eastman School of Music
  Rochester, New York
Rogaland Musikkonservatorium
  N-4000 Stavanger, Norway
Royal Academy of Music
  London NW1 5HT, United Kingdom
Royal Scottish Academy of Music and
Drama
  Glasgow G2 1BS, United Kingdom
Rutgers, The State University of New Jersey
  Department of Music
  New Brunswick, New Jersey
St. Cloud State University
  Department of Music
  St. Cloud, Minnesota
Saint Louis Conservatory of Music
  St. Louis, Missouri
St. Olaf College
  Music Department
  Northfield, Minnesota
Samford University
  School of Music
  Birmingham, Alabama
San Diego State University
  Music Department
  San Diego, California
San Francisco Conservatory of Music
  San Francisco, California
San Jose State University
  Department of Music
  San Jose, California
University of Saskatchewan
  Department of Music
  Saskatoon, Saskatchewan, Canada
Smith College
  Department of Music
  Northampton, Massachusetts
University of South Dakota
  Music Department
  Vermillion, South Dakota
Southeast Missouri State University
  Department of Music
  Cape Girardeau, Missouri
Southern Illinois University at Carbondale
  School of Music
  Carbondale, Illinois
Southern Illinois University at Edwardsville
  Department of Music
  Edwardsville, Illinois
Southern Methodist University
  Meadows School of the Arts
  Dallas, Texas
University of Southern Mississippi
  School of Music
  Hattiesburg, Mississippi
Southwest Texas State University
  Department of Music
  San Marcos, Texas

University of Southwestern Louisiana
  School of Music
  Lafayette, Louisiana
Southwestern Oklahoma State University
  Department of Music
  Weatherford, Oklahoma
Staatliche Hochschule für Musik Freiburg
  D-7800 Freiburg i. Br., Federal Republic
  of Germany
Staatliche Hochschule für Musik Rheinland
- Wuppertal
  Institut Wuppertal
  Wuppertal, Federal Republic of Germany
Staatliche Hochschule für Musik Ruhr
  4300 Essen 16, Federal Republic of
  Germany
Staatliche Hochschule für Musik Trossingen
  D-7218 Trossingen 1, Federal Republic of
  Germany
Staatliche Hochschule für Musik
Westfalen-Lippe
  4930 Detmold, Federal Republic of
  Germany
Staatliche Hochschule für Musik
Westfalen-Lippe
  Institut Dortmund
  D-4600 Dortmund 1, Federal Republic of
  Germany
Stanford University
  Department of Music
  Stanford, California
State University of New York at
Binghamton
  Department of Music
  Binghamton, New York
State University of New York College at
Potsdam
  Crane School of Music
  Potsdam, New York
State University of New York College at
Purchase
  Division of Music
  Purchase, New York
Stephen F. Austin State University
  Department of Music
  Nacogdoches, Texas
Stetson University
  School of Music
  Deland, Florida
Syracuse University
  School of Music
  Syracuse, New York
Teachers College of Columbia University
  Department of Music and Music
  Education
  New York, New York
Tel Aviv University
  Faculty of Fine Arts
  Tel-Aviv, Israel
University of Tennessee at Knoxville
  Department of Music
  Knoxville, Tennessee
University of Texas at Austin
  Department of Music
  Austin, Texas
University of Texas at San Antonio
  Division of Music
  San Antonio, Texas
Texas Christian University
  Music Department
  Fort Worth, Texas
Texas Tech University
  Department of Music
  Lubbock, Texas
The Tokyo College of Music
  Tokyo 171, Japan

Tonlistarskolinn i Reykjavik
105 Reykjavik, Iceland
University of Toronto
Faculty of Music
Toronto, Ontario, Canada
Ueno Gakuen College
Tokyo 110, Japan
University of Utah
Department of Music
Salt Lake City, Utah
Valparaiso University
Department of Music
Valparaiso, Indiana
University of Vermont
Department of Music
Burlington, Vermont
University of Victoria
School of Music
Victoria, British Columbia, Canada
University of Virginia
McIntire Department of Music
Charlottesville, Virginia
Vysoká Skola Mûzickych Umeni v Praha
Academy of Music and Dramatic Arts
1101 00 Prague 1, Czechoslovakia
University of Washington
School of Music
Seattle, Washington
Washington University
Department of Music
St. Louis, Missouri
West Virginia University
Division of Music
Morgantown, West Virginia
University of Western Ontario
Faculty of Music
London, Ontario, Canada
Wheaton College
Conservatory of Music
Wheaton, Illinois
University of Windsor
School of Music
Windsor, Ontario, Canada
University of Wisconsin - Eau Claire
Department of Music
Eau Claire, Wisconsin
University of Wisconsin - Milwaukee
Music Department
Milwaukee, Wisconsin
Wright State University
Department of Music
Dayton, Ohio
University of Wyoming
Music Department
Laramie, Wyoming
Yale College (Yale University)
Department of Music
New Haven, Connecticut
Yale University
School of Music
New Haven, Connecticut
Youngstown State University
Dana School of Music
Youngstown, Ohio

HISTORICAL INSTRUMENTS

University of British Columbia
School of Music
Vancouver, British Columbia, Canada
University of Maryland - College Park
Department of Music
College Park, Maryland

HORN

University of Arizona
School of Music
Tucson, Arizona
Baylor University
School of Music
Waco, Texas
Bowling Green State University
College of Musical Arts
Bowling Green, Ohio
The Catholic University of America
The Benjamin T. Rome School of Music
Washington, District of Columbia
Central Missouri State University
Department of Music
Warrensburg, Missouri
Central Washington University
Department of Music
Ellensburg, Washington
The Claremont Graduate School
Music Department
Claremont, California
Cleveland State University
Department of Music
Cleveland, Ohio
University of Colorado at Boulder
College of Music
Boulder, Colorado
Conservatorio di Musica "Santa Cecilia"
00187 Rome, Italy
The Curtis Institute of Music
Philadelphia, Pennsylvania
University of Denver
Lamont School of Music
Denver, Colorado
Duquesne University
School of Music
Pittsburgh, Pennsylvania
Eastern Illinois University
Department of Music
Charleston, Illinois
Emporia State University
Division of Music
Emporia, Kansas
Florida State University
School of Music
Tallahassee, Florida
George Mason University
Department of Performing Arts - Music
Division
Fairfax, Virginia
Hermann-Zilcher-Konservatorium
D-8700 Würzburg, Federal Republic of
Germany
Indiana State University
Department of Music
Terre Haute, Indiana
University of Iowa
School of Music
Iowa City, Iowa
James Madison University
Department of Music
Harrisonburg, Virginia
The Juilliard School
New York, New York
Kansas State University
Department of Music
Manhattan, Kansas
Lawrence University
Conservatory of Music
Appleton, Wisconsin
Louisiana Tech University
Department of Music
Ruston, Louisiana

University of Louisville
School of Music
Louisville, Kentucky
Loyola University
College of Music
New Orleans, Louisiana
Mansfield University
Department of Music
Mansfield, Pennsylvania
University of Maryland - College Park
Department of Music
College Park, Maryland
University of Minnesota - Duluth
Department of Music
Duluth, Minnesota
University of Missouri - Kansas City
Conservatory of Music
Kansas City, Missouri
Morehead State University
Department of Music
Morehead, Kentucky
National Institute of the Arts
Music Department
Taipei County, Taiwan (Republic of
China)
University of North Carolina at Greensboro
School of Music
Greensboro, North Carolina
Northwestern University
School of Music
Evanston, Illinois
Oklahoma Baptist University
Department of Music
Shawnee, Oklahoma
Pittsburg State University
Department of Music
Pittsburg, Kansas
University of Redlands
School of Music
Redlands, California
University of Regina
Department of Music
Regina, Saskatchewan, Canada
Rice University
Shepherd School of Music
Houston, Texas
University of Rochester
Eastman School of Music
Rochester, New York
St. Olaf College
Music Department
Northfield, Minnesota
San Francisco State University
Department of Music
San Francisco, California
University of South Dakota
Music Department
Vermillion, South Dakota
Southeast Missouri State University
Department of Music
Cape Girardeau, Missouri
Southern Illinois University at Carbondale
School of Music
Carbondale, Illinois
Southern Methodist University
Meadows School of the Arts
Dallas, Texas
University of Southern Mississippi
School of Music
Hattiesburg, Mississippi
Staatliche Hochschule für Musik Trossingen
D-7218 Trossingen 1, Federal Republic of
Germany
State University of New York at Stony
Brook
Department of Music

583

Stony Brook, New York
State University of New York College at
Potsdam
Crane School of Music
Potsdam, New York
State University of New York College at
Purchase
Division of Music
Purchase, New York
Stephen F. Austin State University
Department of Music
Nacogdoches, Texas
University of Tennessee at Knoxville
Department of Music
Knoxville, Tennessee
University of Texas at El Paso
Music Department
El Paso, Texas
Troy State University
Department of Music
Troy, Alabama
Virginia Polytechnic Institute and State
University
Department of Music
Blacksburg, Virginia
Washington State University
Department of Music
Pullman, Washington
West Virginia University
Division of Music
Morgantown, West Virginia
Western Illinois University
Department of Music
Macomb, Illinois
Western Kentucky University
Department of Music
Bowling Green, Kentucky
Wiesbadener Konservatorium und staatliche
anerkannte private Fachschule für
Musikerzieher e.V.
(Conservatory and Seminary for Music
Education)
6200 Wiesbaden, Federal Republic of
Germany
University of Wisconsin - Madison
School of Music
Madison, Wisconsin
University of Wisconsin - Stevens Point
Department of Music
Stevens Point, Wisconsin
Wright State University
Department of Music
Dayton, Ohio

INDIAN FLUTE

California Institute of the Arts
School of Music
Valencia, California

JAPANESE MUSIC

Osaka Ongaku Daigaku
(Osaka College of Music)
Osaka 561, Japan

JAPANESE TRADITIONAL INSTRUMENTS

The Tokyo College of Music
Tokyo 171, Japan

JAVANESE GAMELAN

University of California, Berkeley
Department of Music
Berkeley, California
University of California, Santa Cruz
Music Board, Division of the Arts

Santa Cruz, California
University of Hawaii at Manoa
Music Department
Honolulu, Hawaii

Wesleyan University
Department of Music
Middletown, Connecticut

JAZZ DRUMS

Cleveland State University
Department of Music
Cleveland, Ohio
Rutgers, The State University of New Jersey
Department of Music
New Brunswick, New Jersey

JAZZ GUITAR

University of Redlands
School of Music
Redlands, California
Rutgers, The State University of New Jersey
Department of Music
New Brunswick, New Jersey

KALINGA

University of the Philippines
College of Music
Quezon City, The Philippines

KANTELE

Pohjois-Kymen Musiikkiopisto
(North Kymi Music Institute)
45100 Kouvola, Finland

KENDHANG

Wesleyan University
Department of Music
Middletown, Connecticut

KEYBOARD

Hochschule für Musik - München
8000 München 2, Federal Republic of
Germany

KEYBOARD INSTRUMENTS

Royal Irish Academy of Music
Dublin 2, Ireland

KEYBOARDS

Staatliche Hochschule für Musik
Heidelberg-Mannheim
Friedrich-Ebert-Anlage 62, Federal
Republic of Germany

KOTO

George Mason University
Department of Performing Arts - Music
Division
Fairfax, Virginia
Osaka Ongaku Daigaku
(Osaka College of Music)
Osaka 561, Japan

KRAR

Yared National Institute of Music
Addis Ababa, Ethiopia

KULINTANG

University of the Philippines
College of Music
Quezon City, The Philippines

LUTE

Akademia Muzyczna w Krakowie
31-038 Kraków, Poland
Boston University
School of Music
Boston, Massachusetts
University of California, Irvine
School of Fine Arts
Irvine, California
University of California, Los Angeles
Department of Music
Los Angeles, California
University of California, Riverside
Department of Music
Riverside, California
Dalhousie University
Department of Music
Halifax, Nova Scotia, Canada
University of Evansville
Music Department
Evansville, Indiana
University of Hartford
Hartt School of Music
West Hartford, Connecticut
Hermann-Zilcher-Konservatorium
D-8700 Würzburg, Federal Republic of
Germany
Hochschule für Musik - München
8000 München 2, Federal Republic of
Germany
Hochschule für Musik und Darstellende
Kunst Frankfurt am Main
6000 Frankfurt am Main 1, Federal
Republic of Germany
New England Conservatory
Boston, Massachusetts
Norges Musikkhøgskole
(The Norwegian State Academy of
Music)
N-0130 Oslo 1, Norway
Oakland University
Department of Music, Theatre and
Dance
Rochester, Michigan
Oberlin College
Conservatory of Music
Oberlin, Ohio
Queen's University
School of Music
Kingston, Ontario, Canada
Real Conservatorio Superior de Música de
Madrid
(Royal Academy of Music)
Madrid 13, Spain
Saint Louis Conservatory of Music
St. Louis, Missouri
Shenandoah College and Conservatory
Winchester, Virginia
Staatliche Hochschule für Musik Karlsruhe
7500 Karlsruhe 1, Federal Republic of
Germany
Staatliche Hochschule für Musik Rheinland
- Aachen
Grenzland-Institut Aachen
Aachen, Federal Republic of Germany
University of Toronto
Faculty of Music
Toronto, Ontario, Canada
Ueno Gakuen College
Tokyo 110, Japan
Université de Montréal
Faculty of Music
Montréal, Québec, Canada

MALLETS

Berklee College of Music
Boston, Massachusetts

MANDOLIN

Hermann-Zilcher-Konservatorium
*D-8700 Würzburg, Federal Republic of
Germany*
Staatliche Hochschule für Musik Rheinland
- Wuppertal
Institute Wuppertal
Wuppertal, Federal Republic of Germany

MARIMBA

Southeastern Oklahoma State University
Department of Music
Durant, Oklahoma
University of Southwestern Louisiana
School of Music
Lafayette, Louisiana

MASINKO

Yared National Institute of Music
Addis Ababa, Ethiopia

NON-WESTERN INSTRUMENTS

University of Pittsburgh
Department of Music
Pittsburgh, Pennsylvania

OBOE

Acadia University
School of Music
Wolfville, Nova Scotia, Canada
Akademia Muzyczna w Krakowie
31-038 Kraków, Poland
University of Alabama
School of Music
University, Alabama
University of Alaska
Music Department
Fairbanks, Alaska
American Conservatory of Music
Chicago, Illinois
University of Arizona
School of Music
Tucson, Arizona
University of Arkansas
Department of Music
Fayetteville, Arkansas
Arkansas Tech University
Department of Music
Russellville, Arkansas
Austin Peay State University
Department of Music
Clarksville, Tennessee
Baldwin-Wallace College
Conservatory of Music
Berea, Ohio
Baylor University
School of Music
Waco, Texas
Berklee College of Music
Boston, Massachusetts
Bob Jones University
Division of Music
Greenville, South Carolina
Boston University
School of Music

Boston, Massachusetts
Bowling Green State University
College of Musical Arts
Bowling Green, Ohio
Bradley University
Division of Music and Theatre Arts
Peoria, Illinois
University of British Columbia
School of Music
Vancouver, British Columbia, Canada
Bulgarian State Conservatoire
Sofia 1505, Bulgaria
Butler University
Jordan College of Fine Arts
Indianapolis, Indiana
University of California, Irvine
School of Fine Arts
Irvine, California
University of California, Los Angeles
Department of Music
Los Angeles, California
University of California, Riverside
Department of Music
Riverside, California
University of California, San Diego
Department of Music
La Jolla, California
University of California, Santa Barbara
Department of Music
Santa Barbara, California
University of California, Santa Cruz
Music Board, Division of the Arts
Santa Cruz, California
California State University, Hayward
Department of Music
Hayward, California
California State University, Sacramento
Department of Music
Sacramento, California
The Catholic University of America
The Benjamin T. Rome School of Music
Washington, District of Columbia
University of Central Arkansas
Department of Music
Conway, Arkansas
University of Central Florida
Department of Music
Orlando, Florida
Central Missouri State University
Department of Music
Warrensburg, Missouri
Central Washington University
Department of Music
Ellensburg, Washington
University of Cincinnati
College-Conservatory of Music
Cincinnati, Ohio
The Claremont Graduate School
Music Department
Claremont, California
Cleveland State University
Department of Music
Cleveland, Ohio
University of Colorado at Boulder
College of Music
Boulder, Colorado
Colorado State University
Department of Music, Theatre, and
Dance
Fort Collins, Colorado
University of Connecticut
Department of Music
Storrs, Connecticut
Conservatorio di Musica "Santa Cecilia"
00187 Rome, Italy

Conservatorio Nacional de Musica - La Paz
(National Conservatory of Music - La
Paz)
La Paz, Bolivia
The Curtis Institute of Music
Philadelphia, Pennsylvania
Delta State University
Department of Music
Cleveland, Mississippi
University of Denver
Lamont School of Music
Denver, Colorado
DePaul University
School of Music
Chicago, Illinois
DePauw University
School of Music
Greencastle, Indiana
Drake University
Department of Music
Des Moines, Iowa
Duquesne University
School of Music
Pittsburgh, Pennsylvania
East Carolina University
School of Music
Greenville, North Carolina
Eastern Illinois University
Department of Music
Charleston, Illinois
Eastern Michigan University
Department of Music
Ypsilanti, Michigan
Emporia State University
Division of Music
Emporia, Kansas
Escuela Nacional de Música
Universidad Nacional Autónoma de
México
Mexico City, D.F. 04100, Mexico
Escuela Universitaria de Música -
Montevideo
Montevideo, Uruguay
University of Florida
Department of Music
Gainesville, Florida
Florida State University
School of Music
Tallahassee, Florida
George Mason University
Department of Performing Arts - Music
Division
Fairfax, Virginia
University of Hartford
Hartt School of Music
West Hartford, Connecticut
University of Hawaii at Manoa
Music Department
Honolulu, Hawaii
Hermann-Zilcher-Konservatorium
*D-8700 Würzburg, Federal Republic of
Germany*
Hofstra University
Department of Music
Hempstead, New York
Howard University
Department of Music
Washington, District of Columbia
University of Idaho
School of Music
Moscow, Idaho
University of Illinois
School of Music
Urbana, Illinois
Illinois Wesleyan University
School of Music

Bloomington, Illinois
Indiana State University
  Department of Music
    Terre Haute, Indiana
Indiana University - Bloomington
  School of Music
    Bloomington, Indiana
Institute of Fine Arts
  Faculty of Music
    Rangoon, Burma
University of Iowa
  School of Music
    Iowa City, Iowa
Iowa State University
  Department of Music
    Ames, Iowa
Ithaca College
  School of Music
    Ithaca, New York
Jackson State University
  Department of Music
    Jackson, Mississippi
Jacksonville State University
  Department of Music
    Jacksonville, Alabama
James Madison University
  Department of Music
    Harrisonburg, Virginia
Jersey City State College
  Music Department
    Jersey City, New Jersey
The Juilliard School
    New York, New York
University of Kansas
  School of Fine Arts
    Lawrence, Kansas
Kansas State University
  Department of Music
    Manhattan, Kansas
Kent State University
  School of Music
    Kent, Ohio
University of Kentucky
  School of Music
    Lexington, Kentucky
Lamar University
  Department of Music
    Beaumont, Texas
Lawrence University
  Conservatory of Music
    Appleton, Wisconsin
Louisiana Tech University
  Department of Music
    Ruston, Louisiana
University of Louisville
  School of Music
    Louisville, Kentucky
Loyola University
  College of Music
    New Orleans, Louisiana
University of Maine
  School of Performing Arts
    Orono, Maine
Mandalay School of Music, Dance,
  Painting, and Sculpture
    Mandalay, Burma
Marshall University
  Department of Music
    Huntington, West Virginia
University of Maryland - College Park
  Department of Music
    College Park, Maryland
Marywood College
  Music Department
    Scranton, Pennsylvania

University of Massachusetts at Amherst
  Department of Music and Dance
    Amherst, Massachusetts
University of Miami
  School of Music
    Coral Gables, Florida
Miami University
  Department of Music
    Oxford, Ohio
University of Michigan
  School of Music
    Ann Arbor, Michigan
Middle Tennessee State University
  Department of Music
    Murfreesboro, Tennessee
Millikin University
  School of Music
    Decatur, Illinois
Mills College
  Music Department
    Oakland, California
University of Minnesota - Duluth
  Department of Music
    Duluth, Minnesota
University of Minnesota - Twin Cities
  School of Music
    Minneapolis, Minnesota
University of Missouri - Kansas City
  Conservatory of Music
    Kansas City, Missouri
Moorhead State University
  Music Department
    Moorhead, Minnesota
Morehead State University
  Department of Music
    Morehead, Kentucky
Musikschule und Konservatorium
  Schaffhausen
    Schaffhausen, Switzerland
National Institute of the Arts
  Music Department
    Taipei County, Taiwan (Republic of China)
University of Nebraska - Lincoln
  School of Music
    Lincoln, Nebraska
University of Nebraska - Omaha
  Department of Music
    Omaha, Nebraska
University of Nevada, Las Vegas
  Department of Music
    Las Vegas, Nevada
New England Conservatory
    Boston, Massachusetts
University of New Orleans
  Department of Music
    New Orleans, Louisiana
Norfolk State University
  Department of Music
    Norfolk, Virginia
University of North Carolina at Chapel Hill
  Department of Music
    Chapel Hill, North Carolina
University of North Carolina at Greensboro
  School of Music
    Greensboro, North Carolina
North Texas State University
  School of Music
    Denton, Texas
Northeast Louisiana University
  School of Music
    Monroe, Louisiana
Northern Arizona University
  Music Department
    Flagstaff, Arizona

University of Northern Iowa
  School of Music
    Cedar Falls, Iowa
Northwestern State University of Louisiana
  Department of Music
    Natchitoches, Louisiana
Northwestern University
  School of Music
    Evanston, Illinois
Oakland University
  Department of Music, Theatre and Dance
    Rochester, Michigan
Oberlin College
  Conservatory of Music
    Oberlin, Ohio
Ohio Wesleyan University
  Department of Music
    Delaware, Ohio
University of Oregon
  School of Music
    Eugene, Oregon
University of the Pacific
  Conservatory of Music
    Stockton, California
Pacific Lutheran University
  Department of Music
    Tacoma, Washington
Peabody Institute of The Johns Hopkins
 University
    Baltimore, Maryland
Pennsylvania State University
  School of Music
    University Park, Pennsylvania
Philadelphia College of the Performing Arts
  School of Music
    Philadelphia, Pennsylvania
Pittsburg State University
  Department of Music
    Pittsburg, Kansas
University of Pittsburgh
  Department of Music
    Pittsburgh, Pennsylvania
Pomona College
  Music Department
    Claremont, California
Queen's University
  School of Music
    Kingston, Ontario, Canada
University of Redlands
  School of Music
    Redlands, California
University of Regina
  Department of Music
    Regina, Saskatchewan, Canada
University of Rhode Island
  Department of Music
    Kingston, Rhode Island
Rice University
  Shepherd School of Music
    Houston, Texas
University of Rochester
  Eastman School of Music
    Rochester, New York
Rutgers, The State University of New Jersey
  Department of Music
    New Brunswick, New Jersey
St. Cloud State University
  Department of Music
    St. Cloud, Minnesota
Saint Louis Conservatory of Music
    St. Louis, Missouri
St. Olaf College
  Music Department
    Northfield, Minnesota

San Diego State University
Music Department
San Diego, California
San Francisco Conservatory of Music
San Francisco, California
San Francisco State University
Department of Music
San Francisco, California
San Jose State University
Department of Music
San Jose, California
University of Saskatchewan
Department of Music
Saskatoon, Saskatchewan, Canada
Smith College
Department of Music
Northampton, Massachusetts
University of South Dakota
Music Department
Vermillion, South Dakota
University of South Florida
Department of Music
Tampa, Florida
Southeast Missouri State University
Department of Music
Cape Girardeau, Missouri
Southeastern Oklahoma State University
Department of Music
Durant, Oklahoma
Southern Illinois University at Carbondale
School of Music
Carbondale, Illinois
Southern Illinois University at Edwardsville
Department of Music
Edwardsville, Illinois
University of Southern Mississippi
School of Music
Hattiesburg, Mississippi
University of Southwestern Louisiana
School of Music
Lafayette, Louisiana
Staatliche Hochschule für Musik Trossingen
D-7218 Trossingen 1, Federal Republic of Germany
State University of New York at Stony Brook
Department of Music
Stony Brook, New York
State University of New York College at Fredonia
School of Music
Fredonia, New York
State University of New York College at Potsdam
Crane School of Music
Potsdam, New York
State University of New York College at Purchase
Division of Music
Purchase, New York
Stephen F. Austin State University
Department of Music
Nacogdoches, Texas
Syracuse University
School of Music
Syracuse, New York
Teachers College of Columbia University
Department of Music and Music Education
New York, New York
Temple University
Esther Boyer College of Music
Philadelphia, Pennsylvania
University of Tennessee at Knoxville
Department of Music
Knoxville, Tennessee

University of Texas at El Paso
Music Department
El Paso, Texas
Texas Christian University
Music Department
Fort Worth, Texas
Toho Gakuen School of Music
Tokyo, Japan
University of Toronto
Faculty of Music
Toronto, Ontario, Canada
Troy State University
Department of Music
Troy, Alabama
University of Tulsa
Faculty of Music
Tulsa, Oklahoma
Universidad de Antioquía
Facultad de Artes, Departamento de Música
Medellín, Colombia
Universidade do Rio de Janeiro
Letters and Arts Center - Music Course
22290 Rio de Janeiro, Brazil
Université de Montréal
Faculty of Music
Montréal, Québec, Canada
Valparaiso University
Department of Music
Valparaiso, Indiana
VanderCook College of Music
Chicago, Illinois
Virginia Polytechnic Institute and State University
Department of Music
Blacksburg, Virginia
Vysoká Skola Mûzickych Umeni v Praha
Academy of Music and Dramatic Arts
1101 00 Prague 1, Czechoslovakia
Washington State University
Department of Music
Pullman, Washington
West Chester University of Pennsylvania
School of Music
West Chester, Pennsylvania
West Virginia University
Division of Music
Morgantown, West Virginia
Western Illinois University
Department of Music
Macomb, Illinois
Western Michigan University
School of Music
Kalamazoo, Michigan
Wichita State University
School of Music
Wichita, Kansas
Wiesbadener Konservatorium und staatliche anerkannte private Fachschule für Musikerzieher e.V.
(Conservatory and Seminary for Music Education)
6200 Wiesbaden, Federal Republic of Germany
Wilfrid Laurier University
Faculty of Music
Waterloo, Ontario, Canada
William Carey College
Winters School of Music
Hattiesburg, Mississippi
University of Windsor
School of Music
Windsor, Ontario, Canada
University of Wisconsin - Eau Claire
Department of Music
Eau Claire, Wisconsin

University of Wisconsin - Madison
School of Music
Madison, Wisconsin
University of Wisconsin - Milwaukee
Music Department
Milwaukee, Wisconsin
University of Wisconsin - Stevens Point
Department of Music
Stevens Point, Wisconsin
Wright State University
Department of Music
Dayton, Ohio
University of Wyoming
Music Department
Laramie, Wyoming
Yale College (Yale University)
Department of Music
New Haven, Connecticut
Yale University
School of Music
New Haven, Connecticut
Youngstown State University
Dana School of Music
Youngstown, Ohio

OBOE D'AMORE

Staatliche Hochschule für Musik Freiburg
D-7800 Freiburg i. Br., Federal Republic of Germany

OPERA

Osaka Ongaku Daigaku
(Osaka College of Music)
Osaka 561, Japan
Yale University
School of Music
New Haven, Connecticut

ORCHESTRAL INSTRUMENTS

Alma-Ata Kurmangazy State Conservatory
480091 Alma-Ata 91, Kazahskaja SSR, U.S.S.R.
American Conservatory of Music
Chicago, Illinois
Astrakhan State Conservatory
414000 Astrakhan, Rossiskaja SFSR, U.S.S.R.
Azerbaijan S.S.R. U. Gajibekov State Conservatory
370014 Baku, Azerbajdžanskaja SSR, U.S.S.R.
Byelorussian State Conservatory
220030 Minsk, Belorusskaja SSR, U.S.S.R.
Donetsk Musical-Pedagogical Institute
340086 Donetsk, Ukrainskaja SSR, U.S.S.R.
The East Helsinki Music Institute
SF-00820 Helsinki, Finland
Erevan Komitas State Conservatory
375009 Erevan 9, Armjanskaja SSR, U.S.S.R.
Fachakademie für Music - Augsburg
Leopold Mozart-Konservatorium der Stadt Augsburg
Augsberg, Federal Republic of Germany
Fachakademie für Musik - München
Richard Strauss-Konservatorium der Stadt

München 80, Federal Republic of
Germany
Fachakademie für Musik - Nürnberg
Konservatorium der Stadt Nürnberg
Nürnberg, Federal Republic of Germany
Far-Eastern Pedagogical Institute of the
Arts
690678 Vladivostok, Rossiskaja SFSR,
U.S.S.R.
Gnessinsky State Musical and Pedagogical
Institute
121069 Moscow G-69, Rossiskaja SFSR,
U.S.S.R.
Gorky M.I. Glinka State Conservatory
603005 Gorky, Rossiskaja SFSR, U.S.S.R.
Hochschule der Künste Berlin
1000 Berlin 10, Federal Republic of
Germany
Hochschule für Music und Darstellende
Kunst Hamburg
2000 Hamburg 13, Federal Republic of
Germany
Hochschule für Musik - München
8000 München 2, Federal Republic of
Germany
Hochschule für Musik und Darstellande
Kunst "Mozarteum" Salzburg
(College of Music and Dramatic Art
"Mozarteum")
5020 Salzburg, Austria
Hochschule für Musik und Darstellende
Kunst Frankfurt am Main
6000 Frankfurt am Main 1, Federal
Republic of Germany
Hochschule für Musik und Darstellende
Kunst Graz
A-8010 Graz, Austria
Hochschule für Musik und Darstellende
Kunst Wien
(College of Music and Dramatic Art)
1030 Wien, Austria
Kazan State Conservatory
420015 Kazan 15, Rossiskaja SFSR,
U.S.S.R.
Kharkov State Institute of Arts
310003 Kharkov, U.S.S.R.
Kiev P.I. Tchaikovsky Conservatory
252001 Kiev, Ukrainskaja SSR, U.S.S.R.
Konservatorium für Musik und Theater
CH-3011 Berne, Switzerland
Latvian S.S.R. Y. Vitol State Conservatory
226050 Riga, Latvijskaja SSR, U.S.S.R.
Lvov M.V. Lysenko State Conservatory
290005 Lvov, Ukrainskaja SSR, U.S.S.R.
Moldavian S.S.R. G. Musichesku State
Conservatory
277014 Kishinev, Moldavskaja SSR,
U.S.S.R.
Musikhochschule des Saarlandes
6600 Saarbrücken 3, Federal Republic of
Germany
Musikhochschule Lübeck
Grosse Petersgrube 17-29
2400 Lübeck, Federal Republic of
Germany
Novosibirsk M.I. Glinka State Conservatory
630099 Novosibirsk 99, Rossiskaja SFSR,
U.S.S.R.
Royal Irish Academy of Music
Dublin 2, Ireland
Saratov L.V. Sobinov State Conservatory
410000 Saratov, Rossiskaja SFSR,
U.S.S.R.
Staatliche Hochschule für Musik Karlsruhe
7500 Karlsruhe 1, Federal Republic of
Germany

Staatliche Hochschule für Musik Rheinland
- Aachen
Grenzland-Institut Aachen
Aachen, Federal Republic of Germany
Staatliche Hochschule für Musik Rheinland
- Wuppertal
Institute Wuppertal
Wuppertal, Federal Republic of Germany
Staatliche Hochschule für Musik Ruhr
4300 Essen 16, Federal Republic of
Germany
Staatliche Hochschule für Musik
Westfalen-Lippe
4930 Detmold, Federal Republic of
Germany
Tallinn State Conservatory
200015 Tallinn, Estonskaja SSR, U.S.S.R.
Tashkent State Conservatory
700000 Tashkent, Uzbekskaja SSR,
U.S.S.R.
Tbilisi V. Sarajishvili State Conservatory
380004 Tbilisi 4, Gruzinskaja SSR,
U.S.S.R.
Tonlistarskolinn i Reykjavik
105 Reykjavik, Iceland
Ufa State Institute of Fine Arts
450025 Ufa, Bashkir ASSR, U.S.S.R.
Urals M.P. Mussorgsky State Conservatory
620014 Sverdlovsk, Rossiskaja SFSR,
U.S.S.R.

ORGAN

Acadia University
School of Music
Wolfville, Nova Scotia, Canada
Akademia Muzyczna w Krakowie
31-038 Kraków, Poland
Akademia Muzyczna w Lódź
(Academy of Music of Lódź)
90-716 Lódź, Poland
Akademia Muzycznaj im. Fryderyka
Chopina w Warzawie
(Frederic Chopin Academy of Music of
Warsaw)
00-368 Warsaw, Poland
Akademie voor Musiek
Hilversum Postkode 1217 KR,
Netherlands
University of Akron
Department of Music
Akron, Ohio
University of Alabama
School of Music
University, Alabama
Alabama State University
School of Music
Montgomery, Alabama
University of Alaska
Music Department
Fairbanks, Alaska
University of Alberta
Department of Music
Edmonton, Alberta, Canada
American Conservatory of Music
Chicago, Illinois
Andrews University
Department of Music
Berrien Springs, Michigan
Appalachian State University
Department of Music
Boone, North Carolina
University of Arizona
School of Music
Tucson, Arizona

Arizona State University
School of Music
Tempe, Arizona
University of Arkansas
Department of Music
Fayetteville, Arkansas
Arkansas State University
Department of Music
State University, Arkansas
Arkansas Tech University
Department of Music
Russellville, Arkansas
Auburn University
Department of Music
Auburn, Alabama
Austin Peay State University
Department of Music
Clarksville, Tennessee
Azusa Pacific University
School of Music
Azusa, California
Baldwin-Wallace College
Conservatory of Music
Berea, Ohio
Ball State University
School of Music
Muncie, Indiana
Baylor University
School of Music
Waco, Texas
Bemidji State University
Music Department
Bemidji, Minnesota
Biola University
Department of Music
La Mirada, California
Bob Jones University
Division of Music
Greenville, South Carolina
Boise State University
Music Department
Boise, Idaho
Boston Conservatory of Music
Boston, Massachusetts
Boston University
School of Music
Boston, Massachusetts
Bowling Green State University
College of Musical Arts
Bowling Green, Ohio
Bradley University
Division of Music and Theatre Arts
Peoria, Illinois
Brandeis University
Department of Music
Waltham, Massachusetts
Brandon University
School of Music
Brandon, Manitoba, Canada
Brigham Young University
Department of Music
Provo, Utah
University of British Columbia
School of Music
Vancouver, British Columbia, Canada
Bulgarian State Conservatoire
Sofia 1505, Bulgaria
Butler University
Jordan College of Fine Arts
Indianapolis, Indiana
University of Calgary
Department of Music
Calgary, Alberta, Canada
University of California, Berkeley
Department of Music
Berkeley, California

University of California, Davis
  Department of Music
  Davis, California
University of California, Los Angeles
  Department of Music
  Los Angeles, California
University of California, Riverside
  Department of Music
  Riverside, California
University of California, Santa Barbara
  Department of Music
  Santa Barbara, California
California State University, Chico
  Department of Music
  Chico, California
California State University, Fresno
  Department of Music
  Fresno, California
California State University, Fullerton
  Department of Music
  Fullerton, California
California State University, Hayward
  Department of Music
  Hayward, California
California State University, Long Beach
  Department of Music
  Long Beach, California
California State University, Los Angeles
  Department of Music
  Los Angeles, California
California State University, Sacramento
  Department of Music
  Sacramento, California
Carnegie-Mellon University
  Department of Music
  Pittsburgh, Pennsylvania
Case Western Reserve University
  Department of Music
  Cleveland, Ohio
The Catholic University of America
  The Benjamin T. Rome School of Music
  Washington, District of Columbia
University of Central Arkansas
  Department of Music
  Conway, Arkansas
University of Central Florida
  Department of Music
  Orlando, Florida
Central Michigan University
  Department of Music
  Mount Pleasant, Michigan
Central Missouri State University
  Department of Music
  Warrensburg, Missouri
Central Washington University
  Department of Music
  Ellensburg, Washington
University of Cincinnati
  College-Conservatory of Music
  Cincinnati, Ohio
City of Leeds College of Music
  Leeds LS2 8BH, United Kingdom
City University of New York - Brooklyn
College
  Conservatory of Music
  Brooklyn, New York
City University of New York - Queens
College
  The Aaron Copland School of Music
  Flushing, New York
The Claremont Graduate School
  Music Department
  Claremont, California
Cleveland Institute of Music
  Cleveland, Ohio

Cleveland State University
  Department of Music
  Cleveland, Ohio
University of Colorado at Boulder
  College of Music
  Boulder, Colorado
Colorado State University
  Department of Music, Theatre, and
  Dance
  Fort Collins, Colorado
Columbia University
  Department of Music
  New York, New York
Combs College of Music
  Philadelphia, Pennsylvania
University of Connecticut
  Department of Music
  Storrs, Connecticut
Conservatorio di Musica "Claudio
Monteverdi"
  I-39100 Bolzano, Italy
Conservatorio di Musica "Santa Cecilia"
  00187 Rome, Italy
Converse College
  School of Music
  Spartanburg, South Carolina
Cornell University
  Department of Music
  Ithaca, New York
The Curtis Institute of Music
  Philadelphia, Pennsylvania
Dalhousie University
  Department of Music
  Halifax, Nova Scotia, Canada
University of Delaware
  Department of Music
  Newark, Delaware
Delta State University
  Department of Music
  Cleveland, Mississippi
University of Denver
  Lamont School of Music
  Denver, Colorado
DePaul University
  School of Music
  Chicago, Illinois
DePauw University
  School of Music
  Greencastle, Indiana
Drake University
  Department of Music
  Des Moines, Iowa
Duke University
  Department of Music
  Durham, North Carolina
Duquesne University
  School of Music
  Pittsburgh, Pennsylvania
East Carolina University
  School of Music
  Greenville, North Carolina
East Texas State University
  Department of Music
  Commerce, Texas
Eastern Illinois University
  Department of Music
  Charleston, Illinois
Eastern Kentucky University
  Department of Music
  Richmond, Kentucky
Eastern Michigan University
  Department of Music
  Ypsilanti, Michigan
Elizabeth University of Music
  Hiroshima 730, Japan

Emporia State University
  Division of Music
  Emporia, Kansas
Escuela Nacional de Música
  Universidad Nacional Autónoma de
  México
  Mexico City, D.F. 04100, Mexico
Escuela Universitaria de Música -
Montevideo
  Montevideo, Uruguay
Evangelische Kirchenmusikschule der
Kirchenprovinz Sachsen
  (Evangelical Church Music School of the
  Church Province Saxony)
  *DDR-4020 Halle (Saale), German
  Democratic Republic*
University of Evansville
  Music Department
  Evansville, Indiana
Ferenc Liszt Academy of Music
  Budapest VI, Hungary
University of Florida
  Department of Music
  Gainesville, Florida
Florida State University
  School of Music
  Tallahassee, Florida
George Mason University
  Department of Performing Arts - Music
  Division
  Fairfax, Virginia
University of Georgia
  School of Music
  Athens, Georgia
Georgia Southern College
  Department of Music
  Statesboro, Georgia
Georgia State University
  School of Music
  Atlanta, Georgia
Glassboro State College
  Department of Music
  Glassboro, New Jersey
Guildhall School of Music and Drama
  London EC2Y 8DT, United Kingdom
Hardin-Simmons University
  School of Music
  Abilene, Texas
University of Hartford
  Hartt School of Music
  West Hartford, Connecticut
Harvard University
  Department of Music
  Cambridge, Massachusetts
University of Hawaii at Manoa
  Music Department
  Honolulu, Hawaii
Henderson State University
  Department of Music
  Arkadelphia, Arkansas
Hermann-Zilcher-Konservatorium
  *D-8700 Würzburg, Federal Republic of
  Germany*
Hochschule für Music Franz Liszt
  *DDR 5300 Weimar, German Democratic
  Republic*
Hochschule für Musik - München
  *8000 München 2, Federal Republic of
  Germany*
Hochschule für Musik Carl Maria von
Weber
  *DDR 8010 Dresden, German Democratic
  Republic*
Hochschule für Musik Felix
Mendelssohn-Bartholdy
  7010 Leipzig, German Democratic

Republic
Hochschule für Musik und Darstellande
Kunst "Mozarteum" Salzburg
(College of Music and Dramatic Art
"Mozarteum")
5020 Salzburg, Austria
Hochschule für Musik und Darstellende
Kunst Graz
A-8010 Graz, Austria
Hochschule für Musik und Darstellende
Kunst Wien
(College of Music and Dramatic Art)
1030 Wien, Austria
Hochschule für Musik und Theater
Hannover
*3000 Hannover 1, Federal Republic of
Germany*
Hofstra University
Department of Music
Hempstead, New York
The Hong Kong Academy for Performing
Arts
School of Music
Wanchai, Hong Kong
University of Houston
School of Music
Houston, Texas
Howard University
Department of Music
Washington, District of Columbia
University of Idaho
School of Music
Moscow, Idaho
University of Illinois
School of Music
Urbana, Illinois
Illinois State University
Department of Music
Normal, Illinois
Illinois Wesleyan University
School of Music
Bloomington, Illinois
Indiana University - Bloomington
School of Music
Bloomington, Indiana
Instituto Superior de Arte
Facultad de Música
Playa, Cuba
University of Iowa
School of Music
Iowa City, Iowa
Iowa State University
Department of Music
Ames, Iowa
Ithaca College
School of Music
Ithaca, New York
Jackson State University
Department of Music
Jackson, Mississippi
Jacksonville State University
Department of Music
Jacksonville, Alabama
James Madison University
Department of Music
Harrisonburg, Virginia
Jersey City State College
Music Department
Jersey City, New Jersey
The Jerusalem Rubin Academy of Music
and Dance
Jerusalem, Israel
The Juilliard School
New York, New York
University of Kansas
School of Fine Arts

Lawrence, Kansas
Kansas State University
Department of Music
Manhattan, Kansas
Kent State University
School of Music
Kent, Ohio
University of Kentucky
School of Music
Lexington, Kentucky
Kenya Conservatoire of Music
Nairobi, Kenya
Koninklijk Muziekconservatorium van
Brussel
1000 Brussels, Belgium
Konservatorium für Musik und Theater
CH-3011 Berne, Switzerland
Konzervatoř v Praze
(State Conservatory Prague)
Praha 110 00, Czechoslovakia
Konzervatorium - Bratislava
Bratislava 811 06, Czechoslovakia
Kuopion Konservatorio
70100 Kuopio, Finland
Lamar University
Department of Music
Beaumont, Texas
Lawrence University
Conservatory of Music
Appleton, Wisconsin
Leningrad N.A. Rimsky-Korsakov State
Conservatory
*192041 Leningrad, Rossiskaja SFSR,
U.S.S.R.*
Long Island University - C.W. Post Campus
Music Department
Greenvale, New York
Louisiana State University
School of Music
Baton Rouge, Louisiana
Louisiana Tech University
Department of Music
Ruston, Louisiana
University of Louisville
School of Music
Louisville, Kentucky
University of Lowell
College of Music
Lowell, Massachusetts
Loyola University
College of Music
New Orleans, Louisiana
University of Maine
School of Performing Arts
Orono, Maine
University of Manitoba
School of Music
Winnipeg, Manitoba, Canada
Mankato State University
Department of Music
Mankato, Minnesota
Mannes College of Music
New York, New York
Mansfield University
Department of Music
Mansfield, Pennsylvania
Marshall University
Department of Music
Huntington, West Virginia
University of Maryland - College Park
Department of Music
College Park, Maryland
Marywood College
Music Department
Scranton, Pennsylvania

University of Massachusetts at Amherst
Department of Music and Dance
Amherst, Massachusetts
McGill University
Faculty of Music
Montreal, Québec, Canada
Memphis State University
Music Department
Memphis, Tennessee
University of Miami
School of Music
Coral Gables, Florida
Miami University
Department of Music
Oxford, Ohio
University of Michigan
School of Music
Ann Arbor, Michigan
Michigan State University
School of Music
East Lansing, Michigan
Middle Tennessee State University
Department of Music
Murfreesboro, Tennessee
Millikin University
School of Music
Decatur, Illinois
Mills College
Music Department
Oakland, California
University of Minnesota - Duluth
Department of Music
Duluth, Minnesota
University of Minnesota - Twin Cities
School of Music
Minneapolis, Minnesota
University of Mississippi
Department of Music
University, Mississippi
University of Missouri - Columbia
Department of Music
Columbia, Missouri
University of Missouri - Kansas City
Conservatory of Music
Kansas City, Missouri
University of Montana
Department of Music
Missoula, Montana
Montclair State College
Department of Music
Upper Montclair, New Jersey
University of Montevallo
Department of Music
Montevallo, Alabama
Morehead State University
Department of Music
Morehead, Kentucky
Moscow P.I. Tchaikovsky State
Conservatory
*103009 Moscow K-9, Rossiskaja SFSR,
U.S.S.R.*
Musik-Akademie der Stadt Basel
(Konservatorium)
Konservatorium (Musikhochschule)
Basel, Switzerland
Musikhochschule des Saarlandes
*6600 Saarbrücken 3, Federal Republic of
Germany*
Musikhochschule Lübeck
Grosse Petersgrube 17-29
*2400 Lübeck, Federal Republic of
Germany*
University of Nebraska - Lincoln
School of Music
Lincoln, Nebraska

University of Nebraska - Omaha
Department of Music
Omaha, Nebraska
Nederlands Instituut voor Kerkmuziek
Utrecht, Netherlands
University of Nevada, Las Vegas
Department of Music
Las Vegas, Nevada
University of Nevada, Reno
Department of Music
Reno, Nevada
New England Conservatory
Boston, Massachusetts
University of New Hampshire
Department of Music
Durham, New Hampshire
University of New Mexico
Department of Music
Albuquerque, New Mexico
New South Wales State Conservatorium of
Music
Sydney NSW 2000, Australia
New York University - School of Education,
Health, Nursing, and Arts Professions
Department of Music and Music
Education
New York, New York
Nikos Skalkotas Conservatory
Athens 11141, Greece
Norfolk State University
Department of Music
Norfolk, Virginia
University of North Carolina at Chapel Hill
Department of Music
Chapel Hill, North Carolina
University of North Carolina at Greensboro
School of Music
Greensboro, North Carolina
North Carolina School of the Arts
School of Music
Winston-Salem, North Carolina
University of North Dakota
Department of Music
Grand Forks, North Dakota
North Texas State University
School of Music
Denton, Texas
Northeast Louisiana University
School of Music
Monroe, Louisiana
Northern Arizona University
Music Department
Flagstaff, Arizona
University of Northern Colorado
School of Music
Greeley, Colorado
Northern Illinois University
School of Music
DeKalb, Illinois
University of Northern Iowa
School of Music
Cedar Falls, Iowa
Northwestern State University of Louisiana
Department of Music
Natchitoches, Louisiana
Northwestern University
School of Music
Evanston, Illinois
University of Notre Dame
Department of Music
Notre Dame, Indiana
Oakland University
Department of Music, Theatre and
Dance
Rochester, Michigan

Oberlin College
Conservatory of Music
Oberlin, Ohio
The Ohio State University
School of Music
Columbus, Ohio
Ohio University
School of Music
Athens, Ohio
Ohio Wesleyan University
Department of Music
Delaware, Ohio
University of Oklahoma
School of Music
Norman, Oklahoma
Oklahoma Baptist University
Department of Music
Shawnee, Oklahoma
Oklahoma City University
School of Music and Performing Arts
Oklahoma City, Oklahoma
University of Oregon
School of Music
Eugene, Oregon
Osaka Ongaku Daigaku
(Osaka College of Music)
Osaka 561, Japan
Ouachita Baptist University
School of Music
Arkadelphia, Arkansas
University of the Pacific
Conservatory of Music
Stockton, California
Pacific Lutheran University
Department of Music
Tacoma, Washington
Peabody Institute of The Johns Hopkins
University
Baltimore, Maryland
University of Pennsylvania
Department of Music
Philadelphia, Pennsylvania
Pennsylvania State University
School of Music
University Park, Pennsylvania
Pittsburg State University
Department of Music
Pittsburg, Kansas
University of Pittsburgh
Department of Music
Pittsburgh, Pennsylvania
Pohjois-Kymen Musiikkiopisto
(North Kymi Music Institute)
45100 Kouvola, Finland
Pomona College
Music Department
Claremont, California
Pontifical Institute of Sacred Music
I - 00165 Roma, Italy
Portland State University
Department of Music
Portland, Oregon
Princeton University
Department of Music
Princeton, New Jersey
University of Puget Sound
School of Music
Tacoma, Washington
Queen's University
School of Music
Kingston, Ontario, Canada
Radford University
Department of Music
Radford, Virginia
Real Conservatorio Superior de Música de
Madrid

(Royal Academy of Music)
Madrid 13, Spain
University of Regina
Department of Music
Regina, Saskatchewan, Canada
University of Rhode Island
Department of Music
Kingston, Rhode Island
Rice University
Shepherd School of Music
Houston, Texas
University of Rochester
Eastman School of Music
Rochester, New York
Rogaland Musikkonservatorium
N-4000 Stavanger, Norway
Roosevelt University
Chicago Musical College
Chicago, Illinois
Royal Academy of Music
London NW1 5HT, United Kingdom
Royal College of Music
London, SW7 2BS, United Kingdom
Royal Scottish Academy of Music and
Drama
Glasgow G2 1BS, United Kingdom
Rutgers, The State University of New Jersey
Department of Music
New Brunswick, New Jersey
St. Cloud State University
Department of Music
St. Cloud, Minnesota
Saint Louis Conservatory of Music
St. Louis, Missouri
St. Olaf College
Music Department
Northfield, Minnesota
Sam Houston State University
Department of Music
Huntsville, Texas
Samford University
School of Music
Birmingham, Alabama
San Diego State University
Music Department
San Diego, California
San Francisco Conservatory of Music
San Francisco, California
San Francisco State University
Department of Music
San Francisco, California
San Jose State University
Department of Music
San Jose, California
University of Saskatchewan
Department of Music
Saskatoon, Saskatchewan, Canada
Shenandoah College and Conservatory
Winchester, Virginia
Shorter College
Department of Music
Rome, Georgia
Smith College
Department of Music
Northampton, Massachusetts
University of South Dakota
Music Department
Vermillion, South Dakota
University of South Florida
Department of Music
Tampa, Florida
Southeast Missouri State University
Department of Music
Cape Girardeau, Missouri
Southeastern Louisiana University
Department of Music

Hammond, Louisiana
Southeastern Oklahoma State University
  Department of Music
  Durant, Oklahoma
Southern Baptist Theological Seminary
  School of Church Music
  Louisville, Kentucky
University of Southern California
  School of Music
  Los Angeles, California
Southern Illinois University at Carbondale
  School of Music
  Carbondale, Illinois
Southern Illinois University at Edwardsville
  Department of Music
  Edwardsville, Illinois
Southern Methodist University
  Meadows School of the Arts
  Dallas, Texas
University of Southern Mississippi
  School of Music
  Hattiesburg, Mississippi
Southwest Texas State University
  Department of Music
  San Marcos, Texas
Southwestern Baptist Theological Seminary
  School of Church Music
  Fort Worth, Texas
University of Southwestern Louisiana
  School of Music
  Lafayette, Louisiana
Southwestern Oklahoma State University
  Department of Music
  Weatherford, Oklahoma
Staatliche Hochschule für Musik Freiburg
  *D-7800 Freiburg i. Br., Federal Republic
  of Germany*
Staatliche Hochschule für Musik Rheinland
  - Köln
  *D-5000 Köln 1, Federal Republic of
  Germany*
Staatliche Hochschule für Musik Rheinland
  - Wuppertal
  Institute Wuppertal
  Wuppertal, Federal Republic of Germany
Staatliche Hochschule für Musik Trossingen
  *D-7218 Trossingen 1, Federal Republic of
  Germany*
Staatliche Hochschule für Musik
  Westfalen-Lippe
  *4930 Detmold, Federal Republic of
  Germany*
Staatliche Hochschule für Musik
  Westfalen-Lippe
  Institut Dortmund
  *D-4600 Dortmund 1, Federal Republic of
  Germany*
Stanford University
  Department of Music
  Stanford, California
State University of New York at
  Binghamton
  Department of Music
  Binghamton, New York
State University of New York at Buffalo
  Department of Music
  Buffalo, New York
State University of New York College at
  Fredonia
  School of Music
  Fredonia, New York
State University of New York College at
  New Paltz
  Department of Music
  New Paltz, New York

State University of New York College at
  Potsdam
  Crane School of Music
  Potsdam, New York
State University of New York College at
  Purchase
  Division of Music
  Purchase, New York
Stedelijke Muziekpedagogische Akademie
  Leeuwarden, Netherlands
Stephen F. Austin State University
  Department of Music
  Nacogdoches, Texas
Stetson University
  School of Music
  Deland, Florida
Syracuse University
  School of Music
  Syracuse, New York
Tampereen Konservatorio
  33230 Tampere, Finland
Tasmanian Conservatorium of Music
  Hobart, Tasmania 7001, Australia
Teachers College of Columbia University
  Department of Music and Music
  Education
  New York, New York
Temple University
  Esther Boyer College of Music
  Philadelphia, Pennsylvania
University of Tennessee at Chattanooga
  Cadek Department of Music
  Chattanooga, Tennessee
University of Tennessee at Knoxville
  Department of Music
  Knoxville, Tennessee
University of Texas at Arlington
  Department of Music
  Arlington, Texas
University of Texas at Austin
  Department of Music
  Austin, Texas
University of Texas at El Paso
  Music Department
  El Paso, Texas
University of Texas at San Antonio
  Division of Music
  San Antonio, Texas
Texas Christian University
  Music Department
  Fort Worth, Texas
Texas Southern University
  Department of Music
  Houston, Texas
Texas Tech University
  Department of Music
  Lubbock, Texas
The Tokyo College of Music
  Tokyo 171, Japan
Tonlistarskolinn i Reykjavik
  105 Reykjavik, Iceland
Towson State University
  Department of Music
  Towson, Maryland
Trinity College of Music
  London W1M 6AQ, United Kingdom
Troy State University
  Department of Music
  Troy, Alabama
University of Tulsa
  Faculty of Music
  Tulsa, Oklahoma
Ueno Gakuen College
  Tokyo 110, Japan
Université de Montréal
  Faculty of Music

Montréal, Québec, Canada
Université Laval
  Ecole de Musique
  Ste. Foy, Québec, Canada
Valdosta State College
  Department of Music
  Valdosta, Georgia
Valparaiso University
  Department of Music
  Valparaiso, Indiana
University of Vermont
  Department of Music
  Burlington, Vermont
University of Victoria
  School of Music
  Victoria, British Columbia, Canada
University of Virginia
  McIntire Department of Music
  Charlottesville, Virginia
Virginia Commonwealth University
  Department of Music
  Richmond, Virginia
Virginia State University
  Department of Music Education
  Petersburg, Virginia
Vysoká Skola Mûzickych Umeni v Praha
  Academy of Music and Dramatic Arts
  1101 00 Prague 1, Czechoslovakia
University of Washington
  School of Music
  Seattle, Washington
Washington State University
  Department of Music
  Pullman, Washington
Washington University
  Department of Music
  St. Louis, Missouri
Wayne State University
  Department of Music
  Detroit, Michigan
Webster University
  Department of Music
  St. Louis, Missouri
Welsh College of Music and Drama
  Cardiff, CF1 3ER, United Kingdom
Wesleyan University
  Department of Music
  Middletown, Connecticut
West Chester University of Pennsylvania
  School of Music
  West Chester, Pennsylvania
West Georgia College
  Department of Music
  Carrollton, Georgia
West Texas State University
  Department of Music
  Canyon, Texas
West Virginia University
  Division of Music
  Morgantown, West Virginia
Western Illinois University
  Department of Music
  Macomb, Illinois
Western Michigan University
  School of Music
  Kalamazoo, Michigan
University of Western Ontario
  Faculty of Music
  London, Ontario, Canada
Western Washington University
  Department of Music
  Bellingham, Washington
Westminster Choir College
  Princeton, New Jersey
Wheaton College
  Conservatory of Music

Wheaton, Illinois
Wichita State University
  School of Music
  Wichita, Kansas
Wiesbadener Konservatorium und staatliche
anerkannte private Fachschule für
Musikerzieher e.V.
  (Conservatory and Seminary for Music
  Education)
  6200 Wiesbaden, Federal Republic of
  Germany
Wilfrid Laurier University
  Faculty of Music
  Waterloo, Ontario, Canada
Willamette University
  Department of Music
  Salem, Oregon
William Carey College
  Winters School of Music
  Hattiesburg, Mississippi
William Paterson College
  Department of Music
  Wayne, New Jersey
University of Windsor
  School of Music
  Windsor, Ontario, Canada
Winthrop College
  School of Music
  Rock Hill, South Carolina
University of Wisconsin - Eau Claire
  Department of Music
  Eau Claire, Wisconsin
University of Wisconsin - Madison
  School of Music
  Madison, Wisconsin
University of Wisconsin - Oshkosh
  Department of Music
  Oshkosh, Wisconsin
University of Wisconsin - Stevens Point
  Department of Music
  Stevens Point, Wisconsin
University of Wisconsin - Whitewater
  Department of Music
  Whitewater, Wisconsin
Wright State University
  Department of Music
  Dayton, Ohio
University of Wyoming
  Music Department
  Laramie, Wyoming
Yale College (Yale University)
  Department of Music
  New Haven, Connecticut
Yale University
  School of Music
  New Haven, Connecticut
Youngstown State University
  Dana School of Music
  Youngstown, Ohio

P'HIPAD

University of the Philippines
  College of Music
  Quezon City, The Philippines

PERCUSSION

Acadia University
  School of Music
  Wolfville, Nova Scotia, Canada
Akademia Muzyczna w Krakowie
  31-038 Kraków, Poland
Akademia Muzyczna w Lódź
  (Academy of Music of Lódź)
  90-716 Lódź, Poland

Akademia Muzycznaj im. Fryderyka
  Chopina w Warzawie
  (Frederic Chopin Academy of Music of
  Warsaw)
  00-368 Warsaw, Poland
Akademie voor Musiek
  Hilversum Postkode 1217 KR,
  Netherlands
University of Akron
  Department of Music
  Akron, Ohio
University of Alabama
  School of Music
  University, Alabama
Alabama State University
  School of Music
  Montgomery, Alabama
University of Alberta
  Department of Music
  Edmonton, Alberta, Canada
American Conservatory of Music
  Chicago, Illinois
Andrews University
  Department of Music
  Berrien Springs, Michigan
Appalachian State University
  Department of Music
  Boone, North Carolina
University of Arizona
  School of Music
  Tucson, Arizona
Arizona State University
  School of Music
  Tempe, Arizona
University of Arkansas
  Department of Music
  Fayetteville, Arkansas
Arkansas State University
  Department of Music
  State University, Arkansas
Arkansas Tech University
  Department of Music
  Russellville, Arkansas
Auburn University
  Department of Music
  Auburn, Alabama
Austin Peay State University
  Department of Music
  Clarksville, Tennessee
Azusa Pacific University
  School of Music
  Azusa, California
Baldwin-Wallace College
  Conservatory of Music
  Berea, Ohio
Ball State University
  School of Music
  Muncie, Indiana
Baylor University
  School of Music
  Waco, Texas
Bemidji State University
  Music Department
  Bemidji, Minnesota
Bennington College
  Music Department
  Bennington, Vermont
Biola University
  Department of Music
  La Mirada, California
Bob Jones University
  Division of Music
  Greenville, South Carolina
Boise State University
  Music Department
  Boise, Idaho

Boston Conservatory of Music
  Boston, Massachusetts
Boston University
  School of Music
  Boston, Massachusetts
Bowling Green State University
  College of Musical Arts
  Bowling Green, Ohio
Brandon University
  School of Music
  Brandon, Manitoba, Canada
Brigham Young University
  Department of Music
  Provo, Utah
University of British Columbia
  School of Music
  Vancouver, British Columbia, Canada
Brown University
  Department of Music
  Providence, Rhode Island
Bulgarian State Conservatoire
  Sofia 1505, Bulgaria
Butler University
  Jordan College of Fine Arts
  Indianapolis, Indiana
University of Calgary
  Department of Music
  Calgary, Alberta, Canada
University of California, Davis
  Department of Music
  Davis, California
University of California, Irvine
  School of Fine Arts
  Irvine, California
University of California, Los Angeles
  Department of Music
  Los Angeles, California
University of California, Riverside
  Department of Music
  Riverside, California
University of California, Santa Barbara
  Department of Music
  Santa Barbara, California
University of California, Santa Cruz
  Music Board, Division of the Arts
  Santa Cruz, California
California Institute of the Arts
  School of Music
  Valencia, California
California State University, Chico
  Department of Music
  Chico, California
California State University, Fresno
  Department of Music
  Fresno, California
California State University, Fullerton
  Department of Music
  Fullerton, California
California State University, Hayward
  Department of Music
  Hayward, California
California State University, Long Beach
  Department of Music
  Long Beach, California
California State University, Los Angeles
  Department of Music
  Los Angeles, California
California State University, Northridge
  Music Department
  Northridge, California
Carnegie-Mellon University
  Department of Music
  Pittsburgh, Pennsylvania
Case Western Reserve University
  Department of Music
  Cleveland, Ohio

The Catholic University of America
The Benjamin T. Rome School of Music
Washington, District of Columbia
University of Central Arkansas
Department of Music
Conway, Arkansas
Central Conservatory of Music
Beijing, People's Republic of China
University of Central Florida
Department of Music
Orlando, Florida
Central Michigan University
Department of Music
Mount Pleasant, Michigan
Central Missouri State University
Department of Music
Warrensburg, Missouri
Central State University
Department of Music
Edmond, Oklahoma
Central Washington University
Department of Music
Ellensburg, Washington
University of Cincinnati
College-Conservatory of Music
Cincinnati, Ohio
City of Leeds College of Music
Leeds LS2 8BH, United Kingdom
City University of New York - Brooklyn
College
Conservatory of Music
Brooklyn, New York
City University of New York - City College
Department of Music
New York, New York
City University of New York - Hunter
College
Department of Music
New York, New York
City University of New York - Queens
College
The Aaron Copland School of Music
Flushing, New York
Cleveland Institute of Music
Cleveland, Ohio
Cleveland State University
Department of Music
Cleveland, Ohio
University of Colorado at Boulder
College of Music
Boulder, Colorado
University of Colorado at Denver
College of Music
Denver, Colorado
Colorado State University
Department of Music, Theatre, and
Dance
Fort Collins, Colorado
Columbia University
Department of Music
New York, New York
Columbus College
Department of Music
Columbus, Georgia
Combs College of Music
Philadelphia, Pennsylvania
University of Connecticut
Department of Music
Storrs, Connecticut
Conservatoire de Musique de La
Chaux-de-Fonds - Le Locle
2300 La Chaux-de-Fonds, Switzerland
Conservatorio di Musica "Claudio
Monteverdi"
I-39100 Bolzano, Italy

Conservatorio Nacional de Música
(National Conservatory of Music)
Lima 1, Peru
Conservatorio Nacional de Musica - La Paz
(National Conservatory of Music - La
Paz)
La Paz, Bolivia
Converse College
School of Music
Spartanburg, South Carolina
Cornell University
Department of Music
Ithaca, New York
The Curtis Institute of Music
Philadelphia, Pennsylvania
Dalhousie University
Department of Music
Halifax, Nova Scotia, Canada
University of Delaware
Department of Music
Newark, Delaware
Delta State University
Department of Music
Cleveland, Mississippi
University of Denver
Lamont School of Music
Denver, Colorado
DePaul University
School of Music
Chicago, Illinois
DePauw University
School of Music
Greencastle, Indiana
Drake University
Department of Music
Des Moines, Iowa
East Carolina University
School of Music
Greenville, North Carolina
East Texas State University
Department of Music
Commerce, Texas
Eastern Illinois University
Department of Music
Charleston, Illinois
Eastern Kentucky University
Department of Music
Richmond, Kentucky
Eastern Michigan University
Department of Music
Ypsilanti, Michigan
Eastern New Mexico University
School of Music
Portales, New Mexico
Eastern Washington University
Department of Music
Cheney, Washington
Emporia State University
Division of Music
Emporia, Kansas
Escuela de Música - Heredia
Universidad Nacional
Heredia, Costa Rica
Escuela Nacional de Música
Universidad Nacional Autónoma de
México
Mexico City, D.F. 04100, Mexico
Escuela Universitaria de Música -
Montevideo
Montevideo, Uruguay
University of Evansville
Music Department
Evansville, Indiana
University of Florida
Department of Music
Gainesville, Florida

Florida State University
School of Music
Tallahassee, Florida
Fort Hays State University
Department of Music
Hays, Kansas
George Mason University
Department of Performing Arts - Music
Division
Fairfax, Virginia
University of Georgia
School of Music
Athens, Georgia
Georgia Southern College
Department of Music
Statesboro, Georgia
Georgia State University
School of Music
Atlanta, Georgia
Glassboro State College
Department of Music
Glassboro, New Jersey
Guildhall School of Music and Drama
London EC2Y 8DT, United Kingdom
Hardin-Simmons University
School of Music
Abilene, Texas
University of Hartford
Hartt School of Music
West Hartford, Connecticut
University of Hawaii at Manoa
Music Department
Honolulu, Hawaii
Henderson State University
Department of Music
Arkadelphia, Arkansas
Hermann-Zilcher-Konservatorium
*D-8700 Würzburg, Federal Republic of
Germany*
Hochschule für Musik - Würzburg
*D-8700 Würzburg, Federal Republic of
Germany*
Hochschule für Musik Felix
Mendelssohn-Bartholdy
*7010 Leipzig, German Democratic
Republic*
Hochschule für Musik und Theater
Hannover
*3000 Hannover 1, Federal Republic of
Germany*
Hofstra University
Department of Music
Hempstead, New York
The Hong Kong Academy for Performing
Arts
School of Music
Wanchai, Hong Kong
University of Houston
School of Music
Houston, Texas
Howard University
Department of Music
Washington, District of Columbia
University of Idaho
School of Music
Moscow, Idaho
University of Illinois
School of Music
Urbana, Illinois
Illinois State University
Department of Music
Normal, Illinois
Illinois Wesleyan University
School of Music
Bloomington, Illinois

Indiana State University
  Department of Music
  Terre Haute, Indiana
Indiana University - Bloomington
  School of Music
  Bloomington, Indiana
Indiana University of Pennsylvania
  Department of Music
  Indiana, Pennsylvania
Instituto Superior de Arte
  Facultad de Música
  Playa, Cuba
University of Iowa
  School of Music
  Iowa City, Iowa
Iowa State University
  Department of Music
  Ames, Iowa
Ithaca College
  School of Music
  Ithaca, New York
Jackson State University
  Department of Music
  Jackson, Mississippi
Jacksonville State University
  Department of Music
  Jacksonville, Alabama
James Madison University
  Department of Music
  Harrisonburg, Virginia
Jersey City State College
  Music Department
  Jersey City, New Jersey
The Jerusalem Rubin Academy of Music
  and Dance
  Jerusalem, Israel
The Juilliard School
  New York, New York
University of Kansas
  School of Fine Arts
  Lawrence, Kansas
Kansas State University
  Department of Music
  Manhattan, Kansas
Kent State University
  School of Music
  Kent, Ohio
University of Kentucky
  School of Music
  Lexington, Kentucky
Konzervatoř v Praze
  (State Conservatory Prague)
  Praha 110 00, Czechoslovakia
Konzervatorium - Bratislava
  Bratislava 811 06, Czechoslovakia
Kuopion Konservatorio
  70100 Kuopio, Finland
Lamar University
  Department of Music
  Beaumont, Texas
Lawrence University
  Conservatory of Music
  Appleton, Wisconsin
Leningrad N.A. Rimsky-Korsakov State
  Conservatory
  *192041 Leningrad, Rossiskaja SFSR,
  U.S.S.R.*
Lewis and Clark College
  Music Department
  Portland, Oregon
Louisiana State University
  School of Music
  Baton Rouge, Louisiana
Louisiana Tech University
  Department of Music
  Ruston, Louisiana

University of Louisville
  School of Music
  Louisville, Kentucky
University of Lowell
  College of Music
  Lowell, Massachusetts
Loyola University
  College of Music
  New Orleans, Louisiana
University of Maine
  School of Performing Arts
  Orono, Maine
Manhattan School of Music
  New York, New York
University of Manitoba
  School of Music
  Winnipeg, Manitoba, Canada
Mankato State University
  Department of Music
  Mankato, Minnesota
Mannes College of Music
  New York, New York
Mansfield University
  Department of Music
  Mansfield, Pennsylvania
Marshall University
  Department of Music
  Huntington, West Virginia
University of Maryland - Baltimore County
  Department of Music
  Catonsville, Maryland
University of Maryland - College Park
  Department of Music
  College Park, Maryland
Marywood College
  Music Department
  Scranton, Pennsylvania
University of Massachusetts at Amherst
  Department of Music and Dance
  Amherst, Massachusetts
McGill University
  Faculty of Music
  Montreal, Québec, Canada
McMaster University
  Department of Music
  Hamilton, Ontario, Canada
McNeese State University
  Department of Music
  Lake Charles, Louisiana
Memphis State University
  Music Department
  Memphis, Tennessee
University of Miami
  School of Music
  Coral Gables, Florida
Miami University
  Department of Music
  Oxford, Ohio
University of Michigan
  School of Music
  Ann Arbor, Michigan
Michigan State University
  School of Music
  East Lansing, Michigan
Middle Tennessee State University
  Department of Music
  Murfreesboro, Tennessee
Millikin University
  School of Music
  Decatur, Illinois
Mills College
  Music Department
  Oakland, California
University of Minnesota - Duluth
  Department of Music
  Duluth, Minnesota

University of Minnesota - Twin Cities
  School of Music
  Minneapolis, Minnesota
University of Mississippi
  Department of Music
  University, Mississippi
University of Missouri - Columbia
  Department of Music
  Columbia, Missouri
University of Missouri - Kansas City
  Conservatory of Music
  Kansas City, Missouri
University of Montana
  Department of Music
  Missoula, Montana
Montana State University
  ·Department of Music
  Bozeman, Montana
Montclair State College
  Department of Music
  Upper Montclair, New Jersey
University of Montevallo
  Department of Music
  Montevallo, Alabama
Moorhead State University
  Music Department
  Moorhead, Minnesota
Morehead State University
  Department of Music
  Morehead, Kentucky
Moscow P.I. Tchaikovsky State
  Conservatory
  *103009 Moscow K-9, Rossiskaja SFSR,
  U.S.S.R.*
Musik-Akademie der Stadt Basel
  (Konservatorium)
  Konservatorium (Musikhochschule)
  Basel, Switzerland
Musikhögskolan i Stockholm
  National College of Music
  115 31 Stockholm, Sweden
Musikschule und Konservatorium
  Schaffhausen
  Schaffhausen, Switzerland
National Institute of Music - Sana'a
  Sana'a, Yemen Arab Republic
National Institute of the Arts
  Music Department
  *Taipei County, Taiwan (Republic of
  China)*
University of Nebraska - Lincoln
  School of Music
  Lincoln, Nebraska
University of Nebraska - Omaha
  Department of Music
  Omaha, Nebraska
University of Nevada, Las Vegas
  Department of Music
  Las Vegas, Nevada
University of Nevada, Reno
  Department of Music
  Reno, Nevada
New England Conservatory
  Boston, Massachusetts
University of New Hampshire
  Department of Music
  Durham, New Hampshire
University of New Mexico
  Department of Music
  Albuquerque, New Mexico
New Mexico State University
  Department of Music
  Las Cruces, New Mexico
University of New Orleans
  Department of Music
  New Orleans, Louisiana

New South Wales State Conservatorium of
Music
Sydney NSW 2000, Australia
New York University - School of Education,
Health, Nursing, and Arts Professions
Department of Music and Music
Education
New York, New York
Nikos Skalkotas Conservatory
Athens 11141, Greece
Norges Musikkhøgskole
(The Norwegian State Academy of
Music)
N-0130 Oslo 1, Norway
University of North Carolina at Chapel Hill
Department of Music
Chapel Hill, North Carolina
University of North Carolina at Greensboro
School of Music
Greensboro, North Carolina
North Carolina School of the Arts
School of Music
Winston-Salem, North Carolina
University of North Dakota
Department of Music
Grand Forks, North Dakota
North Texas State University
School of Music
Denton, Texas
Northeast Louisiana University
School of Music
Monroe, Louisiana
Northeast Missouri State University
Division of Fine Arts
Kirksville, Missouri
Northeastern Illinois University
Department of Music
Chicago, Illinois
Northern Arizona University
Music Department
Flagstaff, Arizona
University of Northern Colorado
School of Music
Greeley, Colorado
Northern Illinois University
School of Music
DeKalb, Illinois
University of Northern Iowa
School of Music
Cedar Falls, Iowa
Northwestern State University of Louisiana
Department of Music
Natchitoches, Louisiana
Northwestern University
School of Music
Evanston, Illinois
University of Notre Dame
Department of Music
Notre Dame, Indiana
Oakland University
Department of Music, Theatre and
Dance
Rochester, Michigan
Oberlin College
Conservatory of Music
Oberlin, Ohio
The Ohio State University
School of Music
Columbus, Ohio
Ohio University
School of Music
Athens, Ohio
Ohio Wesleyan University
Department of Music
Delaware, Ohio

University of Oklahoma
School of Music
Norman, Oklahoma
Oklahoma Baptist University
Department of Music
Shawnee, Oklahoma
Oklahoma City University
School of Music and Performing Arts
Oklahoma City, Oklahoma
Oregon State University
Department of Music
Corvallis, Oregon
Osaka Ongaku Daigaku
(Osaka College of Music)
Osaka 561, Japan
Ouachita Baptist University
School of Music
Arkadelphia, Arkansas
University of the Pacific
Conservatory of Music
Stockton, California
Pacific Lutheran University
Department of Music
Tacoma, Washington
Peabody Institute of The Johns Hopkins
University
Baltimore, Maryland
Pennsylvania State University
School of Music
University Park, Pennsylvania
Philadelphia College of the Performing Arts
School of Music
Philadelphia, Pennsylvania
University of the Philippines
College of Music
Quezon City, The Philippines
University of Pittsburgh
Department of Music
Pittsburgh, Pennsylvania
Pohjois-Kymen Musiikkiopisto
(North Kymi Music Institute)
45100 Kouvola, Finland
Pomona College
Music Department
Claremont, California
Portland State University
Department of Music
Portland, Oregon
Princeton University
Department of Music
Princeton, New Jersey
University of Puget Sound
School of Music
Tacoma, Washington
Queen's University
School of Music
Kingston, Ontario, Canada
Radford University
Department of Music
Radford, Virginia
Real Conservatorio Superior de Música de
Madrid
(Royal Academy of Music)
Madrid 13, Spain
University of Redlands
School of Music
Redlands, California
University of Regina
Department of Music
Regina, Saskatchewan, Canada
University of Rhode Island
Department of Music
Kingston, Rhode Island
Rice University
Shepherd School of Music
Houston, Texas

University of Rochester
Eastman School of Music
Rochester, New York
Rogaland Musikkonservatorium
N-4000 Stavanger, Norway
Roosevelt University
Chicago Musical College
Chicago, Illinois
Royal Academy of Music
London NW1 5HT, United Kingdom
Royal College of Music
London, SW7 2BS, United Kingdom
Royal Northern College of Music
Manchester M13 9RD, United Kingdom
Rutgers, The State University of New Jersey
Department of Music
New Brunswick, New Jersey
St. Cloud State University
Department of Music
St. Cloud, Minnesota
Saint Louis Conservatory of Music
St. Louis, Missouri
St. Olaf College
Music Department
Northfield, Minnesota
Sam Houston State University
Department of Music
Huntsville, Texas
Samford University
School of Music
Birmingham, Alabama
San Diego State University
Music Department
San Diego, California
San Francisco Conservatory of Music
San Francisco, California
San Francisco State University
Department of Music
San Francisco, California
San Jose State University
Department of Music
San Jose, California
University of Santo Tomas
Conservatory of Music
Manila, The Philippines
University of Saskatchewan
Department of Music
Saskatoon, Saskatchewan, Canada
Shenandoah College and Conservatory
Winchester, Virginia
Smith College
Department of Music
Northampton, Massachusetts
University of South Carolina
School of Music
Columbia, South Carolina
University of South Dakota
Music Department
Vermillion, South Dakota
University of South Florida
Department of Music
Tampa, Florida
Southeast Missouri State University
Department of Music
Cape Girardeau, Missouri
Southeastern Louisiana University
Department of Music
Hammond, Louisiana
Southeastern Oklahoma State University
Department of Music
Durant, Oklahoma
Southern Baptist Theological Seminary
School of Church Music
Louisville, Kentucky
University of Southern California
School of Music

Los Angeles, California
Southern Illinois University at Carbondale
School of Music
Carbondale, Illinois
Southern Illinois University at Edwardsville
Department of Music
Edwardsville, Illinois
Southern Methodist University
Meadows School of the Arts
Dallas, Texas
University of Southern Mississippi
School of Music
Hattiesburg, Mississippi
Southwest Texas State University
Department of Music
San Marcos, Texas
Southwestern Baptist Theological Seminary
School of Church Music
Fort Worth, Texas
University of Southwestern Louisiana
School of Music
Lafayette, Louisiana
Southwestern Oklahoma State University
Department of Music
Weatherford, Oklahoma
Staatliche Hochschule für Musik Freiburg
D-7800 Freiburg i. Br., Federal Republic
of Germany
Staatliche Hochschule für Musik Rheinland
- Köln
D-5000 Köln 1, Federal Republic of
Germany
Staatliche Hochschule für Musik Trossingen
D-7218 Trossingen 1, Federal Republic of
Germany
Staatliche Hochschule für Musik
Westfalen-Lippe
Institut Dortmund
D-4600 Dortmund 1, Federal Republic of
Germany
Stanford University
Department of Music
Stanford, California
State University of New York at
Binghamton
Department of Music
Binghamton, New York
State University of New York at Buffalo
Department of Music
Buffalo, New York
State University of New York at Stony
Brook
Department of Music
Stony Brook, New York
State University of New York College at
Fredonia
School of Music
Fredonia, New York
State University of New York College at
New Paltz
Department of Music
New Paltz, New York
State University of New York College at
Purchase
Division of Music
Purchase, New York
Stedelijke Muziekpedagogische Akademie
Leeuwarden, Netherlands
Stephen F. Austin State University
Department of Music
Nacogdoches, Texas
Stetson University
School of Music
Deland, Florida
Syracuse University
School of Music

Syracuse, New York
Tampereen Konservatorio
33230 Tampere, Finland
Tasmanian Conservatorium of Music
Hobart, Tasmania 7001, Australia
Teachers College of Columbia University
Department of Music and Music
Education
New York, New York
Tel Aviv University
Faculty of Fine Arts
Tel-Aviv, Israel
Temple University
Esther Boyer College of Music
Philadelphia, Pennsylvania
University of Tennessee at Chattanooga
Cadek Department of Music
Chattanooga, Tennessee
University of Tennessee at Knoxville
Department of Music
Knoxville, Tennessee
University of Texas at Arlington
Department of Music
Arlington, Texas
University of Texas at Austin
Department of Music
Austin, Texas
University of Texas at El Paso
Music Department
El Paso, Texas
University of Texas at San Antonio
Division of Music
San Antonio, Texas
Texas Christian University
Music Department
Fort Worth, Texas
Texas Southern University
Department of Music
Houston, Texas
Texas Tech University
Department of Music
Lubbock, Texas
Texas Woman's University
Department of Music and Drama
Denton, Texas
Toho Gakuen School of Music
Tokyo, Japan
The Tokyo College of Music
Tokyo 171, Japan
University of Toronto
Faculty of Music
Toronto, Ontario, Canada
Towson State University
Department of Music
Towson, Maryland
Trenton State College
Music Department
Trenton, New Jersey
Trinity College of Music
London W1M 6AQ, United Kingdom
Troy State University
Department of Music
Troy, Alabama
Tulane University
Newcomb College
New Orleans, Louisiana
University of Tulsa
Faculty of Music
Tulsa, Oklahoma
Ueno Gakuen College
Tokyo 110, Japan
Universidade do São Paulo
Department of Music
05508 São Paulo, Brazil
Université Laval
Ecole de Musique

Ste. Foy, Québec, Canada
University of Utah
Department of Music
Salt Lake City, Utah
Valdosta State College
Department of Music
Valdosta, Georgia
Valparaiso University
Department of Music
Valparaiso, Indiana
VanderCook College of Music
Chicago, Illinois
University of Vermont
Department of Music
Burlington, Vermont
University of Victoria
School of Music
Victoria, British Columbia, Canada
University of Virginia
McIntire Department of Music
Charlottesville, Virginia
Virginia Commonwealth University
Department of Music
Richmond, Virginia
Virginia Polytechnic Institute and State
University
Department of Music
Blacksburg, Virginia
Virginia State University
Department of Music Education
Petersburg, Virginia
University of Washington
School of Music
Seattle, Washington
Washington State University
Department of Music
Pullman, Washington
Washington University
Department of Music
St. Louis, Missouri
Wayne State University
Department of Music
Detroit, Michigan
Webster University
Department of Music
St. Louis, Missouri
Welsh College of Music and Drama
Cardiff, CF1 3ER, United Kingdom
Wesleyan University
Department of Music
Middletown, Connecticut
West Chester University of Pennsylvania
School of Music
West Chester, Pennsylvania
West Texas State University
Department of Music
Canyon, Texas
West Virginia University
Division of Music
Morgantown, West Virginia
Western Illinois University
Department of Music
Macomb, Illinois
Western Kentucky University
Department of Music
Bowling Green, Kentucky
Western Michigan University
School of Music
Kalamazoo, Michigan
University of Western Ontario
Faculty of Music
London, Ontario, Canada
Western Washington University
Department of Music
Bellingham, Washington

Wheaton College
  Conservatory of Music
  Wheaton, Illinois
Wichita State University
  School of Music
  Wichita, Kansas
Wiesbadener Konservatorium und staatliche
anerkannte private Fachschule für
Musikerzieher e.V.
  (Conservatory and Seminary for Music
  Education)
  *6200 Wiesbaden, Federal Republic of
  Germany*
Wilfrid Laurier University
  Faculty of Music
  Waterloo, Ontario, Canada
Willamette University
  Department of Music
  Salem, Oregon
William Carey College
  Winters School of Music
  Hattiesburg, Mississippi
William Paterson College
  Department of Music
  Wayne, New Jersey
University of Windsor
  School of Music
  Windsor, Ontario, Canada
Winthrop College
  School of Music
  Rock Hill, South Carolina
University of Wisconsin - Eau Claire
  Department of Music
  Eau Claire, Wisconsin
University of Wisconsin - La Crosse
  Department of Music
  La Crosse, Wisconsin
University of Wisconsin - Madison
  School of Music
  Madison, Wisconsin
University of Wisconsin - Milwaukee
  Music Department
  Milwaukee, Wisconsin
University of Wisconsin - Oshkosh
  Department of Music
  Oshkosh, Wisconsin
University of Wisconsin - Stevens Point
  Department of Music
  Stevens Point, Wisconsin
University of Wisconsin - Whitewater
  Department of Music
  Whitewater, Wisconsin
Wright State University
  Department of Music
  Dayton, Ohio
University of Wyoming
  Music Department
  Laramie, Wyoming
Yale University
  School of Music
  New Haven, Connecticut
York University
  Department of Music
  North York, Ontario, Canada
Youngstown State University
  Dana School of Music
  Youngstown, Ohio
Zeneiskolai Tanárkepzó Intézet
  (Music Teachers Training Institute of the
  Liszt Academy of Music)
  Budapest 1052, Hungary

PIANO

Acadia University
  School of Music
  Wolfville, Nova Scotia, Canada
Akademia Muzyczna w Krakowie
  31-038 Kraków, Poland
Akademia Muzyczna w Lódź
  (Academy of Music of Lódź)
  90-716 Lódź, Poland
Akademia Muzycznaj im. Fryderyka
  Chopina w Warzawie
  (Frederic Chopin Academy of Music of
  Warsaw)
  00-368 Warsaw, Poland
Akademie voor Musiek
  *Hilversum Postkode 1217 KR,
  Netherlands*
University of Akron
  Department of Music
  Akron, Ohio
University of Alabama
  School of Music
  University, Alabama
Alabama State University
  School of Music
  Montgomery, Alabama
University of Alaska
  Music Department
  Fairbanks, Alaska
University of Alberta
  Department of Music
  Edmonton, Alberta, Canada
Alma-Ata Kurmangazy State Conservatory
  *480091 Alma-Ata 91, Kazahskaja SSR,
  U.S.S.R.*
American Conservatory of Music
  Chicago, Illinois
Andrews University
  Department of Music
  Berrien Springs, Michigan
Appalachian State University
  Department of Music
  Boone, North Carolina
University of Arizona
  School of Music
  Tucson, Arizona
Arizona State University
  School of Music
  Tempe, Arizona
University of Arkansas
  Department of Music
  Fayetteville, Arkansas
Arkansas State University
  Department of Music
  State University, Arkansas
Arkansas Tech University
  Department of Music
  Russellville, Arkansas
Auburn University
  Department of Music
  Auburn, Alabama
Austin Peay State University
  Department of Music
  Clarksville, Tennessee
A.V. Nezhdanova Odessa Conservatory
  *270000 Odessa, Ukrainskaja SSR,
  U.S.S.R.*
Azerbaijan S.S.R. U. Gajibekov State
  Conservatory

*370014 Baku, Azerbajdžanskaja SSR,
  U.S.S.R.*
Azusa Pacific University
  School of Music
  Azusa, California
Baldwin-Wallace College
  Conservatory of Music
  Berea, Ohio
Ball State University
  School of Music
  Muncie, Indiana
Baylor University
  School of Music
  Waco, Texas
Bemidji State University
  Music Department
  Bemidji, Minnesota
Bennington College
  Music Department
  Bennington, Vermont
Berklee College of Music
  Boston, Massachusetts
Biola University
  Department of Music
  La Mirada, California
Bob Jones University
  Division of Music
  Greenville, South Carolina
Boise State University
  Music Department
  Boise, Idaho
Boston Conservatory of Music
  Boston, Massachusetts
Boston University
  School of Music
  Boston, Massachusetts
Bowling Green State University
  College of Musical Arts
  Bowling Green, Ohio
Bradley University
  Division of Music and Theatre Arts
  Peoria, Illinois
Brandeis University
  Department of Music
  Waltham, Massachusetts
Brandon University
  School of Music
  Brandon, Manitoba, Canada
Brigham Young University
  Department of Music
  Provo, Utah
University of British Columbia
  School of Music
  Vancouver, British Columbia, Canada
Brown University
  Department of Music
  Providence, Rhode Island
Bulgarian State Conservatoire
  Sofia 1505, Bulgaria
Butler University
  Jordan College of Fine Arts
  Indianapolis, Indiana
Byelorussian State Conservatory
  *220030 Minsk, Belorusskaja SSR,
  U.S.S.R.*
University of Calgary
  Department of Music
  Calgary, Alberta, Canada
University of California, Berkeley
  Department of Music
  Berkeley, California
University of California, Davis
  Department of Music
  Davis, California
University of California, Irvine
  School of Fine Arts

Irvine, California
University of California, Los Angeles
  Department of Music
  Los Angeles, California
University of California, Riverside
  Department of Music
  Riverside, California
University of California, San Diego
  Department of Music
  La Jolla, California
University of California, Santa Barbara
  Department of Music
  Santa Barbara, California
University of California, Santa Cruz
  Music Board, Division of the Arts
  Santa Cruz, California
California Institute of the Arts
  School of Music
  Valencia, California
California State University, Chico
  Department of Music
  Chico, California
California State University, Fresno
  Department of Music
  Fresno, California
California State University, Fullerton
  Department of Music
  Fullerton, California
California State University, Hayward
  Department of Music
  Hayward, California
California State University, Long Beach
  Department of Music
  Long Beach, California
California State University, Los Angeles
  Department of Music
  Los Angeles, California
California State University, Northridge
  Music Department
  Northridge, California
California State University, Sacramento
  Department of Music
  Sacramento, California
Carnegie-Mellon University
  Department of Music
  Pittsburgh, Pennsylvania
Case Western Reserve University
  Department of Music
  Cleveland, Ohio
The Catholic University of America
  The Benjamin T. Rome School of Music
  Washington, District of Columbia
University of Central Arkansas
  Department of Music
  Conway, Arkansas
Central Conservatory of Music
  Beijing, People's Republic of China
University of Central Florida
  Department of Music
  Orlando, Florida
Central Michigan University
  Department of Music
  Mount Pleasant, Michigan
Central Missouri State University
  Department of Music
  Warrensburg, Missouri
Central State University
  Department of Music
  Edmond, Oklahoma
Central Washington University
  Department of Music
  Ellensburg, Washington
University of Cincinnati
  College-Conservatory of Music
  Cincinnati, Ohio

City of Leeds College of Music
  Leeds LS2 8BH, United Kingdom
City University of New York - Brooklyn
  College
  Conservatory of Music
  Brooklyn, New York
City University of New York - City College
  Department of Music
  New York, New York
City University of New York - Hunter
  College
  Department of Music
  New York, New York
City University of New York - Queens
  College
  The Aaron Copland School of Music
  Flushing, New York
The Claremont Graduate School
  Music Department
  Claremont, California
Cleveland Institute of Music
  Cleveland, Ohio
Cleveland State University
  Department of Music
  Cleveland, Ohio
University of Colorado at Boulder
  College of Music
  Boulder, Colorado
University of Colorado at Denver
  College of Music
  Denver, Colorado
Colorado State University
  Department of Music, Theatre, and
  Dance
  Fort Collins, Colorado
Columbia University
  Department of Music
  New York, New York
Columbus College
  Department of Music
  Columbus, Georgia
Combs College of Music
  Philadelphia, Pennsylvania
University of Connecticut
  Department of Music
  Storrs, Connecticut
Conservatoire de Musique de La
  Chaux-de-Fonds - Le Locle
  2300 La Chaux-de-Fonds, Switzerland
Conservatorio di Musica "Claudio
  Monteverdi"
  I-39100 Bolzano, Italy
Conservatorio di Musica "Santa Cecilia"
  00187 Rome, Italy
Conservatorio Nacional de Música
  (National Conservatory of Music)
  Lima 1, Peru
Converse College
  School of Music
  Spartanburg, South Carolina
Cornell University
  Department of Music
  Ithaca, New York
The Curtis Institute of Music
  Philadelphia, Pennsylvania
Dalhousie University
  Department of Music
  Halifax, Nova Scotia, Canada
University of Delaware
  Department of Music
  Newark, Delaware
Delta State University
  Department of Music
  Cleveland, Mississippi
University of Denver
  Lamont School of Music

Denver, Colorado
DePaul University
  School of Music
  Chicago, Illinois
DePauw University
  School of Music
  Greencastle, Indiana
Drake University
  Department of Music
  Des Moines, Iowa
Duke University
  Department of Music
  Durham, North Carolina
Duquesne University
  School of Music
  Pittsburgh, Pennsylvania
East Carolina University
  School of Music
  Greenville, North Carolina
East Texas State University
  Department of Music
  Commerce, Texas
Eastern Illinois University
  Department of Music
  Charleston, Illinois
Eastern Kentucky University
  Department of Music
  Richmond, Kentucky
Eastern Michigan University
  Department of Music
  Ypsilanti, Michigan
Eastern New Mexico University
  School of Music
  Portales, New Mexico
Eastern Washington University
  Department of Music
  Cheney, Washington
Emporia State University
  Division of Music
  Emporia, Kansas
Erevan Komitas State Conservatory
  *375009 Erevan 9, Armjanskaja SSR,
  U.S.S.R.*
Escuela de Música - Heredia
  Universidad Nacional
  Heredia, Costa Rica
Escuela Nacional de Música
  Universidad Nacional Autónoma de
  México
  Mexico City, D.F. 04100, Mexico
Escuela Universitaria de Música -
  Montevideo
  Montevideo, Uruguay
Evangelische Kirchenmusikschule der
  Kirchenprovinz Sachsen
  (Evangelical Church Music School of the
  Church Province Saxony)
  *DDR-4020 Halle (Saale), German
  Democratic Republic*
University of Evansville
  Music Department
  Evansville, Indiana
Fachakademie für Music - Augsburg
  Leopold Mozart-Konservatorium der
  Stadt Augsburg
  Augsberg, Federal Republic of Germany
Fachakademie für Musik - München
  Richard Strauss-Konservatorium der
  Stadt
  *München 80, Federal Republic of
  Germany*
Fachakademie für Musik - Nürnberg
  Konservatorium der Stadt Nürnberg
  Nürnberg, Federal Republic of Germany
Far-Eastern Pedagogical Institute of the
  Arts

690678 Vladivostok, Rossiskaja SFSR,
U.S.S.R.
Ferenc Liszt Academy of Music
Budapest VI, Hungary
University of Florida
Department of Music
Gainesville, Florida
Florida State University
School of Music
Tallahassee, Florida
Fort Hays State University
Department of Music
Hays, Kansas
George Mason University
Department of Performing Arts - Music
Division
Fairfax, Virginia
University of Georgia
School of Music
Athens, Georgia
Georgia Southern College
Department of Music
Statesboro, Georgia
Georgia State University
School of Music
Atlanta, Georgia
Glassboro State College
Department of Music
Glassboro, New Jersey
Gnessinsky State Musical and Pedagogical
Institute
121069 Moscow G-69, Rossiskaja SFSR,
U.S.S.R.
Gorky M.I. Glinka State Conservatory
603005 Gorky, Rossiskaja SFSR, U.S.S.R.
Guildhall School of Music and Drama
London EC2Y 8DT, United Kingdom
Hardin-Simmons University
School of Music
Abilene, Texas
University of Hartford
Hartt School of Music
West Hartford, Connecticut
Harvard University
Department of Music
Cambridge, Massachusetts
University of Hawaii at Manoa
Music Department
Honolulu, Hawaii
Henderson State University
Department of Music
Arkadelphia, Arkansas
Hochschule der Künste Berlin
1000 Berlin 10, Federal Republic of
Germany
Hochschule für Music Franz Liszt
DDR 5300 Weimar, German Democratic
Republic
Hochschule für Music und Darstellende
Kunst Hamburg
2000 Hamburg 13, Federal Republic of
Germany
Hochschule für Musik - Würzburg
D-8700 Würzburg, Federal Republic of
Germany
Hochschule für Musik Carl Maria von
Weber
DDR 8010 Dresden, German Democratic
Republic
Hochschule für Musik Felix
Mendelssohn-Bartholdy
7010 Leipzig, German Democratic
Republic
Hochschule für Musik und Darstellande
Kunst "Mozarteum" Salzburg
(College of Music and Dramatic Art

"Mozarteum")
5020 Salzburg, Austria
Hochschule für Musik und Darstellende
Kunst Frankfurt am Main
6000 Frankfurt am Main 1, Federal
Republic of Germany
Hochschule für Musik und Darstellende
Kunst Graz
A-8010 Graz, Austria
Hochschule für Musik und Darstellende
Kunst Wien
(College of Music and Dramatic Art)
1030 Wien, Austria
Hochschule für Musik und Theater
Hannover
3000 Hannover 1, Federal Republic of
Germany
Hofstra University
Department of Music
Hempstead, New York
The Hong Kong Academy for Performing
Arts
School of Music
Wanchai, Hong Kong
University of Houston
School of Music
Houston, Texas
Howard University
Department of Music
Washington, District of Columbia
University of Idaho
School of Music
Moscow, Idaho
University of Illinois
School of Music
Urbana, Illinois
Illinois State University
Department of Music
Normal, Illinois
Illinois Wesleyan University
School of Music
Bloomington, Illinois
Indiana State University
Department of Music
Terre Haute, Indiana
Indiana University - Bloomington
School of Music
Bloomington, Indiana
Indiana University of Pennsylvania
Department of Music
Indiana, Pennsylvania
Institute of Fine Arts
Faculty of Music
Rangoon, Burma
Instituto Superior de Arte
Facultad de Música
Playa, Cuba
University of Iowa
School of Music
Iowa City, Iowa
Iowa State University
Department of Music
Ames, Iowa
Ithaca College
School of Music
Ithaca, New York
Jackson State University
Department of Music
Jackson, Mississippi
Jacksonville State University
Department of Music
Jacksonville, Alabama
James Madison University
Department of Music
Harrisonburg, Virginia

Jersey City State College
Music Department
Jersey City, New Jersey
The Jerusalem Rubin Academy of Music
and Dance
Jerusalem, Israel
The Juilliard School
New York, New York
University of Kansas
School of Fine Arts
Lawrence, Kansas
Kansas State University
Department of Music
Manhattan, Kansas
Karol Szymanowski Academy of Music of
Katowice
Katowice, Poland
Kazan State Conservatory
420015 Kazan 15, Rossiskaja SFSR,
U.S.S.R.
Kent State University
School of Music
Kent, Ohio
University of Kentucky
School of Music
Lexington, Kentucky
Kenya Conservatoire of Music
Nairobi, Kenya
Kharkov State Institute of Arts
310003 Kharkov, U.S.S.R.
Kiev P.I. Tchaikovsky Conservatory
252001 Kiev, Ukrainskaja SSR, U.S.S.R.
Koninklijk Muziekconservatorium van
Brussel
1000 Brussels, Belgium
Konservatorium für Musik und Theater
CH-3011 Berne, Switzerland
Konzervatoř v Praze
(State Conservatory Prague)
Praha 110 00, Czechoslovakia
Konzervatorium - Bratislava
Bratislava 811 06, Czechoslovakia
Kuopion Konservatorio
70100 Kuopio, Finland
Lamar University
Department of Music
Beaumont, Texas
Latvian S.S.R. Y. Vitol State Conservatory
226050 Riga, Latvijskaya SSR, U.S.S.R.
Lawrence University
Conservatory of Music
Appleton, Wisconsin
Leningrad N.A. Rimsky-Korsakov State
Conservatory
192041 Leningrad, Rossiskaja SFSR,
U.S.S.R.
Levinsky Teachers College
Music Teachers Seminary
Tel-Aviv, Israel
Lewis and Clark College
Music Department
Portland, Oregon
Lithuanian State Conservatory
232001 Vilnius, Litovskaja SSR, U.S.S.R.
Long Island University - C.W. Post Campus
Music Department
Greenvale, New York
Louisiana State University
School of Music
Baton Rouge, Louisiana
Louisiana Tech University
Department of Music
Ruston, Louisiana
University of Louisville
School of Music
Louisville, Kentucky

University of Lowell
  College of Music
  Lowell, Massachusetts
Loyola University
  College of Music
  New Orleans, Louisiana
Lvov M.V. Lysenko State Conservatory
  290005 Lvov, Ukrainskaja SSR, U.S.S.R.
University of Maine
  School of Performing Arts
  Orono, Maine
Mandalay School of Music, Dance,
  Painting, and Sculpture
  Mandalay, Burma
Manhattan School of Music
  New York, New York
University of Manitoba
  School of Music
  Winnipeg, Manitoba, Canada
Mankato State University
  Department of Music
  Mankato, Minnesota
Mannes College of Music
  New York, New York
Mansfield University
  Department of Music
  Mansfield, Pennsylvania
Marshall University
  Department of Music
  Huntington, West Virginia
University of Maryland - Baltimore County
  Department of Music
  Catonsville, Maryland
University of Maryland - College Park
  Department of Music
  College Park, Maryland
Marywood College
  Music Department
  Scranton, Pennsylvania
University of Massachusetts at Amherst
  Department of Music and Dance
  Amherst, Massachusetts
McGill University
  Faculty of Music
  Montreal, Québec, Canada
McMaster University
  Department of Music
  Hamilton, Ontario, Canada
McNeese State University
  Department of Music
  Lake Charles, Louisiana
Memphis State University
  Music Department
  Memphis, Tennessee
University of Miami
  School of Music
  Coral Gables, Florida
Miami University
  Department of Music
  Oxford, Ohio
University of Michigan
  School of Music
  Ann Arbor, Michigan
Michigan State University
  School of Music
  East Lansing, Michigan
Middle Tennessee State University
  Department of Music
  Murfreesboro, Tennessee
Millikin University
  School of Music
  Decatur, Illinois
Mills College
  Music Department
  Oakland, California

University of Minnesota - Duluth
  Department of Music
  Duluth, Minnesota
University of Minnesota - Twin Cities
  School of Music
  Minneapolis, Minnesota
University of Mississippi
  Department of Music
  University, Mississippi
University of Missouri - Columbia
  Department of Music
  Columbia, Missouri
University of Missouri - Kansas City
  Conservatory of Music
  Kansas City, Missouri
Moldavian S.S.R. G. Musichesku State
  Conservatory
  *277014 Kishinev, Moldavskaja SSR,
  U.S.S.R.*
University of Montana
  Department of Music
  Missoula, Montana
Montana State University
  Department of Music
  Bozeman, Montana
Montclair State College
  Department of Music
  Upper Montclair, New Jersey
University of Montevallo
  Department of Music
  Montevallo, Alabama
Moorhead State University
  Music Department
  Moorhead, Minnesota
Morehead State University
  Department of Music
  Morehead, Kentucky
Moscow P.I. Tchaikovsky State
  Conservatory
  *103009 Moscow K-9, Rossiskaja SFSR,
  U.S.S.R.*
Musik-Akademie der Stadt Basel
  (Konservatorium)
  Konservatorium (Musikhochschule)
  Basel, Switzerland
Musikhochschule des Saarlandes
  *6600 Saarbrücken 3, Federal Republic of
  Germany*
Musikhögskolan i Stockholm
  National College of Music
  115 31 Stockholm, Sweden
Musikschule und Konservatorium
  Schaffhausen
  Schaffhausen, Switzerland
National Institute of Music - Sana'a
  Sana'a, Yemen Arab Republic
National Institute of the Arts
  Music Department
  *Taipei County, Taiwan (Republic of
  China)*
University of Nebraska - Lincoln
  School of Music
  Lincoln, Nebraska
University of Nebraska - Omaha
  Department of Music
  Omaha, Nebraska
Nederlands Instituut voor Kerkmuziek
  Utrecht, Netherlands
University of Nevada, Las Vegas
  Department of Music
  Las Vegas, Nevada
University of Nevada, Reno
  Department of Music
  Reno, Nevada
New England Conservatory
  Boston, Massachusetts

University of New Hampshire
  Department of Music
  Durham, New Hampshire
University of New Mexico
  Department of Music
  Albuquerque, New Mexico
New Mexico State University
  Department of Music
  Las Cruces, New Mexico
University of New Orleans
  Department of Music
  New Orleans, Louisiana
New South Wales State Conservatorium of
  Music
  Sydney NSW 2000, Australia
New York University - School of Education,
  Health, Nursing, and Arts Professions
  Department of Music and Music
  Education
  New York, New York
Nikos Skalkotas Conservatory
  Athens 11141, Greece
Norfolk State University
  Department of Music
  Norfolk, Virginia
Norges Musikkhøgskole
  (The Norwegian State Academy of
  Music)
  N-0130 Oslo 1, Norway
University of North Carolina at Chapel Hill
  Department of Music
  Chapel Hill, North Carolina
University of North Carolina at Greensboro
  School of Music
  Greensboro, North Carolina
North Carolina School of the Arts
  School of Music
  Winston-Salem, North Carolina
University of North Dakota
  Department of Music
  Grand Forks, North Dakota
North Texas State University
  School of Music
  Denton, Texas
Northeast Louisiana University
  School of Music
  Monroe, Louisiana
Northeast Missouri State University
  Division of Fine Arts
  Kirksville, Missouri
Northeastern Illinois University
  Department of Music
  Chicago, Illinois
Northern Arizona University
  Music Department
  Flagstaff, Arizona
University of Northern Colorado
  School of Music
  Greeley, Colorado
Northern Illinois University
  School of Music
  DeKalb, Illinois
University of Northern Iowa
  School of Music
  Cedar Falls, Iowa
Northwestern State University of Louisiana
  Department of Music
  Natchitoches, Louisiana
Northwestern University
  School of Music
  Evanston, Illinois
University of Notre Dame
  Department of Music
  Notre Dame, Indiana
Novosibirsk M.I. Glinka State Conservatory
  630099 Novosibirsk 99, Rossiskaja SFSR,

U.S.S.R.

Oakland University
Department of Music, Theatre and
Dance
Rochester, Michigan
Oberlin College
Conservatory of Music
Oberlin, Ohio
The Ohio State University
School of Music
Columbus, Ohio
Ohio University
School of Music
Athens, Ohio
Ohio Wesleyan University
Department of Music
Delaware, Ohio
University of Oklahoma
School of Music
Norman, Oklahoma
Oklahoma Baptist University
Department of Music
Shawnee, Oklahoma
Oklahoma City University
School of Music and Performing Arts
Oklahoma City, Oklahoma
University of Oregon
School of Music
Eugene, Oregon
Oregon State University
Department of Music
Corvallis, Oregon
Osaka Ongaku Daigaku
(Osaka College of Music)
Osaka 561, Japan
Ouachita Baptist University
School of Music
Arkadelphia, Arkansas
University of the Pacific
Conservatory of Music
Stockton, California
Pacific Lutheran University
Department of Music
Tacoma, Washington
Peabody Institute of The Johns Hopkins
University
Baltimore, Maryland
University of Pennsylvania
Department of Music
Philadelphia, Pennsylvania
Pennsylvania State University
School of Music
University Park, Pennsylvania
Philadelphia College of the Performing Arts
School of Music
Philadelphia, Pennsylvania
University of the Philippines
College of Music
Quezon City, The Philippines
Pittsburg State University
Department of Music
Pittsburg, Kansas
University of Pittsburgh
Department of Music
Pittsburgh, Pennsylvania
Pohjois-Kymen Musiikkiopisto
(North Kymi Music Institute)
45100 Kouvola, Finland
Pomona College
Music Department
Claremont, California
Pontifical Institute of Sacred Music
I - 00165 Roma, Italy
Portland State University
Department of Music
Portland, Oregon

Princeton University
Department of Music
Princeton, New Jersey
University of Puget Sound
School of Music
Tacoma, Washington
Queen's University
School of Music
Kingston, Ontario, Canada
Radford University
Department of Music
Radford, Virginia
Real Conservatorio Superior de Música de
Madrid
(Royal Academy of Music)
Madrid 13, Spain
University of Redlands
School of Music
Redlands, California
University of Regina
Department of Music
Regina, Saskatchewan, Canada
University of Rhode Island
Department of Music
Kingston, Rhode Island
Rice University
Shepherd School of Music
Houston, Texas
University of Rochester
Eastman School of Music
Rochester, New York
Rogaland Musikkonservatorium
N-4000 Stavanger, Norway
Roosevelt University
Chicago Musical College
Chicago, Illinois
Royal Academy of Music
London NW1 5HT, United Kingdom
Royal College of Music
London, SW7 2BS, United Kingdom
Royal Northern College of Music
Manchester M13 9RD, United Kingdom
Royal Scottish Academy of Music and
Drama
Glasgow G2 1BS, United Kingdom
Rutgers, The State University of New Jersey
Department of Music
New Brunswick, New Jersey
St. Cloud State University
Department of Music
St. Cloud, Minnesota
Saint Louis Conservatory of Music
St. Louis, Missouri
St. Olaf College
Music Department
Northfield, Minnesota
Sam Houston State University
Department of Music
Huntsville, Texas
Samford University
School of Music
Birmingham, Alabama
San Diego State University
Music Department
San Diego, California
San Francisco Conservatory of Music
San Francisco, California
San Francisco State University
Department of Music
San Francisco, California
San Jose State University
Department of Music
San Jose, California
University of Santo Tomas
Conservatory of Music
Manila, The Philippines

Saratov L.V. Sobinov State Conservatory
*410000 Saratov, Rossiskaja SFSR,
U.S.S.R.*
University of Saskatchewan
Department of Music
Saskatoon, Saskatchewan, Canada
Shanghai Conservatory of Music
Shanghai, People's Republic of China
Shenandoah College and Conservatory
Winchester, Virginia
Shengyang Conservatory of Music
*Shengyang, Liaoning Province, People's
Republic of China*
Shorter College
Department of Music
Rome, Georgia
Sichuan Conservatory of Music
*Chengdu, Sichuan, People's Republic of
China*
Smith College
Department of Music
Northampton, Massachusetts
University of South Carolina
School of Music
Columbia, South Carolina
University of South Dakota
Music Department
Vermillion, South Dakota
University of South Florida
Department of Music
Tampa, Florida
Southeast Missouri State University
Department of Music
Cape Girardeau, Missouri
Southeastern Louisiana University
Department of Music
Hammond, Louisiana
Southeastern Oklahoma State University
Department of Music
Durant, Oklahoma
Southern Baptist Theological Seminary
School of Church Music
Louisville, Kentucky
University of Southern California
School of Music
Los Angeles, California
Southern Illinois University at Carbondale
School of Music
Carbondale, Illinois
Southern Illinois University at Edwardsville
Department of Music
Edwardsville, Illinois
Southern Methodist University
Meadows School of the Arts
Dallas, Texas
University of Southern Mississippi
School of Music
Hattiesburg, Mississippi
Southwest Texas State University
Department of Music
San Marcos, Texas
Southwestern Baptist Theological Seminary
School of Church Music
Fort Worth, Texas
University of Southwestern Louisiana
School of Music
Lafayette, Louisiana
Southwestern Oklahoma State University
Department of Music
Weatherford, Oklahoma
Staatliche Hochschule für Musik Freiburg
*D-7800 Freiburg i. Br., Federal Republic
of Germany*
Staatliche Hochschule für Musik Rheinland
- Köln
D-5000 Köln 1, Federal Republic of

Germany
Staatliche Hochschule für Musik Rheinland
- Wuppertal
Institute Wuppertal
Wuppertal, Federal Republic of Germany
Staatliche Hochschule für Musik Ruhr
4300 Essen 16, Federal Republic of Germany
Staatliche Hochschule für Musik Trossingen
D-7218 Trossingen 1, Federal Republic of Germany
Staatliche Hochschule für Musik
Westfalen-Lippe
4930 Detmold, Federal Republic of Germany
Staatliche Hochschule für Musik
Westfalen-Lippe
Institut Dortmund
D-4600 Dortmund 1, Federal Republic of Germany
Stanford University
Department of Music
Stanford, California
State University of New York at
Binghamton
Department of Music
Binghamton, New York
State University of New York at Buffalo
Department of Music
Buffalo, New York
State University of New York at Stony
Brook
Department of Music
Stony Brook, New York
State University of New York College at
Fredonia
School of Music
Fredonia, New York
State University of New York College at
New Paltz
Department of Music
New Paltz, New York
State University of New York College at
Potsdam
Crane School of Music
Potsdam, New York
State University of New York College at
Purchase
Division of Music
Purchase, New York
Stedelijke Muziekpedagogische Akademie
Leeuwarden, Netherlands
Stephen F. Austin State University
Department of Music
Nacogdoches, Texas
Stetson University
School of Music
Deland, Florida
Syracuse University
School of Music
Syracuse, New York
Tashkent State Conservatory
700000 Tashkent, Uzbekskaja SSR, U.S.S.R.
Tasmanian Conservatorium of Music
Hobart, Tasmania 7001, Australia
Tbilisi V. Sarajishvili State Conservatory
380004 Tbilisi 4, Gruzinskaja SSR, U.S.S.R.
Teachers College of Columbia University
Department of Music and Music
Education
New York, New York
Tel Aviv University
Faculty of Fine Arts
Tel-Aviv, Israel

Temple University
Esther Boyer College of Music
Philadelphia, Pennsylvania
University of Tennessee at Chattanooga
Cadek Department of Music
Chattanooga, Tennessee
University of Tennessee at Knoxville
Department of Music
Knoxville, Tennessee
University of Texas at Arlington
Department of Music
Arlington, Texas
University of Texas at Austin
Department of Music
Austin, Texas
University of Texas at El Paso
Music Department
El Paso, Texas
University of Texas at San Antonio
Division of Music
San Antonio, Texas
Texas Christian University
Music Department
Fort Worth, Texas
Texas Southern University
Department of Music
Houston, Texas
Texas Tech University
Department of Music
Lubbock, Texas
Texas Woman's University
Department of Music and Drama
Denton, Texas
Toho Gakuen School of Music
Tokyo, Japan
The Tokyo College of Music
Tokyo 171, Japan
Tonlistarskolinn i Reykjavik
105 Reykjavik, Iceland
University of Toronto
Faculty of Music
Toronto, Ontario, Canada
Towson State University
Department of Music
Towson, Maryland
Trenton State College
Music Department
Trenton, New Jersey
Trinity College of Music
London W1M 6AQ, United Kingdom
Troy State University
Department of Music
Troy, Alabama
Tulane University
Newcomb College
New Orleans, Louisiana
University of Tulsa
Faculty of Music
Tulsa, Oklahoma
Ueno Gakuen College
Tokyo 110, Japan
Universidad de Antioquía
Facultad de Artes, Departamento de
Música
Medellín, Colombia
Universidad de Concepción
Departamento de Arte
Concepción, Chile
Universidade do Rio de Janeiro
Letters and Arts Center - Music Course
22290 Rio de Janeiro, Brazil
Universidade do São Paulo
Department of Music
05508 São Paulo, Brazil
Université de Montréal
Faculty of Music

Montréal, Québec, Canada
Université Laval
Ecole de Musique
Ste. Foy, Québec, Canada
Urals M.P. Mussorgsky State Conservatory
620014 Sverdlovsk, Rossiskaja SFSR, U.S.S.R.
University of Utah
Department of Music
Salt Lake City, Utah
Valdosta State College
Department of Music
Valdosta, Georgia
Valparaiso University
Department of Music
Valparaiso, Indiana
VanderCook College of Music
Chicago, Illinois
University of Vermont
Department of Music
Burlington, Vermont
University of Victoria
School of Music
Victoria, British Columbia, Canada
University of Virginia
McIntire Department of Music
Charlottesville, Virginia
Virginia Commonwealth University
Department of Music
Richmond, Virginia
Virginia Polytechnic Institute and State
University
Department of Music
Blacksburg, Virginia
Virginia State University
Department of Music Education
Petersburg, Virginia
Vysoká Skola Mûzickych Umeni v Praha
Academy of Music and Dramatic Arts
1101 00 Prague 1, Czechoslovakia
University of Washington
School of Music
Seattle, Washington
Washington State University
Department of Music
Pullman, Washington
Washington University
Department of Music
St. Louis, Missouri
Wayne State University
Department of Music
Detroit, Michigan
Webster University
Department of Music
St. Louis, Missouri
Welsh College of Music and Drama
Cardiff, CF1 3ER, United Kingdom
Wesleyan University
Department of Music
Middletown, Connecticut
West Chester University of Pennsylvania
School of Music
West Chester, Pennsylvania
West Georgia College
Department of Music
Carrollton, Georgia
West Texas State University
Department of Music
Canyon, Texas
West Virginia University
Division of Music
Morgantown, West Virginia
Western Illinois University
Department of Music
Macomb, Illinois

Western Kentucky University
Department of Music
Bowling Green, Kentucky
Western Michigan University
School of Music
Kalamazoo, Michigan
University of Western Ontario
Faculty of Music
London, Ontario, Canada
Western Washington University
Department of Music
Bellingham, Washington
Westminster Choir College
Princeton, New Jersey
Wheaton College
Conservatory of Music
Wheaton, Illinois
Wichita State University
School of Music
Wichita, Kansas
Wiesbadener Konservatorium und staatliche
anerkannte private Fachschule für
Musikerzieher e.V.
(Conservatory and Seminary for Music
Education)
*6200 Wiesbaden, Federal Republic of
Germany*
Wilfrid Laurier University
Faculty of Music
Waterloo, Ontario, Canada
Willamette University
Department of Music
Salem, Oregon
William Carey College
Winters School of Music
Hattiesburg, Mississippi
William Paterson College
Department of Music
Wayne, New Jersey
University of Windsor
School of Music
Windsor, Ontario, Canada
Winthrop College
School of Music
Rock Hill, South Carolina
University of Wisconsin - Eau Claire
Department of Music
Eau Claire, Wisconsin
University of Wisconsin - La Crosse
Department of Music
La Crosse, Wisconsin
University of Wisconsin - Madison
School of Music
Madison, Wisconsin
University of Wisconsin - Milwaukee
Music Department
Milwaukee, Wisconsin
University of Wisconsin - Oshkosh
Department of Music
Oshkosh, Wisconsin
University of Wisconsin - Stevens Point
Department of Music
Stevens Point, Wisconsin
University of Wisconsin - Whitewater
Department of Music
Whitewater, Wisconsin
Wright State University
Department of Music
Dayton, Ohio
University of Wyoming
Music Department
Laramie, Wyoming
Yale College (Yale University)
Department of Music
New Haven, Connecticut

Yale University
School of Music
New Haven, Connecticut
York University
Department of Music
North York, Ontario, Canada
Youngstown State University
Dana School of Music
Youngstown, Ohio
Zeneiskolai Tanárkepző Intézet
(Music Teachers Training Institute of the
Liszt Academy of Music)
Budapest 1052, Hungary

PIANO PEDAGOGY

DePauw University
School of Music
Greencastle, Indiana

PICCOLO

Bob Jones University
Division of Music
Greenville, South Carolina
University of British Columbia
School of Music
Vancouver, British Columbia, Canada
East Carolina University
School of Music
Greenville, North Carolina
Hofstra University
Department of Music
Hempstead, New York
Indiana University - Bloomington
School of Music
Bloomington, Indiana
Middle Tennessee State University
Department of Music
Murfreesboro, Tennessee
St. Cloud State University
Department of Music
St. Cloud, Minnesota
Samford University
School of Music
Birmingham, Alabama
San Jose State University
Department of Music
San Jose, California
Southeastern Oklahoma State University
Department of Music
Durant, Oklahoma
William Carey College
Winters School of Music
Hattiesburg, Mississippi

PIPA

University of the Philippines
College of Music
Quezon City, The Philippines

RECORDER

University of Arkansas
Department of Music
Fayetteville, Arkansas
Bradley University
Division of Music and Theatre Arts
Peoria, Illinois
University of California, Riverside
Department of Music
Riverside, California
Case Western Reserve University
Department of Music
Cleveland, Ohio
University of Central Florida
Department of Music
Orlando, Florida

Central Washington University
Department of Music
Ellensburg, Washington
Dalhousie University
Department of Music
Halifax, Nova Scotia, Canada
Eastern Illinois University
Department of Music
Charleston, Illinois
Escuela Nacional de Música
Universidad Nacional Autónoma de
México
Mexico City, D.F. 04100, Mexico
University of Hartford
Hartt School of Music
West Hartford, Connecticut
University of Hawaii at Manoa
Music Department
Honolulu, Hawaii
Hermann-Zilcher-Konservatorium
*D-8700 Würzburg, Federal Republic of
Germany*
Hochschule für Music und Darstellende
Kunst Hamburg
*2000 Hamburg 13, Federal Republic of
Germany*
Kenya Conservatoire of Music
Nairobi, Kenya
Lewis and Clark College
Music Department
Portland, Oregon
New England Conservatory
Boston, Massachusetts
University of North Carolina at Chapel Hill
Department of Music
Chapel Hill, North Carolina
Northeast Louisiana University
School of Music
Monroe, Louisiana
Oakland University
Department of Music, Theatre and
Dance
Rochester, Michigan
Oberlin College
Conservatory of Music
Oberlin, Ohio
University of Oregon
School of Music
Eugene, Oregon
University of Rhode Island
Department of Music
Kingston, Rhode Island
University of Saskatchewan
Department of Music
Saskatoon, Saskatchewan, Canada
Smith College
Department of Music
Northampton, Massachusetts
Southern Illinois University at Carbondale
School of Music
Carbondale, Illinois
Staatliche Hochschule für Musik Trossingen
*D-7218 Trossingen 1, Federal Republic of
Germany*
Teachers College of Columbia University
Department of Music and Music
Education
New York, New York
Toho Gakuen School of Music
Tokyo, Japan
University of Toronto
Faculty of Music
Toronto, Ontario, Canada
Ueno Gakuen College
Tokyo 110, Japan

Universidad de Concepción
Departamento de Arte
Concepción, Chile
Wiesbadener Konservatorium und staatliche
anerkannte private Fachschule für
Musikerzieher e.V.
(Conservatory and Seminary for Music
Education)
*6200 Wiesbaden, Federal Republic of
Germany*
Wilfrid Laurier University
Faculty of Music
Waterloo, Ontario, Canada

RENAISSANCE INSTRUMENTS

Bowling Green State University
College of Musical Arts
Bowling Green, Ohio
Case Western Reserve University
Department of Music
Cleveland, Ohio
Columbia University
Department of Music
New York, New York
Mannes College of Music
New York, New York
Stanford University
Department of Music
Stanford, California
Teachers College of Columbia University
Department of Music and Music
Education
New York, New York

RENAISSANCE WINDS

Oakland University
Department of Music, Theatre and
Dance
Rochester, Michigan

SAXOPHONE

Acadia University
School of Music
Wolfville, Nova Scotia, Canada
Akademia Muzyczna w Krakowie
31-038 Kraków, Poland
University of Alabama
School of Music
University, Alabama
University of Alaska
Music Department
Fairbanks, Alaska
American Conservatory of Music
Chicago, Illinois
University of Arizona
School of Music
Tucson, Arizona
Arkansas Tech University
Department of Music
Russellville, Arkansas
Austin Peay State University
Department of Music
Clarksville, Tennessee
Baldwin-Wallace College
Conservatory of Music
Berea, Ohio
Baylor University
School of Music
Waco, Texas
Boston University
School of Music
Boston, Massachusetts
Bowling Green State University
College of Musical Arts
Bowling Green, Ohio

Bradley University
Division of Music and Theatre Arts
Peoria, Illinois
University of British Columbia
School of Music
Vancouver, British Columbia, Canada
Butler University
Jordan College of Fine Arts
Indianapolis, Indiana
University of California, Los Angeles
Department of Music
Los Angeles, California
University of California, Riverside
Department of Music
Riverside, California
University of California, San Diego
Department of Music
La Jolla, California
California State University, Hayward
Department of Music
Hayward, California
The Catholic University of America
The Benjamin T. Rome School of Music
Washington, District of Columbia
University of Central Arkansas
Department of Music
Conway, Arkansas
University of Central Florida
Department of Music
Orlando, Florida
Central Missouri State University
Department of Music
Warrensburg, Missouri
Central Washington University
Department of Music
Ellensburg, Washington
University of Cincinnati
College-Conservatory of Music
Cincinnati, Ohio
City of Leeds College of Music
Leeds LS2 8BH, United Kingdom
The Claremont Graduate School
Music Department
Claremont, California
Cleveland State University
Department of Music
Cleveland, Ohio
University of Colorado at Boulder
College of Music
Boulder, Colorado
Colorado State University
Department of Music, Theatre, and
Dance
Fort Collins, Colorado
University of Connecticut
Department of Music
Storrs, Connecticut
Delta State University
Department of Music
Cleveland, Mississippi
University of Denver
Lamont School of Music
Denver, Colorado
DePaul University
School of Music
Chicago, Illinois
Drake University
Department of Music
Des Moines, Iowa
Duquesne University
School of Music
Pittsburgh, Pennsylvania
East Carolina University
School of Music
Greenville, North Carolina

Eastern Illinois University
Department of Music
Charleston, Illinois
Eastern Michigan University
Department of Music
Ypsilanti, Michigan
Emporia State University
Division of Music
Emporia, Kansas
Escuela Nacional de Música
Universidad Nacional Autónoma de
México
Mexico City, D.F. 04100, Mexico
University of Florida
Department of Music
Gainesville, Florida
Florida State University
School of Music
Tallahassee, Florida
George Mason University
Department of Performing Arts - Music
Division
Fairfax, Virginia
University of Hartford
Hartt School of Music
West Hartford, Connecticut
Hochschule der Künste Berlin
*1000 Berlin 10, Federal Republic of
Germany*
Hofstra University
Department of Music
Hempstead, New York
Howard University
Department of Music
Washington, District of Columbia
University of Idaho
School of Music
Moscow, Idaho
University of Illinois
School of Music
Urbana, Illinois
Illinois Wesleyan University
School of Music
Bloomington, Illinois
Indiana State University
Department of Music
Terre Haute, Indiana
Indiana University - Bloomington
School of Music
Bloomington, Indiana
Instituto Superior de Arte
Facultad de Música
Playa, Cuba
University of Iowa
School of Music
Iowa City, Iowa
Iowa State University
Department of Music
Ames, Iowa
Ithaca College
School of Music
Ithaca, New York
Jackson State University
Department of Music
Jackson, Mississippi
Jacksonville State University
Department of Music
Jacksonville, Alabama
James Madison University
Department of Music
Harrisonburg, Virginia
Jersey City State College
Music Department
Jersey City, New Jersey
University of Kansas
School of Fine Arts

Lawrence, Kansas
Kansas State University
  Department of Music
  Manhattan, Kansas
Kent State University
  School of Music
  Kent, Ohio
University of Kentucky
  School of Music
  Lexington, Kentucky
Koninklijk Muziekconservatorium van
  Brussel
  1000 Brussels, Belgium
Lamar University
  Department of Music
  Beaumont, Texas
Lawrence University
  Conservatory of Music
  Appleton, Wisconsin
Louisiana Tech University
  Department of Music
  Ruston, Louisiana
University of Louisville
  School of Music
  Louisville, Kentucky
Loyola University
  College of Music
  New Orleans, Louisiana
University of Maine
  School of Performing Arts
  Orono, Maine
Mansfield University
  Department of Music
  Mansfield, Pennsylvania
Marshall University
  Department of Music
  Huntington, West Virginia
University of Maryland - College Park
  Department of Music
  College Park, Maryland
Marywood College
  Music Department
  Scranton, Pennsylvania
University of Massachusetts at Amherst
  Department of Music and Dance
  Amherst, Massachusetts
Memphis State University
  Music Department
  Memphis, Tennessee
University of Miami
  School of Music
  Coral Gables, Florida
Miami University
  Department of Music
  Oxford, Ohio
University of Michigan
  School of Music
  Ann Arbor, Michigan
Middle Tennessee State University
  Department of Music
  Murfreesboro, Tennessee
Millikin University
  School of Music
  Decatur, Illinois
Mills College
  Music Department
  Oakland, California
University of Minnesota - Duluth
  Department of Music
  Duluth, Minnesota
University of Minnesota - Twin Cities
  School of Music
  Minneapolis, Minnesota
University of Missouri - Kansas City
  Conservatory of Music
  Kansas City, Missouri

Moorhead State University
  Music Department
  Moorhead, Minnesota
Morehead State University
  Department of Music
  Morehead, Kentucky
University of Nebraska - Lincoln
  School of Music
  Lincoln, Nebraska
University of Nebraska - Omaha
  Department of Music
  Omaha, Nebraska
University of Nevada, Las Vegas
  Department of Music
  Las Vegas, Nevada
University of New Orleans
  Department of Music
  New Orleans, Louisiana
Norfolk State University
  Department of Music
  Norfolk, Virginia
University of North Carolina at Chapel Hill
  Department of Music
  Chapel Hill, North Carolina
University of North Carolina at Greensboro
  School of Music
  Greensboro, North Carolina
North Texas State University
  School of Music
  Denton, Texas
Northeast Louisiana University
  School of Music
  Monroe, Louisiana
Northern Arizona University
  Music Department
  Flagstaff, Arizona
University of Northern Iowa
  School of Music
  Cedar Falls, Iowa
Northwestern State University of Louisiana
  Department of Music
  Natchitoches, Louisiana
Northwestern University
  School of Music
  Evanston, Illinois
Oakland University
  Department of Music, Theatre and
  Dance
  Rochester, Michigan
Ohio Wesleyan University
  Department of Music
  Delaware, Ohio
University of Oregon
  School of Music
  Eugene, Oregon
University of the Pacific
  Conservatory of Music
  Stockton, California
Pacific Lutheran University
  Department of Music
  Tacoma, Washington
Peabody Institute of The Johns Hopkins
  University
  Baltimore, Maryland
Pennsylvania State University
  School of Music
  University Park, Pennsylvania
Philadelphia College of the Performing Arts
  School of Music
  Philadelphia, Pennsylvania
Pittsburg State University
  Department of Music
  Pittsburg, Kansas
University of Pittsburgh
  Department of Music
  Pittsburgh, Pennsylvania

Pomona College
  Music Department
  Claremont, California
Queen's University
  School of Music
  Kingston, Ontario, Canada
University of Redlands
  School of Music
  Redlands, California
University of Regina
  Department of Music
  Regina, Saskatchewan, Canada
University of Rhode Island
  Department of Music
  Kingston, Rhode Island
University of Rochester
  Eastman School of Music
  Rochester, New York
Rutgers, The State University of New Jersey
  Department of Music
  New Brunswick, New Jersey
St. Cloud State University
  Department of Music
  St. Cloud, Minnesota
St. Olaf College
  Music Department
  Northfield, Minnesota
Samford University
  School of Music
  Birmingham, Alabama
San Diego State University
  Music Department
  San Diego, California
San Francisco State University
  Department of Music
  San Francisco, California
San Jose State University
  Department of Music
  San Jose, California
University of Saskatchewan
  Department of Music
  Saskatoon, Saskatchewan, Canada
University of South Dakota
  Music Department
  Vermillion, South Dakota
University of South Florida
  Department of Music
  Tampa, Florida
Southeast Missouri State University
  Department of Music
  Cape Girardeau, Missouri
Southeastern Oklahoma State University
  Department of Music
  Durant, Oklahoma
Southern Illinois University at Carbondale
  School of Music
  Carbondale, Illinois
Southern Illinois University at Edwardsville
  Department of Music
  Edwardsville, Illinois
Southern Methodist University
  Meadows School of the Arts
  Dallas, Texas
University of Southern Mississippi
  School of Music
  Hattiesburg, Mississippi
University of Southwestern Louisiana
  School of Music
  Lafayette, Louisiana
Staatliche Hochschule für Musik Karlsruhe
  *7500 Karlsruhe 1, Federal Republic of
  Germany*
Staatliche Hochschule für Musik Rheinland
  - Köln
  *D-5000 Köln 1, Federal Republic of
  Germany*

State University of New York College at
Fredonia
  School of Music
  Fredonia, New York
Stephen F. Austin State University
  Department of Music
  Nacogdoches, Texas
Teachers College of Columbia University
  Department of Music and Music
  Education
  New York, New York
Temple University
  Esther Boyer College of Music
  Philadelphia, Pennsylvania
University of Tennessee at Knoxville
  Department of Music
  Knoxville, Tennessee
Texas Christian University
  Music Department
  Fort Worth, Texas
Toho Gakuen School of Music
  Tokyo, Japan
University of Toronto
  Faculty of Music
  Toronto, Ontario, Canada
Troy State University
  Department of Music
  Troy, Alabama
University of Tulsa
  Faculty of Music
  Tulsa, Oklahoma
Université de Montréal
  Faculty of Music
  Montréal, Québec, Canada
Valparaiso University
  Department of Music
  Valparaiso, Indiana
VanderCook College of Music
  Chicago, Illinois
Virginia Polytechnic Institute and State
University
  Department of Music
  Blacksburg, Virginia
Washington State University
  Department of Music
  Pullman, Washington
West Chester University of Pennsylvania
  School of Music
  West Chester, Pennsylvania
West Virginia University
  Division of Music
  Morgantown, West Virginia
Western Illinois University
  Department of Music
  Macomb, Illinois
Western Kentucky University
  Department of Music
  Bowling Green, Kentucky
Western Michigan University
  School of Music
  Kalamazoo, Michigan
Wichita State University
  School of Music
  Wichita, Kansas
Wilfrid Laurier University
  Faculty of Music
  Waterloo, Ontario, Canada
William Carey College
  Winters School of Music
  Hattiesburg, Mississippi
University of Windsor
  School of Music
  Windsor, Ontario, Canada
University of Wisconsin - Eau Claire
  Department of Music
  Eau Claire, Wisconsin

University of Wisconsin - Madison
  School of Music
  Madison, Wisconsin
University of Wisconsin - Milwaukee
  Music Department
  Milwaukee, Wisconsin
University of Wisconsin - Stevens Point
  Department of Music
  Stevens Point, Wisconsin
Wright State University
  Department of Music
  Dayton, Ohio
University of Wyoming
  Music Department
  Laramie, Wyoming
Youngstown State University
  Dana School of Music
  Youngstown, Ohio

SITAR

Bhavan's Bharatiya Sangeet and Nartan
Skikshapeeth
  (Academy of Music and Dance)
  Bombay 4000007, India
California Institute of the Arts
  School of Music
  Valencia, California
City of Leeds College of Music
  Leeds LS2 8BH, United Kingdom
Indira Kala Sangit Vishwavidyalaya
  (University of Music and Fine Arts)
  Madhya Pradesh 491881, India
Institute of Aesthetic Studies
  Colombo 7, Sri Lanka
University of the Philippines
  College of Music
  Quezon City, The Philippines
Prayag Sangit Samiti
  Allahabad 211001, India
Visva-Bharati
  Sangit-Bhavana (College of Music and
  Dance)
  West Bengal 731235, India

SOPRANO RECORDER

Conservatorio Nacional de Musica - La Paz
  (National Conservatory of Music - La
  Paz)
  La Paz, Bolivia

SPINET

Musik-Akademie der Stadt Basel
  Schola Cantorum Basiliensis
  CH-4051 Basel, Switzerland

STRING BASS

Northwestern University
  School of Music
  Evanston, Illinois
Youngstown State University
  Dana School of Music
  Youngstown, Ohio

STRINGED INSTRUMENTS

Akademia Muzyczna w Lódź
  (Academy of Music of Lódź)
  90-716 Lódź, Poland
Akademia Muzycznaj im. Fryderyka
Chopina w Warzawie
  (Frederic Chopin Academy of Music of
  Warsaw)
  00-368 Warsaw, Poland
Akademie voor Musiek
  *Hilversum Postkode 1217 KR,
  Netherlands*

University of Akron
  Department of Music
  Akron, Ohio
Alabama State University
  School of Music
  Montgomery, Alabama
University of Alberta
  Department of Music
  Edmonton, Alberta, Canada
Andrews University
  Department of Music
  Berrien Springs, Michigan
Appalachian State University
  Department of Music
  Boone, North Carolina
Arizona State University
  School of Music
  Tempe, Arizona
Arkansas State University
  Department of Music
  State University, Arkansas
Auburn University
  Department of Music
  Auburn, Alabama
A.V. Nezhdanova Odessa Conservatory
  *270000 Odessa, Ukrainskaja SSR,
  U.S.S.R.*
Azusa Pacific University
  School of Music
  Azusa, California
Ball State University
  School of Music
  Muncie, Indiana
Bemidji State University
  Music Department
  Bemidji, Minnesota
Bennington College
  Music Department
  Bennington, Vermont
Biola University
  Department of Music
  La Mirada, California
Bob Jones University
  Division of Music
  Greenville, South Carolina
Boston Conservatory of Music
  Boston, Massachusetts
Brandeis University
  Department of Music
  Waltham, Massachusetts
Brandon University
  School of Music
  Brandon, Manitoba, Canada
Brigham Young University
  Department of Music
  Provo, Utah
Brown University
  Department of Music
  Providence, Rhode Island
University of Calgary
  Department of Music
  Calgary, Alberta, Canada
University of California, Berkeley
  Department of Music
  Berkeley, California
University of California, Davis
  Department of Music
  Davis, California
California Institute of the Arts
  School of Music
  Valencia, California
California State University, Chico
  Department of Music
  Chico, California
California State University, Fresno
  Department of Music

Fresno, California
California State University, Fullerton
  Department of Music
  Fullerton, California
California State University, Long Beach
  Department of Music
  Long Beach, California
California State University, Los Angeles
  Department of Music
  Los Angeles, California
California State University, Northridge
  Music Department
  Northridge, California
Carnegie-Mellon University
  Department of Music
  Pittsburgh, Pennsylvania
Case Western Reserve University
  Department of Music
  Cleveland, Ohio
Central Conservatory of Music
  Beijing, People's Republic of China
Central Michigan University
  Department of Music
  Mount Pleasant, Michigan
Central State University
  Department of Music
  Edmond, Oklahoma
City of Leeds College of Music
  Leeds LS2 8BH, United Kingdom
City University of New York - Brooklyn
College
  Conservatory of Music
  Brooklyn, New York
City University of New York - City College
  Department of Music
  New York, New York
City University of New York - Hunter
College
  Department of Music
  New York, New York
City University of New York - Queens
College
  The Aaron Copland School of Music
  Flushing, New York
University of Colorado at Denver
  College of Music
  Denver, Colorado
Columbia University
  Department of Music
  New York, New York
Columbus College
  Department of Music
  Columbus, Georgia
Combs College of Music
  Philadelphia, Pennsylvania
Conservatoire de Musique de La
Chaux-de-Fonds - Le Locle
  2300 La Chaux-de-Fonds, Switzerland
Conservatorio di Musica "Claudio
Monteverdi"
  I-39100 Bolzano, Italy
Conservatorio Nacional de Música
  (National Conservatory of Music)
  Lima 1, Peru
Converse College
  School of Music
  Spartanburg, South Carolina
Cornell University
  Department of Music
  Ithaca, New York
Dalhousie University
  Department of Music
  Halifax, Nova Scotia, Canada
University of Delaware
  Department of Music
  Newark, Delaware

Duke University
  Department of Music
  Durham, North Carolina
East Texas State University
  Department of Music
  Commerce, Texas
Eastern Kentucky University
  Department of Music
  Richmond, Kentucky
Eastern New Mexico University
  School of Music
  Portales, New Mexico
Eastern Washington University
  Department of Music
  Cheney, Washington
University of Evansville
  Music Department
  Evansville, Indiana
Ferenc Liszt Academy of Music
  Budapest VI, Hungary
Fort Hays State University
  Department of Music
  Hays, Kansas
University of Georgia
  School of Music
  Athens, Georgia
Georgia Southern College
  Department of Music
  Statesboro, Georgia
Georgia State University
  School of Music
  Atlanta, Georgia
Glassboro State College
  Department of Music
  Glassboro, New Jersey
Guildhall School of Music and Drama
  London EC2Y 8DT, United Kingdom
Hardin-Simmons University
  School of Music
  Abilene, Texas
Harvard University
  Department of Music
  Cambridge, Massachusetts
Hochschule für Music Franz Liszt
  *DDR 5300 Weimar, German Democratic
  Republic*
Hochschule für Musik - Würzburg
  *D-8700 Würzburg, Federal Republic of
  Germany*
Hochschule für Musik Carl Maria von
Weber
  *DDR 8010 Dresden, German Democratic
  Republic*
Hochschule für Musik Felix
Mendelssohn-Bartholdy
  *7010 Leipzig, German Democratic
  Republic*
Hochschule für Musik und Theater
Hannover
  *3000 Hannover 1, Federal Republic of
  Germany*
The Hong Kong Academy for Performing
Arts
  School of Music
  Wanchai, Hong Kong
Hoschschule für Music Hans Eisler
  *DDR Berlin 1080, German Democratic
  Republic*
University of Houston
  School of Music
  Houston, Texas
Illinois State University
  Department of Music
  Normal, Illinois
Indiana University of Pennsylvania
  Department of Music

Indiana, Pennsylvania
Institute of Fine Arts
  Faculty of Music
  Rangoon, Burma
Instituto Superior de Arte
  Facultad de Música
  Playa, Cuba
The Jerusalem Rubin Academy of Music
and Dance
  Jerusalem, Israel
Karol Szymanowski Academy of Music of
Katowice
  Katowice, Poland
Koninklijk Muziekconservatorium van
Brussel
  1000 Brussels, Belgium
Konzervatoř v Praze
  (State Conservatory Prague)
  Praha 110 00, Czechoslovakia
Konzervatorium - Bratislava
  Bratislava 811 06, Czechoslovakia
Kuopion Konservatorio
  70100 Kuopio, Finland
Leningrad N.A. Rimsky-Korsakov State
Conservatory
  *192041 Leningrad, Rossiskaja SFSR,
  U.S.S.R.*
Lewis and Clark College
  Music Department
  Portland, Oregon
Long Island University - C.W. Post Campus
  Music Department
  Greenvale, New York
Louisiana State University
  School of Music
  Baton Rouge, Louisiana
University of Lowell
  College of Music
  Lowell, Massachusetts
Mandalay School of Music, Dance,
Painting, and Sculpture
  Mandalay, Burma
Manhattan School of Music
  New York, New York
University of Manitoba
  School of Music
  Winnipeg, Manitoba, Canada
Mankato State University
  Department of Music
  Mankato, Minnesota
Mannes College of Music
  New York, New York
University of Maryland - Baltimore County
  Department of Music
  Catonsville, Maryland
McGill University
  Faculty of Music
  Montreal, Québec, Canada
McMaster University
  Department of Music
  Hamilton, Ontario, Canada
McNeese State University
  Department of Music
  Lake Charles, Louisiana
Memphis State University
  Music Department
  Memphis, Tennessee
University of Miami
  School of Music
  Coral Gables, Florida
Michigan State University
  School of Music
  East Lansing, Michigan
University of Mississippi
  Department of Music
  University, Mississippi

University of Missouri - Columbia
Department of Music
Columbia, Missouri
University of Montana
Department of Music
Missoula, Montana
Montana State University
Department of Music
Bozeman, Montana
Montclair State College
Department of Music
Upper Montclair, New Jersey
University of Montevallo
Department of Music
Montevallo, Alabama
Moscow P.I. Tchaikovsky State
Conservatory
*103009 Moscow K-9, Rossiskaja SFSR,
U.S.S.R.*
Musik-Akademie der Stadt Basel
(Konservatorium)
Konservatorium (Musikhochschule)
Basel, Switzerland
Musikhögskolan i Stockholm
National College of Music
115 31 Stockholm, Sweden
Musikschule und Konservatorium
Schaffhausen
Schaffhausen, Switzerland
National Institute of the Arts
Music Department
*Taipei County, Taiwan (Republic of
China)*
University of Nevada, Reno
Department of Music
Reno, Nevada
New England Conservatory
Boston, Massachusetts
University of New Mexico
Department of Music
Albuquerque, New Mexico
New Mexico State University
Department of Music
Las Cruces, New Mexico
New York University - School of Education,
Health, Nursing, and Arts Professions
Department of Music and Music
Education
New York, New York
Nikos Skalkotas Conservatory
Athens 11141, Greece
Norges Musikkhøgskole
(The Norwegian State Academy of
Music)
N-0130 Oslo 1, Norway
North Carolina School of the Arts
School of Music
Winston-Salem, North Carolina
University of North Dakota
Department of Music
Grand Forks, North Dakota
Northeast Missouri State University
Division of Fine Arts
Kirksville, Missouri
Northeastern Illinois University
Department of Music
Chicago, Illinois
University of Northern Colorado
School of Music
Greeley, Colorado
Northern Illinois University
School of Music
DeKalb, Illinois
The Ohio State University
School of Music
Columbus, Ohio

Ohio University
School of Music
Athens, Ohio
Oklahoma Baptist University
Department of Music
Shawnee, Oklahoma
Oklahoma City University
School of Music and Performing Arts
Oklahoma City, Oklahoma
Oregon State University
Department of Music
Corvallis, Oregon
Osaka Ongaku Daigaku
(Osaka College of Music)
Osaka 561, Japan
Ouachita Baptist University
School of Music
Arkadelphia, Arkansas
University of the Philippines
College of Music
Quezon City, The Philippines
Pohjois-Kymen Musiikkiopisto
(North Kymi Music Institute)
45100 Kouvola, Finland
Portland State University
Department of Music
Portland, Oregon
Princeton University
Department of Music
Princeton, New Jersey
University of Puget Sound
School of Music
Tacoma, Washington
Rogaland Musikkonservatorium
N-4000 Stavanger, Norway
Roosevelt University
Chicago Musical College
Chicago, Illinois
Royal Academy of Music
London NW1 5HT, United Kingdom
Royal College of Music
London, SW7 2BS, United Kingdom
Royal Northern College of Music
Manchester M13 9RD, United Kingdom
Royal Scottish Academy of Music and
Drama
Glasgow G2 1BS, United Kingdom
Sam Houston State University
Department of Music
Huntsville, Texas
Shanghai Conservatory of Music
Shanghai, People's Republic of China
Shenandoah College and Conservatory
Winchester, Virginia
Shengyang Conservatory of Music
*Shengyang, Liaoning Province, People's
Republic of China*
Sichuan Conservatory of Music
*Chengdu, Sichuan, People's Republic of
China*
University of South Carolina
School of Music
Columbia, South Carolina
Southeastern Louisiana University
Department of Music
Hammond, Louisiana
Southern Baptist Theological Seminary
School of Church Music
Louisville, Kentucky
University of Southern California
School of Music
Los Angeles, California
Southwest Texas State University
Department of Music
San Marcos, Texas

Southwestern Baptist Theological Seminary
School of Church Music
Fort Worth, Texas
Southwestern Oklahoma State University
Department of Music
Weatherford, Oklahoma
Staatliche Hochschule für Musik Rheinland
- Köln
*D-5000 Köln 1, Federal Republic of
Germany*
Staatliche Hochschule für Musik
Westfalen-Lippe
Institut Dortmund
*D-4600 Dortmund 1, Federal Republic of
Germany*
Stanford University
Department of Music
Stanford, California
State University of New York at
Binghamton
Department of Music
Binghamton, New York
State University of New York at Buffalo
Department of Music
Buffalo, New York
State University of New York College at
New Paltz
Department of Music
New Paltz, New York
Stedelijke Muziekpedagogische Akademie
Leeuwarden, Netherlands
Stetson University
School of Music
Deland, Florida
Tampereen Konservatorio
33230 Tampere, Finland
Tasmanian Conservatorium of Music
Hobart, Tasmania 7001, Australia
Tel Aviv University
Faculty of Fine Arts
Tel-Aviv, Israel
University of Tennessee at Chattanooga
Cadek Department of Music
Chattanooga, Tennessee
University of Texas at Arlington
Department of Music
Arlington, Texas
University of Texas at Austin
Department of Music
Austin, Texas
University of Texas at San Antonio
Division of Music
San Antonio, Texas
Texas Southern University
Department of Music
Houston, Texas
Texas Tech University
Department of Music
Lubbock, Texas
Texas Woman's University
Department of Music and Drama
Denton, Texas
The Tokyo College of Music
Tokyo 171, Japan
Towson State University
Department of Music
Towson, Maryland
Trenton State College
Music Department
Trenton, New Jersey
Trinity College of Music
London W1M 6AQ, United Kingdom
Tulane University
Newcomb College
New Orleans, Louisiana

Ueno Gakuen College
  Tokyo 110, Japan
Universidade do São Paulo
  Department of Music
  05508 São Paulo, Brazil
Université Laval
  Ecole de Musique
  Ste. Foy, Québec, Canada
University of Utah
  Department of Music
  Salt Lake City, Utah
Valdosta State College
  Department of Music
  Valdosta, Georgia
University of Vermont
  Department of Music
  Burlington, Vermont
University of Victoria
  School of Music
  Victoria, British Columbia, Canada
University of Virginia
  McIntire Department of Music
  Charlottesville, Virginia
Virginia Commonwealth University
  Department of Music
  Richmond, Virginia
Virginia State University
  Department of Music Education
  Petersburg, Virginia
University of Washington
  School of Music
  Seattle, Washington
Washington University
  Department of Music
  St. Louis, Missouri
Wayne State University
  Department of Music
  Detroit, Michigan
Webster University
  Department of Music
  St. Louis, Missouri
Welsh College of Music and Drama
  Cardiff, CF1 3ER, United Kingdom
Wesleyan University
  Department of Music
  Middletown, Connecticut
West Georgia College
  Department of Music
  Carrollton, Georgia
West Texas State University
  Department of Music
  Canyon, Texas
University of Western Ontario
  Faculty of Music
  London, Ontario, Canada
Western Washington University
  Department of Music
  Bellingham, Washington
Wheaton College
  Conservatory of Music
  Wheaton, Illinois
Willamette University
  Department of Music
  Salem, Oregon
William Paterson College
  Department of Music
  Wayne, New Jersey
Winthrop College
  School of Music
  Rock Hill, South Carolina
University of Wisconsin - La Crosse
  Department of Music
  La Crosse, Wisconsin
University of Wisconsin - Oshkosh
  Department of Music
  Oshkosh, Wisconsin

University of Wisconsin - Whitewater
  Department of Music
  Whitewater, Wisconsin
Yale College (Yale University)
  Department of Music
  New Haven, Connecticut
Yale University
  School of Music
  New Haven, Connecticut
Zeneiskolai Tanárkepző Intézet
  (Music Teachers Training Institute of the
  Liszt Academy of Music)
  Budapest 1052, Hungary

TABLA

Bhavan's Bharatiya Sangeet and Nartan
Skikshapeeth
  (Academy of Music and Dance)
  Bombay 4000007, India
California Institute of the Arts
  School of Music
  Valencia, California
City of Leeds College of Music
  Leeds LS2 8BH, United Kingdom
Indira Kala Sangit Vishwavidyalaya
  (University of Music and Fine Arts)
  Madhya Pradesh 491881, India
Institute of Aesthetic Studies
  Colombo 7, Sri Lanka
Prayag Sangit Samiti
  Allahabad 211001, India
Visva-Bharati
  Sangit-Bhavana (College of Music and
  Dance)
  West Bengal 731235, India

TENOR SAXOPHONE

Berklee College of Music
  Boston, Massachusetts

TIMPANI

The Claremont Graduate School
  Music Department
  Claremont, California
New South Wales State Conservatorium of
Music
  Sydney NSW 2000, Australia
Oakland University
  Department of Music, Theatre and
  Dance
  Rochester, Michigan

TRAVERSO

Bradley University
  Division of Music and Theatre Arts
  Peoria, Illinois

TROMBONE

Acadia University
  School of Music
  Wolfville, Nova Scotia, Canada
Akademia Muzyczna w Krakowie
  31-038 Kraków, Poland
University of Alabama
  School of Music
  University, Alabama
University of Alaska
  Music Department
  Fairbanks, Alaska
American Conservatory of Music
  Chicago, Illinois
University of Arizona
  School of Music
  Tucson, Arizona

University of Arkansas
  Department of Music
  Fayetteville, Arkansas
Arkansas Tech University
  Department of Music
  Russellville, Arkansas
Austin Peay State University
  Department of Music
  Clarksville, Tennessee
Berklee College of Music
  Boston, Massachusetts
Bob Jones University
  Division of Music
  Greenville, South Carolina
Boise State University
  Music Department
  Boise, Idaho
Boston University
  School of Music
  Boston, Massachusetts
Bowling Green State University
  College of Musical Arts
  Bowling Green, Ohio
Bradley University
  Division of Music and Theatre Arts
  Peoria, Illinois
University of British Columbia
  School of Music
  Vancouver, British Columbia, Canada
Butler University
  Jordan College of Fine Arts
  Indianapolis, Indiana
University of California, Irvine
  School of Fine Arts
  Irvine, California
University of California, Los Angeles
  Department of Music
  Los Angeles, California
University of California, Riverside
  Department of Music
  Riverside, California
University of California, San Diego
  Department of Music
  La Jolla, California
University of California, Santa Barbara
  Department of Music
  Santa Barbara, California
University of California, Santa Cruz
  Music Board, Division of the Arts
  Santa Cruz, California
California State University, Hayward
  Department of Music
  Hayward, California
California State University, Sacramento
  Department of Music
  Sacramento, California
The Catholic University of America
  The Benjamin T. Rome School of Music
  Washington, District of Columbia
University of Central Florida
  Department of Music
  Orlando, Florida
Central Missouri State University
  Department of Music
  Warrensburg, Missouri
Central Washington University
  Department of Music
  Ellensburg, Washington
University of Cincinnati
  College-Conservatory of Music
  Cincinnati, Ohio
The Claremont Graduate School
  Music Department
  Claremont, California
Cleveland State University
  Department of Music

Cleveland, Ohio
University of Colorado at Boulder
  College of Music
  Boulder, Colorado
Colorado State University
  Department of Music, Theatre, and
  Dance
  Fort Collins, Colorado
University of Connecticut
  Department of Music
  Storrs, Connecticut
Conservatorio di Musica "Santa Cecilia"
  00187 Rome, Italy
The Curtis Institute of Music
  Philadelphia, Pennsylvania
Delta State University
  Department of Music
  Cleveland, Mississippi
University of Denver
  Lamont School of Music
  Denver, Colorado
DePaul University
  School of Music
  Chicago, Illinois
DePauw University
  School of Music
  Greencastle, Indiana
Drake University
  Department of Music
  Des Moines, Iowa
Duquesne University
  School of Music
  Pittsburgh, Pennsylvania
East Carolina University
  School of Music
  Greenville, North Carolina
Eastern Illinois University
  Department of Music
  Charleston, Illinois
Eastern Michigan University
  Department of Music
  Ypsilanti, Michigan
Emporia State University
  Division of Music
  Emporia, Kansas
Escuela Nacional de Música
  Universidad Nacional Autónoma de
  México
  Mexico City, D.F. 04100, Mexico
Escuela Universitaria de Música -
  Montevideo
  Montevideo, Uruguay
University of Florida
  Department of Music
  Gainesville, Florida
Florida State University
  School of Music
  Tallahassee, Florida
George Mason University
  Department of Performing Arts - Music
  Division
  Fairfax, Virginia
University of Hartford
  Hartt School of Music
  West Hartford, Connecticut
University of Hawaii at Manoa
  Music Department
  Honolulu, Hawaii
Hofstra University
  Department of Music
  Hempstead, New York
Howard University
  Department of Music
  Washington, District of Columbia
University of Idaho
  School of Music

Moscow, Idaho
University of Illinois
  School of Music
  Urbana, Illinois
Illinois Wesleyan University
  School of Music
  Bloomington, Illinois
Indiana State University
  Department of Music
  Terre Haute, Indiana
Indiana University - Bloomington
  School of Music
  Bloomington, Indiana
University of Iowa
  School of Music
  Iowa City, Iowa
Iowa State University
  Department of Music
  Ames, Iowa
Ithaca College
  School of Music
  Ithaca, New York
Jackson State University
  Department of Music
  Jackson, Mississippi
Jacksonville State University
  Department of Music
  Jacksonville, Alabama
James Madison University
  Department of Music
  Harrisonburg, Virginia
Jersey City State College
  Music Department
  Jersey City, New Jersey
The Juilliard School
  New York, New York
University of Kansas
  School of Fine Arts
  Lawrence, Kansas
Kansas State University
  Department of Music
  Manhattan, Kansas
Kent State University
  School of Music
  Kent, Ohio
University of Kentucky
  School of Music
  Lexington, Kentucky
Lamar University
  Department of Music
  Beaumont, Texas
Lawrence University
  Conservatory of Music
  Appleton, Wisconsin
Louisiana Tech University
  Department of Music
  Ruston, Louisiana
University of Louisville
  School of Music
  Louisville, Kentucky
Loyola University
  College of Music
  New Orleans, Louisiana
University of Maine
  School of Performing Arts
  Orono, Maine
Mansfield University
  Department of Music
  Mansfield, Pennsylvania
University of Maryland - College Park
  Department of Music
  College Park, Maryland
Marywood College
  Music Department
  Scranton, Pennsylvania

University of Massachusetts at Amherst
  Department of Music and Dance
  Amherst, Massachusetts
University of Miami
  School of Music
  Coral Gables, Florida
Miami University
  Department of Music
  Oxford, Ohio
University of Michigan
  School of Music
  Ann Arbor, Michigan
Middle Tennessee State University
  Department of Music
  Murfreesboro, Tennessee
Millikin University
  School of Music
  Decatur, Illinois
University of Minnesota - Duluth
  Department of Music
  Duluth, Minnesota
University of Minnesota - Twin Cities
  School of Music
  Minneapolis, Minnesota
University of Missouri - Kansas City
  Conservatory of Music
  Kansas City, Missouri
Moorhead State University
  Music Department
  Moorhead, Minnesota
Morehead State University
  Department of Music
  Morehead, Kentucky
National Institute of the Arts
  Music Department
  *Taipei County, Taiwan (Republic of
  China)*
University of Nebraska - Lincoln
  School of Music
  Lincoln, Nebraska
University of Nebraska - Omaha
  Department of Music
  Omaha, Nebraska
University of Nevada, Las Vegas
  Department of Music
  Las Vegas, Nevada
University of New Orleans
  Department of Music
  New Orleans, Louisiana
New South Wales State Conservatorium of
  Music
  Sydney NSW 2000, Australia
Norfolk State University
  Department of Music
  Norfolk, Virginia
North Texas State University
  School of Music
  Denton, Texas
Northeast Louisiana University
  School of Music
  Monroe, Louisiana
Northern Arizona University
  Music Department
  Flagstaff, Arizona
Northwestern State University of Louisiana
  Department of Music
  Natchitoches, Louisiana
Northwestern University
  School of Music
  Evanston, Illinois
Oakland University
  Department of Music, Theatre and
  Dance
  Rochester, Michigan
Oberlin College
  Conservatory of Music

Oberlin, Ohio
Ohio Wesleyan University
  Department of Music
  Delaware, Ohio
Oklahoma Baptist University
  Department of Music
  Shawnee, Oklahoma
University of Oregon
  School of Music
  Eugene, Oregon
University of the Pacific
  Conservatory of Music
  Stockton, California
Pacific Lutheran University
  Department of Music
  Tacoma, Washington
Peabody Institute of The Johns Hopkins
  University
  Baltimore, Maryland
Pennsylvania State University
  School of Music
  University Park, Pennsylvania
Philadelphia College of the Performing Arts
  School of Music
  Philadelphia, Pennsylvania
Pittsburg State University
  Department of Music
  Pittsburg, Kansas
University of Pittsburgh
  Department of Music
  Pittsburgh, Pennsylvania
Pomona College
  Music Department
  Claremont, California
Queen's University
  School of Music
  Kingston, Ontario, Canada
University of Redlands
  School of Music
  Redlands, California
University of Regina
  Department of Music
  Regina, Saskatchewan, Canada
University of Rhode Island
  Department of Music
  Kingston, Rhode Island
Rice University
  Shepherd School of Music
  Houston, Texas
University of Rochester
  Eastman School of Music
  Rochester, New York
Rutgers, The State University of New Jersey
  Department of Music
  New Brunswick, New Jersey
St. Cloud State University
  Department of Music
  St. Cloud, Minnesota
Saint Louis Conservatory of Music
  St. Louis, Missouri
St. Olaf College
  Music Department
  Northfield, Minnesota
Samford University
  School of Music
  Birmingham, Alabama
San Diego State University
  Music Department
  San Diego, California
San Francisco Conservatory of Music
  San Francisco, California
San Francisco State University
  Department of Music
  San Francisco, California
San Jose State University
  Department of Music

San Jose, California
University of Saskatchewan
  Department of Music
  Saskatoon, Saskatchewan, Canada
Smith College
  Department of Music
  Northampton, Massachusetts
University of South Dakota
  Music Department
  Vermillion, South Dakota
University of South Florida
  Department of Music
  Tampa, Florida
Southeast Missouri State University
  Department of Music
  Cape Girardeau, Missouri
Southeastern Oklahoma State University
  Department of Music
  Durant, Oklahoma
Southern Illinois University at Carbondale
  School of Music
  Carbondale, Illinois
Southern Illinois University at Edwardsville
  Department of Music
  Edwardsville, Illinois
Southern Methodist University
  Meadows School of the Arts
  Dallas, Texas
University of Southern Mississippi
  School of Music
  Hattiesburg, Mississippi
University of Southwestern Louisiana
  School of Music
  Lafayette, Louisiana
Staatliche Hochschule für Musik Trossingen
  D-7218 Trossingen 1, Federal Republic of
  Germany
State University of New York at Stony
  Brook
  Department of Music
  Stony Brook, New York
State University of New York College at
  Fredonia
  School of Music
  Fredonia, New York
State University of New York College at
  Purchase
  Division of Music
  Purchase, New York
Stephen F. Austin State University
  Department of Music
  Nacogdoches, Texas
Teachers College of Columbia University
  Department of Music and Music
  Education
  New York, New York
Temple University
  Esther Boyer College of Music
  Philadelphia, Pennsylvania
University of Tennessee at Knoxville
  Department of Music
  Knoxville, Tennessee
University of Texas at El Paso
  Music Department
  El Paso, Texas
Texas Christian University
  Music Department
  Fort Worth, Texas
Toho Gakuen School of Music
  Tokyo, Japan
University of Toronto
  Faculty of Music
  Toronto, Ontario, Canada
Troy State University
  Department of Music
  Troy, Alabama

University of Tulsa
  Faculty of Music
  Tulsa, Oklahoma
Université de Montréal
  Faculty of Music
  Montréal, Québec, Canada
Valparaiso University
  Department of Music
  Valparaiso, Indiana
VanderCook College of Music
  Chicago, Illinois
Virginia Polytechnic Institute and State
  University
  Department of Music
  Blacksburg, Virginia
Vysoká Skola Mûzickych Umeni v Praha
  Academy of Music and Dramatic Arts
  1101 00 Prague 1, Czechoslovakia
Washington State University
  Department of Music
  Pullman, Washington
West Chester University of Pennsylvania
  School of Music
  West Chester, Pennsylvania
West Virginia University
  Division of Music
  Morgantown, West Virginia
Western Illinois University
  Department of Music
  Macomb, Illinois
Western Kentucky University
  Department of Music
  Bowling Green, Kentucky
Western Michigan University
  School of Music
  Kalamazoo, Michigan
Wichita State University
  School of Music
  Wichita, Kansas
Wiesbadener Konservatorium und staatliche
  anerkannte private Fachschule für
  Musikerzieher e.V.
  (Conservatory and Seminary for Music
  Education)
  6200 Wiesbaden, Federal Republic of
  Germany
Wilfrid Laurier University
  Faculty of Music
  Waterloo, Ontario, Canada
William Carey College
  Winters School of Music
  Hattiesburg, Mississippi
University of Windsor
  School of Music
  Windsor, Ontario, Canada
University of Wisconsin - Eau Claire
  Department of Music
  Eau Claire, Wisconsin
University of Wisconsin - Madison
  School of Music
  Madison, Wisconsin
University of Wisconsin - Milwaukee
  Music Department
  Milwaukee, Wisconsin
University of Wisconsin - Stevens Point
  Department of Music
  Stevens Point, Wisconsin
Wright State University
  Department of Music
  Dayton, Ohio
University of Wyoming
  Music Department
  Laramie, Wyoming
Yale College (Yale University)
  Department of Music
  New Haven, Connecticut

Yale University
  School of Music
  New Haven, Connecticut
Youngstown State University
  Dana School of Music
  Youngstown, Ohio

TRUMPET

Acadia University
  School of Music
  Wolfville, Nova Scotia, Canada
Akademia Muzyczna w Krakowie
  31-038 Kraków, Poland
University of Alabama
  School of Music
  University, Alabama
University of Alaska
  Music Department
  Fairbanks, Alaska
American Conservatory of Music
  Chicago, Illinois
University of Arizona
  School of Music
  Tucson, Arizona
University of Arkansas
  Department of Music
  Fayetteville, Arkansas
Arkansas Tech University
  Department of Music
  Russellville, Arkansas
Austin Peay State University
  Department of Music
  Clarksville, Tennessee
Baldwin-Wallace College
  Conservatory of Music
  Berea, Ohio
Baylor University
  School of Music
  Waco, Texas
Berklee College of Music
  Boston, Massachusetts
Bob Jones University
  Division of Music
  Greenville, South Carolina
Boise State University
  Music Department
  Boise, Idaho
Boston University
  School of Music
  Boston, Massachusetts
Bowling Green State University
  College of Musical Arts
  Bowling Green, Ohio
Bradley University
  Division of Music and Theatre Arts
  Peoria, Illinois
University of British Columbia
  School of Music
  Vancouver, British Columbia, Canada
Bulgarian State Conservatoire
  Sofia 1505, Bulgaria
Butler University
  Jordan College of Fine Arts
  Indianapolis, Indiana
University of California, Irvine
  School of Fine Arts
  Irvine, California
University of California, Los Angeles
  Department of Music
  Los Angeles, California
University of California, Riverside
  Department of Music
  Riverside, California
University of California, San Diego
  Department of Music

La Jolla, California
University of California, Santa Barbara
  Department of Music
  Santa Barbara, California
University of California, Santa Cruz
  Music Board, Division of the Arts
  Santa Cruz, California
California State University, Hayward
  Department of Music
  Hayward, California
California State University, Sacramento
  Department of Music
  Sacramento, California
The Catholic University of America
  The Benjamin T. Rome School of Music
  Washington, District of Columbia
University of Central Arkansas
  Department of Music
  Conway, Arkansas
University of Central Florida
  Department of Music
  Orlando, Florida
Central Missouri State University
  Department of Music
  Warrensburg, Missouri
Central Washington University
  Department of Music
  Ellensburg, Washington
University of Cincinnati
  College-Conservatory of Music
  Cincinnati, Ohio
The Claremont Graduate School
  Music Department
  Claremont, California
Cleveland State University
  Department of Music
  Cleveland, Ohio
University of Colorado at Boulder
  College of Music
  Boulder, Colorado
Colorado State University
  Department of Music, Theatre, and
  Dance
  Fort Collins, Colorado
University of Connecticut
  Department of Music
  Storrs, Connecticut
Conservatorio di Musica "Santa Cecilia"
  00187 Rome, Italy
The Curtis Institute of Music
  Philadelphia, Pennsylvania
Delta State University
  Department of Music
  Cleveland, Mississippi
University of Denver
  Lamont School of Music
  Denver, Colorado
DePaul University
  School of Music
  Chicago, Illinois
DePauw University
  School of Music
  Greencastle, Indiana
Drake University
  Department of Music
  Des Moines, Iowa
Duquesne University
  School of Music
  Pittsburgh, Pennsylvania
East Carolina University
  School of Music
  Greenville, North Carolina
Eastern Illinois University
  Department of Music
  Charleston, Illinois

Eastern Michigan University
  Department of Music
  Ypsilanti, Michigan
Emporia State University
  Division of Music
  Emporia, Kansas
Escuela Nacional de Música
  Universidad Nacional Autónoma de
  México
  Mexico City, D.F. 04100, Mexico
University of Florida
  Department of Music
  Gainesville, Florida
Florida State University
  School of Music
  Tallahassee, Florida
George Mason University
  Department of Performing Arts - Music
  Division
  Fairfax, Virginia
University of Hartford
  Hartt School of Music
  West Hartford, Connecticut
University of Hawaii at Manoa
  Music Department
  Honolulu, Hawaii
Hermann-Zilcher-Konservatorium
  *D-8700 Würzburg, Federal Republic of
  Germany*
Hofstra University
  Department of Music
  Hempstead, New York
Howard University
  Department of Music
  Washington, District of Columbia
University of Idaho
  School of Music
  Moscow, Idaho
University of Illinois
  School of Music
  Urbana, Illinois
Illinois Wesleyan University
  School of Music
  Bloomington, Illinois
Indiana State University
  Department of Music
  Terre Haute, Indiana
Indiana University - Bloomington
  School of Music
  Bloomington, Indiana
University of Iowa
  School of Music
  Iowa City, Iowa
Iowa State University
  Department of Music
  Ames, Iowa
Ithaca College
  School of Music
  Ithaca, New York
Jackson State University
  Department of Music
  Jackson, Mississippi
Jacksonville State University
  Department of Music
  Jacksonville, Alabama
James Madison University
  Department of Music
  Harrisonburg, Virginia
Jersey City State College
  Music Department
  Jersey City, New Jersey
The Juilliard School
  New York, New York
University of Kansas
  School of Fine Arts
  Lawrence, Kansas

Kansas State University
Department of Music
Manhattan, Kansas
Kent State University
School of Music
Kent, Ohio
University of Kentucky
School of Music
Lexington, Kentucky
Kuopion Konservatorio
70100 Kuopio, Finland
Lamar University
Department of Music
Beaumont, Texas
Lawrence University
Conservatory of Music
Appleton, Wisconsin
Louisiana Tech University
Department of Music
Ruston, Louisiana
University of Louisville
School of Music
Louisville, Kentucky
Loyola University
College of Music
New Orleans, Louisiana
University of Maine
School of Performing Arts
Orono, Maine
Mansfield University
Department of Music
Mansfield, Pennsylvania
Marshall University
Department of Music
Huntington, West Virginia
University of Maryland - College Park
Department of Music
College Park, Maryland
Marywood College
Music Department
Scranton, Pennsylvania
University of Massachusetts at Amherst
Department of Music and Dance
Amherst, Massachusetts
University of Miami
School of Music
Coral Gables, Florida
Miami University
Department of Music
Oxford, Ohio
University of Michigan
School of Music
Ann Arbor, Michigan
Middle Tennessee State University
Department of Music
Murfreesboro, Tennessee
Millikin University
School of Music
Decatur, Illinois
Mills College
Music Department
Oakland, California
University of Minnesota - Duluth
Department of Music
Duluth, Minnesota
University of Minnesota - Twin Cities
School of Music
Minneapolis, Minnesota
University of Missouri - Kansas City
Conservatory of Music
Kansas City, Missouri
Moorhead State University
Music Department
Moorhead, Minnesota
Morehead State University
Department of Music

Morehead, Kentucky
National Institute of the Arts
Music Department
Taipei County, Taiwan (Republic of China)
University of Nebraska - Lincoln
School of Music
Lincoln, Nebraska
University of Nebraska - Omaha
Department of Music
Omaha, Nebraska
University of Nevada, Las Vegas
Department of Music
Las Vegas, Nevada
University of New Orleans
Department of Music
New Orleans, Louisiana
New South Wales State Conservatorium of Music
Sydney NSW 2000, Australia
Norfolk State University
Department of Music
Norfolk, Virginia
University of North Carolina at Chapel Hill
Department of Music
Chapel Hill, North Carolina
University of North Carolina at Greensboro
School of Music
Greensboro, North Carolina
North Texas State University
School of Music
Denton, Texas
Northeast Louisiana University
School of Music
Monroe, Louisiana
Northern Arizona University
Music Department
Flagstaff, Arizona
University of Northern Iowa
School of Music
Cedar Falls, Iowa
Northwestern State University of Louisiana
Department of Music
Natchitoches, Louisiana
Northwestern University
School of Music
Evanston, Illinois
Oakland University
Department of Music, Theatre and Dance
Rochester, Michigan
Oberlin College
Conservatory of Music
Oberlin, Ohio
Ohio Wesleyan University
Department of Music
Delaware, Ohio
Oklahoma Baptist University
Department of Music
Shawnee, Oklahoma
University of Oregon
School of Music
Eugene, Oregon
University of the Pacific
Conservatory of Music
Stockton, California
Pacific Lutheran University
Department of Music
Tacoma, Washington
Peabody Institute of The Johns Hopkins University
Baltimore, Maryland
Pennsylvania State University
School of Music
University Park, Pennsylvania

Philadelphia College of the Performing Arts
School of Music
Philadelphia, Pennsylvania
Pittsburg State University
Department of Music
Pittsburg, Kansas
University of Pittsburgh
Department of Music
Pittsburgh, Pennsylvania
Pomona College
Music Department
Claremont, California
Queen's University
School of Music
Kingston, Ontario, Canada
University of Redlands
School of Music
Redlands, California
University of Regina
Department of Music
Regina, Saskatchewan, Canada
University of Rhode Island
Department of Music
Kingston, Rhode Island
Rice University
Shepherd School of Music
Houston, Texas
University of Rochester
Eastman School of Music
Rochester, New York
Rutgers, The State University of New Jersey
Department of Music
New Brunswick, New Jersey
St. Cloud State University
Department of Music
St. Cloud, Minnesota
Saint Louis Conservatory of Music
St. Louis, Missouri
St. Olaf College
Music Department
Northfield, Minnesota
Samford University
School of Music
Birmingham, Alabama
San Diego State University
Music Department
San Diego, California
San Francisco Conservatory of Music
San Francisco, California
San Francisco State University
Department of Music
San Francisco, California
San Jose State University
Department of Music
San Jose, California
University of Saskatchewan
Department of Music
Saskatoon, Saskatchewan, Canada
Smith College
Department of Music
Northampton, Massachusetts
University of South Dakota
Music Department
Vermillion, South Dakota
University of South Florida
Department of Music
Tampa, Florida
Southeast Missouri State University
Department of Music
Cape Girardeau, Missouri
Southeastern Oklahoma State University
Department of Music
Durant, Oklahoma
Southern Illinois University at Carbondale
School of Music
Carbondale, Illinois

Southern Illinois University at Edwardsville
Department of Music
Edwardsville, Illinois
Southern Methodist University
Meadows School of the Arts
Dallas, Texas
University of Southern Mississippi
School of Music
Hattiesburg, Mississippi
University of Southwestern Louisiana
School of Music
Lafayette, Louisiana
Staatliche Hochschule für Musik Trossingen
*D-7218 Trossingen 1, Federal Republic of
Germany*
State University of New York at Stony
Brook
Department of Music
Stony Brook, New York
State University of New York College at
Fredonia
School of Music
Fredonia, New York
State University of New York College at
New Paltz
Department of Music
New Paltz, New York
State University of New York College at
Potsdam
Crane School of Music
Potsdam, New York
State University of New York College at
Purchase
Division of Music
Purchase, New York
Stephen F. Austin State University
Department of Music
Nacogdoches, Texas
Syracuse University
School of Music
Syracuse, New York
Teachers College of Columbia University
Department of Music and Music
Education
New York, New York
Temple University
Esther Boyer College of Music
Philadelphia, Pennsylvania
University of Tennessee at Knoxville
Department of Music
Knoxville, Tennessee
University of Texas at El Paso
Music Department
El Paso, Texas
Texas Christian University
Music Department
Fort Worth, Texas
Toho Gakuen School of Music
Tokyo, Japan
University of Toronto
Faculty of Music
Toronto, Ontario, Canada
Troy State University
Department of Music
Troy, Alabama
University of Tulsa
Faculty of Music
Tulsa, Oklahoma
Université de Montréal
Faculty of Music
Montréal, Québec, Canada
Valparaiso University
Department of Music
Valparaiso, Indiana
VanderCook College of Music
Chicago, Illinois

Virginia Polytechnic Institute and State
University
Department of Music
Blacksburg, Virginia
Vysoká Skola Mûzickych Umeni v Praha
Academy of Music and Dramatic Arts
1101 00 Prague 1, Czechoslovakia
Washington State University
Department of Music
Pullman, Washington
West Chester University of Pennsylvania
School of Music
West Chester, Pennsylvania
West Virginia University
Division of Music
Morgantown, West Virginia
Western Illinois University
Department of Music
Macomb, Illinois
Western Kentucky University
Department of Music
Bowling Green, Kentucky
Western Michigan University
School of Music
Kalamazoo, Michigan
Wichita State University
School of Music
Wichita, Kansas
Wiesbadener Konservatorium und staatliche
anerkannte private Fachschule für
Musikerzieher e.V.
(Conservatory and Seminary for Music
Education)
*6200 Wiesbaden, Federal Republic of
Germany*
Wilfrid Laurier University
Faculty of Music
Waterloo, Ontario, Canada
William Carey College
Winters School of Music
Hattiesburg, Mississippi
William Paterson College
Department of Music
Wayne, New Jersey
University of Windsor
School of Music
Windsor, Ontario, Canada
University of Wisconsin - Eau Claire
Department of Music
Eau Claire, Wisconsin
University of Wisconsin - Madison
School of Music
Madison, Wisconsin
University of Wisconsin - Milwaukee
Music Department
Milwaukee, Wisconsin
University of Wisconsin - Stevens Point
Department of Music
Stevens Point, Wisconsin
Wright State University
Department of Music
Dayton, Ohio
University of Wyoming
Music Department
Laramie, Wyoming
Yale College (Yale University)
Department of Music
New Haven, Connecticut
Yale University
School of Music
New Haven, Connecticut
Youngstown State University
Dana School of Music
Youngstown, Ohio

TUBA

Acadia University
School of Music
Wolfville, Nova Scotia, Canada
Akademia Muzyczna w Krakowie
31-038 Kraków, Poland
University of Alabama
School of Music
University, Alabama
University of Alaska
Music Department
Fairbanks, Alaska
University of Arizona
School of Music
Tucson, Arizona
University of Arkansas
Department of Music
Fayetteville, Arkansas
Arkansas Tech University
Department of Music
Russellville, Arkansas
Austin Peay State University
Department of Music
Clarksville, Tennessee
Baldwin-Wallace College
Conservatory of Music
Berea, Ohio
Baylor University
School of Music
Waco, Texas
Berklee College of Music
Boston, Massachusetts
Bob Jones University
Division of Music
Greenville, South Carolina
Boise State University
Music Department
Boise, Idaho
Boston University
School of Music
Boston, Massachusetts
Bowling Green State University
College of Musical Arts
Bowling Green, Ohio
Bradley University
Division of Music and Theatre Arts
Peoria, Illinois
University of British Columbia
School of Music
Vancouver, British Columbia, Canada
Butler University
Jordan College of Fine Arts
Indianapolis, Indiana
University of California, Irvine
School of Fine Arts
Irvine, California
University of California, Los Angeles
Department of Music
Los Angeles, California
University of California, Santa Cruz
Music Board, Division of the Arts
Santa Cruz, California
California State University, Hayward
Department of Music
Hayward, California
The Catholic University of America
The Benjamin T. Rome School of Music
Washington, District of Columbia
University of Central Arkansas
Department of Music
Conway, Arkansas
University of Central Florida
Department of Music
Orlando, Florida

Central Missouri State University
  Department of Music
  Warrensburg, Missouri
Central Washington University
  Department of Music
  Ellensburg, Washington
University of Cincinnati
  College-Conservatory of Music
  Cincinnati, Ohio
The Claremont Graduate School
  Music Department
  Claremont, California
Cleveland State University
  Department of Music
  Cleveland, Ohio
University of Colorado at Boulder
  College of Music
  Boulder, Colorado
Colorado State University
  Department of Music, Theatre, and
  Dance
  Fort Collins, Colorado
University of Connecticut
  Department of Music
  Storrs, Connecticut
The Curtis Institute of Music
  Philadelphia, Pennsylvania
Delta State University
  Department of Music
  Cleveland, Mississippi
University of Denver
  Lamont School of Music
  Denver, Colorado
DePaul University
  School of Music
  Chicago, Illinois
DePauw University
  School of Music
  Greencastle, Indiana
Drake University
  Department of Music
  Des Moines, Iowa
Duquesne University
  School of Music
  Pittsburgh, Pennsylvania
East Carolina University
  School of Music
  Greenville, North Carolina
Eastern Illinois University
  Department of Music
  Charleston, Illinois
Eastern Michigan University
  Department of Music
  Ypsilanti, Michigan
Emporia State University
  Division of Music
  Emporia, Kansas
Escuela Nacional de Música
  Universidad Nacional Autónoma de
  México
  Mexico City, D.F. 04100, Mexico
University of Florida
  Department of Music
  Gainesville, Florida
Florida State University
  School of Music
  Tallahassee, Florida
University of Hartford
  Hartt School of Music
  West Hartford, Connecticut
University of Hawaii at Manoa
  Music Department
  Honolulu, Hawaii
Hermann-Zilcher-Konservatorium
  *D-8700 Würzburg, Federal Republic of
  Germany*

Hofstra University
  Department of Music
  Hempstead, New York
Howard University
  Department of Music
  Washington, District of Columbia
University of Illinois
  School of Music
  Urbana, Illinois
Illinois Wesleyan University
  School of Music
  Bloomington, Illinois
Indiana State University
  Department of Music
  Terre Haute, Indiana
Indiana University - Bloomington
  School of Music
  Bloomington, Indiana
University of Iowa
  School of Music
  Iowa City, Iowa
Iowa State University
  Department of Music
  Ames, Iowa
Ithaca College
  School of Music
  Ithaca, New York
Jackson State University
  Department of Music
  Jackson, Mississippi
Jacksonville State University
  Department of Music
  Jacksonville, Alabama
James Madison University
  Department of Music
  Harrisonburg, Virginia
Jersey City State College
  Music Department
  Jersey City, New Jersey
The Juilliard School
  New York, New York
University of Kansas
  School of Fine Arts
  Lawrence, Kansas
Kansas State University
  Department of Music
  Manhattan, Kansas
Kent State University
  School of Music
  Kent, Ohio
University of Kentucky
  School of Music
  Lexington, Kentucky
Lamar University
  Department of Music
  Beaumont, Texas
Lawrence University
  Conservatory of Music
  Appleton, Wisconsin
Louisiana Tech University
  Department of Music
  Ruston, Louisiana
University of Louisville
  School of Music
  Louisville, Kentucky
Loyola University
  College of Music
  New Orleans, Louisiana
University of Maine
  School of Performing Arts
  Orono, Maine
Mansfield University
  Department of Music
  Mansfield, Pennsylvania
Marshall University
  Department of Music

Huntington, West Virginia
University of Maryland - College Park
  Department of Music
  College Park, Maryland
Marywood College
  Music Department
  Scranton, Pennsylvania
University of Massachusetts at Amherst
  Department of Music and Dance
  Amherst, Massachusetts
University of Miami
  School of Music
  Coral Gables, Florida
Miami University
  Department of Music
  Oxford, Ohio
University of Michigan
  School of Music
  Ann Arbor, Michigan
Middle Tennessee State University
  Department of Music
  Murfreesboro, Tennessee
Millikin University
  School of Music
  Decatur, Illinois
University of Minnesota - Duluth
  Department of Music
  Duluth, Minnesota
University of Minnesota - Twin Cities
  School of Music
  Minneapolis, Minnesota
University of Missouri - Kansas City
  Conservatory of Music
  Kansas City, Missouri
Moorhead State University
  Music Department
  Moorhead, Minnesota
Morehead State University
  Department of Music
  Morehead, Kentucky
National Institute of the Arts
  Music Department
  *Taipei County, Taiwan (Republic of
  China)*
University of Nebraska - Lincoln
  School of Music
  Lincoln, Nebraska
University of Nebraska - Omaha
  Department of Music
  Omaha, Nebraska
University of Nevada, Las Vegas
  Department of Music
  Las Vegas, Nevada
University of New Orleans
  Department of Music
  New Orleans, Louisiana
New South Wales State Conservatorium of
Music
  Sydney NSW 2000, Australia
Norfolk State University
  Department of Music
  Norfolk, Virginia
University of North Carolina at Chapel Hill
  Department of Music
  Chapel Hill, North Carolina
University of North Carolina at Greensboro
  School of Music
  Greensboro, North Carolina
North Texas State University
  School of Music
  Denton, Texas
Northeast Louisiana University
  School of Music
  Monroe, Louisiana
Northern Arizona University
  Music Department

Flagstaff, Arizona
University of Northern Iowa
  School of Music
  Cedar Falls, Iowa
Northwestern State University of Louisiana
  Department of Music
  Natchitoches, Louisiana
Northwestern University
  School of Music
  Evanston, Illinois
Oakland University
  Department of Music, Theatre and
  Dance
  Rochester, Michigan
Oberlin College
  Conservatory of Music
  Oberlin, Ohio
Ohio Wesleyan University
  Department of Music
  Delaware, Ohio
Oklahoma Baptist University
  Department of Music
  Shawnee, Oklahoma
University of Oregon
  School of Music
  Eugene, Oregon
University of the Pacific
  Conservatory of Music
  Stockton, California
Pacific Lutheran University
  Department of Music
  Tacoma, Washington
Peabody Institute of The Johns Hopkins
  University
  Baltimore, Maryland
Pennsylvania State University
  School of Music
  University Park, Pennsylvania
Philadelphia College of the Performing Arts
  School of Music
  Philadelphia, Pennsylvania
Pittsburg State University
  Department of Music
  Pittsburg, Kansas
Pomona College
  Music Department
  Claremont, California
Queen's University
  School of Music
  Kingston, Ontario, Canada
University of Redlands
  School of Music
  Redlands, California
University of Regina
  Department of Music
  Regina, Saskatchewan, Canada
University of Rhode Island
  Department of Music
  Kingston, Rhode Island
Rice University
  Shepherd School of Music
  Houston, Texas
University of Rochester
  Eastman School of Music
  Rochester, New York
St. Cloud State University
  Department of Music
  St. Cloud, Minnesota
Saint Louis Conservatory of Music
  St. Louis, Missouri
St. Olaf College
  Music Department
  Northfield, Minnesota
Samford University
  School of Music
  Birmingham, Alabama

San Diego State University
  Music Department
  San Diego, California
San Francisco Conservatory of Music
  San Francisco, California
San Francisco State University
  Department of Music
  San Francisco, California
University of Saskatchewan
  Department of Music
  Saskatoon, Saskatchewan, Canada
Smith College
  Department of Music
  Northampton, Massachusetts
University of South Dakota
  Music Department
  Vermillion, South Dakota
University of South Florida
  Department of Music
  Tampa, Florida
Southeast Missouri State University
  Department of Music
  Cape Girardeau, Missouri
Southeastern Oklahoma State University
  Department of Music
  Durant, Oklahoma
Southern Illinois University at Carbondale
  School of Music
  Carbondale, Illinois
Southern Illinois University at Edwardsville
  Department of Music
  Edwardsville, Illinois
Southern Methodist University
  Meadows School of the Arts
  Dallas, Texas
University of Southern Mississippi
  School of Music
  Hattiesburg, Mississippi
University of Southwestern Louisiana
  School of Music
  Lafayette, Louisiana
State University of New York at Stony
  Brook
  Department of Music
  Stony Brook, New York
State University of New York College at
  Fredonia
  School of Music
  Fredonia, New York
State University of New York College at
  Potsdam
  Crane School of Music
  Potsdam, New York
State University of New York College at
  Purchase
  Division of Music
  Purchase, New York
Stephen F. Austin State University
  Department of Music
  Nacogdoches, Texas
Syracuse University
  School of Music
  Syracuse, New York
Teachers College of Columbia University
  Department of Music and Music
  Education
  New York, New York
Temple University
  Esther Boyer College of Music
  Philadelphia, Pennsylvania
University of Tennessee at Knoxville
  Department of Music
  Knoxville, Tennessee
University of Texas at El Paso
  Music Department
  El Paso, Texas

Texas Christian University
  Music Department
  Fort Worth, Texas
Toho Gakuen School of Music
  Tokyo, Japan
University of Toronto
  Faculty of Music
  Toronto, Ontario, Canada
Troy State University
  Department of Music
  Troy, Alabama
University of Tulsa
  Faculty of Music
  Tulsa, Oklahoma
Université de Montréal
  Faculty of Music
  Montréal, Québec, Canada
Valparaiso University
  Department of Music
  Valparaiso, Indiana
VanderCook College of Music
  Chicago, Illinois
Washington State University
  Department of Music
  Pullman, Washington
West Chester University of Pennsylvania
  School of Music
  West Chester, Pennsylvania
West Virginia University
  Division of Music
  Morgantown, West Virginia
Western Illinois University
  Department of Music
  Macomb, Illinois
Western Kentucky University
  Department of Music
  Bowling Green, Kentucky
Western Michigan University
  School of Music
  Kalamazoo, Michigan
Wichita State University
  School of Music
  Wichita, Kansas
Wilfrid Laurier University
  Faculty of Music
  Waterloo, Ontario, Canada
William Carey College
  Winters School of Music
  Hattiesburg, Mississippi
University of Windsor
  School of Music
  Windsor, Ontario, Canada
University of Wisconsin - Eau Claire
  Department of Music
  Eau Claire, Wisconsin
University of Wisconsin - Madison
  School of Music
  Madison, Wisconsin
University of Wisconsin - Milwaukee
  Music Department
  Milwaukee, Wisconsin
University of Wisconsin - Stevens Point
  Department of Music
  Stevens Point, Wisconsin
Wright State University
  Department of Music
  Dayton, Ohio
University of Wyoming
  Music Department
  Laramie, Wyoming
Yale University
  School of Music
  New Haven, Connecticut
Youngstown State University
  Dana School of Music
  Youngstown, Ohio

VIBRAHARP

University of Southwestern Louisiana
  School of Music
  Lafayette, Louisiana

VIOLA

Acadia University
  School of Music
  Wolfville, Nova Scotia, Canada
Akademia Muzyczna w Krakowie
  31-038 Kraków, Poland
University of Alabama
  School of Music
  University, Alabama
University of Alaska
  Music Department
  Fairbanks, Alaska
American Conservatory of Music
  Chicago, Illinois
University of Arizona
  School of Music
  Tucson, Arizona
University of Arkansas
  Department of Music
  Fayetteville, Arkansas
Arkansas Tech University
  Department of Music
  Russellville, Arkansas
Austin Peay State University
  Department of Music
  Clarksville, Tennessee
Baldwin-Wallace College
  Conservatory of Music
  Berea, Ohio
Baylor University
  School of Music
  Waco, Texas
Berklee College of Music
  Boston, Massachusetts
Boise State University
  Music Department
  Boise, Idaho
Boston University
  School of Music
  Boston, Massachusetts
Bowling Green State University
  College of Musical Arts
  Bowling Green, Ohio
Bradley University
  Division of Music and Theatre Arts
  Peoria, Illinois
University of British Columbia
  School of Music
  Vancouver, British Columbia, Canada
Bulgarian State Conservatoire
  Sofia 1505, Bulgaria
Butler University
  Jordan College of Fine Arts
  Indianapolis, Indiana
University of California, Irvine
  School of Fine Arts
  Irvine, California
University of California, Los Angeles
  Department of Music
  Los Angeles, California
University of California, Riverside
  Department of Music
  Riverside, California
University of California, Santa Barbara
  Department of Music
  Santa Barbara, California
University of California, Santa Cruz
  Music Board, Division of the Arts
  Santa Cruz, California

California State University, Hayward
  Department of Music
  Hayward, California
California State University, Sacramento
  Department of Music
  Sacramento, California
The Catholic University of America
  The Benjamin T. Rome School of Music
  Washington, District of Columbia
University of Central Arkansas
  Department of Music
  Conway, Arkansas
University of Central Florida
  Department of Music
  Orlando, Florida
Central Missouri State University
  Department of Music
  Warrensburg, Missouri
Central Washington University
  Department of Music
  Ellensburg, Washington
University of Cincinnati
  College-Conservatory of Music
  Cincinnati, Ohio
The Claremont Graduate School
  Music Department
  Claremont, California
Cleveland Institute of Music
  Cleveland, Ohio
Cleveland State University
  Department of Music
  Cleveland, Ohio
University of Colorado at Boulder
  College of Music
  Boulder, Colorado
Colorado State University
  Department of Music, Theatre, and
  Dance
  Fort Collins, Colorado
University of Connecticut
  Department of Music
  Storrs, Connecticut
Conservatorio di Musica "Santa Cecilia"
  00187 Rome, Italy
Conservatorio Nacional de Musica - La Paz
  (National Conservatory of Music - La
  Paz)
  La Paz, Bolivia
The Curtis Institute of Music
  Philadelphia, Pennsylvania
Delta State University
  Department of Music
  Cleveland, Mississippi
University of Denver
  Lamont School of Music
  Denver, Colorado
DePaul University
  School of Music
  Chicago, Illinois
DePauw University
  School of Music
  Greencastle, Indiana
Drake University
  Department of Music
  Des Moines, Iowa
Duquesne University
  School of Music
  Pittsburgh, Pennsylvania
East Carolina University
  School of Music
  Greenville, North Carolina
Eastern Illinois University
  Department of Music
  Charleston, Illinois
Eastern Michigan University
  Department of Music

Ypsilanti, Michigan
Emporia State University
  Division of Music
  Emporia, Kansas
Escuela Nacional de Música
  Universidad Nacional Autónoma de
  México
  Mexico City, D.F. 04100, Mexico
Escuela Universitaria de Música -
  Montevideo
  Montevideo, Uruguay
University of Florida
  Department of Music
  Gainesville, Florida
Florida State University
  School of Music
  Tallahassee, Florida
George Mason University
  Department of Performing Arts - Music
  Division
  Fairfax, Virginia
University of Hartford
  Hartt School of Music
  West Hartford, Connecticut
Hermann-Zilcher-Konservatorium
  *D-8700 Würzburg, Federal Republic of
  Germany*
Hofstra University
  Department of Music
  Hempstead, New York
Howard University
  Department of Music
  Washington, District of Columbia
University of Idaho
  School of Music
  Moscow, Idaho
University of Illinois
  School of Music
  Urbana, Illinois
Illinois Wesleyan University
  School of Music
  Bloomington, Illinois
Indiana State University
  Department of Music
  Terre Haute, Indiana
Indiana University - Bloomington
  School of Music
  Bloomington, Indiana
University of Iowa
  School of Music
  Iowa City, Iowa
Iowa State University
  Department of Music
  Ames, Iowa
Ithaca College
  School of Music
  Ithaca, New York
Jackson State University
  Department of Music
  Jackson, Mississippi
James Madison University
  Department of Music
  Harrisonburg, Virginia
Jersey City State College
  Music Department
  Jersey City, New Jersey
The Juilliard School
  New York, New York
University of Kansas
  School of Fine Arts
  Lawrence, Kansas
Kansas State University
  Department of Music
  Manhattan, Kansas
Kent State University
  School of Music

Kent, Ohio
University of Kentucky
  School of Music
  Lexington, Kentucky
Lamar University
  Department of Music
  Beaumont, Texas
Lawrence University
  Conservatory of Music
  Appleton, Wisconsin
University of Louisville
  School of Music
  Louisville, Kentucky
Loyola University
  College of Music
  New Orleans, Louisiana
University of Maine
  School of Performing Arts
  Orono, Maine
Mansfield University
  Department of Music
  Mansfield, Pennsylvania
Marshall University
  Department of Music
  Huntington, West Virginia
University of Maryland - College Park
  Department of Music
  College Park, Maryland
Marywood College
  Music Department
  Scranton, Pennsylvania
University of Massachusetts at Amherst
  Department of Music and Dance
  Amherst, Massachusetts
University of Miami
  School of Music
  Coral Gables, Florida
Miami University
  Department of Music
  Oxford, Ohio
University of Michigan
  School of Music
  Ann Arbor, Michigan
Middle Tennessee State University
  Department of Music
  Murfreesboro, Tennessee
Millikin University
  School of Music
  Decatur, Illinois
Mills College
  Music Department
  Oakland, California
University of Minnesota - Duluth
  Department of Music
  Duluth, Minnesota
University of Minnesota - Twin Cities
  School of Music
  Minneapolis, Minnesota
University of Missouri - Kansas City
  Conservatory of Music
  Kansas City, Missouri
Moorhead State University
  Music Department
  Moorhead, Minnesota
Morehead State University
  Department of Music
  Morehead, Kentucky
National Institute of the Arts
  Music Department
  Taipei County, Taiwan (Republic of China)
University of Nebraska - Lincoln
  School of Music
  Lincoln, Nebraska
University of Nebraska - Omaha
  Department of Music

Omaha, Nebraska
University of Nevada, Las Vegas
  Department of Music
  Las Vegas, Nevada
University of New Hampshire
  Department of Music
  Durham, New Hampshire
University of New Orleans
  Department of Music
  New Orleans, Louisiana
New South Wales State Conservatorium of Music
  Sydney NSW 2000, Australia
Norfolk State University
  Department of Music
  Norfolk, Virginia
University of North Carolina at Chapel Hill
  Department of Music
  Chapel Hill, North Carolina
University of North Carolina at Greensboro
  School of Music
  Greensboro, North Carolina
North Texas State University
  School of Music
  Denton, Texas
Northeast Louisiana University
  School of Music
  Monroe, Louisiana
Northern Arizona University
  Music Department
  Flagstaff, Arizona
University of Northern Iowa
  School of Music
  Cedar Falls, Iowa
Northwestern State University of Louisiana
  Department of Music
  Natchitoches, Louisiana
Northwestern University
  School of Music
  Evanston, Illinois
Oakland University
  Department of Music, Theatre and Dance
  Rochester, Michigan
Oberlin College
  Conservatory of Music
  Oberlin, Ohio
Ohio Wesleyan University
  Department of Music
  Delaware, Ohio
University of Oklahoma
  School of Music
  Norman, Oklahoma
University of Oregon
  School of Music
  Eugene, Oregon
University of the Pacific
  Conservatory of Music
  Stockton, California
Pacific Lutheran University
  Department of Music
  Tacoma, Washington
Peabody Institute of The Johns Hopkins University
  Baltimore, Maryland
University of Pennsylvania
  Department of Music
  Philadelphia, Pennsylvania
Pennsylvania State University
  School of Music
  University Park, Pennsylvania
Philadelphia College of the Performing Arts
  School of Music
  Philadelphia, Pennsylvania
Pittsburg State University
  Department of Music

Pittsburg, Kansas
University of Pittsburgh
  Department of Music
  Pittsburgh, Pennsylvania
Pomona College
  Music Department
  Claremont, California
Queen's University
  School of Music
  Kingston, Ontario, Canada
Real Conservatorio Superior de Música de Madrid
  (Royal Academy of Music)
  Madrid 13, Spain
University of Redlands
  School of Music
  Redlands, California
University of Regina
  Department of Music
  Regina, Saskatchewan, Canada
University of Rhode Island
  Department of Music
  Kingston, Rhode Island
Rice University
  Shepherd School of Music
  Houston, Texas
University of Rochester
  Eastman School of Music
  Rochester, New York
Rutgers, The State University of New Jersey
  Department of Music
  New Brunswick, New Jersey
St. Cloud State University
  Department of Music
  St. Cloud, Minnesota
Saint Louis Conservatory of Music
  St. Louis, Missouri
St. Olaf College
  Music Department
  Northfield, Minnesota
Samford University
  School of Music
  Birmingham, Alabama
San Diego State University
  Music Department
  San Diego, California
San Francisco Conservatory of Music
  San Francisco, California
San Francisco State University
  Department of Music
  San Francisco, California
University of Santo Tomas
  Conservatory of Music
  Manila, The Philippines
University of Saskatchewan
  Department of Music
  Saskatoon, Saskatchewan, Canada
Shenandoah College and Conservatory
  Winchester, Virginia
Smith College
  Department of Music
  Northampton, Massachusetts
University of South Florida
  Department of Music
  Tampa, Florida
Southeast Missouri State University
  Department of Music
  Cape Girardeau, Missouri
Southern Illinois University at Carbondale
  School of Music
  Carbondale, Illinois
Southern Illinois University at Edwardsville
  Department of Music
  Edwardsville, Illinois
Southern Methodist University
  Meadows School of the Arts

Dallas, Texas
University of Southern Mississippi
School of Music
Hattiesburg, Mississippi
University of Southwestern Louisiana
School of Music
Lafayette, Louisiana
Staatliche Hochschule für Musik Freiburg
D-7800 Freiburg i. Br., Federal Republic of Germany
Staatliche Hochschule für Musik Trossingen
D-7218 Trossingen 1, Federal Republic of Germany
State University of New York at Stony Brook
Department of Music
Stony Brook, New York
State University of New York College at Fredonia
School of Music
Fredonia, New York
State University of New York College at Purchase
Division of Music
Purchase, New York
Stephen F. Austin State University
Department of Music
Nacogdoches, Texas
Syracuse University
School of Music
Syracuse, New York
Teachers College of Columbia University
Department of Music and Music Education
New York, New York
Temple University
Esther Boyer College of Music
Philadelphia, Pennsylvania
University of Tennessee at Knoxville
Department of Music
Knoxville, Tennessee
University of Texas at El Paso
Music Department
El Paso, Texas
Texas Christian University
Music Department
Fort Worth, Texas
Toho Gakuen School of Music
Tokyo, Japan
University of Toronto
Faculty of Music
Toronto, Ontario, Canada
Troy State University
Department of Music
Troy, Alabama
University of Tulsa
Faculty of Music
Tulsa, Oklahoma
Université de Montréal
Faculty of Music
Montréal, Québec, Canada
Valparaiso University
Department of Music
Valparaiso, Indiana
VanderCook College of Music
Chicago, Illinois
Virginia Polytechnic Institute and State University
Department of Music
Blacksburg, Virginia
Vysoká Skola Mûzickych Umeni v Praha
Academy of Music and Dramatic Arts
1101 00 Prague 1, Czechoslovakia
Washington State University
Department of Music
Pullman, Washington

West Chester University of Pennsylvania
School of Music
West Chester, Pennsylvania
West Virginia University
Division of Music
Morgantown, West Virginia
Western Illinois University
Department of Music
Macomb, Illinois
Western Kentucky University
Department of Music
Bowling Green, Kentucky
Western Michigan University
School of Music
Kalamazoo, Michigan
Wichita State University
School of Music
Wichita, Kansas
Wilfrid Laurier University
Faculty of Music
Waterloo, Ontario, Canada
William Carey College
Winters School of Music
Hattiesburg, Mississippi
University of Windsor
School of Music
Windsor, Ontario, Canada
University of Wisconsin - Eau Claire
Department of Music
Eau Claire, Wisconsin
University of Wisconsin - Madison
School of Music
Madison, Wisconsin
University of Wisconsin - Milwaukee
Music Department
Milwaukee, Wisconsin
University of Wisconsin - Stevens Point
Department of Music
Stevens Point, Wisconsin
Wright State University
Department of Music
Dayton, Ohio
University of Wyoming
Music Department
Laramie, Wyoming
Yale University
School of Music
New Haven, Connecticut
York University
Department of Music
North York, Ontario, Canada
Youngstown State University
Dana School of Music
Youngstown, Ohio

VIOLA D'AMORE

Staatliche Hochschule für Musik Freiburg
D-7800 Freiburg i. Br., Federal Republic of Germany

VIOLA DA GAMBA

Akademia Muzyczna w Krakowie
31-038 Kraków, Poland
Bradley University
Division of Music and Theatre Arts
Peoria, Illinois
University of California, Los Angeles
Department of Music
Los Angeles, California
University of California, Riverside
Department of Music
Riverside, California
George Mason University
Department of Performing Arts - Music Division

Fairfax, Virginia
University of Hawaii at Manoa
Music Department
Honolulu, Hawaii
Hermann-Zilcher-Konservatorium
D-8700 Würzburg, Federal Republic of Germany
Hochschule für Music und Darstellende Kunst Hamburg
2000 Hamburg 13, Federal Republic of Germany
Kansas State University
Department of Music
Manhattan, Kansas
Memphis State University
Music Department
Memphis, Tennessee
New England Conservatory
Boston, Massachusetts
Norges Musikkhøgskole
(The Norwegian State Academy of Music)
N-0130 Oslo 1, Norway
University of North Carolina at Greensboro
School of Music
Greensboro, North Carolina
Oakland University
Department of Music, Theatre and Dance
Rochester, Michigan
Oberlin College
Conservatory of Music
Oberlin, Ohio
St. Olaf College
Music Department
Northfield, Minnesota
Smith College
Department of Music
Northampton, Massachusetts
Staatliche Hochschule für Musik Freiburg
D-7800 Freiburg i. Br., Federal Republic of Germany
Staatliche Hochschule für Musik Rheinland - Köln
D-5000 Köln 1, Federal Republic of Germany
Texas Christian University
Music Department
Fort Worth, Texas
Toho Gakuen School of Music
Tokyo, Japan
Ueno Gakuen College
Tokyo 110, Japan

VIOLIN

Acadia University
School of Music
Wolfville, Nova Scotia, Canada
Akademia Muzyczna w Krakowie
31-038 Kraków, Poland
University of Alabama
School of Music
University, Alabama
University of Alaska
Music Department
Fairbanks, Alaska
American Conservatory of Music
Chicago, Illinois
University of Arizona
School of Music
Tucson, Arizona
University of Arkansas
Department of Music
Fayetteville, Arkansas

Arkansas Tech University
Department of Music
Russellville, Arkansas
Austin Peay State University
Department of Music
Clarksville, Tennessee
Baldwin-Wallace College
Conservatory of Music
Berea, Ohio
Baylor University
School of Music
Waco, Texas
Berklee College of Music
Boston, Massachusetts
Boise State University
Music Department
Boise, Idaho
Boston University
School of Music
Boston, Massachusetts
Bowling Green State University
College of Musical Arts
Bowling Green, Ohio
Bradley University
Division of Music and Theatre Arts
Peoria, Illinois
University of British Columbia
School of Music
Vancouver, British Columbia, Canada
Bulgarian State Conservatoire
Sofia 1505, Bulgaria
Butler University
Jordan College of Fine Arts
Indianapolis, Indiana
University of California, Irvine
School of Fine Arts
Irvine, California
University of California, Los Angeles
Department of Music
Los Angeles, California
University of California, Riverside
Department of Music
Riverside, California
University of California, San Diego
Department of Music
La Jolla, California
University of California, Santa Barbara
Department of Music
Santa Barbara, California
University of California, Santa Cruz
Music Board, Division of the Arts
Santa Cruz, California
California State University, Hayward
Department of Music
Hayward, California
California State University, Sacramento
Department of Music
Sacramento, California
The Catholic University of America
The Benjamin T. Rome School of Music
Washington, District of Columbia
University of Central Arkansas
Department of Music
Conway, Arkansas
University of Central Florida
Department of Music
Orlando, Florida
Central Missouri State University
Department of Music
Warrensburg, Missouri
Central Washington University
Department of Music
Ellensburg, Washington
University of Cincinnati
College-Conservatory of Music
Cincinnati, Ohio

The Claremont Graduate School
Music Department
Claremont, California
Cleveland Institute of Music
Cleveland, Ohio
Cleveland State University
Department of Music
Cleveland, Ohio
University of Colorado at Boulder
College of Music
Boulder, Colorado
Colorado State University
Department of Music, Theatre, and
Dance
Fort Collins, Colorado
University of Connecticut
Department of Music
Storrs, Connecticut
Conservatorio di Musica "Santa Cecilia"
00187 Rome, Italy
Conservatorio Nacional de Musica - La Paz
(National Conservatory of Music - La
Paz)
La Paz, Bolivia
The Curtis Institute of Music
Philadelphia, Pennsylvania
Delta State University
Department of Music
Cleveland, Mississippi
University of Denver
Lamont School of Music
Denver, Colorado
DePaul University
School of Music
Chicago, Illinois
DePauw University
School of Music
Greencastle, Indiana
Drake University
Department of Music
Des Moines, Iowa
Duquesne University
School of Music
Pittsburgh, Pennsylvania
East Carolina University
School of Music
Greenville, North Carolina
Eastern Illinois University
Department of Music
Charleston, Illinois
Eastern Michigan University
Department of Music
Ypsilanti, Michigan
Emporia State University
Division of Music
Emporia, Kansas
Escuela Nacional de Música
Universidad Nacional Autónoma de
México
Mexico City, D.F. 04100, Mexico
Escuela Universitaria de Música -
Montevideo
Montevideo, Uruguay
University of Florida
Department of Music
Gainesville, Florida
Florida State University
School of Music
Tallahassee, Florida
George Mason University
Department of Performing Arts - Music
Division
Fairfax, Virginia
University of Hartford
Hartt School of Music
West Hartford, Connecticut

University of Hawaii at Manoa
Music Department
Honolulu, Hawaii
Hermann-Zilcher-Konservatorium
*D-8700 Würzburg, Federal Republic of
Germany*
Hofstra University
Department of Music
Hempstead, New York
Howard University
Department of Music
Washington, District of Columbia
University of Idaho
School of Music
Moscow, Idaho
University of Illinois
School of Music
Urbana, Illinois
Illinois Wesleyan University
School of Music
Bloomington, Illinois
Indiana State University
Department of Music
Terre Haute, Indiana
Indiana University - Bloomington
School of Music
Bloomington, Indiana
Indira Kala Sangit Vishwavidyalaya
(University of Music and Fine Arts)
Madhya Pradesh 491881, India
Institute of Aesthetic Studies
Colombo 7, Sri Lanka
University of Iowa
School of Music
Iowa City, Iowa
Iowa State University
Department of Music
Ames, Iowa
Ithaca College
School of Music
Ithaca, New York
Jackson State University
Department of Music
Jackson, Mississippi
James Madison University
Department of Music
Harrisonburg, Virginia
Jersey City State College
Music Department
Jersey City, New Jersey
The Juilliard School
New York, New York
University of Kansas
School of Fine Arts
Lawrence, Kansas
Kansas State University
Department of Music
Manhattan, Kansas
Kent State University
School of Music
Kent, Ohio
University of Kentucky
School of Music
Lexington, Kentucky
Kenya Conservatoire of Music
Nairobi, Kenya
Lamar University
Department of Music
Beaumont, Texas
Lawrence University
Conservatory of Music
Appleton, Wisconsin
University of Louisville
School of Music
Louisville, Kentucky

Loyola University
  College of Music
  New Orleans, Louisiana
University of Maine
  School of Performing Arts
  Orono, Maine
Mansfield University
  Department of Music
  Mansfield, Pennsylvania
Marshall University
  Department of Music
  Huntington, West Virginia
University of Maryland - College Park
  Department of Music
  College Park, Maryland
Marywood College
  Music Department
  Scranton, Pennsylvania
University of Massachusetts at Amherst
  Department of Music and Dance
  Amherst, Massachusetts
University of Miami
  School of Music
  Coral Gables, Florida
Miami University
  Department of Music
  Oxford, Ohio
University of Michigan
  School of Music
  Ann Arbor, Michigan
Middle Tennessee State University
  Department of Music
  Murfreesboro, Tennessee
Millikin University
  School of Music
  Decatur, Illinois
Mills College
  Music Department
  Oakland, California
University of Minnesota - Duluth
  Department of Music
  Duluth, Minnesota
University of Minnesota - Twin Cities
  School of Music
  Minneapolis, Minnesota
University of Missouri - Kansas City
  Conservatory of Music
  Kansas City, Missouri
Moorhead State University
  Music Department
  Moorhead, Minnesota
Morehead State University
  Department of Music
  Morehead, Kentucky
National Institute of Music - Sana'a
  Sana'a, Yemen Arab Republic
National Institute of the Arts
  Music Department
  Taipei County, Taiwan (Republic of China)
University of Nebraska - Lincoln
  School of Music
  Lincoln, Nebraska
University of Nebraska - Omaha
  Department of Music
  Omaha, Nebraska
University of Nevada, Las Vegas
  Department of Music
  Las Vegas, Nevada
New England Conservatory
  Boston, Massachusetts
University of New Hampshire
  Department of Music
  Durham, New Hampshire
University of New Orleans
  Department of Music

New Orleans, Louisiana
New South Wales State Conservatorium of Music
  Sydney NSW 2000, Australia
Norfolk State University
  Department of Music
  Norfolk, Virginia
University of North Carolina at Chapel Hill
  Department of Music
  Chapel Hill, North Carolina
University of North Carolina at Greensboro
  School of Music
  Greensboro, North Carolina
North Texas State University
  School of Music
  Denton, Texas
Northeast Louisiana University
  School of Music
  Monroe, Louisiana
Northern Arizona University
  Music Department
  Flagstaff, Arizona
University of Northern Iowa
  School of Music
  Cedar Falls, Iowa
Northwestern State University of Louisiana
  Department of Music
  Natchitoches, Louisiana
Northwestern University
  School of Music
  Evanston, Illinois
University of Notre Dame
  Department of Music
  Notre Dame, Indiana
Oakland University
  Department of Music, Theatre and Dance
  Rochester, Michigan
Oberlin College
  Conservatory of Music
  Oberlin, Ohio
Ohio Wesleyan University
  Department of Music
  Delaware, Ohio
University of Oklahoma
  School of Music
  Norman, Oklahoma
University of Oregon
  School of Music
  Eugene, Oregon
University of the Pacific
  Conservatory of Music
  Stockton, California
Pacific Lutheran University
  Department of Music
  Tacoma, Washington
Peabody Institute of The Johns Hopkins University
  Baltimore, Maryland
University of Pennsylvania
  Department of Music
  Philadelphia, Pennsylvania
Pennsylvania State University
  School of Music
  University Park, Pennsylvania
Philadelphia College of the Performing Arts
  School of Music
  Philadelphia, Pennsylvania
Pittsburg State University
  Department of Music
  Pittsburg, Kansas
University of Pittsburgh
  Department of Music
  Pittsburgh, Pennsylvania
Pomona College
  Music Department

Claremont, California
Prayag Sangit Samiti
  Allahabad 211001, India
Queen's University
  School of Music
  Kingston, Ontario, Canada
Radford University
  Department of Music
  Radford, Virginia
Real Conservatorio Superior de Música de Madrid
  (Royal Academy of Music)
  Madrid 13, Spain
University of Redlands
  School of Music
  Redlands, California
University of Regina
  Department of Music
  Regina, Saskatchewan, Canada
University of Rhode Island
  Department of Music
  Kingston, Rhode Island
Rice University
  Shepherd School of Music
  Houston, Texas
University of Rochester
  Eastman School of Music
  Rochester, New York
Rutgers, The State University of New Jersey
  Department of Music
  New Brunswick, New Jersey
St. Cloud State University
  Department of Music
  St. Cloud, Minnesota
Saint Louis Conservatory of Music
  St. Louis, Missouri
St. Olaf College
  Music Department
  Northfield, Minnesota
Samford University
  School of Music
  Birmingham, Alabama
San Diego State University
  Music Department
  San Diego, California
San Francisco Conservatory of Music
  San Francisco, California
San Francisco State University
  Department of Music
  San Francisco, California
San Jose State University
  Department of Music
  San Jose, California
University of Santo Tomas
  Conservatory of Music
  Manila, The Philippines
University of Saskatchewan
  Department of Music
  Saskatoon, Saskatchewan, Canada
Shenandoah College and Conservatory
  Winchester, Virginia
Smith College
  Department of Music
  Northampton, Massachusetts
University of South Dakota
  Music Department
  Vermillion, South Dakota
University of South Florida
  Department of Music
  Tampa, Florida
Southeast Missouri State University
  Department of Music
  Cape Girardeau, Missouri
Southern Illinois University at Carbondale
  School of Music
  Carbondale, Illinois

Southern Illinois University at Edwardsville
  Department of Music
  Edwardsville, Illinois
Southern Methodist University
  Meadows School of the Arts
  Dallas, Texas
University of Southern Mississippi
  School of Music
  Hattiesburg, Mississippi
University of Southwestern Louisiana
  School of Music
  Lafayette, Louisiana
Staatliche Hochschule für Musik Freiburg
  *D-7800 Freiburg i. Br., Federal Republic
  of Germany*
Staatliche Hochschule für Musik Trossingen
  *D-7218 Trossingen 1, Federal Republic of
  Germany*
State University of New York at Stony
  Brook
  Department of Music
  Stony Brook, New York
State University of New York College at
  Fredonia
  School of Music
  Fredonia, New York
State University of New York College at
  Potsdam
  Crane School of Music
  Potsdam, New York
State University of New York College at
  Purchase
  Division of Music
  Purchase, New York
Stephen F. Austin State University
  Department of Music
  Nacogdoches, Texas
Syracuse University
  School of Music
  Syracuse, New York
Teachers College of Columbia University
  Department of Music and Music
  Education
  New York, New York
Temple University
  Esther Boyer College of Music
  Philadelphia, Pennsylvania
University of Tennessee at Knoxville
  Department of Music
  Knoxville, Tennessee
University of Texas at El Paso
  Music Department
  El Paso, Texas
Texas Christian University
  Music Department
  Fort Worth, Texas
Toho Gakuen School of Music
  Tokyo, Japan
University of Toronto
  Faculty of Music
  Toronto, Ontario, Canada
Troy State University
  Department of Music
  Troy, Alabama
University of Tulsa
  Faculty of Music
  Tulsa, Oklahoma
Universidad de Antioquía
  Facultad de Artes, Departamento de
  Música
  Medellín, Colombia
Universidade do Rio de Janeiro
  Letters and Arts Center - Music Course
  22290 Rio de Janeiro, Brazil
Université de Montréal
  Faculty of Music

Montréal, Québec, Canada
Valparaiso University
  Department of Music
  Valparaiso, Indiana
VanderCook College of Music
  Chicago, Illinois
Virginia Polytechnic Institute and State
  University
  Department of Music
  Blacksburg, Virginia
Vysoká Skola Mûzickych Umeni v Praha
  Academy of Music and Dramatic Arts
  1101 00 Prague 1, Czechoslovakia
Washington State University
  Department of Music
  Pullman, Washington
West Chester University of Pennsylvania
  School of Music
  West Chester, Pennsylvania
West Virginia University
  Division of Music
  Morgantown, West Virginia
Western Illinois University
  Department of Music
  Macomb, Illinois
Western Kentucky University
  Department of Music
  Bowling Green, Kentucky
Western Michigan University
  School of Music
  Kalamazoo, Michigan
Wichita State University
  School of Music
  Wichita, Kansas
Wiesbadener Konservatorium und staatliche
  anerkannte private Fachschule für
  Musikerzieher e.V.
  (Conservatory and Seminary for Music
  Education)
  *6200 Wiesbaden, Federal Republic of
  Germany*
Wilfrid Laurier University
  Faculty of Music
  Waterloo, Ontario, Canada
William Carey College
  Winters School of Music
  Hattiesburg, Mississippi
William Paterson College
  Department of Music
  Wayne, New Jersey
University of Windsor
  School of Music
  Windsor, Ontario, Canada
University of Wisconsin - Eau Claire
  Department of Music
  Eau Claire, Wisconsin
University of Wisconsin - Madison
  School of Music
  Madison, Wisconsin
University of Wisconsin - Milwaukee
  Music Department
  Milwaukee, Wisconsin
University of Wisconsin - Stevens Point
  Department of Music
  Stevens Point, Wisconsin
Wright State University
  Department of Music
  Dayton, Ohio
University of Wyoming
  Music Department
  Laramie, Wyoming
Yale University
  School of Music
  New Haven, Connecticut
York University
  Department of Music

North York, Ontario, Canada
Youngstown State University
  Dana School of Music
  Youngstown, Ohio

VIOLONCELLO

Acadia University
  School of Music
  Wolfville, Nova Scotia, Canada
Akademia Muzyczna w Krakowie
  31-038 Kraków, Poland
University of Alabama
  School of Music
  University, Alabama
University of Alaska
  Music Department
  Fairbanks, Alaska
University of Arizona
  School of Music
  Tucson, Arizona
University of Arkansas
  Department of Music
  Fayetteville, Arkansas
Arkansas Tech University
  Department of Music
  Russellville, Arkansas
Austin Peay State University
  Department of Music
  Clarksville, Tennessee
Baldwin-Wallace College
  Conservatory of Music
  Berea, Ohio
Baylor University
  School of Music
  Waco, Texas
Berklee College of Music
  Boston, Massachusetts
Boise State University
  Music Department
  Boise, Idaho
Boston University
  School of Music
  Boston, Massachusetts
Bowling Green State University
  College of Musical Arts
  Bowling Green, Ohio
Bradley University
  Division of Music and Theatre Arts
  Peoria, Illinois
Bulgarian State Conservatoire
  Sofia 1505, Bulgaria
University of California, Irvine
  School of Fine Arts
  Irvine, California
University of California, Los Angeles
  Department of Music
  Los Angeles, California
University of California, Riverside
  Department of Music
  Riverside, California
University of California, San Diego
  Department of Music
  La Jolla, California
University of California, Santa Barbara
  Department of Music
  Santa Barbara, California
University of California, Santa Cruz
  Music Board, Division of the Arts
  Santa Cruz, California

California State University, Hayward
Department of Music
Hayward, California
California State University, Sacramento
Department of Music
Sacramento, California
The Catholic University of America
The Benjamin T. Rome School of Music
Washington, District of Columbia
University of Central Arkansas
Department of Music
Conway, Arkansas
University of Central Florida
Department of Music
Orlando, Florida
Central Missouri State University
Department of Music
Warrensburg, Missouri
Central Washington University
Department of Music
Ellensburg, Washington
The Claremont Graduate School
Music Department
Claremont, California
Cleveland Institute of Music
Cleveland, Ohio
Cleveland State University
Department of Music
Cleveland, Ohio
University of Colorado at Boulder
College of Music
Boulder, Colorado
Colorado State University
Department of Music, Theatre, and
Dance
Fort Collins, Colorado
University of Connecticut
Department of Music
Storrs, Connecticut
Conservatorio di Musica "Santa Cecilia"
00187 Rome, Italy
Conservatorio Nacional de Musica - La Paz
(National Conservatory of Music - La
Paz)
La Paz, Bolivia
The Curtis Institute of Music
Philadelphia, Pennsylvania
Delta State University
Department of Music
Cleveland, Mississippi
University of Denver
Lamont School of Music
Denver, Colorado
DePaul University
School of Music
Chicago, Illinois
DePauw University
School of Music
Greencastle, Indiana
Drake University
Department of Music
Des Moines, Iowa
Duquesne University
School of Music
Pittsburgh, Pennsylvania
East Carolina University
School of Music
Greenville, North Carolina
Eastern Illinois University
Department of Music
Charleston, Illinois
Eastern Michigan University
Department of Music
Ypsilanti, Michigan
Emporia State University
Division of Music

Emporia, Kansas
Escuela Nacional de Música
Universidad Nacional Autónoma de
México
Mexico City, D.F. 04100, Mexico
Escuela Universitaria de Música -
Montevideo
Montevideo, Uruguay
George Mason University
Department of Performing Arts - Music
Division
Fairfax, Virginia
University of Hartford
Hartt School of Music
West Hartford, Connecticut
University of Hawaii at Manoa
Music Department
Honolulu, Hawaii
Hermann-Zilcher-Konservatorium
*D-8700 Würzburg, Federal Republic of
Germany*
Hofstra University
Department of Music
Hempstead, New York
Howard University
Department of Music
Washington, District of Columbia
University of Idaho
School of Music
Moscow, Idaho
University of Illinois
School of Music
Urbana, Illinois
Illinois Wesleyan University
School of Music
Bloomington, Illinois
Indiana State University
Department of Music
Terre Haute, Indiana
Indiana University - Bloomington
School of Music
Bloomington, Indiana
University of Iowa
School of Music
Iowa City, Iowa
Iowa State University
Department of Music
Ames, Iowa
Ithaca College
School of Music
Ithaca, New York
Jackson State University
Department of Music
Jackson, Mississippi
James Madison University
Department of Music
Harrisonburg, Virginia
Jersey City State College
Music Department
Jersey City, New Jersey
The Juilliard School
New York, New York
University of Kansas
School of Fine Arts
Lawrence, Kansas
Kansas State University
Department of Music
Manhattan, Kansas
Kent State University
School of Music
Kent, Ohio
University of Kentucky
School of Music
Lexington, Kentucky
Kenya Conservatoire of Music
Nairobi, Kenya

Lamar University
Department of Music
Beaumont, Texas
Lawrence University
Conservatory of Music
Appleton, Wisconsin
University of Louisville
School of Music
Louisville, Kentucky
Loyola University
College of Music
New Orleans, Louisiana
University of Maine
School of Performing Arts
Orono, Maine
Mansfield University
Department of Music
Mansfield, Pennsylvania
Marshall University
Department of Music
Huntington, West Virginia
University of Maryland - College Park
Department of Music
College Park, Maryland
Marywood College
Music Department
Scranton, Pennsylvania
University of Massachusetts at Amherst
Department of Music and Dance
Amherst, Massachusetts
University of Miami
School of Music
Coral Gables, Florida
Miami University
Department of Music
Oxford, Ohio
University of Michigan
School of Music
Ann Arbor, Michigan
Middle Tennessee State University
Department of Music
Murfreesboro, Tennessee
Millikin University
School of Music
Decatur, Illinois
Mills College
Music Department
Oakland, California
University of Minnesota - Duluth
Department of Music
Duluth, Minnesota
University of Minnesota - Twin Cities
School of Music
Minneapolis, Minnesota
University of Missouri - Kansas City
Conservatory of Music
Kansas City, Missouri
Moorhead State University
Music Department
Moorhead, Minnesota
Morehead State University
Department of Music
Morehead, Kentucky
Musikschule und Konservatorium
Schaffhausen
Schaffhausen, Switzerland
National Institute of Music - Sana'a
Sana'a, Yemen Arab Republic
National Institute of the Arts
Music Department
*Taipei County, Taiwan (Republic of
China)*
University of Nebraska - Lincoln
School of Music
Lincoln, Nebraska

University of Nebraska - Omaha
  Department of Music
  Omaha, Nebraska
University of Nevada, Las Vegas
  Department of Music
  Las Vegas, Nevada
University of New Hampshire
  Department of Music
  Durham, New Hampshire
University of New Orleans
  Department of Music
  New Orleans, Louisiana
New South Wales State Conservatorium of
  Music
  Sydney NSW 2000, Australia
University of North Carolina at Chapel Hill
  Department of Music
  Chapel Hill, North Carolina
University of North Carolina at Greensboro
  School of Music
  Greensboro, North Carolina
North Texas State University
  School of Music
  Denton, Texas
Northeast Louisiana University
  School of Music
  Monroe, Louisiana
Northern Arizona University
  Music Department
  Flagstaff, Arizona
University of Northern Iowa
  School of Music
  Cedar Falls, Iowa
Northwestern State University of Louisiana
  Department of Music
  Natchitoches, Louisiana
Northwestern University
  School of Music
  Evanston, Illinois
University of Notre Dame
  Department of Music
  Notre Dame, Indiana
Oakland University
  Department of Music, Theatre and
  Dance
  Rochester, Michigan
Oberlin College
  Conservatory of Music
  Oberlin, Ohio
Ohio Wesleyan University
  Department of Music
  Delaware, Ohio
University of Oklahoma
  School of Music
  Norman, Oklahoma
University of Oregon
  School of Music
  Eugene, Oregon
Pacific Lutheran University
  Department of Music
  Tacoma, Washington
Peabody Institute of The Johns Hopkins
  University
  Baltimore, Maryland
University of Pennsylvania
  Department of Music
  Philadelphia, Pennsylvania
Pennsylvania State University
  School of Music
  University Park, Pennsylvania
Philadelphia College of the Performing Arts
  School of Music
  Philadelphia, Pennsylvania
Pittsburg State University
  Department of Music
  Pittsburg, Kansas

University of Pittsburgh
  Department of Music
  Pittsburgh, Pennsylvania
Pomona College
  Music Department
  Claremont, California
Queen's University
  School of Music
  Kingston, Ontario, Canada
Radford University
  Department of Music
  Radford, Virginia
Real Conservatorio Superior de Música de
  Madrid
  (Royal Academy of Music)
  Madrid 13, Spain
University of Redlands
  School of Music
  Redlands, California
University of Regina
  Department of Music
  Regina, Saskatchewan, Canada
University of Rhode Island
  Department of Music
  Kingston, Rhode Island
Rice University
  Shepherd School of Music
  Houston, Texas
University of Rochester
  Eastman School of Music
  Rochester, New York
Rutgers, The State University of New Jersey
  Department of Music
  New Brunswick, New Jersey
St. Cloud State University
  Department of Music
  St. Cloud, Minnesota
Saint Louis Conservatory of Music
  St. Louis, Missouri
St. Olaf College
  Music Department
  Northfield, Minnesota
Samford University
  School of Music
  Birmingham, Alabama
San Francisco Conservatory of Music
  San Francisco, California
San Francisco State University
  Department of Music
  San Francisco, California
San Jose State University
  Department of Music
  San Jose, California
University of Saskatchewan
  Department of Music
  Saskatoon, Saskatchewan, Canada
Shenandoah College and Conservatory
  Winchester, Virginia
Smith College
  Department of Music
  Northampton, Massachusetts
University of South Dakota
  Music Department
  Vermillion, South Dakota
University of South Florida
  Department of Music
  Tampa, Florida
Southeast Missouri State University
  Department of Music
  Cape Girardeau, Missouri
Southern Illinois University at Carbondale
  School of Music
  Carbondale, Illinois
Southern Illinois University at Edwardsville
  Department of Music
  Edwardsville, Illinois

Southern Methodist University
  Meadows School of the Arts
  Dallas, Texas
University of Southern Mississippi
  School of Music
  Hattiesburg, Mississippi
University of Southwestern Louisiana
  School of Music
  Lafayette, Louisiana
Staatliche Hochschule für Musik Freiburg
  *D-7800 Freiburg i. Br., Federal Republic
  of Germany*
Staatliche Hochschule für Musik Trossingen
  *D-7218 Trossingen 1, Federal Republic of
  Germany*
State University of New York at Stony
  Brook
  Department of Music
  Stony Brook, New York
State University of New York College at
  Fredonia
  School of Music
  Fredonia, New York
State University of New York College at
  Potsdam
  Crane School of Music
  Potsdam, New York
State University of New York College at
  Purchase
  Division of Music
  Purchase, New York
Stephen F. Austin State University
  Department of Music
  Nacogdoches, Texas
Syracuse University
  School of Music
  Syracuse, New York
Teachers College of Columbia University
  Department of Music and Music
  Education
  New York, New York
Temple University
  Esther Boyer College of Music
  Philadelphia, Pennsylvania
University of Tennessee at Knoxville
  Department of Music
  Knoxville, Tennessee
University of Texas at El Paso
  Music Department
  El Paso, Texas
Texas Christian University
  Music Department
  Fort Worth, Texas
Toho Gakuen School of Music
  Tokyo, Japan
University of Toronto
  Faculty of Music
  Toronto, Ontario, Canada
Troy State University
  Department of Music
  Troy, Alabama
University of Tulsa
  Faculty of Music
  Tulsa, Oklahoma
Universidad de Antioquía
  Facultad de Artes, Departamento de
  Música
  Medellín, Colombia
Universidade do Rio de Janeiro
  Letters and Arts Center - Music Course
  22290 Rio de Janeiro, Brazil
Université de Montréal
  Faculty of Music
  Montréal, Québec, Canada
Valparaiso University
  Department of Music

Valparaiso, Indiana
VanderCook College of Music
Chicago, Illinois
Virginia Polytechnic Institute and State
University
Department of Music
Blacksburg, Virginia
Vysoká Skola Mûzickych Umeni v Praha
Academy of Music and Dramatic Arts
1101 00 Prague 1, Czechoslovakia
Washington State University
Department of Music
Pullman, Washington
West Chester University of Pennsylvania
School of Music
West Chester, Pennsylvania
West Virginia University
Division of Music
Morgantown, West Virginia
Western Illinois University
Department of Music
Macomb, Illinois
Western Kentucky University
Department of Music
Bowling Green, Kentucky
Western Michigan University
School of Music
Kalamazoo, Michigan
Wichita State University
School of Music
Wichita, Kansas
Wiesbadener Konservatorium und staatliche
anerkannte private Fachschule für
Musikerzieher e.V.
(Conservatory and Seminary for Music
Education)
6200 Wiesbaden, Federal Republic of
Germany
Wilfrid Laurier University
Faculty of Music
Waterloo, Ontario, Canada
William Carey College
Winters School of Music
Hattiesburg, Mississippi
University of Windsor
School of Music
Windsor, Ontario, Canada
University of Wisconsin - Eau Claire
Department of Music
Eau Claire, Wisconsin
University of Wisconsin - Madison
School of Music
Madison, Wisconsin
University of Wisconsin - Milwaukee
Music Department
Milwaukee, Wisconsin
University of Wisconsin - Stevens Point
Department of Music
Stevens Point, Wisconsin
Wright State University
Department of Music
Dayton, Ohio
University of Wyoming
Music Department
Laramie, Wyoming
Yale University
School of Music
New Haven, Connecticut
York University
Department of Music
North York, Ontario, Canada
Youngstown State University
Dana School of Music
Youngstown, Ohio

VOICE

The Academy of Vocal Arts
Philadelphia, Pennsylvania
Acadia University
School of Music
Wolfville, Nova Scotia, Canada
Akademia Muzyczna w Lódź
(Academy of Music of Lódź)
90-716 Lódź, Poland
Akademia Muzycznaj im. Fryderyka
Chopina w Warzawie
(Frederic Chopin Academy of Music of
Warsaw)
00-368 Warsaw, Poland
University of Akron
Department of Music
Akron, Ohio
University of Alabama
School of Music
University, Alabama
Alabama State University
School of Music
Montgomery, Alabama
University of Alberta
Department of Music
Edmonton, Alberta, Canada
American Conservatory of Music
Chicago, Illinois
Andrews University
Department of Music
Berrien Springs, Michigan
Appalachian State University
Department of Music
Boone, North Carolina
University of Arizona
School of Music
Tucson, Arizona
Arizona State University
School of Music
Tempe, Arizona
University of Arkansas
Department of Music
Fayetteville, Arkansas
Arkansas State University
Department of Music
State University, Arkansas
Arkansas Tech University
Department of Music
Russellville, Arkansas
Auburn University
Department of Music
Auburn, Alabama
Austin Peay State University
Department of Music
Clarksville, Tennessee
A.V. Nezhdanova Odessa Conservatory
270000 Odessa, Ukrainskaja SSR,
U.S.S.R.
Azusa Pacific University
School of Music
Azusa, California
Baldwin-Wallace College
Conservatory of Music
Berea, Ohio
Ball State University
School of Music
Muncie, Indiana
Baylor University
School of Music
Waco, Texas
Bemidji State University
Music Department
Bemidji, Minnesota
Bennington College
Music Department

Bennington, Vermont
Berklee College of Music
Boston, Massachusetts
Bhavan's Bharatiya Sangeet and Nartan
Skikshapeeth
(Academy of Music and Dance)
Bombay 4000007, India
Biola University
Department of Music
La Mirada, California
Bob Jones University
Division of Music
Greenville, South Carolina
Boise State University
Music Department
Boise, Idaho
Boston University
School of Music
Boston, Massachusetts
Bowling Green State University
College of Musical Arts
Bowling Green, Ohio
Bradley University
Division of Music and Theatre Arts
Peoria, Illinois
Brandeis University
Department of Music
Waltham, Massachusetts
Brandon University
School of Music
Brandon, Manitoba, Canada
Brigham Young University
Department of Music
Provo, Utah
University of British Columbia
School of Music
Vancouver, British Columbia, Canada
Brown University
Department of Music
Providence, Rhode Island
Butler University
Jordan College of Fine Arts
Indianapolis, Indiana
University of Calgary
Department of Music
Calgary, Alberta, Canada
University of California, Berkeley
Department of Music
Berkeley, California
University of California, Irvine
School of Fine Arts
Irvine, California
University of California, Los Angeles
Department of Music
Los Angeles, California
University of California, Riverside
Department of Music
Riverside, California
University of California, San Diego
Department of Music
La Jolla, California
University of California, Santa Barbara
Department of Music
Santa Barbara, California
University of California, Santa Cruz
Music Board, Division of the Arts
Santa Cruz, California
California Institute of the Arts
School of Music
Valencia, California
California State University, Chico
Department of Music
Chico, California
California State University, Fresno
Department of Music
Fresno, California

California State University, Fullerton
  Department of Music
  Fullerton, California
California State University, Hayward
  Department of Music
  Hayward, California
California State University, Long Beach
  Department of Music
  Long Beach, California
California State University, Northridge
  Music Department
  Northridge, California
California State University, Sacramento
  Department of Music
  Sacramento, California
Carnegie-Mellon University
  Department of Music
  Pittsburgh, Pennsylvania
Case Western Reserve University
  Department of Music
  Cleveland, Ohio
The Catholic University of America
  The Benjamin T. Rome School of Music
  Washington, District of Columbia
University of Central Arkansas
  Department of Music
  Conway, Arkansas
University of Central Florida
  Department of Music
  Orlando, Florida
Central State University
  Department of Music
  Edmond, Oklahoma
Central Washington University
  Department of Music
  Ellensburg, Washington
University of Cincinnati
  College-Conservatory of Music
  Cincinnati, Ohio
City of Leeds College of Music
  Leeds LS2 8BH, United Kingdom
City University of New York - Brooklyn
College
  Conservatory of Music
  Brooklyn, New York
City University of New York - City College
  Department of Music
  New York, New York
City University of New York - Hunter
College
  Department of Music
  New York, New York
City University of New York - Queens
College
  The Aaron Copland School of Music
  Flushing, New York
The Claremont Graduate School
  Music Department
  Claremont, California
Cleveland Institute of Music
  Cleveland, Ohio
Cleveland State University
  Department of Music
  Cleveland, Ohio
University of Colorado at Boulder
  College of Music
  Boulder, Colorado
University of Colorado at Denver
  College of Music
  Denver, Colorado
Colorado State University
  Department of Music, Theatre, and
  Dance
  Fort Collins, Colorado
Columbus College
  Department of Music

Columbus, Georgia
Combs College of Music
  Philadelphia, Pennsylvania
University of Connecticut
  Department of Music
  Storrs, Connecticut
Conservatorio di Musica "Santa Cecilia"
  00187 Rome, Italy
Conservatorio Nacional de Música
  (National Conservatory of Music)
  Lima 1, Peru
Converse College
  School of Music
  Spartanburg, South Carolina
Cornell University
  Department of Music
  Ithaca, New York
The Curtis Institute of Music
  Philadelphia, Pennsylvania
Dalhousie University
  Department of Music
  Halifax, Nova Scotia, Canada
University of Delaware
  Department of Music
  Newark, Delaware
Delta State University
  Department of Music
  Cleveland, Mississippi
University of Denver
  Lamont School of Music
  Denver, Colorado
DePaul University
  School of Music
  Chicago, Illinois
DePauw University
  School of Music
  Greencastle, Indiana
Drake University
  Department of Music
  Des Moines, Iowa
Duke University
  Department of Music
  Durham, North Carolina
Duquesne University
  School of Music
  Pittsburgh, Pennsylvania
East Carolina University
  School of Music
  Greenville, North Carolina
East Texas State University
  Department of Music
  Commerce, Texas
Eastern Illinois University
  Department of Music
  Charleston, Illinois
Eastern Kentucky University
  Department of Music
  Richmond, Kentucky
Eastern Michigan University
  Department of Music
  Ypsilanti, Michigan
Eastern New Mexico University
  School of Music
  Portales, New Mexico
Eastern Washington University
  Department of Music
  Cheney, Washington
Elizabeth University of Music
  Hiroshima 730, Japan
Emporia State University
  Division of Music
  Emporia, Kansas
Escuela de Música - Heredia
  Universidad Nacional
  Heredia, Costa Rica

Escuela Nacional de Música
  Universidad Nacional Autónoma de
  México
  Mexico City, D.F. 04100, Mexico
Evangelische Kirchenmusikschule der
  Kirchenprovinz Sachsen
  (Evangelical Church Music School of the
  Church Province Saxony)
  *DDR-4020 Halle (Saale), German
  Democratic Republic*
University of Evansville
  Music Department
  Evansville, Indiana
Fachakademie für Music - Augsburg
  Leopold Mozart-Konservatorium der
  Stadt Augsburg
  Augsberg, Federal Republic of Germany
Ferenc Liszt Academy of Music
  Budapest VI, Hungary
University of Florida
  Department of Music
  Gainesville, Florida
Florida State University
  School of Music
  Tallahassee, Florida
Fort Hays State University
  Department of Music
  Hays, Kansas
George Mason University
  Department of Performing Arts - Music
  Division
  Fairfax, Virginia
University of Georgia
  School of Music
  Athens, Georgia
Georgia Southern College
  Department of Music
  Statesboro, Georgia
Georgia State University
  School of Music
  Atlanta, Georgia
Glassboro State College
  Department of Music
  Glassboro, New Jersey
Guildhall School of Music and Drama
  London EC2Y 8DT, United Kingdom
Hardin-Simmons University
  School of Music
  Abilene, Texas
University of Hartford
  Hartt School of Music
  West Hartford, Connecticut
Harvard University
  Department of Music
  Cambridge, Massachusetts
Henderson State University
  Department of Music
  Arkadelphia, Arkansas
Hermann-Zilcher-Konservatorium
  *D-8700 Würzburg, Federal Republic of
  Germany*
Hochschule für Music Franz Liszt
  *DDR 5300 Weimar, German Democratic
  Republic*
Hochschule für Musik Carl Maria von
  Weber
  *DDR 8010 Dresden, German Democratic
  Republic*
Hochschule für Musik Felix
  Mendelssohn-Bartholdy
  *7010 Leipzig, German Democratic
  Republic*
Hochschule für Musik und Theater
  Hannover
  *3000 Hannover 1, Federal Republic of
  Germany*

Hofstra University
  Department of Music
  Hempstead, New York
The Hong Kong Academy for Performing
Arts
  School of Music
  Wanchai, Hong Kong
Hoschschule für Music Hans Eisler
  *DDR Berlin 1080, German Democratic
  Republic*
University of Houston
  School of Music
  Houston, Texas
Howard University
  Department of Music
  Washington, District of Columbia
University of Idaho
  School of Music
  Moscow, Idaho
University of Illinois
  School of Music
  Urbana, Illinois
Illinois State University
  Department of Music
  Normal, Illinois
Illinois Wesleyan University
  School of Music
  Bloomington, Illinois
Indiana State University
  Department of Music
  Terre Haute, Indiana
Indiana University - Bloomington
  School of Music
  Bloomington, Indiana
Indiana University of Pennsylvania
  Department of Music
  Indiana, Pennsylvania
Institute of Fine Arts
  Faculty of Music
  Rangoon, Burma
Instituto Superior de Arte
  Facultad de Música
  Playa, Cuba
University of Iowa
  School of Music
  Iowa City, Iowa
Iowa State University
  Department of Music
  Ames, Iowa
Ithaca College
  School of Music
  Ithaca, New York
Jackson State University
  Department of Music
  Jackson, Mississippi
Jacksonville State University
  Department of Music
  Jacksonville, Alabama
James Madison University
  Department of Music
  Harrisonburg, Virginia
Jersey City State College
  Music Department
  Jersey City, New Jersey
The Jerusalem Rubin Academy of Music
and Dance
  Jerusalem, Israel
The Juilliard School
  New York, New York
University of Kansas
  School of Fine Arts
  Lawrence, Kansas
Kansas State University
  Department of Music
  Manhattan, Kansas

Karol Szymanowski Academy of Music of
Katowice
  Katowice, Poland
Kent State University
  School of Music
  Kent, Ohio
University of Kentucky
  School of Music
  Lexington, Kentucky
Kenya Conservatoire of Music
  Nairobi, Kenya
Konservatorium für Musik und Theater
  CH-3011 Berne, Switzerland
Konzervatoř v Praze
  (State Conservatory Prague)
  Praha 110 00, Czechoslovakia
Konzervatorium - Bratislava
  Bratislava 811 06, Czechoslovakia
Kuopion Konservatorio
  70100 Kuopio, Finland
Lamar University
  Department of Music
  Beaumont, Texas
Lawrence University
  Conservatory of Music
  Appleton, Wisconsin
Lewis and Clark College
  Music Department
  Portland, Oregon
Long Island University - C.W. Post Campus
  Music Department
  Greenvale, New York
Louisiana State University
  School of Music
  Baton Rouge, Louisiana
University of Louisville
  School of Music
  Louisville, Kentucky
University of Lowell
  College of Music
  Lowell, Massachusetts
Loyola University
  College of Music
  New Orleans, Louisiana
University of Maine
  School of Performing Arts
  Orono, Maine
Mandalay School of Music, Dance,
Painting, and Sculpture
  Mandalay, Burma
Manhattan School of Music
  New York, New York
University of Manitoba
  School of Music
  Winnipeg, Manitoba, Canada
Mankato State University
  Department of Music
  Mankato, Minnesota
Mannes College of Music
  New York, New York
Mansfield University
  Department of Music
  Mansfield, Pennsylvania
Marshall University
  Department of Music
  Huntington, West Virginia
University of Maryland - Baltimore County
  Department of Music
  Catonsville, Maryland
University of Maryland - College Park
  Department of Music
  College Park, Maryland
Marywood College
  Music Department
  Scranton, Pennsylvania

University of Massachusetts at Amherst
  Department of Music and Dance
  Amherst, Massachusetts
McGill University
  Faculty of Music
  Montreal, Québec, Canada
McMaster University
  Department of Music
  Hamilton, Ontario, Canada
McNeese State University
  Department of Music
  Lake Charles, Louisiana
Memphis State University
  Music Department
  Memphis, Tennessee
University of Miami
  School of Music
  Coral Gables, Florida
Miami University
  Department of Music
  Oxford, Ohio
University of Michigan
  School of Music
  Ann Arbor, Michigan
Middle Tennessee State University
  Department of Music
  Murfreesboro, Tennessee
Millikin University
  School of Music
  Decatur, Illinois
Mills College
  Music Department
  Oakland, California
University of Minnesota - Duluth
  Department of Music
  Duluth, Minnesota
University of Minnesota - Twin Cities
  School of Music
  Minneapolis, Minnesota
University of Mississippi
  Department of Music
  University, Mississippi
University of Missouri - Columbia
  Department of Music
  Columbia, Missouri
University of Missouri - Kansas City
  Conservatory of Music
  Kansas City, Missouri
University of Montana
  Department of Music
  Missoula, Montana
Montana State University
  Department of Music
  Bozeman, Montana
Montclair State College
  Department of Music
  Upper Montclair, New Jersey
University of Montevallo
  Department of Music
  Montevallo, Alabama
Moorhead State University
  Music Department
  Moorhead, Minnesota
Morehead State University
  Department of Music
  Morehead, Kentucky
Moscow P.I. Tchaikovsky State
Conservatory
  *103009 Moscow K-9, Rossiskaja SFSR,
  U.S.S.R.*
Musik-Akademie der Stadt Basel
  Schola Cantorum Basiliensis
  CH-4051 Basel, Switzerland
Musik-Akademie der Stadt Basel
  (Konservatorium)
  Konservatorium (Musikhochschule)

Basel, Switzerland
Musikhochschule Lübeck
Grosse Petersgrube 17-29
*2400 Lübeck, Federal Republic of
Germany*
Musikhögskolan i Stockholm
National College of Music
115 31 Stockholm, Sweden
Musikschule und Konservatorium
Schaffhausen
Schaffhausen, Switzerland
National Institute of the Arts
Music Department
*Taipei County, Taiwan (Republic of
China)*
University of Nebraska - Lincoln
School of Music
Lincoln, Nebraska
University of Nebraska - Omaha
Department of Music
Omaha, Nebraska
University of Nevada, Las Vegas
Department of Music
Las Vegas, Nevada
University of Nevada, Reno
Department of Music
Reno, Nevada
New England Conservatory
Boston, Massachusetts
University of New Hampshire
Department of Music
Durham, New Hampshire
University of New Mexico
Department of Music
Albuquerque, New Mexico
New Mexico State University
Department of Music
Las Cruces, New Mexico
University of New Orleans
Department of Music
New Orleans, Louisiana
New South Wales State Conservatorium of
Music
Sydney NSW 2000, Australia
New York University - School of Education,
Health, Nursing, and Arts Professions
Department of Music and Music
Education
New York, New York
Norfolk State University
Department of Music
Norfolk, Virginia
Norges Musikkhøgskole
(The Norwegian State Academy of
Music)
N-0130 Oslo 1, Norway
University of North Carolina at Chapel Hill
Department of Music
Chapel Hill, North Carolina
University of North Carolina at Greensboro
School of Music
Greensboro, North Carolina
North Carolina School of the Arts
School of Music
Winston-Salem, North Carolina
University of North Dakota
Department of Music
Grand Forks, North Dakota
North Texas State University
School of Music
Denton, Texas
Northeast Louisiana University
School of Music
Monroe, Louisiana
Northeast Missouri State University
Division of Fine Arts

Kirksville, Missouri
Northeastern Illinois University
Department of Music
Chicago, Illinois
Northern Arizona University
Music Department
Flagstaff, Arizona
University of Northern Colorado
School of Music
Greeley, Colorado
Northern Illinois University
School of Music
DeKalb, Illinois
University of Northern Iowa
School of Music
Cedar Falls, Iowa
Northwestern State University of Louisiana
Department of Music
Natchitoches, Louisiana
Northwestern University
School of Music
Evanston, Illinois
University of Notre Dame
Department of Music
Notre Dame, Indiana
Novosibirsk M.I. Glinka State Conservatory
*630099 Novosibirsk 99, Rossiskaja SFSR,
U.S.S.R.*
Oakland University
Department of Music, Theatre and
Dance
Rochester, Michigan
Oberlin College
Conservatory of Music
Oberlin, Ohio
The Ohio State University
School of Music ⸱
Columbus, Ohio
Ohio University
School of Music
Athens, Ohio
Ohio Wesleyan University
Department of Music
Delaware, Ohio
University of Oklahoma
School of Music
Norman, Oklahoma
Oklahoma Baptist University
Department of Music
Shawnee, Oklahoma
Oklahoma City University
School of Music and Performing Arts
Oklahoma City, Oklahoma
University of Oregon
School of Music
Eugene, Oregon
Oregon State University
Department of Music
Corvallis, Oregon
Osaka Ongaku Daigaku
(Osaka College of Music)
Osaka 561, Japan
Ouachita Baptist University
School of Music
Arkadelphia, Arkansas
University of the Pacific
Conservatory of Music
Stockton, California
Peabody Institute of The Johns Hopkins
University
Baltimore, Maryland
University of Pennsylvania
Department of Music
Philadelphia, Pennsylvania
Pennsylvania State University
School of Music

University Park, Pennsylvania
Philadelphia College of the Performing Arts
School of Music
Philadelphia, Pennsylvania
Pittsburg State University
Department of Music
Pittsburg, Kansas
University of Pittsburgh
Department of Music
Pittsburgh, Pennsylvania
Portland State University
Department of Music
Portland, Oregon
Princeton University
Department of Music
Princeton, New Jersey
University of Puget Sound
School of Music
Tacoma, Washington
Queen's University
School of Music
Kingston, Ontario, Canada
Radford University
Department of Music
Radford, Virginia
Real Conservatorio Superior de Música de
Madrid
(Royal Academy of Music)
Madrid 13, Spain
University of Redlands
School of Music
Redlands, California
University of Regina
Department of Music
Regina, Saskatchewan, Canada
University of Rhode Island
Department of Music
Kingston, Rhode Island
Rice University
Shepherd School of Music
Houston, Texas
University of Rochester
Eastman School of Music
Rochester, New York
Rogaland Musikkonservatorium
N-4000 Stavanger, Norway
Roosevelt University
Chicago Musical College
Chicago, Illinois
Royal Academy of Music
London NW1 5HT, United Kingdom
Royal College of Music
London, SW7 2BS, United Kingdom
Royal Northern College of Music
Manchester M13 9RD, United Kingdom
Royal Scottish Academy of Music and
Drama
Glasgow G2 1BS, United Kingdom
Rutgers, The State University of New Jersey
Department of Music
New Brunswick, New Jersey
St. Cloud State University
Department of Music
St. Cloud, Minnesota
Saint Louis Conservatory of Music
St. Louis, Missouri
St. Olaf College
Music Department
Northfield, Minnesota
Sam Houston State University
Department of Music
Huntsville, Texas
Samford University
School of Music
Birmingham, Alabama

San Diego State University
  Music Department
  San Diego, California
San Francisco Conservatory of Music
  San Francisco, California
San Francisco State University
  Department of Music
  San Francisco, California
San Jose State University
  Department of Music
  San Jose, California
University of Saskatchewan
  Department of Music
  Saskatoon, Saskatchewan, Canada
Shenandoah College and Conservatory
  Winchester, Virginia
Shengyang Conservatory of Music
  *Shengyang, Liaoning Province, People's
  Republic of China*
Shorter College
  Department of Music
  Rome, Georgia
Sichuan Conservatory of Music
  *Chengdu, Sichuan, People's Republic of
  China*
Smith College
  Department of Music
  Northampton, Massachusetts
University of South Carolina
  School of Music
  Columbia, South Carolina
University of South Dakota
  Music Department
  Vermillion, South Dakota
University of South Florida
  Department of Music
  Tampa, Florida
Southeast Missouri State University
  Department of Music
  Cape Girardeau, Missouri
Southeastern Louisiana University
  Department of Music
  Hammond, Louisiana
Southeastern Oklahoma State University
  Department of Music
  Durant, Oklahoma
Southern Baptist Theological Seminary
  School of Church Music
  Louisville, Kentucky
University of Southern California
  School of Music
  Los Angeles, California
Southern Illinois University at Carbondale
  School of Music
  Carbondale, Illinois
Southern Illinois University at Edwardsville
  Department of Music
  Edwardsville, Illinois
Southern Methodist University
  Meadows School of the Arts
  Dallas, Texas
University of Southern Mississippi
  School of Music
  Hattiesburg, Mississippi
Southwest Texas State University
  Department of Music
  San Marcos, Texas
Southwestern Baptist Theological Seminary
  School of Church Music
  Fort Worth, Texas
University of Southwestern Louisiana
  School of Music
  Lafayette, Louisiana
Southwestern Oklahoma State University
  Department of Music
  Weatherford, Oklahoma

Staatliche Hochschule für Musik Freiburg
  *D-7800 Freiburg i. Br., Federal Republic
  of Germany*
Staatliche Hochschule für Musik
  Heidelberg-Mannheim
  *Friedrich-Ebert-Anlage 62, Federal
  Republic of Germany*
Staatliche Hochschule für Musik Rheinland
  - Aachen
    Grenzland-Institut Aachen
    Aachen, Federal Republic of Germany
Staatliche Hochschule für Musik Rheinland
  - Köln
    *D-5000 Köln 1, Federal Republic of
    Germany*
Staatliche Hochschule für Musik Rheinland
  - Wuppertal
    Institute Wuppertal
    Wuppertal, Federal Republic of Germany
Staatliche Hochschule für Musik Trossingen
  *D-7218 Trossingen 1, Federal Republic of
  Germany*
Staatliche Hochschule für Musik
  Westfalen-Lippe
    Institut Dortmund
    *D-4600 Dortmund 1, Federal Republic of
    Germany*
State University of New York at Buffalo
  Department of Music
  Buffalo, New York
State University of New York at Stony
  Brook
    Department of Music
    Stony Brook, New York
State University of New York College at
  Fredonia
    School of Music
    Fredonia, New York
State University of New York College at
  New Paltz
    Department of Music
    New Paltz, New York
State University of New York College at
  Potsdam
    Crane School of Music
    Potsdam, New York
State University of New York College at
  Purchase
    Division of Music
    Purchase, New York
Stedelijke Muziekpedagogische Akademie
  Leeuwarden, Netherlands
Stephen F. Austin State University
  Department of Music
  Nacogdoches, Texas
Stetson University
  School of Music
  Deland, Florida
Teachers College of Columbia University
  Department of Music and Music
  Education
  New York, New York
Tel Aviv University
  Faculty of Fine Arts
  Tel-Aviv, Israel
Temple University
  Esther Boyer College of Music
  Philadelphia, Pennsylvania
University of Tennessee at Chattanooga
  Cadek Department of Music
  Chattanooga, Tennessee
University of Tennessee at Knoxville
  Department of Music
  Knoxville, Tennessee
University of Texas at Arlington
  Department of Music

Arlington, Texas
University of Texas at Austin
  Department of Music
  Austin, Texas
University of Texas at San Antonio
  Division of Music
  San Antonio, Texas
Texas Christian University
  Music Department
  Fort Worth, Texas
Texas Southern University
  Department of Music
  Houston, Texas
Texas Tech University
  Department of Music
  Lubbock, Texas
Texas Woman's University
  Department of Music and Drama
  Denton, Texas
Tonlistarskolinn i Reykjavik
  105 Reykjavik, Iceland
University of Toronto
  Faculty of Music
  Toronto, Ontario, Canada
Towson State University
  Department of Music
  Towson, Maryland
Trenton State College
  Music Department
  Trenton, New Jersey
Trinity College of Music
  London W1M 6AQ, United Kingdom
Troy State University
  Department of Music
  Troy, Alabama
Tulane University
  Newcomb College
  New Orleans, Louisiana
University of Tulsa
  Faculty of Music
  Tulsa, Oklahoma
Ueno Gakuen College
  Tokyo 110, Japan
Universidade do Rio de Janeiro
  Letters and Arts Center - Music Course
  22290 Rio de Janeiro, Brazil
Université de Montréal
  Faculty of Music
  Montréal, Québec, Canada
University of Utah
  Department of Music
  Salt Lake City, Utah
Valdosta State College
  Department of Music
  Valdosta, Georgia
Valparaiso University
  Department of Music
  Valparaiso, Indiana
VanderCook College of Music
  Chicago, Illinois
University of Vermont
  Department of Music
  Burlington, Vermont
University of Victoria
  School of Music
  Victoria, British Columbia, Canada
University of Virginia
  McIntire Department of Music
  Charlottesville, Virginia
Virginia Commonwealth University
  Department of Music
  Richmond, Virginia
Virginia Polytechnic Institute and State
  University
    Department of Music
    Blacksburg, Virginia

Virginia State University
Department of Music Education
Petersburg, Virginia
Vysoká Skola Mûzickych Umeni v Praha
Academy of Music and Dramatic Arts
1101 00 Prague 1, Czechoslovakia
University of Washington
School of Music
Seattle, Washington
Washington State University
Department of Music
Pullman, Washington
Washington University
Department of Music
St. Louis, Missouri
Wayne State University
Department of Music
Detroit, Michigan
Webster University
Department of Music
St. Louis, Missouri
Welsh College of Music and Drama
Cardiff, CF1 3ER, United Kingdom
Wesleyan University
Department of Music
Middletown, Connecticut
West Chester University of Pennsylvania
School of Music
West Chester, Pennsylvania
West Georgia College
Department of Music
Carrollton, Georgia
West Texas State University
Department of Music
Canyon, Texas
West Virginia University
Division of Music
Morgantown, West Virginia
Western Illinois University
Department of Music
Macomb, Illinois
Western Michigan University
School of Music
Kalamazoo, Michigan
University of Western Ontario
Faculty of Music
London, Ontario, Canada
Western Washington University
Department of Music
Bellingham, Washington
Westminster Choir College
Princeton, New Jersey
Wheaton College
Conservatory of Music
Wheaton, Illinois
Wichita State University
School of Music
Wichita, Kansas
Wiesbadener Konservatorium und staatliche
anerkannte private Fachschule für
Musikerzieher e.V.
(Conservatory and Seminary for Music
Education)
*6200 Wiesbaden, Federal Republic of
Germany*
Wilfrid Laurier University
Faculty of Music
Waterloo, Ontario, Canada
Willamette University
Department of Music
Salem, Oregon
William Carey College
Winters School of Music
Hattiesburg, Mississippi
William Paterson College
Department of Music

Wayne, New Jersey
University of Windsor
School of Music
Windsor, Ontario, Canada
Winthrop College
School of Music
Rock Hill, South Carolina
University of Wisconsin - Eau Claire
Department of Music
Eau Claire, Wisconsin
University of Wisconsin - La Crosse
Department of Music
La Crosse, Wisconsin
University of Wisconsin - Madison
School of Music
Madison, Wisconsin
University of Wisconsin - Milwaukee
Music Department
Milwaukee, Wisconsin
University of Wisconsin - Oshkosh
Department of Music
Oshkosh, Wisconsin
University of Wisconsin - Stevens Point
Department of Music
Stevens Point, Wisconsin
University of Wisconsin - Whitewater
Department of Music
Whitewater, Wisconsin
Wright State University
Department of Music
Dayton, Ohio
Yale College (Yale University)
Department of Music
New Haven, Connecticut
Yale University
School of Music
New Haven, Connecticut
York University
Department of Music
North York, Ontario, Canada
Youngstown State University
Dana School of Music
Youngstown, Ohio

WASHINT

Yared National Institute of Music
Addis Ababa, Ethiopia

WIND INSTRUMENTS

A.V. Nezhdanova Odessa Conservatory
*270000 Odessa, Ukrainskaja SSR,
U.S.S.R.*
Moscow P.I. Tchaikovsky State
Conservatory
*103009 Moscow K-9, Rossiskaja SFSR,
U.S.S.R.*
Sichuan Conservatory of Music
*Chengdu, Sichuan, People's Republic of
China*

WOODWINDS

Akademia Muzyczna w Lódź
(Academy of Music of Lódź)
90-716 Lódź, Poland
Akademia Muzycznaj im. Fryderyka
Chopina w Warzawie
(Frederic Chopin Academy of Music of
Warsaw)
00-368 Warsaw, Poland
Akademie voor Musiek
*Hilversum Postkode 1217 KR,
Netherlands*
University of Akron
Department of Music
Akron, Ohio

Alabama State University
School of Music
Montgomery, Alabama
University of Alberta
Department of Music
Edmonton, Alberta, Canada
Andrews University
Department of Music
Berrien Springs, Michigan
Appalachian State University
Department of Music
Boone, North Carolina
Arizona State University
School of Music
Tempe, Arizona
Arkansas State University
Department of Music
State University, Arkansas
Auburn University
Department of Music
Auburn, Alabama
Azusa Pacific University
School of Music
Azusa, California
Ball State University
School of Music
Muncie, Indiana
Bemidji State University
Music Department
Bemidji, Minnesota
Bennington College
Music Department
Bennington, Vermont
Biola University
Department of Music
La Mirada, California
Boise State University
Music Department
Boise, Idaho
Boston Conservatory of Music
Boston, Massachusetts
Brandon University
School of Music
Brandon, Manitoba, Canada
Brigham Young University
Department of Music
Provo, Utah
Brown University
Department of Music
Providence, Rhode Island
University of Calgary
Department of Music
Calgary, Alberta, Canada
University of California, Berkeley
Department of Music
Berkeley, California
University of California, Davis
Department of Music
Davis, California
California Institute of the Arts
School of Music
Valencia, California
California State University, Chico
Department of Music
Chico, California
California State University, Fresno
Department of Music
Fresno, California
California State University, Fullerton
Department of Music
Fullerton, California
California State University, Long Beach
Department of Music
Long Beach, California
California State University, Los Angeles
Department of Music

Los Angeles, California
California State University, Northridge
　Music Department
　Northridge, California
Carnegie-Mellon University
　Department of Music
　Pittsburgh, Pennsylvania
Case Western Reserve University
　Department of Music
　Cleveland, Ohio
Central Conservatory of Music
　Beijing, People's Republic of China
Central Michigan University
　Department of Music
　Mount Pleasant, Michigan
Central State University
　Department of Music
　Edmond, Oklahoma
City of Leeds College of Music
　Leeds LS2 8BH, United Kingdom
City University of New York - Brooklyn
College
　Conservatory of Music
　Brooklyn, New York
City University of New York - City College
　Department of Music
　New York, New York
City University of New York - Hunter
College
　Department of Music
　New York, New York
City University of New York - Queens
College
　The Aaron Copland School of Music
　Flushing, New York
Cleveland Institute of Music
　Cleveland, Ohio
University of Colorado at Denver
　College of Music
　Denver, Colorado
Columbia University
　Department of Music
　New York, New York
Columbus College
　Department of Music
　Columbus, Georgia
Combs College of Music
　Philadelphia, Pennsylvania
Conservatoire de Musique de La
　Chaux-de-Fonds - Le Locle
　2300 La Chaux-de-Fonds, Switzerland
Conservatorio di Musica "Claudio
　Monteverdi"
　I-39100 Bolzano, Italy
Conservatorio Nacional de Música
　(National Conservatory of Music)
　Lima 1, Peru
Converse College
　School of Music
　Spartanburg, South Carolina
Cornell University
　Department of Music
　Ithaca, New York
Dalhousie University
　Department of Music
　Halifax, Nova Scotia, Canada
University of Delaware
　Department of Music
　Newark, Delaware
Duke University
　Department of Music
　Durham, North Carolina
East Texas State University
　Department of Music
　Commerce, Texas

Eastern Kentucky University
　Department of Music
　Richmond, Kentucky
Eastern New Mexico University
　School of Music
　Portales, New Mexico
Eastern Washington University
　Department of Music
　Cheney, Washington
Escuela de Música - Heredia
　Universidad Nacional
　Heredia, Costa Rica
University of Evansville
　Music Department
　Evansville, Indiana
Ferenc Liszt Academy of Music
　Budapest VI, Hungary
University of Florida
　Department of Music
　Gainesville, Florida
Fort Hays State University
　Department of Music
　Hays, Kansas
University of Georgia
　School of Music
　Athens, Georgia
Georgia Southern College
　Department of Music
　Statesboro, Georgia
Georgia State University
　School of Music
　Atlanta, Georgia
Glassboro State College
　Department of Music
　Glassboro, New Jersey
Guildhall School of Music and Drama
　London EC2Y 8DT, United Kingdom
Hardin-Simmons University
　School of Music
　Abilene, Texas
Harvard University
　Department of Music
　Cambridge, Massachusetts
Henderson State University
　Department of Music
　Arkadelphia, Arkansas
Hochschule für Music Franz Liszt
　*DDR 5300 Weimar, German Democratic
　Republic*
Hochschule für Music und Darstellende
Kunst Hamburg
　*2000 Hamburg 13, Federal Republic of
　Germany*
Hochschule für Musik - Würzburg
　*D-8700 Würzburg, Federal Republic of
　Germany*
Hochschule für Musik Carl Maria von
Weber
　*DDR 8010 Dresden, German Democratic
　Republic*
Hochschule für Musik Felix
Mendelssohn-Bartholdy
　*7010 Leipzig, German Democratic
　Republic*
Hochschule für Musik und Theater
Hannover
　*3000 Hannover 1, Federal Republic of
　Germany*
The Hong Kong Academy for Performing
Arts
　School of Music
　Wanchai, Hong Kong
Hoschschule für Music Hans Eisler
　*DDR Berlin 1080, German Democratic
　Republic*

University of Houston
　School of Music
　Houston, Texas
Illinois State University
　Department of Music
　Normal, Illinois
Indiana University - Bloomington
　School of Music
　Bloomington, Indiana
Indiana University of Pennsylvania
　Department of Music
　Indiana, Pennsylvania
Instituto Superior de Arte
　Facultad de Música
　Playa, Cuba
The Jerusalem Rubin Academy of Music
and Dance
　Jerusalem, Israel
Karol Szymanowski Academy of Music of
Katowice
　Katowice, Poland
Koninklijk Muziekconservatorium van
Brussel
　1000 Brussels, Belgium
Konzervatoř v Praze
　(State Conservatory Prague)
　Praha 110 00, Czechoslovakia
Konzervatorium - Bratislava
　Bratislava 811 06, Czechoslovakia
Kuopion Konservatorio
　70100 Kuopio, Finland
Leningrad N.A. Rimsky-Korsakov State
Conservatory
　*192041 Leningrad, Rossiskaja SFSR,
　U.S.S.R.*
Lewis and Clark College
　Music Department
　Portland, Oregon
Long Island University - C.W. Post Campus
　Music Department
　Greenvale, New York
Louisiana State University
　School of Music
　Baton Rouge, Louisiana
University of Lowell
　College of Music
　Lowell, Massachusetts
Manhattan School of Music
　New York, New York
University of Manitoba
　School of Music
　Winnipeg, Manitoba, Canada
Mankato State University
　Department of Music
　Mankato, Minnesota
Mannes College of Music
　New York, New York
University of Maryland - Baltimore County
　Department of Music
　Catonsville, Maryland
McGill University
　Faculty of Music
　Montreal, Québec, Canada
McMaster University
　Department of Music
　Hamilton, Ontario, Canada
McNeese State University
　Department of Music
　Lake Charles, Louisiana
Memphis State University
　Music Department
　Memphis, Tennessee
University of Miami
　School of Music
　Coral Gables, Florida

Michigan State University
  School of Music
  East Lansing, Michigan
University of Mississippi
  Department of Music
  University, Mississippi
University of Missouri - Columbia
  Department of Music
  Columbia, Missouri
University of Montana
  Department of Music
  Missoula, Montana
Montana State University
  Department of Music
  Bozeman, Montana
Montclair State College
  Department of Music
  Upper Montclair, New Jersey
University of Montevallo
  Department of Music
  Montevallo, Alabama
Moscow P.I. Tchaikovsky State
  Conservatory
  103009 Moscow K-9, Rossiskaja SFSR,
  U.S.S.R.
Musik-Akademie der Stadt Basel
  (Konservatorium)
  Konservatorium (Musikhochschule)
  Basel, Switzerland
Musikhögskolan i Stockholm
  National College of Music
  115 31 Stockholm, Sweden
Musikschule und Konservatorium
  Schaffhausen
  Schaffhausen, Switzerland
National Institute of the Arts
  Music Department
  Taipei County, Taiwan (Republic of
  China)
University of Nevada, Reno
  Department of Music
  Reno, Nevada
New England Conservatory
  Boston, Massachusetts
University of New Hampshire
  Department of Music
  Durham, New Hampshire
University of New Mexico
  Department of Music
  Albuquerque, New Mexico
New Mexico State University
  Department of Music
  Las Cruces, New Mexico
New South Wales State Conservatorium of
  Music
  Sydney NSW 2000, Australia
New York University - School of Education,
  Health, Nursing, and Arts Professions
  Department of Music and Music
  Education
  New York, New York
Nikos Skalkotas Conservatory
  Athens 11141, Greece
Norges Musikkhøgskole
  (The Norwegian State Academy of
  Music)
  N-0130 Oslo 1, Norway
North Carolina School of the Arts
  School of Music
  Winston-Salem, North Carolina
University of North Dakota
  Department of Music
  Grand Forks, North Dakota
Northeast Missouri State University
  Division of Fine Arts
  Kirksville, Missouri

Northeastern Illinois University
  Department of Music
  Chicago, Illinois
University of Northern Colorado
  School of Music
  Greeley, Colorado
Northern Illinois University
  School of Music
  DeKalb, Illinois
University of Notre Dame
  Department of Music
  Notre Dame, Indiana
The Ohio State University
  School of Music
  Columbus, Ohio
Ohio University
  School of Music
  Athens, Ohio
University of Oklahoma
  School of Music
  Norman, Oklahoma
Oklahoma City University
  School of Music and Performing Arts
  Oklahoma City, Oklahoma
Oregon State University
  Department of Music
  Corvallis, Oregon
Osaka Ongaku Daigaku
  (Osaka College of Music)
  Osaka 561, Japan
Ouachita Baptist University
  School of Music
  Arkadelphia, Arkansas
University of Pennsylvania
  Department of Music
  Philadelphia, Pennsylvania
University of the Philippines
  College of Music
  Quezon City, The Philippines
Pohjois-Kymen Musiikkiopisto
  (North Kymi Music Institute)
  45100 Kouvola, Finland
Portland State University
  Department of Music
  Portland, Oregon
Princeton University
  Department of Music
  Princeton, New Jersey
University of Puget Sound
  School of Music
  Tacoma, Washington
Radford University
  Department of Music
  Radford, Virginia
Rogaland Musikkonservatorium
  N-4000 Stavanger, Norway
Roosevelt University
  Chicago Musical College
  Chicago, Illinois
Royal Academy of Music
  London NW1 5HT, United Kingdom
Royal College of Music
  London, SW7 2BS, United Kingdom
Royal Northern College of Music
  Manchester M13 9RD, United Kingdom
Royal Scottish Academy of Music and
  Drama
  Glasgow G2 1BS, United Kingdom
Sam Houston State University
  Department of Music
  Huntsville, Texas
University of Santo Tomas
  Conservatory of Music
  Manila, The Philippines
Shenandoah College and Conservatory
  Winchester, Virginia

Shengyang Conservatory of Music
  Shengyang, Liaoning Province, People's
  Republic of China
University of South Carolina
  School of Music
  Columbia, South Carolina
Southeastern Louisiana University
  Department of Music
  Hammond, Louisiana
Southern Baptist Theological Seminary
  School of Church Music
  Louisville, Kentucky
University of Southern California
  School of Music
  Los Angeles, California
Southwest Texas State University
  Department of Music
  San Marcos, Texas
Southwestern Baptist Theological Seminary
  School of Church Music
  Fort Worth, Texas
Southwestern Oklahoma State University
  Department of Music
  Weatherford, Oklahoma
Staatliche Hochschule für Musik Freiburg
  D-7800 Freiburg i. Br., Federal Republic
  of Germany
Staatliche Hochschule für Musik Rheinland
  - Düsseldorf
  (State College of Music)
  D-4000 Düsseldorf, Federal Republic of
  Germany
Staatliche Hochschule für Musik Rheinland
  - Köln
  D-5000 Köln 1, Federal Republic of
  Germany
Staatliche Hochschule für Musik
  Westfalen-Lippe
  Institut Dortmund
  D-4600 Dortmund 1, Federal Republic of
  Germany
Stanford University
  Department of Music
  Stanford, California
State University of New York at
  Binghamton
  Department of Music
  Binghamton, New York
State University of New York at Buffalo
  Department of Music
  Buffalo, New York
State University of New York College at
  New Paltz
  Department of Music
  New Paltz, New York
Stedelijke Muziekpedagogische Akademie
  Leeuwarden, Netherlands
Stetson University
  School of Music
  Deland, Florida
Tampereen Konservatorio
  33230 Tampere, Finland
Tasmanian Conservatorium of Music
  Hobart, Tasmania 7001, Australia
Tel Aviv University
  Faculty of Fine Arts
  Tel-Aviv, Israel
University of Tennessee at Chattanooga
  Cadek Department of Music
  Chattanooga, Tennessee
University of Texas at Arlington
  Department of Music
  Arlington, Texas
University of Texas at Austin
  Department of Music
  Austin, Texas

University of Texas at San Antonio
  Division of Music
  San Antonio, Texas
Texas Southern University
  Department of Music
  Houston, Texas
Texas Tech University
  Department of Music
  Lubbock, Texas
Texas Woman's University
  Department of Music and Drama
  Denton, Texas
Towson State University
  Department of Music
  Towson, Maryland
Trenton State College
  Music Department
  Trenton, New Jersey
Trinity College of Music
  London W1M 6AQ, United Kingdom
Tulane University
  Newcomb College
  New Orleans, Louisiana
Ueno Gakuen College
  Tokyo 110, Japan
Universidade do São Paulo
  Department of Music
  05508 São Paulo, Brazil
Université Laval
  Ecole de Musique
  Ste. Foy, Québec, Canada
University of Utah
  Department of Music
  Salt Lake City, Utah
Valdosta State College
  Department of Music
  Valdosta, Georgia
University of Vermont
  Department of Music
  Burlington, Vermont
University of Victoria
  School of Music.
  Victoria, British Columbia, Canada
University of Virginia
  McIntire Department of Music
  Charlottesville, Virginia
Virginia Commonwealth University
  Department of Music
  Richmond, Virginia
Virginia State University
  Department of Music Education
  Petersburg, Virginia
Washington University
  Department of Music
  St. Louis, Missouri
Wayne State University
  Department of Music
  Detroit, Michigan
Webster University
  Department of Music
  St. Louis, Missouri
Welsh College of Music and Drama
  Cardiff, CF1 3ER, United Kingdom
Wesleyan University
  Department of Music
  Middletown, Connecticut
West Georgia College
  Department of Music
  Carrollton, Georgia
West Texas State University
  Department of Music
  Canyon, Texas
University of Western Ontario
  Faculty of Music
  London, Ontario, Canada

Western Washington University
  Department of Music
  Bellingham, Washington
Wheaton College
  Conservatory of Music
  Wheaton, Illinois
Willamette University
  Department of Music
  Salem, Oregon
William Paterson College
  Department of Music
  Wayne, New Jersey
Winthrop College
  School of Music
  Rock Hill, South Carolina
University of Wisconsin - La Crosse
  Department of Music
  La Crosse, Wisconsin
University of Wisconsin - Madison
  School of Music
  Madison, Wisconsin
University of Wisconsin - Oshkosh
  Department of Music
  Oshkosh, Wisconsin
University of Wisconsin - Whitewater
  Department of Music
  Whitewater, Wisconsin
Yale College (Yale University)
  Department of Music
  New Haven, Connecticut
Yale University
  School of Music
  New Haven, Connecticut
York University
  Department of Music
  North York, Ontario, Canada
Zeneiskolai Tanárkepzó Intézet
  (Music Teachers Training Institute of the
  Liszt Academy of Music)
  Budapest 1052, Hungary

XYLOPHONE

Institute of Fine Arts
  Faculty of Music
  Rangoon, Burma
Mandalay School of Music, Dance,
  Painting, and Sculpture
  Mandalay, Burma

APPENDIX

International Telephone Codes

Algeria   213
Argentina   54
Australia   61
Austria   43
Belgium   32
Bolivia   591
Brazil   55
Bulgaria   359
Chile   56
China, People's Republic of   86
Colombia   57
Costa Rica   506
Czechoslovakia   42
Denmark   45
Dominican Republic   809
East Germany (German
    Democratic Republic)   37
Ecuador   593
Egypt   20
El Salvador   503
Ethiopia   251
Federal Republic of Germany
    (West Germany)   49
Finland   358
France   33
German Democratic Republic
    (East Germany)   37
Greece   30
Guatemala   502
Haiti   509

Honduras   504
Hong Kong   852
Hungary   36
Iceland   354
India   91
Indonesia   62
Iran   98
Iraq   964
Ireland   353
Israel   972
Italy   39
Ivory Coast   225
Jamaica   809
Japan   81
Kenya   254
Korea, Republic of   82
Kuwait   965
Liberia   231
Luxembourg   352
Mexico   52
Monaco   33
Morocco   212
Netherlands   31
New Caledonia   687
New Zealand   64
Nicaragua   505
Nigeria   234
Norway   47
Oman   968
Panama   507
Paraguay   595

Peru   51
Philippines   63
Poland   48
Portugal   351
Qatar   974
Romania   40
Saudi Arabia   966
Senegal   221
South Africa, Republic of   27
Spain   34
Sri Lanka   94
Sweden   46
Switzerland   41
Taiwan (Republic of
    China)   886
Tanzania   255
Thailand   66
Tunisia   216
Turkey   90
Uganda   256
United Kingdom   44
Uruguay   598
Venezuela   58
West Germany (Federal Republic
    of Germany)   49
Yemen Arab Republic   967
Yugoslavia   38
Zaire   243
Zambia   260
Zimbabwe   263